Michaël N. van der Meer, Ph. D. (2001) in Theology at the Free University Amsterdam and Leiden University, currently teaches religion at a secondary school in Amstelveen and publishes articles in the field of textual criticism of the Hebrew Bible.

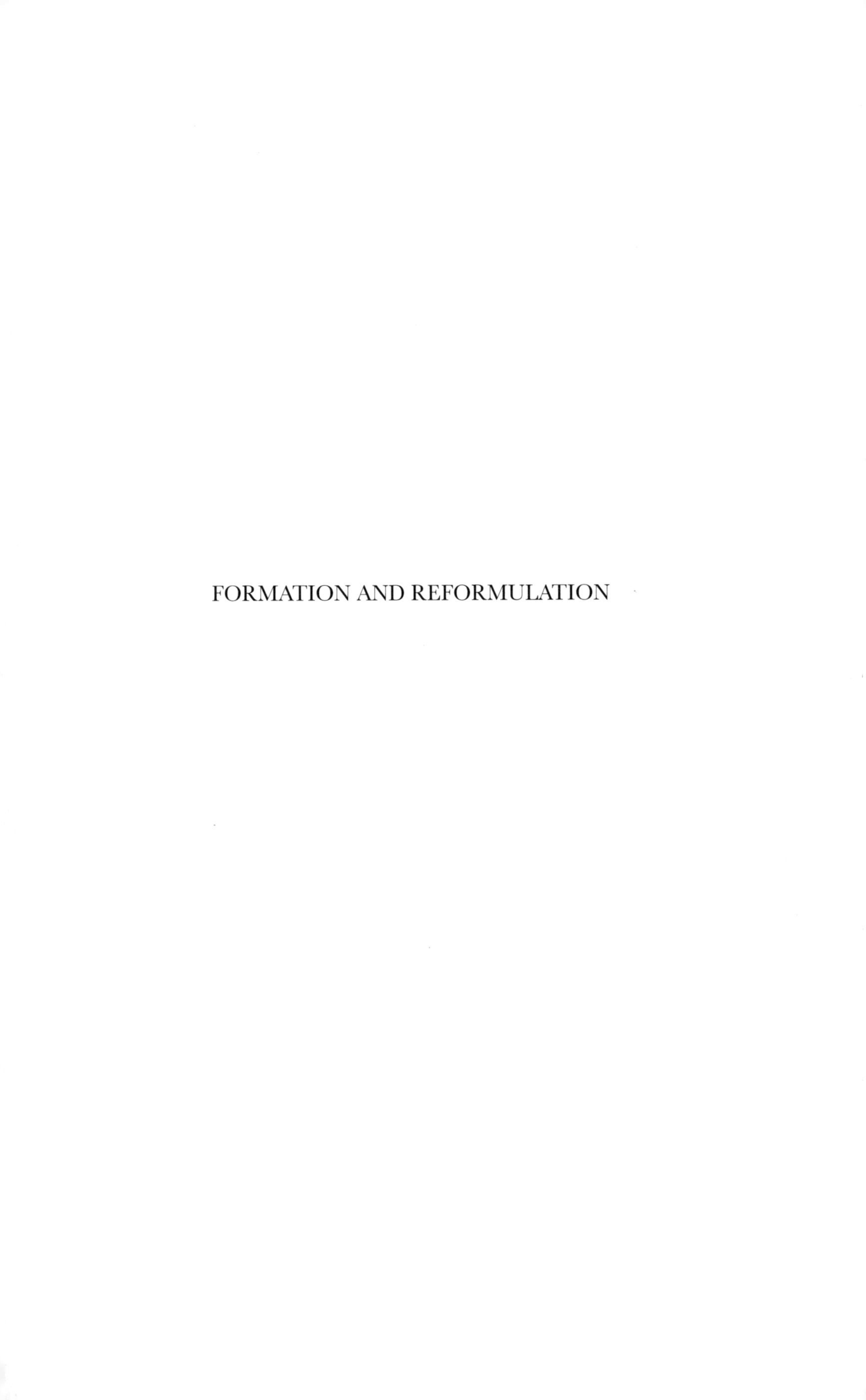

FORMATION AND REFORMULATION

SUPPLEMENTS

TO

VETUS TESTAMENTUM

VOLUME CII

FORMATION AND REFORMULATION

THE REDACTION OF THE BOOK OF JOSHUA IN THE LIGHT OF THE OLDEST TEXTUAL WITNESSES

BY

MICHAËL N. VAN DER MEER

BRILL
LEIDEN · BOSTON
2004

This book is printed on acid-free paper.

Library of Congress Cataloging-in-Publication Data

Meer, Michaël N. van der.
Formation and reformulation : the redaction of the book of Joshua in the light of the oldest textual witnesses / by Michaël N. van der Meer.
p. cm. — (Supplements to Vetus Testamentum, ISSN 0083-5889 ; v. 102).
Includes bibliographical references (p.) and indexes.
ISBN 90-04-13125-6 (alk. paper)
1. Bible. O.T. Joshua—Criticism, Redaction. 2. Bible. O.T. Joshua—Criticism, Textual. I. Title. II. Supplements to Vetus Testamentum ; v. 102.

BS410.V452 v. 102
[BS1295.52]
222'.2066—dc22

2003065322

ISSN 0083-5889
ISBN 90 04 13125 6

PRINTED IN THE NETHERLANDS

To Charlotte
To Jonathan and Joram

CONTENTS

PREFACE

This book is a revision of my dissertation with the same title submitted to the Theological Faculty of Leiden University in March 2001. For the present edition, the monograph has been shortened, updated and re-arranged. Since a number of recent publications (de Vos, de Troyer) refer to the first edition of this book, it is important to note that the page-numbering has been changed. Previous section I.4.3 has become chapter 5, while chapters II.1–4 have become chapters 6–10. Chapter II.3.B and II.3.C have become chapter 8 and 9 respectively. Where possible, new finds (XJoshua, Schøyen Septuagint manuscript 2648) and new insights (Rösel, De Vos) have been incorporated.

It is my pleasant duty to thank all who have contributed to the completion of this work. First of all, I want to express my deep gratitude to my *Doktervater* Arie van der Kooij who supervised my work with his constant gentle and very professional coaching. I am also indebted to professor dr. E. Tov, who introduced my in the field of Qumran biblical studies during his stay at the Free University Amsterdam and remained interested in my work since, in spite of the differences in opinion.

I am very grateful for the constructive discussions with many scholars during the last years. I would like to mention here the names of drs. M.F.J. Baasten, drs. C. van Bekkum, B. Bredereke-Lucassen, dr. J.E. Erbes, professor F. García Martínez, professor dr. L.J. Greenspoon, dr. C.G. den Hertog, dr. K.D. Jenner, dr. P.S.F. van Keulen, professor dr. H. Leene, professor dr. E. Noort, dr. E.J.C. Tigchelaar, dr. J.C. de Vos, dr. S. Sipilä, dr. K. Spronk, and professor dr. A.S. van der Woude.

The book has benefitted much from the critical remarks by professor dr. Johan Lust, professor dr. T. Muraoka, U. Quast, dr. J. Tromp, and professor dr. D. Walter. I owe a special debt to dr. E. Tigchelaar for his extensive reply to earlier versions of chapters 8 and 9 and to dr. C.G. den Hertog for his many written remarks on Joshua 5 (chapter 7).

I would like to express my gratitude to professor L. Greenspoon, who kindly granted me permission to study the unpublished monograph

Andreas Masius and His Commentary on the Book of Joshua written by M.L. Margolis and dr. L. Mazor for providing me with a copy of her unpublished dissertation *The Septuagint Translation of the Book of Joshua.*

I am much indebted to Ch.E. Smit, M.A., for her thorough, critical and quick correction of the English of the entire study, and further to my mother, drs. J. van der Meer-Sauer, dr. J. Tromp, and professor dr. D. Walter for additional corrections. Of course, I remain responsible for all remaining imperfections.

Finally, I thank professor dr. A. Lemaire for accepting my book in the *Supplements to Vetus Testamentum* series and his valuable suggestions.

This study is dedicated to my wife Charlotte Andringa, and our two sons, Jonathan and Joram, who have continuously supported me in the process of formation and reformulation of this book.

CONVENTIONS, SIGLA, AND ABBREVIATIONS

Conventions

Where variants between the Hebrew and Greek texts are discussed, a synopsis of the relevant texts have been offered. The Hebrew text has been divided in clauses according to the system used by N. Winther-Nielsen, E. Taltra, *A Computational Display of the Book of Joshua.* (Applicatio 13) Amsterdam 1995. Ketib-Qere variants in MT have been indicated by respectively one and two asterikses (*). Transcription of the text of the Dead Sea Scrolls is according to the system followed *inter alia* by F. García Martínez, E.J.C. Tigchelaar (eds.), *The Dead Sea Scrolls Study Edition. Volume One 1Q1–4Q273.* Leiden/New York/Köln 1997, p. xx, and E. Tov, *The Texts from the Judaean Desert. Indices and an Introduction to the Discoveries in the Judaean Desert Series.* (DJD 39) Oxford 2002, pp. 18–21. Variants in the Qumran texts *vis-à-vis* the MT have been underlined. In order to highlight the physically attested letters on the Qumran scrolls, the text of the lost letters and lines have been been printed in outline font. Unless otherwise indicated, the Greek text is taken from the Rahlfs edition (see section 2.1 below). Minuses in the Greek text have been indicated by three hyphens per word. Pluses and quantitative variants in the Greek text *vis-à-vis* MT have been indicated by italics.

References to secondary literature have been provided with full title, name of the series and place and date of the publication only the first time the study is mentioned. Further references are by name of the author and short title only. Full information can be gathered from the select bibliography at the end of this study.

Sigla

1. *Textual Witnesses*

4QApocrJosh[a–c]	4QApocryphon of Joshua[a–c] (see sections 3.5.3–5)
4QJosh[a]	4QJoshua[a] (4Q47) (see section 3.2)
4QJosh[b]	4QJoshua[b] (4Q48) (see section 3.3)
4QpaleoParaJosh	4QpaleoParaJoshua (4Q123) (see section 3.5.2)

4QTest	4QTestimonia (4Q175)
5Q9	5QWork with place names (see section 3.5.5)
α'	The Greek revision by Aquila
Arm	Armenian version of the Bible
CD	The Damascus Document
CG	The Cairo Genizah fragments
Eth	Ethiopian version of the Bible
Fragm.Tg	Fragmentary Targum
K or *	Ketib
Ken.	Kenicott (Masoretic manuscript number)
LXX	The Septuagint or Old Greek version of the Hebrew Bible (see section 2.1)
LXX^{A}	Septuagint Codex Alexandrinus
LXX^{B}	Septuagint Codex Vaticanus
LXX^{W}	Septuagint Codex Washingtonianus
MasApocrJosh	Masada Apocryphon of Joshua (see section 3.5.5)
ms.	manuscript
mss.	manuscripts
MT	The Masoretic Text
OG	The Old Greek translation of the Hebrew Bible in contrast to the younger revisions
οἱ λ̣	The three younger revisers
Peš	The Pešiṭta version of the Old Testament
ק or **	Qere
XJosh	XJoshua (see section 3.4)
σ'	The Greek revision by Symmachus
sa	Sahidic version of the Bible (see section 2.1)
SamP	The Samaritan Pentateuch
Syh	Syro-Hexapla
Syh^{L}	Lagarde's edition of the Syro-Hexapla (see section 2.1)
Syh^{M}	Masius' Syro-Hexapla manuscript (see section 2.1)
θ'	The Greek revision by Theodotion
Tg	Targum
TgNF	Targum Neofyti
TgOnq	Targum Onqelos
TgPsJon	Targum Pseudo-Jonathan
VetLat	Vetus Latina
Vg	The Vulgate version of the Old Testament

2. *Qumran Transcriptions*

א̊	possible reconstruction
א̇	plausible reconstruction
[אאא]	text restoration
vacat	space left blank in the manuscript
].[	illegible letter

3. *Literary strata*

DtrH (or DtrG)	The Deuteronomistic History (see section 4.2.1)
DtrN	The nomistic redaction of DtrH (see section 4.2.2)
DtrP	The prophetic redaction of DtrH (see section 4.2.4.2)
DtrL	The *Landnahme* stratum within DtrH (see section 4.2.4.1)
DtrR	The Reuben-Gad-half-Manasseh redaction of DtrH (see section 4.2.4.2)
Dtr_1	The first, Josianic edition of DtrH (see section 4.2.4.1)
Dtr_2	The second, Exilic edition of DtrH (see section 4.2.4.1)
D^2	The historical framework of the book of Deuteronomy
RedP	The Priestly redaction
P^G	The Priestly Code (*Grundschrift* of the *Priesterschrift*)
P^S	Supplements to P^G
P^{SS}	secondary supplements to P^G and P^S
Pent.	Pentateuch

Abbreviations

AASF	Annales Academiae Scientarum Fennicae
AB	The Anchor Bible
ABD	Anchor Bible Dictionary
AGJU	Arbeiten zur Geschichte des antiken Judentums und des Urchristentums
AGSU	Arbeiten zur Geschichte des Spätjudentums und Urchristentums
AHw	Akkadisches Handwörterbuch

AJSL	The American Journal of Semitic Languages and Literatures
AnBibl	Analecta Biblica
AOAT	Alter Orient und Altes Testament
ARM(T)	Archives royales de Mari
ATD	Das Alte Testament Deutsch
AThANT	Abhandlungen zur Theologie des Alten und Neuen Testaments
BASOR	Bulletin of the American School of Oriental Research
BBB	Bonner Biblische Beiträge
BDB	F. Brown, S.R. Driver, C.A. Briggs, *A Hebrew and English Lexicon of the Old Testament with an appendix containing the Biblical Aramaic.* Oxford 1906
BEATAJ	Beiträge zur Erforschung des Alten Testaments und des antiken Judentum
BETL	Bibliotheca Ephemeridum Theologicarum Lovaniensium
BHS	Biblia Hebraica Stuttgartensia
Bib	Biblica
BiOr	Bibliotheca Orientalis
BIOSCS	Bulletin of the International Organization for Septuagint and Cognate Studies
BKAT	Biblischer Kommentar Altes Testament
BOT	De Boeken van het Oude Testament
BWANT	Beiträge zur Wissenschaft vom Alten und Neuen Testament
BZ	Biblische Zeitschrift
BZAW	Beiheft zur Zeitschrift für die alttestamentliche Wissenschaft
CAD	The Assyrian Dictionary of the Oriental Institute of the University of Chicago
CAT	Commentaire de l'ancien Testament
CBET	Contributions to Biblical Exegesis and Theology
CB.OTS	Coniectanea Biblica. Old Testament Series
CBQ	Catholic Biblical Quarterly
COT	Commentaar op het Oude Testament
CRINT	Compendia Rerum Iudaicarum ad Novum Testamentum
CSCO	Corpus scriptorum christianorum orientalium
CSEL	Corpus scriptorum ecclesiasticorum latinorum
DBAT	Dielheimer Blätter zum Alten Testament und seiner Rezeption in der Alten Kirche

DJD	Discoveries in the Judaean Desert
DSD	Dead Sea Discoveries
EB	Echter Bibel
EdF	Erträge der Forschung
ETL	Ephemerides theologicae lovaniensis
FRLANT	Forschungen zur Religion und Literatur des Alten und Neuen Testaments
FS	Festschrift
FzB	Forschung zur Bibel
GCS	Die griechische christliche Schriftsteller der ersten (drei) Jahrhunderte
GELS[2]	T. MURAOKA, *A Greek-English Lexicon of the Septuagint Chiefly of the Pentateuch and the Twelve Prophets*. Louvain/Paris/Dudley, MA 2002
HALOT	L. KOEHLER, W. BAUMGARTNER, J.J. STAMM, B. HARTMANN, Z. BEN-HAYYIM, E.Y. KUTSCHER, P. REYMOND, M.E.J. RICHARDSON, *The Hebrew and Aramaic Lexicon of the Old Testament*. Leiden/New York/Köln 1994–2000
HAT	Handbuch zum Alten Testament
HCOT	Historical Commentary on the Old Testament
HKAT	(Göttinger) Handkommentar zum Alten Testament
HR	E. HATCH, H.A. REDPATH, *A Concordance to the Septuagint and the Other Greek Versions of the Old Testament (including the Apocryphal Books) in Three Volumes*. Oxford 1897, reprinted in Grand Rapids, Michigan 1987
HSM	Harvard Semitic Monographs
HSS	Harvard Semitic Studies
HTR	Harvard Theological Review
HUCA	Hebrew Union College Annual
ICC	International Critical Commentary
IEJ	Israel Exploration Journal
IOSCS	International Organization for Septuagint and Cognate Studies
IOSOT	International Organization for the Study of the Old Testament
JAOS	Journal of the American Oriental Society
JBL	Journal of Biblical Literature
JBS	Jerusalem Biblical Studies
JPOS	Journal of the Palestine Oriental Society
JQR	Jewish Quarterly Review

JQR.NS	Jewish Quarterly Review New Series (nr. 1 in 1910)
JSOT	Journal for the Study of the Old Testament
JSOTS	Journal for the Study of the Old Testament. Supplement Series
JSS	Journal of Semitic Studies
JSS.M	Journal of Semitic Studies Monograph
JThSt	Journal of Theological Studies
KAI	H. DONNER, W. RÖLLIG, *Kanaanäische und aramäische Inschriften*. Wiesbaden 1966–1969
KAT	Kommentar zum Alten Testament
KeH	Kurzgefasstes exegetisches Handbuch zum Alten Testament
KHCAT	Kurzer Hand-Commentar zum Alten Testament
KKANT	Kurzgefaßter Kommentar zu den heiligen Schriften Alten und Neuen Testaments sowie zu den Apokryphen
LCL	Loeb Classical Library
LEH	J. LUST, E. EYNIKEL, K. HAUSPIE, *A Greek—English Lexicon of the Septuagint. Part 1. A—I; Part II. K—W.* Stuttgart 1992, 1996
LSJ	H.G. LIDDELL, R. SCOTT, H.S. JONES, R. MCKENZIE, *A Greek-English Lexicon. With a revised Supplement 1996.* Oxford 1996.
MM	Michaël van der Meer
MSU	Mitteilungen des Septuaginta-Unternehmens
NCB	New Century Bible
OBO	Orbis biblicus et orientalis
OLZ	Orientalistische Literaturzeitung
OTL	The Old Testament Library
OTS	Oudtestamentische Studiën
PEQ	Palestine Exploration Quarterly
PG	Patrologia Graeca
PJB	Palästinajahrbuch
PL	Patrologia Latina
P-S	J. PAYNE SMITH (MRS. MARGOLIOUTH), *A Compendious Syriac Dictionary. Founded upon the Thesaurus Syriacus by R. Payne Smith.* Oxford 1903, reprinted in Winona Lake, Indiana 1998
PVTG	Pseudepigrapha Veteris Testamenti Graece
RB	Revue biblique

RdQ	Revue de Qumran
SBAB	Stuttgarter biblische Aufsatzbände
SBL	Society of Biblical Literature
SBLSBS	Society of Biblical Literature Sources for Biblical Study
SBLSCS	Society of Biblical Literature Septuagint and Cognate Studies
SBS	Stuttgarter Bibel-Studien
SC	Sources chrétiennes
SCS	Septuagint and Cognate Studies
SEÅ	Svensk Exegetisk Årsbok
SFEG	Schriften der Finnischen Exegetischen Gesellschaft
SJOT	Scandinavian Journal of the Old Testament
SSN	Studia semitica neerlandica
STDJ	Studies on the Texts of the Desert of Judah
SVT	Supplements to Vetus Testamentum
SVTG	Septuaginta Vetus Testamentum Graecum Auctoritate Academiae Scientiarum Gottingensis editum
SVTP	Studia in Veteris Testamenti pseudepigraphica
TANZ	Texte und Arbeiten zum neutestamentlichen Zeitalter
TB	Theologische Bücherei
ThHAT	E. Jenni, C. Westermann (Hg.), *Theologisches Handwörterbuch zum Alten Testament*. I–II. München 1971–1976
ThR	Theologische Rundschau
ThWAT	G.J. Botterweck, H. Ringgren, G.W. Anderson, H. Cazelles, D.N. Freedman, S. Talmon, G. Wallis, H.-J. Fabry (Hg.), *Theologisches Wörterbuch zum Alten Testament*. Stuttgart/Berlin/Köln/Mainz 1973–
ThWNT	G. Kittel (Hg.), *Theologisches Wörterbuch zum Neuen Testament*. Stuttgart 1933–
TOTC	Tyndale Old Testament Commentaries
TSAJ	Texte und Studien zum antiken Judentum
TZ	Theologische Zeitschrift
VT	Vetus Testamentum
WBC	Word Biblical Commentary
WdF	Wege der Forschung
WMANT	Wissenschaftliche Monographien zum Alten und Neuen Testament
WUANT	Wissenschaftliche Untersuchungen zum Alten und Neuen Testament

ZAW	Zeitschrift für die Alttestamentliche Wissenschaft
ZDMG	Zeitschrift der Deutschen Morgenländischen Gesellschaft
ZDPV	Zeitschrift des Deutschen Palästina-Verein
ZThK	Zeitschrift für Theologie und Kirche
ZNTW	Zeitschrift für die neuttestamentliche Wissenschaft

CHAPTER ONE

GENERAL INTRODUCTION

1.1 Variant Versions of the Books of the Hebrew Bible

The impact of the discovery of the so-called 'Dead Sea Scrolls' found in the caves around Khirbet Qumran (1–11Q) and other sites close to the Dead Sea (Masada, Wadi Murabbaʿat, Naḥal Ḥever) on the study of the Hebrew Bible can hardly be overestimated.[1] These scrolls, or rather what has been preserved of them in fragments of varying size, date from the period of roughly 250 BCE to about 100 CE. They have offered us a rare glimpse into the religious pluriformity of Early Judaism, the socio-religious background of the world of the New Testament, the literary creativity of that period, and perhaps most importantly, the development of the books that came to constitute the canon of the Hebrew Bible or Old Testament.[2] Of the circa

---

[1] Among the numerous valuable surveys of these scrolls and their relevance to biblical studies are: F.M. Cross jr., *The Ancient Library of Qumran and Modern Biblical Studies*. New York 1958[1], 1961[2], 1995[3]; G. Vermes, *The Dead Sea Scrolls. Qumran in Perspective*. London 1977[1], 1994[3]; and P.W. Flint, J.C. VanderKam, *The Dead Sea Scrolls After Fifty Years. A Comprehensive Assessment*. Leiden/Boston/Köln 1998–1999.

[2] The question whether or not it is historically accurate to speak of a Hebrew Bible as a canonised entity in the period before 70 CE is a matter of the history of the canon; see e.g. E. Ulrich, The Canonical Process, Textual Criticism, and Latter Stages in the Composition of the Bible, in M. Fishbane, E. Tov (eds.), *Shaʿarei Talmon. Studies in Bible, Qumran, and the Ancient Near East Presented to Shemaryahu Talmon*. Winona Lake 1992, pp. 267–291, reprinted in E. Ulrich, *The Dead Sea Scrolls and the Origins of the Bible*. Grand Rapids/Cambridge/Leiden/Boston/Köln 1999, pp. 51–78, who denies the existence of such a fixed list before the late first century CE. For a different view see: R.T. Beckwith, Formation of the Hebrew Bible, in M.J. Mulder, H. Sysling (eds.), *Mikra. Text, Translation, Reading and Interpretation of the Hebrew Bible in Ancient Judaism and Early Christianity*. (CRINT II/1) Assen/Maastricht/Philadelphia 1988, pp. 39–86, who argues for a Hasmonean date of the canon. See also the various contributions on this subject in A. van der Kooij, K. van der Toorn (eds.), *Canonization and Decanonization. Papers Presented to the International Conference of the Leiden Institute for the Study of Religion (LISOR) held at Leiden 9–10 January 1997*. Leiden/Boston/Köln 1998; and L.M. McDonald, J.A. Sanders (eds.), *The Canon Debate*. Peabody 2002. For the sake of convenience I use the terms 'Bible' and 'biblical books' in order to refer to those Hebrew and Aramaic compositions that now form part of this canon.

eight hundred different scrolls, more than two hundred are copies of the books that are now found in the Hebrew Bible. Some of these manuscripts differ significantly from the standard version of that particular book. Hence, it is no exaggeration to state that the study of the history of the text of the Hebrew Bible, or in short textual criticism, has been revolutionised by the discovery of these scrolls.[3]

Before this find, the oldest manuscripts of the Hebrew Bible that had survived until the present day were no more than some thousand years old. Although this is still a considerable age for a manuscript, there is still a gap of circa 1500 years between the time when most of the books of the Hebrew Bible were written down and these manuscripts. The oldest complete manuscript of the entire Hebrew Bible, the Leningrad Codex, dates from 1008/1009 CE, and is still the basis for all modern scholarly editions of the Hebrew Bible. Other Hebrew manuscripts are somewhat older, but have not been preserved completely, such as the Aleppo Codex (circa 925 CE), the Cairo Codex (896 CE) and more fragmentary manuscripts from the Cairo Geniza (600–900 CE). All these Hebrew manuscripts differ from the Leningrad Codex only in details of vocalisation, accentuation and occasionally division into paragraphs. They are the product of very careful transmission (*masora* in Hebrew), and hence designated as a uniform, standardised entity, called the Masoretic Text (hereafter: MT).

Already before the discovery of the biblical scrolls in the caves of Qumran, Masada, Wadi Murabbaʿat, and Naḥal Ḥever, scholars assumed that in the period before circa 100 CE there must have been manuscripts or versions of the biblical books that differed from this standardised text. The Bible used by the Samaritan community (which comprises only the five books of Moses or 'Pentateuch', hereafter SamP) contains various additions as compared to MT, such as a different tenth commandment in Exod. 20/Deut. 5, based on a conflation of texts from Deut. 27:2–8 and 11:29–30, to offer sacrifices on Mount Gerizim, which happens to be the sacred mountain for this community. The Old Greek translation (named after the first translation project, i.e. that of the Pentateuch by allegedly seventy-two or seventy translators, hence the Latin name 'Septuaginta', here-

[3] See the introductions on the witnesses and the textual history of the Hebrew Bible, e.g. E. WÜRTHWEIN, *Der Text des Alten Testaments. Eine Einführung in die Biblia Hebraica*. Stuttgart 1952[1], 1988[5]; and E. Tov, *Textual Criticism of the Hebrew Bible*. Minneapolis/Assen/Maastricht 1992[1], 2001[2].

after LXX) of the various biblical books at times differs considerably from the MT. Since these translations are usually very literal and date from the period of roughly 250 BCE–100 CE,[4] the same period in which the Qumran biblical scrolls were copied, it has long been generally accepted that the Hebrew manuscript from which these Greek translations were made (designated as the Hebrew *Vorlage*) must from time to time have differed from the MT.

Since most of the biblical scrolls from Qumran date from before that period (circa 100 CE), they constitute direct witnesses to the text of the biblical books in their original languages (Hebrew and Aramaic).[5] Although the majority of the biblical scrolls found west of the Dead Sea still correspond closely to MT, there are nevertheless several fragments that differ significantly from MT and agree with LXX.

A well-known small but significant example is offered by the song of Moses in Deuteronomy 32, where in verses 8 and 43 two fragmentary Qumran-scrolls, 4QDeut[j] and 4QDeut[q], support the old Greek translation of an older variant version of the text that contained the more original reference to the 'sons of God' (בני אלהים/υἱοί θεοῦ), which for theological concerns has been omitted (verse 43) or altered in MT into the 'sons of Israel' (verse 8).[6] Whereas the MT in 32:8 states that the highest God (עליון) divided the nations 'according to the number of the sons of Israel', the tiny fragment from Qumran

---

[4] See the introductions to the LXX: H.B. SWETE, *An Introduction to the Old Testament in Greek*. Cambridge 1914², reprint Peabody 1989; S. JELLICOE, *The Septuagint and Modern Study*. Oxford 1968; and G. DORIVAL, M. HARL, O. MUNNICH, *La Bible grecque des Septante. Du judaïsme hellénistique au christianisme ancien*. Paris 1994²; and N. FERNÁNDEZ MARCOS, *The Septuagint in Context. Introduction to the Greek Versions of the Bible*. Leiden/Boston/Köln 2000.

[5] Surveys of the biblical scrolls and their importance for the study of the text of the Hebrew Bible are offered by the various contributions in F.M. CROSS, S. TALMON (eds.), *Qumran and the History of the Biblical Text*. Cambridge, Massachusetts/London 1975. See further A.S. VAN DER WOUDE, Pluriformity and Uniformity. Reflections on the Transmission of the Text of the Old Testament, in J.N. BREMMER, F. GARCÍA MARTÍNEZ (eds.), *Sacred History and Sacred Texts in Early Judaism. A Symposium in Honour of A.S. van der Woude*. (CBET 5) Kampen 1992, pp. 151–169; J. TREBOLLE BARRERA, *The Jewish Bible and the Christian Bible. An Introduction to the History of the Bible*. Grand Rapids/Cambridge/Leiden/Boston/Köln 1998; and É. PUECH, Qumrân et le texte de l'Ancien Testament, in A. LEMAIRE, M. SÆBØ (eds.), *Congress Volume. Oslo 1998*. (SVT 80) Leiden/Boston/Köln 2000, pp. 437–464.

[6] The text of 4QDeut[j] (Deut. 32:7–8) and 4QDeut[q] (Deut. 32:43) has been published by J.A. DUNCAN and P.W. SKEHAN and E. ULRICH in E. ULRICH, F.M. CROSS, S.W. CRAWFORD, J.A. DUNCAN, P.W. SKEHAN, E. TOV, J. TREBOLLE BARRERA (eds.), *Qumran Cave 4.IX. Deuteronomy, Joshua, Judges, Kings*. (DJD 14) Oxford 1995, pp. 75–92, 137–142. For a discussion of the relevance of these readings, see O. EIßFELDT, El and Yahweh, in *JSS* 1 (1956), pp. 25–37; D. BARTHÉLEMY, Les tiqquné sopherim

Cave 4, designated as 4QDeut[j], and the Greek text state that the nations were divided 'according to the number of the sons of the gods' (בני אלוהים). In verse 9 of the song, Yhwh is mentioned as the one to whom Israel was alloted. It is therefore not impossible that the text originally portrayed Yhwh as one of these deities, albeit the most prominent one, just as Baʿal figures in the Ugaritic myths as the most prominent of the deities (*bn ʾil*) that are under the ultimate authority of the father-god El. In another fragment of the same Song of Moses (Deut. 32:43), 4QDeut[q], these divine beings (כל אלהים) return in a passage in which they are commanded to bow before Yhwh, whereas in the shorter MT, it is the nations (גוים) that are admonished to bow down.

Apparently, the Qumran fragments and the Hebrew original or *Vorlage* from which the Greek translation of Deuteronomy was made attest to an older version of the song of Moses which was later adjusted in order to eliminate the heterodox concepts. This adjusted version came to supersede and replace the older version, and is attested by the MT and the younger Greek translations by Theodotion (θ'), Aquila (α'), and Symmachus (σ'), by the Targumim (Tg),[7] the Pešiṭta (Peš), and the Vulgate (Vg).

---

et la critique textuelle de l'Ancien Testament, in *Congress Volume. Bonn 1962.* (SVT 9) Leiden 1963, pp. 285–304; and the literature mentioned by P. Sanders, *The Provenance of Deuteronomy 32.* (OTS 37) Leiden/New York/Köln 1996, pp. 76–80, 154–160, 248–255, 426–429.

Barthélemy argued that the number of Jacob's sons in Gen. 46:19–27 and Exod. 1:5 were corrected from 75 (thus the Greek version, 4QGen-Exod[a], 4QExod[b] and Acts 7:15) to 70 as a result of the scribal correction in Deut. 32:8 by which the number of seventy was transferred from the 70 sons of El (cf. KTU 1.4:vi.46, which mentions the *šbʿm bn ʾṯrt*) to the sons of Israel/Jacob. In the most recent contribution to this issue, I. Himbaza, Dt 32,8, une correction tardive des scribes. Essai d'interprétation et de datation, in *Biblica* 83 (2002), pp. 527–548, contests this thesis. In his view, the corrections in Gen. 46:27 and Exod. 1:5 were made on the basis of Deut. 10:22. Himbaza does not contest the originality of the Qumran versions of Deut. 32:8.43, but argues that the motive behind the alteration was the wish to avoid the mythological motife of the mixture of mortals and heavenly beings (Gen. 6:1–4). The original polytheistic notion in Deut. 32:8.43 would already have been neutralized by the interpretation of the 'sons of God' as 'angels' (cf. Philo, Josephus, Ethiopian Enoch 6:2; Greek Enoch 18:4, Jubilees 5:1, Testament of Naphtali 3:5). Yet, the relation Himbaza sees between Gen. 6:1–4 and Deut. 32:8.43, was not made by the ancient interpreters of both texts. Furthermore, Himbaza's dating of the correction in Deut. 32 (first century CE), seems implausible, since already the Samaritan Pentateuch (generally assumed to have branched off the main textual tradition in the last century BCE) already contains the revised text of Deut. 32:8.43.

[7] Targum Jonathan seems to combine both traditions, see J.H. Tigay, *Deuteronomy.* (The JPS Torah Commentary) Philadelphia/Jerusalem 1996, pp. 513–518: 'Excursus 31: Text and Theology in Deuteronomy 32:8 and 43'.

More substantial are the large-scale additions to the text of the books of Exodus and Numbers as found in the MT, in both the Qumran scrolls 4QpaleoExod^{m} and 4QNum^{b} and the Samaritan Pentateuch. As stated, the Samaritan Pentateuch contains large additions to the text as found in MT, consisting of parallel material from other parts of the Pentateuch (such as the Samaritan tenth commandment in Exod. 20:17b). Before the discovery of the Qumran biblical scrolls it was generally assumed that these additions were the product of Samaritan scribes, since they created their own tenth commandment in Exod. 20:17 on the basis of passages from Deut. 27:2–8 and 11:29–30. Two Qumran scrolls, 4QpaleoExod^{m} and 4QNum^{b}, contain most of these additions, but interestingly enough lack this specific Samaritan commandment (4QpaleoExod^{m} column XXI). Since most of these additions do not express particular Samaritan interests, it is now generally assumed that these additions were made to the biblical text before the Samaritans adopted it and altered it for their own purposes.[8]

In the case of the book of Jeremiah the situation seems to be reversed. Here the MT is considerably longer than the text of the old Greek translation. Viewed in its entirety, LXX-Jeremiah not only lacks a large number of phrases, clauses and verses, but the material contained in the book is also arranged in a different order. Most conspicious is the fact that the oracles against the nations, Jer. 46–51, are in LXX-Jeremiah found in the middle of the book (LXX-Jer. 25:14–31), comparable to the structure of Isaiah, Ezekiel and Zephaniah, where the clusters of oracles against the nations are in the central sections of those books (Isa. 13–23; Ezek. 25–32; Zeph. 2). LXX-Jeremiah thus differs from MT-Jeremiah both in a quantitative (absence of passages) and a qualitative sense (different order of material). These two phenomena now seem to be supported by the evidence of two—be it exceedingly small—Qumran-scrolls, 4QJer^{b}

[8] See for instance the examples from the Samaritan Pentateuch of Exodus, discussed by J.H. Tigay, Conflation as a Redactional Technique, in J.H. Tigay (ed.), *Empirical Models for Biblical Criticism.* Philadelphia 1985, pp. 53–95. See for a general survey of the Samaritan Pentateuch J.D. Purvis, Samaritan Pentateuch, in *The Interpreter's Dictionary of the Bible. Supplementary Volume.* Nashville 1976, pp. 772–775, reprinted in F. Dexinger, R. Pummer (Hg.), *Die Samaritaner.* (WdF 604) Darmstadt 1992, pp. 408–417; E. Tov, Proto-Samaritan Texts and the Samaritan Pentateuch, in A.D. Crown (ed.), *The Samaritans.* Tübingen 1989, pp. 307–407; idem, *Textual Criticism of the Hebrew Bible*, pp. 80–100; idem, Rewritten Bible Compositions and Biblical Manuscripts, with Special Attention to the Samaritan Pentateuch, in *Dead Sea Discoveries* 5 (1998), pp. 334–354.

and 4QJer[d]. On the basis of these agreements it is likely that most of the other places where LXX-Jeremiah deviates from MT-Jeremiah—including the more substantial transposition of the whole complex of the oracles against the nations, and the substantial minus of MT-Jer. 33:14–26 in LXX-Jeremiah—, the Greek version likewise reflects a Hebrew text different from that preserved in MT-Jeremiah and all other textual witnesses, including the other Qumran-Jeremiah scrolls, 2QJer, 4QJer[a], 4QJer[c] (4QJer[e]?).

1.2 The Relevance to the History of the Text of the Hebrew Bible

One might add similar examples[9] from books such as Judges, Samuel, Kings, Ezekiel,[10] Psalms, Job,[11] Song of Songs, Esther[12] and Daniel. What is becoming increasingly clear is that within the study of the Hebrew Bible the traditional distinction between the two disciplines that focus on the history of the text, i.e., on the one hand, textual

---

[9] See for the following examples and relevant literature E. Tov, *Textual Criticism of the Hebrew Bible*, chapter 7 'Textual and Literary Criticism', Part B. 'The Evidence', pp. 319–349. Valuable surveys of the large-scale differences with MT presented by the various Greek 'LXX' translations are offered by H.B. Swete, *An Introduction to the Old Testament in Greek*, pp. 231–264; G. Dorival, M. Harl, O. Munnich, *La bible grecque des Septante*, pp. 173–182; J. Trebolle Barrera, *The Jewish and Christian Bible*, pp. 268–332, 368–404.

[10] LXX-Ezekiel lacks a number of small elements present in MT-Ezekiel. Moreover, in the oldest extant witness to this Greek translation, papyrus 967, the theologically important section Ezek. 36:23b–38 is absent, and chapters 36–40 have a different order, i.e. LXX-Ezek. 36:1–23, 38–39, 37, 40–48, see J. Lust, Ezekiel 36–40 in the Oldest Greek Manuscript, in *CBQ* 43 (1981), pp. 517–533; M.N. van der Meer, A New Spirit in an Old Corpus? Text-critical, Literary-Critical and Linguistic Observations regarding Ezekiel 36:16–38, in F. Postma, K. Spronk, E. Talstra (eds.), *The New Things. Eschatology in Old Testament Prophecy. Festschrift for Henk Leene.* (Amsterdamse Cahiers voor Exegese van de Bijbel en zijn Tradities. Supplement Series 3) Maastricht 2002, pp. 147–158.

[11] In the original Greek version of Job large parts of the poetic sections are absent, see e.g. the 'Studies in the LXX of the Book of Job' by H.M. Orlinsky, in *HUCA* 28 (1957), pp. 53–74; *HUCA* 29 (1958), pp. 229–271; *HUCA* 30 (1959), pp. 153–167; *HUCA* 32 (1961), pp. 239–268; *HUCA* 33 (1962), pp. 119–151; *HUCA* 35 (1964), pp. 57–78; *HUCA* 36 (1965), pp. 37–47.

[12] The Old Greek version of Esther contains long additional narratives as compared to MT-Esther, numbered A–F. The different models that seek to describe the literary development of the book of Esther are presented and critically reviewed by K. de Troyer, *The End of the Alpha-Text of Esther: translation and narrative technique in MT 8:1–17, LXX 8:1–17 and AT 7:14–41.* (SBL-SCS 48) Atlanta 1999; see further R. Kossmann, *Die Esthernovelle. Vom Erzählten zur Erzählung.* (VTS 79) Leiden/Boston/Köln 2000.

criticism, which concentrates on the transmission of the text, and on the other hand literary criticism,[13] which concentrates on the literary formation of the text, is fading. Instead, a new area of research is emerging that focuses on the overlap and interplay between these two aspects of the textual history of the biblical compositions. A short sketch of the models for this relationship as presented by two leading scholars in this field, Emanuel Tov and Eugene Ulrich, contrasted with the traditional model, may suffice.[14]

1.2.1 *The Traditional Model*

In the traditional model the textual development of biblical books is viewed as a process in which these two stages (textual and literary criticism) are clearly divided by a stage in which the literary development of the composition has culminated in the version that can be equated with the source common to all textual witnesses, the so-called *Urtext* of the book.

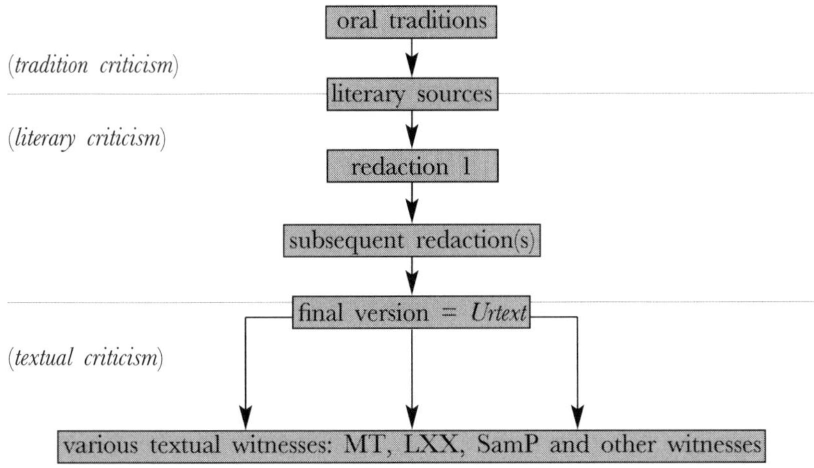

[13] I use the term 'literary criticism' diachronically to refer to the study of the historical development of the text of a composition from the Hebrew Bible, as opposed to 'tradition criticism', which concentrates on the earlier oral stages behind the text. In this study the term 'literary criticism' thus equals the German 'Literarkritik' and refers to that discipline that 'is concerned with most of the essential questions pertaining to the biblical books (origin, date, structure, authorship, authenticity, and uniformity), and it thus deals with various presumed stages in the development of the biblical books', thus E. Tov, *Textual Criticism of the Hebrew Bible*, p. 313. See further e.g. H. Barth, O.H. Steck, *Exegese des Alten Testaments*[9], pp. 30–39: '§ 4. Literarkritik'.

[14] See further e.g. H.-J. Stipp, Das Verhältnis von Textkritik und Literarkritik in

According to this model, the aim of textual criticism is to reconstruct the original text of a biblical composition on the basis of the extant textual witnesses or on the basis of conjectural emendation, with as central underlying assumption the idea that all textual variation can ultimately be reduced to one single hypothetical original text or *Urtext*.[15] The pluriformity of textual witnesses is usually explained as the result of a long process of manifold scribal errors and incidental manipulations of this common source text.[16] Once the secondary elements and scribal corruptions have been removed and the 'original text' has been restored, a second phase of 'higher' critical investigation, that is of the overall historical process of literary formation of the book ('literary criticism'), or more in particular its distinctive redactions ('redaction criticism'),[17] can be carried out.

Although few scholars would argue that the *Urtext* could be fully identified with the text as it was originally conceived and first formulated by its original author(s), most scholars nevertheless regard the hypothetical *Urtext* from which all textual variants ultimately stem as the final product or stage in which the formative process has been closed. As a result, textual criticism and literary criticism are here clearly distinguishable areas of research, and refer to separate phases of the development of the text.

This model may still be valid for those books in which the divergencies between the oldest textual witnesses are only minor com-

---

neueren alttestamentlichen Veröffentlichungen, in *BZNF* 34/1 (1990), pp. 16–37; idem, Textkritik—Literarkritik—Textentwicklung. Überlegungen zur exegetischen Aspektsystematik, in *ETL* 66 (1990), pp. 143–159, who challenges this bipartite division.

[15] See for example the definition of 'Das Ziel der Textkritik' by E. WÜRTHWEIN, *Der Text des Alten Testaments*, p. 102: 'In der Arbeit der Textkritik sucht sie [d.h. die Wissenschaft vom Alten Testament] alle Änderungen aufzuspüren und den ältesten erreichbaren Text wiederherzustellen.' (in the fifth edition significantly modified). See further E. Tov, *Textual Criticism of the Hebrew Bible*, chapter 5: 'Aim and Procedures of Textual Criticism', pp. 287–291.

[16] See the introductions on textual criticism of the Hebrew Bible, e.g. E. Tov, *Textual Criticism of the Hebrew Bible*, chapter 4: 'The Copying and Transmitting of the Biblical Text', pp. 199–285. Exemplary for this approach to textual criticism of the Hebrew Bible is F. DELITZSCH, *Die Lese- und Schreibfehler im Alten Testament nebst den dem Schrifttexte einverleibten Randnoten Klassifiziert*. Berlin/Leipzig 1920.

[17] See H. BARTH, O.H. STECK, *Exegese des Alten Testaments*[9], pp. 50–55: '§ 6 Redaktionsgeschichtliche Fragestellung', and R. KNIERIM, Criticism of Literary Features, Form, Tradition, and Redaction, in D.A. KNIGHT, G.M. TUCKER (eds.), *The Hebrew Bible and its Modern Interpreters*. Philadelphia 1985, pp. 123–165, especially pp. 150–153.

pared to the divergencies described above (Genesis for example), or evidently the result of a secondary reformulation[18] of the older composition (as in LXX-Isaiah).[19] The large-scale variants presented above, however, are clearly not the result of incidental scribal corruptions or manipulations, but amount to different editions of the same composition. In other words, the process of literary formation was not completely closed at the time when the oldest extant textual witnesses were written. By establishing the chronological relation between these distinct editions, textual scholarship finds itself operating in the realm of literary criticism, in which a glimpse is offered of the fascinating process of the literary development of these books.

Whereas in the case of the conflated version of the Pentateuch as attested by SamP and 4QpaleoExod[m] and 4QNum[b] the relative priority of the shorter text as contained in MT and all other textual witnesses is obvious, the intruiging question arises whether there are books in which the received proto-MT can be held to be the younger re-edition, and whether some of the Qumran scrolls together with the Old Greek translation can be held to reflect the older edition of the biblical book.

1.2.2 *The Theory of E. Tov*

Emanuel Tov argues that the literary history of the book of Jeremiah presents evidence to the latter category.[20] In his view the process of literary growth of the book is attested by the considerable quantitative difference between the older and shorter edition reflected in LXX-Jeremiah, 4QJer[d] and 4QJer[b] and the younger expanded edition reflected in MT-Jeremiah and already in the oldest extant witness of that book, 4QJer[a].

[18] I use the term 'reformulation' for a relatively modest alteration of the older text in which the structure and contents of the older text have basically been left intact as opposed to a 'rewritten version', which in my vocabulary points to a more severe alteration of either structure or contents of the older text.

[19] See e.g. A. van der Kooij, *The Oracle of Tyre. The Septuagint of Isaiah 23 as Version and Vision.* (SVT 71) Leiden/Boston/Köln 1998.

[20] See especially E. Tov, *Textual Criticism of the Hebrew Bible*, pp. 313–349; idem, *The Text-critical Use of the Septuagint.* Jerusalem 1997², pp. 237–263: chapter 8: 'The Contribution of the LXX to the Literary Criticism of the Bible'.

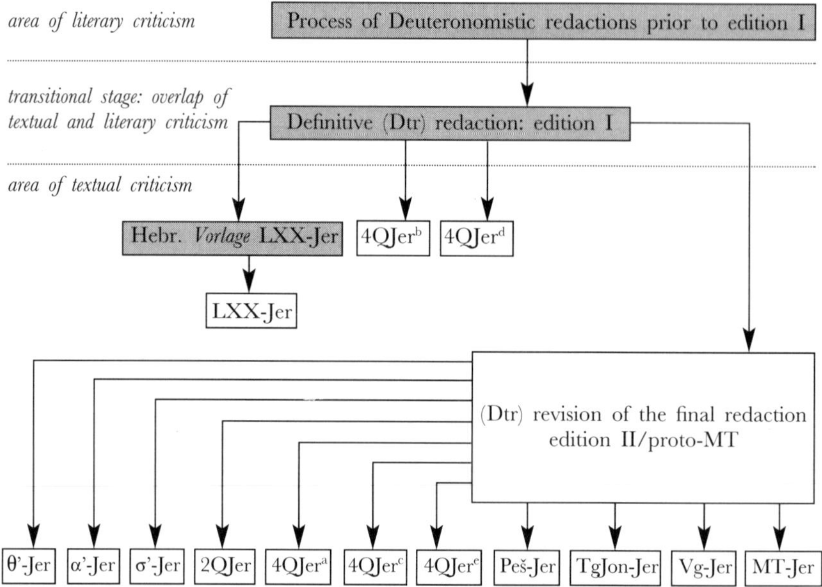

According to Tov, the Second Temple scribes responsible for the transmission of the text of that composition allowed themselves to introduce some—usually minor—elements for the sake of clarification and emphasis, adding headings, new details, such as the proper names and appositions, and in the case of Jer. 33:14–26 incorporating authentic material of the prophet.[21] Since a number of the pluses of the presumed edition II as opposed to the earlier edition can be termed Deuteronomistic formulaic language,[22] Tov sees a point of

---

[21] E. Tov, L'incidence de la critique textuelle sur la critique littéraire dans le Livre de Jérémie, in *RB* 79 (1972), pp. 189–199; idem, Some Aspects of the Textual and Literary History of the Book of Jeremiah, in P.-M. Bogaert (éd.), *Le livre de Jérémie. Le prophète et son milieu, les oracles et leur transmission.* (BETL 54) Leuven 1981[1], 1997[2], pp. 145–167; and idem, The Literary History of the Book of Jeremiah in the Light of Its Textual History, in J.-H. Tigay (ed.), *Empirical Models for Biblical Criticism*, pp. 211–237, reprinted in E. Tov, *The Greek and Hebrew Bible. Collected Essays on the Septuagint.* (SVT 72) Leiden/Boston/Köln 1999, pp. 363–384.

The number of studies on this subject has grown enormously since the early seventies, see C. Dogniez (ed.), *Bibliographie de la Septante (1970–1993).* (SVT 60) Leiden/New York/Köln 1995, pp. 259–266; H.-J. Stipp, *Das masoretische und alexandrinische Sondergut des Jeremiabuches. Textgeschichtlicher Rang, Eigenarten, Triebkräfte.* (OBO 136) Freiburg/Göttingen 1994; and P.-M. Bogaert, Le Livre de Jérémie en perspective: Les deux rédactions antiques selon les travaux en cours, in *RB* 101 (1994), pp. 363–406.

[22] Hence the title 'L'incidence de la critique textuelle sur la critique littéraire' See the list of examples collected under this heading in E. Tov, L'incidence, pp.

contact, or rather *overlap* between these textual data and the commonly accepted thesis of a Deuteronomistic redaction of the book of Jeremiah.[23] There is thus some form of continuity between the Deuteronomistic edition(s) preceding the final edition I and the second edition, the latter being a last product of the Deuteronomistic School, or merely that of an epigone of that school.[24]

In his view, a similar model could be applied to the literary history of the books of Samuel, Ezekiel and Joshua, since in all these cases the LXX reflects an edition that *preceded* the edition as attested by MT and other witnesses. Developments *subsequent* to MT, such as reflected by the Samaritan Pentateuch and its Qumran parallels, 4QpaleoExod^{m} and 4QNum^{b}, or additions of new material to the Greek versions of the books of Esther and Daniel should in his view not be termed 'editions' but rather described as 'harmonizing or midrashic developments.'

1.2.2 *The Theory of E. Ulrich*

This last point of view is contested by Eugene Ulrich, who envisages a process of consecutive variant literary editions, in which the literary edition that eventually became the authoritative one is just one item in a long sequence. Ulrich refers to commonly accepted views concerning the formation of the biblical books as a long dialectical process from experience to textual fixation and reformulation, in order to accommodate the older text to new experiences.[25] The multiple literary editions of the biblical books attested by the Qumran, Old Greek, and Samaritan evidence are only the continuation of this 'canonical' process. The edition reflected by MT was just one of the many successive literary editions which happened to become the authoritative 'canonical' version after the destruction of the Second Temple and the Qumran community, and after the creative process of reworking the bibical text came to an abrupt halt by the fixation

196ff.; idem, Some Aspects, p. 164; idem, The Literary History of Jeremiah, p. 233 (= *The Greek and Hebrew Bible*, pp. 379–380).

[23] See e.g. S. Herrmann, *Jeremia. Der Prophet und das Buch.* (EdF 271) Darmstadt 1990, chapter III: 'Die kritische Analyse des Jeremiabuches', pp. 53–181.

[24] See e.g. E. Tov, L'incidence, pp. 198–199; and idem, The Literary History of Jeremiah, p. 220.

[25] See the essays collected in E. Ulrich, *The Dead Sea Scrolls and the Origins of the Bible.*

of a canon.[26] Thus, with respect to the development of the book of Exodus, for instance, the following editorial stages may be distinguished:

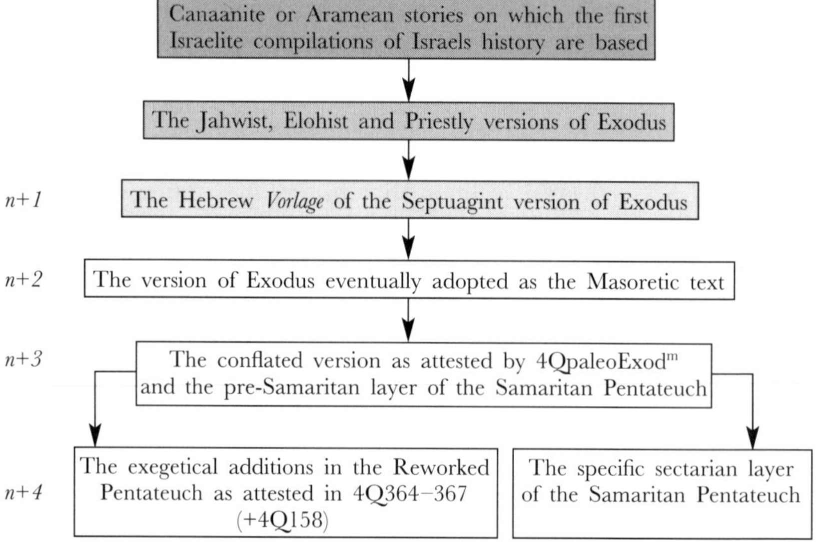

Since the composition designated as 4QReworked Pentateuch repeats substantial parts of the text of the Pentateuch, especially in the version attested by SamP, and weaves in a large number of exegetical elements, Ulrich is inclined to consider this new composition yet another literary variant of the *torah*.[27] As a result, the traditional border lines between 'lower' (i.e. textual) criticism and 'higher' (i.e. literary) criticism and between biblical compositions and rewritten or

[26] E. Ulrich, Multiple Literary Editions: Reflections toward a Theory of the History of the Biblical Text, in D.W. Parry, S.D. Ricks (eds.), *Current Research and Technological Developments on the Dead Sea Scrolls. Conference on the Texts from the Judaean Desert, Jerusalem, 30 April 1995.* (STDJ 20) Leiden/New York/Köln 1996, pp. 78–105, especially p. 90 (= *The Origins of the Bible*, pp. 103–104).

[27] E. Ulrich, The Dead Sea Scrolls and the Biblical Text, in P.W. Flint, J.C. VanderKam (eds.), *The Dead Sea Scrolls after Fifty Years*, pp. 88–89. Ulrich uses the siglum *n*+ in order to indicate that the process of re-editing the biblical compositions is not restricted to the editions still preserved in Qumran, LXX and SamP, but preceded by an unknown number of editions (a–m) no longer extant, see E. Ulrich, Pluriformity in the Biblical Text, Text Groups, and Questions of Canon, in J. Trebolle Barrera, L. Vegas Montaner (eds.), *The Madrid Qumran Congress: Proceedings of the International Congress on the Dead Sea Scrolls, Madrid, 18–21 March 1991.* (STDJ 11) Leiden/Madrid 1992, pp. 23–41, p. 39ff., especially note 49. (= *The Origins of the Bible*, p. 97).

para-biblical compositions should make way for a long historical continuum of successive fixations and reformulations of the sacred narratives and themes.

1.3 The Relevance to the Literary History of the Biblical Books: Challenges and Obstacles

The important consequence of these theories is that the variant editions provide an 'empirical basis' for the otherwise speculative and controversial diachronic 'biblical criticism'.[28] If these variant versions of the biblical composition presented the missing links between, on the one hand, the process of compilation and extensive editing of these books and on the other hand the process of meticulous copying of these writings, such an overlap of data from textual criticism and literary criticism would allow for a more solid and verifiable description of the literary history of the biblical books. To put it still differently: where previous biblical scholarship had to operate on the basis of internal criteria such as consistency, coherence of a text, similar and contrastive idioms and concepts etc. in order to explain the irregularities and contradictions in the biblical compositions resulting from a complex formation process, it would now possess evidence vindicating the theories about the literary growth of the biblical books.

Nevertheless, such far-reaching conclusions cannot be drawn without tackling a number of difficulties and problems.

For one thing, the evidence on which these theories of textual evidence for literary-critical models are built, is not unambiguous: almost all of the Qumran material is extremely scanty and many of the alleged variant versions are based on reconstructions of the scrolls. In the case of the literary history of the book of Jeremiah, the longest book of the Hebrew Bible, the Qumran evidence for a Hebrew version deviating from MT is based on no more than 111 and 213 identifiable extant characters for 4QJer^{b} and 4QJer^{d}, respectively.

The LXX version of the biblical books has been preserved completely, but here we are dealing with the problem that the oldest complete codex of most of the Septuagint books (Codex Vaticanus)

---

[28] After the title of the collection of important essays dealing with this topic edited by J.H. Tigay, *Empirical Models for Biblical Criticism.*

is half a millennium younger (fourth century CE) than the original translation of the oldest translated books (the Pentateuch, which was translated most probably during the third century BCE). As we know from many data (among which the Greek biblical texts found at Qumran and Naḥal Ḥever), the text of the Greek biblical books was altered and revised in order to adapt the Greek text to the then current standard Hebrew text. Among them are the Kaige-Theodotion revision around the turn of the era, the Greek revision amounting to a new translation by Aquila in the first century CE, and the Hexaplaric revision by Origen in the third century CE. Another tendency observable in the transmission of the Greek version(s) of the Hebrew Bible was the wish to improve the literary quality of the stilted translations of several books (by Symmachus in the second century CE or Lucian in the fourth century CE). As a consequence, the original text of the Greek translation has to be reconstructed before assertions concerning its Hebrew *Vorlage* can be made.

Even more problematic is the *evaluation of the (original) Greek translation* and the degree of faithfulness with which the translator rendered his Hebrew parent text. The level of literalness in the translation of the biblical books varies from book to book and occasionally from section to section within the book (for instance in the books of Samuel-Kings and Jeremiah and Ezekiel, where the hands of different translators can be detected). The reconstruction of a Hebrew *Vorlage* differing from the MT becomes more problematic as the translation ostentatively departs from the Hebrew text in order to produce a coherent and dynamic equivalent reformulation, as required by the translation of a Semitic text into a Indo-European language and culture,[29] or in order to apply the old text to the socio-religious context of the translator (as can be observed in the Greek translation of the book of Isaiah).[30]

Even when a deviant Hebrew text can be reconstructed with certainty behind the Greek version, some questions still remain. For one thing, only in a few exceptional cases does the assumed edito-

---

[29] See e.g. J.W. WEVERS, The Interpretative Character and Significance of the Septuagint Version, in M. SÆBØ, C. BREKELMANS, M. HARAN (eds.), *Hebrew Bible/Old Testament. The History of Its Interpretation. Volume I.* Göttingen 1996, pp. 84–107 (with full bibliography), and the introductory statements by the same author to his several notes to the Greek Pentateuch.

[30] See e.g. A. VAN DER KOOIJ, *Die alten Textzeugen des Jesajabuches* (OBO 35) Göttingen/Fribourg 1981.

rial activity reflected by the textual data take the shape of a clearly recognizable large-scale quantitative reworking of the older material. In the case of the book of Jeremiah, for instance, the alternative edition attested by LXX (with support of 4QJer^{d}) is said to be some 7% shorter than the longer MT version, but one can only reach this figure by counting a large number of isolated pluses in MT of only a few words each. The question then arises what constitutes the binding element between these isolated elements, or: how can we be sure that the isolated pluses in MT are the result of a comprehensive project of re-editing the biblical book rather than an elusive process of interpolation of these elements over a long period of time?

Another question is that of the *chronological priority* among the alleged variant versions of the same composition, and the validity of the criteria to determine whether a version of a biblical composition not only differs on an editorial level from the edition as attested in MT, but also precedes that edition. When compared with the MT (and LXX) edition of the Pentateuch, the Samaritan Pentateuch and its pre-Samaritan forerunners 4QpaleoExod^{m} and 4QNum^{b}, as well as the reworking of the material in 4QReworked Pentateuch, undeniably attest to a process of editorial activity of the material in Genesis–Deuteronomy, but in all these cases it is clear that the version of the Pentateuch as contained in MT is the more original. If for instance one can indeed reconstruct two variant editions of a book like Jeremiah, how can one be sure that the canonical version as contained in MT resulted *from* rather than *in* the version attested by LXX and 4QJer$^{b.d}$?[31]

Tov provides an answer to these questions by means of a model of literary growth in which the more expanded version is the younger.

---

[31] Recently a number of studies have appeared in which the *communis opinio* concerning the textual history of the book of Jeremiah is challenged and reversed, see e.g. C.R. Seitz, The Prophet Moses and the Canonical Shape of Jeremiah, in *ZAW* 101 (1989), pp. 3–27; A. Rofé, The Arrangement of the Book of Jeremiah, in *ZAW* 101 (1989), pp. 390–398; and idem, Not Exile but Annihilation for Zedekiah's People: The Purport of Jeremiah 52 in the Septuagint, in L.J. Greenspoon, O. Munnich (eds.), *VIII Congress of the International Organization for Septuagint and Cognate Studies. Paris 1992.* (SBL-SCS 41) Atlanta 1995, pp. 165–170; G. Fischer, Zum Text des Jeremiabuches, in *Bib* 78 (1997), pp. 305–328; and idem, Jeremia 52—Ein Schlüssel zum Jeremiabuch, in *Bib* 79 (1998), pp. 333–359; and A. van der Kooij, Zum Verhältnis von Textkritik und Literarkritik. Überlegungen anhand einiger Beispiele, in J.A. Emerton (ed.), *Congress Volume. Cambridge 1995.* (SVT 66) Leiden/New York/Köln 1997, pp. 185–202.

Although this criterion offers a plausible explanation for the various stages in the Pentateuch (MT—conflated version as attested by SamP, 4QpaleoExod[m], 4QNum[b]—specific pro-Samaritan redaction) and books such as Daniel and Esther, there is also textual evidence for a deliberate shortening the biblical text, as attested not only by Deut. 32:8.43, but also by Canticles[32] in 4QCant[a] and 4QCant[b], and on the level of the translation of the biblical books into Greek by LXX-Job, where long difficult poetic Hebrew sections were not translated in the first instance.[33]

Ultimately, the question of the *relation between textual criticism and literary criticism* is at stake. Since there is a wide variety of theories concerning the origin and development of the biblical books, one may ask to which theory of literary development the textual data offer evidence. Should theories concerning the development of the biblical books be made dependent upon the often scanty and ambiguous textual evidence? Or conversely, should the diffuse variety of textual data be explained on the basis of a well-tested theory of literary developments leading up to their final form? Or: do both methods of approaching the literary/textual development of the same composition remain valid in their own right, and should the results of these distinct approaches be compared only at a second stage?

In any case, no version of—for example—the book of Isaiah has been found among the Dead Sea Scrolls or preserved in an ancient translation without the chapters that are generally ascribed to Deutero-Isaiah (40–55) or Trito-Isaiah (56–66). By the time the Qumran scrolls of Isaiah were copied and the book had been translated into Greek, the long and complex formative process was already completed. As for the book of Jeremiah, in which scholars since the end of the 19th century have detected a secondary, Deuteronomistic stratum, it is evident that not only the longer MT-version, but also the shorter LXX and 4QJer[b.d] versions reflect this secondary stratum. The same can be said of the historical books, starting with the Pentateuch and its commonly accepted Priestly and Deuteronomistic strata. Does the fact that these broad theories find no support in

[32] See E. Tov, Excerpted and Abbreviated Biblical Texts from Qumran, in *RdQ* 16 (1995), pp. 581–600.

[33] Thus according to the *communis opinio*, voiced by G. Dorival, M. Harl, O. Munnich, *La Bible grecque des Septante*, p. 179.

textual evidence invalidate these theories, or conversely render the textual witnesses basically insignificant with respect to the question of the process of literary formation of these books? Or is it possible to offer a reconstruction of the history of the biblical text which takes into account both the data from the textual witnesses and those based upon literary-critical observations of the same text?

One thing is clear: the situation differs from composition to composition. No uniform model can be applied to all books of the Hebrew Bible and their ancient witnesses. For that reason, each biblical composition should first be studied in its own right before parallels with the history of the text of another biblical composition are drawn. This study will therefore concentrate on one composition from the Hebrew Bible not explicitely mentioned above, i.e. the book of Joshua.

1.4 The Textual History of the Book of Joshua as a Test Case

The text of the book of Joshua provides a fascinating but complex test case to the theory of coalescence of data derived from the oldest extant witnesses, and literary-critical observations and theories. The Old Greek translation of that book differs from the MT in numerous instances. Not only are relatively large segments absent from LXX (e.g. MT-Josh. 6:3b–4.7; 8:11b–13.26; 20:4–6), the Greek version also contains sizable passages absent from MT (e.g. LXX-Josh. 6:26b, 16:10b, 24:33a–b), or has a content strikingly different from the MT version (Josh. 5:2–9, to be discussed in chapter 7 below). The section narrating Joshua's erection of an altar on Mount Ebal and the proclamation of the *torah* (MT-Josh. 8:30–35) is of special interest, since the passage is found at different positions in both LXX (after 9:2) and, as has recently become clear, in 4QJosh[a] before Josh. 5:2 (to be discussed in chapter 9 below). Textual and literary-critical data seem to overlap here, since its position between Josh. 8:29 and 9:1 in MT disturbs the context and the sequence of Josh. 8:29 to 9:1 (9:3). The latter example especially makes clear that there is every reason to assume that the divergencies between the oldest textual witnesses of this biblical composition, LXX-Joshua, 4QJosh[a], and MT-Joshua, are the result of editorial activity. On the basis of these data and their analogies with the textual data from the book of Jeremiah, E. Tov refers to the book of Joshua as a second example of overlap between textual and literary criticism.[34] In the same way E. Ulrich views the editions of the book as attested in 4QJosh[a] and LXX-Joshua as redactional precursors of the MT version.[35]

Still, as the following discussion of previous research on the redaction-critical value of especially LXX-Joshua and 4QJosh[a] will make clear, it is not altogether evident that these witnesses can without reservations be held to represent an older stage in the formation process of the book, since the character of the translation is not strictly literal and since the relative chronological priority among the versions is disputable from passage to passage. Thus, the question that the present study addresses, is the following: *Do the oldest extant witnesses of the book of Joshua reflect a stage in the formation of that book both different from and anterior to the version that came to be the canonised Masoretic text of the book?*

This question is a rather recent one within the study of the Hebrew Bible in general and the book of Joshua in particular, especially since one of the major deviations from MT, i.e. the different position of MT-Josh. 8:30–35, has become known only recently (1992).[36] The last decade has witnessed a rapidly growing number of studies (both articles and dissertations) devoted to this question. As a result, this recent type of research in the book of Joshua is still in its initial stages. Of course the differences between LXX-Joshua and MT-Joshua had been noted before and evaluated in different ways during previous generations of biblical scholarship, but studies addressing the question of the redaction-critical value of this witness remained restricted in number, have been written in hardly accessible publications, and up to now have not been collected in a comprehensive history of research.

For that reason it is necessary and illuminating to present a critical review of previous research regarding our topic. Insights from scholars of these previous generations are still valuable, indispensable, and sometimes decisive for recent assessments. Their studies will be presented and discussed in the following chapter (chapter 2.2), after a paragraph devoted to the reconstruction of the original

[34] E. Tov, *Textual Criticism of the Hebrew Bible*, pp. 327–332.

[35] See e.g. E. Ulrich, The Dead Sea Scrolls and the Biblical Text, p. 85, 89–90.

[36] In that year E. Ulrich presented his preliminary publication of 4QJoshua[a] to the First Meeting of the International Organization for Qumran Studies; it was published two years later in G.J. Brooke, F. García Martínez (eds.), *New Qumran Texts and Studies.* (STDJ 15) Leiden/New York/Köln 1994, pp. 89–104.

text of LXX-Joshua, an indispensable related but distinct field of research (chapter 2.1). In the absence of a modern critical *editio maior* of LXX-Joshua in the standard Göttingen edition of the Septuagint, the current editions of LXX-Joshua will be discussed and evaluated. A description of the Qumran material for the book of Joshua will be offered in chapter 3. Chapters 4 and 5 further develops the method by which several relevant passages from the book (Joshua 1, 5:2–12, 8:1–29, 8:30–35) may be assessed (chapters 6–9). The final chapter offers conclusions with respect to the history of the text of Joshua and the relation between textual and literary criticism.

CHAPTER TWO

THE SEPTUAGINT OF JOSHUA

In the study of the relation between textual and literary criticism in the book of Joshua, the Old Greek or Septuagint version of that book takes a prominent place. Unlike the scanty 4QJosh[a], 4QJosh[b], and XJoshua fragments, which together do not even make up 0.5% of the whole text of the book (see chapter 3 below), it has been preserved completely, and unlike the other ancient Versions of the book, such as the revisions of the Greek text by Aquila, Symmachus, and Theodotion,[1] and the Aramaic (Targum Jonathan),[2] Syriac (Pešiṭta)[3]

---

[1] Pending a new publication of the Hexaplaric material (see R.B. ter Haar Romeny, P.J. Gentry, Towards a New Collection of Hexaplaric Material for the Book of Genesis, in B.A. Taylor (ed.), *X Congress of the International Organization for Septuagint and Cognate Studies. Oslo, 1998.* (SBL-SCS 51) Atlanta 2001, pp. 285–299), the most complete collection of the remains of these Greek versions is the one by F. Field, *Origenis Hexaplorum quae supersunt; sive veterum interpretum graecorum in totus Vetus Testamentum fragmenta* I–II. Oxford 1875. For a discussion of the revisions of the Old Greek version of Joshua by Theodotion, Aquila, and Symmachus, see L.J. Greenspoon, *Textual Studies in the Book of Joshua.* (HSM 28) Chico 1983; idem, Theodotion, Aquila, Symmachus, and the Old Greek of Joshua, in *Eretz-Israel* 16 (H.M. Orlinsky Volume) Jerusalem 1982, pp. 82*–91*; and K. Bieberstein, *Lukian und Theodotion im Josuabuch. Mit einem Beitrag zu den Josuarollen von Ḫirbet Qumrān.* (Biblische Notizen. Beihefte 7) München 1994.

[2] A. Sperber (ed.), *The Bible in Aramaic based on Old Manuscripts and Printed Texts. Volume II. The Former Prophets according to Targum Jonathan.* Leiden/New York/Köln 1992. An introduction to Targum Jonathan of Joshua is provided by D.J. Harrington, s.j., A.J. Saldarini, *Targum Jonathan of the Former Prophets. Introduction, Translation and Notes.* (The Aramaic Bible 10) Edinburgh 1987, pp. 1–15. Among the mediaeval Hebrew manuscripts found in the Cairo Geniza, fragments of another Targum has been found, see H. Fahr, U. Glessmer, *Jordandurchzug und Beschneidung als Zurechtweisung in einem Targum zu Josua 5 (Edition des MS T.-S. B 13,12).* (Orientalia Biblica et Christiana 3) Glückstadt 1991. This Targum offers a paraphrase of Josh. 5:2–6:1 and is probably of a relatively young date, although Fahr and Gleßmer argue for a pre-Christian origin of the Targum.

[3] J. Erbes (ed.), *Joshua.* (The Old Testament in Syriac according to the Peshiṭta Version; Part II, fascicle 1b) Leiden 1991. The Pešiṭta of Joshua has been examined by H. Mager, *Die Peschiṭṭho zum Buche Josua.* (Freiburger Theologische Studien 9) Freiburg im Breisgau 1916. Differences between Peš-Josh. 1–5 and the other ancient versions have been examined in full detail by J.E. Erbes, *The Peshitta and the Versions. A Study of the Peshitta Variants in Joshua 1–5 in Relation to Their Equivalents in the Ancient Versions.* (Studia Semitica Upsaliensia 16) Uppsala 1999, see also the critical review article by C.G. den Hertog in *OLZ* 95 (2000), col. 446–452.

and Latin (Vulgate)[4] translations, which all follow the Masoretic text closely, LXX-Joshua contains large and significant variants with MT. For that reason, LXX-Joshua is together with 4QJosh[a] the most important witness to a possible stage in the textual history of Joshua that would precede the stage attested by MT and the other younger Versions. These variants have been discussed ever since the Dutch humanist scholar Andreas Masius published in 1573 a commentary on the book of Joshua in which he printed the Hebrew and Greek text next to each other, and studied the divergencies between these two texts.[5] Especially since the end of the nineteenth century, the redaction-critical value of LXX-Joshua has been the subject of several studies, which will be presented below (section 2.2). Nevertheless, before the character of this version and its redaction-critical value can be assessed, it is necessary to reconstruct the original Greek text itself, since the oldest manuscripts of LXX-Joshua are some five centuries younger than the alleged original Greek translation as it left the hands of the translator.[6]

2.1 Editions of the Septuagint of Joshua

Apart from the recently discovered manuscript Schøyen 2648 (Rahlfs number 816) that probably dates from the beginning of the third century AD and contains the LXX text of Josh. 9:27–11:3,[7] and a

---

[4] The manual edition by R. Weber, o.s.b. (ed.), *Biblia iuxta vulgatam versionem*. Stuttgart 1983[3] has been used in this study. Occasionally the *editio maior*: *Biblia sacra iuxta latinam vulgatam versionem ad codicum fidem iussu Pii PP. XI cura et studio monachorum abbatiae pontificae sancti Hieronymi in urbe ordinis sancti Benedicti edita: Libri Iosue Iudicum Ruth ex interpretatione sancti Hieronymi cum praefatione et variis capitulorum seriebus*. Roma 1939 has been consulted (section 7.6.8.1).

[5] A. Masius, *Josuae imperatoris historia illustrata atque explicata*. Antverpiae 1573. This commentary is divided into two parts, [1] a text-critical section in which the Hebrew and Greek texts of Joshua have been printed on opposite pages (pp. 10–117), followed by a large section of 'Annotationes quibus editionis graecae historiae Iosuae ratio modusque omnis, per capita et versus explicatur', in which Masius offered text-critical remarks on the reconstruction of the original Greek text on the basis of a manuscript of the Syro-Hexapla that has been lost since Masius' days (see below), and [2] an exegetical part with separate page numbering (pp. 1–350). This second part has been incorporated into the Catholic *Scripturae Sacrae Cursus Completus* series in volumes 7 and 8 (Paris 1838). References in this study to the second section are made on the basis of this more accessible re-edition.

[6] It is assumed throughout this study that the Greek version of Joshua is the product of a single translator, as is the common view with respect to LXX-Joshua.

[7] See K. de Troyer, The Schøyen Papyrus of Joshua, in R. Pintaudi (ed.), *Greek*

small papyrus fragment that contains only remains of LXX-Josh. 4:23–5:1,[8] the oldest complete manuscript of Joshua in Greek is the fourth-century CE Codex Vaticanus (B). The text of Joshua of this witness has remained relatively free from the Hexaplaric and Lucianic revisions and has served as the basis of most of the editions of the Septuagint. Although this manuscript is generally recognized to be the most important witness to the original Greek text of Joshua, it is not free from textual corruptions. The original Greek text must therefore be reconstructed on the basis of all extant witnesses.[9] In the case of the Greek Joshua these witnesses include some eight majuscule manuscripts,[10] some 100 minuscule manuscripts, quotations in patristic literature (especially the works of Justin, Eusebius, Origen, Theodoret,[11] and further John Chrysostom),[12] and the daughter translations, i.e. the Sahidic (Sah or sa) version,[13] the Old Latin

Papyri in the Schøyen Collection. Volume 1: Literary Texts. Oslo (Hermes Academic Publishing) forthcoming.

[8] The fourth-century CE Oxyrhynchus Papyrus no. 1168, published by A.S. HUNT (ed.), *The Oxyrhynchus Papyri. part IX.* London 1914, pp. 4–5.

[9] A list of these witnesses with a synsopsis of the sigla used for them in the various critical editions is offered by K. BIEBERSTEIN, *Lukian und Theodotion im Josuabuch. Mit einem Beitrag zu den Josuarollen von Hirbet Qumran.* (Biblische Notizen. Beihefte 7) München 1994. The now authoritative system of sigla and numbers developed by A. RAHLFS, *Verzeichnis der griechischen Handschriften des Alten Testaments.* (MSU 2) Berlin 1915 and used in the Göttingen editions, has been adopted here as well.

[10] These majuscles are codex Vaticanus [B], the most important witness, and further the codices Alexandrinus [A], Ambrosianus [F], Colberto-Sarravianus [G], Lipsiensis/Tischendorfianus [K], Coislinianus [M], Basiliano-Vaticanus [V], and finally the Washington [W] manuscript.

[11] See S. SIPILÄ, Theodoret of Cyrrhus and the Book of Joshua—Theodoret's *Quaestiones* Revisited, in *Textus* 19 (1998), pp. 157–170.

[12] See S. SIPILÄ, John Chrysostom and the Book of Joshua, in B. TAYLOR (ed.), *IX. Congress of the International Organization for Septuagint and Cognate Studies. Cambridge 1995.* (SBL-SCS 45) Atlanta 1997, pp. 329–354.

[13] See K.-H. SCHÜSSLER (Hg.), *Das sahidische Alte und Neue Testament.* Wiesbaden 1995ff. His notation has been adopted here. For the present discussion only the codices sa 18, sa 19 and sa 20 are relevant:

[sa 18] the fourth century CE Joshua-Tobit Codex now divided over the Irish Chestter Beatty (no.1389) and the Swiss Bodmer (no. xxi) libraries, published by A.F. SHORE (ed.), *Joshua i-vi and other passages in Sahidic, edited from a fourth century Sahidic codex in the Chester Beatty Library.* (Chester Beatty Monographs 9) Dublin 1963; and R. KASSER (ed.), *Papyrus Bodmer XXI. Josué VI,16–25, VII,6–XI,23, XXII,1–2, 19–XIII,7, 15–XXIV,23.* (Bibliotheca Bodmeriana) Cologne/Genève 1965; R. KASSER, *L'évangile selon saint Jean et les versions coptes de la Bible.* Neuchâtel/Paris 1966, pp. 90–167, offers a complete re-edition of both the Bodmer and Chester Beatty parts of the codex;

[sa 19] a seventh century CE manuscript edited by H. THOMPSON (ed.), *A Coptic Palimpsest containing Joshua, Judges, Ruth, Judith and Esther in the Sahidic Dialect.* London 1911; and

or 'Vetus Latina' (VetLat),[14] the Ethiopian (Eth), the Armenian (Arm), and the Syriac translation of the Hexapla, the 'Syro-Hexapla' (Syh).[15]

The *Septuaginta-Unternehmen* of the Göttingen Academy in Germany has been working on such a reconstruction for the whole Greek Bible, but unfortunately the edition for LXX-Joshua is still under preparation. Therefore, scholars have to rely on three older critical editions, i.e. those by [1] Brooke-McLean, [2] Rahlfs, and [3] Margolis, which will be reviewed here briefly.[16]

2.1.1 *The Larger Cambridge Edition*[17]

The edition by Alan England Brooke and Norman McLean is a diplomatic edition: it presents the text of Codex Vaticanus with a collection of variant readings from a large number of other textual witnesses in the apparatus. For LXX-Joshua some 30 out of the circa 100 minuscules have been selected for collation. It thus represents an existing text (Codex Vaticanus) rather than a reconstructed one,

[sa 20] a Joshua-Tobit Codex dating from 1003 CE, now divided over various libraries.

[14] Apart from quotations in the Latin patristic literature and incidental marginal gloses in Vulgate manuscript only the Lyon codex 'Codex Lugdunensis', published by U. ROBERT (ed.), *Heptateuchi partis posterioris versio latina antiquissima e codice Lugdunensi. Version latine du Deutéronome, de Josué en des Juges antérieure à Saint Jérôme publiée d'après le manuscrit de Lyon avec un fac-simile, des observations paléographiques et philologiques sur l'origine et la valeur de ce texte.* Lyon 1900, offers a text of the Vetus Latina of Joshua.

[15] For the history of the Syro-Hexapla see S. JELLICOE, *The Septuagint and Modern Study.* Oxford 1968, pp. 124–127, W. BAARS (ed.), *New Syro-Hexaplaric Texts. Edited, Commented upon and Compared with the Septuagint.* Leiden 1968, pp. 1ff. and A. VÖÖBUS, *The Hexapla and the Syro-Hexapla. Very Important Discoveries for Septuagint Research.* (Papers of the Estonian Theological Society in Exile 22) Stockholm 1971. For the present discussion the following sources are of relevance: [1] Syh^{L}: the fragments that have been published by P. DE LAGARDE (ed.), *Bibliothecae syriacae, quae ad philologiam sacram pertinent.* Gottingae 1892; and [2] Syh^{M}: references to a now-lost complete Syh-manuscript which was available to Andreas Masius and used by him for his commentary (see above). Additional Syh fragments have been published by W. BAARS, *New Syro-Hexaplaric Texts* (Syh^{B}: Josh. 6:16–20) and M. GOSHEN-GOTTSTEIN, Neue Syrohexaplafragmente, in *Biblica* 37 (1956), pp. 162–183 (Syh^{G}: Josh. 7:6–9).

[16] For a discussion of these editions, see C.G. DEN HERTOG, *Studien zur griechischen Übersetzung des Buches Josua.* Gießen 1996, pp. 24–29: 'Die Textausgaben'; J. MOATTI-FINE, *Josué.* (La Bible d'Alexandrie 6) Paris 1996, pp. 39–42: 'Les éditions modernes du texte grec'. See further the detailed study by K. BIEBERSTEIN, *Lukian und Theodotion.*

[17] A.E. BROOKE, N. MCLEAN (eds.), *The Old Testament in Greek. According to the Text of Codex Vaticanus Supplemented from Other Uncial Manuscripts, with a Critical Apparatus Containing the Variants of the Chief Ancient Authorities for the Text of the Septuagint.* The text of LXX-Joshua appeared as Part IV. *Joshua, Judges and Ruth* of *Volume I. The Octateuch.* Cambridge 1917.

and in the apparatus offers the variant readings without a preliminary classification, thus enabling users to make their own choice in reconstructing the original Greek text of a given passage. The disadvantage of such a policy is that the reader will have to decide whether or not the reading presented by Codex Vaticanus represents the original Greek text or whether the more original reading has to be extracted out of the wealth of details in the apparatus. Although this diplomatic Cambridge edition was meant to be an improvement on the older diplomatic Oxford edition by R. Holmes and J. Parsons (1798–1827),[18] it is not free of errors, as shown by M.L. Margolis' list of circa 900 corrections to the apparatus for LXX-Joshua.[19]

2.1.2 *M.L. Margolis' Edition of* The Book of Joshua in Greek[20]

A complete reconstruction of the original text of Joshua in Greek was carried out by Max L. Margolis.[21] As the subtitle of his edition of *The Book of Joshua in Greek, According to the Critically Restored Text with an Apparatus Containing the Variants of the Principal Recensions and of the Individual Witnesses* indicates, Margolis not only reconstructed 'the nearest approach to the Greek original as it left the hands of the

[18] R. Holmes, J. Parsons (eds.), *Vetus Testamentum Graecum cum variis lectionibus* I–V. Oxford 1798–1827.

[19] M.L. Margolis, Corrections in the Apparatus of the Book of Joshua in the Larger Cambridge Septuagint, in *JBL* 49 (1930), pp. 234–264.

[20] M.L. Margolis (ed.), *The Book of Joshua in Greek according to the Critically Restored Text with an Apparatus Containing the Variants of the Principal Recensions and of the Individual Witnesses*. This opus magnum of Margolis appeared in several fascicles. The first four fascicles, containing LXX-Josh. 1:1–19:38, were published between 1931 and 1938 in Paris. The fifth fascicle containing the rest of the book (LXX-Josh. 19:39–24:33) was thought to have been lost during the Second World War, but rediscovered on photostat negatives in 1981 by E. Tov and published in Philadelphia in 1992, see E. Tov, The Discovery of the Missing Part of Margolis' Edition of Joshua, in *BIOSCS* 14 (1981), pp. 17–21; E. Tov, The Fifth Fascicle of Margolis' The Book of Joshua in Greek, in *JQR* 74 (1984), pp. 397–407 (= *The Greek and Hebrew Bible*, pp. 21–30).

[21] Biographical and bibliographical information on this Jewish-American (Russian-born) scholar (1866–1932) and his scientific contributions are provided by *Max Leopold Margolis. Scholar and Teacher. Alumni Association Dropsie College for Hebrew and Cognate Learning*. Philadelphia 1952, and by L. Greenspoon, *Max Leopold Margolis. A Scholar's Scholar*. Atlanta 1987. On the relation between Margolis' project and that of the *Septuaginta-Unternehmen*, see the correspondence between Margolis and Rahlfs published by C.G. den Hertog, Einige Briefe von Max Leopold Margolis an K. Marti und A. Rahlfs, in *ZAW* 111 (1999), pp. 234–252.

translator(s)',[22] but also the text of the subsequent recensions of this original text, in the conviction that only after the alterations, omissions and additions resulting from these recensions have been identified, it would be possible to restore this original text. On the basis of frequently recurring agreements between individual witnesses, especially with respect to the unfamiliar geographical names in Josh. 13–21, Margolis was able to distinguish five main families of manuscripts and daughter Versions, which he identified both with the different areas in which the text of the Septuagint was transmitted and the different stages in the transmission of this text, and called these groups [1] an Egyptian recension, [2] the Syrian (or 'Lucianic' or 'Antiochian') recension, [3] the Palestinian recension (i.e., the result of the text-critical efforts by Origen), [4] a Constantinopolitan recension, and [5] a group of Mixed manuscripts.

The Palestinian recension is characterised by Origen's aim to bring the Old Greek translation into conformity with the standardized (proto-MT) text on the basis of the younger Greek translations by Aquila, Symmachus and Theodotion.[23] According to Margolis, Origen executed his project in two stages. In the first stage of his text-critical work on the Septuagint, Origen left the order of the LXX text intact, but incorporated (after an asteriskos, ※ – ↙) in the LXX text passages from the other Greek translations where the LXX presented a shorter text, and marked the passages where the LXX presented a longer

[22] M.L. Margolis, *The Book of Joshua in Greek*, Prefatory Note, p. 1. Unfortunately, the introduction to his edition has not yet been published. Information about Margolis' views on the textual history of LXX-Joshua can be gathered from the many small articles he published. Most important of these is M.L. Margolis, Specimen of a New Edition of the Greek Joshua, in *Jewish Studies in Memory of Israel Abrahams*. New York 1927, pp. 307–323, reprinted in S. Jellicoe (ed.), *Studies in the Septuagint: Origins, Recensions and Interpretations*. New York 1973, pp. 434–450; and M.L. Margolis, Textual Criticism of the Greek Old Testament, in *Proceedings of the American Philosophical Society Held at Philadelphia for Promoting Useful Knowledge* 67 (1928), pp. 187–197.

[23] M.L. Margolis, Hexapla and Hexaplaric, in *AJSL* 32 (1916), pp. 126–140. See further S. Sipilä, Max Leopold Margolis and the Origenic Recension in Joshua, in A. Salvesen (ed.), *Origen's Hexapla and Fragments. Papers presented at the Rich Seminar on the Hexapla, Oxford Centre for Hebrew and Jewish Studies, 25th–3rd* [sic] *August 1994*. Tübingen 1998, pp. 16–38.

An exhaustive investigation of the changes introduced by Origen is offered by G.V. Smith, *An Introduction to the Greek Manuscripts of Joshua. Their Classification, Characteristics and Relationships*. (Dissertation submitted in partial fulfillment of the requirements for the degree of doctor of philosophy. The Dropsie University for Hebrew and Cognate Learning) Philadelphia 1973, chapter 5: 'The Characteristics and Relationships of Family 2' [= Margolis' Palestinian recension], pp. 50–100.

text with an obelos (÷ — ↙). Representative of this first stage, which Margolis identified with the Hexapla, is group $\underline{P}_1$. In a second stage, represented by group $\underline{P}_2$, the text was further brought into conformity with the proto-Masoretic text by transposition of those passages in which the order of the Old Greek differed from MT. This second stage Margolis identified with the Tetrapla.[24]

The tendency to correct the Hellenistic Greek language to the standard Attic Greek dialect is one of the main characteristics of the family of witnesses which Margolis called the 'Syrian recension'.[25] Other features of this family are the replacement of unfamiliar words, especially place names, by more familiar ones, the omission of repetitive pronouns and unnecessary prepositions, harmonisation, conflation and the clarification of the text by means of adding small elements to the text.[26]

---

[24] M.L. MARGOLIS, Hexapla and Hexaplaric, p. 131, Textual Criticism, p. 193. The main representatives of this subgroup $\underline{P}_2$ (Tetrapla) are ms.426 and the Syro-Hexapla, of which only fragments have been preserved.

The complete Syro-Hexapla manuscript used by Masius for his restoration of the original Greek text of Joshua has disappeared after Masius' death, see W. BAARS, *New Syro-Hexplaric Texts*, pp. 1–4. Margolis devoted a special study to this lost Syro-Hexapla manuscript of Joshua and hoped to publish it in the Harvard Theological Review, which, however, never took place. The unpublished typescript for this monograph, M.L. MARGOLIS, *Andreas Masius and His Commentary on the Book of Joshua*, was finished June 15, 1923, and recovered recently by L.J. Greenspoon, see L.J. GREENSPOON, A Preliminary Publication of Max Leopold Margolis's *Andreas Masius*, together with His Discussion of Hexapla-Tetrapla, in A. SALVESEN (ed.), *Origen's Hexapla and Fragments*, pp. 39–69. Professor Greenspoon kindly gave me permission to study the typescript document.

[25] M.L. MARGOLIS, Specimen, p. 313 [440]. This recension of the Old Greek was previously identified as that by the third century CE bishop and martyr Lucian of Antioch. Margolis himself avoided speaking of a 'Lucianic text', see M.L. MARGOLIS, Man by Man, in *JQR NS* 3 (1912), p. 332.

According to Margolis, this recension consists of two subgroups, $\underline{S}_a$ and $\underline{S}_b$, which can be further subdivided into smaller subgroups. Among the witnesses of the first subgroup, $\underline{S}_a$ are the Leipzig codex (K [see Margolis' detailed study of the Joshua portions of this seventh century witness, M.L. MARGOLIS, The K Text of Joshua, in *AJSL* 28 (1911), pp. 1–55]) and the Old Latin translation which has mainly been preserved in the fifth or sixth century Lyons palimpsest ('La' or 'VetLat', Codex Lugdunensis [see Margolis' study Additions to Field from the Lyons Codex of the Old Latin, in *JAOS* 33 (1917), pp. 254–258.]).

[26] See the detailed study of the characteristics of this recension in G.V. SMITH, *Introduction to the Greek Manuscripts of Joshua*, chapter 6: 'The Characteristics and Relationships of Family 3' [= Margolis' Syrian recension], pp. 101–154. A few individual witnesses which belong to this family reveal a drastic condensation of the geographical chapters, see M.L. MARGOLIS, Specimen, p. 312 [439].

Apart from these two familiar main recensions of the Septuagint text of Joshua and a group of relatively young mixed manuscripts,[27] Margolis' grouping of the textual witnesses on the basis of the different transcriptions of the place names brought to light a hitherto unrecognized distinct family of witnesses, to which Margolis allocated the important codices Alexandrinus, Coislinianus, Basiliano-Vaticanus, Washingtonianus and the Armenian translation. The main characteristic of this recension is its omission of the asterisked elements of the Palestinian recension, whilst leaving the tacit changes made by Origen intact. Though this characterisation would drastically reduce the text-critical value of this recension, the transcriptions of the geographical names have been preserved in their original, that is prehexaplaric *and* uncorrupted form.[28]

The unrevised Greek text, that is the Greek text that was not or only incidentally affected by one of these Palestinian, Syrian or Constantinopolitan recensions, is attested by only a few witnesses, of which Codex Vaticanus is undoubtedly the most important.[29] Other witnesses belonging to this group, although not completely free from Hexaplaric influence, are the Coptic-Bohairic, Coptic-Sahidic, and Aethiopian translations. Together these witnesses point to the Egyptian provenance of this textual family. The original text has been preserved in its relatively purest form in this family of witnesses, although the proper names have been subject to extensive corruption in the transmission of this Egyptian text type.

Therefore, in Margolis' view, the original Greek translation 'as it left the hands of the translator(s)' has to be distilled from all these witnesses together and can be restored in many cases only with the aid of emendation. This original Greek translation is characterised by Margolis as a free rendering. The translator's aim was to curtail the repetitive style of the Hebrew rather than reproduce it slavishly. The Hebrew *Vorlage* of this Greek translation differed only occasionally from the MT, so that the MT may be used to restore the Old Greek text.[30] Margolis' handling of the proper names, which

---

[27] Hence the siglum M̲. This family, to which the fifth century Codex Ambrosianus belongs, does not constitute a recension proper.

[28] M.L. MARGOLIS, Specimen, p. 311 [438]; idem, Presidental Address, p. 62.

[29] Other witnesses that belong to this family are the fourth-century Oxyrhynchus papyrus fragment, parts of Codex 55 (from LXX-Josh. 8:24 onwards), Codex 82 (only in LXX-Josh. 10:4–14:15 and 20:8–24), Codex 120 and Codex 129.

[30] M.L. MARGOLIS, Textual Criticism of the Greek Old Testament, p. 196.

are often restored either on the basis of witnesses that—according to his overview of the textual history of the Greek Joshua—belong to very late stages, or merely on the basis of pure conjecture, makes this clear.[31]

Although it must be noted that it was not Margolis' aim to restore the Hebrew *Vorlage* of LXX-Joshua, but the original Greek translation, it is evident that his easy identification of the Hebrew *Vorlage* of LXX-Joshua with a Hebrew text that is very close to the Masoretic text is certainly the weakest point in his whole reconstruction of the Greek Joshua. In a sense this assumption undermines the value of his whole enterprise. It is especially this point that has been criticised most often in Margolis' work.[32]

Margolis has filled the gap that the diplomatic edition by Brooke-McLean had left, by presenting a critical restoration of the original Greek Joshua, based on a comprehensive study of a large number of relevant witnesses and a reconstruction of the textual history of the Greek text. With his five groups of these textual witnesses, Margolis has laid the basis for subsequent studies in the textual history of the Greek Joshua. His reconstruction of the textual history of LXX-Joshua has been affirmed by the important 1928 study by O. Pretzl which was carried out independently from Margolis research,[33] and corroborated in the studies by G.V. Smith, K. Bieberstein and C.G. den Hertog.[34] Den Hertog compared the classification of the same witnesses in the books of the Greek Bible immediately preceding or following the Greek Joshua,[35] i.e. Wevers' classification of the witnesses

[31] See e.g. the criticism by L. Mazor, The Curse upon the Rebuilder of Jericho, in *Textus* 14 (1988), pp. 10ff. on Margolis' conjectural reconstruction in LXX-Josh. 6:26b of the name ὁ Χαιαηλ on the basis of MT-1 Kgs. 16:34, whereas the witnesses to LXX-Josh. 6:26b reflect the name Οζαν (M.L. Margolis, *The Book of Joshua in Greek*, pp. 100–101).

[32] See already the criticism from Margolis' pupil H. Orlinsky, The Hebrew *Vorlage* of the Septuagint of the Book of Joshua, in *Congress Volume. Rome 1968.* (SVT 17) Leiden 1969, pp. 187–195; L.J. Greenspoon, *Textual Studies in the Book of Joshua*, p. 1; and C.G. den Hertog, Anmerkungen zu Margolis' The Book of Joshua in Greek, in *BIOSCS* 28 (1995), pp. 51–56, especially p. 54.

[33] O. Pretzl, Die griechischen Handschriftengruppen im Buche Josua untersucht nach ihrer Eigenart und ihrem Verhältnis zueinander, in *Biblica* 9 (1928), pp. 377–427.

[34] G.V. Smith, *An Introduction to the Greek Manuscripts*; K. Bieberstein, *Lukian und Theodotion*; and C.G. den Hertog, *Studien zur griechischen Übersetzung*. § 2: 'Die Handschriftengruppen', pp. 3–23.

[35] See C.G. den Hertog, *Studien zur griechischen Übersetzung*, § 2, especially. § 2.2: 'Der Vergleich Margolis—Rahlfs (Ruth)—Wevers (Deuteronomium)', pp. 15–23.

of the Greek Deuteronomy[36] and Rahlfs' grouping of the witnesses of LXX-Ruth,[37] and concluded that the classification of the same witnesses by these three outstanding Septuagint scholars are in remarkable agreement.

It should be noted, however, that despite the consensus among the contemporary scholars regarding the five groups of witnesses on the synchronic level, the diachronic arrangement by Margolis, and his identifications with certain localities (Egypt, Syria, Palestine and especially Constantinople) or known or assumed recensional activities have been called in question.[38] For instance, Margolis' identification of his subgroup $\underline{P}_2$ with Origen's Tetrapla becomes problematic once the Tetrapla is called a 'scholarly fiction'.[39] Moreover, Margolis' view of the text of family $\underline{C}$ as a post-hexaplaric recension has been rejected by the European scholars Pretzl, Bieberstein, and Den Hertog, who propose a much earlier *pre*-Hexaplaric date of this textual family.[40] Apart from these issues, it has been noted several times that Margolis' complex apparatus, the fact that he developed his own set of sigla, and his conjectural placing of some Aristarchian signs, do not enhance the accessibility of this edition.[41] Finally, even this meticulous work has fallen victim to some textual errors.[42]

---

[36] J.W. Wevers, *Text History of the Greek Deuteronomy.* (MSU XIII) Göttingen 1978.

[37] A. Rahlfs, *Studie über den griechischen Text des Buches Ruth.* (MSU III) Göttingen 1922.

[38] C.G. den Hertog, *Studien zur griechischen Übersetzung*, pp. 26–29.

[39] See C.G. den Hertog, *Studien zur griechischen Übersetzung*, pp. 11–12. H.M. Orlinsky, Origen's Tetrapla—A Scholarly Fiction? in *Proceedings of the First World Congress of Jewish Studies 1947.* I Jerusalem 1952, pp. 173–182; D. Barthélemy, Origène et le texte de l'Ancien Tetsament, in J. Fontaine, Ch. Kannensieger (eds.), *Epektasis. Mélanges patristiques offerts au Cardinal Jean Daniélou.* (Paris 1972), pp. 247–261, reprinted in D. Barthélemy, *Études d'histoire du texte de l'ancien testament.* (OBO 21) Fribourg/Göttingen 1978, pp. 203–261; and S. Sipilä, The Tetrapla—Is It All Greek to Us?, in *SJOT* 10 (1996), pp. 169–182.

[40] O. Pretzl, Die Handschriftengruppen, pp. 412–421, 426; K. Bieberstein, *Lukian und Theodotion*, pp. 32–36; C.G. den Hertog, *Studien zur griechischen Übersetzung*, pp. 13–14.

[41] See S. Jellicoe, *The Septuagint and Modern Study*, p. 279; and C.G. den Hertog, Anmerkungen zu Margolis' The Book of Joshua in Greek, in *BIOSCS* 28 (1995), pp. 51–56.

[42] See the lists of errors in Margolis' edition by E. Tov, The Fifth Fascicle of Margolis' The Book of Joshua in Greek, in *JQR* 74 (1984), pp. 398–399; S. Sipilä, A Note to the Users of Margolis' Joshua Edition, in *BIOSCS* 26 (1993), pp. 17–21; K. Bieberstein, *Lukian und Theodotion*, pp. 22–27: 'Corrigenda et Addenda zur Textausgabe von Margolis'; and C.G. den Hertog, *Studien zur griechischen Übersetzung*, p. 185: 'Anhang: Korrekturen zur Textausgabe von Margolis', which also

2.1.3 *The Manual Edition of A. Rahlfs*

The manual Septuagint edition by the first director of the Septuagint Institute in Göttingen, Alfred Rahlfs, is the one that is used most often by modern scholars.[43] It offers an eclectic edition of the complete Old Testament in Greek based on the most important uncial manuscripts, Vaticanus, Alexandrinus and Sinaiticus (not extant for LXX-Joshua). Rahlfs made no attempt to reconstruct the original Greek text in the place name sections LXX-Josh. 15:21–62 and 18:22–19:45, but simply printed the text of his main witnesses B and A alongside each other. Compared to the edition by Margolis, Rahlfs' is a rather faithful edition of the text of Vaticanus, without its most obvious errors, and does not contain the problematic conjectures present in Margolis' edition. For that reason, this edition is still the most reliable source for the text of LXX-Joshua.

2.1.4 *The Critical Editions by Rahlfs and Margolis Compared*

Recently, C.G. den Hertog has brought together all passages where the two eclectic editions of LXX-Joshua by Rahlfs and Margolis differ, apart from the proper names. He concludes that since Margolis' edition contains a high number of conjectural readings and since Margolis evaluated the C-witnesses as a relatively late stage, Rahlfs' edition is preferable to that by Margolis in more than half of the cases where the two editions differ.[44] These differences between the

appeared in his article Anmerkungen zu Margolis' The Book of Joshua in Greek, in *BIOSCS* 28 (1995), pp. 55–56.

[43] A. Rahlfs (ed.), *Septuaginta. Id est Vetus Testamentum graece iuxta LXX interpretes*. Stuttgart 1935.

[44] C.G. den Hertog, *Studien zur griechischen Übersetzung*, § 4. 'Die Abweichungen Rahlfs-Margolis', pp. 30–109, discusses circa 270 passages. In some 170 of these 270 cases, preference should be given, according to Den Hertog, to the reconstruction by Rahlfs. This applies, for example, to the passages where the E and younger witnesses present a double translation of one Hebrew expression. Margolis, following Hollenberg (see following paragraph) considered the more literal of the two renderings to be early additions to the original Greek translation and adopted only the freer rendering, while Rahlfs adopted both translations. Den Hertog argues that the double translations should be regarded as supplementary midrash-type renderings from the first translator(s), rather than competitive, and refers to those passages where both Rahlfs and Margolis have adopted a seeming doublet as the original Greek text, see C.G. den Hertog, *Studien zur griechischen Übersetzung*, pp. 81–91: 'Scheinbare Dubletten'. The remaining 100 passages where preference should be given to Margolis' reconstruction usually apply to very small details that do not affect the meaning of the text, such as the correction of the case of a noun, the addition of an article and so forth.

two editions are usually very small and the agreements between the two reconstructions are therefore all the more significant.[45]

One may conclude from the above that some caution is required when using one of the three editions discussed. All of them have their shortcomings and textual errors. Nevertheless, the differences between the editions are still very small, because they all take the text of Codex Vaticanus as their basis. Since Margolis' edition contains a rather high number of conjectural readings, and since the reconstruction of the original Greek text in the end remains a matter of individual decison and hypothesis, Rahlfs' edition has been taken in this study as the point of departure for further study whereas the data from the other two editions have been taken into account as much as possible.

2.2 The Redaction-Critical Value of LXX-Joshua

2.2.1 *The Character of the Greek Translation (J. Hollenberg)*

The first systematic attempt to investigate the character of the old Greek translation of Joshua was made by Johannes Hollenberg in his concise but meticulous 1876 study *Der Charakter des alexandrinischen Übersetzung des Buches Josua und ihr textkritischer Werth.*[46] According to Hollenberg, the Greek version can be classified as a fairly intelligent rendering which aimed at an eloquent Greek style, rather than a concordant rendering of its Hebrew *Vorlage*. Most of the divergencies between MT and LXX can be attributed to this translation technique, whereas in a few cases the variants should be attributed to inner-Greek corruptions, or an occasional hiatus in the Greek translator's knowledge of Hebrew. Variants that can not be assigned to one of these three categories, according to Hollenberg reflect a different Hebrew *Vorlage*, although that does not necessarily imply

[45] C.G. den Hertog, *Studien zur griechischen Übersetzung*, p. 109.

[46] Published as a 'Wissenschaftliche Beilage zu dem Oster-Programm des Gymnasiums zu Moers', where Hollenberg taught German and Latin. This study contains no more than 20 pages, but discusses hundreds of divergencies between LXX-Joshua and MT-Joshua. Hollenberg's investigations of LXX-Joshua were based on the Tischendorf's manual edition of the Septuagint, although he was aware of the need of a more critical evaluation of all the available textual witnesses of LXX-Joshua (op. cit., p. 1) and which he reported to have started working on himself, see J. Hollenberg, Zur Textkritik des Buches Josua und des Buches der Richter, in *ZAW* 1 (1881), pp. 97–105.

that the Hebrew text reflected by LXX is older than that attested by MT. Since most of his observations still remain valid, it is worthwile to present several of them as a first general introduction to the Greek Joshua.

On the basis of numerous examples, Hollenberg made clear that the Greek translator sought to bring variation in his text, in order to avoid the monotonous and repetitive style of the Hebrew. An example of this tendency is offered by the two translations of the same Hebrew phrase לא־נפל דבר אחד, *he has not failed one thing*, in Josh. 23:14. The first time the phrase is rendered literally by οὐ διέπεσεν εἷς λόγος, *he has not dropped one word*, the second time more paraphrastically by οὐ διεφώνησεν, *there will not be missing (one word)*.[47] Just as the Greek translator omitted unnecessary elements to avoid repetition, he could also add small elements to enhance a better understanding of the text. One of his 59 examples can be found in LXX-Josh. 5:3, where the words ἐπὶ τοῦ καλουμένου τόπου, *on the place called (hill of the foreskins)* clarify the place where Joshua circumcised the Israelites.[48]

Whereas such renderings merely rephrase the Hebrew text and hardly alter its meaning, the Greek translator did not shrink from using equivalents that added another nuance to the text which would fit the larger context. An interesting example of such a *contextual* translation is, for instance, the rendering of וילחם בישׂראל, *he (i.e. Balak) fought with Israel*, in Josh. 24:9 by καὶ παρετάξατο τῷ Ισραηλ, *he set up the army in array against Israel*, in order to account for the fact that Num.22–24 does not report a direct confrontation between Balak and Israel.[49]

Although the Greek translator did not strive for a literal translation of the Hebrew text, he did aim at a faithful *ad sensum* translation, thus Hollenberg. With the exception of the hypotactical constructions, the Hebrew syntax has been left intact in the process of translation.[50] Another indication of the faithfulness of translation is the fact that one will look in vain for tendentious alterations of the text. The only exception to this rule is the tendency of the Greek translator (shared with the other ancient translations) to render the

[47] J. Hollenberg, *Der Charakter*, p. 5.
[48] See the discussion of this variant in chapter 7 below.
[49] See J. Hollenberg, *Der Charakter*, pp. 5–6.
[50] See J. Hollenberg, *Der Charakter*, p. 11.

Hebrew idiomatic anthropomorphic expressions literally, see e.g. the translation of the phrase פי יהוה, *the mouth of Yhwh*, as πρόσταγμα κυρίου, *the ordinance of the Lord*.[51]

Although the phenomena described above testify to the translator's great expertise, skill, and intelligence, a small number of renderings betray—according to Hollenberg—the limits of the translator's knowledge of the Hebrew language[52] and especially a lack of precise knowledge of geographical names.[53] The Greek translator's solution to this problem was either to leave the word(s) in question untranslated or guess at their meaning.[54]

Once the intention of the Greek translator has been characterised as an *ad sensum rephrasing* of the text rather than a literal rendering, it becomes possible to draw conclusions with respect to the textual development of the book of Joshua, both as regards the transmission of the Greek text and the preservation of the Hebrew text. Those passages in the Greek text that form a more literal duplication of a less literal translation of the same Hebrew text are identified by Hollenberg as secondary intrusions.[55] In Josh. 1:8, for instance, two Greek phrases (τότε εὐοδωθήσῃ, *then you will be succesful* and καὶ εὐοδώσεις τὰς ὁδούς σου, *and you will make your ways prosperous*) occur as translations of one Hebrew phrase, the second being the more literal, and therefore—according to Hollenberg—the later addition.

---

[51] Thus in Josh. 15:13, 17:4, 19:50, 21:3, 22:9. Other examples of the same tendency are the translation of the Hebrew expression קול יהוה, *the voice of Yhwh*, with αἱ ἐντολαί τοῦ θεοῦ, *the commandments of God* (Josh. 5:6) and יד יהוה, *the hand of Yhwh*, with ἡ δύναμις τοῦ κυρίου, *the power of God* (Josh. 4:24) see J. Hollenberg, *Der Charakter*, p. 9.

[52] J. Hollenberg, *Der Charakter*, p.9: 'Wenn wir die Schwierigkeiten erwägen, mit welchen der Ueb. bei seiner Aufgabe zu kämpfen hatte, wenn wir bedenken, daß er einen vokallosen Text, geschrieben in einer aussterbenden Sprache, vor sich hatte, ohne daß dieser Mangel durch eine grammatische Wissenschaft ergänzt wurde, so werden wir uns wundern, daß der Fälle, wo er das Original gänzlich misverstanden hat, doch verhältnißmäßig wenige sind.'

[53] J. Hollenberg, *Der Charakter*, p. 10: 'Mangel an Klarheit beobachten wir in den Uebersetzung der geographischen Stellen; diese boten allerdings für einen Mann, dem es offenbar an genauerer Kenntnis des heiligen Landes fehlte, besondere Schwierigkeiten dar. Auch mochten ihm diese Partien weniger wichtig erscheinen.' This seems to concur with Hollenberg's presupposition that the Greek translation of the book of Joshua was made in Alexandria, Egypt.

[54] An example is found in Josh. 7:5, where the words עד־השברים, *as far as the ravines* have been left untranslated, see J. Hollenberg, *Der Charakter*, pp. 9–10. See, however, the discussion in chapter 8 below.

[55] See P.A. de Lagarde, *Anmerkungen zur griechischen Uebersetzung der Proverbien*. Leipzig 1863, p. 3.

Nevertheless, there remains a certain number of divergencies between LXX and MT that cannot be explained as inner-Greek textual corruptions, *ad sensum* renderings, or misinterpretations of a difficult Hebrew text; these reflect a different Hebrew text.[56] This is true for those passages where LXX has preserved the original text that had been lost in the MT due to homoioteleuton, as is the case in Josh. 13:7–8.[57]

The opposite phenomenon, an omission in the Hebrew *Vorlage* of LXX-Joshua, can be discerned in Josh. 14:2–3, where the clause *Because Moses had given the inheritance of the two tribes and the half tribe*... has fallen out of the Hebrew *Vorlage* of LXX-Joshua, resulting in an incomprehensible text, which places the nine tribes in the Trans-Jordanian area.[58]

Whereas these divergencies should be ascribed to unconscious errors in one of the two Hebrew texts (MT-Joshua and the Hebrew *Vorlage* of LXX-Joshua), there are also several variants that reflect deliberate alterations that must have taken place on the Hebrew level, for which the Greek translator cannot be held responsible. This applies, according to Hollenberg, to the expansions in LXX-Joshua which have a counterpart in other passages in the same or other biblical books, such as Josh. 6:26a, where LXX-Joshua contains a plus that corresponds to MT-1 Kgs. 16:34, or Josh. 21:42a–d, where LXX-Joshua repeats most of Josh. 19:49–50.[59]

[56] J. Hollenberg, *Der Charakter*, pp. 19–20: 'Wenn wir die Fehler der griech. Abschreiber entfernten, die Freiheiten des Uebersetzers und die aus mangelhafter Sprachkenntniß entsprungenen Abweichungen in Rechnung zogen, wenn wir dem Uebers. noch so scharf in's Gericht gingen: immer blieb ein Rest von Verschiedenheiten übrig, welcher nur durch die Annahme eines von der Massora abweichenden Textes erklärt werden konnte.'

[57] Here, the eye of the scribe responsible for the text preserved by MT must have jumped from the first occurrence of the words וחצי השבט המנשה, *and half the tribe of Manasseh* (Josh. 13:7) to the second occurrence of the same phrase (LXX-Josh. 13:8), thus omitting the three clauses in between (*from the Jordan until the great sea where the sun sets you will give it [i.e. this land], the great sea being its border. To the two tribes and half of the tribe of Manasse*...), see J. Hollenberg, *Der Charakter*, pp. 13–14. The same phenomenon of *parablepsis* in the Masoretic tradition is observable in 15:59a, where a list of eleven Judaean cities—including Bethlehem—have been lost in the Masoretic tradition, and 21:36–37, where the list of the four Reubenite Levitical cities are absent from some Masoretic manuscripts. In these passages the LXX has preserved the original text, whereas the MT is the result of textual corruption.

[58] J. Hollenberg, *Der Charakter*, p. 19.

[59] J. Hollenberg, *Der Charakter*, pp. 17–18.

According to Hollenberg, a similar instance of secondary addition, but this time in the MT, is visible in chapter 20, where Yhwh commands Joshua to designate cities of refuge. In the Greek text, verses 4–5 and parts of verse 6 are lacking. These are, according to Hollenberg, Deuteronomic additions to a shorter version reflected in the Hebrew *Vorlage* of LXX-Joshua, which contains only a description of the execution of commands concerning the cities of refuge in Numbers 35. Hollenberg considered this to be further proof of Wellhausen's thesis that the process of formation of the historical books of the Old Testament was still not completely finished at the time the Greek translation was made.[60] The remarkable coincidence of textual history and redaction history, however, seems to be restricted to this passage only, while many other different readings of the Hebrew *Vorlage* reflect secondary changes of the original text reflected in the MT.

Thus, both the MT and the Hebrew *Vorlage* of LXX not only show traces of textual corruption of the original text of Joshua, but also reflect later additions to the final redaction of Joshua, bearing witness to the phenomenon of the overlap of redaction history and textual history. On the whole, Hollenberg argued, the MT of Joshua is closer to this original text than the Hebrew *Vorlage* of LXX. He described the latter text as a *vulgar* text, inferior to the MT, though occasionally exhibiting the original text of Joshua.[61] The text-critical value of the Septuagint is thus rather restricted, but nevertheless invaluable. The picture of the Greek translator that emerges from the wealth of examples adduced by Hollenberg is that of a learned scribe, well versed in both the Hebrew and Greek language and literature. His aim is to present to his Greek audience an interpretative translation of a venerated book.

Hollenberg has offered a very well-balanced and exhaustive study of the differences between the Hebrew and Greek texts of the book of Joshua. His study may adequately be termed a 'pioneer study', since for the first time in the study of the text of Joshua not only almost all the divergencies between the Greek and Masoretic texts

---

[60] J. Hollenberg, *Der Charakter*, p. 15; see further J. Hollenberg, Die deuteronomistischen Bestandtheile des Buches Josua, in *Theologische Studien und Kritiken* 47 (1874), pp. 462–507, especially p. 503; J. Wellhausen, *Der Text der Bücher Samuelis*. Göttingen 1871, p. ix.

[61] J. Hollenberg, *Der Charakter*, p. 20.

of Joshua were explored, but also well-balanced explanations were offered for them. Unlike later scholars who explained the divergencies one-sidedly on the basis of one dominant model, Hollenberg offered a very balanced view: some of the deviations can be ascribed to later additions to the Greek text, some to the translation technique, still others to shortcomings in the Greek translator's knowledge of the Hebrew language, and a fourth category to a different Hebrew *Vorlage*. The question of course remains how to decide which variant falls into which category. Despite the large numbers of examples adduced for the various categories into which Hollenberg classified the individual deviations, the decision how to classify each variant remained subjective. Although insight in the character of the Greek translation, its shortcomings and subsequent accretions, helps us to discern more clearly those deviations that do not belong in one of the first three categories and are therefore probably the result of a different Hebrew *Vorlage*, Hollenberg did not provide strict criteria for assigning a variant to one of his categories.[62] Due to the conciseness of his study, however, a large number of deviations are placed in one category or another without further commentary.

2.2.2 *The Greek Text as the Product of Systematic Curtailment (A. Dillmann)*

Whereas Hollenberg argued that both MT and LXX contain secondary elements, the subsequent discussion has tended to favour one of the two versions as the original one. August Dillmann, on the one hand, expressed a rather negative view of the text-critical value of the LXX in his commentary on Joshua which appeared ten years after Hollenberg's pioneer study. In his opinion, almost all LXX deviations from MT, including Joshua 20, are to be ascribed to the translator's tendency to curtail, and create deliberate changes, transpositions

[62] Cf. his own remarks, J. Hollenberg, *Der Charakter*, p. 12: 'Können wir denn überhaupt wissen, ob dem Ueb. an einer abweichenden Stelle ein anderer Text vorgelegen hat oder nicht? Es ist von vornherein zuzugeben, daß dies nicht in allen Fällen endgültig und mit völliger Sicherheit bestimmt werden kann. Aber die Kenntniß der Principien unsers Uebers. und die Einsicht in seine Sprachkenntnisse geben doch wichtige Hülfsmittel an die Hand, welche die Entscheidung in der Mehrzahl sehr erleichtern. Mit ihrer Hülfe kann man sehen, ob eine Abweichung bloß der Freiheit des Uebers. entspringt, ob ein Zusatz von ihm herrühren kann, ob er absichtlich etwas aus seinem Original weggelassen hat, oder ob vielmehr die Verschiedenheit auf Rechnung eines anderen ihm vorliegenden Textes zu setzen ist.'

and additions. He argued that if it is evident that the LXX contains many textual errors and later additions from other biblical books, it is likely that in those places where the question of the priority between LXX and MT is disputable, it is more likely that in those cases MT stands closer to the original final edition of Joshua too.[63] Carl Steuernagel, on the other hand, stressed the fluidity of the boundaries between the (many) stages in the formation of Joshua and its textual transmission.[64] Commentators such as S. Oettli[65] and H. Holzinger[66] took an intermediate position, pointing to the textual corruption underlying both the Greek and Masoretic texts, which compared with the transmission of the Pentateuch testify to a less careful tranmission of this biblical book.

2.2.3 *The Hebrew Text as the Product of Systematic Expansion (S. Holmes)*

While scholars such as Dillmann, Oettli and Holzinger emphasised the large number of textual errors in the Hebrew text underlying the Greek translation, Samuel Holmes in his 1914 study *Joshua. The Hebrew and Greek Texts* pointed to the fact that several divergencies between the two texts show remarkable coherence. The two versions are not just the result of a process of textual corruption, but reflect two different versions of the book, one of them being a systematic revision of the other. Since the LXX version is in many places shorter

---

[63] A. Dillmann, *Die Bücher Numeri, Deuteronomium und Josua.* (Kurzgefaßtes exegetisches Handbuch zum Alten Testament) Leipzig 1886², p. 690: 'Die Güte des LXX-Textes ist, wie bei anderen, so auch bei diesem Buch in neuerer Zeit viel überschätzt worden. Im allgemeinen ist der LXX-Text der kürzere; dass darum auch der ursprünglichere, verstehe sich nicht von selbst. Andererseits bleibt aber doch noch eine Menge Stellen, wo die LXX entschieden bessere Lesarten bieten, als der hebr. Text'. For his discussion of LXX-Josh. 20, see A. Dillmann, *Die Bücher Numeri, Deuteronomium und Josua*, p. 568.

[64] C. Steuernagel, *Übersetzung und Erklärung der Bücher Deuteronomium und Josua.* (Handkommentar zum Alten Testament I/3) Göttingen 1900, p. 148: 'Der Text des Buches Josua ist damit [i.e., after its final redaction—MM] noch keineswegs endgültig fixiert gewesen; vielmehr lehrt der Vergleich mit LXX, dass noch später mancherlei Zusätze in den Text eingedrungen sind. . . . Die Grenze zwischen dem, was der Redaktions- und was der Textgeschichte angehört, ist hier wie überall eine fliessende.'

[65] S. Oettli, *Das Deuteronomium und die Bücher Josua und Richter mit einer Karte Palästinas.* (Kurzgefaßter Kommentar zu den Heiligen Schriften Alten und Neuen Testaments sowie zu den Apokryphen A.2) München 1893, p. 127.

[66] H. Holzinger, *Das Buch Josua.* (Kurzer Hand-Commentar zum Alten Testament 6) Tübingen/Leipzig 1901, pp. xiv–xv.

than the MT, and since—according to Holmes—it is 'a tendency of all LXX scribes to amplify',[67] Holmes argued that the MT is the result of a deliberate and systematic revision.

In Josh. 2:17, for instance, the words אשר השבעתנו, *which you have made us swear*, are absent from the LXX. Since the same omission occurs in verse 20, Holmes found it highly unlikely that this was the result of textual corruption. As the translator's tendency towards amplification is demonstrated by the addition in Josh. 2:19 of the words τῷ ὅρκῳ σου τούτῳ, *(we will be free) from this oath*, the words אשר השבעתנו must be the result of a later revision of the Hebrew text.[68]

Having established the priority of LXX over MT in these (and many other) cases, Holmes concluded that Dillmann's contention that in a number of cases the minuses in LXX were 'entschieden fehlerhaft' (such as the long minuses in 6:3–4, 7:25 and 8:12–13) should be dismissed.[69] Holmes attempted to prove that in these cases it was more likely that the Greek text represented the original (Hebrew) text, while the MT was the result of subsequent additions. Against Dillmann's assertion that the Greek translator curtailed the text of Josh. 8:12–18 in order to get rid of the discrepancy in the number of the men in ambush (verse 3 mentions 30,000 men, verse 12 [MT only] no more than 5,000 men),[70] Holmes objected that the Greek translator could easily have altered this figure, and if this was his main difficulty, he would not have left the rest of verses 12–13 untranslated.[71]

A final problem for Holmes' thesis of the priority of LXX is posed by those pluses in LXX-Joshua that have a counterpart in other biblical books and are generally held to be later additions from these books, i.e. LXX-Josh. 6:26, 16:10, 19:47a–48a, and 24:33a–b. Holmes argued that the shorter text of MT in those passages could be explained as the result of omitting offensive ideas,[72] or of later additions

---

[67] S. Holmes, *Joshua. The Hebrew and Greek Texts*. Cambridge 1914, p. 3.

[68] S. Holmes, *Joshua*, p. 3.

[69] A. Dillmann, *Die Bücher Numeri, Deuteronomium und Josua*, p. 690; S. Holmes, *Joshua*, p. 10.

[70] A. Dillmann, *Die Bücher Numeri, Deuteronomium und Josua*, p. 474.

[71] S. Holmes, *Joshua*, pp. 13–14. See the discussion in chapter 8 below.

[72] The omission of LXX-Josh. 16:10 by the Hebrew reviser is, according to Holmes (p. 64), due to the fact that 'the Hebrew reviser no doubt objected to the statement that Gezer kept its independence till the time of Solomon'. The mention of the flint knives in LXX-Josh. 21:42d and 24:31a, and their reference to the

to the Hebrew text of the parallel passages. In LXX-Josh. 19:47a–48a (the migration of the tribe of Dan to the north), the Greek text, according to Holmes, reflects the older combination of the Priestly list of the Danite cities and the Jahwistic narrative of the capture of the city Laish. Holmes deemed it incredible that a Greek scribe would have skilfully gathered the Priestly elements together (in LXX, verse 48 [MT] follows right after verse 46), thus ignoring the intervening Jahwistic narrative (MT verse 47), and subsequently would have placed the missing verse between the two verses from Judg. 1:34–35. The order of LXX-Josh. 19:47–48a is the more logical one. The motive for the Hebrew revision behind the MT would have been the objection to mentioning the failure of Dan (LXX-Josh. 19:47a) and the mention of the Amorites remaining in Elon (LXX-Josh. 19:48a).[73]

As a result, Dillmann's thesis of a deliberate curtailing of the Hebrew text by the Greek translator should be replaced, according to Holmes, by the thesis of a systematic expansion by a Hebrew revisor of an original Hebrew text attested by LXX. On this basis, Holmes offered a running commentary on the whole book of Joshua.

The merit of Holmes' contribution is that he has drawn attention to the fact that many divergencies between LXX and MT are interrelated and therefore point to a systematic revision, rather than to a chain of textual corruptions. Nevertheless, whereas Dillmann placed exclusive emphasis on the priority of MT, Holmes seems to have taken the other extreme position in order to defend the priority of the postulated Hebrew *Vorlage* of LXX-Joshua. True, he admitted that the Greek texts ocassionaly also contained secondary readings, as for instance the change of Shechem into Shiloh in 24:1.25,[74] but he did not systematically examine the character of the Greek translation in the way Hollenberg had done, but simply contented himself with the rather general statement that it is the tendency of all LXX scribes to amplify, rather than to shorten the Hebrew text.[75]

---

offensive ideas related in LXX-Josh. 5:4–9, probably caused their omission by the Hebrew reviser responsible for the shorter Masoretic text.

[73] S. Holmes, *Joshua*, pp. 14–16.

[74] S. Holmes, *Joshua*, pp. 8–9. Holmes explained the difference between the Hebrew and Greek texts as a harmonistic alteration on the part of the Greek translator with Shiloh in mind, which is mentioned eight times in the previous chapters (18:1.8.9.10, 1951, 21:2, 22:9.12) as central sanctuary. See further W.T. Koopmans, *Joshua 24 as Poetic Narrative*. (JSOTS 93) Sheffield 1990, pp. 259–261.

[75] S. Holmes, *Joshua*, p. 3.

Besides that, he made no effort to explain the motives on the part of the Hebrew reviser for his expansions of the text.

Holmes did not make any explicit statements about the textual history of Joshua. His thesis presupposes a two-stage model: an original Hebrew text, still represented by the Greek text, was later revised by a Hebrew scribe. G.A. Cooke in his small 1918 Cambridge commentary on Joshua formulated this model as follows:[76]

> Apparently the Hebr. text of Joshua was once current in two forms: the one which lay before the Gk. translators, and perhaps was generally accepted in Egypt; the other which is represented by the M.T., and perhaps was best known in Palestine. The latter form of the text remained open, possibly as late as 200 BC, to additions which never found a place in the text used by the LXX.

With the positions presented by Dillmann on the one hand and Holmes on the other, the boundaries for subsequent research on the relation between the Greek and Hebrew texts of Joshua had been set. A number of scholars would follow Dillmann's more cautious line, such as M. Noth in his standard commentary on Joshua,[77] while modern text critics in the Qumran era considered Holmes and Cooke unconventional prophets, whose results were to be confirmed by the Hebrew texts from Qumran.

2.2.4 *The 'Gloss' Model (C.D. Benjamin)*

In his 1921 dissertation Charles Dow Benjamin[78] developed the thesis that the quantitative divergencies between MT and LXX are to

[76] G.A. Cooke, *The Book of Joshua.* (The Cambridge Bible for Schools and Colleges) Cambridge 1918, pp. ix–x. In his commentary, Cooke adopted a number of Holmes' suggestions (e.g. on p. 14 [Joshua 2:15], pp. 40–52 [Joshua 6], p. 187 [Josh. 19:47–48]), though in a number of other passages Cooke did not mention Holmes or even rejected his proposals, e.g. regarding the pluses in LXX-Josh. 16:10b and 6:26b (p. 157).

[77] M. Noth, *Das Buch Josua.* (HAT I/7) Tübingen 1938[1], 1953[2], p. 7: 'Die alten Übersetzungen, voran 𝔊, zeigen vielerlei Textabweichungen . . ., die aber wohl nur zum kleineren Teile auf einen abweichenden und gegenüber 𝔐 ursprünglicheren hebräischen Text zurückgehen, meist jedoch—das scheint mir eine Durcharbeitung des Materials zu ergeben—Glättungen und Vereinfachungen des durch seine literarische Vorgeschichte stellenweise kompliziert gewordenen hebräischen Textes seitens der Übersetzer darstellen.'

[78] C.D. Benjamin, *The Variations between the Hebrew and Greek Texts of Joshua: Chapters 1–12.* (Dissertation of the University of Pennsylvania) Leipzig 1921. The second half of this concise study, pp. 23–46, contains a running textual commentary to

be seen as a series of *glosses* or short explicative interpolations into the main body of the text.[79] The aim of these glossators was to give the reader or hearer a better understanding of the text and to that end they expanded the text by short phrases. According to Benjamin, both MT and LXX reflect such glosses, although the Hebrew language was more suited to this kind of scribal intervention, so that the bulk of the glosses are to be found in MT.

An example of such an interpolation in the Greek text is offered by Josh. 2:4(.21). The Hebrew text merely has ותאמר, *she (i.e. Rahab) said*, while the Greek text adds (καὶ εἶπεν) αὐτοῖς λέγουσα, *(and she said) to them saying.*[80] According to Benjamin, an example of a gloss in the Hebrew text can be found in Josh. 1:2, where MT has the gloss לבני ישׂראל, *to the children of Israel*, as an explication of the previous phrase להם, *to them.* The Greek translator found only the first phrase, while the gloss was added to the Hebrew text at a subsequent stage.[81] According to Benjamin, the secondary nature of the gloss is ocasionally proven by its contents. In Josh. 10:37 the Hebrew gloss ואת־מלכה, *and her* [*i.e. Hebron's*] *king*, contradicts the preceding verses 21–27, where the execution of the king of Hebron together with the four other kings has already been narrated.[82]

In order to support his thesis that many of the quantitative differences between LXX-Joshua and MT-Joshua could be regarded as secondary glosses in one of the two texts, Benjamin pointed to the history of the text of the book of Sirach, where many phrases from the Greek and Syriac versions appeared in the Hebrew manuscripts from the Cairo Geniza as marginal glosses.[83]

Whereas Dillmann and Holmes approached the differences between the Greek and Hebrew texts systematically and were therefore able to point to certain common traits and interrelated deliberate tendencies (be it on the part of the Greek translator or the Hebrew reviser), Benjamin reduced the differences to isolated individual instances of either textual corruption or glossation. Though several

---

Joshua 1–12, while the first half of this work combines an introduction to and conclusions from the textual analysis of these 12 chapters.

[79] This definition is taken from E. Tov, *Textual Criticism*, p. 277. Benjamin did not provide a definition of a gloss.

[80] C.D. Benjamin, *The Variations*, pp. 25–26.

[81] For a discussion of the variant see chapter 6 below.

[82] C.D. Benjamin, *The Variations*, pp. 21, 44.

[83] C.D. Benjamin, *The Variations*, p. 18.

glosses convey the same idea or have an anticipatory intention, i.e. to explain to the reader or hearer what is to come, there is no indication that the glosses in both the Hebrew and Greek texts were introduced systematically at a specific discernible stage. The model that seems to lie behind Benjamin's succinct statements is that of a process of continuing accretion of small elements, rather than a comprehensive deliberate reworking of one of the two texts. Furthermore, it remains unclear on what grounds Benjamin was able to classify the variants as glosses. In his commentary one often finds no more than the apparently arbitrary ad-hoc formula '∧ B. H +. Explanatory.' without any grounds as to why a particular plus in MT should be regarded as an explanatory gloss, or without any reference to the opinions of earlier scholars.

2.2.5 *The Hebrew* Vorlage *of LXX*

2.2.5.1 *M.L. Margolis*

As noted above, Max Leopold Margolis held the Hebrew *Vorlage* of LXX-Joshua to be more or less identical with the Hebrew text of MT. In that respect he differed drastically from his contemporaries Samuel Holmes and Charles Benjamin. Although he did not devote a special study to the relation between MT and LXX of Joshua and the redaction-critical value of LXX-Joshua, we find numerous remarks in the ninth apparatus of his critical edition.[84] With respect to the quantitative variants, which played such an important role in the theses of Holmes (revision on the Hebrew level) and Benjamin (individual glosses), Margolis usually simply stated: 'G om' which stands for 'the Greek translator omitted'. Only in a few cases Margolis explicitely employed the opposite formulation: 'om. H[ebrew]' (in the case of LXX-Josh. 13:7–8), 'the verse is missing in H' (LXX-Josh. 15:59a) and 'G found the plus which was omitted in H through homoioteleuton' (LXX-Josh. 21:36–37).

2.2.5.2 *H.M. Orlinsky*

Interestingly it was Margolis' own pupil Harry Orlinsky who swung the pendulum in the opposite direction. In his 1968 lecture for the

[84] See also his remarks in M.L. Margolis, Specimen of a New Edition of the Greek Joshua, p. 318: 'A few comments on the translator's manner of operation. He was apparently given to curtailments.'

IOSOT Rome Congress,[85] Orlinsky argued that in the cases where LXX has a minus and where Margolis explained the variant as 'G omits', one should rather assume that the Hebrew *Vorlage* lacked the word(s) absent in LXX. Orlinsky took the example of the apposition עבד יהוה, *servant of Yhwh*, which has no counterpart in the very first clause of LXX-Joshua (1:1) and in three of the seventeen other instances where the phrase recurs in MT-Joshua.[86]

In order to support this claim, Orlinsky adduced two main arguments, one based on the translation technique, the other based on parallells from the Qumran scrolls. In contrast to Margolis' opinion, Orlinsky held the Greek translator to be 'most faithful' to his Hebrew *Vorlage*, since the Greek translation shows no signs of avoiding anthropopathistic statements, which for Orlinsky formed an important criterion to judge the character of a Greek translation.[87] Anthropopathisms like the קֶצֶף, *wrath*, and יִרְאָה, *fear*, of Yhwh, have not been omitted or watered down in the Greek translation. Orlinsky furthermore referred to the biblical scrolls of Qumran from cave 4, which had shown that the emendations proposed by J. Wellhausen and S.R. Driver for the book of Samuel were now vindicated by the readings from 4QSam[a]. As a result, similar conclusions could be drawn for other books as well. This implied that for the critical study of the text of Joshua, scholarship should return to the work of S. Holmes.[88] It is important to note that Orlinsky did not speak in terms of literary priority between the two Hebrew readings (MT and the alleged Hebrew *Vorlage*), but only argued in favour of a different—not necessarily earlier—Hebrew *Vorlage* for LXX-Joshua.

Orlinsky's study marked the beginning of the 'Qumran era' in the study of the Septuagint of Joshua. Already in 1956 F.M. Cross had argued that the study of the textual history of the Hebrew Bible and its Old Greek translation had been revolutionised by the Dead Sea discoveries,[89] but it was Orlinsky who developed these ideas for the

[85] H.M. Orlinsky, The Hebrew *Vorlage* of the Septuagint of the Book of Joshua, in *Congress Volume. Rome 1968.* (SVT 17) Leiden 1969, pp. 187–195.

[86] H.M. Orlinsky, The Hebrew *Vorlage*, p. 193. See the discussion in chapter 6 below.

[87] H.M. Orlinsky, The Hebrew *Vorlage*, pp. 192–193.

[88] H.M. Orlinsky, The Hebrew *Vorlage*, p. 195.

[89] F.M. Cross jr., *The Ancient Library of Qumran*, chapter 4: 'The Old Testament at Qumrân.', pp. 161–194, especially p. 180. Compare also his article, The Evolution of a Theory of Local Texts, in F.M. Cross, S. Talmon (eds.), *Qumran and the History of the Biblical Text*, p. 311.

question of the divergencies between the Greek and Hebrew texts of Joshua. A painful handicap, however, was posed by the fact that it would take some forty years after their discovery before the scrolls were published, leaving the scholarly world in the meantime with some rather rough impressions concerning their alignment.[90] For this reason, Orlinsky had to argue on the basis of analogies, i.e. the text of Jeremiah and Job, where in Orlinsky's view, the shorter Greek text faithfully reflects a shorter Hebrew *Vorlage*.[91] Although few scholars today would contest that there are indeed remarkable correspondencies in lenght and arrangement between LXX-Jeremiah and 4QJer[b], few scholars would follow Orlinsky's claim that the shorter Greek text of the book of Job faithfully reflects a shorter Hebrew *Vorlage* rather than the translators' aim to avoid the translation of too difficult passages.[92] Each book should therefore be studied on its own, which brings us back to the question of the faithfulness of the Greek translation of Joshua.

Here too, Orlinsky's argumentation is not very convincing. The examples Orlinsky adduced for unaltered anthropopathisms for the larger part do not refer to Yhwh's emotions, but rather to human emotions provoked by or directed towards Yhwh.[93] Where the Hebrew text seems to refer to Yhwh's anger, i.e., in Josh. 22:18, the Greek text presents an interesting modification, probably inspired by verse 20. Instead of MT's assertion *And tomorrow he [i.e., Yhwh] will rage against the whole congregation of Israel*, LXX presents this anger in a less direct and more impersonal way: *And tomorrow there will be anger against whole Israel*.[94] Although the possibility that the Hebrew *Vorlage* had

---

[90] For this reason, a number of different and confusing general statements were made, like for instance in J.A. Soggin, *Le livre de Josué*, p. 21: 'On peut trouver le texte de LXX-B en hébreu dans deux manuscrits de Qumran qui n'ont pas encore été publiés ni étudiés à fond.'

[91] H. Orlinsky, The Hebrew *Vorlage*, p. 194.

[92] Thus already M. Pope, *Job*. (AB 15) New York 1965, p. xliv.

[93] In my view this applies not only to his examples mentioned on pp. 193–194, such as *to destroy Israel* (האביד, השמיד, החרים), *to deliver Israel into the hands of* (נתן . . . ביד), *to wage war for Israel* (נלחם לישׂראל), *to throw the enemy into panic* (ויהמם יהוה), *to stiffen the heart* (לחזק את־לב), *to rebel against the Lord* (למרד ביהוה), or *to refuse a portion in the Lord* (אין לנו חלק ביהוה), but also to the concept of the fear of God. Where the root ירא, *to fear*, occurs in the Hebrew text in conjunction with Yhwh, the latter is always object and nowhere subject of the fearing (Josh. 4:24, 22:25, 24:14).

[94] MT: ומחר אל־כל־עדת ישׂראל יקצף—LXX καὶ αὔριον ἐπὶ πάντα Ισραηλ ἔσται ἡ ὀργή. Compare also the similar translations offered by the Targum, ומחר על כל כנשתא דישׂראל יהי רגזא, and the Pešiṭta, ܘܡܚܪ ܥܠ ܟܠܗ ܗܘ ܟܢܘܫܬܐ ܕܐܝܣܪܝܠ ܢܗܘܐ ܪܘܓܙܐ.

the same expression in verse 18 as in verse 20 cannot be excluded, one should at least admit that the Greek text does not represent an anthropopathistic expression. Besides that, Orlinsky too, had to admit that the Greek translator modified anthropomorphic expressions, such as the rendering of פי יהוה, *the mouth of Yhwh*, by πρόσταγμα κυρίου, *the ordinance of the Lord*. As a result, a close examination of only one aspect of the translation technique employed by LXX-Joshua already makes clear that one cannot simply jump from the Greek text to a Hebrew *Vorlage* deviating from MT.

2.2.5.3 *E.A. Chesman*

In his relatively short contribution Orlinsky referred to the Master's and Ordination thesis of his student, rabbi Edward A. Chesman, who had completed his thesis *Studies in the Septuagint Text of the Book of Joshua* a year earlier (1967).[95] Owing to the limited size of of a Masters' thesis, the scope of this study was restricted to a selection of some ten Hebrew words or phrases that (in some cases) lacked a counterpart in the Greek text.[96] In his discussion of the divergencies between MT and LXX, Chesman followed a standard procedure, i.e. determining whether the variant could be due to *parablepsis* in the Hebrew text or in the Greek text, to *glossation* in the Hebrew text, *intentional alteration* on the part of the Greek translator, or—finally—to a Hebrew *Vorlage* that differed from MT. Here Chesman offered an interesting correction to the work of Benjamin (to whom he does not refer), by pointing out that if the pluses in MT were the result of glosses, they would have to clarify an obscure statement, which is almost never the case. Since the majority of the quantitative divergencies between MT and LXX cannot be attributed to scribal error either, they must reflect two different Hebrew texts.

---

[95] E.A. Chesman, *Studies in the Septuagint Text of the Book of Joshua*. (Thesis Submitted in Partial Fulfillment of Requirements for the Master of Arts in Hebrew Literature Degree and Ordination) [New York?] 1967. See H.M. Orlinsky, The Hebrew *Vorlage*, p. 192.

[96] The words and phrases selected by Chesman are [chapter 1] משה עבד יהוה (dealing especially with 1:1, 13:33, 14:2–3, 24:5, 1:15, 12:6 and 22:4), [2] הזה, זה (1:2.4, 7:25.26, 2:14), [3] גדול (10:2, 18:27, 14:15, 24:17), [4] תורה (1:7), [6] עבר הירדן (1:14), [7] חרש (2:1), [8] ידעתי (2:4.5.9), [9] מהר, האנשים, שער לסגור (2:5, 23:16, 2:9, 18:9), [10] מצרים (2:10, 5:4.4.6, 24:7.17), [11] ארון ברית יהוה (4:5, 6:4.6.7, 7:6, 24:33a). As Chesman pointed out on p. iii, the passages were 'chosen according to their order of appearance in the text rather than according to a specific system'.

In order to dismiss the other possibility, viz. that the Greek translator should be held responsible for the quantitative variants, Chesman discussed those passages where Margolis had claimed that the minus in LXX is due to condensation on the part of the Greek translator. In Josh. 7:2, for instance, the phrases מִירִיחוֹ and עִם־בֵּית אָוֶן in MT do not have a counterpart in the Greek version, which according to Margolis is the result of deliberate curtailment by the Greek translator.[97] Chesman objected that Margolis did not provide arguments for his contention, and that in 18:12–13, where Beth-El and Beth-Aven recur, no condensation has taken place in the Greek translation. Moreover, if condensation had been a major device by the Greek translator, one would expect to find similar cases of condensation in the Greek text, where the Hebrew phrasing is unnecessarily wordy. In Josh. 2:11, the Greek text duly reflects the synonymous clauses וַיִּמַּס לְבָבֵנוּ וְלֹא־קָמָה עוֹד רוּחַ בְּאִישׁ מִפְּנֵיכֶם—ἐξέστημεν τῇ καρδίᾳ ἡμῶν, καὶ οὐκ ἔστη ἔτι πνεῦμα ἐν οὐδενὶ ἡμῶν ἀπὸ προσώπου ὑμῶν.[98] The conclusion regarding the passages discussed by Chesman should therefore be that not the Greek translator, but a Hebrew *Vorlage* which often differed from MT should be held responsible for the many variants. This explanation could then be extrapolated for (almost) all the divergencies between the MT and LXX.[99]

Chesman in many cases rightly rejected the option of scribal error or glossation, which in his case is only plausible when 'it serves a definite purpose, whether for reasons of clarity, grammar or theology'[100] and gives an interesting treatment of the problem of the alleged condensation. Nevertheless, his often repeated claim that 'all problems are resolved if we accept that the translator's *Vorlage* differed from our received text', does not solve the problem of the relation between this alleged different Hebrew *Vorlage* and the Hebrew text of MT, and only seems to shift a problem from the Greek stage to the Hebrew.

2.2.6 *Progressive Supplementation (A.G. Auld)*

Orlinsky's appeal to return to the approach as advocated by S. Holmes received a positive response from the Britisch scholar A. Graeme

[97] M.L. Margolis, *The Book of Joshua in Greek*, p. 103 [lines 21–24].
[98] E.A. Chesman, *Studies*, p. 117.
[99] E.A. Chesman, *Studies*, in his chapter 'Conclusions' pp. 119–121.
[100] E.A. Chesman, *Studies*, p. 38.

Auld. In one of his studies Auld explicitly referred to Holmes by giving it the same title.[101] The main focus of his studies is on in the literary-critical problems of Joshua, and the literary relations between Joshua and the Pentateuch on the one hand, and the book of Chronicles on the other.[102] These literary-critical problems, however, cannot be studied without taking into account the many text-critical data presented by LXX Joshua, which disqualify the MT of Joshua as the basis for literary criticism.[103] In Auld's view, the MT of Joshua has been expanded by all kinds of secondary accretions, which are to be identified with the aid of the shorter LXX.

In order to support his thesis of the superiority of LXX-Joshua over MT-Joshua, Auld points to those passages where the LXX has preserved the longer, more original text, i.e. in Josh. 13:7–8, 15:59a, 21:36–37. More important for him is the fact that the LXX text is considerably shorter than MT, which—in his formulation—attests to a process of 'progressive supplementation'[104] or 'expansion'[105] of the Hebrew text culminating into the present MT.

According to Auld, adopting the Hebrew *Vorlage* of LXX-Joshua as the more original text instead of the MT, has some far-reaching consequences for literary criticism. It would solve several of the literary problems in Joshua 13–21, Auld's main area of research. It would also undermine the basis for classical literary criticism to attribute Josh. 5:10–12 to the Priestly codex (P^G). In this passage the LXX lacks the phrases ממחרת הפסח and ממחרת, which were added, according to Auld, by a later scribe who brought the older Deuteronomistic narrative of the celebration of Passover into conformity with the Priestly calendar of Leviticus 23.[106]

---

101 A.G. Auld, Joshua. The Hebrew and Greek Texts, in J. Emerton (ed.), *Studies in the Historical Books of the Old Testament.* (SVT 30) Leiden 1979, pp. 1–14, reprinted in A.G. Auld, *Joshua Retold. Synoptic Perspectives* (Old Testament Studies 1) Edinburgh 1998, pp. 7–24. The essay is an elaboration of chapter 4: 'Joshua: The Text' of his doctoral dissertation A.G. Auld, *Studies in Joshua: Text and Literary Relations* (thesis presented for the Degree of Ph.D. to the University of Edinburgh) Edinburgh 1976, pp. 95–151.

102 A.G. Auld, *Studies in Joshua*, revised into A.G. Auld, *Joshua, Moses and the Land. Tetrateuch-Pentateuch-Hexateuch in a Generation since 1938.* Edinburgh 1980.

103 A.G. Auld, *Studies in Joshua*, pp. 150–151; A.G. Auld, Textual and Literary Studies in the Book of Joshua, *ZAW* 90 (1978), pp. 412–417, especially p. 413 (= *Joshua Retold*, pp. 19–24); A.G. Auld, Joshua. The Hebrew and Greek Texts, p. 7 (= *Joshua Retold*, p. 11).

104 A.G. Auld, Textual and Literary Studies, p. 417 (= *Joshua Retold*, p. 24).

105 A.G. Auld, *Studies in Joshua*, p. 119.

106 A.G. Auld, *Studies in Joshua*, pp. 106–108; idem, The Hebrew and Greek texts, p. 8 (= *Joshua Retold*, pp. 12–13). See the discussion in chapter 7 below.

The relation between textual and literary criticism in the studies of A.G. Auld is somewhat ambiguous. On the one hand he criticizes literary critics who do not take into account the differences between LXX and MT and argues that not the MT of Joshua, but the (shorter) LXX version should be taken as basis of a literary analysis of Joshua. On the other hand he, too, recognizes secondary elements in LXX. In the case of Joshua 13 he prefers the longer text of LXX in verses 7–8, but also the shorter LXX text at the end of the chapter (without verse 33). But then, he also holds the longer LXX introduction in verses 14–15 to be a secondary addition to verses 15–32, which themselves are already a younger addition. As a result, both MT and LXX contain secondary elements.

If one is therefore not to follow the testimony of LXX blindly, the question arises what then are the criteria for determining the more original reading. This question can also be applied to his treatment of the problem of deliberate alterations of geographical names. On the one hand he argued that LXX in 15:59 the otherwise unknown locality Βαιθαναμ reflects a Hebrew name בית ענון or בית ענם, from which the corresponding name in MT בֵּית עֲנוֹת, *house of (the godess) ʾAnath*, referring to a non-Yahwistic (Judaean) sanctuary, is nothing more than the result of a scribal error.[107] On the other hand, with respect to the variant Shechem (MT)—Shiloh (LXX) in Josh. 24:1.25, he admitted that the LXX reading is secondary, without explaining how and why this secondary reading had come into being.[108] If LXX-Josh. reflects secondary traits such as the notorious Shechem—Shiloh question, how can we be sure that in other cases the LXX should be seen as a more reliable witness to the book of Joshua? Regrettably, Auld hardly pays any attention to the translation technique of LXX-Joshua, but simply assumes a deviating Hebrew *Vorlage* behind almost all of the divergencies between MT and LXX.

Although in Auld's model textual and literary criticism overlap, Auld does not take into account the possibility that the secondary elements should be seen as an editorial stage. Whereas he distinguishes no fewer than nine stages in the development of Josh. 13–21,

[107] A.G. Auld, A Judaen Sanctuary of 'Anat (Josh 15:59)? in *Tel Aviv* 4 (1977), pp. 85–86 (= *Joshua Retold*, pp. 61–62).

[108] A.G. Auld, Joshua. The Hebrew and Greek Texts, p. 14; 'I am not yet persuaded that its 'Shiloh' should be preferred to Massoretic 'Shechem' at the beginning of ch. xxiv—that would entail the rewriting of too many books.'

the MT additions, e.g. those in Josh. 20:4–6, are not regarded as an independent final edition of the book. Basically, therefore, the additions are isolated features of a refined process of progressive supplementation. This takes Auld's approach to the pluses in MT close to the gloss model employed by Benjamin, the distinction between the two being gradual rather than fundamental. The classical distinction, however, between literary or redaction history as designation of the period in which the book of Joshua attained its final compository stage, and on the other hand the history of the transmission of the text is maintained in these two models.

2.2.7 *Textual and Literary Criticism*

As we have seen in the first chapter of this study, it is this distinction between textual criticism and literary criticism that has been queried in modern research, especially in the publications by Emanuel Tov, and other scholars from the Hebrew University in Jerusalem, such as Alexander Rofé and Lea Mazor.

2.2.7.1 *E. Tov*

Like Orlinsky before him, Tov discusses the divergencies between the LXX and MT of Joshua in the broader context of the whole complex of questions and phenomena concerning the transmission and development of the books of the Hebrew Bible.[109] Just as two subsequent literary stages can be discerned in the book of Jeremiah, and other biblical books (Ezekiel, Judges, Samuel), according to Tov, two subsequent literary editions can be discerned in the book of Joshua. Of special importance is Tov's essay 'The Growth of of the Book of Joshua in the Light of the Evidence of the LXX Translation', originally published in 1986.[110] In Tov's view, the numerous divergencies between MT and LXX in this book should not be approached in an atomistic way, but viewed together as the result of a re-edition

---

[109] See E. Tov, *Textual Criticism of the Hebrew Bible*, pp. 313–349: 'Chapter 7: Textual Criticism and Literary Criticism'; and E. Tov, *The Text-critical Use of the Septuagint in Biblical Research.* (JBS 8) Jerusalem 1997², pp. 237–263: 'Chapter 7: The contribution of the LXX to the Literary Criticism of the Bible'.

[110] E. Tov, The Growth of the Book of Joshua in the Light of the Evidence of the LXX Translation, in S. Japhet (ed.), *Studies in Bible 1986.* (Scripta Hierosolymitana 31) Jerusalem 1986, pp. 321–339 (= *The Greek and Hebrew Bible*, pp. 385–396).

of the book of Joshua. In this way, Tov's approach to the variants is a continuation of Holmes' thesis.[111]

This second edition of the book of Joshua mainly consists of the numerous pluses in MT *vis-à-vis* LXX. They can be classified under such headings as 'small elucidations', 'harmonizing additions', 'contextual additions', 'emphasis', 'theological corrections', and 'influence of Deuteronomy'. For instance, the plus in MT-Josh. 4:10 ככל אשר־צוה משה את־יהושע, *in accordance with everything that Moses had commanded to Joshua, vis-à-vis* LXX is designated as part of this edition II, 'whose secondary nature is evident from the context.' According to Tov, this clause is a secondary addition to the Hebrew text attested by LXX based on Deut. 3:28. The shorter LXX text is more logical than MT, where Joshua first has been commanded by Yhwh, while this second clause places the authority in the hands of Moses.[112] The tensions within the logic and syntax of MT are thus to be explained on the basis of textual data.

In cases like in 1:1 (the addition of the apposition עבד יהוה), 1:7 (the addition of כל־התורה), 1:11 (the plus לרשתה), and especially in Josh. 20:4–6, it is also possible to detect the influence of Deuteronomy. According to Tov, there would thus be some continuity between the Deuteronomistic editions preceding the first final edition and this re-edition of the book of Joshua, in the same way the second edition of the books of Jeremiah and Ezekiel reflect the influence of the book of Deuteronomy. This is a very important observation, since it is generally assumed that the book of Joshua in its present form has undergone a Deuteronomistic revision. Contrary to the relatively harmless and insignificant pluses labeled as 'emphasis' (such as מאד in 1:7) and 'small elucidations' (such as the plus לבני־ישראל in 1:2),[113] these Deuteronomistic pluses, according to Tov, offer a clear point of overlap between text-critical and literary-critical observations.

---

[111] See E. Tov, The Growth, pp. 322–323 (= *The Greek and Hebrew Bible*, pp. 385–386).

[112] E. Tov, The Growth, pp. 329–330 (= *The Greek and Hebrew Bible*, p. 389). See also E. Tov, *Textual Criticism*, pp. 327–328, and H.-J. Stipp, Textkritik-Literarkritik-Textentwicklung, p. 145, who presents this passage as a first piece of evidence for his thesis of the inextricability of textual and literary criticism. See further K. Bieberstein, *Josua-Jordan-Jericho*, p. 163, and the discussion in section 6.4.1 below.

[113] E. Tov, The Growth, p. 332 (= *The Greek and Hebrew Bible*, p. 391). See chapter 6 below.

The leading principle is thus one of literary growth.[114] The shorter text underlying the Hebrew *Vorlage* of LXX has been expanded, mainly by small elucidations, to a fuller text underlying the MT. Nevertheless, the LXX of Joshua also contains a number of significant pluses (6:26, 16:10, 19:47–48, 21:42a–d, 24:31a, 33a–b) that, according to the model of literary growth, point to later expansion in the LXX and thus disturb this model. Therefore, the (Hebrew *Vorlage* of) LXX should not be completely identified with this first edition. The pluses were added to the Hebrew *Vorlage* of LXX mainly from parallel passages (LXX-Josh. 21:42a–d from Josh. 19:49–50, LXX-Josh. 19:47a–48a from Judg. 1:34–35, LXX-Josh. 16:10 from 1 Kgs. 9:16 and LXX-Josh. 6:26 from 1 Kgs. 16:10) and subsequently omitted in MT or added to edition I independently of the additions found in edition II.[115] Nevertheless, one of these pluses, i.e. the second conclusion of the passage about the division of the land in LXX-Josh. 21:42a–d, may be fitted into the model of literary growth, if one considers the text between this second and the first conclusion in 19:49–51, i.e., chapters 20 (cities of refuge) and 21 (Levitical cities) to be secondary. After they had been added to the completed narrative of the land divison, a second conclusion had become necessary and consequently was drawn from the first one.[116]

The Septuagint of Joshua shares with LXX-Jeremiah and LXX-Ezek. 7:3–9[117] the phenomenon of a significant difference in sequence *vis-à-vis* MT. The passage concerning the building of an altar on

---

[114] Hence the title of Tov's principal article on this topic 'The Growth of the Book of Joshua in the Light of the LXX Evidence.' See his remarks there, p. 329 (= *The Greek and Hebrew Bible*, p. 389): 'a working hypothesis is formulated according to which a short text *like* the LXX was expanded to a long text *like* MT. The use of the word 'like' enables us to account also for pluses of the LXX.' See also the preliminary methodological remarks to chapter 7 in E. Tov, *Textual Criticism*, p. 314: 'Our working hypothesis is to separate the two types of evidence with a quantitative criterion which also has qualitative aspects. It is assumed that large-scale differences displaying a certain coherence were created at the level of the literary growth of the books by persons who considered themselves actively involved in the literary process of composition.'

[115] E. Tov, The Growth, pp. 336–338 (= *The Greek and Hebrew Bible*, pp. 394–395). Since the diction of these pluses is clearly Hebraistic, and since Tov deems it illogical that translators would create these Hebraisms (p. 328), he considers these pluses to be indications of a Hebrew *Vorlage* different from MT.

[116] E. Tov, The Growth, p. 337 (= *The Greek and Hebrew Bible*, p. 395).

[117] See E. Tov, Recensional Differences between the MT and LXX of Ezekiel, in *ETL* 62 (1986) pp. 89–101 (= *The Greek and Hebrew Bible*, pp. 397–410); and

mount Ebal disturbs the sequence of the story of the fall of Ai (7–8:29) and the reaction of the Cisjordanian Amorite kings to this event (9:1–2), as well as the geographical setting of the surrounding narratives (Josh. 5–8:29 and 9–10 are all situated in the south, while the Shechem area is far more north, i.e. the area that is to be conquered no earlier than in chapter 11). The fact that LXX has the passage after the reaction of the Amorite kings (9:2a–f) is hardly more original (it only solves the first of the two problems) points to a very late date of composition. Its pervasive Deuteronomistic language is another indication of its secondary character. After the passage had been drafted, it was inserted into the main frame of the story by different scribes at slightly different points in the already finished composition.[118] A *qualitative* difference has thus been transformed into a *quantitative* difference that accommodates the model of literary growth.

Whereas the Qumran scrolls of Jeremiah play a principal role in his model of two distinct editions of that book, Tov bases his ideas about the textual history of the book of Joshua principally on the LXX, partly because not all details about the Qumran scrolls of that book were known at the time when he first formulated his ideas, partly because these scrolls in his view do not support the LXX text.[119] This brings Tov to the preliminary problem of evaluating the extent of freedom with which the Greek translator handled his Hebrew text. The question is important, since, 'if the tranlation technique of the book can be recognized as reliable, the minuses should be attributed to the *Vorlage* of the translation rather than to the translator himself.'[120] At this point, Tov has to admit, the Greek translation of

further J. LUST, The Use of Textual Witnesses for the Establishment of the Text. The Shorter and Longer Texts of Ezekiel; and P.M. BOGAERT, Les deux rédactions conservées (LXX et TM) d'Ézéchiel 7, in J. LUST (ed.), *The Book of Ezekiel. Textual and Literary Criticism and their Interrelation.* (BETL 74) Leuven 1986, pp. 7–20, and 21–47.

[118] See E. TOV, Some Sequence Differences Between the MT and LXX and their Ramifications for the Literary Criticism of the Bible, in *JNSL* 13 (1987), pp. 151–160 (= *The Greek and Hebrew Bible*, pp. 411–418); E. TOV, The Growth, p. 326 (= *The Greek and Hebrew Bible*, p. 388); and E. TOV, *Textual Criticism*, pp. 338–340.

[119] His two principal studies on this subject, E. TOV, The Growth, and *Textual Criticism*, date from 1986 and 1992 respectively.

[120] E. TOV, The Growth, p. 327. See further E. TOV, B.G. WRIGHT, Computer-Assisted Study of the Criteria for Assessing the Literalness of Translation Units in the LXX, in *Textus* 12 (1985), pp. 149–187 (= *The Greek and Hebrew Bible*, pp. 219–237).

Joshua is less reliable than those of Jeremiah and Samuel, but should rather be qualified as ranging from 'relatively free' to 'relatively literal', thus reducing the extent of initiatives undertaken by the Greek translator.[121]

Unlike scholars such as Holmes, Benjamin, and Auld, Tov has paid considerable attention to the translation technique of LXX-Joshua and is for that reason in a far better position to evaluate the character of the Greek translation and its redaction-critical value. Nevertheless, it is interesting to note that in an early article Tov has collected an impressive number of cases where the Greek translation reflects a specific type of interpretation of the Hebrew text as preserved by MT, for which Tov employs the term 'Midrash-type Exegesis'.[122] In this study he develops the approach of G.W. Gooding and older Jewish Septuagint scholars like L. Prijs and Z. Frankel, who had stressed the (Jewish) interpretative character of the Greek translation of the Pentateuch, and the books of Kings, Isaiah, and Job.[123] Tov makes use of the term 'midrash-*type* exegesis' in order to focus on those elements 'which deviate from the plain sense of the MT and either reflect exegesis actually attested in Rabbinic sources or resemble such exegesis but are not found in any Midrashic source.'[124]

The question that presents itself is then whether a more general description of these secondary elements reflected in LXX-Joshua as 'interpretative' would not have been more appropriate, since only in a few cases is Tov able to adduce a parallel to the variant reading from the medieval (and therefore many centuries younger) rabbinic literature, whereas for most of his examples an explanation of the variant is derived from the context within the Hebrew Bible. Another problem is that of determining whether the interpretative element was introduced by the Greek translator, or at an earlier stage by a Hebrew scribe. Since, however the Hebrew *Vorlage* of LXX-Joshua

[121] E. Tov, The Growth, pp. 326–329 (= *The Greek and Hebrew Bible*, pp. 388–389); idem, *Textual Criticism*, pp. 327–328.

[122] E. Tov, Midrash-Type Exegesis in the LXX of Joshua, in *RB* 85 (1978), pp. 50–61 (= *The Greek and Hebrew Bible*, pp. 153–164).

[123] See E. Tov, Midrash-Type Exegesis, p. 50, notes 1–2 (= *The Greek and Hebrew Bible*, p. 153). The view of D.W. Gooding, Traditions of Interpretation of the Circumcision at Gilgal, in A. Shinan (ed.), *Proceedings of the Sixth World Congress of Jewish Studies*. (Jerusalem 1977), pp. 149–164, will be discussed in chapter 7 below.

[124] E. Tov, Midrash-type Exegesis, p. 50 (= *The Greek and Hebrew Bible*, p. 153).

is an uncertain factor in itself, attribution to one of the two stages is 'based mainly on intuition'.[125]

In his first category of 'midrash-type exegesis which was probably introduced by the translator' Tov places translations such as אשר הכין by τῶν ἐνδόξων (Josh. 4:4),[126] the addition in LXX-Josh. 5:3 of καὶ ἔθηκεν θιμωνίας ἀκροβυστίων,[127] and the rendering of MT-Josh. 2:1 and 6:22 אנשים, *men*, by νεανίσκοι, *youths*, which is based on the designation of the two men in MT 6:23 as נערים, *youths*.[128] In the second category, i.e. exegetical elements that might reflect a Hebrew variant, Tov places the temporal phrase ἡμέραι θερισμοῦ πυρῶν, *the days of the wheat-harvest*, where the plus *vis-à-vis* MT πυρῶν reflects a Hebrew reading ימי קציר חטים, rather than the shorter MT ימי קציר, *the days of the harvest* (Josh. 3:15). Interestingly, the existence of a Hebrew text containing the plus חטים, has been vindicated by 4QJosh[b], where it was added supralinearly.[129]

As a possible source of some secondary elements in LXX-Joshua Tov mentions the Passover Hagaddah. Thus, the plus in LXX-Josh. 24:4–5, which was taken from the parallel historical retrospect in Deut. 26:5–6, might have entered the Hebrew *Vorlage* of LXX-Joshua via the Passover Haggadah, in which Deuteronomy 26 takes a central

---

[125] Instructive are Tov's remarks, Midrash-type Exegesis, pp. 51–52 (= *The Greek and Hebrew Bible*, p. 154): 'ideally a distinction should be made between (1) Midrashic elements which were introduced by the Greek translator, and (2) Midrashic elements which belonged to the Hebrew *Vorlage* of the LXX. Such a distinction should be based on an analysis which is particularly difficult in the case of Joshua . . . *Hence, overall theories such as in the case of Jeremiah on the one hand and Job on the other hand cannot be applied to the book of Joshua.* [italics MM] The analysis of midrashic elements in Joshua is thus more complicated than the description of similar elements in Isaiah, Daniel, Job and Proverbs. As a result, the *ideal* analysis outline above cannot be maintained. For no good distinction can be made between Midrashic elements presumably found in Hebrew MSS of Joshua and Midrash-type exegesis introduced by the translator. Nevertheless some examples of the latter type are adduced, when our analysis is based mainly on intuition.'

[126] E. Tov, Midrash-type Exegesis, pp. 52–53 (= *The Greek and Hebrew Bible*, p. 155). See already M.L. Margolis, τῶν ἐνδόξων—Josh. 4,4, in *Studies in Jewish Literature in Honor of Professor Kaufmann Kohler Ph.D.* Berlin 1913, pp. 204–209; and the discussion in chapter 9 below.

[127] E. Tov, Midrash-type Exegesis, pp. 53–54 (= *The Greek and Hebrew Bible*, p. 156). See the discussion of this variant in chapter 7 below.

[128] E. Tov, Midrash-type Exegesis, p. 52 (cf. *The Greek and Hebrew Bible*, p. 155): 'If one were to employ a hermeneutical term, one would say that the translator used the system of *g^ezerah šavah*. The spies are described in vi 23 as 'youths', and hence they are to be depicted similarly in other places in the book.'

[129] E. Tov, Midrash-type Exegesis, pp. 55–56 (= *The Greek and Hebrew Bible*, p. 158, where Tov has added the reference to 4QJosh[b]).

place. Since the plus in LXX-Joshua deviates from LXX-Deuteronomy, the addition must have taken place at the Hebrew level.[130] In the same way, Tov proposes to ascribe the change from plural to singular in the children's question in Josh. 4:6 (MT: כי־ישאלון בניכם מחר, *when your children will ask tomorrow* . . . to LXX ἵνα ὅταν ἐρωτᾷ σε ὁ υἱός σου αὔριον, *when your son will ask you tomorrow* . . .) to the influence of the Passover Haggadah upon a Hebrew scribe responsible for the Hebrew *Vorlage* of LXX. Tov admits the speculative character of this suggestion and the question must be asked whether the Passover Haggadah already existed as early as the third or second century BCE, the time when the Greek translation came into being. Since the singular formulation כי־ישאלך בנך מחר already occurs in the parallel passages Exod. 14:14 and Deut. 6:20, it might further be asked whether one really needs the Passover Haggadah as an intermediary between these texts and LXX-Josh. 4:6. One furthermore wonders in what respect the plus in LXX-Josh. 24:4 differs from those in LXX-Josh. 6:26 (= MT-1 Kgs. 16:34), 16:10 (= MT-1 Kgs. 9:16), 19:47–48 (= MT-Judg. 1:34–35).

Apparently, Tov attributes a secondary reading to the Hebrew *Vorlage* when the source from which the variant was drawn was available in Hebrew (1 Kgs. 16:34 as source for the plus in the Hebrew *Vorlage* of LXX-Josh. 6:26, the text of Deut. 26:5–6 as source for the Hebrew *Vorlage* of LXX-Josh. 24:4–7, the occurrence of Shiloh in the list of legitimate cultic places in Mishna *Zebaḥim* 14:6 etc.). Since, however, Tov ascribes some seven examples of his 'midrash-type exegesis' to the interpretation skills of the Greek translator, he appears to attribute more freedom to the Greek translator than he does in his later studies. One might ask then: how are we to determine whether a variant between LXX and MT should be defined as a secondary deviation from proto-MT reflected in LXX, or as a secondary re-edition of a text similar to the Hebrew *Vorlage* of LXX to a text like the MT?

With his thesis that divergencies between LXX and MT offer a textual basis for the study of the literary growth of the book of Joshua, Tov has placed the LXX of Joshua in a more prominent position and in a far broader context than had been done before. Whereas in Hollenberg's view, the primary value of the LXX of

[130] E. Tov, Midrash-type Exegesis, p. 60 (= *The Greek and Hebrew Bible*, pp. 161–162).

Joshua is basically that of a tool for incidental text-emendations, and whereas in Auld's view the LXX primarily serves as a tool to relieve the expansionistic MT from individual secondary accretions, in Tov's model the LXX serves as an empirical basis for reconstructing the literary formation of Joshua.

Nevertheless, many questions remain that deal with the preliminary question of the evaluation of the text-critical value of the Septuagint, and the proper relation between textual criticism and literary criticism: How are we to ascertain that minuses in LXX in fact reveal the later accretions now found in MT? How can we verify Tov's view, against Auld, that the alleged pluses in MT are not the result of an extensive process of incidental additions but stem from the same editorial hand? How can we account for both the alleged primary readings and the many secondary readings in LXX? Are there valid criteria for attributing a variant to an exegetical change introduced by the Greek translator, his Hebrew predecessor, or to a re-edition reflected in MT? Is Tov's model of literary growth, in which the longer text more or less automatically is viewed as part of the re-edition such a valid criterion, and if so, at what stage were the important pluses in LXX-Joshua introduced?

Since Tov draws upon existing literary theories concerning Deuteronomistic additions in a rather broad sense, in order to support his theory of two literary strata evidenced by textual data, one might wonder whether one should submit the literary criticism to textual criticism—that is place the deviations of MT *vis-à-vis* LXX in a framework of textual expansion—or whether an independent literary analysis focussing on the Deuteronomistic and post-Deuteronomistic strata arrives at approximately the same conclusions. Here again we may ask some questions: How does Tov's model of the two literary final editions relate to existing theories of the literary formation of Joshua preceding the common base of both LXX and MT (i.e., edition I)? Does the hypothesis that many Deuteronomistic elements in MT-Joshua are to be seen as part of edition II imply that we should consider the book of Joshua as a book that has undergone a Deuteronomistic redaction or even a large number of subsequent Deuteronomistic redactions of which MT happens to be the final, standardised stage, rather than the literary work that in its present form was created from the outset as a unified Deuteronomistic composition?

In the light of these questions it may be safer to study the Greek translation of Joshua on its own along the lines set out by Tov in his 'Midrash-type Exegesis' essay, and separate the text-critical and literary-critical questions and observations in order to see whether they produce the same results, as will be argued in chapter 5 below.

2.2.7.2 *A. Rofé*

Two important arguments in Tov's thesis concerning the two subsequent editions of the book of Joshua have not been mentioned so far. They are based on two articles written by Tov's Jerusalem colleague Alexander Rofé in 1977 (1982) and 1983 (1985) concerning two significant deviations of LXX from MT, i.e. the plus in LXX-Josh. 24 at the end of Joshua,[131] and the minus in LXX-Josh. 20.[132]

In the latter article, Rofé—like Hollenberg a century before him—points to the fact that the quantitative difference between MT and LXX (where most of verses 4–6 is lacking) corresponds to the difference between Priestly vocabulary (P, 20:1–3 [בשׁגגה], 7–9) and Deuteronomistic vocabulary (D, 20:3b [בבלי־דעת], 4–6) and the two different P and D sets of regulations concerning the cities of refuge (P in Num. 35:9–34 and D in Deut. 19:1–13).[133] The LXX version attests to an earlier version of the execution of Moses' commands by Joshua in Num. 35:9–34, while the MT represents a secondary stage in which a second author supplemented the P text by D elements. As a result two tensions came into existence, both dealing with the question of competent authority in the case of capital crimes. According to the shorter version (verse 6a) *the manslayer will remain in the city of refuge until his case has come before the congregation*, while the second expanded edition has: *until the death of the high priest.* According to the first version the question whether or not the manslaughter was intentional is to be determined by the congregation according

---

[131] A. Rofé, The End of the Book of Joshua according to the Septuagint, in *Henoch* 4 (1982), pp. 17–35. An earlier Hebrew version of this article appeared in *Shnaton* 2 (1977), pp. 217–227. In this study I refer to the English version.

[132] A. Rofé, Joshua 20: Historico-Literary Criticism Illustrated, in J.H. Tigay (ed.), *Empirical Models for Biblical Criticism.* Philadelphia 1985, pp. 131–147. An earlier Hebrew version appeared in A. Rofé, Y. Zakovitch (eds.), *Isac Leo Seeligmann Volume. Essays on the Bible and the Ancient World.* Jerusalem 1983, pp. 137–150; reprinted in A. Rofé, עיונים בשאלת חיבורם של ספרי תורה ונביאים. Jerusalem 1985, pp. 27–40. Again, I refer to the English version.

[133] An elaboration of his ideas regarding the history of the legislation concerning the cities of refuge is presented in A. Rofé, The History of the Cities of Refuge in Biblical Law, in S. Japhet (ed.), *Studies in Bible. Scripta Hierosolymitana* 31 (1986) Jerusalem 1986, pp. 205–239.

to the shorter version in verse 6, while according to the secondary version the elders at the gate have already determined this matter in verse 4. Apparently, the editor intended to define the authority (the shorter text mentions only the community, while in the plus the elders are explicitly mentioned), and to interpret the necessary stay of the unintentional killer as a period of detention. As a result a purely descriptive text became a prescriptive one.[134] Since the editor employed Deuteronomistic vocabulary and conceptions, he should be seen as a late representative of the Deuteronomistic school, which apparently then 'flourished for almost three hundred years, from the mid-seventh to the fourth century BCE',[135] rather than a predecessor of Halakic legal activity, which employed contemporary language and presented different solutions to the problem.[136]

One may question Rofé's conclusion that one should stretch out the Deuteronomistic school over such a long period, especially since the plus in MT-Josh. 20:6 contains the Priestly element of specifying the duration of the stay in the asylum of the refugee *until the death of the High Priest* (עד־מות הכהן הגדול) which has its parallel only in Num. 35:25.28 (כי בעיר מקלטו ישב עד־מות הכהן הגדל 35:28), as pointed out by A. van der Kooij.[137] It is nevertheless important to

---

[134] A. Rofé, Joshua 20, pp. 145–146.

[135] A. Rofé, Joshua 20, p. 145.

[136] A. Rofé, Joshua 20, p. 146: 'In rabbinic sources the manslayer is judged by a court of his own city, who bring him back to the city of refuge for this purpose (*m.Mak.*2:6). The elders of the city of refuge play no role in the judicial proceedings, and their only role is to qualify the city to be a place of refuge. On the stylistic plane, Halacha does not attempt to imitate biblical diction. It uses contemporary language with its own distinctive terminology, unlike the epigonic author of Josh. 20:4–6. It is interesting to note that legal terminology attempting to imitate a biblical model does appear elsewhere from the middle of the Second temple period on—in the book of Jubilees and in Qumran literature.'

Nevertheless, the conception of predestination in the Qumran literature leaves no room for unintentional actions and for this reason the topic is absent from the Temple scroll, which makes it implausible that the editor of Josh. 20 should be sought among the members of the Qumran community, see A. Rofé, The Cities of Refuge, p. 228, n. 50.

[137] A. van der Kooij, Zum Verhältnis von Textkritik und Literarkritik, p. 190: 'Es handelt sich offenbar um einen Autor, der sowohl P als D kannte, sodass man die Zusätze als nachpriesterlich und/oder als nachdeuteronomistisch bezeichnen kann. Wir haben es hier also mit einer Bearbeitung zu tun, ausgeführt von einem schriftgelehrten Autor, für den es kein "P" und "D" mehr gab. Das führt zu einer relativ späten Periode. Man vergleiche zum Beispiel die Tempelrolle, in der Texte des Pentateuch, die einmal verschiedenen Kreisen (P und D) entstammten, ohne Unterschied im Rahmen einer Neukomposition verwendet werden.'

note that text-critical and literary-critical observations *independently from each other* produce the same results: the plus in MT is an addition to the shorter Priestly text as attested by LXX, which transforms the description of Joshua's assignment of the cities of refuge into a prescriptive text, to which the legislation concerning the cities of refuge from both Deut. 16 and Num. 35 has been added. This makes this article very important from a methodological point of view. The convergence of textual and literary data thus validate the historical-criticism of the Hebrew Bible.[138] Yet, the case itself seems to be a unique one, since thus far no similar case, where textual criticism and literary criticism confirm each other so clearly have been adduced for the book of Joshua.

Less clear-cut, but more far-reaching is Rofé's discussion of the end of the book of Joshua in LXX-Josh. 24:33a–b. Although the LXX presents a plus *vis-à-vis* MT, Rofé argues that this passage should be seen as the original transition from the pre-Deuteronomistic version of Joshua to the pre-Deuteronomistic version of Judges. Since this plus begins with the death of Joshua, narrated in Josh. 24:31, and ends with the oppression of the Israelites, narrated in Judges 3:12–30, it is the present text of Judg. 1:1–3:11 that in fact constitutes the plus as opposed to this earlier version.[139] The originality of this plus finds support in the Hebraistic diction of the Greek text.[140] Rofé points to some other significant divergencies between LXX and MT in Josh. 24 in order to support his thesis of the originality of this Greek text. LXX-Josh. 24:31a presents another plus in which the flint knives with which Joshua had circumcised the Israelites in Josh. 5:2–9, are mentioned again and which reappear in the plus LXX-Josh. 21:42d, two pluses that may equally easily be retroverted into Hebrew.

---

[138] Hence the subtitle: Historico-Literary Criticism Illustrated. The article serves as a main argument in Tigay's program for an empirical basis of literary criticism, J.H. Tigay, *Empirical Models*.

[139] A. Rofé, The End of the Book of Joshua. For a similar view, see already E. Nielsen, *Shechem. A Traditio-Historical Investigation*. Copenhagen 1955, pp. 134–137. A recent contribution to this issue along the lines set out by Rofé has been offered by B. Lucassen, *Josua, Richter* und *CD*, in *RdQ* 18 (1998), pp. 373–396.

[140] See A. Rofé, The End of the Book of Joshua, pp. 21ff. with notes and comments on the retroversion. In his adaptation of this retroversion, E. Tov, *Textual Criticism*, p. 331, and E. Tov, *The Text-critical Use of the Septuagint*², p. 247, presents some minor modifications and alternative retroversions.

In Rofé's view these short notes have been deliberatedly removed from the original text, since they were felt to be offensive for two reasons: [1] the flint knives came to be understood and venerated as *reliquiae*, comparable to the bronze serpent made by Moses, and therefore had to be deleted from the biblical accounts,[141] and [2] the plus in LXX-Josh. 24:31a seems to suggest that it was Joshua and not Moses who had led the Israelites out of Egypt (ὅτε ἐξήγαγεν αὐτοὺς ἐξ Αἰγύπτου/בהוציאו אותם ממצרים). This idea finds support in the circumstance that the phrase in MT-Josh. 24:5 ואשלח את־משה ואת־אהרן lacks a counterpart in LXX, and thus appears to be an addition to the original text of Josh. 24, which sought to harmonize the unorthodox historiography to the normative one.[142]

The elements mentioned in LXX-Josh. 33a–b, the ark, the deaths of Eleazar, Joshua, the elders and the subsequent worship of the Ashtaroth, are to be found in the same order in the Damascus Document V:1–5. Rofé infers from the biblical allusion that the scribe of CD must have had knowledge of an ancient Hebrew scroll containing the plus Josh. 24:33a–b,[143] so that the existence of a deviant Hebrew *Vorlage* behind LXX-Josh. 24:33a–b would be supported by this text. Nevertheless, it is important to note that this passage in CD V contains only an allusion to the events that took place from the time of the Joshua's death to David. This Hebrew text does not correspond to Rofé's reconstruction of the Hebrew *Vorlage* of LXX-Josh. 24:33a–b. One may wonder, therefore, whether CD V really attests to such a deviant version of Joshua 24.

The implication of Rofé's 'restoration' of the original sequence of Josh. 24–Judg. 3:11ff. is that part of a pre-Deuteronomistic 'Ephraimite

[141] A. Rofé, The End of the Book of Joshua, pp. 24–25, p. 35. See also his remarks concerning 'Legenda and Reliquiae' in A. Rofé, *The Prophetical Stories. The Narratives about the Prophets in the Hebrew Bible. Their Literary Types and History*. Jerusalem 1988, pp. 22–26, where Rofé draws parallels between these passages and those concerning the hidden burial site of Moses (perhaps destroyed by Mesha, king of Moab, as related in the Moabite Mesha-stele), the bronze serpent smashed by Hezekiah (2 Kgs. 18:4), and the bones of Elisha that revived a dead man (2 Kgs. 13:20–21). Conversely, the priority of MT over LXX in Josh. 24:32 is supported by Rofé for the same reason: MT ויהיו לבני־יוסף לנחלה, *and these (i.e. the bones of Joseph) became an inheritance for the children of Joseph, vis-à-vis* LXX καὶ ἔδωκεν αὐτὴν Ιωσηφ ἐν μερίδι, *and he [i.e., Jacob] gave it [i.e., the piece of land which the latter had acquired from the Amorites] to Joseph in inheritance*, would represent the older rejected idea of Joseph's bones as *reliquiae*, A. Rofé, The End of the Book of Joshua, p. 25.

[142] A. Rofé, The End of the Book of Joshua, pp. 23–24.

[143] A. Rofé, The End of the Book of Joshua, pp. 28–29, 32.

History' has been recovered. The text of Judges without these additions is, according Rofé, the opening of an old eight-century BCE Ephraimite Historical work (EphrH), which is a purely north-Israelite pre-Deuteronomistic book of Judges that extends to 1 Sam. 12. Its ideology can be described as anti-monarchistic, theocratic (Yhwh does battle for Israel, while Israel remains passive) in line with the prophecies of Hosea, as opposed to the ideology of the younger seventh-fifth century BCE Deuteronomistic History, where the central focus is on the unification of the (now aniconic) worship of Yhwh and the importance of the *torah* (as in the DtrH).[144] Although the view that Judg. 1–3:6 contains Deuteronomistic material that is younger than the remainder of Judges is commonly accepted,[145] it should be noted that these Deuteronomistic (DtrH and DtrN) passages overlap the alleged plus Judg. 1:1–3:11 only partially.

Whereas for Tov the quantitative aspect is the main criterion for establishing the chronological priority between two alleged editions of the same book (the longer version is the later), Rofé stresses the ideological intention behind the textual developments. As a result, in Rofé's model secondary textual developments not only result in additions, but also in alterations or omissions of offensive texts. In a lecture at the 1989 Groningen Qumran Symposium, Rofé introduced the concept of 'Nomistic Correction' as the binding principle behind a large number of textual alterations.[146] In his view, one should not draw a sharp line between the copyists of biblical text in the Second Temple Period and the authors of the literary works that were composed during the same period. Such compositions as Tobit, Judith, Chronicles and Jubilees reflect the fundamental transformation of the Jewish people into a people of the *torah*.[147] These

---

[144] A. Rofé, Ephraimite versus Deuteronomistic History, in D. Garrone, F. Israel (eds.), *Storia e Tradizione di Israele. Scritti in Onore di J. Alberto Soggin*. Brescia 1991, pp. 221–235. Rofé has revived the old hypothesis of C.F. Burney, *The Book of Judges*. London 1920², pp. xli–l, who designated the work as that of an heir of the Elohistic source, and hence termed it E².

[145] See chapter 4 below, and further B. Lucassen, *Josua, Richter* und *CD*.

[146] A. Rofé, The Nomistic Correction in Biblical Manuscripts and Its Occurrence in 4QSam^a, in *RdQ* 14/2 (1989), pp. 247–254.

[147] A. Rofé, The Nomistic Correction, pp. 248–249. Rofé refers briefly to a number of indications that confirm this general picture, such as the writings of Ezra and Nehemiah, the Passover letter from Elephantine, 'the democratization of religion' in which the Torah is no longer the legacy of priests but of scribes, and the emergence of the exegetical method of *midraš-hălākâ*.

author-scribes were equally responsible for a number of minor alterations introduced at various stages in the transmission of biblical books, hence they are attested by different textual witnesses of the same biblical composition and to a large extent concern the accentuation of the pious character of important heroes in the biblical narratives such as Moses, Joshua and Samuel.[148]

In this light the alleged addition in Josh. 1:7 of the words כל־התורה, as well as the addition of Josh. 1:8 to the two texts, are to be explained.[149] Since this ideal of daily *torah*-study and the corresponding terminology appear only in Ps. 1:2 and Isa. 59:21,[150] and since both Joshua 1 and Psalm 1 mark the beginning of a new section of the Hebrew canon (Prophets and Writings, respectively), the insertion of these two nomistic or legalistic interpolations must be dated to one of the last stages of the formation of the Hebrew Bible, more specifically the period of canonisation.[151]

Rofé considers this 'nomistic correction' to be the result of a general movement, rather than the intention of a particular editor. These nomistic corrections can be found equally in MT, (the Hebrew *Vorlage* of) LXX, the Samaritan Pentateuch, and the biblical texts from Qumran. For example, the mentioning of Moses building a מצבה (MT-Exod. 24:4) was 'corrected'—because of the Deuteronomists verdict on building a מצבה (Deut. 16:22)—to the more neutral and nomistically inoffensive designation אבנים (SamP and LXX λίθους).[152]

The theories of the two scholars, Tov and Rofé, have apparently influenced one another, as is evident from the cross-references to each other's studies.[153] Nevertheless, there is a difference in scope

---

[148] A. Rofé, The Nomistic Correction, p. 250.

[149] A. Rofé, The Nomistic Correction, p. 248. See the discussion of this variant in chapter 6 below.

[150] A. Rofé, The Piety of the Torah-Disciples: Josh. 1:8; Ps. 1:2; Isa. 59:21, in H. Merklein, K. Müller, G. Stemberger (Hg.), *Bibel in jüdischer und christlicher Tradition. FS J. Maier.* Frankfurt am Main 1993, pp. 73–85 = A. Rofé, המסירות ללימוד התורה בשלהי התקופה המקראית, in S. Japhet (ed.), *The Bible in the Light of Its Interpreters. Sarah Kamin Memorial Volume.* Jerusalem 1994, pp. 622–628.

[151] A. Rofé, From Tradition to Criticism: Jewish Sources as an Aid to the Critical Study of the Hebrew Bible, in J.A. Emerton (ed.), *Congress Volume. Cambridge 1995,* p. 235.

[152] A. Rofé, The Nomistic Correction, p. 249.

[153] See for instance Tov's references to Rofé's studies and private comunications, in E. Tov, Midrash-type Exegesis, p. 54 and p. 59, n. 14, *The Text-Critical Use*[1], pp. 300–301; The Growth, pp. 324–325; *Textual Criticism*, pp. 329–332; *The Text-Critical Use*[2], pp. 246–248; and conversely Rofé's references to Tov's article, L'incidence,

between these two theories: whereas Tov emphasizes the quantitative element inherent in a model of literary growth, Rofé apparently argues on the basis of ideological motives behind the textual alterations. For instance, Tov places the nomistic corrections in the area of textual transmission and designates them as (minor) readings intentionally created by scribes,[154] but considers the substantial change in order concerning MT-Josh. 8:30–35 as a part of differences created at the preceding literary level. Rofé, on the other hand, does not seem to distinguish between the size of his nomistic corrections. Besides that, the observation that older elements might as well have been omitted as altered or neutralized by additions, constitutes an important correction to the linear model of *progressive supplementation* or *literary growth.* Since this nomistic ideal was rather an unconcious concept in the minds of the author-scribes of the Second Temple Period, it accounts for secondary elements in all textual witnesses that originated from that period and thus provides a flexible framework for the evaluation of the intentional variants. The consequence of this model is that it frees the scholar of forcing a specific textual witness into one particular stage of the development of a given book.

Another important aspect, in my view, is that this theory provides opportunities to tie in textual differences with contemporary Jewish literature and thus offers an opportunity to place textual developments not only in a relative chronological sequence (as does Tov's theory with regard to the subsequent editions), but also in a historical context. At the same time, questions arise when Rofé attempts to interpret the variants within the context of rabbinical (Halakic or Midrashic) literature.[155] Is the assumption of an intermediary stage of Pharisaic and Rabbinical literature, such as the case of *Mishna Zebaḥim* for the alteration Shechem-Shiloh, between the older reading and the younger really necessary? If the concept of the placing of the tabernacle at Shiloh in Josh. 18:1.9.9.10, and in the corresponding

in A. Rofé, The End of the Book of Joshua, p. 18, n. 2 (p. 35, n. 46); and to Tov's article, Midrash-type Exegesis, in A. Rofé, The Nomistic Correction, p. 249, n. 12.

[154] E. Tov, *Textual Criticism*, pp. 272–274.

[155] Thus in his lecture at the IOSOT 1995 Cambridge Congress, published as A. Rofé, From Tradition to Criticism: Jewish Sources as an Aid to the Critical Study of the Hebrew Bible, in J.A. Emerton (ed.), *Congress Volume. Cambridge 1995*, pp. 235–247, where he identified the nomistic or legalistic corrections as Proto-Pharisaic.

passages in Josh. 19:51, 21:2, 22:9.12 belongs to a Priestly stratum of Joshua, the alteration of Shechem to Shiloh in Josh. 24:1.25 may then be qualified as an attempt to conform the older text of Joshua 24 to the Priestly concept which was inserted in the text passages preceding chapter 24.

2.2.7.3 *L. Mazor*

A combination of the theories of the two Jerusalem scholars is offered by the dissertation by Lea Mazor, so far the most extensive discussion of the textual-literary problems presented by LXX-Joshua. In her Hebrew thesis *The Septuagint Translation of the Book of Joshua*,[156] she presents an analysis of the translation technique of LXX-Joshua and a discussion of both minor and major divergencies between MT-Joshua and the Hebrew *Vorlage* of LXX-Joshua.

In her view, only a limited number of the divergencies between LXX and MT are to be attributed to the Greek translator. The majority of textual divergencies had already taken place on the Hebrew level before the Greek translator produced his version of the book. In her view the Greek translation can be qualified as 'neither fully literal nor fully free'.[157] The free element in the translation is expressed by the rich Greek vocabulary which the translator employed in order to avoid monotony, the use of synonymous Greek expressions for the same Hebrew words or formularic Hebrew expressions, variation in Greek prefixes, variation between literal and free renderings of the same Hebrew expression, or, conversely, the use of the same Greek word for synonymous Hebrew expressions, and subtle changes in word-order.[158] On the other hand, statistical study of the translation technique with respect to syntactical elements, as

---

[156] L. Mazor, עיונים בתרגום השבעים לספר יהושע—תרומתו להכרת המסירה הטקסטואלית של הספר ולהתפתחותו הספרותית והרעיונית [*The Septuagint Translation of the Book of Joshua—Its Contribution to the Understanding of the Textual Transmission of the Book and Its Literary and Ideological Development*]. (Thesis Submitted for the Degree of Doctor of Philosophy under the supervision of prof. E. Tov) Jerusalem 1994. The author kindly provided me with a copy of her unpublished thesis. An English abstract has been published in *BIOSCS* 27 (1994), pp. 29–38.

[157] L. Mazor, עיונים, pp. 27–73; chapter 1: 'The Text-critical Evaluation of LXX'. See the abstract of this chapter in *BIOSCS* 27 (1994), pp. 32–33.

[158] Most of these observations had already been noted and collected by J. Hollenberg in his 1876 study, but they now find support through computer-assisted statistical investigations, such as the Computer Assisted Tools for Septuagint Study project of E. Tov and others, see e.g. G. Marquis, CATSS-Base: Computer Assisted Tools for Septuagint and Bible Study For All—Transcript of a Demonstration, in

executed by I. Soisalon-Soininen regarding the translation of Hebrew constructions with infinitive construct,[159] by R. Sollamo regarding the handling of Hebrew semiprepositions,[160] and by J. Bajard and R.-F. Poswick concerning the Hebrew *parataxis*,[161] reveal far more consistency, and thus demonstrate, according to Mazor,[162] the relative literalness and hence the fidelity and reliability of the Greek translation of Joshua.

Although LXX-Joshua contains some examples of Midrash-type exegesis, their number is limited and they originate in part from exegesis already introduced at the Hebrew level.[163] Likewise, Mazor admits the presence in LXX-Joshua of what she terms as 'paraphrastic renderings', i.e., translations that depart from the plain sense of the Hebrew text. She hastens to add, however, that these non-literal renderings were only introduced when a straightforward translation of the Hebrew idiom would result in a uncomprehensible, or stylistically unsatisfactory Greek expression, such as, for instance, the translation of the Hebrew clause ולא־היה בהם ידים לנוס הנה והנה, *there was no strength in them to flee hither or tither* (Josh. 8:20) by καὶ οὐκέτι εἶχον ποῦ φύγωσιν ὧδε ἢ ὧδε, *and they were no longer able to flee hither and tither.* One may wonder, however, whether a Greek translator willing and able to introduce such qualitative changes should not be held responsible for a number of quantitative changes as well.

According to Mazor, the Qumran finds of Joshua support the existence of a Hebrew version of Joshua that differs significantly from

C.E. Cox (ed.), *VII Congress of the International Organization for Septuagint and Cognate Studies. Leuven 1989.* Atlanta 1991, pp. 165–203. In the same congress volume Bajard and Poswick present their statistical analyses, which, among other things, demonstrate that the lexical variety of LXX-Joshua as compared with MT is far greater than that of any other Greek translation of a book of the Hebrew Bible, see J. Bajard, R.-F. Poswick, Aspects statistiques des rapports entre la Septante et le texte massorétique, in C.E. Cox (ed.), *VII Congress of the IOSCS*, pp. 123–156, especially p. 131.

[159] I. Soisalon-Soininen, *Die Infinitive in der Septuaginta.* (AASF B 132,1) Helsinki 1965.

[160] R. Sollamo, *Renderings of Hebrew Semiprepositions in the Septuagint.* (AASF 19) Helsinki 1979.

[161] J. Bajard – R.-F. Poswick, Aspects statistiques, found that translations of the paratactical -ו with καί amount to 96.6% of the total, against 3.2% rendered by δέ.

[162] L. Mazor, עיונים, pp. 33–37. She also refers to the study by E. Tov, B.G. Wright, Computer-Assisted Study of the Criteria for Assessing the Literalness of Translation Units in the LXX, in *Textus* 12 (1985), pp. 149–187 (= *The Greek and Hebrew Bible*, pp. 219–238), but unfortunately the authors did not include LXX-Joshua in their investigation.

[163] L. Mazor, עיונים, pp. 31–33.

MT-Joshua.[164] 4QJosh[a] would support the shorter LXX-version of Josh. 8:11–14,[165] 4QTestimonia supports the absence of the words את־יריחו from LXX, CD V would support the alternative version of Joshua's death and the period of the first judges as presented by LXX-Josh. 24:28–33b, and the fact that MT-Josh. 8:30–35 has a different location in both LXX-Joshua (after 9:2) and 4QJosh[a] (after 5:1) would also point to textual differentiation at the Hebrew level. Yet, the Qumran texts receive no study of their own, and the fact that the 4QJosh[a] and 4QJosh[b] texts reflect the longer MT text in almost all quantitative variants is not accounted for in her discussion.[166] She adds to these examples some additional minor agreements between LXX and 4QJosh[a.b], variants that do attest to some scribal variation on the Hebrew level, but which can hardly be taken to support the thesis of an editorial reworking of one text into the other.

The same can be said for the examples Mazor adduces for inner-Hebrew genetic variants reflected by LXX, a third line of argument Mazor employs in favor of her thesis that most of the variants are to be attributed to the process of literary development of Joshua instead of creative initiatives by the Greek translator. In this category she places variants such as those originating from an exchange of letters,[167] substitution of graphically similar letters,[168] synonymous phrases,[169] a different spelling[170] or the elision of gutturals.[171] Among all scholars there is a widespread consensus that the Hebrew *Vorlage* of LXX-Joshua was not completely identical with MT-Joshua, just as not all Masoretic manuscripts attest to hundred percent uniformity, but the fact that minor unconscious scribal variations are attested

---

[164] See chapter 3 below.

[165] See chapter 8 below.

[166] See chapter 3 below.

[167] See for example the exchange of ה and ח in Josh. 8:29 between פתח, *entrance* (MT) and פחת (βόθρος LXX) in the clause describing the fate of the king of Ai's dead body, discussed in chapter 8 below.

[168] L. Mazor, עיונים, p. 61, mentions the divergence between MT-Ketib והים הגבול (15:47) and LXX καὶ ἡ θάλασσα ἡ μεγάλη, which reflects a Hebrew variant הים הגדול (cf. MT-Qere).

[169] See L. Mazor, עיונים, pp. 63–64, as well as chapter 2: 'Minor Variants: Moveable Elements as Evidence of Scribal Activity.'

[170] L. Mazor, עיונים, p. 61, refers to Josh. 5:14 where LXX ὁ δὲ εἶπεν *αὐτῷ*, *and he said to him*, reflects a Hebrew text ויאמר לו rather than MT ויאמר לא, *and he said: No.*

[171] L. Mazor, עיונים, p. 62, takes the variant in Josh. 6:27 τὸ *ὄνομα* αὐτου, *his name*, to reflect a Hebrew *Vorlage* שמו rather than MT שמעו, *his rumour/fame.*

in the textual witnesses does not bear evidence to the claim that these witnesses reflect drastic conscious editorial activity, in spite of Mazor's claim that the difference between the two should be seen as one of degree rather than kind.[172]

Mazor furthermore points to the Hebraistic style of four of the six large pluses in LXX-Josh. 6:26, 16:10, 19:47–48, 21:42a–d and 24:31a, 33a–b, which makes it improbable that these passages were introduced by the Greek translator. Yet, the Hebraistic style can easily be explained by the fact that they have a counterpart in the Hebrew text of MT-1 Kgs. 16:34, 16:10, MT-Judg. 1:34–35 and MT-Josh. 19:49–51, respectively.

Mazor argues that the variants between the two Hebrew versions of Joshua, the MT and the alleged Hebrew *Vorlage* of LXX, reflect independent editorial reshaping of individual passages.[173] Neither of the two versions consistently reflects the older version, but both the MT and the Hebrew *Vorlage* of LXX contain editorial reworking of earlier material, and for that reason are held to be *separate recensions* that developed independently from a common source. Within the process of literary development attested by the variants, Mazor makes a distinction between redactional and ideological variants, in order to differentiate between those variants that were introduced for the sake of the coherence of the book and those inserted because of ideological conceptions relating to theology, cult, law (Josh. 20), territory (Josh. 13–9) and national history (Josh. 24:28–33b).

In the first category of redactional variants Mazor places the difference in sequence regarding the passage of the altar and *torah*-reading at Mount Ebal, the ending of the book (Josh. 24:28–31), the second conclusion of the passage about the division of the land (i.e., the duplication of Josh. 19:49–51 in LXX-Josh. 21:42a–d), and some 'brief literary links designed to strengthen the interconnection between the separate traditions of which the book of Joshua is composed.' Most of these redactional additions were introduced in the MT of Josh. 1–12 for the purpose of presenting the various conquest narratives as a unified Israelite campaign with Gilgal as base for the military operations; hence the contextually intrusive additions

[172] L. Mazor, עיונים, pp. 146–148, see the abstract in *BIOSCS* 27 (1994), pp. 33–34.

[173] L. Mazor, עיונים, pp. 163–170. Part of this central paragraph has appeared in an English translation in the abstract in *BIOSCS* 27 (1994), pp. 35–38.

in MT-Josh. 10:15.43, which are contradicted in verse 21 by the reference to a camp at Makkedah.[174]

Apart from these redactional links, Mazor discerns a series of ideological variants, which constitute the central focus of her interest. According to Mazor, an example of such an ideological variant is offered by the different views of the two editors behind the two recensions with respect to the boundaries of the territory of Israel.[175] In Josh. 1:4 the MT presents, in her opinion, a more expansionistic description of Israel, in which 'the whole Hittite country' is included in the Promised Land. Her thesis that in the tradition behind LXX the territory of Israel did not yet extend as far north as presented by the editor behind MT, would be supported by the divergecies between the two versions of Josh. 19:47(48), where LXX still locates the territory of Dan in the centre of Israel, whereas in MT it is situated in the northern region. Related to this difference in conception is the more hostile perception of the editor behind MT with respect to the Trans-Jordanian part of Israel: in MT-Josh. 22:19 this region is considered to be impure (טמאה), whereas LXX simply speaks of a land that is too small (μικρά) which reflects the Hebrew reading מעטה.[176] Like Holmes before her, Mazor stresses the coherence among the divergencies between the two versions. In this case she leaves both the question of priority and the question of the motives and historical background of this ideological change open for further research.

In Mazor's view, the ideological development evidenced by the textual witnesses did not only result in a process of linear growth, as would have been the case in Josh. 8:1–29,[177] but could equally have resulted in the omission of offensive textual elements, or transposition of historical information.[178] In the case of the plus in LXX-Josh. 6:26, which narrates the fulfilment of Joshua's curse upon whoever will rebuild the city of Jericho, Mazor inverts the current consensus that the plus is a secondary expansion based on 1 Kgs. 16:10, where the fulfillment of this curse in the days of Ahab is narrated:[179]

---

[174] L. Mazor, עיונים, pp. 167–168; *BIOSCS* 27, p. 37. See the discussion of these variants in chapter 8 below.

[175] L. Mazor, עיונים, pp. 161–162, 165; *BIOSCS* 27, p. 37. See further chapter 6 below.

[176] See chapter 6 below.

[177] See chapter 8 below.

[178] L. Mazor, עיונים, p. 169, translated in the abstract in *BIOSCS* 27 (1994), p. 38.

[179] L. Mazor, עיונים, chapter 5. An English version of this chapter has been

LXX-Josh. 6:26b	LXX-3 Reg. 16:34	MT-1 Kgs. 16:34
καὶ οὕτως	ἐν ταῖς ἡμέραις αὐτοῦ	בְּיָמָיו
ἐποίησεν Οζαν	ᾠκοδόμησεν Αχιηλ	בָּנָה חִיאֵל
ὁ ἐκ Βαιθηλ·	ὁ Βαιθηλίτης	בֵּית הָאֱלִי
	τὴν Ιεριχω·	אֶת־יְרִיחֹה
ἐν τῷ Αβιρων	ἐν τῷ Αβιρων	בַּאֲבִירָם
τῷ πρωτοτόκῳ	τῷ πρωτοτόκῳ αὐτοῦ	בְּכֹרוֹ
ἐθεμελίωσεν αὐτὴν	ἐθεμελίωσεν αὐτὴν	יִסְּדָהּ
καὶ ἐν τῷ ἐλαχίστῳ	καὶ τῷ Σεγουβ	**וּ**בִ**שְׂגוּב
διασωθέντι	τῷ νεωτέρῳ αὐτοῦ	צְעִירוֹ
ἐπέστησεν τὰς πύλας	ἐπέστησεν θύρας αὐτῆς	הִצִּיב דְּלָתֶיהָ
αὐτῆς.	κατὰ τὸ ῥῆμα κυρίου	כִּדְבַר יְהוָה
	ὃ ἐλάλησεν ἐν χειρὶ	אֲשֶׁר דִּבֶּר בְּיַד
	Ιησου υἱοῦ Ναυη	יְהוֹשֻׁעַ בִּן־נוּן׃

In her view, this story, which narrates the building of a city in relation to the death of two sons, contains a reminiscence of a tradition concerning events of the tribe of Ephraim (i.e. the tribe of Joshua) during the period of conquest and settlement, which has been preserved more explicitly in the distinctly literary shaping of the same event preserved in the Hebrew *Vorlage* of LXX-1 Chron. 7:21b–24.[180] According to Mazor, the tradition in 1 Chron. 7:21b–23 originally dealt with the building of a city linked to a father's loss of two sons, and has been inserted between two genealogical lists of Ephraim (7:20–21a) and 'Uzzen (24b–28). The correspondence between the two historical acounts (1 Chron. 7:21b–24a and LXX-Josh. 6:26) has been obscured by a number of textual corruptions in 1 Chron. 7, but can be restored with the aid of the LXX of that passage.[181]

---

published separately as L. Mazor, The Origin and Evolution of the Curse upon the Rebuilder of Jericho. A Contribution of Textual Criticism to Biblical Historiography, in *Textus* 14 (1988), pp. 1–26, which was based on a 1986 symposium presentation. I will quote from this English version.

[180] L. Mazor, The Curse upon the Rebuilder, p. 21.

[181] Mazor's argumentation runs as follows: The original heading of the second list in verse 24, ובני אזן, *and the sons of 'Uzzen*, preserved in LXX καὶ υἱοὶ Οζαν, has disappeared before the insertion of verses 21b–24a, as the result of haplography ושותלח בנו : ובני אזן, *and Shutelach his son. The sons of 'Uzzen are*: . . . The otherwise unknown city in MT *'Uzzen-She'erah* would then be a corruption of a father 'Uzzen and a son She'erah. This father 'Uzzen is identical with the father Οζαν in LXX-Josh. 6:26, the name of his son is to be re-established after the LXX translation διασωθέντι, *surviving (son)*, which is an interpretative rendering of the proper name שׂארה. Due to this secondary insertion into the framework of the genealogical lists, the account of Ozan's building of cities in the Ephraimite territory has been attributed to Ephraim. As a result of the dittography of (כי ברעה היתה) בביתי (ובשארה), *because (in) evil has been in my house and in the remnants* (LXX καὶ ἐν ἐκείνοις τοῖς καταλοίποις) into MT כי ברעה היתה בביתו : ובתו שׂארה, *because (in) evil has been in his house;*

Once the historical tradition behind Josh. 6:26 was recovered, its textual development could be reconstructed. Originally, according to Mazor, this historical note did not deal with the rebuilding of Jericho, as is evidenced by LXX-Josh. 6:26 and 4QApocryphon of Joshua[b], and 4QTestimonia, where the second, redundant object את־יריחו is lacking. Mazor infers from these data that the words את־יריחו are a secondary interpolation, and that originally this historical note had nothing to do with Jericho but referred to an anonymous locality in the territory of Ephraim. The editor deemed it suitable to append the text after the account of the fall of Jericho, since no other place in the book would be appropriate.[182]

A third and final stage in the history of the narrative of ʾUzzen's building activities and the death of his two sons Abiram and Sheʾerah, involved the splitting up of the notice in LXX-Josh. 6:26 into two parts, according to Mazor. The second half was transferred to the contextually not very appropriate place in 1 Kings 16:34, in order to fit in the historiographer's framework of prediction and fulfilment.[183] Mazor points to the absence of this verse in the Lucianic text of LXX-3 Regum, which is supported by Josephus' *Jewish Antiquities* VIII.318, the absence of historical data confirming the account of 1 Kings 16:34, and the problematic place of this verse in the context of 1 Kings 16–17, in order to support her claim that this verse was added to the text of Kings at a later stage. With the adaptation of this historical note to a prophetic context, the original name Ozan (LXX-Josh. 6:26) was altered into Hiel and the name of his son Sheʾerah into Segub (1 Kgs. 16:34) with the intention to conceal the origin of the tradition.

In this way Mazor is able to argue for the literary priority of LXX over MT and the reversal of the *communis opinio* regarding the relative

---

and his daughter was Sheʾerah, a daughter was created, who after the subsequent change of ויבן, *and he built*, into MT ותבן, *and she built*, could now be considered the builder of an Israelite city.

[182] L. Mazor, The Curse upon the Rebuilder, p. 22, n. 41.

[183] L. Mazor, The Curse upon the Rebuilder, pp. 23–24. Mazor speaks of a conception of the Deuteronomistic *redactor* [italics MM] of Josh–Kgs. who 'wanted to demonstrate that history is a continuous line of fulfillments of ancient prophecies' and refers here to studies by G. von Rad, Die deuteronomistische Geschichtstheologie in den Königsbüchern, in G. von Rad, *Gesammelte Studien zum Alten Testament* I. (TB 8) München 1958, pp. 189–204; and I. Seeligmann, Aetiological Elements in Biblical Historiography, in *Zion* 28 (1961), pp. 167–169. A similar statement about the relation between LXX-Josh. 6:26 and (LXX[Luc]-) 1 Kgs. 16:34 was made by A. Rofé, *The Prophetical Stories. The Narratives about the Prophets in the Hebrew Bible. Their Literary Types and History*. Jerusalem 1988, p. 184.

priority between MT-Joshua, LXX-Joshua, and the passages in Kings and Chronicles. It should be noted, however, that so far her thesis has not been adopted,[184] probably because it is based on a long chain of complicated and conjectural reconstructions.[185] Furthermore, 'Uzzen and Joshua are mentioned together in this Chronicles text, but they seem to be separated from one another by some eight generations. Apart from the conjectured identical names 'Uzzen and She'erah, there are hardly any common traits in 1 Chron. 7:21b–24 and Josh. 6:26. It remains problematic to consider a secondary addition to the genealogical lists in a composition dating from probably fourth century BCE to be a reminiscence of historical information regarding the premonarchic period.[186] And finally, the fact that the plus in Josh. 6:26 has a parallel in the following historical books (i.e. MT-1 Kgs. 16:10) is not an unusual phenomenon in LXX-Joshua (cf. LXX-Josh. 16:10 and 19:47a–48a with MT-1 Kgs. 9:16 and Jdg. 1:34–35) and it is far from self-evident that duplications in LXX-Joshua are more original than the shorter MT in these passages (compare LXX-Josh. 21:42a–d with Josh. 19:49–51).[187]

According to Mazor, a case of ideological development of the original narrative resulting in drastic reduction of the text is presented by the passage immediately preceding Josh. 6:26. The LXX version of the account of the fall of Jericho, especially Josh. 6:1–20, lacks equivalents for at least 92 words out of a total of approximately 350 words. The LXX thus presents a text which is some 30% shorter

---

[184] E. Tov, *Text-critical Use of the Septuagint*², pp. 245–249, does not discuss her theory at this point and already S. Japhet, *I & II Chronicles.* (OTL) London 1993, p. 183, has not accepted her exegesis of 1 Chron. 7:21b–24.

[185] For example, whereas Mazor criticizes Margolis for reconstructing the proper name of the father in LXX-Josh. 6:26 as ὁ Χαιαηλ as the result of a long chain of corruptions in order to conform LXX-Josh. 6:26 to 1 Kgs. 16:34, she herself has to resort to no fewer than seven emendations in the text of 1 Chron. 7:21b–24 in order to conform this narrative to LXX-Josh. 6:26.

[186] Z. Kallai, *Historical Geography of the Bible. The Tribal Territories of Israel.* Jerusalem/Leiden (1967) 1986, p. 484, dates the episode to the premonarchical period. Most scholars, however, regard the data provided by the short narrative as too scanty to establish a historical background for it, see e.g. W. Rudolph, *Chronikbücher.* (HAT I/21) Tübingen 1955, pp. 72–73. M.J. Mulder, 1 Chronik 7,21b–23 und die rabbinische Tradition, in *JSJ* 6 (1979), pp. 141–166, proposed to regard the passage as an anti-Ephraimite midrashic narrative that has its origin in the post-exilic controverse between Judah and Samaria.

[187] In this particular case, Mazor acknowledges the secondary nature of LXX, see L. Mazor, עיונים, pp. 249–263.

than MT, a rate that is even higher than that of Josh. 8:1–29, where LXX is some 20% shorter than MT. Unlike Josh. 8:1–29, however, the textual data do not point to a process of accumulative growth, but, in Mazor's words, to 'a Second Temple period re-working of the narrative aimed at harmonising the figure of Joshua with the nomistic ideal.'[188]

The problem the editor behind the (Hebrew *Vorlage* of the) LXX tradition sought to resolve was the fact that the original source attested by MT speaks of lay people sounding the trumpet, while according to the legislation of Num. 10:8–9 this right was reserved for the Aaronide priests. The concern of the nomistic editor of the Joshua narrative becomes evident in Josh. 6:9.13, where it is made clear that the rear-guard (המאסף) blowing the shofar, mentioned in MT, consists of priests. Since the same phenomenon also occurs in Targum Jonathan in these passages, the correction had taken place at the Hebrew level and not just at the moment the text was translated into Greek:[189]

LXX-Josh. 6	Tg.Jon-Josh. 6	MT-Josh. 6
καὶ οἱ ἑπτὰ ἱερεῖς	וְשִׁבְעָה כָהֲנַיָּא	וְשִׁבְעָה הַכֹּהֲנִים
οἱ φέροντες	נְסִיבוּ שִׁבְעָה	נֹשְׂאִים שִׁבְעָה
τὰς σάλπιγγας τὰς ἑπτὰ --- ---	שׁוֹפְרַיָּא דְקֶרֶן	שׁוֹפְרוֹת הַיּֽוֹבְלִים
	דִּכְרַיָּא	
προεπορεύοντο ἐναντίον	קֳדָם אֲרוֹנָא	לִפְנֵי אֲרוֹן
--- κυρίου,	דַּייָ	יְהוָה
--- ---	אָזְלִין מֵיזָל	הֹלְכִים הָלוֹךְ
--- --- --- ---	וְתָקְעִין בְּשׁוֹפָרַיָּא	וְתָקְעוּ בַּשּׁוֹפָרוֹת
καὶ *μετὰ ταῦτα* εἰσεπορεύ		
οντο οἱ μάχιμοι --- ---	וּמְזָרְזֵי חֵילָא אָזְלִין	וְהֶחָלוּץ הֹלֵךְ לִפְנֵיהֶם
	קֳדָמֵיהוֹן	
καὶ ὁ *λοιπὸς ὄχλος*	וְשִׁבְטָא דְבֵית דָּן אָזֵיל	וְהַמְאַסֵּף הֹלֵךְ
ὄπισθε τῆς κιβωτοῦ	בָּתַר אֲרוֹנָא	אַחֲרֵי אֲרוֹן
τῆς διαθήκης κυρίου·	דַּייָ	יְהוָה
καὶ *οἱ ἱερεῖς*	וְכָהֲנַיָּא אָזְלִין	*הוֹלֵךְ **הָלוֹךְ
ἐσάλπισαν ταῖς σάλπιγξι,	וְתָקְעִין בְּשׁוֹפָרַיָּא:	וְתָקוֹעַ בַּשּׁוֹפָרוֹת:

---

[188] L. Mazor, A Nomistic Re-Working of the Jericho Conquest Narrative Reflected in LXX to Joshua 6:1–20, in *Textus* 18 (1995), pp. 47–62. An earlier discussion of the passage was published in her dissertation as chapter 8, paragraph 1 'The Priests and the Sacred Horns in the LXX Account of the Conquest of Jericho', L. Mazor, עיונים, pp. 381–387. References are to the English version.

[189] L. Mazor, A Nomistic Reworking, pp. 56–57. She also refers to Flavius Josephus, *Jewish Antiquities* V.22–23.27 as an additional witness.

The original idea, still preserved in MT, that lay people sounded the shofar, was by later generations adapted to the prescripts in the Pentateuch (i.e. Num. 10:8–9) in different ways. The nomistic redactor behind LXX-Joshua and Targum Jonathan explicitly stated that it was the priests who blew the trumpets. The rabbis (Midrash Tanchuma, Beha'aloteka 18) on the other hand, restricted the law of Num. 10:8–9 to the period of Moses only, while the author of the Qumran War Scroll, on the other hand, assigned the sounding of the חצצרות to the priests and the sounding of the shofar to the Levites.[190] Part of the same nomistic reworking is the designation of the shofars in LXX-Josh. 6:8 as *sacred trumpets* (καὶ ἐσάλπισαν ταῖς σάλπιγγας ἱεράς), and the explicit mentioning of the priests in LXX-Josh. 6:20 as well, where the MT states that the people was sounding the shofar (וירע העם ויתקעו בשׁפרות).

In line with her overall model in which all editorial activity took place at the *Hebrew* level, Mazor argues for a Hebrew *Vorlage* of LXX in which the nomistic correction had already been executed. She does so on the basis of the rendering in 6:8 καὶ σημαινέτωσαν *εὐτόνως*, *they shall give a signal vigourously* for MT ותקעו שׁופרות, *they blew on the shofars*, which is the result of a replacing of בשׁופרות by the synonymous בכלי עז, *on mighty instruments*, an expression that has a parallel only in the phrase in 2 Chron. 30:21 ומהללים ליהוה יום ביום הלוים והכהנים בכלי־עז ליהוה, *and the Levites and priests praised Yhwh day by day on mighty instruments to Yhwh*. After the inadvertent omission of the *yod* from the phrase בכלי עז which then became בכל עז, *with all might*—an expression that occurs in 2 Sam. 6:14 ודוד מכרכר בכל־עז לפני יהוה, *and David danced before Yhwh with all might* (LXX-2 Reg. 6:14 καὶ Δαυιδ ἀνεκουέτο *ἐν οργάνοις ἡρμοσμένοις* presupposes בכלי עז here as well)—the reading בכל־עז had come into existence, which was then faithfully rendered by the Greek translator by the Greek adverb *εὐτόνως* in LXX-Josh. 6:8.

Mazor's interpretation of the addition of 'the priests' in the Old Greek and Aramaic versions of Josh. 6:9.13.20 and the addition of the element 'sacred' in LXX-Josh. 6:8 on the basis of Num. 10:8–9, and her exegesis of the various contemporary interpretations in Targum Jonathan and Josephus is very convincing. Less convincing, to my mind, is her thesis that these adaptations should be ascribed

---

[190] L. MAZOR, A Nomistic Reworking, pp. 58–60.

to Hebrew scribes, rather than the Greek and Aramaic translators. In a sense, her arguments in favour of a Hebrew *Vorlage* different from MT are illustrative for her perception of the Greek translator as a relatively faithful, unimaginative dragoman, who obedient to his Hebrew *Vorlage* refrained from all literary initiative unless severe syntactical or semantical difficulties forced him to a more paraphrastic rendering. If, however, the Hebrew *Vorlage* of LXX-Josh. 6:8 indeed had been have the result of the corruption of the unique expression תקע בכלי עז into בכל עז, why then did the translator not render this by the literal Greek phrase ἐν πάσῃ δυνάμει (thus LXX-1 Chron. 13:8), but instead chose an adverb that is unique in the Greek Old Testament?[191] As far as the expression σάλπιγγας ἱεράς is concerned, Mazor has to admit that her retroversion into שופרות הקודש finds no support in a similar expression in the Hebrew Bible.[192] It seems more likely, therefore, to think of a literary initiative on the part of the Greek translator in these cases. Besides that, there are quite a number of other features in the Greek text of Joshua 6 that point to a thoughtful reformulation of the Hebrew text into well-chosen Greek formulations, for instance the use of third-person imperative forms in verses 8 and 9, which transform the narrative section (MT-Josh. 6:8–9) into an extension of the direct speech of Joshua to the priests (Josh. 6:7),[193] and the subtle use of Greek prefixes in the verbs rendering the colourless Hebrew verb הלך, *to go*: παρα-πορεύω (6:9), πορεύω (6:9), προ-πορεύω (6:13) and εἰσ-πορεύω (6:13).[194]

Another argument for Mazor to place all editorial activity and literary initiatives on the Hebrew level is based on the correspondence in ideological motivation which Mazor detects between the variants and the rabbinical literature. In this way, she explaines the absence in (her reconstruction of the Hebrew *Vorlage* of) LXX-Josh. 22:23.29 of an equivalent for מִנְחָה, *(grain) offering*, as an attempt to comply

[191] See HR I, p. 581a. The corresponding noun εὐτονία, *vigour*, occurs only once in the Greek Old Testament, Eccl. 7:7, the adjective εὔτονος, *vigorous* only in 2 Macc. 12:23 and 4 Macc. 7:10.

[192] L. Mazor, A Nomistic Reworking, p. 54.

[193] Her translation of the Greek καὶ σημαινέτωσαν εὐτόνως by 'and sounded vigorously' (L. Mazor, A Nomistic Reworking, p. 55) instead of something like 'they *shall* sound vigorously', seems to indicate that she has failed to take notice of this feature.

[194] L. Mazor, עיונים, pp. 45–46, notes the variation, but does not draw consequences from this free rendering.

with rabbi Yehuda's verdict on such offerings: רבי יהודה אמור, אין מנחה בבמה, recorded in *Mishna Zebaḥim* 14:10.[195] If indeed the Greek text is to be understood in this way, we would be dealing with a halakic correction. The purpose, however, of this halakhic correction remains unclear, since all cultic functions are denied to this altar (מִזְבֵּחַ *not* בָּמָה). Besides that, there is a lapse of some four centuries between the time of rabbi Yehuda (second century CE) and the *terminus ad quem* of the revision of the Hebrew text behind LXX-Joshua, i.e. the alleged date of the Greek translation of Joshua during the third or second century BCE. This exegesis of the Greek text presupposes a mechanical view of the procedure followed by the Greek translator as a word-for-word dragoman. The fact that the Greek translator took recourse to a translation θυσία plus specification (σωτηρίου/ὁλοκαυτωμάτων) instead of one Greek equivalent for one Hebrew word renders such a mechanical view problematic.

Mazor deals with some other alleged or generally acknowledged secondary elements in LXX-Joshua in a similar way, such as the Shiloh–Shechem variant in Josh. 24:1.25, which together with the absence of a rendering of the element בית in the expression בית־יהוה, *house of Yhwh* in Josh. 6:24 and 9:23, reflect the rabbinical view stated in *Mishna Zebaḥim* 14:4–10, in which the successive but exclusive legitimaticy of the cultic places in Gilgal, Shiloh, Nob, Gibeon and Jerusalem are acknowledged.[196] In this case, however, the LXX text shows affinities not only with the post-biblical rabbinic conceptions, but also with the inner-biblical Priestly view. The Priestly codex allows for only one cultic place of worship with the אהל מועד, or later the temple, as centre (cf. Josh. 18:1ff.), whereas the older literature or literary strata in the book of Joshua allow pluriformity of such cultic places. It would appear, then, that the older text preserved in MT has been adjusted by the Hebrew editor behind LXX-Joshua to comply with the Priestly conception.

Such Priestly conceptions are equally discernible in the LXX-expressions οἱ ἱερεῖς *καὶ* οἱ Λευεῖται (the corresponding expression in MT-Josh. 3:3 and 8:33 lacks the conjunction and refers to הכהנים הלוים, *the Levitical priests*),[197] and the additive element τῆς διαθήκης in

---

[195] L. Mazor, עיונים, pp. 390–392.

[196] L. Mazor, עיונים, pp. 392–397; see also A. Rofé, The Nomistic Correction, p. 249.

[197] L. Mazor, עיונים, pp. 388–390.

the references to the ark.[198] In both cases, the MT reflects the older, pre-Priestly conception. In the first case the expression הכהנים הלוים, *the Levitical priests*, preserved in MT, represents the older Deuteronomistic conception in which priesthood and Leviticism are merged, whereas LXX represents the younger Priestly conception in which priesthood is claimed for a specific group within the group of Levites. Again Mazor refers to rabbinical literature (*Talmud babli Soṭah* 32a) in order to support her thesis that the editorial activity already took place at the Hebrew level, but again one wonders if this relatively late work is necessary as intermediary stage between the the older text attested by MT and the adaptation to the Priestly view attested by LXX.[199]

It is to be regretted that Mazor has limited her textual studies to establishing the relative chronology between the two editions, without elucidating her views on the absolute chronology and the religious and historical contexts of the various editions. Neither does she explain her views regarding the nature of the Deuteronomistic and Priestly elements present in both versions and, more importantly, the relation between these editorial elements and the editorial development attested by the textual evidence. Her remarks about the origin of the traditions concerning the rebuilder of Jericho and about the brief literary-redactional links that tie up the different units of the conquest narrative, seem to imply that she regards the formation of Joshua as a process of reworking of premonarchic historical notes rather than as a part of a Deuteronomistic comprehensive reformulation of the older traditions after the fall of Jerusalem, as is the currently generally adopted literary model for the book of Joshua.

This leads me to the broader question of the relation between textual and literary criticism in her studies. In her approach, the reconstruction of the literary development of the book of Joshua has been made almost completely dependent upon the textual data provided by MT, LXX, or occasionally by the Qumran scrolls (4QJosh[a], 4QJosh[b], 4QApocrJosh[b] 4QTest, CD). She makes use of literary-critical observations independent of the textual variants, such as Deuteronomistic and Priestly concepts, but only in a very selective way. Since by her introduction of these elements, she implicitly acknowledges the results of historical-literary criticism procured inde-

---

[198] L. Mazor, עיונים, pp. 397–408.
[199] See chapter 9 below.

pendently of the textual data from which she proceeds, one wonders whether a reconstruction of the literary development of Joshua that takes as its point of departure criteria derived from literary-critical observations such as a pattern of coherent distinctive formulations and concepts (such as for instance the Priestly and Deuteronomistic designations of the ark) would arrive at the same conclusions as those which Mazor reached departing from the textual data. In my view, both textual and literary criticism should be carried out on their own terms, before one of the two approaches is made dependent upon the other.

Since Mazor regards neither of the two versions (MT and LXX) as consistently reflecting the older composition, and since she has not adopted a model of accumulative literary growth as a criterion for distinguishing between primary and secondary elements in a given passage, the question arises what then are valid criteria for determining the relative chronology between the alleged variant editorial formulations of the same unit? According to Mazor's treatment of the relevant passages, these criteria are provided by ideological motives such as adapting older divergent historical traditions to the dominant Pentateuchal portrait of Israel's past (MT-Josh. 5:2–9),[200] stressing the divine providence (MT-Josh. 8:1–29),[201] balancing prediction and fulfilment (MT-Josh. 6:26) or nomistic and halakic interests (secondary elements in LXX). Yet, with the exception of the secondary elements reflected by LXX, these ideological developments seem to have taken place in splendid isolation, since no similar phenomena can be adduced outside the passages in which these ideological developments are held to have taken place.

2.2.8 *Competence and Creativity of the Greek Translator of Joshua*

Recently a number of studies have appeared in which special attention is devoted to the Greek version in its own right. Contrary to the approach of scholars such as Holmes, Benjamin, Orlinsky, Chesman, Auld, Tov, Rofé, and Mazor, these scholars from the Europeaen continent place more stress on the competence and creativity of the Greek translator of Joshua. Although their studies only discuss specific aspects of LXX-Joshua, their observations have a direct bearing on

[200] See chapter 7 below.
[201] See chapter 8 below.

our subject, since they make clear that the Greek translation of Joshua is a well-considered and creative translation which cannot simply be retroverted into a deviant Hebrew *Vorlage*.

2.2.8.1 *K. Bieberstein*

In his extensive and thorough study *Josua-Jordan-Jericho*, Klaus Bieberstein not only provides a painstaking literary-critical analysis of the first six chapters of the book of Joshua, but also a detailed discussion of and commentary on the textual problems involved in these chapters.[202] Unlike several of his predecessors, Bieberstein pays full attention to the different scholarly views regarding these problems, and provides helpful surveys of previous research.

Although Bieberstein does not exclude *a priori* the possibility that textual data may point to editorial activity in line with the theories of Tov, Rofé, and Mazor, his own analysis of the variants in Josh. 1–6 leads him to the conclusion that the traditional distinction between literary and textual criticism as two separate disciplines with their own criteria and aims, and applying *de facto* to successive stages in the literary development of the book, remains valid.[203] According to Bieberstein, the aim of textual criticism is not to establish a fixed original *Urtext*, but rather to reconstruct by its own methods the latter part of the continuing process of the development of the text.[204]

According to Bieberstein, the numerous quantitative and qualitative divergencies in Joshua 6 between MT (supported by fragments 3–8 of 4QJosh[a])[205] and LXX are the result of a comprehensive and deliberate reformulation of the narrative on the part of the Greek translator.[206] The aim of this rewriting was twofold, i.e. first to present a more coherent and fluid narrative, and second to give a more prominent role to the priests. The text-critical value of the Septuagint is thus minimal.[207]

---

[202] K. Bieberstein, Josua-Jordan-Jericho. Archäologie, Geschichte und Theologie der Landnahme-erzählungen Josua 1–6. (OBO 143) Freiburg/Göttingen 1995.

[203] K. Bieberstein, *Josua-Jordan-Jericho*, pp. 72–74.

[204] K. Bieberstein, *Josua-Jordan-Jericho*, p. 72, notes 2 and 3.

[205] K. Bieberstein, *Josua-Jordan-Jericho*, pp. 240–241.

[206] K. Bieberstein, *Josua-Jordan-Jericho*, p. 230: 'freie und teilweise bewußt bearbeitende Nacherzählung' See also the discussion of the variants by E. Otto, *Das Mazzotfest in Gilgal.* (BWANT 107) Stuttgart/Berlin/Köln/Mainz 1975, pp. 65–68.

[207] K. Bieberstein, *Josua-Jordan-Jericho*, p. 267.

In order to substantiate these conclusions, Bieberstein starts his discussion with some observations regarding the translation technique of LXX-Joshua 6. Whereas the MT is characterised by repetition of the same word or phrase, the Greek text shows a remarkable variation in expression which can hardly be considered to point to a variety of different Hebrew lexemes reflecting a different Hebrew *Vorlage*, or to a secondary process on the Hebrew level of standardisation of synonymous expressions. For example, for the seven instances of the Hebrew verb סבב, *to encircle*, the Greek text has no less than four different Greek equivalents: περι-ίστημι (verse 3), κυκλόω (verse 7), περι-έρχομαι (verse 11.15), and περι-κυκλόω (verse 14).[208] The different renderings of the Hebrew syntagma ויהי plus temporal specification make clear that the free element in the translation of Joshua 6 was not restricted to the lexical level only.[209] Bieberstein furthermore points to the prominent role the priests play in the procession according to the Septuagint. As a result of the restructuring of the redundant Hebrew *Vorlage*, the Greek text not only presents the priests as the only group that blows the shofar, but also as the group that leads the whole procession rather than forming the centre of it. Likewise, with the omission of the introduction to the direct speech in MT-Josh. 6:7 (the instructions to the people concerning the procession around Jericho), the Greek text has the priests rather than Joshua issue these orders.[210]

The restructuring of the narrative is also apparent in the amplification of the chronology in LXX-Josh. 6:12, where the temporal indication 'on the second day' from MT-Josh. 6:14 has been placed right at the beginning of the part of the narrative that concerns this day.[211] Likewise, then, the information regarding the number of circumambulations around Jericho has been levelled in verses 15–16

[208] K. Bieberstein, *Josua-Jordan-Jericho*, pp. 241–242: 'konkordante Lexeme—inkonkordante lexematische Äquivalenten.'

[209] K. Bieberstein, *Josua-Jordan-Jericho*, p. 242: 'konkordante Syntax—inkonkordante syntaktische Äquivalenten'. In verse 8 the ויהי-clauses have no equivalent in LXX; in verses 15 and 16 the clauses ויהי ביום השביעי and ויהי בפעם השביעית have been translated by καὶ τῇ ἡμέρᾳ τῇ ἑβδόμῃ and καὶ τῇ περιόδῳ τῇ ἑβδόμῃ respectively, whereas in 6:20 the formula ὡς δέ has been chosen as a rendering for ויהי כשמע העם את־קול השופר.

[210] Thus according to MT-Qere: ויאמר אל־העם, supported by various MT-mss. (see J.B. de Rossi, *Variae Lectiones* II, p. 78), 4QJosh[a] ויאמר] יהושע אל העם, TgJon וַאֲמַר לְעַמָא, Peš ܘܐܡܪ ܠܥܡܐ, and Vg 'ad populum quoque ait'; see K. Bieberstein, *Josua-Jordan-Jericho*, pp. 244–254: 'Tendenziöse Bearbeitungen.'

[211] K. Bieberstein, *Josua-Jordan-Jericho*, pp. 254–257.

of the Greek version. As a result, verse 16 in the Greek version now narrates the events during the seventh time the Israelites encircled Jericho, while the preceding verse 15 reports the six previous processions, in contrast with MT where the seventh time is already included in the two repetititive clauses. The redundant final clause of MT-Josh. 6:15 as well as the anaphoric phrase כמשפט הזה have thus been omitted, while the adverbial phrase in the Hebrew text שֶׁבַע פעמים, *seven times*, has neatly been changed to ἑξάκις, *six times*.[212]

According to Bieberstein, the divergencies between LXX and MT in Joshua 6 are for these reasons to be ascribed to a deliberate and well-thought-out restructuring and reformulation of the Hebrew text as present in MT on the part of the Greek translator. Bieberstein's analysis of the MT–LXX variants has made clear that it is worthwhile and necessary to discuss variants of a passage in context, and that qualitative variants (unusual Greek renderings) should not be strictly separated from the quantitative variants (minuses in the Greek text), as has been done by Holmes, Auld, Tov, and Mazor. A study of the Greek version of the entire passage makes this clear. Therefore, this approach deserves to be applied to other passages as well.

2.2.8.2 *C.G. den Hertog*

Cees den Hertog's 1996 Gießen dissertation *Studien zur griechischen Übersetzung des Buches Josua*[213] does not directly address the problem of the redaction-critical value of the Septuagint of Joshua. Nevertheless his studies deal with related preliminary questions regarding LXX-Joshua, such as the date and provenance of the translation, the canonical status of the Hebrew version and the translation technique used in the Greek version.

One of these questions concerns the date and origin of the Greek translation.[214] Whereas most scholars have merely speculated—because of a lack of positive evidence—that the Greek translation of the book of Joshua must have followed the translation of the Pentateuch rather

[212] K. Bieberstein, *Josua-Jordan-Jericho*, p. 257.

[213] C.G. den Hertog, *Studien zur griechischen Übersetzung des Buches Josua*. (Inaugural-Dissertation zur Erlangung des Doktorgrades der Philosophie des Fachbereichs 07 des Justus-Liebig-Universität Gießen). Gießen 1996. The author kindly provided me with a copy of his dissertation.

[214] C.G. den Hertog, *Studien*, pp. 110–144, chapter 5: 'Datierung und Lokalisierung der Übersetzung.'

quickly,[215] Den Hertog attempts to substantiate this supposition by looking for indications of the Ptolemaic administration of Coele-Syria (between circa 285–189 BCE) in the geographical sections of LXX-Joshua. Thus, the use of the endings -ῖτις for geographical areas in Palestine reflects the administrative division introduced by the Ptolemies after the definitive establishment of their control of Coele-Syria around 285 BCE. On the other hand, the designation of Bashan as Βασανῖτις rather than Βαταναία, as well as the more general use of the term παραλία in contrast with the exact designation for the whole coastal plain of Palestine,[216] would point to a *terminus ante quem* of 198 BCE. In this year Palestine became part of the empire of the Seleucids, who introduced an administrative reorganisation, by which Βαταναία and παραλία became designations of provinces in Coele-Syria. This third century BCE date for the Greek Joshua would correspond well with the relative chronology obtained by an analysis of the parallel passages in LXX-Joshua and LXX-Pentateuch on the one hand, and LXX-Judges on the other hand. Den Hertog argues that LXX-Joshua is dependent on the LXX-Pentateuch (more in particular LXX-Deuteronomy), while LXX-Judges presupposes LXX-Joshua. As a result, the book of Joshua must have been one of the first Hebrew biblical books to have been translated after the Pentateuch (which probably took place around 282 BCE).[217]

At the same time, the unusual Greek geographical references in LXX-Joshua, such as the illogical designation in Josh. 11:2 of the παραλίους Χαναναίους *ἀπὸ ἀνατολῶν, the coastal (i.e. western) Canaanites from the east*, the strange and otherwise unknown area of Μαδβαρῖτις (LXX-Josh. 5:6, 15:61* and 18:12),[218] as well as the sparse use of Hellenised Greek toponyms,[219] reveal the deficiencies in the Greek

---

[215] See e.g. G. Dorival, M. Harl, O. Munnich, *La Bible grecque des Septante*, pp. 83–111.

[216] See C.G. den Hertog, *Studien*, p. 122, n. 21, p. 141.

[217] See G. Dorival, M. Harl, O. Munnich, *La Bible grecque des Septante*, p. 58.

[218] Den Hertog adopts Margolis' emendation of the corrupted form Βαδδαργις (B, ed. Rahlfs) into καὶ Μαδβαρεις (his S-family reads καὶ ἐν τῇ Μαδβαριτιδι, see M.L. Margolis, *The Book of Joshua in Greek*, p. 319). See further the discussion in section 7.6.4.1 below.

[219] Only the Hellenised proper and place names Αἰγύπτος, Ἀντιλίβανος, Βασανῖτις, Γάζα, Γαλααδῖτις, Γάλγαλα, Γαλιλαία, Ἰδουμαία, Ἰόππη, Καρμήλος, Λίβανος, Μαδβαρῖτις, Σίδων, Σίκιμα, Τύρος and Φοινίκη occur, while the names Ἰταβύριον for Tabor, Πτολεμαίς for Acco and Σκυθόπολις for Beth-Shean are absent, C.G. den Hertog, *Studien zur griechischen Übersetzung*, pp. 142–144.

translator's knowledge of the precise topography and geography of Palestine, which renders it unlikely that the Greek Joshua originated from Palestine. Moreover, the use of the word μητρόπολις as a designation for Hebron (Josh. 14:15, 15:13, 21:11 and the cities of the same rank as Gibeon, Josh. 10:2) points to the Egyptian administrative system.[220] The Greek translation of Joshua should thus both in time and space be placed in the proximity of the Greek translation of the Pentateuch.

The fact that the Greek translator of Joshua made several attempts to explain the Hebrew text and adopted the Greek vocabulary of the translators of the Pentateuch, make him a theologian rather than a neutral dragoman.[221] Den Hertog points to the deliberatedly varied renderings of the Hebrew word מזבח in Joshua 22 by βωμός as illegitimate altar in the first part of that chapter, and subsequently by θυσιαστήριον in the last part of the same chapter, once the legitimacy of the altar as a non-sacrificial memorial has been acknowledged,[222] as well as to the differentation between λαός as designation for Israel and ἔθνος as designation of either non-Israelite *or* Israelite (LXX-Josh. 24:4) people, even where the Hebrew text does not make a similar distinction between עם and גוי. Likewise, the use of the Greek verb τελευτάω exclusively with respect to Moses and the priest Eleazar (LXX-Josh. 24:30 describes the death of Joshua with the verb ἀποθνήσκω) reveals a deliberate choice between Greek equivalents. The plus in LXX-Josh. 24:27 ἐπ' ἐσχάτων τῶν ἡμερῶν, (ἡνίκα ἐὰν ψεύσησθε . . .), *(this stone will be a testimony against you) in the final days, whenever (you will betray Joshua's God)*, in Den Hertogs view, even reveals an eschatologizing translation.[223] Since the the eschatological

[220] C.G. den Hertog, *Studien*, pp. 142–143.

[221] C.G. den Hertog, *Studien*, p. 159.

[222] C.G. den Hertog, *Studien*, pp. 180–183, paragraph 7.3: 'Inhaltsbezogene Aspekte der Übersetzungstechnik'.

[223] C.G. den Hertog, *Studien*, p. 183: 'Ein schlagendes Beispiel für eine eschatologisierend-aktualisierende Übersetzung findet sich schließlich in Jos 24:27: Der Stein, der die Selbstverpflichtung des Volkes auf den JHWH-Dienst gehört, soll—so MT—Zeuge gegen Israel sein, *damit* sie ihren Gott nicht verleugnen. Er wird—so Jos^{gr}—*in den letzten Tagen* Zeuge sein gegen Israel, *immer dann, wenn* sie Josuas Gott verleugnen. Hier hat sich Jos^{Übs} zu einer kaum verhüllten Aussage vorgewagt.' See further C.G. den Hertog, Eschatologisierung in der griechischen Übersetzung des Buches Josua, in F. Postma, K. Spronk, E. Talstra (eds.), *The New Things*, pp. 107–117.

role of this stone is not explained in more detail, and since the plus deliberatedly creates a link with Deut. 31:29, which contains the same themes of a farewell discourse with predictments and exhortations, one wonders whether the classification of this plus as 'eschatological' is really appropriate.

Den Hertog opens his final chapter about the translation technique of LXX-Joshua with the statement that a purely lexical study of the Greek translation is insufficient to characterise the extent of freedom with which the translator approached his Hebrew *Vorlage*.[224] For this reason he investigates the translator's handling of some specific Semitic syntactical features, such as the declination in Greek of indeclinable Hebrew proper names, the various renderings of Hebrew construct state combinations and thirdly, taking a reverse approach, the Hebrew equivalents for the Greek participial and hypotactical constructions.[225] The picture of the Greek translator that emerges from these detail studies is one of a competent translator, who nevertheless led himself be guided by the macro-syntax of the Hebrew text. Since he made only sparse use of Greek subordinate temporal or conditional clauses introduced by ἐπεί (4:1, 7:8, 10:24, 17:13), ἡνίκα (10:12, 22:7, 24:20.37), ὅταν (3:3, 4:6.21, 17:18), and ὡς (21 times), and since he occasionally made the stylistic error to rendering the clause-initial *waw* of the Hebrew text by καί in an apodosis (4:1, 8:24, 10:20), the Greek translator must have worked on the principle of first dividing the Hebrew text into relatively short segments (clauses rather than sentences) and subsequently translating these segments more or less independently.[226]

---

[224] C.G. den Hertog, *Studien*, p. 160.

[225] C.G. den Hertog, *Studien*, pp. 160–180, chapter 7: 'Die Übersetzungstechnik des griechischen Josuabuches, § 7.1. Der Gebrauch des Artikels bei Eigennamen, § 7.2. Die Wiedergabe von *Status-constructus*-Verbindungen, § 7.3. Partizipialkonstruktionen und die Bildung von Haupt- und Nebensätzen.' These studies have been published separately as C.G. den Hertog, Drei Studien zur Übersetzungstechnik des griechischen Josuabuches, in *BIOSCS* 29 (1996), pp. 22–52.

[226] C.G. den Hertog, *Studien*, pp. 179–180. Den Hertog here refers to I. Soisalon-Soininen, Beobachtungen zur Arbeitsweise der Septuaginta-Übersetzer, in A. Rofé, Y. Zakovitch (eds.), *Isac Leo Seeligmann Volume* III. Jerusalem 1983, pp. 319–329, reprinted in A. Aejmelaeus, R. Sollamo (eds.), I. Soisalon-Soininen, *Studien zur Septuaginta-Syntax. Gesammelte Aufsätze*. Helsinki 1987, pp. 28–39.

2.2.8.3 *J. Moatti-Fine*

The appreciation for the Greek translation of Joshua as not merely a colourless extract of a deviant Hebrew text but as an intelligent literary work that merits to be studied on its own, is the main focus of the French translation of LXX-Joshua by Jacqueline Moatti-Fine.[227] In line with the interest of the Paris Septuagint school in reading the Greek Old Testament as a literary work for its own sake,[228] Moatti-Fine provides her translation with copious notes and introductions in which she recorded in which way the Greek Joshua was read in Antiquity, and in which she presents an extensive investigation of the vocabulary of LXX-Joshua. Adopting a post-LXX-Pentateuch, Ptolemaic-Egyptian background for LXX-Joshua, she compares the lexical choices made by the Greek translator of Joshua with those of his predecessors, the Greek translators of the Pentateuch.[229]

Compared to LXX-Pentateuch, LXX-Joshua is not only characterized by a number of lexical innovations, but even more by its lexical richness. The abundance of various terms from the field of military vocabulary for stereotyped Hebrew expressions attests to the translator's profound knowledge of both the rare Hebrew terms as well as the classical and koine Greek military vocabulary.[230] Illuminating are the thirteen, seven and five Greek different renderings, respectively, of the frequent Hebrew expressions נכה, *to strike*,[231] לחם, *to*

---

[227] J. Moatti-Fine, *Jésus (Josué). Traduction du texte grec de la Septante, Introduction et notes*. (La Bible d' Alexandrie 6) Paris 1996.

[228] See e.g. the programme for the series set out in the 'Avant-Propos' in M. Harl, *La Genèse*. (La Bible d'Alexandrie 1) Paris 1986, pp. 7–13, as well as the introductory statements under § 2 in J.W. Wevers' commentaries to the Greek Pentateuch, e.g., J.W. Wevers, *Notes on the Greek Text of Exodus*. (SCS 30) Atlanta 1990, pp. xiv–xvi.

[229] J. Moatti-Fine, *Josué*, pp. 42–68: Chapter D. 'La Traduction de *Josué*: Le vocabulaire grec'—Chapter E. 'La tâche du traducteur'. Some of her lexical studies with a number of conclusions regarding the character of the Greek translation have been presented in J. Moatti-Fine, La 'Tâche du Traducteur' de Josué/Jésus, in G. Dorival, O. Munnich (éds.), *Κατα τους Ο'. Selon les Septante. Trente études sur la Bible grecque des Septante en hommage à Marguerite Harl.* Paris 1995, pp. 321–330.

[230] J. Moatti-Fine, *Josué*, p. 55. For similar conclusions, see J. Hollenberg, *Der Charakter*, p. 5.

[231] Thus for נכה: [1] ἀναιρέω (11:12.17, 12:1.7), [2] ἀποκτείνω (7:5, 10:26.41, 11:11), [3] ἐκκόπτω (15:16), [4] ἐκπολεμέω (10:4), [5] ἐκπολιορκέω (10:5.34; outside LXX-Joshua the verb occurs only in 4 Macc. 18:4), [6] ἐξολεθρεύω (11:14), [7] κατακόπτω (10:10, 11:8), [8] κόπτω (10:20, 11:8), [9] μάχομαι (9:18), [10] παίω (20:9), [11] πατάσσω (12 or 13 times in LXX-Joshua: 8:21.22.24, 10:33.37.39.40, 12:6, 13:12.21, 19:47, 20:3.[A5]), [12] συντρίβω (7:5, 10:10[.12.12]), and [13] φονεύω,

fight,[232] and מסס לב, *become fearful*,[233] some of which occur only in this book in the Greek translation of the Hebrew Bible (ἐκπολιορκέω, καταπολεμέω, συμπολεμέω).

Beyond this concern for rendering stereotyped Hebrew phrases καλῶς καὶ ὁσίως and rare expressions ἠκριβωμένως (thus the qualifications given to the Greek Pentateuch in the Aristeas letter 310), Moatti-Fine observes special tendencies demonstrated by the Greek translator's lexical choices. Thus, the Hebrew root חרם, *to devote*, is translated by the Greek noun ἀνάθεμα, *offrande*, and by the verb ἀναθεματίζω, only with respect to the conquest of Jericho, while everywhere else the same Hebrew root is expressed by ἐξολεθρεύω, *exterminer*, and φονεύω, *tuer*. The theological intention of the Greek translator has been to present the conquest of Jericho purely in terms of a divine gift introduced by a theophany (Josh. 5:13–15) and a divine offering by Joshua, as opposed to all subsequent conquests.[234] Alternatively, by adopting the lexical choice made by the Greek translator of Numbers in Joshua 20 in order to explain to a Hellenistic audience the unique Hebrew institution of the city of refuge by means of the Greek neologism φυγαδευτήριον, the Greek translator remained faithful to the options chosen by the Greek translators of the Pentateuch.[235]

These and other lexical observations make the Greek translation a thoughtful version, marked by both 'lisibilité' and 'littéralité'. In light of these observations, phenomena such as Hebraistic syntactical features and the absence of attempts to avoid anthropopathisms (cf. Orlinsky) should not be taken as shortcomings of the Greek translation and constraints posed by a Hebrew text which the Greek

---

(10:28.30.21.35, [A]20:5.6). See for similar observations J. Hollenberg, *Der Charakter*, p. 5.

[232] Translations of לחם are [1] πολεμέω, [2] συμπολεμέω (the verb occurs in the Greek Old Testament only in LXX-Josh. 10:14.42), [3] καταπολεμέω (only in LXX-Josh. 10:25), [4] ἐκπολεμέω, [5] περικαθίζω, [6] ἐκπολιορκέω, [7] παρατάσσω; J. Moatti-Fine, *Josué*, p. 54.

[233] The Hebrew expression is rendered by [1] ἐξίστημι (2:11), [2] μεθίστημι (14:8), [3] πτοέω (7:5), [4] τήκω (5:1) and [5] καταπλήσσω (5:1) as the second rendering of the same Hebrew phrase; J. Moatti-Fine, *Josué*, p. 53; see also J. Hollenberg, *Der Charakter*, p. 5.

[234] J. Moatti-Fine, *Josué*, p. 52. See also J. Moatti-Fine, La 'tâche du traducteur', pp. 325–328.

[235] J. Moatti-Fine, *Josué*, p. 45. See also J. Moatti-Fine, La 'tâche du traducteur', pp. 321–323.

translator attempted to render as faithfuly as possible, but rather as deliberate attempts to leave an 'impression d'étrangeté.'[236]

Due to her unreserved emphasis on LXX-Joshua as a Hellenistic document in its own right, the question of the relation between the Greek and Hebrew versions of Joshua takes a secondary place in Moatti-Fine's commentary. She duly notes all deviations from MT-Joshua and informs the reader of current theories by Orlinsky, Tov, Rofé and Mazor,[237] but refrains from offering a judgement of her own in the individual cases. As a result, the Greek version has become an object of study for its own sake, without specific relation to textual and literary questions.

2.2.8.4 *S. Sipilä*

A very detailed investigation of two aspects of the translation technique of LXX-Joshua has been offered by Seppo Sipilä in his dissertation *Between Literalness and Freedom.*[238] In line with the Finnish approach to the Septuagint developed by I. Soisalon-Soininen and his pupils R. Sollamo and A. Aejmelaeus, Sipilä concentrates on the translation in LXX-Joshua and LXX-Judges of the clause connections introduced in the Hebrew text by -ו and כי and compares the results with the data from the Greek Pentateuch, as examined by A. Aejmelaeus.[239] Compared with LXX-Judges and LXX-Pentateuch, the Greek version of Joshua may—once more—be classified 'between literalness (LXX-Judges) and freedom (LXX-Pentateuch)', although several refinements of this general characterisation are necessary and possible on the basis of Sipilä's study.

---

[236] J. Moatti-Fine, *Josué*, pp. 66–68, p. 67. With respect to the argument advanced by Orlinsky that LXX-Joshua retains the antropopathisms, she remarks (p. 50): 'Ainsi, aux anthropomorphismes de l'hébreu, le traducteur préfère des expressions plus abstraites pour parler de Dieu. Il est vrai, comme le fait remarquer H.M. Orlinsky ('The Hebrew Vorlage', p. 193), qu'il laisse à Dieu des sentiments (surtout de colère: *Jos* 7, 1.26; 22, 18) et des conduites humaines (faire la guerre aux côtés d'Israël, livrer l'ennemi entre ses mains, semer la panique). Mais pouvait-il traduire autrement?'

[237] J. Moatti-Fine, *Josué*, pp. 32–38: 'Le texte grec et le texte hébreu.'

[238] S. Sipilä, *Between Literalness and Freedom. Translation technique in the Septuagint of Joshua and Judges regarding the clause connections introduced by* ו *and* כי. (Publications of the Finnish Exegetical Society 75) Göttingen 1999.

[239] A. Aejmelaeus, *Parataxis in the Septuagint. A Study of the Renderings of the Hebrew Coordinate Clauses in the Greek Pentateuch.* (AASF Dissertationes humanarum litterarum 31) Helsinki 1982.

According to Sipilä, 716 out of 807 Hebrew clauses that open with the conjunction -ו have been translated by the Greek clause coordinator καί (i.e. 88.7%) as opposed to 39 passages where the Greek conjunction δέ has been used (4.8%). Since this heavy use of καί as clause connector differs from genuine Greek, where constructions with δέ or a *participium coniunctum* are far more frequent, the Greek translation of Joshua may with respect to this particular aspect be called 'fairly literal'[240] as opposed to very literal translation of Judges (where the ratio ו – καί is 97.6%). The reason for these unusually high ratios is, according to Sipilä, the 'easy technique' by which the Greek translators produced their translation.[241] According to Sipilä and others (Soisalon-Soininen, Den Hertog), the Greek translators of the books of the Hebrew Bible divided the Hebrew text in short segments (usually a clause), and then translated segment by segment.

Unlike Bajard and Poswick, who do not distinguish between the various uses of the clause-initial ו,[242] Sipilä makes a distinction between the conjunction ו appearing in the Hebrew text at the beginning of an ordinary main clause; in the formulas ויהי, והיה, והנה; and ועתה, at the beginning of an apodosis, and at the beginning of a subordinate clause. The effect of the narrow segmentation in the translation process becomes clearly visible in the renderings of the clause-initial ו by καί in an apodosis. In a few cases (Josh. 4:14; 8:20; 10:19; and 22:30) the Greek translator correctly rendered the protasis of a Hebrew sentence by a *participium coniunctum*, but then also rendered the ו at the beginnning of the apodosis by καί, whereas, according to the rules of classical Greek style and syntax, he should have omitted the conjunction.[243] Equally unidiomatic are the literal renderings of the Hebrew macro-syntactical markers ויהי and והיה by καὶ ἐγένετο/καὶ ἐγενήθη and καὶ ἔσται, respectively,[244] as is the rendering καὶ ἰδοῦ for the Hebrew formula והנה, which in classical Hebrew

---

[240] S. Sipilä, *Between Literalness and Freedom*, pp. 24–82: Chapter 2.2: 'The Hebrew conjunction ו at the beginning of an ordinary main clause.'

[241] S. Sipilä, *Between Literalness and Freedom*, p. 79.

[242] J. Bajard, R.-F. Poswick, Aspects statistiques.

[243] S. Sipilä, *Between Literalness and Freedom*, pp. 57, 109–129.

[244] S. Sipilä, The Renderings of ויהי and והיה as Formulas in the LXX of Joshua, in L. Greenspoon, O. Munnich (eds.), *VIII Congress of the International Organization for Septuagint and Cognate Studies. Paris 1992.* (SCS 41) Atlanta 1995, pp. 273–289; S. Sipilä, *Between Literalness and Freedom*, pp. 82–97.

marks a surprise or climax.[245] Nevertheless, the contextually appropriate translations of the Hebrew conjunction by οὖν (e.g. Josh. 23:5–6), ἀλλά (Josh. 6:17–18), or ἵνα (Josh. 20:9) point in the opposite direction, and make clear that the Greek translator did pay attention to the context of the segment being translated.[246] In a similar vein, the idiomatic translation of the formula ועתה by νῦν οὖν (Josh. 1:2; 22:4) demonstrate the Greek translator's 'ability to use natural Greek expressions.'[247]

In the case of the translation of the Hebrew particle כי, to which Sipilä assigns four major functions: [1] causal כי, [2] circumstantial כי, [3] nominalising כי, and [4] marking a positive alternative, the Greek translation of Joshua reveals an even greater variety in renderings and awareness of the context.[248] The relatively frequent use of the conjunction γάρ for the Hebrew causal כי, which is more idiomatic Greek than the literal rendering by ὅτι, places the Greek translation of Joshua on a par with the idiomatic Greek translations of Genesis and Exodus.[249] Likewise, the contextually appropriate rendering of כי marking a positive alternative by ἀλλά also reveal the Greek translator's ability to survey the literary context beyond the narrow segment being translated.[250]

Sipilä's study has made clear that the general qualifications 'literal' and 'free' can and should be refined, and applied to various aspects of the translation of Hebrew into Greek. Sipilä also makes clear that several cases of unidiomatic Greek renderings (apodotic καί for instance) should be ascribed to the Greek translator's 'easy technique' and 'high tolerance for non-genuine Greek expressions'. What should be kept in mind, is that Sipilä has focussed on only two aspects of the translation technique of LXX-Joshua. Furthermore, the evaluation of the translation technique for these syntactical elements does not need to correspond to an evaluation of the Greek translator's treatment of lexemes. In Joshua 10, for instance, the Greek translator seems to have made no attempt to stylize the rather dull and repetitive Hebrew clause-structure. On the lexical level, however, several literary initiatives (mainly varying translations of the

[245] S. Sipilä, *Between Literalness and Freedom*, pp. 97–102.
[246] S. Sipilä, *Between Literalness and Freedom*, pp. 50–54.
[247] S. Sipilä, *Between Literalness and Freedom*, pp. 105–106.
[248] S. Sipilä, *Between Literalness and Freedom*, pp. 140–192.
[249] S. Sipilä, *Between Literalness and Freedom*, pp. 142–168, 198–199.
[250] S. Sipilä, *Between Literalness and Freedom*, pp. 189–192.

same Hebrew lexeme) can be observed, which points in another direction. It should also be noted that Sipilä excludes from his discussion those passages where MT and LXX differ, so that his research would not be burdened with the question of whether the Greek translator worked from a different Hebrew *Vorlage*.[251] Yet, this approach also excludes beforehand the possibility that the variants are the result of a somewhat freer rendering than the other parts of the book. It is interesting in this respect to note that in LXX-Josh. 5:2–9, which differs significantly from MT, the Greek clause coordinator δέ (5:2.4.7.8) occurs as often as the conjunction καί (5:2.3.3.9).[252]

2.2.8.5 *M. Rösel*

The most recent contribution to date to the Greek Joshua is a short article by Martin Rösel.[253] Rösel argues that some of the long pluses in LXX-Joshua (6:26; 16:10; 21:42; 24:31.33) were introduced by the translator/redactor in order to tie the book of Joshua closer to the historical books (Judges and Kings), which in all likelihood had not yet been translated at the time the Greek translation of Joshua was made (circa 200 BCE).[254] One wonders, however, why such a redactor would have refrained from hinting at important persons such as David and Solomon, as the Joshua narrative 4Q522 seems to do,[255] but instead chose to highlight only the relatively unimportant events of the reconstruction of Jericho (6:26) and the destruction of Gezer (16:10). Rösel also discusses some of the theological peculiarties already noted in earlier studies (Hollenberg, Mazor, Den Hertog).

2.2.9 *Evaluation*

The study of the Greek version of Joshua has gained momentum during the last decade. No less than five dissertations, the present

---

[251] S. SIPILÄ, *Between Literalness and Freedom*, p. 17.
[252] See chapter 7 below.
[253] M. RÖSEL, Die Septuaginta-Version des Josuabuches, in H.-J. FABRY, U. OFFERHAUS (Hg.), *Im Brennpunkt: Die Septuaginta. Studien zur Entstehung und Bedeutung der Griechischen Bibel.* (BWANT 153) Stuttgart/Berlin/Köln 2001, pp. 197–211. The English translation appeared as M. RÖSEL, The Septuagint-Version of the Book of Joshua, in *SJOT* 16/1 (2002), pp. 5–23. I refer to the English version.
[254] M. RÖSEL, The Septuagint-Version of the Book of Joshua, pp. 18–19.
[255] See section 3.5.5 below.

study included, have been devoted to it. Although many aspects of the Greek version have been studied in great detail (text history, translation technique, relation with the Qumran scrolls), the question of the redaction-critical value remains basically the same since the much neglected pioneer study by Hollenberg appeared more than 125 years ago. On the one hand, most scholars seem to agree that in the case of Joshua 20, the Greek version reflects a Hebrew version of Joshua that differs drastically from MT and possibly antedates the now standardized longer version. On the other hand, there is also overwhelming evidence that the Greek translator introduced many variations from the MT for various reasons. Therefore, the methodological question posed at the beginning of this section 2.2 how to decide whether a variant in the Greek version really has redaction-critical value, still remains undecided, in spite of the efforts made by in the studies discussed above to argue either in favour or against such a position. Scholars such as Cross, Orlinksy, Auld, and Mazor held high expectations of the Qumran scrolls of the book. The next chapter will show that what has now become available of these scrolls does not help to formulate a definitive answer to this question.

CHAPTER THREE

THE QUMRAN SCROLLS OF JOSHUA

3.1 Introduction

The text of Joshua is attested by a few fragments of three different Qumran scrolls, which is a rather modest number compared to the 27 Qumran Deuteronomy or the 39 Psalm scrolls found in the various Qumran caves as well as in other sites.[1] Two of them were found in the fourth cave of Qumran (4Q47 [4QJosh[a]] and 4Q48 [4QJosh[b]]). During the final stages of the publication of the *Discoveries in the Judaean Desert* series in 1998 fragments of another Joshua scroll were purchased by M. Schøyen and made public to the scholarly world. Its provenance (probably also Qumran cave four) is uncertain, hence it is designated XJoshua.[2]

Although the scrolls 4Q47 and 4Q48 were found in September 1952, it took four decades before the scrolls were properly published.[3] In the meantime the scholary world had to be content with vague remarks by F.M. Cross that 'The Joshua manuscripts at Qumrân are systematically "Septuagintal" in character',[4] which resulted in a statement made by Woudstra in his commentary to Joshua that 'among the discoveries at Qumran are two manuscripts of the Vaticanus'.[5] A first presentation of these two Qumran scrolls with far more sober conclusions regarding their textual affiliation was

[1] See E. Tov, E. Ulrich, The Biblical Texts from the Judaean Desert, in E. Tov (ed.), *The Texts from the Judaean Desert. Indices and An Introduction to the Discoveries in the Judaean Desert Series.* (DJD 39) Oxford 2002, pp. 165–202.

[2] J. Charlesworth, XJoshua, in J. Charlesworth, N. Cohen, H. Cotton, E. Eshel, H. Eshel, P. Flint, H. Misgav, M. Morgenstern, K. Murphy, M. Segal, A. Yardeni, B. Zissu (eds.), *Miscellaneous Texts from the Judaean Desert.* (DJD 38) Oxford 2000, pp. 231–239.

[3] See K. Bieberstein, *Lukian und Theodotion*, pp. 75–77: 5.1. 'Der Streit um die Josuarollen von Ḫirbet Qumrān' and (the same text) K. Bieberstein, *Josua-Jordan-Jericho*, pp. 74–77.

[4] F.M. Cross, *The Ancient Library of Qumran*, p. 151 [n. 84], pp. 180–181; and idem, The Evolution of a Theory of Local Texts, in F.M. Cross, S. Talmon (eds.), *Qumran and the History of the Biblical Text*, p. 311.

[5] M. Woudstra, *Joshua.* Grand Rapids 1981, p. 40.

offered by Greenspoon in 1990,[6] followed by the preliminary publication of first 4QJosh[b] by E. Tov in 1992,[7] and subsequently 4QJosh[a] by E. Ulrich in the same year, for the first Meeting of the International Organization for Qumran Studies in Paris 1992.[8] Unaware of this latter contribution (which appeared in published form in 1994), K. Bieberstein presented his own transcription with analysis of the two texts in 1994,[9] based on Tov's 1993 microfiche edition of all the photographs of the Dead Sea Scrolls.[10] The final *editio princeps* of the two scrolls in the official *Discoveries of the Judaean Desert* series appeared one year later (1995),[11] 43 years after their discovery. As a result, these scrolls have only very recently become available to scholarship.

Contrary to the Septuagint version of Joshua the scrolls are direct witnesses to the text of the book. They are half a millenium older than the oldest textual witnesses of LXX-Joshua,[12] and thereby the oldest extent textual witnesses of Joshua in any language.[13] Unfortunately, however, they have been preserved in a very fragmentary state. 4QJoshua[a] has preserved remains of Josh. 8:34–35, 5:2–7, 6:5–10, 7:12–17, 8:3–14.18(?) and 10:2–5.8–11. 4QJoshua[b] contains fragments of Josh. 2:11–12, 3:15–4:3 and 17:1–5.11–15. XJoshua now consists of fragments of Josh. 1:9–12 and 2:4–15. Much of what can be deduced from the text of these scrolls depends on a hypothetical reconstruction of the missing parts.

[6] L. Greenspoon, The Qumran Fragments of Joshua: Which Puzzle are They Part of and Where Do They Fit? in G.J. Brooke, B. Lindars (eds.), *Septuagint, Scrolls and Cognate Writings: Papers Presented to the International Symposium on the Septuagint and Its Relations to the Dead Sea Scrolls and Other Writings. Manchester 1990.* Atlanta 1992, pp. 159–194.

[7] E. Tov, 4QJosh[b], in Z.J. Kapera, *Intertestamental Essays in Honour of Józef Tadeusz Milik.* (Qumranica Mogilanensia 6) Kraków 1992, pp. 205–212.

[8] E. Ulrich, 4QJoshua[a] and Joshua's First Altar in the Promised Land; see section 1.4.

[9] K. Bieberstein, *Lukian und Theodotion im Josuabuch*, pp. 75–93: 'Die Josuarollen von Ḫirbet Qumrān.'

[10] E. Tov, S.J. Pfann (eds.), *The Dead Sea Scrolls on Microfiche. A Comprehensive Facsimile Edition of the Texts from the Judean Desert.* Leiden/New York/Köln 1993.

[11] E. Ulrich, 4QJosh[a], and E. Tov, 4QJosh[b], in E. Ulrich, F.M. Cross, S.W. Crawford, J.A. Duncan, P.W. Skehan, E. Tov, J. Trebolle Barrera (eds.), *Qumran Cave 4.IX. Deuteronomy, Joshua, Judges, Kings.* (DJD 14) Oxford 1995, pp. 143–152, 153–160.

[12] These are the fourth-century CE witnesses Codex Vaticanus B, papyri 946 and 816 (third century CE ?) and the Sahidic codex Bodmer 21/Chester Beatty 1389.

[13] E. Ulrich, 4QJosh[a] (DJD 14), p. 143.

3.2 4QJoshua[A]

Twenty-two different fragments belong to this scroll, which together constitute parts of five different columns (numbered I, II, IV, V and VII or VIII by its editor, E. Ulrich). On paleographic grounds, the scroll is dated to the second half of the second century BCE or the first half of the first century BCE.[14] The orthography, though slightly fuller than that of MT,[15] does not display the characteristics of what Tov calls the 'Qumran scribal practice',[16] and may have been written outside the Qumran community.

With the possible exception of Josh. 8:10–17 (Column V consisting of fragments 9 ii, 13–16), the extant text presents no large-scale quantitative differences with MT. The agreements between 4QJosh[a] and LXX-Joshua against MT-Joshua concern two variants in number of suffix or verb (7:13–14), one variant in the stem of the verb ראה (4QJosh[a]/LXX?: Qal; MT: Hiph'il), and two minuses *vis-à-vis* MT-Josh. 8:10.14 (the word ישראל), and the plus in 8:35 in 4QJosh[a] and LXX-Joshua of the object את יהושע:[17]

5[6]	μὴ *ἰδεῖν* αὐτοὺς τὴν γῆν,	[לב]לתי ראות את ה[ארץ]	לְבִלְתִּי הַרְאוֹתָם אֶת־הָאָרֶץ
7[13]	Τὸ ἀνάθεμα ἐν *ὑμῖν* ἐστιν,	חרם בקרבכם	חֵרֶם בְּקִרְבְּךָ
7[13]	ἀπέναντι τῶν ἐχθρῶν *ὑμῶν*,	לפני אויביכם	לִפְנֵי אֹיְבֶיךָ
7[14]	προσάξετε κατ' οἶκον·	תקריבו [ל]בתים	תִּקְרַב לַבָּתִּים
8[10]	καὶ οἱ πρεσβύτεροι ---	[ו]הזקנים [---]	וְזִקְנֵי יִשְׂרָאֵל
8[14]	εἰς συνάντησιν *αὐτοῖς* *ἐπ' εὐθείας*	[לק]ראתם ---	לִקְרַאת־יִשְׂרָאֵל
8[35]	ὧν ἐνετείλατο Μωυσῆς *τῷ Ἰησοῖ*,	מכל צוה משה [את יה]ושוע	אֲשֶׁר־צִוָּה מֹשֶׁה

---

[14] E. Ulrich, 4QJosh[a] (DJD 14), p. 143. E. Ulrich, Joshua's First Altar, p. 89, n. 2, refers to the confirmation of the results for dating Dead Sea Scrolls retrieved from the paleographic system by the radiocarbon dating of several scrolls, although the 4QJoshua-scrolls have not been subjected to the Carbon 14 investigation.

[15] E. Ulrich, 4QJosh[a] (DJD 14), pp. 144–145, counts 14 orthographic divergencies between 4QJosh[a] and MT.

[16] L. Greenspoon, The Qumran Fragments of Joshua, p. 161. See further E. Tov, *Textual Criticism of the Hebrew Bible*, pp. 108–109.

[17] As will be argued in chapter 8, the examples from Josh. 8:10 and 8:14 probably do not belong here, which makes the list even shorter. The first variant (Josh. 5:6) will be discussed in chapter 7 below. Reconstructed elements are given in outline font.

These variants have hardly any bearing on the meaning of the text, and already Greenspoon made the somewhat sobering statement that 'there are no qualitatively important readings definitely shared by the LXX and 4QJoshua.'[18]

More striking, however, are the agreements between 4QJosh[a] and MT-Joshua as opposed to LXX-Joshua. Thus, where LXX-Josh. 5:2–9 presents a version that is markedly different from MT, the preserved Qumran fragments appear to follow MT-Joshua.[19] Likewise, the plus in MT-Josh. 6:6 *vis-à-vis* LXX-Joshua (6:7) finds support in 4QJosh[a]:

6[7]	καὶ εἶπεν αὐτοῖς	[ויאמ]ר אל[יהם]	וַיֹּאמֶר אֲלֵהֶם
	λέγων		
	--- --- --- --- ---	שאו א[ת ארון הברית]	שְׂאוּ אֶת־אֲרוֹן הַבְּרִית
	--- --- --- ---	ושבעה כהנים ישא[ו	וְשִׁבְעָה כֹהֲנִים יִשְׂאוּ
	--- ---	שבעה שופרות יוב]לים	שִׁבְעָה שׁוֹפְרוֹת יוֹבְלִים
	--- --- --- --- ---	לפני א[רון יהוה	לִפְנֵי אֲרוֹן יְהוָה׃
	Παραγγείλατε	ויאמר] יהושע	*וַ*יֹּאמְרוּ **וַ**יֹּאמֶר
	τῷ λαῷ	אל העם	אֶל־הָעָם
	περιελθεῖν	[עברו]	עִבְרוּ

The possible exception to this rule of quantitative 4QJosh[a]-MT agreement would be the text of Josh. 8:10–18 in column V of 4QJosh[a]. According to Ulrich[20] and Mazor, a reconstruction on the basis of the extant fragments of this column would leave no room for 8:7b ונתנה יהוה אלהיכם בידכם, a clause which is also absent from LXX-Joshua, and, more importantly, the whole of verses 11b–13, also absent from LXX-Joshua. Since the plus in MT concerns a literary redundant text, providing a duplicate of Joshua's stationing a group of men in ambush, a coalescence of textual and literary data might be assumed, as L. Mazor has done. Anticipating a more extensive discussion of this passage in chapter 8 below, it should be pointed out here that the alleged shorter text of Josh. 8:11–18 in 4QJosh[a] and LXX-Joshua is a hypothetical reconstruction based on a combination of various fragments and, secondly, that MT-Josh. 8:8a, absent from LXX, finds support in 4QJosh[a]:

---

[18] L. Greenspoon, The Qumran Fragments of Joshua, p. 164. Likewise, Ulrich classifies these agreements 'insignificant', E. Ulrich, 4QJosh[a] (DJD 14) p. 145.
[19] See chapter 7 below.
[20] E. Ulrich, 4QJosh[a] (DJD 14), pp. 150–151, and p. 145.

8[8]	--- ---	]והיה	וְהָיָ֗ה
	--- --- --- ---	כתפשכם את העיר	כְּתָפְשְׂכֶ֣ם אֶת־הָעִ֔יר
	--- --- --- --- ---	תציתו את הע]יׄר באשׄ	תַּצִּ֤יתוּ אֶת־הָעִיר֙ בָּאֵ֔שׁ

Besides these variants, 4QJosh[a] has a number of readings that do not align with either MT or LXX and are therefore termed 'unique readings'. Again, most of the unique readings of 4QJosh[a] *vis-à-vis* both MT and LXX definitely do not point to an editorial reworking of the text of Joshua, but do attest to scribal phenomena such as *homoioteleuton* (7:14), interchange of synonymous phrases (-לְ and אֶל in 8:4), addition (7:12) or omission (7:15) of the conjunctive *waw*, or contextual elucidations, such as the explicative mention of the subject 'Joshua' in 6:7, supporting MT-Qere against MT-Ketib.[21]

6[5]	καὶ εἰσελεύσεται *πᾶς* ὁ λαὸς	ועלה העםׄ	וְעָל֥וּ הָעָ֖ם
6[7]	Παραγγείλατε	[ויאמר] יהושע	*וַ**יֹּאמְרוּ **וַ**יֹּאמֶר֙
7[12]	αὐχένα ἐπιστρέψουσιν ἔναντι	[יפנו לפ]נ[י]	עֹ֚רֶף יִפְנוּ֙ לִפְנֵ֣י
	τῶν ἐχθρῶν αὐτῶν,	אׄיׄבׄיׄו	אֹֽיְבֵיהֶ֔ם
		ולא פנים	
7[12]	οὐ προσθήσω ἔτι	ולא אוסיף	לֹ֤א אוֹסִיף֙
7[14]	καὶ ἔσται ἡ φυλή,	ו]הׄוה השבט	וְהָיָ֞ה הַשֵּׁ֠בֶט
	ἣν ἂν δείξῃ κύριος,	אשר ילכדנו יהוה	אֲשֶׁר־יִלְכְּדֶ֨נּוּ יְהוָ֜ה
	προσάξετε κατὰ δήμους·	--- ---	יִקְרַ֣ב לַמִּשְׁפָּח֗וֹת
	καὶ τὸν δῆμον,	---	וְהַמִּשְׁפָּחָ֞ה
	ὃν ἐὰν δείξῃ κύριος,	--- --- ---	אֲשֶׁר־יִלְכְּדֶ֤נָּה יְהוָה֙
	προσάξετε κατ' οἶκον·	תקריבו [ל]בׄתים	תִּקְרַ֣ב לַבָּתִּ֔ים
7[15]	καὶ --- ὃς ἂν ἐνδειχθῇ --- --- ---,	והיה הנלכד בהם	וְהָיָה֙ הַנִּלְכָּ֣ד בַּחֵ֔רֶם
7[15]	καὶ ἐποίησεν ἀνόμημα	-כי עשה [נבלה]	וְכִֽי־עָשָׂ֥ה נְבָלָ֖ה
7[16]	καὶ ἐνεδείχθη	וילכד אתׄ	וַיִּלָּכֵ֖ד
	ἡ φυλὴ Ιουδα·	[שבט יהודה]	שֵׁ֥בֶט יְהוּדָֽה׃
8[4]	Ὑμεῖς ἐνεδρεύσατε --- ---	[אתם ארבים]	אַתֶּ֗ם אֹרְבִ֤ים
		אל העיר	לָעִיר֙
10[4]	καὶ πρὸς τοὺς υἱοὺς Ισραηλ.	ואת --- ישראל	וְאֵ֖ת בְּנֵ֥י יִשְׂרָאֵֽל׃
10[9]	ὅλην τὴν νύκτα εἰσεπορεύθη	כל הלילה הׄלׄ[ך [22]	כָּל־הַלַּ֖יְלָה עָלָ֥ה
10[11]	λίθους *χαλάζης*	אבניםׄ --- [23]	אֲבָנִ֧ים גְּדֹל֛וֹת

[21] See the discussion of all variants known to Bieberstein in the 'Auswertung' of the MT-LXX-4QJosh[a] variants in his *Lukian und Theodotion*, pp. 83–85. Besides these textual variants there are two metatextual variants in 4QJosh[a]: [1] a short interval in 7:13 before כי כה אמר יהוה whereas MT[L.A] do not present a *setumah*; and [2] as a possible interval in 4QJosh[a] before 10:3 where a reconstruction of the first line of fragments 17–18 leaves room for some 10 letterspaces.

[22] Of this word, only the right stroke of the first letter and the top stroke of the *lamed* have been preserved. Since this right stroke of the first letter is vertical, rather than diagonal, the reconstruction made by Ulrich, הׄלׄ[ך, seems more plausible than that of Bieberstein, p. 83: עׄלׄ[ה.

[23] The reconstruction of the link of fragment 22 to fragment 21 in lines 4 and 5

The most striking feature of this scroll is the fact that the text of Josh. 5:2ff. is preceded by the last words of Josh. 8:34–35 followed by some words that seem to reflect an editorial link between Josh. 8:35 and 5:2. The case will be discussed in chapters 7 and 8 below.

3.3 4QJoshua[b]

Compared to 4QJoshua[a] the second Joshua scroll from Qumran is even more fragmentary. Its text is even closer to MT than that of 4QJosh[a].[24] Six fragments have been preserved, containing remnants of Josh. 2:11–12 (frg. 1), 3:15–4:3 (frg. 2–3), 17:1–5 (frg. 4), 11–15 (frg. 5) and some unidentified signs (frg. 6, col. i and ii).[25] On the basis of the late-Hasmonean handwriting, the manuscript is dated to the middle of the first century BCE. The text of this manuscript corresponds closely to MT, also in passages where MT differs from LXX.[26]

2[11]	ἐν *οὐδενὶ ἡμῶν*	באיש	בְּאִישׁ
3[15]	τὴν κιβωτὸν *τῆς διαθήκης κυρίου*	נשאי הארון	נֹשְׂאֵי הָאָרוֹן
3[15]	τοῦ ὕδατος *τοῦ Ιορδάνου*	[המי]ם	הַמַּיִם
3[16]	*ἕως μέρους Καριαθιαριμ*	העיר אשר	הָעִיר אֲשֶׁר
		מצד צ[רתן]	מִצַּד צָרְתָן
3[16]	τὸ δὲ καταβαῖνον κατέβη	[27] [והירדים]	וְהַיֹּרְדִים
3[16]	*ἕως εἰς τὸ τέλος*	תמו	תַּמּוּ
17[1]	--- ---- --- *ἐν τῇ* Γαλααδίτιδι	ויהי לו ה[ג]לעד	וַיְהִי־לוֹ הַגִּלְעָד
	καὶ *ἐν τῇ* Βασανίτιδι.	[והבשן]	וְהַבָּשָׁן׃
17[2]	--- --- --- ---	[ולבני חפר]	וְלִבְנֵי־חֵפֶר

---

provides a good connection between ב[נ̊סם (fragm. 22) and ויה]י (fragm. 21). This connection, however, leaves no room for the word גדלות in MT-Josh. 10:11 between מן השמ]ים (fragm. 22) and the preceding word אבנים̊ (fragm. 21), see the discussion in Bieberstein, p. 83. Ulrich does not discuss this reconstruction, but merely mentions this difference between 4QJosh[a] and MT/LXX as a variant reading.

[24] A preliminary edition of this manuscript has been offered by E. Tov, 4QJosh[b], in Z.J. KAPERA (ed.), *Intertestamental Essays in Honour of Józef Tadeusz Milik.* (Qumranica Mogilanensia 6) Kraków 1992, part I, pp. 205–212. See also K. BIEBERSTEIN, *Lukian und Theodotion im Josuabuch*, pp. 85–93. The official publication appeared in 1995 as E. Tov, 4QJosh[b], in DJD 14, pp. 153–160. A discussion of the text was already presented in 1990 by L.J. GREENSPOON, The Qumran Fragments of Joshua, pp. 159–194.

[25] On the basis of the difference in line length (frg. 1–3: 7–8 mm.; 4–5:5–6 mm.), the difference in ink between these two groups of fragments, transparency, and the absence (frg. 1–3) and presence (frg. 4–50 of orthographic variants, K. BIEBERSTEIN, *Lukian und Theodotion*, p. 86, wonders whether the two parts really belong to the same manuscript.

[26] See also the discussion in K. BIEBERSTEIN, *Lukian und Theodotion*, pp. 91–93.

[27] E. Tov, 4QJosh[b] (DJD 14), p. 157 lists this possible variant, but adds: '4QJosh[b] could have had here an additional word, like 𝕮 (ירדו according to Margolis).'

	καὶ τοῖς υἱοῖς *Συμαριμ*	[ולבני שמיד]ע	וְלִבְנֵי שְׁמִידָע
	καὶ τοῖς υἱοῖς Οφερ·		
17[2]	οὗτοι --- --- --- ---	אלה בני מנש[ה	אֵלֶּה בְּנֵי מְנַשֶּׁה
		בן יוסף]	בֶּן־יוֹסֵף
17[3]	--- --- --- ---	[בן]גלעד בן מכ[יר	בֶּן־גִּלְעָד בֶּן־מָכִיר
	--- ---	בן מנשה	בֶּן־מְנַשֶּׁה
17[3]	τῶν θυγατέρων *Σαλπααδ·*	בנתיו	בְּנֹתָיו
17[4]	καὶ ἐναντίον Ἰησοῦ --- ---	ולפני יהו[שע	וְלִפְנֵי יְהוֹשֻׁעַ
		בן נון][28]	בִּן־נוּן
17[11]	*καὶ τὸ τρίτον τῆς Ναφετα*[29]	שלשת הנפות	שְׁלֹשֶׁת הַנָּפֶת
17[14]	*καὶ ὁ θεὸς* εὐλόγησέν με.	ברכני יהוה	בֵּרְכַנִי יְהוָה׃
17[15]	καὶ *ἐκκάθαρον* σεαυτῷ ---,	[ובראת לך שם	וּבֵרֵאתָ לְךָ שָׁם
	--- --- --- --- --- --- ---	בארץ]הפ[רזי	בְּאֶרֶץ הַפְּרִזִּי
		והרפאים]	וְהָרְפָאִים

In three cases 4QJosh[b] appears to agree with LXX-Joshua against MT-Joshua. Whereas MT-Josh. 3:15 explains in a circumstantial clause that *the Jordan happened to flow over all its borders during all the days of the harvest*, in order to give supernormal proportions to the otherwise rather modest stream, both the supralinear addition in 4QJosh[b] and the paraphrase of this passage in 4QApocryphon of Joshua[b],[30] agree in specifying this (harvest) time as the period of the wheat harvest:[31]

MT-Josh. 3:15	והירדן מלא על־כל־גדותיו כל ימי קציר ----
4QJosh[b]	בימי קציר(חטים)
4QApocrJosh[b]	והיורדן מלא מי[ם] על כל גדותיו
	ושוטף [ב]מימיו מן החדש ה[ ]י עד חדש קציר חטים
LXX-Josh. 3:15	*ὡσεὶ ἡμέραι θερισμοῦ πυρῶν*

According to Tov, a more significant and extensive correspondance to a shorter LXX-text can be recovered on the basis of a reconstruction of line 7 in the combination of fragments 2 and 3. A reconstruction

[28] Although the apposition בן נון, absent from LXX, is not physically attested in 4QJosh[b], it is unlikely that these words were missing in 4QJosh[b]-frg. 4, line 7, because a reconstruction of the line without the phrase would be too short compared to the other lines.

[29] The reading Ναφετα is a conjectural emendation by Rahlfs. B has Μαφετα. Margolis, *The Book of Joshua in Greek*, p. 338, made the same reconstruction.

[30] Edited by C. Newsom, 4QApocryphon of Joshua[b], in G.J. Brooke, J. Collins, T. Elgvin, P. Flint, J. Greenfield, E. Larson, C. Newsom, E. Puech, L.H. Schiffmann, M. Stone, J. Trebolle Barrera, J. VanderKam (eds.), *Qumran Cave 4. XVII. Parabiblical Texts, Part 3*. (DJD 22) Oxford 1996, pp. 263–288.

[31] See the discussion in K. Bieberstein, *Josua-Jordan-Jericho*, pp. 152–154, with full references to previous opinions.

of fragment 3 according to MT would result in a line which is far too long (81 letterspaces) compared to both the last lines of fragment 3 (66 lines) and the preceding lines of fragment 2 (49–55 lines). In order to accommodate the length of the reconstructed lines to the length of the preceding lines, Tov proposes to omit the underlined elements.[32]

4QJoshua[b] Fragments 2–3: Reconstruction after MT:

number of letterspaces		text line
49	נשאי הארון נטבלו בקצ[ה המים והירדן מלא על כל גדותיו]	1
	חטים	
50	בימי קציר 16ויעמדו המים הירדים מל[מעלה קמו נד אחד הרחק]	2
45?	מאד<מאׄ[ד]>באדם העיר אשר מצד צ[רתן והירדים על ים הערבה]	3
55	[י]ם המלח תמו נכרת[ו והעם עברו נגד יריחו 17ויעמדו הכהנים נשאי]	4
52	[הארון בר]ית יהוה ב[חרבה בתוך הירדן הכן וכל ישראל עברים]	5
	יהוש[ע	
49	[בחרבה עד אשר]ת[מו וכל הגוי לעבר את הירדן 4:1ויהי כאשר תמו]	6
81	[כל הגוי לעבור את הירדן ויאמר יהוה]אל יהוש[ע לאמר 2קחו לכם מן העם שנים עשר אנשים איש]	7
66	[אחד איש אחד משבט 3וצוו אותם לאמר שאו]לכם מתוך ה[ירדן ממצב רגלי הכהנים]	8
66	[הכין שתים עשרה אבנים והעברתם אותם ע]מכם והנ[ח]תם א[ותם במלון אשר תלינו]	9

In order to support his reconstruction of these lines in 4QJosh[b], Tov refers to the LXX of the passage, in which a number of these elements (among which the word מזה noted above) are absent, although he admits the tentative nature of this reconstruction, 'since it goes against the general character of the scroll'.[33] It is important, however, to note [1] that we are dealing here with a reconstruction based on a combining of separate fragments (2 and 3), [2] that the extant text contains some scribal errors and corrections,[34] [3] that

---

[32] The reconstruction of the Qumran text offered here makes use of the following conventions: reconstructed text has been marked by outline font and placed between square brackets. The measuring unit for determining the length of a line includes both letters and spaces, hence the term 'letterspaces'. My own count has been done done manually and hence may contain some minor aberrations. The contours of the fragments have been simulated by a computer drawing.

[33] E. Tov, 4QJosh[b], pp. 154, 156–157.

[34] See the supralinear additions in line 2 and line 6 (both of them not attested in MT) and the errors that resulted in מאד<מאׄ[ד]>באדם, line 3, and possibly in the Ketib-Qere variation in MT קמו נד־אחד הרחק מאד (כ) באדם (ק) מאדם העיר, *the waters were standing like a wall far removed at* (Ketib) *the city Adam/from* (Qere) *the city Adam*; see further the discussion of this passage in E. Tov, 4QJosh[b] (DJD 14), pp. 155, 157; and K. Bieberstein, *Josua-Jordan-Jericho*, pp. 154–157.

LXX does contain several elements that should be deleted as well in order to accommodate the length of line 7 to that of the other lines, and [4] that one has to take into account the character of the Greek translation. The latter methodological point is stressed by Bieberstein, who points out that, although the short expression איש אחד *vis-à-vis* the more common longer expression איש אחד איש אחד does occur in Deut. 1:23, the longer expression is consistently rendered by the Greek translators of Num. 13:2, and Josh. 3:12 by the shorter, not repetitive Greek expression ἕνα ἀφ' *ἑκάστης* (φυλῆς). This makes it problematic to adduce the Greek version of Josh. 4:1–3 to solve a textual problem in the reconstruction of 4QJosh[b].

4QJoshua[b] Fragments 2–3: Reconstruction after Tov:

number of letterspaces	text	line
49	נשאי הארון נטבלו בקׄצ[ה המי]ם ו̇ה̇[ירדן מלא על כל גדותיו] חטים	1
50	בימי קציר 16ויעמדו המים הירדים מלׄ[מעלה קמו נד אחד הרחק]	2
45?	מאד<מאׄ[ד]>ס̇אדם העיר אשר̇ מצד צ[רתן והירדים על ים הערבה]	3
55	[י]ם̇ המלח תמו נכרת[ו והעם עברו נ]ג̇ד יריחו 17ויעמדו הכהנים נשאי]	4
52	[הארון בר]ית יהוה ב[חרבה בתוך הירדן הכן וכל ישראל עברים] יהוש[ע	5
49	[בחרבה עד אשר]ת̇[מ]ו ו̇כל הגוי לעבר את הירדן 4:1ויהי כאשר תמו]	6
54	[לעבור את הירדן ויאמר יהוה]א̇ל יהוש[ע לאמר 2קחו לכם מן העם]	7
51	[איש אחד משבט 3וצוו אותם שא]ו̇ לכם מתוך ה̇[ירדן הכין שתים]	8
56	[עשרה אבנים והעברתם אותם ע]מ̇כם והנ[ח]תׄם א̇[ותם במלון אשר תלינו]	9

A less problematic solution to the problem was offered already in 1990 by L.J. Greenspoon, who reconstructed lines 7–8 in 4QJosh[b] without the phrases איש אחד איש אחד משבט and ממצב רגלי הכהנים, which, in his opinion, were 'short lines' which 'were occasionally overlooked by the 4Q(Josh[b]) scribe'.[35]

[35] L.J. Greenspoon, The Qumran Fragments of Joshua, p. 167.

4QJoshua[b] Fragments 2–3: Reconstruction after Greenspoon:

number of letterspaces	text	line
	חטים	
49	נשאי הארון נטבלו בקצ[ה המי]ם וה[ירדן מלא על כל גדותיו]	1
50	בימי קציר 16ויעמדו המים הירדים מל[מעלה קמו נד אחד הרחק]	2
45	מאד<מא[ד]>מאדם העיר אשר מצד צ[רתן והירדים על ים הערבה]	3
55	[י]ם המלח תמו נכרת[ו והעם עברו נגד יריחו 17ויעמדו הכהנים נשאי]	4
	יהוש[ע	
52	[הארון ברי]ת יהוה ב[חרבה בתוך הירדן הכן וכל ישראל עברים]	5
49	[בחרבה עד אשר]ת[מו וכל הגוי לעבר את הירדן 4:1ויהי כאשר תמו]	6
59	[כל הגוי לעבור את הירדן ויאמר יהוה]אל יהוש[ע לאמר 2קחו לכם מן]	7
49	[העם שנים עשר אנשים 3וצוו אותם לאמר שאו]לכם מתוך ה[ירדן]	8
50	[הכין שתים עשרה אבנים והעברתם אותם ע]מכם והנ[ח]תם א[ותם]	9

In a recent contribution to this problem B. Lucassen suggested that the scribe of 4QJosh[b] passed over the last eight words of Josh. 3:17, which are practically identical to the first eight words of the following verse, Josh. 4:1, and did not include the words כל הגוי as subject of the remaining (single) clause, but only Joshua, as is evident from the supralinear addition in line 6.[36] Lucassen also alters the number of the imperatives קחו and וצוו in Josh. 4:2–3 from plural to singular, to the effect that only Joshua is addressed by Yhwh. Lucassen furthermore not only deletes (with Tov) the second phrase איש אחד, but also tacitly leaves out the phrases שנים עשר אנשים and ממצב רגלי הכהנים. The text of fragments 2–3 could then be reconstructed as follows:

4QJoshua[b] Fragments 2–3: Reconstruction after Lucassen:

number of letterspaces	text	line
	חטים	
49	נשאי הארון נטבלו בקצ[ה המי]ם וה[ירדן מלא על כל גדותיו]	1
50	בימי קציר ויעמדו המים הירדים מל[מעלה קמו נד אחד הרחק]	2
45?	מאד<מא[ד]>מאדם העיר אשר מצד צ[רתן והירדים על ים הערבה]	3
55	[י]ם המלח תמו נכרת[ו והעם עברו נגד יריחו ויעמדו הכהנים נשאי]	4
	יהוש[ע	
52	[הארון ברי]ת יהוה ב[חרבה בתוך הירדן הכן וכל ישראל עברים]	5

[36] B. Lucassen, Possibility and Probability of Textual Reconstruction: The Transition from 4QJosh[b], frg. 2 to frg. 3 and the Transit of the Israelites through the Jordan, in *Textus* 20 (2000), pp. 71–81.

54	[בחרבה עד אשר]תׄ[ם לעבר את הירדן ויאמר יהוה]אל יהוש[ע לאמר]	6
58	[קח לך מן העם איש אחד משבט וצו אותם לאמר שאו]לכם מתוך ה[ירדן]	7
56	[הכין שתים עשרה אבנים והעברתם אותם ע]מׄכם והנ[ח]תׄם א[ותם במלון]	8

Although the possibility of a *parablepsis* with respect to Josh. 3:17–4:1 is very plausible, the present solution leaves open the problem of the reconstruction of the last line. With the phrase ממצב רגלי הכהנים the line would be too long, but without it the words עמכם (line 8) and לכם (line 7) no longer stand on a vertical axis. The reconstruction of these lines thus remains problematic.[37] It is, however, clear, that 4QJosh[b], cannot be simply equated to a non-masoretic Hebrew *Vorlage* of the LXX. In any case, from a redaction-critical point of view, it is difficult to see what could have motivated the addition of the elements Tov proposed to skip.

Apart from these (possible) alignments of 4QJosh[b] readings with (basically) MT or (incidentally) LXX, there are a few non-aligned readings, which, like the preceding variants, have no (significant) bearing on the meaning of the text:

2:12	καὶ νῦν	[ותאמ]ר[38]	וְעַתָּה
17:11	*καὶ τὸ τρίτον τῆς Ναφετα*	שלשת הנפות	שְׁלֹשֶׁת הַנָּפֶת׃
17:13	οὐκ ἐξωλέθρευσαν.	[לא]הורישהו	לֹא הוֹרִישׁוֹ׃
17:14	*Αντεῖπαν* δὲ οἱ υἱοὶ Ιωσηφ τῷ Ἰησοῦ	[וידברו בני יו]סף אל י[ה]ושע	וַיְדַבְּרוּ בְּנֵי יוֹסֵף אֶת־יְהוֹשֻׁעַ
17:14	--- --- --- ---	---אשר --- כה	עַד אֲשֶׁר־עַד־כֹּה

In Josh. 17:11, 4QJosh[b] presents a difference in the sequence of the villages belonging to Manasseh in the territory of Issachar and Aser. According to MT-Josh. 17:11 these cities are [1] Beth-She'an, [2] Ible'am, [3] the inhabitants of Dor, [4] the inhabitants of 'En-Dor,

[37] Thus K. Bieberstein, *Lukian und Theodotion*, pp. 88–89, who arrives at a *non liquet* conclusion: 'Offenbar sind im nicht mehr enthaltenen Text zwischen der ersten und zweiten Zeile kürzere Lesarten anzunehmen, die *nicht* mit G* übereinstimmen und sich *nicht* mit einem einfachen Hinweis auf G* rekonstruieren lassen.'

[38] The variant is based on a reconstruction of the final letter of this word. Tov, 4QJosh[b] (DJD 14), p. 154, reconstructs [ותאמ]ר[12], where MT has ועתה and LXX καὶ νῦν. K. Bieberstein, *Lukian und Theodotion*, p. 86, however, disagrees with Tov: 'doch kann es sich nach Ausweis der klaren Aufnahmen ebenso auch um ein ה handeln, was M ועתה und G*escp και νυν entspräche.' Since the ה of the scribe of 4QJosh[b] does not have the upward edge that is visible on the fragment, while the ר does have such an edge, Tov's reconstruction is preferable.

[5] the inhabitants of Taʿanach, and [6] the inhabitants of Megiddo. In 4QJosh[b], group [4] is placed before groups [2] and [3]. G. Dahl has argued that the final phrase שלשת הנפת in MT should be regarded as a *Glosse* originally intended to designate the third city of the list as Naphath-Dor (שְׁלִשׁתה נפת, *the third is Naphath*), known from Josh. 11:2, 12:23, 1 Kgs. 4:11.[39] In that case, the MT preserves the original order. The different sequence in 4QJosh[b] may then be regarded as an (unconscious?) interpretation of the obscure phrase by taking הנפת as a plural of נפה, *height*, by adding a *waw*: שְׁלֹשֶׁת הַנְּפוֹת, *the three hill(-countrie)s*, corresponding to the form נפות דור in Josh. 11:2 and parallel to the interpretation offered by Targum Onqelos (תְּלָתָה פַּלְכִין, *three districts*) and Pešiṭta (ܬܠܬ ܙܘܝܢ, *three corners*). Judg. 1:27–28 and 1 Chron. 7:29 offer the same list, and here, too, MT and LXX differ. In the light of these variations in the same list it seems likely that the qualitative variant between MT and 4QJosh[b] in 17:11 is not the result of a redactional effort, but of scribal confusion. 4QJosh[b] does not support the shorter LXX-Josh. 17:11 version, in which the cities Ibleam, ʿEn Dor and Taʿanach are not mentioned, and in which the *crux* is rendered by 'a third part of the Naphath' (understood as a place name).

3.4 XJoshua

The fragment designated as XJoshua contains remants of circa 46 words from Josh. 1:9–12 and 2:4–5 in two columns. On the basis of palaeography (late formal Herodian bookhand) and carbon-14 analysis, the manuscript is dated to the first century AD.[40] The text contains no deviations from MT and supports its text *vis-à-vis* LXX:

1^{11}	Ἑτοιμάζεσθε ---	הֹכינו [לֹ]כֹם	הָכִ֥ינוּ לָכֶ֖ם
	ἐπισιτισμόν	צ[ידה]	צֵידָ֑ה
1^{11}	δίδωσιν ὑμῖν	נתֹ[ן] לֹכם	נֹתֵ֥ן לָכֶ֖ם
	--- --- ---.	לֹרשֹׁתֹה	לְרִשְׁתָּֽהּ׃
2^{4}	τοὺς --- ἄνδρας	אֹתֹ ש[נ]י	אֶת־שְׁנֵ֥י הָאֲנָשִׁ֖ים

[39] Thus G. Dahl, The 'Three Heights' of Joshua 17_{11}, in *JBL* 53 (1934), pp. 281–283, whose exegsis is generally accepted, see, e.g., M. Noth, *Das Buch Josua*[2], p. 98; D. Barthélemy, *Critique textuelle de l'Ancien Testament* 1 (OBO 50/1) Göttingen/Fribourg 1983, pp. 47–48; T.C. Butler, *Joshua*. (WBC 7) Waco 1983, p. 182; R.D. Nelson, *Joshua*, pp. 199–200.

[40] J. Charlesworth, XJosh (DJD 38), pp. 232–236.

A reconstruction of the complete text of the first columns of XJoshua reveals no quantitative deviation from MT.[41]

3.5 Parabiblical Joshua Texts

3.5.1 *Introduction*

The circumstance that the Joshua scrolls from Qumran have been preserved in such a deplorable state is somewhat compensated by the fact that fragments of other Hebrew texts from the same period have been found among the Qumran and Masada scrolls that resemble phrases, themes and passages from the book of Joshua. These texts include [1] a text in paleo-Hebrew script resembling Josh. 21, 4QpaleoParaJosh (4Q123), [2–3] two different scrolls containing paraphrases of the Joshua narratives, previously designated as 'Psalms of Joshua', now termed 'Apocryphon of Joshua' (4Q378–379) by their editor C. Newsom. Recently some other fragmentary texts have been identified as paraphrases of Joshua, including [4] 4Q522, a text containing Psalm 122, a number of toponyms, and references to the branch of Jesse (David) and to the rock Zion, [5] another text with toponyms, 5Q9, and [6] a fragmentary text found in Masada (casemate 1039) with allusions to Josh. 23 (Mas 1039–211).

While the possibility that (some of) these texts represent variant editions of Joshua cannot be completely excluded, especially in the case of very fragmentary texts, it is most likely that they should be regarded as 'rewritten version(s)' of Joshua or as *parabiblical texts*, a genre to which a considerable number of Second Temple Judaism compositions within and outside the Qumran community are reckoned, e.g. Chronicles, Jubilees, the Genesis Apocryphon, the Reworked Pentateuch, the TempleScroll, the Moses Apocrypha (1QDibrei Moshe, 4Q374–375, 387–390), and in the Greek language for instance the historical work 'On the Kings in Judea' by Eupolemos, and the Jewish Antiquities by Josephus.[42]

---

[41] J. Charlesworth, XJosh (DJD 38), pp. 236–239.

[42] The list is far from exhaustive. See further G.W.E. Nickelsburg, The Bible Rewritten and Expanded, in M.E. Stone (ed.), *Jewish Writings of the Second Temple Period. Apocrypha, Pseudepigrapha, Qumran Sectarian Writings, Philo, Josephus.* (CRINT II/2) Assen/Philadelphia 1984, pp. 89–156.

If the qualification of these texts as paraphrases of the older Joshua composition holds true, they are only of indirect relevance to the history of that book before the MT version of Joshua. Unfortuntately these texts, too, have suffered much from physical corruption, so that in most cases it is difficult, if not impossible, to determine the nature and scope of these works and the relation between these fragments and the text of Joshua as found in MT, LXX and 4QJosh$^{a.b}$. For instance, the four fragments that make up 4Q123 contain no more than 71 identifiable letters; 5Q9 some 100 identifiable letters; and the Masada fragment some 138 letters.

Nevertheless, since some fragments follow the Joshua text fairly closely (thus 4Q378–379) they might be used as indirect Hebrew witnesses to the text of Joshua (for instance regarding the absence of the words את־יריחו in the actualisation of Josh. 6:26 in 4Q379, frg. 22 ii l.8, or with respect to the presence of the word חטים in 4Q379, frg. 12, l.7). Moreover, they occasionally provide a glimpse of how the Joshua narratives were adapted to the present situation of the authors of these new compositions (such as for instance the application of the curse upon the rebuilder of Jericho [Josh. 6:26] in 4Q379, frg. 22 ii, cited in 4QTestimonia).[43]

3.5.2 *4QpaleoParaJoshua (4Q123)*

Four tiny fragments, together containing no more than 71 identifiable letters, are the sad remains of what once might have been a paraphrase of Joshua in palaeo-Hebrew script.[44] The combination of the words and phrases that can be identified on these scraps, i.e. [1] מגרש, *pasture-ground*, [2] [קר]ית[ ]ארבע, *[Qir]yat-ʿArba*, [3] ביד משה עבד[ו ?], *by the hand of Moses, the servant [of Yhwh?]*, and [4] ערים אר[בע], *[four] cities*, has its parallel in the Hebrew Bible only in Josh. 21.[45] There

---

[43] See the short characterisation by E. Noort, *Das Buch Josua. Forschungsgeschichte und Problemfelder.* (EdF 292) Darmstadt 1998, pp. 55–56: 'wichtig für die Rezeptionsgeschichte Josuas, weniger aber für die Textgeschichte des biblischen Buches.'

[44] E. Ulrich, 4QpaleoParaJoshua, in P.W. Skehan, E. Ulrich, J.E. Sanderson (eds.), *Qumran Cave 4.IV. Palaeo-Hebrew and Greek Biblical Manuscripts.* (DJD 9) Oxford 1992 (1993), pp. 201–203.

[45] The leading term of these fragments, מגרשׁ, occurs 59 times in Josh. 21, and 42 times and 5 times respectively in the parallel passages that deal with the cities of the Levites, 1 Chron. 6:39–66 and Num. 35:1–8; also Lev. 25:34, Ezek. 45:2, 48:15.17, 1 Chron. 5:6, 13:2; 2 Chron. 11:14. In 4QpaleoParaJoshua the word occurs three or four times in fragment 1, lines 2 and 4; fragment 2, line 2 and fragment 4, line 1. Josh. 21 is the only passage in which the phrases [קר]ית[ ]ארבע

is, however, no possible reconstruction of Josh. 21 that fits the text on these fragments.

The fact that this text was written in palaeo-Hebrew script is remarkable, since among the manuscripts found at Qumran this script is used, besides this scroll and some unidentified fragments (4Q124–125), only for the books of the Pentateuch[46] and the book of Job. J. Trebolle Barrera and E. Tov connect this phenomenon of writing the most venerated books (Pentateuch) in the outdated ancient paleo-Hebrew script with the Sadduccean party, which would imply that 4Q123 had belonged to the Sadduccee canon.[47]

Ulrich associates the paleo-Hebrew script with the Samaritan practice to use this script for their canonical books, and, more in particular with the Samaritan version of the Joshua narrative in the so-called Samaritan book of Joshua.[48] Yet, the authenticity of the Hebrew version of this composition *vis-à-vis* the Arabic version is contested, while the alleged pre-13th century CE date of this composition has proven to be unlikely.[49] Furthermore, there are no clear links between the two compositions, since the list of the cities for the Levites (Josh. 21) is completely absent in this Samaritan version (Gaster's chapter XIV).

3.5.3 *4QApocryphon Joshua[a] (4Q378)*

Slightly more extensive is the text of 4Q378, of which 29 fragments have been preserved.[50] The scroll was probably written in the first

---

(Josh. 21:11; cf. 4QpaleoParaJoshua fragment 1, line 5) and ביד־משה (Josh. 21:2, but without the apposition [? עבד]ו; cf 4QpaleoParaJoshua, fragment 2, line 1) occur.

[46] 6QpaleoGen, 4QpaleoGen-Exod[l.m], 4QpaleoExod[m], 1QpaleoLev, 2QpaleoLev, 6QpaleoLev, 11QpaleoLev[a], 1QpaleoNum, 4QpaleoDeut[r.s], and 4QpaleoJob[c].

[47] J. TREBOLLE BARRERA, *La Biblia judía y la Biblia christiana*. Madrid 1993, pp. 227–229 (English Translation: J. TREBOLLE BARRERA, *The Jewish Bible and the Christian Bible*, pp. 219–221), and E. TOV, The Socio-Religious Background of the Paleo-Hebrew Biblical Texts Found at Qumran, in H. CANCIK, H. LICHTENBERGER, P. SCHÄFER (Hg.), *Geschichte—Tradition—Reflexion, Festschrift für Martin Hengel zum 70. Geburtstag. Band I. Judentum*. Tübingen 1996 (pp. 353–374).

[48] See M. GASTER, Das Buch Josua in hebräisch-samaritanischer Rezension, in *ZDMG* 62 (1908), pp. 209–279, 494–549, and a more critical introduction by P. STENHOUSE, Samaritan Chronicles, in A.D. CROWN (ed.), *The Samaritans*, pp. 218–265; and E. NOORT, *Das Buch Josua.*, pp. 58–59.

[49] P. STENHOUSE, Samaritan Chronicles, in A.D. CROWN (ed.), *The Samaritans*, pp. 218–264.

[50] Edited by C. Newsom in preliminary form in: C.A. NEWSOM, The 'Psalms of Joshua' from Qumran Cave 4, in *Journal of Jewish Studies* 39 (1988), pp. 56–73, and in the official DJD series, C. NEWSOM, Apocryphon of Joshua, in G.J. BROOKE,

century CE,[51] possibly by a scribe from the Qumran community.[52] The text on most of these fragments is too marginal to allow for any positive connections with the biblical narratives.[53] Fragment 14 alludes to the death of Moses by paraphrasing Deut. 34:8 and Num. 33:48–49. Fragment 3 ii–4 echo expressions found in Josh. 1:5–6.17–18, but the patchy state of the fragments does not allow any statements to be made other than pointing out to the correspondences between the two texts:

	MT-Joshua	4QApocrJosh[a] fragments 3ii–4
1[17]	כְּכֹל אֲשֶׁר־שָׁמַעְנוּ אֶל־מֹשֶׁה כֵּן נִשְׁמַע אֵלֶיךָ	[ו]שמענו למושה כ[ן]
1[9]	הֲלוֹא צִוִּיתִיךָ חֲזַק וֶאֱמָץ אַל־תַּעֲרֹץ וְאַל־תֵּחָת	ואל תחת חזק וא[מץ]
1[6]	חֲזַק וֶאֱמָץ כִּי אַתָּה תַּנְחִיל אֶת־הָעָם הַזֶּה	[כ]י תנחיל את[העם הזה]
1[5]	אֶהְיֶה עִמָּךְ לֹא אַרְפְּךָ	ירפכה ולוא יעזב[כה]
	וְלֹא אֶעֶזְבֶךָּ׃	ת]חזקנה ידיך[

The other relatively sizable fragments (3 i, 6 i, 6 ii, 11, 22 i, 26) seem to contain discursive texts dealing with the themes of curse (frg. 3 i), which seems to be related to Deut. 28 (frg. 3 i), guilt, sin (frg. 6 i perhaps to be connected with the sin of Achan, Josh. 7, see also frg. 22 i) and trial (frg. 6 ii), and the promise to the patriarchs (frg. 11 referring to Deut. 8:7–9?), but the absence of a clear context does not allow for more precise formulations.

3.5.4 *4QApocryphon Joshua[b] (4Q379)*

Of the parabiblical Joshua texts, this scroll with its 41 fragments is the most extensive and interesting. The scroll antedates 4Q378 and lacks the Qumran scribal features, which together with the use of divine names that are explicitely not used in the sectarian compositions, makes it likely that this scroll was written outside the Qumran community.[54] Three fragments are of interest to our study. In fragment 12, the date of Israel's crossing is not only specified as the

J. Collins, T. Elgvin, P. Flint, J. Greenfield, E. Larson, C. Newsom, É. Puech, L.H. Schiffmann, M. Stone, J. Trebolle Barrera, J. VanderKam (eds.), *Qumran Cave 4. XVII. Parabiblical Texts, Part 3.* (DJD 22) Oxford 1996, pp. 241–262.

[51] C. Newsom, 4Q378 (DJD 22), p. 241: '4Q378 is written in a fully developed Herodian formal hand'.

[52] C. Newsom, 4Q378 (DJD 22), p. 238.

[53] Thus fragments 1–2, 5, 7–10, 12–13 ii, 15–21, 22ii–25, 27–29.

[54] C. Newsom, 4QApocryphon of Joshua[a–b], (DJD 22), p. 238.

period of the *wheat* harvest (see the variant חטים/πυρῶν in 4QJosh[b] and LXX-Joshua, discussed above), but also as the first year of a new jubilee, which corresponds to the fifty-first jubilee according to the chronology of the book of Jubilees.[55]

In fragments 16, a liturgical act of blessing and praising seems to be connected with the event of Israel's crossing of the river Jordan.[56] Newsom connects this fragment with Joshua 4, in which the crossing of the Jordan is followed by the commemorative act of raising twelve stones for the twelve tribes,[57] although the verbs ברך, הלל, and רנן do not occur in that context. E. Tov, on the other hand, regards these fragments (15–17) as a paraphrase of MT-Josh. 8:30–35, where the act of blessing (ברך) does play a prominent role (MT-Josh. 8:33).[58] The ceremony described in this passage, however, is a solemn one, in which Joshua reads the book of the Law, including both blessing and curse. It is difficult to reconcile this with the praising and shouting in this tiny fragment.

Whereas almost all fragments of 4Q379 can be linked only tentatively to passages from Joshua, fragment 22 ii, lines 7–15 clearly contains a citation from Joshua, i.e. Joshua's curse upon the rebuilder of Jericho, Josh. 6:26. The passage that follows seems to describe the fulfillment of this curse by a man of Belial, and resembles the *pesher*-genre. Interestingly, the same passage is found in 4QTestimonia (4Q175), a single-page anthology of the first half of SamP-Exod.

---

[55] C. Newsom, 4Q379 (DJD 22), pp. 270–271. The narrated time covered by the book of Jubilees does not go beyond the period of the forty days that Moses spent on Mount Sinai which forms the narrative framework of this composition. Since this event took place 'forty-nine jubilees from the days of Adam until this day and one week and two years' with 'still forty years to learn the commands of the Lord until they cross over the shore of the land of Canaan, crossing over the Jordan to its western side' to come (Jubilees 50:4), the chronology of 4Q379 perfectly fits that of Jubilees. See further O.S. Wintermute, Jubilees, in J.H. Charlesworth (ed.), *The Old Testament Pseudepigrapha. Volume 2. Expansions of the 'Old Testament' and Legends, Wisdom and Philosophical Literature, Prayers, Psalms, and Odes, Fragments of Lost Judeo-Hellenistic Works*. New York/London/Toronto/Sydney/Auckland 1985, pp. 35–142.

[56] See fragments 15 and 17, where the root ברך occurs in frg. 15, line 1]בכ̊ל ברכו̊ת, line 2? כל ומבר̊[כים, frg. 17, line 2] ומברכים י̊ם[ ). Fragment 17, line 3 has:]ו עבר[י]ם̊[.

[57] C. Newsom, 4Q379 (DJD 22), p. 273.

[58] E. Tov, The Rewritten Book of Joshua as Found at Qumran and Masada, in M.E. Stone, E.G. Chazon (eds.), *Biblical Perspectives: Early Use and Interpretation of the Bible in Light of the Dead Sea Scrolls. Proceedings of the First International Symposium of the Orion Center for the Study of the Dead Sea Scrolls and Associated Literature, 12–14 May, 1996.* (STDJ 27) Leiden/Boston/Köln 1998, pp. 233–256, especially p. 253.

20:21b (i.e., a combination of Deut. 5:28b–29 and Deut. 18:18–19) (lines 1–8), Num. 24:15–17 (lines 9–13), Deut. 33:8–11 (lines 14–20) and this interpretation of Josh. 6:26 (lines 21–30), dating from the first quarter of the first century BCE.

The historical interpretation of these allusions as well as the literary priority between the two texts are matters of dispute. In a recent contribution to the discussion that followed the preliminary publication of 4QTestimonia in 1956 by J.M. Allegro,[59] H. Eshel argues that this *pesher* of Josh. 6:26 fits the character of 4QTestimonia better than 4Q379, and that 4Q379 quotes from 4QTestimonia (as evidenced by the scribal error in 4Q379 lines 12–14)[60] rather than vice-versa (as was the current consensus)[61]. On the basis of archaeological data Eshel argues that this *pesher* refers to the rebuilding of Jericho under John Hyrcanus I.[62] In that case the two brothers are to be identified with his sons Aristobulus I and Antigonus who captured Samaria (hence the allusion to Gen. 49:5; see Josephus, *Jewish Antiquities* XIII.275–283), who died soon after one another in the years 104–103 BCE (although not in the vicinity of Jericho, see *Jewish Antiquities* XIII.307–319). This interpretation has now gained wide acceptance.[63]

---

[59] J.M. ALLEGRO, Further Messianic references in Qumran Literature, in *JBL* 75 (1956), pp. 182–187, and in the 'official' DJD publication in J.M. ALLEGRO, A.A. ANDERSON (eds.), *Qumrân Cave 4.I (4Q158–4Q186).* (DJD 5) Oxford 1968.

[60] H. ESHEL, The Historical Background of the Pesher Interpreting Joshua's Curse on the Rebuilder of Jericho, in *RdQ* 15 (1991–1992), pp. 409–420, especially pp. 410–412. On the following pages, 413–414, Eshel provides a helpful survey of the discussion from 1956 until 1988, including the positions of [1] J.T. MILIK, *Ten Years of Discovery in the Wilderness of Judaea.* London 1959, pp. 61–63, who connects the events with the fortification of Jerusalem by the Hasmonean sons Jonathan and Simon of Mattathias before 146 BCE (cf. 1 Macc. 10:45, FLAVIUS JOSEPHUS, *Jewish Antiquities* XIII.57), [2] F.M. CROSS, *The Ancient Library of Qumran*, pp. 147–152 who explaines the allusion on the basis of 1 Macc. 16:11–22 (cf. FLAVIUS JOSEPHUS, *Jewish Antiquities* XIII.228–235), where the murder of Simon and his sons Matthatias and Judah, in Doq-Jericho around 135/134 BCE is recorded, and [3] C. NEWSOM, The 'Psalms of Joshua', pp. 71–73, who cautiously suggests a fourth century BCE setting, against the background of a destruction of Jericho by Artaxerxes III in 344–343 BCE, mentioned (solely) by the third century (?) CE Latin author Solinus (see M. STERN, *Greek and Latin authors on Jews and Judaism.* II. Jerusalem 1974, pp. 418–420; and further H. ESHEL, H. MISGAV, A Fourth Century BCE. Document from Ketef Yeriḥo, in *IEJ* 28 (1988), pp. 158–176).

[61] Thus C. NEWSOM, 4Q379 (DJD 22), p. 179; F.M. CROSS, *The Ancient Library of Qumran*, p. 148.

[62] H. ESHEL, The Historical Background, p. 415ff.

[63] Thus J.J. COLLINS, 'He Shall Not Judge by What His Eyes See': Messianic Authority in the Dead Sea Scrolls, in *DSD* 2/2 (1995), pp. 145–164, especially

3.5.5 *Additional Joshua Paraphrases? (4Q522, 5Q9, Mas 1039–211)*

Whereas the mentions of Joshua in 4Q378 (frg. 22 i, lines 2–3) and 4Q379 (frg. 22 ii, line 7) and the quotes from and allusions to the Joshua narratives leave no doubt that these texts are related to the book of Joshua, this relation is less evident for three other fragmentary texts, where a relation with Joshua can only be assumed. Among them is a first-century BCE manuscript, containing remnants of Psalm 122 (4Q522).[64] Whereas most of the other 21 fragments are too small to allow for any possible identification, fragment 9 ii offers an interesting parallel to this hymn of ascent to Jerusalem in that it refers in a discursive text to the 'rock of Zion' (line 4: סלע ציון).

Phrases in the following lines 5–11, which speak of the (future?) birth of a son of Jesse (i.e. David), who will expel the Amorites from Jerusalem, in order to build the house for Yhwh, the God of Israel, led Émile Puech in his preliminary 1992 publication of this fragment to the conclusion that the text deals with the building of the temple by David and Solomon (ובנו הקטן], line 6), and the priesthood of David (based on the reconstruction of lines 6–7 [והואה/דויד] יכהן שם ראישון).[65] Yet, scholars such as R. Eisenmann and M. Wise,[66] E. Qimron,[67] H. Eshel,[68] and E. Tov[69] all point to the echoes of the book of Joshua, for instance the setting up of the Tent of Meeting (להשכין שם את אהל מו[עד], line 2; ועתה נ[ש]כינה את א[הל מו]עד, line 12,

p. 150; and idem, *The Scepter and the Star: The Messiahs of the Dead Sea Scrolls and Other Ancient Literature.* New York/London/Toronto/Sydney/Auckland, 1995, pp. 94–95.101.

[64] The official DJD edition has been provided by É. Puech, 4QProphétie de Josué (4QapocrJosué[c]?), in É. Puech (ed.), *Qumrân Grotte 4. XVIII. Textes Hébreux (4Q521–4Q528, 4Q576–4Q579).* (DJD 25) Oxford 1998, pp. 39–74. The Psalm 122 fragments (22–24) had already been published by Puech in 1978, see É. Puech, Fragments du Psaume 122 dans un manuscrit hébreu de la grotte IV, in *RdQ* 9 (1978), pp. 547–554.

[65] É. Puech, La pierre de Sion et l'autel des holocaustes d'après un manuscrit hébreu de la grotte 4 (4Q522), in *RB* 99 (1992), pp. 676–696, especially pp. 683–685 and the 'sommaire', p. 676.

[66] R.H. Eisenmann, M. Wise, *The Dead Sea Scrolls Uncovered. The First Complete Translation and Interpretation of 50 Key Documents Withheld for Over 35 Years.* Shaftesbury, Dorset/Rockport, Massachusetts/Brisbane, Queensland 1992, pp. 89–92; 'Joshua Apocryphon (4Q522)'

[67] E. Qimron, (522ק4) על 'קורות יהושע' מקומראן. ['Concerning Joshua circles from Qumran'] in *Tarbiz* 63 (1995), pp. 503–508.

[68] H. Eshel, A Note on a Recently Published Text: The 'Joshua Apocryphon', in M. Poorthuis, Ch. Safrai (eds.), *The Centrality of Jerusalem. Historical Perspectives.* Kampen 1996, pp. 89–93.

[69] E. Tov, The Rewritten Book of Joshua, pp. 233–256, especially pp. 235–250.

cf. Josh. 18:1 (19:51), and, also, the mentioning of Eleazer and Joshua (line 13: אלעזר̊] וישׁ[ו]ע and line 14: ישׁוׄע]). In first instance, Puech reconstructed this phrase as ישׁוׄע]ת ישׂראל[, *the salvation of Israel*,[70] which resulted in a completely different interpretation and reconstruction of the text. As the remaining fragments repeatedly mention names of places and tribes, which abound in the book of Joshua (especially in fragments 9i–10, further fragments 7, 8, 13), the final 1998 DJD publication of this text by Puech appeared under the title '4QapocrJosué[c]?', which indicates that this text may be seen as a(nother) paraphrase of Joshua, possibly belonging to the same composition as 4QApocryphonJoshua[a-b].

If the general interpretation of 4Q522 is correct, this fragment would, like the prediction about the rebuilder of Jericho (4Q379 22 ii/4QTest), present another prophecy of Joshua in which the future conquest of Zion-Jerusalem by the son of Jesse and the building of the temple are foretold. The reason why Joshua himself is not able to accomplish this is given in lines 9–11: the Amorites had caused Israel to sin, including Joshua, who is to be blamed for not having consulted the judgement (of the Urim?), which may allude to the ruse of the Gibeonites (Josh. 9).[71]

As a result of this new interpretation of 4Q522, the related fragmentary text with toponymes 5Q9,[72] which also seems to contain an allusion to Joshua in fragment 1, line 1: [ ]והיה ישׁוע, is now seen as another exemplar of the Joshua Apocryphon.[73]

Equally uncertain is the interpretation of ten lines with some 138 identifiable letters on the two fragments that make up Masada 1039–211. Their editor, Shemaryahu Talmon, considers them to be fragments of a Joshua Apocryphon dating from the turn of the era.[74]

---

[70] É. Puech, Le pierre de Sion et l'autel, p. 689.

[71] É. Puech, DJD 25, p. 61; E. Tov, The Rewritten Book of Joshua, pp. 244–247.

[72] Edited by J.T. Milik, 5Q9. Ouvrage avec toponymes, in M. Baillet, J.T. Milik, R. de Vaux (éds.), *Les petites grottes de Qumrân.* (DJD 3) Oxford 1962, pp. 179–180. The text consists of nine very small fragments, together containing no more than some 100 identifiable letters. The 'écriture tardive' points to a first century CE date of the manuscript.

[73] E. Tov, The Rewritten Book of Joshua. See also D. Dimant, The Apocryphon of Joshua—4Q522 9ii: A Reappraisal, in S.M. Paul, R.A. Kraft, L.H. Schiffman, W.W. Fields (eds.), *Emanuel. Studies in Hebrew Bible, Septuagint, and Dead Sea Scrolls in Honor of Emanuel Tov.* (SVT 94) Leiden/Boston 2003, pp. 179–204.

[74] S. Talmon, 1039–211; Mas 11; Joshua Apocryphon (MasapocrJosh, final photo 5254), in S. Talmon, *Hebrew fragments from Masada.* (Masada 6) Jerusalem 1999, pp.

Expressions such as [א]שׁר בעבר הׄיׄרׄדׄ[ן], *which is on the other side of the Jordan* (fragment B, line 1), [ואלוהים נ]לחם לעמו באויביהם ולוא [ ], *[And God (?) is fi]ghting for his people against their enemies* (fragment A, line 5), and [וכול אשר] דבר עליהם בא להם ולוא [נפ]ל דבר ארצה, *[everything he had] promised them came to them and not one word fell to the ground* (fragment A, line 7), have their parallels in Joshua (especially Josh. 21:43–45), but little more can be said on the scope of these phrases and their relation to the biblical text.

3.5.6 *Evaluation*

It is obvious from what can be gained from the six texts discussed above (4Q123, 4Q378, 4Q379, 4Q522, 5Q9, Mas1039–211), is that these texts might have offered a valuable contribution to the question of the continuing rewriting of the narratives contained in Joshua, had they been preserved in a less deplorable state. Given the very fragmentary state of these scrolls and the absence of textual overlaps, it is not possible to determine whether they are copies of a single 'Rewritten version of the Book of Joshua', as E. Tov has argued,[75] different paraphrases of Joshua,[76] or fragments of other compositions that happened to contain an allusion to passages in Joshua.

Under the given circumstances, however, all one can say with respect to the process of re-editing the book of Joshua is that these texts attest to at least one rewritten version of Joshua, dating from the first or second century BCE, and that in this period Joshua was portayed as gifted with prophetic powers (4QTest/4Q379 22 ii, 4Q522 9 ii?, cf. the characterisation of Joshua by Sirach 46:1 as Moses' sucessor in prophecy)[77] and that Joshua's curse (6:26) was believed to have come true during the Hasmonean period.[78]

105–116; earlier publication: idem, Fragments of a Joshua Apocryphon. Masada 1039–211, in *JJS* 47 (1996), pp. 128–139. Initially the text was identified by Y. Yadin as an Apocryphon of Samuel.

[75] E. Tov, The Rewritten Book of Joshua, pp. 233–256.

[76] Thus É. Puech, in DJD 25, p. xv, pp. 70–72, with respect to the question whether 4Q522 and 4Q378–4Q379 belong to the same composition.

[77] Hebrew text Ms. B (P.C. Beentjes (ed.), *The Book of Ben Sira in Hebrew. A Text Edition of all Hebrew Manuscripts and A Synopsis of all Parallel Hebrew Ben Sira Texts.* (VTS 68) Leiden/New York/Köln 1997) נבור בן חיל יהושע בן נון משרת משה בנבואה—LXX καὶ *διάδοχος* Μωυσῆ ἐν προφητεὶαις.

[78] See E. Noort, Joshua. The History of Reception and Hermeneutics, in J.C. de Moor, H.F. van Rooy (eds.), *Past, Present, Future. The Deuteronomistic History and the Prophets.* (OTS 44) Leiden/Boston/Köln 2000, pp. 199–215.

From a broader perspective, it is interesting to note that the narratives contained in Joshua like those of other biblical books, were rewritten for new purposes and that by the time these works were composed (from the second century BCE onwards)[79] such reformulations were no longer primarily realized by re-editing the older biblical text—adding passages throughout the book that convey the specific intentions, ideology and theology of the editor(s)—but rather by producing new compositions based on the authoritative texts. It seems, therefore, that these compositions form indirect proof that the process of formation of Joshua had already been completed by the time these reformulations of the Joshua narratives were created. In that sense they also form additional support for the thesis that Joshua had already gained an authoritative or canonical status in the final centuries before the common era.

---

[79] On paleographical grounds the oldest of the texts mentioned is 4Q123, dated by M.D. McLean, *The Use and Development of Palaeo-Hebrew* (not available to me), pp. 63–66, to 'the last half of the second century, but prior to 100 BCE.'

CHAPTER FOUR

THE REDACTION OF THE BOOK OF JOSHUA

4.1 Reconsideration of the Problem

The first chapter of this study ended with the question whether it is possible to regard the oldest extant textual witnesses of Joshua (LXX, 4QJosh[a], 4QJosh[b] and XJoshua) as vestiges of a phase in the history of literary formation of that book preceding the redaction of Joshua as canonised in MT. If anything has become clear from chapters 2 and 3 dealing with the history of research with respect to this redaction-critical value of the Septuagint and the Qumran material, respectively, it is that we are dealing with complex and divergent data and a wide spectrum of interpretations based on these data.

Whereas the search for the oldest attainable form of the original Greek text of LXX-Joshua seems to be drawing to a conclusion with the forthcoming Göttingen edition of LXX-Joshua (section 2.1), the debate with respect to the character of the Greek translation, the freedom and manner in which the translator rendered his Hebrew parent text, the extent and character of the interpretation present in this Greek translation is still far from closed (section 2.2). Unlike the divergencies between MT-Pentateuch and the Samaritan Pentateuch and its Qumran precursors, the quantitative divergencies between LXX and MT do not constitute a clearly recognizable pattern of large-scale additions with a similar intention, but rather a large number of isolated small-scale variants. Are we dealing here with a subtle project of amplification of the older edition as attested by the 'expansionist' MT-version (thus Tov 1986), separate instances of individual younger interpolations (thus Benjamin, Auld), or with stylistic shortenings (thus Dillmann, and to some extent Hollenberg and Bieberstein) and interpretative renderings by the Greek translator (thus Hollenberg, Margolis, Bieberstein, Moatti-Fine, and Den Hertog) of a redundant Hebrew text, consisting of various literary layers, as found in MT?

Although the possibility of reconstructing an editorially different Hebrew version behind LXX-Joshua 20 seems to be commonly acknowledged (Hollenberg, Rofé), other attempts have not been very convincing (Bieberstein, Den Hertog, and Moatti-Fine *pace* Holmes, Auld, Mazor). Even in those cases, however, where a Hebrew text behind the Greek text deviating from MT can be reconstructed with some degree of certainty, the question of relative chronological priority between the two Hebrew versions (MT and Hebrew *Vorlage* of LXX-Joshua) still remains open. Thus, whereas in the case of Joshua 20 the LXX seems to reflect an editorial stratum older than the longer MT-version, the reverse situation appears to be the case with respect to the second conclusion of the land distribution passage in LXX-Josh. 21:42a–d, where according to the current consensus the Greek text (or probably already its Hebrew *Vorlage*) represents a stage in the development of that book subsequent to MT.[1] At least it has become clear that one cannot force all divergencies between MT and LXX into a single one-way genetic model and claim an editorial priority of LXX over MT in all cases; rather, a differentiation within these variants per passage is needed (thus Auld, Rofé, Tov, Mazor). In the light of the open questions posed above, it remains doubtful to postulate the existence of a penultimate stage in the redaction of Joshua solely on the basis of data from LXX.

The Qumran scrolls have not presented a definitive answer to these questions by offering a Hebrew text aligning with LXX-Joshua. For one thing, the fragments of 4QJoshua[a], 4QJoshua[b], and XJoshua are very scanty. More importantly, even if the shorter LXX-version of Josh. 8:1–29 found support in 4QJosh[a], this scroll and the other Joshua scrolls support MT too often to call them 'Septuagintal' (sections 3.2–4). Nevertheless, 4QJoshua[a] has provided clear evidence of editorial activity on the Hebrew level as far as the position of the passage in MT-Josh. 8:30–35 is concerned. The Dead Sea Scrolls discussed in section 3.5 offer some fascinating glimpses of early reception and adaptation of the Joshua narratives, but in all likelihood should be classified as new compositions rather than variant literary editions of the book of Joshua.

Thus, the oldest extant witnesses of Joshua do reflect several striking and puzzling deviations from the standardised version as attested

[1] Thus e.g., J. Hollenberg, *Der Charakter*, pp. 17–18; further E. Tov, The Growth of the Book of Joshua, p. 33; A. Rofé, The End of the Book of Joshua, pp. 34–35: 'Appendix. Joshua 21:42a–d in LXX'; L. Mazor, עיונים, chapter 7.1: 'The Difference Between LXX and MT in the Conclusion of the Section', pp. 249–260.

by MT that are clearly not the result of simple scribal errors but rather point to intentional alterations of the text. It is, however, far from self-evident that (all) these data reflect one or more stages in the history of literary formation *preceding* the edition of the book as preserved in MT. For that reason, the original question of this study, that is *Do the oldest extant witnesses of Joshua reflect a stage in the development of the formation of that book different from and anterior to the version that came to be the canonized Masoretic text of Joshua?* should be modified and replaced by more differentiated questions such as:

* How should variant readings from the Greek version be evaluated?
* What are valid criteria to distinguish the variants created at the literary stages of the book from the variants resulting from the processes of translating and transmitting the book?
* How to ascertain that individual variants are in fact part of a comprehensive re-edition (Holmes, Tov) instead of separate instances of *glossation* (Benjamin, Auld)?
* How to establish the chronological priority between the reconstructed variant versions of a given passage within the book?
* Do the textual alterations fit into the profile of a recognizable and distinguishable redaction of Joshua?
* How do the alleged Deuteronomistic (Tov), nomistic (Rofé, Mazor) and Priestly (Auld) additions and alterations correlate with the Deuteronomistic (DtrH), nomistic (DtrN) and Priestly (RedP) strata of the book?
* Where in the history of the literary formation of the book is the editorial activity attested by the versions to be placed?
* What is the proper relation between textual criticism and literary criticism? Is textual criticism only a stepping stone for the 'higher literary criticism'? Should literary criticism be (entirely or primarily) based on textual data? Or do both approaches maintain their own value?

In the light of these questions, the approach followed by A. Rofé with respect to Joshua 20 and advocated by A. van der Kooij for the Hebrew Bible in general,[2] seems to me the most prudent and

[2] A. van der Kooij, Zum Verhältnis von Textkritik und Literarkritik. See further the discussion in section 1.2 above.

promising. For this reason I propose in the first instance to disconnect the two areas disciplines concerning the textual history of Joshua, that is textual criticism and literary criticism, and compare the results of these approaches only after text-critical and literary-critical investigations of the same passage have been carried out in their own right. If textual data pointed to subsequent redactions of a particular passage in Joshua (e.g. Josh. 1, in which Tov detects a high number of Deuteronomistic pluses, or Josh. 8:1–29, where both 4QJosh[a] and LXX seem to be considerably shorter than MT), it would only be natural that a literary-critical analysis in its own right of the passage involved would result in the same conclusions as those derived from an interpretation of the textual data. In this way it may be surmised that an independent literary-critical analysis not only helps to shed more light on the assumed editorial activity behind the textual data, by placing these phenomena in the wider context of the literary development of the book, but also helps to establish the relative chronology between the variant literary editions of a given passage from the book of Joshua.

Interestingly, in spite of the repeated claim made by Ulrich, Mazor, and others that the borders between textual and literary criticism should be razed, a comprehensive discussion between the two areas of research into the history of the text of Joshua is still in an initial stage. Although in those studies arguing in favour of the originality of LXX-Joshua we find extensive discussions of the scope and limits of the freedom of the Greek translator towards his parent text (e.g., Tov and Mazor), the questions posed above have received little attention so far. Rather, we find a selective use of some generally accepted notions concerning the history of the formation of Joshua prior to the alleged editions attested by the textual witnesses, such as 'Deuteronomistic redactions' (thus e.g. Tov, Mazor). Studies that do approach the problem of redactional variants presented by the textual witnesses along the two lines of independent literary-critical and text-critical evaluations, are relatively modest (thus e.g. Rofé with respect to Joshua 20 and Bieberstein). It is to be hoped that the discussion between the two disciplines can be established without subordinating one approach to the other.

4.2 The Redaction History of the Book of Joshua

For these reasons, it may be helpful to turn to some generally accepted theories concerning the redaction history of Joshua in order to get a clearer picture of how to discern various literary strata in the book, and how to fit the distinct editorial layers attested by the textual witnesses into the broader picture of the formation and redaction processes behind the book of Joshua and thus establish the relative chronological priority between these redactions as represented by LXX, MT and the Qumran scrolls.

This is not to say that the matter of the overall literary history of Joshua is less complex or less disputed than the evaluation of the variant readings of the ancient witnesses of the book. On the contrary, there is a wide variety of opinions and models attempting to reconstruct the prehistory and protohistory of Joshua. This is not the place to discuss all these theories, all the more since excellent surveys of the history of this type of research already exist,[3] let alone to develop independently my own model for the complete history of the oral and literary processes of formation and development of Joshua. For our purpose only those stages in the literary development of the book are relevant that are more or less commonly accepted in critical scholarship as revealing a comprehensive and distinguishable modification of an older complete composition, and only in as far as they would offer possible points of contact with the editorial variants reflected by LXX, MT, and 4QJosh[a]. Interesting and challenging as the quest for oral, historical and literary origins of the material contained in the book may be,[4] these stages in the development of Joshua fall outside the scope of our investigation. For the

[3] The most recent and comprehensive survey of the history of research on the book of Joshua (with respect to both diachronic, synchronic, textual, theological and archeological problems) is offered by E. Noort, *Das Buch Josua*, with full bibliographic references. See further e.g. R. Smend, *Die Entstehung des Alten Testaments*. Stuttgart 1989[4], pp. 110–125; A.H.W. Curtis, *Joshua* (Old Testament Guides) Sheffield 1994; V. Fritz, *Das Buch Josua* (HAT I/7) Tübingen 1994; and K. Bieberstein, *Josua-Jordan-Jericho*, pp. 35–54: chapter II.2: 'Zur Literargeschichte der Landnahmeerzählungen'.

[4] See e.g. the survey in K. Bieberstein, *Josua-Jordan-Jericho*, pp. 54–71: 'Zur Überlieferungsgeschichte der Landnahmeerzählungen.' Bieberstein himself offers a well-balanced and challenging reconstruction of the literary history of Josh. 1–6, and traces the literary origins of the larger pre-Deuteronomistic complex, to which the original narratives of crossing of the Jordan and conquest of Jericho belong, to the Assyrian period, in which theological reflection on the possession of the land became

present study it may suffice to take as point of departure those major stages in the literary history of the book which are generally recognized in critical scholarship. Modern historical-critical research discerns basically the following three stages in the process of literary formation of the book of Joshua:

[0] a pre-Deuteronomistic layer,
[1] the basic Deuteronomistic narrative (part of Noth's Deuteronomistic History [DtrH]),[5]
[2] a nomistic-Deuteronomistic redaction ([DtrN] based on the theory of R. Smend Jr.),[6] and
[3] a Priestly redactional layer (RedP).[7]

---

acute. In this way the origin of the Joshua narratives no longer need to be sought in [1] historical events during the Late Bronze Age-Early Iron Age as has been the traditional view (still upheld by scholars of a more orthodox signature, see e.g. Y. Kaufman, *The Biblical Account of the Conquest of Palestina.* Palestina 1953; M. Woudstra, *The Book of Joshua.* (New International Commentary on the Old Testament). Grand Rapids 1981; and R.S. Hess, *Joshua* (TOTC 6) Leicester/Downers Grove 1996); nor in [2] aetiological sagas (such as for instance A. Alt, Josua, in P. Volz, F. Stummer, J. Hempel (Hg.), *Werden und Wesen des Alten Testaments.* (BZAW 66) Berlin 1936, pp. 13–29, reprinted in his *Kleine Schriften* I. München 1953, pp. 176–192, and M. Noth, *Das Buch Josua*); nor in [3] an alleged cultic festival at Gilgal (thus e.g. H.J. Kraus, Gilgal. Ein Beitrag zur Kultusgeschichte Israels, in *VT* 1 (1951), pp. 181–199; and E. Otto, *Das Mazzotfest in Gilgal*); or [4] simply be dated *in toto* to the Hasmonean period (thus J. Strange, The Book of Joshua: A Hasmonean Manifesto? in A. Lemaire, B. Otzen (eds.), *History and Traditions of Early Israel. Studies Presented to Eduard Nielsen.* (SVT 50) Leiden/New York/Köln 1993; idem, The Book of Joshua-Origin and Dating, in *SJOT* 16/1 (2002), pp. 44–51.)

Similar recent attempts to place the literary origin of (parts of) the Joshua narratives in the Assyrian period have been made by e.g. L. Perlitt, *Bundestheologie im Alten Testament.* (WMANT 36) Neukirchen 1969 with respect to Joshua 24 and the origins of the Deuteronomic covenant theology; and more recently by N. Na'aman, The 'Conquest of Canaan' in the Book of Joshua and in History, in I. Finkelstein, N. Na'aman (eds.), *From Nomadism to Monarchy. Archaeological and Historical Aspects of Early Israel.* Jerusalem/Washington 1994, pp. 218–281, who adduces some strong historical and archeological arguments for dating the basic composition after Sennacherib's conquest of Palestine.

[5] M. Noth, *Überlieferungsgeschichtliche Studien.* Halle 1943[1], Tübingen 1957[2].

[6] R. Smend (jr.), Das Gesetz und die Völker. Ein Beitrag zur deuteronomistischen Redaktionsgeschichte, in H.W. Wolff (ed.), *Probleme biblischer Theologie. Gerhard von Rad zum 70. Geburtstag.* München 1971, pp. 494–509; and idem, *Die Entstehung des Alten Testaments.*

[7] For the 'canonisation' of these literary strata and the theories of their 'geistige Väter', Noth and Smend, see the introductions to Joshua in recent commentaries on the book and recent general introductions to the Old Testament, e.g. O. Kaiser, *Einleitung in das Alte Testament.* Gütersloh 1984[5]; idem, *Grundriß der Einleitung in die kanonischen und deuterokanonischen Schriften des Alten Testaments. Band 1. Die erzählenden*

Issues such as the question whether to what extent pre-Deuteronomistic literary strata, implied by the reference in Josh. 10:13 (MT) to a book of Jashar,[8] can be reconstructed as well as the question whether or not these pre-DtrH Joshua texts form a continuation of ('Jahwistic' and/or 'Elohistic') material from the Pentateuch,[9] fall beyond the limited scope of this presentation of the main stages in the redaction process of Joshua. Alternative redactional strata will be discussed briefly.

4.2.1 *The Deuteronomistic Framework of the Book of Joshua (DtrH)*

Already at an early stage of critical research the many literary affiliations between Joshua and Deuteronomy were noted.[10] Not only does the opening of Joshua form a direct continuation of the narrative Deuteronomistic frame around the Deuteronomic laws in Deut. 1–3, 31–34, throughout the book of Joshua quotations and expressions, phrases and concepts occur that are characteristic of the rhetorical

Werke. Gütersloh 1992, pp. 88–89, 100, 103ff.; R. RENDTORFF, *Das Alte Testament. Eine Einführung*. Neukirchen 1983; and H.-J. ZOBEL, Josua/Josuabuch, in *TRE* 17/1–2. Berlin 1985, pp. 269–278. See also A.D.H. MAYES, *The Story of Israel between Settlement and Exile. A Redactional Study of the Deuteronomistic Hypothesis*. London 1983; M.A. O'BRIEN, *The Deuteronomistic History Hypothesis: A Reassessment* (OBO 92) Freiburg/ Göttingen 1989; E. CORTESE, Theories Concerning Dtr; A Possible Rapprochement, in C. BREKELMANS, J. LUST (eds.), *Pentateuchal and Deuteronomistic Studies. Papers Read at the XIIIth IOSOT Congress. Leuven 1989*. (BETL 94) Leuven 1990, pp. 179–190; and K. BIEBERSTEIN, *Josua-Jordan-Jericho*, p. 48ff. A recent synthesis of these theories has been offered by V. FRITZ, *Das Buch Josua*, pp. 2–9: 'Die literarische Vorgeschichte des Josuabuches', where basically these three literary layers are recognized, [1] a *Grundschicht* (DtrH), [2] a *deuteronomistische Redaktion* (RedD//DtrN), and [3] a *nachpriesterschriftliche Redaktion* (RedP).

[8] A very cautious and even sceptical view concerning the possibility to go beyond the first Deuteronomistic layer of Joshua is expressed by V. FRITZ, *Das Buch Josua*, p. 4ff., where he allows for a pre-DtrH origin of only Josh. 2:1–3.4b.5–7.15–17a.18–19.21–23, 8:10–12.14–15.19.21.23.29, 10:16–23a.24–27, and the lists of tribal territories only.

[9] The assumption that the literary layers recovered in the Pentateuch (J, E, D and P) all find their conclusion in the account of the gift to Israel of the Promised Land forms the basic premise of the classical source criticism of the Hexateuch, as developed by for instance A. Kuenen, J. Wellhausen, and G. von Rad. See further below.

[10] See the surveys of the critical research on the book from the late 16th (Calvin and Masius) until the late 19th century in J. HOLLENBERG, Die deuteronomischen Bestandtheile des Buches Josua, in *Theologische Studien und Kritiken* 47/1 (1874), pp. 462–506, especially pp. 462–467; and E. NOORT, *Das Buch Josua*, pp. 59ff.

style and distinctive ideology of Deuteronomy and are largely absent from the preceding books Genesis—Numbers.[11]

Thus the opening chapter of Joshua not only takes up the narrative line from Deuteronomy 34 (Josh. 1:1 refers to the death of Moses, Deut. 34:5), but also continues with a quotation of Moses' address to the people (Deut. 11:24–25), now spoken by Yhwh to Joshua (Josh. 1:3–5), a divine confirmation of Joshua's 'installation' (Josh. 1:5–6.9) parallel to that in Deut. 3:21–22, 31:7–8) and a renewal of the Trans-Jordanian tribes' pledge of loyalty (Josh. 1:13–15—Deut. 3:18–20). This Deuteronomistic ouverture presents the leading themes of the whole composition,[12] which are [1] a successful conquest (ירשׁ)[13] of all of Cisjordanian Palestine (1:3.5a) [2] by a unified Israel including the Trans-Jordanian tribes (1:12–15) [3] under the sole and unchallenged leadership of Joshua as [4] the ideal and divinely appointed successor of Moses (1:2.5b, 16–18), and [5] the subsequent distribution (נחל)[14] of the land, as [6] a gift (נתן) and

---

[11] See e.g., the detailed surveys in J.W. Colenso, *The Pentateuch and Book of Joshua Critically Examined. Part V.* London 1865, pp. 3–11: 'Chapter 1. The Deuteronomistic Portions of the Book of Joshua'; J. Hollenberg, Die deuteronomischen Bestandtheile; A. Kuenen, *Historisch-critisch onderzoek naar het ontstaan en de verzameling van de Boeken des Ouden Verbonds. Tweede, geheel omgewerkte uitgave. Eerste deel. De Thora en de historische Boeken des Ouden Verbonds.* Leiden 1887, pp. 128–135; C. Steuernagel, *Übersetzung und Erklärung der Bücher Deuteronomium und Josua.* Gottingen 1900, pp. 135–140; and M. Weinfeld, *Deuteronomy and the Deuteronomic School.* Oxford 1972, especially pp. 320ff:. Appendix A: 'Deuteronomistic Phraseology'.

[12] T.C. Butler, *Joshua*, pp. xxvff., summarizes the recurring (Deuteronomistic) themes under the headings 'land, leadership, law, and Lord'; R.D. Nelson, *Joshua*, pp. 15–20, discerns five themes: land, conquest, the enemy, the ban, and obedience. See further V. Fritz, *Das Buch Josua*, pp. 14–17 'Komposition und Intention des Josuabuches'; and G.J. Wenham, The Deuteronomic Theology of the Book of Joshua, in *JBL* 90 (1971), pp. 140–148, who investigates the terminological and conceptual affinities between Deuteronomy and Joshua according to five theological *Leitmotifs*: holy war, the land and its distribution, the unity of all Israel, the role of Joshua, and the covenant and the Law of Moses.

[13] The root occurs five times in Josh. 1 (1:11.11.15.15.15) and 25 times in the remaining chapters of the book. A third of the remaining 218 occurrences throughout the Hebrew Bible are to be found in Deuteronomy (78x). On the distribution of the root and its predominance in Deuteronomy and Deuteronomistic literature, see the statistics in H.H. Schmid, ירשׁ *jrš* beerben, in *ThHAT* I, col. 778–781; N. Lohfink, יָרַשׁ *jāraš* יְרֵשָׁה *j^erešāh*, יְרֻשָּׁה *j^eruššāh*, מוֹרָשׁ *môrāš*, מוֹרָשָׁה *môrašāh*, in *ThWAT* III, col. 953–985; and M. Weinfeld, *Deuteronomy and the Deuteronomic School*, Oxford 1972, p. 341ff.

[14] Of these 281 times the root נחל occurs in the Hebrew Bible, there are 60 occurences are in the book of Joshua and 33 in the book of Deuteronomy; see further G. Wanke, נַחֲלָה *naḥ^alā* Besitzanteil, in *ThHAT* II, col. 55–59.

[7] fulfilment by Yhwh of his promise to the patriarchs (in the formula 1:6 הארץ אשר־נשבעתי יהוה לאבותם לתת להם).[15]

Corresponding to this Deuteronomistic opening chapter, we find a short passage near the end of the book that can be viewed as the central *kerygma* and 'theological climax'[16] of the Deuteronomistic layer of the book of Joshua, a passage in which the narrator clearly states that all Yhwh's promises have been fulfilled (21:43–45),[17] i.e. that all the land promised by Yhwh to the fathers has been given by him to Israel (21:43//Josh. 1:3–6), and that Yhwh has granted rest to Israel now that all its enemies are subdued:

---

[15] The combination of אדמה/ארץ followed by a clause with the verb שבע Niph'al with Yhwh as subject and the אבות as indirect object occurs—according to my count—32 times in the Hebrew Bible, half of them in the book of Deuteronomy, three times in Joshua (1:6; 5:6 and 21:43), twice in Gen. (26:3 and 50:24), four times in Exod. (13:5.11, 32:13, 33:1), four times in Num. (11:12, 14:16.23, 32:11), once in Judg. (2:1) and twice in Jer. (11:5, 32:22).

[16] Thus T.C. Butler, *Joshua*, p. 235.

[17] The Deuteronomistic character of the passage is universally recognised, see already J. Hollenberg, Die deuteronomische Bestandtheile, p. 504; A. Kuenen, *Historisch-critisch onderzoek*, p. 129, p. 134; C. Steuernagel, *Deuteronomium und Josua*, p. 235; M. Noth, *Das Buch Josua*, first 1938 edition, pp. xiii, 101ff.; and S. Mowinckel, *Tetrateuch-Pentateuch-Hexateuch. Die Berichte über die Landnahme in den drei israelitischen Geschichtswerken*. (BZAW 90) Berlin 1964, p. 49.

Nevertheless, an external problem is posed by the fact that the chapters to which this passage forms a conclusion (20, 21:1–42) are ascribed to a younger Priestly redaction, and that a corresponding closure of the land distribution chapters is found in 19:49–51. Hence M. Noth, *Überlieferungsgeschichtliche Studien*, pp. 45–46 (followed by V. Fritz, *Das Buch Josua*, p. 217), considered the passage Josh. 21:43–45 to be a product of late redactor who wished to integrate the secondary chapters 20 and 21 into the whole composition. In the second edition, however, of his commentary on *Das Buch Josua* (HAT 1/7) 1953^2, p. 9, Noth returned to his 1938 view in which he included this passage, together with Josh. 1, 22:1–6 and 23, in the Deuteronomistic framework of the book.

To my mind, this problem rests on the dating and interpretation of Josh. 20, 21:1–42 rather than literary-critical observations regarding style and intentions of the passage Josh. 21:43–45 itself, which perfectly fits the DtrH-layer of the book. When one adopts R. Smend's thesis (see section 4.2.2 below) that Joshua 23 presents a modification of Josh. 21:43–45, the latter passage must belong to an older literary stratum than that of Joshua 23. See also M.A. O'Brien, *The Deuteronomistic History Hypothesis*, p. 74. J.C. de Vos, *Das Los Judas. Über Entstehung und Ziele der Landbeschreibung in Josua 15*. (SVT 95) Leiden/Boston 2003, pp. 214–217, argues that the absence of some main DtrH themes, i.e. the distribution of the land (נחל) and the leading role of Joshua are not mentioned in this passage pleads against the attribution of Josh. 21:43–45 to DtrH. Yet, De Vos does not demonstrate the ideological and formularic contrasts between this passage and other DtrH-passages, but only the variation in wording.

Josh. 1^{5} לא־יתיצב איש לפניך
10^{8} לא־יעמד איש מהם בפניך
21^{44} ולא־עמד איש בפניהם מכל־איביהם

Likewise, the subsequent narrative of the dismissal of the Trans-Jordanian tribes, corresponds closely to their pledge of loyalty in 1:12–18, bound together—*inter alia*—by the theme of 'rest' (נוח Hiphʿil I):[18]

Deut. 3^{20} עד אשר־יניח יהוה לאחיכם ככם
וירשו גם־הם את־הארץ אשר־יהוה אלהיכם נתן להם
Josh. 1^{13} יהוה אלהיכם מניח לכם ונתן לכם את־הארץ הזאת
1^{15} עד אשר־יניח יהוה לאחיכם ככם
וירשו גם־המה את־הארץ אשר־יהוה אלהיכם נתן להם
21^{44} וינח יהוה להם מסביב ככל אשר־נשבע לאבותם
22^{4} ועתה הניח יהוה אלהיכם לאחיכם כאשר דבר להם

The Deuteronomistic themes and expressions are not restricted to this framework of the book, but recur—though in varying degree—in the intermediate chapters that describe the conquest and division of the land leading up to the complete fulfilment of Yhwh's promises.[19] These themes apply, among other things, to the reaction of the Canaanite peoples (Josh. 2:10–11//Deut. 3:6, 4:39; Josh. 9), the ban on the indigenous Canaanite population (Josh. 9, 10:28–43, 11, cf. Deut. 20),[20] and the violation of the war law in Deut. 20:10–18 by Achan in Josh. 7, the execution of the Canaanite kings in Josh 8:29 according to Deut. 21:22–23, the presentation of Caleb's request and land grant in Josh 14:6–15 (corresponding with Deut. 1:19–46 *vis-à-vis*

---

[18] See also the significant places Deut. 12:9–10 (connected with the cult centralisation law), Deut. 25:19, 2 Sam. 7:1.11 (Nathan's oracle) and 1 Kgs. 8:56 (Solomon's temple dedication prayer). See further the discusison of the theme in DtrH and Chronicles, in G. von Rad, Es ist noch eine Ruhe vorhanden dem Volke Gottes. Eine biblische Begriffsuntersuchung, *Zwischen den Zeiten* 11 (1933), pp. 104–11, reprinted in idem, *Gesammelte Studien zum Alten Testament.* (TB 8) München 1971[2], pp. 101–108; M. Weinfeld, *Deuteronomy and the Deuteronomic School*, p. 343; and H.-D. Preuß, נוּחַ *nûaḥ* מְנוּחָה *mᵉnûḥāh*, in *ThWAT* V, col. 297–307.

[19] See the discussion of the Deuteronomistic presentation of 'Die Landnahme im Westjordanland', in M. Noth, *Überlieferungsgeschichtliche Studien* I, pp. 40–47; and A.D.H. Mayes, *The Story of Israel between Settlement and Exile*, pp. 40–57: 'The Deuteronomistic Editing of Joshua', and further the older detailed investigations by J. Hollenberg, Die deuteronomische Bestandtheile; and A. Kuenen, *Historisch-critisch onderzoek*[2], pp. 129–135.

[20] Out of the 70 times the root חרם (nominal and verbal forms, i.e. Hiphʿil and Hophʿal) occurs, 27 instances are to be found in Joshua, and some 10 times in Deuteronomy, see further N. Lohfink, חָרַם *ḥāram* חֵרֶם *ḥeræm*, in *ThWAT* III, col. 192–213.

the competing Caleb narrative in Josh. 15:13–19//Judg. 1:11–15.20), and to the special status of the tribe of Levi as carriers of the ark (Josh. 3–4).

The classic explanation for these literary affinities was formulated in 1943 by Martin Noth in his model of a Deuteronomistic History (DtrH), ranging from Deuteronomy to 2 Kings, in which an author in the Exilic period (circa 560 BCE) sought to explain the fall of Jerusalem by presenting Israel's history so far as a coherent account of Israel's loyalty and disloyalty to Yhwh. The composition thus served as a theodicy for the punishment inflicted by Yhwh, interpretated and evaluated on the basis of the Deuteronomistic Code and ideology. To this end the Deuteronomistic author (not redactor) created a continuous historical narrative, based on various older literary documents and traditions, and interspersed this compilation with speeches held by the leading figures Moses (Deuteronomy), Joshua (Josh. 23), Samuel (1 Sam. 12), Solomon (1 Kgs. 8), or by the Deuteronomistic narrator himself—in the absence of a suitable spokesman for the given period—as in 2 Kgs. 17:7–23.[21] In the second, revised edition of his epoch-making commentary on Joshua,[22] Noth reconstructed basically three stages in the literary history of the book, i.e. a pre-Deuteronomistic, a Deuteronomistic and a post-Deuteronomistic stage. The sources from which the Exilic Deuteronomistic author drew originally consisted of independent material: [1] a compilation of of aetiological legends (Josh. 2–11) tied together by short narrative links between the separate stories (Josh. 5:1, 6:27, 9:3.4a, 10:2.5.40–42, 11:1–2, 16–20) written by a compiler ('*Sammler*') from the sanctuary of Gilgal, [2] a pre-monarchical document in which the boundaries of the Israelite tribes were fixed and laid down (Josh. 13–19) and subsequently expanded by a document containing the names of the Judaean districts during the reign of king Josiah (Josh. 15:20–62), and [3] an independent account of the establishment of an Israelite amphictyony under the charismatic leadership of an originally local Ephraimite leader Joshua (Josh. 24:1–28).[23]

---

[21] M. NOTH, *Überlieferungsgeschichtliche Studien*, pp. 3ff.: 'Merkmale der planvollen Geschlossenheit'.

[22] M. NOTH, *Das Buch Josua*[2]. On the importance of M. Noth for the study of Joshua, see E. NOORT, *Das Buch Josua*, pp. 92ff., who divides the history of research in a pre-Noth and post-Noth period.

[23] Thus M. NOTH, *Das System der zwölf Stämme Israels*. (BWANT 6) Stuttgart 1930; see further the various studies by A. ALT collected in his *Kleine Schriften zur Geschichte*

As a result, the Joshua narratives were no longer to be seen as the 'Hexateuchal' narrative conclusion to the themes from the Pentateuch and their literary formulations in the successive self-contained Pentateuchal sources or documents[24] underlying these books (Genesis-Deuteronomy), as was the dominant view held by scholars adhering to the now classical 'Newer Documentary hypothesis'.[25] Literary affinities with the non-Deuteronomistic parts of the Pentateuch (either J, E, or P) for that reason had to be denied almost beforehand, and were considered by Noth to be post-Deuteronomistic additions.[26] Apart from the problem of the relation between the Joshua narratives and the themes of the Tetrateuch (Genesis-Numbers), a special problem in Noth's original draft of his DtrH-account of the Joshua

des Volkes Israel. München 1953–1959; and E. NOORT, *Das Buch Josua*, pp. 92ff.: 'Der Wendepunkt: Alt und Noth.'

[24] These are: [1] a Jahwistic account, traditionally taken to consist of a very modest account of the conquest, as preserved in Judges 1 and its parallels in the short notices of Palestinian areas not conquered by Israel, Josh. 15:63, 16:10, 17:12–13, 19:47, [2] an Elohistic account, primarily thought to consist of Joshua 24 and to originate from North-Israel, and [3] Priestly narrative, preserved mainly in the second half of the book.

[25] See E. NOORT, *Das Buch Josua*, pp. 59–91. On the so-called 'neuere Urkundenhypothese', see H.-J. KRAUS, *Geschichte der historisch-kritischen Erforschung des Alten Testaments*. Neukirchen 1988[4], pp. 242–274. The main studies with respect to Joshua from the last quarter of the nineteenth century and the first quarter of the twentieth century are: J.W. COLENSO, *The Pentateuch and Book of Joshua Critically Examined. Part VI*. London 1872, pp. 1–11; J. HOLLENBERG, Die deuteronomischen Bestandtheile des Buches Josua, who gave a detailed investigation of the Deuteronomistic elements present in the book of Joshua and argued that they must be seen as the continuation of the Deuteronomistic frame (Deut. 1–4, 29–30) around the Deuteronomic core (Deut. 5–28); A. KUENEN, *Historisch-critisch onderzoek*, pp. 5–331; J. WELLHAUSEN, *Die Composition des Hexateuchs und der historischen Bücher des Alten Testaments*. Berlin 1876–1877[1]; A. DILLMANN, *Die Bücher Numeri, Deuteronomium und Josua*; E. ALBERS, *Die Quellenberichte in Josua I–XII. Beitrag zur Quellenkritik des Hexateuchs*. Bonn 1891; C. STEUERNAGEL, *Deuteronomium und Josua*. Although after the publication of Noth's *Überlieferungsgeschichtliche Studien* most critical scholars dismissed the classical Newer Documentary hypothesis, several scholars still adhered to it, see e.g., G. VON RAD, *Das formgeschichtliche Problem des Hexateuch*. (BWANT 4/26) Stuttgart 1938, reprinted in G. VON RAD, *Gesammelte Studien zum Alten Testament*, pp. 9–86; and idem, *Theologie des Alten Testaments. Band I. Die Theologie der geschichtlichen Überlieferungen Israels*. München 1959, pp. 309–317; and especially S. MOWINCKEL, *Tetrateuch-Pentateuch-Hexateuch*.

[26] The discussion centered especially on the original conclusion of the Priestly document (Priesterschrift understood as literary independent composition), which the older four-sources hypothesis looked for in Joshua 13–21, but which, according to Noth, had no interest in the theme of land distribution at all, see M. NOTH, *Überlieferungsgeschichtliche Studien*, pp. 180–217: 'Anhang. Die 'Priesterschrift' und die Redaktion des Pentateuch'.

narratives was posed by Joshua 23. This chapter duplicates both the introduction to the passsage dealing with the distribution of the land (Josh. 13–19)—by repeating 13:1 in 23:1—and the chapter which in the present context appears to be Joshua's second valedictory address with a similar theme and audience (Josh. 24):

Josh. 13^{1} ויהושע זקן בא בימים
ויאמר יהוה אליו אתה זקנתה באת בימים...
23^{1} ויהושע זקן בא בימים
ויקרא יהושע לכל־ישראל לזקניו ולראשיו ולשפטיו ולשטריו
ויאמר אלהם אני זקנתי באתי בימים...
24^{1} ויאסף יהושע את־כל־שבטי ישראל שכמה
ויקרא לזקני ישראל ולראשיו ולשפטיו ולשטריו...

The literary connections and duplications point to literary dependence. Since in Noth's DtrH model Joshua 23 formed one of the main unifying Deuteronomistic contibutions, Noth was forced to consider both the whole of Josh. 13–19 and Josh. 24 as later insertions in DtrH of pre-Deuteronomistic compositions.[27] Thus, in order to maintain the unity of the DtrH-composition, Noth had to postulate two successive stages in the DtrH-presentation of the Joshua-narratives, in which the older material was incorporated into the main DtrH-composition.[28]

4.2.2 *A Nomistic Deuteronomistic Redaction (DtrN)*

The problem was solved in a more convincing way by Rudolf Smend (junior).[29] Central to his thesis is that the Deuteronomistic theme of complete conquest, as articulated so clearly in Josh. 21:43–45, is balanced by a contrasting theme of partial or negative conquest, as formulated in Joshua 23. In his view, this chapter forms a later Deuteronomistic addition to the first Deuteronomistic layer comprising Joshua 13–21 and Joshua 24. In this younger chapter Joshua

[27] M. Noth, *Überlieferungsgeschichtliche Studien*, p. 9, n. 1; and idem, *Das Buch Josua*^{2}, p. 10: 'Wir haben also mit einem planvoll angelegten deuteronomistischen Josuabuche zu rechnen, dem dann noch in einer sekundären deuteronomistischen Bearbeitung ein großer (13_{1}–21_{42}) und ein kleinerer (24_{1-33}) Abschnitt hinzugefügt worden ist.'

[28] M. Noth, *Das Buch Josua*, p. 10.

[29] R. Smend jr., Das Gesetz und die Völker. This thesis was further developed in R. Smend jr., *Die Entstehung des Alten Testaments*; and idem, Das uneroberte Land, in G. Strecker (Hg.), *Das Land Israel in biblischer Zeit. Jerusalem-Symposium 1981 der Hebräischen Universität und der Georg-August-Universität*. Göttingen 1983, pp. 91–102.

23 the theological summary of Josh. 21:43–45 (*none of Israels enemies has remained*) is modified with the temporal restriction 'until the present day' that is: 'so far, as yet':[30] history is not yet finished with Israel's peaceful dwelling in the Promised Land, but by means of *resumptive repetition* ('Wiederaufnahme') the author of Joshua 23 (DtrN) introduces the possibility of a pessimistic, dark sequel:

Deut.	7^{24}	לא־יתיצב איש בפניך
	11^{25}	לא־יתיצב איש בפניכם
Josh-DtrH	1^{5}	לא־יתיצב איש לפניך
	10^{8}	לא־יעמד איש מהם בפניך
	21^{44}	ולא־עמר איש בפניהם מכל־איביהם
Josh-DtrN	23^{9}	לא־עמד איש בפניהם עד היום הזה

True, according to this author-redactor, Israel may have conquered the Promised Land and a number of these peoples may have been dealt with by Yhwh (23:3), but apparently a remnant of them have remained (v. 12 יתר הגוים האלה הנשארים האלה אִתְּכֶם), posing a serious threat and test to Israel's lasting faithfulness. Here the theme of Joshua 24, on which this chapter 23 is modelled,[31] has been modified from an appeal to choose Yhwh as Israel's God into an appeal not to interfere with the remaining non-Israelite peoples (23:7.12), not to intermarry (23:12 והתחתנתם בהם ובתם בהם והם בכם),[32] and not to worship their gods (23:7). This redactor furthermore laid great stress on the theme of the faithful observance of the *torah* of Moses (23:6 וחזקתם מאד לשמר ולעשות את כל־הכתוב בספר תורת משה).[33] In other words: a condition for lasting peace is made dependent upon strict

[30] R. Smend, Das Gesetz und die Völker, p. 502; R. Smend, Das uneroberte Land, p. 218. See further A.D.H. Mayes, *The Story of Israel*, pp. 48ff.; and E. Noort. Land in zicht...? Geloofsvisie, werkelijkheid en geschiedenis in het oudtestamentische spreken over het land. Enkele opmerkingen naar aanleiding van Jozua 21:43–45, in *Tussen openbaring en ervaring. Studies aangeboden aan prof.dr. G.P. Hartvelt.* Kampen 1986, pp. 94–113.

[31] R. Smend, Das Gesetz und die Völker, pp. 503–504.

[32] Cf. Deut. 7:1–3 where the same topic is discussed and condemned (ולא תתחתן בם). The same verb occurs in the same negative context in Ezra 9:14.

[33] The translation of תורה by 'law' may be somewhat legalistic and hence misleading. The alternative translation 'instruction' has too many wisdom overtones for the specific use made of the term in Deuteronomistic writing, where תורה denotes a specific body of divine instructions mediated to the people by Moses and fixed in a particular book, i.e. the book of Deuteronomy (and not yet the Pentateuch, which may be suggested by a transliteration of the Hebrew word, which is a post-Deuteronomistic development, see e.g., G. Liedke, C. Petersen, תּוֹרָה *tōrāh* Weisung, in *ThHAT* II, col. 1032–1043, especially col. 1040ff.; and F. García López, תּוֹרָה *tôrāh* in *ThWAT* VIII, col. 597–637, especially col. 634ff.

observance of the law, with the prospect that the ideal situation sketched in 21:45 can easily be reverted into a very negative future (23:13, and after a second reference to Joshua's imminent death in 23:14–16):

DtrH 21[45]	לא־נפל דבר מכל הדבר הטוב
	אשר־דבר יהוה אל־בית ישראל הכל בא
DtrN 23[14]	כי לא־נפל דבר אחד מכל הדברים הטובים
	אשר דבר יהוה אלהיכם עליכם הכל באו לכם
	לא־נפל ממנו דבר אחד
23[15]	והיה כאשר־בא עליכם כל־הדבר הטוב
	אשר דבר יהוה אלהיכם אליכם
	כן יביא יהוה עליכם את כל־הדבר הרע
	עד־השמידו אותכם מעל האדמה הטובה הזאת

Thus, according to Smend, Joshua 23 forms a later addition to the book. The chapter is modelled on Josh. 13:1, 21:43–45, and 24, but modifies the general scope of this older Deuteronomistic literary stratum into a conditional theology that introduces the alternative: 'Gesetz' or 'Völker': the *torah* of Moses as opposed to the threat posed by the remaining non-Israelite inhabitants. This conditional and more negative prospect has been prepared in two other passages at decisive places in the book, i.e. at the beginning of the conquest narratives (Josh. 1:7–8.9) and at the start of the land distribution chapters (13:1b–6).

Between the close of the conquest narratives (Josh. 11:23, 12) and the chapters about the land division (Josh. 13:8ff.), we find a short passage in which the original introduction to this second part of the book, with the original reference to Joshua's advanced age (Josh. 13:1) and its logical sequence (Josh. 13:7), corresponds closely in content and structure to the introduction to the first half of the book (Josh. 1:1–2: Moses is dead, Yhwh speaks and introduces the command by ועתה, runs parallel to Josh. 13:1: Joshua is old, Yhwh speaks to him and introduces his commands by ועתה 13:7). This passage, Josh. 13:1.7ff., is interrupted by another passage (Josh. 13:2–6) in which the original meaning of the phrase 'the remaining land (הארץ נשארה הרבה־מאד)' has been transformed from the DtrH-perspective in which the land has been completely conquered and now awaiting its proper distribution among the tribes into the view that the land still has to be conquered. In conformity with this modification, the borders of the land are inflated to unusually large proportions in which the peripheral non-Israelite areas (including the Philistine

Gaza strip 13:2–3 and the Phoenician coast and Libanon 13:4–6) are incorporated, with the apparent intention to make clear that not all the land has been conquered.[34] The tension between this younger addition and the older text is evident in the transition from verse 6 to 7, where Yhwh's command to allocate this remaining part of the land to (all of) Israel is duplicated by the more original command to divide the country between the nine-and-half (Cisjordanian) tribes who had not yet received their territory:

DtrN 13^{6}	רק הפלה לישׂראל בנחלה כאשר צויתיך
DtrH 13^{7}	ועתה חלק את־הארץ הזאת
	בנחלה לתשׁבע השׁבטים וחצי השׁבט המנשׁה

In Josh. 1:7–9 the older DtrH command from Yhwh to Joshua to remain courageous in the coming conquest (Josh. 1:5–6, compare Deut. 3:21–22.28, 31:7–8.23) has been bent towards an admonition to remain steadfast in observing the *torah* by repeating the imperatives of the older DtrH-text (Josh. 1:6) but modifying them by the restrictive particle רק and the assertive particle מאד. As a result, the promise of the gift of the land is made dependent on the strict observance of the *torah*.[35] The same concept can be found in Josh. 22:5, where Joshua's dismissal of the East Jordanian tribes (22:1–4) is followed by a similar restriction,[36] and moreover in Joshua 23, where

DtrH Deut. 31^{7}	חזק ואמץ כי אתה תבוא את־העם הזה אל־הארץ
	אשר נשבע יהוה לאבתם לתת להם . . .
Josh. 1^{6}	חזק ואמץ כי אתה תנחיל את־העם הזה את־הארץ
	אשר־נשבעתי לאבותם לתת להם
DtrN Josh. 1^{7}	רק חזק ואמץ מאד לשמר לעשות ככל־התורה
	אשר צוך משה עבדי אל־תסור ממנו ימין ושמאול
Josh. 22^{5}	רק שמרו מאד לעשות את־המצוה ואת־התורה
	אשר צוה אתכם משה עבד־יהוה
Josh. 23^{6}	וחקתם מאד לשמר ולעשות את כל־
	הכתוב בספר תורת משה לבלתי סור ממנו ימין ושמאול

---

[34] R. Smend, Das Gesetz und die Völker, pp. 497–500; idem, Das uneroberte Land. There is some discussion whether Josh. 13:1b already belongs to DtrN, see e.g. J.C. de Vos, *Das Los Judas*, pp. 211–213. I consider 13:2–6 to be the nomistic addition to the DtrH version in Josh. 13:1.7ff.

[35] R. Smend, Das Gesetz und die Völker, pp. 494–497; idem, *Die Entstehung des Alten Testaments*, pp. 114–115. Smend refers to Noth's earlier designation of Josh. 1:7–9 as 'späteren Zusatz' in the first edition of his commentary on Joshua, p. 7: 'sicher sekundär ist $_{7-9}$' and his *Überlieferungsgeschichtliche Studien*, p. 41, n. 4. See further the discussion in section 6.4.5 below.

[36] R. Smend, Das Gesetz und die Völker, p. 501, n. 29.

the continuation in verse 7 of the same expressions as found in Josh. 23:6 make clear that observance of 'all that is written in the book of the *torah* of Moses' (verse 6) is to be equated with abstaining from contacts with the foreign nations and their gods.

This redaction of the older Deuteronomistic History can be traced in the following books as well, and also solves other literary-critical problems, such as those inherent in the opening chapters of Judges. Here we find Joshua 24:28–31 repeated in Judges 2:6–9. Judges 1 as a whole seems to present an account of the conquest that rivals that of the book of Joshua (for which reason this chapter was attributed unanimuously to the oldest literary conquest narrative in the J-source by scholars working within the classical four-sources Hexateuchal model).[37] According to Smend[38] and A. Graeme Auld,[39] these problems can be solved if the intrusive chapter Judg. 1:1–2:5 is attributed to the same redactional stratum as Joshua 23, Josh. 1:7–8, and Josh. 13:1b–6. Although Judg. 1:1–2:5 may very well contain older, perhaps pre-DtrH material,[40] and contains only few literary links with Joshua 23,[41] it shares with this redactional layer in Joshua the concept of the incomplete conquest of the land (Judg. 1:21.27–35) understood in terms of sin and punishment (Judg. 2:3), i.e. the execution of the sentence pronounced in Josh. 23:13. The same ideas are continued in the secondary verses 2:17.20–21.[22]23:[42]

DtrN Josh. 23[13]	ידוע תדעו כי לא יוסיף יהוה אלהיכם
	להוריש את־הגוים האלה מלפניכם
	והיו לכם לפח ולמוקם ולשטט בצדיכם ולצננים בעיניכם
Josh. 23[16]	עד־אבדכם מעל האדמה הטוב הזאת
	אשר נתן לכם יהוה אלהיכם
	בעברכן את־ברית יהוה אלהיכם אשר צוה אתכם
	והלכתם ועבדתם אלהים אחרים והשתחויתם להם
	וחרה אף־יהוה בכם ואבדתם מהרה מעל הארץ הטובה אשר נתן לכם

[37] Thus from E. MEYER, Kritik der Berichte über die Eroberung Palaestinas (Num. 20, 14 bis Jud. 2,5), in *ZAW* 1 (1881), pp. 117–146; and K. BUDDE, Richter und Josua, in *ZAW* 7 (1887), pp. 93–16, to S. MOWINCKEL, *Tetrateuch-Pentateuch-Hexateuch*.

[38] R. SMEND, Das Gesetz und die Völker, pp. 506–509.

[39] A. GRAEME AULD, Judges 1 and History: A Reconsideration, in *VT* 25 (1975), pp. 261–285. According to the preface of his 1976 dissertation, *Studies in Joshua: Text and Literary Relations*, p. iii, Auld received his inspiration on how to read the book of Joshua at the 1967/1968 Münster seminars given by R. Smend, see R. SMEND, Das Gesetz und die Völker, p. 509, n. 57.

[40] R. SMEND, Das Gesetz und die Völker, p. 508; A. GRAEME AULD, Judges 1 and History, pp. 284–285.

[41] The image of the foreign nations as a trap [מוֹקֵשׁ] in Josh. 23:13 recurs in Judg. 2:3.

[42] R. SMEND, Das Gesetz und die Völker, pp. 504–506. For a different view, see

DtrN Judg. 2[3]	וגם אמרתי לא־אגרש אותם מפניכם
	והיו לכם לצדים ואלהיכם יהיו לכם למוקש
Judg. 2[20]	ויחר־אף יהוה בישראל
	ויאמר יען אשר עברו הגוי הזה את־בריתי
	אשר צויתי את־אבותם ולא שמעו לקולי
Judg. 2[21]	גם־אני לא אוסיף להוריש איש מפניהם
	מן־הגוים אשר־עזב יהושע וימת

Smend and scholars from his so-called 'Göttingen school', among whom A. Graeme Auld, W. Dietrich and T. Veijola may be reckoned, have attempted to trace this redaction throughout the subsequent books of the Deuteronomistic History, and identified passages such as Judg. 6:7–10, 1 Sam. 12, 1 Kgs. 2:2–4, 1 Kgs. 9:1–9 as similar additions.[43] What can be observed throughout these passages is a pattern of additions to the original Deuteronomistic composition that take the older text as point of departure, but proceed to modify its original intention to fit in with a very specific aim in language which is related to that of the Deuteronomistic original, but nevertheless remains clearly distinguishable. Because of this redactor's interest in the *torah*, Smend designated this literary stratum as *nomistic*, indicated by the siglum DtrN. The redactor's historical back projection of a συν-οίκησις of Israel and the foreign nations,[44] his theology of disillusionment and punishment as sequel to a Deutero-Isaiah-type theology of hope, and his nomistic ideals, especially those directed against intermarriage, place him in the context of the (early?) post-Exilic period of Ezra and Nehemia.

Two issues with respect to DtrN need to be raised here. For Smend, the DtrN-passages need not necessarily stem from one hand. Rather, literary-critical tensions within Josh. 1:7–9, 13:1b–6 and 23 seem to point to several subsequent nomistic hands.[45] More recent studies tend to describe DtrN rather as a 'process' (E. Noort)[46] or

A. VAN DER KOOIJ, 'And I also said': A New Interpretation of Judges ii 3, in *VT* 45 (1995), pp. 294–306.

[43] R. SMEND, *Die Entstehung des Alten Testaments*, pp. 110–125; W. DIETRICH, *Prophetie und Geschichte: Eine redaktionsgeschichtliche Untersuchung zum deuteronomistischen Geschichtswerk* (FRLANT 108) Göttingen 1972; T. VEIJOLA, *Die ewige Dynastie: David und die Entstehung seiner Dynastie nach der deuteronomistischen Darstellung* (AASF B/193) Helsinki 1975. See further the studies by A.D.H. MAYES, *The Story of Israel*; and M.A. O'BRIEN, *The Deuteronomistic History Hypothesis*, mentioned above.

[44] Thus R. SMEND, Das uneroberte Land, p. 101.

[45] Thus R. SMEND, *Die Entstehung des Alten Testaments*, p. 115: 'Es gibt Anzeichen dafür, daß diese Ergänzung in mehreren Stadien erfolgerte, die man konsequent mit DtrN[1] usw. bezeichnen müßte (vgl. bereits die Aufeinanderfolge von Jos 1,7 und 8).'

[46] E. NOORT, Josua und seine Aufgabe: Bemerkungen zu Josua 1:1–4, in H.M.

continuous rewriting (*Fortschreibung*, K. Latvus,[47] J.C. de Vos),[48] which would imply that the clear redaction-historical contrast between DtrH and DtrN should make way for a highly sophisticated and hardly recoverable gradual process of subsequent minor textual alterations. So far, however, a systematic approach to the literary history of the book of Joshua has not been carried out.[49]

Furthermore, Smend leaves open the question with respect to the extent of this nomistic redaction. In his pioneer 1971 article he simply stated that space and time did not permit him to trace this redaction fully throughout DtrH, not even throughout Joshua and Judges.[50] Yet, although in his later publications he traced DtrN throughout Judges, Samuel, and Kings, and conjectured that Deuteronomistic elements in the Tetrateuch may be due to the reworking of DtrN,[51]

NIEMANN (Hg.), *Nachdenken über Israel. FS K.-D. Schunck.* (BEATAJ 37) Frankfurt am Main 1994, pp. 69–87, especially p. 85, n. 21: 'Von einem einheitlichen Siglum DtrN kann nicht mehr die Rede sein. Wenn wir alle Unterschiede en detail diachron orten wollen, reicht, so fürchte ich, das Alphabet nicht aus. Denn die an sich stimmige Ausgangsposition: hier unkonditionierte Landzusage, Landzusage ohne Gesetz, Erfüllung dieser Landzusage in aller Totalität und dort übriggebliebene Völker erweist sich mir zunehmend als eine zu starke Schwarz-Weiß-Gegenüberstellung. DtrN, wenn wir das Siglum so mißbrauchen dürfen, hat nicht nur mehrere Hände, sondern ist auch ein Prozeß.'

[47] K. LATVUS, *God, Anger and Ideology. The Anger of God in Joshua and Judges in Relation to Deuteronomy and the Priestly writings.* (JSOTS 279) Sheffield 1998, p. 86. The scope of this study is not the redaction history of the book of Joshua, but rather the place of the theme of divine anger within the historical development of that book.

[48] J.C. DE VOS, *Das Los Judas*, especially pp. 245–307. According to De Vos the first of a series of six subsequent redactions of Joshua 13–21, his 'Israeliten-Bearbeitung', consisting of Josh. 14:1a.5; 15:1–12*.21–44.48–59*.59LXX.61–62*; 16:5–9*; 17:7–10; 18:11–28*; 19:1–48*.49a, depends already on a third Priestly redaction of the Pentateuch and for that reason could be labeled as P-quartair. Passages that are usually attributed to DtrH, such as Josh. 13:1.7; 18:3–4; 14:6–15, are in his viewn part of a second redaction, labelled 'Josua-Bearbeitung', whereas the DtrN passages 13:2–6; 15:63; 16:10; 17:11–13 would belong to a fourth stage, called 'Korrekturnachtrag'. Hence, De Vos concludes (p. 304): 'In Jos 13–21 findet sich weder authentische Sprache von P^G oder P^S noch von Dtr (mit Ausnahme von 14,6–15*), vielmehr sind zahlreiche Texte *im Stil* von P und Dtr gehalten.'

[49] To my mind, a *Fortschreibungs*-model that is so subtle that literary-critical and redaction-historal contrasts have completely vanished, may in the end result in the complete rejection of the possibility of reconstructing redactional layers at all, see B.S. CHILDS, Retrospective Readings of the Old Testament Prophets, in *ZAW* 108 (1996), pp. 362–377. It is therefore worth mentioning that redaction-critical studies by M.A. O'BRIEN, *The Deuteronomistic History Hypothesis*, pp. 67ff.; and K. BIEBERSTEIN, *Josua-Jordan-Jericho*, pp. 95ff. see no reason to take recourse to this solution in their reconstructions of the literary history of Joshua 23 and Joshua 1, respectively.

[50] R. SMEND, Das Gesetz und die Völker, p. 509, note 59: 'Es erschöpft nicht einmal im Buch Josua das Material.'

[51] R. SMEND, *Die Entstehung des Alten Testaments*, p. 125.

he did not extend the DtrN-corpus in Joshua beyond the passages discussed above (Josh. 1:7–9, 13:1b–6, 23). A. Graeme Auld, however, argues that if one of the main themes of DtrN was the failure to conquer the whole land, the isolated references to failed land conquest ('das negative Besitzverzeichnis') throughout Josh. 13–19 (Josh. 13:13; 15:63; 16:10; 17:11–13) should likewise be ascribed to the same DtrN-hand.[52] L. Schwienhorst, in his discussion of the literary history of Josh. 6, takes the next step by ascribing the verses that explicitely deal with the continued existence of a non-Israelite group such as that of Rahab's family (Josh. 6:17b.25) to this same redaction. Following the proposal made by N. Lohfink to detect the hand of DtrN in Deut. 6:17–19, 8:1 and 11:8.22–25,[53] K. Bieberstein argues that the passage corresponding with Deut. 11:24–25, i.e. Josh. 1:3–5, should also be ascribed to the nomistic redaction of Joshua that sought to expand the boundaries of the land to idealistic proportions in order to stress both the culpability of Israel and future possibilities.[54] In Fritz's 1994 commentary the clear profile of this second Deuteronomistic layer, characterized by the two themes 'Gesetz' and 'Völker', is completely submerged in a broad second Deuteronomistic redaction (RedD in his terminology) of the original Deuteronomistic composition.[55]

4.2.3 *A Priestly Redaction of the Book of Joshua (RedP)*

Clearly distinguishable in terms of phraseology and ideology from the Deuteronomistic and nomistic layers of the book of Joshua are

---

[52] A. GRAEME AULD, *Studies in Joshua*, pp. 229–234.

[53] N. LOHFINK, Kerygmata des deuteronomistischen Geschichtswerks, in J. JEREMIAS, L. PERLITT (Hg.), *Die Botschaft und die Boten. FS H.W. Wolff.* Neukirchen 1981, pp. 87–100, especially pp. 98–99; reprinted in idem, *Studien zum Deuteronomium und zur deuteronomistischen Literatur* 2. Stuttgart 1991, pp. 125–142.

[54] K. BIEBERSTEIN, *Josua-Jordan-Jericho*, pp. 392–394. See also the cautious remarks in the same direction by E. NOORT, Land in zicht . . . ? p. 110, n. 28: 'Deze koppeling tussen de buitensporige grootte van het beloofde land en het naleven van de thora heeft gevolgen voor de omvang en intentie van de nomistische redactie van het deuteronomistische geschiedwerk, zoals die blootgelegd is door R. Smend en T. Veijola. Exemplarisch is deze verbinding zichtbaar in Deut. 11:22–25. Wanneer deze verzen tot DtrN zouden horen, moet de verhouding tot Jozua 1:4 (DtrH) opnieuw worden bezien.' See the discussion in section 6.4.4 below.

[55] V. FRITZ, *Das Buch Josua*, pp. 3–4. Fritz ascribes to RedD: Josh. 1:7–9; 2:8.9a.10a.11a.12.13.14a.24a; 3:10–11.13.14b.17; 4:9–10; 5:1.4–7.9.10a.11*.12a; 6:7b.11; 8:1–9.22.24–25.28.30–31.34; 9:1–2.16–17.22–26; 11:16–20; 12:1*.2.5.7 (not 13:1b–6, see p. 141), 14:6a.7–10a.12a.13; 15:13.15–19; 20:1–5.7.8; 23; 24:19–24.26–27.32.33.

a number of passages that reveal close affinities with those passages from the Pentateuch that are attributed to a Priestly literary stratum.[56] Characteristic for these passages in Joshua—as well as those in the preceding books—are a strong interest in the role and position of the (Aaronic) priests in society, the cult, and the systematization of society, time and space: themes and interests that are usually considered to be back projections of a the ideals and interests of Judaism during the post-Exilic, Persian period.[57]

Illuminating is the way in which the Israelite society is presented in these passages:[58] Israel is designated as a *congregation* (עֵדָה),[59] rather than as a *national* (עַם) or *ethnic* (גּוֹי)[60] *entity*. Unlike the Deuteronomistic/

---

[56] A general characterisation of Priestly theology and terminology is offered by the introductions to the Old Testament, see e.g. S.R. DRIVER, *An Introduction to the Literature of the Old Testament*. Edinburgh 1909[8], pp. 126–159, with a helpful list of Priestly phrases (pp. 131–135). M. WEINFELD, *Deuteronomy 1–11*. (AB 5) New York 1991, p. 36, offers a basic list of characteristic contrasts in phraseology between D and P. A general description of the theology of the Priestly scribes is offered by G. VON RAD, *Theologie des Alten Testaments* I, pp. 245–293.

[57] Thus since J. WELLHAUSEN, *[Prolegomena zur] Geschichte Israels*. Berlin 1878. See for a recent discussion for instance R. ALBERTZ, *Religionsgeschichte Israels in alttestamentlicher Zeit Teil 2: Vom Exil bis zu den Makkabäern*. Göttingen 1997[2], pp. 472ff.; and further J.G. VINK, *The Date and Origin of the Priestly Code in the Old Testament*, in P.A.H. DE BOER (ed.), *The Priestly Code and Seven Other Studies*. (OTS 15) Leiden 1969, pp. 1–144. Y. KAUFMAN, תולדות האמונה הישראלית. Tel Aviv 1937–1956, and other Israeli scholars, like such as M. WEINFELD, *Deuteronomy 1–11* (see also T.M. KRAPF, *Die Priesterschrift und die vorexilische Zeit. Yehezkel Kaufmanns vernachlässigter Beitrag zur Geschichte der biblischen Religion*. (OBO 122) Freiburg/Göttingen 1992) argue for a pre-Deuteronomistic, hence pre-Exilic origin of the Priestly corpus, but so far the discussion has remained restricted to the Pentateuchal laws. An exception is M. OTTOSON, Tradition History, with Emphasis on the Composition of the Book of Joshua, in K. JEPPESEN, B. OTZEN (eds.), *The Production of Time: Tradition History in Old Testament Scholarship. A Symposium at Sandbjerg Manor, Denmark May 1982*. Sheffield 1984, pp. 81–106, especially pp. 89–90; and idem, *Josuaboken. En programskrift för davidisk restauration*. (Acta Universitatis Upsaliensis. Studia Biblica Upsaliensia 1) Uppsala 1991, especially pp. 56–57. For Ottoson, however, P stands for the whole Tetrateuch, whereas D stands for the whole Deuteronomistic History understood as a unity. See further section 7.4.3.2 below.

[58] See e.g. E. CORTESE, *Josua 13–21. Ein priesterschriftlicher Abschnitt im deuteronomistischen Geschichtswerk*. (OBO 94) Freiburg/Göttingen 1990, pp. 24–26. 'Die Gliederung des Volkes'.

[59] Josh. 9:15.18.18.19.21.27; 18:1; 20:6.9; 22:12.16.17.18.20.30, see S.R. DRIVER, *Introduction*, p. 133; E. CORTESE, *Josua 13–21*, p. 24; and V. FRITZ, *Das Buch Josua*, p. 98.

[60] The designation of Israel as גּוֹי occurs in MT-Josh. 3:17; 4:1; 5:6.8, 10:13. R.E. CLEMENTS, גּוֹי, in *ThWAT* I, col. 965–973, has pointed out that the Priestly writers deliberatedly avoided this term, since Israel in the post-Exilic period no longer formed an independent political entity (col. 971).

nomistic-Deuteronomistic portrait of the structure of Israelite society in the conquest period (see Josh. 8:33, 23:2, 24:1, Deut. 31:28 *et aliter*) as *tribes* (שֵׁבֶט),[61] governed by *elders* (זְקֵנִים),[62] *judges* (שֹׁפְטִים), *scribes* (שֹׁטְרִים),[63] and *leaders* (רָאשִׁים), according to the Priestly ideology the *tribes* (indicated preferably by the word מַטֶּה rather than שֵׁבֶט)[64] are presided by *heads of the father's houses* ([רָאשֵׁי אֲבוֹת [הַמַּטּוֹת)[65] and represented by a (single) *chief* or *ruler* (נָשִׂיא).[66] The first place in this congregation is no longer held by Joshua, but by the descendant(s) of Aaron, Eleazar and Phinehas, as is evident in the framework of the chapters on the division of the land in 14:1–5, 19:51, where Eleazar has taken over Joshua's role as land distributor,[67] in accordance with the Priestly passage Num. 34:16–29. Another small, but significant modification can be observed in the change from the Deuteronomistic expression 'The Levitical priests', הכהנים הלוים, to 'The priests *and* the Levites', הכהנים וְלוים, by which a distinction between the lower class of Levites and the descendents of Aaron is made.[68]

---

[61] The word שֵׁבֶט occurs in Josh. 1:12; 3:12.12; 4:2.4.5.8.12; 7:14.16; 11:23; 12:6.7; 13:7.7.14.29.33; 18:2.4.7; 21:16; 22:7.9.10.11.13.15.21; 23:4; 24:1, that is 31 times in all, and 18 times in Deuteronomy out of a total of some 190 instances throughout the whole Hebrew Bible; see further E. Cortese, *Josua 13–19*, p. 25.

[62] The זְקֵנִים are mentioned in Josh. 7:6, 8:10.33; 9:11 [20:4] 23:2; 24:1.31, see further J. Conrad, זָקֵן *zāqen*, זֹקֶן *zoqæn*, זִקְנָה *ziqnāh*, זְקֻנִים *zequnîm* in *ThWAT* II, col. 639–650.

[63] The term שֹׁטֵר occurs in Josh. 1:10; 3:2; 8:33; 23:2; 24:1, further only in Exod. 5:6.10.14.15.19; Num. 11:16; Deut. 1:15; 16:18; 20:5.8.9.9; 31:28; Prov. 6:7; 1 Chron. 23:4; 26:29; 27:1, 2 Chron. 19:11; 26:11; 34:13.

[64] The designation מַטֶּה for *tribe* occurs 59 times in Joshua, predominantly (27x) in Josh. 21:1–42 and in the framework of, and superscriptions and subscriptions to, the lists of the tribal territories in Josh. 13–19 [13:15.24.29; 14:1.2.2.3.34; 15:1.20.21; 16:8; 17:1; 18:11.21; 19:1.8.23.24.31.39.40.48.50.51] plus three times in Josh. 20:8. The remaining occurrences are in Josh. 7:1.18 and 22:1.14, frequently in Numbers and Chronicles and never in Deuteronomy, see further S.R. Driver, *Introduction*, p. 134; E. Cortese, *Josua 13–19*, p. 25.

[65] Thus in Josh. 14:1, 19:51, 21:1 and 22:14, see S.R. Driver, *Introduction*, p. 133; E. Cortese, *Josua 13–21*, pp. 25–26.

[66] Thus in Josh. 9:15.18.18.19.21.21; 13:21; 17:4; 22:14.14.30.32, further in Exod. 16:22; 35:27; Lev.4:22; and especially (60x) in Numbers, and Ezekiel (36 instances of which 20 in Ezek. 40–48). See S.R. Driver, *Introduction*, p. 134; and H. Niehr, נָשִׂיא *nāśî'* in *ThWAT* V, col. 647–657.

[67] In the DtrH passages Josh. 1:6, 13:1a.6, 14:6–15, and possibly 17:14–18 (pre-DtrH?), 18:2–10? Joshua figures as the sole leader invested with the authority to divide the land. Eleazar also appears as the principal authority in the chapter about the Levitical cities (21:1–42), and in the chapter on the function of the altar at the Jordan, 22:9–34, where Joshua is absent altogether.

[68] See R. de Vaux, o.p., *Les institutions de l'ancien Testament* II (Paris 1960), pp. 195–277.

The land to be divided primarily by Eleazar in Josh. 13–19 is restricted to the Cisjordanian land, whereas the Trans-Jordanian area, an integral part of the land in the conception of the DtrH-author, may even be termed טְמֵאָה, *unclean*, as opposed to *the land of Yhwh's possession* (אֶרֶץ אֲחֻזַּת יְהוָה) (Josh. 22:19).[69] Whereas the Deuteronomistic authors preferred to refer to the land by means of the divine promise (ארץ אשר נשבע יהוה לאבותהם לתת להם Josh. 1:5, 5:6 and 21:43), the Priestly scribes preferred the colourless designation *land of Canaan*, אֶרֶץ כְּנַעַן.[70] Moreover, the preferred term for occupation of this land is not ירשׁ (as in the Deuteronomistic strata), but אחז, *to take hold of*, more particularly the noun אֲחֻזָּה.[71] Furthermore, in 18:1 we find yet another verb with a similar connotation, i.e. the verb כבשׁ, *to subdue*, which marks a link with Gen. 1:28, and Num. 32:22.29, the chapter that describes the land distribution to the tribes of Reuben, Gad, and half Manasseh (cf. Josh. 13):[72]

Gen. 1^{28} (P)	ויברך אתם אלהים ויאמר להם אלהים פרו ורבו ומלאו את־הארץ וכבשה ורדו בדגת הים ובעוף השמים ובכל־חיה הרמשת על־הארץ׃
Num. 32^{29} (P)	ויאמר משה אלהם אם־יעברו בני־גד ובני־ראובן אתכם את־הירדן כל־חלוץ למלחמה לפני יהוה ונכבשה הארץ לפניכם ונתתם להם את־ארץ הגלעד לאחזה׃

[69] Thus M. WEINFELD, The Extent of the Promised Land—The Status of Transjordan, in G. STRECKER (Hg.), *Das Land in biblischer Zeit*, pp. 59–75; and V. FRITZ, *Das Buch Josua*, pp. 223–224.

[70] Thus in Josh. 5:12; 14:1, 21:2 22:9.10.11.32, and also in the non-Priestly passage 24:3. See further H.-J. ZOBEL, כְּנַעַן *k^{e}na‘an* כְּנַעֲנִי *k^{e}na‘^{a}nî ThWAT* IV, col. 224–243.

[71] The noun אֲחֻזָּה occurs in Josh. 21:12.41; and 22:4.9.19.19, outside Joshua mostly in passages characterised by Priestly theology: Gen. 17:8, 23:4.9.20, 36:43, 47:11, 48:4, 49:30, 50:13; Lev. 14:34.34, 25 (13 times); 27 (5 times); Num. 27:4.7.24; 32:5.22.29.32; 35:2.8.28; Deut. 32:49; Ezek. 44:28.28; 45:5.6.7.7.8; 46 (8 times); Ps. 2:8; Neh. 11:3; 1 Chron. 7:28; 9:2 and 2 Chron. 11:14; 31:1.

E. CORTESE, *Josua 13–19*, pp. 26–28, argues that the alternative preferred by P for the D term ירשׁ is the verb נחל Qal, whereas D would use only the Hiph‘il form of נחל.

[72] Another interesting place is 1 Chron. 22:18 where the theme of the subdual of the land is combined with the (Deuteronomistic) theme of the pacification of the land (נוח Hiph‘il 1) and the building of the Temple by Solomon. In most of the other occurrences the verb כבשׁ is used in profane terms, 2 Sam. 8:11, Jer. 34:11.16, Mic. 7:19, Zech. 9:15, Esther 7:8, Neh. 5:5.5, 2 Chron. 28:10; see further S. WAGNER, כָּבַשׁ *kābaš* כֶּבֶשׁ *kæbæš*, כִּבְשָׁן *kibšān* in *ThWAT* IV, col. 54–60, and the conclusions based on the specific use of this verb by N. Lohfink and J. Blenkinsopp, discussed below.

Josh. 18[1] (RedP)	ויקהלו כל־עדת בני־ישׂראל שׁלה וישׁכינו שׁם את־אהל מועד והארץ נכבשׁה לפניהם׃

The reason for the qualitative distinction between Cisjordanian soil and external territories is given in 22:19a: it is the land *in which the tabernacle abode of Yhwh abides* (אֲשֶׁר שָׁכַן־שָׁם מִשְׁכַּן יְהוָה). This phrase harks back to Josh. 18:1, where an important set of Priestly concepts is introduced in the book, that is that of the transferral by the Israelite congregation of the tent of Meeting (אֹהֶל מוֹעֵד) to Shiloh.[73] The Tent of Meeting represents the divine theophany and immanence before the period of the Temple, and thereby covers the function of the ark (אֲרוֹן) in the older literary layers (in DtrH usually termed אֲרוֹן הַבְּרִית), which in the Priestly terminology then becomes *the ark of the Testimony*, אֲרוֹן הָעֵדוּת.[74] This central moving sanctuary finds its first permanent place—according to this Priestly layer of the book of Joshua (18:1; 19:51)—at Shiloh, anticipating of the references to the sanctuary at Shiloh in the Samuel narratives.[75] This shrine is held by the Priestly scribes to be the sole legitimate sanctuary, and the mere suggestion of another altar at the border of the Land already seems to justify a civil war among the western and eastern tribes (Josh. 22:9–34). The building of such an(other) altar is seen as outright apostasy from Yhwh, comparable to the sin of Israel at Peor (22:16, cf. Num. 25:1–18) and that of Achan (22:20, cf. Joshua 7), and runs the risk of arousing the divine anger (קֶצֶף־יהוה,[76] as opposed

[73] The אֹהֶל מוֹעֵד occurs in Joshua only in 18:1, 19:51, further in Deut. 31:14–15, six times in Chronicles and predominantly—although not exclusively—in the Priestly legislation Exod. 25–Num. 10. See further G. VON RAD, *Theologie des Alten Testaments* I, pp. 247–254, K. KOCH, אֹהֶל אָהַל, in *ThWAT* I, col. 128–141. The Priestly writer(s) adopted a pre-Priestly concept found in Exod. 33, and Num. 11–12.

[74] The אֲרוֹן occurs 31 times in Joshua, only in Josh. 3–4 [18 times], Josh. 6 [10 times], and Josh. 7:6 and 8:33.33. In Joshua, the (Deuteronomistic) combination אֲרוֹן הַבְּרִית occurs some seven times in Josh. 3:8.(11.)14.17; 4:9.18, 6:8, 8:33, the Priestly expression אֲרוֹן הָעֵדוּת only once in 4:16, and further in Exod. 25:22; 26:33.34; 30:6.26; 39:35; 40:3.5.21; Num. 4:5; 7:89; see further H.-J. ZOBEL, אֲרוֹן, in *ThWAT* I, col. 391–404.

[75] Thus Judg. 18:31, 21:12.19.21.21; 1 Sam. 1:3.9.24; 2:14; 3;21.21; 4:3.4.12; 14:3. See further B. HALPERN, Shiloh, in D.N. FREEDMAN (ed.), *The Anchor Bible Dictionary* V. New York 1992, pp. 1213–1215; and J. BRIEND, Silo, in *Supplément au dictionnaire de la Bible. Fascicule 71. Sichem-Songe.* Paris 1996, col. 1330–1341.

[76] The root קצף occurs in Josh. 9:20; 22:18.20. See further G. VON RAD, *Theologie des Alten Testaments* I, p. 282; G. SAUER, קצף *qsp* zornig sein, in *ThHAT* II, col. 663–

to the Deuteronomistic formulation—חרה אַף בְּ)[77] over the whole congregation. The parallels from the Priestly passages in Numbers (and Leviticus) show that the divine anger functions as punishment for cultic transgressions:

Josh. 9[20]	זאת נעשׂה להם והחיה אותם ולא־יהיה עלינו קצף על־השׁבועה אשׁר־נשׁבענו להם:
22[18]	ואתם תשׁבו היום מאחרי יהוה והיה אתם תמרדו היום ביהוה ומחר אל־כל־עדת ישׂראל יקצף:
22[30]	הלוא עכן בן־זרח מעל מעל בחרם ועל־כל־עדת ישׂראל היה קצף והוא אישׁ אחד לא גוע בעונו:
Num. 1[53]	והלוים יחנו סביב למשכן העדה ולא־יהיה קצף על־עדת בני ישׂראל ושׁמרו הלוים את־משׁמרת משׁכן העדות:
16[22]	ויפלו ויאמרו אל אלהי הרוחת לכל־בשׂר האישׁ אחד יחטא ועל כל־העדה תקצף:
18[5]	ושׁמרתם את משׁמרת הקדשׁ ואת המשׁמרת המזבח ולא־יהיה עוד קצף על־בני ישׂראל:

Here another distinctive feature of the Priestly theology becomes visible. Whereas in the Deuteronomistic theology the foreign nations with their foreign gods present the main threat to Israel, according to the Priestly theology it is tensions within the Israelite community and priesthood, that endanger Israel's existence. Or, as Kari Latvus puts it succinctly: 'According to the dtr-theology the main issue *was to serve the right God*, Yahweh, but the P-circle focuses on *the right way of serving God.*'[78] Likewise the Priestly scribes make use of their own vocabulary to formulate the themes of opposition to Yhwh and his ministers, i.e. לון, *to protest*,[79] מָעַל מַעַל, *to commit a treacherous act*,[80] and

666; F.V. Reiterer, קצף *qāṣap̱* קֶצֶף *qæṣæp̱* in *ThWAT* VII, col. 95–104; R. Albertz, *Religionsgeschichte Israels in alttestamentlicher Zeit 2*. Göttingen 1997², pp. 524–525; and especially K. Latvus, *God, Anger and Ideology*.

[77] The root חרה used for the anger of Yhwh occurs in Josh. 7:1, 26 (חָרוֹן) and 23:16. See further K. Latvus, *God, Anger and Ideology*, pp. 25–26.

[78] K. Latvus, *God, Anger, and Ideology*, p. 62.

[79] The verb לון (Niphʿal/Hiphʿil) occurs in Josh. 9:18 and further in Exod. 15:24; 16:2.2.7.7.8; 17:3; Num. 14:2.27.27.29.36.36; 16:11.11; and 17:6.20. The derivative noun תְּלֻנּוֹת, *murmuring*, occurs in the same text segments: Exod. 16:7.8.8.9.12; Num. 14:27; 17:20.25. Although not all these passages can be considered to have a Priestly origin (Exod. 15:24 and 17:3 are the non-Priestly exceptions), the theme figures predominantly in Priestly passages. See further R. Knierim, לון *lūn* rebellieren, in *ThHAT* I, col. 870–872; and K.-D. Schunck, לון *lūn* תְּלֻנּוֹת *tᵉlunnôṯ*, in *ThWAT* IV, col. 527–530.

[80] Josh. 7:1, 22:16.20.22. See S.R. Driver, *Introduction*, p. 134; V. Fritz, *Das Buch Josua*, p. 79; R. Knierim, מעל *mʿl* treulos sein, in *ThHAT* I, col. 920–922; and H. Ringgren, מָעַל *māʿal* מַעַל *māʿal*, in *ThWAT* IV, col. 1038–1042.

מרד, *to revolt*,[81] *vis-à-vis* the more Deuteronomistically coloured expressions לא שמע בקול and מרה, *to rebel*.[82]

Whereas the Deuteronomistic parts of Joshua form a continuation of the themes of Deuteronomy, these Priestly segments correspond closely to the final chapters of Numbers (Num. 25–36). Besides the links between the execution of the allotment of the land by a special committee headed by an Aaronic priest (Josh. 14:1ff., 19:51, 18:1, compare Num. 33:50–56, 34), we find links between the Priestly description of the Trans-Jordanian territory (Josh. 13:15ff. cf. Num. 32:33–39, 31:8), and the special arrangement for an exclusively female clan such as that of the daughters of Zelophehad (Josh. 17:3–4, cf. Num. 27:1–11, 36:1–13). The chapters narrating the special provisions made by Joshua and Eleazar with respect to the cities for refugees from blood revenge and for Levites (Joshua 20* and 21:1–42) have their corresponding parts in Numbers 35.

Hence, most of these Priestly passages are to be found in the second half of Joshua (13:15ff. 14:1–5, 17:3–4, 18:1, 19:51, 20:1–3.9, 21:1–42 and 22:9–34). Apart from the ideological themes described above, these passages are marked by a pronounced systematisation (as becomes evident in the rather unrealistically strict division of the land in Josh. 21:1–42)[83] and provide a structure to the whole complex of land division chapters (13–19 with 14:1–5, 19:51 as framework). Occasionally we find the same themes, vocabulary and systematization in the first half of the book, i.e. in the re-interpretation of the events with respect to the Gibeonites in Joshua 9 as a designation of this group as lower cult personnel, and by laying the blame for their continued presence with the lay authorities of the people (נשׂאים, 9:14.15b.[17?]18–21.27).[84] The fact that the Priestly

[81] Josh. 22:16.18.19.19.29. The verb further occurs some 25 times in the Hebrew Bible, predominantly in Exilic or post-Exilic literature: Gen. 14:4; Num. 14:9; 2 Kgs. 18:7.20 [//Isa. 36:5] 24:1.20 [//Jer. 52:3//2 Chron. 36:13] Ezek. 2:3.3; 17:15; 20:38; Job 24:13; Dan. 9:5.9; Neh. 2:19; 6:6; 9:26, 2 Chron. 13:6. See R. Knierim, מרד *mrd* sich auflehnen, in *ThHAT* I col. 925–928; L. Schwienhorst, מרד *māraḏ* מֶרֶד *mæræḏ* מַרְדּוּת *mardûṯ*, *THWAT* V, col. 1–6.

[82] Josh. 1:18; 5:6; 22:2, and 1:18. See Joshua 23 for the numerous Deuteronomistic expressions for loyalty and disloyalty to Yhwh and the collection of Deuteronomistic expressions for these themes in M. Weinfeld, *Deuteronomy and the Deuteronomic School*, pp. 332–341.

[83] See V. Fritz, *Das Buch Josua*, pp. 206–216.

[84] See e.g., V. Fritz, *Das Buch Josua*, pp. 99–107; K. Latvus, *God, Anger and Ideology*, pp. 64–66.

writers did not adapt the conquest narratives may be explained by their need to adapt to the *Pax persica*. If this group were to maintain their power in the face of the Persian authorities, they had no need to revive the ancient conquest narratives.[85]

The Priestly character of these passages in Joshua is fairly generally recognized in critical scholarship, but the precise literary extent and origin of these passages have been a matter of much dispute. Pioneers of Hexateuchal criticism worked on the assumption of a Priestly codex which in its basic form or 'Grundschrift' formed one of the four sources or 'Quellen' from which the Hexateuch was compiled; hence, the Priestly passages in Joshua were considered to be remnants of this originally independent literary work P^{G}.[86] Although the scarcity of the Priestly elements in the first half of the book was unanimuously recognized, it was generally assumed that the Priestly headings of the lists in Joshua 13–21 must have had a content, and that, as a result, the whole of the lists of place names and border lines should be ascribed to the Priestly basic document ($P^{G(rundschrift)}$ as opposed to secondary Priestly additions $P^{s(ekundär)}$).[87]

With the historical-topographical studies of A. Alt and M. Noth[88] this thesis became untenable and in his epoch-making *Überlieferungsgeschichtliche Studien*, M. Noth systematically assigned the Priestly passages Joshua discussed above to a 'nachpriesterschriftliche' redaction based on the Priestly Codex (P^{G}), and likewise the corresponding chapters in the book of Numbers to a secondary Priestly redaction.[89] In spite of the rescue operations by S. Mowinckel[90] and recent

---

85 See S. McEvenue, *The Narrative Style of the* Priestly *Writer*. (AnBibl 50) Roma 1971; and N. Lohfink, Die Priesterschrift und die Geschichte, in *Congress Volume. Göttingen 1977*. (SVT 29) Leiden 1979, p. 212.

86 Thus e.g. J. Wellhausen, *Die Composition des Hexateuchs*, pp. 116–134; A. Kuenen, *Historisch-critisch onderzoek*², pp. 102–106; C. Steuernagel, *Deuteronomium und Josua*, pp. 140–142; H. Holzinger, *Das Buch Josua*, pp. ix–xxi.

87 Thus e.g. J. Wellhausen, *Die Composition des Hexateuchs*, pp. 127ff.; C. Steuernagel, *Deuteronomium und Josua*, pp. 140–142 (with the proviso that the Priestly segments in Joshua 13–19 may contain ancient material, part of which might reflect real territorial delimitations); and H. Holzinger, *Das Buch Josua*, pp. xi–xxi.

88 See the collected essays of A. Alt in his *Kleine Schriften zur Geschichte des Volkes Israel* I–III. München 1953–1959, M. Noth, *Das Buch Josua*, pp. 13–15, and E. Noort, *Das Buch Josua*, pp. 92–98, 173ff.

89 M. Noth, *Überlieferungsgeschichtliche Studien*, pp. 180–217: 'Anhang: Die 'Priesterschrift' und die Redaktion des Pentateuch', especially pp. 182–190: 'Die Priesterschrift im Buche Josua'.

90 S. Mowinckel, *Zur Frage nach dokumentarischen Quellen in Josua 13–19*. Oslo 1946, and idem, *Tetrateuch-Pentateuch-Hexateuch*. Mowinckel accepted the existence of the

attempts to reinstate a Priestly *Grundschrift* extending from Gen. 1 to Joshua 18 (linked by the rare verb כבשׁ, see above),[91] the characterisation of the Priestly passages in Joshua as redactional extensions has become the current consensus,[92] especially since the existence of an independent Priestly *Grundschrift* underlying the Pentateuch itself is increasingly questioned,[93] or—by others who wish to adhere to a P^G—at least drastically reduced to Genesis and Exodus.[94] A. Graeme Auld—in response to S. Mowinckel—even declares the alleged Priestly passages in Joshua 13–21 to reflect the influence of the theology of Chronicles, which he substantiates by arguing a literary dependence of Joshua 20, 21:1–42 on the parallel material in 1 Chronicles 6.[95]

---

boundaries document and the list of Judah's districts as recovered by Alt and Noth, but contested Noth's statement that P had no interest in the theme 'land' at all, and reasoned that the pre-Exilic documents could not have survived the burning of the tempel in 587 BCE. Hence the actual 'tribal territories' passages in Josh. 13–21, should be ascribed to the Priestly record of these pre-Priestly documents, which must have been preserved by oral tradition.

[91] Thus e.g. N. Lohfink, Die Priesterschrift und die Geschichte, pp. 189–225. See also J.G. Vink, *The Date and Origin of the Priestly Code in the Old Testament*, pp. 63–80, who ascribes to the Priestly Code (P^G) Josh. 18:1–10 *in toto*, Josh. 22:9–34, and even Josh. 8:30–35 because of its use of the Priestly formula כַּגֵּר כָּאֶזְרָח (see chapter 9 below). Vink considers these passages as narrative propagande in support of Ezra's mission to formulate a legislative compromise between the southern and northern Israelite post-Exilic communities ('Judah' and 'Joseph' in Josh. 18:5, who had been holding their territories for a long time, halfway between which [Shiloh, i.e. at equal distances from Jerusalem and Samaria] the sanctuary is set up) and between the Palestinian and Elephantine communities (Josh. 22:9–34 would mirror then the arrangements made for the re-instalment of the Israelite sanctuary at Elephantini, see B. Porten, A. Yardeni (eds.), *Textbook of Aramaic Documents from Ancient Egypt. 1 Letters.* Jerusalem 1986, nrs. A4.7–A4.10). This view is accepted by K. Latvus, *God, Anger and Ideology*, pp. 58ff., but already rejected with some strong arguments by V. Fritz, *Das Buch Josua*, p. 227. See further section 9.4 below.

[92] See e.g. J. Blenkinsopp, The Structure of P, in *CBQ* 38 (1976), pp. 275–292; R. Smend, *Die Entstehung des Alten Testaments*, pp. 58, 114; V. Fritz, *Das Buch Josua*, pp. 2ff.; K. Bieberstein, *Josua-Jordan-Jericho*, pp. 412–413: 'Die Priesterschrift im Josuabuch?'; and K. Latvus, *God, Anger and Ideology*.

[93] See e.g. F.M. Cross, *Canaanite Myth and Hebrew Epic*. Cambridge, Massachusetts/London 1973, pp. 293–325: 'The Priestly Work'; J. van Seters, *Abraham in History and Tradition*. New Haven/London 1975; R. Rendtorff, *Das überlieferungsgeschichtliche Problem des Pentateuch*. (BZAW 147) Berlin 1977; and E. Blum, *Studien zur Komposition des Pentateuch*. (BZAW 189) Berlin/New York 1990; See further the older literature mentioned in N. Lohfink, Die Priesterschrift und die Geschichte, p. 197, n. 28.

[94] Thus e.g. E. Otto, Forschungen zur Priesterschrift, in *ThR* 62 (1997), pp. 1–50, following the research into the ending of the original Priestly document (P^G) with the Sinai pericope by Th. Pola, *Die ursprüngliche Priesterschrift. Beobachtungen zur Literarkritik und Traditionsgeschichte von P^G*. (WMANT 70) Neukirchen 1995.

[95] Thus his dissertation, A.G. Auld, *Studies in Joshua*, and its revision *Joshua, Moses and the* Land, pp. 93ff. 'Priestly Joshua?' as well as the various essays from the same author collected in his *Joshua Retold*.

This line of reasoning has met with vehement opposition by E. Cortese,[96] and thus far has gained little adherence.[97]

Therefore, it seems safe to conclude that we can speak of a commonly accepted *redaction* of Joshua breathing the spirit of Priestly ideology, aimed at introducing into the book distinctive concepts (such as the אהל מועד in 18:1, 19:51), interests (such as the prominence of Eleazar in 14:1, 19:51, 22:9–34, the uniqueness of the central sanctuary in 22:9–34 and the special arrangements for the Levitical priests in 21:1–42), and occasionally bending the original narrative for a specific purpose (for instance in the story of the Gibeonites, Josh. 9). Questions concerning the homogenity of this layer in Joshua, its literary relations to the Deuteronomistic layers of the book of Joshua,[98] and the chronological sequence (RedP after DtrN or before?), the literary relations with the Priestly portions of the Pentateuch and with the books of Chronicles, are relevant, but not essential for our investigation and thus need not be solved here.

4.2.4 *Remaining Questions with Respect to the Redaction History of the Book of Joshua*

On the basis of the redaction-critical observations presented above we may thus discern three major phases in the redaction history of the book of Joshua: [0] a stage preceding the Deuteronomistic reworking, [1] the stage in which the Deuteronomistic author reshaped pre-Deuteronomistic Joshua narratives into a coherent narrative framed by a Deuteronomistic introductory chapter and a corresponding summary, [2] a group of additions to this Deuteronomistic layer in which the promises of DtrH are made dependent on the strict observance of the *torah* (DtrN) and [3] a layer of passages that introduce specifically Priestly concepts and interest into the book (RedP). This does not mean, however, that the debate concerning the literary stratification of Joshua has come to a standstill and has been described exhaustively on the basis of these three stages. Far from that: a large number

---

[96] E. Cortese, Gius. 21 e Giud. 1 (TM o LXX?) e l 'abbottonatura' del 'Tetrateuco' con l' 'Opera Deuteronomistica' in *Rivista Biblica* 33 (1985), pp. 375–394; and especially his *Josua 13–21.*

[97] V. Fritz, *Das Buch Josua*, e.g. p. 210.

[98] E. Noort, *Das Buch Josua*, p. 181, suggests that from a certain stage in the continuous development of the book onwards, the distinctive D and P layers are no longer discernible and hence the P passages can be seen as part of the Deuteronomistic *Fortschreibungs*-process.

of issues are the subject of ongoing debates. These issues, however, seem to be of only indirect relevance to the main focus of the present chapter, and will therefore be discussed only briefly.

Owing to Noth's radical re-arrangement of Israel's Primary History into a Deuteronomistic History and a truncated Tetrateuch, scholars have sought to overcome this anomaly by either returning to some form of Hexateuchal model, by which parts of the Joshua-Judges narratives are rescued to form a conclusion of the otherwise unfinished Jahwistic narratives,[99] or conversely by developing models in which the pre-Priestly or so-called Jahwistic passages from the Pentateuch are in fact a secondary extension of DtrH. In these designs, the Joshua narratives are not the continuation of the Jahwistic parts of the Pentateuch, but rather their source.[100] Alternatively, proposals to dismiss the so-called 'Deuteronomistic History' altogether are becoming more and more numerous.[101] Still, these models have no direct bearing on the stratification within Joshua. The situation differs in the case of the literary models which allow for alternative or additional redactional layers in Joshua, such as the alleged Dtr_2, DtrP, DtrR, and other redactions.

[99] See e.g. S. Mowinckel, *Tetrateuch-Pentateuch-Hexateuch*; E. Otto, *Das Mazzotfest in Gilgal*. See further the survey in K. Bieberstein, *Josua-Jordan-Jericho*, pp. 40–42: 'Rückkehr zum Hexateuch?'

[100] See the various publications by J. van Seters in which this thesis is developed, e.g. J. van Seters, Joshua 24 and the Problem of Tradition in the Old Testament, in J. Barrick, J.R. Spencer (eds.), *In the Shelter of Elyon. Essays on Palestinian Life and Literature in Honor of G.W. Ahlström.* (JSOTS 31) Sheffield 1984, pp. 139–158. See further M. Rose, *Deuteronomist und Jahwist. Untersuchungen zu den Berührungspunkten beider Literaturwerke.* (AThANT 67) Zürich 1981; A.D.H. Mayes, *The Story of Israel*, pp. 139ff.; R. Rendtorff, *Das Alte Testament*, pp. 166–173; E. Blum, *Studien zur Komposition des Pentateuch*; J. Wagenaar, Crossing of the Sea of Reeds (Exod. 13–14) and the Jordan (Josh. 3–4). A Priestly Framework for the Wilderness Wandering, in M. Vervenne (ed.), *The Book of Exodus. Redaction-Reception-Interpretation.* (BETL 126), Leuven 1996, pp. 461–470; and further the thematic survey 'Der Jahwist als Vorhalle des dtr Geschichtswerkes?' in K. Bieberstein, *Josua-Jordan-Jericho*, pp. 42–47.

[101] Thus C. Westermann, *Die Geschichtsbücher des Alten Testaments. Gab es ein deuteronomistisches Geschichtswerk?* (TB 87) Gütersloh 1994; E.A. Knauf, L''Historiographie deutéronomiste' (DtrG) existe-t-elle? in A. de Pury, Th. Römer. J.-D. Macchi (éds.), *Israël construit son histoire. L'historiographie deutéronomiste à la lumière des recherches récentes* (Le Monde de la Bible 34) Genève 1996, pp. 409–418; and H.N. Rösel, *Von Josua bis Jojachin. Untersuchungen zu den deuteronomistischen Geschichtsbüchern des Alten Testaments.* (SVT 75) Leiden/New York/Köln 1999.

4.2.4.1 *An Exilic Dtr_2-Redaction of a Pre-Exilic Dtr_1 (or DtrL) Composition?*

Whereas for M. Noth the whole DtrH was an aetiology of the Exile, F.M. Cross argues that the Exile is only a sub-theme alongside the main themes of Kings, i.e. the exaltation of the house of David, which finds a first crystallisation in Nathan's oracle (2 Sam. 7) and its climax in the description of the reign of king Josiah as contrasted (see already 1 Kgs. 13:2–3) with the rejection of the house of Jeroboam and Northern Israel, culminating into 2 Kgs. 17:7–23.[102] As a result, the bulk of DtrH must have been written during the reign of king Josiah, whereas a second Deuteronomistic edition of this work (Dtr_2) must be held responsible for bringing the work up to date with the Exile and for a minimal retouching of the first edition (Dtr_1) in which the theme of the exile was interspersed.[103]

R.D. Nelson applied this thesis to Joshua and finds in the presentation of the figure of Joshua a thinly disguised allusion to King Josia.[104] He bases his argument on the thematic connections with respect to [1] the very prominent role of the book of the *torah* in Josh. 1:7–8, 8:30–35, 23, Deut. 17:18–19 (the law for the King to read continously from the copy of the book of the *torah*), 1 Kgs. 2:3 (David's testament to Solomon), and especially 2 Kgs. 22–23,[105] [2] the king-like portayal of Joshua in the passages describing his smooth

[102] F.M. Cross, *Canaanite Myth and Hebrew Epic*, pp. 274–289: Chapter 10: 'The Themes of the Book of Kings and the Structure of the Deuteronmistic History.' A similar view had already been proposed by A. Kuenen, *Historisch-critisch onderzoek*², pp. 448ff. See further the recent reviews of critical scholarship with respect to the DtrH in the review articles in *Theologische Rundschau* by H. Weippert, Das deuteronomistische Geschichtswerk: Sein Ziel und Ende in der neueren Forschung, *ThR* 50 (1985), pp. 213–249; and by H.D. Preuß, Zum deuteronomistischen Geschichtswerk, in *ThR* 58 (1993), pp. 226–264, 341–395; and E. Noort, *Das Buch Josua*, pp. 36–42: '3.1.2. Das deuteronomistische Geschichtswerk.'

[103] Thus, according to F.M. Cross, The Themes of the Book of Kings, p. 287: Deut. 4:27–31; 28:36f.63–66; 29;27; 30:1–10; Josh. 23:11–13, 15–16; 1 Sam. 12:25; 1 Kgs. 2:4; 6:11–13; 8:25b, 46–53; 9:4–9; 2 Kgs. 17:19; 20:17ff.; 21:2–15.

[104] R.D. Nelson, Josiah in the Book of Joshua, in *JBL* 100 (1981), pp. 531–540. Recent support of this thesis, has been offered by L.L. Rowlett, *Joshua and the Rhetoric of Violence. A New Historicist Analysis.* (JSOTS 226) Sheffield 1996, who draws parallels between the חזק ואמץ-expressions and Neo-Assyrian military vocabulary; see, however, the criticism of E. Noort, *Das Buch Josua*, p. 124.

[105] Apart from the nine occurrences in Joshua (1:7.8; 8:31.32.34; 22:5, 23:6 and 24:26) and the four times in 2 Kgs. 22–23 (22:8.11, 23:24.25), the *torah* is mentioned in Deuteronomy—2 Kings some 22 times in Deuteronomy, and elsewhere only sporadically, i.e. in 2 Sam. 7:19, 1 Kgs. 2:3, 2 Kgs. 10:31, 14:6; 17:13.34.37.

'dynastic' succession in Moses' role as leader of the people and his installation (Josh. 1:1–9), and the subsequent loyalty pledge of the people (Josh. 1:16–18), [3] his leading role in mediating the covenant during the Ebal-Gerizim episode (Josh. 8:30–35, to be compared with Josiah's covenant mediation between Yhwh and the people, 2 Kgs. 23:1–3), and [4] the exclusive connection between Joshua and Josiah with respect to the celebration of the Passover festival (in Deuteronomy—2 Kings only in Deut. 16, Josh. 5:10–12 and 2 Kgs. 23:21–23). Yet, as Bieberstein has pointed out in his discussion of Nelson's thesis,[106] this argument is to some extent based on a theory developed outside the book of Joshua (i.e. the book of Kings) and to a large extent on passages that are not integral part of the DtrH, but are later DtrN (Josh. 1:7–8, 8:30–35?, 23, 1 Kgs. 2:3) and RedP (Josh. 5:10–12) additions.[107]

Nevertheless, the age of Josiah with the possible expansion of Judah into the former Assyrian provinces Samaria and Gileʿad and beyond as attempts to restore the ideal of the Davidic empire after the collapse of the Assyrian empire,[108] the restructuring of Judah's districts under Josiah's rule which seems to be crystallised in parts of the lists of Judah and Benjamin in Joshua 15:20–63, 18:21–28, (19),[109] as well as the policy of unification of the cult might well provide a historical context for the Deuteronomistic presentation of the Joshua narratives as a succesful conquest by a unified Israel under the sole pious leadership of Joshua, as plausible as the age of the Exile in which the DtrH version of Joshua is understood as an optimistic,

---

[106] K. Bieberstein, *Josua-Jordan-Jericho*, pp. 53–54, 384–386: 'Josua als Spiegelbild Josias?'

[107] One might add that even if Joshua is portrayed by the Deuteronomistic author after the model of King Josiah, this does not necessarily imply that the Deuteronomistic Joshua layer was contemporaneous with its actual model. One would expect to find a Deuteronomistic evaluation of Joshua in which these links are made explicit, rather than a series of covert allusions.

[108] Thus according to 2 Kgs. 23, which describes Josiah's cult-reforming activities in Bethel and the province of Samaria, and his opposition in Megiddo. This might presuppose that he had reconquered these territories, although caution is necessary. See the introductions to the history of Israel in the pre-Christian period, e.g. H. Donner, *Geschichte des Volkes Israel und seine Nachbarn in Grundzugen* 2. Göttingen 1986, pp. 349–350; and J.A. Soggin, *An Introduction to the History of Israel and Judah.* London 1993², p. 256ff.

[109] A. Alt, Judas Gaue unter Josia, in *Palästina-Jahrbuch* 21 (1925), pp. 100–116, reprinted in idem, *Kleine Schriften* II, pp. 76–89; M. Noth, *Das Buch Josua*², pp. 13–15.

but irrealistic program of restoration. Nevertheless, a full assessment of these questions is clearly beyond the scope of this study.[110]

More important for our investigation concerning the literary stratification and possible redaction-historical background for the editorial differences between the ancient textual witnesses of Joshua, is the distinction between the two literary layers Dtr_1 and Dtr_2 within the book. Whereas Cross ascribes to the Exilic update of Dtr_1 only those passages that blatantly reflect the Exilic situation and found such a passage in Joshua only in 23:11–13.15–16,[111] other American scholars such as R.G. Boling[112] and B. Peckham[113] have developed a double-redaction model that assigns far more portions to Dtr_2. Unfortunately, this alleged Exilic second Deuteronomistic update of the pre-Exilic Deuteronomistic version of the Joshua narratives lacks a recognizable ideological, thematic and idiomatic profile as far as Joshua is concerned, and as a result, the two models differ drastically from one another.[114]

---

[110] Recent studies increasingly tend to combine the Harvard and Göttingen schools by dating DtrH to the age of Josiah (cf. Dtr_1) while allowing for an Exilic or post-Exilic DtrN redaction, thus e.g. A.D.H. Mayes, *The Story of Israel*, p. 136; R. Rendtorff, *Das Alte Testament*, p. 198; M.A. O'Brien, *The Deuteronomistic History Hypothesis*, pp. 288ff.; E. Cortese, Theories Concerning Dtr: A Possible Rapprochment, in C. Brekelmans, J. Lust (eds.), *Pentateuchal and Deuteronomistic Studies*, pp. 179–189. K. Bieberstein, *Josua-Jordan-Jericho*, p. 386, also leaves open the possiblity of a late pre-Exilic date of the first Deuteronomistic layer.

[111] F.M. Cross, The Themes of the Book of Kings, p. 287; Cross' view has been accepted by R.E. Friedman, *The Exile and Biblical Narrative. The Formation of the Deuteronomistic and* Priestly *Works*. (HSM 22) Chico 1981.

[112] R.G. Boling, (G.E. Wright), *Joshua* (AB 6) New York/London/Toronto/Sydney/Auckland 1982, pp. 133–134; and R.G. Boling, Joshua, Book of, in D.N. Freedman, G.A. Merion, D.F. Graf, J.D. Pleins, A.B. Beck (eds.), *The Anchor Bible Dictionary. Vol. 3. H.-J.* New York/London/Toronto/Sydney 1992, pp. 1002–1014.

[113] B. Peckham, The Composition of Joshua 3–4, in CBQ 46 (1984), pp. 413–431; and idem, The *Composition of the Deuteronomistic History*. (HSM 35) Atlanta 1985.

[114] R.G. Boling, *Joshua*, p. 133, and Joshua (1992), pp. 1013ff. ascribes Dtr_2 to Levitical refugees from the North after 721 BCE, who introduced supplementary (in part northern) historical material into the Dtr_1 version of Joshua, and altered the southern Aaronic Dtr_1 version from a straightforward propaganda document for King Josiah into a tragi-comical work. Boling ascribes the following passages from Joshua to Dtr_2: Josh. 1:12–2:24; 3:17–4:9; 4:12–5:12; 6:22–25; 8:3–11.20–25.30–35; 9:16–27; 10:12–15; 12–14; 17:3–6; 19:51–21:42; 22–23.

To B. Peckham, *The Composition of the Deuteronomistic History*, Dtr_1 was the successor of J. The work was composed during the reign of king Hezekiah and antedates P, whereas Dtr_2 comes very close to M. Noth's Exilic final compiler of all Israelitic pre-Exilic historical material. Peckham ascribes to Dtr_2: Josh. 1:1b^{b}.5b^{b}.6–18; 2:9b–11.12b^{b}.17–21.24b; 3:1–4.6–10a.11–16a; 4:1–24; 5:1–15; 6:1.3–16a.17–19.20a^{b}.b^{a}.21.23a^{b}.24.25a^{b}.26–27; 7:1–26; 8:2a^{b}.3b^{b}.5b.6a^{b}.8.9a^{b}.9–10.11b–15.17–18?.19a^{a}*.19b–35; 9:1–2.6–7.9a^{b}–11.14.15a^{b}.15b–27; 10:1a^{a}*.4b.6–7.9b.10b–43; 11:2–4;

A variant of this American model of a Josianic Dtr_1 edition of Joshua, possibly augmented by an Exilic Dtr_2 edition, has been offered by N. Lohfink who reconstructs a Deuteronomistic *Landnahme* layer (DtrL), ranging from Deut. 1—Josh. 22, based on the combination of the laws from Deuteronomy with the theme of the conquest of the land as expressed by a distinctive use of the verb ירשׁ Qal with the Promised Land as object.[115] According to Lohfink, this text segment dates from the reign of Josiah and was intended to offer a theological legitimation of Josiah's cult reform and northern conquests, composed as counterpropaganda to the Assyrian conquest ideology. Still during Josiah's reign, according to Lohfink, it was incorporated into a DtrH that extended to 2 Kgs. 23:25. This pristine DtrH was on its turn edited by DtrN, in which Lohfink includes the book of Deuteronomy (e.g., Deut. 6:17–19; 8:1, 11:8.22–25).[116] Lohfink's model can be viewed as a balanced compromise between the Göttingen (Smend) and Harvard (Cross) schools. Since this DtrL coincides with the DtrH layer (i.e. without the DtrN additions), Lohfink's DtrL model has more implications for the literary stratification of the whole of the Deuteronomistic history than for the stratification in Joshua. Unfortunately, the basis for this distinctive layer is not very large: a single, though dominant expression (ירשׁ Qal). The exclusive usage in Deut. 1—Josh. 22 happens to concur with the character of the narratives, in which the conquest of the land is more or less confined to this text segment.

11:6b.8*.9–17.19–22.23ab[b] as well as the whole of chapters 12–24 (and the complete book of Judges). As H.-D. Preuß, in his review article on recent studies 'Zum deuteronomistischen Geschichtswerk', pp. 250–251, remarks, Peckham's work is thetic and lacks argumentation.

Interestingly, in his recent 1997 commentary on Joshua for the Old Testament Library series, R.D. Nelson dismisses the possibility of a second Deuteronomistic redaction of Joshua and leaves open the question of the date of the single Deuteronomistic Joshua composition, see R.D. Nelson, *Joshua* (OTL) Louisville 1997, pp. 5ff., and p. 259, n. 6, where Cross' stratification of Josh. 23 is dismissed.

[115] N. Lohfink, Kerygmata des deuteronomistischen Geschichtswerks, in J. Jeremias, L. Perlitt (Hg.), *Die Botschaft und die Boten. FS H.W. Wolff.* Neukirchen 1981, pp. 87–100, reprinted in idem, *Studien zum Deuteronomium und zur deuteronomistischen Literatur* 2. Stuttgart 1991, pp. 125–142; N. Lohfink, יָרַשׁ *jāraš* יְרֵשָׁה *j^e^rešāh*, יְרֻשָּׁה *j^e^ruššāh*, מוֹרָשׁ *môrāš*, מוֹרָשָׁה *môrašāh*, in *ThWAT* III, col. 953–985. See further K. Bieberstein, *Josua-Jordan-Jericho*, pp. 49–50; E. Noort, *Das Buch Josua*, p. 38.

[116] N. Lohfink, Kerygmata, pp. 98ff. (= 138ff.). Within Deuteronomy, Lohfink (pp. 100ff. = 141ff.) detects an even younger, post-DtrN redactor, DtrÜ (berarbeiter) in Deut. 7, 8, and 9:1–8.22–24 reacting to DtrN.

4.2.4.2 *Additional (Post-)Deuteronomistic Redactions?*

Another redactional layer, reconstructed basically on the basis of the book of Kings, but compatible with the DtrH and DtrN stages, and an integral part of the Göttingen model, is that of a prophetic Deuteronomistic layer (DtrP), developed by a student of R. Smend Jr., W. Dietrich.[117] Within the books of Samuel and Kings Dietrich discerns a layer distinct from both the original DtrH composition and the younger DtrN layer. According to Dietrich, the aim of this redactor was to connect prophecy with history. As for Joshua, Dietrich ascribes only the short notice containing Joshua's curse over the rebuilder of Jericho, Josh. 6:26, which prepares for 1 Kgs. 16:34, to this DtrP.[118] In spite of recent support for this assigning Josh. 6:26 to DtrP,[119] the DtrP-thesis itself is increasingly called into question.[120]

Recent redaction-critical studies of Joshua 6 by L. Schwienhorst and K. Bieberstein have tried to identify additional minor redactions of DtrH, which likewise have a relatively small textual and conceptual basis and which have not yet received much acclaim in critical scholarship. Bieberstein discerns an independent literary stratum in the passages dealing with the participation of the Trans-Jordanian tribes, Reuben, Gad and half-Manasseh in Deut. 3:18–20, Josh. 1:12–15, 4:12–13 and 22:1–4.6 (hence DtrR[euben]) and in the theme of divine rest (מְנוּחָה), already established by Joshua's dismissal of these tribes in Josh. 22 as opposed to the rival DtrH conception in which the verb נוח Hiph'il finds its climax in the dedication of the temple of Solomon (Deut. 12:9–10—1 Kgs. 8:56).[121] Whereas in the older DtrH-presentation of the land the Jordan was considered the real

[117] W. Dietrich, *Prophetie und Geschichte*. Important foundations for this thesis were laid by G. von Rad, Die deuteronomistische Geschichtstheologie in den Königsbüchern, in idem, *Deuteronomium-Studien. Teil B.* (FRLANT 40) Göttingen 1947, pp. 52–64, reprinted in idem, *Gesammelte Studien zum Alten Testament* I, pp. 189–204; and A. Jepsen, *Die Quellen des Königsbuches*. Halle 1956².

[118] W. Dietrich, *Prophetie und Geschichte*, pp. 110–112.

[119] Hence L. Schwienhorst, *Die Eroberung Jerichos*, pp. 99–103, extends the DtrP-layer of the chapter to verse 21b and 24a. K. Bieberstein, *Josua-Jordan-Jericho*, p. 290, pp. 394–397: V.4.4. 'Der Fluch über den Wiederbauer von Jericho (DtrP)' ascribes only Josh. 6:26 to DtrP.

[120] Thus e.g. H.D. Preuß, Zum deuteronomistischen Geschichtswerk, pp. 388ff.

[121] K. Bieberstein, *Josua-Jordan-Jericho*, pp. 387–390: '4.2. Die Beteiligung von Ruben, Gad und Halb-Manasse (DtrR)' based on the semantic study of נוח Hiph'il I by G. Braulik, Zur deuteronomistischen Konzeption von Freiheit und Frieden, in J.A. Emerton (ed.), *Congress Volume. Salamanca 1983* (SVT 36) Leiden 1985, pp. 29–39.

border of Israel (throughout Deuteronomy and Joshua), this layer of additions seeks to re-integrate the Trans-Jordanian territories that had been lost to the Assyrians since 733 BCE.[122] Although Bieberstein underpins his redaction by literary-critical observations,[123] a real and overall ideological distinction between the main Deuteronomistic layer and these passages seems to be absent.

Bieberstein has offered another original contribution to the study of the literary history of Joshua by describing a number of aetiological phrases and passages in the book, not as the tradition-historical nucleus from which basically a-historical narratives developed (as had been the dominant view concerning the origins of the narratives of Josh. 2–11 since Gressmann, Alt and Noth),[124] but as the result of a minimal, late, post-RedP redaction.[125] Bieberstein traces this redaction in [1] Josh. 4:9 (the relocation of the stones from outside the Jordan [4:8//4:20] into the midst of the Jordan), [2] Josh. 5:9 (the connection of the circumcision with Gilgal), [3] Josh. 6:25, [4] Josh. 7:24.25ab$^{\alpha}$.26a$^{\alpha}$.b, [5] Josh. 8:28–29, [6] 9:27, and [7] 10:27. Marked by the aetiological formula עד היום הזה, a post-exilic redaction dating from the time of Nehemiah and Ezra sought to connect localities constituting the Judaean territory in the Persian period (as reflected by the lists of returning exiles [Ezra 2/Neh. 7] and participants in the rebuilding of the walls of Jerusalem [Neh. 3]), with the ancient conquest narratives. In doing so, this very late redactor initiated a trend to aetiologize originally non-aetiological narratives, a trend that can be traced troughout the ancient textual witnesses (LXX and Targumim) and early Christian pelgrimage accounts.

Yet another marginal, late redaction, according to Schwienhorst and Bieberstein, seeks to anchor the institution of the temple treasure into the narrative of the fall of Jericho (6:19.24). The separation of these verses, to which Schwienhorst assigned a few additional phrases from Joshua 6 with the expression תקע הַכֹּהֲנִים בַּשּׁוֹפָרוֹת (Josh. 6:4b, 16aß. and 20aß) as well, is based on the observation that the

[122] K. Bieberstein, *Josua-Jordan-Jericho*, pp. 387–388.

[123] K. Bieberstein, *Josua-Jordan-Jericho*, pp. 98–99 (Josh. 1:12–15), and 182–183 (Josh. 4:12–13).

[124] H. Gressmann, *Die Anfänge Israels 2. Von 2 Mose bis Richter und Ruth* (SAT I.2) Göttingen 1914; A. Alt, Josua, in idem, *Kleine Schriften* I, pp. 176–192; and M. Noth, *Das Buch Josua*, pp. 11–13. See further the thematic survey in K. Bieberstein, *Josua-Jordan-Jericho*, pp. 58–63: '3.2. Die Landnahmeerzählungen als Ätiologien'.

[125] K. Bieberstein, *Josua-Jordan-Jericho*, pp. 418–427.

theme of the temple treasure features almost exclusively in Ezra, Nehemia and Chronicles.[126] Finally, an even younger, relatively substantial redaction (of Joshua 6) is postulated by Schwienhorst, in which concepts from the tradition behind the Qumran War Scroll are introduced into the Jericho narrative.[127] Such a redaction, however, can only be postulated if one is willing to place the origins of the War Scroll early in the second century BCE[128] and allows for a younger date of LXX-Joshua, since most of these alleged additions are reflected by the Greek Joshua.

Apart from the last problem, the recognition of these late marginal redactions is problematic because these theories have been developed on the basis of a relatively small text segment within Joshua (Schwienhorst's layers are reconstructed solely on the basis of Josh. 6, DtrP is found in Joshua only in a single verse), because they are supported by only a limited number of distinctive interests (e.g. the integration of the Trans-Jordanian territories and tribes in the case of DtrR) concepts and expressions (אוצר יהוה in the case of Red-Chron, ירש Qal in the case of DtrL and נוח in the case of DtrR), while clear contrasts with other redactional layers (for example regarding the organisation of the people in RedP *vis-à-vis* DtrH) are absent. So far, these alleged additional layers have been recognized by only a single scholar or small group of scholars, and thus lack support from a large group of scholars. For our purpose it may

---

[126] L. SCHWIENHORST, *Die Eroberung Jerichos*, pp. 125–135; K. BIEBERSTEIN, *Josua-Jordan-Jericho*, pp. 427–430.

[127] In Josh. 6:4a^{a}.5a^{a}.6b.8–9.10a^{β}.13.15$a^{\beta *}$.b.

[128] The original composition, scope and date of the War Scroll is disputed. Y. YADIN, *The Scroll of the Sons of Light against the sons of Darkness*. Oxford 1962, saw Roman warfare practices reflected in this Qumran composition, and as a consequence dated the War Scroll to the end of the first century BCE. Yet, among the 4Q scrolls manuscripts of this composition dating from the first half of the first century BCE came to light, which required an adjustment of Yadin's theory; see D. DIMANT, Qumran Sectarian Literature, in M.E. STONE (ed.), *Jewish Writings of the Second Temple Period. Apocrypha, Pseudepigrapha, Qumran Sectarian Writings, Philo, Josephus*. (CRINT II/2) Assen/Philadelphia 1984, pp. 483–550, especially 516–517; and J. DUHAIME, War Scroll (1QM = 1Q33, 4Q491–496 = 4QM1–6; 4Q397), in J.H. CHARLESWORTH (ed.), *The Dead Sea Scrolls. Hebrew, Greek, and Aramaic Texts with English Translation. Volume 2. Damascus Document, War Scroll, and Related Documents*. Tübingen/Louisville 1995, pp. 80–203, especially pp. 83–84. H. STEGEMANN, *The Library of Qumran. On the Essenes, Qumran, John the Baptist, and Jesus*. Grand Rapids/Cambridge/Leiden/New York/Köln 1998, pp. 102–104, dates the core of this composition to the years after 170 BCE.

be sufficient to have noted these theories and discuss them further only where needed in the following chapters.

4.3 Conclusion

It seems safe to conclude that the redaction of the book of Joshua consisted of basically three stages: [1] a Deuteronomistic reformulation of older pre-Deuteronomistic (written ?) narratives, [2] a nomistic redaction of the Deuteronomistic sections, and [3] a Priestly redaction. Although the number of these and additional literary stages differ in the various redaction-critical models discussed above, and the attribution of individual sections in Joshua to one of these layers may not always be the same in all redaction-critical studies, it is possible to point to a consensus among modern critical scholars with respect to the existence of these three layers. For the sake of clarity with respect to the further discussion, I will give a short, not exhaustive list of the passages attributed to these three redactions, based on the previous discussion. The following discussion in chapters 6–9 will bring some additions to this list.

DtrH Josh. 1:1–6.9.10–18;[129] 10:28–43; 11:16–20; 12:1–6;[130] 14:6–15;[131] 18:2–10?;[132] 22:1–4.6–8.

DtrN Josh. 1:7–8; 13:2–6; 22:5; 23:1–16.[133]

RedP Josh. 4:19; 7:1.10–26; 9:14.15b; 17:3–6; 18:1; 19:51; 20:1–3.9; 21:1–42; 22:9–34; 24:33.

---

[129] See sections 6.3–4 below.

[130] On the Deuteronomistic (DtrH) origin of Joshua 12, see J. Hollenberg, Die deuteronomische Bestandtheile, p. 499ff.; A. Kuenen, *Historisch-critisch onderzoek*², pp. 129, 132–133; M. Noth, *Überlieferungsgeschichtliche Studien*, pp. 44–45, idem, *Das Buch Josua*, pp. 9, 69ff.; S. Mowinckel, *Tetrateuch-Pentateuch-Hexateuch*, pp. 48ff. ascribed the list of the defeated kings to P, as did H. Holzinger, *Das Buch Josua*, pp. xiiff., 46ff. Conversely, V. Fritz, *Das Buch Josua*, pp. 126ff. ascribes Josh. 12:1a.9–24 to DtrH, and ascribes the intermediary verses 12:1b.2.4–5.7 to his RedD, whereas verses 1bß.3.6.8 would in his view consitute even younger redactional additions. Scholars who deny the DtrH character of verses 1–8 do so on the basis of the alleged tension between these verses and the preceding Deuteronomistic conclusion in Joshua 11, although they have to acknowledge the DtrH idiom (e.g., ירשה in 12:6.7).

[131] Because of its Deuteronomistic expressions and its explicit connections with the Deuteronomistic version of the spy narrative in Deut. 1:19–46, the first Caleb narrative, Josh. 14:6–15, is generally recognized as the Deuteronomistic parallel to the probably pre-Dtr. rival account in Josh. 15:13–19 [*]//Judg. 1:11–15.20, thus e.g. A. KUENEN, *Historisch-critisch onderzoek*[2], (1886), p. 129, 134; M. NOTH, *Überlieferungsgeschichtliche Studien*, p. 44 (Noth placed 14:6aßb–15 between 11:21–23a and 11:23b [= 14:15b]); S. MOWINCKEL, *Tetrateuch-Pentateuch-Hexateuch*, (1964), p. 44; A.G. AULD, *Studies in Joshua* (1976), pp. 210–214 (DtrN); E. CORTESE, *Josua 13–19*, (1990), pp. 87–88; and V. FRITZ, *Das Buch Josua* (1994), pp. 149–154 (RedD).

[132] The proper redaction-historical background of Josh. 18:2–10 is hard to determine; see the commentaries and monographs mentioned in the previous note and the extensive recent discussion by J.C. DE VOS, *Das Los Judas*, pp. 185–208. Priestly language and concepts are clearly discernible only in verse 18:1, whereas the other verses clearly employ Deuteronomistic expressions (e.g., verse 3). For these reasons, I tentatively ascribe only verse 1 to RedP, and the other verses to DtrH.

[133] See section 4.2.2 above.

CHAPTER FIVE

TEXTUAL AND LITERARY CRITICISM

5.1 A STUDY OF THE LITERARY FORMATION OF THE HEBREW TEXT *IN ITS OWN RIGHT*

The basic premise of the present study is that if textual and literary criticism would overlap, as argued by Tov, Ulrich, Mazor, Rofé and others (see sections 1.2 and 2.2), such an overlap should be demonstrated on the basis of independent textual and literary analyses of the same section. If textual data point to subsequent redactions of a given text, it might be expected that a literary-critical analysis of the same passage *in its own right* results in the same conclusions as those reached by an interpretation of the textual data. Textual and literary criticism should be iuxtaposed, not subordinated to one another.

It is this convergence of the two sets of data that make the case of Joshua 20 such an important example for the possibility of such an overlap, as demonstrated by Hollenberg, Rofé and others. Yet, most of the other passages in Joshua, for which such an overlap between textual and literary criticism has been claimed, are less clear-cut. Since the textual data in Joshua are no less problematic and ambiguous than the literary-critical information provided by literary tensions and distinctive sets of ideas and phraseology (see sections 2.2 and 3.2), the oldest textual witnesses of the book, LXX and 4QJoshua[a], can not simply be regarded as starting point for redaction-critical operations in the MT.[1] Nor is a selective use of redaction-critical data, provided by relatively old studies of Driver and Weinfeld,[2] sufficient to demonstrate the secondary character of a plus in MT. As Bieberstein makes clear, textual and literary criticism are two distinct approaches to the text:[3]

---

[1] See sections 2.2.3–7 above.

[2] Thus E. Tov, The Growth of the Book of Joshua.

[3] K. BIEBERSTEIN, *Josua-Jordan-Jericho*, pp. 72–73.

> Denn es handelt sich bei der Abgrenzung zwischen Text- und Literarkritik weder um eine Abgrenzung verschiedener Perioden noch um eine Klassifizierung verschieden motivierter Veränderungen, sondern um Arbeitstechniken (denn Methoden sind nichts anderes als Arbeitstechniken, die durch Kriterien und Fragehinsichten definiert werden können), weshalb ihre gegenseitige Abgrenzung auch allein unter dem Aspekt verschiedener Arbeitstechniken erfolgen muß.

As stated in section 4.1 above, a real discussion between the two disciplines still lies ahead. Modern literary-critical scholars, perhaps puzzled by the confusing amount of data and theories coming up from the field of textual criticism, tend to ignore the new text-critical insights. Recent German commentaries to Joshua by Görg and Fritz simply disregard the data from LXX and Qumran.[4] On the other hand, scholars like Tov, Rofé and Mazor make use of redaction-critical terms like 'Deuteronomistic', 'Priestly', and 'nomistic', without taking into account modern developments in redaction-critical research. If the final edition of Joshua attested by MT *vis-à-vis* LXX would contain Deuteronomistic and nomistic additions, the question arises how this nomistic-Deuteronomistic redaction relates to the nomistic (DtrN) and Deuteronomistic (DtrH) literary strata of the book.

A literary-critical analysis of the book of Joshua as a whole has shown that it is possible to discern at least three clearly distinctive literary strata of the book: [0] a pre-Deuteronomistic layer, [1] a Deuteronomistic layer (DtrH; see section 4.2.1 above), [2] a nomistic redaction (DtrN; see section 4.2.2 above), and [3] a Priestly redaction (RedP; see section 4.2.3 above). The first sobering statement to be made here is, that these strata are by and large attested by all extent textual witnesses. It is clear that these main literary strata formed part of the book of Joshua long before the alleged re-edition (Holmes, Tov) attested by MT *vis-à-vis* LXX and 4QJosh[a] took place. Relatively late additions such as Joshua 17 (RedP) Joshua 21 (RedP) and Joshua 23 (DtrN) are by and large represented by LXX and 4QJosh[b]. Ideally, the Qumran scrolls would contain a version of Joshua without these literary strata, just as the claim of an overlap between textual and literary data would have been strengthened, had we had possession of a version of the Pentateuch without the

[4] M. Görg, *Josua.* (Die neue Echter Bibel) Würzburg 1991; V. Fritz, *Das Buch Josua*, p. 2.

Priestly additions, or a version of Isaiah without the Deutero- and Trito-Isaian additions (Isaiah 40–66), which is evidently not the case.

Nevertheless, it may be possible that the ancient witnesses attest to a literary stratum that came after these main literary strata. If that were the case, it should be possible to detect a coherent pattern of distinctive ideas and interests expressed by a distinctive vocabulary, in the same way as the DtrH, DtrN, and RedP strata in the book are traceable on the basis of their distinctive theology and phraseology. In this sense, the preceding chapter has helped us to formulate an answer to the question of valid literary-critical criteria for distinguishing a separate literary stratum. Not every instance of literary tension or repetition in the text points to a redactional expansion. This is only the case when a coherent pattern of distinctive ideas and interests expressed by a distinctive vocabulary is apparent. If the variants do not reflect a coherent pattern, there is no way of telling whether they are individual textual alterations or elements of an otherwise unidentifiable redaction. If the pluses in MT do not express a distinctive theology and phraseology it becomes hard to argue that they are part of a literary stratum that should be distinguished from their context.

It should be noted that Tov and others do not employ the term 'redaction', but rather 'edition'. Yet, Tov's definition of an edition as a set of 'large-scale differences displaying a certain coherence . . . created at the level of the literary growth of the books by persons who considered themselves actively involved in the literary process of the composition'[5] corresponds closely to that of a 'redaction' as formulated above. The preceding paragraph may also help us to obtain a clearer picture of the literary formation of the passages that will be discussed below.

In the following chapters, four passages from Joshua have been selected as test cases: Joshua 1 is supposed to contain a large amount of smaller Deuteronomistic pluses in MT *vis-à-vis* LXX and therefore provides an interesting case to start with (chapter 6). The wide divergencies between MT—LXX—4QJosh[a] in Josh. 5:2–9 serve as one of the main pillars for Samuel Holmes' thesis of a revision of a Hebrew text attested by LXX towards the present MT. The passage has received considerable attention by the scholars mentioned

[5] E. Tov, *Textual Criticism of the Hebrew Bible*, p. 314.

in section 2.2, and presents another interesting test case. In Josh. 5:10–12, Auld detects Priestly additions in MT, so that these verses will be included in the discussion in chapter 7 below. Because 4QJoshua[a] seems to differ markedly from MT in Josh. 8:1–29 and from LXX in 8:30–35, these passages will be discussed in chapters 8 and 9 below.

The method followed in these sections is that of keeping text-critical and literary-critical hypotheses separate as long as possible, in order to find out whether or not the results of an autonomous literary-critical analysis of the passages confirm the hypotheses regarding the formation of the passages developed on the basis of the text-critical data. This method develops the approach followed by A. Rofé, A. van der Kooij and K. Bieberstein for Joshua 20 and Joshua 6, respectively.

The procedure in this study is therefore the following: after an introductory passage, presenting the textual and literary problems inherent in the passage and a critical survey of the research by earlier scholars, the Hebrew text of the passage in question is subjected to a literary-critical analysis in its own right. The textual basis for this analysis will be the MT, since this is the only text that has been preserved completely in Hebrew, but for the sake of methodological clarity the disputed elements in those passages (for the most part the pluses in MT) will be left out of consideration. The aim of this first step is to find out whether or not the thesis of redactional activity attested by the ancient textual witnesses (4QJoshua[a], LXX, and MT) is confirmed by an independent literary-crititical analysis.

5.2 A Study of the Ancient Versions (Septuagint and Qumran) *in their Own Context*

At a second stage, the oldest textual witnesses (LXX and 4QJoshua[a]) will be examined in their own context. As the discussion in chapters 2 and 3 have made clear, caution is needed when using data from the oldest textual witnesses of Joshua for redaction-critical purposes. The redaction-critically relevant variants from the Qumran Joshua scrolls (Joshua 4:1–3 in 4QJosh[b], Josh. 5:2; 8:1–29 and 8:30–35 in 4QJosh[a]) have been established on the basis of a reconstruction of the complete text of the now fragmentary scrolls. As section 3.3 has made clear, the interpretation of such a variant (here in 4QJoshua[b]) can be very different depending on the different attempts to reconstruct the complete lines of the colums of which now only small pieces remain. For the same reason, a careful examination of the reconstruction of the complete text of the 4QJoshua[a] scroll is needed, before data from this highly fragmentary scroll can be used for a literary-critical reconstruction of the formation of Joshua 8 (both Josh. 8:1–29 and 8:30–35), as will be demonstrated in chapters 8 and 9 below.

It is also necessary to study the LXX variants within the context of the Greek Joshua as a whole. Of course, LXX-Joshua is a translation document and for that reason cannot be seen as a purely autonomous Greek composition on its own. Nevertheless, scholars such as J. Hollenberg, A. Dillmann, K. Bieberstein, C.G. den Hertog, J. Moatti-Fine, S. Sipilä, and M. Rösel have pointed out that LXX-Joshua reflects enough literary initiatives to justify a careful contextual analysis of the Greek text.[6] As K. Bieberstein has demonstrated with respect to Joshua 6, there is every reason to examine quantitative and qualitative differences between LXX-Joshua and MT-Joshua in coherence and context. Finally, it should not be forgotten that not only is the Hebrew *Vorlage* of LXX-Joshua a hypothetical entity, but the original Greek translation itself is also the product of a reconstruction on the basis of younger textual witnesses (see section 2.1 above). For that reason, the text of LXX-Joshua as edited by A. Rahlfs should be checked against the data provided by the other two editions of the Greek Joshua (i.e., the Larger Cambridge edition and Margolis' edition).

---

[6] See the methodological discussion regarding a 'contextual approach' to the Greek version *in its own right* A. VAN DER KOOIJ, *The Oracle of Tyre*, pp. 8–19.

CHAPTER SIX

JOSHUA 1: MT—LXX

6.1 Introduction

Joshua 1 relates the divine installation of Joshua (1:2–9), in which Yhwh charges Joshua to cross the river Jordan (1:2), to receive the land—sketched in unusually large proportions (1:4)—as a divine gift (1:3), and to redistribute it to the people (1:6); to remain firm in the face of the coming confrontation (1:5–6) and act carefully according to Moses' instructions (1:7–8). In the second half of the chapter (1:10–18) Joshua first addresses the people through their officials (1:10), commanding them to prepare for the crossing of the river (1:11) and secondly the Trans-Jordanian tribes, who have already received their territories (1:13–15), but nevertheless pledge loyalty to Joshua and all their Israelite brothers to take part in the battle at hand (1:16–18).

As noted above in section 3.4 fragments of verses 9–12 have been preserved in XJoshua. This text corresponds completely to MT. As noted in section 3.5.3 above, 4QApocryphon Joshua[a], fragments 3ii–4 seem to contain allusions to Josh. 1:5–17, but due to their fragmentary state, and owing to their character as rewritten Bible, these fragments must be left out of the following text-critical discussion. Only the Greek version is relevant here. Of the circa 460 lexemes of MT, some 45 are not represented in the original Greek version of the chapter, which amounts to some 10 percent of the text. Since no convincing explanation of scribal error can be adduced for these quantitative variants, it is clear that they must be the result of deliberate literary initiatives, either from the part of an expansionistic Hebrew revisor or from the part of the Greek translator.

Besides these purely quantitative data some qualitative aspects are noteworthy, since patterns of identical or related phrases are discernible: the apposition 'servant of Yhwh' (עבד יהוה) for Moses is absent twice (1:1 and 1:15), whereas Moses himself is absent altogether in verse 14. Likewise, the (Deuteronomistic [DtrH or DtrL]) theme of the conquest of the land (ירשׁ Qal, with הארץ as object) is twice missing from LXX, i.e., in verses 11 and 15. Moreover, the theologically important theme of the *torah* of Moses is absent from LXX-Josh. 1:7. LXX furthermore lacks a number of geographical phrases, such as 'the entire land of the Hittites' (כל ארץ החתים) in 1:4, 'on the other side of the Jordan' (בעבר הירדן), the noun ארץ ('to *the land* of their inheritance') in 1:15, as well as the demonstrative pronoun הזה in 1:2 after הירדן ('cross *this* Jordan') and in 1:4 after הלבנון ('*this* Libanon'). Finally, a number of (other) small textual elements form pluses in MT *vis-à-vis* LXX, such as the prepositional phrases -מ (1:4) -כ, and בו (1:8), לכם (1:11), the conjunction in 1:4 (וְעַד־הנהר), the particles מאד (1:7), כי (1:8), and כן (1:17), as well as the word כל in 1:18 and the direct speech marker לאמר in 1:12.

This chapter will focus primarily on these quantitative variants, as they might reflect the editorial activity of a Hebrew redactor. The following text-critical section (6.2) contains a synopsis of the Hebrew (MT) and Greek texts. Since the tiny fragments of XJoshua correspond completely to MT, the Qumran text has been left out of this synopsis. Minuses in the Greek text are indicated by three lines per Hebrew lexeme. Pluses and variants readings of the Greek text are indicated by italics. The text-critical notes to LXX-Joshua account for the choice of either Rahlfs' or Margolis' critical reconstructions of the original Greek text in cases where the two differ. This section is followed by a redaction-critical analysis of the chapter and a discussion of the individual pluses in MT (section 6.4).

6.2 Text-Critical Analysis

	LXX-Joshua 1 (ed. Rahlfs)	MT-Joshua 1 (ed. BHS)
1:1	Καὶ ἐγένετο μετὰ τὴν τελευτὴν	וַיְהִי אַחֲרֵי מוֹת
	Μωυσῆ --- ---	מֹשֶׁה עֶבֶד יְהוָה
	--- εἶπεν κύριος τῷ Ἰησοῖ υἱῷ Ναυη	וַיֹּאמֶר יְהוָה אֶל־יְהוֹשֻׁעַ בִּן־נוּן
	τῷ ὑπουργῷ Μωυσῆ	מְשָׁרֵת מֹשֶׁה
	λέγων	לֵאמֹר׃
1:2	Μωυσῆς ὁ θεράπων μου τετελεύτηκεν·	מֹשֶׁה עַבְדִּי מֵת
	νῦν *οὖν*	וְעַתָּה
	ἀναστὰς	קוּם
	διάβηθι τὸν Ιορδάνην --- ---,	עֲבֹר אֶת־הַיַּרְדֵּן הַזֶּה
	σὺ καὶ πᾶς ὁ λαὸς οὗτος, εἰς τὴν γῆν	אַתָּה וְכָל־הָעָם הַזֶּה אֶל־הָאָרֶץ
	ἣν ἐγὼ δίδωμι αὐτοῖς --- --- ---.	אֲשֶׁר אָנֹכִי נֹתֵן לָהֶם לִבְנֵי יִשְׂרָאֵל׃
1:3	πᾶς ὁ τόπος,	כָּל־מָקוֹם

	ἐφ᾽ ὃν ἂν ἐπιβῆτε *τῷ ἴχνει τῶν* ποδῶν ὑμῶν,	אֲשֶׁר תִּדְרֹךְ כַּף־רַגְלְכֶם בּוֹ
	ὑμῖν δώσω αὐτόν,	לָכֶם נְתַתִּיו
	ὃν τρόπον εἴρηκα τῷ Μωυσῃ,	כַּאֲשֶׁר דִּבַּרְתִּי אֶל־מֹשֶׁה׃
1[4]	--- τὴν ἔρημον καὶ τὸν *Αντιλίβανον* --- ---	מֵהַמִּדְבָּר וְהַלְּבָנוֹן הַזֶּה
	--- ἕως τοῦ ποταμοῦ τοῦ μεγάλου,	וְעַד־הַנָּהָר הַגָּדוֹל
	ποταμοῦ Εὐφράτου,	נְהַר־פְּרָת
	--- --- --- ---	כֹּל אֶרֶץ הַחִתִּים
	καὶ ἕως τῆς θαλάσσης τῆς *ἐσχάτης*	וְעַד־הַיָּם הַגָּדוֹל
	ἀφ᾽ ἡλίου δυσμῶν	מְבוֹא הַשָּׁמֶשׁ
	ἔσται τὰ ὅρια ὑμῶν.	יִהְיֶה גְּבוּלְכֶם׃
1[5]	οὐκ ἀντιστήσεται ἄνθρωπος	לֹא־יִתְיַצֵּב אִישׁ
	κατενώπιον *ὑμῶν*	לְפָנֶיךָ
	πάσας τὰς ἡμέρας τῆς ζωῆς σου,	כֹּל יְמֵי חַיֶּיךָ
	καὶ ὥσπερ ἤμην μετὰ Μωυσῆ,	כַּאֲשֶׁר הָיִיתִי עִם־מֹשֶׁה
	οὕτως ἔσομαι *καὶ* μετὰ σου,	אֶהְיֶה עִמָּךְ
	καὶ οὐκ *ἐγκαταλείψω* σε	לֹא אַרְפְּךָ
	οὐδὲ *ὑπερόψομαί* σε.	וְלֹא אֶעֶזְבֶךָּ׃
1[6]	ἴσχυε	חֲזַק
	καὶ ἀνδρίζου·	וֶאֱמָץ
	σὺ γὰρ *ἀποδιαστελεῖς* τῷ λαῷ τούτῳ	כִּי אַתָּה תַּנְחִיל אֶת־הָעָם הַזֶּה
	τὴν γῆν,	אֶת־הָאָרֶץ
	ἣν ὤμοσα τοῖς πατράσιν *ὑμῶν*	אֲשֶׁר־נִשְׁבַּעְתִּי לַאֲבוֹתָם
	δοῦναι αὐτοῖς.	לָתֵת לָהֶם׃
1[7]	ἴσχυε *οὖν*	רַק חֲזַק
	καὶ ἀνδρίζου ---	וֶאֱמַץ מְאֹד
	φυλάσσεσθαι	לִשְׁמֹר
	καὶ ποιεῖν --- --- --- ---	לַעֲשׂוֹת כְּכָל־הַתּוֹרָה
	καθότι ἐνετείλατό σοι Μωυσῆς ὁ παῖς μου,	אֲשֶׁר צִוְּךָ מֹשֶׁה עַבְדִּי
	καὶ οὐκ ἐκκλινεῖς ἀπ᾽ *αὐτῶν*	אַל־תָּסוּר מִמֶּנּוּ
	εἰς δεξιὰ οὐδὲ εἰς ἀριστερα,	יָמִין וּשְׂמֹאול
	ἵνα *συνῇς* ἐν πᾶσιν,	לְמַעַן תַּשְׂכִּיל בְּכֹל
	οἷς ἐὰν *πράσσῃς*.	אֲשֶׁר תֵּלֵךְ׃
1[8]	*καὶ* οὐκ ἀποστήσεται ἡ βίβλος	לֹא־יָמוּשׁ סֵפֶר
	τοῦ νόμου *τούτου*	הַתּוֹרָה הַזֶּה
	ἐκ τοῦ στόματός σου,	מִפִּיךָ
	καὶ μελετήσεις ἐν αὐτῷ ἡμέρας καὶ νυκτός,	וְהָגִיתָ בּוֹ יוֹמָם וָלַיְלָה
	ἵνα *εἰδῇς*	לְמַעַן תִּשְׁמֹר
	ποιεῖν --- πάντα τὰ γεγραμμένα --- ---·	לַעֲשׂוֹת כְּכָל־הַכָּתוּב בּוֹ
	--- τότε *εὐοδωθήσῃ* --- --- ---	כִּי־אָז תַּצְלִיחַ אֶת־דְּרָכֶךָ
	καὶ τότε *συνήσεις*.	וְאָז תַּשְׂכִּיל׃
1[9]	*ἰδοὺ* ἐντέταλμαί σοι·	הֲלוֹא צִוִּיתִיךָ
	ἴσχυε	חֲזַק
	καὶ ἀνδρίζου,	וֶאֱמָץ
	μὴ δειλιάσῃς	אַל־תַּעֲרֹץ
	μηδὲ φοβηθῇς,	וְאַל־תֵּחָת
	ὅτι μετὰ σου κύριος ὁ θεός σου *εἰς* πάντα,	כִּי עִמְּךָ יְהוָה אֱלֹהֶיךָ בְּכֹל
	οὗ ἐὰν πορεύῃ.	אֲשֶׁר תֵּלֵךְ׃

		פ
1^{10}	καὶ ἐνετείλατο Ἰησοῦς τοῖς	וַיְצַו יְהוֹשֻׁעַ אֶת־שֹׁטְרֵי הָעָם
	γραμματεῦσιν τοῦ λαοῦ	
	λέγων	לֵאמֹר׃
1^{11}	Εἰσέλθατε κατὰ μέσον	עִבְרוּ בְּקֶרֶב
	τῆς παρεμβολῆς *τοῦ λαοῦ*	הַמַּחֲנֶה
	καὶ ἐντείλασθε τῷ λαῷ	וְצַוּוּ אֶת־הָעָם
	λέγοντες	לֵאמֹר
	Ἑτοιμάζεσθε --- --- ἐπισιτισμόν,	הָכִינוּ לָכֶם צֵידָה
	ὅτι ἔτι τρεῖς ἡμέραι	כִּי בְּעוֹד שְׁלֹשֶׁת יָמִים
	καὶ ὑμεῖς διαβαίνετε τὸν Ιορδάνην τοῦτον	אַתֶּם עֹבְרִים אֶת־הַיַּרְדֵּן הַזֶּה
	εἰσελθόντες	לָבוֹא
	κατασχεῖν τὴν γῆν,	לָרֶשֶׁת אֶת־הָאָרֶץ
	ἣν κύριος ὁ θεὸς *τῶν πατέρων* ὑμῶν	אֲשֶׁר יְהוָה אֱלֹהֵיכֶם
	δίδωσιν ὑμῖν.	נֹתֵן לָכֶם
	--- --- ---	לְרִשְׁתָּהּ׃
		ס
1^{12}	καὶ τῷ Ρουβην καὶ τῷ Γαδ	וְלָרֽאוּבֵנִי וְלַגָּדִי
	καὶ τῷ ἡμίσει φυλῆς Μανασση	וְלַחֲצִי שֵׁבֶט הַמְנַשֶּׁה
	εἶπεν Ἰησοῦς	אָמַר יְהוֹשֻׁעַ
	---	לֵאמֹר׃
1^{13}	Μνήσθητε τὸ ῥῆμα *κυρίου,*	זָכוֹר אֶת־הַדָּבָר
	ὃ ἐνετείλατο ὑμῖν Μωυσῆς ὁ παῖς κυρίου	אֲשֶׁר צִוָּה אֶתְכֶם מֹשֶׁה עֶבֶד־יְהוָה
	λέγων	לֵאמֹר
	Κύριος ὁ θεὸς ὑμῶν κατέπαυσεν ὑμᾶς	יְהוָה אֱלֹהֵיכֶם מֵנִיחַ לָכֶם
	καὶ ἔδωκεν ὑμῖν τὴν γῆν ταύτην.	וְנָתַן לָכֶם אֶת־הָאָרֶץ הַזֹּאת׃
1^{14}	αἱ γυναῖκες ὑμῶν *καὶ* τὰ παιδία ὑμῶν	נְשֵׁיכֶם טַפְּכֶם
	καὶ τὰ κτήνη ὑμῶν κατοικείτωσαν	וּמִקְנֵיכֶם יֵשְׁבוּ
	ἐν τῇ γῇ,	בָּאָרֶץ
	ᾗ ἔδωκεν ὑμῖν --- --- --- --- ---·	אֲשֶׁר נָתַן לָכֶם מֹשֶׁה בְּעֵבֶר הַיַּרְדֵּן
	ὑμεῖς δὲ διαβήσεσθε	וְאַתֶּם תַּעַבְרוּ
	εὔζωνοι πρότεροι τῶν ἀδελφῶν ὑμῶν,	חֲמֻשִׁים לִפְנֵי אֲחֵיכֶם
	πᾶς ὁ ἰσχύων	כֹּל גִּבּוֹרֵי הַחַיִל
	καὶ *συμμαχήσετε* αὐτοῖς,	וַעֲזַרְתֶּם אוֹתָם׃
1^{15}	ἕως ἂν καταπαύσῃ κύριος *ὁ θεὸς ὑμῶν*	עַד אֲשֶׁר־יָנִיחַ יְהוָה
	τοὺς ἀδελφοὺς ὑμῶν ὥσπερ *καὶ* ὑμᾶς	לַאֲחֵיכֶם כָּכֶם
	καὶ κληρονομήσωσιν καὶ οὗτοι τὴν γῆν,	וְיָרְשׁוּ גַם־הֵמָּה אֶת־הָאָרֶץ
	ἣν κύριος ὁ θεὸς *ἡμῶν* δίδωσιν αὐτοῖς·	אֲשֶׁר־יְהוָה אֱלֹהֵיכֶם נֹתֵן לָהֶם
	καὶ ἀπελεύσεσθε *ἕκαστος*	וְשַׁבְתֶּם
	εἰς τὴν --- κληρονομίαν *αὐτοῦ,*	לְאֶרֶץ יְרֻשַּׁתְכֶם
	--- --- ---	וִירִשְׁתֶּם אוֹתָהּ
	ἣν ἔδωκεν ὑμῖν Μωυσῆς --- ---	אֲשֶׁר נָתַן לָכֶם מֹשֶׁה עֶבֶד יְהוָה
	εἰς τὸ πέραν τοῦ Ιορδάνου	בְּעֵבֶר הַיַּרְדֵּן
	ἀπ᾽ ἀνατολῶν ἡλίου.	מִזְרַח הַשָּׁמֶשׁ׃
1^{16}	καὶ *ἀποκριθέντες* τῷ Ἰησοῖ	וַיַּעֲנוּ אֶת־יְהוֹשֻׁעַ
	εἶπαν	לֵאמֹר

	Πάντα,	כֹּ֣ל
	ὅσα ἂν ἐντείλῃ ἡμῖν,	אֲשֶׁר־צִוִּיתָ֨נוּ֙
	ποιήσομεν	נַעֲשֶׂ֔ה
	καὶ εἰς πάντα *τόπον*,	וְאֶל־כָּל־
	οὗ ἐὰν ἀποστείλῃς ἡμᾶς,	אֲשֶׁ֥ר תִּשְׁלָחֵ֖נוּ
	πορευσόμεθα·	נֵלֵֽךְ׃
1^{17}	κατὰ πάντα,	כְּכֹ֤ל
	ὅσα ἠκούσαμεν Μωυσῆ,	אֲשֶׁר־שָׁמַ֙עְנוּ֙ אֶל־מֹשֶׁ֔ה
	--- ἀκουσόμεθα σοῦ,	כֵּ֖ן נִשְׁמַ֣ע אֵלֶ֑יךָ
	πλὴν ἔστω κύριος ὁ θεὸς *ἡμῶν* μετὰ σοῦ,	רַ֠ק יִֽהְיֶ֞ה יְהוָ֤ה אֱלֹהֶ֙יךָ֙ עִמָּ֔ךְ
	ὃν τρόπον ἦν μετὰ Μωυσῆ.	כַּאֲשֶׁ֥ר הָיָ֖ה עִם־מֹשֶֽׁה׃
1^{18}	*ὁ δὲ* ἄνθρωπος,	כָּל־אִ֞ישׁ
	ὃς ἐὰν ἀπειθήσῃ *σοι*	אֲשֶׁר־יַמְרֶ֣ה אֶת־פִּ֗יךָ
	καὶ ὅστις μὴ ἀκούσῃ τῶν ῥημάτων σου ---	וְלֹֽא־יִשְׁמַ֧ע אֶת־דְּבָרֶ֛יךָ לְכֹ֥ל
	καθότι ἂν αὐτῷ ἐντείλῃ,	אֲשֶׁר־תְּצַוֶּ֖נּוּ
	ἀποθανέτω.	יוּמָ֑ת
	ἀλλὰ ἴσχυε	רַ֖ק חֲזַ֥ק
	καὶ ἀνδρίζου.	וֶאֱמָֽץ.
		פ

Text-critical remarks with respect to LXX-Joshua

1:1ff. Ναυη (Rahlfs)] Margolis conjectured that the original Greek text must have read Ναυν, which early in the transmission of the Greek text must have been corrupted into Ναυη as a result of the similarity of N and H.[1] C.G. DEN HERTOG, *Studien*, p. 71, however, points first to the consistency of this name throughout the biblical books (i.e., in LXX-Exodus, LXX-Numbers (11:28 etc.), LXX-Deuteronomy (1:38 etc.), LXX-Joshua, LXX-3 Reg. 16:34, LXX-2 Esdr. 18:17, and LXX-Sir. 46:1), and secondly to the unanimity of the oldest textual witnesses in this respect. Hence Rahlfs' reading is to be preferred.

1:6 ἀποδιαστελεῖς (Rahlfs)] Margolis adopted the (uncorrected) reading of Vaticanus διελεῖς (supported by 129 [E], 376 [P_1], and 72 [M-a]) as the original Greek text, whereas Rahlfs adopted the reading of A.F.M.V.W. and the majority of minuscules (C and P). The first and second correctors of B, supported by mss. 19.56.58, and mss. from Margolis' group S, present a conflated form ἀποδιελεῖς. Both ἀποδιαστέλλω and δι-αιρέω mean *to divide* (LEH p. 49b, 103a; GELS[2], pp. 115b–116a), which differs from the Hebrew נחל Hiphʿil, *to*

[1] See also H.B. SWETE, *Introduction to the Old Testament in Greek*, p. 480, n. 2; S. HOLMES, *Joshua*, p. 17; and R. MEYER in the BHS apparatus: 'G ubique Ναυη (false pro Ναυν).'

give in possession. Whereas the first Greek verb occurs only here in the Greek translations of the books of the Hebrew Bible, the second verb occurs frequently in the (whole) Septuagint. Although the equation נחל—δι-αιρέω recurs in LXX-Josh. 18:4 (καθὰ δεήσει διελεῖν αὐτήν as an interpretation of לפי נחלתם?) and 19:51 (אלה הנחלת—Αὗται αἱ διαρέσεις), the fact that Theodotion (according to the marginal notes in 85.344) used this current expression pleads for the originality of the *lectio difficilior* ἀποδιαστελεῖς, thus C.G. den Hertog, *Studien*, p. 33; *aliter* L.J. Greenspoon, *Textual Studies*, p. 38, who follows Margolis and concludes that Theodotion retained the Old Greek.

1:8 εἰδῇς (Margolis)] συνῇς (Rahlfs). The reading adopted by Margolis containing the verb οἶδα, *to know*, is attested by Codex Vaticanus and readings in the margin of M [C] and 85 [M-n]. The reading adopted by Rahlfs containing the verb συν-ίημι, *to understand*, is attested by the majority of witnesses to LXX-Joshua, including P and C witnesses A.F.M (main text) V.W.Syh^L (ܕܬܬܣܟܠ). Neither of the two readings corresponds to MT למען תשמר (supported by TgJon בְּדִיל דְּתִטַּר, *in order that you may be careful to*, Peš, ܘܬܛܪ, *and you will guard*, and Vg, 'ut custodias', *in order that you may guard*). Minuscule 344 contains in the margin the readings of the recentiores, who employed the verb φυλάσσω, *to guard, to be careful to*, in order to conform the Greek text to the (proto-)MT: ἵνα φυλάσσῃς ποιεῖν κατὰ πάντα τὰ γεγραμμένα (σ', θ') and: ὅπως φυλάσσῃς ποιεῖν κατὰ πάν το γεγραμμένον (α') which is also the reading in LXX-witnesses of the S-group; see L.J. Greenspoon, *Textual Studies*, pp. 84–85, who adopts Margolis' reconstruction. The o'-reading according to this ms. (344) is συνῇς, which seems to be an important argument for C.G. den Hertog, *Studien*, pp. 33–34, to give preference to Rahlfs' reconstruction here. Nevertheless he has to admit that the threefold repetition of the same verb συν-ίημι in verses 7–8 does not really match the varying style of the Greek translator. For this reason I prefer to take the *lectio difficilior* of Codex Vaticanus and Margolis as the original Greek text, rather than a 'stilistische Korrektur' (Den Hertog).

1:8 τότε εὐοδωτήσῃ] Codex Vaticanus (followed by the Sahidic translation and manuscripts from Margolis' C, and M-groups) contains two phrases (τότε εὐοδωθήσῃ καὶ εὐοδώσει τὰς ὁδούς σου, *then you will be succesful and you will make prosperous your ways*) corresponding to the single Hebrew clause כי־אז תצליח את־דרכך, *because then you will bring your way to success.* Rahlfs followed this text, but adopted the reading εὐοδώσεις attested by Codices 129 (E).A.F.M.V.W.Arm. (C) and the majority of the minuscules. Margolis considered the first of the two clauses to be an early addition to the original text εὐοδώσει τὰς ὁδούς σου. This reading is attested by witnesses to the ('Lucianic') S-recension, 19.44.54.75.106.134.VetLat.Syh.

Nevertheless, the secondary origin of this reading is made clear by the alteration of the verb into a first person singular εὐοδώσω.[2] C.G. DEN HERTOG, *Studien*, pp. 83–84, argues that Margolis' reconstruction of the second occurrence of the verb as a third person active εὐοδώσει is weakly supported by the manuscript evidence, and prefers Rahlfs' reconstruction. Although he apparently approves of the qualification of this doublet in the Greek text as 'Doppelübersetzung'[3] and discusses a number of other double translations,[4] none of the parallel places in LXX-Joshua contain expressions where twice the same verb has been employed, something that would hardly fit the varying translation style of LXX-Joshua. Moreover, the first part is an intelligible and in itself coherent, relatively free translation.[5] With its subtle employment of the passive form the translation corresponds to the pattern observable throughout several Septuagint books, i.e. to retain in positive statements the active form for God as subject, and employ the medial and passive for human activities containing the verb εὐοδόω.[6] The second part of the Greek sentence corresponds more closely to the Hebrew text, and thus, given the non-literal and varying style of translation in LXX, probably constitutes an early addition to the original text of LXX,

[2] See already the remarks by A. MASIUS, *Josuae imperatoris historia*, Annotationes, pp. 125b–126a: 'pro εὐοδώσεις, reddidit Syrus primam personam, εὐοδώσω. sed id ei non assentiuntur alia exemplaria.'

[3] See also W. MICHAELIS, ὁδός, ὁδηγός, ὁδηγέω, μεθοδία, εἴσοδος, ἔξοδος, διέχοδος, εὐοδόω, *ThWNT* V, pp. 42–117, p. 115, n. 11; and J. MOATTI-FINE, *Josué*, p. 96.

[4] C.G. DEN HERTOG, *Studien*, pp. 81–91 'Scheinbare dubletten'.

[5] Compare the similar option followed in Peš-Josh, where the longer expression כי־אז תצליח את־דרכך has been condensed into the shorter formulation ܘܬܬܟܫܪ, which H. MAGER, *Die Peschittho zum Buche Josua*, p. 47, classified in the category of Peš-Josh's omission of individual expressions, idem J.E. ERBES, *The Peshitta and the Versions*, pp. 93–95.

[6] Thus C.G. DEN HERTOG, *Studien*, p. 84.

possibly deriving from Theodotion or one of the other recentiores of whom no readings for these clauses have been recorded.[7]

1:9 εἰς πάντα, οὗ ἐὰν πορεύῃ (Rahlfs)] Margolis followed the Complutensian edition, which has an additional τόπον: εἰς πάντα τόπον, οὗ ἐὰν πορεύῃ. This reading is supported mainly by manuscripts from the S-group, which is known for its stylistic corrections. Masius already noted the difference, but preferred the shorter reading.[8] The main argument for Margolis seems to be the similar occurrence of the word in Josh. 1:16, where the originality of this free addition is uncontested. The weak support for the word in 1:9 pleads for its secondary, Lucianic, origin, see also K. BIEBERSTEIN, *Lukian und Theodotion* (1994), p. 23. C.G. DEN HERTOG (1996), p. 34, gives preference to Margolis' reconstruction, but apparently provides the arguments in favour of Rahlfs' reconstruction.

1:15 ὁ θεὸς ἡμῶν (Rahlfs)] Margolis adopted the reading with a second person plural possessive pronoun: ὁ θεὸς ὑμῶν (second time in 1:15), which corresponds to the Hebrew אלהיכם, although he did not discuss the issue in his various apparatusses. As C.G. DEN HERTOG, *Studien*, p. 39, points out, the *lectio difficilior* is supported by the important E and S witnesses, whereas the reading as a second person plural is attested mainly by mixed and relatively younger texts (108.426 [P], A.121.Arm-eds. [C], 75 and VetLat).

1:15 ἔδωκεν (Margolis)] The reading with the perfect δέδωκεν (Rahlfs), attested only by Codex Vaticanus, should be replaced by the aorist ἔδωκεν attested by all other witnesses, thus Margolis, approved by C.G. DEN HERTOG, *Studien*, p. 68.

The circumstance that a certain coherence between the individual pluses in MT-Joshua 1 can be discerned, has played an important role in the discussion. For instance, the fact that right at the beginning of the book such a theologically loaded title for Moses as the

---

[7] As suggested already in 1876 by J. HOLLENBERG, *Charakter*, p. 2; and later by S. HOLMES, *Joshua* (1914), p. 18; and C.D. BENJAMIN, *The Variations* (1923), p. 24.

[8] A. MASIUS, *Josuae imperatoris historia*, Annotationes, p. 126a: 'scribunt Complutenses εἰς πάντα τόπον, οὗ ἐὰν πορεύῃ. Sed quando verbum, τόπον, neq. Hebraeum, neq. alii boni libri, nihil muto. Si quis tamen adscribendum putet, is notet obelisco, sicut in extremo huius capitis.'

'servant of the Lord' is missing from the Greek text, combined with the circumstance that similar instances recur in the book (1:15, 12:6 and 22:5) and that none of these variants can be plausibly explained as deriving from scribal error, forms one of the main arguments for Holmes, Orlinsky, Chesman, and Auld to view the pluses in MT as later additions to the Hebrew *Vorlage* of LXX.[9] Additional observations with respect to the syntax of the Hebrew text have been adduced to affirm the secondary origin of the pluses in 1:2 לבני ישׂראל (redundant explication of the preceding phrase להם), כל־התורה in 1:7 (the masculine suffix in ממנו 1:7 seems to imply a shorter text without the feminine antecedent) and 1:15 וירשׁתם אותה (which disturbs and overloads the sequence of the preceding clause ושׁבתם לארץ ירשׁתכם and the following clause אשׁר נתן לכם).[10] Furthermore, some ideological motives for the MT pluses have been adduced, as in the case of the nomistic addition of the words כל־התורה in 1:7 (thus A. Rofé),[11] and the plus in 1:4 כל ארץ החתים as part of an expansionistic tendency in MT *vis-à-vis* the older Hebrew text reflected in LXX (L. Mazor).[12]

Whereas most of these observations, considered separately, pertain to the realm of textual criticism of this chapter only, E. Tov argues that these pluses should collectively be considered the result of a second (final) edition of Joshua. It is in these quantitative divergencies between MT and LXX that we enter the realm of overlap between textual and literary criticism and first encounter the editorial reworking of the book.[13] Although the redaction of Joshua 1 was restricted to the modest and subtle addition of some individual short

---

[9] S. Holmes, *Joshua. The Hebrew and Greek Texts*, pp. 2ff., 17–18, p. 193; H.M. Orlinsky, The Hebrew *Vorlage*; E.A. Chesman, *Studies*, chapter 1, pp. 1–17; A.G. Auld, Joshua: The Hebrew and Greek Texts, p. 3 (= idem, *Joshua Retold*, pp. 8–9. Likewise, J. Hollenberg, *Der Charakter*, attributed several variants to a different (though not necessarily more original) Hebrew *Vorlage*, as no inner-Greek corruptions, lacunae in the translator's knowledge of classical Hebrew, or one of the demonstrated tendencies in the Greek translation can be adduced as plausible explanations. As a result, Hollenberg (p. 17) considered הים האחרון (Hebr. *Vorlage* LXX-Josh. 1:4) to be a *Hebrew* variant reading for MT הים הגדול, and classified (p. 18) the minuses of LXX-Joshua 1 in verses 2 הזה, 2 לבני ישׂראל, 4 כל ארץ החתים, 8 כי, 12 לאמר, and 14 משׁה בעבת הירדן as 'Lücken' in the Hebrew *Vorlage*.

[10] See e.g. E. Tov, The Growth of the Book of Joshua, p. 331 (category 2. 'Additions in MT whose secondariness is evident from their formulation.' = *The Greek and Hebrew Bible*, p. 390)

[11] A. Rofé, The Nomistic Correction, p. 248.

[12] See L. Mazor, עיונים, pp. 161–162, and her abstract in *BIOSCS* 27, p. 37.

[13] E. Tov, *Textual Criticism*, p. 328; idem, The Growth of the Book of Joshua.

elements meant to elucidate or emphasize the existing text (thus the plus מאד in 1:7),[14] or to introduce additions derived from the immediate context (so the plus in MT משה בעבר הירדן in 1:14)[15] or concepts and phrases from Deuteronomy (thus the apposition עבד יהוה in 1:1.15; 12:6 and 22:4, כל־התורה in 1:7 and לרשתה in 1:11),[16] and the possibility of the translator's omissions cannot be ruled out completely, the large proportion of the pluses makes it likely that the isolated pluses in MT (and related witnesses) together constitute an editorial stratum, rather than a series of isolated individual interpolations. Of special interest to our investigation is the observation that some of these pluses draw upon Deuteronomistic concepts and vocabulary, just as the nomistic plus in 1:7 offers a point of contact with the broader nomistic-Deuteronomistic (DtrN) stratum in this chapter.

Recently, K. Bieberstein has offered a comprehensive discussion of the variants.[17] He, too, detects a comparatively high number of additions to a shorter Hebrew text as reflected in LXX-Joshua,[18] but likewise discerns harmonising renderings in LXX in an even higher number of quantitative variants.[19] Although Bieberstein discusses several variants in clusters of related textual phenomena, and gives full attention to the broader history of the literary formation of Joshua 1, he apparently sees no evidence of a common editorial origin of the pluses in MT, hence no overlap between textual criticism and literary criticism, which remain two clearly distinct fields of textual analysis throughout his study.[20]

Reviewing the history of research with respect to the quantitative divergencies between MT and LXX as regards Joshua 1, it is striking that the discussion has been dominated by the two options, scribal

---

[14] E. Tov, The Growth, p. 333 (= *The Greek and Hebrew Bible*, p. 392).

[15] E. Tov, The Growth, p. 333 (= *The Greek and Hebrew Bible*, p. 392).

[16] E. Tov, The Growth, pp. 335–336, with references to the lists of Deuteronomistic vocabulary in S.R. Driver, *Introduction*; and M. Weinfeld, *Deuteronomy and the Deuteronomic School*. See section 4.2.1 above.

[17] K. Bieberstein, *Josua-Jordan-Jericho*, pp. 83–93.

[18] K. Bieberstein, *Josua-Jordan-Jericho*, p. 93, considers the eight pluses in MT to be secondary expansions: עבד יהוה (1:1 and 1:15), לבני ישראל (1:2), כל ארץ החתים (1:4), מאד (1:7), התורה (without כל, 1:7), לרשתה (1:11), and וירשתם אותה (1:15). This is a relatively high number, as compared to the five pluses in larger sections such as Joshua 2 (p. 123), and Josh. 3:1–5:1 (p. 170), respectively.

[19] See K. Bieberstein, *Josua-Jordan-Jericho*, pp. 83–93, sub T 3, T 4, and T 5, to be discussed in more detail below.

[20] See K. Bieberstein, *Josua-Jordan-Jericho*, pp. 72–74.

error versus additions in MT.[21] The possibility that not only the qualitative, but also the quantitative divergencies between LXX and MT are the result of literary initiatives has not yet received full appreciation. Moreover, the quantitative variants have been either discussed exclusively within the realm of textual criticism (Bieberstein), or form the basis of a redaction-critical theory that only very remotedly touches upon literary-critical observations independent of the textual questions (Tov). Thus, the two questions to be addressed in this chapter are the following:

* Do literary-critical and redaction-historical observations confirm the existence of a re-edition of a Hebrew text, as reflected by LXX, to the fuller text of MT? and, conversely:
* Can the quantitative divergencies between MT and LXX be seen as secondary literary initiatives from the Greek translator or a Hebrew predecessor?

In order to find appropriate answers to these questions it is necessary to study the elements that make up this alleged re-edition of the chapter in relation and within the respective Hebrew (MT) and Greek (LXX) contexts.

6.3 Redaction-Critical Analysis of the Hebrew Text Common to MT and LXX

Before examining the individual elements that allegedly constitute the re-edition of the chapter (section 6.4), it is necessary to make a few redaction-critical observations on the presumed first edition, that is the text common to the two versions, in order to obtain a clearer picture of the literary and redaction-historical context of the presumed re-edition of the chapter. As noted in section 4.2.1 above, Joshua 1 in the form attested by both MT and LXX forms a direct continuation of the narrative line Deut. 1–3, 31–34.[22] In these chapters,

[21] Chesman's methodology may serve as illustration for this approach, but as far as Joshua 1 is concerned we find a very similar approach in Bieberstein's discussion of the text-critical issues in this chapter.

[22] See section 4.2.1 above, and further e.g. J. Hollenberg, Die deuteronomische Bestandtheile (1876), especially pp. 473–478; A. Kuenen, *Historisch-critisch onderzoek*[2], p. 129ff.; M. Noth, *Überlieferungsgeschichtliche Studien*; and further N. Lohfink,

the divine installation of Joshua as Moses' successor in Josh. 1:1–6.9 has been prepared.

Already in Deut. 1:38, within the context of the Deuteronomistic version of the spy narrative we find Yhwh's instruction to Moses to encourage Joshua (אתו חזק), because it is he, not Moses who will enter the land (הוא יבא שמה cf. Josh. 1:2) and distribute it (כי־הוא ינחלנה את־ישׂראל cf. Josh. 1:6). After Moses' review of Israel's history from Horeb to Moab (Deut. 1:1–3:17), and Moses' addresses to the Trans-Jordanian tribes (Deut. 3:18–20//Josh. 1:12–15, see below), another passage follows in Deut. 3:21–22, in which Moses admonishes Joshua not to fear the kings on the other side of the Jordan. This section is followed by a short narrative in which Moses asks Yhwh to be allowed to see the land. After his denial of this request (3:23–27), Yhwh again commands Moses (3:28) to confirm Joshua (וחזקהו ואמצהו cf. Josh. 1:6.9.18 חזק ואמץ) as the one who will lead the people into the land (כי־הוא יעבר לפני העם הזה cf. Josh. 1:2 עבר את־הירדן) and allot the land to them (והוא ינחיל אותם את־הארץ cf. Josh. 1:6 אתה תנחיל את־העם הזה את־הארץ). The corresponding execution of these instructions folllows only after the long hortatory and legislative main body of Deuteronomy (Deut. 4–30), in Deut. 31:7–8, where Moses passes on these commands to Joshua, followed by the assertion that Yhwh will assist Joshua (הוא יהיה עמך cf. Josh. 1:5 אהיה עמך), and will not forsake him (לא ירפך ולא יעזבך cf. Josh. 1:5 לא ארפך ולא אעזבך), so that Joshua need not fear (לא תירא ולא תחת cf. Josh. 1:9 אל־תערץ ואל־תחת). This section is followed by a short passage in which Moses writes down the *torah* and instructs the Levites to teach the Israelites from it (31:9–13), and another passage in which Yhwh summons Moses and Joshua to the Tent of Meeting (31:14–15), which finds its logical continuation in 31:23,[23] where Yhwh affirms Moses' words in Deut. 31:7–8.

Die deuteronomistische Darstellung des Übergangs der Führung Israels von Moses auf Josue, in *Scholastik* 37 (1962), pp. 32–44, reprinted in idem, *Studien zum Deuteronomium und zur deuteronomistischen Literatur* I. Stuttgart 1990, pp. 83–98; J.R. Porter, The Succession of Joshua, in J. Durham, J.R. Porter (eds.), *Proclamation and Presence. Old Testament Essays in Honour of Gwyne Henton Davies*. London 1970, pp. 102–132. A compact and lucid history of previous research with respect to Joshua 1 has been offered by K. Bieberstein, *Josua-Jordan-Jericho*, pp. 81–83. See now also J. Nentel, *Trägerschaft und Intentionen des deuteronomistischen Geschichtswerks: Untersuchungen zu den Reflexionsreden Jos 1; 23; 24; 1 Sam 12 und 1 Kön 8*. (BZAW 297) Berlin/New York 2000, pp. 13–37.

[23] Deut. 31:14–15.23 is interrupted (31:16–22) by the introduction to the song of Moses (Deut. 32:1–43). See further the commentaries to Deut. 31, e.g. C. Steuernagel, *Deuteronomium und Josua*, pp. 110–114; and E. Nielsen, *Das Deuteronomium*

Deut. 1^{38}	יהושע בן־נון העמד לפניך הוא יבא שמה אתו חזק כי־הוא ינחלנה את־ישראל:
Deut. 3^{22}	לא תיראום כי יהוה אלהיכם הוא הנלחם לכם:
Deut. 3^{28}	וחזקהו ואמצהו כי־הוא יעבר לפני העם הזה והוא ינחיל אותם את־הארץ אשר תראה:
Deut. 31^{7}	חזק ואמץ כי אתה תבוא את־העם הזה אל־הארץ אשר נשבעתי יהוה לאבותם לתת להם ואתה תנחילנה אותם:
Deut. 31^{8}	ויהוה הוא ההלך לפניך הוא יהיה עמך לא ירפך ולא יעזבך לא תירא ולא תחת:
Deut. 31^{23}	חזק ואמץ כי אתה תביא את־בני ישראל אל־הארץ אשר־נשבעתי להם ואנכי אהיה עמך:

Thus, the narrative of the installation of Joshua by Yhwh in Josh. 1:1–6.9 forms both a direct continuation and an expanded repetition of these passages from Deuteronomy, containing the themes of admonition, encouragement (חזק ואמץ Deut. 1:38, 3:28, 31:7.23, Josh. 1:6(7) 9. 18,[24] and לא תירא Deut. 3:22, 31:8, Josh. 1:9, cf. Josh. 8:1, 10:8.25, 11:6), and divine assistance (Deut. 31:8, Josh. 1:5, cf. Josh. 3:7). Here we also find the two main themes of the book of Joshua, i.e. the crossing of the Jordan plus the conquest of the land (Josh. 1:2 expressed by the verbs עבר and בוא Hiphʿil; cf. Deut. 3:28; 31:7.23 and Josh. 2–12) and the distribution of the land (Josh. 1:6 with the verb נחל Hiphʿil, cf. Deut. 1:38; 3:28; 31:7; and Josh. 13–21).

The links with Deuteronomy are further strengthened by the fact that Joshua 1 contains large segments of citations from Deuteronomy. By means of the clause 'as I have spoken to Moses' (כאשר דברתי אל־משה), Josh. 1:3–5a integrate (with a few modifications) the description of the Promised Land in its Euphratic proportions, as found in Deut. 11:24–25a.[25] Similarly, in Josh. 1:12–15 the pledge of loyalty by which Moses had bound the Trans-Jordanian tribes (Deut. 3:12–15)

(HAT I/6) Tübingen 1995, p. 273ff., who holds Deut. 31:14–15.23 to be the core of these Deuteronomistic succession texts.

[24] See further Josh. 10:25 in the narrative of Joshua's battle with the five southern Canaanite kings. The same formula recurs in Haggai's prophecy to Zerubbabel and high priest Joshua, the Chronicler's version of the installation of Solomon by David (1 Chron. 22:13, 28:10.20), Hezekiah's address to his people in the context of the Assyrian threat (2 Chron. 32:7). E. Nielsen, *Das Deuteronomium*, seeks the original context of this formula in the Psalms (see Pss. 27:14, 31:25). L.L. Rowlett, *Joshua and the Rhetoric of Violence*. (JSOTS 226) Sheffield 1996, analyzes this formula with the aid of a New Historicist methodology against the background of Ancient Near East parallels, and situates it in a Josianic Dtr$_1$-context (see section 4.2.4.1 above).

[25] See D.B. George, Yahweh's Speech at Jos 1,2–6 and Deut 11: Semantics, Intertextuality, and Meaning, in *ZAW* 112 (2000), pp. 356–364, for an examination of the intertextual relation of the passages on a synchronic level.

has been incorporated within the context of Joshua's succession by the explicit cross-reference זכור את־הדבר אשר צוה אתכם משה עבד־יהוה.[26]

Clearly distinguished from this DtrH-portait is the Priestly presentation of Moses' succession by Joshua as formulated in Num. 27:15–23 and Deut. 34:7–9, where instead of this cluster of themes and vocabulary we find the theme of Joshua's ordination through the imposition of Moses' hands (סמך משה את־ידיו עליו Deut. 34:9, cf. Num. 27:18–23), the theme of the *ruaḥ* (Num. 27:18 איש אשר־רוח בו cf. Deut. 34:9 ויהושע בן־נון מלא רוח חכמה), and the prominent place taken by the priest Eleazar (Num. 27:19–22).[27] Less competitive, but equally distinctive is the nomistic (DtrN) blending of the DtrH-theme of the encouragement of Joshua in the face of the conquest of the Promised Land to a nomistically inspired encouragement to persist in the study and strict execution of the *torah* in Josh. 1:7–8 (DtrN),[28] a theme that is absent from the corresponding passages in Deuteronomy and that transforms[29] the 'theology of the promise of the land' into

[26] As described in section 4.2.4.2, K. Bieberstein, *Josua-Jordan-Jericho*, ascribes these texts to a Deuteronomistic substratum DtrR. Since this theory does not affect our argument, there is no need to evaluate this thesis in the present discussion. It may be sufficient to point out that—contrary to the ideological tension between DtrH and DtrN—the alleged DtrR addition does not contain a similar tensions, since already DtrH is concerned with the unity of all Israel (כל־ישראל), which precludes the participation of these tribes. Moreover, if this DtrR-redaction had been aroused by a renewed interest in the lost Trans-Jordanian territories conquered by the Arameans (2 Kgs. 10:32–33) and subsequently by the Assyrians (see the historical survey in K. Bieberstein, *Josua-Jordan-Jericho*, pp. 323–328), one wonders why this interest would have been dressed in the historiographical fiction of the inhabitants of these territories participating in the conquest of a land markedly different from the one under discussion.

[27] See also C. Schäfer-Lichtenberger, *Josua und Salomo. Eine Studie zu Authorität und Legitimität im Alten Testament.* (SVT 58) Leiden/New York/Köln 1995, pp. 105–224: 'Zweiter Teil. Josua—Der Nachfolger Moses.'

[28] Thus according to the redaction-critical theory developed by R. Smend, see section 4.2.2 above. Similar observations with respect to Josh. 1:7–8 had already been made by E. Albers, *Die Quellenberichte in Josua I–XII*, p. 20ff.; C. Steuernagel, *Deuteronomium und Josua*, pp. 154–155; H. Holzinger, *Das Buch Josua*, p. 2. In his 1938 commentary to Joshua, p. 7, and even in his *Überlieferungsgeschichtliche Studien*, p. 41, n. 4, M. Noth had adopted these observations, but abandoned this opinion in favour of a unified Dtr origin of the whole chapter in the second edition of his commentary (M. Noth, *Das Buch Josua*^{2}, pp. 28–29). Smend's DtrN thesis with respect to Josh. 1:7ff. has found common acceptance, see e.g. E. Otto, *Das Mazzotfest in Gilgal*, n. 87; K. Bieberstein, *Josua-Jordan-Jericho*, pp. 95–97, 390–394; E. Noort, Josua und seine Aufgabe. Bemerkungen zu Josua 1:1–4, in H.M. Niemann (Hg.), *Nachdenken über Israel. FS K.-D. Schunck* (BEATAJ 37) Frankfurt am Main 1994, pp. 69–87, especially p. 73ff.

[29] Thus M. Fishbane, *Biblical Interpretation in Ancient Israel.* Oxford 1985, pp.

a 'theology of the observance of the *torah*' as condition for success.[30]

It is important to note that the chapter as a whole, not only in the alleged expanded form of MT, but also in the form attested by both MT and LXX, should be designated as Deuteronomistic.[31] Furthermore, this Deuteronomistic text already underwent a nomistic

384–385, who mentions this transformation of the old military exhortation formula passage as an example of Haggadic theologizing, without referring to Smend.

[30] Thus the distinction between a 'teologia della Promessa' (Josh. 1:1–6) and a 'teologia del Patto' (Josh. 1:7–9) made by P. SACCHI, Giosuè 1,1–9: Dalla critica storica a quella letteraria, in D. GARRONE, F. ISRAEL (eds.) *Storia e tradizione di Israele. Scritti in onore di J. Alberto Soggin.* Brescia 1991, pp. 237–253; similarly P. SACCHI, Considerazioni sulla spiritualità giudaica del secondo templo, in *Henoch* 13 (1991), pp. 3–17. Sacchi does not mention the DtrN-thesis of Smend and his pupils.

Studies that focus more generally on the themes of royal ideology, *torah* and succession tend to regard verses 7–8 as an integral part of the chapter, on the basis of parallel combinations of law and leadership in e.g. Exod. 24; Deut. 17:18–20; 31:9–13; Josh. 24:26; 2 Kgs. 22–23; Neh. 7–8; 1 Chron. 22; see e.g. G. ÖSTBORN, *Tōrā in the Old Testament.* Lund 1945; G. WIDENGREN, King and Covenant, *JSS* 2 (1957), pp. 1–32; R. PORTER, The Succession of Joshua; R.D. NELSON, Josiah in the Book of Joshua; and C. SCHÄFER-LICHTENBERGER, *Josua und Salomo*, especially p. 193ff.

A close examination of these passages, however, on the one hand reveals the distinctions between Josh. 1:7–8 and the alleged parallel: the ספר תורת אלהים mentioned in Josh. 24:26 is apparently an exceptional book, different from the collective body of Moses' *torah* (כל־התורה in Josh. 23 and 1:7–8). On the other hand, the real correspondencies in vocabulary between the passages adduced by these scholars point to their common DtrN bakground. 1 Kgs. 2:2–4, for instance, transforms David's rather rude advices to Solomon with respect to their former enemies into a pious admonition, and for that reason can hardly be claimed to be an original organically integrated element of the text; see e.g. M. FISHBANE, *Biblical Interpretation*, p. 385, and further the commentaries to 1 Kings, e.g. M.J. MULDER, *1 Kings 1–11* (HCOT) Leuven 1998, p. 86ff.

[31] Adherents of the classical four sources hypothesis tended to ascribe the narrative core of the chapter, Josh. 1:1–2a, to a pre-Deuteronomistic, usually Elohistic source, as well as parts of Josh. 1:10–11, which prepares for Josh. 3:1 and forms a rival account to Josh. 2–3:1, thus e.g. J.W. COLENSO, *The Pentateuch and Book of Joshua Critically Examined* VI, p. 112ff. (Josh. 1:1–2 JE); cautiously J. HOLLENBERG, Die deuteronomische Bestandtheile, pp. 473–478, p. 477; A. KUENEN, *Historisch-critisch onderzoek*[2] (1886), p. 156 (1:11 prepares for 3:2); E. ALBERS, *Die Quellenberichte in Josua I–XII*, pp. 8–34. See further H. HOLZINGER, *Das Buch Josua*, pp. 1–3 (Josh. 1:1–2* possibly from JE); R. SMEND SR., *Die Erzählung des Hexateuch.* Berlin 1912, p. 279ff. (Josh. 1:1a: J1; 1:1bß.10–11: E); and O. EIßFELDT, *Hexateuch-Synopse*, pp. 202*–203* (Josh. 1:1–18: E).

This source division was based on external, rather than on internal literary and redaction-critical arguments based on the text of Joshua 1 itself, and hence rejected already by J. WELLHAUSEN, *Die Composition* (1876, [1963]), p. 117; A. DILLMANN, *Die Bücher Numeri, Deuteronomium und Josua.* (1886), p. 442; C. STEUERNAGEL, *Deuteronomium und Josua* (1900), pp. 153–157; M. NOTH, *Das Buch Josua*[1] (1938), pp. 6–7, idem, 2nd. ed. (1953), p. 27, and, very decidedly in his *Überlieferungsgeschichtliche Studien* (1943), p. 41: 'es gibt keinen Grund, in diesem in seiner Sprache durch und durch deuteronomistischen Kapitel einer schon vorher feststehenden literarkritischen

(DtrN) expansion (at least by the addition of verse 8) at a stage in the literary history of the passage before the alleged re-edition underlying MT took place. This implies that the Deuteronomistic (Tov) and nomistic (Rofé) elements in this assumed re-edition have their counterparts and parallels already in the text common to both MT and LXX (the so-called edition I in Tov's terminology). A particular problem in this respect is posed by verse 7, since both the leading nomistic concept contained in the words כל־התורה and the particles רק and מאד in the Hebrew text that mark the conditional transformation of the imperatives חזק ואמץ in verse 6 towards the *torah*-piety in verse 7, are absent from LXX. The absence of these words forms an important argument in favour of A. Rofé's thesis of a relatively late Second Temple period *nomistic* correction in the sense of a subtle proto-Pharisaic textual alteration of a Deuteronomistic passage (חזק ואמץ לשמר לעשות כ[כל] אשר צוך משה עבדי) corresponding closely to 11:15 (כאשר צוה יהוה את־משה עבדו כן־צוה משה את־יהושע וכן עשה יהושע).[32] Nevertheless, the DtrN-expansion of verse 8 is present in both MT and LXX, which would imply that Rofé's nomistic correction in verse 7 belongs to a post-DtrN-redaction.[33]

It is also important to note that already the Hebrew text common to MT and LXX of Joshua 1, a chapter that in its entirety may be called a repetition of passages in Deuteronomy, is characterised by an explicative and verbose style. This expansionistic style becomes very evident when we examine the Deuteronomistic formulations with respect to the theme of the gift (נתן) of the Promised Land (ארץ).[34] Of the seven times the Promised Land is mentioned in MT-Joshua 1, we find only in Josh. 1:13 the simple indication 'this land' (הארץ הזאת), whereas the remaining passages contain long explicative Deuteronomistic formulations:[35]

Hypothese zuliebe das Vorhandensein vordeuteronomistischer Elemente zu postulieren.' This view has become the dominant one in the subsequent studies, see e.g. V. Fritz, *Das Buch Josua*, p. 25ff.; K. Bieberstein, *Josua-Jordan-Jericho*, pp. 81–101. See further the comprehensive review of previous research, in Bieberstein's work, pp. 81–83.

[32] A. Rofé, The Nomistic Correction, p. 248, idem, The Piety of the Torah-Disciples, p. 79, see section 2.2.7.2 above.

[33] Rofé reckons only with a Deuteronomistic and a Priestly stratum in Joshua, and rejects Smend's thesis, thus A. Rofé, The Piety of Torah, p. 79, n. 6. Nevertheless, he, too, considers Josh. 1:7 secondary *vis-à-vis* Josh. 1:1–6.

[34] See e.g. M. Weinfeld, *Deuteronomy and the Deuteronomic School*, p. 341ff. and section 4.2.1 above.

[35] Phrases not reflected by LXX have been bracketed.

1^{2-3} עבר . . . אל־הארץ אשר אנכי נתן להם [לבני ישראל]
³כל־מקום אשר תדרך כף־רגלכם בו לכם נתתיו
1^{6} כי אתה תנחיל את־העם הזה את־הארץ
אשר נשבעתי לאבותם לתת להם
1^{11} לבוא לרשת את־הארץ
אשר יהוה אלהיכם נתן לכם [לרשתה]
1^{13} ונתן לכם את־הארץ הזאת
1^{14} נשיכם טפכם ומקניכם ישבו בארץ
אשר נתן לכם [משה בעבר הירדן]
1^{15} וירשו גם־המה את־הארץ אשר־יהוה אלהיכם נתן להם
1^{15} ושבתם ל[ארץ] ירשתכם [וירשתם אותה]
אשר נתן לכם משה [עבד יהוה] בעבר הירדן מזרח השמש

Likewise, of the (again) seven times Yhwh is mentioned in MT-Joshua 1,[36] five times the divine name is followed by the epithet 'your God' (אלהיכם/אלהיך).[37] The DtrH-admonitions to Joshua not to lose courage[38] have been phrased in several expressions (חזק ואמץ verses 6, 9, and 18; in verse 9 אל־תערץ ואל־תחת). The same applies to DtrN's taking up the observance of Moses instructions, as a condition for success:

1^{7} לשמר לעשות כ[כל־התורה] אל־תסור ממנו ימין ושמאול
אשר צוך משה עבדי למען תשכיל בכל אשר תלך
1^{8} למען תשמר לעשות ככל־[ה]כתוב [בו] כי־אז תצליח את־דרכך ואז תשכיל

Tov describs the accumulation of pluses in MT as an expansion of the text reflected by LXX, but from the above observations it becomes clear that features such as expansionism and amplification are not exclusive traits of this alleged second edition, but common to the supposed preceding literary stratum. Moreover, these features, inherent in the Deuteronomistic nature of Joshua 1, are confirmed by textual evidence for the same formulas in Deuteronomy, where the Greek

---

[36] LXX-Josh. 1:13 has an additional reference to 'the Lord' in the first clause: Μνήσθητε τὸ ῥῆμα *κυρίου* which was obelized in the Hexapla, according to A. Masius, *Josuae imperatoris historia*, Annotationes, p. 126a; it is, however, absent from B.Eth, and attested by ms. 344 (mg.) as a reading of both o' and θ', which is undoubtedly the original LXX-reading; see also L.J. Greenspoon, *Textual Studies*, p. 59.

[37] LXX-Josh. 1:15 has an additional apposition ὁ θεος ὑμῶν (obelized in the Hexapla, according to A. Masius, *Josuae imperatoris historia*, Annotationes, p. 126a, absent only from ms. 58. Moreover, LXX-Josh 1:11 contains the longer phrase κύριος ὁ θεὸς *τῶν πατέρων* ὑμῶν, again obelized in Syh^{M} (A. Masius, *Josuae imperatoris historia*, Annotationes, p. 126a) and omitted by ms. 58, and a change of person from second plural to first person plural in 1:15 and 1:17, possibly originating from the inner-Greek development towards itacism.

[38] See e.g. M. Weinfeld, *Deuteronomy and the Deuteronomic School*, p. 343ff.

text (as well as the Qumran manuscripts of the book) faithfully reflects the repetitive style of the Hebrew text.[39]

The formation process of Joshua 1, as far as the formation of the DtrH and DtrN layers is concerned, had already taken place before the divergencies between MT and LXX came into being. Most of the characteristic (Deuteronomistic and nomistic) elements in the pluses of MT *vis-à-vis* LXX already have their counterpart in the Hebrew text common to MT and LXX, which in itself may be labelled as repetitive and amplifying. In the light of these observations, one must ask what are the specific contrastive nuances added to the alleged base text reflected in LXX by the (layer of) pluses in MT, and whether the possibility of the curtailing of the verbose Deuteronomistic language by either a Hebrew scribe or the Greek translator should not be taken into account more seriously.

6.4 Discussion of the Pluses in MT-Joshua 1

On the basis of this redaction-critical analysis we are now in a position to study more closely the elements in Joshua 1 that allegedly constitute the second edition of Joshua, *in concreto* the more significant pluses of MT *vis-à-vis* LXX. Special attention will be given to the questions whether the pluses form a coherent pattern of distinctive elements introducing a modification of the older text towards identifiable concerns and interests, and how these quantitative variants fit the overall context of the Greek translation.

6.4.1 *The 'Servant of Yhwh' and related variants (Josh. 1:1.15; 4:10.14; 12:6; 22:4)*

The first of a series of significant pluses in MT occurs right at the beginning of the book. In the very first clause of the first verse, the apposition עבד יהוה is absent from LXX, a phenomenon that occurs

[39] See e.g. J.W. Wevers, *Text History of the Greek Deuteronomy*, p. 86. The MT-LXX variants in Deuteronomy discussed by A. Aejmelaeus, Die Septuaginta des Deuteronmiums, in T. Veijola (Hg.), *Das Deuteronomium und seine Querbeziehungen*. (SFEG 62) Helsinki/Göttingen 1996, pp. 1–22, are not on the same quantitative scale as those in Joshua. See further the long list of stereotyped Deuteronomistic phraseology in M. Weinfeld, *Deuteronomy and the Deuteronomic School*, pp. 320–365, and section 4.2.1 above.

also in Josh. 1:15, 12:6, and 22:4, whereas the epithet occurs an additional fourteen times in both MT and LXX.[40]

The fact that the omission occurs right at the beginning of the book combined with the fact that the same omission recurs three more times in the same book makes an unconscious error in the scribal transmission of the text as proposed by R.G. Boling highly unlikely.[41] It presupposes that the same error occurred right at the beginning of the book, and then three more times. Moreover, the *parablepsis* hinges on a single identical letter (ה), rather than on similar phrases.[42] An inner-Greek development by which the phrase was intentionally skipped by Greek copyists, as suggested by J. Erbes, finds no support in the manuscript evidence and therefore—although not impossible—is to be dismissed as too speculative.[43]

As a result, there is a broad consensus among scholars that we are dealing here with secondary expansions.[44] Tov ascribes this plus to 'the influence of Deuteronomy',[45] which is a somewhat unfortunate designation as the epithet occurs only once in Deuteronomy (34:5).[46] He draws a parallel with Josh. 4:10,[47] where the phrase

[40] Thus in Josh. 1:7.13; 8:31 (LXX 9:2b); 8:33 (LXX 9:2d); 11:12; 12:6 (first clause); 13:8; 14:7; 18:7; 22:2.5. The apposition עבדי/עבדו with suffixes referring to Yhwh occurs in 1:2; 9:24; 11:15.

[41] R.G. Boling, *Joshua*, p. 114 (1:1: 'haplography: *mš*[*h ʿbd yhw*]*h*'), 116 (1:15), 321 (12:6) and 505 (22:4).

[42] Thus e.g. E.A. Chesman, *Studies in the Septuagint Text of the Book of Joshua*, pp. 1–17.

[43] J.E. Erbes, *The Peshitta and the Versions*. Uppsala 1999, pp. 56–58.

[44] See, e.g., S. Holmes, *Joshua*, p. 18 (1:1.15); C.D. Benjamin, *Variations*, pp. 23 (1:1), 24 (1:15); P. Andreas Fernández, s.j., *Commentarius in Librum Iosue*, pp. 36 (1:1), 43 (1:15); P.D. Baldi, *Giosuè*. (SB) Torino/Roma 1952, p. 19 (1:1); A.G. Auld, Joshua. The Hebrew and Greek Texts, p. 3 (= *Joshua Retold*, pp. 8–9); T.C. Butler, *Joshua*, p. 133 (12:6), 239 (22:4); L.J. Greenspoon, *Textual Studies*, pp. 309–312; P. Sacchi, Giosuè 1,1–9, pp. 237–238; K. Bieberstein, *Josua-Jordan-Jericho*, pp. 84–85; R.D. Nelson, *Joshua* (1997), pp. 27–28 (1:1.15), 157 (12:6), 243 (22:4); and J. Nentel, *Trägerschaft*, p. 19.

[45] E. Tov, The Growth of the Book of Joshua, pp. 335–336 (= *The Greek and Hebrew Bible*, p. 394)

[46] Thus K. Bieberstein, *Josua-Jordan-Jericho*, p. 85, n. 21.

[47] E. Tov, The Growth of the Book of Joshua, pp. 329–330: 'The formulation of MT is difficult. According to the short formulation of the LXX, Joshua's actions closely followed the command of God, while the plus stresses that the command was by Moses. The juxtaposition of these two commands in the MT is not impossible—after all, God commanded Moses to command Joshua (Deut 3:28)—but it is awkward. It is therefore likely that two different remarks have been combined in MT. Possibly the plus in MT derived from Deut 3:28 or from v 12 in the context.' See further *inter alia* S. Sipilä, The Septuagint Version of Joshua 3–4, in C.E. Cox (ed.), *VII Congress of the IOSCS. Leuven 1989*. (SCS 31) Atlanta 1991, pp. 63–74, especially p. 69; H.-J. Stipp, Textkritik-Literarkritik-Textentwicklung, p. 145. See

כל־הדבר אשר־צוה יהוה את־יהושע is repeated in a MT plus, this time with Moses as the authority: ככל אשר־צוה <u>משה</u> את־יהושע.[48]

4[10]	*εἰστήκεισαν δὲ* οἱ ἱερεῖς	וְהַכֹּהֲנִ֞ים
	οἱ αἴροντες τὴν κιβωτὸν *τῆς διαθήκης*	נֹשְׂאֵ֣י הָאָר֗וֹן
	ἐν τῷ --- Ιορδάνῃ,	עֹמְדִים֮ בְּת֣וֹךְ הַיַּרְדֵּן֒
	ἕως οὗ συνετέλεσεν *Ἰησοῦς πάντα,*	עַ֣ד תֹּ֣ם כָּל־הַ֠דָּבָר
	ἃ ἐνετείλατο κύριος --- ---	אֲשֶׁר־צִוָּ֨ה יְהוָ֜ה אֶת־יְהוֹשֻׁ֗עַ
	ἀναγγεῖλαι τῷ λαῷ --- ---	לְדַבֵּ֣ר אֶל־הָעָ֔ם כְּכֹ֛ל
	--- --- --- --- ---	אֲשֶׁר־צִוָּ֥ה מֹשֶׁ֖ה אֶת־יְהוֹשֻׁ֑עַ

Like Orlinksy, Chesman, Tov and others, K. Bieberstein considers the plus עבד יהוה in the four passages to be secondary additions to the shorter text as reflected by MT, influenced by the growing stature of the figure of Moses, and the corresponding increase in the use of this epithet for Moses in post-Exilic literature, such as in the books of Nehemiah,[49] Chronicles,[50] and Daniel.[51]

Although these arguments in favour of the secondariness of the four pluses in MT-Joshua seem rather impressive, there are a number of observations that plead against Tov's theory in this case. For

---

further the discussion and fully documented history of previous research in K. Bieberstein, *Josua-Jordan-Jericho*, p. 163.

[48] E.A. Chesman, *Studies in the Septuagint Text of the Book of Joshua*, pp. 8–10, drew attention to the absence in LXX-Josh. 24:5 of the entire phrase ואשלח את־משה ואת־אהרן, but detached this problem from the present one, since the epithet עבד יהוה does not occur here. Tov does not include this variant in his discussion of the textual history of Joshua. This variant requires a study of its own within the context of Joshua 24. If the plus in MT would be the result of the same editor who allegedly added the epithet עבד יהוה in 1:1.15, 12:6, 22:4, the question remains why this editor did not add it in Josh. 24:5 as well.

[49] Neh. 1:7.8, 9:14, 10:30 (עבד־האלהים).

[50] 1 Chron. 6:34 (עבד האלהים), the LXX plus in 1 Chron. 16:30 (ἐν χειρὶ Μωυσῆ τοῦ θεράποντος τοῦ θεου), 2 Chron. 1:3 and 2 Chron. 24:6 (עבד יהוה, but in LXX ἀνθρώπος τοῦ Θεοῦ) and 24:9 (עבד־האלהים).

[51] Dan. 9:11. One might add to this list Mal. 3:22 (3:24 in LXX). See E.A. Chesman, *Studies in the Septuagint Text of the Book of Joshua*, p. 11. K. Bieberstein, *Josua-Jordan-Jericho*, pp. 84–85, also adduces the evidence of LXX-Jonah 1:9 (Δοῦλος κυρίου ἐγώ εἰμι), but this passage is irrelevant, since the Greek text can plausibly be explained as the result of a scribal error from MT עברי אנכי into עבדי understood as עבד יהוה, as Bieberstein himself, p. 84, n. 18, explains. Bieberstein further adduces the occurrences of this title for Moses and other important figures in Second Temple compositions such as 1 Esdras (6:26 for Zerubbabel), Wis. (2:13; 10:16; 12:7 for Israel) and the other occurrences in Daniel (3:26; 3:85 [θ'] 6:21; 10:17). J. Hollenberg, *Der Charakter*, p. 3, ascribed these variants to his category of glosses in either the Greek text or its Hebrew *Vorlage*: 'Bezeichnungen, wie Knecht des Herrn, Sohn Nuns, Eleazars, Kenas', Jephunnes, gelten den Abschreibern als unwichtig und werden zugesetzt oder weggelassen vgl. 1:1.15; 5:9; 15:14; 17:4; 22:31.32.'

one, his thesis would have been much more convincing, had the epithet been completely absent from the entire Hebrew text of Joshua common to MT and LXX, thereby constituting an exclusive feature of the MT as opposed to the Hebrew *Vorlage* of LXX, or had the phrase had a distinctly different significance in this presumed older layer, and had this alleged older edition been demonstrably pre-Exilic. This, however, is not the case. Apart from the four passages under discussion, the title recurs no less than fourteen times both in the DtrH and DtrN-strata of the book,[52] where the phrase is attested by LXX,[53] that is even more often than in the passages in Nehemia, Chronicles, and Daniel combined. Furthermore, the title occurs right at the very end of the preceding book as a posthumous homage to Moses (Deut. 34:5),[54] in the expressly Deuteronomistic passages 1 Kgs. 8:53:56, 2 Kgs. 18:12, 21:8, and in the pre-Priestly Tetrateuch passages Exod. 14:31 and Num. 12:7–8.[55]

Thus, we find no positive evidence for redactional activity in the four passages under discussion in the sense of an adaptation of the existing authoritative text towards concepts and interests originally alien to this text. Rather, the epithet 'servant of Yhwh' is characteristic for the Deuteronomistic portrait of Moses, especially in the Deuteronomistic (DtrH) stratum of Joshua. This implies that possible insertions of this phrase into these passages do not alter the scope of the text by introducing a distinctive idea or interest,[56] nor do they 'Deuteronomicise' a non-Deuteronomistic passage. It would only add more of the same to an already ponderous Hebrew text. Moreover, if we imagine a redactor taking a special interest in ensuring a proper understanding of Moses as the servant of the Lord, it remains difficult to understand why so many places remain where the epithet has not

---

[52] See E. NOORT, Josua und seine Aufgabe, p. 74.

[53] LXX-Josh. 1:2.7.13; 8:31.33, 9:24; 11:12.15; 12:6; 13:8; 14:7; 18;7; 22:2.5.

[54] Likewise, Joshua receives the title *post mortem* in Josh. 24:29 (LXX 24:30)//Judg. 2:8.

[55] See further the lists of instances of this title for Moses in the commentaries, H. RINGGREN, עָבַד *ʿāḇaḏ*, עֶבֶד *ʿæḇæḏ*, עֲבֹדָה *ʿᵃḇoḏāh*, in *ThWAT* V, col. 982–1012, especially col. 1001; and E. NOORT, Josua und seine Aufgabe, p. 74.

[56] Contrast for instance the emphasis on the prophetic role of Moses in the Arabic translation of Josh. 1:1 as 'prophet of Yhwh' (thus J.A. SOGGIN, *Le livre de Josué*, p. 27) and the title 'lord of the prophets' (אדון הנביאים), which the Samaritan Joshua Chronicle gives to Moses in the parallel to Josh. 1:1. Likewise, Sir.46:1 emphasizes the prophetic aspect in his designation of Joshua as Moses' successor in prophecy: משרת משה בנבואה—διάδοχος Μωυσῆ ἐν προφητείαις.

been added to a reference to Moses (Josh. 1:1 משרת משה; 1:3.5.17.17, or in the 32 occurrences of the name Moses without this epithet throughout the remaining chapters of the book).[57] True, the ancients may not have been as systematic as we would like, and not every occurrence of the name Moses would have been an invitation to a redactor to add this title, but one might expect to have found similar additions in the complex Josh. 13:15–21, where Moses is mentioned no less than 19 times,[58] and where the epithet 'servant of Yhwh' occurs only twice (both in MT and LXX), i.e. in the Deuteronomistic passages 14:7 and 18:7.[59] Likewise, one would expect to find this addition in 14:6, the only place in the book of Joshua where we find an alternative title for Moses as 'man of God' (איש־האלהים/LXX ἄνθρωπος τοῦ θεοῦ).[60] Moreover, if the plus in MT-Josh. 1:14 (בארץ אשר נתן לכם) משה בעבר הירדן had derived from the same redaction, one would expect to find the title עבד יהוה introduced here as well.[61]

Something similar can be said of the plus in Josh. 4:10 ככל אשר־צוה משה את־יהושע, where one would have expected the same title עבד יהוה. What is difficult to imagine is that in this particular case an editor would have wanted to overrule the first statement in Josh. 4:10, reflected by both MT and LXX, where authority is derived directly from Yhwh (כל־הדבר אשר־צוה יהוה את־יהושע/πάντα, ἃ ἐνετέλεσεν κύριος), and relegate this authority to the person of Moses instead ככל אשר־צוה משה את־יהושע. The parallel formulation could have been regarded as an example of the redactional device of resumptive repetition (*Wiederaufnahme*), had it contained some specific additional instructions which a younger editor sought to incorporate into the authoritative text, as is the case, for instance, with the incor-

---

[57] Here only the passages where MT and LXX agree have been counted. In addition, Moses recurs in LXX-Joshua an additional time in 13:14b, the LXX-heading to 13:15ff. (parallelled in MT by verse 13:33, absent from LXX). In MT, Moses occurs another 4 times in Josh. 4:10, 14:2 (where LXX has ἐν χειρὶ Ἰησοῦ for MT ביד־משה) 14:3 (where a clause has dropped out of the Greek text or more probably its Hebrew *Vorlage* due to *homoioteleuton*, see the commentaries) and 24:5.

[58] Josh. 13:15.21.24.29.32.33; 14:2.3.5.6.7.9.10.11; 17:4; 18:7; 20:2; 21:2.8.

[59] See section 4.3 above.

[60] This title for Moses recurs in Ezra 3:2, Ps. 90:1 and LXX-2 Chron. 24:6.

[61] Two medieaval Masoretic manuscripts, Kenicott ms. 128 (*prima manu*) and De Rossi ms. 262 (*prima manu*), did in fact contain this title (see J.B. de Rossi, *Variae Lectiones Veteris Testamenti Librorum* II, p. 72a), but it is evident that we are dealing here with a very young scribal accident.

poration of the Priestly legislation into the Sinai-narrative (Exod. 25–Num. 10). Yet, no extra instructions are referred to in the second clause. The two clauses refer to the same set of instructions with respect to the procedure of the crossing of the Israelite priests and tribes, but whereas the first clause may refer to Yhwh's speech to Joshua in Josh. 4:1–3 and its execution by Joshua in 4:4–8, no specific instructions from Moses to Joshua with respect to the crossing of the Jordan have been recorded in the Pentateuch, which makes it very unlikely that a later editor or interpolator would deliberately have created such incoherence, especially if it had have been for amplifying purposes only.[62]

As a result, the *lectio difficilior* contained in MT-Josh. 4:10 does not support the secondary origin of the pluses עבד יהוה in MT-Josh. 1:1.15, 12:6 and 22:4. Rather, it gives occasion to the supposition that the text reflected by LXX is the result of 'stylistic shortening'. This is the term E. Tov used for a very similar variant only a few verses further on in Joshua 4, i.e. in verse 14,[63] a passage that resembles 1:5.17 and 3:7:

4[14]	ἐν ἐκείνῃ τῇ ἡμέρᾳ	בַּיּוֹם הַהוּא
	ηὔξησεν κύριος τὸν Ἰησοῦν	גִּדַּל יְהוָה אֶת־יְהוֹשֻׁעַ
	ἐναντίον παντὸς *τοῦ γένους* Ισραηλ,	בְּעֵינֵי כָּל־יִשְׂרָאֵל
	καὶ ἐφοβοῦντο αὐτὸν	וַיִּרְאוּ אֹתוֹ
	ὥσπερ --- --- Μωυσῆν,	כַּאֲשֶׁר יָרְאוּ אֶת־מֹשֶׁה
	ὅσον χρόνον ἔζη.	כָּל־יְמֵי חַיָּיו :

[62] See already the succinct remarks by D. Barthélemy, *Critique textuelle de l'ancien Testament* I, pp. 3–4: 'Considérant que Moïse n'a rien ordonné à Josué concernant les événements racontés en ce chapitre, Houbigant conclut qu'il faut omettre avec le *G cette phrase qui lui semble d'ailleurs alourdir inutilement la narration. . . . L'absence de cette phrase dans le *G ne peut s'expliquer par un accident textuel. S'il y a eu omission, ce fut vraisemblablement pour les motifs mis en avant par Houbigant. *On sait en effet que le *G est très soucieux d'éviter tout ce qui semblerait contradictoire dans l'Ecriture.*' Likewise, J. Hollenberg, *Der Charakter* (1876), p. 8, classed the variant in his category 'Zusammenziehung des breiten Ausdrucks' (of the Hebrew text by the Greek translator), although he did not deem the argument advanced by Barthélemy very likely: '4,10 . . . weggelassen, weil unmittelbar vorher ähnliches steht, nicht etwa weil von einem solchen Gebot im Pentateuch nichts bekannt war; so weit dachte der Ueb. gar nicht.'

[63] E. Tov, *Textual Criticism of the Hebrew Bible*, p. 126, and idem, *The Text-critical Use of the Septuagint²*, p. 47. See already J. Hollenberg, *Der Charakter*, p. 6, who classed this variant in his category 'Stellen . . ., an welchen der Ueb. den Text frei wiedergibt, um der Eigenthümlichkeit der griech. Sprache zu genügen.'

According to Tov, the Greek translator considered the second clause containing the verb ירא to be superfluous and, as a result, condensed the two clauses into a single one. One might add to this some other observations regarding the Greek translation that confirm Tov's explanation: [1] The Greek translator specified the more general phrase בעיני כל־ישׂראל, *in the eyes of all Israel*, by rendering it ἐναντίον παντὸς *τοῦ γένους* Ισραηλ, *before the whole nation of Israel.* The noun γένος occurs only here in LXX*-Joshua.[64] [2] The phrase כל־ימי חייו, *all the days of his life*, has been rendered freely by ὅσον χρόνον ἔζη, *as long as he lived*, as opposed to the more literal rendering of the same Hebrew expression in LXX-Josh. 1:5 πάσας τὰς ἡμέρας τῆς ζωῆς σου (likewise in the Greek Pentateuch).[65] [3] Furthermore, the Hebrew verb גדל Piʿel is rendered here by the Greek verb αὐξάνω, *to increase*, as opposed to the rendering of the parallel passage in Josh. 3:7 by the verb ὑψόω, *to exalt*, and, moreover, as opposed to the standard translation of the Hebrew root גדל by μεγαλύνω in the Greek Pentateuch and the rest of the Greek Old Testament.

The logical inference of this explanation, then must be, that in Josh. 4:10 the minus in LXX should likewise be explained in terms of 'stylistic shortening' of a redundant Hebrew text, which in addition removed the problem of a reference to unrecorded commands of Moses regarding the procedure of the crossing of the Jordan. The complex syntactic construction of the Hebrew text of Josh. 4:10 has been smoothed by the Greek translator, who remodelled the contents of this verse. In the first clause of the verse he first changed the order subject-phrase-participle (והכהנים . . . עמדים . . .) to the more usual order verb-subject, while maintaining the background-information character of the clause by employing a perfect tense: εἱστήκεισαν δὲ οἱ ἱερεῖς . . ., *the priests . . . had stood.* The continuation of this clause was likewise altered by the translator who replaced the Hebrew text עד תם כל־הדבר אשׁר־צוה יהוה את־יהושׁע, *until everything that Yhwh had commanded was completed*, by the active formulation in which Joshua is made subject of the action ἕως οὗ συνετέλεσεν Ἰησοῦς πάντα, ἃ ἐνετείλατο κύριος ἀναγγεῖλαι τῷ λαῷ, *until Joshua had completed every-*

[64] The occurrence in E and M witnesses (B.56.120.129.407) of the plus in LXX-Josh. 11:21 καὶ ἐκ παντὸς γένους Ισραηλ must be a scribal corruption from καὶ ἐκ παντὸς ὄρους Ισραηλ (thus Margolis' reconstruction based on the remaining witnesses), as is evident from the context (καὶ ἐκ παντὸς ὄρους Ιουδα). See further S. Sipilä, The Septuagint Version of Joshua 3–4, pp. 67–68.

[65] Thus J. Moatti-Fine, *Josué*, p. 113.

thing that the Lord had commanded to proclaim to the people. The elaborate formulation of the Hebrew text was thus cast into a more condensed Greek formulation, i.e. more in line with the present context of the verse, where there are only divine instructions (4:1–3) transmitted via Joshua (4:4–7).

If we now return to the problem of the 'servant of Yhwh' pluses in the four passages in MT, it is not difficult to detect a very similar concern for avoiding the ponderous Hebrew expressions by means of a stylistic shortening. In Josh. 12:6 we find two clauses with Moses as subject followed by the epithet עבד יהוה, the second being absent from the Greek text.

12[6]	Μωυσῆς ὁ παῖς κυρίου	מֹשֶׁה עֶבֶד־יְהוָה
	καὶ οἱ υἱοὶ Ισραηλ ἐπάταξαν αὐτούς,	וּבְנֵי יִשְׂרָאֵל הִכּוּם
	καὶ ἔδωκεν αὐτὴν Μωυσῆς --- ---	וַיִּתְּנָהּ מֹשֶׁה עֶבֶד־יְהוָה
	ἐν κληρονομίᾳ --- Ρουβην--- καὶ --- Γαδ---	יְרֻשָּׁה לָרְאוּבֵנִי וְלַגָּדִי
	καὶ τῷ ἡμίσει φυλῆς Μανασση.	וְלַחֲצִי שֵׁבֶט הַמְנַשֶּׁה׃

It is not difficult to imagine that either a Hebrew copyist or otherwise a Greek translator would have tried to avoid the redundancy of the Hebrew text, by skipping the second apposition as superfluous and unnecessary. The only reason for not skipping Moses altogether in the second clause is that in the first clause the children of Israel constitute the second part of the subject, which necessitated the repeated mentioning of Moses as distributor of the land in the second clause.[66] Like the first chapter of the book, chapter 12 recapitulates the previously reported events, and aims at completeness by mentioning all the defeated Canaanite kings. The double mentioning of Moses as servant of Yhwh in MT fits the amplifying Deuteronomistic style and content of the chapter. The Greek translator on the other hand, had no need to burden his text with the second apposition and left it out.

[66] The Syriac translator went a step further than the Greek translator, and omitted the second part of the subject phrase 'and the children of Israel' as well, so that the subjects of the two clauses were completely identical and 'Moses' did not need to be mentioned at all in the second clause:

ܘܝܗܒܗ̇ ܡܘܫܐ ܥܒܕܗ ܕܡܪܝܐ --- ܠܗܘܢ. --- ܝܪܬܘܬܐ ܠܪܘܒܝܠ ܘܠܓܕ ܘܠܦܠܓܗ ܕܫܒܛܐ ܕܡܢܫܐ ܀

Jerome followed LXX in his Vulgate translation: 'Moses famulus Domini et filii Israhel percusserunt eos tradiditque terram eorum Moses --- --- in possessionem Rubenitis et Gadditis et dimidiae tribui Manasse'.

A very similar situation occurs in Josh. 22:1–6, the Deuteronomistic narrative of Joshua's dismissal of the same Trans-Jordanian tribes addressed in Josh. 1:12–15, and referred to in Josh. 12:6.[67] Moses is mentioned three times here, each time accompanied in the MT by the apposition 'servant of Yhwh' (22:2.4.5):

22[2]	καὶ εἶπεν αὐτοῖς	וַיֹּאמֶר אֲלֵיהֶם
	Ὑμεῖς *ἀκηκόατε* πάντα,	אַתֶּם שְׁמַרְתֶּם אֵת כָּל־
	ὅσα ἐνετείλατο ὑμῖν	אֲשֶׁר צִוָּה אֶתְכֶם
	Μωυσῆς ὁ παῖς κυρίου,	מֹשֶׁה עֶבֶד יְהוָה
	καὶ ἐπηκούσατε τῆς φωνῆς μου κατὰ πάντα,	וַתִּשְׁמְעוּ בְקוֹלִי לְכֹל
	ὅσα ἐνετειλάμην ὑμῖν.	אֲשֶׁר־צִוִּיתִי אֶתְכֶם׃
22[3]	οὐκ ἐγκαταλελοίπατε τοὺς ἀδελφοὺς ὑμῶν	לֹא־עֲזַבְתֶּם אֶת־אֲחֵיכֶם
	ταύτας τὰς ἡμέρας *καὶ* πλείους	זֶה יָמִים רַבִּים
	ἕως τῆς σήμερον ἡμέρας [·][68]	עַד הַיּוֹם הַזֶּה
	--- ἐφυλάξασθε --- ---	וּשְׁמַרְתֶּם אֶת־מִשְׁמֶרֶת
	τὴν ἐντολὴν κυρίου τοῦ θεοῦ ὑμῶν.	מִצְוַת יְהוָה אֱלֹהֵיכֶם׃
22[4]	νῦν δὲ	וְעַתָּה
	κατέπαυσεν κύριος ὁ θεὸς *ἡμῶν*	הֵנִיחַ יְהוָה אֱלֹהֵיכֶם
	τοὺς ἀδελφοὺς *ἡμῶν*,	לַאֲחֵיכֶם
	ὃν τρόπον εἶπεν αὐτοῖς·	כַּאֲשֶׁר דִּבֶּר לָהֶם
	νῦν οὖν	וְעַתָּה
	ἀποστραφ*έντες*	פְּנוּ
	--- ἀπέλθατε --- εἰς τοὺς *οἴκους* ὑμῶν	וּלְכוּ לָכֶם לְאָהֳלֵיכֶם
	καὶ εἰς τὴν γῆν τῆς κατασχέσεως ὑμῶν,	אֶל־אֶרֶץ אֲחֻזַּתְכֶם
	ἣν ἔδωκεν ὑμῖν Μωυσῆς --- ---	אֲשֶׁר נָתַן לָכֶם מֹשֶׁה עֶבֶד יְהוָה
	ἐν τῷ πέραν τοῦ Ιορδάνου.	בְּעֵבֶר הַיַּרְדֵּן׃
22[5]	ἀλλὰ φυλάξασθε ---	רַק שִׁמְרוּ מְאֹד
	ποιεῖν *σφόδρα τὰς* ἐντολὰς καὶ τὸν νόμον,	לַעֲשׂוֹת אֶת־הַמִּצְוָה וְאֶת־הַתּוֹרָה
	ὃν ἐνετείλατο *ἡμῖν*	אֲשֶׁר צִוָּה אֶתְכֶם
	ποιεῖν Μωυσῆς ὁ παῖς κυρίου,	מֹשֶׁה עֶבֶד־יְהוָה

[67] See sections 4.2.1 on Josh. 22:1–4.6 (DtrH) and 4.2.2 on Josh. 22:5 (DtrN) above.

[68] S. Holmes, *Joshua*, p. 74, pointed to the shift in verbal tense in the Greek text from perfect οὐκ ἐγκαταλελοίπατε, *you have not deserted*, to aorist ἐφυλάξασθε, *you have kept*, and to the fact that the conjunctive *waw* in the corresponding Hebrew ושמרתם *and you have kept*, has no equivalent in the Greek text. In the light of the Greek translator's preference to avoid asyndetic clauses, the Greek text should be understood as follows: *You have not deserted your brothers these many days. Until today you have kept the commandment of the Lord your God.* This means that the prepositional phrase ἕως τῆς σήμερον ἡμέρας, *until this day*, is not to be connected with the previous clause (as Rahlfs and Margolis did by placing a semicolon after the phrase, and as the Masoretes did for MT by placing an *ʾatnaḥ* after עד היום הזה) but with the second clause of the verse. Perhaps this construction reflects the Greek translator's understanding of the phrase as anticipation of the following story (verses 13–34), in which the faithfulness of the Trans-Jordanian tribes has become a matter of dispute.

As in the DtrH-passages Josh. 1:1–6.9.10–18 and Josh. 12, the Hebrew text aims at amplifying and emphasizing the themes of obedience of all Israelite tribes to Joshua as successor of Yhwh's servant Moses (evident in the ponderous formulation in verse 2 which twice contains the expression כל אשר צוה אתכם, and the repetition of the root שמר in Josh. 22:2,[69] and 22:3, where both the verb and the noun משמרת occur),[70] and the theme of the inheritance of the land ארץ אחזתכם אשר נתן לכם משה [עבד יהוה] בעבר הירדן.[71] The explicit threefold mentioning of Moses as Servant of Yhwh fits this Deuteronomistic style. The absence in LXX-Joshua of the second of these three consecutive identical phrases within the same context is thus most plausibly explained as a modest attempt to avoid the repetitiveness of the ponderous text, especially since in verse 2 (MT and LXX) Moses had already been introduced by this title. The third occurrence of the epithet occurs in the DtrN-expansion of Josh. 22:5, in which the theme of reward after obedience is transformed in a renewed appeal to obedience, this time to the *torah* of Moses. Probably

[69] The LXX reflects an even stronger parallellism between Joshua and Moses as a result of the double use of the verb ἀκούω. The Hebrew text has two distinct though graphically similar verbs, שמר and שמע, which fits the overall context of the passage and is thus commonly considered to be the more original reading, see e.g. J. Hollenberg, *Der Charakter*, p. 17 (sub Hebrew variants originating on the Hebrew level); S. Holmes, *Joshua*, p. 74: 'misreading for שמרתם.'; and J. Moatti-Fine, *Josué*, p. 220.

[70] The absence of a counterpart of this noun in the Greek text should with J. Hollenberg, *Der Charakter*, p. 8, be classed in the category 'Zusammenziehung des breiten Ausdrucks' of the long-winded and overloaded Hebrew expression ושמרתם את־משמרת מצות יהוה אלהיכם, *you have observed the observance of the command of Yhwh your God*, into the more sensible and coherent Greek expression ἐφυλάξασθε τὴν ἐντολὴν κυρίου τοῦ θεοῦ ὑμῶν. See also J. Moatti-Fine, *Josué*, p. 220. It seems that not even the recentiores felt the need to restore the redundancy of the Hebrew expression, as no readings corresponding to MT have been recorded in either the margin or in the hexaplaric witnesses. The reverse possibility, that a Hebrew editor would have deliberately added the noun influenced by the language of Deuteronomy, has not yet been defended.

[71] The presence of the typically Priestly term for land-property, אחזה, in Josh. 22:2, rather than the Deuteronomistic term ירשה within this Deuteronomistic passage is problematic. A. Kuenen, *Historisch-critisch onderzoek*², p. 328; A. Dillmann, *Numeri, Deuteronomium, Josua*, p. 575; C. Steuernagel, *Deuteronomium und Josua*, p. 236; and H. Holzinger, *Das Buch Josua*, pp. 90–91, explain this phenomenon as a textual alteration created by the final redactor of the book, whereas V. Fritz, *Das Buch Josua*, p. 226, takes it as an argument to claim a very young redactional origin for the whole of Josh. 22:1–6. Since the passage lacks other Priestly concepts and interests, whereas Deuteronomistic themes characterise the whole passage, probably not too much importance should be attached to a single expression.

because of this shift of focus, the Greek translator did not omit the title in verse 5.

The secondary deliberate omission of a superfluous phrase (in LXX-Josh. 22:4) should in all likelihood be ascribed to the Greek translator, who introduced a few other modest modifications in the same verse 4 as well. First he contracted the paratactic chain of two consecutive imperatives פנו ולכו into a hypotactic construction with a subordinated aorist conjunctive participle followed asyndetically by the (main) imperative ἀποστραφέντες ἀπέλθατε.[72] Likewise, the *dativus ethicus* לכם has not been translated, since a literal translation of this Hebrew idiomatic expression would make no sense in the Greek text. Furthermore, the Greek translator rendered the first occurrence of the temporal adverb ועתה, where it functions to introduce the present situation as opposed to the past events (22:2–3), relatively literally by δέ νῦν, while he employed the coordinate conjunction οὖν in the phrase νῦν οὖν to render the same Hebrew phrase in the second half of the verse, where it marks the transition from description to admonition (imperative)[73]—an appropriate, but relatively free rendering.[74] Interesting is finally the actualisation of the expression 'go to your *tents*, to the land of your possession' (ולכו לכם לאהליכם . . .) into the more 'settled' expression 'go to your *houses* and to the land . . .' (ἀπέλθατε εἰς τοὺς οἴκους ὑμῶν καὶ εἰς τὴν γῆν . . .).[75]

---

[72] See the discussion of participle constructions in C.G. den Hertog, *Studien*, p. 172ff. (= *BIOSCS* 29 (1996), p. 42ff.). See further A. Aejmelaeus, *Participium coniunctum* as a Criterion of Translation Technique, in *VT* 32 (1982), pp. 385–393 (= idem, *On the Trail of the Septuagint Translators*. Kampen 1993, pp. 7–16), where she points out (p. 7) that this Greek construction, common in classical and koine Greek, has no direct Hebrew equivalent, and thus indicates the relative freedom of the translator and his ability to master larger Hebrew units beyond the word-for-word-level, and secondly (p. 14), that the Greek translation of Joshua belongs to the group of translated Old Testament books where the conjunctive participle appears most frequently.

[73] Thus W. Schneider, *Grammatik des biblischen Hebräisch*. München 1985[6], § 54 ('Übergangssignal').

[74] See A. Aejmelaeus, *Parataxis in the Pentateuch*, p. 56ff.; and S. Sipilä, *Between Literalness and Freedom*, pp. 105–106.

[75] The same translation appears in Josh. 22:6.7.8, and occasionally in the Greek Pentateuch, see LXX-Gen. 9:21.27; 24:67; 31:33 (5 times), LXX-Lev. 14:8, LXX-Num. 9:15; 19:18, 24:5; LXX-Deut. 5:30; 16:7, and further; and outside the Greek Hexateuch, only in the free Greek rendering of Job (12:5(6); 15:34; 20:26, 29:4). The standard equivalent for אהל is of course σκηνή (cf. LXX-Josh. 7:21.22.23.24 and 18:1. 19:51; 22:19.29; 24:25), whereas οἶκος normally represents the Hebrew noun בית; see further J. Moatti-Fine, *Josué*, pp. 220–221; J.W. Wevers, *Notes on the Greek Text of Deuteronomy*. (SBL-SCS 39) Atlanta 1995, p. 109.

In the passage corresponding to this DtrH-narrative, Josh. 1:12–15, the situation is no different: again the Hebrew text is overloaded with Deuteronomistic themes, of which Moses' designation as 'servant of Yhwh' is one of several word repetitions in this segment, for instance the threefold occurrence of the combination נתן with ארץ followed by a further specification (see above), and the repetition of the root ירש in verse 15 (see further below). Again, at the beginning of this new segment in Joshua 1, the first of the two consecutive occurrences of the same epithet in MT (1:13; 1:15) is also present in LXX-Joshua and sufficient for a proper understanding of the figure of Moses throughout these verses. As a result, the second occurrence in MT-Josh. 1:15, is quite superfluous within this context and could for that reason be missed.

So far, three weighty Deuteronomistic passages have been discussed, where at a secondary stage the verbose Hebrew text has been slightly stylised by omitting the second occurrence within the same context of the title 'servant of Yhwh' (Josh. 12:6; 22:4, 1:15), possibly by a Hebrew copyist, but more probably (at least in the case of Josh. 22:4) by the Greek translator, who (as he did in Josh. 4:10 and 4:14) employed the device of 'stylistic shortening' for the sake of a smooth, intelligible and elegant Greek text. In Joshua 1:1 the situation differs only inasmuch as the first of the two consecutive titles for Moses is absent from LXX, whereas the epithet is attested by both MT and LXX two clauses further on in Josh. 1:2, with the minor difference that it is Yhwh himself who designates Moses as 'My servant' (עבדי/ὁ θεράπων μου).

The apposition occurs in MT exactly where one would expect it, i.e. at the beginning of a new text segment, which would argue for its originality. One could reverse this statement by arguing that this was the very reason for its secondary addition in Joshua 1. In that case we would be dealing with an incidental interpolation rather than an element of a comprehensive re-edition, since in the other three cases (1:15, 12:6 and 22:4) the absence of the phrase is secondary to the more original redundant Hebrew text as preserved in MT. In the light of the previous observations, however, it is plausible to assume that the absence of the epithet עבד־יהוה in LXX-Josh. 1:1 must be ascribed to the same tendency of 'stylistic shortening'. By retaining this title at the beginning of Yhwh's direct speech and omitting it from the narrative introduction (Josh. 1:1) a few things have been accomplished: whereas the opening statement in the second verse (משׁה עבדי מת—Μωυσῆς ὁ θεράπων μου τετελεύτηκεν) is succinct enough, the preceding bulky narrative introduction is now somewhat relieved, so that all emphasis in the narrative introduction to the divine spreech (Josh. 1:1) now falls on the hero of the book and the addressee of the subsequent discourse, and more particularly, on his relation to Moses as the latter's assistant. The epithet for Moses has kept its full weight and importance since it is God himself who uses this designation ('My servant').

As we have seen, the relation between Yhwh and Moses is amplified throughout the Deuteronomistic (DtrH and DtrN) portions of the book, as is the stress (in the DtrH-stratum) on the (more or less) equal status of Moses and Joshua (1:5, 16–18, 3:7, 4:10.14; 11:15). The title מְשָׁרֵת, (*personal*) *servant*,[76] for Joshua, however, occurs only here in the book of Joshua. The Greek translator employed the noun ὑπουργός,[77] *assistant, somebody working under* (*the supervision of a master*),[78] which is a word that occurs only here in the whole Greek Bible.[79]

---

[76] See C. Westermann, שׁרת *šrt* dienen, in *ThHAT* II, col. 1019–1022.

[77] Thus the most important witnesses B.129 (<u>E</u>), and further a number of <u>S</u> (54.Tht) and <u>M</u> (F*.56.85 [in the margin]) witnesses, as well as ms. 19 (<u>P</u>$_1$); cf. the attribution to ο' in the margin of 344. The remaining <u>P</u> and <u>C</u> witnesses (A.F^{b} ^{mg}.M.V.W. 85 [main text] and the majority of minuscules) read the standard equivalent λειτουργός, *servant, minister* (see further below), see S. Daniel, *Recherches sur le vocabulaire du culte dans la Septante.* Paris 1966, p. 93ff., especially p. 95, and 97 (n. 18). The daughter translations VetLat. (*successorem Moysi* 'successor'), Syh (ܡܫܡܫܢܗ ܕܡܘܫܐ. 'servant' [identical with Peš-Josh. 1:1]) and Arm. employ their own vocabulary.

The recentiores replaced the LXX-rendering of the same epithet for Joshua in Exod. 24:13 (Ἰησοῦς ὁ παρεστηκὼς αὐτῷ [sc. Moses]) by the same noun λειτουργός (compare also the replacement of LXX-Gen. 40:4 καὶ παρέστη αυτοῖς—MT וישׁרת אתם [said of Joseph's service to Pharao's baker in prison] by ἐλειτούργει [α' according to M]/ἐλιτούργει [σ' according to 939]). For this reason, Margolis in his unpublished monograph on *Andreas Masius and His Commentary on the Book of Joshua* § 10, note 143, argued that the origin of the Hexaplaric reading in Josh. 1:1 must derive from the recentiores (possibly Aquila) as well:

> It is to be noted that in the three places of the Pentateuch where Joshua is spoken of as the משׁרת of Moses, <u>G</u> uses Ex 33:11 θεραπων (but F^{bm} υπουργος) and Ex. 24:13, Num. 11:28 the paraphrase: ο παρεστηκως αυτω (μωυση); comp. also Ge 40:4 of Joseph: και παρεστη αυτοις. The aim is apparently to express the meaning of 'attendant', and to preclude the notion that Priestly or Levitical functions attached to his ministry (contrast Wellhausen, Composition, 90, n. 1), such as were associated with λειτουργος (compare λειτουργειν in the Pentateuch; Deissmann, Bibelstudien 137). (. . .)

[78] LEH, p. 496a; LSJ, p. 1900b; S. Daniel, *Recherches sur le vocabulaire du culte.* Paris 1966, p. 97ff. The term is used for a doctor's assistant (Hippocrates, *Acute Diseases* 67, fifth century BCE) or workmen (Cairo Zenon Papyrus 59176, lines 220–235, dated July 255 BCE; C.C. Edgar (ed.), *Zenon Papyri* II. Caire 1926).

[79] See HR, p. 1417c.

This title differs from those employed by the Greek translators of Exodus and Numbers, where the same Hebrew noun מְשָׁרֵת is paraphrased by ὁ παρεστηκώς, *attendant, somebody standing besides*,[80] in those cases where Joshua attends Moses on mount Sinai (LXX-Exod. 24:13)[81] or stands at the entrance of the Tent of Meeting (LXX-Num. 11:28),[82] or rendered (LXX-Exod. 33:11)[83] by the title which is used here in Josh. 1:1 for Moses, θέραπων, *servant, attendant* or *companion*.[84]

The Greek translator of Joshua, however, shared with these two translators the concern to reserve the use of the otherwise standard translations of the derivates of the Hebrew root שׁרת by derivatives of the Greek verb λειτουργέω, *to perform a religious service*, exclusively for cultic services (of the Levite and Aaronic priests),[85] and thus reveals the same concern to grant Joshua an adequate and honorary title, which here expresses the positive notion of Joshua being Moses' *fellow* or *partner*.[86]

---

[80] LEH, p. 359. The only parallel to this equation in the Septuagint appears in LXX-2 Reg. 13:17, where Amnon's מְשָׁרֵת has been rendered by ὁ προεστηκώς.

[81] MT: ויקם משה ויהושע משׁרתו—LXX: καὶ ἀναστὰς Μωυσῆς καὶ Ἰησοῦς ὁ παρεστηκὼς αὐτῷ. The younger Greek versions (α', σ', θ') used the standard equivalent λειτουργός.

[82] MT: ויען יהושע בן־נון משרת משה מבחריו—LXX: καὶ ἀποκριθεὶς Ἰησοῦς ὁ τοῦ Ναυὴ ὁ παρεστηκὼς ὁ ἐκλεκτὸς. No readings of the recentiores have been recorded in the Greek manuscripts.

[83] MT: ודבר יהוה אל־משה פנים אל־פנים (. . .) ומשׁרתו יהושע בן־נון נער לא ימישׁ מתוך האהל LXX: καὶ ἐλάλησεν κύριος πρὸς Μωυσῆν ἐνώπιος ἐνωπίῳ (. . .) ὁ δὲ θεράπων Ἰησους υἱος Ναυη νέος οὐκ ἐξεπορεύετο ἐκ τῆς σκηνῆς. The three younger Greek versions (α', σ', θ') departed from the policy to render שׁרת by λειτουργ- and replaced this title by the one occurring in LXX-Josh. 1:1 ὁ ὑπουργός.

[84] Thus LEH, p. 204a; LSJ, p. 793a; GELS², p. 259a; S. Daniel, *Recherches sur le vocabulaire du culte*, p. 103, n. 38; M. Harl, *La Genèse*. (La Bible d'Alexandrie 1) Paris 1986, p. 202; 'L'usage en grec classique est noble, c'est 'le suivant' des dieux.'

[85] See HR, pp. 872b–873c; S. Daniel, *Recherches sur le vocabulaire du culte*, pp. 93–117: 'Chapître IV. La notion de service (suite) III. Le verbe *š-r-t*.'; G. Dorival, *Les Nombres*. (La Bible d'Alexandrie 4) Paris 1994, p. 88. Ten of the twenty times the noun מְשָׁרֵת occurs in the Hebrew Bible, this standard equivalent λειτουργός is employed, thus: LXX-2 Reg. 13:18; LXX-3 Reg. 10:5; LXX-4 Reg. 4:43; 6:15; LXX-Isa. 61:6, LXX-Ps. 102 (103):21, 103 (104):21, LXX-1 Chron. 16:4; LXX-2 Chron. 9:4; 23:6.

[86] See the lucid interpretation provided as early as the late 16th century by A. Masius, *Josuae imperatoris historia*, Commentary (1838), col. 872: 'Sed observandum est, eum non vocari servum Mosis, sed ministrum. Neque enim vir inter suos tribules primarius servitutem Mosi servierat, sed eum officiosè comitatus, observaverat. Unde à Septuag. interpretibus nunc ὑπουργός, alibi θεράπων, semel atque iterùm παρεστηκώς pro vocabulo מְשָׁרֵת redditum est. Haec eò moneo, ne quis Mosis exemplo, cum servitis reipub. consilia communicanda putet, quae prudentissimi homines existimant; his clàm habere debet. *Servus enim*, inquit Christus, *nescit quid faciat dominus ipsius*.'

A similar well-considered interpretation of the Hebrew idiom is apparent in the presentation of the figure of Moses in LXX-Josh. 1:2, where the Greek noun θέραπων conveys the notion of the intimate relation between the Lord and the lawgiver, in clear contradistinction to the plain meaning of the Hebrew noun עֶבֶד, *servant* or *slave*. This title for Moses occurs in the Greek Bible already in LXX-Exod. 14:31 and LXX-Num. 12:7–8; elsewhere only in the LXX plus in 1 Chron. 16:30, and within LXX-Joshua in 9:2b and 2d (MT-Josh. 8:31.33), varying the more frequent and neutral term παῖς in the sense of 'servant',[87] or in LXX-Deut. 34:5 οἰκέτης, which denotes a slave with a prominent status in the household.[88]

Again, LXX-Joshua follows the well-considered device employed by the Greek translators of the Pentateuch to interpret the epitheton as a honorary title, and to avoid the Greek notion of δουλεύω, *to be a slave*, and δοῦλος, *slave*, which in the Hellenistic world refers to a very specific social group and for that reason was regarded as an inappropriate for Israel's great hero Moses.[89]

---

[87] Thus within the same first chapter of the Greek book of Joshua in verses 7 and 13, and further in LXX-Josh. 9:24; 11:12.15; 12:6; 13:8; 14:7 (ὁ παῖς τοῦ θεοῦ for MT עבד־יהוה); 18:7; 22:2.5. Further in LXX-2 Esdr. 11:7–8 (MT-Neh. 1:7–8), LXX-2 Chron. 1:3 and in the phrase παῖς τοῦ θεοῦ for the corresponding Hebrew title עבד (ה)אלהים in LXX-Dan. 9:11 (replaced by θ' by δουλος), LXX-1 Chron. 6:34, 2 Chron. 24:9. Compare also the variation in renderings of the designation of the Gibeonites as עֶבֶד in LXX-Josh. 9 (verses 8, 9, 11 and 23—in verse 24 the Hebrew noun is finally left untranslated). The Gibeonites present themselves as οἰκέται or παῖδές to Joshua and the Israelites (again in 10:6), but when their ruse is discovered, they are convicted to become δοῦλοι, see J. Moatti-Fine, *Josué*, pp. 141, 146.

[88] LEH, p. 325a; S. Daniel, *Recherches sur le vocabulaire du culte*, pp. 103–104. J.W. Wevers, *Notes on the Greek Text of Deuteronomy*, p. 559, discerns a dramatic notion behind the choice for this translation: 'Throughout Deut the therm οἰκέτης has been reserved for Israel's status of slavery in Egypt, except for 15:17 where the literal meaning of 'household servant' is intended for the Hebrew servant who refuses to leave his master after the six years of servitude. The translator, by this choice of the term, dubs Moses as the involuntary slave of the Lord, one chosen by him, even against his will, according to Exod 4.'

[89] See e.g. S. Daniel, *Recherches sur le vocabulaire du culte*, p. 103; B.G. Wright, Δοῦλος and Παῖς as Translations of עבד: Lexical Equivalences and Conceptual Transformations, in B.A. Taylor (ed.), *IX Congress of the IOSCS. Cambridge 1995* (SBL-SCS 45) Atlanta 1997, pp. 263–277. Likewise in LXX-Num. 14:24 Caleb receives the title παῖς for MT עבד. Remarkably, the Greek translator of Joshua had no problems using the word δοῦλος or οἰκέτης with respect to Joshua in LXX-Josh. 5:14 and 24:30. Compare also the parallel passage in LXX-Judg. 2:8 (no variants recorded for the Greek texts), see further J. Moatti-Fine, *Josué*, p. 25ff.: 'Le personnage de Josué'.

In the light of the preceding observations with respect to the redaction-historical background of the Hebrew text, and the well-considered strategies with which the Greek translator transformed the Hebrew text into a more stylized, coherent Greek text, it is very plausible that the plus in MT-Josh. 1:1 is not to be seen as a secondary addition, but rather as a deliberate reformulation of the redundant Hebrew text by the Greek translator.[90]

6.4.2 *'This Jordan' (Josh. 1:2; 4:22)*

The pronoun הזה after 'Jordan' is absent in LXX-Josh. in Josh. 1:2 as well as in 4:22. Again a mechanical copying error as cause for these variants is highly implausible,[91] as is the assumption of an inner-Septuagintal omission.[92]

4[22]	*ἀναγγείλατε* τοῖς υἱοῖς ὑμῶν	וְהוֹדַעְתֶּם אֶת־בְּנֵיכֶם
	ὅτι	לֵאמֹר
	Ἐπὶ ξηρᾶς διέβη Ισραηλ	בַּיַּבָּשָׁה עָבַר יִשְׂרָאֵל
	τὸν Ιορδάνην --- [93]	אֶת־הַיַּרְדֵּן הַזֶּה׃
4[23]	*ἀποξηράναντος κυρίου τοῦ θεοῦ ἡμῶν*	אֲשֶׁר־הוֹבִישׁ יְהוָה אֱלֹהֵיכֶם
	τὸ ὕδωρ τοῦ Ιορδάνου	אֶת־מֵי הַיַּרְדֵּן
	ἐκ τοῦ ἔμπροσθεν *αὐτῶν*	מִפְּנֵיכֶם

Tov describes the pluses as 'small elucidations' introduced by the re-edition of the book.[94] One wonders, however, what constitutes the elucidating element, since there is only one river Jordan. A deliberate addition of the pronoun '*this* Jordan' would imply that a scribe

---

[90] Likewise with respect to Josh. 1:1, but without substantial argumentation and more tentatively: H. Holzinger, *Das Buch Josua*, p. 1; G.A. Cooke, *The Book of Joshua*, p. 2; T.C. Butler, *Joshua*, p. 3.

[91] Thus H.M. Orlinsky, The Hebrew Vorlage, p. 193; E.A. Chesman, *Studies in the Septuagint*, pp. 18–26; and R.G. Boling, *Joshua*, p. 114, who classes the variant in 1:2 with 'traditional variants, since there is no mechanism to explain introduction of the pronoun into one text or loss of it from the other', without explaining the genetic relation between these traditions and without taking into account the possibility of literary initiatives.

[92] Thus J.E. Erbes, *The Peshitta and the Versions*, p. 65. He regards the absence of the pronoun in 1:4 (both LXX and Vg *a deserto et libano*) an intentional removal of information irrelevant to the Greek or Latin readership (pp. 78–79).

[93] The reconstruction of the original Greek text is somewhat problematic since the longer version is attested by B, whereas the shorter version is supported mainly by the younger C [A.M.V.W. 29.55.59.82.121. Arm.] and M [15.58.72.509] witnesses. The Syh (ܕܗܐ ܒܝܒܫܐ ܥܒܪ ܐܝܣܪܝܠ ܠܝܘܪܕܢܢ ※ ܗܢܐ ↙) and the references to οι λ̣ τοῦτον in M and 344 make clear that Origen did not find the pronoun in his Greek *Vorlage*, hence both Rahlfs and Margolis reconstruct LXX* without the pronoun.

[94] E. Tov, The Growth, p. 332 (= *The Greek and Hebrew Bible*, p. 391). These minor variants are largely ignored in the commentaries and text-critical investigations

or editor wanted to distinguish between various rivers with the same name. This is highly unlikely. Moreover, if the MT plus in Josh. 1:2 and 4:22 were the result of a re-edition as reflected by MT, one would expect to find a shorter text in LXX-Josh. 1:11 as well. Here, however, we find the longer expression 'this Jordan' both in MT and LXX (ὑμεῖς διαβαίνετε τὸν Ιορδάνην τοῦτον).

The expression *this Jordan*, הירדן הזה, is found also in Gen. 32:11 and Deut. 3:27 and 31:2.[95] Here the pronoun הזה has the same deictic function as in Josh. 1:2.11, 4:22: *this river Jordan which you see here right before your eyes.*[96]

Gen. 32[10]	ἐν γὰρ τῇ ῥάβδῳ μου διέβην τὸν Ἰορδάνην τοῦτον,	כִּי בְמַקְלִי עָבַרְתִּי אֶת־הַיַּרְדֵּן הַזֶּה
Deut. 3[27]	ὅτι οὐ διαβήσῃ τὸν Ιορδάνην τοῦτον.	כִּי־לֹא תַעֲבֹר אֶת־הַיַּרְדֵּן הַזֶּה׃
Deut. 31[2]	κύριος *δὲ* εἶπεν πρός με Οὐ διαβήσῃ τὸν Ἰορδάνην τοῦτον.	וַיהוָה אָמַר אֵלַי לֹא תַעֲבֹר אֶת־הַיַּרְדֵּן הַזֶּה׃

The pronoun in the Deuteronomistic passages (Deuteronomy 3, 31 and Joshua 1) thus strengthens the fictitious setting of Deuteronomy at the border of the Promised Land.[97] In other words, from a

(including BHS ad 4:22). K. Bieberstein, *Josua-Jordan-Jericho*, p. 87, argues in an extensive discussion of the variant in Josh. 1:2 in conjunction with the MT-plus הזה in 1:4 (see below) and the preposition-phrase בו in 1:3 and 1:8, which is likewise without equivalent in LXX (the variant in 4:22 is noted [p. 87, n. 27], but not discussed separately), that a backwards revision starting from 1:11 where the phrase 'this Jordan' is attested by all extant witnesses, is highly unlikely. He finds it more likely that the Greek translator did not always render the demonstrative pronouns for topographica.

[95] The Jordan (without עבר[ב]) occurs 16 times in Deuteronomy: Deut. 2:29; 3:17.27; 4:21.22.26; 9;1; 11:31; 12:10; 27:2.4.12; 30:18; 31:2.13; 32:47, see further M. Görg, יַרְדֵּן *jarden*, in *ThWAT* III, col. 901–909.

[96] See e.g. W. Schneider, *Grammatik des biblischen Hebräisch* § 52.4, and further the commentaries to Joshua, e.g. P.D. Baldi, o.f.m., *Giosuè*, p. 18: 'G om. il demonstrativo 'questo'. Rientrando il Giordano nella sfere visuale, il demonstrativo dà maggior vivezza al discorso: 'il Giordano che vedi là.'; J.H. Kroeze, *Het boek Jozua*. (COT) Kampen 1968, p. 28.

[97] Gen. 32:11 refers to Jacob's immanent encounter with his brother after he will have crossed the Jordan. Interestingly, Josh. 1:2 shares with the passages in Deut. 3:27 and 31:2 the theme of Moses' fate: not to be allowed by Yhwh to cross the Jordan. Influenced by these passages the pronoun was added to the references to the Jordan in Deut. 4:21 and 22 in LXX*, Peš and MT-ms. Kennicott 605 in Deut. 4:21 and in the original text of B (only) in LXX-Deut. 9:1, see J.W. Wevers, *Notes to the Greek Text of Deuteronomy*, pp. 78–79. Other examples of such deictic ele-

redaction-historical point of view, there is no reason to assume that the pronoun הזה in Josh. 1:2 (and 1:11) belongs to a post-DtrH redaction, since it perfectly fits the Deuteronomistic character of the narrative line Deuteronomy 3–31—Joshua 1.[98]

The absence of these deictic elements from LXX-Josh. 1:2 and 4:22 may therefore be explained in terms of stylisation of the redundant Hebrew text.[99] Since there was only one river Jordan, the Greek translator had no need to translate this element. Perhaps the reason why he retained it in Josh. 1:11 was his wish to visualise the distance between Jordan and the people's camp, which was removed from the place where Joshua and the officials were located (Josh. 1:11), and which according to Josh. 3:1 was a full marching day removed from the Jordan.

6.4.3 *The Receivers of the Divine Gift of the Land (Josh. 1:2)*

MT-Josh. 1:2 contains the plus לבני ישׂראל *vis-à-vis* LXX after the phrase אשׁר אנכי נתן להם. The plus would have provided an interesting example of a subtle redactional blending—ideologically or theologically motivated—of the original expression, had the suffix in the first of the two prepositional phrases להם referred to a group other than the Israelites.[100] The preceding clauses (עבר . . . אתה וכל־העם הזה . . .), however, leave no doubt about the identity of this group, since the suffix can only refer to 'this people', understood as a collectivum. The plus in MT is merely redundant and superfluous. For this reason it is hard to see why an editor (Tov)[101] or an interpolator (as is the general consensus)[102] would have wanted to elucidate a shorter text that in itself is already crystal-clear.

---

ments in Deuteronomy are found, for instance, in Deut. 1:19 המדבר . . . אשׁר ראיתם (cf. 1:31), and 1:31 עד־באכם עד־המקום הזה.

[98] On the Deuteronomistic background of Josh. 4:21–24, see section 7.4.3.2 below.

[99] Jerome followed the opposite way. He rendered the phrases in 1:2 and 4:22 (*Iordanem istum*), but left it untranslated in 1:11 (*post diem tertium transibitis Iordanem*).

[100] Again the possibility of an unconscious scribal error as origin of the variant is most unlikely, see R.G. Boling, *Joshua*, p. 115.

[101] E. Tov, The Growth, p. 332 (= *The Greek and Hebrew Bible*, p. 391), classes this MT plus under 'small elucidations' (introduced by the second edition of the Book of Joshua).

[102] Thus BHS *ad loco* and further e.g. A. Dillmann, *Die Bücher Numeri, Deuteronomium und Josua*, p. 443; C. Steuernagel, *Das Buch Josua*, p. 154; H. Holzinger, *Das Buch Josua*, p. 1; A.B. Ehrlich, *Randglossen zur hebräischen Bibel Dritter Band*. Leipzig 1910,

The additional argument put forward by Holmes and Benjamin,[103] that the construction is Aramaic, rather than classical Hebrew is untenable, since we are not dealing here with a genitive construction formed with a proleptic suffix,[104] which is a common Aramaic construction. According to the rules of classical Hebrew a construction containing a double indirect object with the same preposition is superfluous, but by no means impossible or unique, see Num. 32:33 ויתן להם משה לבני־גד ולבני ראובן ולחצי שבט מנשה (supported by all witnesses) or 2 Sam. 7:8 כה־תאמר לעבדי לדויד . . . להיות נגיד על־עמי על־ישראל.[105] Within the context of Joshua 1, one might compare this expression with the equally redundant one in verse 6, where the indirect object has been realized twice with the same preposition as well תנחיל את־העם הזה את־הארץ אשר־נשבעתי לאבותם לתת להם, although the order preposition *le-* plus suffix; preposition *le-* plus noun has been inverted and the parts have been separated from one another by a verb (לתת). Interestingly, the redundancy in Josh. 1:2 was also felt by Jerome (*in terram quam ego dabo filiis Israhel*) and some Masoretic scribe(s) who omitted the first phrase in Josh. 1:2 (Kenn. 50, 109, 111, 187, 244, de Rossi 443).[106] The absence of the phrase לבני ישׂראל is thus the result of a shortening of a superfluous Hebrew expression, either effected by a Hebrew scribe at a stage preceding the Hebrew *Vorlage* of LXX,[107] but in the light of the preceding observations more likely the enterprise of the Greek translator.[108]

---

p. 1; G.A. Cooke, *The Book of Joshua*, p. 3; M. Noth, *Das Buch Josua*², p. 20; P.D. Baldi, *Giosuè*, p. 18; H.W. Hertzberg, *Die Bücher Josua, Richter, Ruth*, p. 13, n. 1; J.H. Kroeze, *Het boek Jozua*, p. 28; J.A. Soggin, *Le livre de Josué*, p. 27; P. Sacchi, Giosuè 1,1–9, p. 238; V. Fritz, *Das Buch Josua*, p. 26; K. Bieberstein, *Josua-Jordan-Jericho*, p. 86; and J. Nentel, *Trägerschaft*, p. 19.

[103] S. Holmes, *Joshua*, p. 17; C.D. Benjamin, *The Variations*, p. 23.

[104] See e.g. F. Rosenthal, *A Grammar of Biblical Aramaic* Wiesbaden 1963² § 48.

[105] Already Holmes referred to the observations made by S.R. Driver, *Notes on the Hebrew Text of the Books of Samuel*. Oxford 1890, pp. 140–141 (ad 1 Sam. 21:14). See further the examples mentioned by P. Joüon, s.j.—T. Muraoka, *A Grammar of Biblical Hebrew*. Roma 1991, § 146e observation 2: Judg. 21:7; Jer. 41:3; 51:56; Dan. 11:11; 1 Chron. 4:42; and 2 Chron. 26:14.

[106] J.B. de Rossi, *Variae lectiones veteris testamenti librorum* II, p. 71a.

[107] J. Hollenberg, *Der Charakter der alexandrinischen Uebersetzung des Buches Josua*. Moers 1876, p. 18, classed the minus of LXX under 'Lücken' (i.e. in the Hebrew *Vorlage*).

[108] Thus already A. Masius, *Josuae imperatoris historia*, Commentary (1838), col. 877: 'Quod in verborum sacrorum ordine sequitur, *ipsis filiis Israel*, hebraismus est; dum ἐξηγητίκως ea nomina in oratione adduntur, quae alioqui per posita ante, ipsorum loco, pronomina satis expressa videri poterant; qualis est illa quoque in Exodo, 2,6, phrasis: *Et vidit ipsum, puerum*, in quo loquendi genere vulgus solet apud

6.4.4 *The Extent of the Promised Land (Josh. 1:3–4)*

The MT of Josh. 1:4 contains a number of pluses *vis-à-vis* LXX: [1] the preposition מִן, *from*, in front of המדבר, *the desert*, [2] the demonstrative pronoun הזה after הלבנון, *this Lebanon*,[109] [3] the conjunction -וְ before the first occurrence of the preposition עַד, *until*, and [4] most strikingly, the phrase כל ארץ החתים, *all the land of the Hittites*. Whereas the addition or omission of the one-letter elements -מ and -ו could be the result of scribal neglect, such an explanation is again unlikely in the case of the pluses הזה[110] and the phrase כל ארץ החתים. The situation is complicated by the fact that this passage quotes from Deut. 11:24, where the latter two phrases are also absent and which reads מן־הנהר rather than ועד־הנהר (MT-Josh. 1:4):

Deut. 11:24	מן־המדבר והלבנון [112]מן־הנהר[111]
Josh. 1:4	מהמדבר והלבנון הזה ועד־הנהר הגדול
Deut. 11:24	נהר־פרת ועד הים האחרון
Josh. 1:4	נהר־פרת כל ארץ החתים ועד־הים הגדול מבוא השמש

These discrepancies between these two related passages have occasioned numerous scholars to regard the pluses of MT-Josh. 1:4 as compared to LXX-Joshua and the Deuteronomy text as interpolations in MT-Joshua. As a result, these scholars propose to reconstruct the original wording of Josh. 1:4 more or less in accordance with the Deuteronomy text.[113] Influence of the Greek text of Deuteronomy on the Joshua parallel is not very likely in the light of the divergencies between the two texts:

Latinos addere particulam, *scilicet*. Septuag. interpretes, ut supervacaneum, non reddiderunt illud.' See further T.C. Butler, *Joshua*, p. 3: 'LXX omits 'to the sons of Israel', a phrase as unnecessary in the original Heb. construction as it is in the English translation.'

[109] The recentiores furnished the missing word τοῦτον (thus the reading in the margin of M: οι λ̣ τουτον) which found its way into the Hexaplaric (376.426.Syh), S_b (44.106.134) and younger (F.V.344.509) witnesses. The shorter LXX text is followed by Jerome's Vulgate: *a deserto et Libano*.

[110] Thus E.A. Chesman, *Studies in the Septuagint Text of the Book of Joshua*, pp. 20–22.

[111] The plus in MT-Josh. *vis-à-vis* MT-Deut. הגדול is attested for Deuteronomy by LXX (τοῦ ποταμοῦ) *τοῦ μεγάλου*, a Cairo Genizah fragment, ms.i (Brit.Mus. 2228–2230), of Targum Onqelos, and Targum Pseudo-Jonathan and Neofiti (ימא רבא), and the Vulgate (*a flumine magno Eufraten*).

[112] Some MT-Mss, SamP, LXX-Deut (καὶ ἀπὸ τοῦ ποταμοῦ), and Peš-Deut. (ܘܡܢ ܢܗܪܐ) have an additional conjunction in front מן־הנהר, which corresponds to MT-Josh. 1:4.

[113] Thus e.g. BHS, and further A. Dillmann, *Die Bücher Numeri, Deuteronomium und Josua*, p. 443; C. Steuernagel, *Das Buch Josua*, p. 154; H. Holzinger, *Das Buch Josua*, p. 1.

Deut. πάντα τὸν τόπον, οὗ ἐὰν πατήσῃ τὸ ἴχνος τοῦ ποδὸς ὑμῶν,
Josh. πᾶς ὁ τόπος, ἐφ' ὃν ἂν ἐπιβῆτε τῷ ἴχνει τῶν ποδῶν ὑμῶν,

Deut. ὑμῖν ἔσται·
Josh. ὑμῖν δώσω αὐτόν, ὃν τρόπον εἴρηκα τῷ Μωυσῃ,

Deut. ἀπὸ τῆς ἐρήμου καὶ *Αντιλιβάνου καὶ* ἀπὸ τοῦ
Josh. τὴν ἔρημον καὶ τὸν *Αντιλίβανον* --- ἕως τοῦ

Deut. ποταμοῦ τοῦ *μεγάλου*, ποταμοῦ Εὐφράτου, καὶ ἕως τῆς
Josh. ποταμοῦ τοῦ μεγάλοῦ, ποταμοῦ Εὐφράτου, καὶ ἕως τῆς

Deut. θαλάσσης *τῆς ἐπὶ δυσμῶν* ἔσται τὰ ὅριά ὑμῶν.
Josh. θαλάσσης τῆς *ἐσχάτης* ἀφ' ἡλίου δυσμῶν ἔσται τὰ ὅρια ὑμῶν.

The first of the two main pluses הלבנון הזה, *this Lebanon*, is a unique expression within the Hebrew Bible. Unlike the deictic use of the pronoun after 'Jordan' in order to situate the narrative on the border of that stream, a deictic function is less evident in Josh. 1:4 הלבנון הזה, since the Lebanon mountain range falls outside the field of vision from the plains of Moab/Shittim, where the narrative of Joshua 1 is located (Deut. 34:8, Josh. 2:1).[114] Sacchi's suggestion that the longer MT text is reflected in the condensed Greek designation 'Anti-Lebanon', i.e. 'this Lebanon' is the part of the mountain range that runs in line with *this* (east) side of the river Jordan,[115] is refuted by the fact that within LXX-Joshua (as well as in LXX-Deuteronomy) the Greek geographical name ὁ Αντιλίβανος occurs as a standard rendering of the Hebrew name הלבנון without the pronoun (thus e.g. LXX-Deut. 11:24).[116] Most scholars propose to delete the pronoun as an element that disturbs the more original text to be recovered on the basis of LXX and the parallel text in Deuteronomy,[117] but

[114] Thus e.g. G.A. Cooke, *The Book of Joshua*, p. 4; T.C. Butler, *Joshua*, p. 4.

[115] P. Sacchi, Giosuè 1,1–9, p. 238: 'Inoltre l'ebraico aggiunge un 'questo' riferto a 'Libano', che non trova riscontro nelle traduzioni, a meno che non si voglia vedere nella traduzione greca 'Antilibano' per 'Libano' una certa interpretazione del 'questo'.'

[116] Thus e.g. A. Graeme Auld, Joshua. The Hebrew and Greek Texts, p. 3 (= *Joshua Retold*, pp. 8–9). The Greek name ὁ 'Αντιλίβανος appears also in LXX-Deut. 1:7; 3:25; 11:24; LXX-Josh. 1:4; 9:1 and LXX-Judith 1:7, see further below.

[117] Thus e.g., BHS *ad loco*; see further C. Steuernagel, *Deuteronomium und Josua*, p. 154; H. Holzinger, *Das Buch Josua*, p. 3; M. Noth, *Das Buch Josua²*, p. 20; V. Fritz, *Das Buch Josua*, p. 26; R.D. Nelson, *Joshua*, p. 27. H.W. Hertzberg, *Die Bücher Josua, Richter, Ruth*, p. 15, note 1, suggested that the pronoun originally referred to the first word of the clause, i.e. 'the desert': 'Eigenartig ist das von Auslegern meist nach LXX gestrichene Wort 'dieser' hinter Libanon'. Vermutlich gehört es zur 'Steppe'.

from a text-critical perspective this is an unjustified smoothening of the *lectio difficilior* contained in MT-Josh. 1:4. Tov classes the plus with the 'small elucidations' introduced by the second editor, but one wonders what constitutes the clarifying element in the newly created unique expression. One might argue that this editor was too enthousiastic to be fully aware of the results of his elucidating re-edition, but it is difficult to reconcile such an explanation with the general view on scribes and editors of the Hebrew Scriptures.

The somewhat problematic presence of the pronoun in the Hebrew text does make sense, to my mind, if understood from the perspective of the Deuteronomistic portrait of the Promised Land, which extended far beyond the traditional territory, which ranged 'only' 'from Dan to Bersheba' (thus e.g. in the preceding narrative Deut. 34:1–3).[118] This utopian extent of the Promised Land recurs in Deuteronomistic passages such as Deut. 1:7, 3:25, 11:24–25, and Gen. 15:18–21, Exod. 23:31,[119] and find their purported realisation in the era of David and Solomon (2 Sam. 8:3ff., 1 Kgs. 5:1):[120]

Gen. 15^{18}	לזרעך נתתי את־הארץ הזאת מנהר מצרים <u>עד־הנהר הגדול נהר פרת</u>:
Exod. 23^{31}	ושתי את־גבלך מים־סוף ועד־ים פלשתים <u>וממדבר עד־הנהר</u>
Deut. 1^{7}	פנו וסעו לכם ובאו הר האמרי . . .
	ארץ הכנעני <u>והלבנון עד־הנהר הגדול נהר־פרת</u>:
Deut. 3^{25}	אעברה־נא ואראה את־הארץ הטובה
	אשר בעבר הירדן ההר הטוב הזה <u>והלבנון</u>:
1 Kgs. 5^{1}	ושלמה היה מושל בכל־הממלכות <u>מן־הנהר</u>
	ארץ פלשתים ועד גבול מצרים . . .

In the imaginary motion of the hand 'from the desert' 'to the river Euphrates', the Lebanon mountains form the centre of this extended Israel, rather than a territory beyond its northern borders. Seen within this context, the pronoun הזה after הלבנון aims to integrate this territory within the expansionistic view of a 'Euphratic Israel'.[121]

---

[118] The tension between this portrait and that in Deut. 11:24, as well as the passages cited above, has been harmonized in SamP-Deut. 34:1b, where the detailed description of the land has been replaced by an adaptation of Gen. 15:18: מנהר מצרים עד הנהר הגדול נהר פרת ועד הים האחרון. Exactly the same description has again in SamP replaced the more precise Priestly description of the territory of Canaan in Gen. 10:19 (MT and remaining witnesses). Interestingly TgPsJon. and TgNF to Num. 34:7–9 extend the northern border of the Promised Land beyond Antiochia.

[119] These passages (Gen. 15:18–21 and Exod. 23:31) have many affinities with Deuteronomistic phraseology and concepts, see R. SMEND, *Die Entstehung des Alten Testament*, pp. 62–69.

[120] On these descriptions of Euphratic Israel, see e.g. L. PERLITT, *Deuteronomium.* (BKAT V/1), p. 47ff.; and E. NOORT, Josua und seine Aufgabe, pp. 79–80.

[121] E. NOORT, Josua und seine Aufgabe, pp. 77–80, charges the pronoun with

Again, redaction-critical observations support the originality of the longer MT text.

Similar remarks can be made with respect to the phrase כל ארץ החתים, *all the land of the Hittites*, a plus that is generally considered a secondary amplifying gloss,[122] occasionally with reference to the corresponding standard designation of this territory as *mat Ḫatti* in Assyrian royal inscriptions.[123] Mazor attributes the plus to the MT redaction of the Joshua, which allegedly held a negative view towards the Trans-Jordanian territory and instead had expansionist aspirations towards the northern territories.[124] In her view, this tendency is also evident in MT-Josh. 19:47–48, where, contrary to the LXX narrative of a conquest of Lachish in the centre of the land Israel (between the tribal territories of Judah, Joseph and Benjamin), MT reports the Danite conquest of the northern territories between Lake Huleh and Mount Hermon.

The suggestion that the plus in MT was added for amplifying purposes, however, does not make much sense, since apart from the reference to the Hittites in the formula of the seven autochthonous nations inhabiting the Promised Land (e.g. Gen. 15:20; Exod. 3:10, 13:5, 23:23.28; Num. 13:29, Deut. 7:1, 20:17, Josh. 3:10, 9:1, 11:3, 12:8, 24:11), the mention of a political, geographical and ethnic

---

the theological interpretation of offering a qualitative dimension to the land, by taking recourse to the mythical and metaphorical dimensions of these mountains in the poetic and prophetic literature (Ps. 104, Ezek. 31, Zech. 10:10, Cant.), p. 75: 'Zum Jordan, Libanon, zum Volk und zum Gesetzbuch sowie zum Land gibt es Jos.1 weder eine alternative noch eine explizite Vor- oder Rückschau. Hier scheinen die Demonstrativa eher qualitativ eingesetzt zu werden.' See further M.J. Mulder, לְבָנוֹן *l^e^bānôn*, in *ThWAT* V, col. 461–471. These metaphorical overtones for Lebanon, however, are not discernible in Deuteronomy and Joshua, where this area is mentioned only as part of Euphratic Israel (Deut. 1:7, 3:25 [here in addition to and thus distinguished from ההר הטוב הזה = Israel], 11:24, Josh. 1:4, 11:17, 12:7), or in geographical lists (Josh. 9:1, 13:5.6).

[122] Thus BHS *ad loco*; A. Dillmann, *Die Bücher Numeri, Deuteronomium und Josua*, p. 443; C. Steuernagel, *Deuteronomium und Josua*, p. 154; H. Holzinger, *Das Buch Josua*, p. 1; S. Holmes, *Joshua*, p. 17: 'Not in LXX or the parallel passage Deut. xi.24. To be omitted therefore as a late insertion.'; T.C. Butler, *Joshua*, p. 4; and K. Bieberstein, *Josua-Jordan-Jericho*, p. 86.

[123] C.D. Benjamin, *The Variations*, p. 23; M. Noth, *Das Buch Josua*², p. 20: 'dl c G^BAL^ 'das ganze Land der Hethiter', Glosse auf Grund der in den assyrischen Königsinschriften üblichen Bezeichnung von Syrien als Hethiterland' (cf wieder Dt 11_{24}).' adopted by V. Fritz, *Das Buch Josua*, p. 26. See further B.J. Alfrink, *Josue uit de grondtekst vertaald en ingeleid.* (BOT) Roermond/Maaseik 1952, p. 20; P.D. Baldi, *Giosuè*, p. 18; J.A. Soggin, *Le livre de Josué*, p. 27.

[124] L. Mazor, עיונים, pp. 161–162, see also the abstract in *BIOSCS* 27 (1994), p. 37.

Hittite entity is very rare in the Hebrew Bible. Only Judg. 1:26 mentions this territory in passing in the short, undoubtedly ancient, pre-Deuteronomistic narrative of the fall of Beth-El (Judg. 1:22–25),[125] after which the anonymous person who betrayed his city to the Josephites, migrates to the land of the Hittites and there builds another city called 'Luz'.[126]

Moreover, mention of Hittites is made only in 1 Kgs. 10:29 (2 Chron. 1:17), where it is said that Solomon traded Egyptian horses with Hittite kings, and 2 Kgs. 7:6, in the narrative of the wonderous withdrawal of the Syrians from Samaria. If in the narrative of Joab's census (2 Sam. 24:6) the unintelligible MT reading ויבאו הגלעדה ואל־ארץ תחתים חדשי should be corrected on the basis of LXX* καὶ ἔρχονται εἰς Γαλαὰδ καὶ εἰς γῆν Χεττιεὶμ Κάδης (represented here by the Antiochene or 'Lucianic' manuscripts 19.82.93.108)[127] into ויבאו הגלעדה ואל־ארץ החתים קדשה,[128] the implication would be that not only all Israel from Dan to Bersheba (so 2 Sam. 24:2), but also the northern coastal territories including Sidon and Tyre (24:6–7), as far as the Hittite land around Qadesh at the Orontes were tributary to David, according to the author of 2 Samuel 24. In that case the

---

[125] See the commentaries to this passage as well as R. SMEND JR., Das Gesetz und die Völker, pp. 506–509, who ascribes the composition and interpolation of Judg. 1:1–2:5 to DtrN, but nevertheless argues that the passage was compiled from ancient pre-DtrH material (p. 508).

[126] MT-Judg. 1:26 וילך האיש ארץ החתים ויבן עיר ויקרא שמה לוז הוא שמה עד היום הזה. See the commentaries to Judges, e.g., B. LINDARS, *Judges 1–5*, pp. 55–56.

[127] Edition: N. FERNÁNDEZ MARCOS, J.R. BUSTO SAIZ, *El Texto Antioqueno de la Biblia Griega. 1. 1–2 Samuel.* (Textos y estudios 'Cardenal Cisneros' 50) Madrid 1989. Codex Vaticanus here (2 Reg. 24:6) reads καὶ ἦλθον εἰς τὴν Γαλααδ καὶ εἰς γῆν Θαβασων, ἥ ἐστιν Ναδασαί, the N being a dittography for *ἐστιν Αδασαι* (so Rahlfs). The other witnesses to LXX show a wide variety of variations on this B-reading, originating from the obscurity of the names, see the apparatus *ad loco* in the Brooke-McLean-Thackeray edition. Symmachus translated this passage by τὴν κατωτέραν ὁδόν according to Eusebius' *Onomasticon* (ad Αεθθὰν Αδασαί).

Interestingly, the Pešiṭta paraphrase of 2 Sam. 24:6–7 also refers to this Hittite country:

ܘܐܬܘ ܥܕܡܐ ܠܨܘܪ ܘܠܨܝܕܢ ܠܐܪܥܐ ܕܟܢܥܢܝܐ ܘܠܐܪܥܐ ܕܚܬܝܐ ܘܠܐܪܥܐ ܕܝܒܘܣܝܐ, *and they went as far as Tyre and Sidon and to the land of the Canaanites and to the land of the Hittites and to the land of the Jebusites*, but not to the city Qadesh.

Jacob of Edessa combined the traditions in his Samuel manuscript (text and translation: A. SALVESEN, *The Books of Samuel in the Syriac Version of Jacob of Edessa.* (MPI Leiden 10) Leiden/Boston/Köln 1999):

ܘܐܬܘ ܠܓܠܥܕ ܘܠܐܪܥܐ ܕܚܬܝܐ: ܘܠܐܪܥܐ ܕܛܒܝܨ. ܗܝ ܕܩܕܫ., *they came to Gal'ad and the land of the Hittites, and the land of Tabiṣ, which is Qadesh.*

[128] Thus e.g. S.R. DRIVER, *Notes on the Hebrew Text of the Books of Samuel*, p. 286; D. BARTHÉLEMY, *Critique textuelle 1*, pp. 324–325 with full discussion and references.

divine promise of Josh. 1:4 would find its postponed fulfillment during David's and Solomon's reign (cf. 1 Kgs. 5:1).

On the basis of this rather scanty information, mainly from old, pre-Deuteronomistic sources,[129] the picture of a Hittite territory emerges that corresponds closely to that retrieved from extra-biblical sources, i.e. the royal Assyrian inscriptions. From these documents it is clear that the area designated as 'land of the Hittites' (*mat Ḫatti*) is that of north-west Syria between the Mediterranean Sea and the river Euphrates, where in the first half of the first millenium BCE a number of city-states formed the remains of the large second millenium BCE empire. Interesting in this respect is the Assyrian parallel to the description of Josh. 1:4 offered by the Calah Slab (ANET 281) which reports Adad-Nirari III's conquest in the early years of the eighth century BCE:[130]

> [10] (. . .) as far as the great sea [11] of the rising sun; from the banks of the Euphrates, Ḫatti [KUR ḫat-ti], Amurru in its totality, [12] Tyre, Sidon, [Bit-]Ḫumri, Edom, Philistia, [13] as far as the great sea of the setting sun (. . .)

What is important for our discussion is the fact that these Hittite states had disappeared from the international scene already by the end of the eighth century BCE after the repeated campaigns under the Neo-Assyrian kings from Shalmaneser III (858 BCE) until Sargon II (708 BCE).[131] Although Akkadian scribes continued to employ this name in their cuneiform documents until the period of Antiochus I

---

[129] See e.g. M. NOTH, *Überlieferungsgeschichtliche Studien*, p. 211 (with respect to Judg. 1: 'nachträglich in das werk von Dtr eingefügten alten Erzählungen'), p. 71 (1 Kgs. 10:29), and idem, *Könige* (BKAT IX/1), p. 208 ('Der Komplex 9_{10}–10_{29} ist fast durchweg vordeuteronomistisch').

[130] Text and translation taken from J. KAH-JIN KUAH, *Neo-Assyrian Historical Inscriptions and Syria-Palestine. Israelite/Judaean-Tyrian-Damascene Political and Commercial Relations in the Ninth-Eighth Centuries BCE.* Hong Kong 1995, pp. 81–84. See also M. WEINFELD, Zion and Jerusalem as Religious and Political Capital: Ideology and Utopia, in R.E. FRIEDMAN (ed.), *The Poet and the Historian. Essays in Literary and Historical Biblical Criticism.* (HSM 26) Chico 1983, pp. 75–115, especially pp. 98–99.

[131] See e.g., H.A. HOFFNER JR., Hittites, in A.J. HOERTH, G.L. MATTINGLY, E.M. YAMAUCHI (eds.), *Peoples of the Old Testament World.* Grand Rapids/Cambridge 1994, pp. 127–155; and especially the survey of the history of the Hittite area during the Assyrian period in J.D. HAWKINS, Ḫatti, in D.O. EDZARD (Hg.), *Reallexikon der Assyriologie* IV. Berlin/New York 1975, pp. 152–159. See further the commentaries to Josh. 1:4 and E. NOORT, Josua und seine Aufgabe, p. 81: ''Hethiter' umfassen aus assyrischer Sicht alles Aufständische westlich des Euphrat bis zum Mittelmeer.'

Soter (ca. 275 BCE), this archaising anachronism had been replaced since the Persian period by the name *ʿeber nāri* (Akkadian), and עבר נהרא (Aramaic) or עבר הנהר (Hebrew),[132] and had completely lost its referential function in the second half of the first millenium BCE.[133]

Two conclusions with respect to the variant in Josh. 1:4 can be drawn from these observations. First, the extension of the land promised by Yhwh to Joshua introduced by the alleged re-edition of the book of Joshua as reflected by MT (Mazor) would have meant an enormuous expansion of this territory, if the older edition common to MT and LXX had only spoken of an Israelite territory within its usual boundaries, i.e. from Dan to Bersheba (as we find in e.g. MT-Deut. 34:1–3).[134] Both MT and LXX in Josh. 1:4, however, extend the boundaries of the land to the river Euphrates. In the MT formulation, the phrase functions as a specification of the territory from 'this' Lebanon to the river Euphrates, hence the asyndesis.[135]

Secondly, the phrase would have made sense as an explanatory gloss or as element of a more comprehensive re-edition of the book, if the MT edition had dated from the seventh century BCE or earlier, when the memory of a Hittite area in North Syria was still alive, and if the older edition as reflected by LXX had dated from an even earlier period, so that the plus could be seen as an actualisation of the area involved. Such an early pre-Exilic date for the two alleged editions is not claimed by Mazor. Rather, it seems more likely that the phrase was omitted from the text in a post-Exilic or, even more probable, Hellenistic period, when it had lost its referential function.[136]

---

[132] J.D. HAWKINS, Ḫatti, pp. 155b–156a.

[133] This seems to be confirmed by the fact that in the very similar portrait of the Promised Land in 1QGenesis Apocryphon (column xxi, lines 10–12), which presents an extension of Yhwh's promise to Abraham of the land and Abraham's subsequent travel through the entire territory, the same locations 'river of Egypt', 'Lebanon', 'Qadesh', and 'Euphrates' appear, but where this North-Syrian area is designated as 'land of Gebal', rather than 'land of the Hittites'.

[134] Mazor's interpretation of the variants in Josh. 19:47–48 requires a discussion of its own. Her argumentation would have been more impressive, had LXX-Josh. 11:16ff. not reported Joshua's conquest of these territories. See further the discussion in section 6.4.6 below.

[135] The Pešiṭta translator of Josh. 1:4 was not sensible to this nuance and added the conjunctive ܘ in his rendering of the verse: ܘܥܕܡܐ ܠܦܪܬ ܢܗܪܐ ܪܒܐ. ܘܟܠܗ ܐܪܥܐ ܕܚܬܝܐ ܘܥܕܡܐ ܠܝܡܐ ܪܒܐ.

[136] Thus H.W. HERTZBERG, *Die Bücher Josua, Richter, Ruth*, pp. 14–15; J.H. KROEZE, *Het boek Jozua*, p. 29; and R.G. BOLING, *Joshua* (1982), p. 115. P. SACCHI, Giosuè 1,1–9, p. 239, offers the novel explanation that, for the reasons described above,

If we study the variants within the broader Greek context of Josh. 1:3–4, it is significant to note the different arrangement of this sentence, which in LXX starts a little further than in MT. Whereas in the MT the description of the land starts in 1:4 with the preposition מִן, *from* (*the desert* . . .), the Greek text not only lacks such a preposition, but moreover employs the accusative for 'desert' and 'Anti-Lebanon'. In this way, these areas are presented as complements to the object in the preceding clause: πᾶς ὁ τόπος, . . ., ὑμῖν δώσω αὐτόν, . . ., τὴν ἔρημον καὶ τὸν Αντιλίβανον. *every place, . . . I will give it to you, (including) the desert as well as Antilebanon.*[137] The presentation of the land plus (Anti-)Lebanon resembles that of Deut. 3:25. The next words are not preceded by a conjunction, as in the Hebrew text (וְעַד־הַנָּהָר הַגָּדוֹל), but form the beginning of a new clause. As a result, the remainder of verse 4 in the Greek text only describes the borders of the Promised Land: ἕως . . . καὶ ἕως . . . ἔσται τὰ ὅρια ὑμῶν, *Until (the Euphrates) and until (the sea) will be your boundaries.* Whereas the Hebrew text describes in a somewhat complicated manner the imaginary motion from desert (south), Lebanon (centre) to the Euphrates (north-east) and back again to the Mediterranean Sea (west) via the northern Hittite countries (north-west), the Greek text displays a more stylised description of the land: [1] it includes the desert and the Lebanon, and [2] its borders are the river and the sea.

In this re-organisation of the description of the land, the Hebrew pronoun הזה after 'Lebanon' completely lost its function as an overstating and thus somewhat artificial attempt to include the Lebanon-area into the Promised Land, now that the Lebanon no longer functioned as an interim station between desert and Euphrates. As in verse 2, the Greek adverb ὧδε would have hindered the Greek reader from understanding this sense of the Hebrew text; while a translation τὸν Αντιλίβανον τοῦτον would distract the reader's attention from the main land promised by the Lord. Furthermore, a

---

the original wording of the gloss was not כל ארץ החתים, but rather כל ארץ הכִתים and thus contained an allusion to the Greek or Roman invaders, for whom the name had become a common pseudonym (see e.g. 4QpešNah, 1 Macc. 1:1, and the interpretation in Dan. 11:30 of Num. 24:1, explicitly in the Greek (o') translation of Daniel [Ρωμαῖοι *vis-à-vis* θ'-Dan. 11:30 Κίτιοι], see further A. van der Kooij, *The Oracle of Tyre*, p. 77ff.), which subsequently had been disguised into the MT-reading. This is a rather complicated theory. Moreover, it remains difficult to understand why a scribe would have wanted to include this territory into that of the Promised Land.

[137] See e.g. J.A. Soggin, *Le livre de Josué*, p. 27.

description of the territory in-between Lebanon, Euphrates and Mediterranean Sea, which in the Hebrew text occurs as a specifying apposition parallel to the phrase מבוא השמש that specifies the location הים הגדול, has also become superfluous in the new presentation of the Promised Land (LXX). Although it is not impossible that a defective Hebrew copy of Josh. 1:4, without the preposition -מ and the subsequent conjunction -ו prompted this re-arrangement reflected by the Greek text, it seems more simple to attribute these changes to the Greek translator.[138]

Another literary initiative on the part of the Greek translator is demonstrated by the significant rendering הלבנון, *the Lebanon*, by Αντιλίβανος, *Anti-Lebanon*. Although the latter name is certainly no unusual geographical designation of the eastern Lebanon range in classical and Hellenistic Greek geographical descriptions,[139] the Greek name Αντιλίβανος occurs in the Greek Old Testament only five times, i.e., in Deut. 1:7; 3:25; 11:24; Josh. 9:1;[140] and further in Judith 9:1. The reason for this scarcity is evident: it is an interpretative rendering of the classical Hebrew expression לבנון, which does not differentiate between a western Lebanon and an eastern Anti-Lebanon range.[141] Hence in all other cases where in the Hebrew Bible the name 'Lebanon' occurs, the Greek translators employed the corresponding Greek designation ὁ Λίβανος.[142] In the description

---

[138] Cf. J. NENTEL, *Trägerschaft*, p. 19.

[139] See e.g. the rather incidental references in THEOPHRASTUS, *Enquiry into Plants* IX.7 (fourth–third century BCE) and the more detailed, but more recent descriptions in the geographical work of STRABO, *Geography* XVI.16 (first century BCE–first century CE). See further the article 'Libanos' (by HONIGMANN), in G. WISSOWA, W. KROLL, *Paulys Real-encyclopädie der classischen Altertumswissenschaft* 25. Stuttgart 1926, col. 1–11.

[140] The S manuscripts 44.54.75.106.134.314 as well as the Sahidic translation replace the LXX reading by the general τῷ Λιβάνῳ. The S-witness VetLat. conflates two versions of LXX-Josh. 9:1–2, one before the Ebal-Gerizim passage (LXX-Josh. 2a–f), one after it (cf. MT-Josh. 8:30–35); the former contains *ab Antelibum*, the second *contra facie Libani*. M.L. MARGOLIS, Additions to Field from the Lyons Codex, pp. 254–258, identified the second version as a Latin translation of the version by Theodotion.

[141] M.J. MULDER, לְבָנוֹן *lᵉbānôn*, in *ThWAT* IV, col. 461–471, mentioned the name of the שִׂרְיֹן mountain in Ps. 29:6, which on the basis of Ugaritic (KTU 1.4.VI.8ff.) and Akkadian (Gilgamesh Epic, a Treaty in the Boghazköi archive) parallels might point to a particular Hebrew name for the Anti-Lebanon. If that were the case, the name was only seldomly used, since it recurs only in Deut. 3:29 as the name which the inhabitants of Sidon give to the Hermon, parallel to the Amorite name Sinir (שְׂנִיר).

[142] See HR III, p. *102a*.

of the land from southern desert to Euphrates as in LXX-Deut. 1:7, 11:24 and LXX-Josh. 1:4, the mentioning of Anti-Lebanon rather than Lebanon fits well, as both Lebanon and Euphrates are located north-east of Canaan, even though a translation of לבנון by the common term ὁ Λίβανος would not have disturbed the context.

All the more surprsing, then, is the fact that the Greek translator of Joshua employed the term ὁ Λίβανος for the Hebrew לבנון in Josh. 13:5–6, where a translation of the Hebrew phrase לבנון מזרח השמש, *the Lebanon on the side where the sun rises*, i.e., *the eastern part of the Lebanon mountains*, would have been far more approriate and even necessary:

13[5]	καὶ *πᾶσαν* τὴν γῆν Γαλιλαθ	וְהָאָרֶץ הַגִּבְלִי
	[Ra: Γαβλι][143] *Φυλιστιιμ*	
	καὶ πάντα τὸν Λίβανον ἀπὸ ἀνατολῶν ἡλίου	וְכָל־הַלְּבָנוֹן מִזְרַח הַשֶּׁמֶשׁ
	ἀπὸ Βααλγαδ [Ra: *Γαλγαλ*][144]	מִבַּעַל גָּד
	ὑπὸ τὸ ὄρος τὸ Αερμων	תַּחַת הַר־חֶרְמוֹן
	ἕως *τῆς εἰσόδου* Εμαθ·	עַד לְבוֹא חֲמָת׃
13[6]	πᾶς *ὁ* κατοικ*ῶν* τὴν ὀρεινὴν	כָּל־יֹשְׁבֵי הָהָר
	ἀπὸ τοῦ Λιβάνου	מִן־הַלְּבָנוֹן
	ἕως *τῆς* Μασερεφωθμαιμ,	עַד־מִשְׂרְפֹת מַיִם
	πάντας *τοὺς* Σιδωνίους,	כָּל־צִידֹנִים
	ἐγὼ αὐτοὺς ἐξολεθρεύσω	אָנֹכִי אוֹרִישֵׁם
	ἀπὸ προσώπου --- Ισραηλ·	מִפְּנֵי בְּנֵי יִשְׂרָאֵל
	ἀλλὰ *διάδος* αὐτὴν ἐν κλήρῳ τῷ Ισραηλ,	רַק הַפִּלֶהָ לְיִשְׂרָאֵל בְּנַחֲלָה
	ὃν τρόπον σοι ἐνετειλάμην.	כַּאֲשֶׁר צִוִּיתִךָ׃

According to Holmes, this alternation in equivalents marks the change in translator of the two sections,[145] a thesis developed by H.St.J. Thackeray for other Septuagintal books, and extrapolated rather than substantiated for the Greek Joshua.[146] To my mind, an alternative solution for this rather remarkable shift within the Greek Joshua is

---

[143] Rahlfs adopted the Hexaplaric P and C reading [A.G.N.W. 15.29 (mg.). 82.85 (mg.). 344 (mg.). Eusebius' *Onomasticon*] corresponding to MT, as the more original LXX-reading. Margolis assumed a Hebrew *Vorlage* corresponding to the phrase in Josh. 13:2 גלילות פלשתים and adopted the reading Γαλιλαθ Φυλιστιειμ, primarly reflected by the S-witnesses as the original. The E-reading Γαλιὰθ (B. 407) would be a slight corruption of this form.

[144] Rahlfs adopted the C-reading Γαλγαλ (A.N.W.VetLat *sub Galgal* and the majority of minuscules). Margolis considered both this reading and that of the E family (B. Sah) Γαλαα to be corruptions of Βααλγαδ, also reflected by the P (and S)-witnesses (44.106.134.376.426; with orthographical variations in G etc.).

[145] S. Holmes, *Joshua*, p. 16.

[146] H.St.J. Thackeray, *Grammar of the Old Testament in Greek according to the Septuagint*. Cambridge 1909, p. 13, only held LXX-Josh. 21:2–11.34–42 to be the result of Aquila's version, and classed part of the Greek Joshua as a good koine translation, without further specifying which parts and on what grounds. The second part of

possible, when one takes into account the redaction-historical background of the two Hebrew passages. The specific use of 'Lebanon' here as well as 'Anti-Lebanon' in Josh. 1:4 reflects a well-considered exegesis of the tension between the DtrH stratum and the DtrN redaction of Joshua caused by the two different and conflicting concepts of the extent of the Promised Land and its conquest by Joshua. In the DtrH-passage Josh. 1:3–4,[147] the extent of the Promised Land is sketched as extending as far as the Euphrates, in line with Gen. 15:18, Exod. 23:31, Deut. 1:7, 11:24–25. In Josh. 11:16–20 and Joshua 12, the DtrH conclusions to the conquest narratives, we find the corresponding statements that Joshua took all the land from the desert (Josh. 11:16) until Baʿal-Gad in the Lebanon valley behind Mount Hermon (11:17), likewise Josh. 12:7, in the reverse order. Since the Hebrew text here speaks of the Beqaʿa-valley בעל גד (ב)בקעת הלבנון, the Greek translator employs the Greek expression τὰ πεδία τοῦ Λιβάνου.

11:16	Καὶ ἔλαβεν Ἰησοῦς	וַיִּקַּח יְהוֹשֻׁעַ
	πᾶσαν τὴν γῆν . . .	אֶת־כָּל־הָאָרֶץ הַזֹּאת
11:17	καὶ ἕως Βααλγαδ	וְעַד־בַּעַל גָּד
	καὶ τὰ πεδία τοῦ Λιβάνου	בְּבִקְעַת הַלְּבָנוֹן
	ὑπὸ τὸ ὄρος τὸ Αερμων	תַּחַת הַר־חֶרְמוֹן
	καὶ πάντας τοὺς βασιλεῖς αὐτῶν ἔλαβεν	וְאֵת כָּל־מַלְכֵיהֶם לָכַד
12:7	Καὶ οὗτοι οἱ βασιλεῖς τῶν Αμορραίων,	וְאֵלֶּה מַלְכֵי הָאָרֶץ
	οὓς ἀνεῖλεν Ἰησοῦς	אֲשֶׁר הִכָּה יְהוֹשֻׁעַ
	καὶ οἱ υἱοὶ Ισραηλ	וּבְנֵי יִשְׂרָאֵל
	ἐν τῷ πέραν τοῦ Ιορδάνου	בְּעֵבֶר הַיַּרְדֵּן
	παρὰ θάλασσαν--- Βααλγαδ	יָמָּה מִבַּעַל גָּד
	ἐν τῷ πεδίῳ τοῦ Λιβάνου	בְּבִקְעַת הַלְּבָנוֹן

LXX-Joshua is more literal than the first, but this is due to the geographical subject matter. P.-M. Bogaert, Septante, *Supplément au Dictionnaire de la Bible*, fasc. 68, Paris 1991, col. 587, adduces the circumstance that the fourth-century Sahidic papyrus (sa 18) contains only Joshua 1–11, and 22–24, which might reflect one of the two distinct translation units. It seems more likely, however, that the absence of the list material contained in Josh. 12–21 in this codex is the result of a deliberate curtailment and omission of material held to be no longer relevant enough to be transmitted, as happened occasionally within the transmission of the text of LXX-Joshua, as in the case of ms. 118, see M.L. Margolis, The K Text of Joshua, pp. 28–30.

[147] E. Noort, Josua und seine Aufgabe (1994), p. 83; and K. Bieberstein, *Josua-Jordan-Jericho* (1995), p. 393, ascribe these verses to a post-DtrH literary stratum (Noort), or to DtrN (Bieberstein). According to the latter, the aim of portraying the Promised Land in these unrealistically large proportions was to increase Israel's guilt not to have conquered these territories as well. Nevertheless, the negative tones so

In the DtrN survey in Josh. 13:2–6[148] of the territories not (yet) conquered, a list follows to which—apart from the Philistine Gaza-strip (Josh. 13:2–3)—the Lebanon area from Baʿal-Gad behind the Mount Hermon as far as Leboʾ-Hamath is reckoned. By avoiding the use of the word Antilebanon, the Greek translator is in the position to neutralize the tension between the positive and negative statements with respect to the conquest of the land: it was the Antilebanon range running as far as the Euphrates that had been promised by Yhwh (LXX-Deut. 1:7, 3:25, 11:24, LXX-Josh. 1:4), a promise that indeed had been fulfilled in LXX-Josh. 11:17 and 12:7 as a result of the Antilebanon kings' own foolishness in offering opposition to Joshua (LXX-Josh. 9:1–2, the only other place in Joshua where the name Antilebanon occurs). The western Lebanon mountains, however, had not been included in the divine promise, according to this interpretation, and could therefore figure as ὁ Λίβανος in the list of areas not conquered by Israel. As a result, the translation of הלבנון הזה in Josh. 1:4 by ὁ Αντιλίβανος reflects a concern to reserve 'Antilebanon' for the area promised by God, and 'Lebanon' for the unconquered territory.[149]

The discussion above, however, does not necessarily imply that the Hebrew *Vorlage* of LXX-Josh. 1:3–4 in all other details exactly agreed with MT, only that there is not sufficient reason to assume that the pluses in MT are the result of a re-edition of the chapter. The variant in 1:4 ἡ θαλάσση ἡ ἐσχάτης, *the farthest sea*, for MT הים הגדול, *the great sea*, can hardly be ascribed to a literary initiative by the Greek translator, since the expression *uttermost sea* is even more problematic and unusual in Greek than in Hebrew. The common Greek

clearly audible in Joshua 23 and Judges 2 are completely absent from Josh. 1:3–5a. Moreover, Josh. 1:3–4 is not formulated in imperatives, but with the governing verb: *I will give it*. This implies that if somebody is to be blamed, when at the end of the story not all of this territory has become Israelite, it would be Yhwh himself! The literary links rather point to the idealized portrait of the era of David and Solomon (including the phrase דרך כף־רגל in Josh. 1:3, which has a clear parallel in 1 Kgs. 5:17).

[148] Thus R. Smend, Das Gesetz und die Völker, p. 497ff., see the discussion in section 4.2.2 above.

[149] In his second homily on Joshua (II.4), Origen detected a similar qualitative distinction between Lebanon and the Anti-Lebanon, and applied these two entities to the old Israel (Lebanon) and new Christian Israel (Anti-Lebanon), see A. Jaubert, *Origène. Homélies dur Josué.* (SC 71) Paris 1960, pp. 122–123.

designation for the Mediterranean Sea is ἡ θάλασσα ἡ παρ' ἡμῖν,[150] common names for the Atlantic ocean ἡ θάλασσα ἡ ἔξω, ἡ ἔσω θάλασσα, or ἡ Ατλαντικὴ θάλασσα. Therefore, the Greek translator in all probability rendered the phrase הים האחרון as we find it in MT-Deut. 11:24, rather than that of MT-Josh. 1:4 הים הגדול. In the present context, both expressions are synonymous, and the MT could be the result of a replacement of the more original expression as found in Deut. 11:24, which recurs in the Hebrew Bible only in Deut. 34:2 as well as in Joel 2:20 and Zech. 14:8 (thus Holmes and Benjamin).[151]

In the latter three instances, however, the use of the expression הים האחרון is well defined by the context. In the two prophetic oracles (Joel 2:20 and Zech. 14:8) the הים האחרון is opposed to the phrase הים הקדמוני, which denotes the sea in front of the speaker oriented towards the east, i.e. the Dead Sea. In Deut. 34:2 this orientation is 180 degrees reversed, i.e. from the east side (of the Promised Land) towards the west, but here the 'hinder sea' refers to the sea *behind* the Jordan and the mountain area of Judah and Ephraim-Manasseh. Although the perspective is not very much different in Deut. 11:24 and Josh. 1:4, the phrase הים האחרון does not occur in these passages in a context of an actual view of the land (so Deut. 34:1: ויראהו יהוה את־כל־הארץ). Therefore the phrase is less dictated by the context.

There is, however, a significant difference between Deut. 11:24 and Josh. 1:4, caused by the apposition phrase in Josh. 1:4 מבוא השמש, which is also relatively rare within the Hebrew Bible (elsewhere only in Deut. 11:30, Josh. 23:4, Zech. 8:7, and in the phrase ממזרח־שמש עד־מבואו in Mal. 1:11, Ps. 50:1, 113:3). The phrase is absent from MT-Deut. 11:24, in all probability because the location of the sea mentioned is already well determined by the adjective אחרון. In that case the reading of the *Vorlage* of LXX ועד־הים האחרון מבוא השמש is more superfluous than the MT text הים הגדול מבוא השמש, which moreover nicely balances the text regarding the other extreme of the Promised Land ועד־הנהר הגדול. The double use by the DrH

150 See LSJ, p. 781b; C. Dogniez, M. Harl, *Le Deutéronome*, p. 100.

151 S. Holmes, *Joshua*, p. 17: 'הגדול was probably an explanatory gloss, as הים האחרון occurs only four times Deut. xi.24, xxxiv.2, Joel ii.20, Zech. xiv.8.' C.D. Benjamin, *The Variations*, p. 23: 'Harmonistic revision. The Greek here goes back to the older term.'

author of Josh. 1:4 of the adjective גדול adds to the notion of magnitude of the land contained between these two great waters, and again corresponds closely to the descriptions of this area in the Neo-Assyrian accounts, as far instance the Calah Slab (see above). Since the phrase מבוא השמש is well reflected by LXX (ἀφ' ἡλίου δυσμῶν), the reconstruction proposed by Dillmann, by which an expression in Josh. 1:4 identical with Deut. 11:24 was supplemented by the phrase מבוא השמש and afterwards altered into the present MT, is unnecessarily complicated.

It would seem therefore, that like the other MT—LXX variants in Josh. 1:3–4 discussed above, the MT here too has preserved the more original text. Unlike the other, quantitative variants, however, in this particular case the Greek text is not the result of a particular interpretation of the more original Hebrew text, but reflects a different, though secondary Hebrew *Vorlage*.[152] A similar instance of influence from the text of Deut. 11:24 on the parallel passage in Josh. 1:3 is offered by the replacement of the phrase לכם נתתיו, *I will give it to you*, by the phrase לכם יהיה (thus Deut. 11:24) in a few mediaeval Masoretic manuscripts (Ken. 93, 196, De Rossi 665) and the Pešiṭta version ܠܟܘܢ ܢܗܘܐ.[153] Here, too, the reading in MT probably represents the older text, since the notion of the divine gift of the land fits the general character of the DtrH stratum of the chapter, with its eight occurrences of the verb נתן, better.

6.4.5 *Moses' Commands to Joshua (Josh. 1:7)*[154]

The MT presents a significant plus *vis-à-vis* LXX in verse 7, where for the first time in the book of Joshua the theme of the *torah* is introduced. Whereas in MT, within the narrative context of Yhwh's 'installation' discourse, Joshua is summoned to persist in strictly

[152] Likewise J. Hollenberg, *Der Charakter*, p. 17; C. Steuernagel, *Das Buch Josua* (1900), p. 154; L. Mazor, עיונים, pp. 134–135.

[153] So K. Bieberstein, *Josua-Jordan-Jericho*, p. 88, see J.B. de Rossi, *Variae Lectiones* II, p. 71a V. Aptowitzer, *Das Schriftwort in der rabbinischen Literatur* IV, p. 243. The Pešiṭta variant is discussed by J.E. Erbes, *The Peshitta and the Versions*, pp. 71–73.

[154] Part of this section has been presented at the Tenth Congress of the International Organization for Septuagint and Cognate Studies, held in Oslo, 1 August 1998, and has been published as M.N. van der Meer, Textual Criticism and Literary Criticism in Joshua 1:7 (MT and LXX), in B.A. Taylor (ed.), *X Congress of the International Organization for Septuagint and Cognate Studies. Oslo, 1998.* (SBL-SCS 51) Atlanta 2001, pp. 355–371.

observing *the whole torah* enjoined by Moses,[155] LXX simply contains an admonition in more general terms to execute carefully what Moses had commanded to Joshua.

The originality of this shorter reading without the nomistic concept seems to be corroborated by the syntactic circumstance that the masculine suffix in the prepositional phrase in the subsequent clause אל־תסור ממנו, *do not deviate from him*, does not correspond to the feminine gender of the alleged antecedent תּוֹרָה. The Masoretes already noted this problem, but placed the *sebirin* note ו׳ סביר ממנה in the margin with references to five parallel passages (Lev. 6:8, 27:9, Judg. 11:34, 1 Kgs. 22:43, 2 Kgs. 4:39)[156] in order to safegard the *lectio difficilior.*

Factors causing inner-Greek or inner-Hebrew scribal corruptions are absent,[157] hence we are dealing here with an intentional textual alteration. As a result, there is a widespread consensus among scholars that the plus in MT *vis-à-vis* LXX presents a secondary addition, usually designated as a *Glosse* or interpolation with an explanatory or emphatic intention, introduced in verse 7 under the influence of the next verse, where the same formulations occur (both in MT and LXX).[158]

---

[155] See section 4.2.2 for my choice to translitterate rather than translate the Hebrew noun תורה.

[156] Thus according to Masorah magna no. 2038. These five parallel passages are far from homogeneous. In two cases (Lev. 6:8, 27:9 and 1 Kgs. 22:43) the masculine suffix in ממנו is syntactically correct. There the *sebirin* serves only as a caveat for copyists to avoid confusion with nearby feminine forms (אתה in Lev. 6:7?, ממנה in Lev. 27:9 first clause). In two other cases the *sebirin* note points to variation in gender of the Hebrew nouns דרך in 1 Kgs. 22:43 and גפן in 2 Kgs. 4:39. Only in Judg. 11:34 אֵין־לוֹ מִמֶּנּוּ בֵּן אוֹ־בַת, *besides him there was no son or daughter to him* (*i.e., Jephta*) the masculine suffix is as problematic as it is in Josh. 1:7, since it can only refer to Jephta's daughter. Most scholars explain this as the result of a scribal corruption influenced by the preceding masculine suffix in לו, thus G.F. MOORE, *Judges* (ICC) Edinburgh 1895, p. 303; C.F. BURNEY, *The Book of Judges*. London 1920, p. 321; R.G. BOLING, *Judges* (AB 6) New York 1975, p. 208; J.A. SOGGIN, *Judges* (OTL) London 1981, p. 214. On the proper understanding of the *sebirin* notations, see E. TOV, *Textual Criticim of the Hebrew Bible*, p. 64.

[157] Thus extensively argued by E.A. CHESMAN, *Studies in the Septuagint Text of the Book of Joshua*, pp. 37–45: 'Chapter 4: תורה.' In this particular case, Chesman saw no solution to the problem by postulating a different Hebrew *Vorlage*, but after a discussion of related problems concluded that 'the problem must be left in abeyance.' (p. 45). Equally inconclusive and unsatisfactory is suggestion made by R.G. BOLING, *Joshua*. p. 116, to place the problem in the domain of oral transmission: 'LXX lacks *the entire Treaty-Teaching*. The differences are possibly to be resolved into two variants stemming from oral tradition.'

[158] See e.g. R. MEYER in BHS: 'G καθότι, 1 כַּאֲשֶׁר (cf. ממנו)'; Similar remarks can be found in the commentaries by C. STEUERNAGEL, *Deuteronomium und Josua*, p. 154;

1:7 לשמר לעשות כ[כל־התורה] אשר צוך משה עבדי
1:8 לא ימוש ספר התורה הזה מפיך והגית בו יומם ולילה
למען תשמר לעשות ככל־הכתוב בו

For E. Tov, the plus originated with the re-edition of the book and reflects the influence of Deuteronomy on that re-edition.[159]

More than any of the other MT pluses in Joshua 1, this plus has implications for the redaction history of this first chapter of the book, since it conveys the central theme of the nomistic (DtrN) redaction of the whole segment 1:7–8.[160] R. Smend considers the text of verse 7 without these words a DtrN[1]-addition supplemented by a DtrN[2] addition of verse 8, which in turn resulted in the interpolation in verse 7.[161] One wonders, however, whether such a *Fortschreibungs*-model does not undermine the DtrN-thesis and whether one should really designate this shorter text of verse 7 as nomistic.

H. Holzinger, *Das Buch Josua*, p. 1; A.B. Ehrlich, *Randglossen*, p. 2; S. Holmes, *Joshua*, p. 17: 'LXX omits. The LXX reading together with ממנו makes it almost certain that התורה is a late addition and that the original reading was simply ככל אשר.'; C.D. Benjamin, *The Variations*, p. 23; and even M.L. Margolis, *The Book of Joshua in Greek*, p. 6: 'αυτων neut.pl. = ממנו hence כל התורה a gloss.' See further M. Noth, *Das Buch Josua*[1], p. 4, (= 1953[2], p. 22); P.D. Baldi, *Giosuè*, p. 22; H.W. Hertzberg, *Die Bücher Josua, Richter, Ruth*, p. 15; J. Gray, *Joshua, Judges, Ruth.* (NCB) London 1967, p. 50; J.A. Soggin, *Le livre de Josué*, p. 31; P. Sacchi, Giosuè 1,1–9, pp. 240–241; E. Noort, Josua und seine Aufgabe, p. 72: 'sicherlich späte Glosse'; R.D. Nelson, *Joshua*, p. 28; J. Nentel, *Trägerschaft*, p. 20. K. Bieberstein, *Josua-Jordan-Jericho*, pp. 89–90, n. 40, mentions several other scholars as well. In his view, the Hebrew construction לעשות כאשר, postulated by most scholars, is not attested elsewhere in the Hebrew Bible, and since the Greek word καθότι also occurs as a rendering of ככל, the Greek text reflects a *Vorlage* in which only the noun תורה was absent (and added secondarily to MT).

[159] E. Tov, The Growth of the Book of Joshua, p. 331 (= *The Greek and Hebrew Bible*, p. 390), classes the variant in the category 'Additions in MT whose secondariness is evident from their formulation)' and p. 336 (= *The Greek and Hebrew Bible*, p. 394) sub 'Influence of Deuteronomy'.

[160] On the DtrN character of the 7–8 verses, see sections 6.3 and 4.2.2 above. Whether verse 9 (completely or in part) belongs to DtrN as well is debatable. This verse lacks the nomistic themes evident in the preceding verses, whereas the final clauses (אל־תערץ ואל־תחת and further) rather formulate the DtrH-themes. R. Smend, Das Gesetz und die Völker, p. 496, and others interpreted verse 9 as a deliberate attempt on the part of DtrN to return to the DtrH themes, in order to make clear that earlier commands still remained valid. K. Bieberstein, *Josua-Jordan-Jericho*, p. 95ff., considers only the resumptive repetition of the imperatives הלוא צויתיך חזק ואמץ to be part of the DtrN addition, whereas the rest of the verse is seen as part of the older (DtrA in his termonology) text. If the first clause הלוא צויתיך is understood as a reference to Deut. 31:23, it appears more plausible to ascribe the verse to DtrH. See further J. Nentel, *Trägerschaft*, pp. 24–26.

[161] R. Smend, Das Gesetz und die Völker, p. 494, n. 3: 'כל־התורה ist spätere Einfügung, wie sich anerkanntermaßen aus dem Fehlen in der LXX und dem folgenden ממנו ergibt.' See further R. Smend, *Die Entstehung des Alten Testaments*, p. 115.

For these reasons A. Rofé reserves the term 'nomistic' for the alleged addition of only these words in MT-Josh. 1:7, along with the whole of verse 8 which blends Deuteronomistic phrases with late Wisdom ideas found only in Ps. 1:2:[162]

Josh. 1[8]	לא ימוש ספר התורה הזה מפיך והגית בו יומם ולילה. . . כי־אז תצליח את־דרכך ואז תשכיל
Ps. 1[2-3]	כי אם בתורת יהוה חפצו ובתורתו יהגה יומם ולילה [3]. . . וכל אשר־יעשה יצליח

Without these nomistic additions the admonition to Joshua in verse 7 corresponds closely to the concluding statement in Josh. 11:15 that Joshua carefully executed what Moses had commanded him:[163]

Josh. 1[7*] (according to Rofé)	לשמר לעשות כאשר צוך משה עבדי אל־תסור ממנו ימין ושמאול
Josh. 11[15]	כאשר צוה יהוה את־משה עבדו כן־צוה משה את־יהושע וכן עשה יהושע לא־הסיר דבר מכל אשר צוה יהוה את־משה:

According to Rofé, the stress on Joshua's direct obedience to Moses and Yhwh fits the Deuteronomistic concept, though the parallel passages to which Rofé refers are mostly DtrN-passages in Smend's model (Josh. 22:5, 23:6–8, 1 Kgs. 2:3). The portrait of Joshua in 1:8 as the ideal *talmid-ḥăkāmîm* devoted to daily study of the *torah* (והגית בו יומם ולילה) is extraneous to the Deuteronomistic concepts, and, moreover, unnecessary within the book of Joshua, since Joshua receives commands directly from Yhwh (Josh. 4:2–3.15–16; 5:2; 6:2–5; 7:10–15; 8:1–2, 10:8; 11:6 etc.). The closest parallel to this passage, the law for the king, Deut. 17:18–19, only sketches a picture of a king acquainted with the *torah* by reading it all his life:[164]

> It shall be when he (i.e. the king) sits on the throne of his kingdom, that he shall write for himself a copy of this *torah* (וכתב לו את־משנה התורה הזאת על־ספר) in a *book* in front of the Levitical priests. It will be with him and he will read in it all the days of his life (וקרא בו כל־ימי חייו) in order that he may learn to fear Yhwh, his God, by

[162] A. Rofé, The Nomistic Correction, p. 248; and idem, The Piety of the Torah-disciples. See further section 2.2.7.2 above.

[163] A. Rofé, The Piety of the Torah-Disciples, pp. 79, 81–82. See further the commentaries to the Psalter, e.g. H.-J. Kraus, *Psalmen.* (BKAT XV/1) Neukirchen 1978[5], pp. 131–142.

[164] A. Rofé, The Piety of the Torah-Disciples, p. 80; idem, The Nomistic Correction, p. 248.

> observing all the words of this torah (לשמר את־כל־דברי התורה הזאת) and these statutes by doing them.

Although Rofé acknowledges the secondary character of verse 7 (without the MT-plus) *vis-à-vis* verse 6,[165] he nevertheless holds that both verse 8 and the plus in MT verse 7 form the nomistic correction proper. This addition must have taken place, according to Rofé, at a rather late stage in the Second Temple period[166] along with the last stages in the formation of the canon of the Hebrew Bible, as is evidenced by the fact that after the first part of the Hebrew canon (the Torah proper), both the second and third divisions (Prophets and Writings) open with the ideal of observance of the Torah (Joshua 1, Psalm 1).[167] These textual alterations should be seen in relation to other nomistic corrections, including the transposition of the narrative of Joshua's reading of the *torah* near Mount Ebal from its MT position (8:30–35) to the position before 5:2 in 4QJosh[a].[168] These alterations reflect the development in Early Judaism in which the study of the Torah became 'democratized'. According to Rofé the textual changes express (proto-) Pharisaic interests.[169]

At first sight it would seem that this particular case in MT-Josh. 1:7 has all the characteristics of a re-edition of the book: the plus introduces for a clear purpose a concept into the text that is markedly different from its context, and that is embedded within a broader religion historical development. Nevertheless, when both the Hebrew and Greek texts are studied within their own context first, a different picture emerges.

The plus in MT-Joshua 1:7 is unique within the whole book of Joshua, as well as within the broader context of Genesis-2 Kings.[170]

---

[165] A. Rofé, The Piety of the Torah-Disciples, pp. 78–79.

[166] This in opposition to the early post-Exilic date of Smend's DtrN-stratum (see R. Smend, *Die Entstehung des Alten Testaments*, pp. 124–125, see further section 4.2.2 above). Rofé does not recognize such a DtrN-layer; see his The Piety of the Torah-Disciples, p. 79, n. 6.

[167] A. Rofé, The Piety of the Torah-Disciples, p. 82; idem, From Tradition to Criticism: Jewish sources as an Aid to the Critical Study of the Hebrew Bible, in J.A. Emerton (ed.), *Congress Volume. Cambridge 1995.* (SVT 66) Leiden/New York/Köln 1997, p. 235 (ff.).

[168] A. Rofé, The Editing of the Book of Joshua; idem, From Tradition to Criticism, p. 235, idem, The Onset of Sects in Postexilic Judaism: Neglected Evidence from the Septuagint, Trito-Isaiah, Ben Sira, and Malachi, in J. Neusner, P. Borgen, E.S. Frerichs, R. Horsley (eds.), *The Social World of Formative Christianity and Judaism. Essays in Tribute to Howard Clark Kee.* Philadelphia 1988, pp. 39–49.

[169] A. Rofé, The Nomistic Correction, pp. 247–248.

[170] G. Östborn, *Tōrā in the Old Testament*, pp. 172–178. 'Appendix: The occur-

The textual witnesses do not (directly) attest to the explicit addition of the related passage within the book about Joshua's reading the *torah* to the people, since the text of MT-Josh. 8:(30–)34–35 is attested by all witnesses, only at different locations in the book.[171] This leaves the alleged addition of the nomistic concept in Josh. 1:7 without a parallel. Moreover, the first half of the next verse (Josh. 1:8a), where the theme of the *torah* is further developed and which to a large extent forms the basis of Rofé's view, is fully attested by the LXX, which undermines the text-critical proposal made by Rofé that one scribe added verse 8 and another the MT-plus in verse 7. On literary-critical grounds it appears to be more plausible to regard verses 7 and 8 as a unit, since the two verses share not only the theme of the *torah*, but also that of its 'careful observance' (שׁמר לעשׂות) and that of its subsequent 'success' (השׂכיל), the latter occurring only here in Joshua:

1⁷ לשׁמר לעשׂות ככל־התורה אשׁר צון משׁה עבדי למען תשׂכיל בכל אשׁר תלך
1⁸ למען תשׁמר לעשׂות ככל־הכתוב בו כי־אז תצליח את־דרכך ואז תשׂכיל

The theme in verse 8 of the continuous study (והגית בו יומם ולילה) of what is written in the book of the *torah*, may be extraneous to the main DtrH presentation of Joshua, but it suits this context of Joshua 1:7–8 well. Furthermore the theme functions as the centre of verses 7–8 rather than as an addition that incorporates an idea extraneous to this particular context.[172] Therefore, there is no reason to distinguish between two stages in this DtrN-addition.[173]

---

rence of הורה, 'to impart *tōrā*' and תורה *tōrā* in 𝔐 and SamP, and their Renderings in 𝔊, A', Θ', Σ', ℭ, 𝔖, and 𝔙', p. 174, n. 2, mentions three more passages where the Hebrew noun תורה is not reflected by the standard Greek equivalent νόμος (191 times of the total of 219 occurrences in MT) or cognate nouns: In Ezek. 43:12b LXX καὶ τὴν διαγραφὴν τοῦ οἴκου and Peš ܗܘ ܒܝܬܐ ܨܘܪܬܐ reflect a Hebrew *Vorlage* זאת/ואת צֻורת הבית, which undoubtedly is a scribal error secondary to MT זאת תֹורת הבית; see W. ZIMMERLI, *Ezechiel* (BKAT XIII/2, p. 1073). In Jer. 44:10 (LXX 51:10) and Neh. 12:44 (LXX-2 Esdras 22:44) the noun תורה likewise lacks a counterpart in the respective Old Greek translations.

[171] See the discussion in chapter 9 below.

[172] See K. BIEBERSTEIN, *Josua-Jordan-Jericho*, p. 390ff. who detects a concentric structure in the DtrN-addition Josh. 1:7–9c, consisting of the themes [A] 'encouragement' (7//9a–c חזק ואמץ), [B1] obedience to the *torah*, [B2] the road metaphor (אל תסור ממנו verse 7, אז תצליח דרכך verse 8), [B3] success (השׂכיל, verse 7–8) around the first two clauses of verse 8, which form its core ([C] study of the *torah*).

[173] R. SMEND, Das Gesetz und die Völker, p. 496, only cautiously mentions this possibility, but stresses the correspondences between verses 7 and 8.

In passing it may be noted that in the DtrN-concept the *torah* is seen as a completed entity, referred to as ספר התורה הזה (Josh. 1:8), כל הכתוב בספר התורה (Josh. 8:34) and כל הכתוב בספר התורת משה (Josh. 23:6). All these expressions are grammatically masculine phrases. Perhaps this circumstance explains the somewhat unexpected—although by no means impossible—incongruity[174] between the masculine suffix in ממנו and its—strictly speaking feminine—antecedent כל־התורה, if we assume that the DtrN-redactor (or a later copyist) had in mind the longer grammatically masculine concept כל הכתוב בספר התורה. In that case the *lectio difficilior* ממנו should be interpreted as an *ad sensum* reference to this idea, as suggested already by David Qimchi.[175] Moreover, it is hardly plausible that an editor would so carefully weave into the existing text the object of his interest, and at the same time be careless enough to forget to make the minor adaptation of altering the ו of ממנו into the more appropriate ה of ממנה.[176]

The real literary-critical seam is not to be found in the Hebrew text between verses 7 and 8, but between verses 6 and 7. Here we

---

[174] See W. Gesenius, E. Kautzsch, *Hebräische Grammatik* Leipzig 1902[27] § 135o, § 145.

[175] See already the explanations by the mediaeval Jewish commentators, who adduce alternative antecedents as well: D. Qimchi אל תסור ממנו ־ שב אל משה, ופירושו מדרכו הטובה או פירוש ממנו ־ מספר התורה, *'do not deviate from him', refers to 'Moses', and the explanation of it is: from his good way (example), or the explanation of 'from him' is: from the Book of the Torah*; and Josef ibn Kaspi: ממנו—כנוי אל כל ונכון גם כן לתורה, כי היא ספר וגם היא נשם *from him' refers to 'all', and certainly also to torah as well, since that is a book and also a substance.'*

A. Masius, *Josuae imperatoris historia*, Commentary (1838), col. 900, mentioned Qimchi's explanations and demonstrates on the basis of Ps. 45:17 that incongruity between suffix and antecedent is not without analogy in classical Hebrew: 'Illud porro, *ab ea*, quia masculino genere dictum est, non videtur ad nomen, *legem*, referri posse, cum hoc sit generis feminini. R. David Kimchi ergo, Mosen in eo spectari autumat, ac si dicat Deus: Ne divertas a Mose, hoc est, Mosis praescripto: vel, librum legis, per synecdochen. Sed non est insolens in sacris litteris ea generis mutatio. Nam David filiam regis, hoc est, feminam, consolatus, ait: *Pro patribus tuis erunt filii tui*; ubi utrumque, pronomen est generis masculini. Sin autem, Davidem hic ad regem ipsum retulisse sermonem mavis existimare, quem in psalmi initio alloquebatur, certe vetus Hebraeorum observatio, sive traditio, quam vocant, מסורה, notavit ממני, pro ממנה, positum hoc loco esse.'

For similar solutions see the modern commentators A. Dillmann, *Die Bücher Numeri, Deuteronomium und Josua.*, p. 443; S. Oettli, *Das Deuteronomium und die Bücher Josua und Richter*, p. 130; J.H. Kroeze, *Het boek Jozua*, p. 30. K. Bieberstein, *Josua-Jordan-Jericho*, p. 90, n. 39, rejects this explanation with the argument that in classical Hebrew a suffix never has a kataphoric function, but does not take an *ad sensum* formulation into consideration. He likewise dismisses the alternative solution that the suffix is congruent with כל, because in classical Hebrew the suffix as a rule corresponds to the noun following that word; see W. Gesenius, E. Kautzsch, *Hebräische Grammatik* § 146c.

[176] Thus C. Schäfer-Lichtenberger, *Josua und Salomo*, pp. 192–193.

find the repetition of the imperatives of verse 6 חזק ואמץ, which make sense only as a redactional device, and which have no other function than to transform the more or less positive and unconditional, stereotypical encouragement formula[177] into a restrictive condition formulated by the infinitives immediately following these imperatives. Throughout the Hebrew Bible these imperatives normally occur in the context of encouragement (and are thus accompanied by reverse admonitions not to fear, thus e.g. אל־תיראו ואל־תחתו in Josh. 10:25, elsewhere Deut. 31:8, Josh. 1:9,18, 1 Chron. 22:13, 28:20, 2 Chron. 32:7). Likewise the two additional particles רק and מאד in verse 7, which modify the two imperatives, stress the Janus-aspect of the beginning of verse 7: the particle רק, *only, however*, introduces a restriction, the particle מאד, *very much*, stresses the previous statement. In other words, the shift in the presentation of Joshua from an obedient and successful military leader, with whom Yhwh apparently maintains a direct contact, towards a devout observer of the *torah*, takes place not in verse 8, but already here in verse 7. Other DtrN-additions employ the same vocabulary as the whole of Josh. 1:7–8, as the following comparison makes clear:

Josh. 1^{7}	רק חזק ואמץ מאד לשמר לעשות ככל־התורה אשר צוך משה עבדי אל־תסור ממנו ימין ושמאול
Josh. 22^{5}	רק שמרו מאד לעשות את־המצוה ואת־התורה אשר צוה אתכם משה עבד־יהוה
Josh. 23^{6}	וחזקתם מאד לשמר ולעשות את כל־הכתוב בספר תורת משה לבלתי סור ממנו ימין ושמאול
1 Kgs. 2^{2-3}	וחזקת... לשמר חקתיו... ככתוב בתורת משה למען תשכיל את כל־אשר תעשה
2 Kgs. 21^{8}	רק אם־ישמרו לעשות ככל אשר צויתם ולכל־התורה אשר־צוה אתם עבדי משה

The goal of this redactional moulding is the mentioning of the *torah* in MT-Josh. 1:7: it expresses the main object of interest of the editor and thus suits the DtrN context of verses 7–8. Literary-critical observations therefore support the secondary nomistic character of verses 7–8 *in toto*, not only the plus in verse 7. In other words, it is not the presence of the central concern of the nomistic editor (the

[177] Deut. 3:20; 31:3.7.23; Josh. 1:6.9.18; 10:25, 1 Chron. 22:13; 28:20; 2 Chron. 32:7; elsewhere (without אמץ) 2 Sam. 10:12, 1 Kgs. 2:2, Hag. 2:4, Ezra 10:42, 2 Chron. 19:11. See N. Lohfink, Die deuteronomistische Darstellung des Übergangs der Führung Israels von Mose auf Josue; and K. Bieberstein, *Josua-Jordan-Jericho*, p. 377ff.: 'Zur Amtseinsetzungsformular.'

words כל־התורה) which is problematic, but it is the absence of these words in LXX which is unexpected and which requires explanation.

If we now examine the minus in its Greek context we have to take into consideration a few other deviations in LXX from MT as well. Where in the Hebrew text the caesura between the DtrH (Josh. 1:1–6) and DtrN (Josh. 1:7–8) layers is marked by the particles רק and מאד, we find no equivalent for the latter in the Greek text. Furthermore, the transition of verse 6 to 7 is in the Greek text not marked by a conjunction expressing the same notion of contrast as the Hebrew particle רק, which is normally rendered by either πλήν or ἀλλά (preferably in variation),[178] but rather by the inferential conjunction οὖν, *thus, therefore*.[179] The fact that the Greek translator used precisely this conjunction is significant, not only because it is an unique rendering for the Hebrew particle,[180] but also because it lacks a Hebrew counterpart and thus points to a literary initiative on the part of the Greek translator.[181] Moreover, his intention is contrary

---

[178] Πλήν for רק occurs in 1:17; 6:17.24; 8:27; 13:14; ἀλλά for רק in 1:18; 6:18; 11:13; 13:6; 22:5, together they appear as ἀλλὰ πλῆν in 11:22. Note the variation between the two Greek equivalents in 1:17–18; 6:17–18.24 and 13:6.14.

[179] See LSJ, pp. 1271a–1272a; LEH, p. 342b; GELS², p. 422b; F. Blass, A. Debrunner, F. Rehkopf, *Grammatik des neutestamentlichen Griechisch* § 451.1.

[180] In LXX-Joshua and often elsewhere the Greek conjunction occurs in the phrase νῦν οὖν as an adequate rendering of the Hebrew transition marker ועתה (LXX-Josh. 1:2, 22:4); see S. Sipilä, *Between Literalness and Freedom*, p. 102ff. Elsewhere in LXX-Joshua, i.e. 14:12, 22:29 and 23:6 (κατισχύσατε οὖν σφόδρα φυλάσσειν καὶ ποιεῖν πάντα τὰ γεγραμμένα ἐν τῷ βιβλίῳ του νόμου Μωυσῆ) this conjunction marks the transition to a new text segment containing the main statement of the larger discursive passage.

[181] A. Aejmelaeus, *Parataxis in the Septuagint*, p. 59, in her discussion of the various renderings of the Hebrew conjunction *waw*, considers the use of οὖν 'an indication of considerable freedom in translation technique, for οὖν can by no means be said to be an obvious equivalent of ו. As a matter of fact, there is no Hebrew word which actually corresponds to οὖν, and this is enough to make it rare at least in the translated parts of the Septuagint.'

Most commentators do not discuss or mention this unusual rendering. S. Holmes, *Joshua*, p. 17, noted the two variants and suggested that 'the translator may not have been consistent in the retention or omission of small words.' P. Sacchi, Giosuè 1,1–9, p. 240, suggests that the Greek translator—as well as Jerome who with his Latin rendering *confortare igitur* followed the Greek version (cf. also VetLat: *inualesce itaque*)—had problems with the translation of the Hebrew *Vorlage* (identical with MT here), but this view is clearly contradicted by the correct rendering of these Hebrew particles throughout the rest of the book. R.G. Boling, *Joshua*, p. 115, supposes that οὖν renders the second particle מאד, which would be as unusual as is the equation οὖν—רק, and that the first particle had fallen out of the Hebrew text due to *homoioteleuton*, apparently on the basis of the double occurrence of the *qof*. Both suggestions are not convincing and have not found approval so far.

to that of the Hebrew DtrN redactor: the Greek conjunction does not reflect a restrictive condition, but rather stresses the logical continuity between the two segments beginning with the imperatives to remain courageous, verses 6 and 7: ἴσχυε καὶ ἀνδρίζου·. . . . ἴσχυε *οὖν* καὶ ἀνδρίζου. The absence of an equivalent for מאד serves the same purpose of linking, rather than separating the two verses. Therefore, this minus does not point to a secondary interpolation (either from a glossator [scholarly consensus][182] or a second editor [Tov]),[183] but rather stems from the same harmonising interpretation by the Greek translator of the Hebrew text.[184]

If the translator deliberately intended to take verse 7 as the logical sequence to verse 6 rather than the introduction of a new segment, the absence of an equivalent for the Hebrew words כל־התורה becomes understandable. The Greek text of verse 7a as it stands ἴσχυε οὖν καὶ ἀνδρίζου φυλάσσεσθαι καὶ ποιεῖν καθότι ἐνετείλατό σοι Μωυσῆς can only refer to Moses' commands to Joshua as we find them in Deut. 3:21–22(.28); 31:7–8, i.e. the instruction to remain courageous and fearless, and assured of the divine assistance, to take the people into the Promised Land, to conquer it and to give it to the people as their property. In other words, the Greek texts refers to all the themes we find in the DtrH-part of Yhwh's installation speech

---

[182] Thus e.g. C. STEUERNAGEL, *Deuteronomium und Josua*, 1923² p. 210; C.D. BENJAMIN, *The Variations*, p. 23: 'Intensificatory [gloss]'; V. FRITZ, *Das Buch Josua*, p. 26; K. BIEBERSTEIN, *Josua-Jordan-Jericho*, pp. 88–89: 'stilistisch motivierte Zufügung' (i.e. in the Hebrew text).

[183] E. TOV, The Growth, p. 333 (= *The Greek and Hebrew Bible*, p. 392); L. MAZOR, עיונים, p. 101.

[184] Thus without arguments J. HOLLENBERG, *Der Charakter*, p. 8 (listed as an example of the translator's tendency to omit words in order to improve the Greek text); and T.C. BUTLER, *Joshua*, p. 4: 'no reason for the addition or omission of the particle is apparent, unless it is another attempt to maintain consistency by reproducing exactly the formula of v.6.'

The Greek translation of 2 Kings 21:8 offers an interesting parallel to this phenomenon. Here too we find a DtrN-addition in the Hebrew text (see e.g. P.S.F. VAN KEULEN, *Manasseh through the Eyes of the Deuteronomists*. (OTS 38) Leiden/New York/Köln 1996, pp. 161–164, 189–191) to Yhwh's promise of the election of Jerusalem (21:7), in a formulation which corresponds closely to the DtrN-addition in Josh. 1:7: רק אם־ישמרו לעשות ככל אשר צויתים ולכל־התורה אשר־צוה אתם עבדי משה, which forms a restrictive condition to the preceding promise to Israel of secure habitation in the land: ולא אסיף להניד רגל ישראל מן־האדמה אשר נתתי לאבותם. The Greek translator modified this transition by deviating from his policy to render the Hebrew particle רק consistently by the Greek πλήν and translated the particle by οἵτινες. As a result the unconditional promise in the first half of the verse was restricted to only those pious Israelites who strictly observed Moses' commands.

in the preceding verses, Josh. 1:1–6. For that reason the Greek translator understood the problematic preposition phrase ממנו as a plural: καὶ οὐκ ἐκκλινεῖς ἀπ' αὐτῶν, *and you shall not deviate from them.*[185]

Nowhere in these DtrH passages or elsewhere in the Pentateuch do we find a passage that relates the specific instruction of *all the torah* or a particular book of the *torah* by Moses to Joshua. Moses expounds the *torah* to all the people (Deut. 1:5 and further), he writes it down and gives it in custody to the Levite priests and elders (Deut. 31:9–13.24ff.), but not explicitly to Joshua.[186] For that reason, the Greek translator felt the Hebrew text of verse 7 to be somewhat problematic, as he interpreted *all that Moses has commanded you* in the light of the preceding commands in the DtrH-passages mentioned above. A slavish rendering of the first half of the verse by the Greek term νόμος, the standard equivalent of תורה (LXX-Josh. 1:8; 9:2 b.c.e.; 22:5, 23:6, 24:26),[187] would have been inconsistent with this interpretation. This noun is predominantly used by the Greek translators not as a rendering of profane commands, but rather as the term to indicate 'a body of normative rules prescribing men's conduct',[188] hence the divine Law as found in the Pentateuch.[189] It is to be under-

---

[185] The plural has not been retained in the daughter translations of VetLat (*et non declinabis ex illa*) Arm. (codd.), Eth., and in an quotation of the text by Lucifer of Cagliari. In LXX-Josh. 23:6, the Greek translator omitted the preposition phrase ממנו in the similar phrase לבלתי סור־ממנו ימין ושמאול altogether: ἵνα μὴ ἐκκλίνητε --- --- εἰς δεξιὰν ἢ εὐώνυμα.

[186] Thus already A. Masius, *Josuae imperatoris historia*, Commentary (1838), col. 898: 'Sed enim quid sibi vult, quod ait Deus, *quam imperavit tibi Moses*? Non enim lex singulariter Josuae, sed universe populo Israelitico imperata est. Et ipse legis liber primum est sacerdotibus portantibus arcam sacram traditus, atque commendatus' and the commentary on verses 7–8 by G.A. Cooke, *The Book of Joshua*, pp. 5–6: 'Although *this book of the law*, i.e., the legislation embodied in Dt.xii-xxvi, is mentioned several times in Deut. (e.g. xxviii.58, 61, xxix 21), nothing is said about Moses committing it to Joshua's special charge.'

[187] According to G. Östborn, *Tōrā in the Old Testament*, p. 174, this Hebrew noun has been rendered 191 times by the Greek equivalent νόμος. Exceptions to this stereotypical equation are the Greek terms νόμιμον (LXX-Gen. 26:5, LXX-Prov. 3:1, LXX-Hos. 8:12, LXX-Jer. 33[26]:4; LXX-Ezek. 43:11, 44:5.24), ἐντολή (LXX-Deut. 17:19, LXX-4 Reg. 21:8, LXX-2 Chron. 12:1; 30:16), πρόσταγμα (LXX-Jer. 32[39]:23; 44[51]:23; LXX-2 Chron. 19:10), θεσμός (LXX-Prov.1:8; 6:20), διαγραφή (LXX-Ezek. 43:12a), διαθήκη (LXX-Dan. 9:13), ἐξηγορία (LXX-Job 22:22), λόγος (LXX-Prov. 7:2), and τάξις (LXX-Prov. 31:26[25]).

[188] GELS², pp. 388b–389a.

[189] LSJ, p. 1180; LEH, p. 318. See further L. Monsengwo Pasaniya, *La notion de nomos dans le Pentateuque grec.* (AB 52) Rome 1972; F. García López, תּוֹרָה *tôrāh*, in *ThWAT* VIII, col. 634ff.; and, with due caution, W. Gutbrod, νόμος in der Septuaginta, in *ThWNT* IV, col. 1039–1040.

stood in a collective sense, as is evident from the preference of the translators for the singular form, even where the Hebrew has the plural תורות.[190] The νόμος in this sense, that is a Law Code to be studied continuously (μελετάω), figures in the next verse. Here the Greek translator introduced this text segment as an independent command marked by a conjunction: καὶ οὐκ ἀποστήσεται ἡ βίβλος τοῦ νόμου τούτου, where the Hebrew text has an asyndetic construction לא־ימוש ספר.

The Greek translator thus interpreted the layered Hebrew text (DtrH in 1:2–6 plus DtrN 1:7–8) synchronically and understood the contents of Moses instruction(s) to Joshua in the light of the preceding verses (Josh. 1:2–6) and the parallel passages in Deuteronomy (3; 31) and faithfully rendered the Hebrew text of verse 7a according to his interpretation of the text, that is, he marked the transition from verse 6 to verse 7 by οὖν and passed over the Hebrew words מאד and כל־התורה.[191] The Greek translation of Joshua 1:7 thus reflects the same concern for coherence between the book of Joshua and the Pentateuch as we have seen above (section 6.4.1) in LXX-Josh. 4:10, where the Hebrew text mentions specific commands from Moses to Joshua about the manner of the Isrealites' crossing of the river Jordan, for which no specific corresponding command in the Pentateuch can be found.

---

[190] Thus for instance in Dan. 9:9, ללכת בתורתיו, which has been rendered by a singular in the OG κατακολουθῆσαι τῷ νόμῳ σου, *vis-à-vis* the translation by θ' πορεύεσθαι ἐν τοῖς νόμοις αὐτοῦ; see further LXX-Exod. 16:28; 18:16.20; LXX-Lev. 26:46, LXX-Isa. 24:5, LXX-Ps. 104[105]:45. Another expression of the same tendency to maintain the collective, hence singular, notion of νόμος is the use of the substantivized form τὰ νόμιμα, *the lawful things*, derived from the adjective νόμιμος (LXX-Gen. 26:5, LXX-Ezek. 43:11; 44:5.24) as translation of the Hebrew plural תורות. The reverse development (plural νόμοι for the singular תורה) occurs only in LXX-4 Reg. 14:6, possibly influenced by the fact that the construct state of the Hebrew noun (תורת) occurs here, and in this case reference is made to a particular law (Deut. 24:16). Apart from the few literal renderings of תורות by νόμοι in LXX-2 Esdr. 19:13 (Neh. 9:13), Jer. 38[31]:33 (in verse 37 the Greek plural corresponds to MT החקים), and θ'-Dan. 9:10, the plural νόμοι is used only for profane laws or directives (thus particularly in LXX-Esther for the Hebrew/Aramaic דת, 1:15.19; 3:8.8.16.17; 8:11.17). Only in original Greek compositions such as 2 Maccabees and Wisdom of Solomon the plural νόμοι frequently designates divine laws (2 Macc. 2:22; 3:1; 4:2.17; 5:8.15; 6:1.1.5.28; 7:2.9.11.23.37; 8:21.36; 11:31; 13:14, Sap.Sal.6:18.18; 9:5).

[191] Thus already without arguments J. HOLLENBERG, *Der Charakter der alexandrinischen Uebersetzung*, p. 8, where this variant is classed in the category 'Zusammenziehung des breiten Ausdrucks' (of the Hebrew text by the Greek translator).

In short, the Hebrew text of Joshua 1:1–9 shows the signs of a nomistic re-edition of the Deuteronomistic (DtrH) composition, but this nomistic editing was not confined to the MT plus כל־התורה in 1:7, but constitutes the whole segment verses 7–8. The tension created by this redactional moulding of the original meaning of the text was smoothened by the Greek translator, who had before him a Hebrew *Vorlage* identical with MT. Thus, the contents of Moses' commands were not understood as a reference to the body of laws presented in Deuteronomy or the whole Pentateuch, since nowhere in the Pentateuch a specific commisioning of the *torah* to Joshua by Moses is reported. Rather, the phrase *according to all the torah that Moses had commanded Joshua* was interpreted in the light of the more specific commands of Moses to Joshua with respect to DtrH-themes expressed in the preceding verses 2–6, and in Deut. 3:21–22 and 31:7–8: encouragement, crossing of the Jordan, conquest of the land and its subsequent division among all Israelite tribes. The omission of the particle מאד and the use of the conjunction οὖν instead of a more literal rendering of the Hebrew particle רק give expression to this harmonizing interpretation of the Hebrew text.

The incongruity on the Hebrew level between the masculine suffix in ממנו and its formally feminine antecedent כל־התורה should be seen in its Hebrew context only, and does not support a hypothetical shorter Hebrew *Vorlage* underlying the Greek text, all the more since the Greek text renders this prepositional phrase by a plural form (ἀπ' αὐτῶν). Both the Hebrew and Greek texts should be studied in their own contexts before they are confronted with redaction-critical theories. As a result, textual and literary criticism do not overlap, but illuminate one another.

6.4.6 *The Occupation of the Land (Josh. 1:11; 1:15)*

MT twice contains a plus *vis-à-vis* LXX consisting of a clause with the verb ירש Qal[192] followed by 'the land' as object, in 1:11[193] and

[192] The meaning of ירש Qal comprises both the annexation aspect of *to take into possession, to occupy*, and the hereditary aspect of the passing of real property from one person to another; *inheritance*, thus H.H. Schmid, ירשׁ *jrš* beerben, in *ThHAT* I, col. 778–781. N. Lohfink, יָרַשׁ *jāraš* יְרֵשָׁה *j'rešāh*, יְרֻשָּׁה *j'ruššāh*, מוֹרָשׁ *môrāš*, מוֹרָשָׁה *môrašāh*, in *ThWAT* III, col. 953–985, distinguishes another, post-Exilic component with a more passive dimension: *to possess, to enjoy the usufruct of one's property*, see section 4.2.4.1 above.

[193] The Vulgate also lacks a Latin equivalent for this clause: *et intrabitis ad possidendam terram quam Dominus Deus vester daturus est vobis.*

15. Again it is unlikely that these minuses in LXX are the result of scribal error, and Boling's suggestions in that direction have not been very convincing.[194] Since the theme of the inheritance or occupation of the land is expressed by the root ירשׁ, which figures pre-dominantly in the book of Deuteronomy and Deuteronomistic literature,[195] Tov places these pluses together with the עבד יהוה pluses (see section 6.4.1 above) in his category 'Influence of Deuteronomy'.[196] The second plus in MT (verse 15) disturbs the correspondance between the antecedent ארץ (second occurrence) and the following relative clause אשׁר נתן לכם משׁה, and is thus regarded as a secondary interpolation by a large number of scholars.[197] Most of these scholars apply a similar label for the first plus in 1:11.[198] With respect to this second plus, N. Lohfink adds the argument that, since in his opinion the original meaning of the root ירשׁ Qal is 'to take possession of', the clause implies that the Trans-Jordanian area had not yet been conquered. This idea is contrary to the original presentation of the history by DtrH in which the whole of the Trans-Jordanian

---

194 R.G. Boling, *Joshua*, p. 116, ascribes the minus in 1:11 to haplography on the basis of the repetition of the *lamedh* in 1:11 and 1:12: לְ[רשׁה ולְ]ראובני. In his view the second omission can be explained in terms of a partial dittography of the preceding adjective ירשׁתכם; thus also J.A. Soggin, *Le livre de Josué*, p. 28. For S. Holmes, *Joshua*, p. 18, the repetition of the same word(s) as plus in MT was one of the main arguments in favour of the literary priority of LXX, but in this particular case he was more cautious and opted for the same scribal accident explanation, p. 18: 'The expression must be compared with וירשׁתם אתה in *v*. 15 which is also absent from LXX. As pointed out in the Introduction, the fact that two similar expressions in M.T. are omitted from LXX, raises the suspicion that they are insertions by a later hand. It must however be admitted that לרשׁתה is used as in the text, in Deut. $3^{18.31}$, 9^{6}, 12^{1}, $19^{2.4}$, 21^{1} (LXX omits in 19^{2}), so that the omission here may, as in Deut. 19^{2}, have been an accident.'

195 See previous discussion, section 4.2.1.

196 E. Tov, The Growth of the Book of Joshua, p. 336 (= *The Greek and Hebrew Bible*, p. 394), and idem, *Textual Criticism of the Hebrew Bible*, p. 328, where he adduces this clause as prime example of the alleged re-edition of the book of Joshua.

197 A. Dillmann, *Die Bücher Numeri, Deuteronomium und Josua*, p. 444; H. Holzinger, *Das Buch Josua*, p. 2; S. Holmes, *Joshua*, p. 18; M. Noth, *Das Buch Josua*^{1}, p. 6 (1953^{2}, p. 22); J.H. Kroeze, *Het boek Jozua*, p. 33; J.A. Soggin, *Le livre de Josué*, p. 28; R. Meyer, critical apparatus in BHS; V. Fritz, *Das Buch Josua*, p. 26; K. Bieberstein, *Josua-Jordan-Jericho*, pp. 90–91 (with an extensive survey of the scholarly discussion); J. Nentel, *Trägerschaft*, p. 20 For the same syntactical reasons H.W. Hertzberg, *Die Bücher Josua, Richter, Ruth*, p. 13, prefers to move the clause to the end of the verse.

198 E. Albers, *Die Quellenberichte in Josua I–XII*, p. 29; H. Holzinger, *Das Buch Josua*, p. 2; C.D. Benjamin, *The Variations*, p. 24. Likewise K. Bieberstein, *Josua-Jordan-Jericho*, pp. 90–91, with full bibilographical references.

area was conquered by Moses, but corresponds to the view of DtrN in which only parts of the land were conquered by the Israelites.[199]

A quick glance through the contexts of these pluses makes clear that one does not need to go as far back as the book of Deuteronomy to find parallels for the Deuteronomistic expressions, since these may be found in the immediate context, attested both by MT and LXX. This is particularly evident in 1:11 where the final clause in the Hebrew text לרשתה repeats the preceding clause לרשת את־הארץ, *to occupy the land.* The repetition of this clause underscores the intention of both Yhwh's gift and the immediate crossing of the Jordan, i.e. the occupation of the land. The plus does not introduce a new concept or idiomatic expression into the text, not even an aftertought, but fits the overall emphatic and repetitive style of this Deuteronomistic chapter.

The absence of the phrase likewise corresponds to the stylising Greek translation, evident also in the omission of the *dativus ethicus* phrase לכם in הכינו לכם צידה, *prepare for yourselves provision* in its Greek reformulation: Ἑτοιμάζεσθε --- ἐπισιτισμόν, *prepare provision,*[200] as well as in the hypotactic rendering of the two asyndetic Hebrew infinitives לבוא לרשת, *to come to inherit,* by εἰσελθόντες κατασχεῖν, *having entered to gain possession of.* Bieberstein dismisses the possibility of a curtailing translation on the grounds that elsewhere the double occurrence of the verb ירשׁ Qal has been duly represented by either the Greek verbs κληρονομέω, κατα-κληρονομέω, *to inherit, to gain possession*, or κτάομαι, *to acquire.*[201] Only here in the book of Joshua, however, we find this concentration of ירשׁ Qal,[202] and the choices made by the translators of other books with respect to similar verbose constructions are of course only of relative relevance. Precisely this variation in Greek equivalents and the unusual employment of the Greek verb

[199] N. Lohfink, Textkritisches zu jrš im Alten Testament, in P. Casetti, O. Keel, A. Schenker (éd.), *Mélanges Dominique Barthélemy.* (OBO 38) Fribourg/Göttingen 1981, p. 278.

[200] E. Tov, The Growth, p. 332, (= *The Greek and Hebrew Bible*, p. 391) ranks this plus as well as the similar plus in MT-Josh. 4:2 (קחו לכם מן־העם שנים עשׂר אנשׁים—Παραλαβὼν --- --- --- ἄνδρας ἀπὸ τοῦ λαοῦ) as small elucidations introduced by the second editor of the book. Nevertheless, the construction כון Hiph'il + obj. + -ל is completely normal in classical Hebrew (thus e.g. BDB, p. 466), whereas the Greek text without the phrase is equally smooth and intelligible.

[201] K. Bieberstein, *Josua-Jordan-Jericho*, p. 91.

[202] The verb ירשׁ Qal occurs in Joshua in 1:11.11.15.15; 12:1; 13:1; 18:3; 19:47; 21:43; 23:5; 24:4.8.

κατ-έχω, *to occupy*, as yet another equivalent for the Hebrew verb ירש Qal,[203] as well as the variation in equivalents for the same Hebrew verb עבר with either εἰσ-έρχομαι, *to go inside*, or δια-βαίνω, *to cross*, all make clear that the Greek translator was more concerned with a contextually appropriate rendering than a concordant representation of every word of his Hebrew original. Hence, the absence of a phrase corresponding to the Hebrew לרשתה is the result of a literary initiative on the part of the Greek translator, and was not caused by a Hebrew editor.[204]

In Josh. 1:15 the situation is not much different. The Hebrew root ירש occurs no less than three times in the same verse and serves to emphasize the importance of the theme of the complete occupation of the land on the two sides of the Jordan. Once the task of the Trans-Jordanian tribes will be fulfilled, they are allowed to return to the territory that had already been granted to them by Moses, where their relatives and possessions had settled already (ישבו verse 14), and which they may finally take into possession themselves: וירשתם.

The syntactical construction ושבתם לארץ ירשתכם וירשתם אותה אשר נתן לכם משה, *then you may return to the land of your possession—and you will take it into possession—which Moses has given to you*, in which the topic of the land is first mentioned, then realized in an anaphoric suffix phrase (אותה), and subsequently specified in a relative clause, is ponderous but certainly not impossible from a syntactic point of view. Rather, the position of the clause וירשתם אותה is emphatic, intended to stress the notion that after their support the Trans-Jordanian tribes may take full occupation of their property. One might compare the Hebrew construction of verse 3 as a similar case

[203] The Greek verb κατ-έχω occurs no more than 52 times in the whole Greek Old Testament, and only in LXX-Ezek. 33:34 as a rendering of the same Hebrew verb ירש. J. Moatti-Fine, *Josué*, pp. 57–58, explains this unusual rendering as a conscious attempt to mark the beginning of the theme of the occupation of the land, as does the equally unusual translation of נחל by ἐμβατεύω near the ending of the book (LXX-Josh. 19:49.51).

[204] Likewise: A. Masius, *Josuae imperatoris historia*, Commentary (1838), col. 913–914; J. Hollenberg, *Der Charakter*, p. 8, where the variant has been classified sub 'einzelne Wörter, welche er (d.h. der griechische Übersetzer) übergeht' (weil) 'bereits durch κατασχειν ausgedrückt.'; further N. Lohfink, Textkritisches zu jrš im Alten Testament, p. 278. L. Mazor, עיונים, p. 426 (note 34), before mentioning Tov's opinion, leaves open the possibility of a deliberate curtailment of what she regards to be a conflation of two Deuteronomistic formulations containing לרשתה, but apparently only on the level of the Hebrew text.

of an embedded construction where the sequence proleptic object + relative אשר-clause + main clause with verb and suffixed object also serves the purpose of emphasis intrinsic to the main DtrH 'land occupation' theme of this chapter.

The logical tension detected by Lohfink between a DtrH layer without the plus in which the Trans-Jordanian tribes are promised the land already given to them preliminarily by Moses on the one hand, and a DtrN-inspired correction that postpones the conquest of Trans-Jordanian to the future on the other, exists only when one allows for a very strict interpretation of ירשׁ Qal as 'to conquer' only. The semantic spectrum of this Hebrew verb, however, is broader than that, and if interpreted as 'to take into (full) possession', the perceived incoherence dissolves. Moreover, if the phrase was meant to correct the DtrH-view, one wonders why it has remained so cryptic and concise. Moreover, the main concern of the DtrN ideology, i.e. to make the complete conquest of the land dependent on a strict observance of the *torah*, is completely absent here. Also, the areas in Josh. 13:2–6 left to be conquered in the DtrN presentation include those territories that never formed part of the Israelite territory, i.e. the coast areas around Gaza, Sidon, and Tyre. Nowhere (else) in the DtrN passages do we find the idea that the Trans-Jordanian area still remains to be conquered.

Thus, if the clause in 1:15 were the result of a secondary addition, it would only add to the redundancy of the Hebrew text, and would not introduce a new concept extraneous to the original DtrH concepts. Of course, the possibility cannot be ruled out completely that somebody at the beginning of the transmission process of Joshua explicitly wanted to underline the main themes of these verses, but if this had been a conscious effort of a retouching editor, one wonders why other passages, where the theme of the gift of the land also figures, remained untouched by such a 'ירשׁ-revision', as e.g. verses 3–4, 6.

In the light of the preceding observations it is more plausible that here, too, we are faced with a deliberate stylistic shortening by the Greek translator: the redundancy of the threefold occurrence of the theme of ירשׁ Qal/κληρονομ- has been reduced to two statements, in which the Trans-Jordanian tribes are allowed to return to their own κληρονομία when the remaining Cisjordanian tribes will also have taken possession of the Promised Land (καὶ κληρονομήσωσιν καὶ οὗτοι τὴν γῆν).[205] The notion of a return to their own property had already been expressed in the clause καὶ ἀπελεύσεσθε ἕκαστος εἰς τὴν κληρονομίαν αὐτοῦ, which corresponds to the Hebrew text of the parallel in Deut. 3:20: ושבתם איש לירשתו, rather than to that of MT-Josh. 1:15 ושבתם לארץ ירשתכם.[206] As the MT clause is the *lectio difficilior*, the LXX version may well reflect a Hebrew *Vorlage* influenced by the parallel text from Deuteronomy. The Hebrew text of Joshua stresses the idea of the land as a whole and that of the Trans-Jordanian area as an integral part of Israel, whereas the text in Deuteronomy places more emphasis on the individual territories, a phenomenon that is also observable in the divergence between Deut. 3:19 (נשׁיכם . . . ישבו בעריכם, *your wives etc. will live in your cities*) and Josh. 1:14 (נשׁיכם . . . ישבו בארץ/κατοικείτωσαν ἐν τῇ γῇ, *your wives etc. . . . will live in the land*). In both the readings in Joshua and Deuteronomy, the Trans-Jordanian teritory is designated as Israel's יְרֻשָּׁה, so that the emphatic clause immediately following, וירשתם אותה, could be left untranslated. As a result of this, the correspondence between the two halves of the verse (occupation of the territory west of the Jordan as gift of Yhwh corresponding to the occupation of the territory east of the Jordan already given by Moses) has become even closer in the Greek text than it is in the Hebrew text.

6.4.7 *Introductions to Direct Discourse and Related Variants (Josh. 1:12)*

The absence of an equivalent in the Greek text for the Hebrew direct discourse marker לאמר in 1:12 is not discussed by most modern commentators, since the variant has no bearing on the content of the text.[207] Similar omissions in LXX occur in Josh. 3:6; 4:3.22; 9:22; 17:17; 22:24. To this list one may add those passages in which the Hebrew narrative clause introducing direct discourse ויאמר (+

---

[205] Likewise: J. Hollenberg, *Der Charakter*, p. 8, who ranked the variant sub 'Zusammenziehung des breiten Ausdrucks'; and D. Barthélemy, *Critique textuelle* I, p. 1.

[206] Since the Greek translator employed the root κληρονομ- for both the Hebrew roots נחל and ירש (see HR I, pp. 768–770; and J. Moatti-Fine, *Josué*, pp. 57–58), there is no reason to assume a still different Hebrew expression ושבתם איש לנחלתו (cf. MT-Josh. 24:28//Judg. 2:6 (further 21:24), as L. Mazor, עיונים, p. 90, does.

[207] Thus e.g. R. Meyer in BHS; further A. Dillmann, *Die Bücher Numeri, Deuteronomium und Josua*; C. Steuernagel, *Deuteronomium und Josua*; H. Holzinger, *Das Buch Josua*; C.D. Benjamin, *The Variations*; R.G. Boling, *Joshua*; T.C. Butler, *Joshua*; E. Tov, The Growth; K. Bieberstein, *Josua-Jordan-Jericho*; J. Moatti-Fine, *Josué*.

subject + address) is absent from LXX (i.e. in 3:10, 4:21, 9:21, 10:24 22:8, and 24:22). In most of the following cases, the Pešiṭta and the Vulgate also lack an equivalent for the direct discourse marker:[208]

1[12]	καὶ τῷ Ρουβην καὶ τῷ Γαδ	וְלָרְאוּבֵנִי֙ וְלַגָּדִ֔י
	καὶ τῷ ἡμίσει φυλῆς Μανασση	וְלַחֲצִ֖י שֵׁ֣בֶט הַמְנַשֶּׁ֑ה
	εἶπεν Ἰησοῦς ---[209]	אָמַ֥ר יְהוֹשֻׁ֖עַ לֵאמֹֽר׃
3[6]	καὶ εἶπεν Ἰησοῦς τοῖς ἱερεῦσιν ---[210]	וַיֹּ֣אמֶר יְהוֹשֻׁ֗עַ אֶל־הַכֹּהֲנִים֙ לֵאמֹ֔ר
3[9–10]	καὶ εἶπεν Ἰησοῦς	וַיֹּ֥אמֶר יְהוֹשֻׁ֖עַ
	τοῖς υἱοῖς Ισραηλ	אֶל־בְּנֵ֣י יִשְׂרָאֵ֑ל
	Προσαγάγετε ὧδε	גֹּ֣שׁוּ הֵ֔נָּה
	καὶ ἀκούσατε τὸ ῥῆμα	וְשִׁמְע֕וּ אֶת־דִּבְרֵ֖י
	κυρίου τοῦ θεοῦ ἡμῶν.	יְהוָ֥ה אֱלֹהֵיכֶֽם׃
	--- --- ---[211]	וַיֹּ֣אמֶר יְהוֹשֻׁ֔עַ
4[3]	--- σύνταξον αὐτοῖς	וְצַוּ֨וּ אוֹתָ֜ם
	Καὶ [Ra: λέγων][212]	לֵאמֹ֗ר
4[21–22]	--- --- --- --- --- --- λέγων	וַיֹּ֛אמֶר אֶל־בְּנֵ֥י יִשְׂרָאֵ֖ל לֵאמֹ֑ר
	Ὅταν ἐρωτῶσιν *ὑμᾶς* οἱ υἱοὶ ὑμῶν	אֲשֶׁר֩ יִשְׁאָל֨וּן בְּנֵיכֶ֤ם
	-- --- --- --- λέγοντες	מָחָר֙ אֶת־אֲבוֹתָ֣ם לֵאמֹ֔ר
	Τί εἰσιν οἱ λίθοι οὗτοι;	מָ֖ה הָאֲבָנִ֥ים הָאֵֽלֶּה׃
	[22] *ἀναγγείλατε* τοῖς υἱοῖς ὑμῶν *ὅτι*	וְהוֹדַעְתֶּ֖ם אֶת־בְּנֵיכֶ֣ם לֵאמֹ֑ר
	Ἐπὶ ξηρᾶς διέβη Ισραηλ	בַּיַּבָּשָׁה֙ עָבַ֣ר יִשְׂרָאֵ֔ל
	τὸν Ιορδάνην ---,[213]	אֶת־הַיַּרְדֵּ֖ן הַזֶּֽה׃

[208] See J.E. Erbes, *The Peshitta and the Versions*, for the Pešiṭta variants.

[209] The LXX has a parallel in the Pešiṭta (--- ܘܠܦܠܓܗ ܕܫܒܛܐ ܕܡܢܫܐ ܐܡܪ ܝܫܘܥ. ܘܠܪܘܒܝܠ ܘܠܓܕ.) and the even shorter Vulgate (*Rubenitis quoque et Gadditis et dimidiae tribui Manasse ait* ---) versions.

[210] See J.E. Erbes, *The Peshitta and the Versions*, pp. 185–186, for the isolated and erased Peš. 7g1 variant ܕܫܩܘܠܘ where the *dalath* marks the transition to direct discourse.

[211] In this case Peš (ܘܐܡܪ ܝܫܘܥ.) and TgJon (וַאֲמַר יְהוֹשֻׁעַ) follow MT, whereas Vg introduces the word *rursum* in *et rursum in hoc inquit.*

[212] Rahlfs adopted the reading corresponding to MT λέγων, which is attested by A.F.M.N.Arm.Syh and minuscules from the S (without 54.75.127.VetLat), P, C, and M (without 53.669) families, as well as 129 (E). Codex Vaticanus, supported by the remaining witnesses including the Coptic versions, has Καὶ ἀνέλεσθε. Margolis, p. 49, followed B and explained: 'G ignores לאמר. Καὶ of eager appeal.' C.G. den Hertog, *Studien*, p. 56, supports Margolis' view as the *lectio difficilior*; 'So ist die von *E* gebotene Lesart καί auffällig, λέγων *C P* sowie große Teile der Gruppe *S* hingegen das Übliche. Vom Kern der Gruppe *S* (k [= 54.75.127]. VetLat) wurde es ausgelassen (stilistische Erleichterung). Mayser 1934, 145, bietet einige Belege für ein καί mit konsekutiver Bedeutung (und Subjektswechsel) nach einem Imperativ (vgl. Blass/Debrunner/Rehkopf 1990 § 442). In diesem Sinne läßt sich auch unsere Stelle deuten (Vgl. auch 8:29 und 10:27, Befehlsverb + καί).' Margolis' reconstruction is therefore to be preferred. Again Peš. (ܘܦܩܕ ܐܢܘܢ ܘܐܡܪ ܠܗܘܢ.) and Vg (*et ait ad sacerdotes*) also omit the Hebrew word.

[213] In Josh. 4:21 Peš. renders the opening clause and omits the לאמר (ܘܐܡܪ ܠܒܢܝ̈

6[7]	καὶ εἶπεν αὐτοῖς *λέγων* . . .[214] *Παραγγείλατε* τῷ λαῷ	וַיֹּאמֶר אֲלֵהֶם . . . *וַ*יֹּאמְרוּ **וַ**יֹּאמֶר אֶל־הָעָם
7[2]	--- --- --- --- λέγων[215]	וַיֹּאמֶר אֲלֵיהֶם לֵאמֹר
9[19ff.]	καὶ εἶπαν οἱ ἄρχοντες πάσῃ τῇ συναγωγῇ	וַיֹּאמְרוּ כָל־הַנְּשִׂיאִים אֶל־כָּל־הָעֵדָה
	[9[21]]--- --- --- --- --- ---	וַיֹּאמְרוּ אֲלֵיהֶם הַנְּשִׂיאִים
	[9[22]] καὶ συνεκάλεσεν αὐτοὺς Ἰησοῦς καὶ εἶπεν αὐτοῖς ---[216]	וַיִּקְרָא לָהֶם יְהוֹשֻׁעַ וַיְדַבֵּר אֲלֵיהֶם לֵאמֹר
10[24]	καὶ συνεκάλεσεν Ἰησοῦς πάντα --- Ισραηλ καὶ --- --- τοὺς *ἐναρχομένους* --- τοῦ πολέμου τοὺς συμπορευομένους αὐτῷ *λέγων αὐτοῖς*[217]	וַיִּקְרָא יְהוֹשֻׁעַ אֶל־כָּל־אִישׁ יִשְׂרָאֵל וַיֹּאמֶר אֶל־קְצִינֵי אַנְשֵׁי הַמִּלְחָמָה הֶהָלְכוּא אִתּוֹ
17[17]	καὶ εἶπεν Ἰησοῦς *τοῖς υἱοῖς* Ιωσηφ --- --- --- --- --- ---[218]	וַיֹּאמֶר יְהוֹשֻׁעַ אֶל־בֵּית יוֹסֵף לְאֶפְרַיִם וְלִמְנַשֶּׁה לֵאמֹר
22[24]	*ἀλλ᾽* ἕνεκεν εὐλαβείας ῥήματος ἐποιήσαμεν τοῦτο λέγοντες *Ἵνα μὴ* εἴπωσιν αὔριον τὰ τέκνα ὑμῶν τοῖς τέκνοις ἡμῶν ---[219]	וְאִם־לֹא מִדְּאָגָה מִדָּבָר עָשִׂינוּ אֶת־זֹאת לֵאמֹר מָחָר יֹאמְרוּ בְנֵיכֶם לְבָנֵינוּ לֵאמֹר
24[22]	--- --- ---[220]	וַיֹּאמְרוּ עֵדִים׃

ܐܝܣܪܝܠ.), as does Vg (*et dixit ad filios Israhel*). In the following verse Peš. (ܘܐܡܪܘ ܠܗܘܢ. [illegible]) and Vg (*docebitis eos atque dicetis*) make no effort either to render the Hebrew idiom literally.

[214] 4QJosh[a] adds the subject 'Joshua': [ ] יהושע אל העם [ויאמר]. Peš. simplifies the statement to ܘܐܡܪ ܠܗܘܢ. ܐܟܪܙܘ ܠܥܡܐ cf. Vg (*ad populum quoque ait*).

[215] Peš. renders the introductory narrative clause, but skips the לאמר (ܘܐܡܪ ܠܗܘܢ.), as does Vg (*dixit eis ascendite*).

[216] Peš. (ܘܐܡܪ ܠܗܘܢ.) and Vg (*vocavit Gabaonitas Iosue et dixit eis*) again side with LXX.

[217] Peš. also has the *verbum dicendi* immediately before the direct discourse: ܘܩܪܐ ܝܫܘܥ ܠܟܠܗܘܢ ܓܒܪ̈ܝ ܐܝܣܪܝܠ ܘܠܪ̈ܫܝ ܚܝܠܐ ܕܡܗܠܟܝܢ ܥܡܗ ܘܐܡܪ ܠܗܘܢ., whereas TgJon and Vg follow the uniform MT tradition.

[218] Again Peš. (ܘܐܡܪ ܝܫܘܥ ܠܒܝܬ ܝܘܣܦ. ܠܒܢܝ̈ ܐܦܪܝܡ ܘܡܢܫܐ.) and Vg (*dixitque Iosue ad domum Ioseph Ephraim et Manasse*) omit the redundant direct discourse marker.

[219] Peš. (ܕܠ ܡܚܪ ܒܢܝ̈ܟܘܢ ܠܒܢܝ̈ܢ. ܡܢܐ . . .) and Vg (*ut diceremus cras dicent filii vestri filiis nostris quid vobis et Domino Deo Israhel*) likewise lack a formal equivalence.

[220] Peš. (ܘܐܡܪܝܢ ܠܗ ܣܗܕ̈ܝܢ), TgJon (וַאֲמַרוּ סָהֲדִין) and Vg (*responderuntque testes*) follow MT.

For S. Holmes, the fact that these minuses occur consistently throughout LXX, combined with the fact that in the majority of the other cases where לאמר occurs in MT the Greek translator duly rendered it by λέγων, formed a strong indication of a Hebrew revision of the shorter Hebrew *Vorlage* of LXX-Joshua.[221] Lea Mazor more moderately refers to scribal activity (on the Hebrew level), as an aspect of the numerous small alterations introduced, according to Mazor, by Hebrew scribes. Nevertheless, this type of minor alteration of the text is not to be separated from more substantial editorial changes, thus Mazor.[222] This scribal activity is not restricted to the MT of Joshua only, she argued, but is also reflected by pluses in LXX-Joshua, as in 22:21 (as well as in 6:7 and 10:24), and numerous other divergencies between MT and LXX in other biblical books as well:[223]

22[21] Καὶ ἀπεκρίθησαν οἱ υἱοὶ Ρουβην	וַיַּעֲנוּ בְּנֵי־רְאוּבֵן
καὶ οἱ υἱοὶ Γαδ	וּבְנֵי־גָד
καὶ τὸ ἥμισυ φυλῆς Μανασση	וַחֲצִי שֵׁבֶט הַמְנַשֶּׁה
καὶ ἐλάλησαν τοῖς χιλιάρχοις Ισραηλ	וַיְדַבְּרוּ אֶת־רָאשֵׁי אַלְפֵי יִשְׂרָאֵל׃
λέγοντες	

The fact that in classical Hebrew the shift from narrative to direct discourse was not always marked by the word לאמר but could be realized with other forms of the same verb אמר or to a lesser extent by other *verba dicendi* as well, undoubtedly gave rise to these minor changes in the process of textual transmission. Therefore, there is no reason to doubt that there existed some variation in the biblical manuscripts regarding the introduction of direct speech in the pre-Masoretic and proto-Masoretic period.

The importance of these variants, however, does not extend beyond that of the variant in MT-manuscript Kenicott 113, where in Josh. 4:13 the subject 'Joshua' has been added,[224] and similiar minor vari-

---

[221] S. Holmes, *Joshua*, p. 6: 'Lastly לאמר, which occurs 43 times in M.T., is absent from LXX four times, I.13, III.6, IV.3 and IV.22. Here, very strong evidence indeed can be adduced in support of the faithfulness of LXX in two of these places.' Holmes mistakenly referred to Josh. 1:13 instead of 1:12 and failed to mention 9:22, 17:17 and 22:24.

[222] L. Mazor, The Septuagint Translation of the Book of Joshua, in *BISOCS* 27 (1994), p. 34: 'The difference between major and minor variants here is one of degree and not of essence . . .' See further the introduction to chapter 3 in her עיונים, pp. 146–148.

[223] L. Mazor, עיונים, Chapter 2, part III, pp. 102–105.

[224] See J.B. de Rossi, *Variae Lectiones* II, p. 76a.

ants offered by the witnesses of the (proto-)MT of Joshua. Far more problematic seems to me the conclusion drawn by Holmes (and, with the reservations mentioned above, indirectly also by Mazor), that these variants in the passages cited above resulted from a deliberate and comprehensive effort, constituting an ideologically motivated intervention in the text of Joshua, which are the main characteristics of editorial endeavour. In Josh. 3:9–10 both speaker (Joshua) and addressees (Israelites) remain the same, as is the case in 9:21 (chiefs [נשׂיאים] of the community of Israelites, see 9:19). If the MT-pluses in these passages were the result of a conscious enterprise, we are forced to believe that a later scribe deliberately broke up a segment of direct discourse with the sole purpose to re-emphasize the identity of speaker and addressees.[225] Furthermore, the pluses in MT cited above are not identical, which would imply that the alleged editor(s) randomly interpolated phrases introducing the direct speech.

More plausible is the opposite view that the word לאמר and related phrases were occasionally, either unconsciously or deliberately, passed over, since the information provided by these phrases is far from indispensable, especially in those cases where MT contains double formulations (1:12; 3:6; 4:3; 4:21.21.22; 7:2; 9:22; 17:17; 22:24). This omission of redundant phrases may incidentally have already taken place on the Hebrew level, but since the Greek language does not require an introduction to mark direct discourse similar to the Hebrew לאמר, we are in most of the cases probably dealing with the Greek translator's device of stylising the redundant Hebrew text. In Josh. 4:21–22, for example, the Hebrew text contains three consecutive clauses in direct discourse introduced by לאמר. The first time the translator omitted the preceding phrase ויאמר אל־בני ישׂראל, since this information is clear from the context and the Greek direct discourse introduction λέγων would suffice, while in the third case he employed the ὅτι *recitativum*, a Greek mode of expression that has no parallel in classical Hebrew and as a result was employed only rarely by the Greek translators of the Hebrew Bible[226] in order to avoid the redundancy of the Hebrew text.[227]

---

[225] Thus with respect to Josh. 3:10, J. HOLLENBERG, *Der Charakter*, p. 8; S. SIPILÄ, The Septuagint Version of Joshua 3–4, p. 70.

[226] See A. AEJMELAEUS, OTI *recitativum* in Septuagintal Greek, in D. FRANKEL, U. QUAST, J.W. WEVERS (Hg.), *Studien zur Septuaginta—Robert Hanhart zu Ehren.* (MSU XX) Göttingen 1990, pp. 74–82, reprinted in idem, *On the Trail of the Septuagint Translators*, pp. 37–48, especially pp. 45–46. Aejmelaeus points out that the Greek

Some of the other variants relating to the introduction of direct discourse may also be explained in terms of a modest stylistic reorganisation of the text. The two relevant variants in 10:24 (minus ויאמר אל in the second line, plus λέγων αὐτοῖς in line four) can also be explained in terms of a stylistic condensation of the two groups of Joshua's addressees ('all Israel' and 'chiefs of the men of war') into one object clause in the Greek version, and relocation of the direct discourse marker to a position after this first clause. In Joshua 22:24 the second לאמר introduces a short question embedded in a larger discursive segment. Here the omission of the Hebrew phrase improves the fluidity of the text. Finally, in Joshua 24:22 not only the introduction to the direct discourse (ויאמרו) but also its short contents (עדים) are absent from LXX. Verse 23 immediately continues with a part of speech in which Joshua is apparently the speaker, as in the first half of verse 22. Here the omission of the two words mitigates the text and collects the two pieces of direct speech spoken by Joshua to the people into one discourse.[228] We may conclude therefore, that Holmes' firm assertion that we have 'strong evidence . . . in support of the faithfulnesss of LXX' in the cases discussed above,[229] should be altered into 'strong evidence for the stylistic reorganisation of the Hebrew text by the Greek translator'. The fact that the Greek translator in many other cases duly rendered the Hebrew word לאמר and related phrases only indicates that he did not make a systematic attempt to pass over this Hebrew idiomatic expression. In conclusion, the absence of לאמר in LXX-Josh. 1:12 does not point to a conscious editorial expansion of the Hebrew text, but to the stylistic adaptation of the Hebrew idiom by the Greek translator.

6.4.8 *Moses and the Trans-Jordanian Territory (Josh. 1:14)*

In verse 14 MT-Josh. contains the plus משה בעבר הירדן *vis-à-vis* LXX. As a result, the subject of the phrase נשיכם . . . ישבו בארץ אשר נתן לכם,

construction has no real Hebrew equivalent and that it is employed as a rendering for the Hebrew direct discourse marker לאמר only four times in the translated books of the Septuagint.

[227] Thus already J. Hollenberg, *Der Charakter*, p. 8.

[228] Thus e.g. G. Schmitt, *Der Landtag von Sichem.* (Arbeiten zur Theologie I/15) Stuttgart 1964, p. 9; and W.T. Koopmans, *Joshua 24 as Poetic Narrative.* (JSOTS 93) Sheffield 1990, pp. 99–101. Peš-Josh. solves the tension in the opposite direction by adding the direct speech introduction ܐܡܪ ܠܗܘܢ ܝܫܘܥ. J. Hollenberg, *Der Charakter*, p. 19, classed the minus in the category of lacunae in the Hebrew *Vorlage.*

[229] S. Holmes, *Joshua*, p. 6.

your wives . . . may settle in the land which he has given to you, is different in the two versions: the subject of verse 13b, i.e. Yhwh, remains subject of this clause in LXX verse 14 as well. Thus in LXX-Josh. 1:14 the land remains a gift of Yhwh, whereas in MT-Josh. 1:14 it is expressly said that it is Moses who gave the Trans-Jordanian land to the tribes of Reuben, Gad and half-Manasseh. In addition, the plus specifies the place where Moses gave this land as the area *on the (other) side of the Jordan*. The plus in MT-Josh. 1:14 is also a plus *vis-à-vis* the corresponding text in Deut. 3:19, where the clause occurs in the context of a direct speech by Moses to these two-and-a-half tribes, and where, moreover, the territory for the wives and children is not indicated by the word ארץ as in Josh. 1:14 (MT and LXX), but by *cities* (ערים/πόλεις):

Deut. 3[19]	רק נשיכם וטפכם ומקנכם ידעתי כי־מקנה רב לכם ישבו בעריכם אשר נתתי לכם:
Josh. 1[14]	נשיכם טפכם ומקניכם ישבו בארץ אשר נתן לכם משה בעבר הירדן:

A scribal error explanation for the minus in LXX can easily be dismissed.[230] Holmes, Benjamin and others considered the plus in MT-Josh. 1:14 to be a secondary addition adapted from the parallel (but somewhat longer) formulation in verse 15b:[231]

1[14a]	ישבו בארץ אשר נתן לכם משה
1[15b]	ושבתם לארץ ירשתכם וירשתם אותה אשר נתן לכם משה עבד יהוה

Tov ascribes the plus to the second edition of the book rather than to a more anonymous incidental interpolator.[232] Departing from this relatively harmless characterization, L. Mazor detects a more ideological interest behind the MT-edition, viz. that of a negative attitude towards the Trans-Jordanian territory, which according to Mazor, is also discernible in the change in Josh. 22:19 of the designation of

---

[230] As argued extensively in a chapter 6 entirely devoted to this variant by E.A. CHESMAN, *Studies in the Septuagint Text of the Book of Joshua*, pp. 49–52, leading to his standard deviating Hebrew *Vorlage* solution, p. 52. Apparently J. HOLLENBERG, *Der Charakter* (1876), p. 18, followed a similar line of reasoning, since he likewise classed the plus in his category 'Lücken' in the Hebrew *Vorlage* rather than in the category of Greek condensations.

[231] S. HOLMES, *Joshua*, p. 18; C.D. BENJAMIN, *The Variations*, p. 24. See further the authors mentioned by K. BIEBERSTEIN, *Josua-Jordan-Jericho*, p. 92, n. 51, and recently: R.D. NELSON, *Joshua*, p. 28.

[232] E. TOV, The Growth (1986), p. 333 (= *The Greek and Hebrew Bible*, p. 392).

this territory as 'too small' (according to the Hebrew *Vorlage* of LXX אם־מעטה ארץ אחזתכם retroverted from LXX$^{B/Rahlfs}$ εἰ μικρὰ ὑμῖν ἡ γῆ τῆς κατασχέως ὑμῶν) to the negative characterisation 'unclean' (MT טמאה).[233]

22[19]	καὶ *νῦν*	וְאַךְ
	εἰ *μικρὰ* ὑμῖν ἡ γῆ	אִם־טְמֵאָה אֶרֶץ
	τῆς κατασχέσεως ὑμῶν,	אֲחֻזַּתְכֶם
	διάβητε --- εἰς τὴν γῆν	עִבְרוּ לָכֶם אֶל־אֶרֶץ
	τῆς κατασχέσεως κυρίου,	אֲחֻזַּת יְהוָה
	οὗ κατασκηνοῖ ἐκεῖ ἡ σκηνὴ κυρίου,	אֲשֶׁר שָׁכַן־שָׁם מִשְׁכַּן יְהוָה
	καὶ κατακληρονομήσατε ἐν ἡμῖν·	וְהֵאָחֲזוּ בְּתוֹכֵנוּ

Bieberstein, on the other hand, points to the well-considered systematic structure of the speech in MT-Joshua (and its Deut. 3:18–20 parallel): Yhwh and Moses appear in turn in the descriptions of the land, with the subtle difference that the gift of the land in its totality is ascribed to Yhwh (note the inversion subject-verb instead of the usual order verb-subject), whereas Moses is mentioned only in the more specific context of the regulations with respect to the wives, children and cattle of the tribes of Reuben, Gad and half-Manasseh.[234]

Deut. 3:18–20	Josh. 1:12–15
יהוה אלהיכם נתן לכם את־הארץ הזאת לרשתה...	יהוה אלהיכם מניח לכם ונתן לכם את־הארץ הזאת...
רק נשיכם... ישבו בעריכם אשר נתתי לכם...	נשיכם... ישבו בארץ אשר נתן לכם משה...
וירשו גם־הם את־הארץ אשר יהוה אלהיכם נתן...	וירשו גם־המה את־הארץ אשר יהוה אלהיכם נתן...
ושבתם איש לירשתו אשר נתתי לכם	ושבתם לארץ ירשתכם... אשר נתן לכם משה

In Bieberstein's view, not the Hebrew text, but the Greek version presents an adaptation—although only partially successful—to the parallel in verse 15, with the additional aim to retain verse 14 as part of a quotation of the words of Moses (see verse 13), where the reference to Moses in the third person would be out of place. In verse 15, however, the translator apparently abandoned this principle already, since Moses is mentioned there in the Greek text as well.[235]

---

[233] L. Mazor, The Septuagint Translation of the Book of Joshua, in *BIOSCS* 27 (1994), pp. 29–38, p. 37: 'LXX seems to exhibit a less hostile view of the Trans-Jordanian territory than that shown by MT, lacking reference to 'impure land' (MT 22:19) and reporting that the territory east of the Jordan was given to the Israelites not by Moses but by God himself (LXX 1:4–15).' See further L. Mazor, עיונים, p. 162.

[234] K. Bieberstein, *Josua-Jordan-Jericho*, pp. 91–92.

[235] K. Bieberstein, *Josua-Jordan-Jericho*, p. 92, note 51: 'Möglicherweise war die Tilgung der Worte auch von dem Bemühen getragen, die Worte, in denen Mose

Mazor's characterisation of this variant would fit in well with our understanding of a redactional alteration as a deliberate modification inspired by a distinctive and clearly discernable ideological motive. The question immediately arises, however, if the replacement of Yhwh by Moses as the authority for the gift of the land really implies a degradation of this territory, since Moses figures in both the Hebrew and Greek texts of Joshua and almost everywhere else in the Jewish literature as Yhwh's intermediary. As in the case of the LXX minus in Josh. 4:10 discussed above (section 6.4.1), a sort of hidden polemics between Yhwh and Moses appears unlikely as there are no parallels for this in contemporary Jewish literature.

It is true that the MT of Josh. 22:19 voices a remarkably negative attitude to the Trans-Jordanian area by presenting it as impure, and distinct from the presentation of the Cisjordanian area as the land of Yhwh's holding. This designation of the Trans-Jordanian area, however, is not restricted to the word טמאה in MT only, but is rather presupposed by the whole of the narrative in Josh. 22:9–34, which in its entirety can be characterized as a 'Priestly' (RedP) passage.[236] Already the distinction (also reflected by LXX) between 'land of your possession' (ארץ אחזתכם) and 'land of Yhwh's holding' (ארץ אחזת יהוה), i.e. 'where the abode of Yhwh abides' (אשר שכן־שם משכן יהוה), presupposes a negative evaluation in cultic respect of the territory on the other side of the Jordan. The reading of LXX^{B} and all other LXX-witnesses μικρά, *(too) small* in all likelihood reflects an early corruption in the textual transmission of the Greek text from the graphically similar but rarely used word μι<u>α</u>ρά, *polluted*, influenced by the adjective μικρός in verse 17, as conjectured already by Andreas Masius and since accepted by Margolis and other scholars:[237]

---

in der 3. Person begegnet, auszugrenzen, um den Vers besser als Zitat von Mose-Worten verstehbar zu machen. Wie kurzsichtig dieses Vorgehen indes war, läßt sich Jos 1,15f entnehmen, wo Mose erneut in der 3. Person begegnet, aber in der Tilgung übersehen wurde.' Compare also H. Holzinger, *Das Buch Josua*, p. 2.

[236] See section 4.2.3 above.

[237] See A. Masius, *Iosuae imperatoris historia*, Annotationes, p. 151: 'xix. καὶ νύν εἰ μικρὰ ὑμῖν. auferatur Pronomen ὑμῖν. In Hebraeo est polluta, loco μικρὰ unde coniuncio scriptum olim fuisse ab ipsis interpretibus, μιαρὰ. Certè Aquilas dixit ἀκάθαρτος; Symmachus βεβήλη. et nemo nescit illos interpretes saepe uti verbis parum aptis.' (cf. Syh^{L} which contains in the margin the reading of Symmachus ܣ. ܐܢ ܡܣܝܒܐ.) The other *versiones* likewise support MT (Tg וּבְרַם אִם מְסָאֲבָא אֲרַע אַחסָנַתכוֹן, Peš ܒܪܡ ܕܝܢ ܐܢ ܡܛܠܫܐ ܗܝ ܐܪܥܐ ܕܝܪܬܘܬܟܘܢ, Vg *quod si putatis inmundam esse terram possessionis vestrae*). See further M.L. Margolis, *The Book of Joshua in Greek*, p. 434, who adopted the conjecture in his main text, and recently C.G. den Hertog, *Studien zur griechischen Übersetzung*, pp. 78–79.

22:17 μὴ <u>μικρὸν</u> ἡμῖν τὸ ἁμάρτημα Φογωρ; הַמְעַט־לָנוּ אֶת־עֲוֹן פְּעוֹר

The Deuteronomistic (DtrH) parts of Joshua lack such a negative view on the Trans-Jordanian territories. On the contrary, the stress on the participation of the tribes of Reuben, Gad and half-Manasseh (Josh. 1:12–15; 4:12, 22:1–4.6 in both MT and LXX) and the deliberate juxtaposition of the conquest of the Cisjordanian land by Joshua and the conquest of the Trans-Jordanian area by Moses (Josh. 12:1–8, 13:8–14 in both MT and LXX) emphasize the view that this Trans-Jordanian land forms an integral part of the Promised Land. The tension between the two concepts of the extent of the land is therefore not one between MT and LXX, but one between the literary strata of the book underlying both MT and LXX.

The more harmless view that the plus in Josh. 1:14 is an editor's or interpolator's adaptation of the stereotypical language found in verse 15 is contradicted by the circumstance that MT-Josh. 1:15 contains two pluses *vis-à-vis* MT-Josh. 1:14: the first containing the עבד־יהוה epithet for Moses, the second the narrower definition of the allotment of the land to the tribes of Reuben, Gad and half-Manasseh. The absence of the epithet in MT-Josh. 1:14 argues against Tov's view that the pluses of MT are part of a comprehensive re-edition of the book, since in that case one would have expected the same title to have been introduced in verse 14 as well (see section 6.4.1 above).

Moreover, the absence in MT-Josh. 1:14 of the second phrase, in which the side of the Jordan (עבר הירדן) is specified as the eastern side, i.e. where the sun rises (מזרח השמש), is even more significant, since the text without this qualifying apposition suggests that the land was given to the Trans-Jordanian tribes on the opposite side of the Jordan, i.e. the western side. This is problematic, since in chapter one of the book, Joshua and the Israelite tribes are located on the same eastern side of the Jordan where the Trans-Jordanian tribes received their territory.[238] It is therefore difficult to see why an editor

---

[238] The problematic character of this unspecified phrase has been noted by some commentators, among whom already some mediaeval Jewish scholars, as for instance Levi ben Gerson in his paraphrase of these verses explained ...הארץ אשר מעבר הירדן <u>לפאת מזרח</u>, and Josef Ibn Kaspi: וטעם 'בעבר הירדן'—אותו העבר שהיו יושבים שם היום, כי עדין לא עברו את הירדן.' (cited from M. Cohen (ed.), *Mikra'ot Gedolot 'Haketer'. Joshua-Judges*. Jerusalem 1992, p. 5.) Even the South-African commentator J.H. Kroeze, in his rather conservative commentary *Het Boek Jozua*, p. 33, noted

or incidental interpolator responsible for the addition of the phrase בעבר הירדן would have deliberately created this logical tension. If his purpose was only to amplify the shorter text attested by LXX with stereotypical language, he would have added the phrase מזרח השמש or a comparable expression (such as מזרחה, see Josh. 13:8.27.32, 18:7, 20:8) as well. Therefore, on text-critical grounds it seems far more plausible that LXX-Josh. 1:14 reflects a deliberate avoidance of the *lectio difficilior* present in the Hebrew (MT) text. The phrase in the Hebrew text probably came into existence at the moment when Deut. 3:18–20 was taken up in the context of Joshua 1. Since the phrase בעבר הירדן and its Priestly counterpart מעבר לירדן[239] predominantly refer to the eastern Trans-Jordanian area,[240] the DtrH author of Josh. 1:14 overlooked the circumstance that the geographical setting of Joshua 1 is situated in the same Trans-Jordanian area, so that the phrase בעבר הירדן in this context suggest the opposite of what the author actually intended.

By the same token the absence of Moses as the subject of the clause can be explained in terms of a smoothening of the text. Throughout Joshua the idea of the inheritance of the land is presented as an exclusive gift from Yhwh, thus e.g. in the frequently recurring Deuteronomistic formula הארץ אשר נשבע יהוה לאבותם לתת להם (thus 1:2–4.6.11.13.15a, 21:43–45, 24:13).[241] Moses may occur as a mediator reponsible for the distribution of individual parts of land (e.g. ויתנה משה עבד־יהוה ירשה לראבני ולגדי ולחצי שבט המנשה, Josh. 12:6 see also 13:8.15.24), but nowhere in the book do we find the express idea of the possession of the land as a gift of Moses. It is probably

---

the problem and its historical-critical implications: 'Ditzelfde gebied heet in v. 14 בעבר הירדן = het Overjordaanse. . . . De vaste betekenis van Oost-Jordaanland krijgt deze uitdrukking eerst na de vestiging in West-jordaanland. Daaruit blijkt dat de schrijver van deze verzen na die vestiging leefde en wel in West-Jordaanland . . .' See further C. Steuernagel, *Deuteronomium und Josua*, p. 155, B.J. Alfrink, *Josue*, p. 21.

[239] Within Joshua this designation occurs only in passages that are on the basis of several idiomatic expressions attributed to RedP: Josh. 13:32; 14:3; 17:5; 18:7; 20:8. For that reason the phrase can be seen as an additional criterion for isolating P-material in Joshua, as argued by E. Cortese, *Josua 13–21*, p. 23.

[240] Thus, apart from the RedP-passages mentioned in the previous footnote, in Josh. 1:15; 2:10; 7:7; 9:10; 12:1; 13:8.27; 22:4; 24:8. The few passages where the phrase refers to the area west of the Jordan are in most cases accompanied by the specification ימה *in the direction of the sea*: 5:1 (but absent from LXX); 12:7 and 22:7 (where a deliberate equation with statements regarding Trans-Jordan has been effected).

[241] See section 4.2.1 above.

for this reason that the parallel text in Deut. 3:19 only mentions the Trans-Jordanian *cities* given by Moses (עריכם אשר נתתי לכם).[242]

If we now take a look at the Greek version of the alleged Hebrew source for the presumed MT expansion in verse 14, i.e. verse 15b, we may note several related phenomena: The Greek text of Josh. 1:15 does not reflect the word ארץ in ושבתם לארץ ירשתכם,[243] but instead here contains the formulation in Deut. 3:19: *and you will return everyone to his own inheritance, which Moses gave to you; i.e., towards the other side of the Jordan where the sun rises*: καὶ ἀπελεύσεσθε ἕκαστος εἰς τὴν κληρονομίαν αὐτοῦ, ἣν δέδωκεν ὑμῖν Μωυσῆς εἰς τὸ πέραν τοῦ Ιορδάνου ἀπ' ἀνατολῶν ἡλίου:

Deut. 3[19] ושבתם איש לירשתו אשר נתתי לכם
Josh. 1[15] ושבתם לארץ ירשתכם וירשתם אותה
אשר נתן לכם משה עבד יהוה בעבר הירדן מזרח השמש

Here, too, the variants can be explained in terms of a deliberate avoidance of the idea that Moses gave the Trans-Jordanian land to the tribes of Reuben, Gad and half-Manasseh, by replacing the expression *land of your possession* by the more restricted *every individual piece of inheritable land*. The repetition of the preposition εἰς instead of the expected preposition ἐν[244] might be understood as a specification of these individual properties rather than an adverbial phrase qualifying the preceding words (*which Moses has given to you*). The translation thus forms a deliberate attempt to avoid the problem that the geographical setting of the words spoken to the Trans-Jordanian tribes in the narrative world (east side of the Jordan) of Joshua 1 differs from that of the (DtrH) narrator (west side).

In conclusion, the LXX reflects the concern to attribute the gift of the land exclusively to Yhwh and to remove the ambiguities of the Hebrew text. For this reason the mentioning of Moses in verse 14 has been suppressed in order to adapt this statement to its context (verses13 and 15b). Likewise, the general designation of the

[242] Cf. T.C. Butler, *Joshua*, p. 19; and M. Rösel, The Septuagint-Version, p. 21.

[243] The phrase ארץ ירשה- recurs only in Deut. 2:12, where it refers to the Promised Land in general. The LXX renders the phrase duly by γῆ τῆς κληρομίας. The noun ירשה occurs in the Hebrew Bible only in Deut. 2:5.9.12.19; 3:20 and Josh. 1:15, 12:6.7, and further in Judg. 21:17; Jer. 32:8; Ps. 61:6 and 2 Chron. 20:11, see further section 4.2.1 above.

[244] The priority of εἰς τὸ over ἐν τῷ is supported by the important E witnesses B.129 and furthermore the M-n witnesses 52.53.57.85.344 (txt). The remaining (Greek) witnesses read conform MT ἐν τῷ.

Trans-Jordanian territory in the Hebrew text of verse 15b has been replaced by a more specific one. Since the subject of the clause in verse 14 is no longer Moses but Yhwh, the problematic geographical phrase 'on the other side of the Jordan' has lost its function: Yhwh's gift of the land is not bound to a specific side of the Jordan. In the absence of variations within the Greek equivalents or of particular Greek constructions, these changes may have been effected already at the Hebrew level, though the more economical solution is to attribute them to the Greek translator. In any case, the idea that these pluses in MT are deliberate additions by a Hebrew editor remains without support.

6.5 The Greek Version of Joshua 1

In the preceding section it was shown that the significant quantitative variants between MT and LXX in Joshua 1 should be ascribed to intentions and interpretations by the Greek translator. Already several qualitative variants have been discussed in order to support this thesis. In this section a discussion follows of a number of other Greek renderings where the question of a Hebrew *Vorlage* different from MT is not at stake and where it is evident that the Greek text is not merely a slavish translation of the Hebrew, but reflects a well-considered literary initiative, however modest.

6.5.1 *LXX-Josh. 1:7–8*

In Josh. 1:7 the Greek translator did not interpret the Hebrew verb שׂכל Hiphʿil as 'to be successful' as most modern lexicons and translations do,[245] but as συν-ίημι, *to understand, to do intelligently*,[246] and thus preserved the original sense of the Hebrew root שׂכל, *to be prudent*.[247]

[245] See e.g. BDB, p. 968b; HALOT, pp. 1328–1329.

[246] Thus LSJ, p. 1718; LEH, pp. 458b–459a. In the Greek Old Testament, this verb is mainly used to render the Hebrew verbs שׂכל (33 times) and בין, *to discern, have insight* (18 times), see HR, pp. 1316–1317. Occasionally this Greek verb appears as an equivalent for the Hebrew verbs חוש, *to haste* (once in Job 20:2), ידע, *to know* (once in Exod. 36:1), כון, *to be firm* (once in Ketib-Prov. 21:29—The Qere has יבין), ראה, *to see* (twice in 2 Reg. 12:19) and שׁמר, *to guard* (once in Josh. 1:8).

[247] T.C. Butler, *Joshua*, p. 5: 'The Hebrew root שכל means: 'to be wise, clever, to understand, to have success.' The translation attempts to incorporate the breadth of the semantic field of the Hebrew.'

The same equation occurs at the end of verse 8, where the synonymous verb οἶδα (according to Margolis' edition)[248] appears as a translation of the Hebrew verb שׁמר.

The Greek translator transformed the nomistic concept of the observance of the *torah* as *conditio sine qua non* for future success into a more sapiential presentation in which faithful observance leads to insight, similar to the idea found in Psalm 1.[249] This might be regarded as another deliberate attempt on the part of the Greek translator to smoothen the tension between the concepts of the unconditionality of Yhwh's gift of the land (DtrH), and the restrictive concept of obedience to the *torah* as condition for success (DtrN). Throughout the Greek Old Testament, however, this Hebrew verb has been understood in its primary sense of 'to understand' and rendered accordingly by συν-ίημι and synonymous Greek verbs,[250] for instance in Deut. 29:8 (29:9 in LXX):

29[9]	καὶ φυλάξεσθε	וּשְׁמַרְתֶּם אֶת־דִּבְרֵי הַבְּרִית הַזֹּאת
	ποιεῖν πάντας	וַעֲשִׂיתֶם אֹתָם
	τοὺς λόγους τῆς διαθήκης ταύτης,	
	ἵνα *συνῆτε* πάντα,	לְמַעַן תַּשְׂכִּילוּ אֵת כָּל־
	ὅσα ποιήσετε.	אֲשֶׁר תַּעֲשׂוּן׃

1 Kings 2:3 offers an even closer parallel to Josh. 1:7 as the DtrN Hebrew text introduces the same nomistic concept:[251]

2[3]	καὶ φυλάξεις τὴν φυλακὴν	וְשָׁמַרְתָּ אֶת־מִשְׁמֶרֶת
	κυρίου τοῦ θεοῦ σου	יְהוָה אֱלֹהֶיךָ
	τοῦ πορεύεσθαι ἐν ταῖς ὁδοῖς αὐτοῦ	לָלֶכֶת בִּדְרָכָיו
	φυλάσσειν τὰς ἐντολὰς αὐτοῦ	לִשְׁמֹר חֻקֹּתָיו מִצְוֺתָיו
	καὶ τὰ δικαιώματα καὶ τὰ κρίματα	וּמִשְׁפָּטָיו וְעֵדְוֺתָיו
	τὰ γεγραμμένα ἐν νόμῳ Μωυσέως,	כַּכָּתוּב בְּתוֹרַת מֹשֶׁה
	ἵνα *συνίῃς* ---	לְמַעַן תַּשְׂכִּיל אֵת כָּל־
	ἃ ποιήσεις	אֲשֶׁר תַּעֲשֶׂה
	κατὰ πάντα,	וְאֵת כָּל־
	ὅσα ἂν ἐντείλωμαί σοι,	אֲשֶׁר תִּפְנֶה שָׁם׃

[248] See the extensive discussion of the difference between the reconstructions of Margolis εἰδῇς and Rahlfs συνῇς in section 6.2 above.

[249] See M. Rösel, The Septuagint-Version, p. 22.

[250] See T. Muraoka, *Hebrew/Aramaic Index to the Septuagint. Keyed to the Hatch-Redpath Concordance.* Grand Rapids 1998, p. 143b.

[251] For the DtrN background of this passage see section 4.2.2. The corresponding Antiochene text of LXX-Regum (here LXX-2 Reg. 26:2 in the minuscules 19.82.93.127.243 [margin] and in Theodoret's text) employs the Greek verb εὐοδόω:

Yet, the use in LXX-Josh. 1:7 of the verb πράσσω, *to accomplish, to do*, following συν-ίημι does point to a modest but significant literary initiative of the Greek translator. The Hebrew text further develops the imagery of the road למען תשׂכיל בכל אשׁר תלך, *do not deviate from it to the right or left in order that you may have success everywhere you go*, and therefore employs the verb הלך rather than the verb עשׂה, as we find it in the parallel passages Deut. 29:8, 1 Kgs. 2:3. and apparently in LXX-Josh. 1:7. Since the phrase בכל אשׁר תלך recurs in verse 9, Margolis, Bieberstein, and others assume that MT-Josh. 1:7 is the result of 'aberration to verse 9', which would imply that the Greek text contains the older text.[252]

Nevertheless, even if the Greek word πράσσῃς would reflect a Hebrew *Vorlage* תעשׂה deviating from and prior to MT, the use of precisely this Greek verb would still point to a well-considered decision by the Greek translator, since it occurs only sporadically throughout the Greek Old Testament[253] and then predominantly in the free translations (LXX-Job, 8 times; LXX-Proverbs, 9 times) or 'free' Greek compositions (2–4 Maccabees, 6 times). Therefore it seems that this unusual rendering should rather be seen in conjunction with and as the logical result of the translation of the Hebrew השׂכיל by συν-ίημι: in line with this understanding of the Hebrew text in the sense of 'to understand, to have insight', it would be more appropriate to describe the contents of this insight as 'all the things you might accomplish' than to render the Hebrew text slavishly by 'so that you will have insight in everywhere you go.'

If we are dealing in these final clauses of verse 7 with a 'deliberate alteration induced by the preceding mistake' as noted—remarkably—by S. Holmes,[254] the logical inference must be that the analoguous

ὅπως εὐοδωθῇ πάντα ἃ ποιήσεις, see N. Fernández Marcos, J.R. Busto Saiz, *El Texto Antioqueno de la Biblia Griega I*, p. 172.

[252] M.L. Margolis, *The Book of Joshua in Greek, ad loco*. Likewise C.D. Benjamin, *The Variations*, p. 23; L.J. Greenspoon, *Textual Studies*, pp. 123–124; and K. Bieberstein, *Josua-Jordan-Jericho*, p. 90: 'Die M-Lesart 1,7f בכל אשׁר תלך lässt sich leicht als Anpassung sowohl an die Metaphorik des vorangegangenen Satzes 1,7d אל תסור ממנו ימין ושמאול als auch an die Parallelle der folgenden Sätze 1,9fg בכל אשׁר תלך erklären. . . .'

[253] See HR, p. 1201a; and the statistics in LEH, p. 392, who count a total of 41 occurrences in the whole Septuagint, 19 times of which in the sections 'Writings', and 19 times in the deuterocanonical section, where we also find the composites δια-πράσσομαι and προ-πράσσω. In the historical books, the Greek verb appears only in LXX-Gen. 31:28.

[254] S. Holmes, *Joshua*, p. 18.

qualitative variant in LXX *vis-à-vis* MT in verse 8 should also be attributed to a modification of the original Hebrew text by the translator. In the Hebrew text the mention of careful *torah* study as a condition for future success is repeated (למען תשמר לעשות ככל־הכתוב בו) for the purpose of underlining of what had been said at the beginning of verse 7 (לשמר לעשות ככל־התורה). In line with his understanding of the νόμος as a source of insight, the Greek translator no doubt refrained from offering a strictly literal rendering of this Deuteronomistic formula,[255] and presented a Greek text in which the logical connection between meditation (μελετάω), knowledge (οἶδα) and action (ποιέω) is maintained. Thus, the variant תשמר—εἰδῇς fits well the Greek context well and should therefore not be explained on the basis of a different Hebrew *Vorlage* תשׂכיל (Holmes, Benjamin)[256] or תשמע (Margolis).[257] Such reconstructions not only disregard the interpretative character of the Greek translation, but moreover do not fit the Deuteronomistic character of the Hebrew phrase, and either require some unusual scribal errors as the interchange of both כ and מ as well as ל and ר (in addition to the omission of the י) or presuppose the equation of שמע with οἶδα which would be as unique as the present rendering.[258]

6.5.2 *LXX-Josh. 1:14b*

Finally, there are a number of other examples of (modest) interpretative Greek renderings in Joshua 1 in the second half of verse 14, where Joshua obliges the Trans-Jordanian tribes to participate in the conquest of the west side of the Jordan. From a quantitative point of view, the two versions hardly differ and so far no deviating Hebrew *Vorlage* has been postulated for the Greek text. Nevertheless, it is significant to note the manner in which the Hebrew text has been translated into Greek.

---

[255] See section 4.2 above and further *inter alia* M. Weinfeld, *Deuteronomy and the Deuteronomic School*, p. 346; T.C. Butler, *Joshua*, p. 5.

[256] S. Holmes, *Joshua. The Hebrew and Greek Texts*. Cambridge 1914, p. 18: 'LXX most probably misread the word as תשכיל and as this had just been translated by συνῇς just before, varied with εἰδῇς.'; C.D. Benjamin, *The Variations*, p. 24: 'Perhaps the translator read תשכיל.'

[257] M.L. Margolis, *The Book of Joshua in Greek*. Paris 1931–1992, p. 7.

[258] Thus only in MT-1 Kgs. 20:31: ...ויאמרו אליו עבדיו הנה־נא שמענו כי—3 Reg. 21:31 καὶ εἶπεν τοῖς παισὶν αὐτοῦ Οἶδα ὅτι ...

The rare Hebrew word חֲמֻשִׁים, which occurs in the Hebrew Bible only in Exod. 13:18, Josh. 4:12 and Judg. 7:11 (possibly also in Num. 32:17) and which is understood by modern scholars in a military sense as *in battle array*,[259] has here been rendered by the Greek translator of Joshua by εὔζωνοι, *well-girded, well-equipped*.[260] The Greek translator of Joshua did not take up the etymological exegesis of the word adopted by the Greek translators of Exodus and Judges, where the noun has been connected with חמשׁ in the sense of '*five*'.[261] Instead he offered a well-considered and contextually appropriate rendering that stresses the military function of the Trans-Jordanian tribes as a vanguard for the Israelite army, in line with Num. 32 and Josh. 4:13, where in the Hebrew text the (apparently synonymous) word חלוצים, *equipped for war*,[262] occurs.

4[12]	καὶ διέβησαν οἱ υἱοὶ Ρουβην	וַיַּעַבְרוּ בְּנֵי־רְאוּבֵן
	καὶ οἱ υἱοὶ Γαδ	וּבְנֵי־גָד
	καὶ οἱ ἡμίσεις φυλῆς Μανασση	וַחֲצִי שֵׁבֶט הַמְנַשֶּׁה
	διεσκευασμένοι ἔμπροσθεν	חֲמֻשִׁים לִפְנֵי
	τῶν υἱῶν Ισραηλ,	בְּנֵי יִשְׂרָאֵל
	καθάπερ *ἐνετείλατο* αὐτοῖς Μωυσῆς.	כַּאֲשֶׁר דִּבֶּר אֲלֵיהֶם מֹשֶׁה׃
4[13]	τετρακισμύριοι εὔζωνοι *εἰς μάχην*	כְּאַרְבָּעִים אֶלֶף חֲלוּצֵי הַצָּבָא
	διέβησαν ἐναντίον κυρίου εἰς πόλεμον	עָבְרוּ לִפְנֵי יְהוָה לַמִּלְחָמָה
	πρὸς *τὴν* --- Ιεριχω *πόλιν*.	אֶל עַרְבוֹת יְרִיחוֹ׃

259 BDB, p. 332b; HALOT, p. 331a.

260 LEH, p. 185b. According to LSJ, p. 712b this Greek adjective already occurs in the *Illias* (1.429) and the Homeric *Hymn to Demeter* 255, first only as an epithet for women: *well-girded*. In XENOPHON, *Anabasis* 7.3.46, the word is used to designate the hoplites without their heavy shields. In a metaphorical sense the word is used for 'unencumbered'.

261 Thus in LXX-Exod. 13:18, where the Hebrew word has been interpreted in the sense of 'fifth generation': *πέμπτῃ δὲ γενεᾷ* ἀνέβησαν οἱ υἱοὶ Ἰσραὴλ—וחמשים עלו בני־ישׂראל. See the remarks by J.W. WEVERS, *Notes on the Greek Text of Exodus*, p. 204: 'Exod's interpretation is consistent with the tradition of four generations of Israel's stay in Egypt; cf. 6:16ff.' The etymological exegesis of the crux as a derivation from חמשׁ, *five*, is to some extent parallelled by SamP-Exod. manuscripts ABC-INPQW[3] that have וחמישים, and Theodotion's translation πεμπταίζοντες [according to M 57' 85'–344], *on the fifth day* (LSJ, p. 1359a). The Greek translator of Judg. 7:11 (according to both the B and A texts including the other witnesses) likewise understood the word as a derivation from חמשׁ, *five*: καὶ κατέβη αὐτὸς καὶ Φαρα τὸ παιδάριον αὐτοῦ εἰς μέρος τῶν πεντήκοντα—וירד הוא ופרה נערו אל־קצה החמשים.

262 BDB, p. 322b; HALOT, pp. 321b–322a. In Num. 32:27.29.30.32 as well as in Deut. 3:18, the Greek word ἐνωπλισμένος has been used to render the Hebrew word חלוץ, in alteration with πᾶς ὁ ὁπλίτης in Num. 31:21. In Chronicles, where the Hebrew noun occurs five times, synonymous Greek expressions occur: δυνατοὶ παρατάξεως (1 Chron. 12:25), δυνατοὶ πολέμου (2 Chron. 17:18), οἱ πολεμισταὶ (2 Chron. 28:14); (further 1 Chron. 12:24, 2 Chron. 20:21).

Both the Greek adjective εὔζωνός (4:13) and the verb διασκευάζομαι, *to be equipped*,[263] (4:12) occur only once outside the context of LXX-Joshua, i.e. in LXX-Sir. 36:26 (τίς γὰρ πιστεύσει εὐζώνῳ λῃστῇ, *for who will trust a well-equipped robber?* for Hebrew מי יאמין נדוד צבא, *who willl trust a troop of the army?*) and 1 Macc.6:33, respectively. In LXX-Josh. 6:7.9.13, where the חלוץ appears in the Hebrew text as a collective body of people walking in front of the priests carrying the ark, the Greek translator employs yet another Greek adjective, μαχίμος, *fit for battle, war-like*, a word that also occurs rarely outside LXX-Joshua.[264]

Both the variation in Greek equivalents and the low frequencies of these lexemes elsewhere in the Septuagint make clear that the Greek translator commanded a rich vocabulary of Greek military terms, as noted already by J. Moatti-Fine.[265] Moreover, he apparently did not strive for a standardisation in translation equivalents, but opted for contextually appropriate renderings. Hence it need not surprise us that the Greek translator took the liberty to introduce two other minor modifications of the Hebrew text. First, he condensed the apposition phrase כל גבורי החיל, *all the mighty heroes* or perhaps *elite troops*,[266] into πᾶς ὁ ἰσχύων, *every strong one*, in order to stress the contrast with the wives and children allowed to remain on the east side of the Jordan, and to emphasize that every able-bodied man was urged to participate in the conquest of West Jordan. It is evident that the shorter Greek text offers an adequate idiomatic rendering, even if in other passages in the book (6:2; 8:3; 10:7) the more literal rendering δυνατὸς ἐν ἰσχύϊ was chosen for the same Hebrew phrase.[267]

Finally, the Hebrew clause ועזרתם אותם, usually understood as *you will aid them*, appears in the Greek version as καὶ *συμμαχήσετε* αὐτοῖς, *you will fight alongside with them*. Again a Greek verb has been employed

---

[263] LEH, p. 108b; LSJ, p. 411b.

[264] LEH, p. 292b; LSJ, p. 1085b. In LXX-Josh. 5:6 and 6:3, the word renders the Hebrew phrase אנשי המלחמה, *men of war*. The Greek word occurs in the Septuagint only in LXX-4 Reg. 19:25 for the unique expression גַּלִּים נִצִּים, *ruined heaps* (= Isa. 37:26) and LXX-Prov. 21:19, γυναικὸς μαχίμου καὶ γλωσσώδους καὶ ὀργίλου, corresponding to the Hebrew אשת מדונים/מדינים וכעס, *a contentious and fretful woman* (HR 901b).

[265] J. Moatti-Fine, *Josué*, p. 53ff. 'Une plus grande initiative dans les domaines militaire et géographique', see further section 2.2.8.3 above.

[266] See e.g. HALOT, p. 172a; and R. Nelson, *Joshua*, p. 28, note h.

[267] Thus J. Moatti-Fine, *Josué*, p. 98.

that appears only rarely in the Septuagint, predominantly in 2 Maccabees, which is a genuine Greek composition.[268] The Greek rendering in Josh. 1:14 has been used as an argument in favour of the existence of a second Hebrew root עזר (II), cognate with the Ugaritic *ǵzr, warrior, hero,* frequently the epithet of the hero Dan'il (KTU 1.17–19).[269] Yet, apart from the problem that no verbal forms have been identified in Ugaritic literature, this argumentation disregards the fact that both the Hebrew and Greek versions of the clause in Josh. 1:14 make good sense and are understandable in their respective contexts. The Hebrew text presents an admonition to the Transjordanain tribes to aid the rest of Israel, so that the unity of all Israel can be maintained. Since this aid implies participation in the coming battle, the Greek translator produced a successful *ad sensum* rendering with καὶ *συμμαχήσετε* αὐτοῖς.

6.6 Concluding Remarks

6.6.1 *Conclusions Regarding the Formation of Joshua 1*

As we have seen in the preceding paragraphs, the various pluses in MT *vis-à-vis* LXX in the first chapter of Joshua do not constitute a distinctive re-edition of that specific chapter, nor a random collection of individual interpolations into a shorter Hebrew text that would be reflected by LXX-Joshua 1. Seen in their Hebrew context, these pluses fit their respective Deuteronomistic (DtrH) and nomistic (DtrN) literary contexts (section 6.3), which are both characterized by an amplifying, redundant style, inherent in the fact that in its first DtrH version this overture to the book is a recapitulation of passages from Deuteronomy (Deut. 3:18–20//Josh. 1:12–15; Deut. 11:24–25//Josh. 1:3–5a; Deut. 31:7–8.23//Josh. 1:1–2.6.9). There are convincing indications of a re-edition of this chapter inspired by a nomistic ideal,

[268] LEH, p. 449a. The verb recurs in LXX-1 Chron. 12:22 καὶ αὐτοὶ συνεμάχησαν τῷ Δαυιδ as a translation of MT-1 Chron. 22:22 והמה עזרו עם־דויד, and further in 1 Macc. 8:25.27.28; 10;47; 11:43; 15:19.26; 2 Macc. 11:13; 3 Macc. 7:6, and 4 Macc. 3:4. The corresponding noun συμμαχία and adjective σύμμαχος mainly occur in the books of (1–4) Maccabees, see HR, p. 1304a–b.

[269] T. Muraoka, The Semantics of the LXX and Its Role in Clarifying Ancient Hebrew Semantics, in T. Muraoka (ed.), *Studies in Ancient Hebrew Semantics.* (Abr-Nahrain Supplement Series 4) Louvain 1995, pp. 19–32, especially pp. 24–25; P.D Miller, Ugaritic *ǵzr* and Hebrew *ʿzr* II, in *UF* 2, pp. 159–175.

but these redaction-critical observations do not match the text-critical data, since the most outspoken nomistic part of the chapter, verse 8, is already fully attested by LXX-Joshua.

6.6.2 *Conclusions Regarding the Greek Version of Joshua 1*

Once this Greek text is studied in its own context, it becomes clear that most if not all of its minuses *vis-à-vis* MT are the result of a conscious attempt to streamline the redundant and layered Hebrew text for the sake of a coherent and stylised Greek text and in that sense reflect the attempt of the Greek translator to produce a faithful, though not literal translation of the Hebrew original.

Several of these minuses are the result of such a stylistic shortening of the redundant Hebrew text by the Greek translator, e.g. in LXX-Josh. 4:10 (section 6.4.1). In passages such as 1:15, 12:16, 22:4, where the Hebrew text presents repetitions of the same Deuteronomistic epithet עבד יהוה for Moses, the translator offered a condensed rendering (section 6.4.1). Right at the beginning of the book in 1:1, the epithet has not been incorporated in the Greek *prostasis*, in order to concentrate the attention on the living hero of the book, characterized by well-considered Greek terms, and in order to reserve the appellation for Yhwh's own words in 1:2 (section 6.4.1). The absence of a literal rendering for the pronoun הזה in 1:2, 1:4, 4:22 (sections 6.4.2 and 6.4.4), the explicative clause לבני ישראל in 1:2 (section 6.4.3), the clause לרשתה in 1:11 and וירשתם אותה (section 6.4.6), and the direct discourse marker לאמר in 1:12 (section 6.4.7), are best explained as the result of the Greek translator's concern to avoid redundancy. A contextual approach to the divergencies between MT and LXX in Josh. 1:3–4 makes clear that the Greek translator rationalized the description of the land, and consequently passed over the archaic description of the northern Syrian territory still preserved in MT: כל ארץ החתים (section 6.4.4)

Furthermore, occasionally a phrase or clause has not been rendered literally, because their contents were felt to be problematic by the Greek translator. Thus, a reference in 4:10 to instructions from Moses to Joshua regarding the procedure of the Israelites' crossing of the Jordan were disregarded the sake of consistency, since the statement that Moses gave specific commands how to cross the Jordan has no parallel in the Pentateuch (section 6.4.1). Since we also do not find in the Pentateuch a reference to a specific *torah* commanded by Moses to Joshua, the Greek translator understood the phrase לעשות ככל־התורה אשר צוך משה עבדי (Josh. 1:7) in the light of the preceding passage and its parallels in Deuteronomy 3:21–22 and 31:7–8. As a result, he smoothened the transition from DtrH (1:1–6) to DtrN (1:7–8) by rendering רק by οὖν and omitting both the phrases מאד and כל־התורה (section 6.4.5). The Greek translator furthermore avoided the tension between the two contrasting concepts of 'the land as divine gift' and 'the land given by Moses to the Trans-Jordanian tribes' by leaving out the subject 'Moses' in 1:14, and by adopting the formulation of Deut. 3:18–20 in which Moses' donation to the Trans-Jordanian tribes is presented as individual possessions (ירשה/κληρονομία) (section 6.4.8).

Following his understanding of verses 7–9 in general and the Hebrew verb שׂכל Hiph'il in particular, the Greek translator chose the word πράσσω in order to produce a logical and coherent translation of the final clauses in verse 7. Owing to the sapiental understanding of the *torah* evoked by the first clause in verse 8, he also altered the Hebrew wording in following clauses by using the expression *knowing what to do* (οἶδα) instead of a more litteral translation of the Hebrew *to be careful to do* (שׁמר) (section 6.5.1). In Josh. 1:14, he used the unusual rendering εὐζωνός for the Hebrew word חמשים, followed in 4:12 by another unusual equation διασκευασμένοι for the same Hebrew word. The Greek translator also did not bother to render the idiomatic Hebrew expression כל גבורי החיל literally, but chose the less literal rendering πᾶς ὁ ἰσχύων instead. Another *ad sensum* rendering is offered in the same verse by the equation עזר—συμμαχέω (section 6.5.2).

The modifications of the Hebrew text by the Greek translator discussed so far are relatively modest. They do not introduce new ideologies or philosophical systems extraneous to the Hebrew text. The aim behind these changes was rather to make the Hebrew text clear and comprehensible to the Greek audience. The method, however, to attain this goal is not a slavish and literal rendering for every Hebrew word, but rather a translation that occasionally allowed for adequate *ad sensum* renderings, lexical variety, restructuring of the clauses and omission of redundant or problematic details.

6.6.3 *Conclusions Regarding the Method*

The quantitative and qualitative variants of the Greek translation *vis-à-vis* the Hebrew text should not be studied and evaluated in isolation, but in their mutual relationship. Especially those cases where no deviating Hebrew *Vorlage* can be postulated behind a Greek interpretative rendering (e.g. in Josh. 1:7 οὖν instead of רק) argue for literary initiatives by the Greek translator also in cases where one can reconstruct a Hebrew text different from MT (e.g., in Josh. 1:7 כאשׁר for ככל־התורה אשׁר). The thesis that such reconstructions did actually exist once and, furthermore, reflect an older literary edition, requires corroboration from an independent redaction-critical analysis of the Hebrew text. As for the first chapter of the book of Joshua with its numerous small variations between the Hebrew and Greek texts, the results of such an investigation are negative. Study of the individual quantitative variants in their respective Hebrew and Greek contexts clearly demonstrates that the Hebrew text of MT, itself a product of a nomistic (DtrN) redaction of an older (DtrH) text, was (almost completely) identical with the Hebrew *Vorlage* of the Greek translation. The divergencies between MT and LXX are therefore the result of literary initiatives by the Greek translator, not of an expansionistic re-edition of the Hebrew text. Study of other relevant passages in the book of Joshua will have to make clear whether the general observations and preliminary conclusions reached in this chapter find further support or require adjustment.

CHAPTER SEVEN

JOSHUA 5:2–12: MT—4QJOSHUA[a]—CD—LXX

7.1 Introduction

Joshua 5 narrates the first acts of the Israelite people in the Promised Land, which consist of the reinstatement of the rite of circumcision (5:2–8) and the celebration of Passover (5:10–12). The entry into the Promised Land is further marked by the cessation of the manna (5:12), which had been the nourishment for the Israelite people during the period of their wanderings through the desert (Exod. 16). These cultic acts (circumcision and celebration of the Passover) are possible thanks to the fact that the hostile forces are paralysed because of the supernatural event at the river Jordan (Josh. 3–4, 5:1). Verse 9 explains the name of the site Gilgal as a reference to the divine act of rolling away (גלל) the humiliation of Egypt. The final verses of the chapter (5:13–15) describe an encounter between Joshua and the commander of Yhwh's army, which breaks off abruptly after their first acquaintance.

As noted above in section 2.2, the Hebrew and Greek texts of Joshua 5:2–12 are strongly divergent. In verses 1, and 13–15, MT and LXX correspond more closely, and for that reason are of less importance for our discussion. In verses 2–12, MT and LXX offer self-consistent variant versions of the same passage. In verse 2, for instance, the word שֵׁנִית, *a second time*, is absent from LXX and the corresponding verb וְשׁוּב, *do again* (MT) has been understood by the LXX as וְשֵׁב/καθίσας, *and sit.* Verses 4–7, narrating the who and why of Joshua's act of circumcision, are formulated differently in the two versions. Here among other things, the Hebrew lacks the notion present in LXX that not all Israelites had been circumcised in Egypt, a notion that, moreover, is strongly denied in the Hebrew formulation of verse 4. In verse 11 the phrase ממחרת הפסח, *on the day after Passover*, as well as the phrase ממחרת, *on the following day*, in verse 12, is absent from LXX. Another temporal phrase בעצם היום הזה, *on the very day*, marks in LXX the moment of cessation of the manna (ἐν ταύτῃ τῇ ἡμέρα ἐξέλιπεν τὸ μαννα, *on that day the manna ceased*), whereas in the MT is underscores the preceding plus ממחרת הפסח *vis-à-vis* LXX, in order to stress the preceding statement that the Israelites ate *maṣṣot* on the day after Passover. Furthermore, fragments of the first verses of this chapter (verses 2–7) have been preserved on the 4QJoshua[a] scroll, which because of their fragmentary character require a study on their own. Another document related to Qumran, the Damascus Document (CD XX), contains an allusion to Josh. 5:6 which may reflect a different Hebrew text. For the sake of convenience a synopsis of the three textual witnesses, MT-Josh. 5:2–12, 4QJosh[a] frg. 1–2 with Josh. 5:2–6 and LXX-Josh. 5:2–12, is presented below:[1]

5[2]	*Ὑπὸ δὲ τοῦτον τὸν καιρὸν*	[בעת]ההיא	בָּעֵ֣ת הַהִ֗יא	5[2]
	εἶπεν κύριος τῷ Ἰησοῖ	אמר יהוה אליהש[ע	אָמַ֤ר יְהוָה֙ אֶל־יְהוֹשֻׁ֔עַ	
	Ποίησον σεαυτῷ	ע]שׂ[ה לך	עֲשֵׂ֥ה לְךָ֖	
	μαχαίρας πετρίνας	חרבות צרים	חַֽרְב֣וֹת צֻרִ֑ים	
	ἐκ πέτρας ἀκροτόμου			
	καὶ *καθίσας*	ושוב	וְשׁ֛וּב	
	περίτεμε τοὺς υἱοὺς Ισραηλ	חל את בני ישראל	מֹ֥ל אֶת־בְּנֵֽי־יִשְׂרָאֵ֖ל	
	---.	---?	שֵׁנִֽית׃	
5[3]	καὶ ἐποίησεν --- Ἰησοῦς	ויעשׂ]ל[ו י]הֹשע	וַיַּֽעַשׂ־ל֥וֹ יְהוֹשֻׁ֖עַ	5[3]
	μαχαίρας πετρίνας *ἀκροτόμους*	ח]רבות צ]רֹ[ים	חַֽרְב֣וֹת צֻרִ֑ים	
	καὶ περιέτεμεν τοὺς υἱοὺς Ισραηλ	וימל את בני ישראל	וַיָּ֙מָל֙ אֶת־בְּנֵ֣י יִשְׂרָאֵ֔ל	
	ἐπὶ τοῦ καλουμένου τόπου			
	Βουνὸς τῶν ἀκροβυστιῶν.	אל גבעת הערלות	אֶל־גִּבְעַ֖ת הָעֲרָלֽוֹת׃	
5[4]	*ὃν δὲ τρόπον περιεκάθαρεν*	וזה הדבר	וְזֶ֥ה הַדָּבָ֖ר	5[4]
	Ἰησοῦς τοὺς υἱοὺς *Ισραηλ*,	אשר מל יהושע	אֲשֶׁר־מָ֣ל יְהוֹשֻׁ֑עַ	
	--- --- ---	כ]ל[frg. 2]הֹעֹםֹ	כָּל־הָעָ֨ם	
	--- --- --- ---	היֹצֹ[א ממצרים	הַיֹּצֵ֜א מִמִּצְרַ֣יִם	
	---	הזכרים	הַזְּכָרִ֗ים	
	--- --- --- --- ---	כל אנשי המלחמה	כֹּ֚ל אַנְשֵׁ֣י הַמִּלְחָמָ֔ה	
	--- --- --- --- --- ---	מתו במדבר בדרך	מֵ֤תוּ בַמִּדְבָּר֙ בַּדֶּ֔רֶךְ	
	--- --- --- --- ---	בצאתם]מֹמצֹרֹים	בְּצֵאתָ֖ם מִמִּצְרָֽיִם׃	
	--- --- --- --- --- ---	כיֹ[מלים היו כל העם	כִּֽי־מֻלִ֣ים הָי֔וּ כָּל־הָעָ֖ם	5[5]
	--- ---	היצאים	הַיֹּֽצְאִ֑ים	
	ὅσοι ποτὲ	וכל העם	וְכָל־הָעָ֡ם	
	ἐγένοντο --- --- ἐν τῇ ὁδῷ	הילדים במדבר בדרך	הַיִּלֹּדִ֨ים בַּמִּדְבָּ֤ר בַּדֶּ֙רֶךְ֙	
	--- --- --- --- ---	בצ]אֹתם ממצֹ[רים	בְּצֵאתָ֣ם מִמִּצְרַ֔יִם	
	--- ---	לא מלו	לֹא־מָֽלוּ׃	

[1] The LXX text is taken from the Rahlfs edition; text-critical notes to this text are offered in section 7.6 below.

	καὶ ὅσοι ποτὲ ἀπερίτμητοι ἦσαν			
	τῶν ἐξεληλυθότων ἐξ Αἰγύπτου,			
5[5]	*πάντας τούτους περιέτεμεν Ἰησοῦς·*			
5[6]	τεσσαράκοντα γὰρ καὶ δύο ἔτη	כי ארבעים שנה	כִּי אַרְבָּעִים שָׁנָה	5[6]
	ἀνέστραπται --- Ισραηλ	הלכו בני ישראל	הָלְכוּ בְנֵי־יִשְׂרָאֵל	
	ἐν τῇ ἐρήμῳ τῇ Μαδβαρίτιδι,	במדבר	בַּמִּדְבָּר	
	διὸ ἀπερίτμητοι ἦσαν οἱ πλεῖστοι	עד תם כל הגוי]	עַד־תֹּם כָּל־הַגּוֹי	
	αὐτῶν τῶν --- *μαχίμων*	אנשי המלח[מה	אַנְשֵׁי הַמִּלְחָמָה	
	τῶν ἐξεληλυθότων ἐκ γῆς Αἰγύπτου	היצאים ממצרים	הַיֹּצְאִים מִמִּצְרַיִם	
	οἱ *ἀπειθήσαντες*	אשר לא שמעו	אֲשֶׁר לֹא־שָׁמְעוּ	
	τῶν ἐντολῶν τοῦ θεοῦ,	בקול יהוה	בְּקוֹל יְהוָה	
	οἷς *καὶ διώρισεν* --- ---	אשר נשבע יהוה להם	אֲשֶׁר נִשְׁבַּע יְהוָה לָהֶם	
	μὴ ἰδεῖν αὐτοὺς	לב]לתי ראות	לְבִלְתִּי הַרְאוֹתָם	
	τὴν γῆν,	את ה[ארץ	אֶת־הָאָרֶץ	
	ἣν ὤμοσεν κύριος	אשר נשבע יהוה	אֲשֶׁר נִשְׁבַּע יְהוָה	
	τοῖς πατράσιν αὐτῶν	לאבותם	לַאֲבוֹתָם	
	δοῦναι ἡμῖν,	לתת לנו	לָתֶת לָנוּ	
	γῆν ῥέουσαν γάλα καὶ μέλι.	ארץ זבת חלב ודבש	אֶרֶץ זָבַת חָלָב וּדְבָשׁ׃	
5[7]	ἀντὶ δὲ τούτων *ἀντικατέστησεν*	ואת בני]הם הק[ים	וְאֶת־בְּנֵיהֶם הֵקִים	5[7]
	τοὺς υἱοὺς αὐτῶν,		תַּחְתָּם	
	--- οὓς Ἰησοῦς περιέτεμεν		אֹתָם מָל יְהוֹשֻׁעַ	
	διὰ τὸ αὐτοὺς γεγενῆσθαι		כִּי־עֲרֵלִים הָיוּ	
	κατὰ τὴν ὁδὸν ἀπεριτμήτους.			
	--- --- --- --- --- --- ---		כִּי לֹא־מָלוּ אוֹתָם בַּדָּרֶךְ׃	
5[8]	--- ---		וַיְהִי	5[8]
	--- --- --- ---		כַּאֲשֶׁר־תַּמּוּ כָל־הַגּוֹי	
	περιτμηθέντες δὲ		לְהִמּוֹל	
	ἡσυχίαν εἶχον			
	αὐτόθι καθήμενοι ἐν τῇ παρεμβολῇ,		וַיֵּשְׁבוּ תַחְתָּם בַּמַּחֲנֶה	
	ἕως *ὑγιάσθησαν.*		עַד חֲיוֹתָם׃	
			פ	
5[9]	καὶ εἶπεν κύριος τῷ Ἰησοῖ *υἱῷ Ναυη*		וַיֹּאמֶר יְהוָה אֶל־יְהוֹשֻׁעַ	5[9]
	Εν τῇ σήμερον ἡμέρᾳ ἀφεῖλον		הַיּוֹם גַּלּוֹתִי	
	τὸν ὀνειδισμὸν Αἰγύπτου ἀφ᾽ ὑμῶν,		אֶת־חֶרְפַּת מִצְרַיִם מֵעֲלֵיכֶם	
	καὶ ἐκάλεσεν τὸ ὄνομα τοῦ τόπου ἐκείνου		וַיִּקְרָא שֵׁם הַמָּקוֹם הַהוּא	
	Γαλγαλα.		גִּלְגָּל	
	--- --- --- --- ---		עַד הַיּוֹם הַזֶּה׃	
	--- --- --- --- --- --- ---		וַיַּחֲנוּ בְנֵי־יִשְׂרָאֵל בַּגִּלְגָּל	5[10]
5[10]	Καὶ ἐποίησαν *οἱ υἱοὶ Ισραηλ* τὸ πασχα		וַיַּעֲשׂוּ אֶת־הַפֶּסַח	
	τῇ τεσσαρεσκαιδεκάτῃ ἡμέρᾳ τοῦ μηνὸς		בְּאַרְבָּעָה עָשָׂר יוֹם לַחֹדֶשׁ	
	ἀπὸ ἑσπέρας		בָּעֶרֶב	
	ἐπὶ δυσμῶν Ιεριχω		בְּעַרְבוֹת יְרִיחוֹ׃	
	ἐν τῷ πέραν τοῦ Ιορδάνου ἐν τῷ πεδίῳ			

5^{11}	καὶ ἐφάγοσαν ἀπὸ τοῦ *σίτου* τῆς γῆς	וַיֹּאכְלוּ מֵעֲבוּר הָאָרֶץ	5^{11}
	--- --- --- ---	מִמָּחֳרַת הַפֶּסַח	
	ἄζυμα καὶ *νέα*.	מַצּוֹת וְקָלוּי	
5^{12}	ἐν ταύτῃ τῇ ἡμέρᾳ	בְּעֶצֶם הַיּוֹם הַזֶּה׃	
	--- ἐξέλιπεν τὸ μαννα --- ---	וַיִּשְׁבֹּת הַמָּן מִמָּחֳרָת	5^{12}
	μετὰ τὸ βε*βρωκέναι* αὐτοὺς ἐκ τοῦ *σίτου* τῆς γῆς,	בְּאָכְלָם מֵעֲבוּר הָאָרֶץ	
	καὶ οὐκέτι ὑπῆρχεν τοῖς υἱοῖς Ισραηλ μαννα·	וְלֹא־הָיָה עוֹד לִבְנֵי יִשְׂרָאֵל מָן	
	ἐκαρπίσαντο δὲ --- --- ---	וַיֹּאכְלוּ מִתְּבוּאַת	
	τὴν χώραν τῶν Φοινίκων	אֶרֶץ כְּנַעַן	
	ἐν τῷ ἐνιαυτῷ ἐκείνῳ.	בַּשָּׁנָה הַהִיא׃	
			ס

Consistent divergences such as those mentioned above, make clear that the variants do not originate in a series of unconscious scribal corruptions, but rather reflect a well-considered reworking of one version into the other. Therefore we have reason to assume that we are dealing here with editorial activity and intentional literary initiatives reflected by at least one of the two versions.[2] For this reason the present passage holds a prominent place in studies that concentrate on the relation and overlap between textual criticism and literary and redaction criticism. Richard Nelson, for instance, in his recent commentary,[3] presents the LXX and MT versions of this chapter as the unrevised and revised editions of this chapter, respectively, and comments upon these independently. The differences between the Hebrew and Greek texts of this chapter play a prominent role in A. Graeme Auld's argumentation of the literary priority of the text of Joshua as reflected by LXX as opposed to the MT,[4] as given in the opening essay of his recent collection of essays on the book of Joshua.[5] Likewise, for Emanuel Tov in his essay 'The Growth of the Book of Joshua',[6] these quantitative divergencies between LXX and MT point to editorial activity on the Hebrew level. Nevertheless, the Greek text also reflects several cases of reinterpretation by the Greek translator of his Hebrew *Vorlage* and thus points to literary initiatives on the Greek level.

---

[2] See e.g., E.A. Chesman, *Studies in the Septuagint Text of the Book of Joshua*, pp. 81–85.

[3] R.D. Nelson, *Joshua*, pp. 71–83. J.A. Soggin, *Le livre de Josué*, pp. 58–60, followes a similar procedure.

[4] See section 2.2.6 above.

[5] A.G. Auld, Joshua. The Hebrew and Greek Texts, see section 2.2.6 above.

[6] E. Tov, The Growth of the Book of Joshua (= *The Greek and Hebrew Bible*, pp. 385–396) see section 2.2.7.1 above and section 7.2.5 below.

7.2 Critical Review of Previous Research

Before we start a new investigation of the Hebrew and Greek texts of these problematic verses, it is necessary to review the long and complex history of research on the significant variation between the two versions. In the course of more than a century of study, several aspects of the versions have been investigated and different positions have been defended. A critical review of these studies will help us to see more clearly the problems and their possible explanations.[7]

7.2.1 *Deuteronomistic Corrections (J. Hollenberg)*

Although most of these contemporary scholars take S. Holmes' thesis of a deliberate reworking of a Hebrew text reflected by LXX towards the more 'orthodox' and redundant text of MT as the starting-point for their line of research, it was in fact J. Hollenberg who, in 1874, for the first time brought together observations from the fields of textual criticism and literary criticism, although in a somewhat implicit manner.[8] In his search for Deuteronom(ist)ic elements in the book of Joshua, he assigned the whole segment 5:4–7 to the Deuteronomic redactor of the book of Joshua.[9] In his view, the *crux interpretum* חרפה מצרים, 'Die Schmach Aegyptens', refers to the simple fact that none of the Israelites had been circumcised in Egypt, and that this situation apparently had served as a reason for the Egyptians to deride the Israelites.[10] This uncomplicated state of affairs, however, is in defiance of the law on the circumcision of each Israelite male as found in Genesis 17.[11]

A later redactor therefore added the whole of verses Josh. 5:4–7 as well as the element of repetition in verse 2: שׁוב and שׁנית, in order

[7] A full *status quaestionis* regarding textual and literary critical issues of Josh. 5:2–12 is offered by K. Bieberstein, *Josua-Jordan-Jericho*, p. 194ff. (5:2–9), p. 210ff. (5:10–12). A helpful and comprehensive discussion of all texts from Antiquity dealing with the theme of circumcision (Hebrew Bible, Septuagint, Targumim, Jubilees, Qumran sectarian writings, Philo, Josephus, other Jewish writings from the second Temple period, New Testament, rabbinical literature, early Christian Church fathers and [pagan] Greek and Latin authors) is offered by A. Blaschke, *Beschneidung. Zeugnisse der Bibel und verwandter Texte.* (TANZ 28) Tübingen 1998.

[8] J. Hollenberg, Die deuteronomischen Bestandtheile, pp. 462–507, especially pp. 493–495.

[9] See section 4.2.1 above.

[10] J. Hollenberg, Die deuteronomischen Bestandtheile, pp. 493–495.

[11] See the discussion in A. Blaschke, *Beschneidung*, pp. 79–92.

to harmonise this older circumcision narrative (5:2*.3.8–9) with that of Genesis 17. On the basis of the parallels between Josh. 5:6 and Deut. 1:35 and 2:14.16, Hollenberg identified this redactor with the Deuteronomistic redactor (D^{2}) of both the book of Joshua and the legislative core of the book of Deuteronomy (D^{1}).

Josh. 5^{6}	כי ארבעים שנה הלכו בני־ישראל במדבר
	עד־תם כל־הגוי אנשי המלחמה היצאים ממצרים
	אשר לא־שמעו בקול יהוה
	אשר נשבע יהוה להם לבלתי הראותם את־הארץ
	אשר נשבע יהוה לאבותם לתת לנו ארץ זבת חלב ודבש:
Deut. 1^{35}	אם־יראה איש באנשים האלה הדור הרע הזה את הארץ הטובה
	אשר נשכעתי לתת לאכתיכם:
2^{14}	והימים אשר־הלכנו . . . שלשים ושמנה שנה
	עד־תם כל־הדור אנשי המלחמה . . .
	כאשר נשבע יהוה להם:
2^{16}	ויהי כאשר־תמו כל־אנשי המלחמה למות מקרב העם:

Although Hollenberg did not explicitly refer to the LXX version of this passage, the connection between literary-critical and text-critical data was made soon afterwards by J. Wellhausen.[12] Scholars like A. Kuenen. A. Dillmann, C. Steuernagel, H. Holzinger, R. Smend sr. and S.R. Driver adopted this view, but were compelled to ascribe this redaction of Josh. 5 to a post-Priestly hand ('R' or 'RP'), in order to uphold on the one hand the basic thesis of the newer documentary hypothesis in which the Priestly stratum of the Hexateuch was seen as its completion rather than its groundwork (so Nöldeke),[13] and on the other hand the older thesis by Hollenberg, who simply understood the redaction as a Deuteronomistic harmonisation of the older narrative with the Priestly account of Gen. 17 (which he placed before the Deuteronomic redaction).[14] In his systematic investigation of the character of the Greek version of Joshua (1876), Hollenberg did not (yet) make the synthesis proposed by Wellhausen (1876–77),

[12] J. Wellhausen, *Die Composition des Hexateuchs*, pp. 122–123.

[13] T. Nöldeke, *Untersuchungen zur Kritik des Alten Testaments*. Kiel 1869. Nöldeke, p. 95, did not discuss the relation between Josh. 5:4–7 and Gen. 17, but see section 7.4.3.2 below.

[14] A. Kuenen, *Historisch-critisch onderzoek*², pp. 131–132; A. Dillmann, *Die Bücher Numeri, Deuteronomium und Josua*, pp. 457–460; S. Oettli, *Das Deuteronomium und die Bücher Josua und Richter*, p. 140; C. Steuernagel *Deuteronomium und Josua*, pp. 167–168; H. Holzinger, *Das Buch Josua.*, pp. 11–12; R. Smend (sr), *Die Erzählung des Hexateuch*, pp. 289–290; S.R. Driver, *Introduction*, p. 106. See further section 7.4.2.3 below.

but rather pointed to a number of small literary initiatives by the Greek translator on the one hand, while on the other hand he saw in the Greek text of Josh. 5:4–7 a hopelessly confused text full of internal contradictions.[15]

7.2.2 *The Special Case of Josh. 5:10–12*

Whereas Hollenberg initially attributed the absence of equivalents for the phrases ממחרת הפסח and ממחרת in LXX-Josh. 5:11–12 to the Greek translator's lack of knowledge of the Hebrew lexeme (the word מחרת occurs only here in the Hebrew text of Joshua),[16] he later adopted the view that the MT reflects a secondary expansion *vis-à-vis* the Hebrew *Vorlage* of the original Greek text.[17] The pluses in MT should be seen in relation to the parallel text in Leviticus 23, where we find regulations with respect to the cultic calendar, in which the feast of *maṣṣot* is placed directly behind that of Passover with explicit temporal prescriptions (verses 4–6). In the same context the phrase ממחרת השבת has been employed to indicate the proper time for the wave-offering by the priest of the first sheaf of the harvest (verse 11), when the Israelites will have settled in the land (verse 10), and as starting-point for the counting of the seven weeks from this specific day until the new offering on the feast of Pentecost (verse 16):

> [23[4]] These are the appointed times of sacred convocations, that you shall proclaim at their appointed times: [23[5]] In the first month on the 14th day of the month (בחדשׁ הראשׁון בארבעה עשׂר לחדשׁ) in the evening twilight (בין הערבים): Passover for Yhwh (פסח ליהוה). [23[6]] and on the 15th day of this month (ובחמשׁה עשׂר יום לחדשׁ הזה) the feast of unleavened breads for Yhwh (חג המצות ליהוה). Seven days you shall eat unleavened breads (שׁבעת ימים מצות תאכלו). [23[7]] On the first day there shall be a sacred convocation for you, no laborious work whatsoever you shall perform. [23[8]] You shall present a fire(offering) for Yhwh 7 days; on the seventh day (there is) a sacred convocation, no

[15] J. Hollenberg, *Der Charakter*, p. 18: '5,4–8 enthält die LXX einen ganz andern Text, völlig fehlt 4b; 5 und 6 stehen beinahe in umgekehrter Ordnung, anderes dagegen ist zugestetzt. Offenbar war an der sachlich schwierigen Stelle vielfach korrigiert worden, aber der den LXX vorliegende Text macht die Sache noch dunkler. Fast scheint es als ob die LXX hier noch nicht unversehrt geblieben ist, denn was wir jetzt lesen, ist geradezu unsinnig und voller Widersprüche.'

[16] J. Hollenberg, *Der Charakter*, p. 18.

[17] J. Hollenberg, Zur Textkritik des Buches Josua, pp. 97–98.

> laborious work whatsoever you shall perform.' [23[9]] Yhwh said to Moses as follows: [23[10]] 'Say to the children of Israel and speak to them: 'When you will come into the land that I give to you, (כי־תבאו אל־הארץ אשר אני נתן לכם) you will gather in the harvest, bring the the first sheaf of your harvest to the priest, [23[11]] and he shall wave the sheaf before Yhwh in favour of you, on the day after the shabbat the priest shall wave it. (ממחרת השבת יניפנו הכהן) . . . [23[14]] Bread, roasted (grain), and new corn you shall not eat (ולחם וקלי וכרמל לא תאכלו) until that very day, (עד־עצם היום הזה) until you will bring the sacrifice. (This is) an eternal ordinance throughout your generations in all your habitations. [23[15]] You shall count from the day after the shabbat (וספרתם לכם ממחרת השבת) from the day you will bring the sheaf of the wave offering seven complete weeks it shall be, [23[16]] until the day after the seventh shabbat (עד ממחרת השבת השביעת) you shall count fifty days, then you shall present a new cereal offering for Yhwh.

This Priestly legislation of Leviticus 23 shares with Josh. 5:10–12 [1] the mentioning of both Passover and *maṣṣot* in direct sequence as opposed to the older traditions in which these festivals were less related to one another (Exod. 23:15; 34:18–24.25; Deut. 16:1–2.5–7; 3–4.8),[18] [2] the almost exclusive mentioning of קָלִי/קָלוּי, *roasted (grain)*,[19] [3] the notion of entry into the land (Lev. 23:10), [4] the stress on the particular day (עצם היום הזה) on which the roasted grain may be consumed (Lev. 23:14, MT-Josh. 5:11), and [5] the temporal designation ממחרת, *on the following day* (Lev. 23:11.15.16, MT-Josh. 5:11.12). In Leviticus 23, however, the phrase ממחרת השבת marks

[18] See the commentaries on Joshua 5 and Leviticus 23 and the studies devoted to the Israelite, Jewish and Christian Passover festivals, e.g., G. Beer, *Die Mischna II/3. Pesachim.* Gießen 1912; J. Jeremias, πάσχα, in *ThWNT* V, pp. 895–903; R. de Vaux, *Les Institutions* II. Paris 1960, pp. 383–394; H. Haag, *Vom alten zum neuem Pascha. Geschichte und Theologie des Osterfestes.* (SBS 49) Stuttgart 1971; and E. Otto, פָּסַח *pasaḥ* פֶּסַח *pæsaḥ*, in *ThWAT* VI, col. 659–682.

[19] See HALOT 1102b. The word קָלוּי is the passive participle Qal of the verb קלה I, which recurs in the Hebrew Bible only three times, in Lev. 2:14 אביב קלוי באש, *grain parched with fire*, Jer. 29:22 קלם מלך־בבל באש, *the king of Babel roasted them [i.e., Zedekiah and Ahab] in the fire*, and Ps. 38:8 כי־כסלי מלאו נקלה, *my loins are filled with burning* (image of distress), see Lisowsky, *Konkordanz zum hebräischen Bibel.* Stuttgart 1981², p. 1259b. The nominal form קָלִי or קָלִיא occurs five times in the Hebrew Bible, apart from Lev. 23:14, in 1 Sam. 17:17; 25:18; 2 Sam. 17:28 and Ruth 2:14. See the explanatory note in H.J. Stoebe, *Das erste Buch Samuelis.* (KAT VIII/1) Gütersloh 1973, p. 323, note b: 'Unzerkleinerte, geröstete Getreidekörner, sowohl eine besondere Delikatesse als auch für Marschverpflegung gut geeignet; noch jetzt gebräuchlich.'

the proper moment for bringing the first offering of the harvest (verse 11) as well as the starting point for calculating the proper time of the festival of Pentecost (verses 15 and 16). The present context of these phrases suggest a relation between this day and the Passover—*maṣṣot* festival, but is not specific about that relation. As a result, from the period of Early Judaism onward there has been a variety of interpretations of and corresponding diverging calendrical calculations for the Pentecost (so e.g., the Sadducean group of Boethusians, the Samaritans, the Falashas and the Karaites).[20]

Elaborating on observations made by Wellhausen and others, Hollenberg argued that the Hebrew text of Joshua already reflects a harmonising interpretation of this problem by combining the two traditions of Passover (Lev. 23:4–8) and the tradition of the first harvest (Lev. 23:9–14) on the one hand, and the Pentecost festival (Lev. 23:15–22) on the other, into the phrase ממחרת הפסח. Thus, the phrases in MT-Josh. 5:11.12 should be regarded as the result of a late interpretation of the Leviticus text. The LXX text would still attest to an earlier stage in this development.[21] As a result, the two pluses in MT would reflect a conscious elaboration of an older version of the book. Interestingly, however, with respect to Josh. 5:10–12 Wellhausen had argued that this passage in its entirety reflects an elaboration of the legislative complex in Lev. 23, with the argument that the Priestly writer of Josh. 5:10–12 had to introduce the Passover dates both in 5:10 and in 4:19 (the date of the crossing of the Jordan being the tenth of the first month), in order that the Israelites might eat from the produce of the land Canaan without violating the laws in Leviticus 23.[22] In that case, not only the pluses in MT, but a

[20] See the ancient versions of Lev. 23:11.16 (e.g., LXX-Lev. 23:11 τῇ ἐπαύριον *τῆς πρώτης* but see LXX verse 15 ἀπὸ τῆς ἐπαύριον τῶν σαββάτων) and the modern commentaries on Leviticus, e.g., A. Bertholet, *Leviticus* (KHCAT III) Tübingen/Leipzig 1901, p. 80; J.E. Hartley, *Leviticus.* (WBC 4) Waco 1992, pp. 385–386; J. van Goudoever, *Biblical Calendars.* Leiden 1959, pp. 17–29; and M. Fishbane, *Biblical Interpretation*, pp. 145–151.

[21] J. Hollenberg, Zur Textkritik des Buches Josua, pp. 97–98.

[22] J. Wellhausen, *Composition*[2], p. 123: 'Die Verse 5,10–12 hängen zusammen mit 4,19 und mit Q. Da man von der Frucht des Landes nicht essen darf, ohne die Erstlingsgarbe dargebracht zu haben, so war es eine Notwendigkeit, dass die Israeliten gerade zu Ostern in Kanaan einrückten.'

larger text-segment of these verses would be dependent upon the Leviticus text.[23]

Nevertheless, with this combination of text-critical and literary-critical observations, Hollenberg initiated a long and complex discussion regarding the proper interpretation of these verses.[24] A. Dillmann refuted Hollenberg's suggestions by pointing out that none of the ancient versions of Lev. 23:11.15.16 interpreted the phrase ממחרת השבת in the sense of ממחרת הפסח, and that not the MT but rather the LXX reflects a secondary harmonisation of the Joshua narrative with the legislation in Leviticus, by omitting the problematic phrases.[25]

C. Steuernagel, however, pointed out that the purpose of the pluses in MT was rather to combine the originally independent spring festivals Passover and *maṣṣot*, which in his view is secondary to the original legislation of the Priestly code. Without the pluses in MT and the date at the beginning of verse 10, the original P text did not mention any cultic festival at all, but simply the fact that at this time in the narrative, the Israelites started to eat from the produce of the land. Since the Israelites did not yet have any leaven, the products happened to be unleavened. That the original Priestly author had no cultic meaning of מצות in mind,[26] is demonstrated, according to Steuernagel, by the unique combination of מצות and קלוי. Recently C. Brekelmans has also argued for a non-cultic background of these verses.[27] In his view, the מצות in verse 11 do not point to the festival of the unleavened bread but simply mention the first products of the new land for which no dough to leaven the breads were available. Only later was the verse seen as a reference to that festival

---

[23] See section 7.4.5 below.

[24] See for a similar argumentation, e.g., S. Holmes, *Joshua*, pp. 3–4.31; C.D. Benjamin, *The Variations*, p. 33; A.G. Auld, Joshua. The Hebrew and Greek Texts, pp. 7–8 (= *Joshua Retold*, pp. 12–13).

[25] A. Dillmann, *Die Bücher Numeri, Deuteronomium und Josua*, p. 460.

[26] C. Steuernagel, *Deuteronomium und Josua*, pp. 168–169.

[27] C. Brekelmans, Joshua V 10–12. Another Approach, in A.S. van der Woude (ed.), *New Avenues in the Study of the Old Testament. FS M.J. Mulder* (OTS 25) Leiden 1989, pp. 89–95. For a comparable view see already the explanation of the passage in the commentary of the Jewish scholar Tanchum Ben Josef ha-Jerushalmi († 1291 ce); ed. H.-G. von Mutius, *Der Josua-Kommentar des Tanchum Ben Josef ha-Jeruschalmi. Neu herausgegeben, übersetzt und mit ausführlichen Erläuterungen versehen.* (Judaistische Texte und Studien 9) Hildesheim/Zürich/New York 1983, pp. 37–39.

and supplemented accordingly with the temporal elements in verses 11–12 and the whole of verse 10.[28]

Thus, for Steuernagel the original account of a secular event was already a product of the Priestly author, while the alterations that transformed the narrative into a cultic event were attributed to a post-Priestly editor. M. Noth, however, used this literary stratification in order to attribute the P-like elements in Joshua to a later redaction of his DtrH-edition of the book in the style of P.[29] In his view, the combination of מצות and קלוי is *atypical* of the Priestly code (P^{G}), and only the temporal indications in this text-segment, i.e., the date in verse 10, the two pluses in MT, and the phrase בעצם היום הזה are later Priestly additions to an ancient pre-Deuteronomistic account produced by his *Sammler*.[30] H.J. Kraus, E. Otto and others then used this argumentation for their recovery of a pre-monarchical cultic celebration in Gilgal.[31] From the outset it is important to note, that this literary-critical hypothesis is only *partially* supported by the text-critical data, since the date in Josh. 5:10, which is generally seen as an imprint of Priestly origin, is attested both in MT and LXX.

7.2.3 *A Full Synthesis of Textual and Literary Criticism (S. Holmes)*

Samuel Holmes assigned a central role to the MT—LXX variants in verses 2–9 in his thesis of a revision of a superior Hebrew text reflected by LXX towards the secondary, expanded MT.[32] Like Hollenberg, Wellhausen, and Kuenen before him, he regarded the

---

[28] See also T.C. Butler, *Joshua*, p. 55, 60; V. Fritz, *Das Buch Josua*, pp. 59–63; and R.D. Nelson, *Joshua*, pp. 79–80.

[29] M. Noth, *Überlieferungsgeschichtliche Studien*, p. 183.

[30] M. Noth, *Das Buch Josua*², p. 39.

[31] A. George, Les récits de Gilgal en Josué (V,2–15), in *Memorial J. Chaine*. Lyon 1950, pp. 169–186; H.J. Kraus, Gilgal; J.A. Soggin, Gilgal, Passah und Landnahme. Eine neue Untersuchung des kultischen Zusammenhangs der Kap. III–VI des Josuabuches, in *Volume du Congrès. Genève 1965*. (SVT 15) Leiden 1966, pp. 263–277; J. Wilcoxen, Narrative Structure and Cult Legend. A Study of Joshua 1–6, in R.C. Rylaarsdam (ed.), *Transitions in Biblical Scholarship*. Chicago/London 1968, pp. 43–70; F.M. Cross, *Canaanite Myth and Hebrew Epic*, pp. 103–105; J. Halbe, Erwägungen zu Ursprung und Wesen des Massotfestes, in *ZAW* 87 (1975), pp. 324–346; E. Otto, *Das Mazzotfest in Gilgal*; R. Schmitt, *Exodus und Passa. Ihr Zusammenhang im Alten Testament*. (OBO 7) Freiburg/Göttingen 1982², pp. 49–52; and G. Kuhnert, *Das Gilgalpassah. Literarische, überlieferungsgeschichtliche und geschichtliche Studien zu Josua 3–6*. Mainz 1981. See further the detailed surveys in K. Bieberstein, *Josua-Jordan-Jericho*, pp. 63–71; and E. Noort, *Das Buch Josua*, pp. 147–164.

[32] S. Holmes, *Joshua*, pp. 2, 9–10, 29–31, see further section 2.2.3 above.

shorter text of verse 2 without the element of a *second* circumcision (as reflected by LXX) followed by verses 3 and 8 as the original version of the narrative, but argued that the Septuagint version of the verses reflects a first and unsuccessful addition, whereas the Masoretic text of the passage would reflect the final redaction of the text.[33] The redundancy of the MT—according to Holmes—was intended to conceal the statements reflected by LXX that not every Israelite had been circumcised in Egypt, as becomes evident by the very striking contradiction between the statement in MT verse 5a and LXX verse 4b:

MT 5:5a כי־מלים היו כל־העם היצאים,

because circumcised were all the people that left (Egypt).

LXX 5:4b καὶ ὅσοι ποτὲ ἀπερίτμητοι ἦσαν τῶν ἐξεληλυθότων ἐξ Αἰγύπτου, πάντας τούτους περιέτεμεν Ἰησους,

and as many as were uncircumcised of those who had gone out of Egypt, all these Joshua circumcised.

Whereas MT and LXX agree on the statement that Joshua circumcised all those male Israelites that were born in the desert (LXX 5:4a ὅσοι ποτὲ ἐγένετο ἐν τῇ ὁδῷ), the LXX mentions (in verse 4b) another category of male Israelites to be circumcised, whose very existence is strongly denied in the Hebrew text of MT. According to Holmes, the only plausible explanation for this contradiction must be that the original Hebrew text still reflected by LXX was reworked by a later Hebrew scribe who could not and would not accept that the law in Gen. 17 on circumcision was not universally practised in Egypt. According to Holmes, the references to the flint knives in the pluses of LXX in Josh. 21:42d and 24:31a were deleted for the same purpose.[34]

[33] S. Holmes, *Joshua*, p. 31: 'Here as elsewhere LXX appears to give an intermediate stage in the history of the text. As Dillmann (p. 459) says, the section 4–7 is an endeavour to bring the account of the circumcision at Gilgal into harmony with Genesis xvii. In LXX we have the record of an attempt that was not drastic enough for subsequent editors: in M.T. we have the final endeavour of one or more scribes to achieve the impossible.'

[34] S. Holmes, *Joshua*, p. 9: 'The text was revised from a religious standpoint. The Reviser's overworking here and his omissions in xxi.42d and xxiv.30a, where the mention of the 'flint knives' would have called to mind the circumcision at Gilgal, are all due to the same motive. If the LXX text is original the Hebrew reviser

21[42d] καὶ ἔλαβεν Ἰησοῦς τὰς μαχαίρας τὰς πετρίνας, ἐν αἷς περιέτεμεν τοὺς υἱοὺς Ισραηλ τοὺς γενομένους ἐν τῇ ὁδῷ ἐν τῇ ἐρήμῳ, καὶ ἔθηκεν αὐτὰς ἐν Θαμνασαραχ.

And Joshua took the rocky knives, with which he had circumcised the sons of Israel that were born on the way in the desert, and placed them in Tamnasarach.

24[31a] ἐκεῖ ἔθηκαν μετ' αὐτοῦ εἰς τὸ μνῆμα, εἰς ὃ ἔθαψαν αὐτὸν ἐκεῖ, τὰς μαχαίρας τὰς πετρίνας, ἐν αἷς περιέτεμεν τοὺς υἱοὺς Ισραηλ ἐν Γαλγαλοις, ὅτε ἐξήγαγεν αὐτοὺς ἐξ Αἰγύπτου, καθὰ συνέταξεν αὐτοῖς κύριος, καὶ ἐκεῖ εἰσιν ἕως τῆς σήμερον ἡμέρας.

And they placed with him in the grave, in which they buried him, the rocky knives, with which he had circumcised the sons of Israel in Galgala, when he had brought them out of Egypt, as the Lord had ordered them, and there they are until the present day.

The question, however, immediately arises why a reviser, responsible for such drastic measures in Josh. 21:42d and 24:31a would not have simply excised the whole of Josh. 5:2–9 from the book as well or at least only the offensive verse 4b (LXX) and why this orthodox reviser was not offended by the ideas expressed in Josh. 24:2, 15–22, which speak of the foreign worship of Israel's fathers beyond the river and in Egypt.

According to Holmes, the variants in verse 2 (καθίσας instead of שׁוב . . . שׁנית), as well as the plus כל הגוי in MT-Josh. 5:8b, should be seen in relation to these textual changes. The reviser introduced them in order to account for those Israelites that were not yet twenty years old at the time Yhwh pronounced his sentence of the forty years wandering through the desert as narrated in Numbers 14. With the alterations in verse 2, this reviser expressed his view that those Israelites were also included in Joshua's act of circumcision, so that the conclusion was that *all the nation* was circumcised (in MT-Josh. 5:8b). Since in the perception of this orthodox reviser this group could not have been uncircumcised when they had left Egypt, they were now physically circumcised for a second time, thus Holmes.[35]

would have the strongest motive for alteration: he would be most reluctant to admit that any of the Israelites in Egypt were uncircumcised. On the other hand the hypothesis of deliberate alteration from M.T. seems hopeless. The LXX translator could not possibly have gone out of his way to make a statement which implied that the Israelites did not universally practise circumcision while in Egypt. If probability is to be any guide it must be admitted that LXX here had a very different text from ours and one that was earlier in point of time.'

[35] S. Holmes, *Joshua*, pp. 30–31.

Again, one wonders from the outset why such a Hebrew reviser would not have made things clearer and simpler, if he had just altered his alleged Hebrew text into ושב מל את־בני־ישראל הילדים במדבר בדרך?

Holmes' thesis offers an explanation in which several variants are brought together under a single religious motivation. Nevertheless, the thesis has a number of weaknesses, which become apparent when one studies his commentary on this specific chapter in more detail.[36] If the MT is the result of a Hebrew revision, this intervention is rather half-hearted and unclear, as pointed out above. Furthermore, Holmes' approach accounts for only a small number of divergencies between MT and LXX in this chapter and, moreover, presupposes a rather mechanical Greek translator. Apparently, for Holmes there seem to be only two main solutions for explaining the divergencies between the Hebrew and Greek texts: they either display a certain coherence and are therefore to be attributed to literary activity on the Hebrew level (thus the pluses in 5:11.12), or the variants result from scribal errors (e.g. the LXX minus in verses 9–10 עד היום הזה בגלגל (5:10) ויחנו בני־ישראל as an example of parablepsis resulting from the *homoioteleuton* 'Gilgal' (verse 9.10a).[37]

Nevertheless, in the cases of the Greek plus in 5:3b τοῦ καλουμένου [τόπου] which he described as an 'explanatory addition',[38] the 'paraphrastic' rendering of the verb מול in 5:4 by περικαθαίρω, or the 'idiomatic rendering' in verse 12 of the phrase ויאכלו מתבואת with the highly unusual Greek verb καρπίζομαι,[39] Holmes too acknowledged a non-mechanical but well-considered *translation technique* underlying the Greek version. On the other hand, Holmes explained the Greek rendering in 5:4 ὃν δε τρόπον for the MT וזה הדבר as a misreading of this original Hebrew phrase as וכה הדבר, even though such an expression is without parallel in the Hebrew Bible and moreover only roughly approximates the Greek counterpart, whereas a mechanical-literal rendering of such a Hebrew phrase would have been something like οὗτος ὁ λόγος. Likewise, Holmes explained the shorter *ad sensum* Greek clause in 5:7b διὰ τὸ αὐτοὺς γεγενῆσθαι κατὰ τὴν ὁδὸν ἀπεριτμήτους, *vis-à-vis* the two clauses כי־ערלם היו כי לא־מלו

[36] S. Holmes, *Joshua*. pp. 28–31.

[37] S. Holmes, *Joshua*, p. 31.

[38] S. Holmes, *Joshua*, p. 28. Holmes apparently overlooked the word τόπου, which has no counterpart in the MT either.

[39] S. Holmes, *Joshua*, p. 31. This Greek verb recurs within the Septuagint only in LXX-Prov. 8:19, see section 7.6.8.1 below.

אותם בדרך in MT as a faithful, though not completely successful rendering of the original Hebrew clause כי הילורים בדרך היו ערלים, or otherwise כי ערלים היו כי יִלְּדו בדרך.[40] The former retroversion, however, defies the normal Hebrew word order, while the second does not fully correspond to the Greek text. Moreover, it remains completely unclear why a Hebrew reviser would have wanted to change such constructions to the present MT version. Holmes thus showed a somewhat ambivalent evaluation of the Greek translation and occasionally took recourse to unusual Hebrew constructions in order to uphold his thesis of the literary priority of LXX.

Similar remarks can be made about Holmes' solution with respect to the beginning of verse 6 in the Greek version, which differs strikingly from the MT:

MT כי ארבעים שנה הלכו בני־ישראל במדבר
עד־תם כל־הגוי אנשי המלחמה היצאים ממצרים
אשר לא שמעו בקול יהוה אשר נשבע להם לבלתי הראותם את הארץ

> Because for forty years the children of Israel had wandered in the desert, until the entire nation, all the men of war that had left Egypt, had come to an end, who had not listened to the voice of Yhwh, to whom Yhwh had sworn not to show them the land . . .

LXX[B] τεσσαράκοντα γὰρ καὶ δύο ἔτη ἀνέστραπται Ισραηλ ἐν τῇ ἐρήμῳ τῇ Μαδβαρίτιδι, διὸ ἀπερίτμητοι ἦσαν οἱ πλεῖστοι αὐτῶν τῶν μαχίμων τῶν ἐξεληλυθότων ἐκ γῆς Αἰγύπτου οἱ ἀπειθήσαντες τῶν ἐντολῶν τοῦ θεοῦ, οἷς καὶ διώρισεν μὴ ἰδεῖν αὐτοὺς τὴν γῆν, . . .

> Because for forty-*two* years Israel had dwelt in the desert *of Madbaritidis, on which account most of them*, of the warriors of the ones that had gone out of the land of Egypt, *were uncircumcised*, the ones that had *disobeyed the commandments of God*, to whom *he moreover, had determined*, that they would not see the land, . . .

According to Holmes, the Greek text is 'unanimously admitted to be wrong'. The problem with the Greek text is that on the one hand it seems to give an explanation for the fact that not everyone was circumcised (διὸ ἀπερίτμητοι ἦσαν οἱ πλεῖστοι αὐτῶν), while on the other the text immediately continues with the statement that this group had been disobedient to God, which resulted in their wanderings through the desert. Therefore, the fact that the majority of this older generation was uncircumcised is irrelevant here, since they

---

[40] S. Holmes, *Joshua*, p. 30.

are supposed to have passed away at the time Israel has entered the Promised Land. Holmes proposed to solve the problem of this inconsistency by postulating a Hebrew *Vorlage* different from MT which had been rendered mechanically by the Greek translator:[41]

כי ארבעים <u>ושנים</u> שנה הלכו בני־ישׂראל במדבר
<u>לכן ערלים היו רבים מהם</u> אנשי המלחמה היצאים ממצרים
אשר לא שמעו בקול יהוה אשר נשבע להם לבלתי הראותם את הארץ

The Hebrew reviser behind the MT reworking would have had a strong objection to this statement and altered it into our familiar Hebrew text. Nevertheless, this solution only transfers the problem to the Hebrew level. Holmes therefore had to postulate a stop behind the word מהם and proposed to delete the word אשׁר before נשׁבע, in order to make a sharp distinction between the group that was uncircumcised and the older generation that was responsible for the journey through the wilderness. There are, however, no indications neither in this reconstructed Hebrew text, nor in the transmitted Greek text for such a distinction between the subject ערלים / ἀπερίτμητοι and the following οἱ ἀπειθήσαντες. Furthermore, it remains doubtful whether the phrase οἱ πλεῖστοι αὐτῶν can be held to be a mechanical rendering of a Hebrew phrase רבים מהם,[42] since this phrase rather conveys the meaning 'many of them', whereas there appears to be no direct equivalent in the Hebrew Bible for this Greek expression 'most of them'.

Classical Hebrew is well capable of expressing the superlative by qualifying the adjective by the article, a determinate noun, or a suffix.[43] Nevertheless, parallels to the expression 'most of them' as found in the Greek text of Joshua 5:6 by which a certain number of persons within a larger entity is indicated, are extraordinarily rare in the Hebrew Bible.

The parallel in 1 Kgs. 18:25 אַתֶּם הָרַבִּים only expresses the idea that the Baʿal priests outnumber the Yhwh followers (*in casu* Elijah) and was understood accordingly by the Greek translator: ὅτι πολλοὶ ὑμεῖς. In 2 Chron. 25:9 יֵשׁ לַיהוָה לָתֶת לְךָ הַרְבֵּה מִזֶּה, the idea expressed

[41] S. Holmes, *Joshua*, pp. 29–30.
[42] Idem R.D. Nelson, *Joshua*, p. 73, note j.
[43] So P. Joüon, s.j., T. Muraoka, *A Grammar of Biblical Hebrew*, § 141j.

is not that Yhwh is capable of giving Amaziah the largest part of the hundred talents mentioned in the previous verse (thus LXX-B.A.V.60.127.158.243.489 Ἔστιν τῷ κυρίῳ δοῦναί σοι πλεῖστα τούτων), but that Yhwh is capable of giving far *more* (comparative) than that amount (thus the remaining LXX-2 Chron. 25:9 witnesses: πλεῖον[α]). Likewise, in other cases where in the Septuagint the Greek expression οἱ πλεῖστοι / τὸ πλεῖστον recurs, the corresponding Hebrew phrase appears to express the notion of 'a large number', rather than a certain percentage. In 2 Chron. 13:18 the noun מַרְבִּית refers to a multitude of people[44] (LXX-B.V ὅτι πλεῖστον τοῦ λαοῦ).

The Hebrew retroversion proposed by S. Holmes may not be impossible, from a grammatical point of view, but it is not a common and plausible one either. In any case, his suggestion that the Greek translation is merely a mechanical rendering of a Hebrew *Vorlage* different from MT is not very convincing.

As for the variant between LXX τεσσαράκοντα γὰρ *καὶ δύο* ἔτη, *forty-two years*, for MT ארבעים שנה, Holmes took recourse to a scribal error model by explaining the postulated Hebrew *Vorlage* of LXX as a corruption from the original MT by dittography of the word שנה,[45] although in that case the Hebrew text must have read ארבעים ושנים שנה. Nevertheless, it must be admitted that the Greek text is cryptic and problematic here, but a sound approach to this problem would be to study the Greek text in its own context first, in order to understand the Greek text in its own right before distilling a hypothetical Hebrew *Vorlage* that would reflect an older redaction of the passage.

7.2.4 *Septuagint and Midrash (D.W. Gooding)*

A position diametrically opposed to that of S. Holmes was defended by D.W. Gooding in 1973.[46] Gooding points to an inconsistency in Holmes' hypothesis: if a Hebrew editor had wanted to conceal the notion that—in spite of the legislation found in Genesis 17 that every Israelite man has to be circumcised—the practice of circumcision had been abandoned in Egypt, he would not have added in verse 8 the words כל־הגוי, *the entire nation*, in the MT plus ויהי כשר־תמו

---

[44] See HALOT, p. 631b.
[45] S. Holmes, *Joshua*, p. 30.
[46] D.W. Gooding, The Circumcision at Gilgal.

כל־הגוי להמול, *it happened when the entire nation had completely been circumcised*, as opposed to the shorter LXX reading περιτμηθέτες δὲ, *having been circumcised* . . ., as Holmes had claimed,[47] but would rather have tried to obscure these words as well, if he had found this Hebrew text before him.[48] Thus, the Hebrew revisers would have been a group of 'hopelessly incompetent bunglers',[49] which is rather improbable. Furthermore, according to Gooding, Holmes interpreted the second circumcision of the MT redaction in a literal sense, i.e., as a physical second circumcision of those Israelites that had been circumcised in Egypt,[50] and had survived the journey through the wilderness because they were still too young (i.e., under twenty years of age) to be sentenced to die in the desert after the events at Kadesh Barnea (Numbers 14). In Gooding's view, however, the Hebrew text of MT-Josh. 5:2 does not support such an interpretation, but rather refers to the reinstatement of the rite of circumcision for the Israelite people,[51] as suggested already by rabbi Nehemiah in *Pesikta rabbati* 52.4,[52] and the Church Fathers Augustine[53] and Išoʿdad of Merv.[54]

---

[47] S. Holmes, *Joshua*, pp. 30–31. Holmes, however, interpreted these clauses not as the result of Joshua's activities, but rather as a general concluding statement in the sense of: 'now that the entire nation was finally circumcised', that is, now that the Israelites who had been born in the desert were finally circumcised as well . . .' For this reason, Holmes could claim that the Greek text is consistent here.

[48] D.W. Gooding, The Circumcision at Gilgal, pp. 154–157.

[49] D.W. Gooding, The Circumcision at Gilgal, p. 155.

[50] Thus some rabbinical traditions in—*inter alia*—*Talmud babli Yebamoth* 71b and *Pirqe de Rab Eliezer* chapter 29, where a distinction is made between two stages of circumcision, the latter of which, the פריעה, is the more definitive. See further section 7.4.1 below and A. Blaschke, *Beschneidung*, pp. 259–266.

[51] D.W. Gooding, The Circumcision at Gilgal, pp. 156–157

[52] The *Pesikta rabbati* homily for the eighth day in the cycle of homilies for festival days dating from the seventh—ninth century CE (text: M. Friedmann, *Pesikta rabbati, Midrasch für den Fest-Cyclus und die ausgezeichneten Sabbathe.* Wien 1880 [numbered as additional *pisqa* 4]; translation: W.G. Braude, *Peskita rabbati. Discourses for Feasts, Fasts, and Special Sabbaths.* New Haven/London 1968 [numbered as *pisqa* 52]) contains a midrash ascribed to rabbi Nehemiah (third generation of Tannaim, mid second century CE) on Qoh. 11:2 ('give a portion to seven, or even to eight') applied to the seven, or eight generations between the circumcision carried out by Abraham (Gen. 17) and those by Moses (Exod. 4:24–26?) and Joshua (Josh. 5:2), respectively:

> R. Nehemiah said: The words *Give a portion* [*of prosperity*] *to seven* allude to the generation which Moses circumcised—the seventh generation [from Abraham]. The words *and also because of eight* refer to the generation which Joshua circumcised—the eighth generation [from Abraham]. The Holy One, blessed be He, said to Joshua: Israel's master, Moses, circumcised them in the seventh generation from Abraham, and thou didst circumcise them in the eighth, as is said *At that time the Lord said unto Joshua*: "*Make thee knives of flint, and circumcise again the children of Israel a second time*, and bring them into the covenant."

Gooding's most important point of criticism is Holmes' supposition that the later Hebrew editors responsible for the MT version must have felt the notion expressed in the (*Vorlage* of) LXX, i.e., that circumcision was not commonly practised by the Israelites in Egypt, to be offensive enough to alter the biblical text, finds no support in rabbinical literature. On the contrary, the theme of the negligence of circumcision in Egypt is well attested in this corpus, e.g. in Midrash rabbah on Exod. 1:8:[55]

> (Exod. 1:8) '*Now there arose a new king*'. The rabbis commenced this discourse with this verse: (Hos. 5:7) '*They have acted treacherously against the Lord, for they have begotten strange children, now shall the new moon devour them with their portions.*' This teaches you that when Joseph died, they abolished the covenant of circumcision, saying: 'Let us become like the Egyptians.' You can infer that from the fact that Moses had to circumcise them on their departure from Egypt.

Underlying both this tradition and the Greek translation of Josh. 5:2–9 is an ancient *midrash* on Exod. 12:43–49, where we find the additional prescriptions that foreigners have to be circumcised if they

---

> The words *second time* intimate that God was saying, "Circumcise them once again; thou shalt not have to circumcise them a third time."

[53] AUGUSTINE, *Quaestionum in Heptateuchum Liber Sextus. Quaestiones Iesu Nave* VI (CCSL 33/5) Turnhout 1958:

> One might ask why it is stated in this commandment 'again': not because a single person is circumcised twice, but because there was one people among whom some were circumcised, and others not. Therefore it is said 'again', so that not a person, but a people is circumcised again, as the following text shows.

[54] Text and translation: C. VAN DEN EYNDE, *Commentaire d'Išoʿdad de Merv sur l'ancien Testament. III. Livres des sessions.* (CSCO 229/230. Scriptores Syri 96/97) Louvain 1962–1963):

> 'A second time': not that he would have circumcised those that had already been circumcised, but because He had ordered the circumcision a first time and (because) it was abandoned in the desert. Presently he ordered it to them a second time because of its novelty.

[55] The text is taken from A. SHINAN, *Midrash Shemot Rabbah, Chapters I–XIV. A Critical Edition Based on a Jerusalem Manuscript with Variants, Commentary and Introduction.* Tel Aviv 1984; the translation is taken from S.M. LEHRMAN, *Midrash Rabbah. Exodus.* London 1951, p. 10. Parallels are to be found—according to D.W. GOODING, The Circumcision at Gilgal, p. 157, note 6—in *Midrash Rabbah* on Genesis XLIV.6; Exodus XIX.5; Numbers XI.3; XIV.12; and Ecclesiastes XI.2.1. See further A. BLASCHKE, *Beschneidung*, pp. 217–219: 'Exkurs 5: Das Unbeschnittensein der Israeliten in Ägypten.' Apparently inspired by LXX-Josh. 5, PHILO too stated that the Israelites in Egypt did not circumcise their sons, *Questions and Answers on Exodus* 2:2: ἐν Αἰγύπτῳ γὰρ τὰ Ἑβραῖον γένος οὐ περιτέτμητο (R. MARCUS, *Philo Supplement II. Questions and Answers on Exodus.* Cambridge, Massachusetts/London 1953).

want to partake in the Passover celebration. The midrash as found in *Midrash Rabbah* on Song of Songs I 12,3 (נג)[56] infers from the repeated statement that no uncircumcised foreigner is allowed to eat the Paschal lamb, that the Israelites were not circumcised in the Passover night:[57]

> This made them long to eat, and they said to him: 'Our master Moses, give us to eat.' Said Moses to them: 'Thus has God said to me, *There shall no alien eat thereof* (Exod. 12:43).' They went and removed the aliens from among them, and they still fainted for food. They said to him: 'Our master Moses, give us to eat.' He said to them: 'Thus has God said to me: *Every man's servant that is bought for money, when thou hast circumcised him, then he shall eat thereof* (Exod. 12:44). They went and circumcised their servants, and still fainted for food, so they said to him, 'Give us to eat.' He said to them: 'Thus has God said to me, in one word: *No uncircumcised person shall eat thereof* (Exod. 12:48).' Forthwith each one put his sword on his thigh and circumcised himself. Who circumcised them? R. Berakiah said: 'Moses circumcised them and Aaron turned back the flesh and Joshua gave them to drink.' Some, however, say that Joshua circumcised them and Aaron turned back the flesh and Moses gave them to drink, wherefore it is written, *At that time the Lord said unto Joshua Make thee knives of flint, and circumcise again the children of Israel the second time.* (Josh. 5:2) Why '*second time*'? This shows that *he* circumcised them the first time. Straightway, *Joshua made knives of flint, and circumcised the children of Israel at Gibeath-ha-ʿaraloth* (Josh. 5:3). Rabbi said: Thence we infer that they made a hill of foreskins.

According to Gooding, the Greek version of Joshua 5:2–9 reflects the same midrashic exegesis of Exod. 12:43–49.[58] The Greek sentence in 5:4 should then be understood as a statement in which this second act of circumcision (5:4b as *apodosis*) by Joshua is compared to this first act in Egypt on the night of the Passover (5:4a as *protasis*):[59]

---

[56] Text S. Donski (ed.), *Midrash Rabbah Shir haShirim. Midrash Chazit.* Tel Aviv 1980, translation M. Simon, *Midrash Rabbah. Song of Songs.* London/Bournemouth 1951, pp. 80–81.

[57] On the combination of the themes Passover—Exodus–Circumcision see R. le Déaut C.S.Sp, *La nuit pascale. Essai sur la signification de la Pâque juive à partir du Targum d'Exode XII 42.* (AnBibl 22) Rome 1963, pp. 209–212; and A. Blaschke, *Beschneidung*, pp. 277–278: 'Exkurs 8: Beschneidung, Passah und der Auszug aus Ägypten.'

[58] D.W. Gooding, The Circumcision at Gilgal, pp. 161–162.

[59] D.W. Gooding, The Circumcision at Gilgal, pp. 159–160: 'The Greek sentence states a correlation and is of a basic form: And in what way Joshua did x, he also did y. . . . The sentence is an almost perfect chiasm, which thus serves to emphasise the correlation . . .'

(relative clause:) And in the way Joshua purified the children of Israel as many as were born in the way,
(main clause) thus also as many as were uncircumcised of those who came out of Egypt, all these Joshua circumcised.'

In that case, the Greek sentence forms an explanation of the 'second circumcision' mentioned in verse 2. As a consequence, one has to postulate that the absence of the element of repetition ἐκ δευτεροῦ in a number of Greek witnesses (B. 19.108.407. Eth^{C}. VetLat. Cyr.)[60] is an early, but nevertheless secondary deviation from the original Greek text that did contain these words (witnessed by the majority of Greek manuscripts as well as the early patristic citations). The reason for its omission in these witnesses might be sought in Jewish-Christian controversies concerning the literal versus the spiritual meaning of the second circumcision. Such an exegesis of 'the second circumcision'is to be found as early as the second century CE in the work of the Christian author Justin Martyr († 165 CE), *Dialogue with the Jew Tryphon* 113.6.[61]

In order to support his thesis of a midrash-based interpretative rendering of the Greek translator, Gooding points to another parallel between the Greek text and the midrashic literature, where MT has the somewhat cryptic statement וימל את־בני ישראל אל־גבעת הערלות, *and he circumcised the children of Israel to a hill of foreskins.* The Greek text of manuscripts 118, 314, supported by the Vetus Latina,

[60] See section 7.6.1.3 below.

[61] Text: M. MARCOVICH (ed.), *Iustini Martyris Dialogus cum Tryphone.* (Patristische Texte und Studien 47) Berlin/New York 1997:

> This one [i.e. Jesus son of Naue] is said to have circumcised the people with a second circumcision—which was the kerugma of this circumcision with which Jesus Christ himself has circumcised us from the stones and other idols—and he made heaps of the foreskins, which is (made) of those who were circumcised from the error of the world at every place with flint knives, being the words of our Lord Jesus.

Similar allegorical interpretations can be found among many Christian scholars, e.g., ORIGEN, *Homilies on Joshua* V (ed. A. JAUBERT, *Origène. Homélies sur Josué*), and THASCIUS CAECILIUS CYPRIANUS (circa 210/215–258 CE), *Testimonia* (ed. G. HARTEL, CSEL III/1. Vienna 1868) I 8; see further J. MOATTI-FINE, *Josué*, pp. 116–117. The spiritualisation of the circumcision of course has its antecedents in the New Testament and already in the Hebrew Bible, Deut. 10:16, 30:6, Jer. 9:25; see R. MEYER, περιτέμνω, περιτομή, ἀπερίτμητος, in *ThWNT* VI, pp. 72–83; and R. LE DÉAUT, Le thème de la circoncision du coeur (Dt. xxx 6; Jér. iv 4) dans les versions anciennes (LXX et Targum) et a Qumrân, in J.A. EMERTON (ed.), *Congress Volume. Vienna 1980.* (SVT 32) Leiden 1981, pp. 178–205.

the Sahidic manuscripts Sa.19 and Sa.20, and the quotation by Justin Martyr, present the longer text:[62]

> καὶ περιέτεμεν τοὺς υἱοὺς Ἰσραηλ *καὶ ἔθηκεν θιμωνίας ἀκροβυστίων* ἐπὶ τοῦ καλουμένου νῦν τόπου Βουνὸς τῶν ἀκροβυστιῶν,
>
> *et posuit grumos praeputiorum* in loco qui nunc vocatur Collis Praeputiorum
>
> and he circumcised the children of Israel *and formed heaps of foreskins* on the place that is now called Hill of foreskins.

This idea of Joshua heaping up the foreskins of the sons of Israel that he had circumcised, again has several parallels in the midrashic literature,[63] among them the *Midrash rabbah* on Song of Songs, quoted above (אמר רבי: ׳מכאן, שעשו אותה גבעה בערלה) the ninth century haggadic work *Pirqe de rabbi Eliezer* (ויקבץ כל הערלות עד שעשׂה אותם כגבעה),[64] and Rashi's exegesis (על שם המאורע נקראת, שעשאו כמין גבעה, *it was given this appellation to commemorate the events, because the foreskins were made into a sort of mound*).[65]

Without parallels in the midrashic literature but equally interpretative,—according to Gooding—is the Greek translator's alteration of the period of forty years of wandering in the desert (MT) into forty-two years. Holmes' supposition that the Greek is merely a dittographic corruption of the Hebrew text ignores the historiographic interest of the Hellenistic Jewish authors.[66] The number forty-two is, according to Gooding, a combination of the forty years wandering

---

[62] See section 7.6.2 below; pluses of these witnesses over the majority LXX-text are indicated by cursivation.

[63] D.W. Gooding, The Circumcision at Gilgal, pp. 161–162. These correspondences had already been noticed by Margolis in his 1911 article, The K Text of Joshua, p. 5. In his final edition of *The Book of Joshua in Greek*, p. 67, however, Margolis relegated this clause to his seventh apparatus, where he placed the variants within the basic form of any recension, thereby designating these words as a late addition. In *Midrash Rabbah* on Song of Songs 4:6, the notion of circumcision (מול) and the hill of foreskins (גבעת הערלות) seem to be wordplays on the mountain of myrrh (הר מור) and hill of frankincense (גבעת הלבונה), mentioned in that verse.

[64] Traditional text, Warschau 1879; translation: G. Friedlander, *Pirḳê de rabbi Eliezer*. London 1916, p. 212, with references to parallel passages in the rabbinical literature:

[65] Text: M. Cohen (ed.), *Miqra'ot Gedolot 'Haketer'. Joshua-Judges*; translation A.J. Rosenberg, S. Shulman, *The Book of Joshua. A New English Translation of the Text and Rashi with a Commentary Digest*. New York 1984 with references to other mediaeval Jewish interpretations.

[66] D.W. Gooding, The Circumcision at Gilgal, p. 163, note 14, refers to the Greek translator of Exodus 12:40, or the Hellenistic Jewish historian Demetrius.

as punishment (Num. 14:33), and the statement found in Num. 10:11 that Israel had spent already two years in the desert before they set out for Kadesh Barnea.[67]

A major problem for Gooding is the interpretation of the Greek text at the beginning of verse 6, which states that the majority of the warriors that left Egypt were uncircumcised (διὸ ἀπερίτμητοι ἦσαν οἱ πλεῖστοι αὐτῶν τῶν μαχίμων τῶν ἐξεληλυθότων ἐκ γῆς Αἰγύπτου οἱ ἀπειθήσαντες . . .). As the Greek text stands, it appears to explain why the older generation was uncircumcised, which makes no sense in this narrative of Joshua's circumcision of their sons.[68] Gooding rejects Holmes' solution as a too speculative chain of emendations of both the Hebrew and Greek texts, but even his own solution of a two-stage circumcision act by Joshua, one before and one after the journey through the desert, does not make sense of the Greek text of 5:6a. Gooding therefore proposes to take the genitive in the phrase αὐτῶν τῶν μαχίμων as a *possessive* genitive (*of them* [*sons*] *of the warriors that left Egypt*), rather than a *partitive* (*of them, that is of the warriors that had left Egypt*). This interpretation would allow for the shift in generations between the ones circumcised (the younger generation) and those responsible for their uncircumcised state (the older generation). Although this suggestion does not require the textual emendations proposed by Holmes, the problem remains that the 'rescue [of] the Greek sentence from being nonsense' is 'at the expense of somewhat forced grammar.'[69] Furthermore, it is difficult to see why a Greek translator, willing and able to modify the idiom and expressions of the original text for the sake of clarity, consistency,

---

[67] D.W. Gooding, The Circumcision at Gilgal, pp. 163–164. See also D.W. Gooding, On the Use of the LXX for Dating Midrashic Elements in the Targums, in *JThSt* 25 (1974), pp. 1–11.

[68] D.W. Gooding, The Circumcision at Gilgal, p. 164: 'there would still remain what seems to be an insurmountable difficulty. Verse 6 begins with the statement that Israel walked up and down the desert for forty-two years, and then it adds *for that reason* (διό—*wherefore*) the majority of the actual warriors who came out of Egypt were uncircumcised. But that is a nonsense statement: they came out of Egypt *before* they spent forty-two years in the desert. Therefore their forty-two years' wandering in the desert cannot be cited as a reason why they were uncircumcised when they came out of Egypt.'

[69] D.W. Gooding, The Circumcision at Gilgal, p. 164. Gooding therefore prefers yet another solution in which verses 4 and 5 are seen as an *interpolation* 'The more probable explanation is that verse 4 and 5 of the LXX are, as I have argued above, a midrashic interpolation which, when it was incorporated into the text, disturbed the logical flow of the context.'

or style, would have altered the clear and unproblematic Hebrew sentence into such an obscure statement.

In spite of this problem, Gooding's approach does more justice to the Greek text and the interpretative elements in it, as for instance in 5:6 τεσσαράκοντα καὶ δύο, than that of Holmes. Nevertheless, although Gooding places this example of the Greek translator's interpretation in the context of contemporary Hellenistic-Jewish exegetical interests, his appeal to Jewish midrashic literature requires a considerable shift in time from the Hellenistic context in which the LXX came into existence to the later rabbinical circles that produced and compiled the midrashim.[70] As for the plus in verse 3 καὶ ἔθηκεν θιμωνίας ἀκροβυστίων, the parallels between the various witnesses and traditions may just as well be the result of similar independent interpretations of the same exegetical problem.[71]

More importantly, the Greek text lacks any explicit references to an alleged first circumcision-act of the Israelites by Joshua in Egypt, which form the core of Gooding's interpretation of the divergencies between MT and LXX. Moreover, his corresponding interpretation of verses 4–5 in LXX is rather forced. If the Greek translator had wanted to compare this circumcision by Joshua at Gilgal to a previous circumcision in Egypt, it would have been logical to mark this by a ὡς . . . οὕτως construction, and by a differentiation in verbal tense (such as a pluperfect in the first statement allegedly referring to an earlier past event rather than the aorist forms περιεκάθαρεν . . . περιέτεμεν). Instead of this, the Greek text simply mentions two groups of Israelites circumcised by Joshua, formulated in strict parallelism (ὅσοι ποτὲ ἐγένοντο. . . . καὶ ὅσοι ποτὲ ἀπερίτμητοι ἦσαν. . . .) and recapitulated in verse 5 (πάντας τούτους). Reading the late midrash on Song of Songs into this Greek sentence does no justice to the Greek text in its own right. Finally, Gooding's claim that the absence of the words ἐκ δευτεροῦ from LXX-witnesses B.19.108.407. Eth^C. VetLat. Cyr is a secondary omission, disregards the fact that pre-

[70] The oldest of the midrashim that contains (an allusion to) the tradition of a circumcision by Joshua before the Exodus, *Midrash Genesis Rabba*, may be dated to the 5th century CE, *Midrash Shir haShirim* to the 6th century CE, whereas *Midrash Exodus Rabbah* and *Midrash Numbers Rabba* probably date from no earlier than the 11th or 12th century, see H.L. Strack, G. Stemberger, *Einleitung in Talmud und Midrasch*. München 1982, p. 260, 284–287, 289. Nevertheless, the material contained in these collections may be (considerably) older.

[71] See section 7.6.2 below.

cisely these witnesses are the best witnesses to the original Greek text, whereas the secondary character in the younger LXX witnesses is supported by the fact that the other element of repetition in the Hebrew text (ושוב) is not reflected as such in LXX (καθίσας) as well.[72]

7.2.5 *Literary Growth and Midrash-Type Exegesis (E. Tov)*

In one of his earlier articles, E. Tov adopted many of Gooding's views with respect to the evaluation of LXX-Josh. 5, for which he coined the expression 'Midrash-type exegesis' in order to describe those interpretations that are either actually attested within the corpus of midrashic literature, or merely resemble this type of exegesis.[73] In this article, Tov collects some 20 examples of this type of exegesis reflected by the Greek translation of Joshua, but introduced a distinction between cases where—in his view—the translator was responsible for the exegesis (e.g., the plus in some of the LXX-witnesses in 5:3 καὶ ἔθηκεν θιμωνίας ἀκροβυστίων),[74] and those cases of exegesis that might have been introduced already at the Hebrew stage (as e.g., in LXX-5:6 τεσσαράκοντα καὶ δύο ἔτη).[75]

To the latter category, Tov assigned the variant in 5:10 ויעשׂו את־הפסח . . . בערב, *they made the Passover(-offering)* in *the evening*—Καὶ ἐποίησαν οἱ υἱοι Ισραηλ τὸ πάσχα (. . .) ἀπὸ ἑσπέρας, *the sons of Israel kept the Passover* (. . .) from *the evening.* The concept underlying the Greek translation is that of the fusion of the Passover and *maṣṣot* festivals under the single name of 'Passover',[76] whereas the older text reflected by MT still reflects the more original idea of a Passover sacrifice in the evening. Since, however, the Greek text might reflect a Hebrew variant מערב, Tov seems to be reluctant to speak of midrashic exegesis here.[77] One wonders, however, whether an alteration of ב into מ, either in Hebrew manuscripts or in the mind of the Greek translator, would not already reflect a conscious interpretation,

[72] See section 7.6.1.3 below.

[73] E. Tov, Midrash-Type Exegesis, pp. 50–61 (= *The Greek and Hebrew Bible*, pp. 151–163). See further E. Tov, *The Text-critical Use of the Septuagint*², pp. 45–50.

[74] E. Tov, Midrash-Type Exegesis, pp. 53–54 (156–157).

[75] E. Tov, Midrash-Type Exegesis, p. 56 (158).

[76] E. Tov, Midrash-Type Exegesis, pp. 56–57 (159). See further section 7.6.8.1 below.

[77] E. Tov, Midrash-Type Exegesis, p. 57 (159): 'On the other hand, if the translator actually *read* מערב, no midrashic exegesis is involved, unless one describes the very alteration of consonants as 'midrashic' (thus often Prijs, *Tradition*, 54ff.'

since a phrase like מערב . . . עשׂה את־הפסח is not attested in the Hebrew Bible.

Tov's restrained attitude towards the freedom of the Greek translator of Joshua becomes evident in the two (other) examples of midrash-type exegesis which he ascribed directly to the Greek translator. In verses 2 and 3, the MT speaks of 'stone knives' (חַרְבוֹת צֻרִים) with which Joshua circumcised the Israelite people. The LXX specifies these instruments in verse 2 as μαχαίρας πετρίνας ἐκ πέτρας ἀκροτόμου, *rocky knives from a sharp rock*, and in verse 3 as μαχαίρας πετρίνας ἀκροτόμους, *sharp rocky knives*. Tov does not trace the extra element [ἐκ πέτρας] ἀκροτόμου[ς] to a specific tradition in the midrashic literature, but to the lexical choice of the Greek word ἀκρότομος for the Hebrew phrase צור החלמישׁ, *a flinty rock*, the designation in Deut. 8:15 for the rock that produced water for the Israelites.[78] Although it is evident that the phrase in LXX-Josh. 5:2.3 would certainly have formed a literal rendering of a *hypothetical* Hebrew phrase עשׂה לך חרבות צרים החלמישׁ, the implied connection between this tradition of water from the rock and rocky circumcision-knives remains unclear. Tov's proposal does not draw a parallel between the Greek translation and the midrashic literature, nor does it characterise the specific exegesis of the Hebrew text.

Even less exegetical is Tov's explanation of the unusual rendering of the word קָלוּי, *roasted (grain)*, in the clause ויאכלו מעבור הארץ ממחרת הפסח מצות וקלוי, *they ate from the produce of the land the day after Passover unleavened bread and roasted (corn)* by νέα, *new ones*, in καὶ ἐφάγοσαν ἀπὸ τοῦ σίτου τῆς γῆς ἄζυμα καὶ *νέα*, *and they ate from the grain of the land unleavened and new (ones)*. According to Tov, the source for this incorrect rendering must be sought in the Greek translation of Lev. 2:14 where the Hebrew phrase אביב קלוי באשׁ, *new (ears), roasted in the fire*, was rendered by *νέα* πεφρυγμένα, *new, parched* (*grain*):

2[14]	ἐὰν δὲ προσφέρῃς θυσίαν πρωτογενημάτων τῷ κυρίῳ	וְאִם־תַּקְרִיב מִנְחַת בִּכּוּרִים לַיהוָה
	νέα πεφρυγμένα χίδρα ἐρικτὰ *τῷ κυρίῳ*	אָבִיב קָלוּי בָּאֵשׁ גֶּרֶשׂ כַּרְמֶל
	καὶ προσοίσεις τὴν θυσίαν τῶν πρωτογενημάτων, . . .	תַּקְרִיב אֵת מִנְחַת בִּכּוּרֶיךָ׃

[78] E. Tov, Midrash-Type Exegesis, p. 53 (155–156). Tov further refers to Deut. 32:13, Ps. 114:8 and Job 28:9.

According to this 'exegetical procedure', the Greek translator of Joshua, who was not familiar with the word קלוי, used the Greek translation of Leviticus as a sort of lexicon. He erroneously held νέα to be its rendering, instead of the proper Greek equivalent πεφρυγμένα, *parched*, whereas νέα actually reflects the Hebrew word אָבִיב, *new ears*. In that case, it would seem more appropriate to consider the Greek rendering νέα for קָלוּי in Josh. 5:10 to be an erroneous equivalent based on an incorrect use of the Greek translation of Leviticus. Nevertheless, Tov also provides another solution for the Greek word that would approach our understanding of the term 'exegesis' as a well-considered and creative interpretation of the parent text: the Greek word may also be understood in terms of a collective denoting all the 'new produce of the field, which is not permitted to be used before the Omer day' (see Lev. 23:10–14).[79]

Whereas in this earlier study Tov made several restrictions with respect to the creative freedom of the translator, in his later studies he places more emphasis on the possibility of a divergent Hebrew *Vorlage* responsible for the divergencies between MT and LXX. In his essay 'The Growth of the Book of Joshua',[80] Tov detects four examples of editorial activity on the Hebrew level witnessed by minuses in the Greek version. Without further commentary, the plus in 5:2 שנית is categorised in the section of 'additions in MT whose secondariness is evident from their formulation.' To the same category Tov reckons the MT plus יהוה in 5:6,[81] but, seen in context, the absence of a reference to the Deity in this clause might just as well reflect the Greek translator's tendency to avoid the redundancy of the threefold mentioning of Yhwh in this verse, as does the variation in the rendering of the verb נשבע by διορίζω and ὄμνυμι.[82]

[79] E. Tov, Midrash-Type Exegesis, p. 54 (157). Tov erroneously refers to Exod. 23:10–14.

[80] See section 2.2.7.1 above.

[81] The redundant subject has also been omitted in the Vulgate 'et quibus ante iuraverat' and in Rashbam's commentary to Deut. 2:14, thus V. Aptowitzer, *Das Schriftwort in der rabbinischen Literatur* IV, p. 257.

[82] E. Tov, The Growth, p. 331 (391). An additional weakness with respect to this example is posed by the fact that Tov gives his examples primarily in English translation, thus: '5:6 ... because they had not obeyed the Lord who had sworn (the Lord) them.' As a consequence, it remains unclear whether or not Tov considers the word להם, which is not directly reflected in the LXX either, to be part of the MT-revision as well.

Likewise, Tov ascribes the temporal pluses in MT-Josh. 5:11.12 to this second edition of Joshua.[83] Since, however, Tov had ascribed the variant בערב—ἀπὸ ἑσπέρας to a midrash-type exegesis of the Hebrew text as attested by MT,[84] the question arises how to distinguish between those variants that reflect the process of formation of the Hebrew text culminating into MT on the one hand, and variants that reflect reformulation of the Hebrew text as attested by MT.

7.2.6 *A New Synthesis (L. Mazor)*

Lea Mazor's approach to the variant versions of Joshua 5:2–9 is one more step removed from the approach to the Greek text of Joshua as midrash-type exegesis of the Hebrew text. In her discussion of the passage, the Greek text itself has almost completely disappeared in favour of her reconstruction of the alleged Hebrew *Vorlage* underlying the Greek translation.[85] Characteristic for her approach is also her decision to dismiss *a priori* the possibility that the divergencies between the Hebrew and Greek text should be ascribed to a conscious effort of the Greek translator, since such a feature would contradict her overall picture of the Greek translation, which she describes here as 'neither free nor reworking'.[86]

The main point of difference between the two Hebrew versions of Josh. 5:2–9, the extant MT and her reconstruction of the Hebrew *Vorlage* of LXX, does not concern the issue of the *second* circumcision (שׁנית in MT-Josh. 5:2), but rather the contradiction in the presentation of Israel's history from exodus from Egypt to entry into Canaan. If a later reviser had wanted to obscure the idea that circumcision was not universally practised by the Israelites in Egypt (as Holmes and Auld claim), he would have tried to avoid rather than add the notion of repetition in verse 2 (thus Mazor). In her view, Gooding ignores the fact that the best witnesses of LXX do not reflect the words ἐκ δευτέρου for שׁנית. Hence there remains no basis for Gooding's exegesis of the Greek text as a midrashic interpreta-

[83] E. Tov, The Growth, p. 330 (389–390).

[84] See further section 7.6.8.1 below.

[85] L. Mazor, עיונים, pp. 171–190: 'Chapter IV: The Circumcision of the Israelites Upon entering Canaan', summarised in her abstract L. Mazor, The Septuagint Translation of the Book of Joshua, in *BIOSCS* 27 (1994), pp. 29–38, especially p. 36, under the heading 'Historiographical Assumptions'.

[86] L. Mazor, עיונים, pp. 171–174.

tion of this element of repetition in verse 2. In Mazor's view, the original Hebrew text of verse 2 ושׁב מל את בני ישׂראל was interpreted by the Greek translator as וְשֵׁב—καὶ καθίσας in the light of the Egyptian practice to circumcise adults in a sitting position, as attested in an Egyptian relief of the Sixth dynasty from Sakkarah.[87] The MT on the other hand, tried to secure the interpretation of the ambivalent word ושׁב as וְשׁוּב by adding the word שֵׁנִית. This interpretation sought to stress the exceptional character of the circumcision that marked the entry of Israel into the Promised Land.[88]

The real contradiction between the two versions—in Mazor's view—concerns the historiographic assumptions underlying the two versions, as exemplified at the beginning of verse 6. Whereas the MT explicitly states that the entire generation of the men that had left Egypt, had died in the desert (MT-Josh. 5:6a), this notion is absent in the LXX, which she retroverts into the following Hebrew sentence:

MT	כי ארבעים	שׁנה הלכו בני־ישׂראל במדבר
LXX	כי ארבעים ושתים	שׁנה הלך ישׂראל במדבר
MT	עד־תם	כל־הגוי אנשי המלחמה
LXX	לכן ערלים היו,	מרביתם מאנשי המלחמה

In other words, while the Hebrew *Vorlage* of LXX allows for a continuity between the group of Israelites that left Egypt on the one hand and the group that entered the land on the other hand, the MT makes a sharp division in verses 4 and 5: the older generation had died in the desert, the younger generation entered the Promised Land.[89] The *Vorlage* of LXX furthermore contains the notion of a period of forty-*two* years of wandering through the desert, which is unique throughout the Hebrew Bible. Related to this different concept is the more positive evaluation of the wilderness period in the Hebrew *Vorlage* of LXX, which in Mazor's opinion is also present in Jer. 2:2, Deut. 29:4–5 and Neh. 9:15.21, whereas the MT of Josh. 5:6 (עד־תם כל־הגוי) would convey the negative view dominant in the

---

[87] See J.B. Pritchard, *The Ancient Near East in Pictures Relating to the Old Testament.* Princeton/New Jersey 1954, no. 629; H. Gressmann, *Altorientalische Bilder zum Alten Testament.* Berlin/Leipzig 1927², no. 158. See the commentaries to Joshua, and further A. Blaschke, *Beschneidung*, pp. 43–45: 'Exkurs 1. Zum Zusammenhang zwischen ägyptischer und israelitischer Beschneidung.'

[88] L. Mazor, עיונים, pp. 175–179.

[89] L. Mazor, עיונים, pp. 182–185.

Hebrew Bible, as found for instance in Num. 13–14, 32:5–15; Deut. 1:34–39; 2:14–16 and Ps. 95:10.[90]

Contrary to Gooding and Tov, who consider the Greek phrase τεσσαράκοντα καὶ δύο ἔτη to be a reflection of a secondary interpretation of the MT by which the typological number 'forty' for the years of wandering was taken literally and combined with the statement that Israel had been in the desert already for two years (Num. 10:11), Mazor holds this element and the other historiographic divergencies between MT and LXX to be remnants of an older view on Israel's past. Such an apocryphal historiography would also have left its traces in the parenetic passages Deut. 5:1–5, 11:2–10, 29:1–4 and Josh. 24:5–7, in which Moses and Joshua, respectively, remind their audiences of the circumstance that they have seen Yhwh's wondrous acts in Egypt with their own eyes, at the moment when they are about to enter the Promised Land (Deuteronomy) or have even completed the conquest of it (Joshua 24). She furthermore adduces A. Rofé's arguments for a divergent older historiography underlying the plus in LXX-Josh. 24:31a ὅτε ἐξήγαγεν αὐτοὺς ἐξ Αἰγύπτου, and the alleged addition in MT-Josh. 24:5 ואשלח את־משה ואת־אהרן, which would reflect a historiography of the Exodus without Moses.[91]

Thus, whereas Holmes regarded the MT revision as an attempt to suppress the unorthodox view of the uncircumcised state of the Israelites in Egypt, Mazor shifts the emphasis from the variants in verses 4–5 to those at the beginning of verse 6, and interpreted the MT-revision as an attempt to harmonise the deviant historiography reflected by the LXX-*Vorlage* with the standard historiography. Yet, Mazor is silent about the implications of her thesis: does this clash of concepts imply that the LXX reflects a more accurate and historically reliable account of a shady period of Israel's past? Where and when did such an alternative historiography originate, and when and why did it make way for the now prevalent historiography found throughout the Hebrew Bible? Moreover, the basis for such a far-reaching thesis is very slender, and consists of only a few clauses in LXX-Josh. 5:6a, a single clause in the LXX-plus in 24:31a and, conversely, a single clause in the plus MT-Josh. 24:5. The presumably related relics of this alternative historiography outside the book of

---

[90] L. Mazor, עיונים, pp. 185–186.

[91] L. Mazor, עיונים, pp. 187–189. See further A. Rofé, The End of the Book of Joshua, and the discussion above in section 2.2.7.2 above.

Joshua do not lend support to a concept of forty-two years of wandering through the desert, or to the concept of an exodus led by Joshua instead of Moses, or a positive view of the wilderness period. The imagery in Jer. 2:2 (or Hosea) does not aim at an idealisation or positive evaluation of Israel's journey through the wilderness, but functions only as an incidental appeal to repentance.[92] Passages such as Deut. 29:4–5 and Neh. 9:11.15 stress the divine providence during the desert journey, and do not differ from the common presentation of Israel's stay in the wilderness. Studied closely, neither the Greek version nor the reconstructed Hebrew *Vorlage* of LXX-Josh. 5:6, give any evaluation, positive or negative, of the period of Israel's stay in the desert, but simply provides background information to the main narrative line.

As noted above, the major weakness in Mazor's argumentation is her disregard of the Greek text *in its own right.* Although it is evident that her thesis of a secondary MT revision requires a deviant older Hebrew text underlying the LXX, it remains doubtful whether the Greek text lends itself to a straightforward distillation of an unrevised Hebrew text. Not only does this procedure neglect the various nuances, variations and interpretations introduced by the Greek translator as noted by Hollenberg, Gooding and Tov, but occasionally even results into a formulation that is uncommon or impossible in classical Hebrew. For one, she retroverts the Greek phrase οἱ πλεῖστοι (αὐτῶν) to the uncommon Hebrew noun מַרְבִּית, which, however indicates a *multitude*, rather than *the majority of*.[93] Mazor furthermore adapts the syntax of MT-Josh. 5:6 אשׁר נשׁבע יהוה להם to אשׁר להם גם נשׁבע

[92] See S. Talmon, The 'Desert Motif' in the Bible and in Qumran Literature, in A. Altmann (ed.), *Biblical Motifs. Origins and Transformations.* Cambridge, Massachusetts 1966, pp. 31–63, and further the modern commentaries to Jer. 2:2, e.g., S. Herrmann, *Jeremia.* (BKAT XII/2) Neukirchen 1990, p. 114; and P.C. Craigie, P.H. Kelley, J.F. Drinkard, *Jeremiah 1–25.* (WBC 26) Waco 1991, p. 24.

[93] See HALOT, p. 631b and the discussion in section 7.2.3 above. The noun occurs only five times in the Hebrew Bible (G. Lisowsky, *Konkordanz*, p. 862b–c), in the sense of *large part* only in Chronicles. In Lev. 25:37 (ובמרבית לא־תתן אכלך) the noun signifies *interest surcharge*; in 1 Sam. 2:33 (וכל־מרבית ביתך ימותו) the noun is employed in the general sense of *increase, multitude, offspring*. In 2 Chron. 9:6 (לא הגד־לי חצי מרבית חכמתך) the lexeme refers to the *magnitude* of Solomon's wisdom. Only in 2 Chron. 30:18 (כי מרבית העם ... לא הטהרו, *because a large part of the people . . . had not cleansed themselves*), and 1 Chron. 12:30 (ועד־הנה מרביתם שׁמרים משׁמרת בית שׁאול, *and hitherto a large part of them had kept the allegiance with the house of Saul*), does the semantic content of the noun approach the desired meaning '*majority*', and does the Greek translation employ the noun τὸ πλεῖστον.

in order to account for the Greek formulation differing from that in MT οἷς καὶ διώρισεν.[94] Such a reconstructed Hebrew phrase, however, not only produces a highly unusual deviation of the stereotyped Deuteronomistic formula attested by MT,[95] but also results in the anomalous syntactical construction: 'preposition phrase—the particle גם—verb' within a single clause, which is not attested in the Hebrew Bible.[96] Such an adaptation of the Hebrew text of MT is thus unlikely and unnecessary. Moreover, it disregards the distinctive character of the Greek translation, as becomes evident by the use of the emphatic καί, and the unique employment of the rare verb διορίζω as a rendering of the Hebrew נשׁבע.[97]

Less problematic but equally unnecessary is her inversion of the phrases ואת־בניהם הקים תחתם in MT-Josh. 5:7 into a reconstructed Hebrew *Vorlage* of LXX reading תחתם הקים את־בניהם in order to conform the Hebrew text to the Greek diction ἀντὶ δὲ τούτων ἀντικατέστησεν τοὺς υἱοὺς αὐτῶν. Even if the Greek translator had had such a deviating Hebrew formulation before him, his rendering of such a Hebrew phrase by the rarely used verb ἀντι-καθίστημι preceded by an extra occurrence of the preposition ἀντί still reflects a conscious literary initiative.[98] Apparently the aim of these Greek renderings was to stress the notion of substitution (ἀντί) of the older generation, and thus the result of a modification on the level of the Greek translation of the Hebrew text of MT where the accent is placed rather on the new generation itself. Finally, in verse 6 Mazor introduces a clause division between her reconstructed phrases לכן ערלים היו (LXX[B]: διὸ ἀπερίτμητοι ἦσαν) and מרביתם מאנשׁי המלחמה (LXX οἱ πλεῖστοι αὐτῶν τῶν μαχίμων). Nevertheless, neither the extant Greek text nor the Hebrew text of MT contain any marker of a clause division.

[94] L. Mazor, עיונים, p. 172.

[95] See the discussion in sections 4.2.1 and 7.2.1 above.

[96] When the particle גַּם(וְ) precedes a verb rather than a noun or personal pronoun, it is found at the beginning of a clause, not in the middle of it, see BDB, p. 169; HALOT, pp. 195b–196a. A query with the syntax search program Quest does not yield instances of the sequence preposition phrase—גַּם—verbal phrase in a single clause, nor do the examples mentioned in C.J. Labuschange, The emphasising particle *gam* and its connotations, in W.C. van Unnik, A.S. van der Woude (eds.), *Studia Biblica et Semitica. T.C. Vriezen . . . dedicata*. Wageningen 1966, pp. 193–203; T. Muraoka, *Emphatic Words and Structures In Biblical Hebrew*. Jerusalem/Leiden 1985, pp. 143–146; and B.K. Waltke, M. O'Connor, *An Introduction to Biblical Hebrew Syntax*. Winona Lake 1990[6] § 16.3.5b, 35.3.1f, 38n.13, 39.3.4.c–d.

[97] See section 7.6.4.3 below.

[98] See section 7.6.5 below.

Her proposal may offer a solution to the logical problem posed by the context of the Greek text, in which the statement about the uncircumcised state of the majority of the people is followed without interruption by the assertions that these people were no longer present at the time of the act of circumcision by Joshua, but to my mind such a problem should be studied first within the context of the Greek text.[99]

7.2.7 *The Septuagint as Product of Scholarly Research (K. Bieberstein)*

A completely different approach to the text-critical and literary-critical problems of the verses under discussion is offered by Klaus Bieberstein.[100] Unlike Mazor, Bieberstein keeps text-critical matters and literary-critical matters separate, but approaches the several variants separately as well, which leads to a somewhat diffuse picture. With a few exceptions, Bieberstein gives preference to the MT, while the variants in LXX in his view reflect either scribal errors or sophisticated interpretations of the Hebrew text. Bieberstein also pays attention to the circumstance that the fragments of this chapter in the 4QJosh[a] scroll support MT rather than a postulated deviant Hebrew *Vorlage* underlying LXX.[101]

With respect to the deviating number of forty-two years in LXX-Josh. 5:6, Bieberstein fully adheres to the interpretations of Gooding and Tov, which he labels 'Interesse an chronologischen Recherchen', that is, a study of the chronological data found in the Pentateuch.[102] Interestingly, Bieberstein detects the same interest behind the Greek version of verses 4–5, where the Greek translator introduced an additional category of male Israelites circumcised by Joshua, in order to account for either the category of non-Israelite participants of the Exodus mentioned in Exod. 12:38 (וגם־ערב רב עלה אתם—καὶ ἐπίμικτος πολὺς συνανέβη αὐτοῖς) and Num. 11:4 (והאספסף אשר בקרבו—Καὶ ὁ ἐπίμικτος ὁ ἐν αὐτοῖς),[103] or—alternatively—those male Israelites

[99] See section 7.6.4.2 below.

[100] K. Bieberstein, *Josua-Jordan-Jericho*, pp. 194–223, especially pp. 198–206, and pp. 215–220.

[101] K. Bieberstein, *Josua-Jordan-Jericho*, p. 198, with reference to his study of 4QJosh[a] in K. Bieberstein, *Lukian und Theodotion im Josuabuch.*

[102] K. Bieberstein, *Josua-Jordan-Jericho*, p. 201.

[103] The noun עֵרֶב (II) indicates an 'admixture or group of non-Israelites who joined in the Hebrews at the time of the Exodus; further a people of foreign origin in post-exilic Judah (Neh. 13:3); or the mixture of races in the population of

that were under twenty, when the sentence of the forty years of wandering in the desert was pronounced at Kadesh (Numbers 14).[104] Bieberstein thus inverts Holmes' argumentation: not a Hebrew editor, but the Greek translator introduced a correction of the older text, with the aim of harmonising the text with the Pentateuch. With Gooding, Bieberstein is able to explain the absence of a rendering of the words כל־הגוי in 5:9 as a deliberate omission by the Greek translator, for the sake of consistency with the interpretation offered in verses 4–5.[105] Unlike Gooding, however, Bieberstein does not have to take recourse to mediaeval midrashic literature, but explains the two groups circumcised by Joshua on the basis of the data from the Pentateuch only. Hence, Bieberstein characterises the Greek translation as 'basiert auf schriftgelehrten Recherchen und chronologischen Ausgleichsversuchen mit Ex. 12,38 und Num. 10,11; 11,4; 14,29.33–34,'[106]

All the more problematic, then, is the circumstance that verse 6a in the Greek version seems to distort this picture. Here too, Bieberstein gives preference to the MT, but on exactly opposite grounds. The logic of the MT in verses 6–7 is coherent and unproblematic, while the LXX contains some tension as a result of the statement in LXX^{B} διὸ ἀπερίτμητοι ἦσαν οἱ πλεῖστοι αὐτῶν, which would imply that there were still some circumcised males alive at the time of the entry of Israel into the Promised Land and the circumcision by Joshua. This, however, contradicts the statement that God had sworn that they would not see the land (οἷς καὶ διώρισεν μὴ ἰδεῖν αὐτοὺς τὴν γῆν . . .), so that these men must have died in the desert, as stated clearly in MT-Josh. 5:6a עד־תם כל־הגוי. The problem of the logic in these verses poses a serious problem with respect to Bieberstein's estimation of the Greek version: if the Greek translator—for the sake of consistency between this text and the data found in the Pentateuch—slightly altered the meaning of the Hebrew *Vorlage*, in order to account for additional information (i.e., [1] the two extra years preceding the

Babylon (Jer. 50:37), and especially Egypt (Jer. 25:20, Ezek. 30:5)' see HALOT 878b. The hapax legomenon אֲסַפְסֻף probably has a similar meaning, but with a more outspoken pejorative connotation: *a bunch of vagabonds* (HALOT 75a). See for an extensive discussion of the Greek word ἐπίμικτος employed in both instances: G. Dorival, *Les Nombres*, pp. 286–288.

[104] K. Bieberstein, *Josua-Jordan-Jericho*, pp. 199–201.

[105] K. Bieberstein, *Josua-Jordan-Jericho*, p. 203.

[106] K. Bieberstein, *Josua-Jordan-Jericho*, p. 206.

forty years in the desert, and [2] the inclusion of some other males of the present generation that for several reasons had not been circumcised), why then did such a competent and sophisticated scholarly translator allow for such grave inconsistencies in the product of his interpretative translation?

Bieberstein does not extend his conclusions on the interpretative character of the Greek translation of this chapter to the other main variants he discusses. As for the variants in MT-Josh. 5:2 שׁוב—שׁנית, Bieberstein adopts the shorter reading ושׁב reflected by LXX as the older one, with reference both to the Egyptian iconographic evidence of a sitting circumcision rite, and the midrashic interpretation of Exod. 12:43–50.[107] A Greek translator who sought to harmonise the Joshua narratives with the Pentateuch, would not have wilfully avoided this back reference. Therefore, the addition in MT—not the Greek version of the original Hebrew text—reflects, according to Bieberstein, the midrashic interpretation detected by Gooding of the originally ambivalent word ושׁב. Such an interpretation of course presupposes that the phrase in MT must be understood in the literal sense of a second circumcision, and that the midrash on Exod. 12:43–50 in some form was already in vogue in the Hellenistic period, two presuppositions that are open to discussion.

Finally, in a long discussion of the MT-pluses ממחרת הפסח (5:11) and ממחרת (5:12), Bieberstein argues that, if the Greek translator had wanted to harmonise the chronological data in verses 10–12 with the cultic calendar of Leviticus 23, he would not have omitted these phrases, as Dillmann and others have argued,[108] but rather have modified the text to such an extent that the eating of the *maṣṣot* would fall on the fifteenth of the first month (cf. Lev. 23:6) and the eating of the roasted corn on the sixteenth.[109] The MT, on the other hand, reflects, according to Bieberstein, a number of contradictions that point to its secondary character: if in verse 11 the phrase ממחרת הפסח is original, the function of the following temporal phrase בעצם היום הזה remains unexplained. Since in MT the latter phrase refers to the eating of *maṣṣot* and roasted corn, instead of to the day of

[107] K. Bieberstein, *Josua-Jordan-Jericho*, pp. 203–206.

[108] A. Dillmann, *Die Bücher Numeri, Deuteronomium und Josua*, p. 446 (see the discussion in section 7.2.2 above). See further K. Bieberstein, *Josua-Jordan-Jericho*, p. 219, n. 34.

[109] K. Bieberstein, *Josua-Jordan-Jericho*, p. 219.

the cessation of the manna (so LXX), it is difficult to see why the manna would not have stopped already on the same day as the Israelites ate from the produce of the land, instead of the day after (thus MT by means of the plus ממחרת). Bieberstein furthermore finds literary-critical support for his thesis in the position of the phrase ממחרת הפסח, which, in his view, interrupts the sequence of the prepositional phrase מעבור הארץ and its appositional phrase מצות וקליו. Secondly, the sequence of the two preposition phrases מ̱מחרת and the following ב̱אכלם מעבור הארץ would also be a literary-critical indication of the secondary character of the temporal phrase ממחרת.[110]

Contrary to the generation of scholars who sought to detect an ancient premonarchical origin of these verses in a cultic conquest celebration at a sanctuary in Gilgal,[111] Bieberstein sees no convincing reason to ascribe these verses to another literary stratum than the Priestly redaction (RedP) of Joshua.[112] He argues that all clinical surgery on the text in order to excise various admittedly late elements from the text, among which the date בארבעה עשׂר יום לחדשׁ in 5:10 and the other temporal phrase בעצם היום הזה, or one of the elements in the unusual combination קלוי—מצות—פסח, is based on circular reasoning or otherwise dubious literary-critical arguments aimed at providing a literary-critical basis for the thesis of a premonarchical festival at Gilgal.

The question then remains why the other two temporal phrases, which happen to be absent in the LXX, should be seen as Priestly additions to a passage that in itself already is the product of a Priestly redaction. The argument that the phrase ממחרת הפסח interrupts the sequence prepositional phrase—object phrase is only an aesthetic one, as there is no convincing reason why, from a syntactical point of view, such a construction would not be possible in classical Hebrew. The same holds true for the alleged problematic sequence ממחרת—infinitive construct with ב clause. Although there happens to be no direct parallel to this construction within the Hebrew Bible, there is again no convincing syntactical evidence for the impossible or problematic character of such a construction.[113] According to Bieberstein, the pluses obscure the text as they would clash with the phrase בעצם

[110] K. Bieberstein, *Josua-Jordan-Jericho*, pp. 218–219, with reference to G. Kuhnert, *Das Gilgalpassah*, p. 73.

[111] See section 7.2.2 above.

[112] See K. Bieberstein, *Josua-Jordan-Jericho*, pp. 63–71, 220–223.

[113] The noun מָחֳרָת, *the following day*, (BDB, p. 564a; HALOT, p. 572a) occurs 32 times in the Hebrew Bible, predominantly in the construction ויהי ממחרת + *way-*

היום הזה, but he does not explain why a scribe-editor would have wilfully created this *lectio difficilior*. Finally, Bieberstein argues that a competent and creative Greek translator such as the one responsible for the Septuagint of Joshua would have avoided the calender problems by altering the text in such a way that the eating of מצות would fall on the fifteenth and the eating of the קלוי on the sixteenth, but here Bieberstein pays no attention to the fact that the Greek text has no roasted corn at all, but only speaks of ἄζυμα καὶ νέα. Again there is every reason to study the Hebrew and Greek texts in their own context first, before the quantitative variants with respect to MT are used in a literary-critical argument.

7.2.8 *Homoioarcton and Homiletics (C.G. den Hertog)*

Like Gooding and Bieberstein, Kees den Hertog fully recognises the interpretative character of the Greek translation of these verses,[114] but nevertheless argues that the Greek translator cannot be considered responsible for the blatant contradiction between MT and LXX concerning the state of circumcision of the Israelites in Egypt. Rather, the threefold repetition of the phrase כל העם (היצא) in the original text of these verses as reflected by MT must have triggered a scribal error due to homoioarcton. A Hebrew scribe responsible for the Hebrew *Vorlage* of LXX or one of its predecessors would have jumped from the first occurrence of the phrase כל העם (היצא) to the second one.[115] The resulting Hebrew *Vorlage* of LXX would have read as follows:

וזה הדבר אשר מל יהושע ∩ כל העם היצאים
וכל העם הילדים במדבר בדרך בצאתם ממצרים לא מלו

(5:4b) And this is the reason why Joshua had circumcised them: ∩
(5:5a) All the people that had come out and all the people that had been born in the desert on the way when they had come out of Egypt, not had (they) circumcised (them).

---

yiqtol clause (e.g. Gen. 19:34 and 13 other occurrences). The sequence ממחרת + infinitive construct is unique, but that is probably due to the low frequency of occurrences of the noun. C. Steuernagel, *Deuteronomium und Josua*, p. 169, adduces the argument that the more correct Hebrew diction would have been ממחרת לאכלם, but such a construction would be as unique as the one attested in Josh. 5:11.

[114] C.G. den Hertog, *Studien*, pp. 145–149; 'Exkurs: Jos 5:4–6 in der griechischen Übersetzung', published under the same title in *ZAW* 110 (1998), pp. 601–606. Den Hertog points to the non-literal renderings (5:2) מול—περι-καθαίρω, (5:6) הלך—ἀναστρέφω (5:6), לא שמע—ἀπείθω, (5:6) קול יהוה—ἐντόλαι τοῦ θεοῦ, (5:6) נשבע—διορίζω/ὄμνυμι.

[115] C.G. den Hertog, *Studien*, p. 146 (*ZAW* 110, p. 603).

This incomprehensible text urged the Greek translator to the present paraphrastic reinterpretation. Due to this scribal error, the Hebrew *Vorlage* did not contain the statement that all male Israelites that had left Egypt were uncircumcised. The opposite view reflected in the Greek version, that apparently there were a number of Israelites that were uncircumcised when they left Egypt (ὅσοι ποτὲ ἀπερίτμητοι ἦσαν τῶν ἐξεληλυθότων), must be understood, according to Den Hertog, as an admonition of the Greek translator to his (Egyptian) Hellenistic Jewish contemporaries, who no longer had their sons circumcised or even attempted to revert their own circumcision.[116] The basis for this interpretation of the Hebrew text was the enigmatic phrase in Josh. 5:9 חרפת מצרים—ὀνειδισμός Αἰγύπτου, which the Greek translator interpreted in the light of the preceding context as a reference to the uncircumcised state of the Israelites in Egypt, more precisely the abolition of circumcision, rather than as a reference to the disobedient behaviour of the adult Israelite generation at Kadesh Barnea (Numbers 14).[117] The idea the Greek translator read into his Hebrew text, and which he wanted to convey to his readership was, that the wilderness period was also a punishment for the Israelites' disobedience with respect to the law of circumcision. If one adopts the meaning 'because' for the Greek word διό instead of the usual meaning 'wherefore, on which account', which in the present Greek context produces the illogical statement that the wandering through the wilderness was the cause of the Israelites' uncircumcised state, the Greek text of verse 6 would confirm this exegesis.[118]

The great merit of Den Hertog's approach is that it accounts for the qualitative variants of LXX *vis-à-vis* MT in a comprehensive and convincing way, without forcing the Hebrew text into a hybrid of classical Hebrew and classical Greek phraseology and without importing late concepts from a foreign intellectual environment into the Greek version. Nevertheless, not all questions have been answered. For one, Den Hertog dates the Greek Joshua to the end of the

---

[116] C.G. den Hertog, *Studien*, pp. 147–148, (*ZAW* 110, p. 604). See further Jubilees 15:33, 1 Macc. 1:15; Ass. Mos. 8:3; Josephus, *Jewish Antiquities* XII.241; *Mishna Shabbat* 18:3–19:6; Celsus Medicus, *De medicina* 7.25.1; Dioscurides, *De materia medica* 2.101.2; 4.154.4; Soranus, *Gynaecorum libri* 2.34; and the discussion of these passages by A. Blaschke, *Beschneidung*, pp. 133–144, 171–175, 181–183, 229–230, 259–266, 350–355.

[117] C.G. den Hertog, *Studien*, p. 147 (*ZAW* 110, p. 603).

[118] C.G. den Hertog, *Studien*, p. 148 (*ZAW* 110, pp. 604–605).

period of the Ptolemaic rule of Palestine (circa 198 BCE), and thus to a period before the crisis under Antiochus IV Epiphanes, i.e., the events alluded to in 1 Maccabees 1 and Jubilees 15. Furthermore, if laxity by Hellenized Jews with regard to the law of circumcision was felt by the Greek translator to be such a widespread religious problem, that it instigated him to introduce the homiletic undertone in his translation as detected by Den Hertog, he did so in a most concealed manner.

More importantly, Den Hertog gives no evidence for his proposal to twist the meaning of the Greek διό by 180 degrees, from a conjunction that introduces the logical consequence or conclusion of a preceding clause into a conjunction that provides the logical background for the statement made in a subsequent clause. Den Hertog points out that the scribes of the Washington codex and minuscule 29 understood the preposition in this sense when they altered διό into διότι, *because*, but it remains doubtful whether this alteration should not be seen as a scribal error, rather than an intentional amplification of the original meaning of the word. The Greek dictionaries list for διό only the meaning 'wherefore, on which account', but never 'because'.[119] As a result, there seems to be no textual evidence for Den Hertog's thesis that the Greek translator sought to depict the wandering in the wilderness as a punishment for the Israelites' negligence of the circumcision in Egypt, as a concealed exhortation to his contemporary readership.

As stated above, the main problem in LXX-Josh. 5:6 lies in the words διὸ ἀπερίτμητοι ἦσαν, since in the same sentence the subject of this clause is identified with the male Israelites responsible for the uncircumcised state of their sons, who had disobeyed the divine commandments (οἱ ἀπειθήσαντες τῶν ἐντολῶν). Whether or not they themselves were uncircumcised is irrelevant, because they were not allowed to see the Promised Land (οἷς καὶ διώρισεν μὴ ἰδεῖν αὐτοὺς τὴν γῆν). Den Hertog does not solve this problem, so the question with respect to Bieberstein's argumentation remains, i.e., if the Greek version is

[119] See LEH, p. 116b: '*therefore, on which account*'; LSJ, p. 432a: '*wherefore, on which account*', idem the *1998 Supplement*, p. 94a; W. BAUER, *Griechisch-Deutsches Wörterbuch zu den Schriften des Neuen Testaments und der übrigen urchristlichen Literatur*. Berlin/New York 1971[5], col. 394: 'Konjunktion z. folgernden Verknüpfung dienend . . . *deshalb, deswegen, daher*'; E. KIESSLING, H.-A. RUPPRECHT, *Wörterbuch der griechischen Papyrusurkunden. IV. Band*. Wiesbaden 1993, col. 597–598: '*weswegen, daher, demnach*'; See further F. BLASS, A. DEBRUNNER, F. REHKOPF, *Grammatik* § 451.5.

the product of a free and well-considered interpretation of the Hebrew text, why did the Greek translator allow for these obscurities in his rendering?

Den Hertog has given a plausible explanation for the fact that LXX and MT contradict each other so blatantly in verses 4–5. Yet, even without the problematic statement at the beginning of the Hebrew text of Josh. 5:5, the Greek version is far from a direct rendering of this allegedly corrupted Hebrew *Vorlage*, as Den Hertog himself points out. If the reconstructed Hebrew text had been the Greek translator's *Vorlage*, the translator would have inverted the order of the two כל־העם clauses, rendered it freely by ὅσοι ποτέ . . . ὅσοι ποτέ . . . and even introduced freely the whole of the Greek verse 5 πάντας τούτους περιέτεμεν Ἰησοῦς. It would seem, therefore, that the Greek translator was even more creative than Den Hertog would allow for. The question then rises whether we still need the intermediary stage of a corrupted Hebrew *Vorlage*, in order to explain the present Greek paraphrase?

7.3 Method

It has become clear that the divergencies between MT and LXX in Joshua 5:2–12 have attracted the attention of many scholars and are the subject of detailed and extensive discussions. It is remarkable to note not only that the themes of circumcision and Passover described in these verses have gained a place in Israel's *status confessionis*,[120] but also that these divergencies between MT and LXX have taken such a prominent place in the discussion with the result that this passage serves as an example where the differences in approach become most apparent. For scholars who argue in favour of a Hebrew revision of a more original text underlying the LXX, such as Holmes, Auld, and Mazor, the grave divergences in content between MT and LXX serve as a showpiece for their thesis of a revision of the older text reflected by LXX towards a more orthodox and complex MT. On the other hand, scholars such as Gooding, Bieberstein, and Den

[120] See G. von Rad, *Theologie des Alten Testaments*. München 1963[4], p. 92; K. Grünwaldt, *Exil und Identität. Beschneidung, Passa und Sabbat in der Priesterschrift*. (BBB 85) Frankfurt am Main 1992; A. Blaschke, *Beschneidung*.

Hertog have pointed to the numerous initiatives by the Greek translator in his genuine Greek renderings and come to the opposite conclusion that the reformulation is to be found in the LXX. The character of the Greek version and its redaction-critical value are judged in widely divergent ways. Particularly problematic in this respect is the beginning of verse 6. On the one hand, the Greek expression οἱ πλεῖστοι αὐτῶν can hardly be retroverted into a classical Hebrew phrase that precedes the phrase attested by MT (*pace* Holmes and Mazor). On the other hand, the Greek formulation itself is not clear, so that it is problematic to maintain the sophisticated interpretative character of the passage if the result of this interpretation is incoherent (*pace* Gooding, Bieberstein and Den Hertog).

Furthermore, a strong interference between text-critical and literary-critical observations is observable throughout the history of research on these verses. Therefore, it will be necessary to disconnect the two approaches in order to see whether or not they reach the same conclusions independently from one another. So far, no literary-critical analysis has been undertaken aimed at a solution of, but executed independently from, the questions that arise from the textual data. The following section 7.4 will address the literary-critical questions in order to establish the redaction-critical background of the verses in this section and in order to see whether the literary-critical seams between the various redactions correspond with the text-critical variants. After that the fragmentary text of 4QJosh[a] and the allusion to Josh. 5:6 in the Damascus Document (section 7.5) and the Greek text (section 7.6) will be examined in their own respective contexts.

7.4 Redaction-Critical Analysis of the Hebrew Text

Since the alleged re-edition of Joshua 5:2–12 reflected by MT not only consists of quantitative variants, as is the case for Joshua 1, but a combination of quantitative and qualitative variants, the whole of Josh. 5:2–12 has to be taken into account. For the same reason, it is not as easy as it was in the previous chapter to base a redaction-critical analysis on the Hebrew text common to LXX and MT. For the sake of clarity, the present analysis will be based in first instance on the MT, being the sole Hebrew witness to Joshua 5 that has been preserved completely. For the sake of methodological purity, the passages in which MT and LXX differ, are bracketed or italicised in the following synopsis. Each clause is given a letter in order to facilitate further discussion.[121]

5^{2} a At that time Yhwh spoke to Joshua
b ‘Make for yourself flint knives,
c and circumcise *again*
d the children of Israel [*a second time*].’
5^{3} a Joshua made [*for himself*] flint knives
b and circumcised the children of Israel until a hill of the foreskins.
5^{4} a *And this is the reason*
b *why Joshua had circumcised (them)*
c *all the people,*
d *that came out from Egypt,*
e *the males, all the men of war, had died in the desert on the way*
f *when they had come out from Egypt,*
5^{5} a [*since circumcised were all the people*
b *that had come out,*]
c and all the people
d that had been born in the desert on the way
e when they had come out of Egypt,
f not had (they) circumcised (them),
5^{6} a *because* for *forty years* the [*children of*] Israel had wandered in the desert,
b *until* [*all the nation*], the men of war, *was finished off,*
c who had come out of Egypt,
d who had not listened to the *voice of Yhwh,*
e to whom [*Yhwh*] had sworn,
f not to show them the land,
g that Yhwh had sworn to their fathers
h to give it to us,
i a land flowing with milk and honey,
5^{7} a while their children he has raised instead of them,
b these (were the ones) Joshua has circumcised,
c [*because they were uncircumcised,*]
d because (they) had not circumcised them on the way.
5^{8} a It happened
b when [*all the nation*] *had finished*
c being circumcised,
d that they stayed at their place in the camp,
e until their recovery.

[121] See the short discussion of the narrative structure of Josh. 5:2–12 in N. WINTHER-NIELSEN, *A Functional Discourse Grammar of Joshua. A Computer-assisted Rhetorical Structure Analysis.* (CB.OTS 40) Stockholm 1995, pp. 165–168. K. BIEBERSTEIN, *Josua-Jordan-Jericho*, Textheft, adopts a similar system of clause-division, but takes clauses 4c–f, 5a–b, 5d–f, 6a–b, 6e–f, 6g–i as single clauses.

5^{9} a Yhwh spoke to Joshua
b 'Today I have rolled away the humiliation of Egypt from upon you.'
c and he called the name of that place Gilgal [*until the present day*

5^{10} a *The children of Israel encamped in Gilgal*]
b and celebrated the Passover on the fourteenth day of the month *in* the evening in the plains of Jericho.
5^{11} a They ate from the produce of the land [*on the day after Passover*] unleavened bread and *roasted grain at that very day.*
5^{12} a The manna ceased [*on the morrow*]
b when they ate from the produce of the land.
c There was no longer manna for the children of Israel
d while they ate from the yield of the land of Canaan in that year.

Within the Hebrew text of Joshua 5:2–12, two segments can clearly be distinguished from one another: verses 10–12 deal with the celebration of Passover, and the consumption of the produce of the land instead of the manna. Verses 2–8 deal with the circumcision of the Israelite people. Verse 9 comes as an appendix after this segment, separated from it in the Masoretic tradition by a *petuḥah.*[122]

The first segment has a slight outer frame consisting of command (2), execution of that command (3), and a conclusion (8), and a rather complex inner structure offering the background information on the whom and why of Joshua's circumcision (4–7). The outer frame (2–3.8) relates only four actions, for which the narrative form *wayyiqtol*

[122] On the *parašah*-division see J. Oesch, *Petucha und Setuma. Untersuchungen zu einer überlieferten Gliederung im hebräischen text des Alten Testament.* (OBO 27) Freiburg/Göttingen 1979; E. Tov, *Textual Criticism of the Hebrew Bible*, pp. 50–52; M.C.A. Korpel, J.M. Oesch, *Delimitation Criticism. A New Tool in Biblical Scholarship.* (Pericope. Scripture as Written and Read in Antiquity 1) Assen 2000.

The *parašiyyot*-distribution of the chapter in MT is as follows: a ס before 5:1, a ס before 5:2–8, a פ before 5:9–12, and a ס before 5:13–6:1. The same structure, but without a distinction between *setumah* and *petuḥah*, is reflected in the Peshiṭta by means of a so-called 'diamond' (❖) after 4:24, 5:1; 5:8, 5:12 and 6:1. The three oldest Greek uncials Vaticanus, Alexandrinus, and the Washington Codex differ from this system and among themselves. In B the beginning of 5:1, 5:2, 5:3, 5:9 and 6:1 are marked by a protrusion of the first letter to the left of the column margin. The same device is discernible in A, but here the beginnings of 5:1, 5:2, 5:3, 5:4, 5:6, 5:7, 5:8, 5:9, 5:10, 12 (11b in MT), and 6:1 are marked. In W the beginnings of 5:1, 5:2, 5:3, 5:4, 5:7, 5:9 and 5:12 (11b in MT) have been indicated.

has been employed: *Joshua made* (ויעש 3a), *he circumcised* (וימל 3b), *it happened* (ויהי 8a), and *they stayed* (וישבו 8d). These actions are preceded by a succinct instruction from Yhwh to Joshua (אמר יהוה אל־יהושע 2a). The temporal adjunct *at that time* (בעת ההיא 2a) loosely connects this segment with the preceding one in which the temporary suspension of the hostile forces is narrated.

7.4.1 *MT-Josh. 5:2–3*

It is remarkable that the narrator did not mention the command and execution of the circumcision proper immediately, but first mentioned the (flint-)stone knives (חרבות צרים 2b, 3:a) to be made in advance. The background for this motif is not very clear, since such flint knives recur in the Hebrew Bible only in the puzzling passage Exod. 4:24–26,[123] which shares with Josh. 5:2–8 the element of circumcision by means of a stone tool, צֹר. In Josh. 5:2, the explicit command to Joshua to produce such primitive instruments at a time when metal was widely in use is probably intended to give the narrative an archaic character in the sense that a very ancient ritual is being reinstated.[124]

Likewise the elements of repetition in 2c–d שׁוּב . . . שֵׁנִית, absent from LXX, can be understood as the reinstatement of an ancient tradition. Scholars such as Holmes, Auld, Sasson and Finkel[125] interpret these elements literally as *a second circumcision on those males that have been circumcised already* by means of the distinction made between

[123] See the commentaries to Exodus, e.g., W.H. Schmidt, *Exodus 1*. (BKAT II/1) Neukirchen 1988, pp. 216–234; further R. Blum, E. Blum, Zippora und ihr חתן־דמים, in E. Blum (Hg.), *Die hebräische Bibel und ihre zweifache Nachgeschichte. FS für R. Rendtorff zum 65. Geburtstag*. Neukirchen 1990, pp. 41–54; and A. Blaschke, *Beschneidung*, pp. 19–30.

[124] W.H. Schmidt, *Exodus* 1, p. 227: 'Daß die Handlung mit einem scharfkantigen Stein oder wie nach Jos 5,2f. mit einem Steinmesser צר (akkad. *ṣurru* 'Feuerstein[klinge]') vorgenommen wird, gilt durchweg als Hinweis auf das hohe Alter der Beschneidung: Der Ritus bleibt in der Form bewahrt, in der man ihn zunächst, in der Steinzeit, geübt hat.' Idem H.W. Hertzberg, *Die Bücher Josua, Richter, Ruth*, p. 32. See further T.C. Butler, *Joshua*, p. 58; A. Blaschke, *Beschneidung*, pp. 34–45.

[125] S. Holmes, *Joshua*, pp. 30–31 (see section 7.2.3 above); A. Graeme Auld, Joshua: The Hebrew and Greek Texts, pp. 9–10 (= *Joshua Retold*, p. 14); J.M. Sasson, Circumcision in the Ancient Near East, in *JBL* 85 (1966), pp. 473–476; J. Finkel, The Case of the Repeated Circumcision in Josh 5:2–7, in H.L. Silverman (ed.), *Annals of the Jewish Academy of Arts and Sciences*. New York 1974, pp. 177–213, with

the two stages in the rite of circumcision from the rabbinical period onwards. The adverb שֵׁנִית, however, can also be understood in its broader etymological sense of *doing again, repeating.*[126] In that sense, the intention of the clauses in MT is a reinstallation of the rite of circumcision, in the way most modern scholars understand the phrase.[127] Similar ideas of a reinstatement of an ancient rite are to be found within the Hebrew Bible in 2 Kgs. 23:22/2 Chronicles 30 with respect to the reinstatement of the rite of Passover under Josiah (Hezekiah according to Chronicles), which had not been observed since the days of the judges (2 Kgs. 23:22; 'Solomon' according to 2 Chron. 30:26), or alternatively with respect to the reinstatement of the feast of booths under Ezra (Neh. 8:13–18), something that allegedly had been neglected during the days of Joshua. Common to these texts is the idea of a return to the roots by means of a reinstatement of ancient, but forgotten traditions during a period of political restoration (after the Assyrian oppression [2 Kings 23] or Babylonian captivity [Nehemiah 8]). The MT of Josh. 5:2 most likely

references to rabbinical literature and parallels from the Arab customs. A. BLASCHKE, *Beschneidung*, pp. 36, 259–265, further refers to M. MERKER, *Die Masai. Ethnologische Monographie eines ostafrikanischen Semitenvolkes*. Berlin 1904, pp. 318–320. See already the literal interpretation offered by the Syro-Persian sage Aphrahat (fourth century CE), *Demonstrationes XI. De circumcisione* 6 (ed. J. PARISOT, *Patrologia Syriace. Pars Prima*. Paris 1894):

> When they crossed the Jordan, the Lord commanded Joshua son of Nun and said to him (Josh. 5:2): '*Circumcise again the children of Israel for the second time.*' Why did He say to Joshua to circumcise them for the second time? Only because they were already circumcised in their heart, according to what the prophet had said (Deut. 10:16): '*Circumcise the foreskin of your heart, and do not stiffen your neck anymore.*' And Joshua circumcised them again (ܘܦܢ ܬܘܒ ܝܫܘܥ ܓܙܪ ܐܢܘܢ) and inscribed them in their flesh for the second time (ܘܪܫܡ ܐܢܘܢ ܒܒܣܪܗܘܢ ܬܢܝܢܘܬ.).

See for a discussion of this text J. NEUSNER, *Aphrahat and Judaism. The Jewish-Christian Argument in Fourth-Century Iran*. (Studia Post-biblica 11) Leiden 1971, pp. 10–30, 141–143; and M.-J. PIERRE, *Aphraate le sage persan. Tome II. Exposés XI–XXIII*. (Sources chrétiennes 359) Paris 1989, pp. 549–568.

[126] Thus the meaning of the root שׁנה II *to repeat, do again*, see HALOT, pp. 1598b–1599a, pp. 1604b–1605a.

[127] See section 7.2.4 above; R. NELSON, *Joshua*, p. 77: 'Since the exodus generation had all been circumcised, this circumcision of those born on the way is asserted to be a 'second' one (v. 2). It is a 'second time' in the sense of being a reimposition of the rite after it had lapsed after the 'first time'. See further e.g., A. MASIUS, *Josuae imperatoris historia*, Commentary (1838), col. 1037; A. BLASCHKE, *Beschneidung*, pp. 36–37.

has the same purport: the period of slavery in Egypt and wanderings through the desert is closed and the Promised Land is about to be captured. This new start is then marked with the reinstatement of an ancient rite.

The latter part of clause 3b, וימל את־בני ישׂראל אל־גבעת הערלות, *he circumcised the children of Israel towards a hill of foreskins*, i.e., is the preposition אֶל followed by the singular phrase גבעת הערלות, is ambivalent. Many scholars regard this phrase as a geographical designation, which would have been the aetiological point of departure for the present narrative, and translate the preposition אֶל in the sense of עַל: *upon the Hill of Foreskins.*[128] Since nothing of such a hill is known from other sources, one has to assume that in the vicinity of Jericho there was some sort of elevation in the landscape to which this name was attached: because it resembled a heap of foreskins, because foreskins were usually buried there, or because circumcision was usually performed at the time the author wrote this narrative. The alternative solution is that such a mound existed only in the narrative world of Josh. 5:3, and that the preposition אֶל has its normal meaning *towards, into*:[129] *And Joshua circumcised so many Israelites, until a heap as high as a hill could be formed of the foreskins.* In that case, the author only wanted to stress the extraordinary character of the event narrated.[130] The latter interpretation better fits the fictitious character of the entire passage.

---

[128] Thus e.g., A. Masius, *Josuae imperatoris historia*, Commentary (1838), col. 1042; A. Knobel, *Die Bücher Numeri, Deuteronomium und Josua erklärt nebst einer Kritik des Pentateuch und Josua.* Leipzig 1861, p. 377; B. Stade, Der 'Hügel der Vorhäute' Jos 5, in *ZAW* 6 (1886), pp. 132–143; C. Steuernagel, *Deuteronomium und Josua*, p. 168; H. Holzinger, *Das Buch Josua*, p. 12; G.A. Cooke, *The Book of Joshua*, p. 34; M. Noth, *Das Buch Josua*[2], pp. 26–27; J.A. Soggin, *Josué*, p. 58; R. Gradwohl, Der 'Hügel der Vorhäute' (Josua v 3), in *VT* 26 (1976), pp. 235–240; T.C. Butler, *Joshua*, p. 58; V. Fritz, *Das Buch Josua*, p. 58. A. Blaschke, *Beschneidung*, pp. 38–39, favours this interpretation because even a heap of 700,000 foreskins buried with sand only produces a heap of circa 2.8 m^3, i.e., a גַּל, not a גִּבְעָה. This, however, is a far too rationalistic approach to the text.

[129] See HALOT, pp. 50a–51a.

[130] See section 7.2.4 above and further A.B. Ehrlich, *Randglossen*, p. 20: '. . . hier gar kein Eigennamen vorliegt, sondern dass der Sinn eigentlich ist: Und Josua beschnitt die Israeliten bis zu einem Hügel von Vorhäuten, das heisst, bis sich ein Berg von Vorhäuten anhäufte, was bei der Menge der Beschnittenen nicht im mindesten übertrieben wäre.'; H.W. Hertzberg, *Die Bücher Josua, Richter, Ruth*, p. 31.

7.4.2 *MT-Josh. 5:4–7*

According to MT, verses 4–7 offer the reason for the circumcision performed by Joshua: the older generation had died in the desert and had not circumcised their children[131] during the forty years of wandering. The phrase that introduces the long explanation וזה הדבר אשׁר (4a) in the sense of *and this is the reason why* recurs in the Hebrew Bible only in 1 Kgs. 11:26, where information concerning the background to Jeroboam's rebellion against Solomon is given (וזה הדבר אשׁר־הרים יד במלך).[132] The clauses following this introduction consist of three parallel statements about two groups: [1: 4c–f] *the older generation had died in the desert*, [2: 5a–b] *the older generation was circumcised*, [3: 5c–f] *they did not circumcise the younger generation*:

[1] 5[4] [כל־העם היצא ממצרים הזכרים
כל אנשׁי המלחמה מתו במדבר בדרך בצאתם ממצרים
[2] 5[5] כי־מלים היו כל־העם היצאים]
[3] וכל־העם הילדים במדבר בדרך בצתם ממצרים לא־מלו

7.4.2.1 *Exoneration of the Older Generation?*

Statements two and three are formulated as a *chiasmus*: (A) מול, (B) כל־העם, (B') וכל־העם, (A') לא־מלו, and form a literary unity. The second statement is relatively short compared to the other two. It is this statement [2] that creates the contradiction with the parallel in LXX (4b καὶ ὅσοι ποτὲ ἀπερίτμητοι ἦσαν τῶν ἐξεληλυθότων ἐξ Αἰγύπτου).

From a literary-critical perspective of the Hebrew text in its own context, there is little reason to assume that this second statement should be seen as a redactional correction aimed at an exoneration of this older generation (Holmes, Auld, Nelson). The sentence immediately following this statement (5c–f) already contradicts such an allegedly more positive view on this group of men. On the analogy of the formulation in statement [2], one would expect a similar construction with a passive form (Niphʿal) of the verb מול with וכל־העם (5c) as its subject ('and all the people . . . were not circumcised') in the following statement. The Qal pattern, however, has been used

[131] The Masoretes vocalised the word in 5d הילדים as הַיִּלֹּדִים, i.e., as a plural of the relatively rare word יִלּוֹד, a Qal passive participle of ילד *born* (HALOT, pp. 412b–413a). The word recurs in the Hebrew Bible only in Exod. 1:22; 2 Sam. 5:14 and 12:14; and Jer. 16:13.

[132] Another parallel is offered by the Siloam inscription, line 1: [זאת] הנקבה וזה היה דבר הנקבה, *This is the tunnelling and this was the case of the tunnelling.*

in 5f, which implies that the subject of the verb is still the males of the older generation. As a result, this older generation is made directly responsible for the uncircumcised state of their sons.

Within the context of MT-Josh. 5:4–7, there is no contradiction or tension between the two statements [2] and [3], as there are no other indications in MT of an improved opinion on this older generation. On the contrary, in the parallel to these statements in verse 6 (see below), we find a very negative picture of this group of Israelites: they have been disobedient (לא־שמעו בקול יהוה) and because of their disobedience, all of Israel was obliged to wander in the wilderness for forty years. If a later Hebrew scribe had been offended by the idea that his forefathers neglected the practice of circumcision during their stay in Egypt, and therefore changed the text, in order to exonerate this group of Israelites, one would have expected a similar procedure with respect to the statements in 5c–f and 6.

Moreover, outside the context of MT-Josh. 5:2–12 we do not find any trace of such an alleged revaluation of this group of Israelites. Rather, they are depicted throughout the Pentateuch as rebellious, obstinate, and disobedient (so e.g., Exod. 16; 17:1–7; 32–33; Num. 11:4–35; 14; Deut. 9; Ps. 78, 95, 106; Neh. 9:16ff.). In the Qumran literature this group of Israelites is seen as a prototype of the community's adversaries, who will likewise come to an end after a period of about forty years. Thus the Damascus Document CD^B XX 14–15 (see also section 7.5.2 below) compares those that collaborate with the man of lies with the older generation in the desert, who will have to come to an end after 40 years: [133]

> And from the day of the gathering in of the unique teacher until the end of all the men of war (עד תם כל אנשי המלחמה) who turned back with the man of lies, there shall be about forty years (כשנים ארבעים).

Compare also the allusion to the wilderness period in 4QpešerPsalm 37 II, lines 7–9:[134]

> 'I will stare at his place and he will be no longer there' (Ps. 37:10) Its interpretation concerns all the wickedness (פשרו על כול הרשעה) at the end of forty years (לסוף ארבעים השנה), for they will be completed

[133] Text and translation are taken from F. García Martinéz, E. Tigchelaar, *The Dead Sea Scrolls Study Edition. Volume I.* Leiden/New York/Köln 1997, pp. 578–579.
[134] F. García Martínez, E. Tigchelaar, *The Dead Sea Scrolls Study Edition 1*, pp. 342–343.

(אשר יתמו) and upon earth no wicked person will be found (ולוא ימצא בארץ כול איש [ר]שע).

Another interesting parallel is offered by a fragmentary Targum to our Joshua-passage.[135] In this Targum, the theme of *circumcision* (מול) has been completely replaced by *admonishment* (יכח). In the reinterpretation of MT-Josh. 5:4–6, this generation is depicted as an evil generation (T-S B, 13,12, fol. 3b, line 5: הדא דרא בישא) and as a group that practised the idolatry of the pharaoh (fol. 2b):

> This is the people whom Joshua admonished (ודין עמא דאוכאח יהושע): All the people that had served the idolatry of the sinful pharaoh (כל עמא דפאלחין פולחאן טאעותא דפרעה חייבא) and all the men that had not accepted the instruction of the Lord, had died from the pest in the desert after their departure from Egypt.

In this Targum we do not find a reference to the state of circumcision of the older generation, but neither do we find any attempt to smoothen the portrayal of this group. Thus, if MT-Josh. 5:5a–b is read in its own proper context, there is no reason to assume that it presents a redactional correction of another statement aimed at the exoneration of Israel's ancestors. Rather, the function of the short statement is to give background information for the following statement in 5:5c–f, by contrasting the two groups.

Only in Talmud bavli Yebamoth 71b–72a do we find such an exoneration: the fatigue caused by the long wandering or, alternatively, the absence of a refreshing north wind would have prevented the Israelites from circumcising their sons. Nevertheless, even here the punitive character of the wilderness journey is not denied:[136]

> Why were they not circumcised in the wilderness? If you wish I might say: Because of the fatigue of the journey and if you prefer I might say: Because the North wind did not blow upon them. What was the reason? If you wish I might say: Because they were under divine displeasure.

7.4.2.2 *Style, Structure and Integrity of the Hebrew Text of Josh. 5:4–7*

Another important argument in favour of Holmes' thesis of the secondary character of the MT version of Josh. 5:4–7 is its redundancy

---

[135] See H. Fahr, U. Gleßmer, *Jordandurchzug*.

[136] Text: A. Steinsaltz (ed.), *Talmud babli. Yebamoth*. Jerusalem 1986; translation: I. Epstein (ed.), *The Babylonian Talmud. Seder Nashim*. London 1936, p. 485.

and complexity. This style, however, is inherent in the text common to both MT and LXX. Already the style of the three short statements in MT-Josh. 5:4–5 is redundant: the root יצא has been employed four times either to define one of the two generations כל־העם היצא[ים] (4c–d; 5a–b), or to add the temporal element בצאתם ממצרים (4f; 5e) to the geographical phrase במדבר בדרך (4e; 5d). The use of the phrase כל־העם is also emphatic, since in statement [1] this group is further specified as הזכרים כל אנשי המלחמה (4d) and in statement [3] as הילדים במדבר (5d), and could be missed in both cases.[137] These repetitions serve to emphasize the themes of the Exodus (יצא ממצרים), the totality of the people (כל־העם), and circumcision (מול).

These clauses would have been more than sufficient to explain why Joshua performed the act of circumcision, but remarkably enough the Hebrew text continues with a repetition of these statements in verses 6–7. Verse 6 provides additional background information, linked to the preceding passage via the particle כי. The statement in 6a 'for forty years the Israelites had wandered in the desert' does not seem to be an adequate explanation for the fact that the younger

[137] Thus for instance in the Vulgate, where the first כל־העם in 4c has duly been rendered by *omnis populus*, in 5a condensed into *omnes*, in 5c into *populus autem*. In 6b Jerome simply skipped the entire Hebrew phrase כל־הגוי אנשי המלחמה היצאים ממצרים as superfluous information. Jerome's treatment of the entire passage 4–7 provides a fine example of how the redundant Hebrew text may be rearranged and rendered in a more stylised manner:

5[4]	haec autem causa est *secundae circumcisionis*	וְזֶה הַדָּבָר אֲשֶׁר־מָל יְהוֹשֻׁעַ
	omnis populus qui egressus est ex Aegypto	כָּל־הָעָם הַיֹּצֵא מִמִּצְרַיִם
	generis masculini universi	הַזְּכָרִים כֹּל אַנְשֵׁי
	bellatores viri mortui sunt in deserto	הַמִּלְחָמָה מֵתוּ בַמִּדְבָּר
	per *longissimos* viae *circuitus*	בַּדֶּרֶךְ בְּצֵאתָם מִמִּצְרָיִם׃
5[5]	*qui omnes* circumcisi erant.	כִּי־מֻלִים הָיוּ כָּל־הָעָם
	---	הַיֹּצְאִים
	--- --- populus *autem*	וְכָל־הָעָם
	qui natus est in deserto ---	הַיִּלֹּדִים בַּמִּדְבָּר בַּדֶּרֶךְ
	--- --- --- --- ---	בְּצֵאתָם מִמִּצְרַיִם
		לֹא־מָלוּ׃
5[6]	*per* quadraginta annos *itineris latissimae solitudinis*	כִּי אַרְבָּעִים שָׁנָה
	--- --- --- --- ---	הָלְכוּ בְנֵי־יִשְׂרָאֵל בַּמִּדְבָּר
	incircumcisus fuit	
	donec *consumerentur* ---	עַד־תֹּם כָּל־הַגּוֹי
	--- --- --- --- --- ---	אַנְשֵׁי הַמִּלְחָמָה הַיֹּצְאִים מִמִּצְרַיִם
	qui non audierant vocem Domini	אֲשֶׁר לֹא־שָׁמְעוּ בְּקוֹל יְהוָה
	et quibus *ante* iuraverat	אֲשֶׁר נִשְׁבַּע יְהוָה לָהֶם
	ut ostenderet eis	לְבִלְתִּי הַרְאוֹתָם
	--- --- --- --- --- --- --- --- --- ---	אֶת־הָאָרֶץ אֲשֶׁר נִשְׁבַּע יְהוָה לַאֲבוֹתָם לָתֶת לָנוּ
	terram lacte et melle manantem	אֶרֶץ זָבַת חָלָב וּדְבָשׁ.

generation had not been circumcised. What is introduced here by means of the particle כי is not so much an explanation of the state of circumcision, but rather elaborates on the motif of the wandering in the desert as a punishment for disobedience: the older generation had not listened to Yhwh's voice (6d) with regard to the Promised Land (6f–i), hence the Israelites were sentenced to wander in the desert for forty years (6a), until the entire generation of disobedient men had died in the wilderness (6c). The same is true for כי in 5a, where the clause introduced by this particle does not so much provide the strict reason for the statement made in 4c–f, but rather provides additional information about this group.[138]

Clauses 6a–c continue with additional information to statement [1] in 4c–d concerning the older generation and the period in the desert (במדבר 4e; 6a). Here, the appositional phrases אנשי המלחמה (4e, 6b) and היצאים ממצרים (4d, 5b, 6c) recur, but the Israelites are no longer designated by the threefold כל־העם (4c, 5a, 5c), but first by [בני־]ישראל (6a) and then by כל־הגוי (6b). The first term is understandable as an inclusive term for all Israelites, both older and younger males and females, but the second term raises a number of questions. The noun גוי as opposed to עם is usually understood as *population of a territory, nation* as opposed to a *group of people bound together by blood relation*, frequently employed for the non-Israelite foreign nations, and thus often burdened with negative connotations.[139] Butler offers a subtle interpretation for the—in his view deliberate—variation of the two nouns: the two groups of Israelite *goyim* are finished off (תם), the first in the desert, while the second group is transformed in verse 8 from an uncircumcised גוי into a circumcised עם.[140] Still, this interpretation of 8a ויהי כאשר תמו כל־הגוי להמול seems to be a too sophisticated *eisegesis* of a phrase simply narrating the conclusion (תמו) of the period in which the entire people (כל־הגוי) was circumcised by Joshua. Furthermore, in numerous cases it is impossible to make a clear distinction between the two nouns.[141] In MT-Joshua

[138] Thus also P.A. FERNÁNDEZ, S.J., *Commentarius in Librum Iosue*. Paris 1938, p. 71: 'כי non indicat hic causam eorum, quae praecedunt, sed habet vim intensivam et quodammodo coniunctivam'. See further the extensive discussion by K. BIEBERSTEIN, *Josua-Jordan-Jericho*, pp. 207–208.

[139] See the extensive discussion in K. BIEBERSTEIN, *Josua-Jordan-Jericho*, pp. 208–209; and the dictionaries, e.g. HALOT, pp. 182b–183b; R.E. CLEMENTS, גּוֹי in *ThWAT* I, col. 965–973.

[140] T.C. BUTLER, *Joshua*, p. 59.

[141] Thus e.g. A.R. HULST, עַם/גּוֹי *'am/gōj* Volk, *ThHAT* II, col. 316: 'Die beiden

3:14.16 (עם) and 3:17, 4:1 (גוי), both nouns appear synonymously, supported in all cases by LXX ([πᾶς] ὁ λαός).[142] Therefore, there is no reason to regard the use of גוי for Israel as an indication of its secondary character, as Birgit Lucassen has claimed.[143]

The real problem in 6b regarding the phrase כל־הגוי is not the variation with כל־העם in 5:4–5, but in the ambivalent notion that the entire nation had perished in the desert (עד־תם כל־הגוי), since only the male warriors of the disobedient older generation had deserved this punishment. As a matter of fact the appositional phrase after כל־הגוי makes this restriction: כל־הגוי אנשי המלחמה, *the entire people, as far as the men of war are concerned*, but it is clear that the expression used in the parallel passage in Deut. 2:14: כל־הדור, *the entire generation*, is more appropriate and less ambiguous. It is not surprising, then, that this graphically similar reading כל־הדור can be found in a considerable number of mediaeval Masoretic[144] and Targum

---

Wörter werden manchmal im Parallellismus nebeneinander verwendet, ohne daß man von einem klaren und nennenswerten Unterscheid der Bedeutung reden könnte.

[142] In MT-Josh. 10:13 the noun recurs in the phrase עד־יקם גוי איביו, *until the people took vengeance on its enemies.* The main witnesses for LXX (including B) read ἕως ἠμύνατο ὁ θεὸς τοὺς ἐχθροὺς αὐτῶν, but already H. Holzinger, *Das Buch Josua*, p. 35, and M.L Margolis, *The Book of Joshua in Greek*, p. 180, suggested that this reading reflects an early inner-Greek corruption of ΕΘΝΟΣ into ΘΕΟΣ. The same suggestion is even made by A.G. Auld, Joshua: The Hebrew and Greek Texts, p. 13 (= *Joshua Retold*, p. 17) and R.D. Nelson, *Joshua*, p. 137, note k. Contrary to Auld's remark (note 23), S. Holmes, *Joshua: The Hebrew and Greek Texts*, p. 50, did not argue that an original reading גוי was corrupted into יהוה, but rather *vice-versa*, i.e., that the MT גוי is a secondary corruption of the abbreviation for Yhwh י' as attested by the LXX (idem G.A. Cooke, *The Book of Joshua*, p. 89). Yet, there is no direct evidence for the thesis that the divine name was ever abbreviated in biblical manuscripts. C.G. den Hertog, *Studien*, p. 73, sees in the employment of ἔθνος a negative connotation usually employed by the Greek translator for the foreign nations as opposed to the exclusive use of λαός for Israel (ibidem, pp. 181–183), and on the basis of these observations he rejects Margolis' conjecture with the argument that the Greek translator would have had no motive to portray Israel as an ἔθνος. There are, however, within the Greek Joshua some exceptions to this rule (e.g. LXX-Josh. 24:4), that make it likely that the Greek translator employed the noun ἔθνος for Israel here as well. Den Hertog nevertheless holds the MT to be the original Hebrew text. In his view, the Greek translator would have understood the Hebrew phrase גוי איביו as a unity instead of a subject-object chain, in the same way as Aquila and Symmachus (according to Syh[L] (ܐ. ܥܕܡܐ ܕܢܬܒܥ ܥܡܐ ܒܥܠܕܒܒܐ ܕܝܠܗ ܀ ܣ. ܥܕܡܐ ܕܢܬܒܥ ܠܥܡܐ ܕܒܥܠܕܒܒܘܗܝ) interpreted the phrase. An often neglected alternative suggestion was made by J. Hollenberg, *Der Charakter der alexandrinischen Uebersetzung*, p. 19, who regarded ΘΕΟΣ as a corruption from ΛΑΟΣ.

[143] B. Lucassen, Josua, Richter und CD, *RdQ* 18 (1998), p. 377. See section 7.5.2 below.

[144] MT-mss. Kennicott 70, 80, 107, 150, 249, 253 (marg), 337, originally 72, 665. MT-mss. De Rossi 264, 295, 345, 443, 594, originally 260, 266, 373, 405,

manuscripts of Josh. 5:6[145] and a quotation of Josh. 5:6 in *Qohelet zutra*.[146] The *lectio difficilior* כל־הגוי, however, is attested by the three main MT codices, Leningrad, Cairo, and Aleppo, the main witnesses to Targum Jonathan, and furthermore supported by Aquila,[147] Symmachus,[148] and the Pešiṭta.[149] The clauses 6d–f following the statement in 6b introduce the required restriction, so that the phrase in MT is unusual, but not impossible.

The redundant style of verses 4–5 returns in 6e–i with respect to the themes of the promise of Yhwh (אשר נשבע יהוה ל– 6e, g) and the land (ארץ . . . 6f–i). Important for our discussion is the fact that these redundant clauses are also attested by LXX, and thus formed part of its Hebrew *Vorlage*. Furthermore, these clauses stand out for their Deuteronomistic phraseology, as observed by many scholars,[150] and convey the Deuteronomistic topics of disobedience to Yhwh (לא שמע בקול יהוה 6d),[151] the promise of Yhwh to the patriarchs (אשר נשבע יהוה לאבותם 6g),[152] and the gift of the land (ארץ plus נתן 6f–h), which is characterised as 'flowing with milk and honey' (ארץ זבת חלב ודבשׁ 6i).[153] These clauses are reminiscent of Num. 14:22–23, and Deut. 1:35 and 2:14–16:[154]

543, corrected 722, 547 (marg.) and the Biblia Soncino and Soncino Prophets early printed editions, thus J.B. DE ROSSI, *Variae Lectiones Veteris Testamenti Librorum. Volumen II*, p. 76a–b.

[145] See A. SPERBER, *The Bible in Aramaic. Volume II*, where the reading דרא is attested in manuscript Brit.Mus.Or.2210 and the Fragmentary Targum on Joshua 5: הדא דרא בישא.

[146] See V. APTOWITZER, *Das Schriftwort in der rabbinischen Literatur* IV, p. 257: 'Kohelet Zutra ed. Buber S. 85. ומנין שהדור ששים רבוא שנאמר עד תום כל הדור אנשי המלצמה היוצאים וגו'. Diese Lesart wird auch vom Inhalt der Stelle bestätigt, indem aus unserer Stelle dafür ein Beleg gebracht word, daß ein 'Geschlecht' דור 600.000 Seelen umfaßt.'

[147] SyhL: ܐ. ܒܡܕܒܪܐ ܕܣܦܘ ܟܠܗ ܥܡܐ ܕܓܒܪܐ ܕܩܪܒܐ ܕܗܢܘܢ ܕܢܦܩܘ ܡܢ ܡܨܪܝܢ܀.

[148] SyhL: ܣ. ܒܡܕܒܪܐ ܕܐܬܛܠܠ ܟܠܗ ܥܡܐ ܓܒܪܐ ܩܪܒܬܬܢܐ ܗܢܘܢ ܕܢܦܩܘ ܡܢ ܡܨܪܝܢ.

[149] Peš: ܒܡܕܒܪܐ ܕܣܦܘ ܟܠܗ ܥܡܐ ܕܓܒܪܐ ܟܢܫܐ، ܩܪܒܐ. ܕܢܦܩܘ ܡܢ ܡܨܪܝܢ.

[150] See e.g., J. HOLLENBERG, Die deuteronomische Bestandtheile, pp. 493–495; A. DILLMANN, *Die Bücher Numeri, Deuteronomium und Josua*, pp. 458–459; M. NOTH, *Überlieferungsgeschichtliche Studien*, p. 42.

[151] See the various lists of Deuteronomistic phraseology, e.g., A. KUENEN, *Historisch-critisch onderzoek*², p. 110; C. STEUERNAGEL, *Deuteronomium und Josua*, p. xl; M. WEINFELD, *Deuteronomy and the Deuteronomic School*, p. 337.

[152] The promise to the patriarchs recurs in the book of Joshua only in the DtrH-frame, Josh. 1:6 and 21:43.44, see section 4.2.1 above.

[153] See e.g., H. AUSLOOS, 'A Land Flowing with Milk and Honey' Indicative of a Deuteronomistic Redaction? in *ETL* 75 (1999), pp. 297–314. Ausloos considers the phrase only to be an indicator for a Dtr. provenance, when it is occurs among other Dtr. phrases, as is the case in Josh. 5:6 (pp. 309–310).

[154] The relation between Num. 14:11–25 and the Deuteronomistic literature is a

Num. 14[22] כי כל־האנשים הראים את־כבדי ואת־אתתי
אשר־עשיתי במצרים ובמדבר
וינסו אתי זה עשר פעמים ולא שמעו בקולי׃
14[23] אם־יראו את־הארץ אשר נשבעתי לאבתם
וכל־מנאצי לא יראוה׃
Deut. 1[35] אם־יראה איש באנשים האלה הדור הרע האלה
את הארץ הטוב אשר נשבעתי לתת לאבתיכם׃

The object of 7a ואת־בניהם, *their sons*—placed in proleptic position at the beginning of the clause—marks the contrast with the אנשי המלחמה היצאים ממצרים (6), and gives the whole sentence 6–7 its ponderous, theologically-loaded character. This is even further strengthened by the repetition of the proleptic figure in the following clause 7b אתם מל יהושע, which forms an *inclusio* with 4a–b וזה הדבר אשר־מל יהושע. The two following clauses, 7c (כי־ערלים היו) and 7d (כי לא־מלו אותם בדרך) both express the same idea and furthermore form a repetition (or second *inclusio*) of the statement in 5c–f. Although LXX has only one clause here, with elements of both clauses: διὰ τὸ αὐτοὺς γεγενῆσθαι κατὰ τὴν ὁδὸν [בדרך 7d] ἀπεριτμήτους [ערלים היו 7c], it does reflect the doublet 5c–f/7c–d. The redundancy in these verses is therefore inherent in the passage itself as attested by both MT and LXX, and is not characteristic of the pluses in MT. Thus, the structure of verses 4–7 is as follows:

A: *circumcision by Joshua* (5:4a–b)
B: *death of the older generation* (5:4a–f)
C: *circumcised state of this older group* (5:5a–b)
D: *uncircumcised state of the children born on the way* (5:5c–d)
B': *end of the older, disobedient generation* (5:6a–c)
E: *disobedience and punishment* (5:6d–f)
G: *Yhwh's promise of the land* (5:6g–i)
A': *circumcision by Joshua* (5:7a–b)
D' *uncircumcised state of the younger generation* (5:7c–d)

hotly debated issue. Sufficient for our thesis is the *communis opinio* that this passage has more than mere incidental affinities with the Deuteronomistic concepts and phrases, see further R. Smend, *Die Entstehung des Alten Testaments*, p. 68; E. Blum, *Zur Komposition des Pentateuchs*, pp. 33–135, 176–180; P.J. Budd, *Numbers.* (WBC 5) Waco 1984, pp. 152–153; H. Seebass, *Numeri.* (BKAT IV/II/2) Neukirchen 1995, p. 91ff.

One might also characterise this segment as a diptych: 6–7 repeat most of the elements in 4–5:

* Joshua	אשר מל יהושע	4b	אתם מל יהושע	7b
* first generation	כל־העם . . . מתו	4c–e	עד־תם כל־הגוי	6b
	היצא ממצרם הזכרים	4d–e	היצאים ממצרים	6c
	כל אנשי המלחמה	4e	אנשי המלחמה	6b
* second generation	וכל־העם הילדים)	5c–f	כי־ערלים היו	7c
	במדבר) . . . לא מלו		כי לא־מלו אותם בדרך	7d

The logical sequence in this text is retrospective, rather than progressive: the author takes us back in time and space to a point halfway between Egypt and Israel, in order to recall the disobedience of the older generation and their rejection of the Promised Land and to draw a contrast with the present moment in the narrative line, when the younger generation has entered the Promised Land.

7.4.2.3 *Literary-Critical Interpretations of MT-Josh. 5:4–7*

Several scholars have regarded the complex and repetitive character of the text and the problematic logical sequences as indications of the composite or layered origin of the text, but their proposals have not proved convincing. Moreover, they differ widely from one another, since no clear theological motives for the assumed additions, nor a layer-specific vocabulary distinct from the main text can be discerned.

E. Albers sought to restore the original logical coherence of these verses by changing the sequence of the verses 4 and 5 and ascribing the move to their present position to the same Priestly redaction that introduced the doublets 6a–d and 7. The original narrative, preserved in 5.4.6e–i, would be a Deuteronomistic reworking of an originally Jehovistic (JE) narrative.[155] C. Steuernagel, on the other hand, made a distinction between verse 5 on the one hand and verses 4.6–7 on the other, and considered both of them to be independent explanations for Joshua's circumcision.[156] H. Holzinger ascribed 6a–d to a Deuteronomistic-type redaction of his Jehovistic source (JE^{S}), 5 to the redactor of this source (R^{JE}), 6e–i to a redaction

---

[155] E. Albers, *Die Quellenberichte in Josua I–XII*, pp. 79–84.
[156] C. Steuernagel, *Deuteronomium und Josua*, pp. 167–168.

of the Deuteronomistic source (D^S), and verses 4 and 7 (plus אנשי המלחמה in 6b) to a post-Priestly glossator who added his remarks in the margin of the text.[157] This would point to a remarkably complex literary history for such a small piece of text. M. Noth adopted Steuernagel's analysis, but saw verses 5 and 4.6–7 as two successive additions,[158] while E. Otto proposes to regard verses 6–7.8a–b as a secondary addition, characterised by the—in his view—pejorative noun גוי.[159]

The arguments for distinguishing between the supposed layers have not been very convincing or applied consistently. If one criticizes the Hebrew text for presenting an illogical sequence from verse 5 to 6 (Otto), one should make a literary-critical distinction between verse 4 and 5a as well. Steuernagel's proposal to regard both verses 5 and 4.6–7 as independent additions to the text neglects the circumstance that 4e (כל אנשי המלחמה מתו במדבר) and 6b (במדבר עד־תם כל־הגוי . . . אנשי המלחמה) form a doublet within the alleged older layer 4.6–7 as well. The repetitive style is characteristic for the entire passage, and is removed only if one omits either all of 4–5 or 6–7. If one employs the variation between עם and גוי as a literary-critical indicator (Holzinger, Otto), one has to include 8b, 3:17, 4:1, 10:12 with this secondary layer as well, and moreover, one also has to explain the intention and concepts behind this variation. The problem with this and other alleged indicators for literary layers (Albers and Holzinger regard the phrases אנשי המחלמה and זכרים as Priestly terms) is that they are not layer-specific and do not convey the main concepts and interest of the literary layers of Joshua (DtrH, DtrN, RedP), as outlined chapter 4 above. If the sole purpose behind the supposed addition of any of the elements in 4–7 had been to clarify the text (Steuernagel, Holzinger, Noth), one has to conclude that the effort has been less than successful.

Several conclusions can be drawn: [1] the segment 5:4–7 is best understood as a unity (so most scholars, including V. Fritz and K. Bieberstein),[160] [2] the repetitive, ponderous style and logic are inherent in the passage itself, not the result of literary accretion, [3] even if one follows one of the literary-critical models discussed above, there is no (complete) overlap with the text-critical data, and [4] the

[157] H. Holzinger, *Das Buch Josua*, p. 11.
[158] M. Noth, *Das Buch Josua*. 1953², p. 39.
[159] E. Otto, *Das Mazzotfest in Gilgal*, pp. 60–61.
[160] V. Fritz, *Das Buch Josua*, pp. 56–59; K. Bieberstein, *Josua-Jordan-Jericho*, pp. 207–210.

passage and its redundant style are best understood as part of the Deuteronomistic (DtrH) layer of the book of Joshua. As we have seen above, the second half of verse 6 contains an accumulation of Deuteronomistic phrases, and as we have seen in section 6.3, the Deuteronomistic passages stand out for their repetitive style. The phrase in 6b עד־תם כל־הגוי אנשי המלחמה, would fit this picture well, because it takes over the formulations found in Deut. 2:14–16.[161] This would imply that the reading of MT here finds support in literary-critical observations. M. Noth regarded the redundant and repeated phrase in 4f and 5e בדרך בצאתם ממצרים as another indication for the Deuteronomistic provenance of these verses.[162] Although the theme of the exodus from Egypt recurs throughout the Hebrew Bible,[163] it is nevertheless remarkable that eight of twenty-two times the combination ‘יצא’ infinitive construct + the preposition מן + מצרים’ occurs in Deuteronomy (4:45.46; 16:3.6; 23:5; 24:9; 25:17); four other instances (Exod. 13:8,[164] Josh. 2:10,[165] 1 Kgs. 8:9 = 2 Chron. 5:10) have strong affinities with the Deuteronomistic literature. By contrast, in the chronological reports in the Priestly layer of the Pentateuch (Exod. 16:1,[166] Num. 1:1, 9:1),[167] we find the phrase לצאתם מארץ

[161] The verb תמם itself is not layer-specific: it occurs throughout the Hebrew Bible (64 times), but in this phrase only in Deut. 2:14–16 and Josh. 5:6. In the Priestly layer of Num. 14:33 we find the related, but somewhat different expressions עד־תם פגריכם במדבר (verse 33) and במדבר הזה יתמו (verse 35). The verb recurs in Joshua in 3:16 ויעמדו המים . . . תמו נכרתו; 3:17 עד אשר־תמו כל־הגוי לעבר את־הירדן, 4:1 (ויהי כאשר־תמו כל־הגוי לעבר את־הירדן); 4:10 עד תם כל־הדבר; 4:11 (ויהי כאשר־תם כל־הגוי לעבר); 8:24 (ויפלו כלם לפי־חרב עד־תמם) and 10:20 (להכותם מכה גדולה־מאד עד־תמם).

[162] M. Noth, *Das Buch Josua*, p. 39.

[163] See e.g., H. Lubsczyk, *Der Auszug Israels aus Ägypten. Seine theologische Bedeutung in prophetischer und priesterlicher Überlieferung.* (Erfurter Theologische Studien 11) Leipzig 1963.

[164] Exod. 13:1–16 shows much affinity with Deuteronomistic concepts and expressions, and shares with Deut. 6:20–25, Exod. 12:26–27, Josh. 4:6–7, 4:21–24 the *genre* of the children's question. N. Lohfink, *Das Hauptgebot. Eine Untersuchung literarischer Einleitungsfragen zu Dtn 5–11.* (AnBibl. 20) Roma 1963, pp. 121–124, designates the passage as 'proto-Deuteronomistic'. See further the commentaries to Exodus, e.g., B. Baentsch, *Exodus-Leviticus-Numeri.* (HKAT I/2) Göttingen 1903, p. 109ff.; and B.S. Childs, *The Book of Exodus.* (OTL) Philadelphia 1974, p. 180ff.

[165] Rahab's confession in Josh. 2:10–11 contains several parallels with Deuteronomistic phrases and concepts, compare e.g., Josh. 2:11b with Deut. 4:39 and 7:9. See further M. Weinfeld, *Deuteronomy and the Deuteronomic School*, p. 331; A. Kuenen, *Historisch-critisch onderzoek*², p. 131; H. Holzinger, *Das Buch Josua*, pp. 3–4; M. Noth, *Überlieferungsgeschichtliche Studien*, pp. 41–42; R.D. Nelson, *Joshua*, p. 41.

[166] See the commentaries to Exodus, e.g. B. Baentsch, *Exodus-Leviticus-Numeri*, pp. 144ff.; B.S. Childs, *The Book of Exodus*, p. 275.

[167] See e.g. P.J. Budd, *Numbers*, pp. 3, 96.

מצרים. The implication of these observations would be that the phrase in MT-Josh. 5:4f.5e בצאתם ממצרים [בדרך], reflected by LXX 5:4, is another characteristic element of the Deuteronomistic background of the passage, and would thus form a cogent unity with the Deuteronomistic elements in verse 6d–i.

From a literary-critical point of view, MT-Josh. 5:4–7 is best understood as a literary unity characterised by Deuteronomistic phrases and themes and a Deuteronomistic, repetitive and ponderous style. The thesis of a redaction of an alleged Hebrew *Vorlage* towards the present MT does not find support in literary-critical observations, since the doublets in MT are inherent in the passage itself and characteristic for the Deuteronomistic origin of the text that is also reflected by LXX.

7.4.3 *MT-Josh. 5:8.1*

7.4.3.1 *The Wider Deuteronomistic Context*

Verses 4–7 do not stand in isolation. Their purport is to explain the whom and why of this apparently extraordinary circumcision. As Hollenberg already pointed out, these verses are inextricably linked with the elements of repetition in MT-Josh. 5:2c–d שׁוּב—שֵׁנִית. What is narrated here in Joshua 5 is not an ordinary circumcision of a single new-born, but the reinstatement of an ancient religious practice that had become obsolete during the long period of wandering in the inhabitable land. Verses 4–7 presuppose the text of MT. Hollenberg drew the conclusion that the Deuteronomistic reworking of Josh. 5:2–9 consisted of precisely these elements in verse 2 and the entire segment 4–7. In that case, one would have to make a very selective use of the text-critical data by focusing only on the quantitative variants in verse 2c–d, in order to be able to speak of an overlap between textual and literary criticism. Yet, it seems questionable to detach verses 4–7 and the elements שׁוּב–שֵׁנִית from a presumed older shorter circumcision narrative. For one, verse 8b contains the same designation of the Israelites as occurs in 6b כָּל־הַגּוֹי.[168] The function of 8a–c is to return to the main narrative line, as is evident both from the use of the macro-syntactical introduction formula

[168] Thus e.g. K. Bieberstein, *Josua-Jordan-Jericho*, pp. 208–209.

ויהי,[169] the return of *wayyiqtol* forms after the long section with only *qatal* forms, participles and infinitives expressing the background information character of the passage,[170] and the inclusio by means of the verb מול. G. Hölscher and E. Otto judged these clauses to be a an example of the redactional device of resumptive repetition,[171] but in that case the base text without the alleged redactional expansion would become even more minimal than the present narrative frame (2–3.8) already presents. Without the narrative frame the long explanatory segment loses its context, but without these Deuteronomistic clauses, the slight narrative outer frame lacks any substance and purpose.

Furthermore, the temporal setting of the segment introduced in 2a by the vague expression בעת ההיא, *about that time, in that period*, presupposes verse 1. The function of the first verse of the chapter is to create on the narrative level some temporal suspense of the hostile forces, which would allow the Israelites to undergo the painful operation that would render them helpless for some period of time.[172] The description of the paralysis of the autochthonous forces (וימס לבבם) again reveals affinities with the Deuteronomistic literature (Deut. 1:28, 20:8, Josh. 2:11).[173] Furthermore, the verse corresponds closely to the passage immediately preceding, Josh. 4:21–24, where the events at the Jordan are explained as instruction (למען דעת כל־עמי הארץ את־יד יהוה) and a deterrent for the peoples of the earth (למען יראתם את־יהוה אלהיכם...).[174] Taken together, it seems most logical and convincing to regard Josh. 4:21–24 together with 5:1–8 as a literary unit created by the Deuteronomistic author whose purpose it was to introduce the themes of a new start in the Promised Land—expressed by both the miracles of the draining of the Jordan and

---

169 See e.g. W. SCHNEIDER, *Grammatik des biblischen Hebräisch*, § 53.2.

170 See W. SCHNEIDER, *Grammatik des biblischen Hebräisch*, § 48–49.

171 G. HÖLSCHER, *Geschichtsschreibung in Israel. Untersuchungen zum Jahwisten und Elohisten*. Lund 1952, p. 338; E. OTTO, *Das Mazzotfest in Gilgal*, p. 61.

172 Thus for instance A. DILLMANN, *Die Bücher Numeri, Deuteronomium, und Josua*, p. 457; S. OETTLI, *Deuteronomium, Josua und Richter*, p. 140; H. HOLZINGER, *Das Buch Josua*, p. 11; A.B. EHRLICH, *Randglossen*, pp. 18–19; R.G. BOLING, *Joshua*, pp. 187–188; R.S. HESS, *Joshua*, p. 117.

173 See M. WEINFELD, *Deuteronomy and the Deuteronomic School*, p. 344. The verb מסס also occurs in several other, not explicitly Deuteronomistic passages, Exod. 16:21; Josh. 7:5; Judg. 14:14; 1 Sam. 15:9; 2 Sam. 17:10; Isa. 13:7, 19:1, 34:3; Ezek. 21:12; Mic. 1:4; Nah. 2:11; Ps. 22:15, 68:3, 97:5, and 112:10.

174 Cf. A. DILLMANN, *Die Bücher Numeri, Deuteronomium und Josua*, p. 457: 'Der Zweck des Wunders (4,24) erfüllte sich sofort.'

the paralysis of the hostile forces and the circumcision—as contrasted with the sin of the disobedient older generation.[175]

7.4.3.2 *Priestly affinities?*

If Josh. 4:21–5:8 is seen in its entirety as a Deuteronomistic creation, it need not occasion surprise that specific Priestly elements are absent in this passage, since this Priestly literary stratum is generally held to be younger than the Deuteronomistic (DtrH) stratum of the book of Joshua and the Pentateuch.[176] Nevertheless, several scholars have argued that this passage does reflect Priestly influence.

H.-J. Fabry argues that Josh. 4:21–24 consists of a blending of both Deuteronomistic phrases (יראתם יהוה; כי חזקה היא יד יהוה 4:24) and Priestly, late classical Hebrew phrases (אשר [4:21b] instead of כי [4:6], הוביש את־מי [4:22] instead of כרת [4:7], הודע [4:22] instead of אמר [4:7], למען דעת 4:23), and concludes that these verses must be ascribed to a post-Priestly redactor.[177] K. Bieberstein likewise attributes the whole passage Josh. 4:19–5:8, together with the related passage in Josh. 2:10–11, to a 'postpriesterschriftliche Redaktion' of Joshua.[178] In his view, the use of the noun יבשה (4:22) instead of חרבה (3:17) points to a Priestly hand, since in the Priestly version of the Sea Narrative (Exod. 14) we find a similar variation: חרבה Exod. 14:21 (JE) and יבשה Exod. 14:16.22.29 (P).[179] Joshua 5:2–8 would

---

[175] Already J. Hollenberg, Die deuteronomische Bestandtheile, pp. 492–493, argued for a Deuteronom(ist)ic provenance of these verses. See further e.g., A. Kuenen, *Historisch-critisch onderzoek*[2], pp. 129–131; J. Wellhausen, *Composition*, p. 122; A. Dillmann, *Die Bücher Numeri, Deuteronomium und Josua*, p. 457; E. Albers, *Die Quellenberichte in Josua I–XII*, pp. 69–73; C. Steuernagel, *Deuteronomium und Josua*, pp. 160–167; G.A. Cooke, *The Book of Joshua*, pp. 32–33; M. Noth, *Das Buch Josua*[2], p. 39; E. Otto, *Das Mazzotfest in Gilgal*, pp. 44–46, who all regard Josh. 4:21–24 as a Deuteronomistic creation. Otto, however, ascribes Josh. 5:1 to his pre-Deuteronomistic Quelle A, because he perceives a tension between the idea expressed by יראתם (4:21–24), understood as obedience, and paralysis (5:1).

[176] See section 4.2 above.

[177] H.-J. Fabry, Spuren des Pentateuchredaktors in Jos 4,21ff. Anmerkungen zur Deuteronomismus-Rezeption, in N. Lohfink (Hg.), *Das Deuteronomium. Entstehung, Gestalt und Botschaft.* (BETL 68) Leuven 1985, pp. 351–356. A similar view was already expressed by H. Holzinger, *Das Buch Josua*, p. 9: '21–24 ist überflüssige Wiederholung von v. 6f. Auf eine zweite dtn-istische Hand weist die Annäherung an den Sprachgebrauch von P (יַבָּשָׁה v. 22).'

[178] K. Bieberstein, *Josua-Jordan-Jericho*, p. 128ff., 134–135, 185–186, 193–194, 210, 397–418.

[179] For the commonly accepted stratification of the Sea Narrative, see for instance: M. Noth, *Überlieferungsgeschichte des Pentateuch.* Stuttgart 1948, pp. 7–44; B.S. Childs,

be a midrashic tale that presupposes Josh. 5:10–12 and the Halakah of Exod. 12:43–49, which states that no uncircumised person is allowed to eat from the Passover meal.

Whereas for Fabry and Bieberstein Josh. 4:21–24, 5:1–8 is the product of an author that can be labelled both post-Deuteronomistic and post-Priestly, M. Ottoson reverts the commonly accepted order D – P. He, too, considers our passage to be Deuteronomistic, but argues that the whole Deuteronomistic layer is dependent upon and thus later than the Priestly layer of the book of Joshua.[180] Ottoson also argues that the sequence 'entry into the land—circumcision—Passover' reflects the Priestly Halakah of Exod. 12:43–49, with which he also includes Exod. 13:5–6: והיה כי־יביאך יהוה אל־ארץ הכנעני . . . שבעת ימים תאכל מצת. Since in his view P predates D, Ottoson is able to return to Hollenberg's position who had argued that Josh. 5:5 (D) depends on Genesis 17 (P).[181]

Ottoson, however, employes the term 'Priestly' in the very broad sense in which his teacher Ivan Engnell used the terms 'Priestly Work' for the Tetrateuch and 'Deuteronomistic Work' for Deuteronomy—2 Kings.[182] Thus, Ottoson does not discriminate between specifically Priestly parts and allegedly pre-Priestly parts of the Tetrateuch, so that he interprets the intertextuality between Josh. 5:15 and Exod. 3:5 as another indication of the dependence of the 'D Work' (Josh. 5:13–15) upon the 'P Work' (Exod. 3). Yet, from the perspective of consistency in distinctive vocabulary and ideas, there is just as little Deuteronomistic theology to be found in Josh. 5:13–15 as Priestly material in Exod. 3:5 (in contrast with Exod. 6:2–9, which forms the proper Priestly parallel to the vocation narrative).[183]

Furthermore, if one employs the criterion of coherence in distinctive, theologically or ideologically motivated vocabulary expressing

---

Exodus, pp. 215–239; F. Kohata, *Jahwist und Priesterschrift in Exodus 3–14*. (BZAW 166) Berlin/New York 1986, pp. 277–301; M. Vervenne, The 'P' Tradition in the Pentateuch: Document and/or Redaction? The 'Sea Narrative' (Ex. 13,17–14,31) as a Test Case, in C. Brekelmans, J. Lust (eds.), *Pentateuchal and Deuteronomistic Studies*, pp. 67–90 (with full bibliographical references).

[180] M. Ottoson, Tradition History, pp. 89–90; and M. Ottoson, *Josuaboken*, pp. 56–57.

[181] See section 7.2.1 above.

[182] I. Engnell, *A Rigid Scrutiny. Critical Essays on the Old Testament*. Nashville 1969, pp. 50–67: 'The Pentateuch'; M. Ottoson, Tradition History, pp. 82–84.

[183] See the commentaries to Joshua and Exodus. Similar remarks can be made with respect to Exod. 13:1–16, a passage that shares many expressions and concepts with the Deuteronomistic literature, rather than the Priestly literature.

the main interests of a given group (*torah* [DtrN], priests [RedP]), there seems to be little reason to attribute Josh. 2:10–11, 4:21–24, 5:1 to a Priestly layer and no basis at all for taking the Deuteronomistic phrases in these passages as well as in 5:2–8 as indications of a Priestly layer (*pace* Fabry and Bieberstein). The root יבשׁ hardly expresses any theological interests. Even if the passages in Exodus 14 where the root יבשׁ occurs, should be ascribed to a Priestly layer, the variation between חרב and יבשׁ alone does not point to different layers, and could be merely coincidental.[184] Neither do other alleged Priestly formulations such as ידע Hiphʿil, and למען דעת convey any specific Priestly interests or diction. Nowhere in these alleged Priestly passages in Joshua does Eleazar or any other priest play a role, or do we encounter one of the other specifically Priestly interests and formulations as sketched in section 4.2.3 above. On the other hand, the parallels between Josh. 4:21–24 and Deut. 4:9, 6:2.20–23, 8:3, 28:10 strongly point to a Deuteronomistic provenance of these verses as well.

Within Josh. 5:2–12, the circumcision and Passover narratives follow one another without any clear connection. Nowhere in Josh. 5:2–9 is there any hint that the circumcision was performed for the sake of the purity of the Passover festival, nor is there any hint in Exod. 12:43–49 that the regulations regarding the participants in the Passover festival were formulated with the Joshua 5 narratives in mind. Exod. 12:43–49 does not refer to a first circumcision of the Israelites that would correspond with their second circumcision in Joshua 5, but only discusses the problem of the participation of non-Israelite individuals (i.e., the foreigner בן־נכר, the residents תושׁב, and the wage labourer שׂכיר).[185] Only when the Bible is read in a strict synchronic way, as the rabbis did, is there a relation between Exod. 12:43–49 and Josh. 5:2–12.

The same is true for the alleged relation between Josh. 5:5 and Genesis 17. If the purpose of Josh. 5:4–7, either in its entirity (thus

---

[184] H.D. Preuß, יָבֵשׁ *jāḇeš* יַבָּשָׁה *jabbāšāh* יַבֶּשֶׁת *jabbæšæṯ* in *ThWAT* III, col. 400–406, especially col. 405–406, subsumed the passages Exod. 14, Josh. 2:10; 4:22–24; 5:1; Gen. 8:7.14 under his discussion of the use of the root by the Priestly Writer, but also noted that the root occurs in all literary layers of the Hebrew Bible and observed 'daß *jbš* und seine Derivate innerhalb des AT, trotz der zuweilen auftretenden Beziehungen zum Exodusgeschehen, das sich auch in Aussagen über JHWHs Macht über Trockenes und Meer widerspiegelt, kein besonderes und schon gar kein positives theol. Eigengewicht haben.'

[185] See e.g. G. Beer, *Pesachim*, p. 40.

Hollenberg), or only in the parts that constitute the present MT as opposed to LXX (thus Holmes), was to harmonise the older text with the Priestly legislation in Genesis 17, one would have expected to find a clear reference in the text of Joshua 5 to the legislation in Genesis 17. This, however, is not the case. As many scholars have noted, Joshua 5 simply presupposes circumcision as an ancient religious rite, but does not (yet) reflect the late Priestly theological founding narrative in Israel's pre-Sinaitic history as found in Genesis 17.[186]

In conclusion, Josh. 5:1–8 together with Josh. 4:21–24 is best understood as a literary unit created by the Deuteronomist, and thus as part of the DtrH-stratum of the book of Joshua. The passage itself does not yet reflect any influence from the Priestly parts of the Hexateuch, as this Priestly layer is younger than the Deuteronomistic one.

7.4.4 *MT-Josh. 5:9*

By contrast, it seems unlikely to regard the subsequent verse 9 as the logical conclusion of this passage, as was argued by Hollenberg and many others. The verse gives an explanation for the name of the place (שׁם המקום ההוא 9c) Gilgal by means of a wordplay on גלל—גלגל *to roll away*. Although the preceding context almost automatically generates the interpretation of 9b היום גלותי את־חרפת מצרים מעליכם, *Today I* (i.e. Yhwh) *have rolled away the humiliation of Egypt from upon you*, in terms of: *at that time* (בעת ההיא 2a) *Joshua removed the contemptuous uncircumcised state from the Israelites by cutting off their foreskins*, it remains dubious whether one should interpret חרפת מצרים in the light of the preceding context as a reference to the uncircumcised state of the Israelites, either in Egypt or at any moment afterwards. Verses 4–7 in MT mention only the neglect of circumcision during the wilderness wandering, not during the period in Egypt. In the context of MT, the statement in 5a–b כי־מלים היו כל־העם היצאים excludes the possibility that the Egyptians would reproach their slaves for being uncircumcised, since we are told that all males of the Exodus generation were circumcised. Already in the early manuscript tradition this verse was separated from the preceding text by means of a strong caesura or *petuḥa*.

---

[186] Thus e.g. K. Grünwaldt, *Exil und Identität*, pp. 44–46; A. Blaschke, *Beschneidung*, pp. 38–43.

Although there is evidence that circumcision was practised by Egyptians,[187] there is no evidence the Egyptians despised the Israelites in the same way the Israelites held the Philistines in contempt.[188] Moreover, one wonders why the Egyptians would bother about whether or not their former slaves were circumcised, or why the Israelites would care what the Egyptians would think and say of them, forty years after their liberation from Egypt.[189] R.S. Hess argues that the phrase refers to the disobedience of the Israelite generation that left Egypt,[190] but it is difficult to see how the phrase can refer to something else than the 'humiliation coming from (part of) Egypt.'

If read solely within the context of verse 9, the phrase חרפת מצרים, *humiliation of Egypt*, rather seems to refer to a situation of national-political humiliation of Israel by Egypt comparable to the expression חרפת מואב in Zeph. 2:8.[191] In Gen. 34:14 and 1 Sam. 17:26 we find a combination of the roots חרף and ערל, but in these passages it is not the state of being uncircumcised *per se* that is the object of humiliation, but rather the humiliating subjection of Israel to *uncircumcised* foreigners (e.g. Shechem [Gen. 34], or the Philistines [in the David and Goliath passage 1 Sam. 17]). Within the context of only

---

[187] See the commentaries to Josh. 5 and Jer. 9:24–25, and further G. MAYER, מול *mûl* מוּלָה *mûlāh*, in *ThWAT* IV, col. 734–738; W. WESTENDORF, Beschneidung, in W. HELCK, E. OTTO (Hg.), *Lexicon der Ägyptologie. Band I. A—Ernte.* Wiesbaden 1975, col. 727–729; J.M. SASSON, Circumcision in the Ancient Near East, in *JBL* 85 (1966), pp. 473–476; A. BLASCHKE, *Beschneidung*, pp. 43–45, pp. 323–360, where the statements in HERODOTUS, *Histories*, II 35–37.104, DIODORUS SICULUS, *Library of History*, I.28; 55:5; III.32.4; and STRABO, *Geography*, XVII.2.5 are examined.

[188] Thus Judg. 14:3; 15:18; 1 Sam. 14:6; 17:26.36; 18:25–27; 31:4 (= 1 Chron. 10:4); 2 Sam. 1:20; 3:14. See further A. BLASCHKE, *Beschneidung*, pp. 45–48.

[189] So A.B. EHRLICH, *Randglossen*, pp. 20–21, although he still adhered to the interpretation of the phrase as a reference to the state of not being circumcised: 'חרפת מצרים aber besagt nicht, dass die Aegypter den Israeliten das Unbeschnittensein als Schmach anrechneten. Denn soweit die Zeit während der Knechtschaft in Betracht kommt, werden die Aegypter auch ihre nichtisraelitischen Sklaven nicht beschnitten haben, und zur Zeit Josuas gingen die Israeliter die Aegypter nichts an. Am allerwenigsten konnten sich die Aegypter dann dafür interessieren, ob ihre ehemaligen Sklaven beschnitten waren oder nicht. חרפת מצרים kann daher nur heissen die Schmach von Aegypten her, d.i., die Schmach, die seit Aegypten datierte.'

[190] R.S. HESS, *Joshua*, p. 122.

[191] שמעתי חרפת מואב וגדופי בני עמון אשר חרפו את־עמי ויגדילו על־גבולם, *I have heard the humiliation of Moab and the abuses of the Ammonites with which they humiliated my people and enlarged their territory*. See further, for instance, Ezek. 5:14–15; 36:15.30, Joel 2:17 (ואל־תתן נחלתך לחרפה למשל־בם גוים), Lam. 5:1–2 (זכר יהוה מה־היה לנו הביט וראה את־חרפתנו: נחלתנו נהפכה לזרים בתינו לנכרים); and Neh. 5:9 (חרפת הגוים אויבינו); HALOT, p. 356a–b; E. KUTSCH, חרף *ḥrp* II, in *ThWAT* III, col. 223–229; and E. POWER, S.J., Josue 5:9 and the Institution of Circumcision, in *Irish Theological Quarterly* 18 (1951), pp. 368–372.

Josh. 5:9, it remains difficult to assess the precise meaning of the phrase חרפת מצרים. Several scholars regard the expression as a reference to the humiliating state of slavery of the Israelites in Egypt, the בית עבדים, which with the completion of the wanderings through the desert following this period, has finally come to an end.[192] Alternatively, one might regard the phrase as a reference to passages such as Exod. 32:12, Num. 14:13–16 and Deut. 9:28, where Moses persuades Yhwh not to destroy the Israelites, lest the Egyptians ridicule Yhwh's power:[193]

Exod. 32^{12} למה יאמרו מצרים לאמר ברעה הוציאם
להרג אתם בהרים ולכלתם מעל פני האדמה...
Num. 14^{13} ויאמר משה אל־יהוה ושמעו מצרים
כי־העלית בכחך את־העם הזה מקרבו...
14^{16} מבלתי יכלת יהוה להביא את־העם הזה אל־הארץ
אשר־נשבע להם וישחטם במדבר
Deut. 9^{28} פן־יאמרו הארץ אשר הוצאתנו משם מבלי יכלת יהוה
להביאם אל־הארץ אשר־דבר להם
ומשנאתו אותם הוציאם להמתם במדבר

These two explanations need not be mutually exclusive, but can be seen as complementary. In fact, Josephus in his *Jewish Antiquities* V.34 already gave an interpretation of the name 'Gilgal' that comprises

---

[192] Thus already THEODORETUS CYRENSIS, *Quaestiones in Josuam* IV (text: N. FERNÁNDEZ MARCOS, A. SÁENZ-BADILLOS (ed.), *Theodoreti Cyrensis Quaestiones in Octateuchum*. Madrid 1979, p. 276): δηλοῖ δὲ ὁ λόγος τὴν τῆς αἰγυπτιακῆς δουλείας καὶ δυσσεβείας ἀπαλλαγήν. See further e.g. A. KNOBEL, *Die Bücher Numeri, Deuteronomium und Josua erklärt*, pp. 377–378: 'Die *Schmach Aegyptens* ist das von Aegypten her Israel noch anhangende Elend. In Aegypten lebte Israel in unwürdigem Drucke, in schmählichem Elende.... Mit dem Einzuge in Kanaan nahm dies ein Ende.'; S. OETTLI, *Das Deuteronomium und die Bücher Josua und Richter*, p. 139; O. EIßFELDT, *Hexateuch-Synopse*. Leipzig 1922, pp. 31–32; W. RUDOLPH, *Der 'Elohist' von Exodus bis Josua*. (BZAW 68) Berlin 1938, p. 180; P.D. BALDI, *Giosuè*, p. 42; E. KUTSCH, חרף *ḥrp* II, in *ThWAT* III, col. 223–229, especially col. 228; R.G. BOLING, *Joshua*, p. 190; T.C. BUTLER, *Joshua*, p. 59; K. GRÜNWALDT, *Exil und Identität*, p. 9; V. FRITZ, *Das Buch Josua*, p. 59; A. BLASCHKE, *Beschneidung*, p. 38.

[193] Thus already the Mediaeval Jewish commentator DON ISAAK ABRABANEL Jerusalem 1955:

ואחשוב אני בזה, שלפי שהלכו ישראל במדבר ארבעים שנה היו המצריים אומרים מבלתי יכולת ה׳ להביאם אל הארץ אשר נשבע להם וישחטם במדכר, ועתה כאשר העבירם האל ית׳אל הארץ והיו ישראל בגלגל, אמר היום גלותי את חרפת מצרים מעליכם, כי יאמרו שכבר באתם אל הארץ.

See further C.F. Keil, *Biblischer Commentar über die prophetischen Geschichtsbücher des Alten Testament. Erster Band: Josua, Richter und Ruth.* (BCAT II/1) Leipzig 1863, p. 39; A.D.H. MAYES, *The Story of Israel*, p. 44; K. DEURLOO, Spiel mit und Verweis auf Torah-Worte in Jos 2–6; 9, in *Dielheimer Blätter zum Alten Testament und seiner Rezeption in der Alten Kirche* 26 (1989/90 [1992]), pp. 70–80, especially p. 77.

both the liberation from the slavery in Egypt and the miseries in the desert:[194]

> The place where Joshua had established his camp was called Galgala. This name signifies 'freedom' (σημαίνει δὲ τοῦτο ἐλευθέριον ὄνομα·); for, having crossed the river, they felt themselves henceforth free both from the Egyptians and from the miseries in the desert.

Although Josephus did not explicitly connect this interpretation with the phrase 'humiliation of Egypt', it is clear that he elaborates on Josh. 5:9, since nowhere else in the book of Joshua or elsewhere in the Bible an explanation of the name Gilgal is presented.

It is thus very probable that the clause 'today I have rolled away the humiliation of Egypt' does not refer to the circumcision mentioned in the preceding verses 5:2–9. Rather, the rolling away of this humiliation marks the end of the period of slavery and wandering in the desert, and forms a connection with the erection of the twelve stones at Gilgal as narrated in Josh. 4:20: ואת שתים עשׂרה האבנים האלה אשר לקחו מן הירדן הקים יהושע בגלגל, *The twelve stones which they had taken from the Jordan, Joshua erected at Gilgal.* The prominent temporal phrase in 5:9b היום, *today*, may be seen in conjunction with the similar statement in Josh. 3:7: ויאמר יהוה אל־יהושע היום הזה אחל גדלך בעיני כל־ישראל, *Yhwh said to Joshua: 'This very day I have started to exalt you in the eyes of all Israel'.* The two passages mark the beginning (3:7) and the end (5:9) of the crossing of the border of the Promised Land and deal with status (exaltation [3:7] versus humiliation [5:9]). If Josh. 5:9 is to be read in conjunction with Joshua 4 (verses 18–19) rather than the preceding verses dealing with a different topic (circumcision), the most logical literary-critical solution would be, that the Deuteronomistic verses in between (Josh. 4:21–5:8) form a Deuteronomistic addition to a pre- or proto-Deuteronomistic stratum.[195]

---

[194] Text and translation: H.St.J. Thackeray, R. Marcus, *Josephus V. Jewish Antiquities, Books V–VIII.* Cambridge, Massachusetts/London 1934. The editors considered the rendering of Galgala by ἐλευθερία to be 'one of the historian's "free" etymologies.' (p. 17, note e). This remark in V. 34 provides Josephus' readers with background information on the place where Achar hid his stolen objects (V. 33), as Josephus did not adopt the circumcision narrative in his rewritten composition (see section 7.6.3.2 below).

[195] Thus W. Rudolph, *Der 'Elohist'*, p. 180; and E. Power, Josue 5:9 and the Institution of Circumcision.

Hertzberg suggested that verse 5:9 was transposed from an earlier position after 4:19, but failed to find a motivation for the transposition.[196] Bieberstein, on the other hand, regards the verse to be a very young addition to the complex 4:19–5:8 which he regards as a Priestly addition (see above), and ascribes 5:9 to a post-Priestly aetiological redaction ($\text{Red}_{\text{ätiol}}$).[197] Yet, if the purpose of this alleged—admittedly heterogeneous—redaction had been to connect the *realia* of the land of Israel as found by the remigrants under Ezra and Nehemiah (Ezra 2/Neh. 7) with the localities in the ancient scriptures,[198] and if this redactor held the toponym Beth-haGilgal (mentioned only in Neh. 12:29) to be identical with the pre-Exilic place Gilgal,[199] one wonders why the redactor did not append his aetiological note in 5:9b to Josh. 4:19, and why he did not use the name Beth-haGilgal in his addition as well. According to Bieberstein, this redactor sought to underline the importance of circumcision as *nota judaica*, and consequently interpreted the neglect of the circumcision mentioned in the older text, Josh. 5:2–8, as a humiliation.[200] In that case, it remains difficult to see why the redactor would have obscured his intention by designating this situation as 'humiliation *of Egypt*'. Since this theology rather reflects that of the Priestly writer(s), Bieberstein is forced to assume a minimal distance in time and theology between his two post-exilic redactors.

7.4.5 *MT-Josh. 5:10–12*

Verses 10–12 consist of seven clauses, five of which carry the main narrative line as indicated by the *wayyiqtol* form: *they camped in Gilgal* (ויחנו 10a), *they made the Passover* (ויעשׂו את־הפסח 10b), *they ate from the produce of the land* (ויאכלו מעבור הארץ 11a), *the manna ceased* ([וי]שבת המן 12a, change of subject, LXX presupposes a *qatal*-form) and *they ate from the yield of the land* (ויאכלו מתבואת ארץ 12d). In these verses, Joshua has disappeared as the main agent (thus in 2a, 3a, 4b, 7b, 9a), whereas the Israelites are the sole agents (MT-5:10a;[201] 5:12c). This

---

[196] Thus H.W. Hertzberg, *Die Bücher Josua, Richter, Ruth*, p. 32.
[197] Thus K. Bieberstein, *Josua-Jordan-Jericho*, pp. 209ff., 419ff.
[198] K. Bieberstein, *Josua-Jordan-Jericho*, pp. 418–427.
[199] K. Bieberstein, *Josua-Jordan-Jericho*, pp. 403–404.
[200] K. Bieberstein, *Josua-Jordan-Jericho*, p. 420.
[201] The clause is absent from LXX, but this subject is present as an LXX plus in the Greek version of the next clause Καὶ ἐποιήσαν *οἱ υἱοὶ Ισραηλ* τὸ πάσχα.

observation already makes it implausible that the verses should be seen as a prefiguration of the Passover celebrated by Josiah and should therefore be ascribed to a first edition of the Deuteronomistic History (Dtr_1),[202] as argued by R.D. Nelson.[203]

7.4.5.1 *The Camp in Gilgal*

Josh. 5:10a repeats Josh. 4:19b (ויחנו בגלגל בקצה מזרח יריחו), the first place in Joshua where Gilgal is mentioned. There is another connection between the two verses in that both contain an explicit date: *the tenth day of the first month* (והעם עלו מן־הירדן בעשׂור לחדשׁ הראשׁון 4:19a)—*the fourteenth day of the month* (5:10b). The clause in 5:10a not only repeats 4:19b, but is also superfluous after the circumcision episode, 5:2–8, which is located *in the camp* (וישבו תחתם במחנה 5:8d). A.G. Auld makes a connection between this plus in MT and the related pluses in MT *vis-à-vis* LXX in 8:9.13 and 10:15.43, and regards them as examples of a 'pedantic concern for the location of the camp and the precise whereabouts of Joshua himself at any given moment'.[204]

Although it is remarkable that there are a number of pluses in MT *vis-à-vis* LXX with respect to the position of the Israelite camp, there are a number of observations that argue against the view that they reflect a common pedantic redaction. For one, the minus in Josh. 8:13 is part of a larger minus in LXX (and 4QJosh[a]?) that will be discussed in the following chapter. Furthermore, the clause does not deal with the camp in Gilgal, but with a camp in the vicinity of Ai. Josh. 8:9 may implicitly be situated in the camp in Gilgal, but does not mention it. The identical verses in 10:15.43, on the other hand, both absent from LXX, locate the camp in Gilgal, although another verse (10:21) postulates a camp in Makkedah. Here too, the camp is not mentioned in LXX. Holmes,[205] Benjamin,[206] Auld, Mazor,[207] De Troyer,[208] and many other scholars (including

[202] See section 4.2.4.1 above.

[203] R.D. Nelson, Josiah in the Book of Joshua, p. 536. In his recent commentary on Joshua, p. 79, note 11, Nelson is more cautious: 'It must be admitted that Joshua himself is not actually mentioned in this unit.'

[204] A.G. Auld, Joshua. The Hebrew and Greek Texts, p. 5 (= *Joshua Retold*, p. 10).

[205] S. Holmes, *Joshua. The Hebrew and Greek Texts*, pp. 4, 51, 53.

[206] C.D. Benjamin, *The Variations*, pp. 43–44.

[207] L. Mazor, עיונים, pp. 167–168, see section 2.2.7.3 above.

[208] K. de Troyer, Did Joshua Have a Crystal Ball? The Old Greek and the

already Hollenberg)[209] consider the pluses in MT-Josh. 10:15.43 to be late additions to the Hebrew text reflected by LXX. Such a thesis would have gained probability if all references to an Israelite camp in Gilgal were found in pluses in MT *vis-à-vis* LXX, and if some special ideological interest in this locality could be detected. This, however, is not the case. The camp in Gilgal recurs in Josh. 4:19, 9:6, 10:6.7, and is presupposed in 14:6, in all cases attested by LXX as well.

Furthermore, the locality of Gilgal may have been deserted or destroyed as early as the (late) Assyrian period. In the books of the pre-exilic prophets Amos (4:4, 5:5) and Hosea (4:15; 9:15; 12:12), Gilgal is consistently depicted as a place of idolatry. It is therefore hard to imagine that a scribe from the Second Temple period would have wilfully introduced this infamous place name in the book of Joshua, and deliberately created the doublets and tensions between Josh. 5:8 and 10 on the one hand, and 10:15.43 versus 10:21 on the other. If we are to believe that a redactor only for the sake of pedantry at random and without attention to the context interspersed the running text with these references to a camp in Gilgal, one wonders why he did not do so as well in other narrative passages, such as Joshua 7, 11, 14:1–5. Given the circumstance that the Greek translator was prepared to alter geographical indications for the sake of consistency in Josh. 24:1.25 ('Shiloh' for 'Shechem') and 1:3–4, 14 (see sections 6.4.4 and 6.4.8 above), there seems to be no basis for the thesis of a redactional addition of MT-Josh. 5:10a only. The repeated mentioning of the Israelites camping at Gilgal in MT-Josh. 5:10a should be seen as a *Wiederaufnahme* introducing a redactional addition of the whole passage 5:10–12(a–b).[210]

MT of Joshua 10:15, 17 and 23, in S.M. PAUL, R.A. KRAFT, L.H. SCHIFFMAN, W.W. FIELDS (eds.), *Emanuel. Studies in Hebrew Bible, Septuagint, and Dead Sea Scrolls in Honor of Emanuel Tov.* (SVT 94) Leiden/Boston 2003, pp. 571–589.

[209] J. HOLLENBERG, *Der Charakter der alexandrinischen Übersetzung*, p. 19.

[210] M. ANBAR, La 'reprise', *VT* 38 (1998), pp. 385–398, regards the intervening passages Josh. 4:21–24, 5:1, 5:2–8, and 5:9 to be 'interpolations' (pp. 388–389), but in my view, the order of chronological dependence should be inverted: the Priestly redactor (RedP) bracketed these passages with the dates of Passover and the place where the Passover was held. See further H. HOLZINGER, *Das Buch Josua*, p. 12: 'V.10[a], LXX B om., ist neben 4_{19} nicht überflüssig: 4_{19b} sagt, dass die Israeliten am 10. Tag des 1. Monats das Lager in Gilgal bezogen, 5_{10a}, dass sie am 14. Tag d. M. noch dort waren.'

7.4.5.2 *The Priestly Background of Josh. 5:10–12a*

In Josh. 5:10b the celebration of Passover is mentioned in both MT and LXX. As numerous scholars have pointed out, the specific date (*on the fourteenth day of the* [*first*] *month*) in combination with the date of Josh. 4:18 (*on the tenth day of the first month*), as well as the verb employed here (עשׂה את־הפסח attested also by LXX: Καὶ ἐποίησαν . . . τὸ πάσχα), are elements characteristic of the Priestly layer of the Pentateuch and Joshua.[211] The specific dates for the celebration of Passover can be found in Exod. 12:6, Lev. 23:5, Num. 9:5 and 28:16, Ezek. 45:21, Ezra 6:19, 2 Chron. 35:1, passages that are all related to or dependent on the Priestly literature.[212] The sequence 10th day of the first month–14th day of the first month, from entry into the land (Josh. 4:19) to Passover (Josh. 5:10b), corresponds with the introduction of the tenth day of the month as the preparation period for the festival in Exod. 12:3.[213] The mere circumstance that the months are numbered, rather than named by their original Canaanite names (such as Abib in Deut. 16:1) points to an Exilic or post-Exilic date for the passage, since this practice originates from Neo-Babylonian usage and was introduced into the Israelite calendar during or after the period of the Exile.[214]

Although the phrase עשׂה את־הפסח occurs occasionally in Deuteronomistic passages, such as Deut. 16:1, and 2 Kgs. 23:21.22.23, it occurs predominantly in Priestly passages (Exod. 12:48; Num. 9:2.4.5.6.10.13.14.14) or late compositions such as Ezra (6:19), Chronicles (2 Chron. 30:1.2.5; 35:16.17.18.18.19), 11QTemple[a] col. XVII–XVIII, and in the Elephantine Passover Papyrus (recto, line 4) in its Aramaic equivalent עבד פסחא.[215] By contrast, in the Deuteronomistic legislation with respect to Passover (Deut. 16:2.5.6), the domi-

---

[211] See section 7.2.2 above. See further S. MOWINCKEL, *Tetrateuch-Pentateuch-Hexateuch*, p. 57ff.; H. HAAG, *Vom alten zum neuen Pascha*, p. 67; N. LOHFINK, Die Priesterschrift und die Geschichte, p. 198, n. 29; J. BLENKINSOPP, The Structure of P, p. 288; the 'Forschungsgeschichte' in M. ROSE, *Deuteronomist und Jahwist*, pp. 25–28; H. SEEBASS, Josua, *BN* 28 (1985), pp. 53–65, especially p. 64; K. GRÜNWALDT, *Exil und Identität*, pp. 118–121.

[212] See the commentaries and also the studies devoted to the history of the Passover festival mentioned above in section 7.2.2.

[213] E. OTTO, פָּסַח *pāsaḥ* פֶּסַח *pæsaḥ*, in *ThWAT* VI, col. 676.

[214] K. BIEBERSTEIN, *Josua-Jordan-Jericho*, p. 70. See further R. DE VAUX, *Institutions anciennes* I, p. 278ff.

[215] Cowley 21; B. PORTEN, A. YARDENI, *Textbook of Aramaic Documents 1*, no. A.4.1.

nant verb is זבח, *to sacrifice*, and in the oldest legislative regulations regarding Passover, Exod. 12:21 and 34:25, the verb שׁחט, *to slaughter*, has been employed.[216] The Hebrew text underlying both MT and LXX in Josh. 5:10b is unmistakably of Priestly origin.[217]

A. Dillmann and C. Brekelmans, however, have pointed to the fact that the more common temporal phrase בערב, *in the evening*, has been employed here as in Deut. 16:1, whereas in the Priestly prescriptions regarding Passover (Exod. 12:6, Lev. 23:5, Num. 9:3.5.11; 28:4.8), the precise formulation בין הערבים, *between the two evenings, in the evening twilight*, occurs. This would be a contraindication for our ascribing the verse to a Priestly hand.[218] The phrase, however, hardly reflects any distinctive theological interests,[219] and occurs in other contexts (although all Priestly passages) such as the eating of the *manna* (Exod. 16:12), the daily evening offering (Exod. 29:39.41), and the setting up of the lamps (Exod. 30:8) as well. On the other hand, the phrase בערב also occurs in the Priestly legislation with respect to the eating of the *maṣṣot* in Exod. 12:18 (בראשׁן בארבעה עשׂר יום לחדשׁ בערב תאכלו מצת, *in the first month on the fourteenth day of the month in the evening you will eat maṣṣot*). It would seem, therefore, that the Priestly author of Josh. 5:10b was not so much concerned with the precise moment for the slaughtering of the Passover-lamb as with that of the consuming of the *maṣṣot*.

The clauses following this Priestly opening clause in 5:10b contain other elements that also point to a Priestly (RedP) background

---

[216] Further Ezra 6:20, 2 Chron. 35:15.17; 35:1.6.11. See H. HAAG, *Vom alten zum neuen Pascha*.

[217] J. HALBE, Erwägungen zu Ursprung und Wesen des Mazzotfestes, in *ZAW* 87 (1975), pp. 324–346, suggested that the Priestly redactor who added the date (14.1) in verse 10, also changed the original wording concerning the celebration of Passover into the present Priestly formulations. It is clear, however, that the assumption of such an older, now fully eclipsed version, only serves the need to uphold the desired high antiquity of the Josh. 5:10–12 narrative.

[218] A. DILLMANN, *Die Bücher Numeri, Deuteronomium und Josua*, p. 460; C. BREKELMANS, Joshua V 10–12: Another Approach, p. 94; G. KUHNERT, *Das Gilgalpassah*, p. 72.

[219] Thus E. ALBERS, *Die Quellenberichte in Josua I–XII*, p. 84: 'dieses Anzeichen (d.h. einer deuteronomistischen Hand) würde in diesen Versen ganz allein stehen; jede andere deuteronomistische Spur fehlt. Dagegen könnte ein solche Änderung leicht auf irgend eine Art mit Rücksichtnahme auf das folgende fast gleichlautende בערבות entstanden sein.' Idem G.A. COOKE, *The Book of Joshua*, p. 38: 'The alteration here reveals a late hand of the school of P.' and J. WAGENAAR, The Cessation of Manna. Editorial Frames for the Wilderness Wandering in Exodus 16,35 and Joshua 5,10–12, in *ZAW* 112 (2000), pp. 192–209, especially pp. 199–200.

of the passage 5:10–12. Common to the Priestly and post-Exilic passages Exod. 12:1–20 (verse 15–20), Lev. 23 (verses 4–5), Num. 28 (verse 17), Ezek. 45:21, 2 Chron. 30 (verse 13ff.); 2 Chron. 35 (verse 17); Ezra 6 (verse 22), the Passover Papyrus and 11QTemple[a], is the complete fusion of the two originally distinct festivals of the Passover night proper and the feast of Unleavened Breads. In Josh. 5:10b–11a we also find *Passover* and *maṣṣot* in direct sequence, which is another indication of the Priestly origin of the passage underlying both MT and LXX.[220]

7.4.5.3 *The Relation Between Josh. 5:11 and Lev. 23:1–14*

As noted in section 7.2.2 above, the word in MT-Josh. 5:11 קָלוּי, *roasted grain,* links the passage with Lev. 23:14, one of the few places in the Hebrew Bible where the word recurs (besides Lev. 2:14; 1 Sam. 17:17; 25:18; 2 Sam. 17:28; Ruth 2:14). As many scholars since Steuernagel have pointed out, the combination of מצות and קלוי is unique in the Hebrew Bible, but that need not surprise us, given the low frequency of occurrences of the root קלה I.[221] Nevertheless, it can hardly be coincidental that these two terms occur together within the wider context of a Passover festival (Josh. 5:10b, Lev. 23:4–5), which is held at the entry of the Promised Land (Joshua 3–5, Lev. 23:10), and is connected with the (first) consumption of the products of the land (Josh. 5:11–12; Lev. 23:10–14). Whereas in the Leviticus text these elements of Passover and *maṣṣot* (Lev. 23:1–3.4–8) and regulations concerning the first fruits of the harvest (Lev. 23:9–14) form independent segments, separated from one another by a *petuḥah* between 23:8 and 23:9 and a new narrative introduction in Lev. 23:9 (וידבר יהוה אל־משה לאמר cf. 23:1), the Joshua text contains these elements in a single homogeneous passage. Therefore, it seems most likely that Josh. 5:10(b)–12 is dependent on the Leviticus text in its present composite shape. The *roasted corn* (קלוי) eaten by the Israelites upon entering the Promised Land in Josh. 5:11 then *pars pro toto* stands for all the fresh products of the

[220] So also E. Kutsch, Erwägungen zur Geschichte der Passahfeier und des Massotfestes, in *ZThK* 55 (1958), pp. 1–35, especially pp. 20–21; K. Bieberstein, *Josua-Jordan-Jericho* (see section 7.2.7 above).

[221] M. Rose, *Deuteronomist und Jahwist,* p. 39: 'es zeigt sich schon bei diesen Beispielen, daß man mit einer singulären Wendung so ziemlich alles belegen versuchen kann.'

first harvest of the land (עבור הארץ Josh. 5:11.12) to which the legislation in the Holiness Code (Lev. 17–26)[222] refers.

If Josh. 5:10–12 presupposes the composite text of Lev. 23:1–8.9–14, it need not surprise us, that the chronological element in MT-Josh. 5:11 ממחרת הפסח likewise combines two elements from the two passages in Leviticus 23. As noted above, the passage Lev. 23:11(.15) contains the phrase ממחרת השבת, *on the first day after the sabbat*, which has given rise to widely diverging interpretations, because it follows directly after the regulations for another distinct religious activity to be performed in the same period of the first month of the year. i.e., the Passover-*maṣṣot* festival (Lev. 23:4–5). The author of Josh. 5:10–12 read the two successive regulations in Lev. 23:1–8.9–14 in conjunction. As a consequence, he understood them as specifications of the same, single cultic celebration. Hence he interpreted the phrase in Lev. 23:11 ממחרת השבת in the sense of *the first day after the night of Passover proper*, that is ממחרת הפסח, which is the day that coincides with the second part of the combined Passover-*maṣṣot* festival, the feast of unleavened breads lasting for seven days (Lev. 23:6).[223] The emphatic phrase בעצם היום הזה in MT-Josh. 5:11 then corresponds to the statement in Lev. 23:14,[224] in which the first day on which the consuming of the first fruits takes place, has been underlined with the same expression.

The conclusion, then, must be first that both ממחרת הפסח and בעצם היום הזה refer to the same day of the eating of both the unleavened

[222] The possibility of identifying an independent 'Holiness Code' in Leviticus 17–26 is disputed, compare for instance R. Smend, *Die Entstehung des Alten Testaments*, pp. 59–62, with R. Rendtorff, *Das Alte Testament*, p. 154. Likewise the dating of these chapters before Dtr and the Exile (so J. Joosten, *People and Land in the Holiness Code. An Exegetical Study of the Ideational Framework of the Law in Leviticus 17–26*. (SVT 67) Leiden/New York/Köln 1997) or after (thus e.g. K. Grünwaldt, *Das Heiligkeitsgesetz Leviticus 17–26*. (BZAW 271) Berlin/New York 1999) is disputed. An examination of these questions lies beyond the scope of the present study.

[223] Thus M. Fishbane, *Biblical Interpretation*, pp. 145–151; and further already J. Wellhausen, *Die Composition des Hexateuchs*, p. 123; R. Smend sr., *Die Erzählung des Hexateuch*. Berlin 1912, p. 290; G. Beer, *Pesachim*, pp. 39–40, note 1; W. Rudolph, *Der 'Elohist'*, pp. 179–80. B.J. Malina, *The Palestinian Manna Tradition. The Manna Tradition in the Palestinian Targums and Its Relationship to the New Testament Writings*. (AGJU 7) Leiden 1968, p. 30, calls the passage a 'halakic midrash'; M. Rose, *Deuteronomist und Jahwist*, p. 40ff.

[224] With the exception of Josh. 10:27 this exact temporal modifier עצם היום further recurs in the Hebrew Bible only in passages of a distinctly Priestly origin, i.e., in Gen. 7:13; 17:23.26; Exod. 12:17.41.51; Lev. 23:21.28.29.30; Deut. 32:48; Ezek. 2:3; 24:2.2; 40:1.

bread and the roasted grain as first product of the harvest, and secondly that these phrases are best understood within the context of the whole passage Josh. 5:10–12 as a literary creation dependent on Lev. 23:1–8 and Lev. 23:9–14; thus they form an integral part of these verses.

Furthermore, the phrase ממחרת הפסח recurs in the Hebrew Bible only in Num. 33:3, also a passage of distinctively Priestly origin,[225] as an indication of the starting point for Israel's journey through the desert (ממחרת הפסח יצאו בני־ישׂראל). As a result, the use of the exact same phrase in Josh. 5:11–12 also forms an inclusio, on the Priestly level, with this passage in Num. 33:3.

7.4.5.4 *The Relation Between Josh. 5:12 and Exod. 16:35*

In Josh. 5:12 the consuming (אכל 12b.d) of the produce of the land (12b עבור הארץ, 12d תבואת ארץ כנען) replaces that of the *manna* (12a וישבת המן 12c ולא־היה עוד . . . מן). Normal food harvested from the land takes the place of the unusual food of the wilderness. This verse contains a doublet. Clauses 12c–d repeat almost all elements from 12a–b, but mention the recipients of the *manna* (לבני ישׂראל), and the name of the land ארץ כנען (12c):

a–b	ממחרת באכלם מעבור הארץ	וישבת המן
c–d	ויאכלו מתבואת ארץ כנען בשׁנה ההיא	ולא־היה עוד לבני ישׂראל מן

There are two sets of contrasting elements in the two lines: Line 5:12d has the more general temporal indication בשׁנה ההיא, *in that year*, whereas 5:12a contains the more precise temporal phrase ממחרת, *on the following day*. Furthermore, the two clauses contain two synonymous words for *produce* עבור (5:12b, cf. 5:11) and תבואה (5:12d). The former word recurs in the Hebrew Bible only in the preceding verse Josh. 5:11, but is well attested in Semitic languages, from Old-Assyrian and Old-Babylonian Akkadian,[226] Northwest Semitic epi-

---

[225] See e.g. B. BAENTSCH, *Exodus, Leviticus und Numeri*, p. 672ff.; P.J. BUDD, *Numbers*, pp. 347–357.

[226] See HALOT, pp. 777b–778a; M. ROSE, *Deuteronomist und Jahwist*, p. 36, n. 68; I.J. GELB, T. JACOBSEN, B. LANDSBERGER, A.L. OPPENHEIM, *The Assyrian Dictionary of the Oriental Institute of the University of Chicago. Volume 4: E.* Chicago/Glückstadt 1958, pp. 16b–20b: *ebūru: harvest; crop; harvest time; summer.* M. ROSE, *Deuteronomist und Jahwist*, p. 36, n. 68; and J. WAGENAAR, The Cessation of Manna, p. 204, refer to the Old Babylonian phrase *ebūr māt nakrīka takal, you shall eat the produce of the land of your*

graphic languages,[227] and epigraphic Old Hebrew (attested in an Old-Hebrew ostracon from Arad dating from the second half of the seventh century BCE)[228] onwards up to Egyptian Aramaic,[229] Jewish Aramaic,[230] and Syriac.[231] The reverse seems to be the case for the related word תבואה: well attested within the Hebrew Bible (43 times), but without clear cognates in the other Semitic languages.[232] Interestingly, the somewhat general description *there was no more manna* (ולא־היה עוד מן 5:12c) is preceded in 5:12a by the parallel, but stricter expression וישבת המן, *the manna ceased*. The employment of the verb שׁבת, which occurs predominantly in Exilic or post-Exilic texts,[233] may be seen in connection with the phrase ממחרת השבת in Lev. 23:11.15,[234] as well as the interdiction of any strenuous work particularly on this first day of the *maṣṣot*-festival as prescribed in Lev. 23:7.[235]

The verse forms an *inclusio* with the conclusion of the manna narrative in Exod. 16(:35), and thereby establishes a link between the exodus and entry into the desert (Exodus 16) on the one hand and

---

enemies, in an omen text (AO 7033) published by J. NOUGAYROL, Textes héptatoscopiques d'époque ancienne, conservés au Musée du Louvre (II), in *Revue d'Assyriologie et d'archéologie orientale* 40 (1945–46), pp. 56–98, especially p. 85, which presents an interesting parallel to our passage in Josh. 5:10–12.

[227] See J. HOFTIJZER, K. JONGELING, *Dictionary of the North-West Semitic Inscriptions*. II Leiden 1995, pp. 822–823. It is disputed whether the word *lʿbrm* in KTU 1.22.I.15 *k.ksp.lʿbrm.zt.ḫrṣ.lʿbrm.kš* contains the same lexeme, as suggested by C. GORDON, *Ugaritic Textbook*. (Analecta Orientalia) Roma 1965, § 19:1871. G. DEL OLMO LETE, J. SANMARTÍN, W.G.E. WATSON, *A Dictionary of the Ugaritic Language in the Alphabetic Tradition. Part One*. Leiden/Boston 2003, p. 145, list the word under *ʿbr* I 'passenger, guest'.

[228] See J. RENZ, *Die althebräischen Inschriften. Teil I. Text und Kommentar*. Darmstadt 1995, pp. 290–292: Arad Ostracon 31.

[229] See B. PORTEN, A. YARDENI, *Textbook of Aramaic Documents 1*, no. A 6.15, lines 5–6.

[230] See J. LEVY, *Chaldäisches Wörterbuch über die Targumim*. Leipzig 1868, p. 200b; M. JASTROW, *A Dictionary of the Targumim, The Talmud Babli and Yerushalmi, and the Midrashic Literature*, p. 1066a–b; M. SOKOLOFF, *A Dictionary of Jewish Palestinian Aramaic*. Ramat-Gan 1992², p. 393a. See also Targum Jonathan to Josh. 5:11–12 וַאֲכָלוּ מֵעֲבוּרָא דְאַרְעָא.

[231] See P-S p. 398a. See also Peš-Josh. 5:11–12 ܘܐܟܠܘ ܡܢ ܥܒܘܪܐ ܕܐܪܥܐ.

[232] See HALOT, pp. 1678b–1679b. G. LISOWSKY, *Konkordanz*, p. 1505a–b. The noun does not occur in the epigraphic corpus, but occurs once in the (non-biblical) Qumran-manuscripts, i.e., in two copies of the *Sefer ha-Milchamah* 4Q285, frg. 1, line 8 = 11Q14 frg. 1, col. II, line 12 (text and translation: F. GARCÍA MARTÍNEZ, E.J.C. TIGCHELAAR, *The Dead Sea Scrolls Study Edition*. 2, pp. 1210–1211): שדפון וירקון לוא יראה בתבואתיה, *drought and blight will not be seen in its harvests*.

[233] See F. STOLZ, שׁבת *šbt* aufhören, ruhen, in *ThHAT* II, col. 863–869.

[234] M. FISHBANE, *Biblical Interpretation*, p. 148: 'The phrase וישבת המן ממחרת 'and the manna ceased on the morrow' is an unmistakable allusion to the Pentateuchal expression ממחרת השבת in Lev. 23:11.'

[235] So B.J. MALINA, *The Palestinian Manna Tradition*, p. 30.

entry into the land of Israel (Joshua 5) on the other hand. As in Josh. 5:12 the manna-statement occurs twice, the first time with the more general geographical description ארץ נושבת, *inhabitable land*, which does not correspond exactly to the land of Israel, but could include other habitable regions east of the Jordan as well, a second time described very precisely as קצה ארץ כנען, *the border of the land Canaan*. Exod. 16:35b thus represents a secondary correction that sought to secure the proper understanding of Exod. 16:35a.[236]

35a	ובני ישראל אכלו את־המן ארבעים שנה עד־באם אל־ ארץ נושבת
35b	את־המן אכלו עד־באם אל־קצה ארץ כנען

Several scholars have pointed to the correspondence between Exod. 16:35 and Josh. 5:12d with respect to the unambiguous but colourless name of the Promised Land: *land of Canaan*,[237] which has been employed frequently by the Priestly writers in the Pentateuch and Joshua.[238] In that case, the occurrences here in Josh. 5:12d and Exod. 16:35 would be additional indications for the Priestly origin of the passages involved, or in both cases (Exod. 16:35b and Josh. 5:12c–d) a Priestly editing of a pre-Priestly passage (Exod. 16:35a, Josh. 5:12a–b). In the latter case, we would have a contraindication of the Priestly origin of at least Josh. 5:12a–b,[239] or otherwise a succession of post-Priestly layers,[240] or two parallel Priestly narratives.[241]

[236] See M. Rose, *Deuteronomist und Jahwist*, p. 50: 'Dieses Stilmittel [i.e., of a chiastic repetition] wird hier dazu benutzt, in einer Glosse (V.35b) einen korrigierend-weiterführenden Fingerzeig dafür zu geben, wie die Aussage des der Interpretation vorliegenden Textes (V.35a) nun richtig verstanden werden müsse. Der Erläuterer will sicherstellen, daß die ארץ נושבת nicht schon das Ostjordanland meint—dem man die Charakterisierung ארץ נושבת nicht absprechen kann—, sondern daß das Manna als Wüstenspeise bis an den Rand des Landes Kanaan, des Westjordanlands, gereicht hat.'

[237] See e.g. E. Zenger, *Die Sinaitheophanie. Untersuchungen zum jahwistischen und elohistischen Geschichtswerk.* (FzB 3) Würzburg 1971, p. 137; E. Otto, *Das Mazzotfest in Gilgal*, p. 92, who ascribes both Josh. 5:12a–b/5:12c–d and Exod. 16:35b to J; M. Rose, *Deuteronomist und Jahwist*, pp. 36–38; C. Brekelmans, Joshua v 10–12: Another Approach, pp. 92–93; J. Wagenaar, The Cessation of Manna, pp. 195–197.

[238] Gen. 17:8, 23:2.19; 35:6; 48:3.7; Exod. 6:4; Lev. 14:34; 18:3; 25:38; Num. 13:2.17; 26:19; 32:30.32; 33:40.51; 34:2.2.29; 35:10.14; Deut. 32:49; and Josh. 14:1; 21:2; 22:9.10.11.32. See e.g. R. Smend, *Die Entstehung des Alten Testaments*, pp. 47–49, 58. See further section 4.2.3 above.

[239] See e.g. E. Otto, *Das Mazzotfest in Gilgal*, p. 92; G. Kuhnert, *Das Gilgalpassah*, pp. 75–76; V. Fritz, *Das Buch Josua*, p. 61.

[240] H. Holzinger, *Das Buch Josua*, p. 13, ascribed verses 10 and 12b to P^G, 11–12a to P^S and considered the phrases וקלוי, ממחרת הפסח and ממחרת to be even younger interpolations.

[241] Thus G. von Rad, *Die Priesterschrift im Hexateuch.* (BWANT 13) Stuttgart 1934,

Nevertheless, the name alone does not *per se* point to a Priestly hand, since the pre-Priestly author(s) of passages such as Gen. 12:5.5; 13:12; 16:3; 31:18; 33:18; 42:5.7.13.29.32; 44:8; 45:17.25; 46:6.12.31 and Josh. 24:3 also employ the ancient name.[242] It is therefore also possible to regard Josh. 5:12c–d as the original conclusion to Josh. 5:9, which triggered the late Priestly correction of Josh. 5:10(b)–12a–c, as suggested by W. Rudolph.[243] In that case, the use of the rare noun עבור should not be seen as a relic of an ancient term (in spite of the epigraphic evidence), explained by the word תבואה by the Priestly redactor, as Wagenaar has argued,[244] but as an Aramaism and thus a relatively late element.[245] Likewise, the *renominalisation* of the Israelites in 5:12c, which—strictly taken—is unnecessary in the context of Josh. 5:10–12a–b, as there are no other agents, now becomes more functional after Josh. 5:9 where Joshua is the main agent. The phrase בשנה ההיא in 5:12d (pre-P) then refers directly to ארבעים שנה in Exod. 16:35a (likewise pre-P).

If Josh. 5:12a–b is part of a (late) Priestly correction of a pre-Priestly note found in Josh. 5:12c–d, we are not dealing with a geographical correction (*land of Canaan* 5:12d for *land* 5:12b),[246] but rather with a temporal correction, in which the general phrase בשנה ההיא, *in that year*, is corrected to a very specific day: *the following day while they were eating* ממחרת באכלם מעבור הארץ (5:12a–b). Because this phrase

pp. 146–147. His main thesis of two parallel Priestly narratives (P[A] and P[B]) has not convinced other scholars, and even in his later works, (e.g., G. von Rad, *Theologie des Alten Testaments*. I, p. 245ff. ('Die Priesterschrift') Von Rad, no longer upheld his former thesis.

[242] See H.-J. Zobel, כְּנַעַן *k^ena'an* כְּנַעֲנִי *k^ena'^anî*, in *ThWAT* IV, col. 224–243.

[243] W. Rudolph, *Der 'Elohist'*, pp. 179–180: 'v.12 wendet sich gegen Ex 16_{35}: nicht schon an der Grenze von Kanaan, sondern wegen Lev $23_{10ff.}$ erst einige Tage nach dem Betreten des heiligen Landes hörte das Manna auf. [. . .] auf Grund von Ex 16_{35} war zunächst an 5_9 die harmlose Bemerkung $5_{12a\beta.b}$ [5:12c–d] angefügt, daß mit dem Übertritt nach Kanaan das Manna aufhörte. Aber das brachte nun einen genauen Gesetzeskenner in Harnisch: so einfach war die Sache nicht, erst mußte durch die Passahfeier die nach Lev 23 notwendige Vorbedingung für den Genuß der Landesfrucht geschaffen werden, deshalb fügte er davor (4_{19a}+) $5_{10-12a\alpha}$ ein. Da schon Ex 16_{35} und demnach Jos $5_{12a\beta.b}$ später Text ist, muß der davon abhängige Einschub Jos $5_{10-12a\alpha}$ erst recht spät sein, wie er denn auch bereits Lev 23 in seiner heutigen Zusammensetzung voraussetzt.'

[244] J. Wagenaar, The Cessation of Manna, p. 201. Wagenaar ascribes Josh. 5:11 to the Deuteronomist, 5:12aα to the Jahwist, which he considers to be a post-Deuteronomistic redactor, in line with Van Seters' revision of the Newer Documentary hypothesis (see section 4.2.4 above), and 5:12aβb to the Priestly redactor.

[245] Thus also H. Holzinger, *Das Buch Josua*, p. 13; M. Rose, *Deuteronomist und Jahwist*, pp. 35–37; K. Grünwaldt, *Exil und Identität*, p. 119.

[246] So M. Rose, *Deuteronomist und Jahwist*, pp. 37–38.

repeats 5:11 ויאכלו מעבור הארץ, and because the preposition בְּ has been employed here (according to MT) which primarily indicates synchronism (*when*) rather than chronological sequence (*after*),[247] the day indicated by ממחרת must be the same day as the one indicated twice in MT-Josh. 5:11: ממחרת הפסח and בעצם היום הזה, rather than yet a third day, the 16th of the first month.[248] By mentioning this day for a third time, all emphasis in this short passage falls on the proper sequence *Exodus—entry into the desert—consuming of the manna during the desert period—entry into the land of Canaan—Passover—maṣṣot—consuming of the first products of the land.*

The temporal phrases in MT-Josh. 5:11–12 ממחרת באכלם—בעצם היום הזה—ממחרת הפסח all point to the same day: the 15th of Nisan, the day following the nocturnal sacrifice of the Passover lamb, the day that marks the start of the festival of *maṣṣot*, and also the first day of the period in which the eating of the first fruits is allowed. The short passage 5:10–12b should be seen in its entirety as a late Priestly addition to the text of Joshua, created by a scribe that sought to adjust the Joshua narratives to the Priestly legislation of Leviticus 23 in its present composite form. Probably Josh. 5:12c–d should be regarded as the older, pre-Priestly note that triggered the correction of 5:10–12b. In any case, it has become clear that the temporal elements in verses 11–12 which are absent from LXX or reflected in a different way (as far as the position of בעצם היום הזה in verse 11 (MT)/verse 12 (LXX) is concerned), are well understood against this specific background. On the basis of these redaction-critical observations, there is no support for the thesis of a post-Priestly revision of an alleged Hebrew *Vorlage* of the LXX towards the present MT (*pace* Bieberstein). All surgery on the present text that extracts these elements along with other admittedly Priestly elements such as the date in 5:10b (so Noth, Kraus, Soggin, Otto, Kuhnert and others), is biased by a preconceived idea of an ancient cultic festival at Gilgal,[249] disregards the specific purpose of the entire passage, makes only selective use of text-critical data, and is therefore to be dismissed.

---

[247] See BDB, pp. 90b–91a; HALOT, pp. 103a–105b.

[248] See section 7.6.8.1 below.

[249] See the criticism by M. Rose, *Deuteronomist und Jahwist*, pp. 25–45; K. Bieberstein, *Josua-Jordan-Jericho*, pp. 70–71, 210–223.

7.4.6 *Conclusions*

The phrases in MT-Josh. 5:2–12 that are missing or different in LXX-Josh. 5:2–12 cannot be isolated from their immediate literary contexts. Rather, a literary-critical analysis of the verses *in its own right* shows how much phrases such as שוב—שנית (5:2c.d), ממחרת הפסח (5:11), ממחרת (5:12), and כי־מלים היו כל־העם היצאים (5:5a–b), are embedded in their immediate context.

This does not mean that these verses form a single literary entity, but rather that the different literary strata in the Hebrew text do not correspond to the variants posed by the Greek text. We have discerned three literary strata in this segment: [1] (4:21–24–) 5:1–8, which are the product of the Deuteronomistic (DtrH) author/editor of the book (sections 7.4.1–4.3), [2] 5:9, which is to be read independently of the immediately preceding context and possibly reflects remnants of a pre-Deuteronomistic stratum (JE?) to which in all likelihood 5:12c–d should also be ascribed (sections 7.4.4, 7.4.5), and [3] 5:10–12b, a Priestly (RedP) 'halakic midrash' based on Lev. 23:1–8.9–14 (section 7.4.5).

In the oldest layer, 5:9.12c–d, the entry into the land of Canaan is described as the removal of the Egyptian humiliation, which refers to Israel's slavery in Egypt and the humiliation of the Egyptians about Israel's misery in the desert (section 7.4.4). This theological interpretation is presented as an aetiology for the circle of stones at Gilgal (Josh. 4:18–19). Since in the view of the pre-Exilic prophets Amos and Hosea the site was connected with idolatry and since the site was deserted or destroyed perhaps already before the time of the Exile, it is hard to see why a scribe from a later period would have wanted to introduce this place here in Josh. 5:12, as well as in related pluses in MT *vis-à-vis* LXX (Josh. 10:15.43) and thereby wilfully have created the logical tension between Josh. 5:12–5:8 and 10:15.43 versus 10:21, merely for the sake of pedantry (Auld). Furthermore, the entry into the land is accompanied by the change from the miraculous desert food (*the manna*) to the 'normal' food produced by the land (Josh. 5:12c–d).

For the Deuteronomist, the final fulfilment of the divine promise to the patriarchs formed a good opportunity to recall the main Deuteronomistic themes of divine promise and human (dis-)obedience (Josh. 5:6). This new beginning was expressed by means of the reinstatement of the ancient *rite de passage* that marks the transition from infancy to adolescence.[250] The literary phrasing of this act shows the conventional emphatic and redundant Deuteronomistic style and phraseology, with an extensive retrospective section (4–7), and portrays the action of the single leader (Joshua), who circumcises all male Israelites, so that a complete hill of foreskins could be heaped up (3). In order to give this literary fiction some place in a narrative of conquest, the Deuteronomistic writer postponed the threat posed by Israel's enemies by having them paralysed by fear of the Jordan miracle (Josh. 5:1 anticipated by 4:21–24). In order to express this notion of a new start in the Promised Land, the Deuteronomistic writer introduced the notion that the disobedient older generation—though circumcised themselves—neglected the practice of circumcising their sons, so that Joshua is in the position to circumcise the Israelites *anew*. The phrases שׁוב . . . שׁנית fit this idea, as does the simple division of the Israelite male population into [1] an older generation, which happened to be circumcised and found their end in the desert because of their disobedience and [2] the younger generation that was born on the way, whom the older generation did not circumcise. Both groups are alternatingly described as כל־העם (group 1: 4c, 5a; group 2: 5c) and כל־הגוי (group 1: 6b; group 2: 8c). The phrase that forms the sharp contradiction with LXX, MT-Josh. 5:5a–b, does not aim at an exoneration of this disobedient older generation (Holmes, Auld), nor at an orthodoxification of Israel's past (Mazor), but simply provides the background for the subsequent statements, narrating the need for Joshua's circumcision.

A scribe from the Priestly school added his own view on the appropriate entry into the land, i.e. compliance with the Holiness Code, Leviticus 23. Before the Israelites could enjoy the new fruits (including the קלוי) of the land, the festival of Passover—*maṣṣot*—presentation of the first fruits (based on a harmonising reading of Lev. 23:1–8 and 23:9–14) had to be held at the proper times (Josh. 4:19; 5:10). To this end, this late Priestly writer introduced the short segment recording the first Passover in the land, which he connected to the older text by means of the resumptive repetition of Josh. 4:19 ויחנו

[250] See e.g. G.A. Cooke, *The Book of Joshua*, p. 37; C. Westermann, *Genesis II*, pp. 319–320; W.H. Schmidt, *Exodus*, pp. 228–229: 'Exkurs 2. Zur Beschneidung'; K. Grünwaldt, *Exil und Identität*, p. 9: 'Religionsgeschichtlich handelt es sich bei der Beschneidung in Jos 5,2–9 um einen Ritus des Übergangs (rite de passage).' See further *in extenso* A. Blaschke, *Beschneidung*, pp. 12–15, 40–44.

בני־ישׂראל בלגל. The repeated reference to the first day of the *maṣṣot* festival, which corresponds to the first day of freedom from Egyptian slavery (Num. 33:3), ממחרת באכלם מעבור הארץ—בעצם היום הזה—ממחרת הפסח secure that the new generation of Israelites make their start in the new land in a proper manner, in accordance with the ideology of the Holiness Code. The orthodoxification of Israel's past should therefore not be sought in Josh. 5:5a–b, but rather in this segment.

Again, an independent redaction-critical analysis of the Hebrew text does not support the thesis of a revision of the text reflected by the ancient witnesses. By contrast, a study of the passages under discussion within their Hebrew context helps to get a sharper perspective on the character of the Hebrew passages and the underlying process of their formation. Such an analysis makes clear where the real literary-critical 'seams' between the different layers are to be found (5:8–5:9; 5:9–5:10; 5:12b–5:12c). Such fractures call for creative interpretations for people who found the Hebrew text in its present composite state and were unaware (or uninterested) in the formation process of the text, but set themselves the task to create a faithful, but sensible new version of the passage in a completely different language, as the Greek translators of the Hebrew Bible did.

7.5 The Qumran Witnesses: 4QJoshua[A] and the Damascus Document

Before we can proceed to examine the Greek text in its own right (section 7.6), it is necessary to sort out two minor questions with respect to the testimony of the 4QJoshua[a] text and the allusion to Josh. 5:6 in the (Cairo Genizah) Damascus Document CD[B] XX (see section 7.4.2.1 above). In both cases, the Qumran (or Cairo Genizah) texts have been adduced to support the argument in favour of the existence of a Hebrew text deviating from MT and reflected by LXX. A reconstruction of the text of 4QJosh[a] would leave no room for the word שׁנית (Josh. 5:2), whereas CD[B] XX would provide a Hebrew witness to the LXX minus הגוי in Josh. 5:6.

7.5.1 *4QJoshua[a]*

Fragments of the Hebrew text of Josh. 5:2–7 have been preserved on fragments 1 and 2 of 4QJosh[a]. Eugene Ulrich has demonstrated that the small Qumran fragment IAA 329.237 should be connected to the larger fragment containing the text of Josh. 8:34–35; 5:x; 5:2–3 (PAM 41.201).[251] The IAA photograph of fragment 2 is not very clear, but according to Ulrich, the joint between the two fragments has been confirmed by an enhanced digital image of the edges of these fragments, produced by G. Bearman and B. and K. Zuckermann.[252] Ulrich's reconstruction of the complete Hebrew text of the column of 4QJosh[a] to which these two fragments (now labelled 4QJosh[a] fragments 1–2) belong, has been reproduced below. The outline font indicates reconstructed letters. The contours of the extant fragments have been imitated by means of a computer drawing. On the right-hand side the line numbers have been indicated; on the left-hand side a calculation of the length of the line in question is given, as the sum of letters and spaces (labelled 'letterspaces'). A reconstruction of the contours of fragment 2 is not useful here, since the relative position of the words in lines 5–11 do not completely correspond to those preserved on fragment 2.

4QJoshua[a] Column I: Joshua 8:34–35; 5:x; 5:2ff.:
Reconstruction after Ulrich

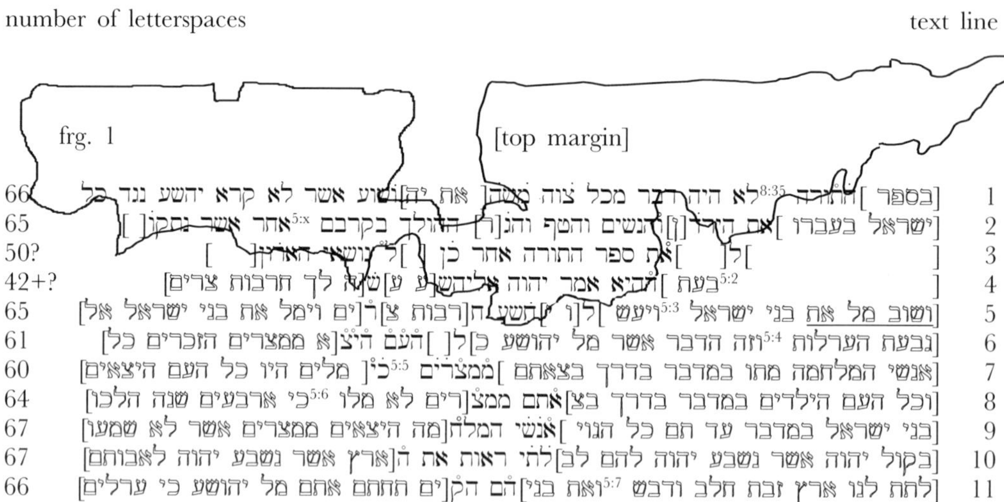
number of letterspaces
text line
frg. 1
[top margin]
66 [בספר]התורה 8:35לא היה דבר מכל צוה משה] את יה]ושע אשר לא קרא יהשע נגד כל 1
65 [ישראל בעברו]את הירד[ן] הנשים והטף והג[ר ההולך בקרבם 5:xאחר אשר נתקו[ ] 2
50? [ ]ל[ ]ל[ ]את ספר התורה אחר כן [ ]ל נושאי הארון[ ] 3
42+? [ ]5:2בעת]ההיא אמר יהוה אל יהושע ע]שה לך חרבות צרים] 4
65 [ושוב מל את בני ישראל 5:3ויעש]ל[ו י]הושע ח[רבות צ]רים וימל את בני ישראל אל] 5
61 [גבעת הערלות 5:4וזה הדבר אשר מל יהושע כ]ל[ ]העם היצ[א ממצרים הזכרים כל] 6
60 [אנשי המלחמה מתו במדבר בדרך בצאתם]ממצרים 5:5כי[מלים היו כל העם היצאים] 7
64 [וכל העם הילדים במדבר בדרך בצ]אתם ממצ[רים לא מלו 5:6כי ארבעים שנה הלכו] 8
67 [בני ישראל במדבר עד תם כל הגוי]אנשי המלח[מה היצאים ממצרים אשר לא שמעו] 9
67 [בקול יהוה אשר נשבע יהוה להם לב]לתי ראות את ה[ארץ אשר נשבע יהוה לאבותם] 10
66 [לתת לנו ארץ זבת חלב ודבש 5:7ואת בני]הם הק[ים תחתם אתם מל יהושע כי ערלים] 11

[251] E. Ulrich, Joshua's First Altar, pp. 89–104, idem, 4QJosh[a], pp. 143–152, and plate XXXII. See further section 3.2 above.

[252] E. Ulrich, 4QJosh[a], p. 145; plate XXXII.

Leaving aside the intriguing opening lines 1–3 containing the text of Josh. 8:34–35+5:x,[253] the complete text of the subsequent lines 4 to 11 may be fully reconstructed on the basis of the Hebrew text of MT, if one postulates a *setumah* at the beginning of line 4.[254]

As noted in section 3.2, 4QJosh[a] supports the MT *vis-à-vis* LXX with the possible exception of the variant ראות (Qal) *vis-à-vis* הראותם (Hiphʿil plus suffix) in MT.[255] An exception to this general characterisation would be posed by lines 4–5, which in Ulrich's view leave no room for the text-critically disputed phrase שֵׁנית in Josh. 5:2.[256] He nevertheless reconstructed the corresponding imperative as ושוב. A reconstruction of the end of line 4 (42 [+?] letterspaces), however, leaves enough room for the short words ושוב מל את, so that in line 5 the words preceding the ל, the stroke of which is clearly visible on the fragment,[257] can be reconstructed as בני ישראל שנית 5:3ויעש, that is, including the disputed word שֵׁנית:

[253] See chapter 9 below.

[254] It is also possible that the editorial bridge between lines 1–2 and Josh. 5:2 (designated by Ulrich as 5:x) continued on line 4. In this reconstruction, however, fragments 1 and 2 do not correspond as neatly as on the photo (DJD XIV, plate XXII), where the *lamedh* of ל[כ] in line 6 is immediately below the *shin* of הושע[י] in line 5. Furthermore, the extant words of lines 5–11 on fragment 2 are right above each other, not in the curve the reconstruction above seems to suggest. This discrepancy between reconstructed and physical text may be the result of the fact that a standard Hebrew font has been used to simulate the extant letters, or the result of physical detoriation of the leather of fragment 2. It is also possible that the first half of line 6 was somewhat shorter than the present reconstructed text (perhaps the subject יהושע was lacking). Since LXX does not contain minuses here, the matter is not relevant for our discussion.

[255] See E. Ulrich, 4QJosh[a], p. 148, and further the discussion in section 7.6.4.4 below.

[256] E. Ulrich, Joshua's First Altar, p. 99: 'The length of the line [line 5] suggests that this MS, like LXX, probably lacked שנית (LXX).'; Idem E. Ulrich, 4QJosh[a] (DJD 14), p. 147.

[257] See DJD 14, plate XXXII, PAM 41.201.

4QJoshua[a] Column I: Joshua 8:34–35; 5:x; 5:2ff.

number of letterspaces | text line

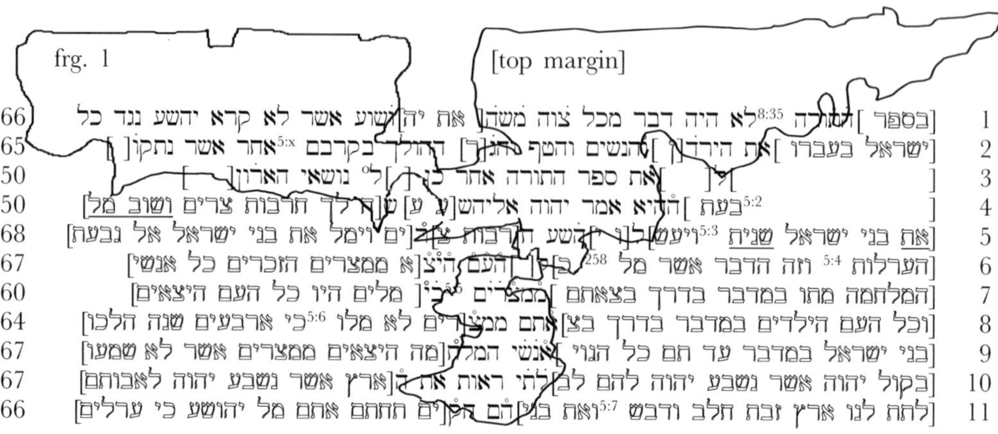

The totals for the letterspaces in lines 4 and 5 (50 and 67 letterspaces respectively) still corresponds to those of lines 1 (66 letterspaces), 2 (65), 7 (65), 9 (67), 10 (67), 11 (66), and 12 (67). In other words, there is no reason to assume that 4QJoshua[a] did not present the text as found in MT for this place as well, that is, including the phrase שֵׁנִית.

With the minor exception of the stem of the verb ראה in Josh. 5:6, the MT of Josh. 5:2ff. is supported by the oldest extant witness to the text of Joshua. The text of 4QJosh[a] does not support the retroversions from LXX to a Hebrew *Vorlage*, as proposed by Holmes, Auld, and Mazor. This does not exclude the possibility that the Greek text reflects another Hebrew text, but it does not support that thesis either.

7.5.2 *The Damascus Document*

In a recent article in *Revue de Qumran*, Birgit Lucassen has drawn attention to the fact that the passage in the Damascus Document, CD[B] Col. XX, lines 14–15: עד תם כל אנשי המלחמה, does not con-

[258] The subject יהושע has been omitted in this reconstruction for reasons given above in note 254.

tain the word הגוי in a phrase that alludes to Josh. 5:6.[259] Since the Greek version of Josh. 5:6 does not reflect the word הגוי either, Lucassen suggests that the text in CD reflects a pre-Masoretic Hebrew text of Josh. 5:6 that is identical with the alleged Hebrew *Vorlage* of LXX-Joshua. Since the period of forty years of penitence corresponds to Josh. 5:6 (MT, not LXX) as opposed to Deut. 2:14, which reckons with thirty-eight years, the allusion in CD^{B} XX must be to Josh. 5:6 rather than to the Deuteronomy text, thus Lucassen:

Josh. 5^{6}	כי ארבעים שנה הלכו בני־ישׂראל במדבר
Deut. 2^{14}	והימים אשר־הלכנו . . . שלשים ושמנה שנה
CD^{B} XX	ומיום $^{1.14}$ האסף יורה היחיד
Josh. 5^{6}	עד־תם כל־הגוי אנשי האלחמה היצאים ממצרים
Deut. 2^{14}	עד־תם כל־הדור אנשי המלחמה . . .
CD^{B} XX	עד תם כל אנשי המלחמה . . . כשנים ארבעים.

Lucassen finds literary-critical support for her thesis that both LXX and CD attest to an original formulation in Josh. 5:6: עד־תם כל אנשי המלחמה היצאים ממצרים in the observation that the noun גוי usually refers to a foreign, non-Israelite nation, a thesis she does not substantiate.[260] The motive for the redactor would have been to portray Israel as a nation.[261]

As we have seen, however, in section 7.4.2.3 above, the word הגוי has no literary-critical value in Josh. 5:6 or elsewhere in the book of Joshua. In Josh. 3:17, 4:1, 5:6.8, and 10:13 it is just a term to designate the entity called Israel. One wonders, furthermore, who would be interested in altering the authoritative text only for the purpose of portraying Israel as a nation with a term that in biblical writing is regarded as somewhat pejorative? Lucassen is cautious enough to stress that this thesis must remain hypothetical because the text in the Damascus Document does not contain a direct quotation, and since the designation of this group of men siding with the wrong party as גוי would be out of place.[262] It thus seems highly

---

[259] B. Lucassen, Josua, Richter und CD, in *Revue de Qumran* 18/3 (1998), pp. 373–396, especially pp. 376–378.

[260] B. Lucassen, Josua, Richter und CD, p. 377: 'Dieser Befund ist insofern interessant, als es auch bei den meisten der restliche Belege, wo die Wendung כל הגוי bezogen auf Israel vorkommt, Hinweise darauf gibt, daß dieser Begriff einen sekundären Zusatz darstellt.'

[261] B. Lucassen, Josua, Richter und CD, p. 377.

[262] B. Lucassen, Josua, Richter und CD, p. 377.

questionable to make such an exclusive connection between Joshua 5 and a text that clearly only alludes to the Hebrew Bible rather than quoting it directly. It would rather seem that the author made a general allusion to the theme of the forty years punishment, in the same way that Deut. 2:16 and Num. 32:13 (a text she did not mention and where we also find the number of 40 years) do:

Deut. 2^{16}	ויהי כאשר־
Num. 32^{13}	ויחר־אף יהוה בישׂראל וינעם במדבר ארבעים שׁנה
Deut. 2^{16}	תמו כל־אנשׁי המלחמה למות מקרב העם:
Num. 32^{13}	עד־תם כל־הדור העשׂה הרע בעיני יהוה:

Finally, in her article Lucassen pays no attention to the Greek text of Joshua itself, which differs from MT in more respects than only this minor qualitative issue, but simply refers to the studies by Holmes and Orlinsky in order to claim an overall fidelity of the Greek translator to his parent text.[263] In fact, the two versions of Josh. 5:6b agree only with respect to the element 'warriors' המלחמה—τῶν μαχίμων. Thus, this text does not provide undisputed evidence of a Hebrew *Vorlage* of LXX differing from MT. The Greek version of Joshua 5 rather deserves a thorough study in its own right before it is used for literary-critical purposes.

7.6 The Greek Version of Joshua 5:2–12

Below follows a literal translation of the Greek version of Joshua 5:2–12. Passages where Margolis' edition differs from Rahlfs' will be discussed below in the following paragraph. Variants of LXX *vis-à-vis* MT are marked in this translation by italics or three hyphens per word in MT absent in LXX.

5^{2} *About this time* the Lord said to Jesous: 'Make for yourself rocky knives *from a sharp rock* and *having sat down*, circumcise the sons of Israel ---.'

5^{3} And Jesous made --- *sharp* rocky knives and circumcised the sons of Israel *at the place called Hill of the Tops of shame* (Foreskins).

---

[263] B. Lucassen, Josua, Richter und CD, p. 377, note 10.

5[4] *Thus* Jesous *purified* the sons of Israel *all around: as many as were born on*
the way and as many as were uncircumcised of those who had gone out of Egypt,
5[5] *all these Jesous circumcised.*
5[6] Since for forty-*two* years --- --- Israel had dwelt in the desert *of Madbaritis,*
on which account were *uncircumcised most of them*, i.e., the warriors --- that
had gone out of *the land of* Egypt, the ones who had *disobeyed the com-*
mandments of God, whom he had *also determined* not to let them see the
land, that the Lord had sworn to their fathers, to give to us, a land
flowing with milk and honey.
5[7] Instead of these he *put* their sons *in their place whom* Jesous circumcised,
because they had been born on the way being uncircumcised. --- ---
--- --- --- --- ---
5[8] Having been circumcised --- ---, *they had rest*, staying there, in the camp,
until they *recovered.*
5[9] The Lord said to Jesous *son of Naue*: 'Today *on this day* I took away
the insult of Egypt from you.' and he called the name of that place
Galgala --- --- ---. --- --- --- --- --- --- --- --- ---
5[10] The *sons of Israel* held the Passover on the fourteenth day of the month
from the evening *in the western* (*region of*) Jericho *at the other side of the*
Jordan in the plain,
5[11] and ate from the *grain* of the land --- --- --- --- unleavened and *new*
(*products*).
5[12] On that day --- --- the manna ceased *after* they had eaten from the
grain of the land, and there was no longer manna at the disposal of
the sons of Israel *but they enjoyed the fruits* of the country *of the Phoenicians*
in that year.

7.6.1 *LXX-Josh. 5:2*

7.6.1.1 *The Temporal Setting*

The Greek text of our passage opens with the phrase ὑπὸ δὲ τοῦτον τὸν καιρόν, *about this time*, which corresponds to the Hebrew phrase בעת ההיא, *at that time.* The particle δέ marks the change of subject. The Greek noun καιρός means *specific time, season, time of festivity, critical time* or *opportunity*,[264] and renders the Hebrew noun עֵת, which signifies a special time of undetermined length.[265] Interestingly, however,

[264] See LEH, p. 222; LSJ, pp. 859b–860a; GELS², pp. 282b–283a; E. Eynikel, K. Hauspie, The Use of καιρός and χρόνος in the Septuagint, in *ETL* 73 (1997), pp. 369–385.
[265] BDB, p. 773; HALOT, pp. 899b–901a.

the Greek translator did not employ the preposition ἐν as a rendering of—בְּ, but used the preposition ὑπό instead, only here in LXX-Joshua employed in a temporal sense. Furthermore, he used the pronoun οὗτος for the Hebrew demonstrative ההיא instead of ἐκεῖνος, as in LXX-Josh. 11:10.21:

11[10]	Καὶ ἀπεστράφη Ἰησοῦς	וַיָּשָׁב יְהוֹשֻׁעַ
	ἐν τῷ καιρῷ ἐκείνῳ	בָּעֵת הַהִיא
11[21]	Καὶ ἦλθεν Ἰησοῦς	וַיָּבֹא יְהוֹשֻׁעַ
	ἐν τῷ καιρῷ ἐκείνῳ	בָּעֵת הַהִיא

The Greek translator did not employ a standard translation for the phrase בעת ההיא either in the four other passages in the book of Joshua where it occurs. In Josh. 8:29 and 10:27 he condensed the phrases referring to sunset:

8[29]	ἕως --- --- ἑσπέρας·	עַד־עֵת הָעֶרֶב
	καὶ ἐπιδύνοντος τοῦ ἡλίου	וּכְבוֹא הַשֶּׁמֶשׁ
10[27]	καὶ ἐγενήθη --- --- πρὸς ἡλίου δυσμὰς	וַיְהִי לְעֵת בּוֹא הַשֶּׁמֶשׁ

In Josh. 11:6, the Greek translator rendered the Hebrew phrase מחר כעת הזאת, *tomorrow at this time*, more precisely by αὔριον ταύτην τὴν ὥραν, *tomorrow at the same time*.[266] Since no different Hebrew *Vorlage* needs to be postulated here,[267] this rendering reflects a literary initiative on the part of the Greek translator, albeit a modest one.[268]

In the passage about Joshua's curse of the person who will rebuild Jericho, Josh. 6:26, we find the Greek phrase ἐν τῇ ἡμέρᾳ ἐκείνῃ for the Hebrew phrase בעת ההיא. Although the possibility of a different Hebrew *Vorlage* ביום ההוא cannot be excluded,[269] it is also possible

[266] GELS[2], p. 610a; LEH, p. 527a with references to the secondary literature. The Greek noun occurs only here in LXX-Joshua. See for comparable formulations LXX-Gen. 18:10, LXX-Exod. 9:18; 10:4; LXX-3 Reg. 19:2; 21(20):6; and LXX-4 Reg. 7:1.18.

[267] Out of 51 times the Greek noun ὥρα is listed in HR 1493b–c as a rendering of a Hebrew noun (the two versions of Daniel counted only once, and the Greek compositions excluded) almost half of them, i.e., 25 times, this Greek noun is the translation of Hebrew עֵת.

[268] See C.G. den Hertog, *Studien*, p. 170.

[269] Thus L. Mazor, The Curse upon the Rebuilder of Jericho, p. 3. She argues that καιρός always represents עת in Joshua, whereas ἡμέρα always represents the Hebrew יום (4:14, 8:25, 9:27, 10:28,35, 14:9.12, 24:25) and that this reconstructed

that the Greek translator rendered the more neutral Hebrew phrase by the more precise Greek formulation, in order to integrate the short note of Joshua's curse more closely into the main narrative of the Fall of Jericho.

In the light of these observations, the rendering of בעת ההיא in Josh. 5:2 by ὑπὸ δὲ τοῦτον τὸν καιρόν should be regarded a successful effort to offer a fitting, though not slavish, rendering of the Hebrew text. By employing this phrase, the Greek translator introduced a certain lapse of time in which the autochthonous kings heard about the Jordan miracle and are temporarily immobilised by fear, in order to allow for the circumcision and the subsequent recovery (section 7.4.1).

7.6.1.2 *The Sharp Flint Knives*

The Greek translator specified the *flint knives* (חרבות צרים) as large knives made from a sharp rock: μαχαίρας πετρίνας ἐκ πέτρας ἀκροτόμου, which contains a double rendering of the single Hebrew word צרים.

Both Rahlfs and Margolis considered the plus in LXX *vis-à-vis* MT ἐκ πέτρας ἀκροτόμου to be part of the original Greek text. Margolis,[270] however, following De Lagarde's second axiom, conjectured that the more literal of the two phrases, πετρίνας, reflects a secondary interpolation derived from the parallel in verse 3 μαχαίρας πετρίνας ἀκροτόμους for the same Hebrew expression חרבות צרים, and reconstructed the original Greek text as: μαχαίρας ἐκ πέτρας ἀκροτόμου. This shorter text is actually attested by several younger C̲ (A.29.82.121. Arm) and P̲$_2$ (19.426.Syh) witnesses, while manuscripts 44 (S̲$_b$) and 72 (M̲) omit the words ἐκ πέτρας, resulting in a similar expression as in verse 3: μαχαίρας πετρίνας ἀκροτόμους. Theodotion (according to 344) apparently opted for this shorter formulation too (compare α' μαχαίρας πετρίνας, σ' μαχαίραν εξ ακροτόμου 344). L. Greenspoon, E. Tov and others have adopted Margolis'

different Hebrew reading is attested by Kennicott's MT-mss. 150 and 336 plus three manuscripts (ד, ל, מ) of *Sifre on Deuteronomy* § 95 (ed. L. Finkelstein. New York 1969).

[270] M.L. Margolis, *The Book of Joshua in Greek*, p. 66; M.L. Margolis, *Andreas Masius and His Commentary on the Book of Joshua* § 17.B.77, discussed the problem posed by the fact that Syh[L] ܥܒܕ ܠܟ ܣܟܝܢܐ ÷ ܡܢ ܟܐܦܐ ܕܓܙܘܪܬܐ ↙ reflects a Greek text Ποίησον σεαυτῷ μαχαίρας ÷ ἐκ πέτρας ἀκροτόμου ↙, which would imply that the original Greek translation had no equivalent for צרים at all.

reconstruction.[271] Since the most important witnesses support the reading edited by Rahlfs, K. Bieberstein suggested that the Greek text originally read μαχαίρας πετρίνας which was later expanded within the Greek textual tradition into the longer expression.[272]

C. den Hertog, however, has drawn attention to the fact that the two phrases are not completely synonymous: the second part provides additional information to the first.[273] In the light of other cases where the Greek translator provided double renderings for a single Hebrew expression, he comes to the conclusion that both the word πετρίνας and the phrase ἐκ πέτρας ἀκροτόμου are the product of the Greek translator who added his 'midrash-type exegesis' to the text in order to specify the circumcision-instruments. This explanation fits the manuscript evidence better, and is therefore to be preferred.

As mentioned in section 7.2.5 above, E. Tov explains the plus in LXX as 'midrash-type exegesis' introduced by the Greek translator on the basis of the phrase צור החלמיש underlying the parallel formulation ἐκ πέτρας ἀκροτόμου in Deut. 8:15, and recurring in Deut. 32:13 and Ps. 114:8.[274] Tov does not, however, explain why the Greek translator introduced this exegetical element, nor does he specify the relation between the tradition of water from the rock and rocky circumcision knives. To my mind there is no logical connection between these passages. It seems more likely that the Greek translator sought to modify the crude notion of a circumcision with such primitive instruments as stone knives. Since the basic meaning of the adjective ἀκρότομος is *cut off* (τέμνω) *sharply, acutely, with a sharp top* (ἀκρο-),[275] the purpose of the phrase is to clarify that the painful

---

[271] L.J. Greenspoon, *Textual Studies*, pp. 62–63; E. Tov, Midrash-type Exegesis, p. 53.

[272] K. Bieberstein, *Lukian und Theodotion im Josuabuch*, p. 24.

[273] C.G. den Hertog, *Studien*, p. 85.

[274] E. Tov, Midrash-Type Exegesis, p. 53 (= *The Greek and Hebrew Bible*, pp. 155–156).

[275] LEH, p. 17b; LSJ, p. 57b; GELS[2], p. 17a. Within the Septuagint, the adjective occurs only 11 times: LXX-Deut. 8:15; LXX-Josh. 5:2.3; LXX-3 Reg. 6:7 (as a rendering for אבן־שלמה, *a pure stone*, from which Solomon's temple was built); LXX-Job 28:9, 40:15(20); LXX-Ps. 113(114):8; Sap.Sal. 11:4 (paraphrase of Deut. 8:15); LXX-Sir. 40:15 and 48:17 (referring to the construction of the tunnel of Hezekiah), see HR, p. 51c. See also Theodotion's rendering of Exod. 4:25 of the

operation on the adult population was at least performed by sharp knives. Interestingly, we find a similar exegesis in TgJon-Josh. 5:2–3, where the Hebrew phrase has been rendered by אִזְמֵילְוָן חֲרִיפִין, *sharp circumcision knives*.[276] Perhaps the related pluses in LXX-Josh. 21:42d, and more in particular 24:31a, should be seen in the same light: These primitive instruments accompany Joshua in the grave (LXX-Josh. 24:31a ἐκεῖ ἔθηκαν μετ᾽ αὐτοῦ εἰς τὸ μνῆμα, . . ., τὰς μαχαίρας τὰς πετρίνας), so that it is clear that the crude practice of circumcising men with these stones was restricted only to the time of Joshua (καὶ ἐκεῖ εἰσιν ἕως τῆς σήμερον ἡμέρας).[277]

7.6.1.3 *The Sitting or Second Circumcision*

The original Greek text lacks the notion of a second circumcision. The text as edited by Rahlfs and Margolis (καὶ καθίσας περιτέμε τοὺς υἱοὺς Ισραηλ ---) has been disputed by Gooding and Otto, who argue that the shorter text is reflected by only a small number of witnesses. The situation is complex, since the element ἐκ δευτέρου reflected by the majority of witnesses was already part of the main LXX tradition preceding the Hexaplaric revision. Origen apparently did not mark it with an asterisk,[278] and already the quotation in Justin Martyr's *Dialogue with Tryphon* 113 presupposes a Septuagint text accepted both by Justin and his Jewish discussion partner that did contain the element of a δευτέρα περιτομή. Nevertheless, the Greek text καθίσας περιτέμε τοὺς υἱοὺς Ισραηλ ἐκ δευτέρου reflects a *conflate* text, since the ἐκ δευτέρου/שֵׁנִית presupposes the MT-reading וְשׁוּב. Moreover,

same Hebrew expression צר by ἀκρότομος *vis-à-vis* LXX-Exod. ψῆφος, *pebble*; Aquila τὸ πέτραν; and Symmachus ψῆφος πετρίνης.

[276] So also A. Blaschke, *Beschneidung*, pp. 115, 310–312.

[277] *Pace* A. Rofé, The End of the Book of Joshua, pp. 34–35 (see section 2.2.7.2 above); A. Blaschke, *Beschneidung*, pp. 116–117. B. Lucassen, *Josua, Richter* und *CD*, pp. 374–396, reckons with the possibility that the pluses in LXX-Josh. 21:42a–d and 24:31a reflect secondary Hebrew expansions. For a very strong view, see A.B. Ehrlich, *Randglossen*, p. 66: 'Dieses Plus, von Driver im Kittels Biblia Hebraica in allem Ernst registriert, rührt im griechischen Texte von irgendeinem witzigen hellenistischen Juden her, den die Beschneidung genierte—vgl. zu Gen. 17,13—und der darum den grotesken Ritus gern mit Josua begraben wissen wollte.' To my mind, Ehrlich's statement is only valid as regards the practice of performing circumcision with stone knives.

[278] Thus already M.L. Margolis, *The Book of Joshua in Greek*, p. 66.

given the weight attached to this element in Christian-Jewish polemics from Justin onwards, it is difficult to see who was willing and authoritative enough to remove this important element from the manuscript tradition.

Furthermore, the LXX version of verse 4 lends support to the shorter formulation in verse 2. The LXX does not contain the statement of MT-Josh. 5:5a–b asserting that all Israelites of the Exodus generation were circumcised, but rather reckons with a group of uncircumcised males who had not been circumcised in Egypt besides the group of children born on the way. As a result, there is no place in the logic of the Greek text for a *second* circumcision (ἐκ δευτέρου) by Joshua, since Joshua circumcised all those (πάντας τούτους 5:5) Israelites (τοὺς υἱοὺς Ισραηλ) that had either been born on the way (ὅσοι ποτὲ ἐγένοντο ἐν τῇ ὁδῷ), or had not been circumcised before in Egypt (καὶ ποτὲ ἀπερίτμητοι ἦσαν τῶν ἐξεληλυθότων ἐξ Αἰγύπτου). Although the Greek text differs from the MT, it is consistent in itself.

The shorter text καὶ καθίσας περίτεμε τοὺς υἱοὺς Ισραηλ, as edited by both Rahlfs and Margolis, is attested by the most important witnesses to the original Greek text B.19.108.407.Eth^C.VetLat (*et sedens circumcide filios Istrahel*) and a quotation from the Alexandrine Church Father Cyrill.[279] Already Aquila and Symmachus felt the need to revise the Old Greek at this point, thus the readings in the margin of ms.344 (α' καὶ ἐπιστρέψας περίτεμε, σ' καὶ πάλιν περίτεμε),[280] ms.108 without attribution (καὶ ἐπιστρέψας περίτεμε), the margin of Syh^L where the variant ܘܗܦܘܟ for ܘܬܘܒ has been recorded, and ms.56, which records the same reading as ἐν τῷ ἰουδ. Interestingly, however, Theodotion maintained the Old Greek at this point (ms.344 θ' και καθίσας περίτεμε).[281]

[279] P.E. Pusey (ed.), *Sancti Patris Nostri Cyrilli Archiepiscopi Alexandrini in D. Joannis Evangelium*. Bruxelles 1965). In S. Joannem Lib. IV, Cap. VII.24 (pp. 637–638):

Γέγραπται δὲ οὕτως περὶ αὐτοῦ "Καὶ εἶπε Κύριος τῷ Ἰησοῦ Ποίησον σεαυτῷ μαχαίρας πετρίνας ἐκ πέτρας ἀκροτόμου, καὶ καθίσας περίτεμε τοὺς υἱοὺς Ἰσραήλ. καὶ ἐποίησεν Ἰησοῦς μαχαίρας πετρίνας, καὶ περιέτεμε τοὺς υἱοὺς Ἰσραήλ."

[280] See also the reading by the ninth century CE Syrian Church Father Išoʿdad of Merv (C. van den Eynde (ed.), *Commentaire d'Išoʿdad de Merv sur l'Ancien Testament. III*, pp. 5–6, transl. (1963), pp. 6–7):

ܥܒܕ ܠܟ ܣܟܝܢܐ ܕܛܪܢܐ : ܘܗܦܘܟ ܓܙܘܪ. ܗܝ ܕܐܬܡܠܬ [. . .]

ܘܗܢܐ: ܥܒܕ ܠܟ ܣܟܝܢܐ ܡܢ ܟܐܦܐ ܕܛܪܢܐ : ܘܬܘܒ ܓܙܘܪ ܐܝܟ ܣܘܡܟܘܣ. ܘܬܘܒ ܓܙܘܪ.

[281] See L.J. Greenspoon, *Textual Studies*, p. 63.

The majority of witnesses to LXX-Josh. 5:2 (including A.M.V.W. Arm. Sah. Eth^{f}. Syh. Origen,[282] Theodoret,[283] Cyprian-cod.)[284] read καὶ καθίσας περίτεμε τοὺς υἱοὺς Ισραηλ ἐκ δευτέρου which forms a quantitative adjustment to MT. Here the phrase שׁנית is reflected by ἐκ δευτέρου, but the reading of ושׁוב as καθίσας has been left unaltered. The few alternative readings (the omission of καθίσας in ms.72, the readings τοῖς υἱοῖς ιηλ ἐκ δευτέρου in ms.72; and τοὺς υἱοὺς Ισραηλ δευτέρον in ms.106^{b}) represent inner-Greek developments.

Interestingly, the Masoretic manuscript Kennicott 90 and the Pešiṭta lectionary 9*l*6 likewise lack the phrase שֵׁנִית (respectively ܬܢܝܢܘܬ), undoubtedly due to inner-Hebrew and inner-Syriac developments.[285] The opposite development can be observed in the addition of the adverbial phrase ἐκ δευτέρου in verse 3 in LXX-manuscripts 44.118. 314.610, sa 19, and the Pešiṭta. Although Erbes holds the Syriac text to be dependent on 'a rare Septuagintal tradition',[286] it would seem more natural to regard these expansions as autonomous developments, introduced independently by one or more Greek and Sahidic (sa 19) scribes on the one hand, and the Syriac Pešiṭta translator on the other hand.

In the light of the numerous modifications presented by the Greek translator in order to deal delicately with the theme of circumcision (see section 7.6.3.2 below), the absence of a rendering for the Hebrew word שׁנית and the corresponding reading of ושׁוב as ושׁב, must be seen as deliberate efforts by the Greek translator to avoid the literal understanding of a second circumcision of adult males that had already been circumcised.

---

[282] Origen's fifth homily on Joshua, see A. JAUBERT (ed.), *Origène. Homélies sur Josué*, pp. 168–169: V.5 'Post haec iubetur filius Nave facere cultros ex petra et sedens circumcidere filios Istrahel *secundo*.'

[283] N. FERNÁNDEZ MARCOS, A. SÁENZ-BADILLOS (eds.), *Theodoreti Cyrensis Quaestiones in Octateuchum*, p. 274.

[284] Thascius Caecilius Cyprianus (210/215–258 CE): Thasci Caecili Cypriani ad Quirinum (Testimoniorum Libri Tres) (ed. G. HARTEL, *S. Thasci Caecili Cypriani Opera Omnia 1*. (CSEL III/1) Vindobonae 1868, p. 45) Test. I, 8: 'Item apud Iesum Naue: Et dixit Dominus ad Iesum: fac tibi cultellos petrinos nimis acutos et adside et circumcide *secundo* filios Israel.'

[285] See the cautious discussion in J.E. ERBES, *The Peshitta and the Versions*, pp. 286–287.

[286] J.E. ERBES, *The Peshitta and the Versions*, pp. 287–289.

7.6.2 *LXX-Josh. 5:3*

In verse three the Greek translator presented the execution of the divine command by Joshua somewhat more concisely by omitting the phrase לו as irrelevant, and using the phrase μαχαίρας πετρίνας ἀκροτόμους for the circumcision knives.[287]

The Greek translator apparently understood the phrase גבעת הערלות as a specific toponym (ἐπὶ . . . τόπου). Unlike his practice with respect to other place names, the Greek translator did not offer a mere transliteration of the site, but a translation in order to reflect the curious name: Βουνὸς τῶν ἀκροβυστιῶν. The addition τοῦ καλουμένου serves to explain this otherwise unknown place. This extra phrase has a striking parallel in TgJon-Josh. 5:3 וּגזַר יָת בְּנֵי יִשְׂרָאֵל בְּגִבעֲתָא וּקרָא לַהּ גִּבעַת עֲרלָתָא:, *and (Joshua) circumcised the children of Israel at the hill and called it hill of foreskins.*[288] Although it is not impossible that the two versions reflect mutual influence, it is more likely that the Greek and Aramaic translators arrived at a similar (but not identical) interpretative formulation independently, resulting from a similar exegesis of the enigmatic text.

As noted in section 7.2.4 above, manuscripts 118 and 314 from the $\underline{S}_a$-family, the Sahidic Manuscripts sa 19 and 20, the Old Latin version (*et posuit grumos praeputiorum in loco qui nunc vocatur Collis Praeputiorum*), and Justin Martyr in a quotation of the passage in his *Dialogue with Tryphon* 113.6 (καὶ ποιήσας τῶν ἀπὸ ἀκροβυστίας), contain a further expansion in the form of the additional clause preceding the plus discussed above: καὶ ἔθηκεν θιμωνίας ἀκροβυστίων, *and he formed heaps of foreskins.* Gooding and Tov hold this plus to be the original Greek text,[289] but the basis for such a claim appears to be too weak.

---

[287] The Greek tradition reflects a few harmonisations with verse 2. A second reviser of ms.106 ($\underline{S}_b$) added [μαχαίρας] ἐξακονήσμενας, *sharpened knives*, whereas ms.72 ($\underline{M}$) reads, in accordance with the longer formulation of verse 2: [πετρίνας] ἐκ πέτρας [ἀκροτόμους]; ms.120 ($\underline{E}$) more properly [πετρίνας] ἐκ πέτρας ἀκροτόμου and 376 ($\underline{P}_1$) [πετρίνας] ἐκ λιθῶν ἀκροτομῶν. Paul of Tella or one of his assistants regarded the entire notion of stone knives as secondary and placed the adjective ܛܢܢܝܬܐ *sub obelo*: ܘܥܒܕ ܠܗ ܝܫܘܥ ܣܟܝܢܐ ÷ ܛܢܢܝܬܐ ⁞, as was done with the phrase in the preceding verse 2: ܥܒܕ ܠܟ ܣܟܝܢܐ ÷ ܡܢ ܟܐܦܐ ܕܛܪܢܝܐ ⁞.

[288] A note in the margin of Codex Reuchlinianus reads here: לאתרא דהוה קרי ליה גבעת עורלתא. The Antwerp Polyglot has דקרו for וקרא. In the FragmTg the phrase וקרא לה גבעת is absent. See further the discussion in J.E. Erbes, *The Peshitta and the Versions*, pp. 290–291.

[289] D.W. Gooding, The Circumcision at Gilgal, p. 162; idem, On the Use of

The Sahidic version is not uniform at this point. The Sahidic witnesses known to Brooke-McLean and Margolis, sa.19 (the seventh-century palimpsest edited by Thompson) and sa.20.2 (dating from 1003 CE),[290] reflect the longer reading of manuscripts 118.314. The oldest witness to the Sahidic version, however, sa.18, the Joshua-Tobit papyrus codex, dating from the first half of the fourth century, and now divided over the Chester Beatty (no. 1389) and Bodmer (XXI) collections, published in 1963, does not contain the plus.[291]

Tov adduces the argument that many unique elements in Vetus Latina and (other) witnesses from the so-called 'Lucianic' tradition (in Margolis' system of sigla, S for 'Syrian recension') reflect the text of the Old Greek.[292] The value, however, of this recension differs from book to book: in the book of Reigns, this recension may reflect a Greek substratum older than the main text (B for instance) for those books, for the Greek Joshua the value of this text is not that important.[293]

Although the Old Latin and Sahidic versions are important and ancient witnesses to the text of LXX-Joshua, they are daughter translations, which implies that a certain amount of reinterpretation is to be expected at the stage of the translation of the Greek text into the Latin, respectively Sahidic. Justin too is a very ancient witness to the text, but nevertheless contains an allusion to the Septuagint text, not a literal quotation. Instead of forcing the witnesses from distinct textual families (E [Sa.19 and 20.2], S_a [118.314.537.VetLat] and Justin) into a strict model of genetic dependence reaching back into the second century CE, one should also reckon with independent similar interpretations of the same enigmatic text.

In section 7.4.1 it was pointed out that the Hebrew phrase וימל . . . אל־גבעת הערלות can be understood in two ways: either Joshua

the LXX for Dating Midrashic Elements in the Targums; E. Tov, Midrash-type Exegesis, pp. 53–54 (= *The Greek and Hebrew Bible*, p. 156; here Tov employs the more cautious formulation: 'This addition may reflect the OG . . .').

[290] See K. Schüssler (Hg.), *Das sahidische Alte und Neue Testament sa 1–20*. Wiesbaden 1995, p. 97ff.

[291] A.F. Shore (ed.), *Joshua I–VI and Other Passages in Coptic*, pp. 35, 58; R. Kasser, *L'évangile selon Saint Jean et les versions coptes de la Bible*, p. 109.

[292] E. Tov, Midrash-type Exegesis, p. 54 (= *The Greek and Hebrew Bible*, p. 156).

[293] See section 2.1 above; K. Bieberstein, *Lukian und Theodotion im Josuabuch*. München 1994.

performed the circumcision at a(n already existing) place that was called *hill of the foreskins*, or, alternatively Joshua circumcised so many Israelites that one could form a hill out of foreskins. We find both interpretations in the Greek tradition. The original Greek text understood the Hebrew phrase in the former 'historical-geographical' sense, whereas Justin, his contemporary rabbi Jehuda ha-Nasi (according to *Midrash Song of Songs* the author of the midrash in question), Rashi and others understood the phrase in the latter sense. What is evident so far is that the fictive setting of the narrative in the Hebrew text gave rise to a number of problems for later generations of exegetes and translators. The Greek translator dealt with these problems in a creative way, just as later interpreters and translators were forced to offer interpretations of the original Hebrew text, as attested by MT, some of which coincide with that of LXX.

7.6.3 *LXX-Josh. 5:4–5*

7.6.3.1 *The Structure of the Greek Text*

The two verses form a new unit, marked by the particle δέ, and describe in detail who are circumcised by Joshua. The Greek text shares with MT only the elements of the circumcision by Joshua (LXX 5:5 περίετεμεν Ἰησοῦς MT 5:4b מל יהושע) and the mentioning of the group of Israelites born on the way (LXX 5:4 ὅσοι ποτὲ ἐγένοντο ἐν τῇ ὁδῷ MT 5:5d הילדים במדבר בדרך), but forms a cogent literary unit in itself.

Whereas in the MT verse 4 marks the beginning of the long retrospective explanation (וזה הדבר אשר, see section 7.4.2 above), in the Greek version this background information does not start until verse 6, marked by the change of verb tense from aorist (εἶπεν [5:2], ἐποίησεν [5:3], περιέτεμεν [5:3], περιεκάθαρεν [5:4], περιέτεμεν [5:5]) to perfect (ἀνέστραπται [5:6]), and the conjunction γὰρ. The structure of the four clauses may be regarded as a chiasm:

5:4 A: verb (περιεκάθαρεν)—B: subject (Ἰησοῦς)—C: object (τοὺς υἱοὺς Ἰσραήλ)—
5:5 C': object (πάντας τούτους)—A' verb (περιέτεμεν)—B' subject (Ἰησοῦς).

The two intervening clauses specify the object: all those (πάντας τούτους) circumcised by Joshua were uncircumcised either because they were born on the way (ὅσοι ποτὲ ἐγένοντο ἐν τῇ ὁδῷ) or because they were uncircumcised when they left Egypt (ὅσοι ποτὲ ἀπερίτμητοι ἦσαν τῶν ἐξεληλυθότων ἐξ Αἰγύπτου).

The passage opens with ὃν δὲ τρόπον περιεκάθαρεν Ἰησοῦς, *accordingly Jesous purified* . . . Out of the 26 times the phrase ὃν . . . τρόπον occurs within LXX-Joshua,[294] it is mainly used in comparisons (e.g. in Josh. 1:17 ἔστω κύριος ὁ θεὸς ἡμῶν μετὰ σοῦ *ὃν τρόπον* ἦν μετὰ Μωυσῆ) or in back references (8:27 κατὰ πρόσταγμα κυρίου *ὃν τρόπον* συνέταξεν κύριος τῷ Ἰησοῖ). In the few other cases in LXX-Joshua where the phrase opens a sentence (11:15; 14:5) it occurs at the beginning of a comparison of which the second part contains the adverb ὡσαυτως (11:15) or οὕτως (14:5). Since such an element is absent in LXX-Josh. 5:4–5, the phrase should be understood absolutely in the sense of 'thus', 'accordingly' or French 'ainsi' (thus J. Moatti-Fine),[295] rather than in the sense of the introduction of a reference to a similar circumcision event before the Exodus, as Gooding argued (see section 7.2.4 above), or otherwise kataphorically.[296] The phrase refers anaphorically to the manner in which Joshua performed the circumcision, i.e., with the unusual instruments made from flint stones. Although the phrase could be retroverted into the classical Hebrew phrase כאשׁר, neither Holmes, Auld, nor Mazor postulate at this point a Hebrew *Vorlage* different from the anaphoric Hebrew phrase וזה הדבר אשׁר preserved in the MT. At this point, too, the freedom should be ascribed to the Greek translator.

7.6.3.2 *Circumcision and Purification*

The same holds true for the unusual rendering of the verb מול by περικαθαίρω, *to purge, purify* [*completely*], *cleanse on all sides*,[297] a verb that recurs within the Greek Bible only in LXX-Deut. 18:10 (οὐχ εὑρεθήσεται ἐν σοὶ περικαθαίρων τὸν υἱὸν αὐτοῦ ἢ τὴν θυγατέρα αὐτοῦ

[294] Josh. 1:3.17; 5:4; 8:2.6.27; 10:1.28.30.32.35.37.39.40; 11:9.12.15.20; 13:6; 14:2.5.12; 21:8; 22:4; 23:15.

[295] J. Moatti-Fine, *Josué*, p. 117.

[296] Thus L.L. Brenton, *The Septuagint Version of the Old Testament with an English Translation*. London 1879, p. 285: 'And *this is* the way in which Joshua purified the children of Israel.'

[297] LSJ, p. 1375b; LEH, p. 369a; GELS², p. 451b; R. le Déaut, Le theme de la circoncision du coeur, pp. 184–185.

ἐν πυρί, as a euphemism for לא־ימצא בך מעביר בנו־ובתו באש),[298] and 4 Macc. 1:29.[299] More relevant to our passage are the renderings of the same Hebrew verb מול by the synonymous Greek verb περικαθαρίζω, *to purge entirely*, in LXX-Lev. 19:23 and LXX-Deut. 30:6.[300] In both cases a straightforward rendering of the verb מול would have been inappropriate, since in the first instance (Lev. 19:23) the verb has been used in the context of pruning trees, which was prohibited for five years after entering the Promised Land (καὶ περικαθαριεῖτε τὴν ἀκαθαρσίαν αὐτοῦ for וערלתם ערלתו),[301] and in the second case (Deut. 30:6) the verb has been used in the metaphorical expression 'circumcision of the heart': (καὶ περικαθαριεῖ κύριος τὴν καρδίαν σου—ומל יהוה אלהיך את־לבבך).[302]

[298] See C. Dogniez, *Le Deutéronome*, p. 229; J.W. Wevers, *Notes on the Greek Text of Deuteronomy*, p. 298.

[299] In a metaphor of a master gardener purifying and pruning the undergrowth of inclinations and passions: ὁ παγγέωργος λογισμὸς περικαθαίρων καὶ ἀποκνίζων . . . τὰς τῶν ἠθῶν καὶ παθῶν ὕλας, see H. Anderson, 4 Maccabees, in J.H. Charlesworth (ed.), *The Old Testament Pseudepigraph* 2, p. 531ff. Contrast the use of the verb περιτέμνω in this same sense of the 'pruning vines' by Hesiod, *Works and Days*, line 570: τὴν φθάμενος οἴνας περιταμνέμεν· ὣς γὰρ ἄμεινον, *before she (i.e. the wailing daughter of Pandion) comes, prune the vines, for it is best so.*

[300] LSJ, p. 1375b; LEH, p. 369a; GELS², p. 452a; R. le Déaut, Le theme de la circoncision du coeur, pp. 184–185. The verb recurs in the Greek Bible only in LXX-Isa. 6:7 καὶ τὰς ἁμαρτίας σου περικαθαριεῖ as translation of the Hebrew וחטאתך תכפר.

[301] The Greek version (*you shall cleanse the fruit trees*) seems to contradict the Hebrew text (*you shall leave its fruits uncircumcised*), but in both cases it is clear that one is not allowed to take off the fruits from the tree, hence the dynamic-equivalent rendering in LXX-Leviticus. The recentiores, by contrast, replaced the words with the root καθαρ- by the literal rendering of ערל by ἀκροβυστ-: ἀκροβυστιεῖτε τὴν ἀκροβυστίαν αὐτου M' 708^comm Cyr C'344–740^-cat 18^cat. See P. Harlé, D. Pralon, *La Bible d' Alexandrie 3. Le Lévitique*. Paris 1988, pp. 169–171; J.W. Wevers, *Notes on the Greek Text of Leviticus* (SBL-SCS 44) Atlanta 1997, pp. 304–305; A. Blaschke, *Beschneidung*, pp. 112–113.

[302] In Deut. 10:16, the Greek translator avoided the same problem of rendering a metaphor literally by using the neologism σκληροκαρδία, *stubbornness* (LEH, p. 429a; GELS², p. 514a): καὶ περιτεμεῖσθε τὴν *σκληροκαρδίαν* ὑμῶν for ומלתם את ערלת לבבכם. This noun recurs only in LXX-Jer. 4:4 (LXX^S.A. ed. Ziegler: περιτμήθητε τῷ θεῷ ὑμῶν καὶ περιέλεσθε τὴν ἀκροβυστίαν τῆς καρδίας ὑμῶν; Rahlfs, following LXX^B, has in the second half: καὶ περιτέμεσθε τὴν σκληροκαρδίαν ὑμῶν for MT המלו ליהוה והסרו ערלות לבבכם) and in LXX-Sir. 16:10 (τοὺς ἐπισυναχθέντες ἐν σκληροκαρδίᾳ αὐτῶν). Aquila (M.108.Syh) employed the literal rendering corresponding to MT [τὴν 108] ἀκροβυστίαν καρδίας [ὑμῶν 108]. See further C. Dogniez, M. Harl, *Le Deutéronome*, pp. 183–184: 'transposition morale du tour imagé du TM'; J.W. Wevers, *Notes on the Greek Text of Deuteronomy*, p. 183; and R. le Déaut, Le thème de la circoncision du coeur, pp. 178–205; A. Aejmelaeus, Die Septuaginta des Deuteronomiums, p. 12ff.; A. Blaschke, *Beschneidung*, pp. 113–114.

The fivefold use of the Greek verb περιτέμνω in LXX-Joshua 5 (verses 2.3.5.7.8) makes clear that the Greek translator of our passage did not intend to avoid the problems of a second circumcision of adult males by a metaphorical rendering of the theme, as in LXX-Deut. 30:6. Nevertheless, if the Greek translator employed the unusual Greek verb περικαθαίρω merely for the sake of stylistic variation in the Greek vocabulary, as most scholars seem to presuppose,[303] it remains difficult to see why in all other cases he rendered the verb מול consistently by περιτέμνω.[304] Moatti-Fine suggests that the Greek verb περικαθαίρω has a moral connotation and correlates with the removal of the ὀνειδισμός in LXX-Josh. 5:9, which she with Philo interpretes as a sign of Egyptian licentiousness.[305] Yet, the verb implies fysical purity rather than moral behaviour. Moreover, it is highly dubious whether one should read Philo's characterisation of Egypt in general into the phrase τὸν ὀνειδισμόν Αἰγύπτου. If the Greek translator had wanted to differentiate between the two groups of Israelites mentioned in verse 4 (those born on the way were purified by Joshua, whereas the older Israelites that had left Egypt uncircumcised were circumcised by Joshua), as Moatti-Fine proposes as an alternative solution to the problem, one would have expected the reverse order (those born on the way were circumcised by Joshua instead of merely purified). Moreover, πάντας τούτους περιέτεμεν Ἰησοῦς excludes the possibility that one of the two groups was 'only' purified.[306]

The variation in rendering of the same Hebrew verb מול could also be explained in terms of a deliberate interpretation of the custom of the circumcision itself, that is: circumcision (περιτέμνω) should according to the Greek translator be seen as an act of purification (περικαθαίρω),[307] rather than an unintelligible, primitive custom. As is well known, the Greeks had little affinity with this practise, which they viewed as mutilation of the body.[308] See for instance the very

---

303 Thus e.g. J. Hollenberg, *Der Charakter*, p. 5; S. Holmes, *Joshua*, p. 29; C.G. den Hertog, *Studien*, p. 146 (*ZAW* 110 [1998], p. 603).

304 Thus J. Moatti-Fine, *Josué*, p. 117: L'emploi exceptionnel dans cette scène de circoncision d'un verbe à valeur morale ne peut s'expliquer ni par a volonté de varier ni par euphémisme.'

305 J. Moatti-Fine, *Josué*, pp. 117–119.

306 *Pace* M. Rösel, The Septuagint-Version, p. 16.

307 See F. Hauck, καθαρός, καθαρίζω, καθαίρω, καθαρότης, ἀκάθαρτος, ἀκαθαρσιά, καθαρισμός, ἐκκαθαίρω, περικάθαρμα, in *ThWNT* III pp. 416–434

308 See e.g. R. Meyer, περιτέμνω, περιτομή, ἀπερίτμητος, in *ThWNT* VI, p. 78, and the extensive discussion by A. Blaschke, *Beschneidung*, pp. 323–360: 'C. Die Beschneidung im Urteil griechischer und lateinischer Autoren.'

negative description of the Judeans precisely on this point of circumcision (in general) by the first century BCE and CE geographer Strabo, *Geography* XVI.37:[309]

> His [i.e., Moses'] successors for some time abided by the same course, acting righteously and being truly pious toward God; but afterwards, in the first place, superstitious men were appointed to the priesthood, and then tyrannical people; and from superstition arose abstinence of the flesh, from which it is their custom to abstain even today, and circumcisions and excisions and other observances of the kind (καὶ αἱ περιτομαὶ καὶ αἱ ἐκτομαὶ και εἴ τινα τοιαῦτα ἐνομίσθη).'

For the Jews, on the other hand, 'being uncircumcised' was equal to 'being unclean', as becomes clear in the idealized description of the new Jerusalem in Deutero-Isaiah 52:1.[310]

---

[309] Text and translation: H.L. JONES, *The Geography of Strabo. VII. Books XV–XVI.* Cambridge, Massachusetts/London 1930, 1983, pp. 284–285.

[310] See also the allusions to this passage in the Qumran literature, 1QH XVI, line 20, 4QH[c], frg. 2, line 5; frg. 4, line 9, 4Q176, frg. 8–11, line 3; frg. 12–13, line 2. See further G. MEYER, עָרַל *'āral* עָרֵל *'ārel*, עָרְלָה *'ŏrlāh*, in *ThWAT* VI, col. 385–387; and A. BLASCHKE, *Beschneidung*, pp. 19–322. 'Teil B. Beschneidung in Israel und im Judentum.' Blaschke, pp. 70–71, stresses the circumstance that within the Hebrew Bible this is the only passage where circumcision and cleanness are so strictly paralleled. Nevertheless, there are enough parallels for this equation in the younger Jewish literature, e.g. LXX-Esther C:26–28 (A. BLASCHKE, *Beschneidung*, pp. 130–131); Jubilees 1:23 (A. BLASCHKE, *Beschneidung*, pp. 131–133); Jubilees 20:1–3 (A. BLASCHKE, *Beschneidung*, pp. 147–148); and FLAVIUS JOSEPHUS, *Jewish Antiquities* XIII.257ff. and XIII.318ff. (A. BLASCHKE, *Beschneidung*, pp. 230–233).

Not discussed by Blaschke, but nevertheless relevant to this issue is Symmachus' treatment of a number of circumcision passages in the Hebrew Bible, mentioned by R. LE DÉAUT, Le thème de la circoncision du coeur, p. 186:

[1] Exod. 6:12 ואני ערל שׂפתים—LXX ἐγω δὲ ἄλογός εἰμι (see A. BLASCHKE, *Beschneidung*, pp. 111–112)—σ' οὐκ εἰμὶ *καθαρὸς* τῷ φθέγματι (M 707 57'458[txt] 85'–344)—contrast α' ἀκρόβυστος χείλεσιν (M 707 57'85'–344') and θ' ἀπερίτμητος τοῖς χείλεσιν (M 57'458[txt] 85'–344). See further A. SALVESEN, *Symmachus in the Pentateuch* (JSS.M 15). Manchester 1991, pp. 77–78.

[2] Jer. 4:4 המלו ליהוה והסרו ערלות לבבכם—LXX (ed. Ziegler) περιτμήθητε τῷ θεῷ ὑμῶν καὶ περιέλεσθε τὴν ἀκροβυστίαν τῆς καρδίας ὑμῶν—σ' *καθαρίσθητε* τῷ κυρίῳ καὶ περιέλεσθε τὰς πονηρίας τῶν καρδιῶν ὑμῶν; retroverted from the Latin quotation *apud* Jerome: *purificamini* Domino et auferte malitias cordium vestrorum.

[3] Jer. 6:10 הנה ערלה אזנם—LXX ἰδοὺ ἀπερίτμητα τὰ ὦτα αὐτῶν—σ'/α' *ἀκάθαρτον* τὸ οὖς αὐτῶν (86).

[4] Ezek. 44:9 כל־בן־נכר ערל לב וערל בשׂר לא יבוא אל־מקדשׁי—LXX Πᾶς υἱὸς ἀλλογενὴς ἀπερίτμητος καρδίᾳ καὶ ἀπερίτμητος σαρκὶ οὐκ εἰσελεύσεται εἰς τὰ ἅγιά μου—σ' *ἀκάθαρτος* καρδίᾳ καὶ *ἀκάθαρτος* σαρκί, from Syh ܣ. ܠܐ ܕܟܝܐ ܒܠܒܐ ܘܠܐ ܕܟܝܐ ܒܒܣܪܐ ܀ see F. FIELD, *Origenis Hexaplorum . . . fragmenta* II, p. 888b. See also the anonymuous reading in

[5] Lev. 26:41 או־אז יכנע לבבם הערל—LXX τότε ἐντραπήσεται ἡ καρδία αὐτῶν ἡ ἀπερίτμητος—ἄλλος ἡ *ἀκάθαρτος* (128).

5 2[1] לא יוסיף יבא־בך עוד ערל וטמא

οὐκέτι διελθεῖν διὰ σοῦ ἀπερίτμητους καὶ ἀκάθαρτος,

no longer shall an uncircumcised and unclean person enter you

According to Herodotus, *History of the Persian Wars* II.37, the Egyptians too regarded circumcision as an act of purification:[311]

> They [i.e., the Egyptians] practice circumcision for cleanliness' sake (τά τε αἰδοῖα περιτάμνονται καθαρειότητος εἵνεκεν); for they set cleanness above seemliness.

In order to defend this ancient Jewish custom, the Alexandrine philosopher Philo in his apologetical work on *The Special Laws* I.1–11 argued *inter alia* that circumcision, an object of derision to many people (ἀπὸ τοῦ γελωμένου παρὰ τοῖς πολλοῖς), should in fact be seen as an act of purification that sanctifies the whole body as befits the consecrated order (τὴν δι' ὅλου τοῦ σώματος *καθαριότητα* πρὸς τὸ ἁρμόττον τάξει ἱερωμένῃ), which is, moreover, also observed by the ancient and prestigious Egyptian people (πρᾶγμα σπουδαζόμενον οὐ μετρίως καὶ παρ' ἑτέροις ἔθνεσι καὶ μάλιστα τῷ Αἰγυπτιακῷ, ὃ καὶ πολυανθρωπότατον καὶ ἀρχαιότατον καὶ φιλοσοφώτατον εἶναι δοκεῖ).[312] Although the work of the other Jewish-Egyptian scholar, the Greek translator of Joshua (circa 200 BCE), precedes Philo's *The Special Laws* (first half first century CE)[313] by two centuries, it displays the same tendency to make this important Jewish custom acceptable for his (Egyptian) Hellenistic readership, the crude idea of a circumcision of adult (occasionally already middle-aged) males by means of such primitive instruments as stone knives is softened in the same way by the assertion that these instruments were at least made of *sharp* stone

Although it is evident that Symmachus sought to offer an idiomatic rendering for those passages in which the Hebrew word ערל was used in a metaphorical sense, it is clear that through his use of the Greek root καθαρ- he presented a very clear understanding of the rite of circumcision itself.

[311] Text and translation: A.D. GODLEY, *Herodotus. Books I–II.* Cambridge, Massachusetts/London 1920. See further the discussion in A. BLASCHKE, *Beschneidung*, pp. 323–326.

[312] Text and translation: F.H. COLSON, *Philo. VII.* London/Cambridge, Massachusetts 1937. Philo offered a similar explanation in his *Questions and Answers on Genesis* 3.48; see further A. BLASCHKE, *Beschneidung*, pp. 193–209.

[313] P. BORGEN, Philo of Alexandria, in M.E. STONE, *Jewish Writings of the Second Temple Period.* (CRINT II/2) Assen/Philadelphia 1984, pp. 233–280.

(ἐκ πέτρας ἀκροτόμου).[314] For probably the same reasons, Josephus entirely omitted Josh. 5:2–9 from his rewritten version in *Jewish Antiquities* V.20–21.[315]

7.6.3.3 *The Two Groups of Israelites Circumcised by Joshua (LXX-Josh. 4b–5)*

Although from a quantitative point of view the Greek text of verses 4–5 is 50% shorter than the redundant Hebrew text of verses 4–5 (27 Greek words as opposed to 55 in MT), from the point of view of contents the Greek version contains a plus. According to MT, Joshua circumcised only those Israelites that were born on the way. The older generation that had left Egypt had completely perished and, moreover, had been circumcised when they left Egypt. According to the Greek text, however, Joshua did not only circumcise this younger generation, but in addition also as many as happened to be *uncircumcised* when they left Egypt, and apparently were still alive. As scholars such as Gooding, Bieberstein and Blaschke have pointed out (see section 7.2), this second group, mentioned only in LXX, refers to those male Israelites that were not yet twenty years old at the time of the events narrated in Numbers 14, and for that reason could both have been born in Egypt (τῶν ἐξεληλυθότων ἐξ Αἰγύπτου) and still be alive at the time of the events narrated in the present story.

The formulation ὅσοι ποτέ is remarkably indefinite: we are not told how many Israelites had not been circumcised among those that left Egypt. The Greek text does not say that *none* of the Israelites that left Egypt had been circumcised, which would have been a complete contradiction with MT-Josh. 5:5a–b; it only states that besides the group mentioned in the previous clause and known also from MT, there was an additional group of Israelites not mentioned in MT. The formulation ὅσοι ποτέ points to an initiative by the Greek translator, since it has no direct equivalent in classical Hebrew. Admittedly, the pronoun ὅσος, *as much as*, occurs relatively frequently in LXX-Joshua (29 times) and throughout the whole LXX (615

---

[314] Thus also A. Blaschke, *Beschneidung*, pp. 115, 321.

[315] Thus P.A. Fernández, s.j., *Commentarius in Librum Iosue*, p. 72: 'Iosephus, cum loquitur de monumento in Gilgal et de celebratione Paschatis (Ant.V.1,4), silet de circumcisione, forsan eo quod ii, pro quibus historiam scribebat, circumcisionem irriderent.'

times). As far as the passages in Joshua are concerned, however, this pronoun always introduces a certain qualification to the general Hebrew phrase אשׁר or כל אשׁר,[316] which strictly speaking, could also be rendered in Greek by the simple relative pronoun ὅς. By contrast, the particle πότε, *once, at one time*, occurs only 24 times in the whole Greek Old Testament, predominantly in original Greek compositions such as 2 Maccabees (10:4; 13:10; 14:32), 4 Maccabees (1:14; 4:1; 7:4), and Sapientia Salomonis (5:4; 14:15; 16:18.19; 17:15). In those cases where the Hebrew text is still extant, the particle always reflects a free rendering of the original Hebrew text.[317] Even if one reconstructs a deviant Hebrew *Vorlage* כל . . . וכל, as Holmes, Auld and Mazor have done, one has to admit that the Greek translation introduces its own nuances here.

Given these and other nuances introduced by the Greek translator, it is likely that the corrective addition of the groups of Israelites to be circumcised by Joshua, mentioned in LXX Josh. 5:4b καὶ ὅσοι πότε ἀπερίτμητοι ἦσαν τῶν ἐξεληλυθότων ἐξ Αἰγύπτου, originates from the same interpretative and creative genius. As Margolis and Den Hertog have already pointed out,[318] the key to the interpretation of this passage lies in verse 9. As we have seen in section 7.4.4 above, the relation between this verse and the preceding verses is not self-evident, and the contents of the phrase 'rolling away of the humiliation of Egypt' are disputed. A close reading of the Hebrew text reveals that verses 2–8 and 9 are not directly related. When the verses are read in conjunction, however, this phrase can only be understood as a reference to the uncircumcised state of the Israelites, which at the very moment (LXX-5:9 ἐν τῇ σήμερον ἡμέρᾳ) the circumcision enterprise is completed (verse 8) has been removed (verse 9

---

[316] The Greek phrase (πᾶς) ὅσος renders כל־אשׁר in Josh. 1:16.17; 2:13.19; 6:17.17.21.22.23; 7:15; 9:9.10; 15:46; 22:2; and 23:3.

[317] Thus in Deut. 1:46 ותשׁבו בקדשׁ ימים רבים כימים אשׁר ישׁבתם—καὶ ἐνεκάθησθε ἐν Καδὴς ἡμέρας πολλάς, *ὅσας ποτὲ* ἡμέρας ἐνεκάθησθε; Josh. 22:28 והיה—ἐὰν γένηταί *ποτε*; 2 Sam. 11:25 כי־כזה וכזה תאכל החרב—ὅτι *ποτὲ* μὲν οὕτως καὶ *ποτὲ* οὕτως φάγεται ἡ μάχαιρα; 1 Esd. 8:69 καὶ ἐπισυνήχθησαν πρός με ὅσοι *ποτὲ* ἐπεκινοῦντο τῷ ῥήματι κυρίου τοῦ Ισραηλ, cf. Ezra 9:4 = II Esd. 9:4 ואלי יאספו כל חרד בדברי אלהי־ישׂראל—καὶ συνήχθησαν πρός με πᾶς ὁ διώκων λόγον θεοῦ Ισραηλ. See further Job 31:16.38; Ps. 94(93):8; Isa. 41:7.

[318] M.L. Margolis, *The Book of Joshua in Greek*, pp. 70–71; '. . . rephrased in G so as to convey the idea that the majority of the יוצאי [מ]מצרים were uncircumcised, circumcision not having been practised by the Israelites in Egypt (hence חרפת מצרים).' C.G. den Hertog, *Studien*, p. 147 (*ZAW* 110 [1998], p. 603). See further section 7.2.8 above.

ἀφεῖλον). As mentioned in sections 7.4.4 and 7.6.3.2 above, circumcision was a well-known and esteemed practice among Egyptian priests, so that the phrase חרפת מצרים could well be interpreted by the Greek translator as reproaches from the Egyptians to the Israelites with respect to their uncircumcised state.[319]

Following this interpretation of the phrase חרפת מצרים, the translator concluded that already in Egypt a certain—undetermined—number of Israelites were object of insults (ὀνειδισμός), because of the fact that their foreskins, the tops (ἀκρο-) of shame (-βυστία/בֹּשֶׁת),[320] had not been removed (ἀφ-αιρέω verse 9). For that reason, he chose the unusual and less specific equivalent ἀφ-αιρέω, *to remove*,[321] for the Hebrew verb גלל, *to roll away*,[322] instead of the more literal rendering κυλίω, *to roll*,[323] as in LXX-Josh. 10:21 and elsewhere in the Septuagint.[324]

The other versions of the book of Joshua followed a similar approach in order to render the verb גלל in a neutral, idiomatic way: Targum Jonathan of Joshua: יוֹמָא דֵין אַעֲדִיתִי יָת חִסוּדֵי מִצְרָאֵי מִנְכוֹן,

[319] This in contrast to the later controversy between Jews and Greeks where the opposite situation, circumcision itself, formed the object of derision.

[320] The use of the word ἀκροβυστία reflects Jewish-Hellenistic idiom for the existing Greek word for foreskin, ἀκροποσθία, based on the combination of the Greek word ἄκρος, *top, utmost*, and the Hebrew word בשת, *shame*, and occurs only in Jewish (LXX, Philo) and Christian literature, thus LEH, p. 17b; LSJ, p. 56b, 57a; K.L. Schmidt, ἀκροβυστία, in *ThWNT* I, pp. 226–227; M. Harl, *La Genèse* (La Bible d' Alexandrie 1) Paris 1994², p. 171.

[321] LEH, p. 72a–b; GELS², p. 77a–b. According to HR, pp. 180a–181a, this Greek verb has been used throughout the Septuagint for a large number (35) of Hebrew verbs, usually only once as is the case with the unique equation גלל—ἀφαιρέω. Thirty-six out of the 168 times ἀφαιρέω occurs in the Greek Old Testament, it has been used to render the Hebrew verb סור, *to remove*, which has been translated in LXX-Josh. by ἐκκλίνω (1:7; 23:6), ἐξαίρω (7:13), παρα-βαίνω (11:15), περιαιρέω (24:14.23).

[322] HALOT, pp. 193b–194a.

[323] LEH, p. 271b; GELS², p. 334b.

[324] The Hebrew verb גלל occurs 17 times in the Hebrew Bible, nine times in the Qal formation (Gen. 29:3.8.10; Josh. 5:9; 10:18; Ps. .22:9; 37:5; Prov. 16:3; 26:17), twice in the Niphʿal (Isa. 34:4; Amos 5:24), once in the Polʿel (Isa. 9:4), twice in the Hitpolʿel (Gen. 43:18; 2 Amos 20:12), once in the Hitpalpʿel (Job 30:14), and once in the Pilpʿel (Jer. 51:25). Seven times, the Greek equivalent is κυλίω (LXX-Josh. 10:18; LXX-Prov. 26:27 and LXX-Amos 5:24) or its composites ἀποκυλίω (a neologism? LXX-Gen. 29:3.8.10) and κατακυλίω (LXX-Jer. 28[51]:25). Other renderings are ἀπο-καλύπτω, *to uncover* (LXX-Ps. 37:5), ἐλίσσομαι, *to be rolled up* (LXX-Isa. 34:4), ἐλπίζω, *to hope* (LXX-Ps. 22:9), ἐπισυνάγω, *to gather together* (LXX-Isa. 9:4), συκοφαντέω, *to slander* (LXX-Gen. 43:18), and φύρω passive, *to be soaked with* (LXX-2 Reg. 20:12; LXX-Job 30:14). MT-Prov. 16:3 has no translation in LXX.

today I have removed the reproaches of the Egyptians from you; Pešiṭta of Joshua ܘܝܘܡܢܐ ܐܥܒܪܬ ܚܣܕܐ ܕܡܨܪܝܢ ܡܢܟܘܢ., *today I have removed the reproach of Egypt from you*, and Vg *hodie abstuli obprobrium Aegypti a vobis*. The Fragmentary Targum goes its own way by interpreting the rolling away of the humiliation of Egypt in terms of the removal of the Egyptian idols יומא דין אסתלאקית טאעואת מצראי מנכון (an allusion to Josh. 24:14.23?).

An interesting parallel to our passage is offered by the translation of Gen. 30:23 where Leah explains the name of her new-born son Joseph אָסַף אֱלֹהִים אֶת־חֶרְפָּתִי, *God has taken away my humiliation*. LXX-Genesis renders this by Αφεῖλεν ὁ θεός μου τὸ ὄνειδος, and Targum Pseudo-Jonathan explicitly links it with our Joshua text:

> The Lord has taken away my disgrace (כנש ייי ית חיסודי). Similarly, Joshua the son of Joseph is destined to take away the disgrace of Egypt from the children of Israel (למכנש ית חיסודי דמצרים מעל בני ישראל) and to circumcise them on the other side of the Jordan.

Likewise in Isa. 4:1, the request of the seven women to the single man אֱסֹף חֶרְפָּתֵנוּ, *take away our disgrace*, is rendered in LXX-Isa. by ἄφελε τὸν ὀνειδισμὸν ἡμῶν, in Tg-Isa. by כנוש בהתתנא, in Peš-Isa. by ܘܐܥܒܪ ܚܣܕܢ, and in Vg-Isa. by *aufer obprobium noster*. Interesting is also the plus in LXX-1 Reg. 17:36 (cf. MT-1 Sam. 17:26) καὶ *ἀφελῶ σήμερον ὄνειδος ἐξ Ισραηλ* διότι τίς ὁ ἀπερίτμητος οὗτος ὃς ὠνείδισεν παράταξιν θεοῦ ζῶντος.[325]

The versions of these passages apparently avoided a literal rendering of the verb גלל. Josh. 5:9 was generally interpreted in the light of the preceding text: the rolling away of the humiliation was interpreted as the removal of the uncircumcised state.

In order to express his interpretation of the passage as a whole, the Greek translator passed over the small statement in MT-Josh. 5:5a–b and created the additional group of uncircumcised Israelites that had not been circumcised in Egypt, had survived the long wilderness period, and were now circumcised by Joshua in Josh. 5:2–9, so that the Lord is able to conclude that now this humiliation had finally

---

[325] In Ps. 119:22 the Masoretes vocalised גל מעלי חרפה as גַּל, i.e. a Piʿel imperative of גלה, *uncover*, but most versions and modern scholars read the word as גֹּל, *roll away*: περίελε ἀπ' ἐμοῦ ὄνειδος (LXX) אעדי מעלי קלנא (Tg), ܐܥܒܪ ܡܢܝ ܚܣܕܐ (Peš), *aufer a me obprobium* (Vg), thus e.g. H.-J. KRAUS, *Psalmen*, p. 994, note g.

been removed. For this reason, the Greek translator employed the rather general terms ὅσοι ποτέ, *as many as once happened to be uncircumcised* in verse 4. The fact that we read nowhere in the Pentateuch that the Israelites circumcised their children (or that they universally abandoned the practice of circumcision), and that even Moses' son had not been circumcised until Zippora did so in Exod. 4:24–26, may have facilitated this interpretation.[326] LXX-Josh. 5:4b thus reflects the pursuit of both inner coherence of the text read synchronically and complete correspondence with the Pentateuch. Not the MT, but the Greek translation reflects harmonisation with the Pentateuch.

On the other hand, it does not seem very likely that this harmonisation with the Pentateuch also pertains to the slaves and foreigners to be circumcised before Passover according to Exod. 12:43–51, as suggested by Den Hertog and Bieberstein, or to the group of non-Israelites mentioned in Exod. 12:38 and Num. 11:4.[327] Nowhere does the Greek text hint at a midrashic interpretation of Exod. 12:43–51, either in the form proposed by Gooding or that proposed by Bieberstein. In both the MT and LXX of Josh. 5:10 it is only the Israelites that take part in the celebration of Passover. For that reason it seems to be too sophisticated to interpret LXX-Josh. 5:4b as a reference to this group of non-Israelites.

Given the relative freedom with which the Greek translator handled his Hebrew parent text, it appears to be superfluous and unnecessary to assume a Hebrew *Vorlage* deviating from MT as a sort of intermediary stage between the present and more original MT and the Greek text, in the manner in which Den Hertog reconstructed a truncated Hebrew text that suffered from *parablepsis* due to *homoioarcton*. According to the exegesis of the Greek text as described above, the Greek version is the result of a coherent and comprehensive effort to interpret the whole of Josh. 5:2–9. A translator capable and willing to paraphrase the redundant and difficult Hebrew text did not only have the possibility to expand, but also to condense the Hebrew parent text. Therefore, rather than postulating such a different Hebrew *Vorlage*, it seems more likely that the Greek translator interpreted MT-Josh. 5:4a–b *anaphorically*, passed over MT-Josh. 5:4c–h

---

[326] See C.G. den Hertog, *Studien*, p. 147 (= *ZAW* 110, p. 603).

[327] C.G. den Hertog, *Studien*, p. 147 (= *ZAW* 110, p. 604); K. Bieberstein, *Josua-Jordan-Jericho*, pp. 199–201. See section 7.2.7 above.

as a redundant parallel to MT-Josh. 5:6a–c, skipped MT-Josh. 5:5a–b as too inaccurate and rendered only the remaining part MT-Josh. 5:5c–d.

Since the Greek translator did not render MT-Josh. 5:5e בצאתם ממצרים which forms a specification of במדבר בדרך in 5:5d, but did reflect this phrase in LXX-Josh. 5:4b τῶν ἐξεληλυθότων ἐξ Αἰγύπτου, it is not impossible that he deliberately interpreted MT 5:5e–f בצאתם ממצרים לא־מלו separately from MT-Josh. 5:5c–d as a second independent group 'that had come out of Egypt had not been circumcised' in order to express his interpretation of the חרפת מצרים.

7.6.4 *LXX-Josh. 5:6*

As stated above, the explanation why Joshua had to perform his unusual circumcision enterprise, is given in verse 6 of the Greek version. The use of the conjunction γὰρ instead of ὅτι already indicates a non-slavish rendering of the Hebrew particle כי.[328] The change from aorist to perfect (ἀναστραπται) marks this transition from narrative to background information. Although the Greek text corresponds more closely to the MT in this verse than it did in the previous two, it abounds with slight deviations, unusual renderings and specific refinings and corrections of the Hebrew text, which reinforce the impression of a well-considered, intelligent and scholarly translation gained in the preceding paragraphs. Nevertheless, the second clause of this verse in the Greek version contains a serious problem with respect to the inner logic of the present Greek text, noted by all scholars mentioned above in section 7.2.

7.6.4.1 *The Forty-Two Years Wandering in the Desert of Madbaritis (LXX-Josh. 5:6a)*

The first of the modest alterations is the more exact specification of the period of the wandering in the wilderness, which according to the calculation of the Greek translator of Joshua lasted not forty but forty-two years: two before and forty after the events at Kadesh

[328] See A. AEJMELAEUS, ὅτι *causale* in Septuagintal Greek, in N. FERNÁNDEZ MARCOS, *La Septuaginta en la investigacion contemporanea (V Congreso de la IOSCS)*. Madrid 1985, pp. 115–132 (= *On the Trail of the Septuagint Translators*, pp. 17–36); and S. SIPILÄ, *Between Literalness and Freedom*, pp. 153–158.

Barnea (Num. 10:11–12, 12:16; 13:3; 14:20ff. 14:33–34).[329] The suggestion that the phrase τεσσεράκοντα γὰρ καὶ δύο actually reflects a different Hebrew *Vorlage* שתים וארבעים שנה (so Margolis)[330] or, alternatively, ארבעים ושנים שנה (Hollenberg, Holmes, Benjamin, Auld, Tov, Mazor and Nelson)[331] cannot be dismissed completely, but given the numerous other alterations introduced at the Greek level, and the preoccupation with chronology in contemporary Jewish-Hellenistic writings such as those by Demetrius and Eupolemos, it seems to be most likely that the alteration should be ascribed to the Greek translator. On the basis of the chronological data from the Pentateuch he corrected the statement concerning the length of time spent in the desert. Since the Israelites did not circumcise their sons during the entire period of wandering in the desert (thus 5:7 διὰ τὸ αὐτοὺς γεγενῆσθαι κατὰ τὴν ὁδὸν ἀπεριτμήτους), there must have been a group of Israelites between 40 and 42 years old, who had been infants (0–2 years) at the time of the events at Kadesh Barnea, and who needed to be circumcised as well.

LXX renders subject and predicate of the same first clause of the verse הלכו בני־ישׂראל by ἀνέστραπται Ισραηλ. The minor difference in number of subject and verb (plural [MT]—singular [LXX]) may reflect scribal variation with respect to synonymous phrases,[332] or perhaps a deliberate attempt (by the Greek translator?) to make clear that the whole Israelite people had to suffer the sentence of forty

---

[329] Thus M.L. Margolis, *The Book of Joshua*, pp. 69–70; D.W. Gooding, The Circumcision at Gilgal, pp. 163–164; E. Tov, Midrash-type Exegesis, p. 56 (*The Greek and Hebrew Bible*, p. 158); T.C. Butler, *Joshua*, p. 55, and K. Bieberstein, *Josua-Jordan-Jericho*, p. 201 ('Interesse an chronologischen Recherchen'); J. Moatti-Fine, *Josué*, p. 118. Mazor's suggestion that the number of forty-two years reflects a deviant historiography which in MT has been adapted to the standard historiography is discussed and rejected in section 7.2.6 above.

[330] M.L. Margolis, *The Book of Joshua in Greek*, p. 69, line 23.

[331] J. Hollenberg, *Der Charakter*, p. 17; S. Holmes, *Joshua*, p. 30; C.D. Benjamin, *The Variations*, p. 33; R.G. Boling, *Joshua*, p. 184; R.D. Nelson, *Joshua*, p. 73, note i, regards this reconstructed Hebrew text to be a scribal error through dittography of שתים שנה, even though the two words only share the initial *šin*. See further E. Tov, Midrash-Type Exegesis, p. 56 (= *The Greek and Hebrew Bible*, p. 158); and L. Mazor, עיונים, pp. 185–186, who reconstructs ארבעים ארבעים שנה, see further section 7.2.6 above.

[332] Thus M.L. Margolis, *The Book of Joshua in Greek*, p. 70: 'G read הלך ישׂראל'. See L. Mazor, עיונים, p. 85ff. for an overview of all examples of divergencies between the two synonymous phrases ישׂראל and בני ישׂראל in Joshua (MT-LXX). See also V. Aptowitzer, *Das Schriftwort in der rabbinischen Literatur* IV, p. 257 for a parallel in *Eshkol ha-Kofer* 112a of the Caraite Jehuda Hadassi.

years in the desert. In that case the phrase כל־הגוי in the next clause in MT may have been reflected in this change of number. Although the Greek verb ἀναστρέφω has regularly been employed by the Greek translators of the Hebrew Bible and occurs 113 times in the Septuagint, it has almost always been used to translate the Hebrew lexeme שׁוב (thus e.g. LXX-Josh. 2:16; 7:3; 19:12.29.29).[333] The rendering of הלך by ἀναστρέφω (passive), *to dwell*,[334] is unusual.[335] The Greek translator probably wanted to stress the idea of the long period of Israel's stay in the desert, and hence corrected the number of years from forty to forty-two years.

The Greek translator specified the area of Israel's dwelling as ἐν τῇ ἐρήμῳ τῇ Μαδβαρίτιδι, *in the desert of Madbaritis*, whereas the Hebrew text simply speaks of *walking in the desert* במדבר. The addition of the name Madbaritis, a Hellenisation of this Hebrew word מִדְבָּר or perhaps the Aramaic מַדְבְּרָא, forms a plus *vis-à-vis* MT.[336]

Margolis considered the Greek phrase ἐν τῇ ἐρήμῳ τῇ Μαδβαρίτιδι to be a conflation of two renderings for the single Hebrew phrase במדבר. The second, unusual element, would constitute the original Greek text, whereas the first (literal) rendering would be a secondary interpolation in the Greek text. The witnesses to LXX, however, all attest to the longer reading of B with several minor scribal variations.[337] The Sahidic and Old Latin translations omit the second part

---

[333] HR, pp. 82b–83a; M.L. Margolis, *The Book of Joshua in Greek*, p. 70, refered to the few parallels for ἀναστρέφω pass for הלך in LXX^A^-3 Reg. 6:12 (ושמרת את־כל־מצותי ללכת בהם—καὶ φυλάσσῃς πασὰς τὰς ἐντολὰς μου ἀναστρεφέσθαι ἐν αὐταῖς); LXX-Prov. 20:7; LXX-Zech. 3:8(7) and LXX-Ezek. 19:6 (ויתהלך בתוך־אריות—ἀναστρεφόμενος ἐν μέσῳ λεοντων).

[334] Thus LSJ 122a; W.F. Arndt, F.W. Gingrich, *A Greek-English Lexicon of the New Testament and Other Early Christian Literature*. Chicago/Cambridge 1957⁴, pp. 60b–61a. GELS², p. 33a–b, lists only the active meanings 1. *to turn back, return*, 2. *to busy oneself*, for the occurrences in LXX-Pentateuch and LXX-Twelve Prophets. LEH, p. 32b, lists the meaning *to wander in* for LXX-Josh. 5:6, but this meaning seems to be provided by the Hebrew equivalent הלך, since no other attestations for ἀναστρέφω passive = *to wander in* are given by LEH or LSJ.

[335] Thus C.G. den Hertog, *Studien zur griechischen Übersetzung*, p. 146 (= Jos 5,4–6 in der griechischen Übersetzung, *ZAW* 110 [1998], p. 603).

[336] C.G. den Hertog, *Studien*, pp. 85, 143; idem, Erwägungen zur Territorialgeschichte Koilesyriens in frühhellenistischer Zeit, in *ZDPV* 111 (1995), pp. 168–184; H.St.J. Thackeray, *A Grammar of the Old Testament in Greek*, § 11.14.

[337] These are: Μαδβαρειτιδι [B*.W.29.56.59.108.376.509], Μαδβαριτιδι [121], Μαγβαριτιδι [118 txt], Μαμβαριτιδι [344], Μανβαριτιδι [the Catena group 52.53.57.85.130] Μαδαριτιδι [16.71], Βαδβαριτιδι [120], Μαβδαριτι [55], Μαβδαριδι [54.75],

[VetLat.: *annis habitauerant filii Istrahel in deserto* . . . [doublet:] *.XL. enim annis conuersatus est Istrahel in deserto*]. Ms. 56 (M) quotes the literal Greek translation of the Hebrew text: ἐν τῳ ἑβραϊκῳ· μ̅ ἔτη ἀνέστραπται ιηλ ἐν τῇ ἐρήμῳ ἕως τοῦ τελέσθηναι τὸ ἐθνος ἅπαν and provides lexical information with respect to this geographical name: λέξις ἑβραϊκή· Μαδβαρίτις ἐρήμος ἑρμηνεύεται. It is evident that the unusual geographical name belongs to the original Greek text, and that there is no basis for Margolis' conjectural solution to the problem posed by the Greek text to assume that the Greek translator originally only transliterated the Hebrew phrase.

The geographical name Μαδβαρῖτις recurs in LXX-Josh. 18:12 (καὶ ἔσται αὐτοῦ ἡ διέξοδος *ἡ Μαδβαρῖτις Βαιθων*—[Qere ק] והיה [Ketib כ]) והיו תצאתיו מדברה בית און and should probably be reconstructed in LXX-Josh. 15:61 after the reading Βαδδαργείς attested by the main E, P_1, C witnesses (MT במדבר).[338] In these geographical lists, however, the context dictates that this toponym refers to the arid area west of the Dead Sea, not the Sinai desert in which Israel dwelt for forty(-two) years according to the traditions from the Pentateuch. In passages related to Josh. 5:6, such as Josh. 14:10 (Kaleb reminds Joshua of Moses' promise) and Josh. 24:7 (the recapitulation of Israel's history from exodus to entrance), the Greek translator offers a straightforward rendering of במדבר by ἐν τῇ ἐρήμῳ.

The name does not occur in any other classical Greek literary or epigraphic source, so that it is highly unlikely that the name of the desert region offers additional information to the Greek translator's readership. The plus in LXX obscures rather than elucidates the text, and for that reason can hardly be ascribed to a deliberate intention on the part of the Greek translator.[339] Probably, then, he already

Μαυαριτιδι [72], Μωαβιτιδι [82.314], Μαβδαρειτιδι [the correctors of B. A.N and other mss.].

[338] The reading attested by the main E, P_1, and C witnesses βαδδαργεῖς probably reflects an early corruption, thus M.L. Margolis, *The Book of Joshua in Greek*, p. 319; and C.G. den Hertog, *Studien*, p. 86, who accepted Margolis' conjectural emendation, but reconstructed Μαδβαριτις instead of Μαδβαρεῖς (Margolis).

[339] C.G. den Hertog, *Studien*, p. 86, and in an extensive private communication dated 17.03.2000, explains the double rendering as an amplification (by means of the phrase ἐν τῇ ἐρήμῳ) of the transliteration of the Hebrew, but does not explain why the Greek translator decided to give a transliteration of such a common word as מדבר in the first place: 'Daß der Übersetzer hier das Bedürfnis hatte, eine hellenisierende Transkription—die auch der wörtlichsten *Übersetzung* an Wörtlichkeit

found the doublet in his Hebrew *Vorlage* במדבר המדבר, which might be the result of dittography, as suggested in 1851 already by Z. Frankel and further by R.G. Boling.[340] Given the Greek translator's relatively weak knowledge of exact historical topography of Palestine,[341] as becomes evident in the Greek text of the topographical lists (Josh. 13–21), including the two 'incorrect' interpretations of מדבר in 15:61 and 18:12, his rendering of such a phrase as we find it in 5:6 belongs in the category of 'misunderstood geographical terms' (thus Benjamin).[342] Nevertheless, in spite of this, the Greek translator still sought to offer a creative interpretation of this unknown toponym by transforming the doublet into a Hellenistic geographical name by means of the addition -ῖτις.

---

noch überlegen ist!—und eine wörtliche Übersetzung nebeneinander zu stellen, mag damit zusammenhangen, daß er mit Μαδβαρῖτις eine Namensbildung eingeführt hat, von der er nicht sicher sein konnte, daß sie ohne Verdeutlichung verstanden werden würde.'

[340] Z. FRANKEL, *Ueber den Einfluss der palästinischen Exegese auf die alexandrinische Hermeneutik*. Leipzig 1851, pp. 205–206, note e: 'Josua 5, 6 ist במדבר übersetzt ἐν τῇ ἐρήμῳ τῇ Μαδβαρίτιδι. Die Bedeutung des so häufig vorkommenden מדבר war unbezweifelt jedem Vertenten bekannt; wenn also doch dieses Μαδβαριτ. als das hebr. Wort (corrumpirt) neben der Uebers. stehet, so kann es nur als Einschiebsel aus einer Randglosse, das dann ein ungewissender Abschreiber gräcisirte, betrachtet werden.' R.G. BOLING, *Joshua*, p. 193.

A. MASIUS, *Josuae imperatoris historia*, Commentary (1838), col. 1045, suggested that the Hebrew noun מדבר might have undergone a semantic transformation from desert to solitude, and therefore constituted a meaningful precision introduced by a later scribe: 'Desertum istud, quasi suo nomine, appellant Septuaginta interpretes, Μαδβαρίτιδα: fortassis vulgus eo seculo quo hi scripsere, hebraeum verbum *Midbar*, quod desertum significat, ei solitudini, ut proprium ejus nomen, attribuerat, quodam loquendi usu, nisi imperiti hominis audacia adscriptum hoc nomen olim in illa editione graeca putemus.' There is, however, no evidence for such a postulated transformation.

[341] C.G. DEN HERTOG, *Studien*, pp. 142–144: '5.3 Die Lokalisierung der Übersetzung'.

[342] C.D. BENJAMIN, *The Variations*, p. 13. Although Den Hertog refutes Benjamin's solution, he offers a very similar one himself: C.G. DEN HERTOG, *Studien*, p. 143: 'Auf Grund der beiden letzteren Belege [15:61, 18:21] könnte man noch fragen, ob Jos[Übs] hier vielleicht aus Kenntnissen über die Verwaltung Palästinas (eigene Verwaltungseinheit am Ostabfall des judäischen Gebirges zwischen En Gedi und der benjaminitischen Nordgrenze—Vorort Jericho?) geschöpft hat. Da er aber in Jos 5:6 den Ort der Wüstenwanderung ebenfalls als Μαδβαρῖτις bezeichnet, liegt es auf der Hand, in diesem außerhalb des Josuabuches nirgendwo belegbaren Toponym eine freie Bildung nach festem Muster zu sehen, die eben keinen genaueren Ortskenntnisse voraussetzt.'

7.6.4.2 *The Fate of the Older Generation*

The second and subsequent clauses of the Greek text of verse 6, διὸ ἀπερίτμητοι ἦσαν οἱ πλεῖστοι αὐτῶν τῶν μαχίμων τῶν ἐξεληλυθότων ἐκ γῆς Αἰγύπτου οἱ ἀπειθήσαντες τῶν ἐντυλῶν τυῦ θευῦ, οἷς καὶ διώρισεν μὴ ἰδεῖν τὴν γῆν, have proved a *crux interpretum* among the exegetes of the Greek text of Joshua. On the one hand, it contains several unusual equivalents for the MT (διό—עד; ἀπερίτμητος—תמם; οἱ πλεῖστοι αὐτῶν—כל־הגוי; τῶν μαχίμων—אנשי המלחמה; ἀπειθέω—לא שמע; αἱ ἐντολαί τοῦ θεοῦ—קול יהוה; the plus καί; διορίζω—נשבע; and the minus יהוה להם in MT-5:6e), which seem to point to a similar creative elaboration of the redundant Hebrew text, while on the other hand the focus of the Greek text as a whole seems to shift from the present generation circumcised by Joshua (διὸ ἀπερίτμητοι ἦσαν) to the older generation that had died in the desert (μὴ ἰδεῖν τὴν γῆν). The text as it stands seems to provide the reasons for the uncircumcised state (5:6b διὸ ἀπερίτμητοι ἦσαν) of the Israelites circumcised by Joshua. The information, however, given in the first clause of the verse, *since for forty-two years Israel had dwelt in the desert of Madbaritis*, does not provide the expected answer to the question why the Israelites had abandoned the practice of circumcision. Although it is not impossible to translate the corresponding statement in verse 7 διὰ τὸ αὐτοὺς γεγενῆσθαι κατὰ τὴν ὁδὸν ἀπεριτμήτους in that sense: *because they* [i.e., the younger generation] *had become uncircumcised on the way*, it is more logical to render the verb γίγνομαι here according to its primary meaning *to be born, to come into being*:[343] *because they had been born on the way being uncircumcised*.[344] The Greek text as its stands is problematic. Below five attempts to solve the problem of the inner logic of the Greek text are offered and rejected in favour of my own proposal.

---

[343] LEH, p. 90a–b; LSJ, pp. 349a–350a. GELS², pp. 97b–99b. Mss. B, 129* (E), 134 (S_b), 376 (P_1), and 509 (M) read in LXX-Josh. 5:7 γεγεννησθαι, i.e., a perfect infinitive medium of γεννάω, *to produce* (LSJ, p. 344a), *to bring forth* (LEH, p. 86b; GELS², p. 95a), but neither Rahlfs nor Margolis adopted this reading in their main text.

[344] See the translations by L.L. BRENTON, *The Septuagint Version. Greek and English*, p. 285: 'because they were uncircumcised, having been born by the way.' and J. MOATTI-FINE, *Josué*, p. 118: 'parce que, nés au cours du voyage, ils étaient restés incirconcis.' See further P. WALTERS (KATZ), *The Text of the Septuagint. Its Corruptions and their emendation*. Cambridge 1973, p. 115.

7.6.4.2.1 *A Caesura?*

In order to solve the problem posed by the logic of the text, several scholars have postulated a clause division somewhere between the statement *on which account most of them were uncircumcised* and the subsequent text dealing with the older generation. Holmes suggested that in the Hebrew *Vorlage* of LXX a stop has to be assumed after רבים מהם (his retroversion of οἱ πλεῖστοι αὐτῶν, see section 7.2.3 above), so that the sentence would read: *For forty-two years Israel had dwelt in the desert, wherefore most of them were uncircumcised.* In that case, the phrase 'most of them' would refer to the two groups of Israelites mentioned in LXX-5:4. The relation, however, between dwelling in the desert and not being circumcised is not very clear. The real problems with this solution come in the remainder of the verse. Holmes suggested that the word אשׁר before נשׁבע להם should be deleted.[345] In that case, however, the phrase אנשׁי המלחמה becomes the object of the clause with Yhwh as implied subject, so that the *nota accusativi* would be required before אנשׁי המלחמה. Moreover, the להם after נשׁבע loses its function as well. It remains difficult to see how such a hybrid Hebrew text could have resulted from the MT or resulted into the present MT. L. Mazor proposes to move the caesura back a bit: לכן ערלים היו, מרביתם מאנשׁי היצאים מארץ מצרים אשׁר לא שׁמעו, but this reconstruction leaves the first clause without a subject and the second without a predicate.[346] These reconstructions are thus problematic from the point of view of classical Hebrew syntax, and, moreover, find no support in the Greek text where the shift in subject is not marked, nor in the Hebrew text of MT, which has a completely clear structure (see section 7.4 above).

What remains problematic in these attempts, is that it remains difficult to see why a Greek translator who introduced so many nuances and unusual renderings in order to clarify the text according to his interpretation, should have abandoned his practice of interpretative translation in the case of this single clause. Even if the Greek translator had found a problematic Hebrew phrase, it would have been his policy to elucidate the text as he did throughout this chapter, rather than to transmit it in the problematic formulation

[345] S. HOLMES, *Joshua*, pp. 29–30; C.D. BENJAMIN, *The Variations*, p. 32, A.G. AULD, Joshua. The Hebrew and Greek Texts, pp. 8–9 (*Joshua Retold*, p. 13); R.D. NELSON, *Joshua*, p. 72ff.

[346] L. MAZOR, עיונים, p. 172. See section 7.2.6 above.

we now find in our oldest extant witnesses. Had the Greek translator found before him such a syntactically awkward Hebrew text as reconstructed by Holmes or Mazor, he would have marked the shift in subject by means of a disjunctive conjunction, such as δέ. The present text does not allow for a distinction between the subjects of the clauses οἱ πλεῖστοι αὐτῶν τῶν μαχίμων τῶν ἐξεληλυθότων ἐκ γῆς Αἰγύπτου and οἱ απειθήσαντες τῶν ἐντολῶν τοῦ θεοῦ, οἷς καὶ διώρισεν μὴ ἰδεῖν τὴν γῆν, and neither does the lay-out of the oldest Greek manuscripts (B.A.W) provide any support for a differentiation between the two nominal clauses.

7.6.4.2.2 *The Conjunction διό*

As stated in section 7.2.8 above, C.G. den Hertog tries to get round the difficulty posed by the Greek text by interpreting the conjunction διό as a *causal conjunction*. The logic of the sentence would then become: *a certain number of Israelites had not been circumcised in Egypt* [verse 4b], *therefore they were humiliated by the Egyptians* [verse 9]; *Israel had wandered 42 years in the desert, because* [διό] *they were uncircumcised* [verse 6]. The wandering would thus be presented as a punishment for the Israelites' laxity with respect to the circumcision law. Although this interpretation would make more sense of the text, διό always introduces a result or conclusion, never a cause.[347] The variants in the Greek tradition, διότι (W.29) and καὶ διὰ τοῦτο (manuscripts 44, 54, 75, 106, 134, 314 and VetLat [second version 'Ideoquae'], all belonging to the S-family) are best understood as secondary, inner-Greek developments. The conjunction thus introduces the logical result of this long wandering in the desert, not the reason for it. Nevertheless, it is interesting to note that within the translated books of the Septuagint, the conjunction occurs only nine times, predominantly as a translation of the Hebrew phrases על־כן or לכן in LXX-Job,[348] which is commonly regarded as a free rendering.[349] Its occurrence here thus points to a well-considered initiative by the Greek translator.

[347] See section 7.2.8 above. See also D.W. Gooding, The Circumcision at Gilgal, p. 164.

[348] That is in LXX^{S}-Job 9:21 without Hebrew equivalent, LXX-Job 9:22 probably as equivalent for Hebrew על־כן; LXX-Job 32:6 idem; 32:10 for לכן; 34:10 idem, 34:34 without Hebrew counterpart; 37:24 for לכן; and 42:6 for על־כן; LXX-Ps. 115:1 corresponding to MT-Ps. 116:10 כי.

[349] See e.g. H.B. Swete, *An Introduction to the Old Testament in Greek*, pp. 255–257; G. Dorival, M. Harl, O. Munnich, *La Bible grecque des Septante*, p. 179.

7.6.4.2.3 *The Construction αὐτῶν τῶν μαχίμων*
Equally unsatisfactory is Gooding's proposal to interpret the genitive [οἱ πλεῖστοι] αὐτῶν τῶν . . . as a possessive (*'most of them* [*sons*] *of the warriors that had left Egypt'*) rather than a partititve genitive (*'most of them, that is of the ones that had left Egypt'*), in order to account for the required shift between the two generations of Israelites. One wonders, however, why the Greek translator would have altered the clear and unproblematic Hebrew sentence into an obscure statement that very easily could be misunderstood.

The pronoun αὐτός in the phrase οἱ πλεῖστοι αὐτῶν τῶν μαχίμων seems to be redundant. For that reason Margolis omitted the pronoun from his critical text: οἱ πλεῖστοι τῶν μαχίμων. The textual basis, however, for this reconstruction, which consists in the manuscripts 53 [M] and 75 [S_a], the Sahidic [E] and Armenian translations [C], is relatively weak, and therefore rejected by several scholars.[350] Moreover, this reconstruction does not solve our problem and does not explain why the Greek formulation should have been corrupted into this *lectio difficilior*.

It seems more likely that the phrase τῶν μαχίμων . . . should be seen as an apposition to the preceding αὐτῶν and should be rendered accordingly: *'most of them, that is/insofar as it concerns, the warriors that had gone out of the land of Egypt . . .'* or *'la plupart d'entre eux, les combattants sortis d'Égypte, ceux qui . . .'* (Moatti-Fine). The function of this construction is thus to make a precision, comparable to the restrictive apposition in MT אנשי המלחמה after כל־הגוי, *the entire people, that is the valiant men*. Those who had been disobedient (5:6c) formed only a part of whole Israel (5:6a). This interpretation would fit the general character of the Greek version of this passage and makes sense of the otherwise redundant Greek expression, but does not yet solve our main problem with the logic of the text.

---

[350] S. Sipilä, A Note to the Users of Margolis' Joshua Edition, p. 19; K. Bieberstein, *Lukian und Theodotion im Josuabuch*, p. 24; C.G. den Hertog, *Studien*, p. 96: 'Für die Beurteilung bleiben somit nur die vier Textzeugen, welche das αὐτῶν auslassen. Es sind 53.75.Co.Arm. Diese Textzeugen gehören in Margolis' Gruppeneinteilung vier verschiedene Textgruppen an! Von Hs 75 hat Margolis selbst (1927, 312) festgestellt, daß sie zu Abkürzungen des Textes neigt.'

7.6.4.2.4 *The Intermediary Generation*

According to A. Blaschke, the Greek translator attempted in this clause to account for the existence of the group of Israelites that had been circumcised in Egypt and left Egypt as children: most of the Israelites had died in the desert (LXX-5:6b), but apparently there were also some sons of the Israelites of the Exodus generation that had been circumcised.[351] The subtle use of the genuine Greek expression οἱ πλεῖστοι αὐτῶν, *most of them*, in the phrase ἀπερίτμητοι ἦσαν *οἱ πλεῖστοι* αὐτῶν τῶν μαχίμων τῶν ἐξεληλυθότων ἐκ γῆς Αἰγύπτου, would then correspond nicely with the other genuine Greek expression in verse 4b *ὅσοι* ποτὲ ἀπερίτμητοι ἦσαν τῶν ἐξεληλυθότων ἐξ Αἰγύπτου. In that case, LXX verse 6 would provide an explanation for the fact that those who left Egypt uncircumcised had remained uncircumcised up until now. One would have expected, however, to find a construction with the verb ὑπομένω, *to remain* (e.g., διὸ ἀπερίτμητοι ὑπέμεινον οἱ πλεῖστοι), as we find it for instance in LXX-Josh. 19:48a (καὶ ὁ Αμμοραῖος *ὑπέμεινεν* τοῦ κατοικεῖν ἐν Ελωμ, cf. MT-Judg. 1:35 ויואל האמרי לשבת בהר־חרס באילון). Furthermore, if verse 6 (LXX) provided background information about the group mentioned in verse 4b (LXX), one would have expected an explanation why they had not yet been circumcised in Egypt, for instance in a statement that the Israelites had neglected to circumcise their children in Egypt (see section 7.6.3.3 above), and why the desert was an unsuitable place to perform circumcision. Perhaps the Greek translator held the desert to be an inappropriate and unhygienic place for the execution of this operation (so Blaschke),[352] but if so, he did not state that explicitly.

The most problematic aspect of this interpretation is the fact that the formulation in verse 6 has a small but important plus compared with the similar one in verse 4: τῶν μαχίμων. The Greek text as it

---

[351] A. Blaschke, *Beschneidung*, p. 116: 'die schon beschnittenen Kinder der Auszugsgeneration sind ja auch noch da.'

[352] A. Blaschke, *Beschneidung*, p. 116: 'Als Grund für das Unterlassen der Beschneidung wird hier ausdrücklich (διό) die Wanderungssituation genannt. Die Mutmaßung, die der MT nur naheliegt, hat die LXX damit zum Faktum gemacht. Daß eine Reisesituation als aufschiebend für die Durchführung der Beschneidung gewertet werden kann, belegen auch die späteren jüdischen Auslegungen zu Ex 4,24–26 in MekhY zu Ex 18,3 und ShemR 5,8: Mose habe wegen des befohlenen Reiseantritts die Beschneidung seines Sohn verschoben.' See further Talmud babli Yebamoth 71b–72a, cited in section 7.4.2.1 above.

stands does not provide additional information concerning the two groups already mentioned in verses 4 and 5, but clearly introduces yet a third, group, i.e. those who left Egypt *as warriors* (τῶν μαχίμων τῶν ἐξεληλυθότων ἐκ γῆς Αἰγύπτου) and were even older than those Israelites that had already been born in Egypt but were not yet eighteen at the time of the Exodus. It is this older group of warriors that had been disobedient (οἱ ἀπειθήσαντες) who for that reason were not allowed to enter the Promised Land (οἷς καὶ διώρισεν μὴ ἰδεῖν αὐτοὺς τὴν γῆν). They had died in the desert before the present moment in the narrative in which Joshua and the remaining Israelites entered the Promised Land. Whether or not all or any of these disobedient Israelites of the older generation were circumcised is irrelevant for the present situation: they had died in the desert and no longer belong to the Israelites that entered the Promised Land. Thus, the correspondence between the verse 4b and 6b in the Greek text is misleading, since it refers to two distinct groups.

7.6.4.2.5 *A Statement About the Older Generation?*

Finally, it could be argued that the Greek translator wanted to state that not even this older generation was circumcised. As we have seen above, the Greek translator inferred from verse 9 that already in Egypt circumcision was no longer carried out, hence those who left Egypt as warriors must have been uncircumcised too. In that case, however, one would have expected to find this view clearly expressed in the Greek text by means of an adverbial καὶ: διὸ ἀπερίτμητοι ἦσαν καὶ οἱ μαχίμοι οἱ ἐξεληλυθόντες . . . Since the Greek translator felt free enough to reformulate the Hebrew text of verses 4 and 5, one wonders why he did not express this view clearly already in these verses in a formulation such as ὅτι οὐ περιετμήθησαν ἐν Αἰγύπτῳ.

In the present narrative, the older generation has only two logical functions: 1. they are responsible for the long wandering in the desert (as the Hebrew text clearly and unproblematically states), and 2. they are responsible for the fact that their sons remained uncircumcised during all these years. The Greek translator, however, did not stress either of the two functions. In verses 5 and 7, the Hebrew text clearly states that the older males did not circumcise their children on the way (לא־מלו אתם), whereas the Greek translator only made a statement about the uncircumcised state (ἀπερίτμητοι ἦσαν) of the younger generation. Likewise, the Hebrew text of verse 6 is completely logical with respect to the first function of this older generation (כי ארבעים שנה הלכו בני־ישראל במדבר עד־תם כל־הגוי אנשי... המלחמה). In the logic of the Greek text one could only expect a statement similar to MT: *those who had left Egypt as warriors and, moreover, had been disobedient, had died in the desert during the long wandering.* If the Greek translator deliberately departed from the clear, coherent and logical Hebrew text in order to present his own exegesis, why, then, did he do so in such an obscure and half-hearted manner?

7.6.4.2.6 *A New Interpretation*

The Greek text thus presents 'a puzzling internal contradiction'[353] that has evoked such evaluations as 'was wir jetzt lesen, ist geradezu unsinnig und voller Widersprüche',[354] 'unanimously admitted to be wrong',[355] 'logical nonsense',[356] and 'eine unsinnige Aussage'.[357] Either the Greek translator had a slip of the mind when he created the present text, or the present Greek text is not the original product of the Greek translator. I prefer the latter option, following the suggestion advanced by Hollenberg: 'Fast scheint es, als ob die LXX hier nicht unverzehrt geblieben ist'.[358]

Entering the realm of conjectural emendation of the extant Greek text, I see three possibilities for restoring the internal logic of the Greek text: [1] Following Den Hertog's analysis, the conjunction διό is altered into διότι. In that case, the problem still remains why we do not find any trace of a similar reinterpretation of the relation between wandering in the desert and laxity with respect to circumcision, either in LXX-Josh. 5:2–9 or elsewhere in contemporaneous literature. [2] By means of a disjunctive particle between the two groups mentioned in LXX-Josh. 5:4–6, a caesura is introduced. Such a particle, for instance δέ, would separate the subject of ἀπερίτμητοι, which must apply to the younger generation, from the nominal phrase οἱ ἀπειθήσαντες, which must apply to the older generation. The question then arises how to reconstruct such a text and where

[353] R.D. Nelson, *Joshua*, pp. 75–76, note 4.
[354] J. Hollenberg, *Der Charakter*, p. 18.
[355] S. Holmes, *Joshua*, pp. 13, 29.
[356] D.W. Gooding, The Circumcision at Gilgal, p. 164.
[357] C.G. den Hertog, *Studien*, p. 148 (= *ZAW* 110, p. 605). See further K. Bieberstein, *Josua-Jordan-Jericho*, p. 202 (see section 7.2.7 above) and R.D. Nelson, *Joshua*, pp. 75–76, note 4.
[358] J. Hollenberg, *Der Charakter*, p. 18.

to put such a particle. Without the predicate ἀπερίτμητοι the verb ἀπειθήσαντες can easily be identified as οἱ πλεῖστοι αὐτῶν τῶν μαχίμων τῶν ἐξεληλυθότων ἐκ γῆς Αἰγύπτου, since only those Israelites older than 20 years were sentenced to die in the desert (Num. 14). In that case, one would have to reconstruct a subject for the predicate ἀπερίτμητοι ἦσαν and a conjunction καί or, more in conformity with the translation technique in this passage, the particle δέ (used in verses 2, 4, 7, 8 as well): διὸ ἀπερίτμητοι ἦσαν πάντες, οὓς Ἰησοῦς περιέτεμεν· οἱ δὲ πλεῖστοι [αὐτῶν?] τῶν μαχιμῶν . . . This emendation is rather drastic, does not give a logical antecedent for the phrase αὐτῶν, does not explain how the present Greek text originated from this longer text, and, moreover, does not solve the logical problem of how many males could have become uncircumcised because of wandering too long in the desert.

[3] It has become increasingly clear that all problems concerning the internal logic of the text are related to the single word ἀπερίτμητοι in verse 6. Since this phrase occurs repeatedly in our passage (verse 4b, 7), and since the corresponding Masoretic text goes to great lengths to explain how it came to be that there were Israelites that had not yet been circumcised, it would not appear so strange to find this phrase here as well. As we have seen above, however, the Greek text does not follow the Hebrew text (as preserved in MT) with respect to the structure of verses 4–7. Verse 4 according to the Greek version forms the continuation of the narrative, not the beginning of a long recapitulation and explanation, which is given only in verse 6. What one would have expected to read at this place in the Greek text is not so much an explanation why several Israelites had not been circumcised, since LXX-4b makes clear that the Greek translator is not so much troubled with that circumstance as the rabbis in Late Antiquity and modern scholars have been; rather, one would expect to read here that this older generation had died in the desert, as the logic of the Greek version of the entire verse 6 dictates, and as we find twice in the Hebrew text (MT-5:4e; 5:6b).

We do find such a statement, if we postulate that the present Greek text (attested by all witnesses to LXX) διὸ ἀπερίτμητοι ἦσαν [οἱ πλεῖστοι αὐτῶν], *wherefore [most of them] were uncircumcised* presents an early corruption in the transmission of the Greek text from the graphically similar phrase διὸ ἀπηρτίσθησαν [οἱ πλεῖστοι αὐτῶν], *wherefore [most of them] were finished off.* This reconstructed rendering would represent a non-stereotypical, but *ad sensum* appropriate rendering of the Hebrew phrase [כל־הגוי] עד־תם, *until* [*the entire nation*] *was finished off*. The Greek verb ἀπαρτίζω (pass.) means *to be completed; to be complete; to be finished; to be brought to perfection*,[359] and corresponds well to the meaning of the verb תמם, *to be complete; to become complete; to come to an end, expire*.[360]

The verb does not occur in LXX-Joshua, nor in any other original 'Septuagint' translation of the books of the Hebrew Bible. Where the Hebrew verb תמם occurs in Josh. (3:16.17; 4:1.10.11; 5:8; 8:24; 10:20), it has either been rendered by the Greek verb συντελέω (3:17; 4:1.10.11), reformulated in the phrase ἕως [εἰς τὸ] τέλος (3:16; 8:24; 10:20), or not rendered at all (as in 5:8, see below). These two observations would discredit my conjectural emendation, if the Greek translation of Joshua were very stereotyped and literal. This, however, is evidently not the case.

The Greek version of Joshua contains many lexemes that are unique within the larger corpus of the Septuagint.[361] Although this circumstance probably applies to many books of the Septuagint, it is nevertheless noteworthy that many of these *hapaxhermeneuta* have been employed for common Hebrew verbs such as בוא, הלך and נכה, which, moreover, have been rendered in LXX-Joshua by a variety of Greek equivalents.[362] Already in our passage we find various translations of for the same Hebrew verb, for instance the renderings of מול by the unusual Greek equivalent περικαθαίρω (5:4) in addition to the standard equivalent περιτέμνω, and שבע translated both by

[359] LSJ, p. 180b, Suppl. 41a; W. Bauer, *Griechisch-Deutsches Wörterbuch*, col. 160–161; F. Preisigke, E. Kiessling, *Wörterbuch der griechischen Papyrusurkunden*. Berlin 1923. col. 157.

[360] BDB, p. 1070a–b; HALOT, pp. 1752–1754.

[361] For instance διεκβάλλω (for יצא in 15:4.9.11; 16:7, עבר in 15:7, עלה in 15:8, and תאר in 15:9.11), ἐκπολιορκέω (7:3 for נכה, and 10:5 for לחם Niphʿal), ἐπιπαραγίνομαι (10:9 for בום), εὐτόνως (6:8 without Hebrew equivalent), καταπελματόομαι (9:5 for the rare Hebrew verb טלא), καταφερής (7:5 for מוֹרָד), καταχαλάω (2:15 for ירד Hiphʿil), κληρωτί (21:4.5.7.8 for בַּגּוֹרָל), λινοκαλάμη (2:6 for בְּפִשְׁתֵּי הָעֵץ, also a *hapax*), λοφιά (15:2.5; 18:19 for לָשׁוֹן), περίοδος (6:16 for פַּעַם), προσανάβασις (15:3 for מַעֲלָה), συγκαταμιγνύμαι (23:12 for בוא), σχοινισμός (17:5 for חֶבֶל), ὑπουργός (1:1 for מְשָׁרֵת, see section 6.4.1 above), χωματίζεσθαι (11:13 as an idiomatic rendering of הָעֹמְדוֹת עַל־תִּלָּם) and χωροβατέω (18:8 for כתב, 18:8 for הלך Hitpaʿel, and 18:9 for עבר).

[362] See e.g. the observation by J. Moatti-Fine, *Josué*, p. 54, that the Hebrew verb נכה has been rendered by 14 different Greek equivalents.

the unique rendering διορίζω (5:6) and the standard equivalent ὄμνυμι (5:6; further 1:6; 2:12; 9:15.18.19.20; 14:9; 21:41.42), as well as the verb ὁρκίζω (6:26 for שׁבע Hiph'il).[363] In fact, the whole passage LXX-Josh. 5:2–12 abounds with unusual translations, as the present chapter attempts to demonstrate.[364]

In other words, the circumstance that the Greek translator does not employ the verb συντελέω here, assuming that his *Vorlage* did not differ from MT, should not trouble us. Rather, the alleged use of the verb ἀπαρτίζω in LXX-Josh. 5:6 not only fits in well the overall context of LXX-Josh. 5:2–9 and the meaning of the corresponding Hebrew verb תמם, but also with the style of varying Greek equivalents for the same Hebrew word and the translator's preference for specific Greek formulations.

7.6.4.2.7 *The Verb ἀπαρτίζω*

In the wider corpus of younger Jewish and Christian Hellenistic writings we find the verb ἀπαρτίζω in readings attributed to Aquila and Symmachus, in the Testament of Levi 9:11,[365] and three times in the writings of the Apostolic Fathers:[366] the letters of Ignatius to the Ephesians 1:1,[367] and his letter to Polycarp 7:3[368] and the Martyrium of Polycarp 6:2.[369] Relevant to our discussion are the readings by

---

[363] Furthermore, the common Hebrew verb הלך has been rendered here by ἀναστρέφω (5:6), in addition to the following 14 equivalents employed in LXX-Joshua for the same verb ἀναβαίνω (2:1), ἀπέρχομαι (2:16; 22:4), ἀποτρέχω (23:14), ἔρχομαι (9:4.6) εἰσπορεύω (6:13), ἐπακολουθέω (6:9), παραγίνομαι (9:12), παραπορεύω (6:9) πορεύω (1:9.16; 2:1.5.22; 3:3.4.6; 4:18; 6:9; 8:9; 9:11, 14:10; 16:8; 17:7; 18:8.8.8.9; 22:5.6.9.9; 23:16; 24:17), πράσσω (1:7) προπορεύω (6:13), προσέρχομαι (5:13), προσπορεύω (8:35/9:2f), συμπορεύομαι (10:24).

[364] See further section 2.2 above, especially sections 2.2.1 and 2.2.8.

[365] T.Levi. 9:11 Καὶ πρὸ τοῦ εἰσελθεῖν εἰς τὰ ἅγια, λούου· καὶ ἐν τῷ θύειν, νίπτου. καὶ ἀπαρτίζων πάλιν τὴν θυσίαν, νίπτου. *and before entering the holy place, bathe, and when you offer (the sacrifice), wash, and when you finish again the sacrifice, wash.*' Text M. DE JONGE (ed.), *The Testaments of the Twelve Patriarchs. A Critical Edition of the Greek Text.* Leiden 1978; Translation by H.W. HOLLANDER, M. DE JONGE, *The Testaments of the Twelve Patriarchs. A Commentary.* (SVTP 8) Leiden 1985.

[366] Texts and translations by K. LAKE, *The Apostolic Fathers* I. Cambridge, Massachusetts/London 1912.

[367] Ignatius to the Ephesians 1:1 μιμηταὶ ὄντες θεοῦ, ἀναζωπυρήσαντες ἐν αἵματι θεοῦ τὸ συγγενικὸν ἔργον τελείως ἀπηρτίσατε· *You are imitators of God, and having kindled your brotherly task by the blood of God, you completed it perfectly.*

[368] Ignatius to Polycarp 7:3.V: τοῦτο τὸ ἔργον θεοῦ ἐστιν καὶ ὑμῶν, ὅταν αὐτὸ ἀπαρτίστητε. *This is the work of God and yourselves, when you complete it.*

[369] Martyrium of Polycarp 6:2 (id.): καὶ ὁ εἰρήναρχος, ὁ εκεληρωμένος τὸ αὐτα ὄνομα, Ἡρώδης ἐπιλεγόμενος, ἔσπευδεν εἰς τὸ στάδιον αὐτὸν εἰσαγαγεῖν, ἵνα ἐκεῖνος μὲν τὸν ἴδιον κλῆρον ἀπαρτίστῃ Χριστοῦ κοινωνος γενόμενος, οἱ δὲ προδόντες αὐτὸν

Aquila and Symmachus. Aquila employed the verb as a standard equivalent for the Hebrew root שׁלם, *to come to a conclusion*,[370] which is a synonym for תמם, whereas Symmachus used the verb to render various Hebrew expressions.[371]

The verb ἀπαρτίζω occurs in Aquila's version five times: [1] In Gen. 34:21 MT states that Hamor and Shechem designate the sons of Jacob as friendly people: האנשׁים האלה שׁלמים הם אתנו. Instead of the LXX rendering of (Οἱ ἄνθρωποι οὗτοι] εἰρηνικοί [εἰσιν μεθ' ἡμῶν·), Aquila (according to Jerome) employed the word ἀπηρτισμένους. [2] In the law of the just and fair weights for measurements, Deut. 25:15, Aquila replaced the LXX rendering (στάθμιον) ἀληθινὸν (καὶ δίκαιον), *a trustful and just weight*, for the Hebrew אבן שׁלמה וצדק, *a complete and righteous stone* by ἀπηρτισμένον (according to ms. M). [3] Likewise in Deut. 27:6, the same Hebrew phrase אבנים שׁלמות, *complete stones*, has been rendered by Aquila by the word ἀπηρτισμένους as opposed to LXX's option for ὁλοκλήρους, *intact*. [4] In Isa. 60:20, Aquila again employed this verb (ἀπαρτισθήσονται according to ms. 86) to render the Hebrew verb שׁלם in the phrase ושׁלמו ימי אבלך, *and completed shall be the days of you mourning*, where LXX-Isa. has καὶ ἀναπληρωθήσονται (αἱ ἡμέραι τοῦ πένθους σου). [5] In Amos 1:6, Aquila restored the original meaning of the Hebrew phrase in MT-Amos: עַל־הַגְלוֹתָם גָּלוּת שְׁלֵמָה, *because they (i.e. the inhabitants of Gaza) carried into exile a whole people*, misunderstood by the LXX-translator, who read שׁלמה as a reference to king Solomon and translated the phrase as ἕνεκεν τοῦ αἰχμαλωτεῦσαι αὐτοὺς αἰχμαλωσίαν τοῦ Σαλωμων, *because of the taking them captive into the captivity of Solomon* by replacing the words τοῦ Σαλωμων by αἰχμαλωσίαν ἀπηρτισμενην.[372]

τὴν αὐτου τοῦ Ἰούδα ὑπόσχοιεν τιμωρίαν, *and the police captain who had been allotted the very name, being called Herod, hastened to bring him to the arena that he might fulfil his appointed lot by becoming a partaker of Christ, while they who betrayed him should undergo the same punishment as Judas.*

[370] HALOT 1532b–1536a.

[371] The Greek verbs employed by Aquila and Symmachus for תמם in Josh. 5:6 are respectively ἐκλείπω, *to forsake, to cease* or (alternatively) by τελειόω, *to finish*, (depending on the retroversion of Syh^{L} ܐ. ܥܕܡܐ ܕܫܠܡ ܟܠܗ ܥܡܐ ܓܒܪ̈ܐ ܕܩܪܒܐ ܗܢܘܢ ܕܢܦܩܘ ܡܢ ܡܨܪܝܢ܀ to ἕως ἐξέλιπεν (thus F. Field, *Origenis Hexaplorum . . . fragmenta* I, p. 344b) or ἕως ἐτελειώθη πᾶν τὸ ἔθνος ἀνδρᾶν πολέμου τῶν ἐξελθόντων ἐξ Αἰγύπτου (thus M.L. Margolis, Additions to Field from the Lyons Codex, p. 256) and ἀναλίσκω, *to spend, consume, to kill, destroy* (σ': ἕως ἀναλώθη [ἀνηλώθη thus M.L. Margolis, Additions to Field, p. 256] πᾶς ὁ λαὸς ἄνδρες πολεμισταὶ οἱ ἐξελθόντες ἐξ Αἰγύπτου— ܣ. ܥܕܡܐ ܕܐܬܚܒܠ ܟܠܗ ܥܡܐ ܓܒܪ̈ܐ ܩܪܒܬܢܐ ܗܢܘܢ ܕܢܦܩܘ ܡܢ ܡܨܪܝܢ.).

[372] Thus Syh ܕܢܫܬܡܠܐ, *to be perfected* (P-S 72b–73a), σ', θ' ܕܡܫܬܡܠܝܢܐ for σ', θ'

Symmachus employed the verb three times. The corresponding noun ἀπάρτισμα occurs once, i.e. [1] in 1 Kgs. 7:9 for the Hebrew hapax legomenon טְפָחוֹת, *cross-beams?*[373] which LXX (3 Reg. 9:46) rendered by ἕως τῶν γεισῶν, *protecting parts of the roof* (LEH, p. 87b). [2] In 1 Sam. 20:7, Jonathan explains to David that if his father Saul reacts negatively to his son's request, David should interpret Saul's behaviour as an expression of Saul's dangerous intentions: ואם־חרה יחרה לו דע כי־כלתה הרעה מעמו, *in case he is angry, know then that evil is intended by him.* LXX-1 Reg. 20:7 rendered the apodosis by γνῶθι ὅτι συντετέλεσται ἡ κακία παρ' αὐτοῦ. Symmachus then replaced the verb by ἀπήρτισται (ms.243, Coislin. 8). [3] In Ps. 7:10 aα, MT reads יגמר־נא רע רשעים, *let the evil of the wicked come to an end,*[374] LXX has συντελεσθήτω δὴ πονηρία ἁμαρτωλῶν, which α' (according to Syh ܐ. ܬܫܬܟܠܠ) changed into ἀπαρτισθήσεται and σ' accordingly (according to Syh ܣ. ܬܫܬܟܠܠ ܗܟܠ ܫܘܚܩܐ ܥܠ ܪ̈ܫܝܥܐ܀) into ἀπαρτισθήτω κάκωσις κατὰ τῶν ἀσεβῶν. [4] In Ps. 118(119):73, finally, we find the verb in the reading of Symmachus (according to Syh ܘܫܟܠܠܘܢܝ): αἱ χεῖρές σου ἐποίσάν με καὶ ἀπήρτισάν με, for MT יָדֶ֣יךָ עָ֭שׂוּנִי וַֽיְכוֹנְנ֑וּנִי—contrast LXX αἱ χεῖρές σου ἐποίσάν με καὶ ἔπλασάν με· and α' αἱ χεῖρές σου ἐποίσάν με καὶ ἥδρασάν με. In all these cases, the verb ἀπαρτίζω has the meaning *to come to an end, to complete.* The overtones may be negative, as in the case of Ps. 7, but the word can have a neutral sense as well.

Although it may appear from this short survey that the occurrences of the verb ἀπαρτίζω are confined to a late, Christian period, we already find the verb well attested in classical Greek literature, e.g., in the writings of Aeschylus (sixth to fifth century BCE), *Seven Against Thebes* 374, Aristoteles (fourth century BCE), *Generation of Animals* 780b 10; *Meteorologica* 340b 35; Polybius (second century BCE), *Histories* 31.12.10; 31.13.10 (all active forms). In the passive form with the temporal meaning *to be completed, to be complete* in the sense

---

αἰχμαλωσίαν τελείαν. Cf. the remarks by Jerome: 'Pro captivitate perfecta LXX captivitatem Salomonis interpretati sunt . . . denique Aq. ἀπηρτισμένην transtulit et ἀναπεπληρωμένην; Sym. et Theod. τελείαν.' See F. Field, *Origenis Hexaplorum . . . fragmenta* II, p. 968a–b.

[373] HALOT 378b: 'unknown architectural tech. term, Akk. *(a)dappu* (AHw. 10b) horizontal crossbeam'; M.J. Mulder, *1 Kings* (HCOT) Leuven 1998, p. 297: 'a vertical construction (composed of large natural stones), which ran up from the foundations to a certain height, be it to the coping, or to 'the tin-like breastwork of the roof', or to a (first?) protruding story.'

[374] HALOT 197b: 'גמר *to requite, avenge* with acc. Ps. 7_{10} (rd. נְמֹר, *y* ditt.)'

of the *end of a period of time*, the verb occurs in the writings of Hippocrates (fifth century BCE), *Diseases* IV.48:[375] ἀπηρτισμένης <τῆς> πρώτης περιόδου, *a first period being completed* and *Epidemics* II.3.17:[376] τῆς δὲ ὀκταμήνου ἀπαρτιζούσης, *when the eight-month period is complete.* Finally, we find the verb attested in several Greek papyri, for instance in P.London XV.10.2, dating from 131–130 BCE (context broken).[377] In these genuine Greek sources, the verb ἀπαρτίζω does not occur very frequently, but often enough to conclude that it formed part of Greek vocabulary already in the early, classical period. It was employed usually to indicate the end or completion of a period of time, a product, or activity. There is no reason why the Greek translator could not have made use of this lexeme.

Once the original wording of the Greek text in Josh. 5:6 has conjecturally been emended, the logic and intention of the whole passage in the Greek text can be restored. The Greek translator found in his Hebrew text the same phrase as we find it in MT (עד־תם), and offered a well-considered and appropriate rendering by the phrase διὸ ἀπηρτίσθησαν. He had no intention to conceal the death (תם MT-6b, מתו MT-4e) of a large number of Israelites resulting from the long period of wandering through the desert, but rather wanted to stress that it was *not* the *entire population* (כל־הגוי thus MT and the Hebrew *Vorlage* of LXX) that had died there—in which case the story would have ended in the book of Numbers—, but only a large part of it (οἱ πλεῖστοι αὐτῶν), that is (. . . αὐτῶν τῶν . . .) those who left Egypt as warriors and who had been disobedient. Because of the striking similarity between this lexical choice ἀπηρτίσθησαν and the phrase ἀπερίτμητοι ἦσαν, which occurs almost immediately before this passage (verse 4b) and recurs as διὰ τὸ αὐτοὺς γεγενῆσθαι . . . ἀπεριτμήτους in verse 7, and because of the fact that the original lexical choice by the translator for the Greek verb ἀπαρτίζω intro-

---

[375] Text: É. Littré, *Oeuvres completes d' Hippocrate. Tome Septième.* Paris 1851 (Amsterdam 1979).

[376] Text and translation: W.D. Smith, *Hippocrates Volume VII.* Cambridge, Massachusetts/London 1994.

[377] F.G. Kenyon, *Greek Papyri in the British Museum. Catalogue with Texts. Volume I.* London 1893. Papyrus XV (frgs. 1–16) Fragments of banking records, dated at 131–130 BCE. See further P.Brem 48, line 25 (Hermoupolis Magna, from the year 118 CE), P.Mich. Vol. 8, 478, line 41; P. Oslo. Vol. 2.36, line 11 (from Theadelphia, from the year 145 CE), P.Oxyrhynchus vol. 33, 2679, line 5.

duced a verb that was not very common in Greek literature in general, the original Greek text suffered from a scribal corruption from the original phrase ΑΠΗΡΤΙΣΘΗΣΑΝ into the graphically similar phrase ΑΠΕΡΙΤΜΗΤΟΙΗΣΑΝ. This corruption must have taken place early in the transmission of the Greek text, since all our extant witnesses—the oldest of which are still half a millennium younger than the original Greek text—contain the error.

7.6.4.3 *The Fate of the Younger Generation*

In addition to this concern on the part of the Greek translator to uphold the inner logic of the text (οἱ πλεῖστοι αὐτῶν instead of כל־הגוי), it is also likely that a certain interest in the theme of the innocence of this younger generation brought him to his translation of verse 6. In his view, it was not the *entire* population (כל־הגוי) that had been punished to die in the desert (תם—ἀπηρτίσθησαν), but only those who had deserved it (αὐτῶν τῶν μαχίμων τῶν ἐξεληλυθότων). As Blaschke has pointed out, the Greek translator provided an answer to the old question of whether the sons deserved punishment for the sins of their fathers (Jer. 31:29–30, Ezek. 18).[378] The picture of the Greek version of Joshua 5 as a product of intensive exegesis, slight harmonisation with the Pentateuch and well-considered translation, is further affirmed by several other literary initiatives introduced into this verse by the Greek translator that serve the same purpose of clearly distinguishing between guilty fathers and innocent children.

The rendering of the Hebrew אשר לא־שמעו, *who did not listen to*, by οἱ ἀπειθήσαντες, *who have disobeyed*, although in this context *ad sensum* identical, presents a unique rendering of a very common Hebrew (Deuteronomistic) construction by the Greek verb ἀπειθέω that lacks a direct equivalent in the Hebrew language.[379] Parallel formulations

---

[378] A. Blaschke, *Beschneidung*, pp. 115–116.

[379] Fourteen out of the 49 instances of the verb ἀπειθέω appear in passages without an (extant) Hebrew substratum. The verb has been used (sporadically) by the Greek translators to translate a large variety of Hebrew expressions, most of them normally rendered by other equivalents: [1] צדל, *to forbear, refrain* (HALOT, p. 292a–b), in LXX-Ezek. 3:27; [2] מאן, *to refuse* (HALOT, p. 540a–b), in LXX-4 Reg. 5:6; LXX-Zech. 7:11; [3] מאס, *to refuse, reject* (HALOT, pp. 540b–541a), in LXX-Lev. 26:15; LXX-Num. 11:20; LXX-Isa. 30:12; [4] מעל, *to violate one's legal obligations* (HALOT, pp. 612b–613a), in LXX-Deut. 32:51; [5] מרד, *to revolt* (HALOT, p. 632a), in LXX-Isa. 36:5; [6] מרה, *to be rebellious* (HALOT, pp. 632b–633a), in LXX-Deut. 1:26; 9:7.23.24; LXX-Josh. 1:18, LXX-Isa. 3:8; 50:5; 63:10; [7] מרר

in MT-Josh. 22:2 (ותשמעו בקולי) and 24:24 (ובקולו נשמע) have been rendered straightforwardly by (ἐπ-)ἀκούω τῆς φωνῆς. The verb ἀπειθέω, by contrast, has been used to render a variety of Hebrew expressions, and thus forms an unidiomatic rendering of the Hebrew phrase here. In LXX-Josh. 1:18 the verb has been used to indicate disobedience as a capital crime.

Interestingly, in both the Pentateuch and Joshua the Greek verb has been employed relatively consistently in the cases of disobedience towards Yhwh in Kadesh Barnea (LXX-Num. 14:43,[380] LXX-Deut. 1:26;[381] 9:23,[382] referring to Num. 14), Moses' and Aaron's disobedience at Meribah (LXX-Deut. 32:51 referring to Num. 20),[383] or disobedience during the desert journey in general (LXX-Deut. 9:7[384] and 9:24[385]).[386] All these passages deal with cases of disobedience resulting in (postponed) death penalties: Moses and Aaron for their sin in Meribah, the older generation for their obstinacy at Kadesh Barnea, and possible rebels against Joshua in Josh. 1:18. By

---

Hiphʿil, *to complain bitterly* (HALOT, p. 638b), in LXX-Exod. 23:21; [8] the noun סרה, *obstinacy* (HALOT, p. 769a), in LXX-Isa. 59:13; [9] סרר, *to be stubborn* (HALOT, p. 770b), in LXX-Deut. 21:20, LXX-2 Esd. 19:29; LXX-Ps. 67(68):18; LXX-Hos. 9:16; LXX-Isa. 1:23; 65:2; [10] לא אבה in LXX-Prov. 1:25 and [11] without any Hebrew counterpart in LXX-Num. 14:43; LXX-Deut. 28:65; LXX-Isa. 1:25; 8:11; 33:2; 66:14; and LXX-Jer. 13:15; see HR, p. 119c.

380 Num. 14:43 MT כי־על־כן שבתם מאחרי יהוה—LXX οὗ εἵνεκεν ἀπεστράφητε *ἀπειθοῦντες* κυρίῳ.

381 Deut. 1:26 MT ותמרו את־פי יהוה אלהיכם—LXX καὶ *ἠπειθήσατε* τῷ ῥήματι κυρίου τοῦ θεοῦ ὑμῶν.

382 Deut. 9:23 MT ותמרו את־פי יהוה אלהיכם—LXX καὶ *ἠπειθήσατε* τῷ ῥήματι κυρίου.

383 Deut. 32:51 MT על אשר מעלתם בי—LXX διότι *ἠπειθήσατε τῷ ῥήματί μου.*

384 Deut. 9:7 MT למן־היום אשר־יצאת מארץ מצרים עד־באכם עד־המקום הזה ממרים הייתם עם־יהוה—LXX ἀφ' ἧς ἡμέρας ἐξήλθετε ἐξ Αἰγύπτου ἕως ἤλθετε εἰς τὸν τόπον τοῦτον, *ἀπειθοῦντες διετελεῖτε τὰ πρὸς* κύριον.

385 Deut. 9:24 MT ממרים הייתם עם־יהוה—LXX διότι *ἠπειθήσατε τῷ ῥήματί* μου.

386 See A. Thibaut o.s.b., *L' infidélité du peuple élu: ἀπειθῶ entre la Bible hebraïque et la Bible Latine.* (Collectanea biblica latina vol. XVII) Roma/Turnhout 1988, p. 288: 'Dans la littérature biblique, ἀπειθῶ ne traduit pas moins de onze mots hébreux, et ces divers mots hébreux à leur tours aboutissent chacun à plusiers mots grecs. On a l'impression d'assister tout ensemble à la dispersion des idées ou des images qu'expriment les racines hébraïques et à un regroupement nouveau de ces concepts, ou éléments de concepts, qui édifieront et présiceront l'idée d' ἀπείθεια. Le fait initial et majeur de cette histoire sémantique si complexe, c'est la présence d' ἀπειθῶ dans deux textes importants du Pentateuque: Mériba (Nm. 20,10) et Cadès (Dt. 1,26 et 9,23).' Thibaut, p. 83, links LXX-Josh. 5:6 with LXX-Deut. 32:51 and LXX-Numbers 20, but from the discussion above it is evident that the Greek translator did not have the sin of Moses and Aaron in mind, but rather that of the older generation at Kadesh Barnea.

employing precisely this expression, the Greek translator created a direct link with these passages in the Pentateuch, intensified the gravity of the sin of the older generation, and at the same time thus explained why these people had to die (ἀπαρτίζω). Whereas the Hebrew expression לא שמע בקול יהוה is strongly embedded in the Deuteronomistic theology, the Greek expression evokes the Pentateuchal theme of the rebellious people and thus serves to stress the distinction between the ignorant and innocent younger Israelites, called ἄπειροι in LXX-Num. 14:23, who happened to be ἀπερίτμητοι on the one hand, and the ἀπειθήσαντες that ἀπηρτίσθησαν on the other.

In line with this exegesis of the Hebrew text, the Greek translator also altered the phrase קול יהוה, *voice of Yhwh*, into ἐντολαί τοῦ θεοῦ, *commandments of the Deity*. The Greek noun ἐντολή served the Greek translators of the Hebrew Bible (including the Greek translator of Joshua) as a stereotyped rendering of the Hebrew מצוה, and in this entire corpus it occurs only here as an equivalent of קול. Remarkably, neither Holmes, Auld or Mazor have proposed a literal retroversion such as אשׁר מרו את מצות האלהים. Auld proposes to reconstruct a Hebrew phrase קול האלהים for the Greek expression with reference to nine similar cases of equations יהוה—ὁ θεος, but does not explain why the Deuteronomistic author of the Hebrew text of the book of Joshua would have wanted to exchange the stereotyped expression קול יהוה[387] for this unique phrase, or why the Greek text could not be secondary.[388] Hollenberg, Moatti-Fine and even Orlinsky consider the Hebrew phrase in MT to be original, and detect behind this Greek rendering an attempt to avoid anthropomorphic expressions for the Deity, comparable to the translation of פי יהוה by προστάγμα κυρίου/θεοῦ[389] and יד יהוה by δύναμις τοῦ κυρίου (4:24),[390]

[387] The phrase קול יהוה occurs 52 times in the Hebrew Bible, predominantly in Deuteronomy (14 times: 5:25; 8:20; 13:19; 15:5; 18:16; 26:24; 27:10; 28:1.2.15.45.62; 30:8.10), [MT-]Jer. (11 times: 3:25; 7:28; 26:13; 38:20; 42:6.13.21; 43:4.7; 44:23), and [MT-]Ps. (11 times: 3:5; 29:3.4.4.5.7.8.9; 106:25; 142:2.2), and further Gen. 3:8; Exod. 15:26; Josh. 5:6; 1 Sam. 12:15 (Dtr); 15:19.20.22; 28:18; 1 Kgs. 20:36; 2 Kgs. 18:12 (Dtr); Isa. 30:12; 66:6; Mic. 6:9; Hag. 1:12, Zech. 6:15 and Dan. 9:10.

[388] A.G. Auld, Joshua. The Hebrew and Greek Texts, pp. 9, 12–13 (= *Joshua Retold*, pp. 13, 16–17).

[389] Thus in Josh. 15:13; 17:4; 19:50; 21:3; 22:9; see also Josh. 9:14 את־פי יהוה לא שׁאלו—κύριον οὐκ ἐπηρώτησαν.

[390] J. Hollenberg, *Der Charakter*, p. 9; C.D. Benjamin, *The Variations*, p. 32; H.M. Orlinsky, The Hebrew *Vorlage* of the Septuagint of the Book of Joshua, p. 193 (see section 2.2.5.2 above); J. Moatti-Fine, *Josué*, pp. 49–50, 118.

and the expression used consistently by the Aramaic *meturgemanim*, as in Targum Jonathan here: דְלָא קַבִּילוּ לְמֵימְרָא דַיְיָ, *who had not accepted the Memra of the Lord.*[391] In Josh. 24:24, however, the Greek translator had no difficulty with translating the same Hebrew phrase שמע בקול literally by ἀκουῶ τῆς φωνῆς (κυρίου), as is the normal rendering employed throughout the Greek Pentateuch and in fact the whole Septuagint.[392]

Therefore it seems more likely that the unusual rendering should be seen as another attempt by the Greek translator to bring out clearly the contrast between the two groups, by specifying the more general statement 'voice of Yhwh' into the more strict 'divine commandments'. On the other hand, there is no indication in the Greek text that the Greek translator intended to refer to a specific group of commandments, such as those pertaining to the circumcision, as implied by Den Hertog's exegesis of the Greek text (see section 7.2.8 above). The use of the plural (αἱ ἐντολαί) rather seems to remind the reader of all the cases of the Israelites' disobedience to the divine commandments during the whole desert period. In that respect, the variants 'forty-two years' and 'disobey the divine commandments' form a coherent pattern of modifications, introduced by the Greek translator for a single purpose.

The Greek translator further pursued his aim to differentiate between the two groups by employing two distinct renderings of the same Hebrew phrase—אשר נשבע יהוה ל, i.e. οἷς καὶ διώρισεν and ἣν ὤμοσεν κυρίος . . . (second time), and the employment of an adverbial καί.[393] As noted in section 7.2.6 above, it is hardly plausible that

---

[391] Thus M.L. Margolis, *The Book of Joshua in Greek*, p. 71, line 17. See further D.J. Harrington, s.j., A. Saldarini, *Targum Jonathan to the Former Prophets* (The Aramaic Bible, Vol. 10) Edinburgh 1987, pp. 279–280. In line with its overall adaptation of this text, the author of the Fragmentary Targum of Josh. 5 transformed the phrase into דלא קבילו באולפאן, *who had not accepted the Instruction*, see H. Fahr, U. Gleßmer, *Jordandurchzug*, pp. 34–35, 79–81.

[392] With the exception of 1 Sam. 15:20, where LXX has φωνὴ τοῦ λαοῦ, the expression φωνὴ κυρίου has been used in all 50 other cases, where the phrase קול יהוה occurs in the Hebrew text. The Greek phrase further appears in LXX-Gen. 15:4 (for דבר־יהוה); LXX-Num. 3:16.39.51; 4:37.41.45.49 (for על־פי יהוה); 7:89 (for MT קול); 9:20; 10:13; 13:3 (for על־פי יהוה); LXX-Deut. 28:9 (ἐὰν εἰσακούσῃς τῆς φωνῆς κυρίου τοῦ θεοῦ σου for MT כי תשמר את־מצות יהוה אלהיך); and Bar.1:18.21; 2:22; and 3:4.

[393] Because of its position in the clause, the word καί cannot be understood as an ordinary conjunction. On this special use of καί see LSJ, p. 857b; F. Blass, A. Debrunner, F. Rehkopf, *Grammatik des neutestamentlichen Griechisch*, § 442; A. Aejmelaeus, *Parataxis in the Septuagint*, pp. 12–13. The manuscript tradition of LXX-Joshua

such a typically Greek construction reflects a Hebrew construction as אשר להם גם נשבע. The verb ὄμνυμι, *to swear*, is the standard equivalent for שׁבע Niphʿal throughout the book of Joshua and the entire Septuagint.[394] By contrast, the equation שׁבע Niphʿal—διορίζω is unique in the Septuagint, and the occurrences of this Greek verb within this corpus are limited to some fifteen places. Only in six of the eight occurrences in LXX-Ezek. 41–42 does it have a clear Hebrew equivalent, although with a different meaning: בִּנְיָה/בִּנְיָן, *building*.[395] The verb διορίζω has a quite distinctive meaning: *to draw a boundary* (literally and metaphorically); *to pronounce clearly; to determine; set a limit; to be distinguished from*.[396] In LXX-Exod. 26:33, LXX-Lev. 20:24,[397] and LXX-Job 35:11, the verb has been used to mark an important qualitative distinction, i.e., between the Holy and the Holy of Holiest (Exod. 26:33),[398] Israel and the nations (Lev. 20:24),[399] and man and beast (Job 35:11):[400] In LXX-Josh. 15:47 and LXX-Ezek. 47:18.20,

---

is rather uniform at these points. Only ms.120 reads οἱ πλειόνες instead of οἱ πλεῖστοι. The *adverbial* καί is attested by all witnesses, including for instance, Syh: ܠܗܘܢ ܕܐܦ ܐܬܦܪܫ ܡܪܝܐ ܠܗܘܢ and VetLat: *quibus et definierat*.

[394] Thus in Josh. 1:6; 2:12; 9:15.18.19.20; 14:9; 21:43.44, see further HR, pp. 991b–992a.

[395] I.e. in LXX-Exod. 26:33; LXX-Lev. 20:24; LXX-Josh. 5:6; 15:47; LXX-2 Chron. 32:4; LXX-Job 35:11; LXX-Isa. 45:18; LXX-Ezek. 41:12.12.13.15; 42:1.10; 47:18.20, see HR, p. 336b. In LXX-Isa. 45:24, Ziegler adopted the reading οἱ ἀφορίζοντες ἑαυτούς instead of οἱ διορίζοντες ἑαυτούς (S* O'-Q^mg-88 L'-233 C 403' Eus.comm.et dem. Tht).

[396] LEH, p. 117a; LSJ, p. 434b; GELS², p. 129b. M.L. Margolis, *The Book of Joshua in Greek*, p. 71, lines 19–25.

[397] In the subsequent verses LXX-Lev. 20:25.26 the corresponding verb ἀφορίζω, *to separate, to set apart*, (GELS², p. 80a–b) has been used in the same context and as a rendering of the same Hebrew verb בדל Hiphʿil, *to separate, to make a distinction* (HALOT, p. 110a–b).

[398] Exod. 26:33 MT והבדילה הפרכת לכם בין הקדשׁ ובין קדשׁ הקדשׁים—LXX καὶ *διοριεῖ* τὸ καταπέτασμα ὑμῖν ἀνὰ μέσον τοῦ ἁγίου καὶ ἀνὰ μέσον τοῦ ἁγίου τῶν ἁγίων.

[399] Lev. 20:24 MT אשׁר־הבדלתי אתכם מן־העמים—LXX ὅς *διώρισα* ὑμᾶς ἀπὸ πάντων τῶν ἐθνῶν.

[400] The MT מלפנו מבהמות ארץ ומעוף השׁמים יחכמנו differs from LXX ὁ *διορίζων* με ἀπὸ τετραπόδων γῆς ἀπὸ δὲ πετεινῶν οὐρανοῦ as regards content. The word מַלְּפֵנוּ is a Piʿel participle from אלף, *to teach* (HALOT, p. 59a–b), which corresponds to the verb חכם Piʿel, *to make wise* (HALOT 314a). The Greek translator interpreted the word as a participle from the root פלה, *to treat specially* (HALOT 930a), thus M.L. Margolis, *The Book of Joshua*, p. 71 (see note above) and the commentaries, e.g. S.R. Driver, G.B. Gray, *The Book of Job* (ICC) Edinburgh 1921, p. 268. Interestingly, 11QtgJob, col. xxvi, lines 5–6 offers an Aramaic version similar to LXX: די פרשׁנא, see further M. Pope, *Job*, p. 264. The Pešiṭta reading ܡܢ ܡܦܪܫ presupposes an understanding of the Hebrew phrase as מִלִּפְנֵי.

the verb has been employed in cases where either the Mediterranean Sea (Josh. 15:47;[401] Ezek. 47:20)[402] or the river Jordan (Ezek. 47:18)[403] marks a distinctive boundary (in all cases reflecting the Hebrew noun גְּבוּל, *boundary*).

Against this background it becomes clear that the Greek translator's choice of this unusual rendering of נשבע not only expresses his preference for stylistic and idiomatic variation, but also adds to the narrative of LXX-Joshua 5 the nuances of a clear qualitative distinction and division: because of their disobedience, the men of the older generation were not allowed to cross the border of the Promised Land and were therefore clearly separated from the younger innocent generation. The latter group are the actual recipients of the divine promise made to the offspring of Israel's forefathers. The Greek translator thus reserved the Greek verb ὄμνυμι for the second statement, and employed the verb διορίζω for the first.

7.6.4.4 *Other Variants*

Thus far we have seen a number of literary initiatives introduced by the Greek translator reflecting his specific exegesis and adaptation of his Hebrew *Vorlage*, which differed only slightly from MT (in casu the postulated dittography of מדבר in 5:6a). Therefore it is only natural to ascribe the other minor quantitative variants in this verse to this same hand.

In the second clause of the verse, the Greek text presents a single word μαχίμος, *warlike, fit for battle*,[404] as a translation of the two words in MT אנשי המלחמה, *men of war*. The Greek translator could have employed the word-for-word translation ἀνήρ/ἄνθρωπος—πολεμιστής/του πολέμου which is the standard equivalent for this Hebrew word throughout the Greek Pentateuch and in fact the whole Septuagint,[405]

---

[401] Josh. 15:47 MT-Qere והים הגדול וגבול—LXX καὶ ἡ θάλασσα ἡ μεγάλη *διορίζει*.

[402] Ezek. 47:20 MT ופאת־ים הים הגדול מגבול עד־נכח לבוא חמת—LXX τοῦτο τὸ μέρος τῆς θαλάσσης τῆς μεγάλης· *διορίζει* ἕως κατέναντι τῆς εἰσόδου Ημαθ.

[403] Ezek. 47:18 MT הירדן מגבול על־הים הקדמוני תמדו—LXX ὁ Ιορδάνης *διορίζει* ἐπὶ τὴν θάλασσαν τὴν πρὸς ἀνατολὰς Φοινικῶνος.

[404] LSJ, p. 1085b; LEH, p. 292b; J. Moatti-Fine, *Josué*, p. 54.

[405] The phrase איש המלחמה has been rendered by ἀνήρ πολεμιστής in LXX-Num. 31:49; LXX-Deut. 2:14.16 [!]; LXX-Josh. 17:1 [!]; LXX^{A}-Judg. 20:17 (LXX^{B} has ἀνὴρ παρατάξεως); LXX-1 Reg. 16:18; 17:33; LXX-2 Reg. 17:8; LXX-4 Reg. 25:4 = LXX-Jer. 52:7; LXX-4 Reg. 25:19 = LXX-Jer. 52:25; LXX-Jer. 30:32 (= MT-

as well as the revisions of Josh. 5:4.6 and 6:3 by the recentiores.[406] He opted, however, for the expression μαχίμος, which occurs regularly in classical Greek works,[407] but within the Septuagint almost exclusively in the Greek version of Joshua, i.e. here in 5:6; further in LXX-Josh. 6:3.7.9.13, in the latter three cases as a rendering of the Hebrew word חָלוּץ, *group of men equipped for war*.[408] The Greek word μαχίμος thus offers—again—an unusual, but idiomatically very appropriate rendering for, and at the same time condensation of, the Hebrew phrase איש המלחמה. In this case, too, it is evident that no shorter Hebrew *Vorlage* should be postulated behind LXX.

In the following clause it is the LXX that contains a minor plus *vis-à-vis* MT: ἐκ γῆς Αἰγύπτου—ממצרים. The two expressions are interchangeable and synonymous. Mazor mentions this variant in her discussion of the many divergencies between MT and LXX with respect to the addition or omission of the element ארץ before the name of the area,[409] e.g. Josh. 2:10 בצאתכם ממצרים—ὅτε ἐξεπορεύεσθε ἐκ γῆς

Jer. 49:26; LXX-Jer. 27:30 (= MT-Jer. 50:30); LXX-Jer. 28:31 (= MT-Jer. 51:32); LXX-Ezek. 27:10.27; 39:20; LXX-Joel 2:7; 4:9; LXX-1 Chron. 12:39; 18:10; LXX-2 Chron. 8:9; 17:13. In LXX-Num. 31:28, LXX-Isa. 3:2; LXX-Jer. 45:4 (= MT-Jer. 38:4); 48:14 (MT 38:14); and LXX-1 Chron. 28:3 the parallel formulation ἄνθρωπος πολεμιστής has been employed. In LXX-Exod. 15:3 and LXX-Isa. 42:13, the metaphor of Yhwh as warrior has been transformed into a more pacifist image: συντρίβων πολέμους. In Jer. 6:23 and 50:42 (LXX 27:42), the Greek translator read כְּאֵשׁ instead of כְּאִישׁ and translated ὡς πῦρ εἰς πόλεμον. In Josh. 10:24, the Greek translator rendered the Hebrew phrase אל־קציני אנשי המלחמה, *to the chiefs of the men of war* by the unique phrase ἐναρχομένοι τοῦ πολέμου, *the officers of war*, using a verb ἐνάρχομαι, *to hold office* (LSJ, p. 557a), that occurs in the Septuagint only 10 other times.

[406] In Josh. 5:4 the reading of VetLat. *viri bellatores* and Syh ܓܒܪܐ ܕܩܪܒܐ probably reflect the text of Symmachus ἄνδρες πολέμου. In 5:6 the Syh gives for σ' ܓܒܪܐ ܡܩܪܒܬܢܐ /VetLat. *viri bellatores* which probably reflects ἄνδρες πολεμισταί, whereas the Syh for α' ܓܒܪܐ ܕܩܪܒܐ again equals the phrase ἄνδρες πολέμου. For Josh. 6:3 the reading οἱ λ̣ παντες ανδρες πολεμου has been preserved in the margin of mss. 85.344.

[407] LSJ, p. 1085b, *inter alia* mentions Herodotus, *History of the Persian Wars* 2.141; 2.165; 3:102; 7.185, Thucydides, *History* 1.110; 6:23, Xenophon, *Cyropaedia* 5.4.46, Plato, *Laws* 830c; *Timaeus* 24a; *Critias* 110c; Aristoteles, *Politics*, 1268a 36; and a second century BCE Papyrus Tebtunis 61(a).109.

[408] See section 6.5.2 above.

[409] L. Mazor, עיונים, ch. 2: 'Minor Variants: Moveable Elements as Evidence of Scribal Activity', section II.4, pp. 83–85: 'שם הארץ + 'ארץ'/שם ארץ'. Mazor refers to the similar variations in the parallel passages such as 1 Kgs. 8:9 (אשר כרת יהוה עם־בני ישראל בצאתם מארץ מצרים) *vis-à-vis* 2 Chron. 5:10 (אשר כרת יהוה עם־בני ישראל בצאתם ממצרים) or, conversely, 1 Kgs. 8:16 (מן־היום אשר הוצאתי את עמי את־ישראל ממצרים) as compared to the slightly different formulation in 2 Chron. 6:5 (מן־היום אשר הוצאתי את־עמי מארץ מצרים).

Αἰγύπτου and Josh. 24:17 מארץ מצרים—ἐξ Αἰγύπτου, and suggests that the variation may have taken place already at the Hebrew level. Nevertheless, in these cases it is equally possible that the Greek translator was responsible for this insignificant variant, either unconsciously or deliberately with the intention to offer a variation on the preceding phrase in 5:4b τῶν ἐξεληλυθότων <u>ἐξ</u> Αἰγύπτου.

In 5:6e LXX has no equivalent for the subject (יהוה) and indirect object (להם) of the Hebrew clause אשר נשבע יהוה להם. As we have seen in section 7.2.5 above, E. Tov considers the pluses of MT to be part of a second edition of the Hebrew text of Joshua, but fails to mention the specific nuances introduced by the Greek translator. In this case the identity of both the subject and the indirect object is sufficiently clear, as already indicated by Margolis.[410] The absence of a reference to Yhwh may well be explained by the fact that he is mentioned both in the preceding and following clauses. The indirect object is realised in the Greek text by the dative of the relative pronoun οἷς. Tov's proposal thus pays insufficient attention to the Greek context here.

Of a different, qualitative, nature is the variant MT לבלתי הראותם את־הארץ, *not to show them the land*—LXX μὴ ἰδεῖν αὐτοὺς τὴν γῆν, *that they would not see the land*, which seems to reflect a Qal formation of the verb ראה instead of the Hiphʿil. Interestingly, 4QJosh^a, frg. 2, line 10, corresponds to this reading: [לב]לתי ראות את ה[ארץ].[411] If, however, the Greek translator had found in his *Vorlage* a text similar to 4QJosh^a (ראות), he deliberately would have added the object αὐτούς.[412] Related to this variation is that attested by the Pešiṭta manuscripts, where the main text has ܕܠܐ ܢܚܘܐ ܐܢܘܢ ܐܪܥܐ, *that he would not show them the land* while 9a1*fam* reads ܕܠܐ ܢܚܘܢ, *that they would not see . . .*[413]

In the Pentateuch both formulations occur, e.g. in Num. 14:23 כל־מנאצי לא יראוה, 32:11 אם־יראו האנשים, Deut. 1:35 אם־יראה איש for

[410] M.L. Margolis, *The Book of Joshua in Greek*, p. 71, lines 21–23.

[411] E. Ulrich, 4QJosh^a, p. 148.

[412] L. Mazor, עיונים, p. 172, 436 (note 7), points to the 4QJosh^a reading, but reconstructs ראות<u>ם</u>, i.e. a hybrid of both MT and 4QJosh^a.

[413] See the extensive discussion in J.E. Erbes, *The Peshitta and the Versions*, pp. 294–295.

the expressions with ראה Qal, and Gen. 12:1 לך־לך . . . אל־הארץ אשר אַרְאֶךָּ, Deut. 34:11, וַיַּרְאֵהוּ, and 34:4 הֶרְאִיתִיךָ for the phrases with the Hiphʿil, although it must be conceded that the passages with the Qal outnumber those with the Hiphʿil. Margolis suspected behind the Greek text an attempt to 'avoid action by the Deity',[414] but such a tendency is not apparent elsewhere in the Greek Joshua. In LXX-Josh. 10:11, for instance, the translator was not bothered by the idea of God throwing stones at Israel's enemies (καὶ κύριος ἐπέρριψεν αὐτοῖς λίθους χαλάζης ἐκ του οὐρανοῦ—ויהוה השליך עליהם אבנים גדלות מן־השמים), as long as it would concern only *hail stones* (λίθους χαλάζης cf. אבני הברד in the same verse) instead of *great stones* (אבנים גדלות). The variation should rather be understood as a subtle correction of the construction with the Hiphʿil to that with the Qal formation. The Hiphʿil of ראה could imply that those to whom the land would (not) be shown would remain outside the land, just as Moses in Deut. 34 sees the land but from a distance. The Qal formation of ראה has been used in the passage referred to above, in cases where 'seeing the land' in fact implies 'entering into the land'. As a result, the change in stem can be explained as independent examples of conformation of the *lectio difficilior* contained in MT to the more common expression using the Qal (4QJosh[a], LXX, Peš-9a1*fam*).

The last variant between MT and LXX in this verse is presented by the B text in 5:6g–h τοῖς πατράσιν ἡμῶν δοῦναι, (*the land that the Lord swore*) *to our fathers to give (it)* for the corresponding phrase in MT לאבותם לתת לנו, *to their fathers to give (it) to us.* The text of LXX-B thus lacks the indirect object for δοῦναι. The manuscript evidence is rather complex here, grouped by Margolis into the following main text types:[415]

family E	τοῖς πατράσιν ἡμῶν δοῦναι
family S	τοῖς πατράσιν ἡμῶν δοῦναι αυτοῖς
family P_1	τοῖς πατράσιν ἡμῶν δοῦναι ἡμῖν
family P_2, C (Rahlfs)	τοῖς πατράσιν αὐτῶν δοῦναι ἡμῖν

[414] M.L. MARGOLIS, *The Book of Joshua in Greek*, p. 71, lines 23–25.

[415] M.L. MARGOLIS, *The Book of Joshua*, p. 72: 'The correction of ημων into ημιν is self-evident. Accordingly G read with H לאבתם לתת לנו; the translator merely ignored ם־ and transposed the indirect object as he does elsewhere.'

The reading of the S̲yrian family of textual witnesses is the *lectio facilior*, with its—undoubtedly independent—parallels in the Pešiṭta ܕܐܝܡܐ ܠܐܒܗܝܗܘܢ ܠܡܬܠ ܠܗܘܢ., a number of mediaeval Masoretic manuscripts לאבותם לתת להם,[416] and the fragmentary Targum לאבהתיהון לאברהם ליצחק וליעקב למתאן להון. Margolis conjectured that the pronoun ἡμῶν in LXX-E̲, S̲, P̲$_1$, and C̲ presents an early corruption from the dative ἡμῶν, so that the original Greek text would have read τοῖς πατράσιν ἡμῖν δοῦναι. Bieberstein rejects this conjectural emendation with the argument that it finds no support in the manuscript evidence, but his own proposal to maintain the text of B (E̲) is not very satisfactory either, since it leaves δοῦναι without the expected indirect object.[417] Den Hertog conjectures that the original Greek text read τοῖς πατράσιν ἡμῶν ἡμῖν δοῦναι, which then suffered from *parablepsis* and resulted in the E̲-text.[418] This suggestion is self-evident and fits the manuscript evidence better than Margolis' conjecture or Rahlfs' adoption of the Hexaplaric text. In that case, the Greek translator would not have tried to avoid the remarkable change in the Hebrew text from third person to first, but would rather have correlated the person of the genitive pronoun to that of the indirect object. This alleged original Greek formulation thus presents another attempt to harmonise MT's *lectio difficilior*.[419]

7.6.5 *LXX-Josh. 5:7*

In line with his aim to differentiate clearly between the two generations, the Greek translator introduced in verse 7 a subtle shift in emphasis from the persons circumcised by Joshua to the idea of substitution of the older generation. In the Hebrew text, the first two clauses open with the object in proleptic position (MT-Josh. 5:7a . . . ואת־בניהם, 5:7b . . . אתם) for the sake of emphasis. In the Greek text, however, the aspect of substitution ἀντὶ δὲ τούτων/תחתם takes the front position in the clause, which is reinforced by means

[416] See J.B. de Rossi, *Variae Lectiones Veteris Testamenti Librorum. Volumen II*, p. 76b: 'Kenn. cod.18, 181, 223, mei 198, 262, 594, primo 2, 265, 419, 721, nunc 716, utrumque primo 264, Targum cod. mei 265 primo, Syrus, Arabs, quorum textum male hic reddit latinus interpres, postposito *patribus eorum*, nec expresso pronomine ܠܗܘܢ.'

[417] K. Bieberstein, *Lukian und Theodotion*, p. 24.

[418] C.G. den Hertog, *Studien*, p. 72.

[419] See also N. Lohfink, *Die Väter Israels im Deuteronomium. Mit einer Stellungnahme von Thomas Römer.* (OBO 111) Freiburg/Göttingen 1991, p. 78.

of the repetition of the preposition ἀντί as composite element in the verb ἀντικαθίστημι, *to raise up instead of, replace.*[420] By contrast, the proleptic object phrase אתם has been rendered by the colourless relative pronoun οὕς instead of the demonstrative pronoun τούτους.

The Greek translator could afford to introduce these modest innovations, since he had already stated clearly *whom* Joshua circumcised in verse 4, and underlined this by the phrase πάντας τούτους in verse 5. For that reason, he made no effort to reintroduce the second group of uncircumcised Israelites (ὅσοι ποτὲ ἀπερίτμητοι ἦσαν τῶν ἐξεληλυθότων ἐξ Αἰγύπτου) responsible for the ὀνειδισμός Αἰγύπτου. Apparently he was not so much interested in the question why several Israelites had not yet been circumcised, but rather in how this omission was now compensated for (i.e. not too crudly, verses 2–4). In this case, the Greek translator sought to clarify the relation between the verses 6 and 7 and avoid the redundancy of the Hebrew text (see section 7.4.2 above).

L. Mazor has attempted to retrovert these Greek formulations into Hebrew and reconstructs a Hebrew *Vorlage* of LXX as follows: ותחתם הקים את בניהם אתם מל יהושע.[421] She too, however, has to concede that a retroversion of the word order subject-predicate in the second clause אתם יהושע מל does not produce a syntactically logical Hebrew construction.[422] Furthermore, the word order in the first clause of MT is supported by 4QJosh[a] (frg. 2, line 11) [ואת בני]הם הק[ים]. Moreover, her retroversion does not account for the repetition of the element ἀντι-. As a matter of fact, the verb ἀντικαθίστημι recurs in the Greek Old Testament only in LXX-Deut. 31:21 καὶ *ἀντικαταστήσεται* ἡ ᾠδὴ αὕτη κατὰ πρόσωπον μαρτυροῦσα, for MT וענתה השירה הזאת לפניו לעד, in the sense of *to stand up against* in 'the legal sense of being set up over against a defendant . . . for the prosecution.'[423] Here the employment of this rather unique verb serves

---

[420] LSJ, p. 156a; LEH, p. 40b. The S̲ witnesses (54, 75) and other Greek manuscripts (120, 129 [E̲], 19 [P̲₁], 55[C̲] and 53, 57, 85, and 130 [M̲]) reflect the slight alterion of the word into ἀντε̲κατέστησεν.

[421] L. Mazor, עיונים, p. 172.

[422] L. Mazor, עיונים, p. 172, 436 note 8.

[423] J.W. Wevers, *Notes on the Greek Text of Deuteronomy*, p. 503. Another occurrence of this verb is in the A″ text of LXX-Micah 2:8 καὶ ἔμπροσθεν ὁ λαός μου εἰς ἔχθραν ἀντικατέστη (B and main text: ἀντέστη), *and before my people withstood enmity* for MT וְאֶתְמוּל עַמִּי לְאוֹיֵב יְקוֹמֵם, which is usually corrected into ואתם לעמי לאויב תקומו, *and you stand up against my people as an enemy* (thus e.g. BHS; RSV; and H.W. Wolff, *Micha.* (BKAT XIV/4), Neukirchen 1982, p. 40; slightly differently A.S. van der Woude, *Micha* (POT) Nijkerk 1976, p. 84.

to underline the idea of substitution,[424] and clearly points to an innovation introduced by the Greek translator.

The third clause of this verse in LXX gives the reason why Joshua circumcised the sons that replaced their fathers: διὰ τὸ αὐτους γεγενῆσθαι κατὰ τὴν ὁδὸν ἀπεριτμήτους, *because they had been born on the way, being uncircumcised.* Whereas LXX has a single clause, MT contains two complementary clauses: [5:7c]כי ערלים היו [5:7d]כי לא מלו אתם בדרך, *because they were uncircumcised because they (i.e., their fathers) had not circumcised them on the way.* As we have seen in section 7.4.2 above, the function of the somewhat redundant last clause in MT is to re-emphasise the laxity of the older generation. The Greek text contains elements of both Hebrew clauses: 5:7c ערלים היו—αὐτους γεγενῆσθαι ἀπεριτμήτους; 5:7d בדרך—κατὰ τὴν ὁδὸν. The most evident conclusion would be to regard the Greek text as a deliberate attempt to condense the redundancy of the Hebrew text.

Nevertheless, Holmes, Benjamin, and Mazor have suggested to regard the Greek text as the rendering of a Hebrew *Vorlage* בדרך היו ערלים or כי ערלים היו כי ילדו בדרך (thus Holmes),[425] or כי הילודים בדרך לא־מלו (thus Benjamin and Mazor).[426] None of these retroversions, however, offer a direct equivalent of the extant Greek text. Literal Greek renderings of these Hebrew formulations would have been ὅτι οἱ γεννηθέντες ἐν τῃ ὁδῷ ἦσαν ἀπεριτμήτοι, or ὅτι ἀπεριτμήτοι ἦσαν ὅτι γεγεννηθήσαν ἐν τῃ ὁδῷ, or ὅτι τοὺς γεννηθέντας ἐν τῃ ὁδῷ οὐκ περιέτεμον/οἱ γεννηθέντες . . . οὐκ περιετμήθησαν. By contrast, the present Greek text does not correspond to any of these Greek re-retroversions but displays a free reformulation based on the LXX rendering of verse 5. Already the rendering of the Hebrew conjunction כי by the construction διὰ τό with an infinitive points to an idiomatic rather than literal translation of the passage.[427]

---

[424] In this sense of *replacement* rather than *opposition* the verb has been employed *inter alia* by Herodotus, *The Persian Wars* 9.93; Thucydides, *History* 2.13, and a fragmentary papyrus from the Zenon archive (P.Cair.Zen. 59.278) dated 251 BCE: [l.1] ···ᾳν λά-[l.2] βωμεν χόρτον στα- [l.3] ···· ληψόμεθα ·· [l.4] ···· ἀντικαταςς-[l.5]τήσομεν εἰς τὰ νέα [. . .]. See further C. Spicq, o.p., *Notes de lexicographie néo-testamentaire. Tome 1.* (OBO 22/1) Fribourg/Göttingen 1978, pp. 102–103.

[425] S. Holmes, *Joshua. The Hebrew and Greek Texts*, p. 30.

[426] C.D. Benjamin, *The Variations*, p. 33; L. Mazor, עיונים, p. 172.

[427] See S. Sipilä, *Between Literalness and Freedom*, pp. 159–160. I counted 46 cases in the Septuagint where this construction διὰ τό plus infinitive occurs, predominantly in original Greek compositions (2 Maccabees [2:11; 3:18; 4:19; 6:11], Sapientia

More important than these observations is the fact that there appears to be no reason why a Hebrew scribe would have wanted to duplicate such a presumed single statement into two more or less synonymous clauses. Benjamin argued that a later scribe wanted to add the word ערלים in order to link this statement with the aetiology offered in verse 3.[428] Yet, it is this word that constitutes the direct equivalent for ἀπεριτμήτους in the Greek text and thus forms part of the older shorter text. Moreover, the aetiology in this passage comes only in verse 9 with an explanation of the name 'Gilgal', whereas the name גבעת הערלות is explained only in the Greek versions (ἐπὶ τοῦ καλουμένου τόπου and καὶ ἔθηκεν θιμωνίας ἀκροβυστίων, see section 7.6.2). For these reasons, it is more reasonable to conclude that we are dealing here with another clear example of the Greek translator's device to condense the redundant Hebrew text.

7.6.6 *LXX-Josh. 5:8*

Out of the eleven phrases in MT, only במחנה has a direct equivalent in the Greek text ἐν τῇ παρεμβολῇ. Although the Greek and Hebrew texts correspond *ad sensum*, the short verse in the Greek text is full of modest innovations that can only be attributed to the Greek translator.

With respect to the protasis of the sentence (MT-8a–c ויהי כאשר־תמו כל־הגוי להמול LXX-Josh περιτμηθέντες δέ) there is some discussion whether the subject 'all the people' has been added in the MT to a presumed shorter *Vorlage* of LXX (Holmes, Benjamin, Auld, Mazor, see section 7.2 above). Nevertheless, there has been no discussion with respect to the fact that the Greek translator condensed this longer Hebrew text ויהי כאשר־תמו ... להמול into a simple, but effective conjunctive participle περιτμηθέντες δέ,[429] comparable to Jerome's

---

Salomonis [14:17], Baruch [4:6]); or idiomatic, non-slavish renderings, such as LXX-Genesis [6:3; 39:23], LXX-Exodus [16:8; 17:7; 19:28; 33:3], LXX-Deuteronomy [1:27.36; 4:37; 28:55], LXX-Isaiah [5:13; 8:6; 36:21; 53:7; 60:15; 63:9]). In LXX-Joshua this construction occurs in 14:14 (διὰ τὸ αὐτὸν ἐπακολουθῆσαι τῷ προστάγματι κυρίου—יען אשר מלא אחרי יהוה) and 22:19 (διὰ τὸ οἰκοδομῆσαι ὑμας βωμὸν ἔξω τοῦ θυσιαστηρίου κυρίου—בבנתכם לכם מזבח מבלעדי מזבח יהוה). See further LXX-Judg(B-A) 3:12; LXX-1 Reg. 15:20; LXX-3 Reg. 10:9; LXX-4 Reg. 19:28; LXX-1 Chron. 13:10; LXX-2 Chron. 13:10; 29:36; LXX-Jer. 7:32; 9:12; 26:19; LXX-Ezek. 33:28; 34:5; 35:10; Jdt.13:1; Tob^S 6:13; 1 Macc. 6:53; 10:42; 10:77; 11:2; 14:35; θ'-Sus. 1:4.39. See also I. Soisalon-Soininen, *Die Infinitive in der Septuaginta.*

[428] C.D. Benjamin, *The Variations*, p. 33.

[429] The proper use of this genuine Greek mode of expression already indicates

omission of the element הם in his Latin version: *postquam autem omnes --- circumcisi sunt.* We will return to the quantitative variant after we have discussed the several qualitative divergencies between MT and LXX in this verse.

The Greek text continues with a plus *vis-à-vis* MT ἡσυχίαν εἶχον, *they got rest,* which stresses the notion of rest in the Hebrew verb וישבו, *they remained.* The Greek translator rendered this connotation, too, but by the participle construction καθήμενοι, in order to express the idea of inactivity. Since the noun ἡσυχία occurs only eight times within the whole corpus of translated books and furthermore renders a wide variety of Hebrew expressions, there is—again—every reason to believe that it originated from the hand of the Greek translator. Although this noun and the related verb ἡσυχάζω appear to have served the Greek translators of the books of the Hebrew Bible as a fixed equivalent of the Hebrew root שקט, *to be at rest, to be peaceful,*[430] it is noteworthy that the two passages where this Hebrew verb occurs in the book of Joshua, i.e. in the identical phrase והארץ שקטה מִמלחמה, *and the earth got rest from war,* it has been rendered by two other different and unique translations: 11:23 καὶ ἡ γῆ *κατέπαυσεν* πολεμουμένη, and 14:15 καὶ ἡ γῆ *ἐκόπασεν* τοῦ πολέμου. The addition of the short clause in 5:8 ἡσυχίαν εἶχον thus points to another innovation introduced by the Greek translator. He probably wanted to emphasise the idea of the recuperation of the Israelite adult war-

---

the relative freedom by which the translator dealt with this text, see e.g. A. Aejmelaeus, *Participium coniunctum* as Criterion of Translation Technique, in *VT* 32 (1982), pp. 385–393 (= idem, *On the Trail of the Translators*, pp. 7–16). In dealing with these syntactical phenomena, S. Sipilä, *Between Literalness and Freedom*, p. 89, wonders whether the Hebrew *Vorlage* lacked the macro-syntactic marker ויהי, but gives no reconstruction of such a shorter Hebrew *Vorlage.*

[430] HALOT, pp. 1641a–1642a. The Greek noun ἡσυχία has been used to render the corresponding Hebrew noun שֶׁקֶט in 1 Chron. 22:9 (*a hapax*), and the verb שקט in LXX-1 Chron. 4:40; LXX-Job 34:29. The noun further appears in LXX-Prov. 7:9 (for אִשׁוּן, *starting time*, instead of MT אִישׁוֹן, ? *pupil of the eye*, thus the commentaries and BHS); LXX-Prov. 11:12 (for חרשׁ Hiph'il) and further (without [extant] Hebrew *Vorlage*) LXX-Est. 4:17; 1 Macc. 9:58; 2 Macc. 12:2; 14:4; LXX-Sir. 28:16. In 21 out of 46 passages where the corresponding noun ἡσυχάζω occurs in the Greek Old Testament, it has been used to render the Hebrew verb שקט, i.e. in LXX[B-A]-Judg. 3:11.30; 5:31(32); 8:28; 18:7.27; LXX-Ruth 3:18; LXX-4 Reg. 11:20; LXX-2 Chron. 14:1 (13:23); 23:21; LXX-Job 3:13.26; 32:17; LXX-Ps. 75(76):8; 106(107):30; LXX-Zech. 1:11; LXX-Isa. 7:4; LXX-Jer. 26(46):47; 29(47):6.7; LXX-Ezek. 38:11. In LXX-Ezek. 32:14, the Greek translator as well as the Aramaic translator read אשקיט instead of אשקיע, see W. Zimmerli, *Ezechiel* (BKAT XIII/2), p. 765. See also C. Spicq, o.p., *Notes de lexicographie néo-testamentaire* 1, pp. 358–364.

riors after such a painful operation. As we learn from Gen. 34:24–25, where the adult male population of Shechem circumcised themselves (וַיִּמֹּלוּ כָּל־זָכָר—καὶ περιετέμοντο τὴν σάρκα τῆς ἀκροβυστίας αὐτῶν, πᾶς ἄρσην), the days immediately afterwards were painful and rendered those operated vulnerable to hostile attacks (וַיְהִי בַיּוֹם הַשְּׁלִישִׁי בִּהְיוֹתָם כֹּאֲבִים—ἐγένετο δὲ ἐν τῇ ἡμέρᾳ τῇ τρίτῃ, ὅτε ἦσαν ἐν τῷ πόνῳ). In Josh. 5:1, the threat of the hostile forces has temporarily been postponed, so that the phrase ἡσυχίαν εἶχον also implies the notion of security.

The Greek translator rendered the preposition phrase תחתם, *at their place; where they were standing*, by the adverb αὐτόθι, *there, on the spot*, which recurs in the Greek Old Testament only seven times.[431] The Greek translator of Joshua was well aware of the different nuances of the Hebrew preposition, and offered various idiomatic renderings such as ἀντί in cases of substitution (2:14; 5:7), ὑπό in cases of altitude (11:3.17; 12:3; 13:5 and 24:26), or other renderings that would fit the context best according to the Greek translator.[432] Here, the use of αὐτόθι underlines the idea that after the severe and painful operation the male Israelites remained inactive (καθήμενοι) at the place where they had been circumcised (αὐτόθι, that is ἐν τῇ παρεμβολῃ).[433]

For the same reasons, a straightforward rendering of the Hebrew phrase עד חיותם by the Greek verb ζάω[434] would have been inappropriate in this specific context of being allowed to recover from the operation. Hence the Greek translator employed the Greek verb ὑγιάζω (passive) *to become healthy, to recover*,[435] comparable to the renderings in Targum Jonathan עַד דְאִתַּסִּיאוּ, Pešiṭta ܥܕܡܐ ܕܐܬܐܣܝܘ, and Vulgate *donec sanarentur*. Although it is evident that the context of this clause called for an idiomatic rendering rather than a literal one, it is still noteworthy that the verb ὑγιάζω recurs only rarely in

---

[431] That is in 1 Esdr. 8:41.61 (cf. MT-Ezra [LXX-II Esdr.] 8:15.32 שָׁם/ἐκεῖ), LXX-Tob. 2:3; 2 Macc. 3:24, 11:8; 12:38; and 15:37.

[432] Cf. Josh. 4:9 [רגלי הכהנים] תחת מצב—ἐν τῷ γενομένῳ τόπῳ ὑπὸ [τοὺς πόδας τῶν ἱερέων]; Josh. 6:5 תחתיה [ונפלה חומת העיר]—[πεσεῖται] αὐτόματα [τὰ τειχη τῆς πόλεως]; and 6:20 תחתיה [ותפל החומה]—[καὶ ἔπεσεν ἅπαν το τεῖχος] κύκλῳ.

[433] Jerome condensed the two phrases תחתם במחנה into a single description of the place: *manserunt in eodem castrorum loco.*

[434] So in 3:10, 4:14 and 8:23 for חי and further 9:21.

[435] See mss. 54, 75 and 314 from the S̲yrian family, which read ὑγιεῖς ἐγενόντο. Mss. 19 (P̲$_l$), 44 (S̲$_b$), 53 (M̲), 58 (M̲), 72 (M̲) and 129 (E̲) read ἑως ἡγιάσθησαν, *until they were sanctified.*

the Septuagint,[436] just as the renderings of the same Hebrew verb חיה in LXX-Joshua by διασῴζω, *to preserve, maintain* (9:15),[437] διατρέφω, *to support* (14:10),[438] ζωγρέω, *to keep alive* (2:13; 6:25; 9:20)[439] and περιποιέω, *to keep alive* (6:17; 9:20) are not stereotyped renderings.[440] The use of the verb ὑγιάζω here reflects an uncommon, but adequate rendering of the Hebrew text, which at the same time reflects the difficulties the Greek translator had with the idea of the painful operation on already adult males. Thus, whereas in the Hebrew text of this verse the emphasis falls on the completion of a rite that marks the new beginning of the people in the Promised Land, the Greek translator stressed the element of rest and recovery of those operated after such an unusual operation.

Given these nuances introduced by the Greek translator, it would seem a hazardous enterprise to reconstruct a deviant Hebrew *Vorlage*

---

[436] That is, in LXX-Lev. 13:18.37 and LXX-Ezek. 47:8.9.11 the Greek verb ὑγιάζω appears as equivalent for the Hebrew רפא, *to heal*, in LXX-4 Reg. 20:7 and LXX-Hos. 6:3(2) for חיה, and in LXX-Lev. 13:24 and LXX-Job 24:23 without Hebrew equivalent, see HR, p. 1380b.

[437] Only here in the whole Septuagint does the verb διασῴζω represent the Hebrew חיה, whereas in the majority of the other 76 cases it has been used predominantly as an equivalent for the Hebrew verbs מלט, פלט, and שרד (thus e.g. in LXX-Josh. 10:20.20.28.30.37.39.40; 11:8) see HR, p. 312a–b.

[438] The verb διατρέφω occurs only 17 times in the Septuagint, predominantly as the equivalent of the Hebrew verb כול Pilpʿel (LXX-Gen. 50:21; LXX-Ruth 4:15; LXX-2 Reg. 19:32(33).33(34); 20:3; LXX-3 Reg. 17:4.9; 18:4; LXX-II Esdr. 19:21; LXX-Ps. 54(55):22). In LXX-Gen. 7:3; 50:20; and Ps. 32(33):19, the verb has been used to render the Hebrew verb חיה. See further Judg. 5:10; and LXX^{B}-Prov. 22:9; and HR, p. 314a.

[439] The Greek verb ζωγρέω, *to save, to preserve alive*, occurs only eight times in the Greek Old Testament, three of which in the Greek Joshua, 2:13 and its parallel in 6:24(25) and further in 9:20. The other passages are LXX-Num. 31:15.18, LXX-Deut. 20:16, LXX-2 Reg. 8:2 and LXX-2 Chron. 25:12, see HR, p. 599b.

In LXX-Josh. 9:20 the verb occurs in the double rendering ζωγρῆσαι αὐτούς, καὶ περιποιησόμεθα αὐτούς, for the single Hebrew clause והחיה אותם. Margolis considered the second part to be the original Greek rendering and the first part to be a secondary interpolation, and reconstructed τοῦτο ποιήσομεν, περιποιησόμεθα αὐτους, on the basis of Codex Lugdunensis *Sed hoc faciamus: adseruemus eos*, see M.L. Margolis, *The Book of Joshua in Greek*, p. 163. With the exception of the Codex Ambrosianus, however, all extant Greek witnesses support this double translation. Moreover, it remains unclear to which Greek verb the Latin asservo, *preserve*, corresponds. Neither of the two Greek verbs reflect a literal, stereotyped rendering of the Hebrew phrase. On these and other grounds C.G. den Hertog, *Studien*, pp. 89–90, considers the doublet to be a double (supplementary) translation.

[440] The verb περιποιέω occurs another 29 times in the Septuagint, eight times as a rendering for חיה: LXX-Gen. 12:12; LXX-Exod. 1:16; 22:18(17); LXX-Num. 22:33; LXX-2 Reg. 12:3; LXX-3 Reg. 18:5; and LXX-Ezek. 13:18.19.

without the words כל־הגוי, which are not explicitly rendered by the Greek translator. For one, a Hebrew text without these words lacks the required subject, which is indispensable after the change in subject in the immediately preceding clause from those circumcised (the younger generation MT-Josh. 5:7c) to those responsible for their uncircumcised state (לא־מלו MT-Josh. 5:7d). Moreover, as Gooding has already pointed out,[441] there would have been no reason for a Hebrew reviser to add these words in Holmes' view. Had there been a Hebrew reviser who had wanted to make the alleged Hebrew *Vorlage* of LXX-Josh. 5:4–5 more orthodox, in the way Holmes and others explain the variants in these verses, he would have had no reason to alter the text here, since the preceding verse (in the alleged shorter version of LXX) mentioned precisely the group of Israelites (i.e. the children born on the way), which is the only group acknowledged by the alleged reviser. As we have seen above, both from a redaction-critical perspective and a study of the Greek text in its own context, there is no reason to assume that the Greek text reflects another, older Hebrew text than MT.

On the other hand, there would have been a clear motive for the Greek translator to deal with the Hebrew text freely, in the same manner as he did with many of the other elements in this verse which he adapted to his interpretation. It was of course not the *entire population* that had been circumcised by Joshua, but only the male part of it, and of these only those either born on the way or not yet circumcised before the exodus in Egypt (LXX-Josh. 5:4). Since the Greek translator had already clearly stated whom Joshua circumcised, and since he did not intend to reflect the change in subject in MT-Josh. 5:7c–d, he could allow for the omission of these words in verse 8 in order to present his own version of the events narrated in the Hebrew text.[442]

---

[441] D.W. Gooding, The Circumcision at Gilgal, pp. 156–157.

[442] See also the long discussion in J.E. Erbes, *The Peshitta and the Versions*, pp. 296–297. In his view 'The origin of the entire omission is evidently an inner-Septuagintal shortening, for the Vulgate a similar partial one.' He does not explain, however, whether the omission should be ascribed to an initiative by the Greek translator or to a scribal corruption in the process of the transmission of the text of the Septuagint.

7.6.7 *LXX-Josh. 5:9*

As described in section 7.6.3.3, the Greek translator inferred from the phrase חרפת מצרים, which he rendered straightforwardly by ὀνειδισμός Αἰγύπτου,[443] that not all Israelites had been circumcised in Egypt, and thus formed an object of scorn for the Egyptians, among whom this custom was well-known and held in esteem. Hence, he rendered the Hebrew verb גלל by ἀφαιρέω, and introduced the category of Israelites that had left Egypt uncircumcised, but had not died in the desert (LXX-5:4b).

Leaving the plus in LXX υἱῷ Ναυη after τῷ Ἰησοῖ *vis-à-vis* MT אל־יהושע aside as irrelevant to our present discussion, the passage that requires our attention is the plus in MT *vis-à-vis* LXX ויקרא] שם המקום ההוא גלגל] עד היום הזה 5:10ויחנו בני־ישראל בגלגל. The minus in LXX is usually regarded as the result of parablepsis through homoioteleuton,[444] and occasionally as an expansion by a Hebrew scribe (see the discussion in section 7.4.5). As E. Otto and others have pointed out,[445] the clause ויחנו בני־ישראל בגלגל is redundant after Josh. 4:19. Since no change of scene is narrated in the verses following 4:19, it is no more than logical to assume that, according to the narrative, the circumcision of the Israelites and their recovery took place in the same camp at Gilgal. Thus there would have been a very clear motive for the Greek translator to pass over these words as redundant and thus confusing information, and add the subject of this clause to that of the second.[446]

As Bieberstein has pointed out, however, the minus in LXX also contains the last words of verse 9, עד היום הזה, for which this thesis does not account.[447] One might argue that the translator omitted these words, since the place Gilgal had ceased to exist perhaps already

[443] Of the 73 times the Hebrew noun חֶרְפָּה occurs in the Hebrew Bible, 45 times the equivalent ὀνειδισμός, *disgrace, insult, reproach* (LEH, p. 333b) has been used, and 22 times the corresponding noun ὄνειδος, *disgrace, object of reproach* (LEH, p. 333b).

[444] Thus e.g. J. Hollenberg, *Der Charakter*, p. 18; S. Holmes, *Joshua*, p. 31; C.D. Benjamin, *The Variations*, p. 74; P.A. Fernández, s.i., *Commentarius in librum Iosue*, p. 71; B.J. Alfrink, *Josue*, p. 36; R.G. Boling, *Joshua*, p. 184; M. Anbar, La reprise, in *VT* 38 (1988), p. 388–389; L. Mazor, עיונים, p. 180; K. Bieberstein, *Josua-Jordan-Jericho*, p. 206; R.D. Nelson, *Joshua*, p. 73, note 1.

[445] E. Otto, *Das Mazzotfest in Gilgal*, p. 62, note 1; G. Kuhnert, *Das Gilgalpassah*, p. 71; T.C. Butler, *Joshua*, p. 55.

[446] Thus M.L. Margolis, *The Book of Joshua in Greek*. Paris 1931–1992, p. 74.

[447] K. Bieberstein, *Josua-Jordan-Jericho*, p. 206.

before the Exile.[448] In that case, however, one would expect a similar procedure from the Greek translator in cases where the same phrase עד היום הזה is connected to other sites that had ceased to exist long before his days, e.g. with the alternative group of stones that were placed according to Josh. 4:9 in the Jordan, Ai (LXX-Josh. 8:28), the grave for the king of Ai (LXX-Josh. 8:29), and the grave of the five kings of the southern coalition (LXX-Josh. 10:27). In all cases, the LXX renders the Hebrew phrase by either ἕως τῆς σήμερον ἡμέρας (4:9; 10:27) or ἕως τῆς ἡμέρας ταύτης (8:28.29). The phrase recurs in other contexts as well within the Hebrew book of Joshua (6:25, 7:26.26; 9:27; 13:13; 14:14; 15:63; 16:10; 22:3.17; 23:8.9) and has consistently been rendered by one of the two phrases (or in the case of LXX-Josh. 15:63 by ἑως τῆς ἡμέρας ἐκείνης). The sole exception forms Josh. 7:26, a passage that shares with our text the reference to a circle of stones (גלגל 5:9; גל־אבנים 7:26) and an aetiological explanation of the name of that place (קרא שם המקום ההוא 5:9; 7:26). In Josh. 7:26 we find the phrase עד היום הזה twice in the Hebrew text, and only once (the second time) in LXX:

7[26]	καὶ ἐπέστησαν αὐτῷ σωρὸν λίθων	וַיָּקִימוּ עָלָיו גַּל־אֲבָנִים
	μέγαν. --- --- --- ---	גָּדוֹל עַד הַיּוֹם הַזֶּה
	καὶ ἐπαύσατο κύριος ---	וַיָּשָׁב יְהוָה
	τοῦ θυμοῦ τῆς ὀργῆς ---.	מֵחֲרוֹן אַפּוֹ
	διὰ τοῦτο ἐπωνόμασεν --- --- --- *αὐτὸ*	עַל־כֵּן קָרָא שֵׁם
	Εμεκαχωρ	הַמָּקוֹם הַהוּא עֵמֶק עָכוֹר
	ἕως τῆς ἡμέρας ταύτης.	עַד הַיּוֹם הַזֶּה׃

Although the plus in MT עד היום הזה is almost unanimously seen as a later expansion of the shorter text reflected by LXX,[449] the reasons for this presumed scribal intervention remain vague. On the other hand it is well conceivable that a Greek translator concerned with style and clarity deliberately omitted the first of the two phrases.

[448] See O. Bächli, Zur Lage des alten Gilgal, in *ZDPV* 83 (1967), pp. 64–71; with some reservations E. Otto, *Das Mazzotfest in Gilgal*, pp. 12–18 (I.2.A. 'Zu Topographie und Archäologie Gilgals bei Jericho'). See further E. Otto, Gilgal, in *TRE* XIII (1985), pp. 268–270; W.R. Kotter, Gilgal (place), in *ABD* II (1992), pp. 1022–1024.

[449] C. Steuernagel, *Deuteronomium und Josua*, p. 180; S. Holmes, *Joshua*, p. 41; C.D. Benjamin, *The Variations*, p. 38; E.A. Chesman, *Studies in the Septuagint Text of the Book of Joshua*, pp. 22–24; R.G. Boling, *Joshua*, p. 220; T.C. Butler, *Joshua*, p. 78; V. Fritz, *Das Buch Josua*, p. 78; R.D. Nelson, *Joshua*, p. 97.

More important for our present discussion, however, is the circumstance that unlike Josh. 5:9 the subject in 7:26 is impersonal: *therefore one calls the name of that place.* Usually in the Hebrew Bible we find the combination of the formula עד היום הזה and the name-giving of a place in a passive or impersonal form (קרא שׁם, or -קרא ל).[450] In Gen. 26:33, for instance, a nominal clause has been used: על־כן שׁם־העיר באר שׁבע עד היום הזה, *therefore the name of the place is Beersheba until the present day*,[451] while in Judg. 1:26 the naming of the city of Luz and the statement that this is its name until today have been formulated as two separate clauses ויקרא שׁמה לוז הוא שׁמה עד היום הזה, *he called the name of the place Luz, and that is its name until the present day.*[452] In Judg. 18:12, the subject of קרא Qal is an impersonal plural form על־כן קראו למקום ההוא מחנה־דן עד היום הזה, *therefore they call that place Camp of Dan until the present day*,[453] while in 2 Sam. 18:18, for instance, the Niphʿal of קרא has been employed: ויקרא למצבת על־שׁמו וַיִּקָּרֵא לה יד אבשׁלם עד היום הזה, *he called the pillar after his name; and it is called Absalom's monument until the present day.*[454]

In Josh. 5:9, however, both the Masoretes and the Greek translator parsed the verb ויקרא as a Qal (וַיִּקְרָא—ἐκάλεσεν), so that either Yhwh or Joshua should be seen as the subject of that verb. Moreover, the combination καλέω plus τόπος recurs in the immediate context of LXX-Josh. 5:9 in verse 3 ἐπὶ τοῦ καλουμένου τόπου Βουνὸς τῶν ἀκροβυστιῶν. There is no change of location in the verses in between; rather, we find explicitly mentioned that everyone stayed at the same place (αὐτόθι καθήμενοι, verse 8). Hence there is every reason to believe that for the Greek translator both names 'Hill of the foreskins' and 'Gilgal' referred to the same place, so that the place known by the former name (see sections 7.4.1, 7.6.2 above), already known to the reader by the latter name in Josh. 4:19, in Josh. 5:9 receives its proper name 'Gilgal' from the mouth of the Deity himself. In

[450] The combination of name-giving (קרא שׁם) and the formula עד היום הזה occurs in Joshua only in 5:9 and 7:26.

[451] The Greek translator of Gen. 26:33 translated this clause in a rather straightforward manner: διὰ τοῦτο ἐκάλεσεν ὄνομα τῇ πόλει Φρέαρ ὅρκου ἕως τῆς σήμερον ἡμέρας.

[452] LXX$^{A.B}$-Judg. 1:26 ἕως τῆς σήμερον ἡμέρας Λουζα· τοῦτο ὄνομα αὐτῆς ἕως τῆς ἡμέρας ταύτης.

[453] LXX$^{A.B}$-Judg. 18:12 διὰ τοῦτο ἐκλήθη τῷ τόπῳ ἐκείνῳ Παρεμβολὴ Δαν ἕως τῆς ἡμέρας ταύτης.

[454] The Greek translator of 2 Reg. 18:18 read the verb as a Qal: καὶ *ἐκάλεσεν* τὴν στήλην Χεὶρ Αβεσσαλωμ ἕως τῆς ἡμέρας ταύτης.

such a context the phrase 'until the present day' (ἕως τῆς σήμερον ἡμέρας) or 'until that day' (ἕως τῆς ἡμέρας ταύτης)[455] would not have been very appropriate, all the more since the Greek translator had already stressed the notion of 'the present day' by his rendering of the Hebrew phrase היום, *today*, by ἐν τῇ σήμερον ἡμέρᾳ, *on the day of today*, in the second clause of the verse. Hence it is well conceivable that the omission of this phrase, too, reflects a literary initiative on the part of the Greek translator, rather than a scribal error by a copyist of either the Hebrew or the Greek text, even though this option still remains plausible.

7.6.8 *LXX-Josh. 5:10–12*

7.6.8.1 *The Temporal Setting*

As noted in section 7.2.2 above, the Greek text of Joshua 5:10[b]–12 differs significantly from MT with respect to chronology and calendar regarding the celebration of Passover-*maṣṣot* and the consumption of the first fruits. The most obvious variants are the minus ממחרת הפסח in verse 11, and the related phrase ממחרת in verse 12. Although the Greek text apparently presents a far less complicated account, it was shown in section 7.4.5.2 above, that the Hebrew text of MT-Josh. 5:10–12a forms a coherent unity, produced by a scribe from the Priestly school who wanted to conform the older text in 5:12b to legislation of the Holiness Code (Leviticus 23) by underlining the proper cultic sequence of the events *entry into the land—Passover—maṣṣot—consuming of the first-fruits of the land.* The pluses in

[455] In the majority of cases (i.e., 67 out of 87 times) when the Hebrew phrase עד היום הזה occurs, it has been rendered literally by ἕως τῆς ἡμέρας ταύτης (thus in LXX-Gen. 32:33; 47:26; 48:15; LXX-Exod. 10:6; LXX-Lev. 23:14; LXX-Deut. 2:22; 3:14; 10:8; 29:3; 34:6; LXX-Josh. 7:26; 8:28.29; 14:14; 16:10; 22:17; 23:8.9; LXX[A/B]-Judg. 1:21.26; 6:24; 10:4; 15:19; 18:12; 19:30; LXX-1 Reg. 5:5; 6:18; 8:8; 12:2; 27:6; 29:3.8, LXX-2 Reg. 4:3; 6:8; 7:6; 18:18; LXX-3 Reg. 9:13; 10:12; 12:19; LXX-4 Reg. 2:22; 8:22; 14:7; 16:6; 17:23.34.41; 20:17; 21:15; LXX-Isa. 39:6; LXX-Jer. 3:25; 7:25; 25:3; 39[32]:20.31; 43[36]:2; 51[44]:10; LXX-II Esdr. 9:7; 19:32 [= MT-Neh. 9:32]; LXX-1 Chron. 4:41.43; 5:26; 13:11; 17:5; LXX-2 Chron. 5:9; 8:8; 10:19 and 21:10). In a few (13) cases the idiomatic rendering ἕως τῆς σήμερον ἡμέρας has been used (LXX-Gen. 26:33; LXX-Num. 22:30; LXX-Deut. 11:4; LXX-Josh. 4:9; 6:25; 9:27; 10:27; 13:13; 22:3; LXX-1 Reg. 29:6; 30:25; LXX-Ezek. 2:3; 20:29) and (only) in LXX-Josh. 15:63 the phrase ἕως τῆς ἡμέρας ἐκείνης. In the remaining 6 passages, LXX-Josh. 5:9; 7:26; LXX-3 Reg. 8:8; 9:21; LXX-Jer. 11:7; 42[35]:14, the phrase lacks a counterpart in the text of the Septuagint.

MT *vis-à-vis* LXX already formed an integral and central part of the Priestly addition to the book of Joshua at the time the Greek translation of that book was produced. Thus, text-critical data and literary-critical observations do not overlap.

Nevertheless, the addition of the Priestly passage with the various temporal specifications—בארבעה עשׂר יום לחדשׁ בערב—ממחרת הפסח בעצם היום הזה—ממחרת to the more general statement of the older text (5:12b 'in that year'), caused confusion by later readers of the text: does the text mention three days (14th Nisan in verse 10–15th Nisan in verse 11–16th Nisan in verse 12)[456] or only two? And in the latter case: which events fall on what day? Does the repetition of the phrase אכל מעבור refer to an event that took place on the same day or not?[457] The younger translations of the Hebrew text, Targum Jonathan, the Fragmentary Targum, the Pešiṭta, and the Vulgate, all struggled with a correct interpretation of the redundant Hebrew text and found various solutions.

The Aramaic versions (Targum Jonathan, the Fragmentary Targum, and Pešiṭta) clearly distinguish between the consuming of the *maṣṣot* and the parched grain—which the Targumim explicitly identify as בִּכרַן, *first-fruits* (Hebrew בִּכּוּרִים)—and the cessation of the manna, by means of the phrases מבראר יומא . . . כד שׁארין דב[תר]והי, בְּיוֹמָא דְבָתְרוֹהִי בְּמֵיכַלהוֹן, and ܡܢ ܒܬܪ ܝܘܡܐ ܟܕ ܐܟܠܘ. The cultic activities of Passover and *maṣṣot*, however, are only loosely distinguished from one another by means of the phrase מִבָּתַר/ܡܢ ܒܬܪ.

MT	5:11	וַיֹּאכְלוּ מֵעֲבוּר הָאָרֶץ מִמָּחֳרַת הַפֶּסַח מַצּוֹת וְקָלוּי
TgJon	5:11	וַאֲכַלוּ מֵעֲבוּרָא דְאַרעָא מִבָּתַר פִּסחָא פַּטִיר וְקַלְיָא בִּכרַן
FrgTg	5:11	ושארין ואכלו מן פתא דארעא מבתאר יומא טבא פטיר וקלי בכראן
Peš	5:11	ܘܐܟܠܘ ܡܢ ܥܒܘܪܐ ܕܐܪܥܐ ܡܢ ܒܬܪ ܦܨܚܐ. ܦܛܝܪܐ ܘܩܠܝܬܐ ܐܟܠܘ.[458]
MT	5:12	בְּעֶצֶם הַיּוֹם הַזֶּה. וַיִּשְׁבֹּת הַמָּן מִמָּחֳרָת בְּאָכְלָם מֵעֲבוּר הָאָרֶץ
TgJon	5:12	יוֹמָא הָדֵין. וּפסַק מַנָא בְּיוֹמָא דְבָתְרוֹהִי בְּמֵיכַלהוֹן מֵעֲבוּרָא דְאַרעָא
FrgTg	5:12	יומא האדין. ופסאק [מנ]א מבראר יומא [. . .] כד שארין דב[תר]והי
Peš	5:12	ܒܗ ܒܝܘܡܐ ܗܢܐ ܘܐܬܦܣܩ ܡܢܢܐ ܡܢ ܒܬܪ ܝܘܡܐ. ܟܕ ܐܟܠܘ ܡܢ ܥܒܘܪܐ ܕܐܪܥܐ.

[456] Thus e.g. C.F. Keil, *Josua, Richter und Ruth*, pp. 40–41.

[457] See sections 7.2.2, 7.4.5.2–3 above and the halakhic discussions by the mediaeval Jewish commentators as summarised by S. Hoenig. A.J. Rosenberg, P. Oratz, S. Shulman, *The Book of Joshua. A New English Translation of the Text and Rashi with a Commentary Digest*. New York 1984, pp. 33–34.

[458] On the plus ܐܟܠܘ and the variant in Peš-mss. 11*l*1 and 11*l*5 ܦܛܝܪܐ ܘܩܠܝܬܐ. ܘܐܟܠܘ, see J.E. Erbes, *The Peshitta and the Versions*, pp. 301–302.

On the other hand, Jerome sought to improve the logic of the text by placing the consuming of the fruits of the land on the *die altero, the following day*, and by omitting in verse 12 the references to a specific day. Instead, he reinterpreted the temporal phrase in the light of that in 5:12b: azymos panes et polentam eisudem anni, *unleavened bread and barley-groats from the same year.*[459]

5^{11}	et comederunt de frugibus terrae	וַיֹּאכְלוּ מֵעֲבוּר הָאָרֶץ
	die altero azymos panes et polentam	מִמָּחֳרַת הַפֶּסַח מַצּוֹת וְקָלוּי
	eiusdem anni	בְּעֶצֶם הַיּוֹם הַזֶּה׃
5^{12}	defecitque manna ---	וַיִּשְׁבֹּת הַמָּן מִמָּחֳרָת
	postquam comederunt de frugibus terrae	בְּאָכְלָם מֵעֲבוּר הָאָרֶץ
	nec *usi* sunt ultra *illo cibo* filii Israhel	וְלֹא־הָיָה עוֹד לִבְנֵי יִשְׂרָאֵל מָן
	sed comederunt de frugibus	וַיֹּאכְלוּ מִתְּבוּאַת
	praesentis anni terrae Chanaan	אֶרֶץ כְּנַעַן בַּשָּׁנָה הַהִיא׃

The Greek translator was faced with the same problems and offered his own solution. He interpreted the references to cultic activities in verses 10 and 11 as elements of a single unified Passover festival. During the Second Temple Period the festivals of Passover and *maṣṣot* had completely fused into a single festival, starting with the Passover night proper and continuing with the seven days' eating of *maṣṣot*, thus e.g. Josephus, *Jewish Antiquities* XIV.21 κατὰ τὸν καιρὸν τῆς τῶν ἀζύμων ἑορτῆς, ἣν πάσχα λέγομεν and Mishna Pesaḥim IX.5 ופסח דורות נוהג כל־שבעה, *the Passover of the generations* (i.e. as distinguished from the Passover night in Egypt) *is practised all seven (days)*.[460] As E. Tov has already pointed out,[461] it is this understanding of Passover that allowed for the subtle change from the Hebrew preposition phrase בערב, (*they celebrated the Passover night proper*) *in the evening* towards the more general and inclusive statement ἀπὸ ἑσπέρας, *from the evening onwards*.[462] But whereas Tov approaches this variant separately from

[459] The Vulgata edition by R. Weber (ed.), *Biblia Sacra iuxta Vulgatam Versionem*. Stuttgart 1994^4, reads (with Vg mss. C Λ^{L*} L* F* X Π^{D} Σ^{TO*} B^2 A T O) *pu̲lentam*, which must be a scribal error for *po̲lentam, hulled and crushed grain; barley-groats, barley-meal* (thus P.G.W. Glare (ed.), *Oxford Latin Dictionary*. Oxford 1982, p. 1396c), attested by mss. B* Φ^{Z*} and adopted in the 'Roman' Benedictine edition *Biblia sacra iuxta latinam vulgatam.*

[460] See further J. Jeremias, πάσχα, *ThWNT* V, p. 897, n. 17 and the literature on the history of the Passover festival mentioned in section 7.2.2 above.

[461] E. Tov, Midrash-Type Exegesis, p. 57 (= *The Greek and Hebrew Bible*, p. 159).

[462] LXX mss. from the $\underline{P}_2$ (426), $\underline{C}$ (A, M, W, 29, 82), and $\underline{M}$ (85 [mg], 344 [mg]) families read ἀπὸ ἑσπερου. Interesting is the fact that the absence of an explicit

the quantitative variants in verses 11 and 12—in his view expansions introduced by editor II of the book of Joshua—,[463] it seems more appropriate to see the qualitative and quantitative variants as related: because the Greek translator took the mentioning of Passover as a reference to the whole seven-days festival, the distinction between the first evening and the following morning became meaningless, unnecessary and redundant. As a result of this subtle change, the Greek translator was free to pass over the confusing phrases ממחרת הפסח and ממחרת. In verse 12 the Greek translator secured the proper sequence of consuming and cessation of the manna by means of the preposition μετά plus accusative:[464] μετὰ τὸ βεβρωκέναι.[465] He did retain the temporal phrase בעצם היום הזה—ἐν ταύτῃ τῇ ἡμέρᾳ, but stripped it of its absolute function, i.e. a reference to the 15th Nisan, and instead gave it the function of clarifying the relation between verses 11 and 12: as soon as the Israelites could *enjoy the fruits* (καρπίζομαι) of the land flowing with milk and honey, the desert nourishment had become obsolete. Contrary to the interpretation by the Aramaic translators, the Greek translator inferred from the sequence in verse 12 'the Israelites ate from the produce of the land'—'the manna ceased', that these verses, where the same expression אכל מעבור הארץ occurs, refer to the same day. As a result, he

---

reference to the month, which is self-evidently the first month, has been compensated for in various traditions. J.B. DE ROSSI, *Variae Lectiones Veteris Testamenti Librorum* II, p. 76b, mentioned some 50 MT-mss. in which the older text בארבעה עשׂר יום לחדשׁ has been supplemented with the explicit statement בראשׁון בארבעה עשׂר. The FragmTg has a similar text בארבעה עשׂר יומא בניסאן. The S manuscripts of LXX add the number of the month: τοῦ πρώτου μηνός S_a (54, 61 [S_b], 75, 128 [M], 314) τοῦ μηνός πρώτου S_b $F^{a\ mg}$ (44, 106, 134, Or-lat.), which corresponds to the Peš text ܒܐܪܒܥܣܪܐ ܒܝܪܚܐ ܩܕܡܝܐ ܒܪܡܫܐ.

463 E. Tov, The Growth of the Book of Joshua, p. 330 (= *The Greek and Hebrew Bible*, pp. 389–390). See section 7.2.5 above.

464 The construction μετά plus accusative, *after*, has been employed 14 times in LXX-Joshua, usually as a translation of the Hebrew prepositions אחר (2:16; 24:5) and אחרי (1:1 καὶ ἐγένετο μετὰ τὴν τελευτὴν Μωυσῆ—ויהי אחרי מות משׁה; 9:2e [MT 8:34], 9:16 μετὰ τὸ διαθέσθαι πρὸς αὐτοὺς διαθήκην—אחרי אשׁר־כרתו להם ברית; 22:27; 24:30). In LXX-Josh. 3:2 and 9:16 the phrase καὶ ἐγένετο μετὰ τρεῖς ἡμέρας renders the Hebrew phrase ויהי מקצה שׁלשׁת ימים, cf. 23:1 καὶ ἐγένετο μεθ' ἡμέρας πλείους—ויהי מימים רבים. LXX-Josh. 6:13 καὶ μετὰ ταῦτα εἰσεπορεύοντο οἱ μάχιμοι—והחלוץ הלך לפניהם forms part of a comprehensive reorganisation of the Hebrew text, see e.g. K. BIEBERSTEIN, *Josua-Jordan-Jericho*, pp. 240–266. In LXX-Josh. 24:33 (Καὶ ἐγένετο μετὰ ταῦτα) the Greek text has no Hebrew counterpart.

465 Thus according to Rahlfs' edition. C.G. DEN HERTOG, *Studien*, p. 72 (= *BIOSCS* 28 [1995], p. 55), has pointed out that the genitive construction μετὰ τοῦ βεβρωκέναι (Margolis) is not supported by the manuscripts and is evidently an error.

slightly modified the syntax of the passage in accordance with this interpretation in order to enhance the logic of the text.

7.6.8.2 *The New Products*

Once it is realised that the Greek translator interpreted the Passover in the broader and inclusive sense of the seven-day festival including both the slaughtering of the Paschal lamb and the consumption of the unleavened bread, the unusual rendering of the Hebrew phrase קלוי, *roasted corn*, by νέα, *new products*, becomes understandable. In all other passages where this Hebrew phrase occurs in the Hebrew Bible it has been rendered literally by either πεφρυγμένα, *parched*,[466] φρυκτόν,[467] or ἄλφιτα, *groats, grain*.[468] Tov has argued that the Greek translator was unacquainted with this rare Hebrew word and consulted the Greek translation of the Pentateuch as a lexicon (viz. Lev. 2:14), but made the wrong equation.[469] Since the various renderings of the Hebrew noun עֲרָבָה III, *steppe, plain*,[470] in verse 10 may indicate that the Greek translator was not completely familiar with its precise meaning (see further below), it is not impossible that he simply guessed the meaning of the rare Hebrew word קלוי. Nevertheless, whereas the proper interpretation of the Hebrew word עֲרָבָה III posed problems for the Greek translators of the Pentateuch and other books of the Hebrew Bible as well,[471] the word קלוי never did. Moreover, the

466 LEH, p. 508b; GELS², p. 588a. The verb φρύγω occurs only in LXX-Lev. 2:14; 23:14 in the Septuagint.

467 The word occurs in the Greek Bible only in α' and σ' in Josh. 5:11; 2 Reg. 17:28; and α' in 1 Reg. 25:18; Ruth 2:14. For Josh. 5:11 ms. 108 contains the reading φρικτόν in the margin, ms. 85 (mg.) more properly: φρυκτόν.

468 LEH, p. 22a. LXX-Ruth 2:14; LXX$^{A.O'}$-1 Reg. 17:17; LXX-1 Reg. 25:18; LXX-2 Reg. 17:28; and Jdt. 10:5.

469 E. Tov, Midrash-Type Exegesis, p. 54 (= *The Greek and Hebrew Bible*, p. 157). See section 7.2.5 above.

470 HALOT, p. 880a–b.

471 In Num. 22:1; 33:48.49.50; 35:1; 36:13; Deut. 1:1; Josh. 11:16; 2 Sam. [4 Reg.] 2:29; 4:7; Amos 6:14; Ps. 68 [LXX 67]:5 the word was interpreted by the Greek translators as a form of the Hebrew noun עֶרֶב and rendered by the Greek noun δυσμαί. In 1 Sam. 23:24 the phrase בערבה has correspondingly been rendered by καθ' ἑσπέραν. In Num. 26:3.63; 31:12; Deut. 1:7; 3:17.17; 4:49; 34:1.8; Josh. 3:16; 11:2; 12:1.3.3.8; 13:32; 18:18.18; 2 Sam. [2 Reg.] 15:28; 17:16; 2 Kgs. [4 Reg.] 14:25; 25:4.5; Isa. 15:7; Jer. 52:7; and Ezek. 47:8 (ἐπὶ τὴν Αραβίαν) the word has simply been transliterated as Araba. Alternative renderings are γῆ ἀβάτος (LXX-Jer. 28 [51]:43), γῆ ἀπείρος (LXX-Jer. 2:6), γῆ διψώση (LXX-Isa. 35:6); ἔρημος (LXX-Jer. 17:6; 50[27]:12; LXX-Zech. 14:10; LXX-Job 39:6), and περάς (Jer. 52:8). The Greek translator of Isaiah seems to have avoided translating this

inclusive term νέα fits the context of the consumption of the first fruits in the Promised Land very well. Whereas the Hebrew term קלוי serves as a *pars pro toto* reference to the first fruits to be consumed after the dedication to the Deity by the priest in Leviticus 23, the rendering of this term by νέα serves as a successful *totum pro parte* translation,[472] comparable to the inclusive interpretation of Passover in the preceding verse 10, as suggested by Tov as alternative solution.[473]

An interesting parallel to our passage is offered by Num. 28:26, a passage that shares with Josh. 5:10–12 and Leviticus 23 the element of the cereal offerings of new grain (here בכורים), but deals with the feast of Weeks (שׁבעתיכם). Here too the general collective Greek term νέα has been used to denote the new cereal products as a whole (בכורים),[474] instead of the more common renderings of this Hebrew word by πρωτογένημα, *first fruits*:[475]

28[26]	Καὶ τῇ ἡμέρᾳ τῶν *νέων*,	וּבְי֤וֹם הַבִּכּוּרִ֗ים
	ὅταν προσφέρητε θυσίαν *νέαν* κυρίῳ	בְּהַקְרִ֨יבְכֶ֜ם מִנְחָ֤ה חֲדָשָׁה֙ לַֽיהוָ֔ה
	τῶν ἑβδομάδων,	בְּשָׁבֻעֹתֵיכֶ֑ם
	ἐπίκλητος ἁγία ἔσται ὑμῖν,	מִקְרָא־קֹ֙דֶשׁ֙ יִהְיֶ֣ה לָכֶ֔ם
	πᾶν ἔργον λατρευτὸν οὐ ποιήσετε.	כָּל־מְלֶ֥אכֶת עֲבֹדָ֖ה לֹ֥א תַעֲשֽׂוּ׃

---

word (thus LXX-Isa. 33:9; 35:1; 40:3; 41:19; 51:3. Wevers stated that the Greek translator of Deuteronomy 'had trouble with the word ערבה whenever it occurred in the book', thus J.W. WEVERS, The Attitude of the Greek Translator of Deuteronomy towards his Parent Text, in H. DONNER (Hg.), *Studien zur Theologie der alttestamentlichen Überlieferungen. FS W. Zimmerli.* Göttingen 1977, pp. 498–506, p. 499. Apparently this applies to the Greek translators of the other biblical books as well. See further C.G. DEN HERTOG, *Studien*, pp. 86–88.

[472] M.L. MARGOLIS, *Andreas Masius and His Commentary on the Book of Joshua.* (unpublished typescript document finished June 15, 1923) § 13, note 112: 'The translator saw in קלוי an abbreviation of the fuller phrase אביב קלוי νεα πεφρυγμενα Le 2:14.— νεα = אביב comp. Exod. 13:4; 23:15; 34:18.18 Deut. 16:1 (but Sir. 50:8 בימי מועד is freely rendered εν ημεραις νεων, contrast Smend) πεφρρυγμενα (+ (εν) πυρι α' σ' θ'. [. . .]'

[473] E. Tov, Midrash-type Exegesis, p. 54 (157).

[474] See G. DORIVAL, *Les Nombres*, pp. 500–501; J.W. WEVERS, *Notes to the Greek Text of Numbers*, p. 480: 'The rendering is unique; the term is a nominalized use of the adjective νέος 'fresh, new', and is intended to refer to the new grain products of the field; in other words, the translation is not incorrect, but merely unusual.'

[475] Thus in LXX-Exod. 23:16.19; LXX-Lev. 2:14.14; 23:17.19.20; LXX-Num. 18:13; LXX-4 Reg. 4:42; LXX-Neh. 10:35[36].

Like the Greek translator of the book of Numbers, our translator refered to the first products of the land mentioned in Leviticus 23 in general terms, as he did in the case of the Passover festival.

7.6.8.3 *The Geographical Setting*

Finally, the Greek translator introduced several minor modifications with respect to the geographical setting of this short narrative. As opposed to the single phrase in MT-Josh. 5:10, which states that the Israelites kept the Passover בערבות יריחו, *in the plains of Jericho*, the Greek translator employed three phrases to designate the same area: [1] ἐπὶ δυσμῶν Ιεριχω, *in the western (region of) Jericho*, [2] ἐν τῷ πέραν τοῦ Ιορδάνου, *at the other side of the Jordan*, and [3] ἐν τῷ πεδίῳ, *in the plain*. The Greek text likewise deviates from MT in verse 12, where it is stated that the Israelites ate from the yield from the ארץ כנען, *land of Canaan*, whereas LXX has ἐκαρπίσαντο δὲ τὴν χώραν τῶν Φοινίκων, *they enjoyed the fruits from the country of the Phoenicians*.[476]

Margolis argued that the phrase 'ἐν τῷ πεδίῳ which P (sub ÷) C retain is a pendant to ἐπὶ δυσμῶν and must be deleted.'[477] Similar proposals had already been made by Masius[478] and Hollenberg.[479] Yet, whereas the preceding plus in LXX ἐν τῷ πέραν τοῦ Ἰορδάνου is omitted in witnesses of the P (19.426.Syh), C (A.M [text]. V.W. 29.55.59.82.121. Arm), M (15.58.72) and occasionally S (314.VetLat) families, this second plus is supported by all witnesses. Therefore, there is no reason to doubt the originality of the Greek text as preserved by the older E family and as edited by Rahlfs.

---

[476] The reading of Vaticanus τὴν κουρὰν, *the shorn wool*, is 'a singular reading', M.L. MARGOLIS, *The Book of Joshua in Greek*, p. 76, line 20, and undoubtedly the result of an inner-Greek scribal error, see L. MAZOR, עיונים, p. 23.

[477] M.L. MARGOLIS, *The Book of Joshua in Greek*, p. 75, lines 21–22.

[478] A. MASIUS, *Josuae imperatoris historia*, Annotationes, p. 130a–b: 'Qua notat insigniuit Syrus etiam illud, quod in extremo versus est ἐν τῷ πεδίῳ ⸔. Nimirum voci Hebraicum בַּעֲרָבוֹת respondet, ἐπὶ δυσμῶν. Meo tamen iudicio hoc potius iugulandum ab Adamantio erat. Nam illud, ἐν τῷ πεδίῳ, magis est ei verbo Hebraico consentaneum. verùm si coniectura uti liceat, dicam: hoc, ἐν τῷ πεδίῳ, ab aliquo Hebraeae linguae perito in margine scriptum fuisse, pro illo, ἐπὶ δυσμῶν; quod ille iudicabat non satis congruere verbo illi Hebraeo. atque ita errore librariorum in ipso texto tandem scribi capisse.'

[479] J. HOLLENBERG, *Der Charakter*, p. 2: 'Der Übersetzer leitete ערבות von ערב (Abend) ab, wie auch 11:16; Also ist ÷ ἐν τῷ πεδίῳ ⸔ zweite Übersetzung.'

As noted above, the precise meaning of the Hebrew word עֲרָבָה III was probably unknown to the early Greek translators. Elsewhere in the book of Joshua, the Greek translator transliterated the word (3:16, 11:2;[480] 12:1.3.3.8; 13:32; 18:18.18), derived it from the Hebrew noun עֶרֶב, *evening* (11:16), or avoided a rendering of this word, as in Josh. 4:13 where the same expression occurs:

4[13]	τετρακισμύριοι	כְּאַרְבָּעִים אֶלֶף
	εὔζωνοι εἰς μάχην	חֲלוּצֵי הַצָּבָא
	διέβησαν ἐναντίον κυρίου	עָבְרוּ לִפְנֵי יְהוָה
	εἰς πόλεμον	לַמִּלְחָמָה
	πρὸς *τὴν* --- Ιεριχω *πόλιν*.	אֶל עַרְבוֹת יְרִיחוֹ׃
11[16]	Καὶ ἔλαβεν Ἰησοῦς	וַיִּקַּח יְהוֹשֻׁעַ
	πᾶσαν τὴν γῆν [. . .]	אֶת־כָּל־הָאָרֶץ הַזֹּאת [. . .]
	καὶ τὴν πεδινὴν	וְאֶת־הַשְּׁפֵלָה
	καὶ τὴν *πρὸς δυσμαῖς*	וְאֶת־הָעֲרָבָה
	καὶ τὸ ὄρος Ισραηλ	וְאֶת־הַר יִשְׂרָאֵל
	καὶ τὰ ταπεινά,	וּשְׁפֵלָתֹה׃

The three Greek phrases that render the problematic phrase in Josh. 5:10 are complementary rather than mere synonyms: the phrase ἐπὶ δυσμῶν Ιεριχω indicates the wind direction *in the western area near Jericho*, the second phrase ἐν τῷ πέραν τοῦ Ιορδάνου denotes the western part of the Jordan and implies the entry into the Promised Land; the phrase ἐν τῷ πεδίῳ designates the arable area where one could cultivate grain. Therefore, there is no need to assume that one or two of these phrases reflect later interpolations into the Greek text, or into the Hebrew text, i.e. בבקעה [3] מעבר לירדן [2], בערבות יריחו [1], as proposed by Den Hertog.[481] Rather, the variants *vis-à-vis* the Hebrew text as preserved by MT should be seen as successful attempts by the Greek translator to provide a sensible translation for a problematic Hebrew phrase.[482]

The rendering of the last clause in our passage ויאכלו מתבואת ארץ כנען בשנה ההיא by ἐκαρπίσαντο δὲ τὴν χώραν τῶν Φοινικῶν ἐν τῷ ἐνιαυτῷ ἐκείνῳ is both remarkable and puzzling. Since no other

---

[480] Here the conjectural emendation by Margolis καὶ εἰς τὴν Αραβα is preferable to Rahlfs' καὶ εἰς τὴν Ραβα [thus B.120.407 and, with variations, most of the other E̲ and C̲ witnesses] for MT ובערבה.

[481] C.G. den Hertog, *Studien*, pp. 86–88.

[482] See J. Moatti-Fine, *Josué*, pp. 112, 119. C.G. den Hertog, *Studien*, p. 88, also provides this solution of a 'verdeutlichende Doppel 'übersetzung''.

Hebrew text than that attested by MT can be reconstructed behind this Greek formulation, it is clear that the Greek text reflects a well-considered, idiomatic rendering. Yet, the motives behind this reformulation are not always easy to recover.

The Greek verb καρπίζομαι, *to enjoy the fruits of*, recurs in the Greek Bible only in LXX-Prov. 8:19 (βέλτιον ἐμὲ καρπίζεσθαι ὑπὲρ χρυσίον, *better than gold it is to enjoy my fruits* [i.e. of wisdom]—טוב פריי מחרוץ, *my fruit is better than gold*). Whereas, for instance, the Greek translator of Lev. 25:22 offered a literal rendering of the same Hebrew expression ואכלתם מן־התבואה by καὶ φάγεσθε ἀπὸ τῶν γενήματων,[483] the Greek translator of Joshua, by contrast, offered a non-literal translation in which the Hebrew phrase has been condensed into a single Greek expression.[484] The rendering of the Hebrew word שׁנה, *year*, by ἐνιαυτός instead of the more common equivalent ἔτος (thus in all other places in Joshua, i.e. 5:6; 14:7.10.10; 24:29[30]) also points to a non-literal rendering of the clause.

The phrase χώρα τῶν Φοινικῶν deserves special attention. Although the Greek word χώρα, *place, region, land, cultivated land*, occurs outside the Greek version of Joshua some 65 times as an alternative rendering of the Hebrew noun ארץ besides the standard equivalent γῆ,[485] the equation is unique in the Greek version of Joshua.[486] Within LXX-Joshua the noun χώρα recurs only in 4:18 ὥρμησεν τὸ ὕδωρ του Ἰορδάνου κατὰ χώραν, *the water of the Jordan set itself in motion along*

[483] See also the renderings by Aquila and Symmachus of Josh. 5:12 καὶ ἔφαγον ἀπὸ γεννήματος τῆς (γῆς) Χαναάν. M.85.344. Theodotion took a middle course by employing the phrase καὶ ἐφάγον ἀπὸ τῶν καρπῶν (καρπωματῶν 344.85) τῆς γῆς Χαναaν M.85.344.

[484] Thus also L.J. GREENSPOON, *Textual Studies*, pp. 91–93: 'Since καρπιζω in the middle may mean 'to enjoy the fruits of', there is no reason to suggest that the Hebrew *Vorlage* of OG was anything other than the Hebrew of MT. Th. produced a more literal translation of the same Hebrew, influenced by the choice of noun by the OG.' Thus even S. HOLMES, *Joshua*, p. 31.

[485] Thus in LXX-Gen. 10:20.31; 41:57; 42:9; LXX-Num. 32:1.1; LXX-4 Reg. 18:33; LXX-1 Chron. 20:1; LXX-2 Chron. 15:5; 32:13; LXX-Job 1:1; LXX-Ps. 104[105]:44; 105[106]:27; 106[107]:3; 114[116]:9; LXX-Prov.8:26; 29:4; LXX-Jona 1:8; LXX-Isa. 2:7; 7:18; 8:8; 9:1[8:23]; 9:2 [9:1]; 13:14; 18:2.3.7; 19:19.20; 21:14; 22:18; 27:13; 28:2; 36:10.18; 37:7.18; LXX-Jer. 16:15; LXX-Ezek. 5:5.6; 6:8; 11:16.17; 12:15; 20:23.34.41; 21:19[24]; 22:4.15; 25:7; 29:12; 30:7.23.26; 34:14; 35:10; 36:19; 39:27; and LXX-Dan. 9:7; 11:16.19.28.28.40.41.42.

[486] Of the 107 times the Hebrew noun ארץ occurs in MT-Joshua, it has 89 times been rendered by the Greek noun γῆ, if one adopts Margolis' conjectural emendation in 7:2 of ΓΑΙ into ΓΗ. In ten cases (1:4 כל ארץ החתים, see section 6.4.4 above]; 2:9; 6:22; 10:41; 17:8.15.16; 18:10; 23:16; 24:17) the word and its immediate context lack an equivalent in LXX. In LXX 1:15 the word has been replaced by κληρονομία (see section 6.4.6 above), in 2:14.16 by πόλις.

the region, in an idiomatic rendering of the Hebrew clause וישבו מי־הירדן למקומם, *the water of the Jordan returned to its place*. This text resembles the narrative of Israel's crossing through the Red Sea (Exod. 14:27) where the Greek translator rendered the corresponding clause וישב הים לפנות בקר לאיתנו, *the water returned to its normal level at daybreak* by καὶ ἀπεκατέστη τὸ ὕδωρ πρὸς ἡμέραν ἐπὶ χώρας, *the water returned to its place towards the day*.[487] The use of the preposition κατά with accusative in LXX-Josh. 4:18, however, rather seems to express the idea of the waters flowing (again) along the Jordan valley, i.e., the same region where the Israelites in Josh. 5:12 enjoy the fruits of the new land.

Whereas the Hebrew words כנען, *Canaan*, and כנעני, *Canaanite*, are usually transliterated in the Greek version as Χαναaν and ὁ Χαναναῖος respectively,[488] it appears that the toponym כנען has been rendered here by the *gentilicum* Φοίνικες, *Phoenicians*. The equation Canaan(ite)—Phoenicia(n) is not unique in the Greek Old Testament, but nevertheless remarkable, since the Greek words Φοινίκη, Φοίνικες, Φοίνισσα usually refer to the coastal area north of the land of the Canaanites, roughly identical with the modern state of Lebanon.[489] It is in this sense that the Greek translator of Joshua employed the name in 5:1 in his interpretative rendering of מלכי הכנעני אשר על־הים—οἱ βασιλεῖς τῆς Φοινίκης οἱ παρὰ τὴν θάλασσαν, i.e. the autochthonous kings along the coast of the Mediterranean Sea. Likewise the Greek translator of Deuteronomy interpreted the reference to the inhabitants of Sidon in 3:9 (צידנים יקראו לחרמון שׂרין, *the Sidonians call the Hermon Sirion*) as a *pars pro toto* reference to all the Phoenicians (οἱ Φοίνικες ἐπονομάζουσιν τὸ Αερμὼν Σανιώρ). A similar equation has been made in Isa. 23:2 where סחר צידון, *the merchants of Sidon*, have been identified as μεταβόλοι Φοινίκης, *the retailers of Phoenicia*.[490] In the same way, the translator of Job 40:30 renders the word כנענים, here in the sense of *merchants*, by Φοίνικες. Thus, when the Greek translators of the books of the Hebrew Bible departed from the standard equation כנען—

[487] So J. Moatti-Fine, *Josué*, p. 113.

[488] So in LXX-Josh. 3:10; 7:9; 9:1; 11:3; 12:8; 13:3.4; 14:1; 16:10; 17:12.13.16.18; 21:1; 22:9.10.11.32; and 24:11. In 24:3 the Greek text lacks an equivalent for Canaan.

[489] See e.g., B. Peckham, Phoenicia, in ABD 5, pp. 349b–357b. See further the ancient Greek authors, such as Herodotus, *History of the Persian Wars* II.104; Strabo, *Geography* XVI.2.2, and the second century BCE Jewish-Hellenistic historian Eupolemos (see C.R. Holladay, *Fragments from Hellenistic Jewish Authors. Volume 1: Historians*. Chico 1983, pp. 93–156).

[490] See A. van der Kooij, *The Oracle of Tyre*, pp. 52–53, 75ff.

Χαναάν,[491] it was because they felt the genuine Greek name Φοινικ- was—given the context—a more appropriate designation of the country and its inhabitants north of Israel/Canaan.[492]

It is evident that the phrase χώρα τῶν Φοινικῶν in LXX-Josh. 5:12 does not reflect a Hebrew text different from that preserved in MT, i.e. ארץ כנען. The reason for this idiomatic rendering, however, is not self-evident since the area where LXX-Josh. 5:12 is situated, i.e. the plain (πεδίον 5:10) in the vicinity of Jericho (ἐπὶ δυσμῶν Ιεριχω 5:10) is far removed from the Phoenician coast (Φοινίκη . . . παρὰ τὴν θάλασσαν 5:1). Nevertheless, this unusual rendering has a striking parallel in Exod. 16:35 (see section 7.4.5.2 above) where the same Hebrew phrase ארץ כנען has been translated by ἡ Φοινίκη:

16[35] οἱ δὲ υἱοὶ Ισραηλ ἔφαγον τὸ μαν	וּבְנֵי יִשְׂרָאֵל אָכְלוּ אֶת־הַמָּן
ἔτη τεσσαράκοντα,	אַרְבָּעִים שָׁנָה
ἕως ἦλθον εἰς γῆν οἰκουμένην·	עַד־בֹּאָם אֶל־אֶרֶץ נוֹשָׁבֶת
τὸ μαν ἐφάγοσαν,	אֶת־הַמָּן אָכְלוּ
ἕως παρεγένοντο εἰς μέρος	עַד־בֹּאָם אֶל־קְצֵה
τῆς --- *Φοινίκης*.	אֶרֶץ כְּנָעַן׃

Both passages deal with the cessation of the manna which was to take place at the border of the land of Canaan. Hence C. den Hertog and J. Moatti-Fine explain the unusual rendering in LXX-Joshua as a case of literary dependency on the choice made by the translator of the book of Exodus.[493] Nevertheless, the rendering in Exod. 16:35 is no less problematic—or 'surprising' as J.W. Wevers has put it—than it is in Josh. 5:12.[494] Therefore, it is difficult to see why the

[491] See HR III, p. 157a–c.

[492] A special case is posed by the Greek author-translator of the book 1 Esdras, who frequently employed the expression (Κοίλη) Συρία καὶ Φοινίκη to denote the area indicated in the Hebrew/Aramaic book of Ezra as עבר נהרה/עבר נהרים (LXX-1 Esdr. 2:19; 4:48; 6:3.7.7.26.26.28; 7:1; 8:19.23.64), which the Greek translator of II Esdras (= MT-Ezra-Nehemiah) rendered more literally by πέραν τοῦ ποταμοῦ (LXX-II Esdr. 4:17; 5:3.6; 6:6; 7:21.25). See J.M. Myers, *1 and 2 Esdras*. (AB 42) New York 1974, p. 12. The combination recurs in 2 Macc. 3:5.8, 4:4.22; 8:8; 10:11; 3 Macc. 3:15 and 4 Macc. 4:2.

[493] C.G. den Hertog, *Studien*, pp. 113–114; J. Moatti-Fine, *Josué*, p. 120.

[494] J.W. Wevers, *Notes on the Greek Text of Exodus*, p. 261. A. le Boulluec, P. Sandevoir, *L'Exode*. (La Bible d'Alexandrie) Paris 1989, p. 188, consider the Greek rendering to be 'une actualisation du lexique géographique' but do not explain the variation in translations between Χαναάν and Φοινίκη.

No less unusual is LXX-Exodus' rendering of the phrase in Exod. 6:15 שאול בן־כנענית, *Saul the son of the Canaanite* (woman married to Judah according to Gen. 38) by Σαουλ ὁ ἐκ τῆς Φοινίσσης. J.W. Wevers, *Notes on the Greek Text of Exodus*, p. 81,

Greek translator of Joshua would have wanted to adopt this lexical choice of LXX-Exodus here in LXX-Josh. 5:12. Furthermore, the Greek version of Joshua does share a large number of stereotyped renderings for important Hebrew expressions with the Greek Pentateuch,[495] but in cases where the Hebrew text of Joshua offers a parallel with Hebrew passages in the Pentateuch, the Greek versions as a rule differ from one another, so for instance in the case of the synoptic passage Josh. 1:12–15 and Deut. 3:18–20 or even in the case of the parallel between Josh. 5:15 and Exod. 3:5, where the two Greek versions of the almost identical Hebrew sentence differ from one another:[496]

Exod. 3[5]	של־נעליך מעל רגליך כי מקום אשר אתה עומד עליו אדמת־קדש הוא
Josh. 5[15]	של־נעלך מעל רגלך כי מקום אשר אתה עמד עליו קדש הוא
Exod. 3[15]	Λῦσαι τὸ ὑπόδημα ἐκ τῶν ποδῶν σου· ὁ γὰρ τόπος
Josh. 5[15]	Λῦσαι τὸ ὑπόδημα ἐκ τῶν ποδῶν σου· ὁ γὰρ τόπος
Exod. 3[15]	<u>ἐν ᾧ σὺ</u> ἕστηκας γῆ ἅγιός ἐστιν.
Josh. 5[15]	<u>ἐφ' ᾧ νῦν</u> ἕστηκας ἅγιός ἐστιν.

In our passage, we do not find an exact correspondence either between the renderings of the same Hebrew phrase ארץ כנען in LXX-Exod. 16:35 ἡ Φοινίκη and LXX-Josh. 5:12 ἡ χώρα τῶν Φοινίκων. This may be due to the Greek translator's preference for variation, but in line with LXX-Josh. 5:1 one would at least have expected a phrase such as ἡ χώρα τῆς Φοινίκης. Therefore, it remains difficult to explain the curious rendering in LXX-Josh. 5:12 on the basis of this parallel passage in LXX-Exod. 16:35.

The present formulation in LXX-Josh. 5:12, however, leaves room for a completely different reading of the same text but without a capital letter: ἡ χώρα τῶν φοινίκων. In that case, the last word is not a genitive plural of the *gentilicum* Φοινίκες, but a genitive plural of

---

argues that 'The name Phoenicia and Canaan were synonymous in ancient times with the name Phoenicia in origin merely a translation of כנען 'place of purple'; see also M. Weippert, Kanaan, in D.O. Edzard (Hg.), *Reallexikon der Assyriologie und Vorderasiatischen Archäologie. Fünfter Band.* Berlin/New York 1976–1980, pp. 352–355; H.-J. Zobel, כְּנַעַן *kᵉnaʿan* כְּנַעֲנִי *kᵉnaʿᵃnᵃ* in *ThWAT* IV, col. 224–243, especially p. 233. Be that as it may, it does not explain why the Greek translator of Exodus chose the alternative rendering Χαναὰν/Χαναναίος in all other passages where the name כנען/כנעני occurs in the Hebrew text of Exodus, i.e. in Exod. 3:8.17; 6:4.15; 13:5.11; 15:15; 23:23.28; 34:11.

495 See J. Moatti-Fine, *Jésus*, pp. 42–53.

496 See C.G. den Hertog, *Studien*, pp. 110–125.

the related noun φοῖνιξ, *date-palm.*[497] Although this reading does not provide a direct link with the Hebrew text of Josh. 5:12, the phrase ἡ χώρα τῶν φοινίκων is a very adequate description of the area around Jericho. Already in the Hebrew Bible we find the epithet 'palm-city' עיר התמרים/πόλις τῶν φοινίκων for Jericho, thus in Judg. 1:16; 3:13, 2 Chron. 28:15, and Deut. 34:3, in the description of the land shown to Moses by Yhwh:

34[3]	καὶ τὴν ἔρημον	וְאֶת־הַנֶּגֶב
	καὶ *τὰ περίχωρα Ἰεριχώ*,	וְאֶת־הַכִּכָּר בִּקְעַת יְרֵחוֹ
	πόλιν φοινίκων, ἕως Σηγωρ.	עִיר הַתְּמָרִים עַד־צֹעַר׃

We find similar descriptions of the area around Jericho in the Strabo's *Geography* (first century BCE or first century CE), XVI.2.41 and 2.16:

2.41 Jericho is a plain (Ἰερικοῦς δ' ἐστὶ πεδίον) surrounded by a kind of mountainous country, which, in a way, slopes towards it like a theatre. Here is the palm-grove (ἐνταῦθα δ' ἐστὶν ὁ φοινικών), which is mixed also with other kinds of cultivated and fruitful trees (μεμιγμένην ἔχων καὶ ἄλλην ὕλην ἥμερον καὶ εὔκαρπον), though it consists mostly of palm trees (πλεονάζων δὲ τῷ φοίνικι).

2.16 Here are two mountains, Libanus and Antilibanus, which form Coele-Syria, as it is called, and are approximately parallel to each other, . . . (the two mountains) terminate in other mountains that are hilly and fruitful (εἰς ἄλλα ὄρη γεώλοφα καὶ καλλίκαρπα). They leave a hollow plain between them (ἀπολείπουσι δὲ μεταξὺ πεδίον κοῖλον), . . . It is intersected with rivers, the Jordan being the largest, which water a country that is fertile and all-productive (χώραν εὐδαίμονα καὶ πάμφορον).

The date palm produced various products and was therefore also very popular in Mesopotamia, thus Strabo, *Geography* XVI.1.14 and Herodotus, *History of the Persian Wars* I.193:

> The country [i.e. Assyria] produces larger crops of barley than any other country (bearing three hunderdfold, they say), and its other needs are supplied by the palm tree (τὰ δὲ ἄλλα ἐκ τοῦ φοίνικος παρέχεται); for this tree yields bread, wine, vinegar, honey, and meal;

[497] LEH, p. 506b; LSJ, p. 1948a–b; GELS[2], pp. 585b–586a.

> There [i.e. Assyria] are palm trees (φοίνικες) growing all over the plain (ἀνὰ πᾶν τὸ πεδίον), most of them yielding fruit, from which food is made and wine and honey.

Likewise, Flavius Josephus in his *Jewish War* IV, 459–475,[498] offers a long eulogy on this specific region (χώρα) in the plain (πέδιον) of the Jordan valley, a garden (παράδεισος) full of date-palms (φοινῖξ) and other fruits (καρπός), which is unique in the habitable world (οἰκουμένη cf. LXX-Exod. 16:35):

> [459] Hard by Jericho, however, is a copious spring of excellent value for irrigation; it gushes up near the old town, which was the first in the land of the Canaanites to fall before the arms of Jesous the son of Naue, general of the Hebrews. . . . [467] Indeed this spring irrigates a larger tract than others, permeating a plain (πεδίον) of seventy furlongs in length and twenty in breadth, and fostering within that area the most charming and luxuriant parks. [468] Of the date-palms watered by it there are numerous varieties (τῶν δὲ φοινίκων ἐπαρδομένων γένη) differing in flavour and in medicinal properties; the richer species of the fruit when pressed under foot emit copious honey, not much inferior to that of bees, which are also abundant in this region (καὶ μελιττοτρόφος δ' ἡ χώρα). . . . [470] For, with regard to its other fruits (τῶν μὲν γὰρ ἄλλων αὐτῷ καρπῶν), it would be difficult to find another region in the habitable world (κλίμα τῆς οἰκουμένης) comparable to this; so manifold are the returns from whatever is sown.

Josephus used the name γῆ Χαναναίων when referring to its conquest by Joshua (IV.459), as he did in his rewritten version of Josh. 5:10–12 in *Jewish Antiquities* V.21:

> They also kept the feast of Passover at that spot (καὶ τὴν φάσκα ἑώρταζον ἐν ἐκείνῳ τῳ χωρίῳ), being now readily provided with all that they had lacked before; for they reaped the corn of the Canaanites, now at its prime, and took any booty they could (τόν τε γὰρ σῖτον ἀκμάζοντα ἤδη τῶν Χαναναίων ἐθέριζον καὶ τὰ λοιπὰ λείαν ἦγον). It was then too that the supply of manna ceased which had served them for forty years.

Although Josephus did not explicitly mention the date-palms in this passage, it is clear that he makes a strong link between the consuming of the first new products of the Promised Land and the region around Jericho. Whereas the Hebrew text of Joshua simply

[498] Text and translation: H. St. J. Thackeray, *Josephus III. The Jewish War. Books IV–VII.* Cambridge, Massachusetts/London 1928.

asserts that the Israelites took this food at the proper time, Josephus offered a vivid portrait of this episode by turning the food into booty.

On the basis of these observations it seems plausible to assume that the Greek translator of Joshua had a similar idea when he produced the Greek version of Josh. 5:10–12. Apparently, he was familiar with the area around Jericho and wove into his version a few of the elements mentioned above. Although geographical knowledge of the land of Israel may not have been the Greek translator's strongest point, the references to the area by Strabo and Josephus make clear that the region around Jericho was famous for its palm-trees all around the inhabitable world. Hence the Greek translator introduced the explicit statement in verse 10 that the narrative took place in a plain (ἐν τῷ πεδίῳ). Since the Israelites did not reap the entire land of Canaan/Israel, but only the area around Gilgal and Jericho, the Greek translator used the specific word χώρα for ארץ instead of the more general standard equivalent γῆ. Since this region was well-known for its fruitful palm trees, the translator found a successful way to reflect the variation in the Hebrew text between אכל מעבור and אכל מתבואה by rendering the first phrase by ἐσθίω ἀπὸ/ἐκ τοῦ σίτου. He applied this to the field produce and interpreted the alternative phrase in the sense of the consumption of the fruits (καρπίζομαι) of the palm trees (τῶν φοινίκων), so abundantly present in that region.

Interestingly, Origen in his sixth homily on Joshua, also provided an allegorical interpretation of the types of nourishment mentioned in Josh. 5:10–12, and apparently read the phrase in LXX-Josh. 5:12 as 'region of the palm-trees:[499]

> He who will deserve to enter into the land of promise, that is those things, that are promised by our Saviour, will eat the fruit of the region of the palms (*e regione palmarum*). Indeed he will find the fruit of the palm (*Vere enim fructus palmae inveniet*), who will attain the promises after the defeat of the enemy.

In short, the historical exegesis of the Hebrew text as proposed by Steuernagel and Brekelmans (see section 7.4.5.2 above) in fact applies better to the Greek version. Here, the central 'H' in this passage no longer stands for 'Holiness Code' (the point of reference for the Hebrew editor) but 'historicity' (the central concern for the Greek

---

[499] A. JAUBERT, *Origène. Homélies sur Josué*, pp. 182–185.

translator). The present text with the capital Φ is the result of the change from uncial to minuscule script that did not take place until the ninth century. Since the Greek translator employed the name Φοινίκη in 5:1 it was only natural for later copyists to interpret the uncial phrase ΧΩΡΑΤΦΝΦΟΙΝΙΚΩΝ in the way the ancient daughter translations and all modern editions do.[500]

7.6.9 *Conclusions with Respect to the Greek Version*

The Greek text of these verses of the book of Joshua is an interpretative version through and through, probably even more so than most scribes, editors, and scholars have realised. Nearly every clause contains one or more literary initiatives introduced by the Greek translator, which reveal his concern for the inner coherence of the passage as a whole, and the historical plausibility of these originally programmatic narratives. The Greek version of these verses can be understood in terms of answers to questions that arise from the text due to the formation process of the passage as a whole (see section 7.4.6 above) and the fictitious and idealized character of the literary creations of the Deuteronomistic author (Josh. 4:21–5:8) and the Priestly redactor (5:10–12b), respectively. This process of the literary formation of the Hebrew text was already finished at the time when the Greek translation of the passage was made. As a result, there is no reason to assume that the Hebrew text underlying the Greek translation differed from that as preserved by MT and 4QJosh[a].

The idea of a collective enterprise by which the entire surviving male population of the Israelite people was circumcised, including not only infants but also adults and even aged people (up to sixty years of age according to the Greek translator), was felt to be problematic by the Greek translator, especially since the authoritative text also contained the curious reference to such outdated circumcision instruments as knives made from stone. For the Greek translator this text must have evoked the idea of a very painful operation. In order to smoothen this notion, he expanded the original Hebrew text, which simply speaks of 'stone knives', into 'sharp knives made from sharp stones' (μαχαίρας πετρίνας ἐκ πέτρας ἀκροτόμου, see section 7.6.1.2). Hence, he avoided a literal interpretation of the Hebrew

---

[500] Thus e.g. Vetus Latina *Possiderunt autem regionem Phoenicum in illo anno*; and the Syro-Hexapla ܘܐܚܕܘ ܕܝܢ ܦܐܬܐ ܕܐܬܪܐ ܕܦܘܢܝܩܐ ܒܗ ܒܫܢܬܐ ܗܝ ܀.

phrases שׁוב–שׁנית by omitting the second element and reading וְשׁוּב as וְשֵׁב (καὶ καθίσας). Likewise, he amplified the short statement in verse 8 that the Israelites remained in their camp until they had revived, into an account of their recuperation after this severe operation, which explicitly mentions a certain period of rest (ἡσυχίαν εἶχον), inactivity (αὐτόθι καθήμενοι ἐν τῇ παρεμβολῇ), and complete recovery (ἕως ὑγιάσθησαν, see section 7.6.5). In order to assure his readership, which most likely consisted of Hellenistic Jews in Egypt and perhaps some local Hellenistic Egyptians and Greeks as well, that this whole exceptional enterprise should be understood in terms of purification, the Greek translator employed the unique rendering περι-καθαίρω for the Hebrew verb מול in addition to the standard equivalent περι-τέμνω (section 7.6.3.2).

Whereas the Deuteronomistic author of the passage stressed the notion that the Israelite people *as a whole* was circumcised when it left Egypt and immediately after the entry into the Promised Land, the Greek translator sought to offer a somewhat more realistic and—in his view—more correct presentation. Since the Israelites used to circumcise only their male children—in contrast to the undoubtedly incorrect statement by Strabo who reported a practice to incise females among the Israelites (see section 7.6.3.2)—the statement כל־הגוי in the Hebrew text in verse 5:8a–c could only apply to the male part of the nation. Instead of stressing this idea, the Greek translator chose to condense the redundant Hebrew text into the self-evident and adequate statement περιτμηθέντες δὲ (section 7.6.6).

Furthermore, he interpreted the enigmatic phrase 'Today I have rolled away the humiliation of Egypt from upon you' (היום גלותי את־חרפת מצרים מעליכם) in the light of the preceding context, and explained this lifting away (ἀφαιρέω, an unusual rendering for the corresponding Hebrew verb גלל) of disgrace in terms of the circumcision of the offensive foreskin (section 7.6.3.3), while in all likelihood in the Hebrew text the disgrace originally referred to the end of the humiliating period of slavery in Egypt and the following wanderings in the desert (section 7.4.4). As a result, the Greek translator inferred that there must have been several Israelites who had not been circumcised in Egypt and were subjected to insults (ὀνειδισμός) by the Egyptians (section 7.6.3.3). This notion, however, clearly contradicts the statement in MT-Josh. 5:5a–b. Helped by the redundant formulations of the Hebrew text in Josh. 5:5, the Greek translator transformed the clauses in MT-Josh. 5:5e–f בצאתם ממצרים לא־מלו

into a separate category of Israelite males that were circumcised by Joshua (LXX-5:4b καὶ ὅσοι ποτὲ ἀπερίτμητοι ἦσαν τῶν ἐξεληλυθότων ἐξ Αἰγύπτου), in order to remove this offensive contradiction (section 7.6.3.3).

It would seem that this idea is repeated in LXX-Josh. 5:6, where the Rahlfs text has διὸ ἀπερίτμητοι ἦσαν οἱ πλεῖστοι αὐτῶν τῶν μαχίμων τῶν ἐξεληλυθότων ἐκ γῆς Αἰγύπτου . . ., following the statement that Israel had wandered in the desert for forty-two years. Since the text continues, however, with the information that this group had been disobedient (οἱ ἀπειθήσαντες τῶν ἐντολῶν τοῦ θεοῦ), and had therefore been forbidden to enter the land (οἷς καὶ διώρισεν μὴ ἰδεῖν αὐτοὺς τὴν γῆν), this group cannot be equated with that introduced by the Greek translator in verse 4b (section 7.6.4.2.4), but must refer to the older generation of Israelites that had been condemned to die in the desert (Numbers 14). The Greek text thus seems to shift from the male Israelites that were still alive at the moment of entry into the Promised Land and were circumcised by Joshua to those who had died before. In order to solve this puzzling contradiction within the Greek text, it is suggested (section 7.6.4.2.6) that the present Greek formulation ἀπερίτμητοι ἦσαν should be seen as an early corruption from the graphically similar phrase ἀπηρτίσθησαν, which is an unusual but idiomatically correct rendering of the corresponding Hebrew verb תמם (see section 7.6.4.2.7).

As a result, the main motive behind the numerous changes introduced by the Greek translator in this verse was not the wish to offer an explanation for the uncircumcised state of so many Israelites, or an attempt to conceal the fact that this older generation had died in the desert, but rather a concern for the individual responsibility for the disobedient behaviour of older generation, and thus for the innocence of the Israelites of the younger generation. To this end, the Greek translator modified the *totum pro parte* statement of the Hebrew text כל־הגוי אנשי המלחמה היצאים ממצרים, *the entire nation, the men of war that had come out of Egypt* (5:6b) into οἱ πλεῖστοι αὐτῶν τῶν μαχίμων τῶν ἐξεληλυθότων ἐκ γῆς Αἰγύπτου, *most of them, in sofar as it concerns the warriors that had come out of Egypt* (section 7.6.4.2.3). By using the verb ἀπειθέω for the phrase אשר לא שמעו, the Greek translator evoked the Pentateuchal theme of the rebellious people and thus underscored the gravity of their sin (section 7.6.4.3). This notion was further accentuated by the translation of the phrase קול יהוה by ἐντολαί τοῦ θεοῦ, and the various renderings of the same Hebrew phrase—אשר נשבע יהוה ל by either the standard equivalent phrase ἣν ὤμοσεν κύριος τοῖς πατράσιν αὐτῶν, in the case of the divine promise of the land, or οἷς καὶ διώρισεν, in the case of the verdict on the older Israelites that they were not to see the land. This Greek verb διορίζω marks an important qualitative distinction, evokes the image of the drawing of a border, and thus points again to the well-considered formulations chosen by the Greek translator (section 7.6.4.3). In verse 7, the Greek translator shifted the stress from the persons circumcised by Joshua (ואת־בניהם . . . אתם) to the notion of the older generation being replaced by the younger (ἀντὶ δὲ τούτων ἀντικατέστησεν section 7.6.5). It is not Israel's fathers who were exonerated by a redactor behind the MT (thus Holmes, sections 7.2.3, 7.4.2.1), but their innocent children who were exonerated by the Greek translator!

Several of the other variants introduced by the Greek translator can be classified under the heading 'concern for coherence and plausibility in temporal and geographical matters'. One of these issues is the correct calculation of the period of Israel's wanderings in the desert. According to the Greek translator, the statement in the Hebrew text that Israel wandered in the desert for forty years (כי ארבעים שנה הלכו בני־ישראל במדבר) required some refinement, since the Israelites had already dwelt in the desert for two years (Num. 10:11–12; 12:16; 13:3) before the sentence of a forty-year period in the desert was pronounced by Yhwh over all of Israel (hence LXX ἀνέστραπται Ισραηλ, see section 7.6.4.1). In order to account for the lapse of time in which the autochthonous kings heard about the Jordan miracle, the Greek translator modified the Hebrew expression בעת ההיא into ὑπὸ δὲ τοῦτον τὸν καιρόν (section 7.6.1.1). Since the Greek translator interpreted the Hebrew verb ויקרא in 5:9 to refer to an act of the Deity (i.e. the subject of the immediately preceding clause), he saw no logical function for the following phrase עד היום הזה and left it untranslated (section 7.6.7).

The Greek translator was probably no less puzzled by the confusing agglomeration of emphatic temporal elements in verses 10–12 as the younger translators (Targum Jonathan, the Fragmentary Targum, the Pešiṭta, and Vulgate) and modern scholars have been. He apparently inferred from the sequence 'consuming of the products of the Promised Land'—'cessation of the manna', that the former must have relieved the latter. Hence he interpreted the phrase בעצם היום הזה in a relative sense, rather than in the absolute sense of another reference to the proper day on which, according to Lev. 23:9–14 the first products of the field were allowed to be consumed, i.e. the sixteenth of the month Nisan. Since the Greek translator understood the Passover in the general post-biblical sense of the whole seven-days spring festival, including both the sacrifice of the Passover-lamb and the feast of the unleavened breads, he altered the preposition -ב (*they celebrated the Passover on the fourteenth Nisan proper*) to ἀπό (*the Israelites held the Passover from the evening onwards*). As a result, the redundant phrases ממחרת הפסח and ממחרת, originally intended to emphasize the proper temporal sequence of the events narrated in Joshua, i.e. consumption of the first fruits (קלוי, properly understood by the translator as a *pars pro toto* expression and hence rendered by νέα section 7.6.8.2) only after the Passover night and the dedication to the priest (Lev. 23:1–8.9–14, see section 7.4.5.3), had become obsolete and were therefore not adopted by the Greek translator in his version, so that his text would not needlessly cause problems with respect to a proper interpretation of the passage (section 7.6.8.1)

With respect to the geographical elements the Greek translation also reveals some surpising initiatives. For the Greek translator the setting for the entire narrative is that of the camp in Gilgal (4:19; 5:8). Hence, he passed over the clause ויחנו בני־ישׂראל בגלגל in 5:10a, which was originally intended by the Priestly redactor to connect his temporal specifications to the older text, but for the Greek translator was no more than a confusing and superfluous piece of information (sections 7.4.5.1, 7.6.7). In the view of the translator, this place only received its name Gilgal/Galgala (καλέω τὸ ὄνομα τοῦ τόπου ἐκείνου Γαλγαλα) in 5:9 from the Deity himself. As a result, he took the ambivalent phrase אל־גבעת הערלות (section 7.4.1) as a reference to the older name of the site (ἐπὶ τοῦ καλουμένου τόπου, section 7.6.2).

It appears that the Greek translator was not thoroughly familiar with the topography of Palestine. Hence to the best of his abilities he created the unique Hellenised toponym ἔρημος Μαδβαρῖτις probably out of a corrupted *Vorlage* במדבר המדבר, i.e. a dittography of MT's במדבר (section 7.6.4.1). Likewise he made the best out of the word ערבה III, which must have been unknown to the early Greek translators (sections 7.6.8.2–3). Nevertheless, he appears to have been well-informed about the region (χώρα) in the plain (πεδίον) around Jericho, which was famous throughout the then known inhabitable world (section 7.6.8.3) for its date-palms. Hence, the Greek translator rephrased the somewhat colourless statement of the Hebrew text ויאכלו מתבואת ארץ כנען to the more vivid and historically plausible statement ἐκαρπίσαντο δὲ τὴν χώραν τῶν φοινίκων, *they enjoyed the fruits of the region of the palm trees*, in order to provide his readership with a plausible setting for the idea in the Hebrew text of an entire people being nourished instantly by the produce of the newly gained territory. Since, however, both the text in LXX-Josh. 5:1 and the corresponding passage in LXX-Exod. 16:35 mention the land of Phoenicia (Φοινίκη), this subtle notion introduced by the Greek translator of Joshua was no longer understood by later generations, and interpreted and edited as χώραν τῶν Φοινίκων, *region of the Phoenicians*, even though this region was far removed from that described in Josh. 5:10–12 (section 7.6.8.3), and even though neither LXX-Exod. 16:35 nor LXX-Josh. 5:1 contain precisely this phrase χώρα τῶν Φοινίκων. Only through a close reading of the Greek text in its own context can the full extent of its rich interpretative value be recovered.

7.7 Conclusions

As was the case with the passages discussed in the preceding chapter, the divergencies between MT and LXX in this passage do not lend support to the thesis of an overlap between textual and literary criticism. The present Hebrew text is likely the result of a process of two subsequent stages: [1] the addition by the Deuteronomist (DtrH) of his ideal of a new start of an entire regenerated people unchallenged by the surrounding nations (Josh. 4:21–5:8) to the older pre-DtrH passage decribing the end of Israel's humiliation (5:9), and [2] the correction of the second part of this oldest attainable literary stratum in 5:12b in which the proper order of entry into the land and consumption of the first-fruits has been adjusted by a Priestly redactor (RedP) to the legislation in Lev. 23:1–8.9–14. None of these stages, however, is attested by the Greek translation, which simply presupposes the Hebrew text in its present, expanded form, as does the text attested by 4QJosh[a] and alluded to by the author of the Damascus Document (section 7.5).

In one or two cases, the Hebrew *Vorlage* may have differed from the Masoretic text best preserved in the Leningrad, Aleppo, and Cairo codices. In the case of the exceptional Greek phrase ἐν τῇ ἐρήμῳ τῇ Μαδβαρίτιδι, the most convincing explanation for this otherwise unknown toponym is to assume that the Hebrew *Vorlage* of LXX-Joshua contained a scribal error resulting from dittography of the Hebrew phrase במדבר into במדבר המדבר (section 7.6.4.1). In the case of Josh. 5:6f, the Greek text μὴ ἰδεῖν αὐτοὺς τὴν γῆν may reflect a Hebrew *Vorlage* where the Qal formation had been used instead of the Hiphʿil as in MT לבלתי הראותם את־הארץ, as was the case with 4QJosh[a] (section 7.6.4.4). In both cases, the MT reflects the older reading. Since this type of variation does not exceed what is witnessed by the younger Masoretic manuscripts, where we find the variants כל־הדור for כל־הגוי (section 7.4.2.2) and אשר נשבע יהוה לאבותם לתת להם for אשר נשבע יהוה לאבותם לתת לנו (section 7.6.4.4), there is no reason to argue that the variants posed by these oldest textual witnesses exceed beyond the realm of the so-called lower (i.e. textual) criticism into that of the higher (i.e. historical-literary) criticism.

By contrast, all (other) divergencies between MT and LXX can be ascribed to the careful and well-considered literary restructuring and reformulation by the Greek translator (section 7.6.9). The Greek version of this passage does not witness the penultimate stage of the formation process of the Hebrew text, but rather the first stage of its reformulation and interpretation. With the exception of the interpretation of circumcision as purification, the Greek translator did not introduce ideas that were completely absent in or contradictory to the older Hebrew text. Apparently, the Greek translator saw as his own task to bring out what was implicit in the text, and smoothen what was held to be offensive or contradictory. For that reason, the extent of the changes introduced by the Greek translator never equals that of a new edition of the older text on the scale of the transformations effected by the Deuteronomistic and Priestly redactors.

Again, it has proven helpful, necessary and illuminating to keep text-critical data and literary-critical observations separate. In cases such as this passage, where text-critical and literary-critical approaches to the history of the text have become entwined in the history of research for such a long period, a strict distinction between the two types of evidence and argumentation has provided new insights and solutions to old problems. Once more, it has become clear that the LXX cannot be used as an empirical basis for literary-critical enterprises, but requires to be studied in its own context. An independent literary-critical approach to the text that leaves the intricate text-critical issues out of sight for a while may free the scientific study of the text from diffuse theories of *Fortschreibung* and progressive supplementation. Again, textual and literary criticism do not overlap, but are nevertheless mutually illuminating.

CHAPTER EIGHT

JOSHUA 8:1–29 MT—4QJOSHUA[a]—LXX

8.1 Introduction

In the previous chapters the main emphasis of the present investigation has been on the relation between MT and LXX. In the following chapters we will turn to the main textual divergencies between MT and 4QJoshua[a]. As stated in section 3.2, the text of this oldest witness of Joshua, where preserved, usually agrees with MT. Where LXX differs significantly from MT, e.g. in Josh. 6:6–7, and even in Josh. 5:2 (see section 7.5.1 above) and 5:6 (section 7.6.4.4), 4QJoshua[a] sides with MT and does not support the theory of a Hebrew *Vorlage* underlying the Greek interpretative version deviating from MT.

In Joshua 8, however, this situation seems to be different. Here we have two passages (8:1–29 and 8:30–35) that have caused the exegetes considerable problems: Josh. 8:1–29, describing the second, successful attack on Ai, contains several duplications, of which that of Joshua's sending a group of men in ambush (8:3–9 versus 8:10–13) is the most prominent; Josh. 8:30–35, dealing with the altar on Mount Ebal and the reading from the *torah* there, clearly disturbs the logical, geographical and theological connection between Josh. 8:1–29 and 9:1–27. In both cases, LXX differs considerably from MT: in LXX-Josh. 8:1–29 almost all of the awkward doublets (including most of MT-Josh. 8:11b–13) are absent, while the location of MT-Josh. 8:30–35 is different in LXX. In the latter text this passage comes only after 9:1–2, which describes the reaction of the autochthonous peoples to Joshua's military successes. 4QJoshua[a] seems to support—indirectly—these major quantitative and qualitative variants in LXX *vis-à-vis* MT: a reconstruction of the text of the fifth column of 4QJoshua[a] does not seem to leave room for the plus in MT-Josh. 8:11b–13. In fragment 1 of this scroll we find the end of the second passage, i.e., Josh. 8:34–35, right before Joshua 5:2ff., which seems to imply that this passage had a different location in this scroll as well, be it at a position deviating from both MT and LXX.

It would seem therefore, that there is strong evidence that these variants cannot be attributed to the Greek translator. This would run counter to the general impression gained in the previous two chapters, where (almost) all divergencies between MT and LXX could be attributed to the Greek translator. Since it is highly implausible that these two main variants, the quantitative one in MT-Josh. 8:11–13 and the qualitative one regarding MT-Josh. 8:30–35, are the result of unconscious scribal errors, it would seem that we have here a firm text-critical basis for a literary-critical reconstruction of the formation of the Hebrew text, as argued by Holmes,[1] Auld,[2] Tov[3] and Ulrich.[4] Nevertheless, a literary-critical analysis of the passages in its own right, and a proper reconstruction of the text of 4QJosh[a] on its own terms point in another direction. These two main differences between MT and 4QJosh[a] will be examined separately in chapters 8 and 9, respectively.

8.1.1 *The Contents of MT-Josh. 8:1–29*

The variant under discussion regards the coherence in the order of events described in Joshua 8:1–29. Since the narrative line of this passage is rather complex, it is necessary to describe its contents briefly.

Joshua 8:1–29 describes the second attack on the city of Ai, after a first unsuccessful attempt (7:2–5). After Joshua's intercessory plea to Yhwh (7:6–9), the interpretation of the failure in terms of Israel's offence (7:1 וימעלו בני־ישׂראל מעל בחרם) against the law of the *ḥerem* (7:1, 10–15) and its expiation (7:16–27), Yhwh assures Joshua of his assistance (8:1–2 אל־תירא ואל־תחת) and the defeat of Ai (8:2 ראה נתתי בידך את־מלך העי), and advises Joshua to use the device of an ambush behind the city (8:2 שׂים־לך ארב לעיר מאחריה). Before Joshua sets out to march on Ai, he selects no less than 30,000 heroes, and orders them to lay in ambush behind the city. Joshua unfolds to them his strategy of a feigned attack and sham flight, so that the city's warriors will be lured out of the city (verses 5–6). After that,

[1] S. Holmes, *Joshua*, pp. 13–14, 42.

[2] A.G. Auld, Joshua. The Hebrew and Greek Texts, pp. 4–5 (= *Joshua Retold*, pp. 9–10).

[3] E. Tov, *The Text-critical Use of the Septuagint*[2], pp. 245–249.

[4] E. Ulrich, The Dead Sea Scrolls and the Biblical Text, in P.W. Flint, J.C. VanderKam (eds.), *The Dead Sea Scrolls after Fifty Years* 1, pp. 79–100.

the men hidden in the ambush are to capture and burn the city according to the divine instructions (8:7 ונתנה יהוה אלהיכם בידכם; 8:8 כדבר יהוה תעשׂו). Having sent these men to their position between Ai and Beth-El, Joshua himself remains among the people during that night (8:9 וילן יהושע בלילה ההוא בתוך העם).

On the following morning Joshua rises and marches with the people in the direction of Ai (8:10). Instead of attacking the city immediately, so that the exceptionally large number of 30,000 men no longer need to hide their presence, Joshua first pitches his camp north of Ai and then again selects a number of men to be placed in ambush, although the number (5,000) is more moderate than the other group (8:12). As in verse 9 this strategy is followed by an action from Joshua, but this time Joshua does not stay overnight amidst the people (8:9), but that night enters the valley (8:13 וילך יהושע בלילה ההוא בתוך העמק), which is presumably identical with the valley (הגי) mentioned in verse 11.

This action does not pass unnoticed by the king of Ai (8:14), who hastily rises with his men (8:14) and leaves the city unprotected, unaware of the ambush behind the city (8:14). Joshua and all of Israel feign defeat and flee in the direction of the desert (8:15 וינגעו יהושע וכל־ישׂראל לפניהם וינסו דרך המדבר).[5] The city's inhabitants encourage their warriors to pursue Joshua (8:16), so that the city is left without any defense (8:17).

At this point in the narrative, the Deity intervenes (again), and commands Joshua to raise the *kidon*—a javelin or scimitar?[6]—(8:18). At this signal (8:19), the men in ambush capture the city and set fire to it (8:19). This signal in turn causes panic in the field among the warriors of Ai on the one hand, and on the other hand serves as the signal for the Israelites to turn around (8:20), so that the roles

---

[5] Labelled by W. GESENIUS, E. KAUTZSCH, *Hebräische Grammatik*[27] § 51c as a *Niphʿal tolerativum*.

[6] The meaning of the Hebrew word כידון is problematic, see HALOT 472a. O. KEEL, *Wirkmächtige Siegeszeichen im Alten Testament.* (OBO 5) Freiburg/Göttingen 1974, pp. 11–88: 'I. Das ausgestreckte Sichelswert des Josua (Jos 8,18.26)', argues in favour of the rendering by 'scimitar' ('Sichelswert') on the basis of Egyptian parallels. The ancient versions, however, render the word by javelin, thus LXX and α' γαῖσος, TgJon רמחא, Peš, ܣܘܟܐ, or 'shield' so σ' ἀσπίς (cf. LXX-1 Reg. 17:6.45) and Vg *clypeus*, see O. KEEL, *Wirkmächtige Siegeszeichen*, p. 32. For a parallel from the Mari archive (ARMT XXVI.169), see M. ANBAR, La critique biblique à la lumièe des Archives royales de Mari: Jos 8*, in *Biblica* 75 (1994), pp. 70–74.

are reversed. Again we are told that Joshua and all of Israel see that the men in ambush have captured the city (8:21) and return (8:21), so that the men of Ai become sandwiched between Israel's main force and the ambush men who have left the city (8:22). The king of Ai is captured alive (8:23), while all other inhabitants of Ai, both outside (8:24) and inside the city (8:24), 12,000 in total (8:25), are killed. Although it has seemed as if the *kidon* only served as a signal for the ambush, and the whole city of Ai had been laid waste at this point in the narrative, in verse 26 we find the statement that Joshua did not lower his hand with the *kidon* until all the inhabitants of Ai had been banned (8:26). The cattle and spoil are spared (8:27) in accordance with Yhwh's instructions to Joshua (8:27 כדבר יהוה אשׁר צוה את־יהושׁע cf. 8:2 רק־שׁללה ובהמתה תבזו לכם) see below. Again, the city is burnt (8:28), but this time in a definitive manner (8:28 וישׂימה תל־עולם שׁממה עד היום הזה). Finally, the king of Ai is hanged on a tree and buried before sunset at the entrance to the city under a large heap of stones (8:29).

8.1.2 *The Exegetical Problems*

Even a brief cursory reading of this passage as presented above reveals the various tensions, duplications and other problems in the MT version of the narrative:

1. Most conspicious is the doublet regarding Joshua's sending a group of men in ambush. Since the second part of the passage only refers to a single group (8:19 והאורב, 8:21 הארב), and since we do not find any hint in 8:12 that the group of 5,000 men in ambush are considered to be some kind of supplementary force to the group of 30,000 mentioned in verses 3–9, it is clear that in verse 11ff. we have a rival account of the narrative in the verses preceding it (8:3–9). As the Hebrew verbs in verses 12–13 (וישׂימו וישׂם, ויקח) are *wayyiqtol* forms instead of *qatal* forms, it is not possible to interpret them as pluperfects.[7] Nor is it plausible to interpret verse 12 as an independent action of the Israelite people, who allegedly had been unaware of the same action by Joshua,

[7] Thus e.g. B.J. ALFRINK, *Josue*, p. 50. R.S. HESS, *Joshua*, p. 164: 'The position of the ambush group is described twice, in verses 9 and 12. . . . Verse 12 adds the information that about *five thousand* were selected by Joshua to make up this group.'

as suggested by Abrabanel,[8] since the verbs in these verses, with העם as subject, are formulated in the plural (8:11 וכל־העם . . . עלו . . . ויבאו . . . ויחנו; 8:13 וישימו העם). According to the first version these men are sent from Jericho or Gilgal, while in the second version the smaller group is sent only after Israel has approached Ai.

2. Related to this doublet is that of the nearly identical phrases in verses 9b and 13b:

וילן יהושע בלילה ההוא בתוך העם, *That night Joshua spent among the people*
וילך יהושע בלילה ההוא בתוך העמק, *That night Joshua went into the valley*

The almost literal repetition of the same clause suggests some kind of literary dependency between the two.[9] The present text clearly refers to two subsequent nights, relieved by the morning in which Joshua rose early in order to march with the people towards Ai (8:10). This situation raises the following questions: how is it possible that such an extraordinarily large group of 30,000 men were able to hide themselves in the vicinity of Ai for a whole day without being noticed? If there is a direct dependence of one version upon the other, which of the two is the more original?

3. The action of the inhabitants of Ai pursuing the Israelites into the open field is narrated three times: in verse 14 ויצאו אנשי־העיר לקראת־ישראל למלחמה, and in almost identical formulations in verse 16 וירדפו אחרי יהושע and verse 18 וירדפו אחרי ישראל.

---

[8] Abrabanel, פירוש על נביאים ראשונים. Jerusalem 1955, p. 42.

[9] In the textual witnesses we find various attempts to harmonise the two almost identical clauses, thus e.g. Peš. 8:13 ܘܐܙܠ ܝܫܘܥ ܒܠܠܝܐ ܗܘ ܠܓܘ ܥܡܩܐ, and a number of mediaeval Masoretic manuscripts, see J.B. de Rossi, *Variae Lectiones Veteris Testamenti Librorum* II, p. 81b: 'וילן—וילך Kenn. cod. 4, 99, 153, 198 marg., 601, nunc 158, cod. mei 20, 226, 295, 663, primo 2, 305, 604, 688, 716, 744, 789, nunc 174, 627, et ut videtur, 701, Bibl. Sonc., Proph. Sonc.1486, Talmud Babylonicum. Lectionem hanc sistunt ad marg. utraque Bibl. Ven.1518, eamque sequitur Kimchius in Josue V 14. Cod meus 341 hispanus habet ad marg, Kerì וילן *lege et pernoctavit.* At vero veteres omnes hodiernum textum confirmant.' V. Aptowitzer, *Das Schriftwort in der rabbinischen Literatur* 268: 'וילן—וילך Erubin 63b, Megillah 3a, Synhed. 44b. וילן folgt auch aus dem Inhalt der Deutung: er (Josua) übernachtete (verharrte) in der Tiefe der Halacha (וילן יהושע בלילה ההוא בתוך העמק מלמד שלן בעמוקה של הלכה). וילן auch Raschi zur Stelle. Einige Kodd. und edd. Manche Kodd. וילן als Q're.' See further R. Meyer in BHS ad 8:9: 'l prb העמק ut 13.' while for Joshua 8:13 וילך he suggested 'l frt c nonn Mss וַיָּלֶן'; A. Tricot, La prise d'Aï (Jos. 7,1–8,29). Notes de critique textuelle et d'histoire biblique, in *Biblica* 3 (1922), pp. 273–300, especially p. 285; D. Barthélemy, *Critique textuelle*, p. 11, J. Gray, *Joshua, Judges and Ruth* (NCB) London 1977, p. 77; A.B. Ehrlich, *Randglossen*, II, p. 16.

4. Verse 14 refers to a מועד, an appointed place, in the direction of the plain (לפני הערבה) to which the king of Ai and his men went to engage Israel in battle. It is unclear, however, what is meant with this appointment, since the logic of the narrative excludes the possibility that the Israelites and the inhabitants of Ai had made an appointment where to meet for battle.[10]
5. Verse 17 all of a sudden includes the inhabitants of the neighbouring city Beth-El into the group of the men that pursued the Israelites along with the inhabitants of Ai. In the present narrative, the place Beth-El occurs only as a geographical point of reference for the position of the men in ambush (8:9 וישבו בין בית־אל ובין העי מים לעי is repeated almost verbatim in 8:12 בין בית־אל ובין העי מים לעיר). Nowhere in the remainder of the narrative do the men of Beth-El and their town appear again, so that the phrase in verse 17 remains an enigmatic and erratic segment.
6. Equally unexpected is the command by Yhwh to Joshua to raise his hand holding a *kidon* in verse 18, since we do not find any anticipation of this in verses 1–2. Only the assurance that Yhwh will give Ai into the hand of Joshua (כי בידך אתננה, the so-called *Übergabe-formel*) has a parallel in verse 1 (נתתי בידך את־מלך העי), but it seems that the two phrases are unrelated. The function of this gesture is also unclear: according to verse 19 it seems to function as a signal for the men in ambush to take action. Although the following verses relate the subsequent actions of Joshua and the people (i.e., return from their feigned flight [verse 21], victory over their pursuers [verse 22], the bringing up of the king of Ai before Joshua [verse 23], the return to the city [verse 24] and its complete destruction [verse 25]), according to verse 26, Joshua was still raising his hand with the *kidon* until all the inhabitants were banned. This motif resembles that of Exod. 17:8–13, where Israel is able to win the battle with Amalek only because Moses with his divine staff (Exod. 17:9 ומטה האלהים בידו) kept his hands raised (Exod. 17:11–13). It would seem, therefore, that the *kidon* in Josh. 8:18.26 also has such a magical function. Furthermore, it seems that the verses preceding 8:26 disturb the logical sequence between 8:18 and 8:26.

---

[10] Thus for instance rabbi Isaiah ben Elijah di Trani in M. Cohen (ed.), *Miqra'ot qedolot 'Haketer'*, p. 31. Targum Jonathan interpreted the phrase as a pre-ordained time for the king. לִזְמַנָא דִמְתַקַן לֵיה קֳדָם מֵישְׁרָא, *at the time that was appointed for him*, idem Rashi, Radaq, Ralbag.

7. We read twice that the roles of pursuer and pursued have been reversed, first in verse 20 והעם הנס המדבר נהפך אל־הרודף, and then again in verse 21 ויהושע וכל־ישׂראל ראו כי־לכד הארב את־העיר וכי עלה עשׁן העיר וישׁבו ויכו את־אנשׁי העי.

The narrative thus presents various tensions and doublets, which have given rise to different exegetical solutions and literary-critical reconstructions.

8.1.3 *A Literary-Critical Solution Offered by LXX?*

Most of the elements that disturb the logical sequence of the narrative are absent from the Greek version. Most conspicuous, again, is the almost complete absence of MT-Josh. 8:11b–13. Both MT-Josh. 8:9b and 8:13b are not present in LXX. As a result, according to the Greek version, all action takes place in one night (verses 1–9 νυκτός LXX-Josh. 8:3) and on the following day (verses 10–29). The main Israelite force does not pitch its camp to the north (thus MT 8:11.13), but simply arrive from the eastern direction, i.e. straight from Gilgal/Jericho, which is the opposite direction from the men in ambush (8:11 ἦλθον ἐξ ἐναντίας τῆς πόλεως *ἀπ' ἀνατολῶν καὶ τὰ ἔνεδρα τῆς πολέως ἀπὸ θαλάσσης*). For this reason, the Greek version does not contain an equivalent for the phrase וישׁכימו, (*the king and inhabitants of Ai*) *rose early*, which in MT corresponds closely to the nocturnal action by Joshua narrated in verse 13b. The Greek text has no reference to the מעוד in verse 14, or to the men of Beth-El in verse 15. The problematic verse 26 is also absent from LXX, while on the other hand a plus in the Greek version containing the Lord's direct speech to Joshua strengthens the function of the *kidon* as a signal (καὶ τὰ ἔνεδρα ἐξαναστήσονται ἐν τάχει ἐκ τοῦ τόπου αὐτῶν, which corresponds strongly to the subsequent narrative clause in verse 19: καὶ τὰ ἔνεδρα ἐξανέστησαν ἐν τάχει ἐκ τοῦ τόπου αὐτῶν). Since the second part of MT 8:20 (והעם הנס המדבר נהפך אל־הרודף) is also absent from LXX, the Greek version does not contain the doublet concerning the reversal of roles either. Furthermore, LXX lacks an equivalent for the problematic second occurrence of the phrase ונסנו לפניהם in verse 6. Also absent from LXX are the last half of MT-Josh. 8:7, and the first half of the next verse 8.

Although it is not my intention to offer an extensive discussion of all the variants, a complete synopsis of the three main witnesses to the text of Joshua 8:1–29, i.e. MT, LXX and 4QJoshua[a], may be helpful for the following discussion. The lay-out conventions used in the previous chapters have been employed here as well. The Greek text is that of Rahlfs, and the few cases where Margolis has reconstructed a different original Greek text are given in the footnotes. Horizontal lines between the verses refer to my proposal for the literary stratification of the Hebrew text (see section 8.4 below).

	MT-Joshua	4QJoshua[a]	LXX-Joshua	
8[1]	Καὶ εἶπεν κύριος πρὸς Ἰησοῦν		וַיֹּאמֶר יְהוָה אֶל־יְהוֹשֻׁעַ	8[1]
	Μὴ φοβηθῇς		אַל־תִּירָא	
	μηδὲ δειλιάσῃ·		וְאַל־תֵּחָת	
	λαβὲ μετὰ σοῦ *τοὺς ἄνδρας*		קַח עִמְּךָ אֵת	
	πάντας τοὺς πολεμιστὰς		כָּל־עַם הַמִּלְחָמָה	
	καὶ ἀναστὰς		וְקוּם	
	ἀνάβηθι εἰς Γαι·		עֲלֵה הָעָי	
	ἰδοὺ		רְאֵה	
	δέδωκα εἰς *τὰς* χεῖράς σου		נָתַתִּי בְיָדְךָ	
	τὸν βασιλέα Γαι		אֶת־מֶלֶךְ הָעַי	
	--- --- --- --- --- ---		וְאֶת־עַמּוֹ וְאֶת־עִירוֹ	
	καὶ τὴν γῆν αὐτοῦ.		וְאֶת־אַרְצוֹ׃	
8[2]	καὶ ποιήσεις τὴν Γαι --- --- --- ---		וְעָשִׂיתָ לָעַי וּלְמַלְכָּהּ	8[2]
	ὃν τρόπον ἐποίησας τὴν Ιεριχω		כַּאֲשֶׁר עָשִׂיתָ לִירִיחוֹ	
	καὶ τὸν βασιλέα αὐτῆς,		וּלְמַלְכָּהּ	
	καὶ τὴν προνομὴν --- *τῶν* κτηνῶν		רַק־שְׁלָלָהּ וּבְהֶמְתָּהּ	
	προνομεύσεις *σεαυτῷ.*		תָּבֹזּוּ לָכֶם	
	κατάστησον δὲ σεαυτῷ ἔνεδρα τῇ πόλει		שִׂים־לְךָ אֹרֵב לָעִיר	
	εἰς τὰ ὀπίσω ---.		מֵאַחֲרֶיהָ׃	
8[3]	καὶ ἀνέστη Ἰησοῦς	יהושוע	וַיָּקָם יְהוֹשֻׁעַ	8[3]
	καὶ πᾶς ὁ λαὸς ὁ πολεμιστὴς	וכל עם המלחמה	וְכָל־עַם הַמִּלְחָמָה	
	ὥστε ἀναβῆναι εἰς Γαι.	לעלות העי [	לַעֲלוֹת הָעָי	
	ἐπέλεξεν *δὲ* Ἰησοῦς	ויבחר יהושע	וַיִּבְחַר יְהוֹשֻׁעַ	
	τριάκοντα χιλιάδας ἀνδρῶν	שלשים אלף איש[	שְׁלֹשִׁים אֶלֶף אִישׁ	
	δυνατοὺς ἐν ἰσχύι	גבורי החיל	גִּבּוֹרֵי הַחַיִל	
	καὶ ἀπέστειλεν αὐτοὺς νυκτός.	וישלחם ל[ילה	וַיִּשְׁלָחֵם לָיְלָה׃	
8[4]	καὶ ἐνετείλατο αὐτοῖς	ויצו אתם	וַיְצַו אֹתָם	8[4]
	λέγων	לאמר	לֵאמֹר	
	---	ראו	רְאוּ	
	Ὑμεῖς ἐνεδρεύσατε --- ---	אתם ארבים] <u>אל</u> העיר	אַתֶּם אֹרְבִים לָעִיר	
	ὀπίσω τῆς πόλεως·	מאח[רי העיר	מֵאַחֲרֵי הָעִיר	
	μὴ *μακρὰν γίνεσθε*	אל תרחיקו	אַל־תַּרְחִיקוּ	
	[ἀπὸ][11] τῆς πόλεως ---	מן העיר מאד	מִן־הָעִיר מְאֹד	
	καὶ ἔσεσθε πάντες --- ἕτοιμοι.	והייתם כלכם נכנים[	וִהְיִיתֶם כֻּלְּכֶם נְכֹנִים׃	

[11] [8:4] Rahlfs adopted the reading μὴ μακρὰν γίνεσθε <u>ἀπὸ</u> τῆς πόλεως attested by B.129. Since classical Greek does not require the preposition ἀπό after μακρὰν (+ gen.), and since Origen placed an asterisk before the preposition (thus Syh

8[5]	καὶ ἐγὼ καὶ πάντες	ואני וכל[העם	וַאֲנִי וְכָל־הָעָם	8[5]
	οἱ μετ' ἐμοῦ	אשר אתי	אֲשֶׁר אִתִּי	
	προσάξομεν πρὸς τὴν πόλιν,	נקרב אל העיר	נִקְרַב אֶל־הָעִיר	
	καὶ ἔσται	והיה	וְהָיָה	
	ὡς ἂν ἐξέλθωσιν *οἱ κατοικοῦντες Γαι*	כי יצאו	כִּי־יֵצְאוּ	
	εἰς συνάντησιν ἡμῖν	לקראתנו	לִקְרָאתֵנוּ	
	καθάπερ καὶ *πρῴην*,	כאשר] בראש[נה	כַּאֲשֶׁר בָּרִאשֹׁנָה	
	καὶ φευξόμεθα ἀπὸ προσώπου αὐτῶν.	ונסנו לפניהם	וְנַסְנוּ לִפְנֵיהֶם׃	
8[6]	καὶ *ὡς ἂν* ἐξέλθωσιν ὀπίσω ἡμῶν,	ויצאו]אחרינו	וְיָצְאוּ אַחֲרֵינוּ	8[6]
	--- --- ἀποσπ*άσομεν* αὐτοὺς	עד[התיקנו אותם	עַד הַתִּיקֵנוּ אוֹתָם	
	[ἀπὸ] τῆς πόλεως·	מן העיר	מִן־הָעִיר	
	καὶ ἐροῦσιν	כי יאמרו	כִּי יֹאמְרוּ	
	Φεύγουσιν *οὗτοι* ἀπὸ προσώπου ἡμῶν	נסים לפנינו	נָסִים לְפָנֵינוּ	
	ὃν τρόπον καὶ ἔμπροσθεν.	כאשר בראשנה	כַּאֲשֶׁר בָּרִאשֹׁנָה	
	--- --- --- --- ---	ונסנו לפניהם	וְנַסְנוּ לִפְנֵיהֶם׃	
8[7]	ὑμεῖς *δὲ ἐξανα*στήσεσθε	ואתם תקמו	וְאַתֶּם תָּקֻמוּ	8[7]
	ἐκ τῆς ἐνέδρας	מהאורב	מֵהָאוֹרֵב	
	καὶ *πορεύσεσθε εἰς* τὴν πόλιν.	והורשתם]את הע[יר	וְהוֹרַשְׁתֶּם אֶת־הָעִיר	
	--- --- --- --- ---	ונתנה יהוה אלהיכם	וּנְתָנָהּ יְהוָה אֱלֹהֵיכֶם	
	--- --- ---	בידכם	בְּיֶדְכֶם׃	
8[8]	--- ---	והיה	וְהָיָה	8[8]
	--- --- --- ---	כתפשכם את העיר	כְּתָפְשְׂכֶם אֶת־הָעִיר	
	--- --- --- --- ---	תציתו את הע]יר באש	תַּצִּיתוּ אֶת־הָעִיר בָּאֵשׁ	
	κατὰ τὸ ῥῆμα *τοῦτο* ποιήσετε·	[כדבר יהוה תעשו	כִּדְבַר יְהוָה תַּעֲשׂוּ	
	ἰδοὺ	ראו	רְאוּ	
	ἐντέταλμαι ὑμῖν.	צויתי אתכם	צִוִּיתִי אֶתְכֶם׃	
8[9]	καὶ ἀπέστειλεν αὐτοὺς Ἰησοῦς,	וישלחם יהושע	וַיִּשְׁלָחֵם יְהוֹשֻׁעַ	8[9]
	καὶ ἐπορεύθησαν εἰς τὴν ἐνέδραν	ויל]כו אל[המארב	וַיֵּלְכוּ אֶל־הַמַּאְרָב	
	καὶ ἐνεκάθισαν ἀνὰ μέσον Βαιθηλ	וישבו בין בית אל	וַיֵּשְׁבוּ בֵּין בֵּית־אֵל	
	καὶ ἀνὰ μέσον Γαι	ובין העי	וּבֵין הָעַי	
	ἀπὸ θαλάσσης τῆς Γαι.	מים לעי	מִיָּם לָעָי	
	--- --- --- --- --- --- ---	וילן יהושע בלילה ההוא	וַיָּלֶן יְהוֹשֻׁעַ בַּלַּיְלָה הַהוּא	
	--- --- --- ---	בתוך העם	בְּתוֹךְ הָעָם׃	

8[10]	καὶ ὀρθρίσας Ἰησοῦς τὸ πρωὶ	וישכם יהושע בבקר	וַיַּשְׁכֵּם יְהוֹשֻׁעַ בַּבֹּקֶר	8[10]
	ἐπεσκέψατο τὸν λαόν·	ויפקד את העם	וַיִּפְקֹד אֶת־הָעָם	
	καὶ ἀνέβησαν αὐτὸς	ויעל הוא	וַיַּעַל הוּא	
	καὶ οἱ πρεσβύτεροι ---	ו]הזקנים [---	וְזִקְנֵי יִשְׂרָאֵל	
	κατὰ πρόσωπον τοῦ λαοῦ ἐπὶ Γαι.	לפני העם העי	לִפְנֵי הָעָם הָעָי׃	

ܠܐ ܪܘܚܩܐ ܬܗܘܘܢ ※ ܡܢ ܡܕܝܢܬܐ ※ ܛܒ.), Margolis omitted the preposition ἀπό from his main text. See further C.G. DEN HERTOG, *Studien*, p. 34, who supports Margolis' reconstruction.

8[11]	καὶ πᾶς ὁ λαὸς ὁ πολεμιστὴς	וכל העם המלחמה	וְכָל־הָעָם הַמִּלְחָמָה	8[11]
	--- μετ᾽ αὐτοῦ	אשר א]תו	אֲשֶׁר אִתּוֹ	
	ἀνέβησαν	וישובו	עָלוּ	
	καὶ *πορευόμενοι*	---	וַיִּגְּשׁוּ	
	--- ἦλθον ἐξ ἐναντίας τῆς πόλεως	[ויבאו נגד] העֹ[ר	וַיָּבֹאוּ נֶגֶד הָעִיר	
	--- --- *ἀπ᾽ ἀνατολῶν* --- ---,		וַיַּחֲנוּ מִצְּפוֹן לָעַי	
	--- --- --- ---		וְהַגַּי *בֵּינוֹ**בֵּינָיו	
	--- --- --- ---		וּבֵין־הָעָי׃	
8[12]	--- --- --- ---- --- ---		וַיִּקַּח כַּחֲמֵשֶׁת אֲלָפִים אִישׁ	8[12]
	καὶ --- --- τὰ ἔνεδρα		וַיָּשֶׂם אוֹתָם אֹרֵב	
	--- --- ---		בֵּין בֵּית־אֵל	
	--- --- --- --- ---		וּבֵין הָעַי	
	τῆς πόλεως ἀπὸ θαλάσσης.		מִיָּם לָעִיר׃	
8[13]	--- --- ---		וַיָּשִׂימוּ הָעָם	8[13]
	--- --- ---		אֶת־כָּל־הַמַּחֲנֶה	
	--- --- --- --- ---		אֲשֶׁר מִצְּפוֹן לָעִיר	
	--- --- --- --- --- --- --- ---		וְאֶת־עֲקֵבוֹ מִיָּם לָעִיר	
	--- --- --- --- --- --- ---		וַיֵּלֶךְ יְהוֹשֻׁעַ בַּלַּיְלָה הַהוּא	
	--- --- --- ---		בְּתוֹךְ הָעֵמֶק׃	
8[14]	καὶ ἐγένετο	ויהי]	וַיְהִי	8[14]
	ὡς *εἶδεν* βασιλεὺς Γαι,	כראות [מלך העי]	כִּרְאוֹת מֶלֶךְ־הָעַי	
	ἔσπευσεν	יֹמהרֹ[ו	וַיְמַהֲרוּ	
	--- ---	וישכימו	וַיַּשְׁכִּימוּ	
	καὶ ἐξῆλθεν --- --- ---	ויצאו אשני העיר	וַיֵּצְאוּ אַנְשֵׁי־הָעִיר	
	εἰς συνάντησιν αὐτοῖς *ἐπ᾽ εὐθείας*	לק]רֹאתם ---	לִקְרַאת־יִשְׂרָאֵל	
	εἰς τὸν πόλεμον,		לַמִּלְחָמָה	
	αὐτὸς καὶ πᾶς ὁ λαὸς *ὁ μετ᾽* αὐτοῦ,		הוּא וְכָל־עַמּוֹ	
	--- --- --- --- --- ---		לַמּוֹעֵד לִפְנֵי הָעֲרָבָה	
	καὶ αὐτὸς οὐκ ᾔδει		וְהוּא לֹא יָדַע	
	ὅτι ἔνεδρα αὐτῷ ἐστιν ὀπίσω τῆς πόλεως.		כִּי־אֹרֵב לוֹ מֵאַחֲרֵי הָעִיר׃	

8[15]	*καὶ εἶδεν*			
	καὶ *ἀνεχώρησεν* Ἰησοῦς καὶ --- Ισραηλ		וַיִּנָּגְעוּ יְהוֹשֻׁעַ וְכָל־יִשְׂרָאֵל	8[15]
	ἀπὸ προσώπου αὐτῶν.		לִפְנֵיהֶם	
	--- --- --- --- ---		וַיָּנֻסוּ דֶּרֶךְ הַמִּדְבָּר׃	

8[16]	--- --- --- --- ---		וַיִּזָּעֲקוּ כָּל־הָעָם	8[16]
	--- --- ---		אֲשֶׁר *בָּ*עִיר **בָּ**עַי	
	--- --- ---		לִרְדֹּף אַחֲרֵיהֶם	
	καὶ κατεδίωξαν ὀπίσω *τῶν υἱῶν Ισραηλ*		וַיִּרְדְּפוּ אַחֲרֵי יְהוֹשֻׁעַ	
	καὶ *αὐτοὶ ἀπέστησαν* ἀπὸ τῆς πόλεως·		וַיִּנָּתְקוּ מִן־הָעִיר׃	

8[17]	οὐ κατελείφθη οὐθεὶς ἐν τῇ Γαι		וְלֹא־נִשְׁאַר אִישׁ בָּעַי	8[17]
	--- ---,		וּבֵית אֵל	
	ὃς οὐ *κατεδίωξεν*		אֲשֶׁר לֹא־יָצְאוּ	
	ὀπίσω Ισραηλ·		אַחֲרֵי יִשְׂרָאֵל	
	καὶ κατέλιπον τὴν πόλιν ἀνεῳγμένην		וַיַּעַזְבוּ אֶת־הָעִיר פְּתוּחָה	
	καὶ κατεδίωξαν ὀπίσω Ισραηλ.		וַיִּרְדְּפוּ אַחֲרֵי יִשְׂרָאֵל׃	
			פ	

8:18	καὶ εἶπεν κύριος	ויאמר יהוה	וַיֹּאמֶר יְהוָה	8:18
	πρὸς Ἰησοῦν	אל יהושע	אֶל־יְהוֹשֻׁעַ	
	Ἔκτεινον *τὴν χεῖρά σου*	נטה	נְטֵה	
	ἐν τῷ γαίσῳ	בכידון	בַּכִּידוֹן	
	τῷ ἐν τῇ χειρί σου ἐπὶ τὴν *πόλιν*	אשר ב]ידך אלהעי	אֲשֶׁר־בְּיָדְךָ אֶל־הָעַי	
	--- εἰς γὰρ *τὰς χεῖράς* σου		כִּי בְיָדְךָ	
	παρα*δέδωκα* αὐτήν ---,		אֶתְּנֶנָּה	
	καὶ τὰ ἔνεδρα ἐξαναστήσονται ἐν τάχει			
	ἐκ τοῦ τόπου αὐτῶν.			
	καὶ ἐξέτεινεν Ἰησοῦς *τὴν χεῖρα αὐτοῦ,*		וַיֵּט יְהוֹשֻׁעַ	
	--- τὸν γαῖσον,[12]		בַּכִּידוֹן	
	--- --- --- --- ἐπὶ τὴν πόλιν,		אֲשֶׁר־בְּיָדוֹ אֶל־הָעִיר׃	
8:19	καὶ τὰ ἔνεδρα ἐξανέστησαν ἐν τάχει		וְהָאוֹרֵב קָם מְהֵרָה	8:19
	ἐκ τοῦ τόπου αὐτῶν		מִמְּקוֹמוֹ	
	καὶ *ἐξῆλθοσαν,*		וַיָּרוּצוּ	
	ὅτε ἐξέτειν*εν* τὴν χεῖρα,		כִּנְטוֹת יָדוֹ	
	καὶ ἤλθοσαν ἐπὶ τὴν πόλιν		וַיָּבֹאוּ הָעִיר	
	καὶ κατελάβοντο αὐτὴν		וַיִּלְכְּדוּהָ	
	καὶ σπεύσαντες		וַיְמַהֲרוּ	
	--- ἐνέπρησαν τὴν πόλιν ἐν πυρί.		וַיַּצִּיתוּ אֶת־הָעִיר בָּאֵשׁ׃	
8:20	καὶ *περιβλέψαντες* οἱ *κάτοικοι* Γαι		וַיִּפְנוּ אַנְשֵׁי הָעַי	8:20
	εἰς τὰ ὀπίσω αὐτῶν		אַחֲרֵיהֶם	
	καὶ ἐθεώρουν		וַיִּרְאוּ	
	--- ---		וְהִנֵּה	
	καπνὸν ἀναβαίνοντα ἐκ τῆς πόλεως		עָלָה עֲשַׁן הָעִיר	
	εἰς τὸν οὐρανόν·		הַשָּׁמַיְמָה	
	καὶ *οὐκέτι εἶχον*		וְלֹא־הָיָה בָהֶם יָדַיִם	
	ποῦ φύγωσιν ὧδε ἢ ὧδε.		לָנוּס הֵנָּה וָהֵנָּה	
	--- --- ---		וְהָעָם	
	--- --- --- ---		הַנָּס הַמִּדְבָּר	
	--- --- --- ---		נֶהְפַּךְ אֶל־הָרוֹדֵף׃	
8:21	καὶ Ἰησοῦς καὶ πᾶς Ισραηλ εἶδον		וִיהוֹשֻׁעַ וְכָל־יִשְׂרָאֵל רָאוּ	8:21
	ὅτι ἔλαβον τὰ ἔνεδρα τὴν πόλιν		כִּי־לָכַד הָאֹרֵב אֶת־הָעִיר	
	καὶ ὅτι ἀνέβη ὁ καπνὸς τῆς πόλεως		וְכִי עָלָה עֲשַׁן הָעִיר	
	εἰς τὸν οὐρανόν,			
	καὶ μεταβαλό*μενοι*		וַיָּשֻׁבוּ	
	ἐπάταξαν τοὺς ἄνδρας τῆς Γαι.		וַיַּכּוּ אֶת־אַנְשֵׁי הָעָי׃	

[12] [8:18] Margolis assumed that the double accusative τὴν χεῖρα αὐτοῦ τὸν γαῖσον was a corruption of the accusative-dative construction as found at the beginning of the verse, and conjecturally reconstructed τὴν χεῖρα αὐτοῦ τῷ γαίσῳ. As C.G. DEN HERTOG, *Studien*, pp. 72–73, has pointed out, the accusative form as attested by all witnesses and adopted by Rahlfs reflects the difficulty the Greek translator had with the Hebrew the double preposition constructions בַכידון אשר בִיד.

8^{22}	καὶ οὗτοι ἐξήλθοσαν ἐκ τῆς πόλεως	וְאֵ֨לֶּה יָצְא֤וּ מִן־הָעִיר֙	8^{22}
	εἰς συνάντησιν ---	לִקְרָאתָ֔ם	
	καὶ ἐγενήθησαν --- --- *ἀνὰ μέσον τῆς παρεμβολῆς*,	וַיִּהְי֤וּ לְיִשְׂרָאֵל֙ בַּתָּ֔וֶךְ	
	οὗτοι ἐντεῦθεν	אֵ֥לֶּה מִזֶּ֖ה	
	καὶ οὗτοι ἐντεῦθεν·	וְאֵ֣לֶּה מִזֶּ֑ה	
	καὶ ἐπάταξαν ---	וַיַּכּ֣וּ אוֹתָ֔ם	
	ἕως τοῦ μὴ καταλειφθῆναι αὐτῶν	עַד־בִּלְתִּ֥י הִשְׁאִֽיר־ל֖וֹ	
	σεσωσμένον καὶ διαπεφευγότα.	שָׂרִ֥יד וּפָלִֽיט׃	
8^{23}	καὶ τὸν βασιλέα τῆς Γαι	וְאֶת־מֶ֥לֶךְ הָעַ֖י	8^{23}
	συνέλαβον ζῶντα	תָּ֣פְשׂוּ חָ֑י	
	καὶ *προσήγαγον* αὐτὸν πρὸς Ἰησοῦν	וַיַּקְרִ֥בוּ אֹת֖וֹ אֶל־יְהוֹשֻֽׁעַ׃	
8^{24}	καὶ ---	וַיְהִ֣י	8^{24}
	ὡς ἐπαύσαντο *οἱ υἱοὶ* Ισραηλ	כְּכַלּ֣וֹת יִ֠שְׂרָאֵל	
	ἀποκτέν*νοντες πάντας τοὺς ἐν* τῇ Γαι	לַהֲרֹ֨ג אֶת־כָּל־יֹשְׁבֵ֜י הָעַ֗י	
	τοὺς ἐν *τοῖς* πεδίοις --- --- ---	בַּשָּׂדֶה֙ בַּמִּדְבָּר֙	
	καὶ ἐν τῷ ὄρει ἐπὶ τῆς καταβάσεως,		
	οὗ κατεδίωξαν αὐτοὺς ἀπ᾽ αὐτῆς	אֲשֶׁ֣ר רְדָפ֣וּם בּ֔וֹ	
	--- --- --- --- --- --- ---	וַיִּפְּל֥וּ כֻלָּ֛ם לְפִי־חֶ֖רֶב	
	εἰς τέλος,	עַד־תֻּמָּ֑ם	
	καὶ ἀπέστρεψεν *Ἰησοῦς* εἰς Γαι	וַיָּשֻׁ֤בוּ כָל־יִשְׂרָאֵל֙ הָעַ֔י	
	καὶ ἐπάταξεν αὐτὴν ἐν στόματι ῥομφαίας.	וַיַּכּ֥וּ אֹתָ֖הּ לְפִי־חָֽרֶב׃	
8^{25}	καὶ ἐγενήθησαν ---	וַיְהִ֨י כָֽל־	8^{25}
	οἱ πεσόντες ἐν τῇ ἡμέρᾳ ἐκείνῃ	הַנֹּפְלִ֜ים בַּיּ֣וֹם הַה֗וּא	
	ἀπὸ ἀνδρὸς καὶ ἕως γυναικὸς	מֵאִ֙ישׁ֙ וְעַד־אִשָּׁ֔ה	
	δώδεκα χιλιάδες,	שְׁנֵ֥ים עָשָׂ֖ר אָ֑לֶף	
	πάντας τοὺς *κατοικοῦντας* Γαι,	כֹּ֖ל אַנְשֵׁ֥י הָעָֽי׃	

8^{26}	--- --- --- --- --- --- ---	וִיהוֹשֻׁ֙עַ֙ לֹא־הֵשִׁ֣יב יָד֔וֹ	8^{26}
	--- --- --- ---	אֲשֶׁ֥ר נָטָ֖ה בַּכִּיד֑וֹן	
	--- --- --- --- --- --- ---	עַ֚ד אֲשֶׁ֣ר הֶחֱרִ֔ים אֵ֖ת כָּל־יֹשְׁבֵ֥י הָעָֽי׃	

8^{27}	πλὴν [τῶν κτηνῶν καὶ][13] τῶν σκύλων	רַ֣ק הַבְּהֵמָ֗ה וּשְׁלַל֙	8^{27}
	τῶν ἐν τῇ πόλει,	הָעִ֣יר הַהִ֔יא	
	πάντα ἃ ἐπρονόμευσαν --- *οἱ υἱοὶ* Ισραηλ	בָּזְז֥וּ לָהֶ֖ם יִשְׂרָאֵ֑ל	
	κατὰ *πρόσταγμα* κυρίου,	כִּדְבַ֣ר יְהוָ֔ה	
	ὃν τρόπον συνέταξεν *κύριος* τῷ Ἰησοῖ.	אֲשֶׁ֖ר צִוָּ֥ה אֶת־יְהוֹשֻֽׁעַ׃	
8^{28}	καὶ ἐνεπύρισεν Ἰησοῦς *τὴν πόλιν ἐν πυρί*·	וַיִּשְׂרֹ֥ף יְהוֹשֻׁ֖עַ אֶת־הָעָ֑י	8^{28}
	--- --- χῶμα ἀοίκητον εἰς τὸν αἰῶνα *ἔθηκεν αὐτὴν*	וַיְשִׂימֶ֤הָ תֵּל־עוֹלָם֙ שְׁמָמָ֔ה	
	ἕως τῆς ἡμέρας ταύτης.	עַ֖ד הַיּ֥וֹם הַזֶּֽה׃	

---

[13] [8:27] The phrase τῶν κτηνῶν καὶ is not present in B.129.344* and Sa, and therefore Margolis did not adopt it in his main text. Nevertheless, as C.G. den Hertog, *Studien*, p. 44, has argued, the sequence of genitive constructions most likely resulted in *parablepsis*, as is evident from the omission of the following phrase τῶν σκύλων in manuscripts of the S̲ family.

	LXX	MT	
8[29]	καὶ τὸν βασιλέα τῆς Γαι ἐκρέμασεν	וְאֶת־מֶלֶךְ הָעַי תָּלָה	8[29]
	ἐπὶ ξύλου *διδύμου*,	עַל־הָעֵץ	
	καὶ ἦν ἐπὶ τοῦ ξύλου ἕως --- --- ἑσπέρας·	עַד־עֵת הָעָרֶב	
	καὶ ἐπιδύνοντος τοῦ ἡλίου	וּכְבוֹא הַשֶּׁמֶשׁ	
	συνέταξεν Ἰησοῦς	צִוָּה יְהוֹשֻׁעַ	
	καὶ *καθείλοσαν* αὐτοῦ τὸ σῶμα ἀπὸ τοῦ ξύλου	וַיֹּרִידוּ אֶת־נִבְלָתוֹ מִן־הָעֵץ	
	καὶ *ἔρριψαν* αὐτὸν	וַיַּשְׁלִיכוּ אוֹתָהּ	
	εἰς τὸν *βόθρον* --- ---	אֶל־פֶּתַח שַׁעַר הָעִיר	
	καὶ ἐπέστησαν αὐτῷ σωρὸν λίθων ---	וַיָּקִימוּ עָלָיו גַּל־אֲבָנִים גָּדוֹל	
	ἕως τῆς ἡμέρας ταύτης.	עַד הַיּוֹם הַזֶּה׃	
		פ	

8.2 Critical Review of Previous Research

8.2.1 *Condensation or Expansion?*

It will not come as a surprise that several scholars have embraced the shorter Greek version as the solution to the literary-critical problems posed by the MT. Already in 1900, Carl Steuernagel argued that the Greek version is a faithful rendering of a shorter and more original Hebrew text than that found in MT. In his view, the pluses in MT *vis-à-vis* LXX are the result of the youngests additions to the book of Joshua.[14] Steuernagel, however, did not explain the motives behind these supposed additions, but simply contented himself with the observation that the narrative thus purged should be seen as the product of the Deuteronomistic historian (D^2 in his terminology).[15] S. Holmes adopted this proposal, but only first after exploring the solution of a haplography in the Hebrew *Vorlage* of LXX from נגד העיר (verse 11) to לעיר (verse 13).[16] In his view, a translator working on verse 11bff. would hardly remember that verse 3ff. is incompatible with the text now under his hands. And if the translator had felt the

[14] C. Steuernagel, *Deuteronomium und Josua*, p. 180.

[15] A similar solution to the problem of the doublet was proposed even earlier by A. Knobel, *Die Bücher Numeri, Deuteronomium und Josua*, p. 389, although Knobel did not refer to the LXX: 'Vermuthlich hat der Jehovist die Stelle [i.e., Josh. 8:12–13—MM] aus seiner ersten Urkunde, die freilich sonst nicht kenntlich ist, entnommen und hier eingefügt.'

[16] S. Holmes, *Joshua*, p. 42. Similar proposals with the same reservations have been advanced by R.G. Boling, *Joshua*, p. 234: 'The bulk of vv 12–13 is not reflected in LXX. Since it is a recapitulation, it might have been intentionally omitted, if it was not the victim of another haplography: *wy*[*qḥ* . . .[14] *wy*]*hy*.'; and R.D. Nelson, *Joshua*, p. 109: 'At this point OG begins a long haplography covering much of vv. 11–13, one triggered by the repetition of "on the north side of Ai/the city" in vv. 11b and 13a.'

problem, he could have simply harmonised the numbers in verses 3 and 12.[17] C.D. Benjamin,[18] A.G. Auld[19] and L.J. Greenspoon[20] faithfully adopt Holmes' thesis. Auld furthermore ascribes the expansion in MT-Josh. 8:11b–13 to what he sees as 'the pedantic concern for the location of the camp and the precise whereabouts of Joshua himself at any given moment' (see section 7.4.5.1 above). In a similar vein, A. Tricot argued in favour of the LXX version of this and the preceding chapter solely on the basis of his *a priori* characterisation of the Greek translation as faithful and literal.[21] P.A. Fernández followed a similar line of reasoning in order to rid the sacred text of a troublesome passage.[22] E. Tov, finally, places the plus in MT in his category 'Additions of MT whose secondary nature is evident from the context' without further argumentation.[23]

The problem with this line of reasoning is that it does not explain why a scribe/redactor from the Late Second Temple Period would deliberatedly have created these tensions in the text either by creating the pluses himself or otherwise incorporating them from a different source, either directly or through the margin.[24] The only motive for

---

[17] S. Holmes, *Joshua*, pp. 13–14, 42–43: 'If the translator had felt the difficulty there was open to him the simple expedient of making the numbers correspond.' (p. 13) In a similar vein, Holmes ascribes the other pluses in MT-Josh. to the Hebrew revisor. The MT plus in verse 1 ואת עמו ואת עירו is 'probably an editorial addition to M.T.' (p. 41); verse 7b–8a 'a harmonising or 'anticipatory' insertion from v. 19' (p. 42), verse 9b and 13b should be seen as 'a case of double insertion' (p. 42), the problematic phrase למועד לפני הערבה in verse 14 are 'the insertion of the revisor who perhaps also altered the next verse with the same end in view, viz. to make it plain that the retreat was premeditated.' (p. 43); verse 15b–16a thus also reflect 'anticipatory insertions' (p. 43), the words in verse 24 ויפלו כלם לפי חרב are 'an awkwardly attached amplification' (p. 45), and verse 26 is 'a gloss on the basis of Ex.xvii.8.'

[18] C.D. Benjamin, *The Variations*, p. 39.

[19] A.G. Auld, Joshua. The Hebrew and Greek Texts, pp. 4–5 (= *Joshua Retold*, pp. 9–10).

[20] L.J. Greenspoon, *Textual Studies*, p. 162.

[21] A. Tricot, La prise d'Aï, pp. 274–275, 293–294.

[22] P.A. Fernández, s.j., *Commentarius in librum Iosue*, p. 109: 'Omissionis fortuitae nulla fuit occasio. Quod scriba integram pericopam expungeret ad contradictionem, quam ibi deprehenderet, vitandam est omnino improbabile: plures sunt interpretes etiam recentiores qui nullam ibi antilogiam videant. Neque ex alia parte existimandum est scribam, licet audaciorem, sententias, quae habentur in TM, proprio marte induxisse. Dicendum ergo hos versus ex documento non inspirato, ubi de pugna contra Hai erat sermo, desumptos esse, et in margine forsan collocatos, unde in textum deinde irrepserint. Textus igitur brevior, scil. LXX est praeferendus.'

[23] E. Tov, The Growth, pp. 330–331 (= *The Greek and Hebrew Bible*, p. 390).

[24] Thus e.g. W. Rudolph, *Der 'Elohist'*, pp. 194–195.

these additions adduced so far is that of A.G. Auld's thesis of a pedantic concern for geographical information, a thesis that rests on a very slender basis (see section 7.4.5.1 above). The other difficulty with this approach is that it *a priori* assumes that the Greek version is the product of a slavish, unintelligent literalist, an assumption that is open to discussion after the observations made in the previous chapters, to say the least. For these two reasons, the majority of scholars regard the minuses in LXX-Josh. 8:1–29 as the result of deliberate omissions on the part of the Greek translator intended precisely to avoid the logical problems posed by the original longer Hebrew text.[25] Scholars such as H.N. Rösel[26] and J. Briend[27] have further pointed out that various topographical elements in the Hebrew text have not been understood by the Greek translator and as a result were either omitted or rendered incorrectly.

8.2.2 *Support from Qumran?*

With the discovery and eventual publication of the Qumran scrolls in general and 4QJosh[a] in particular, the old discussion *pro* or *contra* the priority of the LXX version has received a new impetus. In 1968, J.A. Callaway reported in a footnote the existence of a Qumran scroll of Joshua that would support the thesis of a Hebrew *Vorlage* underlying the LXX version that was both shorter than and superior to the MT.[28] It was not until the preliminary publication of the Qumran fragments by L.J. Greenspoon in 1990, and the subsequent publications by Ulrich and Bieberstein, that the relevant 4QJosh[a]

[25] Thus e.g. J. Wellhausen, *Die Composition des Hexateuchs*, p. 126; A. Dillmann, *Die Bücher Numeri, Deuteronomium und Josua*, pp. 472–477; S. Oettli, *Das Deuteronomium und die Bücher Josua und Richter*, p. 148; H. Holzinger, *Das Buch Josua*, p. 25; E. Albers, *Die Quellenberichte in Josua I–XII*, pp. 108–122; M.L. Margolis, *The Book of Joshua in Greek*, p. 129; M.L. Margolis, Ai or the City? Joshua 8.12.16, in *JQR.NS* 7 (1916), pp. 491–497, especially pp. 495–496; W. Rudolph, *Der 'Elohist'*, p. 195; O. Keel, *Wirkmächtige Siegeszeichen*, p. 18; D. Barthélemy, *Critique textuelle*, p. 11; T.C. Butler, *Joshua*, p. 78; and J. Moatti-Fine, *Josué*, p. 134.

[26] H.N. Rösel, Studien zur Topographie der Kriege in den Büchern Josua und Richter, in *ZDPV* 91 (1975), pp. 159–190, especially pp. 162–163.

[27] J. Briend, *Bible et archéologie en Josué 6,1–8,29. Recherches sur la composition de Josué 1–12.* Paris 1978, pp. 198–199.

[28] J.A. Callaway, New Evidence on the Conquest of 'Ai, in *JBL* 87 (1968), pp. 312–320, especially pp. 319–320, note 35: 'There are unpublished fragments of Josh 8_{3-18} from Qumran Cave IV that Professor Frank M. Cross kindly brought to my attention. He pointed out that verse 9b is omitted with the LXX, and that 4Q has a very short text in the following verses, esp. 10–18.'

fragments were presented to the scholarly world.[29] In the official *editio princeps* by Ulrich in DJD 14 the fragments that contain parts of the text of our passage are the second column of fragment 9, and further fragments 13–16.[30] The first column of fragment 9 contains, together with fragments 10–12, most of the text of Joshua 8:12–17. Here follows Ulrich's transcription with the contours of the fragments in computer-drawn imitation and the reconstructed text in outline font:

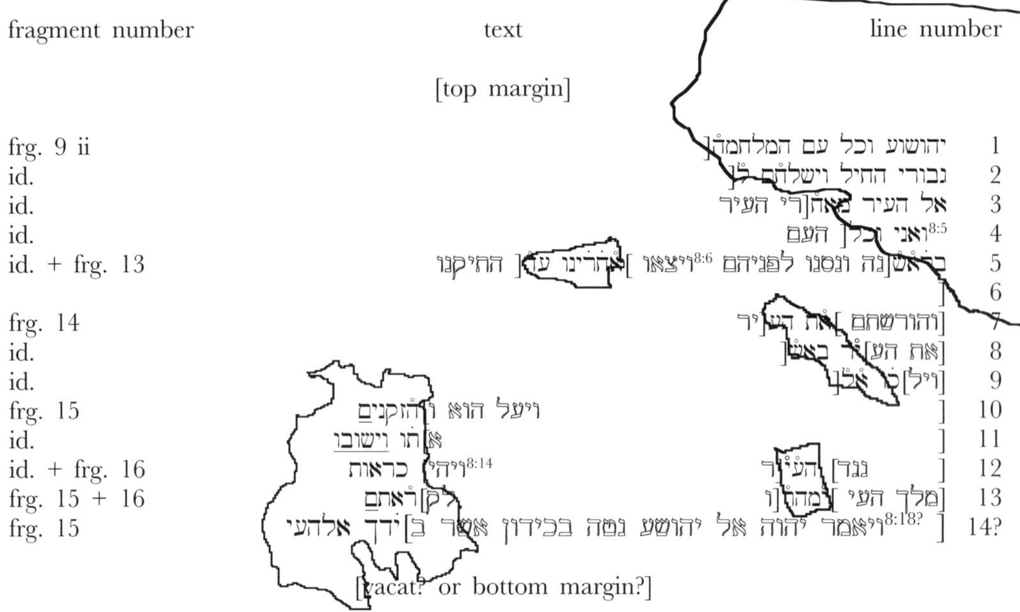

fragment number	text	line number
	[top margin]	
frg. 9 ii	יהושע וכל עם המלחמה[	1
id.	גבורי החיל וישלחם לו[	2
id.	אל העיר מאח[רי העיר	3
id.	8:5 ואני וכל] העם	4
id. + frg. 13	בראש[נה ונסנו לפניהם 8:6 ויצאו]אחרינו עד[התיקנו	5
	]	6
frg. 14	[והורשתם]את הע[יר	7
id.	[את הע]יר באש[	8
id.	[ויל]כו אלנ[	9
frg. 15	] ויעל הוא ו]הזקנים	10
id.	] א]תו וישובו	11
id. + frg. 16	] נגד] העי[ר 8:14 ויהי] כראות	12
frg. 15 + 16	[מלך העי]מהר[ו לק]ראתם	13
frg. 15	] 8:18? ויאמר יהוה אל יהושע נטה בכידון אשר ב]ידך אלהעי	14?
	[vacat? or bottom margin?]	

Together these short fragments constitute column V of 4QJoshua[a]. Line 14 was added by a different and larger second hand from the Herodian period, and does not contain the text of the second part of verse 14, but apparently that of verse 18. Fragment 15 contains both a right and bottom margin. If the complete text of this column is reconstructed after MT, it will be evident that 4QJosh[a] must have had a shorter text than that preserved in MT.

---

[29] See section 3.1 above.

[30] E. Ulrich, 4QJosh[a], p. 150.

If line 12 is reconstructed after MT, it would contain 210 letterspaces, which is almost four times the average number of circa 55 letterspaces per line.[31] Moreover, the fixed relative position of the words contained on frg. 16 seem to make a reconstruction of lines 12–13 after MT impossible. According to Ulrich, 'the fixed relative position of the extant words in lines 7–9 and 10–13 appears to require a shorter text similar to that in the LXX, rather than a longer text as in the MT'.[32] The agreement of 4QJosh[a] with LXX seems to be supported by two minor details: line 10 (Josh. 8:10) [ו]הׄזקנים agrees with LXX(B.129.407.Sah.VetLat) καὶ οἱ πρεσβύτεροι *vis-à-vis* MT וזקני ישראל; and line 13 (Josh. 8:14) [לק]ראׄתם agrees with LXX εἰς συνάντησιν *αὐτοῖς ἐπ' εὐθείας vis-à-vis* MT לקראת־ישראל. Furthermore, lines 7 and 9 with 65 and 70 letterspaces, respectively, are also unusually long, so that for these lines (Josh. 8:7–9) Ulrich suspects a shorter Hebrew text like that reflected in LXX. In this way,

---

[31] For lack of space, this reconstruction has been printed on two lines.

[32] E. Ulrich, Joshua's First Altar, p. 102; E. Ulrich, 4QJosh[a], p. 150. Idem L.J. Greenspoon, The Qumran Fragments of Joshua, pp. 170–171. K. Bieberstein, *Lukian und Theodtion*, pp. 80–81, discusses only fragment 9 ii.

the Qumran scroll would give indirect evidence of the existence of a shorter Hebrew version of Josh. 8:7–18 underlying LXX-Josh. Unfortunately, however, Ulrich has made no attempt to reconstruct the missing text of this fifth column.

8.2.3 *L. Mazor's Theory of the Literary Growth of the Passage*

A full interpretation of the textual differences between these three witnesses has been offered by Lea Mazor.[33] According to Mazor the three witnesses reflect three successive stages in the formation process of this narrative: [1] the oldest and shortest version as preserved in 4QJosh[a], [2] an intermediate stage as reflected by LXX, and [3] the final and most elaborate version attested by MT. In her view, the original narrative was a secular one, which in the final version was expanded into a theological account in which the participation of Yhwh was stressed. Other factors behind this process of literary growth were—according to Mazor—the process of assimilation to the similar, but originally unrelated narrative of the fall of Gibeʿah (Judges 20), and the process of expanding the biblical narrative according to the principle of complete agreement between command and execution as attested for instance by the additions to the plague narrative in the SamP version of Exodus 7–10.

Mazor rejects the possibility of an 'improved redaction' of the layered longer MT as proposed by Wellhausen and many others, on the grounds that the LXX presents a smoother and more logical version of the narrative. If a redactor had wanted to free the longer version from all points of friction, he would have deleted the discrepancy between verse 17 and 24 (attested by both LXX and MT): according to verse 17 Ai was left empty, while verse 24 seems to contradict this. Furthermore, such a redactor would have placed verse 21 before 20, since the clause in verse 20 ולא היה בהם ידים לנוס הנה והנה (attested both by MT and LXX), seems to presuppose the return of the Israelites narrated in verse 21.[34]

---

[33] L. Mazor, עיונים, pp. 210–244 (chapter 6). This chapter has been published separately as L. Mazor, הסיפור אודות הנצחון על העי (יהושע ח) עיוני נוסח וספרות (A Textual and Literary Study of the Fall of Ai in Joshua 8), in S. Japhet (ed.), המקרא בראי מפרשיו, ספר זיכרון לשרה קמין (*The Bible in the Light of Its Interpreters. Sarah Kamin Memorial Volume*). Jerusalem 1994, pp. 73–108.

[34] L. Mazor, הסיפור אודות הנצחון על העי, pp. 84–85.

The motive of stressing the divine participation in the course of events is evident, according to Mazor, in verse 7b, in which the shorter and more neutral Hebrew text of the *Vorlage* of LXX כדבר הזה תעשו, *according to this word you will act*, was altered into a divine command כדבר יהוה תשעו, *according to the word of Yhwh you will act.*[35] According to Mazor, verse 26 was added to the original narrative as attested by LXX in order to reinterpret the function of Joshua's staff from signal to magical instrument, similar to Moses' staff in Exod. 17:8–16. In doing so, the editor not only transformed the secular conquest narrative into a theological one,[36] but also strenghtened the similiarity between the two leaders, Joshua and Moses.[37] The originality of the shorter LXX text is proven, according to Mazor, by the fact that without verse 26 the sequence of events is not interrupted: in the preceding verses the defeat of the men of Ai both in the open field and in the city is narrated (verses 21–25), whereas the next verses continue with an account of the actions after the conquest of the city (verses 27–29), which is the logical continuation of the text without verse 26. Thus the literary-critical problem of the intrusion of verse 26 should be explained on the basis of textual data. Subsequently, the MT editor has tried to resolve this tension by changing 'Joshua' in verse 24 to 'Israel'.

Mazor attempts to explain the plus in MT-Josh. 8:11b–13 *vis-à-vis* LXX and 4QJosh[a] on the basis of the parallels between Joshua 8 and Judges 20. Although the two stories were originally independent narratives about a battle in the same Benjaminite area, won by means of the stratagem of placing an ambush, they gradually became assimilated, according to Mazor.[38] In practice, this means that some

---

[35] L. Mazor, הסיפור אודות הנצחון על העי, pp. 93–94. For a similar view, see W. Rudolph, *Der 'Elohist'*, p. 194: 'Während der Fall Jerichos durch ein göttliches wunder erfolgte, ist die durch eine Kriegslist gelungene Eroberung von Ai eine rein militärische Angelegenheit. Diese Darstellung erschien später zu 'weltlich', und um ihr religiös aufzuhelfen, wurden v. 1f. davorgestetzt. . . . Dadurch wurde der Kampfplan Josuas zu einer göttlichen Eingebung ($1^{a\beta}$ = 3^{a}; 2^{b} = 4^{a}); zugleich wurde damit die Angleichung an Jos 6 hergestellt (1^{b} = 6_{2}); . . . Zu dem religiösen Zusatz darf man wohl noch v. 7^{b} rechnen, ebenso v.8 die Worte כדבר י׳, die, wie 𝔊 zeigt, aus כַּדָּבָר הַזֶּה umgeformt sind.'

[36] L. Mazor, הסיפור אודות הנצחון על העי, pp. 92–94.

[37] L. Mazor, הסיפור אודות הנצחון על העי, pp. 94–97.

[38] For a similar thesis but with a completely different conclusion see W.M. Roth, Hinterhalt und Scheinflucht. Der stammespolemische Hintergrund von Jos 8, in *ZAW* 75 (1963), pp. 296–304.

of the MT pluses can be explained as assimilations to elements from the related narrative (she does not give examples of a possible influence of Joshua 8 upon Judges 20). According to Mazor, the original order of events described in verses 1–13 was simple and coherent: Joshua sent out 30,000 men in ambush at night (verses 1–9), at daybreak Joshua arrived with the main force from the east, opposite to the location of the ambush (ἦλθον ἐξ ἐναντίας τῆς πόλεως ἀπ' ἀνατολῶν καὶ τὰ ἔνεδρα τῆς πόλεως ἀπὸ θαλάσσης, which she retroverts into ויבאו נגד העיר מקדם ומארב העיר מים), and immediately after that the battle started (verse 14). Since in the parallel Judges version several ambushes are placed around the city (וישם ישׂראל ארבים אל־הגבעה סביב Judg. 20:29), the element מקדם was replaced in the MT version by מצפון in order to convey this idea of two ambushes around Ai, one to the east and one to the north.[39] In order to smooth out the discrepancy that had now arisen between the two ambush groups, an even later hand added the pluses in MT 8:9b and 13b which insert an additional night in MT 8:9b in order to account for the two ambush groups, the MT plus in verse 14 וישׂימו, and in order to make clear that Joshua stayed among his people.[40]

Mazor finds other examples of influence of the Judges narrative on the MT edition of Joshua 8 in the change of והלכתם אל העיר (καὶ πορεύσεσθε εἰς τὴν πόλιν) in verse 7 to MT והורשתם את־העיר, which supposedly was inspired by the story of the capture of Gibeʿah by the ambush men והארב החישו ויפשטו אל־הגבעה וימשך הארב ויך את־כל־העיר לפי־חרב (Judg. 20:37).[41] Although without parallel in the Judges narrative, Mazor likewise considers the next addition in MT, 8:8a תציתו את־העיר באשׁ to be an expansion based on verse 19 ויציתו את־העיר באשׁ (= LXX ἐνέπρησαν την πόλιν ἐν πυρί).[42] In the original story (verse 9) the aspect of setting the city on fire was only an initiative of the men in ambush. According to Mazor this phrase is ambiguous, since the burning of the city can be explained either as a signal for the men in the open field, or as the complete destruction

---

[39] L. Mazor, הסיפור אודות הנצחון על העי, pp. 86–91. Mazor, p. 90, note 35, refers to a similar procedure in Josephus' version of the narrative in Flavius Josephus, *Jewish Antiquities* V. 45: Ἰησοῦς δὲ ἁγνίσας τὸν στρατὸν ἐξῆγεν ἐπὶ τὴν Ναϊὰν αὐτοὺς καὶ νυκτὸς τὰ *περὶ τὴν πόλιν ἐνέδραις* προλοχίσας ὑπὸ τὸν ὄρθρον συμβάλλει τοῖς πολεμίοις.

[40] L. Mazor, הסיפור אודות הנצחון על העי, pp. 90–91.

[41] L. Mazor, הסיפור אודות הנצחון על העי, p. 101.

[42] L. Mazor, הסיפור אודות הנצחון על העי, pp. 101–102.

of the city, as was the fate of Jericho, 6:24 והעיר שׂרפו באשׁ and Hazor, 11:11 ואת־חצור שׂרף באשׁ. By adding this element in verse 8, the editor would have wanted to stress this first function. It should be pointed out straightaway, however, that in these two specific cases 4QJosh[a] supports MT: [ו]הורשתם[אֿת הע]יר [(8:7) *vis-à-vis* Mazor's reconstruction behind LXX והלכתם אֿל העיר and [את הע]יׄר באשׁׄ[ ] (8:8).

Since in Judg. 20:38 this stratagem is presented as an appointment between the Israelites and the ambush men והמועד היה לאישׁ ישׂראל עם־הארב הרב להעלותם משׂאת העשׁן מן־העיר, one would have expected to find a similar phrase in its alleged derivative, the MT-edition of Josh. 8:7–8. This, however, is not the case. Nevertheless, Mazor holds the erratic element למועד in the MT-plus in 8:14 to be an unconscious reminiscence of the parallel in Judges.[43] The question then arises, how a word from such a broad context as Judges 20—the chapter contains 48 verses—could turn up in such a misplaced context as Josh. 8:14, where the word occurs in a geographical context.

Other pluses in MT that Mazor explains in the same manner are 8:20b, where the verb הפך which occurs only here as synonym for שׁוב (verse 21.24) should be seen, thus Mazor, as an assimilation of the next verse Josh. 8:20 to Judg. 20:39 ויהפך אישׁ־ישׂראל במלחמה and Judg. 20:41 ואישׁ ישׂראל הפך.[44] In Mazor's view, in the original narrative Joshua did not feign a withdrawal (verse 15 וינגעו יהושׁע וכל־ישׂראל לפניהם), but was really defeated (καὶ εἶδεν καὶ ἀνεχώρησεν Ἰησοῦς καὶ Ισραηλ ἀπὸ προσώπον αὐτῶν, which she retroverts into וירא וינס יהושע וַישׂראל לפניהם). The MT would then be the result of assimilation with Judg. 20:31–32 ויצאו בני־בנימן . . . הנתקו מן־העיר . . . ובני ישׂראל אמרו ננוסה ונתקנהו מן־העיר.[45] One would, however, have expected to find a minus in LXX-Josh. 8:17 (καὶ αὐτοὶ ἀπέστησαν ἀπὸ τῆς πόλεως which corresponds to MT וינתקו מן־העיר) as well. Furthermore, Mazor disregards the fact that the Greek text in verse 15 does not contain the verb φεύγω, which would have been the literal rendering for נוס, but ἀναχωρέω, *to depart, withdraw*, which occurs in the Greek Old Testament only 13 times.[46] Mazor also points to the

---

[43] L. Mazor, הסיפור אודות הנצחון על העי, pp. 105–106.
[44] L. Mazor, הסיפור אודות הנצחון על העי, p. 103.
[45] L. Mazor, הסיפור אודות הנצחון על העי, pp. 102–103.
[46] See section 8.6 below.

threefold plus in MT of the element מדבר in Josh. 8:15b.20.24, which together with Judg. 20:42 (ויפנו לפני איש ישראל אל־דרך המדבר) and 45, 47 (וינסו המדברה אל־סלע הרמון) would be the only reference in the Hebrew Bible to a desert inside Israel.[47] One wonders, however, who would have wanted to harmonise the two narratives on this insignificant point.

Finally, Mazor points to the remarkable sequence in 4QJosh[a] fragment 15 of Josh. 8:14 to 8:18. Although she notes that the element [ב]ידך אלהעי] was added by a later hand, she nevertheless concludes that originally Josh. 8:18 was the immediate sequel to Josh. 8:14a, Therefore, Josh. 8:14b–17 must be seen as an expansion to this shorter text, according to Mazor, which was added prior to the LXX-edition, since it is reflected by LXX as well. In her view this expansion is based on the corresponding passage 8:4–6 and was added in order to balance the instructions by a narrative about their execution, in the same manner as the Samaritan Pentateuch contains expansions of the biblical text based on parallel accounts:[48]

alleged source text	alleged edition II (Hebr. *Vorlage* LXX)	alleged edition I (4QJosh[a])
		8:14 ויהי כראות מלך העי
		וימהר_--- ויצא_לקראתם
	למלחמה הוא וכל העם אשר עמו --- --- ---	
8^4 אתם ארבים --- אחרי העיר	והוא לא ידע כי ארב לו מאחרי העיר	
8^5 ונסנו לפניהם	8:15 וירא וינס יהושע_וישראל מפניהם	
	--- --- --- --- ---	
	8:16 --- --- --- --- --- --- --- ---	
	--- --- --- ---	
	וירדפו אחרי בני ישראל	
8^6 נתיקם --- מן העיר	וינתקו מן העיר	
	8:17 ולא* נשאר איש בעי --- ---	
8^6 וכי_יצאו אחרינו	אשר לא רדפו אחרי ישראל	
	ויעזבו את העיר פתוחה	
	וירדפו אחרי ישראל	
		8:18 ויאמר יהוה אל־יהושע
		נטה בכידון

[47] L. MAZOR, הסיפור אודות הנצחון על העי, pp. 103–105.

[48] L. MAZOR, הסיפור אודות הנצחון על העי, pp. 106–108. The synopsis is based on Mazor's reconstruction of the Hebrew *Vorlage* of LXX, see L. MAZOR, הסיפור אודות הנצחון על העי, pp. 75–82. Variants *vis-à-vis* MT have been marked by underlinings; hyphens indicate minuses.

In this way, the perceived discrepancy between verses 19 and 24 concerning the moment of burning the city can also be ascribed to the alleged formation process of the text, thus Mazor. The element בית אל in the MT plus 8:17 would then be nothing more than the slip of an over-enthousiastic redactor.[49] As a result, all tensions in the text can be explained on the basis of the formation history of the text that itself is based solely on the ancient textual witnesses.

8.3 Questions and Methodological Considerations

Mazor has offered an ingenious, original and painstaking analysis. Yet, although she claims to have solved all the problems related to this passage, her approach also raises several questions and remarks:

* If 4QJosh[a] represents the oldest stage in the formation process, how can it be that this text supports the longer text of MT in verse 8a (and most probably in verse 7b) as well?
* If the final line of 4QJosh[a] fragment 15 was written by another hand than the preceding lines, how is it possible to assume that verse 18a (final line) was the immediate continuation of verse 14a (preceding line). Moreover, from a narrative point of view, these verses cannot readily be missed, as they narrate how the city was left unprotected. Furthermore, the agreements between these verses and the elements from verses 4–6 only account for a few phrases. The expansions found in the Samaritan Pentateuch and pre-Samaritan texts such as 4QpaleoExodus[m] and 4QNumbers[b] always contain completely copied passages from another biblical text with only minor adaptations to the context, but never free elaborations of the kind and size as proposed by Mazor. Her view implies that removing 8:14b–17 frees the narrative of the discrepancy between verses 17 and 24 (was the city abandoned or not?). Verse 17, however,—attested by both MT and LXX, apart from the minor element 'Beth-El'—does not state that the city was completely abandoned, but only that all the valiant men left the city in order to pursue the Israelites. Therefore, there is no contradiction with verse 24, which speaks only in general terms of a massacre of the population of Ai (ויכו אתה לפי־חרב).

[49] L. Mazor, הסיפור אודות הנצחון על העי, pp. 107–108.

* Although it is easy to draw parallels between Joshua 8 and Judges 20, it remains difficult to detect any direct influence of Judges 20 on the alleged pluses in MT-Joshua 8. If the process of assimilation had been an unconscious one, one would rather have expected to find large(r) text segments from Judges 20 conflated with Joshua 8 (and vice versa). The agreement, however, between the two versions never extends beyond word level. By far the majority of instances where Joshua 8 and Judges 20 (especially in the verses 29–44) correspond, the text of Joshua 8 is supported by both MT and LXX.

The various agreements between Judges 20 and the text of Joshua 8 attested by both MT and LXX (and occasionally 4QJosh[a], where extant) makes clear that if the two versions had undergone assimilation, this process must have taken place during a stage in the formation of Joshua 8 preceding the textual variation. In that case, textual and literary criticism do not overlap completely. It would seem, however, more appropriate to ascribe these agreements to the circumstance that both versions happen to describe a similar strategy.[50] One wonders furthermore how isolated expressions such as הפך, מדבר and מועד could have crept into the text of Joshua 8. If the change of the alleged older reading in Josh. 8:7 והלכתם אל to MT והורשתם את (= 4QJosh[a]!) was due to influence of Judges 20, one would expect to find ירש Hiphʿil attested in the parallel passage in Judges 20. Nevertheless, the verb does not occur at all in Judges 20, and the parallel Mazor adduces, Judg. 20:39, is only vaguely related to this expression.

* Moreover, it remains hard to explain the plus in MT-Josh. 8:11b–13 on the basis of Judg. 20:29. If the MT-editor deliberatedly or unconsciously had conformed the Joshua narrative to that verse, one would have expected to find the word סביב there as well. The plus, however, in no way conveys this idea of several ambushes around the city. There is only one specific place where the ambush group is to hide, and that is west of Ai. The element מפצון does not refer to the location of an alleged second ambush group, but to that of the Israelite main force, which moreover does not take a specific position, but only approaches the city in order to attack it straightaway. Therefore, the motive behind the supposed repetition

[50] So also to some extent L. Mazor, הסיפור אודות הנצחון על העי, pp. 99–100.

of the sending of a group in ambush and their location west of Ai remains to be clarified.

* If stress on the divine participation in the order of events had been a motive for expanding the text, it would be logical to find a secular text fully transformed into a more pious theological one, as was the case with the book of Esther. Here, however, Yhwh plays a role in both MT and LXX in verses 1–2, 18 and 27. Only 8:7b is absent in LXX ונתנה יהוה אלהיכם בידכם, and LXX-8a has κατὰ τὸ ῥῆμα τοῦτο ποιήσετε· instead of כדבר יהוה תעשׂו. Thus, textual data and literary-critical observations do not fully overlap.
* Mazor classes the plus in MT-Josh. 8:26 in the same category of stress on the divine participation,[51] but the Deity is not mentioned in this verse. Furthermore, it is hard to find a plausible religion-historical context in the Late Second Temple period for the insertion into the authoritative text of the idea of a magical function of the *kidon*. There is indeed reason to believe that this weapon should be seen as a magical instrument, but in that case one would rather ascribe verse 26 to a relatively early period in the history of the religion of Israel.
* Mazor also detects behind this plus in MT-Josh. 8:26 the wish to correlate the figures of Moses and Joshua. Unlike all other alleged motives behind the pluses in MT, this notion is well attested in the book of Joshua.[52] In all these cases, however, the MT is supported by LXX, and furthermore, the idea of correlation is stated explicitely. If Josh. 8:26 was the result of the same concern, one would have expected similar explicit statements.

Again there is every reason to disentangle the questions related to the formation of the Hebrew text, those concerning the reconstruction of the text of 4QJosh[a], and the question of the evaluation of the character of the Greek translation. These questions will be addressed in this order, although not as exhaustively as the passages discussed in the previous two chapters. Here, I will expand more briefly on the conclusions drawn in those chapters.

---

[51] L. Mazor, הסיפור אודות הנצחון על העי, pp. 95–96.

[52] See Josh. 1:6 כאשר הייתי עם־משה אהיה עמך = 3:7; 1:17 רק יהיה יהוה אלהיך עמך כאשר היה עם־משה, similarly in 4:14 ויראו אתו כאשר יראו את־משה כל־ימי חייו.

8.4 Redaction-Critical Analysis of the Hebrew Text

If the textual witnesses fully covered the literary formation process of our passage, one should be able to arrive at similar conclusions if textual and literary criticism are executed independently of each other. As we have seen already, this is not the case.

If we take as our point of departure the major plus in MT-Josh. 8:11b–13, the first thing to be taken into account is that the doublet is not restricted to the element of the sending of an ambush group. The designation of the position of the group has also been repeated. In fact, the whole of Joshua 8:10–13 constitutes a duplication of verses 3–9, as is evident from the following synopsis:

topic	version 1: Josh. 8:3–9		version 2: Josh. 8:10–13	
Joshua rises	ויקם יהושע וכל־עם המלחמה	3	וישכם יהושע בבקר ויפקד את־העם	10
destination Ai	לעלות העי	3	ויעל הוא וזקני ישראל לפני העם העי וכל־העם המלחמה אשר אתו עלו וינשו ויבאו נגד העיר	10
selection by Joshua	ויבחר יהושע	3	ויקח	12
number of men	שלשים אלף איש גברי החיל	3	כחמשת אלפים איש	12
initial location ambush	(Gilgal or Jericho)	–	מצפון לעי והני [ק] ביניו ובין־העי	11
instructions	verses 4–8		Ø	
sending by Joshua	וישלחם יהושע וילכו אל־המארב	9	וישם אותם ארב	12
location ambush	וישבו בין בית־אל ובין העי מים לעי	9	בין בית־אל ובין העי מים לעיר	12
action by Joshua	וילן יהושע בלילה ההוא בתוך העם	9	וילך יהושע בלילה ההוא בתוך העמק	13

The literary-critical seam between the two rival accounts of the ambush should therefore not be sought in 11b, i.e. the place where the quantitative differences between the versions start, but already in verse 10. From the viewpoint of literary growth, it should be noted that this first version is far more extensive and elaborated than the second. From a military point of view the number of 5,000 men in ambush seems to be more plausible than that of 30,000.

As Hartmut Rösel has demonstrated, this second, shorter version contains specific topographical information, which has been simplified in both the first Hebrew version and the Greek version of the whole chapter.[53] Rösel holds the second version to be the original of the

[53] H.N. Rösel, Studien zur Topographie, pp. 158–171.

two rival accounts and regarded these verses 8:10–13 to be the original continuation of Josh. 7:2–5a. Although in his view this older text should still be seen as a fictitious literary creation, its author must have had a very precise picture and knowledge of the geography around Ai, according to Rösel.[54] Rösel identifies the place where the ambush group were to hide as the hill now known as *Burǧmus*,[55] and the '*quarries*' or '*ravines*' (השברים) mentioned in MT-Josh. 7:5, i.e. the place where the inhabitants of Ai stopped pursuing the first group of Israelites (וירדפום לפני השער עד־השברים ויכום במורד) as the steep rock-formation east of present-day *Dēr Dibwān*, called *Qurnet Šaḥṭūra*.[56] Since the wadi in which Ai/*et-Tell* takes a central strategic position, runs east-west, the idea expressed in MT-Josh. 8:11 that the main Israelite force pitched its camp north of Ai, that is on one of the hills north of the wadi, out of direct sight of the inhabitants of Ai,[57] makes more sense than the simplified idea expressed in LXX, in which the Israelites arrive from the east of the city.[58]

With respect to the topographical information, the Greek text reflects a simplified and smoothened version. In contrast to version 2, the first version is far less specific regarding topography;[59] this information could easily have been taken from the second version.

---

[54] H.N. Rösel, Studien zur Topographie, p. 160: 'Obwohl der Feldzug Josuas gegen die Kanaanäerstadt Ai aller Wahrscheinlichkeit nach also nicht stattgefunden hat, scheint eine klare Konzeption vom topographischen Ablauf dieses fiktiven Feldzugs in der Schilderung niedergeschlagen zu haben.'

[55] H.N. Rösel, Studien zur Topographie, pp. 169–170.

[56] H.N. Rösel, Studien zur Topographie, p. 167. See also plates 16–17 at the end of the journal.

[57] H.N. Rösel, Studien zur Topographie, pp. 167–168: 'Für den Lagerplatz standen zwei Möglichkeiten zur Auswahl. Er konnte an einer geeigneten Stelle am Weg liegen, natürlich außer Sichtweise von Ai. Hier bot sich etwa die Ebene bei *Kafr Nāta* ca. 2 km südöstlich von *Dēr Dibwān* an. Bei dieser Wahl des Lagers wäre ein kompliziertes Umgehensmanöver um die Stadt nicht notwendig gewesen. Auch befände man sich am nächsten Morgen in der denkbar günstigsten Ausgangsposition für den Angriff auf die Stadt, deren Hügel nur gegen den Kessel von *Dēr Dibwān* hin sanft abfällt. Andererseits war ein solches Lager durch seine günstige Lage am Weg von Jericho nach Ai natürlich auch besonders gefährdet. Anscheinend aus diesem Grund ließ die Überlieferung Josua die zweite Möglichkeit wählen: Josua slug sein Lager gegenüber der Stadt auf, und zwar auf einem Hügel nördlich von Ai (8,11). Von hier aus konnte die Stadt gut beobachtet werden, andererseits bot das dazwischenliegende Tal guten Schutz.'

[58] H.N. Rösel, Studien zur Topographie, pp. 162, 167–169.

[59] 8:4 אתם ארבים לעיר מאחרי העיר אל־תרחיקו מן־העיר מאד, 8:9 וישבו בין בית־אל ובין העי מים לעי.

Furthermore, the Greek version of Josh. 7:5 does not contain an equivalent for the characteristic location השברים—*Qurnet Šaḥtūra*,[60] or the geographical phrase in MT-Josh. 8:14 למעוד לפני הערבה. Since the Greek translation was probably produced outside Palestine (Alexandria?), by a scholar who was probably not familiar with all the specific details of the geography of Israel (see section 7.6.4.1 above), it is more logical to ascribe this pattern of variants in geographical details to the ignorance of the Greek translator with respect to these specific toponyms,[61] than to assume that a later editor was overly concerned about the precise whereabouts of the events described in the narrative, as Auld holds (see section 7.4.5.1).

According to the second version, Joshua sent the 5,000 men in ambush at some point before reaching Ai, and with his army climbed some hill north of the wadi (הגי verse 11). By descending into the valley (עמק), again still under cover of the night (verse 13b), Joshua apparently tried to distract the attention of the men of Ai, so that the ambush group could take their position without being noticed. The clause 13b thus fits well in the context of this second version. Moreover, verse 14 perfectly concurs with this version, since it reports that the king of Ai and his men *rose up early* (וישכימו), apparently at daybreak. Since verse 14 marks the point in the present developed version where the two rival ambush accounts come together, it is clear that the originality of the verses 10–13 is supported by the verses immediately following this text.

The alternative (first) version of the story of the ambush is situated in the vicinity of Gilgal or Jericho and suggests that the 30,000 men were able to approach Ai all the way from Jericho and stay in ambush without being noticed for two successive nights, which is rather implausible. The purpose of this alternative narrative, however, is not to offer a narrative which is plausible from a military point of view, but rather to stress the superiority of Israel over its enemies. For that reason, elements from the original narrative are anticipated here, in order to assure the reader of Israel's success.

---

[60] See also J. Hollenberg, *Der Charakter*, pp. 10–11. The other versions also struggled with this name. Jerome transliterated it as *Sabarim*, Targum Jonathan (עַד דְּתַבַרוּנוּן) and Pešiṭta (ܥܕܡܐ ܕܐܬܬܒܪܘ.) tried to make sense out of the phrase by parsing the unvocalized Hebrew text as an infinitive Nipḥʿal with a third person plural suffix עַד הִשָּׁבְרָם, *until their being broken, until they were scattered.*

[61] H.N. Rösel, Studien zur Topographie, pp. 162–163.

These links are not confined to the pluses in MT *vis-à-vis* LXX, but also include phrases that are attested by both MT and LXX:

	Alternative version (Josh. 8:5–8)		Original version (Josh. 8:14–19)
8^{5}	והיה כי־יצאו לקראתנו καὶ ἔσται ὡς ἂν ἐξέλθωσιν *οἱ κατ-οικοῦντες Γαι* εἰς συνάντήιν ἡμῖν	8^{14}	ויצאו אנשי־העיר לקראת־ישראל καὶ ἐξῆλθεν --- --- --- εἰς συν-άντησιν αὐτοῖς *ἐπ᾽ εὐθείας*
8^{5}	ונסנו לפניהם καὶ φευξόμεθα ἀπὸ προσώπου αὐτῶν.	8^{15}	וינסו דרך המדבר --- --- --- --- ---
8^{6}	עד התיקנו אותם מן־העיר --- --- *ἀποσπάσομεν* αὐτοὺς	8^{16}	וינתקו מן־העיר καὶ *αὐτοὶ ἀπέστησαν* ἀπὸ τῆς πόλεως·
8^{7}	ואתם תקמו מהאורב ὑμεῖς *δὲ ἐξαναστήσεσθε* ἐκ τῆς ἐνέδρας	8^{19}	והאורב קם מהרה ממקומו καὶ τὰ ἔνεδρα ἐξανέστησαν ἐν τάχει ἐκ τοῦ τόπου αὐτῶν
8^{8}	תציתו את־העיר באשׁ --- --- --- --- ---	8^{19}	ויציתו את־העיר באשׁ --- ἐνέπρησαν τὴν πόλιν ἐν πυρί.

This redactor embedded the long discursive passage into the original narrative by means of the resumptive repetition וילך יהושע בלילה ההוא בתוך העמק of verse 13b in slightly modified form: וילן יהושע בלילה ההוא בתוך העם: once this group of 30,000 men had been sent, Joshua could spend the night undisturbed amidst the remaining people. The alteration of וילך to וילן is determined by the word וישכם in the original text. The element בלילה ההוא corresponds to that in verse 3 וישלחם לילה. This final clause in verse 9 thus fits in well with the addition of the whole passage Josh. 8:3–9. Therefore, the additional night (and subsequent day) in which the ambush group is to remain out of sight of the men of Ai, is adequately explained if we assume that the editor who created Josh. 8:3–9 carefully tried to integrate his expansion into the text, albeit at the cost of historical plausibility. This plus in MT thus forms part of the whole literary expansion consisting of verses 3–9, and there is no reason to ascribe it to a hand later than that responsible for the addition of whole Josh. 8:3–9.

The addition of verses 3–9 may be ascribed to the DtrH-layer of Joshua. Deuteronomistic concepts and expressions are clearly visible in the beginning and end of the chapter. Fully compliant with the Deuteronomistic law (Deut. 21:22–23) is the execution of the king of Ai and the burial of his corpse before sunset (cf. also Josh. 10:27):

> (21:22) If someone has committed a crime punishable by death and he is put to death, you will hang him on a tree (ותלית אתו על־העץ). (21:23) His body shall not remain overnight on the tree (לא־תלין נבלתו על־העץ), but you shall bury him the same day (כי־קבור תקברנו ביום ההוא), for a hanged man is accursed by God; you shall not defile your land which Yhwh your God is giving you as inheritance.

Equally Deuteronomistic is the divine command to take as booty only the spoil and the cattle and its execution in verses 2 and 27, which reflect the Deuteronomistic legislation found in Deut. 20:12–14:

> (20:12) But if it (i.e., a city under siege by the Israelites) makes no peace with you, but makes war with you (like Ai), then you shall besiege it; (20:13) and when the Lord your God gives it into your hand (ונתנה יהוה אלהיך בידך cf. Josh. 8:1.7.18) you shall put all its males to the sword (והכית את־כל־זכורה לפי־חרב cf. Josh. 8:24); (20:14) but the women and the little ones, the cattle and everything (רק הנשׁים והטף והבהמה וכל) else in the city; all its spoil, you shall take as booty for yourselves (כל־שׁללה תבז לך); and you shall enjoy the spoil of your enemies, which Yhwh your God has given you.

The execution of the command in Josh. 8:27 is expressly linked to the instruction in verse 2, and indirectly to the passage in Deut. 20:13–14 by means of the phrase כדבר יהוה. Another Deuteronomistic parallel to the destruction of the city and its inhabitants, be it in a somewhat different context, is offered by Deut. 13:16–17 (modern versions: Deut. 13:15–16), which orders the complete annihilation of an Israelite city (Deut. 13:13) whose inhabitants preach apostasy from Yhwh (Deut. 13:14):[62]

> (13:15) You shall surely put the inhabitants of that city to the sword הכה תכה את־ישׁבי העיר (cf. Josh. 8:22.24), put it under the ban and all that is in it (החרם אתה ואת־כל־אשׁר־בה cf. Josh. 8:26) and its cattle to the sword (ואת־בהמתה לפי־חרב) (13:16) You shall gather its spoil (ואת־כל־שׁללה תקבץ cf. Josh. 8:2.28) into the midst of its open square and burn the city with fire (ושׂרפת באשׁ את־העיר cf. Josh. 8:28) with all its spoil (ואת־כל־שׁללה) as a whole burnt offering for Yhwh your God;

[62] See e.g. T. Veijola, Wahrheit und Intoleranz nach Deuteronomium 13, in *ZThK* 92 (1995), pp. 287–314, especially pp. 305–306, who points to the literary affinities between the two texts.

it shall be a heap for ever (והיתה תל עולם cf. Josh. 8:28) it shall not be built again (לא תבנה עוד cf. Josh. 6:26).

This law differs from that in Deut. 20:13–14, and the Deuteronomistic narrative in Joshua 8, in that it does not even allow the Israelites to take cattle or spoil as booty, but agrees with the narrative in Joshua 6, where all living beings are put to the sword including even the animals,[63] except for Rahab and her family (6:22–23.25). Unlike the laws in Deut. 20, this passage contains the command to burn the city (שׂרף באשׁ) and turn it into an everlasting ruin (תל עולם), an expression that occurs in the Hebrew Bible only in Deut. 13:17 and Josh. 8:27.[64]

These Deuteronomistic concepts and expressions are not restricted to the first (8:1–2) and final (8:27–29) verses of the chapter, but related phrases are also found in Josh. 8:7–8. The so-called *Übergabeformel* נתן יהוה ביד in 8:7b (ונתנה יהוה אלהיכם בידכם) corresponds directly to verse 1 (נתתי בידך את־מלך העי . . .),[65] while the phrase כדבר יהוה תעשׂו corresponds closely to verse 27 כדבר יהוה. These Deuteronomistic phrases are not attested by LXX, but if textual criticism and literary criticism would coincide fully one would have expected to find Josh. 8:1–2 and 27–29 to be absent from LXX as well, which is not the case. Finally, the repeated stress on *all Israel* (כל־ישׂראל) in Josh. 8:1.3 (כל־עם המלחמה, contrast 8:11 כל־העם המלחמה אשׁר אתו), 8:15 (וינגעו יהושׁע וכל־ישׂראל לפניהם, contrast 8:16 ונתקו מן־העיר), 8:17 (וירדפו אחרי ישׂראל, contrast 8:16 וירדפו אחרי יהושׁע), 8:21 (ויהושׁע וכל־ישׂראל ראו וישׁבו, contrast 8:20 והעם הנס המדבר נהפך אל־הרודף) and 8:24 (וישׁבו כל־ישׂראל העי) may be ascribed to the Deuteronomist's emphasis on a unified Israel under the sole leadership of Joshua.[66]

---

[63] 6:21 ויחרימו את־כל־אשׁר בעיר מאישׁ ועד־אשׁה מנער ועד־זקן ועד שׁור ושׂה וחמור לפי־חרב.

[64] The Hebrew noun תֵּל, *tell, mound, heap of ruins*, elsewhere occurs only in Josh. 11:13, where we are told that the cities standing on their *tells* were spared from destruction by Israel (רק־כל־ערים העמדות על־תלם לא שׂרפם ישׂראל); in Jer. 49:2, which contains a similar formulation in an oracle about Ammon and its citadel Rabbah (והיתה לתל שׁממה ובנתיה באשׁ תצתנה); and Jer. 30:18, where the image of destruction is transformed into restauration: ונבנתה עיר על־תלה.

[65] This formula recurs in Joshua in 2:24; 6:2; 8:18; 10:8.19.30.32; 11:8; 21:44; 24:8.11; in Deuteronomy in 2:24.30; 3:2.3; 20:13; 21:10. See C. STEUERNAGEL, *Deuteronomium und Josua*, p. xxxviii, no. 61.

[66] See section 4.2.1 above. Cf. A. DILLMANN, *Die Bücher Numeri, Deuteronomium und Josua*, pp. 476–477.

On the basis of the criteria of literary-critical tensions and doublets on the one hand, and the occurrence of Deuteronomistic expressions in several verses on the other, it is possible to discern two literary strata in this chapter: [1] a Deuteronomistic layer (DtrH), to which verses 1–2, 3–9, 15, 17, 21–25, and 27–29 belong, and [2] an older pre-Deuteronomistic layer consisting of verses 10–14, 16, 18–20, and 26.

In the older narrative, Joshua and his men approached Ai and encamped north of the city on a hill above the valley (8:10–11). At night-time the people sent a group of men in ambush west of the city (8:12), probably behind the hill now known as *Burǧmus*, while Joshua descended into the valley in order to distract the attention of the men of Ai (8:13b). Thereupon the king of Ai and his men, expecting to defeat Joshua in the same manner as the scout group (Josh. 7:2–5a),[67] left the city early in the morning in eastern direction (לפני הערבה), lured away from the city by the feigned defeat of Joshua (8:16) and unaware of the ambush west of the city (8:14). There is no need to interpret the phrase למועד as term for dusk and alter the phrase לִפְנוֹת עֶרֶב, as suggested by Wellhausen,[68] since without the element למועד the phrases בלילה ההוא (verse 13)—וישכימו (verse 14) and לפני הערבה (verse 14) make perfect sense. Since the corresponding narrative Josh. 7:5a mentions the location of the descent (מורד), the old emendation of למועד into למורד still fits the context best.[69]

Only at this point in the narrative (8:18) does Yhwh intervene and promises the submission of the city (כי בידך אתננה), effected by the gesture of Joshua's raised hand holding the *kidon*. Simultaneously (כִנטות ידו) the men in ambush capture the city and set it on fire (8:19), so that the Israelite people (והעם) in the field can deal with the men of Ai (8:20), while Joshua himself does not lower the *kidon*

[67] Here I adopt the stratification of Josh. 7–8 proposed by H.N. Rösel, Studien zur Topographie, pp. 158–171. The second part of Josh. 7:5 contains the clause וימס לבב־העם, which is also found in the Deuteronomistic passages in the book of Joshua, 2:11 and 5:1, as well as in Deut. 1:28 and 20:8; further Isa. 13:7; 19:1; Ezek. 21:12; and Nah. 2:11; see further M. Weinfeld, *Deuteronomy and the Deuteronomic School*, p. 344, no. 15.

[68] J. Wellhausen, *Die Composition des Hexateuchs*², p. 126.

[69] See e.g. R. Smend sr., *Die Erzählung des Hexateuch*, p. 302, note 1. See further D. Barthélemy, *Critique textuelle* I, pp. 11–12, who preferred the *lectio difficilior*, with M. Noth, *Das Buch Josua*, p. 46; H.W. Hertzberg, *Die Bücher Josua, Richter, Ruth*, p. 58; J.A. Soggin, *Le livre de Josué*, p. 79.

until the inhabitants of the city have been put under the ban, that is: have been killed (8:26). In this narrative Joshua's raising his hand holding the *kidon* does not function primarily as a signal for the men in ambush (Joshua was probably out of sight of these men), but as a magical action that works *ex opere operato*, similar to the actions narrated in the old stories concerning Moses' staff (Exod. 17:8–13), Elijah's mantle (2 Kgs. 2:8), Elisha's arrows (2 Kgs. 13:14–19), the horns of the prophet Micaiah ben Imla (1 Kgs. 22:11) etc.[70]

This original narrative has been taken up by the Deuteronomistic historian, who transformed it into an idealized account of an exemplary victory over an enemy of *all Israel* according to the Deuteronomic Law, led by Joshua under the auspices of Yhwh. To this end the Deuteronomistic author took up the original submission formula כי בידך אתננה in verse 18 and elaborated this into the discursive text in 8:1–2, so that the divine assistance with Joshua and the divine control over the events would be stressed. Since Josh. 7:1.15–26 presents a coherent narrative about the sin of Achan that contains affinities with the Priestly literature (מעל in 7:1, compare Josh. 22:9–34, especially 22:16–20.22;[71] the theme of sin and transgression against Yhwh, 7:11, and also the very systematic procedure ordered and executed in 7:14.17–18), while Josh. 7:5b–9 contains the Deuteronomistic theme of the name (שֵׁם) of Yhwh,[72] it is possible that Josh. 8:1–2 originally formed the (DtrH) answer of Yhwh to Joshua's question in 7:5b–9. By taking up the ambush stratagem, the Deuteronomitic author gave away the plot of the original narrative (Josh. 8:12). The same holds true for the Deuteronomist's adaptation of verses 8:10–13 of the pre-DtrH account, in which the subsequent strategy of the original narrative (8:19) is anticipated (8:7–8).

Although verses 15 and 17 contain hardly any specific Deuteronomistic themes and expressions, they should be ascribed to this second layer as well, since they contain several doublets with verses 14 and 16. Verse 15 (וינגעו יהושע וכל־ישראל לפניהם וינסו דרך המדבר) is

---

[70] See O. Keel, *Wirkmächtige Siegeszeichen*; and further J. Lindblom, *Prophecy in Ancient Israel*. Oxford 1962.

[71] See section 4.2.3 above.

[72] See e.g. G. von Rad, *Das Gottesvolk im Deuteronomium*. (BWANT 11) Stuttgart 1929, p. 37; A.S. van der Woude, שֵׁם *šēm* Name, in *ThHAT* II, col. 935–963, especially col. 953–955.

related to the statement וינתקו מן־העיר in verse 16, the final clause in verse 17 וירדפו אחרי ישראל is a doublet of וירדפו אחרי יהושע in verse 16, and the clauses in verse 17 ולא־נשאר איש בעי ובית אל אשר לא־יצאו אחרי ישראל repeat information already presented in verse 14 ויצאו אנשי־העיר לקראת־ישראל. Common to these alterations is the stress on (all) Israel. If the aim of the DtrH author was to portray Joshua's conquest as complete and unconditional (Josh. 1, 12, 21:43–45), the mentioning of the men of Beth-El in 8:17 might reflect the tendency to transform the older Joshua conquest narratives into a narrative that contained the conquest of all Israelite cities, including Beth-El (Josh. 12:16).

Verses 21–25 do not contain many specific Deuteronomistic themes either, but do interrupt the coherence between verses 18–20 on the one hand and 26 on the other. Whereas 8:21 reports that Israel, including Joshua, turned around as soon as smoke was seen coming from the city (ויהושע וכל־ישראל ראו . . . וישבו ויכו את־אנשי העי), verse 26 presupposes that Joshua remained motionless until the victory was completed. Furthermore, the element וישבו in verse 21 is a repetition of נהפך in verse 20. Since we find the stress on *all Israel* again in verse 21, it is plausible to regard this part of the doublet 8:20.21 as the younger, Deuteronomistic strand. The final clause in verse 22 (עד־בלתי השאיר־לו שריד ופליט) has its parallels in Deut. 2:34; 3:3 (the two Trans-Jordanian territories ruled by Sihon and Og) and Josh. 10:28–43 in particular, where the phrase occurs six times (10:28 [Makkedah], 30 [Libnah], 33 [Lachish], 37 [Hebron], 39 [Debir], and 40 [the southern hill country and the Negeb]) and further in Josh. 11:8 (the northern coalition).[73] Interestingly, Josh. 10:28–43, commonly attributed to DtrH,[74] also frequently contains the phrase יהושע וכל־ישראל.[75] If Josh. 8:21–25 is seen as a secondary addition,

---

[73] See also Num. 21:36 (Heshbon); 2 Kgs. 10:11 (the house of Jehu); contrast Jer. 42:17; 44:14; Obad. 18 and Lam. 2:22, where the expression ולא יהיה שריד ופליט occurs. See further M. Weinfeld, *Deuteronomy and the Deuteronomic School*, p. 344, no. 16a.

[74] See e.g. J. Wellhausen, *Die Composition des Hexateuchs*², pp. 128–129; S.R. Driver, *Introduction*, p. 108; C. Steuernagel, *Deuteronomium und Josua*, p. 190; G.A. Cooke, *The Book of Joshua*, pp. 83–99; V. Fritz, *Das Buch Josua*, pp. 114–118.

[75] Josh. 10:29.31.34.36.38.43 and further Josh. 10:15. The expression כל־ישראל occurs elsewhere in the book of Joshua in 3:7.17; 4:14; 7:24.25; 8:15.21.24; 8:33; and 23:2.

the tension disappears between this version, which states that all inhabitants of Ai, up to 12,000 men (8:25) have been slain by all Israel (8:21 ויכו את־אנשי העי, 8:22 ויכו אותם, 8:24 ויהי ככלות ישׂראל להרג את־כל־ישׁבי העי בשׂדה במדבר אשׁר רדפום בו, 8:24 וישׁבו כל־ישׂראל העי ויכו אתה לפי־חרב), and the version in verse 26, where these inhabitants are killed once more (עד אשׁר החרים את כל־ישׁבי העי).

Although the notion of the חרם plays an important role in the Deuteronomistic conquest ideology (Deut. 2:34; 3:6.6; 7:2; 13:16; 20:17; Josh. 2:10; 6:18.21; 10:1.28.35.37.39.40; 11:11.12.21),[76] the occurrence of the verb חרם in the rival verse 26 in itself does not imply that this verse should also be ascribed to the Deuteronomistic reworking of this chapter, since the idea of consecration occurs in pre-DtrH passages as well (Num. 21:2; Judg. 1:17),[77] and is well-attested in documents from the *Umwelt* of Ancient Israel, including the Mesha stele:[78]

> (line 14) And Chemosh said to me: 'Go, capture Nebo from Israel.' (line 15) So I went by night and fought against it (ואהלך בללה ואלתחם בה) from the break of dawn until noon (מבקע השחרת עד הצהרם) (line 16) taking it and killing all (ואחזה ואהרג כלה), seven thousand men, boys, women, (line 17) girls and maid-servants, for I had devoted them to destruction for Ashtar-Chemosh (כי לעשתר כמש החרמתה).

Rather, the Deuteronomistic writer transformed the notion of the חרם found in the original text into a statement in conformity with the Deuteronomic Law (Deut. 20:14). He further added the notions of the complete and everlasting destruction of the city (8:28) and the proper execution and burial of its king (8:29) to the conclusion of the original narrative.[79]

---

[76] See N. Lohfink, חָרַם *ḥāram* חֵרֶם *ḥæræm*, in *ThWAT* III, col. 192–213, especially col. 209–212.

[77] N. Lohfink, חָרַם *ḥāram* חֵרֶם *ḥæræm*, col. 206–209.

[78] Text H. Donner, W. Röllig, *Kanaanäische und Aramäische Inschriften. Band I: Texte.* Wiesbaden 1962, no. 181; translation based upon that of W.F. Albright, The Palestinian Inscriptions, in J.B. Pritchard (ed.), *The Ancient Near East. An Anthology of Texts and Pictures.* Oxford 1958, pp. 209–210.

[79] N. Na'aman, The 'Conquest of Canaan' in the Book of Joshua and in History, in I. Finkelstein, N. Na'aman, *From Nomadism to Monarchy. Archaeological and Historical Aspects of Early Israel.* Jerusalem/Washington 1994, pp. 218–281, draws parallels between the impalement mentioned in Josh. 8:29 and 10:26–27, and the common Neo-Assyrian method of impalement of executed leaders of cities conquered by the

With this literary stratification the main exegetical problems mentioned in the first paragraph of this chapter can be solved on their own terms. An independent literary-critical analysis of the chapter does not confirm the thesis of literary growth attested by the ancient witnesses. The plus in MT-Josh. 8:11b–13 is part of the older version of the narrative (Josh. 8:10–14.16.18–20.26). The rival version, Josh. 8:3–9, can be placed in the context of the Deuteronomistic reworking of the narrative (Josh. 8:1–9, 15, 17, 21–25, 27–29). Therefore, the old thesis of Julius Wellhausen and others, i.e. that the longer MT is the older text, still remains unchallenged. If there was ever a Hebrew text which lacked MT-Josh. 8:11b–13, it must have been a deliberately condensed and stylized, hence secondary text.

8.5 4QJoshua[a]

But was there ever such an abbreviated Hebrew version of the narrative? A reconstruction of the text of 4QJoshua[a] seems to point in this direction. When, however, this text is reconstructed on its own terms, a completely different picture emerges.[80]

In order to assess the questions concerning the proper reconstruction of the text of 4QJoshua[a], it is necessary to return to the first fragments of this scroll, fragments 1–3, already discussed in section 7.5.1 above. Here follows the text of the first two fragments, constituting the first column of the scroll that has still been preserved (in part). Again, a computer drawing imitates the contours of the fragments:

Assyrians. The narrative of Joshua's conquest of southern Israel, Josh. 10:29–39, would then reflect Sennacherib's campaign to Judah of 701 BCE. If these verses are indeed a Judean answer to the Neo-Assyrian expansions, this would imply that the Deuteronomistic author of Josh. 8:1–9, 15, 17, 21–25, 26–29 and Josh. 10:26–43 should be dated to the period of Josiah rather than that of the Exile, see further section 4.2.4.1 above.

[80] I am indebted to Dr. E.J.C. Tigchelaar of the Qumran Institute, Groningen University, for his many helpful, painstaking and challenging personal comments (written 25 March 1998) on an earlier draft of this paragraph, which I presented as a lecture for the Groninger Oudtestamentische Kring on 15 December 1997.

4QJoshua[a] fragments 1–3

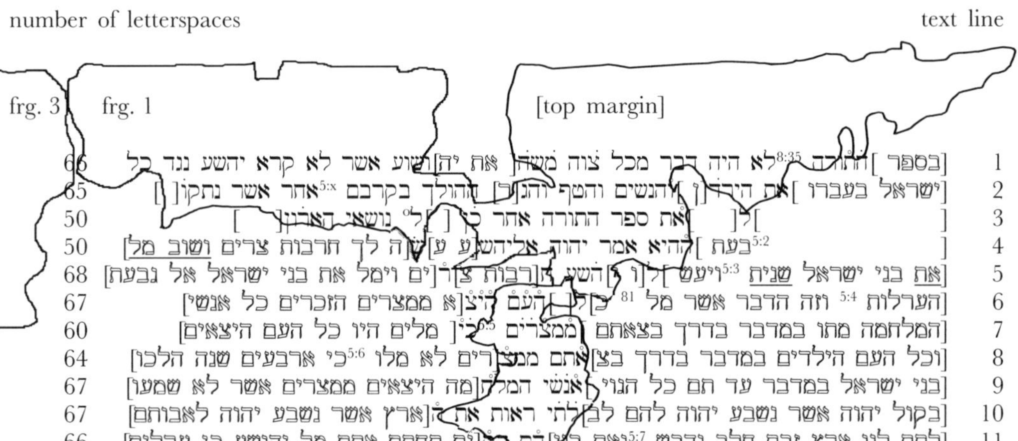

Lines without open (פ) or closed (ס) paragraphs (such as lines 4 and 13) contain 62–67 letterspaces. Since fragment 3 contains the top lines of the next column, it is possible to make a tentative reconstruction of the whole text of the first column preserved in 4QJoshua[a], on the basis of an average number of 65 letterspaces per line. Since the extant text from line 4 onwards corresponds almost completely with MT *vis-à-vis* LXX (see section 7.5.1 above), this reconstruction can be made on the basis of the MT text:

[81] The subject יהושע has been omitted in this reconstruction for reasons described in section 7.5.1 above.

4QJoshua[a] Column I: Joshua 8:34–35; 5:x; 5:2–6:5

frg. 3 frg. 1 [top margin]

number of letterspaces		text line
66	[בספר]התורה [8:35]לא היה דבר מכל צוה משה[את יה]ושע אשר לא קרא יהשע נגד כל	1
65	[ישראל בעברו]את הירד[ן]והנשים והטף והג[ר] ההולך בקרבם [5:x]אחר אשר נתקו[ ]	2
50	[ ]ל[ ]את ספר התורה אחר כן [ ]ל נושאי הארון[ ]	3
50	[ ]בעת [5:2]ההיא אמר יהוה אליהש[ע ע]שה לך חרבות צרים ושוב מל[	4
68	[את בני ישראל שנית [5:3]ויעש]ל[ו י]השע ח[רבות צ]רים וימל את בני ישראל אל גבעת[	5
67	[הערלות [5:4] וזה הדבר אשר מל כ]ל[ ]העם היצ[א ממצרים הזכרים כל אנשי[	6
60	[המלחמה מתו במדבר בדרך בצאתם]ממצרים [5:5]כי[מלים היו כל העם היצאים[	7
64	[וכל העם הילדים במדבר בדרך בצ]אתם ממצ[רים לא מלו [5:6]כי ארבעים שנה הלכו[	8
67	[בני ישראל במדבר עד תם כל הגוי]אנשי המלח[מה היצאים ממצרים אשר לא שמעו[	9
67	[בקול יהוה אשר נשבע יהוה להם לב]לתי ראות את ה[ארץ אשר נשבע יהוה לאבותם[	10
66	[לתת לנו ארץ זבת חלב ודבש [5:7]ואת בני]הם הק[ים תחתם אתם מל יהושע כי ערלים[	11
67	[היו כי לא מלו אותם בדרך [5:8]ויהי כאשר תמו כל הגוי להמול וישבו תחתם במחנה[	12
9	[עד חיותם [	13
66	[[5:9]ויאמר יהוה אל יהושע היום גלותי את חרפת מצרים מעליכם ויקרא שם המקום[	14
69	[ההוא גלגל עד היום הזה [5:10]ויחנו בני ישראל בגלגל ויעשו את הפסח בארבעה עשר[	15
66	[יום לחדש בערב בערבות יריחו [5:11]ויאכלו מעבור הארץ ממחרת הפסח מצות וקלוי[	16
69	[בעצם היום הזה [5:12]וישבת המן ממחרת באכלם מעבור הארץ ולא היה עוד לבני ישראל[	17
60	[מן ויאכלו מתבואת ארץ כנען בשנת ההיא [5:13]ויהי בהיות יהושע ביריחו[	18
73	[וישא עיניו וירא והנה איש עמד לנגדו וחרבו שלופה בידו וילך יהושע אליו ויאמר[	19
69	[לו הלנו אתה אם לצרינו [5:14]ויאמר לא כי אני שר צבא יהוה עתה באתי ויפל יהושע[	20
67	[אל פניו ארצה וישתחו ויאמר לו מה אדני מדבר אל עבדו [5:15]ויאמר שר צבא יהוה[	21
73	[אל יהושע של נעלך מעל רגלך כי המקום אשר אתה עמד עליו קדש הוא ויעש יהושע כן[	22
62	[[6:1]ויריחו סגרת ומסגרת מפני בני ישראל אין יוצא ואין בא [6:2]ויאמר יהוה[	23
70	[אל יהושע ראה נתתי בידך את יריחו ואת מלכה גברי החיל [6:3]וסבתם את העיר כל אנשי[	24
66	[המלחמה הקיף את העיר פעם אחת כה תעשה ששת ימים [6:4]ושבעה כהנים ישאו שבעה[	25
75	[שופרות היובלים לפני הארון וביום השביעי תסבו את העיר שבע פעמים והכהנים יתקעו[	26
68	[בשופרות [6:5]והיה במשך בקרן היובל בשמעכם את קול השופר יריעו כל העם תרועה[	27

Thus, this column contains 27 lines of circa 62–72 letterspaces each (lines containing paragraph endings excluded).[82] The total number of letterspaces in this column is circa 1700.[83] On the basis of these data it is also possible to make a tentative reconstruction of the following column II, of which the upper part has been preserved on fragments 3–8:

[82] Thus also E. Ulrich, 4QJosh[a], p. 144. My reconstruction differs somewhat from his (p. 147).

[83] The counting has been done manually and may contain some minor errors.

4QJoshua[a] Column II: Joshua 6:5–22

frg. 6 · frg. 4 (*top margin*) · frg. 3 · frg. 1

number of letterspaces			text line
52	(frg. 3–6)	גדולה ונפלה חמ°[ת העיר תחתיה]ועלה הע°[ם א]י°ש [נ]גדו [6:6ויקרא]	1
53	(frg. 3–5)	יהושע בן נון אל ה°[כהנים ויאמ]ר א°[ליהם] שאו א[ת ארון הברית]	2
56	(frg. 3, 5)	ושבעה כהנים ישא[ו שבעה שופרות יוב]ל°ים לפני א[רון יהוה 6:7ויאמר]	3
58	(frg. 3, 5, 7)	יהושע אל העם[עברו וסבו את העיר והח]ל°[וץ יעבר לפ]נ°[י ארו]ן° [יהוה]	4
53	(frg. 3, 7)	[6:8ויהי כ]א°מ°ר י[הושע אל העם ושבעה הכהנים נשאים שב]ע°ה שופ°ר[ות]	5
57	(frg. 3, 7–8)	[היובלים]ל°[פני יהוה עברו ותקעו בשופרו]ת וא°ר°[ו]ן ב°רית יה°ו°ה הולך	6
54	(frg. 7–8)	[אחריהם 6:9והחלוץ הלך לפני הכהנים תקעי] השפ°רות והמ°א°[ס]ף° הולך	7
58	(frg. 7–8)	[אחרי הארון הלוך ותקוע בשופרות 6:10ואת העם צוה י]הושע ל°א[מר]ל°[א]	8
55	(frg. 8)	[תריעו ולא תשמיעו את קולכם ולא יצא מפיכם דבר]עד י[ום אמרי]	9
54		[אליכם הריעו והריעתם 6:11ויסב ארון יהוה את העיר הקף פעם אחת]	10
25		[ויבאו המחנה וילינו במחנה]	11
55		[6:12וישכם יהושע בבקר וישאו הכהנים את ארון יהוה 6:13ושבעה הכהנים]	12
56		[נשאים שבעה שופרות היבלים לפני ארון יהוה הלכים הלוך ותקעו]	13
56		[בשופרות והחלוץ הלך לפניהם והמאסף הלך אחרי ארון יהוה הלוך]	14
57		[ותקוע בשופרת 6:14ויסבו את העיר ביום השני פעם אחת וישבו המחנה]	15
56		[כה עשו ששת ימים 6:15ויהי ביום השביעי וישכמו כעלות השחר ויסבו]	16
57		[את העיר כמשפט הזה שבע פעמים רק ביום ההוא סבבו את העיר שבע]	17
55		[פעמים 6:16ויהי בפעם השביעית תקעו הכהנים בשופרות ויאמר יהושע]	18
55		[אל העם הריעו כי נתן יהוה לכם את העיר 6:17והיתה העיר חרם היא]	19
55		[וכל אשר בה ליהוה רק רחב הזונה תחיה היא וכל אשר אתה בבית]	20
55		[כי החבאתה את המלאכים אשר שלחנו 6:18ורק אתם שמרו מן החרם פן]	21
55		[תחרימו ולקחתם מן החרם ושמתם את מחנה ישראל לחרם ועכרתם]	22
57		[אותו 6:19וכל כסף וזהב וכלי נחשת וברזל קדש הוא ליהוה אוצר יהוה]	23
54		[יבוא 6:20וירע העם ויתקעו בשפרות ויהי כשמע העם את קול השופר]	24
54		[ויריעו העם תרועה גדולה ותפל החומה תחתיה ויעל העם העירה]	25
55		[איש נגדו וילכדו את העיר 6:21ויחרימו את כל אשר בעיר מאיש ועד]	26
56		[אשה מנער ועד זקן ועד שור ושה וחמור לפי חרב 6:22ולשנים האנשים]	27

The relative position of the first words on fragment 3, of which both the top margin and the right margin have been preserved shows that these lines were somewhat shorter than the lines of column I and contain circa 52–58 letterspaces each. If one adopts the number of 27 lines from column I, this column stops in Josh. 6:22,[84] and contains some 1463 letterspaces. Again, the Hebrew text of 4QJosh[a] agrees with MT *vis-à-vis* LXX, e.g. in verses 6–7, where LXX has a large minus.[85]

[84] So also E. Ulrich, 4QJosh[a], pp. 143–144. Ulrich does not offer a full reconstruction of this column.

[85] See section 3.2.1 above.

4QJoshua[a] Column III: Josh. 6:22–7:12

number of letterspaces		text line
59	[המרגלים את הארץ אמר יהושע באו בית האשה הזונה והוציאו משם את]	1
54	[האשהו את כל אשר לה כאשר נשבעתם לה 6:23ויבאו הנערים המרגלים]	2
57	[ויציאו את רחב ואת אביה ואת אמה ואת אחיה ואת כל אשר לה ואת]	3
59	[משפחותיה הוציאו ויניחום מחוץ למחנה ישראל 6:24והעיר שרפו באש וכל]	4
58	[אשר בה רק הכסף והזהב וכלי הנחשת והברזל נתנו אוצר בית יהוה]	5
55	[6:25ואת רחב הזונהואת בית אביה ואת כל אשר לה החיה יהושע ותשב]	6
56	[בקרב ישראל עד היוםהזה כי החביאה את המלאכים אשר שלח יהושע]	7
13	[לרגל את יריחו]	8
59	[6:26וישבע יהושע בעת ההיא לאמר ארור האיש לפני יהוה אשר יקום ובנה]	9
63	[את העיר הזאת את יריחו בבכרו ייסדנה ובצעירו יציב דלתיה ויהי יהוה]	10
58	[את יהושע ויהי שמעו בכל הארץ 7:1וימעלו בני ישראל מעל בחרם ויקח]	11
58	[עכן בן כרמי בן זבדי בן זרח למטה יהודה מן החרם ויחר אף יהוה]	12
59	[בבני ישראל 7:2וישלח יהושע אנשים מיריחו העי אשר עם בית און מקדם]	13
62	[לבית אל ויאמר אליהם לאמר עלו ורגלו את הארץ ויעלו האנשים וירגלו]	14
61	[את העי 7:3וישבו אל יהושע ויאמרו אליו אל יעל כל העם כאלפים איש או]	15
61	[כשלשת אלפים איש יעלו ויכו את העי אל תיגע שמה את כל העם כי מעט]	16
61	[המה 7:4ויעלו מן העם שמה כשלשת אלפים איש וינסו לפני אנשי העי 7:5ויכו]	17
62	[מהם אנשי העי כשלשים וששה איש וירדפום לפני השער עד השברים ויכום]	18
60	[במורד וימס לבב העם ויהי למים 7:6ויקרע יהושע שמלתיו ויפל על פניו]	19
61	[ארצה לפני ארון יהוה עד הערב הוא וזקני ישראל ויעלו עפר על ראשם]	20
61	[7:7ויאמר יהושע אהה אדני יהוה למה העברת העביר את העם הזה את הירדן]	21
58	[לתת אתנו ביד האמרי להאבידנו ולו הואלנו ונשב בעבר הירדן 7:8בי אדני]	22
63	[מה אמר אחרי אשר הפך ישראל ערף לפני איביו וישמעו הכנעני וכל ישבי]	23
59	[הארץ ונסבו עלינו והכריתו את שמנו מן הארץ ומה תעשה לשמך הגדול]	24
58	[7:10ויאמר יהוה אל יהושע קם לך למה זה אתה נפל על פניך 7:11חטא ישראל]	25
62	[וגם עברו את בריתי אשר צויתי אותם וגם לקחו מן החרם וגם גנבו וגם]	26
59	[כחשו וגם שמו בכליהם 7:12ולא יכלו בני ישראל לקום לפני איביהם ערף]	27

Although no fragments of this column have been preserved, its text can be reconstructed fairly easily and without difficulties after MT, as the beginning lines of the next column (IV) and part of the preceding column (II) are still extant. Like the preceding two columns this column must have contained 27 lines, with some 1550 letterspaces, one line (8) containing a *petucha* (between 6:25 and 6:26), and one line (24) with a *setumah* (between 7:9 and 7:10) corresponding to the *parasiyyot* division of the Leningrad Codex.[86]

[86] Codex Aleppo seems to have two additional *setumot*, between 6:26 and 6:27 and between 7:1 and 7:2.

4QJoshua[a] Column IV: Joshua 7:12–8:3

number of letterspaces	frg. 9 ii frg. 9 i		text line
		[top margin]	
52	frg. 9 i	[יפנו לפ]נ֯[י] א֯י֯ב֯י֯ו֯ ולא פנים כי היו לחרם ולא אוסיף להיות	1
51	frg. 9 i	[עמכם אם] לא תשמידו החרם מקרבכם [7:13]קום קדש את העם ואמרת	2
51	frg. 9 i	[התקדשו]ל֯מחר כי כה אמר יהוה אלהי ישראל חרם בקרבכם	3
54	frg. 9 i	[ישראל ל]א֯ תוכל ל֯ק֯ו֯ם לפני אויביכם עד [87]הסירכם החרם מקרבכם	4
52	frg. 9 i	[[7:14]ונקרבתם]ב֯ב֯ק֯ר לשבט[יכם ו]ה֯י֯ה֯ השבט אשר ילכדנו יהוה תקריבו	5
55	frg. 9 i–10	[ל]ב֯ת֯י֯ם [והבית]א֯ש֯[ר]ילכדנו יהו[ה]ת֯ק֯רב לגברים [7:15]והיה הנלכד בהם	6
53	frg. 9 i–10	[ש]ר֯ף[ ] באש אתו ואת כל אשר לו כי [ ]ע֯בר את ב֯רית יהוה כי עשה	7
12	frg. 9 i	[נבלה בישראל	8
52	frg. 9 i	[[7:16]וישכם יהושע]בבקר ויקרב את ישר֯אל ל]ש֯ב֯טיו וילכד את֯[שבט]	9
62	frg. 11–12	[יהודה [7:17]וי]ק֯ר֯ב֯[ ]את משפחות יהודה וילכד א֯ת [משפח]ת הזרחי ויקרב את]	10
63	frg. 11	[משפחת]ה֯ז֯ר֯[ח]י לגברים וילכד זבדי [7:18]ויקרב את ביתו לגברים וילכד עכן בן]	11
64		[כרמי בן זבדי בן זרח למטה יהודה [7:19]ויאמר יהושע אל עכן בני שים נא כבוד]	12
69		[ליהוה אלהי ישראל ותן לו תודה והגד נא לי מה עשית אל תכחד ממני [7:20]ויען עכן]	13
65		[את יהושע ויאמר אמנה אנכי חטאתי ליהוה אלהי ישראל וכזאת וכזאת עשיתי]	14
60		[[7:21]וארא בשלל אדרת שנער אחת טובה ומאתים שקלים כסף ולשון זהב אחד]	15
64		[חמשים שקלים משקלו ואחמדם ואקחם והנם טמונים בארץ בתוך האהלי והכסף]	16
65		[תחתיה [7:22]וישלח יהושע מלאכים וירצו האהלה והנה טמונה באהלו והכסף תחתיה]	17
65		[[7:23]ויקחום מתוך האהל ויבאום אל יהושע ואל כל בני ישראל ויצקם לפני יהוה]	18
66		[[7:24]ויקח יהושע את עכן בן זרח ואת הכסף ואת האדרת ואת לשון הזהב ואת בניו]	19
69		[ואת בנתיו ואת שורו ואת חמרו ואת צאנו ואת אהלו ואת כל אשר לו וכל ישראל]	20
64		[עמו ויעלו אתם עמק עכור [7:25]ויאמר יהושע מה עכרתנו יעכרך יהוה ביום הזה]	21
67		[וירגמו אתו כל ישראל אבן וישרפו אתם באש ויסקלו אתם באבנים [7:26]ויקימו עליו]	22
68		[גל אבנים גדול עד היום הזה וישב יהוה מחרון אפו על כן קרא שם המקום ההוא]	23
40		[עמק עכור עד היום הזה [8:1]ויאמר יהוה אל יהושע]	24
65		[אל תירא ואל תחת קח עמך את כל עם המלחמה וקום עלה העי ראה נתתי בידך]	25
63		[את מלך העי ואת עמו ואת עירו ואת ארצו [8:2]ועשית לעי ולמלכה כאשר עשית]	26
68		[ליריחו ולמלכה רק שללה ובהמתה תבזו לכם שים לך ארב לעיר מאחריה [8:3]ויקם]	27

Since fragment 9 contains both the endings of the first lines of column IV and the beginnings of the first lines of the next column (V), which starts with the second word of Josh. 8:3, it is clear that the last word in this column IV must have been the first of Josh. 8:3. If the text between this last word and the words attested in fragments

[87] The transliteration offered by E. Ulrich, 4QJosh[a], p. 149, with a *ḥet*: חסירכם instead of הסירכם with a *he* (thus MT and the *versiones*) no doubt represents a typographical error.

9 i and 10–12 is reconstructed on the basis of the MT, assuming circa 53 letterspaces per line, which is the average number for the first nine lines attested by fragment 9 i, this column must have contained 30 lines instead of the 27 of the preceding three columns.[88] In the present reconstruction, the number of 27 lines per column has been retained. As a consequence, the average number of letterspaces per line has been increased to 65, which corresponds to the size of the first lines in column I. The fixed position of the words on fragment 12 already indicates that line 10 must have been longer than the preceding lines, and that this line must have consisted of 62 letterspaces. In the present reconstruction, the open paragraph ending (פ) between Josh. 7:26 and Josh. 8:1, attested by the three main Masoretic codices (Leningrad, Aleppo, Cairo), has been altered into a closed paragraph ending (ס). It is not impossible either, that the text of 4QJosh[a] was slightly shorter than MT, perhaps due to parablepsis. In line 5 (fragment 9 i), the text of 4QJosh[a] lacks six phrases due to homoioteleuton:[89]

השבט אשר־ילכדנו יהוה [יקרב למשפחות והמשפחה אשר־ילכדנה הוה]

With due caution we may so far conclude, that the columns of 4QJosh[a] once contained circa 27 lines, with circa 50–65 letterspaces per line. With respect to its textual character it should be noted that 4QJosh[a] corresponds closely to MT and does not support the thesis of a shorter Hebrew *Vorlage* behind LXX in passages such as Josh. 5:2–7 (fragment 2, see the discussion in section 7.5.1 above) and Josh. 6:6–7 (fragments 3–6). Where 4QJosh[a] differs from MT it is only in minor matters due to scribal variation or scribal error (like the case of parablepsis mentioned above).[90]

If we now turn to the text of our passage, which in 4QJosh[a] has been preserved in part in column V, we see these observations hold true for the first lines of this column as well. The text of the first five lines, preserved in part in fragments 9 ii and 13, can be reconstructed after MT without difficulties:

---

[88] This is probably how E. Ulrich, 4QJosh[a] reconstructs this column, since he writes (p. 144): 'The number of lines per column can be estimated as *c.* 27–30.'

[89] See section 3.2.1 above.

[90] See section 3.2.1 above.

number of letterspaces		frg. 9 ii	frg. 9 i
		[top margin]	
57	(frg. 9 ii)	יהושע וכל עם המלחמה [לעלות העי ויבחר יהושע שלשים אלף איש]	1
51	(frg. 9 ii)	גבורי החיל וישלחם ל[ילה 8:4ויצו אתם לאמר ראו אתם ארבים]	2
58	(frg. 9 ii)	אל העיר מאח[רי העיר אל תרחיקו מן העיר מאד והייתם כלכם נכנים]	3
59	(frg. 9 ii)	8:5ואני וכל[העם אשר אתי נקרב אל העיר והיה כי יצאו לקראתנו כאשר]	4
55	(frg. 9 ii + 13)	בראשנ[ה ונסנו לפניהם 8:6ויצאו]אחרינו עד[התיקנו אותם מן העיר]	5

Line lenghts range from 51 to 59 letterspaces. The text contains the minor variant אֶל העיר *vis-à-vis* MT לָעיר, while the whole prepositional phrase is absent from LXX. On the other hand, the plus in LXX *vis-à-vis* MT in Josh. 8:5, where the subject of יצאו has been amplified by οἱ κατοικοῦντες Γαι, perhaps under influence of the parallel passage in MT-Josh. 8:14 (ויצאו אנשי־העיר) finds no support in 4QJosh[a], since a reconstruction of the longest of these first five lines in 4QJosh[a] column V leaves no room for the additional eight letterspaces ישבי העי. Moreover, 4QJosh[a] supports MT *vis-à-vis* LXX with respect to the minor quantitative variant concerning the preposition עַד, absent from LXX.

Although the final clause in Josh. 8:6 ונסנו לפניהם in all likelihood represents a doublet inspired by the double occurrence of the phrase כאשר בראשנה in 8:5 and 8:6,[91] it is noteworthy that a reconstruction of line 6 of 4QJosh[a] column V would result in an unusually short line of only 49 letterspaces. Therefore, it is likely that 4QJosh[a] supports the longer MT.[92] With lines 7–9, extant in three lines of fragment 14, some problems arise. According to Ulrich, 'The relative

[91] Thus most of the commentaries ad loco, e.g. J. Hollenberg, *Der Charakter*, p. 19; A. Dillmann, *Die Bücher Numeri, Deuteronomium und Josua*, p. 473; E. Albers, *Die Quellenberichte in Josua I–XII*, p. 111; S. Oettli, *Das Deuteronomium und die Bücher Josua und Richter*, p. 148; H. Holzinger, *Das Buch Josua*, p. 25; S. Holmes, *Joshua*, p. 41; G.A. Cooke, *The Book of Joshua*, p. 64; M.L. Margolis, *The Book of Joshua in Greek*, p. 126; M. Noth, *Das Buch Josua*[2], p. 44; P.D. Baldi, *Giosuè*, p. 62; J.A. Soggin, *Le livre de Josué*, p. 72; R.G. Boling, *Joshua*, p. 233; T.C. Butler, *Joshua*, p. 78; V. Fritz, *Das Buch Josua*, p. 87; L. Mazor, הסיפור אודות הנצחון על העי, p. 77; R.D. Nelson, *Joshua*, p. 108, note e. Although the presence of this clause can only be explained as a dittography from verse 5, this does not imply that the Greek text, in which these words are absent, attests to an earlier stage of the Hebrew text in which these words had not yet entered the text of verse 6; thus e.g. D. Barthélemy, *Critique textuelle*, p. 10. See further below.

[92] E. Ulrich, 4QJosh[a], p. 150, too, includes these words in his reconstruction of the line.

position of the words in these three lines appears to require a shorter text similar to that in 𝔊.'[93] This statement seems to be true only for line 7, which would contain 65 letterspaces, if reconstructed after MT. Line 8, however, counts 54 letterspaces and fits in well with the average of 50–60 letterspaces:

65 [והורשתם]את הע[יר ונתנה יהוה אלהיכם בידכם 8:8 והיה כתפשכם את העיר תציתו] 7
54 [את הע]י֯ר באש֯[כדבר יהוה תעשו ראו צויתי אתכם 8:9 וישלחם יהושע] 8
[ויל]כ֯ו א֯ל֯[ ] 9

The LXX does offer a shorter text here, but lacks the whole of verses 7b–8a. As noted above, 4QJosh[a] contains remnants of the clause [תציתו] line 8 [את הע]י֯ר באש֯, which is absent from LXX. It is thus clear that one cannot reconstruct line 7 of 4QJosh[a] column V mechanically on the basis of the LXX text. Even if only the first half of the minus in LXX *vis-à-vis* MT, i.e. the final clause of Josh. 8:7, was lacking in line 7 of 4QJosh[a]-col. V, this line would be unusually short, i.e. contain only 41 letterspaces:

41 [והורשתם]א֯ת הע[יר 8:8 והיה כתפשכם את העיר תציתו] 7
54 [את הע]י֯ר באש֯[כדבר יהוה תעשו ראו צויתי אתכם 8:9 וישלחם יהושע] 8
[ויל]כ֯ו א֯ל֯[9

In the light of the haplography in line 5 of column IV (fragment 9 i, Josh. 7:14), the suggestion made by L.J. Greenspoon that the text of 4QJosh[a] suffered from haplography due to homoioteleuton from כתפשכם]את העיר תציתו[את העיר, seems to be the more plausible solution to the problem.[94] Without the words את העיר תציתו, the text remains intelligible and results in a line consisting of 51 letterspaces, which corresponds to the length of line 2 in the same column:[95]

---

[93] E. Ulrich, 4QJosh[a], p. 150.

[94] L.J. Greenspoon, The Qumran Fragments of Joshua, p. 170.

[95] In his private communication (25 March 1998), E. Tigchelaar made an alternative suggestion for the reconstruction of this line, i.e. to leave out the words יהוה אלהיכם instead of את העיר תציתו, and take the verb ונתנה as a Niph'al. In that case, the line would contain 53 letterspaces. It remains unclear, however, how these important words יהוה אלהיכם could have dropped from the text, or vice versa why these words were added, if the text attested by MT contains the standard Deuteronomistic expression. For these reasons, the reconstruction proposed by L.J. Greenspoon is preferable.

51 [והורשתם]את העי֯ר ונתנה יהוה אלהיכם בידכם 8:8 והיה כתפשכם] 7
54 [את העי]ר֯ באש[כדבר יהוה תעשו ראו צויתי אתכם 8:9 וישלחם יהושע] 8
[ויל]כ֯ו֯ אל[[9

If the text of 4QJosh[a] is reconstructed properly on its own terms, there is no reason to believe that it was related to a postulated Hebrew *Vorlage* of LXX deviating from MT. This situation would change, if we included fragment 15 in the same column of 4QJoshua[a]. As we have seen in section 8.2.2 above, a reconstruction of line 12 after MT would result into a line that would be four times longer (210 letterspaces) than the surrounding lines (51 to 59 letterspaces). Although less problematic, line 7 would also be unusually long with 70 letterspaces.[96] The quantitative agreement between 4QJosh[a] and LXX would be supported by the double absence of the word ישראל in Josh. 8:10 (lines 10–11) and Josh. 8:14 (lines 13–14).

It should be noted that the whole matter of this alleged 4QJosh[a]—LXX agreement pertains to fragment 15 only. According to Ulrich, the variant Hebrew text of fragment 15 is supported by the tiny fragment 16, which he places on lines 12 and 13.[97]

] [הע֯יר
] י֯מהר[ו

The text contained in this fragment [הע֯י]ר and י֯מהר]ו might just as well reflect Josh. 8:18.19, where we find the same words in the same order:[98]

60 [אתננה ויט יהושע בכידון אשר בידו אל] הע֯י֯ר 8:19 והאורב קם מהרה ממקומו]
57 [וירוצו כנטות ידו ויבאו העיר וילכדוה ו]ימהר[ו ויציתו את העיר]

[96] In his private communication dated 25 March 1998, E. Tigchelaar suggested a *vacat* behind the words בתוך העם in line 10. In that case, fragment 15 would be moved somewhat more to the left, so that the lines following the rather long line 9 would end at more or less the same vertical position as line 9. This, however, only increases the problems of the gaps in the text of lines 11 and 13. Furthermore, none of the extant textual witnesses (MT-Leningrad, Aleppo, Cairo, LXX-mss. and Peš-mss.) contain a *setumah* between 8:9 and 8:10.

[97] E. Ulrich, 4QJosh[a], p. 150.

[98] In his private communication dated 25 March 1998, E. Tigchelaar pointed out to me that after the letters]י֯מהר֯[the remains of the stroke of a *lamedh* is visible on the photo (PAM.43.060). If the dark point between the letters of these lines really points to a reading]י֯מהר֯ ל֯[, this would imply that the fragment should not be identified with Josh. 8:11.14 or Josh. 8:18–19, but with yet another passage. All

Furthermore, a reconstruction of lines 10–14 of 4QJoshua[a] including fragment 14 after LXX may solve the problem of the extraordinary length of line 12, but does not solve all problems. In Ulrich's reconstruction, line 11 would contain only 42 letterspaces and line 13 only 43 letterspaces, which is unusually short as compared to the number of 52 to 59 letterspaces for lines 1–5 of the column:

51	[והורשתם]את הע[יר ונתנה יהוה אלהיכם בידכם [8:8]והיה כתפשכם]	7
54	[את הע]י֯ר ב֯אש[כדבר יהוה תעשו ראו צויתי אתכם [8:9]וישלחם יהושע]	8
70	[ויל]כ֯ו א֯ל[המארב וישבו בין בית אל ובין העי מים לעי ולין יהושע בלילה ההוא]	9
55	[בתוך העם [8:10]וישכם יהושע בבקר ויפקד את העם ויעל הוא ו]הזקנים	10
42	[________לפני העם העי [8:11]וכל העם המלחמה אשר א]תו וישבו	11
210	[<circa 200 additional letterspaces> [8:14]וי]הי כראות	12
43	[מלך העי ימהרו________וישכימו ויצאו אשני העיר לק]ר֯אתם	13
45 (sec. manu)	[[8:18?]ויאמר יהוה אל יהושע נטה בכידון אשר ב]ידך אלהעי	14?

bottom margin

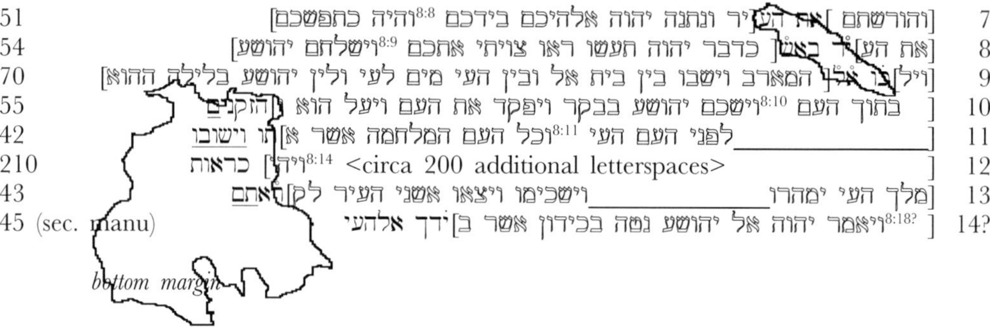

The fixed position of the words on fragment 15 makes clear that if the remaining text were reconstructed after Josh. 8:10–14, this would leave some unexplainable gaps in the text of lines 11 and 13. This problem becomes even graver, if one reconstructs the text of these lines after LXX, as has been done by L. Mazor:[99]

51	[והורשתם]את הע[יר ונתנה יהוה אלהיכם בידכם [8:8]והיה כתפשכם]	7
54	[את הע]י֯ר ב֯אש[כדבר יהוה תעשו ראו צויתי אתכם [8:9]וישלחם יהושע]	8
48	[ויל]כ֯ו א֯ל[המארב וישבו בין בית אל ובין העי מים לעי________]	9
46	[________[8:10]וישכם יהושע בבקר ויפקד את העם ויעל הוא ו]הזקנים	10
42	[________לפני העם העי [8:11]וכל העם המלחמה אשר א]תו וישבו	11
50	[________ויבאו נגד העיר מקדם ומארב העיר מים [8:14]ויה]י כראות	12
25	[מלך העי ימהרו________ויצא לק]ר֯אתם	13
45 (sec. manu)	[[8:18?] ויאמר יהוה אל יהושע נטה בכידון אשר ב]ידך אלהעי	14?

bottom margin

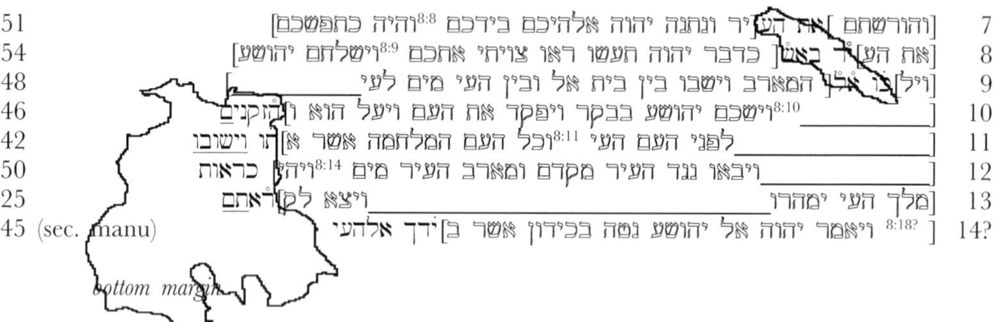

the more reason to question the idea that this fragment supports a shorter Hebrew text of Josh. 8:11–14.

[99] L. Mazor, הסיפור אודות הנצחון על העי, pp. 88–89. She designates this fragment 15 as fragment 14 and seems to have been unaware of the existence of fragment 16.

Even more problematic is the fact that fragment 15 contains a bottom margin. The empty space on the fragment below the last words leaves enough room for the last words of an additional line. Since a paragraph ending (פ or ס) *after* the first words of Josh. 8:18 and onwards is not attested by any textual witness (the Leningrad, Cairo, and Aleppo codices, the lay-out of the Greek manuscripts, and the paragraphing system in the Pešiṭta manuscripts), and would be highly surprising from a narrative point of view, the empty space below the last words can only be interpreted as a bottom margin. The conclusion would be, that this column contains half as many lines (14) as the preceding four columns (27 lines each, column IV perhaps even 30 lines). This would be highly unusual for a Qumran biblical scroll.

Although the variant readings in line 10 ([ו]הׄזקנים]—זקני ישראל MT-Josh. 8:10) and line 13 (לק[ראׄתם]—לקראת־ישראל MT-Josh. 8:14) can be explained with the aid of LXX, the variant reading וישובו in line 11 remains unexplainable. LXX-Joshua (ἀνέβησαν) supports MT (עלו). From a narrative point of view, it remains unaccountable how the verb שׁוב could function in the context of Josh. 8:11, where it is stated that Joshua marched with his warriors to Ai. The mentioning of a return of this army (either from Ai back to Gilgal or from Gilgal back to Ai) makes no sense, since only a group of 30,000 men in ambush has been sent to Ai (verse 9) and a small group of 3,000 men as vanguard (7:4–5) had been in the vicinity of Ai. Moreover, the initial *waw* suggests the beginning of a new clause, rather than the continuation of a previous clause 9 (as in MT and LXX). There is thus every reason to believe that this fragment did *not* belong to 4QJoshua[a] column V, a suggestion already succinctly made by K. Bieberstein.[100]

This of course raises the question where then to place this fragment within or outside 4QJoshua[a], a question I have not been able to answer. The only element in the fragment that links this piece of leather to Joshua 8 is the word that was written by the younger

[100] K. Bieberstein, *Lukian und Theodotion*, p. 81: 'Nach der Ausgabe von Tov beziehe sich ein weiteres Fragment [i.e. Frg. 15?] angeblich ebenfalls auf Jos 8,3–5. Doch ergibt sich nach den auf dem Fragment lesbaren Worten im gesamten Josuabuch keine sinnvolle Rekonstruktion. Vermütlich gehört das Fragment zu einem anderen Werk.'

hand (אלהעי). The words in the preceding lines]ראתם—כראות [ ] הזקנים [ ]—וישׁובו—only suggest that this fragment formed part of a narrative. There is no other passage in Joshua where this combination occurs, nor any other biblical passage, either in MT or in extended versions such as 4QReworkedPentateuch. I know of no Qumran fragment that contains the same combination of these two hand writings. In a private communication Eibert Tigchelaar pointed out to me that both the hand of the first four lines of this fragment and the material (leather) on which these lines were written very much resemble the hand and material of the (other) fragments of 4QJosh[a]. Common to all these fragments is the exceptional feature of unusually large pores in the leather.[101] This would imply that these fragments were written by the same hand on the same type of material, but need not necessarily imply that this fragment belonged to 4QJosh[a] column V. Perhaps this situation can be compared with that of 4Q365a, the hand of which happens to resemble that of our fragments: because of its physical characteristics it has been ascribed to 4QReworkedPentateuch[c], but on the basis of the contents several scholars regard it as a copy of the Temple Scroll.[102]

Notwithstanding the unsolved problem of the proper identification of the text of the first four lines of this fragment and the purpose of the secondary addition of the fifth line, we may still conclude on the basis of [1] the physical restoration of 4QJosh[a] column V, [2] the contents of the extant text, and [3] the general observations that 4QJosh[a] reflects the MT of Joshua with some minor variants—while the Greek translation of Joshua is characterized by many literary initiatives intended to enhance the readability and comprehensibility of the text—this fragment does not belong to 4QJosh[a] column V. 4QJosh[a] does not support the thesis of a shorter Hebrew version of Joshua 8, which would also be reflected by LXX. If this reconstruction is acceptable, it has consequences for the Ebal-passage, as

[101] See E. Ulrich, 4QJosh[a] (DJD XIV), p. 144.

[102] See S. White, 4Q365a (4QTemple?), in H. Attridge, T. Elgvin, J. Milik, S. Olyan, J. Strugnell, E. Tov, J. VanderKam, S. White (eds.), *Qumran Cave 4.VIII. Parabiblical Texts, Part I.* (DJD 13) Oxford 1994, pp. 319–333; and F. García Martínez, New Perspectives on the Study of the Dead Sea Scrolls, in F. García Martínez, E. Noort (eds.), *Perspectives in the Study of the Old Testament and Early Judaism. A Symposium in Honour of Adam S. van der Woude on the Occasion of his 70th Birthday.* (SVT 73) Leiden/Boston/Köln 1998, pp. 230–248.

we shall see in the next chapter. For the sake of completeness, a new reconstruction of column V—that is without fragment 15 and with fragment 16 at a lower position reflecting Josh. 8:18.19 instead of Josh. 8:11–14—is now offered below:

4QJoshua[a] Column V (without fragment 15): Josh. 8:3–21

number of letterspaces		frg. 9 ii / frg. 9 i	
		[top margin]	
57	(frg. 9 i)	יהושע וכל עם המלחמ̊ה [לעלות העי ויבחר יהושע שלשים אלף איש]	1
51	(frg. 9 i)	גבורי החיל וישלח̊ם ל[ילה 8:4 ויצו אתם לאמר ראו אתם ארבים]	2
58	(frg. 9 i)	אל העיר מא̊ח[רי העיר אל תרחיקו מן העיר מאד והייתם כלכם נכנים]	3
59	(frg. 9 i)	8:5 ואני וכל̊[העם אשר אתי נקרב אל העיר והיה כי יצאו לקראתנו כאשר]	4
55	(frg. 9 i + 13)	בר̊אש̊[נה ונסנו לפניהם 8:6 ויצאו]א̊חרינו ע̊ד̊[התיקנו אותם מן העיר]	5
61		[כי יאמרו נסים לפנינו כאשר בראשנה ונסנו לפניהם 8:7 ואתם תקמו מהאורב]	6
51	(frg. 14)	[והורשתם]את הע̊[יר ונתנה יהוה אלהיכם בידכם 8:8 והיה כתפשכם]	7
54	(frg. 14)	[את הע]י̊ר באש̊[כדבר יהוה תעשו ראו צויתי אתכם 8:9 וישלחם יהושע]	8
59	(frg. 14)	[ויל]כו א̊ל̊[המארב וישבו בין בית אל ובין העי מים לעי ולין יהושע]	9
56		[בלילה ההוא בתוך העם 8:10 וישכם יהושע בבקר ויפקד את העם ויעל הוא]	10
58		[וזקני ישראל לפני העם העי 8:11 וכל העם המלחמה אשר אתו עלו וינשו]	11
60		[ויבאו נגד העיר ויחנו מצפון לעי והגי בינו ובין העי 8:12 ויקח כחמשת]	12
59		[אלפים איש וישם אותם ארב בין בית אל ובין העי מים לעיר 8:13 וישימו]	13
59		[העם את כל המחנה אשר מצפון לעיר ואת עקבו מים לעיר וילך יהושע]	14
54		[בלילה ההוא בתוך העמק 8:14 ויהי כראות מלך העי וימהרו וישכימו]	15
57		[ויצאו אנשי העיר לקראת ישראל למלחמה הוא וכל עמו למועד לפני]	16
55		[הערבה והוא לא ידע כי ארב לו מאחרי העיר 8:15 וינגעו יהושע וכל]	17
51		[ישראל לפניהם וינסו דרך המדבר 8:16 ויזעקו כל העם אשר בעיר]	18
53		[לדרף אחריהם וירדפו אחרי יהושע וינתקו מן העיר 8:17 ולא נשאר]	19
58		[איש בעי ובית אלאשר לא יצאו אחרי ישראל ויעזבו את העיר פתוחה]	20
17		[וירדפו אחרי ישראל]	21
56		[8:18 ויאמר יהוה אל יהושע נטה בכידון אשר בידך אל העי כי בידך]	22
60		[אתננה ויט יהושע בכידון אשר בידו אל]הע̊י̊[ר 8:19 והאורב קם מהרה ממקומו]	23
57		[וירוצו כנטות ידו ויבאו העיר וילכדוה ו]י̊מה̊[רו ויציתו את העיר]	24
59		[באש 8:20 ויפנו אנשי העי אחריהם ויראו והנה עלה עשן העיר השמימה ולא]	25
54		[היה בהם ידים לנוס הנה והנה והעם הנס המדבר נהפך אל הרודף]	26
56		[8:21 ויהושע וכל ישראל ראו כי לכד הארב את העיר וכי עלה עשן העיר]	27

8.6 Some Remarks Regarding the Greek Version of Joshua 8:1–29

Before looking at Josh. 8:30–35, it is worthwile to pay some attention to the Greek version of our passage. Since the main emphasis of this chapter is on the relation between 4QJosh[a] and MT, and since it has already been demonstrated that the shorter version of the chapter as attested by LXX must be seen as the condensed, secondary one, we need not go into all the fascinating details of the Greek text in the same extensive and comprehensive manner as was done in the preceding two chapters. Nevertheless, a few remarks should be made with respect to the Greek translation.

What has hindered the discussion so far is a lack of proper understanding of the method employed by the Greek translator and his competence to translate the Hebrew text. Holmes, Tricot, Mazor and others seem to hold the Greek translator as a kind of dragoman, who faithfully rendered what was under his hands, and who concentrated only on the text segment (clause) he was translating, without (precise) knowledge of the preceding or following text segments.[103] For this reason, Holmes found it hard to believe that the Greek translator altered the Hebrew text in verse 11 מצפון to another direction: ἀπ' ἀνατολῶν, skipped over most of verse 11b–12 and retained only the information about the position of the ambush group καὶ τὰ ἔνεδρα τῆς πόλεως ἀπὸ θαλάσσης.[104] Nevertheless, as Arie van der Kooij has demonstrated, it is rather implausible to regard the work of the Greek translators of the Hebrew Bible as the product of a dragoman-style of translating.[105] The translators must have been

[103] The 'dragoman model' was introduced in Septuagint scholarship by E. BICKERMAN, The Septuagint as Translation, in *Proceedings of the American Academy for Jewish Research* 28 (1959), reprinted in E. BICKERMAN, *Studies in Jewish and Christian History. Part One.* (Arbeiten zur Geschichte des Antiken Judentums und des Urchristentums 9) Leiden 1976, pp. 167–200; and C. RABIN, The Translation Process and the Character of the Septuagint, in *Textus* 6 (1968), pp. 1–26, especially p. 21ff.

[104] S. HOLMES, *Joshua*, p. 14: 'Again, the theory of deliberate omission from the text as we now have it ascribes to the translator a performance which seems too ingenious to be true. According to this hypothesis the Greek translator first passed over 29 or 30 words. Then he took the next three words and translated them. Then he omitted the next six words, and afterwards went on with the narrative; i.e. a long piece was omitted, a short piece was translated, and a second short piece omitted. This would be a strange performance, but it is what must have been done if the translator had our M.T. before him.'

[105] A. VAN DER KOOIJ, *The Oracle of Tyre*, pp. 112–123; A. VAN DER KOOIJ, Perspectives on the Study of the Dead Sea Scrolls, in F. GARCÍA MARTÍNEZ, E. NOORT (eds.), *Perspectives in the Study of the Old Testament*, pp. 214–229; A. VAN DER KOOIJ, The Origin and Purpose of Bible Translations in Ancient Judaism: Some Comments, in *Archiv für Religionsgeschichte* 1 (1999), pp. 204–214; A. VAN DER KOOIJ, Zur Frage der Exegese im LXX-Psalter. Ein Beitrag zur Verhältnisbestimmung zwischen Original und Übersetzung, in A. AEJMELAEUS, U. QUAST (Hg.), *Der Septuaginta-Psalter und seine Tochterüberstezungen. Symposium in Göttingen 1997.* (MSU XXIV) Göttingen 2000, pp. 366–379.

skilled scribes and scholars, who had familiarized themselves thoroughly with the authoritative Scriptures and only turned to a translation of this text after they had read it aloud and interpreted the whole text (see the Prologue to Sirach, lines 7–11; the Letter of Aristeas § 305b: ἐτρέποντο πρὸς τὴν ἀνάγνωσιν καὶ τὴν ἑκάστου διασάφησιν). As a result, they must have had a thorough knowledge of both the composition as a whole and the individual text segments.

As we have seen in the preceding chapters, the Greek translation of Joshua 1 and 5 must likewise be considered as the product of an intensive interpretation of these passages as a whole. The variant readings in LXX-Josh. 1:7 (see section 6.4.5) and LXX-Josh. 5:4–5 (see section 7.6.3.3) are best understood as attempts by the Greek translator to understand individual phrases in the Hebrew text in their context and harmonise the tensions in the Hebrew text resulting from the process of literary growth (the DtrN-addition of Josh. 1:7–8 to Josh. 1:1–6.9; and the DtrH-addition of Josh. 5:2–8 to Josh. 5:9). Therefore it is plausible to ascribe the main divergencies in this chapter between the Hebrew (MT and 4QJosh[a]) and Greek texts to the interpretative, harmonising and stylising skills of the Greek translator, as suggested by Wellhausen and many scholars after him.[106]

As we have seen in the preceding paragraphs, the Hebrew text of this chapter contains a relatively large number of doublets, tensions and problems that should be seen as the result of the process of literary growth of the text, that is, the DtrH addition to the older narrative still preserved in Josh. 8:10–14.16.18–20.26 by verses 8:1–9.15.17.21–25.27–29. Since most of this second layer of the chapter is attested by LXX, it is clear that the Greek translator had this expanded text before him. Unaware of the Hebrew text's prehistory but troubled by the duplications and contradictions, the Greek translator sought to produce a coherent and intelligible rendering that—to his mind—offered a faithful version of the contents of the chapter as a whole. In doing so, he mainly followed the text of the second (DtrH) layer at the cost of the older version (8:11b–13, 26).

Once the Greek translator had followed the DtrH-version of Joshua's sending a group of men in ambush, he could adopt only those elements of the older, second version (8:10–13), that would not con-

[106] See section 8.1.3 above.

tradict the former. For that reason, the Greek translator had no difficulty rendering verse 10 and the first part of verse 11, but retained of verse 12 only the information about the position of the ambush group (καὶ τὰ ἔνεδρα τῆς πόλεως ἀπὸ θαλάσσης, a condensation of וישׂם אותם ארב בין בית־אל ובין העי מים לעיר, in which the action שׂים אותם was omitted, since the ambush group had already been sent by Joshua in 8:9). He could not give a logical explanation for the implication in the Hebrew text that the (first) ambush group of 30,000 men would have to spend two nights and a whole day in the vicinity of Ai without being noticed. Therefore he altered the chronology of the narrative to such an extent that only the element of posting the ambush group at night-time (8:3 καὶ ἀπέστειλεν αὐτοὺς νυκτός—וישׁלחם לילה) was retained, while he concentrated all subsequent action (8:10–29) on a single day. For that reason, he had the encounter between Joshua and the men of Ai take place the following day immediately after Joshua's arrival (8:11). As a result, the statement that Israel pitched its camp before the battle took place (MT-Josh. 8:11 ויחנו מצפון לעיר; 8:12 וישׂימו העם את־כל־המחנה אשׁר מצפון לעיר) became a discordant element, which the Greek translator omitted. Since Joshua and his men approached Ai from Jericho and Gilgal, the Greek translator also rationalised the geographical element מצפון into ἀπ' ἀνατολῶν.[107] In the same manner, he skipped the word וישׁכימו in 8:14, because he had already deliberatedly dropped the element בלילה ההוא in verse 13b.

Likewise, the Greek translator reduced the doublet in verses 15–17 to a more coherent, stylised unity. He retained the first part of the DtrH addition 8:15, and added the short clause καὶ εἶδεν before καὶ ἀνεχώρησεν Ἰησοῦς καὶ Ισραηλ ἀπὸ προσώπου αὐτῶν—וינגעו יהושׁע וכל־ישׂראל לפניהם, but passed over the second half of the verse as well as the first three clauses of verse 16, so that the order of events became more transparent in the Greek version: Joshua and his men approach the city from the West (LXX-Josh. 8:11)—the king of Ai sets out to encounter Joshua (LXX-Josh. 8:14)—Joshua withdraws (LXX-Josh. 8:15)—the men of Ai pursue Joshua (LXX-Josh. 8:16)

---

[107] M.L. Margolis, *The Book of Joshua in Greek*, p. 129: 'απ ανατολων is a correction of מצפון לעי, so that main army and ambush are at directly opposite ends. και τα ενεδρα της πολεως απο θαλασσης as if = והאורב מים לעיר sums up v. 12 and v. 13. See Wellhausen, Composition[2], 126. P̲ athetizes απ—θαλασσης and adds sub ※ end of v. 11, 12 and 13.'

and leave the city unprotected (LXX-Josh. 8:17). Although the Greek translator did not merge the duplicate statements in Josh. 8:16 (pre-DtrH) וירדפו אחרי יהושע and 8:17 (DtrH) וירדפו אחרי ישראל, he did harmonise the two parallel clauses by altering the object of the first of the two to 'Israelites': καὶ κατεδίωξαν ὀπίσω *τῶν υἱῶν Ισραηλ*—καὶ κατεδίωξαν ὀπίσω Ισραηλ. At word level, he levelled the number and subject of the first verbs in 8:14: since the Hebrew text of 8:14 starts with the king of Ai as the subject of perceiving the approach of the Israelites (ויהי כראות מלך־העי), the Greek translator altered the number of the subsequent verbs from plural (וימהרו . . . ויצאו) to singular, and omitted the corresponding plural subject (אנשי־העיר), so that the extension of the focus from the king of Ai to all his men is retained for the second part of the verse (הוא וכל־עמו—αὐτὸς καὶ πᾶς ὁ λαὸς *ὁ μετ' αὐτοῦ*).

The Greek translator followed the Deuteronomist's understanding of the raising of Joshua's hand holding the *kidon*. In the context of the expanded text of Joshua 8, the Greek translator could interpret this action only as a sign for the men in ambush, just as Josephus interpreted our passage (*Jewish Antiquities* V. 45–46):

> Joshua, having purified his army (cf. Joshua 7), now led them out against Naia (cf. Josh. 8:10–11), and after posting ambuscades during the night (cf. Josh. 8:3.9.12–13) all about the town, at daybreak (cf. Josh. 8:14) joined battle with the enemy. And when these advanced against them with an assurance begotten of their former victory, Joshua, feigning defeat (cf. Josh. 8:15), drew them in this way to a distance from the town (cf. Josh. 8:16), they imagining themselves in pursuit of a beaten foe and being disdainful of them in anticipation of victory. Then turning his forces around (cf. Josh. 8:21), he made them face their pursuers and, giving the prearranged signals to those in ambush (σημεῖά τε δοὺς ἃ πρὸς τοὺς ἐν ταῖς ἐνέδραις), roused them also to the fight.

In order to stress this function of the *kidon*, the Greek translator incorporated the first action by the men in ambush after Joshua had raised his hand (8:19 καὶ τὰ ἔνεδρα ἐξανέστησαν ἐν τάχει ἐκ τοῦ τόπου αὐτῶν) into the divine instruction, as the plus in LXX-Josh. 8:18 καὶ τὰ ἔνεδρα ἐξαναστή*σονται* ἐν τάχει ἐκ τοῦ τόπου αὐτῶν.[108]

---

[108] J. Hollenberg, *Der Charakter*, p. 18, ascribed the plus to the Greek translator's Hebrew *Vorlage*. In my view, he missed the link between this variant, that in verse 26 (see the next note) and that in 8:24.

As a result, the curious verse 26, remnant of the older narrative, became obsolete and was for this reason omitted.[109] Once Joshua was relieved from his duty to effectuate the fall of Ai by keeping the powerful *kidon* raised, he could take up his military role as leader in verse 24, where the Hebrew phrase וישבו כל־ישראל העי was turned into καὶ ἀπέστρεψεν *Ἰησους* εἰς Γαι. Mazor's argument for the opposite thesis, that the original text reflected by LXX had been reworked into the present MT, would have been convincing if the Greek text had contained the element 'Joshua' in the other DtrH-passages, where Israel figures prominently (8:15; 8:17, see 8:16; 8:24a; 8:27), and if the MT had lacked the element 'Joshua' in 8:21 so that it would have been clear that alleged MT-redaction of the passage had deliberatedly introduced this strange notion in Josh. 8:18–26. Since, however, already the Deuteronomist had Joshua take part of the battle in Josh. 8:21, the Greek translator could only conclude likewise and skip over the enigmatic verse 26 in order to present his readership with a coherent and dignified version of the passage. He furthermore passed over the short clause in 8:24 ויפלו כלם לפי־חרב, which he considered to be redundant, since in the immediately preceding clauses it had already been stated that all of Ai's inhabitants had been killed (ויהי ככלות ישראל להרג את־כל־ישבי העי), and since the enumeration of those who had fallen in battle would follow immediately in verse 25. Likewise, the difference between MT and LXX in 8:29 καὶ *ἔρριψαν* αὐτὸν εἰς τὸν *βόθρον*, *they threw him into a pit*, for MT וישליכו אותה אל־פתח שער העיר, *they placed it (i.e., the corpse of the king of Ai) under the city-gate*, which Lea Mazor ascribes to an exchange with פחת (βόθρος),[110] may be attributed to the reasoning of the Greek translator: since Ai was burnt to the ground (8:28), there could have been no city-gate left to bury the king, so what remained for the king's corpse was nothing more than an anonymous pit.

---

[109] M.L. MARGOLIS, *The Book of Joshua in Greek*, p. 140, considered the minus in LXX to be the result of an inner-Greek corruption triggered by the homoioteleuton πάντας τοὺς κατοικοῦντας Γαι in verses 25 and 26. Thus also J. HOLLENBERG, *Der Charakter*, p. 19. Although this option cannot be dismissed completely, the explanation of the minus as a deliberate omission better fits the character of the Greek version of the passage as a whole as well as that of the entire book.

[110] See L. MAZOR, עיונים, pp. 60–61, where she adduces this case as example for her thesis that most of the divergencies between LXX and MT must have originated on the Hebrew level. For the idea underlying LXX she refers to 1 Sam. 18:17 וישליכו אתו ביער אל־הפחת הגדול ויצבו עליו גל־אבנים גדול מאד, where Absalom's corpse is taken from the tree and thrown into a large pit in the forest and buried under stones.

Another example of how the Greek translator avoided the tensions in the text created during the literary history of the Hebrew text is his handling of the doublet in verses 20–21. The Deuteronomist elaborated the short statement of the older narrative, preserved in 8:20b והעם הנס המדבר נהפך אל־הרודף into the longer sentence in 8:21, in which the Israelites only turned around (וישבו), after they, too, had seen that the city had been captured (ויהושע וכל־ישׂראל ראו כי־לכד הארב את־העיר וכי עלה עשן העיר). The Greek translator rationalised this redundant sequence: 'Israel turns around (MT-Josh. 8:20b)—Israel perceives the capture of the city (MT-Josh. 8:21)—Israel turns around (MT-Josh. 8:21)', by dropping the first of these three elements, so that the new version of the text would present a smoother account.

Some other divergencies between the Hebrew and Greek texts may also be explained in the light of these attempts by the Greek translator to harmonise the tensions of the Hebrew text. The last words in 8:6 ונסנו לפניהם are out of context and no doubt are a dittography from verse 5 triggered by the repetition of the phrase כאשׁר בראשׁנה. As we have seen above, this corruption had taken place at an early stage in the transmission of the Hebrew text, at least in a time before 4QJosh[a] was copied (second half of the second century—first half of the first century BCE). Since the Greek translation of Joshua was produced even (a century?) earlier, the possibility cannot be excluded that this corruption had not yet entered the Hebrew text of the passage from which the Greek translation was made. Nevertheless, if it had formed part of the Greek translator's *Vorlage*, our translator would have had every reason to leave these words untranslated as he did with other large parts of our text.

The variant κατὰ τὸ ῥῆμα *τοῦτο* ποιήσετε·—כדבר יהוה תעשׂו would have been an interesting example of theologising a profane narrative (so Rudolph and Mazor),[111] had verses 1–2 and verse 18 been absent from the Greek version. Since Yhwh in 8:2 (attested by both MT and LXX) only instructed Joshua to place an ambush (שׂים־לך ארב לעיר מאחריה), but did not provide the instructions Joshua gives to the men in ambush (in 8:7–8a) about what to do after they have taken their position, the presentation in MT of these additional com-

[111] W. RUDOLPH, *Der 'Elohist'*, p. 194; L. MAZOR, הסיפור אודות הנצחון על העי, pp. 93–94. M.L. MARGOLIS, *The Book of Joshua*, p. 127; and J. MOATTI-FINE, *Josué*, p. 135, seem to think of a confusion of the two Hebrew expressions.

mands as the word of Yhwh is problematic. For that reason, the Greek translator avoided this problem by interpreting the phrase as כדבר הזה and rendering it correspondingly.

The variants in 8:7–8a can be explained in a similar way. The word והורשתם is somewhat premature in this context, although perfectly justifiable against the background of the Deuteronomistic origin of these verses, in which the theme of conquest (ירשׁ Hiphʿil) plays an important role.[112] The alteration of this verb to καὶ πορεύσεσθε may be regarded as an anticipation of verse 19 (καὶ τὰ ἔνεδρα ἐξανέστησαν ἐν τάχει ἐκ τοῦ τόπου αὐτῶν καὶ *ἐξήλθοσαν*).[113] Before the city could be conquered completely and razed to the ground by Joshua and all Israelites, both main force and ambush, it was first necessary that the men in ambush would leave their position, enter the city, set it on fire, leave the city to enclose the enemy in the field, and defeat the men of Ai there. Only after that could the city be fully captured and conquered. Since the Deity interrupts the sequence of events in 8:18 with an additional command on which the submission of the city seems to be dependent, the Greek translator probably chose to retain the second part of the duplicate submission formula (Josh. 8:7 ונתנה יהוה אלהיכם בידכם [DtrH]—Josh. 8:18 כי בידך אתננה [pre-DtrH]) and reserve that part of the strategy for these verses (8:19), so that full emphasis on the important participatory and leading role of the Deity in the order of events was maintained. Nevertheless, the minus in LXX-Josh. 8:7b–8a may also be explained as the result of a scribal error per homoioteleuton, comparable to the alleged omission of את־העיר תציתו in 4QJosh[a] column V, line 7.

Although most of these variants could have originated already on the Hebrew level (thus e.g. the interchange of כדבר הזה/כדבר יהוה 8:8; אל־פתח/אל־פחת 8:29), the Greek version contains enough non-stereotypical renderings to make it plausible that (nearly) all variants should be ascribed to the same hand, i.e. that of the Greek translator. For one, the Greek translator—again—did not strive for a

[112] See section 4.2.1 above.

[113] Thus M.L. Margolis, *The Book of Joshua in Greek*, p. 126: 'The end of v. 7 and the beginning of v. 8 condensed by the translator. P̲ obelizes και πορευσεσθε εις την πολιν, because it cannot identify it with והורשתם את העיר with which therefore the plus sub ※ sets in. והורשתם cannot be the original reading. Graetz proposes ותפשתם. G̲ translates with a view to v. 19.'

concordant translation as the various Greek renderings of the same Hebrew phrase make clear:

* כאשׁר בראשׁנה (5.6)—καθάπερ καὶ πρῴην (5)—ὃν τρόπον καὶ ἔμπροσθεν (6)
* קום—ἀν-ίστημι (1.3)—ἐξ-αν-ίστημι (7.18.19)—ἐπ-ίστημι (29)
* ראה—ὁράω (1.7.14)—θεωρέω (20)—ἰδού—no translation (4)
* אנשׁי העי—οἱ κάτοικοι (20.25)—ἀνδρές (21)—παντας τούς ἐν τῇ Γαι (24)—no translation (14)[114]
* עם המלחמה—τούς πολεμιστάς (1)—πᾶς ὁ λαὸς ὁ πολεμιστὴς (3.11; 10:7; 11:7)[115]
* (מ)ארב—τά ἔνεδρα (2.12.14)—ἡ ἔνεδρα (7.9)[116]

As scholars such as Hollenberg, Margolis, Den Hertog, Moatti-Fine, and Sipilä have pointed out, the Greek text furthermore contains some other interesting renderings:

* The use of the verbs φοβέω and δειλιάω in LXX-Josh. 8:1 (Μὴ φοβηθῇς μηδὲ δειλιάσῃς) creates a link with LXX-Josh. 1:9 (μὴ δειλιάσῃς μηδὲ φοβηθῇς) that is not so explicit on the Hebrew level (MT-Josh. 1:9 אל־תערץ ואל־תחת—8:1 אל־תירא ואל־תחת).[117]
* The formulation וכל־העם אשׁר אתי has been paraphrased by καὶ πάντες οἱ μετ' ἐμοῦ.[118]
* The sentence ...ויצאו אחרינו עד התיקנו אותם מן־העיר כי יאמרו, *they will come out after us until we will lure them away from the city because they will say* ... has been transformed into a temporal clause, while the כי clause was transformed into the logical continuation of the preceding main clause: καὶ *ὡς ἂν* ἐξέλθωσιν ὀπίσω ἡμῶν, --- --- ἀποσπάσ*ομεν* αὐτοὺς [ἀπο] τῆς πόλεως· καὶ ἐροῦσιν, *and when they*

---

[114] See J. HOLLENBERG, *Der Charakter*, p. 5.
[115] See J. MOATTI-FINE, *Josué*, p. 134.
[116] See J. MOATTI-FINE, *Josué*, p. 135: 'le traducteur établit une distinction entre 'les hommes en embuscade', *[tà] énedra*, mot employé ici et aux v. 12, 14, 18, 19, et 21 comme équivalent du TM, *'ōrēb*, et 'l'embuscade', *hē énedra*, employé uniquement aux v. 7 et 9 correspondant pour le v. 9 au TM *ma'rāb*.' The feminine noun ἡ ἔνεδρα recurs in the LXX only in LXX-Ps. 9:29 [MT-Ps. 10:8], whereas the neuter noun occurs some 41 times in the LXX.
[117] Thus J. MOATTI-FINE, *Josué*, p. 134.
[118] Thus C.G. DEN HERTOG, *Studien*, p. 171.

will come out after us, we will draw them away from the city, and they will say . . .[119]

* The Greek verb ἀναχωρέω, *to depart, to withdraw,* occurs only 14 times in the Greek Bible, where, apart from this place and Tob. 1:19; Prov. 25:8; and 2 Macc. 5:27; 10:13; it renders a variety of Hebrew verbs, i.e. ברח, *to flee,* in Exod. 2:15; Ho. 12:12(13); and Jer. 4:29; נוס, *to flee,* Judg. 4:17; 1 Reg. 19:10; 2 Reg. 4:4; סבב, *to encircle,* Ps. 113(114):5; עלה Niphʿal, *be brought up,* Num. 16:24; and פרץ Hitpaʿel, *to break away,* in 1 Reg. 25:10. The use of this verb for נגע Niphʿal may be classified as a free rendering.[120]

* Although the occurrence of the conjunction καί at the beginning of the apodosis in 8:20 καὶ περιβλέψαντες οἱ κάτοικοι Γαι εἰς τὰ ὀπίσω αὐτῶν <u>καὶ</u> ἐθεώρουν . . ., should be regarded as a stylistic error if one takes classical Greek literature as standard,[121] the lexical choice for the verb θεωρέω, *to behold,* for Hebrew ראה, *to see,* instead of its more common equivalent ὁράω, *to see* (so in 8:1.7.14),[122] again points to a well-considered, non-stereotypical translation. Perhaps the Greek translator wanted to express the idea of the inhabitants of Ai being struck by amazement and fear when they percieved that their city was burning. The omission of the Hebrew word והנה after a verb of seeing must also be ascribed to the Greek translator.[123]

* An example of a successful idiomatic rendering is καὶ οὐκέτι εἶχον ποῦ φύγωσιν ὧδε ἢ ὧδε, *they had no longer (a possibility) where to escape*

[119] Thus M.L. Margolis, *The Book of Joshua in Greek,* p. 126: '<u>G</u> certainly intends the apodosis to begin at αποσπασομεν. The Hebrew is rephrased as if it read ויצאו . . . וְהִתַּקְנוּ . . . ואמרו.'; S. Sipilä, *Between Literalness and Freedom,* p. 162: 'The translator recast the grammatical structure of his parent text. The main clause was turned into a temporal clause and the infinitive construction into a main clause. Thereafter it was probably natural to employ a co-ordinated main clause instead of a causal clause.' On pp. 176–177 Sipilä returns to the passage and classifies it as a 'free rendering'. The Greek verb ἀποσπάω, *to tear away* (LSJ 218a–b; LEH, p. 56a; GELS^2, p. 60a), appears in the LXX only nine times, i.e. in LXX-Lev. 22:24; LXX^B-Judg. 16:9; LXX-Job 41:8(9); LXX-Isa. 28:9; LXX-Jer. 12:14; LXX-Ezek. 19:5; 2 Macc. 12:10.17; 4 Macc. 13:18.

[120] Thus J. Hollenberg, *Der Charakter,* p. 7.

[121] See S. Sipilä, *Between Literalness and Freedom,* pp. 127–129.

[122] The Greek verb θεωρέω occurs in the Septuagint only 75 times as opposed to the 1539 times the Greek verb ὁράω has been used. Of these 75 cases, half of them (35) are found in the Apocrypha, and another 23 instances in LXX/θ'-Daniel as technical term for visions (Aramaic חֲזָה).

[123] Thus S. Sipilä, *Between Literalness and Freedom,* pp. 100–101.

hither or thither, for ולא־היה בהם ידים לנוס הנה והנה, (literally:) *there were in them no hands (guts?) to flee hither or thither.*[124]

* By changing the word-order in 8:28 וישׂימה תל־עולם שׁממה, *he turned it into an everlasting desolate tell*, into the asyndetic clause χῶμα ἀοίκητον εἰς τὸν αἰῶνα ἔθηκεν αὐτὴν, *a ruin uninhabitable forever he made of it*, the Greek translator placed all the stress on the complete destruction of the city.[125] The Greek vocabulary resembles LXX-Deut. 13:17 καὶ ἔσται ἀοίκητος εἰς τὸν αἰῶνα, and LXX-Josh. 11:13 (ἀλλα πάσας τὰς πόλεις τὰς κεχωματισμένας), where the unique Greek verb χωματίζεσθαι[126] forms a remarkably successful *ad sensum* rendering of the Hebrew phrase רק כל־הערים העמדות על־תלם.[127]

* The Greek translator seems to have modernised the impalement of the king of Ai, by rendering the Hebrew phrase תלה על־העץ, *hang on a tree (pale)*, by κρεμάννυμι ἐπὶ ξύλου *διδύμου*, *to hang on a forked piece of wood*. The next plus *καὶ ἦν ἐπὶ τοῦ ξύλου*, *and he was on that wooden (piece)*, probably reflects an expansion introduced by the Greek translator to underline this specific type of punishment.[128]

* The use of the genuine Greek stylistic device of the genitive absolute in LXX-Josh. 8:29 καὶ ἐπιδύνοντος τοῦ ἡλίου for וכבוא השׁמשׁ is another indication of the relative freedom of the Greek translator.[129] The omission of the word עת in the preceding temporal

---

[124] Compare Targum Jonathan וְלָא הֲוָה בְהוֹן חֵילָא לְמִעְרַק לְכָא וּלְכָא, *they had no more power to flee hither or thither*, Pešiṭta ܘܠܐ ܐܫܟܚܘ ܠܡܥܪܩ ܠܟܐ ܘܠܟܐ, *they could not flee hither or thither*, Vulgate 'non potuerunt ultra huc illucque diffugere'. See further J. HOLLENBERG, *Der Charakter*, p. 6; J. MOATTI-FINE, *Josué*, p. 137.

[125] See S. SIPILÄ, *Between Literalness and Freedom*, p. 72: 'The translator composes an ingenious rendering and by changing the word order he is able to use asyndeton. The linkage between the two clauses is clear. The explicit marker of the linkage is the pronoun αὐτήν, which refers backwards to the object of the preceding clause.'

[126] The verb is found, according to LSJ, p. 2014b, only in a first century CE Papyrus published in F. PREISIGKE, *Sammelbuch griechischer Urkunden aus Ägypten* IV. Heidelberg 1931, no. 7376.13 and a second century BCE Tebtunis Papyrus, no. 105.26.

[127] See J. MOATTI-FINE, *Josué*, pp. 138, 159.

[128] See J. HOLLENBERG, *Der Charakter*, p. 7; M.L. MARGOLIS, *The Book of Joshua in Greek*, p. 142: 'διδυμου two-forked—διδυμον ξυλον η παρα Ρωμαιοις φουρκα (furca, fork-shaped gallows) Suidas—added by the translator. He similarly added και ην επι του ξυλου to bring out the pregnant construction.' L. MAZOR, הסיפור אודות הנצחון על העי, p. 81, note 26, also acknowledges the exegetical character of the Greek rendering, but in her opinion, the Greek text reflects a semantic change of the noun עץ from 'tree' to 'wood' in a time when the verb צלב, *to crucify*, had replaced the verb תלה, *to hang*. The Greek version would then reflect a Hebrew *Vorlage* in which the former verb had replaced the latter.

[129] I. SOISALON-SOININEN, Der Gebrauch des *Genitivus absolutus* in der Septuaginta,

phrase must be the result of the condensation of the Hebrew text by the Greek translator.[130]

Given these smaller variants, it is plausible to ascribe the larger variants to the same restructuring and interpretative genius as well.

8.7 Concluding Remarks

The ancient textual witnesses of Joshua 8, i.e. LXX and 4QJoshua[a], do not help us to recover the process of the literary formation of the Hebrew text in a direct manner. When the redaction history of the Hebrew text of the passage is examined on its own terms, independently from the textual data, it becomes evident that the longer version of the passage as attested by MT must have been the basis for the condensed Greek reformulation. This version reflects a far-reaching attempt to harmonise the tensions and doublets in the Hebrew text, which are the result of the addition of Joshua (7:5b–9?–) 8:1–9.15.17.21–25.27–29 by the Deuteronomistic author (DtrH) to an older pre-DtrH account of the conquest of Ai, still preserved in Joshua (7:2–5a–) 8:10–14.16.18–20.26. The Greek translator removed the contradictions and tensions (e.g. in 8:11b–13, 15b–16a, 20b) by following largely the younger literary stratum of the passage.

Nevertheless, the Greek version is of some indirect help to the literary critic, because the literary initiatives introduced by the Greek translator reveal the literary tensions in the Hebrew text. In this way, the ancient witnesses have a hermeneutical value. Furthermore, they reflect the process of reinterpretation and reformulation of the given and grown Hebrew text.

The situation in LXX-Joshua 8 resembles to some extent that of 1 Samuel 17–18, the story of David and Goliath, where, just as in Joshua 8, an original Hebrew text has been expanded by a younger literary strand, and where the Greek translator of that particular passage translated the first and younger of the two versions of David's encounter with Saul and Goliath, and his marriage to one of Saul's

in *VT* 28 (1978), pp. 92–99, (= A. Aejmelaeus, R. Sollamo (Hg.), I. Soisalon-Soininen, *Studien zur Septuaginta-Syntax*, pp. 175–180); C.G. den Hertog, *Studien*, p. 176; S. Sipilä, *Between Literalness and Freedom*, p. 66.

[130] See C.G. den Hertog, *Studien*, pp. 170–171.

daughters.[131] Other parallels to this procedure are offered by Josephus' drastically condensed version of the narrative (*Jewish Antiquities* V. 45–48) and the Samaritan book of Joshua (IX.8–10), where the first seven verses have more or less been retained while the rest of the narrative is subsumed under the following clauses:

> And they did as Joshua son of Nun had commanded them and Yhwh gave it in the hand of Israel. They burned it and all that was in it with fire, according to what Yhwh had commanded to Joshua. This is the city east of the HarGerizim (וזאת העיר היא מקדם להרנריזים), the name of which is Beth-El (אשר שמו בית אל).

The text of 4QJoshua[a], the main focus of the present chapter, does not attest to a Hebrew text of our passage in which verses 11b–13 and 14b–17 had not (yet) been written. Rather, a careful examination of the text preserved on the scattered fragments and a reconstruction of the complete columns of which these tiny fragments once formed part, reveal that the text of 4QJosh[a] follows the MT closely, albeit with some minor variations. In passages where LXX and MT differ considerably, such as Josh. 5:2–8, 6:6–7, 4QJosh[a] supports MT. All problems regarding our passage pertain to a single fragment (15) that from the point of view of a physical reconstruction of the text could not have belonged to column V of 4QJosh[a]. If this fragment is included in 4QJosh[a], as proposed by Ulrich, Mazor, and others, there would not only be the problem of the length of line 12 which would be four times the average length of the surrounding lines, but the column would also contain some lines (11 and 13) that are unexplainably short. Furthermore, since the fragment contains a bottom margin, this reconstruction would imply that the column would have been half as long (14 lines) as the other columns of 4QJosh[a] (27 lines). From the point of view of the contents of the passage, the fragment can only be forced into the context of Josh. 8:10–14 if one disregards the problem that line 2 contains the word וישובו. This

[131] See A. Rofé, The Battle of David and Goliath: Folklore, Theology, Eschatology, in J. Neusner, B.A. Levine, E.S. Frerichs (eds.), *Judaic Perspectives on Ancient Israel*. Philadelphia 1987, pp. 117–151; and A. van der Kooij, The Story of David and Goliath. The Early History of Its Text, in *ETL* 68 (1992), pp. 118–131. Both scholars respond in their own way to the Joint Venture by D. Barthélemy, D.W. Gooding, J. Lust, E. Tov, *The Story of David and Goliath. Textual and Literary Criticism. Papers of a Joint Venture*. (OBO 73) Fribourg/Göttingen 1986.

word cannot be placed in the context of Josh. 8:10, which it is supposted to reflect. Although the question to what part of 4QJosh[a] or to what other composition this fragment should be assigned remains an open one, it remains clear that it cannot have belonged to 4QJosh[a] column V at this point. Thus, 4QJosh[a] does not support the thesis of a deviating Hebrew text underlying LXX, but rather supports MT.

CHAPTER NINE

JOSHUA 8:30–35: MT—4QJOSHUA[a]—LXX

9.1 Introduction

9.1.1 *The Contents of the Passage*

One of the major literary and textual problems of the book of Joshua is posed by the relatively short passage MT-Joshua 8:30–35. The passage describes how Joshua builds an altar on Mount Ebal in accordance with the commandments of Moses (8:31 cf. Deut. 11:29–32), i.e. an altar of unhewn stones (8:31 cf. Deut. 27:5–6 and Exod. 20:25). The Israelites offer burnt-offerings and peace-offerings on it. Joshua writes on the stones a copy of the *torah* of Moses (8:32 cf. Deut. 31:9). All Israel with its elders, officials, and judges is placed around the ark which is carried by the Levitical priests half of them facing Mount Gerizim, half of them facing in the opposite direction Mount Ebal, as prescribed by Moses (8:33 cf. Deut. 11:29–30; 27:11–13) in order to bless the people of Israel in the beginning (8:33 cf. Deut. 27:12). After that, Joshua reads all the words of the *torah*, both blessing and curse as written in the book of the *torah*. Again, it is emphasised that there was not a single word of Moses' commandments that was not read by Joshua in front of all Israel. The passage ends as abruptly as it had started (אז).

For the sake of convenience a synopsis of the three relevant textual witnesses is offered here, although it is not my purpose to deal with the smaller divergencies between LXX and MT. The sole instance of a difference in the reconstruction of the original Greek text by Rahlfs and Margolis will be dealt with in a footnote.[1]

---

[1] [LXX-Josh. 9:2c] Margolis adopted the reading attested by Codex Vaticanus, ms. 72 (M), and Eth[C] without the words ὃν ἔγραψεν (Rahlfs). According to D. Barthélemy, *Critique textuelle* 1, p. 13, the reference to Or-lat (in the Brooke-McLean and Margolis editions) is erroneous. For a proper presentation of the other witnesses, see S. Sipilä, A Note to the Users of Margolis' Joshua Edition, p. 19. The absence of the words are best seen as an inner-Greek stylistic shortening of the longer expression, thus Barthélemy and C.G. den Hertog, *Studien*, p. 68.

	LXX-Josh. 9:2a–f (ed. Rahlfs)	4QJosh[a] (ed. Ulrich)	MT-Josh. 8:30–35 (BHS)	
9^{2a}	Τότε ᾠκοδόμησεν Ἰησοῦς θυσιαστήριον		אָז יִבְנֶה יְהוֹשֻׁעַ מִזְבֵּחַ	8^{30}
	κυρίῳ τῷ θεῷ Ισραηλ		לַיהוָה אֱלֹהֵי יִשְׂרָאֵל	
	ἐν ὄρει Γαιβαλ,		בְּהַר עֵיבָל׃	
9^{2b}	καθότι ἐνετείλατο Μωυσῆς ὁ θεράπων κυρίου		כַּאֲשֶׁר צִוָּה מֹשֶׁה עֶבֶד־יְהוָה	8^{31}
	τοῖς υἱοῖς Ισραηλ,		אֶת־בְּנֵי יִשְׂרָאֵל	
	καθὰ γέγραπται ἐν τῷ --- --- νόμῳ Μωυσῆ,		כַּכָּתוּב בְּסֵפֶר תּוֹרַת מֹשֶׁה	
	θυσιαστήριον λίθων ὁλοκλήρων,		מִזְבַּח אֲבָנִים שְׁלֵמוֹת	
	ἐφ᾽ οὓς οὐκ ἐπεβλήθη σίδηρος,		אֲשֶׁר לֹא־הֵנִיף עֲלֵיהֶן בַּרְזֶל	
	καὶ ἀνεβίβασεν *ἐκεῖ* ὁλοκαυτώματα κυρίῳ		וַיַּעֲלוּ עָלָיו עֹלוֹת לַיהוָה	
	καὶ θυσίαν *σωτηρίου.*		וַיִּזְבְּחוּ שְׁלָמִים׃	
9^{2c}	καὶ ἔγραψεν *Ἰησοῦς* --- ἐπὶ τῶν λίθων		וַיִּכְתָּב־שָׁם עַל־הָאֲבָנִים	8^{32}
	τὸ *δευτερονόμιον,* νόμον Μωυσῆ,		אֵת מִשְׁנֵה תּוֹרַת מֹשֶׁה	
	(ὃν ἔγραψεν) ἐνώπιον υἱῶν Ισραηλ.		אֲשֶׁר כָּתַב לִפְנֵי בְּנֵי יִשְׂרָאֵל׃	
9^{2d}	καὶ πᾶς Ισραηλ καὶ οἱ πρεσβύτεροι αὐτῶν		וְכָל־יִשְׂרָאֵל וּזְקֵנָיו	8^{33}
	καὶ οἱ δικασταὶ καὶ οἱ γραμματεῖς αὐτῶν		וְשֹׁטְרִים וְשֹׁפְטָיו	
	παρεπορεύοντο ἔνθεν		עֹמְדִים מִזֶּה	
	καὶ ἔνθεν τῆς κιβωτου ἀπέναντι,		וּמִזֶּה לָאָרוֹן נֶגֶד	
	καὶ οἱ ἱερεῖς *καὶ οἱ* Λευῖται		הַכֹּהֲנִים הַלְוִיִּם	
	ἦραν τὴν κιβωτὸν τῆς διαθήκης κυρίου,		נֹשְׂאֵי אֲרוֹן בְּרִית־יְהוָה	
	καὶ ὁ προσήλυτος καὶ ὁ αὐτόχθων,		כַּגֵּר כָּאֶזְרָח	
	οἳ ἦσαν ἥμισυ πλησίον ὄρους Γαριζιν,		חֶצְיוֹ אֶל־מוּל הַר־גְּרִזִים	
	καὶ οἳ ἦσαν ἥμισυ πλησίον ὄρους Γαιβαλ,		וְהַחֶצְיוֹ אֶל־מוּל הַר־עֵיבָל	
	καθότι ἐνετείλατο Μωυσῆς ὁ θεράπων κυρίου		כַּאֲשֶׁר צִוָּה מֹשֶׁה עֶבֶד־יְהוָה	
	εὐλογῆσαι τὸν λαὸν --- ἐν πρώτοις.		לְבָרֵךְ אֶת־הָעָם יִשְׂרָאֵל בָּרִאשֹׁנָה׃	
9^{2e}	καὶ μετὰ ταῦτα οὕτως ἀνέγνω *Ἰησοῦς*		וְאַחֲרֵי־כֵן קָרָא	8^{34}
	πάντα τὰ ῥήματα τοῦ νόμου *τούτου,*		אֶת־כָּל־דִּבְרֵי הַתּוֹרָה	
	τὰς εὐλογίας καὶ τὰς κατάρας,		הַבְּרָכָה וְהַקְּלָלָה	
	κατὰ πάντα τὰ γεγραμμένα		כְּכָל־הַכָּתוּב	
	ἐν τῷ --- --- νόμῳ *Μωυσῆ·*	[בספר]התורה	בְּסֵפֶר הַתּוֹרָה׃	
9^{2f}	οὐκ ἦν ῥῆμα ἀπὸ πάντων,	לא היה דבר	לֹא־הָיָה דָבָר מִכֹּל	8^{35}
	ὧν ἐνετείλατο Μωυσῆς	מכל צוה משה	אֲשֶׁר־צִוָּה מֹשֶׁה	
	τῷ Ἰησοῖ,	[את יה]ושוע		
	ὃ οὐκ ἀνέγνω Ἰησοῦς	אשר לא קרא יהשע	אֲשֶׁר לֹא־קָרָא יְהוֹשֻׁעַ	
	εἰς τὰ ὦτα πάσης ἐκκλησίας	נגד כל ---	נֶגֶד כָּל־קְהַל	
	υἱῶν Ισραηλ,	[ישראל	יִשְׂרָאֵל	
		[בעברו]את הירד[ן]		
	τοῖς ἀνδράσιν *καὶ ταῖς γυναιξὶν*	והנשים	וְהַנָּשִׁים	
	καὶ *τοῖς* παιδίοις	והטף	וְהַטַּף	
	καὶ *τοῖς* προσηλύτοις	והג[ר]	וְהַגֵּר	
	τοῖς προσπορευομένοις τῷ Ισραηλ.	ההולך בקרבם	הַהֹלֵךְ בְּקִרְבָּם׃	
		אחר אשר נתקו[ ]		
		[ ]ל[ ]את ספר התורה	פ	
		אחר כן [ ]ל נושאי הארו[ן][ ]		
		[ ]		

9.1.2 *The Exegetical Problems*

The passage does not fit the context in MT. For one, the location where the passage is situated, the area around Shechem, is far removed from the area around Gilgal, Jericho and Ai. It would take at least one day for an army like that of ancient Israel to march from Ai to Shechem. Furthermore, this mountainous area was still unconquered territory, so that this enterprise would have been a hazardous one. The narratives preceding MT-Josh. 8:30–35 (Joshua 5–8:29) and following it (Joshua 9–10) are all situated in the southern part of Israel, in the vicinity of Gilgal. According to Josh. 9:6 Israel was (again) in its camp in Gilgal. We hear nothing of a march up and down Shechem. Moreover, the passages following MT-Josh. 8:30–35, i.e. Josh. 9:1–2, and Josh. 9:3ff. presuppose only Josh. 8:1–29. Josh. 9:3 explicitly refers only to Joshua 6 and 8:1–29 (וישבי גבעון שמעו את אשר עשה יהושע ליריחו ולעי). Although it is not stated explicitly what the Hittite, Amorite, Canaanite, Perizzite, Hivite, and Jebusite kings of the southern coalition heard exactly (9:1 ויהי כשמע כל־המלכים אשר בעבר הירדן), it is clear from the context that this must refer to the fall of Jericho and Ai and not to the events narrated in MT-Josh. 8:30–35. Therefore, Josh. 9:1 is the direct sequel to Josh. 8:29.[2] In LXX the passage is placed between MT-Josh. 9:1–2, a passage that describes the reaction of the Canaanite kings, and 9:3ff., which narrates the subsequent ruse of the Gibeonites. Here too, the passage disturbs the logical connection between Josh. 8:1–29; 9:1–2 and 9:3–27.

What makes the case even more complicated is the circumstance that the corresponding passages in Deuteronomy are enigmatic and far from homogeneous. Most of our passage in Josh. 8:30–35 refers to Deuteronomy 27, where we find two commands by Moses to the Israelites to erect stones after Israel has crossed the river Jordan (Deut. 27:2 and 27:4). One command stresses the temporal element (27:2), while the other does not mention the specific time, but the place instead: 'on Mount Ebal'. The Samaritan Pentateuch here reads: 'on Mount Gerizim',[3] which is the sacred moutain for the

[2] Hence the succinct statement by T.C. BUTLER, *Joshua*, p. 94: 'Joshua 8:30–35 does not fit the present geographical, chronological, or narrative context.'

[3] SamP (A.F. VON GALL (Hg.), *Der hebräische Pentateuch der Samaritaner*. Gießen 1918; A. TAL (ed.), *The Samaritan Pentateuch edited according to MS 6 (C) of the Shekhem Synagogue*. Tel-Aviv 1994) reads בהרגריזים, which is supported by the Greek *Samareitikon* translation

Samaritan community. We also find two commands to write all the words of this *torah* (Deut. 27:3 and 27:8) on the stones. After a short passage of a different signature (27:9–10), we find another short passage (Deut. 27:11–13), which corresponds to MT-Josh. 8:33. Unlike the latter passage we do not find any reference in the Deuteronomy passage to the officials of Israel, the Levitical priests, or the ark, but instead a clearly defined list of six tribes standing on Mount Gerizim standing in for the blessing (?), while the six remaining tribes are to stand on mount Ebal for (?) the curse (27:13). The chapter is concluded by a list of curses (Deut. 27:15–26), which do not seem to be related to either Deut. 27:1–13 or Josh. 8:30–35. Below follows a synopsis of the LXX and MT versions with SamP variants of Deuteronomy 27, 4QDeut^{c} and 4QDeut^{f} being identical to MT:

	LXX-Deut. 27 (ed.Wevers)	SamP-Deut. 27 (ed. Von Gall)	MT-Deut. 27 (BHS)	
27^{1}	Καὶ προσέταξεν Μωυσῆς		וַיְצַו מֹשֶׁה	27^{1}
	καὶ *ἡ* γερουσία Ἰσραὴλ --- ---		וְזִקְנֵי יִשְׂרָאֵל אֶת־הָעָם	
	λέγων		לֵאמֹר	
	Φυλάσσεσθε πάσας *τὰς* ἐντολὰς *ταύτας*,	[שמרו]	שָׁמֹר אֶת־כָּל־הַמִּצְוָה	
	ὅσας ἐγὼ ἐντέλλομαι ὑμῖν σήμερον.		אֲשֶׁר אָנֹכִי מְצַוֶּה אֶתְכֶם הַיּוֹם׃	
27^{2}	καὶ ἔσται ᾗ ἂν ἡμέρᾳ		וְהָיָה בַּיּוֹם	27^{2}
	διαβῆτε τὸν Ἰορδάνην εἰς τὴν γῆν,		אֲשֶׁר תַּעַבְרוּ אֶת־הַיַּרְדֵּן אֶל־הָאָרֶץ	
	ἣν κύριος ὁ θεός σου δίδωσίν σοι,		אֲשֶׁר־יְהוָה אֱלֹהֶיךָ נֹתֵן לָךְ	
	καὶ στήσεις σεαυτῷ λίθους μεγάλους		וַהֲקֵמֹתָ לְךָ אֲבָנִים גְּדֹלוֹת	
	καὶ κονιάσεις αὐτοὺς κονίᾳ·		וְשַׂדְתָּ אֹתָם בַּשִּׂיד׃	
27^{3}	καὶ γράψεις ἐπὶ *τῶν λίθων*		וְכָתַבְתָּ עֲלֵיהֶן	27^{3}
	πάντας τοὺς λόγους τοῦ νόμου τούτου,		אֶת־כָּל־דִּבְרֵי הַתּוֹרָה הַזֹּאת	
	ὡς ἂν διαβῆτε *τὸν Ἰορδάνην*,		בְּעָבְרֶךָ	
	ἡνίκα ἂν εἰσέλθ*ητε* εἰς τὴν γῆν,		לְמַעַן אֲשֶׁר תָּבֹא אֶל־הָאָרֶץ	
	ἣν κύριος ὁ θεὸς *τῶν πατέρων* σου δίδωσίν σοι,		אֲשֶׁר־יְהוָה אֱלֹהֶיךָ נֹתֵן לְךָ	
	γῆν ῥέουσαν γάλα καὶ μέλι,		אֶרֶץ זָבַת חָלָב וּדְבַשׁ	
	ὃν τρόπον εἶπεν κύριος		כַּאֲשֶׁר דִּבֶּר יְהוָה	
	ὁ θεὸς τῶν πατέρων σού σοι·		אֱלֹהֵי־אֲבֹתֶיךָ לָךְ׃	
27^{4}	καὶ ἔσται		וְהָיָה	27^{4}
	ὡς ἂν διαβῆτε τὸν Ιορδάνην,		בְּעָבְרְכֶם אֶת־הַיַּרְדֵּן	
	στήσετε τοὺς λίθους τούτους,		תָּקִימוּ אֶת־הָאֲבָנִים הָאֵלֶּה	
	οὓς ἐγὼ ἐντέλλομαί σοι σήμερον		אֲשֶׁר אָנֹכִי מְצַוֶּה אֶתְכֶם הַיּוֹם	
	ἐν ὄρει Γαιβάλ,	[בהר גריזים]	בְּהַר עֵיבָל	
	καὶ κονιάσεις αὐτοὺς κονίᾳ.		וְשַׂדְתָּ אוֹתָם בַּשִּׂיד׃	

(Pap. Giesen (αρ γαρ[ι]ζιμ) and notes in the Catena Manuscripts (οὐκ ἐν ὄρει Γεβὰλ ἔχει το σαμ' ἀλλ' ἐν τῷ Γαριζείν). Vetus Latina Codex Lugdunensis (*in monte Garzin*) seems to support this reading (but see section 9.4.1).

27^{5}	καὶ οἰκοδομήσεις ἐκεῖ θυσιαστήριον		וּבָנִיתָ שָּׁם מִזְבֵּחַ	27^{5}
	κυρίῳ τῷ θεῷ σου,		לַיהוָה אֱלֹהֶיךָ	
	θυσιαστήριον ἐκ λίθων		מִזְבַּח אֲבָנִים	
	οὐκ ἐπιβαλεῖς ἐπ᾽ αὐτοὺς σίδηρον·		לֹא־תָנִיף עֲלֵיהֶם בַּרְזֶל׃	
27^{6}	λίθους ὁλοκλήρους οἰκοδομήσεις		אֲבָנִים שְׁלֵמוֹת תִּבְנֶה	27^{6}
	τὸ θυσιαστήριον κυρίῳ τῷ θεῷ σου,		אֶת־מִזְבַּח יְהוָה אֱלֹהֶיךָ	
	καὶ ἀνοίσεις ἐπ᾽ αὐτὸ ὁλοκαυτώματα		וְהַעֲלִיתָ עָלָיו עוֹלֹת	
	κυρίῳ τῷ θεῷ σου·		לַיהוָה אֱלֹהֶיךָ׃	
27^{7}	καὶ θύσεις θυσίαν σωτηρίου		וְזָבַחְתָּ שְׁלָמִים	27^{7}
	καὶ φάγῃ		וְאָכַלְתָּ שָּׁם	
	καὶ ἐμπλησθήσῃ ἐκεῖ			
	καὶ εὐφρανθήσῃ ἐναντίον κυρίου τοῦ θεοῦ σου.		וְשָׂמַחְתָּ לִפְנֵי יְהוָה אֱלֹהֶיךָ׃	

27^{8}	καὶ γράψεις ἐπὶ τῶν λίθων		וְכָתַבְתָּ עַל־הָאֲבָנִים	27^{8}
	πάντα τὸν νόμον τοῦτον		אֶת־כָּל־דִּבְרֵי הַתּוֹרָה הַזֹּאת	
	σαφῶς σφόδρα.		בַּאֵר הֵיטֵב׃	

ס

27^{9}	Καὶ ἐλάλησεν Μωυσῆς καὶ οἱ ἱερεῖς οἱ Λευῖται		וַיְדַבֵּר מֹשֶׁה וְהַכֹּהֲנִים הַלְוִיִּם	27^{9}
	παντὶ Ἰσραὴλ		אֶל כָּל־יִשְׂרָאֵל	
	λέγοντες		לֵאמֹר	
	Σιώπα		הַסְכֵּת	
	καὶ ἄκουε,		וּשְׁמַע	
	Ἰσραήλ·		יִשְׂרָאֵל	
	ἐν τῇ ἡμέρᾳ ταύτῃ γέγονας εἰς λαὸν	[לעם קדש]	הַיּוֹם הַזֶּה נִהְיֵיתָ לְעָם	
	κυρίῳ τῷ θεῷ σου·		לַיהוָה אֱלֹהֶיךָ׃	
27^{10}	καὶ εἰσακούσῃ τῆς φωνῆς κυρίου τοῦ θεοῦ σου		וְשָׁמַעְתָּ בְּקוֹל יְהוָה אֱלֹהֶיךָ	27^{10}
	καὶ ποιήσεις πάσας τὰς ἐντολὰς αὐτοῦ		וְעָשִׂיתָ אֶת־מִצְוֺתָו	
	καὶ τὰ δικαιώματα αὐτοῦ,	[חקתיו]	וְאֶת־חֻקָּיו	
	ὅσα ἐγὼ ἐντέλλομαί σοι σήμερον.		אֲשֶׁר אָנֹכִי מְצַוְּךָ הַיּוֹם׃	

ס

27^{11}	Καὶ ἐνετείλατο Μωυσῆς τῷ λαῷ		וַיְצַו מֹשֶׁה אֶת־הָעָם	27^{11}
	ἐν τῇ ἡμέρᾳ ἐκείνῃ		בַּיּוֹם הַהוּא	
	λέγων		לֵאמֹר׃	
27^{12}	Οὗτοι στήσονται		אֵלֶּה יַעַמְדוּ	27^{12}
	εὐλογεῖν τὸν λαὸν ἐν ὄρει Γαριζίν,		לְבָרֵךְ אֶת־הָעָם עַל־הַר גְּרִזִּים	
	διαβάντες τὸν Ἰορδάνην·		בְּעָבְרְכֶם אֶת־הַיַּרְדֵּן	
	Συμεών, Λευί, Ἰουδάς,		שִׁמְעוֹן וְלֵוִי וִיהוּדָה	
	Ἰσσαχάρ, Ἰωσὴφ καὶ Βενιαμίν.		וְיִשָּׂשכָר וְיוֹסֵף וּבִנְיָמִן׃	
27^{13}	καὶ οὗτοι στήσονται *ἐπὶ* τῆς κατάρας		וְאֵלֶּה יַעַמְדוּ עַל־הַקְּלָלָה	27^{13}
	ἐν ὄρει Γαιβάλ·		בְּהַר עֵיבָל	
	Ρουβήν, Γὰδ καὶ Ἀσήρ,		רְאוּבֵן גָּד וְאָשֵׁר	
	Ζαβουλών, Δὰν καὶ Νεφθαλί.		וּזְבוּלֻן דָּן וְנַפְתָּלִי׃	

Even more enigmatic is the circumstance that we find a parallel passage to Deut. 27:11–13 in Deut. 11:29–30. In this passage, however, we find no mention of tribes or Israelites standing on (Deut. 27:12–13) or facing (MT-Josh. 8:33) the twin mountains. Here Moses simply commands the Israelites to place the blessing on Mount Gerizim and the curse on Mount Ebal (11:29). We are not told what is meant by that, but instead, we find a long explanation where the two mountains are located (11:30). This verse, however, obscures rather than clarifies the precise location of the two mountains, since the information in the text refers both to the Gilgal area (הלא־המה בעבר הירדן אחרי דרך מבוא השמש בארץ הכנעני הישב בערבה מול הגלגל, *Are they not beyond the Jordan, behind the road to the West in the land of the Canaanite who lives in the Arabah*) and to the area around Shechem (אצל אלוני מרה, *besides the oak of Moreh*). The Arabah is the plain around the river Jordan, roughly identical with the modern West Bank, and thus indicates the area around Gilgal. According to Gen.12:6, the oak of Moreh was situated in the vicinity of Shechem. Hence we find the addition מול שכם, *towards Shechem* in the Samaritan Pentateuch:

	LXX-Deut. 11:29–32 (ed. Wevers)	SamP variants (ed. Von Gall)	MT-Deut. 11:29–32 (BHS)	
11[29]	καὶ ἔσται		וְהָיָה	11[29]
	ὅταν εἰσαγάγῃ σε κύριος ὁ θεός σου		כִּי יְבִיאֲךָ יְהוָה אֱלֹהֶיךָ	
	εἰς τὴν γῆν,		אֶל־הָאָרֶץ	
	εἰς ἣν διαβαίνεις ἐκεῖ		אֲשֶׁר־אַתָּה בָא־שָׁמָּה	
	κληρονομῆσαι αὐτήν,		לְרִשְׁתָּהּ	
	καὶ δώσεις τὴν εὐλογίαν ἐπ' ὄρος Γαριζὶν		וְנָתַתָּה אֶת־הַבְּרָכָה עַל־הַר גְּרִזִּים	
	καὶ τὴν κατάραν ἐπ' ὄρος Γαιβάλ.		וְאֶת־הַקְּלָלָה עַל־הַר עֵיבָל׃	
11[30]	οὐκ ἰδοὺ ταῦτα	[הלוא הם_]	הֲלֹא־הֵמָּה	11[30]
	πέραν τοῦ Ἰορδάνου		בְּעֵבֶר הַיַּרְדֵּן	
	ὀπίσω ὁδὸν δυσμῶν ἡλίου		אַחֲרֵי דֶּרֶךְ מְבוֹא הַשֶּׁמֶשׁ	
	ἐν γῇ *Χαναaν*,		בְּאֶרֶץ הַכְּנַעֲנִי	
	τὸ κατοικοῦν ἐπὶ δυσμῶν,		הַיֹּשֵׁב בָּעֲרָבָה	
	ἐχόμενον τοῦ Γολγόλ,		מוּל הַגִּלְגָּל	
	πλησίον *τῆς δρυὸς τῆς ὑψηλῆς*;	[אצל אלוני מורא מול שכם [<קצה>]	אֵצֶל אֵלוֹנֵי מֹרֶה׃	

Although the last element seems to defy standard Israelite geography, it does seem to correspond to Deut. 27:2 and MT-Josh. 8:30–35, where the raising of the stones seem to be directly connected to the crossing of the Jordan. On the other hand, there might have been more than one stone circle in ancient Israel, so that the name Gilgal in Deut. 11:30 might just as well fit the context of Shechem. As we have seen above, the Samaritan version of Joshua locates the events described in Josh. 8:1–29 in the vicinity of Ai and proceeds to narrate the fall of Beth-El/Luz, which is identified as the city built on Mount Gerizim (IX.11–14), so that the narrative of the Ebal-Gerizim passage in Joshua fits neatly:

> Joshua went to the city of Luz which is on Mount Gerizim—that is Beth-El—(אשר בהר גריזים אשר הוא בית אל) and slew it. Joshua son of Nun commanded the people that they should camp in Elon Moreh which is next to the city of Shechem (אשר הוא אצל עיר שכם) and they placed the Tent of Meeting there (ונצבו את אהל מועד שם) Joshua son of Nun built an altar of stones (ויבן יהושע בן נון מזבח אבנים) on Mount Gerizim which is Beth-El (בהר גריזים אשר הוא בית אל) as Moses had commanded the Israelites in accordance with the instruction of Yhwh, of unhewn stones (אבנים שלמות).

In modern times, E. Sellin advocated a similar solution,[4] whereas O. Eißfeldt explained the confusing data as a merging of two independent traditions, one centered around Gilgal, the other around Shechem.[5] The complex of questions has been dealt with in several studies by important scholars, but so far, no consensus has been reached.[6]

9.2 Critical Review of Previous Research

With the publication of 4QJosh[a], this old discussion has also received a new impetus. As noted earlier, the last verse of the problematic

---

[4] E. Sellin, *Gilgal.* Leipzig 1917.

[5] O. Eißfeldt, Gilgal or Shechem? in J.L. Durham, J.R. Porter, *Proclamation and Presence*, pp. 90–101.

[6] See e.g. A. Kuenen, Bijdragen tot de critiek van Pentateuch en Jozua. V. De godsdienstige vergadering bij Ebal en Gerizim (*Deut.* XI:29,30; XXVII; *Joz* VIII:30–35) in *Theologisch Tijdschrift* 12 (1878), pp. 297–323; A. Kuenen, *Historisch-critisch onderzoek*[2], pp. 122–128; M. Noth, *Das System der zwölf Stämme Israels.* Stuttgart 1930; and E. Nielsen, *Shechem*; M. Anbar, The Story about the Building of an Altar on Mount Ebal. The History of Its Composition and the Question of the Centralization of the Cult, in N. Lohfink (Hg.), *Das Deuteronomium*, pp. 304–309.

passage in MT-Josh. 8:30–35 appears before Josh. 5:2, with some unidentified short line (5:x) between the two passages.[7] Since the line containg Josh. 8:35 and the last words of 8:34 appear at the top of the column (column I, fragment 1), it seems reasonable to assume that the remainder of the passage was written at the end of the preceding column which has been lost.

9.2.1 *'A latecomer looking for a suitable home' (C. Steuernagel, E. Tov, A.G. Auld)*

One of the conclusions several scholars have drawn form the various positions of the passage in the textual witnesses of Joshua (MT, LXX, and 4QJosh[a]), is that the passage is really a late addition to the book. In fact, it was composed at such a late stage that there was not really a suitable location for the passage, so that different scribes incorporated the passage at different locations. We find this solution already propagated by Carl Steuernagel in 1900 to explain for the difference between MT and LXX.[8] Recently E. Tov has made a similar suggestion and adduced similar cases of sequence differences (1 Kgs. 8:12–13; Num. 10:34–36; 1 Sam. 2:1–10; Ezek. 7:3–9).[9] A. Graeme Auld holds a similar position and has coined an apt title for this interpretation: 'a latecomer looking for a suitable home'.[10] Although the late character of the passage is widely acknowledged by almost all authors,[11] it remains problematic to suppose that the passage was first created independently on a separate sheet of paper without any connection to a specific context within Joshua, and later incorporated into the text of the book by different scribes at different positions at relatively close proximity. If the passage was really composed entirely independent of a specific passage in Joshua, it would have been more natural to find it at the end of the book, where in Joshua 24 we find a chapter that has close affinities with Josh. 8:30–35 (in Joshua 24 Joshua also gathers all the people in Shechem and has them pledge loyalty to Yhwh).[12]

---

[7] See section 7.5.1 above.

[8] C. Steuernagel, *Deuteronomium und Josua*, p. 186.

[9] E. Tov, Some Sequence Differences. See section 2.2.7.1 above.

[10] A.G. Auld, Reading Joshua After Kings, in J. Davies, G. Harvey, W.G.E. Watson (eds.), *Words Remembered, Texts Renewed: Essays in Honour of John F. Sawyer.* (JSOTS 195) Sheffield 1995, pp. 167–181 (= A.G. Auld, *Joshua Retold*, pp. 102–112).

[11] See already J. Hollenberg, Die deuteronomistische Bestandtheile, pp. 478–481.

[12] It was in fact suggested by J.A. Soggin, *Le livre de Josué*, pp. 175–180, that

9.2.2 *Original Conclusion of an Early Version of the Book (A. Kempinski)*

An interesting, but already outdated solution to the problem was offered by Aharon Kempinski in 1993. Whereas Tov reported in 1986 that 'the ending of chapter 8 in that scroll (i.e. 4QJosh[a]) differs much from all other known sources',[13] and Greenspoon in 1990 had to admit that he had 'not been able to identify the source of the longer addition at the close of this section', but speculated on a midrashic extension with a possibe connection to 4QApocrJosh,[14] Kempinksi was able to identify the final lines of the fragment as part of Josh. 5:2ff.[15] He did not, however, draw the obvious conclusion that Josh. 8:(30–)35 was situated between 5:1 and 5:2 in 4QJosh[a], but rather considered the narrative sequence 'building of the altar on Mount Ebal'—'circumcision' as a remnant of the original conclusion of Joshua.

Kempinski compared the literary history of Joshua[16] to the transformation of a historical campaign by Sargon I in northern Mesopotamia[17] into the Akkadian epic composition *Šar tamḫari*.[18] The literary origin of Joshua should then be sought in an original eighth or seventh—century BCE version of the Joshua narratives that only described the victories of a local hero-judge over two cities, Jericho and Ai, resembling the narratives of the Trans-Jordanian Israelite victories over Hesbon and Bashan (Num. 21:21–35), and was concluded by a cultic celebration in Shechem (Josh. 24), which now lay open to the Israelites. Following the proposal made by a number of

MT-Josh. 8:30–35 originally followed Josh. 24:27. None of the extant witnesses, however, support this thesis. Moreover, Josh. 24:1–28 and Josh. 8:30–35 are not complementary, but rather rival versions. See also R.G. BOLING, *Joshua*, p. 246.

[13] E. TOV, The Growth of the Book of Joshua, p. 322.

[14] L. GREENSPOON, The Qumran Fragments of Joshua, p. 173, p. 191, note 51.

[15] A. KEMPINKSI, 'בתנומת ההיסטוריה משנשנת התיאלוניה' הערות על יהושע פרק ח' 30–35 והארכיאולוגיה של תקופת ההתנחלות. ('When History Sleeps, Theology Arises': A Note on Joshua 8:30–35 and the Archaeology of the 'Settlement Period'), in S. AḤITUV, B.A. LEVINE (eds.), *Avraham Malamat Volume.* (Eretz-Israel 24) Jerusalem 1993, pp. 175–183. English abstract, p. 237*.

[16] A. KEMPINSKI, 'בתנומת ההיסטוריה משנשנת התיאלוניה', pp. 180–181.

[17] A. KEMPINSKI, 'בתנומת ההיסטוריה משנשנת התיאלוניה', pp. 175–176, see also A.F. ALBRIGHT, The Epic of the King of Battle: Sargon of Akkad in Cappadocia, in *Journal of the Society of Oriental Research* 7 (1923), pp. 1–20, especially p. 17.

[18] EA 359, see, A.F. RAINEY, *El Amarna Tablets 359–379. Supplement to J.A. Knudtzon Die El-Amarna-Tafeln.* (AOAT 8) Neukirchen 1978², pp. 10–15.

older commentators,[19] Kempinski regarded Josh. 8:30–35 as the original conclusion of this pre-Deuteronomistic passage (Josh. 24), to which an additional circumcision ceremony was attached (Josh. 5:2–9),[20] analoguous to the 'covenant-circumcision' combination found in Gen. 15:12–21 and 17:8–14.[21] Subsequent to this pre-721 BCE, probably northern Israelite composition, the stories of the victories over the two cities were expanded by stories of sweeping campaigns throughout the country (Joshua 9–12), mirroring perhaps the territorial losses suffered by the Assyrians and Babylonians. As a consequence, Joshua 24 was transposed to the end of the book after the newly composed Joshua 23. Kempinksi assumed a Priestly redaction responsible for parts of Joshua 13–21, and a harmonistic redactor, who added Josh. 5:10–12 in order to conform Joshua 5 to the legislation of Exod. 12:43–49. The text found in 4QJosh[a] would thus attest to this theological development of the book; the sequence of passages found in this scroll precedes the sequence of the passages as found in MT and LXX, and can be considered a silent witness to the original shape of the book.

Fascinating as Kempinski's reconstruction of the literary development of Joshua may be, his theory does not explain why the original unit Josh. 24*—Josh. 8:30–35—Josh. 5:2–9 was broken up and dispersed, nor does it clarify the relation between the ratification of the covenant in a book of the *torah* of Yhwh with a large stone as witness (Josh. 24:25–27) and the inscribing of the *torah* on the stones outside Shechem in Josh. 8:32. Moreover, Kempinski's reconstruction proved untenable when Eugene Ulrich established not only the joint of fragment 1 (Josh. 8:34–35—5:x—5:2–3) and fragment 2 (with Josh. 5:4–7), but also that of this first fragment with fragments 3–8, containing Josh. 6:5–10, thus establishing beyond doubt that the fragments 1–2 do not constitute the end of the book of Joshua, but rather the beginning of the extant columns of 4QJosh[a].[22]

---

[19] H. Holzinger, *Das Buch Josua*, p. 29; J.A. Soggin, *Josué*, pp. 175–180; R. Boling, *Joshua*, p. 246.

[20] Kempinski refers to the study by M.J. bin Gurion, *Sinai und Garizim. Über den Ursprung der israelitischen Religion. Forschungen zum Hexateuch auf grund rabbinsicher Quellen*. Berlin 1926, especially pp. 357–388, 416–436, and 438–470 'Die Beschneidung am Berge Garizim', whose speculative thesis would now be vindicated by 4QJosh[a].

[21] A. Kempinski, 'בתנומת ההיסטוריה משנשנת התיאלוניה', pp. 178–179.

[22] E. Ulrich, Joshua's First Altar, p. 91, and idem, 4QJosh[a], p. 145.

9.2.3 *Anti-Samaritan transposition (E. Ulrich)*

Like Kempinski, Ulrich holds the order of passages in 4QJosh[a] to be the oldest of the three texts, but derives his arguments from the parallel passages in Deuteronomy 27 and 11:29–31. According to Ulrich, the newly established order of events as witnessed by 4QJosh[a] solves the problems in the Deuteronomy and Joshua passages: Joshua's first altar in the Promised Land was not built in Shechem, but simply in Gilgal immediately after Israel's crossing of the Jordan (cf. Deut. 27:2). This version, Ulrich argues, is also attested by Josephus' paraphrase in *Jewish Antiquities* V. 20, where the stones taken from the river Jordan explicitly serve as altar for sacrifices, and which expressly ties the building of the altar not to the commands given by God to Joshua during the crossing of the people (Josh. 4:1–3), but to the instructions by the prophet (Moses):

> (V. 20) These, having advanced fifty stades, pitched their camp at a distance of ten stades from Jericho. And Joshua, with the stones which each of the tribal leaders had, by the prophet's orders, taken up from the river-bed (Ἰησοῦς δὲ τόν τε βωμὸν ἐκ τῶν λίθων ὧν ἕκαστος ἀνείλετο τῶν φυλάρχων ἐκ τοῦ βυθοῦ τοῦ προφήτου κελεύσαντος ἱδρυσάμενος, cf. Josh. 4), erected the altar that was to serve as a token of the stoppage of the stream, and sacrificed thereon to God (ἔθυεν ἐπ' αὐτοῦ τῷ θεῷ, absent from Josh. 4–5, 8:30–35). (V. 21) They also kept the feast of Passover at that spot (καὶ τὴν φάσκα ἑώρταζον ἐν ἐκείνῳ τῳ χωρίῳ, cf. Josh. 5:10), being now readily and amply provided with all they had lacked before.

At a second stage, the text of Deuteronomy was conformed to the Samaritan claim by the addition of Deut. 27:4 (as attested by Samaritan Pentateuch and the original Greek text reflected by the Vetus Latina). Out of an anti-Samaritan ideology this text was subsequently altered to בהר עיבל in MT-Deut. 27:4, also reflected in all Greek witnesses of LXX-Deuteronomy 27, which in turn would have prompted the transposition of the passage about Joshua's first altar to its current place in MT-Josh. 8:30–35.[23]

One of the questions related to Ulrich's reconstruction concerns the awkward position of the passage in MT/LXX: if the *torah* passage was transposed from its original position in 4QJosh[a] to its position in MT/LXX, why would a redactor have chosen such an illogical

---

[23] E. ULRICH, 4QJosh[a], pp. 145–146.

and inappropriate position between the narratives of the fall of Ai (Joshua 8) and the treaty with the Gibeonites (Joshua 9)? If the redactor had needed a narrative of the conquest of the Shechemite area (strikingly absent from the whole book of Joshua), would a position after Joshua 11 and 12 not have been a far better position? As a matter of fact, this solution appears to have been already adopted by Josephus, who presents his version of MT-Josh. 8:30–35 in *Jewish Antiquities* V. 68–70, after his recount of Joshua's victory over the northern part of the country (cf. Josh. 11):[24]

> (V. 68) A fifth year had now passed away and there was no longer any Canaanite left (cf. Josh. 12–13), save for such as had escaped through the solidity of their walls. So Joshua moved his camp up from Gilgala (Ἰησους δ' ἐκ τῶν Γαλγάλων cf. MT-Josh. 10:43) into the hill country and set up the holy tabernacle at the city of Shiloh (ἀναστρατοπεδεύσας εἰς τὴν ὄρειον ἱστᾷ τὴν ἱερὰν σκηνὴν κατὰ Σιλοῦν πόλιν cf. Josh. 18:1), since that spot, by its beauty, seemed meet for it, until circumstances should permit them to build a temple. (V. 69) Proceeding thence to Sikima, with all the people (καὶ χωρήσας ἐντεῦθεν ἐπὶ Σικίμων σὺν ἅπαντι τῷ λαῷ cf. MT-Josh. 24:1), he erected an altar (βωμόν τε ἵστησιν cf. MT-Josh. 8:30, absent from Josh. 24) at the spot foreordained by Moses (ὅπου προεῖπε Μωυσῆς cf. MT-Josh. 8:31), and, dividing his army, posted one half of it on mountain Garizin and the other half on Hebel (cf. MT-Josh. 8:33), whereon also stood the altar (ἐν ᾧ καὶ ὁ βωμός, cf. MT-Josh. 8:30), along with the Levites and priests (καὶ τὸ Λευιτικὸν καὶ τοὺς ἱερέας cf. LXX-Josh. 9:2d). (V. 70) After sacrificing (θύσαντες δὲ cf. MT-Josh. 8:31) and pronouncing imprecations (καὶ ἀρὰς ποιησάμενοι cf. MT-Josh. 8:34), which they also left graven upon the altar (καὶ ταύτας ἐπὶ τῷ βωμῷ γεγραμμένας cf. MT-Josh. 8:32), they returned to Shiloh.

9.2.4 *Nomistic Correction (A. Rofé)*

Already at the same 1992 Paris congress, Alexander Rofé defended the opposite position by reversing the priority between the two Hebrew witnesses.[25] In his view the more difficult position of the

---

[24] E. ULRICH, 4QJosh[a], p. 146, rectifies his earlier omission to mention this passage from Josephus in his 1992 preliminary edition of 4QJoshua[a], but does not draw the implications for his thesis.

[25] A. ROFÉ, The Editing of the Book of Joshua in the Light of 4QJosh[a], in G.J. BROOKE, F. GARCÍA MARTÍNEZ (eds.), *New Qumran Texts and Studies*, pp. 73–80. For a comparable view, see H.-J. FABRY, Der Altarbau der Samaritaner—ein Produkt der Text- und Literargeschichte? in U. DAHMEN, A. LANGE, H. LICHTENBERGER

passage in (proto-)MT was the more original, and the transposition of the passage to the position in 4QJosh[a] should be seen as a secondary, *nomistic* alteration.[26] In Rofé's view, the passage, which in itself already reflects a nomistic ideal formulated by a late or post-Deuteronomistic author-editor,[27] was transferred from its awkward but pragmatic position after the story of Israel's gaining a foothold in the hill country (proto-MT-Josh. 8:1–29)[28] to a position before any military campaign had started (4QJosh[a] 5:1–2). This transposition reflects a strong emphasis on the nomistic ideal of Israel's leaders abiding by the law.[29] The arrangement in LXX is in his view the result of 'inaccurate copying of the interpolated passage from one manuscript to another'.[30]

Whereas Ulrich attempts to present Josephus' remodelling of the Joshua narratives in *Jewish Antiquities* V as an additional witness, Rofé points to the exegetical discussion in the rabbinic literature (tractate Soṭa in the *Mishna, Tosefta* and *Talmud yerushalmi*), where we basically find three solutions to the problems posed by the chronology and geography of MT-Josh. 8:30–35. One explanation was that the

(Hg.), *Die Textfunde vom Toten Meer und der Text der Hebräischen Bibel.* Neukirchen 2000, pp. 35–52.

[26] See the previous discussion in section 2.2.7.2.

[27] A. Rofé, The Editing of the Book of Joshua, pp. 76–77: 'This author did not report any living tradition, but just modelled his account after the text of Deuteronomy. Such a literary dependence proves the author of Josh. 8:30–35 to be a late Deuteronomistic (= Dtr) scribe, perhaps even a post-Dtr one. He expresses a nomistic ideal: Joshua, the righteous leader, strictly observes the laws of the Torah, 'as Moses, the servant of the Lord, had commanded the Israelites' (v. 31).'

[28] A. Rofé, The Editing of the Book of Joshua, p. 77: 'One of the editors of the book of Joshua, working on a manuscript that can be defined as proto-MT, chose to insert the Ebal-Gerizim episode after the report of the conquest of Ai (8:1–29). His motives were probably of a topographical strategic nature: Joshua had just conquered a foothold in the hill country. To be sure, the distance between Ai and Shechem is all of 30 km as the crow flies, yet, it is the place nearest to Shechem to be reached by Joshua in his campaigns; later he will go to the south (chaps 9–10) and to the far north (11:1–14). On such practical grounds, the placing of the Ebal-story after 8:29 seems appropriate.'

[29] A. Rofé, The Editing of the Book of Joshua, p. 78: 'Its placement of Joshua's cultic acts and celebration soon after the crossing of the Jordan certainly cannot be attributed to textual mishap. At the root lies a well-planned redaction which discards strategy in favour of another principle—obedience to the laws of the Torah.... Joshua, the leader described by the Dtr author as effecting the commands of D through his military campaigns, is now turned into a devotee who would postpone war for the sake of the Torah. Abiding by the law comes now before warfare. The nomistic ideal has won precedence over statecraft.'

[30] A. Rofé, The Editing of the Book of Joshua, pp. 77–78.

whole sequence of passing through the Jordan, traversing unconquered land, building the altar, reading the *torah* and returning to Gilgal took place in one miraculous day (thus rabbi Simeon on *Tosefta Soṭah* 8:7 and rabbi Yehuda in *Talmud yerushalmi Soṭah* 7:3).

> According to the opinion of rabbi Yehuda they went 120 mile on the same day.

Rabbi Ishmael, on the other hand, regarded the passage as having taken place only after the fourteen years of conquest and land division (ibidem), which would take the passage close to the narrated time of Joshua 24:

> In accord with the view of rabbi Ishmael, for rabbi Ishmael said: all (these passages related to) the entry (into the land) of which the *torah* speaks, refer to (what happened) after fourteen years: seven for its conquest and seven for its partition.

A third tradition (also in *Talmud yerushalmi Soṭah* 7:3) voiced by the Tanaaite rabbi Eliezer ben Hyrcanus reinterpreted the mountains as the 'hills of foreskins' mentioned in Josh. 5:3:

> Rabbi Eliezer said: This is not the Mount Gerizim and the Mount Ebal of the Cuthim (= Samaritans). (. . .) How does rabbi Eliezer uphold Mount Gerizim and the Mount Ebal? They made two heaps and named them Mount Gerizim and Mount Ebal.

On the basis of the latter interpretation, Rofé conjectures that a 4QJosh[a] text might have been known to the Pharisaic masters, which would take the unique order attested by this Qumran manuscript out of its Qumran context into the wider context of Pharisaic circles.[31]

9.2.5 *Nomistic Theology (E. Noort)*

In line with the already old tradition of locating the two mountains Gerizim and Ebal in the vicinity of Gilgal (Deut. 11:30), propagated by rabbi Eliezer ben Hyrcanus, and further the Christian authori-

[31] A. Rofé, The Editing of the Book of Joshua, p. 79: 'The assertion of R. Eliezer ben Hyrcanus may serve us as a terminus ad quem: the accepted Tannaitic ruling had been formulated before the fall of the Second Temple. It therefore is plausible that such a ruling had not originated in order to adhere to the dating contained in Deut 27; rather, it could have been known to the Pharasaic masters.'

ties of Eusebius,[32] Jerome,[33] Procopius,[34] and the Map of Madaba,[35] Ed Noort defends the originality of the position of the passage in 4QJosh[a] by focussing on the theological intention of the passage, and by explaining its origin from the literary and theological developments within the passages in Deuteronomy.[36] In his view, the order of events as presented in 4QJosh[a] is related to Deut. 11:30 and the modification of the older text Deut. 27:4.8.5–7 by Deut. 27:2–3. In all these three passages the two mountains Ebal and Gerizim are moved from their geographical positions towards a theological position, in order to mark not only the entry of Israel into the land, but moreover, the homecoming of yet a third mountain: Mount Sinai.[37]

---

[32] In his Onomasticon of biblical place-names, EUSEBIUS OF CAESAREA considers the usual location of the two mountains around Shechem/Neapolis/Nablus to be a Samaritan perversion (ed. E. KLOSTERMANN, *Eusebius. Das Onomastikon der biblischen Ortsnamen* (GCS 11,I) Leipzig 1904[1], Hildesheim 1966, p. 64:

> Γαιβάλ ὄρος ἐν τῇ γῇ τῆς ἐπαγγελίας, ἔνθα κελεύει Μωϋσῆς στῆσαι θυσιαστήριον. καὶ λέγεται παρακεῖσθαι τῇ Ἱεριχὼ ὄρη δύο κατὰ πρόσωπον ἀλλήλων καὶ πλησίον, ὧν τὸ μὲν εἰναι Γαριζείν, τὸ δὲ Γαιβάλ. Σαμαρεῖται δὲ ἕτερα δεικνύουσιν τὰ τῇ Νέᾳ πόλει παρακείμεμενα, σφαλλόμενοι, ὅτι δὴ πλεῖστον διεστήκασιν ἀλλήλων <τὰ> ὑπ' αυτῶν δεικνύμενα, ὡς μὴ δυνασθαι ἀλλήλων ἀκούειν τοὺς ἑκατέρωθεν βοῶντας.

[33] In his Latin translation of Eusebius' Onomasticon, JEROME follows this view: ed. E. KLOSTERMANN, *Eusebius. Das Onomastikon der biblischen Ortsnamen* (GCS 11,I) Leipzig 1904[1], Hildesheim 1966, p. 65:

> Sunt autem iuxta Iericho duo montes uicini contra se inuicem respicientes, e quibus unus Garizin alter Gebal dicitur. porro Samaritani arbitrantur hos montes iuxta Neapolim esse, sed uehementer errant; plurimum enim inter se distant, nec possunt inuicem benedicentium siue maledictium inter se audiri uoces, quod scriptura commemorat.

[34] Thus PROCOPIUS OF GAZA (ed. E. KLOSTERMANN, *Eusebius. Das Onomastikon der biblischen Ortsnamen* (GCS 11,I) Leipzig 1904[1], Hildesheim 1966, p. 64):

> κεῖται δὲ ταῦτα κατὰ τὸ ἀνατολικὸν μέρος Ἱεριχοῦς ἐπέκεινα τοῦ Γαλγὰλ τόπου. οἱ δὲ Σαμαρεῖται νομίζουσιν αὑτὰ παρακεῖσθαι Σικίμοις πόλει τῇ Συχὴμ . . . η νῦν καλεῖται Νεάπολις.

[35] The map of Madaba combines the two traditions by mentioning ΓΕΒΑΛ and ΓΑΡΙΖΕΙΝ in the vicinity of ΙΕΡΙΧΩ, and by marking ΤΟΥΡΓΩΒΗΛ and ΤΟΥΡΓΑΡΙΖΙΝ in the vicinity of ΝΕΑΠΟΛΙΣ.

[36] E. NOORT, The Traditions of Ebal and Gerizim. Theological Positions in the Book of Joshua, in M. VERVENNE, J. LUST (eds.), *Deuteronomy and Deuteronomic Literature. Festschrift C.H.W. Brekelmans.* (BETL 133) Leuven 1997, pp. 161–180; and E. NOORT, 4QJoshua[a] and the History of Tradition in Joshua, in *JNSL* 24 (1998), pp. 127–144.

[37] E. NOORT, The Traditions of Ebal and Gerizim, p. 178: 'The scene on Mount Ebal transfers the law from Sinai to the promised land itself . . . what was said once far away (Sinai), is said again on the threshold (Deuteronomy/Moab covenant) and is definitely repeated in the land itself. The scene on the Ebal means one thing: Sinai is coming home.' This theological interpretation of MT-Josh. 8:30–35 was

Moses' instructions to build an altar and to read the *torah* (Deut. 27:4–8) corresponds to Exod. 24:4–7, which narrates the building of an altar by Moses, the offerings on that altar and the reading of the *torah*, and thus represents the *Vergegenwärtigung* of the Sinai in the Promised Land.[38] Moreover, the building of an altar right after entering of the land corresponds to the patriarchal narratives in which both Abram (Gen. 12:6) and Jacob (Gen. 33:20) build altars (in Shechem) immediately after their arrival in Canaan.[39] The narrative of the twelve stones from the river Jordan set up in Gilgal as זכרון (Josh. 4:7) may have served as point of attachment for the mountain shift. Together with the narratives of the Passover festival, the cessation of the manna, and the circumcision, this passage, with its full emphasis on the *torah*, marks the ideal beginning of an ideal nation in the ideal land.[40]

The motive for this shift in emphasis is thus to have the *torah* narrated right at the very start of Israel's existence in the Promised Land,[41] rather than an anti-Samaritan ideology, as Ulrich holds. Deut. 27:4–8 itself already contains an anti-Samaritan counterclaim, by placing the altar on Mount Ebal rather than Mount Gerizim.[42] The originality of the MT-reading in Deut. 27:4 'on Mount Ebal'

---

already offered by Noort in his inaugural lecture one year before Ulrich's preliminary publication of 4QJoshua[a] appeared, E. Noort, *Een plek om te zijn. Over de theologie van het land aan de hand van Jozua 8:30–35.* (inaugural lecture, Groningen, 8 June 1993) Kampen 1993.

[38] E. Noort, The Traditions of Ebal and Gerizim, p. 177, with a reference to M. Anbar, The Story about the Building of an Altar on Mount Ebal.

[39] E. Noort, *Een plek om te zijn*, p. 15, Traditions of Ebal and Gerizim, pp. 170–172.

[40] E. Noort, *Een plek om te zijn*, p. 15. Compare his remarks in E. Noort, 4QJoshua[a] and the History of Tradition in Joshua, pp. 134–135: 'Although many problems of the text still remain, there is a high probability that 4QJosh[a], the oldest text witness we have for the book of Joshua, gives (parts of) the scene of MT Joshua 8:30–35 a place after Ch. 4, that is at the beginning of Ch. 5. This is in conformation of my 1993 study of the theology of Joshua 8:30–35 where, unaware of the new Qumran fragments, I wrote: 'There would be an ideal place for Joshua 8:30–35 for this going together of writing down and reciting the law: Joshua 5. There the stopping of the manna, keeping the passover and the circumcision of the people describe an ideal people in an ideal land with an ideal beginning of a life *coram deo* in the promised land.' One year later the prophecy was fulfilled.'

[41] E. Noort, The Traditons of Ebal and Gerizim, p. 177: 'No time must be lost. Israel must not be in the promised land without the law for a single moment.' cf. E. Noort, *Een plek om te zijn*, p. 14.

[42] E. Noort, The Traditions of Ebal and Gerizim, p. 177.

is proven by similar pro-Gerizim alterations in the Samaritan adaptation of Deut. 11:29–30 and 27:2–7 in SamP-Exod. 20:17b, where the command to build an altar on mount Gerizim is presented as the last of the ten commandments, i.e. [1] the alteration of the interrogative opening 'are they not' (הלא־המה, SamP הלא הם) into the affermative 'this mountain is' (ההר ההוא); [2] the change in number from the more ambiguous plural 'oracle oaks' (אלוני מרה SamPDeut = MT) into the oak of Moreh, known from Gen. 12:6, where this oak is obviously linked with Shechem, and, most clearly, [3] the addition of מול שכם, *towards Shechem.*[43]

After this literary stage, in which Deut. 27:2–3, Deut. 11:30, and the passage under discussion were produced, the Ebal passage was moved from its 4QJosh[a]-position to its present position in MT-Josh. 8:30–35, again for theological reasons: in its present MT-position the passage forms the center of chiastic structure of narratives of success (Joshua 6, 8, 10–11) and failure (Joshua 7, 9). Especially the problem of the continued presence of the non-Israelite population, which is presented in the nomistic (DtrN) chapter Joshua 23 as a threat to the faithful observance of the *torah* and to Israel's secure existence in the land (to be realized in Judg. 2:17.20–3:6) may serve to explain this half-hearted secondary shift of the passage from its more original position.[44]

Noort has shown that the relatively straightforward explanation of transposition inpired by nomistic ideals as proposed by A. Rofé can be matched with a redaction-critical model of subsequent nomistic stages in the process of literary formation of Deuteronomy and Joshua. When, however, both the formation of the Ebal passage and its secondary transposition to its present MT-position are the result of purely theological constructs, it might be asked whether the sequence 4QJosh[a]—MT could not just as simply be reverted. If the Ebal passage reflects nomistic interests, and if its admittedly inconclusive position in MT can be equally well explained as a nomistic-redactional view, is it not equally possible that MT preserves the older sequence

[43] E. Noort, The Traditions of Ebal and Gerizim, pp. 167–168.

[44] E. Noort, *Een plek om te zijn*, pp. 14, 18–19; The Traditions of Ebal and Gerizim, p. 178: 'after the gift of the land with the victories at Jericho and Ai, and before the covenant with the Gibeonites, where the theme of the remaining peoples is dealt with, a main theme in the nomistic redactional way of thinking.'

and 4QJosh[a] a secondary movement, reflecting the theological motives explored by Noort? If a redactor had wanted to match or overrule the already lenghty exposition of the *torah* before Israel's crossing the Jordan (the whole of the book of Deuteronomy) by yet another proclamation of the *torah* right after the crossing, why would he have complicated matters by moving mountains to geographically impossible positions?

9.3 Questions and Method

So far, these first attempts to assess the major variant between MT and 4QJosh[a] have shown that there is definite proof for a reworking of the biblical text on the Hebrew level and that a proper assessment of the question of the priority of the three versions cannot be reached without taking into account a wide spectrum of literary problems (in Joshua as well as in Deuteronomy) and (religion-)historical developments during Second Temple Judaism (*torah* theology, controverse between Jerusalem and Samaria). There are still a number of questions that call for an answer:

* If the position of the passage in MT is the result of a secondary transposition, why did the reponsible scribe place it in such an awkward and incomprehensible place? Josephus offers a far better solution by placing it after the conquest narratives (cf. Joshua 1–12). After the publication of 4QJosh[a], the question of the function of the passage in the context of MT has become an even more urgent question.
* None of the various textual witnesses (MT, 4QJosh[a], LXX) and exegetical traditions (Josephus, the rabbis, and also Pseudo-Philo)[45] offer a completely convincing literary context for our passage. 4QJosh[a] too, can only offer a plausible setting for the passage if

[45] Pseudo-Philo, *Liber Antiquitatum Biblicarum* (ed. D.J. Harrington, J. Cazeaux (eds.), *Pseudo-Philon. Les Antiquités Bibliques* I. (SC 229) Paris 1976) 20:7:

> Et descendit Ihesus in Galgala, et edificavit sacrarium lapidibus fortissimis, et non intulit in eos ferrum sicuti praeceperat Moyses. Et statuit lapides magnos in monte Gebal et dealbavit eos et scripsot super eos verba legis manifesta valde. (. . .)

we disregard the mountains mentioned in MT-Josh. 8:30–35, since the context of the passage, Josh. 5:1–2, situating it at the border of the river Jordan deep in the Arabah, does not leave a plausible location for the mountains mentioned in Josh. 8:30.33.

* Fascinating as the various exegetical traditions might be, they are in fact irrelevant to our discussion, since we do have two (ancient) Hebrew textual witnesses of Joshua that differ widely from each other. The paraphrases and interpretations are therefore not vital to our argumentation. Moreover, they deal with the biblical text in a free manner and are also relatively young (first century CE for Josephus and Pseudo-Philo, second century CE for rabbi Ishmael) compared with 4QJosh[a] (ca. 100 BCE), LXX (ca. 200 BCE) and MT. These traditions require a study of their own.[46]
* What makes the passage nomistic? Its position (Rofé) or its contents (Noort), and how does an answer to this question relate to the divergencies between the textual witnesses?
* Is it possible to make a connection between this passage and the main literary strata in Joshua. Is it a creation of the Deuteronomist (J. Hollenberg, M. Noth, R. Smend and others),[47] part of the Priestly Codex (J.G. Vink),[48] or a product from the circle of nomistic Deuteronomists (E. Noort)?
* Is the position of the passage in the context of Joshua 4–5 really the ideal setting for the passage within the Deuteronomistic History, if the Israelite people had heard the entire *torah* read to them by Moses just before they crossed the Jordan, as narrated in Deuteronomy?
* The text of 4QJosh[a] contains some variants with MT and LXX and most notably a complete line that has not been identified. What could its contents be, and what consequences does this have for the discussion of these variants?

[46] See for instance D.A. GLATT, *Chronological Displacement in Biblical and Related Literatures.* (SBL Dissertation Series 139) Georgia 1993, pp. 83–89; C. BEGG, The Cisjordanian Altar(s) and their Associated Rites According to Josephus, in *Biblische Zeitschrift* NF. 41 (1997), pp. 192–211; and C. BEGG, The Ceremonies at Gilgal/Ebal According to Pseudo-Philo, in *ETL* 73 (1997), pp. 72–83.

[47] J. HOLLENBERG, Die deuteronomistische Bestandtheile, pp. 478–481; M. NOTH, *Überlieferungsgeschichtliche Studien.* Tübingen 1953², p. 43; R. SMEND, *Die Entstehung des Alten Testaments*, p. 114: 'Eine Dtr Neubildung'.

[48] J.G. VINK, *The Date and Origin of the Priestly Code in the Old Testament*, pp. 77–80.

Before we allow textual and literary criticism to answer each other's questions, it is necessary to study the various textual witnesses on their own and try to solve the literary-critical issues independently of the textual data. Again, our point of departure will be the MT, since this is the only Hebrew witness that has been preserved completely. In the following paragraph (section 9.4) the questions concerning the literary context of the passage will be dealt with; in the subsequent paragraphs the data from 4QJosh[a] (section 9.5) and LXX (section 9.6) will be discussed.

9.4 Redaction-Critical Analysis of the Hebrew Text

In order to find an answer to the question of the proper literary context of the passage, it is necessary to turn again to the relation between our passage and the parallels in Deuteronomy and try to disentangle the intricate problems in Deuteronomy 27. Here I will follow most of what has been said about the passage by scholars such as A. Kuenen, E. Nielsen, H. Seebass, M. Anbar, and E. Noort.[49]

9.4.1 *The Relation Between MT-Josh. 8:30–35,—Deut. 27:1–8.11–13 and Deut. 11:29–30*

The first thing to be noted in the text of Deuteronomy 27 is the literary-critical tension between verse 2 and verse 4. In these verses we find the same command repeated in almost exactly the same words, but each contains a unique element: verse 2 stresses the time, while verse 4 gives the location:

27²	והיה ביום אשר תעברו את־הירדן . . .
27⁴	והיה בעברכם את־הירדן
27²	והקמת לך אבנים גדלות
27⁴	תקימו את־האבנים האלה אשר אנכי מצוה אתכם היום בהר עיבל

[49] A. Kuenen, Bijdragen tot de critiek van Pentateuch en Jozua. V, pp. 297–323. and A. Kuenen, *Historisch-critisch onderzoek*², pp. 122–128; E. Nielsen, *Shechem*, pp. 75–80; H. Seebass, Garizim und Ebal als Symbole von Segen und Fluch, in *Biblica* 62 (1982). pp. 22–31; M. Anbar, The Story about the Building of an Altar on Mount Ebal; E. Noort, The Traditions of Ebal and Gerizim.

The verses also differ with respect to the function of the stones. According to verses 2–3 they are meant to be plastered (ושׂדת אותם בשׂיד),[50] so that the words of the *torah* can be written on them (וכתבת עליהן את־כל־דברי התורה הזאת); according to verses 4–7 they are intended as an altar for sacrifices. The commands concerning the undamaged state of the stones (27:5 לא־תניף עליהם ברזל; 27:6 אבנים שׁלמות) are in accordance with the Law on altars in the Covenant Code in Exod. 20:25:[51]

> If you make me an altar you will not build it of hewn stones (לא־תבנה אתהן גזית) for if you wield your iron tool upon it (כי חרבך הנפת עליה) you profane it.

Verse 8, however, transforms the altar stones into a stele again via the resumption of verse 4. The addition באר היטב, *very clearly*, links the passage to Deut. 1:5, with Hab.2:2 the only other place where the verb באר occurs:[52]

> On the other side of the Jordan in the land of Moab Moses undertook to expound this torah, saying (האיל משה באר את־התורה הזאת לאמר): . . .

Most plausibly, Deut. 27:2–3.8 is to be seen as a Deuteronomistic correction of an older commandment, changing the instruction to build an altar on Mount Ebal into a command to inscribe the *torah* on stones immediately after the crossing of the Jordan.[53] The motive for this transformation probably lies in a polemic between Judaean scribes and circles around Samaria, perhaps in the period immediately after the return from exile, as has been argued by Horst Seebass.[54]

---

[50] The verb שׂיד occurs only here in the Hebrew Bible.

[51] See P. Heger, *The Three Biblical Altar Laws*. (BZAW 279) Berlin/New York 1999; N. Na'aman, The Law of the Altar in Deuteronomy and the Cultic Site Near Shechem, in S.L. McKenzie, Th. Römer, H.H. Schmid (eds.), *Rethinking the Foundations. Historiography in the Ancient World and in the Bible*. (BZAW 294) Berlin/New York 2000, pp. 141–161.

[52] Thus E. Nielsen, *Shechem*, p. 63.

[53] Thus e.g. N. Na'aman, The Law of the Altar in Deuteronomy and the Cultic Site Near Shechem, pp. 147–151; E. Noort, The Traditions of Ebal and Gerizim, pp. 177–178; M. Anbar, The Story about the Building of an Altar on Mount Ebal. Anbar and Noort stress the seam between Deut. 27:4 and 27:5–7, but to my mind the seam between 27:4–7 and 27:2–3 on the one hand and 27:8 on the other is more important.

[54] H. Seebass, Garizim und Ebal als Symbole von Segen und Fluch, p. 28, bases his dating on a common, but not undisputed anti-Samaritan exegesis of Hag.

In Deut. 27:11–13, Mount Ebal appears as the geographical symbol of the curse (27:13 ואלה יעמדו על־הקללה בהר עיבל) as opposed to Mount Gerizim, on which (if that is the correct translation of עמד על[55] the tribes Simeon, Levi, Judah, Issachar, Joseph and Benjamin are to stand, in order to represent symbolically (?) the blessing for the people (27:12 אלה יעמדו לברך את־העם על־הר גרזים). H. Seebass has convincingly argued that the specific division of the tribes probably reflects the political situation under the expansions of Josiah (whose territory would comprise that of these six tribes).[56] Deut. 11:29–30 (understood as a unit) would be another attempt on the part of the Deuteronomistic author of Deut. 27:1–3.8 to preserve the sacred text (Deut. 27:4–7), but to tone down the importance of the mountains Ebal and Gerizim.[57] Deut. 27:9–10 is probably the original link between Deuteronomy 26 and 28, as argued by A. Kuenen,[58] whereas Deut. 27:15–28 may reflect a Priestly expansion.[59] These verses have no connection with MT-Josh. 8:30–35, and are for that reason not important to our discussion.

On the basis of these observations, the following conclusions with respect to the literary context of MT-Josh. 8:30–35 may be drawn:

* The suggestion advanced by Ulrich that only the words בהר עיבל/בהר הריזרין in Deut. 27:4 are a secondary Samaritan expansion

---

2:10–14, which should enable the historian to date the conflict between Jerusalem and Samaria to the early post-Exilic period; see further J.W. Rothstein, *Juden und Samaritaner. Die grundlegende Scheidung von Judenthum und Heidentum.* (BZAW 3) 1908; and for a different opinion A.S. van der Woude, *Haggai—Maleachi.* (POT) Nijkerk 1982, pp. 58–59. According to E. Noort, The Traditions of Ebal and Gerizim, p. 177, the anti-Samaritan polemic is already visible in the choice of the author of Deut. 27:4 for Mount Ebal instead of Mount Gerizim, but unfortunately Noort does not try to give an absolute chronology for his historical reconstructions.

[55] H. Seebass, Garizim und Ebal als Symbole von Segen und Fluch, p. 23, explains the prepositions in the light of MT-Josh. 8:33 where אל־מול, *towards*, has been used, but it seems to me that here different prepositions and different literary strata are confused. The use of the phrase אל־מול probably reflects a simplification of the idea presented in Deut. 27:11–13, just as the whole passage Deut. 27:11–13 has been transformed into Josh. 8:33, as will be shown below.

[56] H. Seebass, Garizim und Ebal als Symbole von Segen und Fluch, p. 24; See further E. Noort, Traditions of Ebal and Gerizim, p. 175.

[57] So E. Noort, The Traditions of Ebal and Gerizim, pp. 177–178.

[58] A. Kuenen, Bijdragen tot de critiek van Pentateuch en Jozua V, pp. 301–304.

[59] A. Kuenen, Bijdragen tot de critiek van Pentateuch en Jozua V, pp. 306–309.

corrected by Judaean scribes can now be refuted, as has already been argued by Noort.[60] From the outset the idea that Judaean scribes would accept a biblical text altered by Samaritans seems questionable. Moreover, the reading בהרגריזין in the Samaritan sources reflects a secondary, ideologically motivated alteration of בהר עיבל, attested by all other witnesses to Deut. 27:4, including LXX*.

Of the witnesses to LXX-Deut. 27:4 only the fifth or sixth-century CE Lyons manuscript[61] seems to support the reading attested by the Samaritan sources. Wevers characterises its text (designated as Cod. 100) as a witness to the European text,[62] but does not group it among his recensions of LXX-Deuteronomy. For LXX-Joshua its text can be classified as 'Lucianic' or 'Syrian' ($\underline{S}_a$), as labelled by Margolis. Den Hertog points out that the manuscript grouping for LXX-Deuteronomy by Wevers (*n* = W^I.54–75.75–458.767) and that for LXX-Josh. ($\underline{S}_a$ = K.VetLat.54–75.127) by Margolis are by and large identical.[63] Now, one of the characteristics of this group of manuscripts, at least for LXX-Joshua, is the simplification of geographical names. Given the fact that Vetus Latina is a daughter translation of LXX, and the fact that the geographical name Γαιβάλ in LXX-Deut. 27:4 (supported by A B F M V 29–426–707–oI^{-15} 56–129 W^I-54' 130–321–343'–730 121 *z* 55 407 Cyr II 665 Co) has been corrupted into various forms such as γαβαιλ 509; γεβαδ 71; and even γαλααδ 19, it seems plausible that the reading *in monte Garzin* in this particular Codex Lugdunensis reflects a secondary attempt by the Latin translator, or a Greek or Latin copyist, to make sense of a corrupted Greek/Latin *Vorlage*. The reading Γαιβάλ attested by the main witnesses to LXX-Deuteronomy reflects the original Greek translation (thus also Wevers in his main text of LXX-Deuteronomy). As a result, LXX*-Deut. 27:4 does not support the alleged originality of the Samaritan reading.

60 E. Noort, The Traditions of Ebal and Gerizim, p. 176.

61 U. Robert, *Heptateuchi partis posterioris versio latina antiquissima e codici lugdunensi*, p. 30.

62 J.W. Wevers, *Deuteronomium*. (SVTG III,2) Göttingen 1977, p. 20.

63 C.G. den Hertog, *Studien*, pp. 15–17. Wevers avoids the term 'Lucianic', and prefers to speak only of an *n* group of manuscripts, see J.W. Wevers, *Text History of the Greek Deuteronomy*, pp. 17–30.

* In Deut. 27 the various literary layers are still discernible, whereas in MT-Josh. 8:30–35 elements from the various literary strata in Deuteronomy 27 have been merged into a homogeneous passage. Apparently, the late scribe of MT-Josh. 8:30–35 had the text of Deut. 27 in its present layered form in front of him.
* On the other hand, the author of MT-Josh. 8:30–35 introduced his own elements as the following synopsis of MT-Josh. 8:30–35 with the parallel passages from Deuteronomy makes clear:

8^{30}	אז יבנה יהושע מזבח ליהוה אלהי ישראל	ובנית שם מזבח ליהוה אלהיך	27^{5}
	בהר עיבל	תקימו את־האבנים האלה. . . בהר עיבל	27^{4}
8^{31}	כאשר צוה משה עבד־יהוה את בני ישראל	ויצו משה וזקני ישראל את־העם	27^{1}
	ככתוב בספר תורת משה		
	מזבח אבנים שלמות	אבנים שלמות תבנה את מזבח יהוה אלהיך	27^{6}
	אשר לא־הניף עליהן ברזל	לא־תניף עליהם ברזל	27^{5}
	ויעלו עליו עלות ליהוה	והעלית עליו עולת ליהוה אלהיך	27^{6}
	ויזבחו שלמים	וזבחת שלמים	27^{7}
		ואכלת שם	
		ושמחת לפני יהוה אלהיך	
8^{32}	ויכתב־שם על־האבנים את משנה תורת משה	וכתבת עליהן את־כל־דברי התורה הזאת//	27^{3}
		וכתבת על־האבנים את־כל־דברי התורה הזאת	27^{8}
	אשר כתב לפני בני ישראל	[ויכתב משה את־התורה הזאת ?//]	[31^{9}
8^{33}	וכל־ישראל וזקניו שטרים ושפטיו	[Ø Deut. 27; 11:29-30, cf. Josh. 23:2, 24:1]	
	עמדים מזה ומזה לארון		
	נגד הכהנים הלוים נשאי ארון ברית־יהוה		
	כגר כאזרח		
	חציו אל־מול הר־גריזים	אלה יעמדו לברך את־העם על־הר גרזים	27^{12}
		בעברכם את־הירדן	
		שמעון ולוי ויהודה ויששכר ויוסף ובנימן	
	והחציו אל־מול הר־עיבל	ואלה יעמדו על־הקללה בהר עיבל	27^{13}
		ראובן גד ואשר וזבולן דן ונפתלי	
	כאשר צוה מאה עבד־יהוה		
	לברך את־העם ישראל בראשנה	אלה יעמדו לברך את־העם על־הר גרזים	27^{12}
8^{34}	ואחרי־כן קרא את־כל־דברי התורה		
	הברכה וקללה		
	ככל־הכתוב בספר התורה		
8^{35}	לא־היה דבר מכל אשר־צוה משה		
	אשר לא־קרא יהושע נגד כל־קהל ישראל		
	והנשים והטף והגר ההלך בקרבם		

* Elements of the older literary stratum in Deut. 27:4–7 are reflected in MT-Josh. 8:30–31, while elements of the younger literary stratum in Deut. 27:1–3.8 have been taken up in MT-Josh. 8:32.
* The temporal element in Deut. 27:2, on the other hand, has been smoothed to the general and inconclusive word אז, *then.*
* Moreover, all elements that refer to the crossing of the Jordan, so abundantly present in Deut. 11:29; 27:2.3.4.12, are completely absent from MT-Josh. 8:30–35.
* The references to cultic activities seem to have been condensed in MT-Joshua 8 (31). The second part of Deut. 27:7 has not been taken up in Josh. 8:31. Mention of cultic activities such as burnt-offerings and peace-offerings is restricted to a minimum.
* A shift in the position and function of the people of Israel is discernable. In Josh. 8:33 all emphasis falls on the people as a whole as expressed by the word כל in MT-Josh. 8:33 כל־ישׂראל, which is further strengthened in MT-Josh. 8:35 in the phrase כל־קהל ישׂראל. On the other hand, the explicit mentioning of the officials of the people (כל־ישׂראל וזקניו שׁטרים ושׁפטיו) has no counterpart in Deut. 27:11–13, but does have a counterpart in Josh. 23:2 en 24:1, where Joshua also addresses the people.
* The other differences between Deut. 27:11–13 and MT-Josh. 8:33 attest to the same tendency. Whereas in Deut. 27:12–13 we find a specific distribution of the Israelite tribes, half of them symbolising the blessing, the other half symbolising the curse, in Josh. 8:33 it is the entire people that faces the two mountains. The people no longer stand on the mountains (על־הר גריזים en בהר עיבל), but are simply looking towards them (אל־מול). MT-Josh. 8:33 simply speaks of *half of them facing the one mountain, half of them facing the other* (חציו . . . והחציו). Apparently the entire nation receives the blessing *in the beginning* (יעמדו לברך את־העם בראשׁנה).
* Blessing and curse are still present in MT-Joshua 8 (34), but are now written down in the book of the *torah* of Moses, and no longer represent independent entities. In fact the whole ceremony described in Deut. 27:11–13 has been transformed from a visualisation of blessing and curse into a proclamation of the *torah* (which happens to contain some blessing and curse sections).
* MT-Josh. 8:34–35 has no counterpart in Deuteronomy 27. Here the specific character and intention of MT-Josh. 8:30–35 come to light most clearly: the building of an altar, the cultic activities, and the blessing and curse ceremony are completely subordinated to

> the stress on the *torah* being written on the stones by Joshua. We here find the expression 'a copy of the *torah*' (משנה תורת משה אשר כתב לפני בני ישראל), which is another innovation *vis-à-vis* Deut. 27:4.8, where the expression *all the words of this torah* (כל־דברי התורה הזאת) seems to reflect an as yet less unified concept of the *torah*. The notion that Moses wrote the *torah* (MT-Josh. 8:32) occurs in Deuteronomy only in Deut. 31:9 (ויכתב משה את־התורה הזאת).

These observations support the general consensus that MT-Josh. 8:30–35 forms a relatively late composition written by a redactor who had Deut. 27 in its present layered form in front of him. The specific interest of this redactor was to put all emphasis on the *torah* of Moses.

9.4.2 *The Nomistic Character of MT-Josh. 8:30–35*

The word *torah* takes a central position in this passage. It is mentioned no less than four times in this relatively short text (8:31.32.34.34), which constitutes almost half of all the (nine) places where this theologically important word occurs in Joshua (also in Josh. 1:7.8; 22:5; and 23:6, whereas the phrase בספר תורת אלהים in 24:26 clearly differs from the other eight instances). In conformity with Josh. 1:7.8; 22:5; and 23:6 and unlike 24:26, the reference to the *torah* is clearly connected to the person of Moses who figures no less than five times in our passage, which amounts to 10 % of the 49 places in Joshua, where Moses is mentioned. Significant also is the formulation in which Moses is mentioned ((כ)אשר צוה משה (עבד־יהוה) (את־בני ישראל)), which occurs three times in MT-Josh. 8:30–35. In MT-Josh. 8:31, the phrase refers to Moses' command to build an altar (Deut. 27:4); in MT-Josh. 8:33 it refers to Deut. 27:11–13, while in MT-Josh. 8:35, everything Moses has commanded has been subsumed under the word כל, which connects this notion to the כל־דברי התורה and כל הכתוב בספר התורה in MT-Josh. 8:34. We may conclude, therefore, that the nomistic element (if this is a proper way of referring to the concept of *torah*) is inherent in the passage itself and not dependent on its position in the book.

The Greek translator of this passage even intensified the stress on the *torah* and the correspondance between this passage and Deuteronomy by rendering the phrase בספר תורת משה (8:31.34) by ἐν τῷ νόμῳ Μωυσῆ, making a strict rendering of ספר by βίβλιον superfluous. The copy (משנה) of the *torah* (MT-Josh. 8:32) has been explicitly identified with the book of Deuteronomy in LXX-Josh. 9:2c καὶ ἔγραψεν . . . τὸ δευτερονόμιον, νόμον Μωυσῆ (cf. LXX-Deut. 17:18).[64]

The passages in the book of Joshua that show the closest affinities with MT-Josh. 8:30–35, i.e. Josh. 1:7–8, 22:5 and 23, are all redactional expansions to the book, intended to underline the importance of the *torah*:

1^{7}	רק חזק ואמץ מאד לשמר לעשות ככל־התורה אשר צוך משה עבדי אל־תסור ממנו ימין ושמאול	1^{7}
1^{8}	לא־ימוש ספר התורה הזה מפיך . . . למען תשמר לעשות ככל־הכתוב בו . . .	1^{8}
8^{31}	כאשר צוה משה עבד־יהוה את־בני ישראל ככתוב בספר תורת משה . . .	8^{31}
8^{34}	ואחרי־כן קרא את־כל־דברי התורה הברכה והקללה ככל הכתוב בספר התורה:	8^{34}
8^{35}	לא־היה דבר מכל אשר־צוה משה אשר לא־קרא יהושע נגד כל־קהל ישראל . . .	8^{35}
22^{5}	רק שמרו מאד לעשות את־המצוה ואת־התורה אשר צוה אתכם משה עבד־יהוה . . .	22^{5}
23^{6}	וחזקתם מאד לשמר ולעשות את כל־הכתוב בספר תורת משה לבלתי סור־ממנו ימין ושמאול	23^{6}

Although the father of DtrN, Rudolf Smend, considers our passage to be a product of the hand of DtrH, these affinities in concepts and expressions between the passages mentioned above—all secondary additions to the DtrH layer of the book of Joshua—dictate that MT-Josh. 8:30–35 should be ascribed to this same literary layer, that is: DtrN.[65]

This conclusion is corroborated by the fact that the characteristic elements of the other two redactional strata in Joshua, DtrH and RedP, are absent. If one considers the Deuteronomistic parts of Joshua to be the continuation of both the frame of the book of Deuteronomy (Deut. 1–3; 31) and its legislative core (Deut. 12–26), it remains inexplicable how a DtrH author of MT-Josh. 8:30–35 would deliberately have created a passage that would violate one of the basic dogmas of his ideology, i.e., the centralisation of the cult in Jerusalem (Deuteronomy 12).[66] If a Deuteronomistic author had found a passage in an older, pre-DtrH version of Joshua, dealing with an altar outside Jerusalem, even in the center of the apostate Nothern Kingdom, he would certainly have excised the passage.

[64] See e.g. E. Nielsen, *Shechem*, p. 75.

[65] See section 4.2.2 above.

[66] See e.g. O. Eißfeldt, *Hexateuch-Synopse*. Leipzig 1922, p. 281*.

Elements characteristic for the Priestly layer of the book of Joshua are also absent. The people of Israel are presented in MT-Josh. 8:30–35 as עָם (8:33) and קָהָל (8:35), not as עֵדָה, which is the characteristic expression employed by the Priestly writer(s). Joshua is the sole leading person; Eleazar does not figure here; cultic activities such as burnt-offerings and peace-offerings are performed without explicit mention of the intermediary role played by the priests. The typical distinction between priests and Levites is not made here. Instead, we find the Deuteronomistic expression 'Levitical priests', הכהנים הלוים (8:33).[67]

The Greek text does reflect the distinction οἱ ἱερεις <u>καὶ</u> οἱ Λευῖται, but on the other hand (also) changes the number of the verbs ויעלו עליו עלות ליהוה ויזבחו שלמים from plural to singular: καὶ ἀνεβίβασεν ἐκεῖ ὁλοκαυτώματα κυρίῳ καὶ θυσίαν σωτηρίου, so that it becomes even more explicit that not the priests but a lay person, i.e. Joshua, performs the offerings.

The change from the Deuteronomistic expression to the Priestly term in LXX-Josh. (9:2c) to my mind reflects a secondary harmonisation with the Priestly view, and also reflects the restructuring of the Hebrew text by the Greek translator. The Greek translator adopted the list of Israelite functionaries mentioned in MT-Josh. 8:33, but replaced the participial form (עמדים) by the imperfect παρεπορεύοντο, *and all Israel and their elders and the judges and their scribes went along on each side of the ark, and the priests and the Levites carried the ark of the covenant of the Lord*, and after that introduced both the priests and the Levites (*καὶ* οἱ ἱερεῖς *καὶ* οἱ Λευῖται) with the conjunction καί. The Greek translator thus strengthened the stress on the totality of Israel and its ranks. Lea Mazor, too, considers the LXX to be secondary here,[68] although she ascribed the alteration to a Hebrew scribe on the basis of the Hebrew text of *Mishna Soṭah* VII 5b, where an allusion is made to MT-Josh. 8:33, but where we also find the distinction between priests and Levites:[69]

---

[67] See section 4.2.3 above.

[68] Lea Mazor, עיונים, pp. 388–390.

[69] See H. Bietenhard, *Soṭah. (Die des Ehebruchs verdächtige). Text, Übersetzung und Erklärung, nebst einem textkritischen Anhang* (Die Mischna. Text, Übersetzung und ausführliche Erklärung III.6) Berlin 1956.

> Six tribes went up to the top of the mountain Gerizim and six tribes went up to the mountain Ebal and the priests *and* the Levites (והכהנים והלוים) and the ark were standing below in the center. The priests surrounded the ark (הכהנים מקיפים את הארון) and the Levites (surrounded) the priests (והלוים את הכהנים) and all Israel on one side and on the other side (. . .)

Yet, we find a similar adaptation to the Priestly concepts in LXX-Josh. 4:4, where no deviating Hebrew *Vorlage* can be postulated. The twelve men selected by Joshua (אשר הכין) to carry the twelve stones from the river bed are transformed into 'notables' (οἱ ἐνδόξοι) under influence of the Priestly designation of representatives of the twelve tribes as the 'prominent delegates' (נשׂיאים), as demonstrated by Max Margolis:[70]

4[4]	καὶ ἀνακαλεσάμενος Ἰησοῦς	וַיִּקְרָא יְהוֹשֻׁעַ
	δώδεκα ἄνδρας	אֶל־שְׁנֵים הֶעָשָׂר אִישׁ
	τῶν ἐνδόξων ἀπὸ τῶν υἱῶν Ισραηλ,	אֲשֶׁר הֵכִין מִבְּנֵי יִשְׂרָאֵל
	--- ἕνα --- --- ἀφ' *ἑκάστης* φυλῆς,	אִישׁ־אֶחָד אִישׁ־אֶחָד מִשָּׁבֶט׃

We furthermore find a similar contamination of the rival Deuteronomistic and Priestly concepts in Josh. 3:3, where the context of the passage, because of the link with Josh. 1:11 (DtrH), makes clear that the expression 'Levitical priests' must be the older one, whereas the distinction between the 'priests' and 'Levites' likewise reflects an adaptation to the Priestly terminology:

3[3]	καὶ ἐνετείλαντο τῷ λαῷ	וַיְצַוּוּ אֶת־הָעָם
	λέγοντες	לֵאמֹר
	Ὅταν ἴδητε τὴν κιβωτὸν	כִּרְאוֹתְכֶם אֵת אֲרוֹן
	τῆς διαθήκης κυρίου τοῦ θεοῦ *ἡμῶν*	בְּרִית־יְהוָה אֱלֹהֵיכֶם
	καὶ τοὺς ἱερεῖς *ἡμῶν καὶ* τοὺς Λευίτας	וְהַכֹּהֲנִים הַלְוִיִּם
	αἴροντας αὐτήν,	נֹשְׂאִים אֹתוֹ

In Deut. 27:9 we find a similar confusion, but here the distinction is found only in the A and Byzantine text of LXX (καὶ οἱ ἱερεῖς *καὶ* οἱ Λευῖται), and in Peš. ܘܟܗܢܐ ܘܠܘܝܐ.[71]

---

[70] M.L. MARGOLIS, τῶν ἐνδόξων.

[71] See E. NIELSEN, *Shechem*, p. 66; J.W. WEVERS, *Notes on the Greek Text of Deuteronomy*, p. 419.

If MT-Josh. 8:30–35 is to be placed in the literary context of the DtrN-stratum of the book of Joshua, rather than the DtrH or RedP-strata, there remains no basis for the interesting thesis by J.G. Vink, who ascribed our passage to the Priestly Codex (P^G).[72] Vink considered the Priestly Codex, understood as an independent literary work, to be the literary reflection of Ezra's attempt in the Late Persian period (398 BCE) to unite Judaeans (designated by the term אזרח) and Samaritans (designated by גרים) under a single Law Code. MT-Josh. 8:30–35 would then be the fictitious literary wrapping (Joshua proclaims the *torah* at Shechem) of this Judaean religious mission (Ezra propagates his Law Code [P^G] to Samaritan circles). Joshua 18:1–10 and 22:9–34 would reflect the same intention. As noted above, however, the specific Priestly concepts in these passages (such as the אהל מועד and the term כבשׁ for subdual) are absent from MT-Josh. 8:30–35.

Vink, however, attached great value to the phrase כגר כאזרח, *allochthonous and authochthonous alike*, a formula that in the Hebrew Bible appears only in Priestly passages such as Exod. 12:19.48.49 (prescripts concerning Passover), Lev. 16:29 (Day of Atonement), 17:15 (purification after the consuming of a contaminated animal), 18:26 (laws concerning sexual behaviour), 19:34 (command to love the stranger), 24:16 (death penalty for a blasphemer), 24:22 (death penalty for a murderer), Num. 9:14 (prescripts concerning Passover), 15:29–30 (atonement for inadvertent sins, punishment for premeditated sins), and Ezek. 47:22 (where the *gerim* are integrated among the receipients of the redistributed land). Vink, following H. Cazelles en P. Grelot,[73] took the phrase as a covert allusion to the groups in Judaea (אזרחים) and Samaria (גרים) and thus elevated it to one of the most significant characteristics of the Priestly vocabulary. Although the Deuteronomistic (DtrH) phraseology contains a rival expression for the same idea, האח והגר,[74] it seems dubious to me to base the attribution of the passage solely on this expression. If the phrase were connected to the time of Ezra, Nehemiah and the Elephantine papyri,

[72] J.G. VINK, *The Date and Origin of the Priestly Code in the Old Testament*, pp. 77–80.

[73] H. CAZELLES, La mission d'Esdras, *VT* 4 (1954), pp. 113–140; P. GRELOT, Le Papyrus Pascal d'Eléphantine, in *VT* 4 (1954), pp. 349–384; P. GRELOT, Le Papyrus Pascal d'Eléphantine et le problème du Pentateuque, in *VT* 5 (1955), pp. 250–265; and P. GRELOT, Le dernière étape de la rédaction sacerdotale', in *VT* 6 (1956), pp. 174–189.

[74] See e.g., M. WEINFELD, *Deuteronomy 1–11*, p. 36.

one would expect to find this formula in these sources, which is not the case. In MT-Josh. 8:33 the formula can well be understood as part of the intention of the author to portray all branches of the people. As a result, there is no reason to attribute MT-Josh. 8:30–35 to P (either P^G or RedP) instead of to DtrN.

9.4.3 *The Nomistic Position of Josh. 8:30–35 in MT*

Once it has become clear that MT-Josh. 8:30–35 is the product of the nomistic redactor of Joshua, it is also possible to explain the position of the passage in MT. It is clear that one of the motives for DtrN to create this piece must have been the wish to portray Joshua as the ideal follower of the *torah* of Moses, and to create the fulfillment of the commandments in this *torah.* Since the *torah* itself had taken the central position in the ideological framework of the nomistic writer, it was no longer a problem to accept the existence of a cultic site outside Jerusalem. Nevertheless, by placing the passage at this juncture in the book of Joshua, i.e. after the narrative of the fall of Ai, the DtrN redactor remained vague enough to situate the area both in the neighbourhood of the Jordan and the area around Shechem. For that reason no references to the crossing of the Jordan (Deut. 11:29; 27:2.3.4.12) have been adopted from the source text (Deuteronomy) into this DtrN-creation.

More important for the DtrN redactor was his understanding of the essence and function of the *torah.* As R. Smend has demonstrated, the DtrN redactor saw as one of his main concerns the need to keep Israel strictly separated from the foreign peoples.[75] For DtrN, the opposite of following the *torah* was to merge with the foreign nations. A passage from Joshua 23 (also a product of DtrN) makes this very clear:

> [23[6]] You will remain very strong (וחזקתם מאד cf. Josh. 1:7 DtrN) to observe and perform everything that is written in the *book of the torah of Moses* (כל־הכתוב בספר תורת משה Josh. 1:7–8) *in order not* to deviate from it to the right or to the left (לבלתי סור־ממנו ימין ושמאול) [23[7]] *in order not to go to these peoples* (לבלתי־בוא בגוים האלה) *that have remained with you* (הנשארים האלה אתכם) you will not bring into memory the name of their gods you will not swear by them, worship them or bow before

[75] See section 4.2.2 above.

> them in worship. (...) [23[12]] But if you ever turn away and cling to the *remnant* of *these peoples that have remained with you* and *intermarry* with them (והתחתנתם בהם) *so that you will merge with them* (ובאתם בהם) *and they with you*... (והם בכם), [23[13]] be fully aware that Yhwh your God will not continue to disposses these nations from before you. Then they will become for you a trap and a snare a scourge on your sides and thorns in your eyes until you perish from this good land which Yhwh your God is giving to you.

The doom scenario depicted in Josh. 23:13.15–16 may readily be identified with the curse referred to in MT-Josh. 8:34 (cf. Deuteronomy 28). For DtrN, obedience to the *torah* was equal to keeping one's distance from non-Israelite peoples, while intermarriage was equal to disobedience (cf. Ezra 9) and a direct threat to the identity of Israel.[76]

Contrary to the triumphant claim of DtrH in Josh. 21:43–45 that none of the foreign peoples had been able to withstand Joshua, DtrN takes into account a remnant of these foreign peoples, which continue to pose a threat to Israel's faithful observance of the *torah*. The origin of precisely this problem can be found in Joshua 9. This chapter narrates how a non-Israelite people, i.e. the Gibeonites, managed to remain alive and secure in Israel.[77] Unlike Rahab and her family, this group was not restricted to a single family, but constituted a complete population (that of the Hivites according to Josh. 9:7; 11:19). In the view of DtrN, this event must have been something like the primeval Fall.

It is true that MT-Josh. 8:30–35 does not contain these negative overtones. Rather, we only find the statement that Israel received a blessing (לברך את־העם ישׂראל), but significantly—as it deviates from the *Vorlage* in Deut. 27:12—it is qualified by the word בראשׁנה, *in the beginning*. This word introduces a restriction: in the beginning everything might be a blessed situation, but sin and curse are luring. It is the same method DtrN employed when he altered the optimistic statements in Josh. 21:43–45 (DtrH) by adding the small but omi-

[76] R. SMEND, Das Gesetz und die Völker, p. 508; idem, Das unerobertе Land, pp. 100–101; idem, *Die Entstehung des Alten Testaments*, pp. 124–125.

[77] E. NOORT, 4QJoshua[a] and the History of Tradition, p. 141, also suggests a link between the nomistic ideal and the continued presence of the remaining people personified by the Gibeonites, but he does not draw the conclusions I present here.

nous phrase 'until the present day' (עד היום הזה): *so far nobody has been able to withstand you, but . . .* (23:8.9):[78]

DtrH 21[45]
לא־נפל דבר מכל הדבר הטוב
אשר־דבר יהוה אל־בית ישראל הכל בא

DtrN 23[14]
כי לא־נפל דבר אחד מכל הדברים הטובים
אשר דבר יהוה אלהיכם עליכם הכל באו לכם
לא־נפל ממנו דבר אחד

23[15]
והיה כאשר־בא עליכם כל־הדבר הטוב
אשר דבר יהוה אלהיכם אליכם
כן יביא יהוה עליכם את כל־הדבר הרע
עד־השמידו אותכם מעל האדמה הטובה הזאת

For these reasons we may conclude that contents and position of the passage in MT correspond neatly. If the passage is ascribed to DtrN, it is most plausible that this redactor deliberatedly inserted his nomistic passage immediately before Josh. 9, that is at the position where we find it in MT/LXX. Since in the theology of DtrN the theme of the conquest of the land has been made completely subordinate to that of the observance of the *torah*, a position of this passage right at the beginning of the conquest narrative (i.e. before Josh. 5:2) would be anything but ideal and self-evident (*pace* Noort).

9.5 4QJoshua[A]

But what about 4QJoshua[a]? Unlike the case in Josh. 8:11–18 (discussed in the previous chapter) we do find the text of Josh. 8:34–35 physically attested at the beginning of column I. Does this mean that an independent literary-critical investigation supports A. Rofé's thesis? What remains problematic in his view is that there seems to be no motive for a nomistic corrector to transpose this nomistic passage, since the nomistic ideal had already been presented at the beginning of the book, in Josh. 1:7–8. Since the theme of the land

[78] See R. Smend, Das Gesetz und die Völker, pp. 502–504; E. Noort, Land in zicht? Geloofsvisie, werkelijkheid en geschiedenis in het oudtestamentische spreken van het land. Enkele opmerkingen naar aanleiding van Jozua 21:43–45, in *Tussen openbaring en ervaring. Studies aangeboden aan prof.dr. G.P. Hartvelt.* Kampen 1986, pp. 94–113; and further section 4.2.2. above.

was not as important to DtrN as it was to DtrH, there seems to be no clear motive for an even later nomist to mark the entry into the Promised Land by this passage. Moreover, the problem still remains that MT-Josh. 8:30–35 refers to two mountains which cannot be easily stationed somewhere near the border of the river Jordan. Noort emphasizes that the belief of the Deuteronomists was able to move mountains,[79] but what we find in Deut. 11:30 is not a transfer of the mountains Ebal and Gerizim to the river Jordan. Rather they are detached from their geographical position in order to fit both geography (near Shechem) and theology (near the river Jordan).

What has hindered the discussion so far is that the text of 4QJosh[a] has not been approached exclusively on its own terms, but from the outset has served to corroborate existing theories. What we certainly do not find in 4QJosh[a] is 'Joshua's First Altar in the Promised Land',[80] nor do we find in 4QJosh[a] any mountain theologically transposed from its geographical position (Shechem or Sinai). On the contrary, the few lines, that we do posses of this scroll make it impossible that 4QJosh[a] contained a version of MT-Josh. 8:30–35 in which the mountains mentioned in Josh. 8:30.33 figured. 4QJosh[a] contains a small plus in fragment 1, line 2: [בעברו]את הירד[ן], which makes clear that Joshua recited the *torah* (thus fragment 1, line 1 לא היה דבר מכל צוה משה[את יה]ושע אשר לא קרא יהשע נגד כל [ישראל]) while Israel was crossing the river Jordan. Israel does face the two mountains as in MT-Josh. 8:33, but according to this plus in 4QJosh[a] passes through the river Jordan, while Joshua recites from the *torah*. This idea is reinforced by the plus in 4QJosh[a] at the end of the same line 2. The phrase אחר אשר נתקו[ ], part of the editorial plus in 4QJosh[a] (5:x) links the preceding line to Josh. 4:18:

> When the priests bearing the ark of the covenant of Yhwh came up from the midst of the Jordan and the soles of the priest's feet were lifted up (נִתְּקוּ כפות רגלי הכהנים) to dry ground, the waters of the Jordan returned to their place (וישבו מי־הירדן למקומם).

---

[79] See E. Noort, 4QJoshua[a] and the History of Tradition, p. 135ff.; 'all our problems with Jos. 8:30–35, as stated above, have to do with the general presupposition that we know where the 'real' Gerizim and 'real' Ebal are located.' See further the relocation of the mountains by Eusebius, *Onomasticon* sub Γαιβαλ and its Latin translation by Jerome (section 9.2.5 above).

[80] Thus the title of Ulrich's preliminary publication of 4QJosh[a]. See E. Noort, 4QJoshua[a] and the History of Tradition, pp. 132–134: 'It cannot be demonstrated that the whole of the text of Joshua 8:30–35 belongs to the beginning of chapter 5. The text itself proves only the presence of 8:34b–35.'

Since the verb נתק appears in the book of Joshua further only in Josh. 8:6.16, where it has a completely different function, it is most plausible to link the plus in 4QJosh[a] to Josh. 4:18.[81] The conclusion must be, then, that if MT-Josh. 8:30–35 in its entirety had been transposed from its original position to its position in 4QJosh[a], the mountains Ebal and Gerizim could not have stood on their original geographical position, nor on the border of the river Jordan, but would have stood right in the middle of the river itself!

It is now time to rid ourselves of an obstacle to the proper understanding of the character of the difference between MT and 4QJosh[a]. Analogous to difference between MT and LXX, it has always been assumed that this divergence between 4QJosh[a] and MT(-LXX) could also be explained in terms of *transposition*: either the passage was transposed from its original position in 4QJosh[a] to its secondary position in MT-LXX, or vice versa. Nevertheless, the text of Josh. 8:19–Josh. 10:2 has been lost, so that we cannot be sure whether MT-Josh. 8:30–35 was present or absent there (but see below). I propose a different solution to the problem: in my view, Josh. 8:30–35 did form part of the text of 4QJosh[a] in the position as we find it in MT. In 4QJosh[a], however, those verses of this passage that narrate the writing of the *torah* on stones and its recitation (i.e., Josh. 8:32.34–35) were duplicated and added to the text of 4QJosh[a] after Josh. 5:1. The aim of this duplication of existing material was to bring the Joshua narratives in complete accordance with to the two commandments contained in Deut. 27:2 and Deut. 27:4. The scribe responsible for the doublet in 4QJosh[a] must have understood the commandments in Deut. 27:2 and 4 as two separate commands. He found the the second (*you will build an altar on mount Ebal*) fulfilled in Josh. 8:30, but missed the fulfillment of the first command (*on the day you pass over the Jordan you will erect large stones and write the words of the torah on them*). Nevertheless, the scribe did find a point of attachment in Josh. 4:20, where we are told that Joshua raised the twelve stones which the twelve representatives of the tribes had taken from the river bed.[82]

Thus, the scribe responsible for the expanded text as we find it in 4QJosh[a] added Josh. 8:32.34–35 to this passage (Josh. 4:20.21–24,

[81] Thus also A. Rofé, The Editing, p. 78: '... which shows, through its affinity with Josh 4:18 (MT), that the editor figured the ceremony to take place at the very crossing of the Jordan.'

[82] Thus also M. Anbar, The Story about the Building of an Altar on Mount Ebal, p. 307.

5:1), so that the commandment of Deut. 27:2–3 found its fulfillment in the book of Joshua as well. In order to elaborate his view, he added the element [בעברו]את הירד[ן] from Deut. 27:4 and incorporated this extension into the main text by means of the resumptive repetition of Josh. 4:18. In this way the scribe offered his own creative solution to the problems of Deut. 27, which were solved in so many different other ways by later generations (thus the rabbis and modern scholars). As a result, we may continue to trust our atlases regarding the position of the two mountains Ebal and Gerizim: they never left their place around Shechem.

If this interpretation of the plus in 4QJosh^{a} column I holds true, it is also possible to solve the question of the reconstruction of the text of 4QJosh^{a} and that attested on fragments 17–22, which contain remnants of Josh. 10:2–5 and 10:8–11. Fragments 19–22 offer a helpful point of departure since fragment 21, to my mind, preserves a bottom margin:

4QJoshua^{a}, col. VIII, fragments 19–22 [Josh. 10:6–11]

number of letterspaces

vacat

56 [10:8 ויאמר י]הוה אל י[הושע אל תירא מה]ם כי בידך נתתי[ם לא יעמד איש]
59 [מ]הם בפניך 10:9 ויבוא אל[יהם יהושע פתאם] כל הלילה הל[ך מן הגלגל 10:10 ויהמם]
67 [י]הוה לפנ[י י]שראל ויכ[ם מכה גדולה בגבעון וירדפם דרך מעלה בית חורן ויכם]
55 ע[ד עזקה ועד] מקדה 10:11 ויה[י ב]נסם [מפני ישראל הם במורד בית חורן]
59 ויהוה השליך עליהם אבנים מן השמ[ים עד עזקה וימתו רבים אשר מתו]
36 באבני הברד מאשר הרג[ו בני ישראל בחרב] [*vacat?*/

vacat

Both the top of fragment 20 and the bottom of fragment 22 contain empty space. The two *vacats* may refer to paragraph intervals, since Josh. 10:8 (attested by frg. 19–20) in MT is preceded by an open paragraph ending (פ), while Josh. 10:11 (attested by frg. 21–22) is followed in MT by a closed paragraph (ס). Ulrich is therefore reluctant to draw conclusions from these data.[83] The remainder, however,

---

[83] E. Ulrich, 4QJosh^{a}, pp. 151–152: 'The format of this column is difficult to determine. The space at the top of frg. 20 could be the top margin of col. VIII or simply an interval (פ 𝔐). Similarly, the space at the bottom of frg. 21 could be the bottom margin of col. VII or simply an interval (ס 𝔐).'

of the last line on fragment 21 leaves enough room for the interval, so that it is plausible to conclude that the empty space in this fragment does reflect the bottom margin of the column. Since a top margin has been preserved on fragment 9 ii (see the section 8.5), it is possible to reconstruct the text of the columns between these top (frg. 9 ii) and bottom margins (frg. 21), on the basis of the conclusions reached in the preceding section that the first four columns of 4QJosh[a] each contained 27 (possibly 30) lines, and that each regular line (without ס or פ) contained at least 50 letterspaces with a maximum of circa 73 letterspaces (column I). The whole of this last column can be reconstructed as follows:

4QJoshua[a] Colomn VIII (fragments 17–22): Josh. 9:22–10:11

number of letterspaces		text line
54	[רמיתם אתנו לאמר רחוקים אנחנו מכם מאד ואתם בקרבנו ישבים]	1
53	[[9:23]ועתה ארורים אתם ולא יכרת מכם עבד וחטבי עצים ושאבי מים]	2
56	[לבית אלהי [9:24]ויענו את יהושע ויאמרו כי הגד הגד לעבדיך את אשר]	3
53	[צוה יהוה אלהיך את משה עבדו לתת לכם את כל הארץ ולהשמיד]	4
57	[את כל ישבי הארץ מפניכם ונירא מאד לנפשתינו מפניכם ונעשה את]	5
55	[הדבר הזה [9:25]ועתה הננו בידך כטוב וכישר בעיניך לעשות לנו עשה]	6
57	[[9:26]ויעש להם כן ויצל אותם מיד בני ישראל ולא הרגום [9:27]ויתנם יהושע]	7
60	[ביום ההוא חטבי עצים ושאבי מים לעדה ולמזבח יהוה עד היום הזה אל]	8
14	[המקום אשר יבחר]	9
57	[[10:1]ויהי כשמע אדני צדק מלך ירושלם כי לכד יהושע את העי ויחרימה]	10
56	[כאשר עשה ליריחו ולמלכה כן עשה לעי ולמלכה וכי השלימו ישבי]	11
61	[גבעון את ישראל ויהיו בקרבם [10:2]וייראו מאד כי עיר גדולה גבעון כאחת]	12
58	ע֯ר֯י ה֯מ֯[מלכה וכי היא גדולה מ֯ן העי וכל אנשיה גברים [10:3]וישלח אדני]	13
60	צדק מלך [ירושלם אל הוהם]מלך[ח]ב֯ר֯ו[ן ואל פראם מלך ירמות ואל יפיע]	14
61	מלך לכיש ואל ד[ביר] מ[ל]ך עגלון לאמר [10:4]עלו אלי וע֯[ז]רני ונכה את גבעון]	15
62	[כ]י֯ השלימה את י֯[הו]שע ואת ישראל [10:5]ויאספו ויע֯ל[ו] חמשת מלכי האמרי מלך]	16
57	[ירושלם מ֯ל[ך חברו]ן֯ מ[ל]ך֯ י֯[רמות מ]ל[ך]לכי֯[ש מלך עגלון הם וכל מחניהם]	17
59	[וילחמו עליה [10:6]וישלחו אנשי גבעון אל יהושע אל המחנה הגלגלה לאמר]	18
55	[אל תרף ידיך מעבדיך עלה אלינו מהרה והושיעה לנו ועזרנו כי]	19
58	[נקבצו אלינו כל מלכי האמרי ישבי ההר [10:7]ויעל יהושע מן הגלגל הוא]	20
32	[וכל עם המלחמה עמו וכל גבורי החיל *vacat*	21
56	[[10:8]ויאמר י]ה֯ו֯[ה] א֯ל֯ י֯[הושע אל תירא מה]ם֯ כי בידך נתתי֯[ם לא יעמד איש]	22
59	[מ]ה֯ם֯ בפניך֯ [10:9]ויבוא א֯ל֯[י]הם יהושע פתאם] כל הלילה ה֯ל֯[ך מן הגלגל [10:10]ויהמם]	23
67	[י]הוה לפנ[י] ישראל ויכ֯[ם מכה גדולה בגבעון וירדפם דרך מעלה בית חורן ויכם]	24
55	ע֯[ד עזקה ועד] מקדה [11]ויה֯[י ב]נ֯סם [מפני ישראל הם במורד בית חורן]	25
59	ויהוה השליך עליהם אבני֯[ם מן השמ]י֯ם עד עזקה וימתו רבים אשר מתו]	26
36	באבני הברד מאשר הרג֯[ו בני ישראל בחרב *[vacat?/*	27
	[*vacat* = *bottom margin*	

This column would have contained 1414 letterspaces, and a blank line coinciding with the open paragraph endings between Joshua 9 and 10 (line 9). The beginning of this column was probably formed by the text of Josh. 9:22.

Without the disturbing fragment 15 column V can be reconstructed on the same basis: 27 lines of circa 50–60 letterspaces per line:

4QJoshua[a] Column V (fragments 9ii, 13–14, 16, without fragment 15): Josh. 8:3–21

frg. 9 ii frg. 9 i

[top margin]

number of letterspaces		
57	יהושע וכל עם המלחמה [לעלות העי ויבחר יהושע שלשים אלף איש]	1
51	נבורי החיל וישלחם ל[ילה 8:4 ויצו אתם לאמר ראו אתם ארבים]	2
58	אל העיר מא[חרי העיר אל תרחיקו מן העיר מאד והייתם כלכם נכנים]	3
59	8:5 ואני וכל[העם אשר אתי נקרב אל העיר והיה כי יצאו לקראתנו כאשר]	4
55	בראש[נה ונסנו לפניהם 8:6 ויצאו]אחרינו עד[התיקנו אותם מן העיר]	5
61	[כי יאמרו נסים לפנינו כאשר בראשנה ונסנו לפניהם 8:7 ואתם תקמו מהאורב]	6
51	[והורשתם]את הע[יר ונתנה יהוה אלהיכם בידכם 8:8 והיה כתפשכם]	7
54	[את הע]יר באש[כדבר יהוה תעשו ראו צויתי אתכם 8:9 וישלחם יהושע]	8
59	[ויל]כו אל[המארב וישבו בין בית אל ובין העי מים לעי ולין יהושע]	9
56	[בלילה ההוא בתוך העם 8:10 וישכם יהושע בבקר ויפקד את העם ויעל הוא]	10
58	[והזקני ישראל לפני העם העי 8:11 וכל העם המלחמה אשר אתו עלו ויגשו]	11
60	[ויבאו נגד העיר ויחנו מצפון לעי והגי בינו ובין העי 8:12 ויקח כחמשת]	12
59	[אלפים איש וישם אותם ארב בין בית אל ובין העי מים לעיר 8:13 וישימו]	13
59	[העם את כל המחנה אשר מצפון לעיר ואת עקבו מים לעיר וילך יהושע]	14
54	[בלילה ההוא בתוך העמק 8:14 ויהי כראות מלך העי וימהרו וישכימו]	15
57	[ויצאו אנשי העיר לקראת ישראל למלחמה הוא וכל עמו למועד לפני]	16
55	[הערבה והוא לא ידע כי ארב לו מאחרי העיר 8:15 וינגעו יהושע וכל]	17
51	[ישראל לפניהם וינסו דרך המדבר 8:16 ויזעקו כל העם אשר בעיר]	18
53	[לרדף אחריהם וירדפו אחרי יהושע וינתקו מן העיר 8:17 ולא נשאר]	19
58	[איש בעי ובית אלאשר לא יצאו אחרי ישראל ויעזבו את העיר פתוחה]	20
17	[וירדפו אחרי ישראל]	21
56	[8:18 ויאמר יהוה אל יהושע נטה בכידון אשר בידך אל העי כי בידך]	22
60	[אתננה ויט יהושע בכידון אשר בידו אל] העי[ר 8:19 והאורב קם מהרה ממקומו]	23
57	[וירוצו כנטות ידו ויבאו העיר וילכדוה ו]מהר[ו ויציתו את העיר]	24
59	[באש 8:20 ויפנו אנשי העי אחריהם ויראו והנה עלה עשן העיר השמימה ולא]	25
54	[היה בהם ידים לנוס הנה והנה והעם הנס המדבר נהפך אל הרודף]	26
56	[8:21 ויהושע וכל ישראל ראו כי לכד הארב את העיר וכי עלה עשן העיר]	27

The text of this column has been reconstructed here after MT without fragment 15. The text of fragment 16 has been identified as Josh. 8:18–19.[84] If the remainder of the column is reconstructed on the basis of 27 lines of circa 50–60 letterspaces each, the column must have ended somewhere in Josh. 8:21.

Therefore, the text between the column attested by the fragments 17–22 and this column V, attested by fragments 9 ii, 13–14 and 16 must have contained Josh. 8:21–9:22. If we now return to the text preceding column VIII, i.e. column VII, which must have ended with Josh. 9:22, a similar reconstruction of its text on the basis of the same procedure makes clear that this column VII must have started with Josh. 9:3:

4QJoshua[a] Column VII: Josh. 9:3 (?)–22 (?)

number of letterspaces		text line
54	[9:3 וישבי גבעון שמעו את אשר עשה יהושע ליריחו ולעי 9:4 ויעשו גם]	1
55	[המה בערמה וילכו ויצטירו ויקחו שקים בלים לחמוריהם ונאדות]	2
52	[יין בלים ומבקעים ומצררים 9:5 ונעלות בלות ומטלאות ברגליהם]	3
53	[ושלמות בלות עליהם וכל לחם צידם יבש היה נקדים 9:6 וילכו אל]	4
51	[יהושע אל המחנה הגלגל ויאמרו אליו ואל איש ישראל מארץ]	5
54	[רחוקה באנו ועתה כרתו לנו ברית 9:7 ויאמרו איש ישראל אל החוי]	6
54	[אולי בקרבי אתה יושב ואיך אכרות לך ברית 9:8 ויאמרו אל יהושע]	7
53	[עבדיך אנחנו ויאמר אלהם יהושע מי אתם ומאין תבאו 9:9 ויאמרו]	8
53	[אליו מארץ רחוקה מאד באו עבדיך לשם יהוה אלהיך כי שמענו]	9
51	[שמעו ואת כל אשר עשה במצרים 9:10 ואת כל אשר עשה לשני מלכי]	10
57	[האמרי אשר בעבר הירדן לסיחון מלך חשבון ולעוג מלך הבשן אשר]	11
58	[בעשתרות 9:11 ויאמרו אלינו זקינינו וכל ישבי ארצנו לאמר קחו בידכם]	12
57	[צידה לדרך ולכו לקראתם ואמרתם אליהם עבדיכם אנחנו ועתה כרתו]	13
55	[לנו ברית 9:12 זה לחמנו חם הצטידנו אתו מבתינו ביום צאתנו ללכת]	14
54	[אליכם ועתה הנה יבש והיה נקדים 9:13 ואלה נאדות היין אשר מלאנו]	15
55	[חדשים והנה התבקעו ואלה שלמותינו ונעלינו בלו מרב הדרך מאד]	16
53	[9:14 ויקחו האנשים מצידם ואת פי יהוה לא שאלו 9:15 ויעש להם יהושע]	17
54	[שלום ויכרת להם ברית לחיותם וישבעו להם נשיאי העדה 9:16 ויהי]	18
56	[מקצה שלשת ימים אחרי אשר כרתו להם ברית וישמעו כי קרבים הם]	19
56	[אליו ובקרבו הם ישבים 9:17 ויסעו בני ישראל ויבאו אל עריהם ביום]	20
59	[השלישי ועריהם גבעון והכפירה ובארות וקרית יערים 9:18 ולא הכום בני]	21
55	[ישראל כי נשבעו להם נשיאי העדה ביהוה אלהי ישראל וילנו כל]	22
57	[העדה על הנשיאים 9:19 ויאמרו כל הנשיאים אל כל העדה אנחנו נשבענו]	23

[84] See section 8.5 above.

55	[להם ביהוה אלהי ישראל ועתה לא נוכל לנגע בהם 9:20זאת נעשה להם]	24
54	[והחיה אותם ולא יהיה עלינו קצף על השבועה אשר נשבענו להם]	25
60	[9:21ויאמרו אליהם הנשיאים יחיו ויהיו חטבי עצים ושאבי מים לכל העדה]	26
58	[כאשר דברו להם הנשיאים 9:22ויקרא להם יהושע וידבר אליהם לאמר למה]	27

If we then attempt to reconstruct the text of the column between this column VII and column V, it becomes clear that this can only lead to a plausible reconstruction if we retain the text of Joshua 8:30–35 after Joshua 8:29. Without this passage, the text of this column would lack 11 lines and would therefore be unusually short. The present reconstruction on the other hand remains within the parameters gained from a reconstruction of the text of the first four columns:

4QJoshua[a] Column VI: Joshua 8:21–9:2

number of letterspaces		text line
50	[וישבו ויכו את אנשי העי 8:22ואלה יצאו מן העיר לקראתם ויהיו]	1
52	[לישראל בתוך אלה מזה ואלה מזה ויכו אותם עד בלתי השאיר]	2
53	[לו שריד ופליט 8:23ואת מלך העי תפשו חי ויקרבו אתו אל יהושע]	3
51	[8:24ויהי ככלות ישראל להרג את כל ישבי העי בשדה במדבר אשר]	4
52	[רדפום בו ויפלו כלם לפי חרב עד תמם וישבו כל ישראל העי]	5
54	[ויכו אתם לפי חרב 8:25ויהי כל הנפלים ביום ההוא מאיש ועד אשה]	6
51	[שנים עשר אלף כל אנשי העי 8:26ויהושע לא השיב ידו אשר נטה]	7
53	[בכידון עד אשר החרים את כל ישבי העי 8:27רק הבהמה ושלל העיר]	8
53	[ההיא בזזו להם ישראל כדבר יהוה אשר צוה את יהושע 8:28וישרף]	9
52	[יהושע את העי וישימה תל עולם שממה עד היום הזה 8:29ואת מלך]	10
53	[העי תלה על העץ עד עת הערב וכבוא השמש צוה יהושע וירידו]	11
51	[את נבלתו מן העץ וישליכו אותה אל פתח שער העיר ויקימו]	12
30	[עליו גל אבנים גדול עד היום הזה]	13
50	[8:30אז יבנה יהושע מזבח ליהוה אלהי ישראל בהר עיבל 8:31כאשר]	14
54	[צוה משה עבד יהוה את בני ישראל ככתוב בספר תורת משה מזבח]	15
56	[אבנים שלמות אשר לא הניף עליהן ברזל ויעלו עליו עלות ליהוה]	16
52	[ויזבחו שלמים 8:32ויכתב שם על האבנים את משנה תורת משה אשר]	17
55	[כתב לפני בני ישראל 8:33וכל ישראל וזקניו ושטרים ושפטיו עמדים]	18
55	[מזה ומזה לארון נגד הכהנים הלוים נשאי ארון ברית יהוה כגר]	19
53	[כאזרח חציו אל מול הר גרזים והחציו אל מול הר עיבל כאשר]	20
50	[צוה משה עבד יהוה לברך את העם ישראל בראשנה 8:34ואחרי כן]	21
53	[קרא את כל דברי התורה הברכה וקללה ככל הכתוב בספר התורה]	22
50	[8:35לא היה דבר מכל אשר משה אשר לא קרא יהושע נגד כל קהל]	23
33	[ישראל והנשים והטף והגר ההלך בקרבם]	24
50	[9:1ויהי כשמע כל המלכים אשר בעבר הירדן בהר ובשפלה ובכל]	25
57	[חוף הים הגדול אל מול הלבנון החתי והאמרי הכנעני הפרזי החוי]	26
52	[והיבוסי 9:2ויתקבצו יחדו להלחם עם יהושע ועם ישראל פה אחד]	27

This reconstruction of the columns of 4QJosh[a] is of course a tentative one. The amount of text reconstructed is much larger than that physically attested on the remaining fragments. Nevertheless, the aim of this reconstruction is to make plausible my thesis that also in 4QJoshua[a] MT-Joshua 8:30–35 originally was in its proper place, i.e. where the nomistic author had intended it to be placed, that is: before Joshua 9.

9.6 LXX-Joshua

Of course it is impossible to establish whether the passage in 4QJosh[a] was actually placed before Josh. 9:1 (thus MT) or two verses further (thus LXX). From a redaction-critical point of view, both the positions in MT and that in LXX are plausible. If the DtrN-redactor had placed the verses right before Josh. 9:3, the relation between blessing (Josh. 8:30–35) and sin (Joshua 9, according to the view of DtrN) would be even stronger than it is in MT. There are, however, two good reasons to regard the position in LXX as secondary *vis-à-vis* MT. The transposition of the passage from its place in MT to that in LXX was probably motivated by the observation made by the Greek translator that Josh. 9:1 (*when all the kings heard . . .*) can only refer to Josh. 8:1–29, and not to Josh. 8:30–35. Furthermore, as we have seen in section 8.6 above and as demonstrated by J. Moatti-Fine with respect to the numerous lexical innovations *vis-à-vis* LXX-Pentateuch in the area of martial terms,[85] the Greek translator took a keen interest in military affairs. As we have seen in section 7.6.8, he was also concerned about a historically plausible rendering of the parent text. Therefore it is likely that the Greek translator considered the events described in Josh. 9:1–2 as a concentration of the hostile forces, which would allow Joshua and Israel to enter unconquered territory and there perform the prescribed religious duties. As long as the hostile forces were preparing themselves for the battle at hand, they would not pose a threat to Israel. Hence, the Greek translator transferred the problematic passage to a position nearby that would in his view fit better the logical order of events.

[85] J. Moatti-Fine, *Josué*, pp. 53–66.

9.7 Conclusions

Thus, we may discern the following stages in the literary development of the Ebal-Gerizim passages in the versions of Deuteronomy and Joshua:

0. An early version of Deuteronomy contained the passages Deut. 27:4–7 and Deut. 27:11–13. These probably unrelated passages contained Moses' commands to the Israelites to build an altar on Mount Ebal in conformity with the Law in the Covenant Code and another command concerning a ceremony that would reflect the political situation during Josiah's reign.
1. A first redactional (Deuteronomistic?) elaboration of these passages in Deut. 27:2–3.8 altered the injunction in Deut. 27:4–7 from a command to build an altar on Mount Ebal into a command to erect large stones as soon as Israel had crossed the Jordan, and have these stones inscribed by the *torah*. Perhaps this redactor had Joshua 4 in mind.[86] The alteration was probably motivated by a Judaean polemic against (religious) circles in Samaria.
2. Connected with this alteration (perhaps the result of the same hand) is the addition of Deut. 11:29–30, in which the tension between the two commands in Deut. 27:2–4 (Jordan versus mountains) is harmonised by obscuring the location of the two mountains.
3. Whereas the DtrH-author of the book of Joshua avoided the tension between the command in Deut. 27:4 and the main dogma of the centralisation of the worship in Jerusalem by leaving out the former command altogether, the DtrN-redactor of the book of Joshua considered the *torah* more important than the proper place for worship. He created a counterpart to Deuteronomy 27 in its present layered form, but transformed the Deuteronomy texts into a passage that would propagate his own beliefs and interests, by having Joshua recite from the *torah*. Since the text would have to deal with the blessing of the people, he positioned this passage between Joshua 8 and Joshua 9, i.e. where it is still found in MT-Josh. 8:30–35, to mark the point that in his view formed the primeval sin in Israel's history: the alliance with a foreign nation (Joshua 9).

[86] Thus C. Steuernagel, *Deuteronomium und Josua*, p. 96.

4. A Hebrew scholar-scribe of the Late Second Temple period offered his own solution to the tensions in the text of Deuteronomy 27, by reading Deut. 27:2 and 27:4 as two distinct commands. He found the fulfillment of Deut. 27:4 in the DtrN-addition in Josh. 8:30–35, but missed a counterpart for Deut. 27:2–3. As a result, this scribe added a short passage to Josh. 4:20–5:1, based upon Josh. 8:32.34–35 with the addition of a few editorial links (4QJosh[a], frg. 1, line 2 [ן]את הירד[בעברו], and [ ]אחר אשר נתקו) that would help to blend this expansion into the narrative of Israel's crossing of the Jordan. This text is attested by 4QJosh[a], and reflects a secondary development *vis-à-vis* MT. The type of harmonisation by means of duplication is well attested for the period of the first two centuries BCE for the Pentateuch (Samaritan Pentateuch, 4QpaleoExod[m], 4QNum[b], 4QReworkedPentateuch, 4QDeut[n], Papyrus Nash). Interestingly, the Greek version of Joshua contains similar expansions based on parallel biblical passages, such as LXX-Josh. 6:26a (cf. MT-1 Kgs. 16:34), 16:10a (cf. MT-1 Kon. 9:16), 19:47–48 (cf. MT-Judg. 1:34–35), 21:42a–d (cf. MT-Josh. 19:49–50) and 24:33a–b (cf. Judg. 2:6.11–14, 3:12).
5. Nevertheless, the Greek translator did not have this expansion in Josh. 5:1 in front of him, but independenly offered his own solution to the tensions created in the text of Joshua 8–9, by moving the DtrN-addition (MT-Josh. 8:30–35) a few verses further on in the narrative, so that the order of events would gain in historical probability. The verses Josh. 9:1–2 were understood as a sort of suspension of hostilities that would allow the hostile forces to regroup their forces, while Joshua and Israel could perform their religious duties.
6. Neither of these two literary initiatives have become normative in Judaism, but remained individual solutions to the problems posed by the Deuteronomy and Joshua texts. Josephus offered his own independent solution by transforming the stones of Josh. 4:20 into an altar (not into steles on which the *torah* was inscribed as in 4QJosh[a]!) and transposing MT-Josh. 8:30–35 to a point in his rewritten version of the Joshua narratives where the whole country has been conquered, so that the passage lost its ominous function and became an expression of gratitude by the Israelites. Rabbi Ishmael held a similar opinion, whereas rabbi Yehuda took recourse to a supranatural explanation of biblical events. Rabbi Eliezer solved the geographical problems by assuming that Josh. 8:30–35

> should be situated near the river Jordan, as many Christian authorities (Eusebius, Jerome, Procopius, the maker of the Madaba map, E. Noort) have done since, whereas the Samaritans on the other hand identified all locations mentioned in Joshua 8 as places around their sacred centre.

The textual witnesses to the book of Joshua and the exegetical traditions based upon this book thus reflect a welter of solutions to a set of problems that can only be solved on a literary-critical basis. If one is prepared to consider the expansions in the versions of the Pentateuch as part of a comprehensive re-edition of the Pentateuch, one might call 4QJosh[a] a re-edition of the book of Joshua, and part of this comprehensive reworking of the biblical text. Nevertheless, the addition does not introduce a new ideology foreign to the original text, as the DtrN redactor did with his insertion of the passage. For that reason, it may not be helpful to use the word 'redaction' in this context; 'harmonisation' may be the better term. In any case, it is clear that in this particular case too, MT preserves the older text as compared to the other ancient witnesses. LXX and 4QJosh[a] do not take us back to a stage in the formation of the book of Joshua beyond that attested by MT. These versions require a study of their own, just as a literary-critical examination deserves its independent status.

CHAPTER TEN

GENERAL CONCLUSIONS

10.1 Recapitulation

In the present study, several aspects of the textual history of the book of Joshua have been explored. The main question has been that of the possibility of recovering part of the formation process of the book preceding the stage now standardised in the Masoretic text, on the basis of the oldest textual witnesses to that book, 4QJoshua[a] and LXX-Joshua. The answer to this question is a negative one, as far as those parts of Joshua are concerned that have been examined extensively in this study (Joshua 1, 5, and 8). The conclusion of this research must be, that these ancient witnesses do not attest to the process of formation preceding the edition of the book of Joshua as preserved in MT, but to the process of interpretation, harmonisation and reformulation of that version.

In the first chapter the background of this guiding question has been discussed. The discovery of the biblical Dead Sea Scrolls has shed new light on the history of the biblical text. Manuscripts such as 4QpaleoExod[m], 4QNum[b], 4QReworkedPentateuch, 4QDeut[n], 4QDeut[q], 4QSam[a], 4QJer[b], 4QJer[d], 11QPs[a], 4QCant[a] and 4QCant[b] have made it clear that in the centuries before the end of the first century CE versions of the biblical books existed that differed significantly from the Hebrew text that has become standardised in the Masoretic text. Since these manuscripts do not contain specific elements characteristic of the Qumran ideology or scribal practice,[1] there is no reason to believe that this textual pluriformity was restricted to the Qumran community. Given the fact that these biblical texts share specific characteristics and significant variant readings *vis-à-vis* MT with the oldest textual witnesses (Samaritan Pentateuch, Old Greek translations of the biblical books), it is plausible to assume that in those

[1] E. Tov, *Textual Criticism of the Hebrew Bible*, pp. 107–117.

parts of the Hebrew Bible where LXX shows large-scale divergences for which no Qumran material is extant or only very fragmentarily preserved (Joshua, Samuel, 1 Kings, Jeremiah, Ezekiel, Esther, Daniel), the variants do not reflect specific Greek-Hellenistic alterations of the Hebrew text attested by MT, but similar variant Hebrew versions of those books (section 1.1). Whereas the MT version in most cases is older than the variant versions attested by the ancient versions (e.g. the expansions in the Pentateuch attested by 4QpaleoExod[m], 4QNum[b], SamP, and further the expansions in LXX-3 Regum, LXX-Esther, LXX-Daniel, or—alternatively—the condensations of Song of Songs in 4QCant[a] and 4QCant[b]), there are cases where the MT version is possibly younger than the one attested by Qumran or LXX (Jeremiah). In those cases scholars such as E. Tov and E. Ulrich argue that textual data overlap with the literary history of those books (section 1.2).

The oldest textual witnesses to the book of Joshua, i.e. 4QJosh[a] and LXX, reflect similar large-scale variants *vis-à-vis* MT, supported by 4QJosh[b], XJosh, and the other versions (Theodotion, Aquila, Symmachus, Targum Jonathan, the Pešiṭta, and the Vulgate). Since LXX—and in a single case (Josh. 8:10–18) 4QJosh[a]—contains minuses *vis-à-vis* the younger textual witnesses, there is reason to believe that these younger witnesses attest to a later, expansionistic stage in the formation of the book of Joshua, as argued by E. Tov and others (sections 1.4 and 2.2). Although the Greek translation of Joshua may not be very free, it cannot be classified as very literal either, as pointed out already in 1876 by J. Hollenberg (section 2.2.1). Although scholars such as S. Holmes, C.D. Benjamin, H.M. Orlinksy, E.A. Chesman, A.G. Auld, E. Tov, A. Rofé, and L. Mazor (sections 2.2.3–7) still put great confidence in the redaction-critical value of LXX-Joshua, scholars such as A. Dillmann, K. Bieberstein, C.G. den Hertog, J. Moatti-Fine, S. Sipilä, and M. Rösel (sections 2.2.2. and 2.2.8) have pointed to the various literary initiatives on the part of the Greek translator, which to a large extent undermines this redaction-critical value. Furthermore, the Qumran scrolls of Joshua have not presented the expected 'Septuagintal' Hebrew manuscripts, but as far as the texts have been preserved, they closely follow MT, also in cases where LXX offers a strikingly different and shorter text (sections 3.1–3).

For these reasons, it is methodologically wrong to base literary-critical theories on (the final stages of) the formation of the book of

Joshua culminating into the MT version purely or mainly on text-critical data. In chapter 5 it is argued that a proper study of the passages where MT, LXX, and 4QJosh[a] differ, should proceed from two independent approaches, i.e. a literary-critical examination of the passage in its own right and a text-critical examination of the ancient witnesses (LXX and 4QJosh[a]) on their own terms and in their own context. Literary criticism of the text should not be subjugated to text-critical theories, but remains invaluable as an autonomous method to examine the literary history of the text. In order to stimulate the discussion between these related disciplines, a short sketch of the main stages in the literary history of the Hebrew text of Joshua as accepted by most modern critical scholars has been offered in chapter 4. These stages include [0] a pre-Deuteronomistic layer, [1] a Deuteronomistic layer (DtrH), [2] a nomistic redaction (DtrN), and [3] a Priestly redaction (RedP). These literary strata are by and large attested by both MT and LXX. From the outset it is therefore clear that the textual witnesses do not attest to these main stages. If the variants presented by MT *vis-à-vis* LXX and 4QJosh[a] should nevertheless be the result of a redaction of the book of Joshua that took place between these main stages and the version attested by MT (thus Holmes, Tov, Rofé, Mazor), rather than a collection of individual interpolations (thus Benjamin), it is only logical to expect a common ideology and phraseology expressed by these variants, in the same way as the DtrH, DtrN and RedP layers are characterised (and recognisable) by their respective interests (unification, *torah*, and priesthood) and vocabulary (section 4.2).

On the basis of these methodological considerations, a number of passages from the book of Joshua have been selected for further examination. The first chapter of the book (Joshua 1) contains a relatively large number of small quantitative variants (pluses in MT), which according to Holmes, Orlinksy, Chesman, Auld, Tov, and others, are clearly not the result of scribal errors but of a comprehensive re-edition of the chapter (Tov). These variants and related variants throughout the book (3:6.9.10; 4:3.10.14.21–22; 6:7; 7:2; 9:19–22; 10:24; 11:17; 12:6.7; 13:5–6; 17:17; 22:4.24; 24:22) provided a suitable test case for the method outlined above (chapter 6). Although several of the pluses in MT may be labelled Deuteronomistic (the epithet עבד־יהוה for Moses in 1:1.15 [section 6.4.1]; the deictic element הזה in the phrase הירדן הזה 1:2 [section 6.4.2]; the verb ירשׁ

in 1:11.15 [section 6.4.6]; and the phrase משה בעבר הירדן in 1:14 [section 6.4.8]) or nomistic (the MT plus כל־התורה in 1:7 [section 6.4.5]), a literary-critical examination of the chapter on its own terms reveals that these alleged additions are no more Deuteronomistic or nomistic than their respective contexts (Josh. 1:1–6.9–18 DtrH and Josh. 1:7–8 DtrN, see section 6.3).

A close examination of the quantitative variants within the context of the Greek translation of the chapter as a whole showed that these variants should be seen as literary initiatives introduced by the Greek translator, which also become visible in a number of quantitative variants (unusual Greek renderings). In order to produce a smooth and stylised version of the chapter, the Greek translator employed various equivalents for the same Hebrew word (δοῦλος, θεράπων, παῖς for עֶבֶד [section 6.4.1] or κληρονομέω, κατα-κληρονομέω, κατέχω, κτάομαι for ירשׁ Qal [section 6.4.6], or highly unusual words for a common Hebrew expression (ὑπουργός for מְשָׁרֵת [section 6.4.1]; πράσσσω for הלך [section 6.5.1]; and συμμαχέω for עזר [section 6.5.2]), and made stylistic cuts in the redundant text, such as the variants related to the status of Moses and Joshua in LXX-Josh. 4:10.14, 1:1.15; 12:6, and 22:4 (section 6.4.1), the numerous introductions to direct discourse (לאמר in 1:12 and throughout the book [section 6.4.7]). Other examples of this tendency on the part of the Greek translator to curtail the emphatic style inherent in the Deuteronomistic Hebrew text are the omission of the deictic element הזה in 1:2.4; and 4:22 (sections 6.4.2; 6.4.4), the explicative clause לבני ישׂראל after להם in 1:2 (section 6.4.3), and the clauses לרשׁתה and וירשׁתם אותה in 1:11.15 (section 6.4.6). Since the Greek translator slightly modified the description of the extent of the Promised Land and saw no function for the archaic name for the northern Syrian area in 1:4 כל ארץ החתים, he omitted this phrase as well (section 6.4.4).

In a few cases, phrases in the Hebrew text were left untranslated or modified, when their contents could not be fully harmonised with elements from the Pentateuch. For this reason the phrase ככל אשׁר־צוה משׁה את־יהושׁע in Josh. 4:10 was left untranslated in the Greek reformulation of the whole verse, since the Pentateuch does not contain specific commands from Moses to Joshua on how to cross the Jordan (section 6.4.1). Since the Pentateuch does contain specific commands from Moses to Joshua about what to do after his death (Deut. 3:21–22; 31:7–8, parallel to the recapitulation in Josh. 1:1–6), but no specific mention of a *torah* commanded by Moses to Joshua, the Greek translator interpreted the beginning of Josh. 1:7 in the light of the preceding Josh. 1:6, and smoothed the redactional seam between these DtrH and DtrN strata by rendering רק by οὖν, and omitting the phrases מאד and כל־התורה (section 6.4.5). In order to avoid the tension between the two contrasting themes in Josh. 1:12–15 between 'the land as a gift from Yhwh' and 'the land given by Moses to the Trans-Jordanian tribes', and in order to avoid the geographical tension evoked by the phrase 'on the other side of the Jordan', which in the narrative geography of Joshua 1 should have been 'on the same eastern side of the Jordan', the Greek translator omitted the words משה בעבר הירדן (section 6.4.8).

In Joshua 5:2–9, MT and LXX offer strikingly different answers to the question whom and why Joshua circumcised at Gilgal (chapter 7). These variants have been the object of extensive discussions ever since S. Holmes argued that the redundant MT should be seen as an attempt to obliterate the idea (still) expressed by MT that the Halaka to perform circumcision (Genesis 17) was not universally practised by the Israelites during their stay in Egypt (LXX-Josh. 5:4–5 καὶ ὅσοι ποτὲ ἀπερίτμητοι ἦσαν τῶν ἐξεληλυθότων ἐξ Αἰγύπτου, πάντας τούτους περιέτεμεν Ἰησοῦς *versus* MT-Josh. 5:5 כי־מלים היו; כל־העם היצאים see section 7.2.3). The reworking of verses 4 and 5 to the present MT-version, the addition of the words כל־הגוי in MT-Josh. 5:6.8, and the modification of וְשֵׁב מל את־בני־ישׂאל in 5:2 to MT's וְשׁוּב מל את־בני־ישׂראל שֵׁנית would reflect the same tendency (section 7.2.3). In the verses following this passage, Josh. 5:10–12, the pluses in MT ממחרת הפסח and ממחרת are generally held to be additions to the older (Deuteronomistic [Auld] or even pre-Deuteronomistic [Noth, Kraus, Otto and others]) narrative intended to conform the cultic events described in these verses to the Priestly calendar of Leviticus 23 (section 7.2.2).

Yet, a redaction-critical analysis of the passages independent from the text-critical data offers a completely different picture (section 7.4). The pluses in MT-Josh. 5:11.12 are no more Priestly than their context 5:10–12a, as attested by both MT and LXX (section 7.4.5). Furthermore, the redundancy in MT-Josh. 5:2–9 is not restricted to the MT pluses *vis-à-vis* LXX, but inherent in the Deuteronomistic (DtrH) background of the entire passage Josh. 4:21–5:8 (section 7.4.1–3). The aim of MT-Josh. 5:2–9 is not to exonerate the older generation of Israelites in Egypt (section 7.4.2.1), but rather to contrast the themes of divine promise and human disobedience (second half of Josh. 5:6 as attested by both MT and LXX, section 7.4.2.2). The problematic clause in MT-Josh. 5:5 כי־מלים היו כל־העם היצאים should therefore not be seen as a veiled apology for the older Israelites in Egypt, but only serves as a preparation for the negative evaluation of this group expressed by מול Qal—לא: *they had not circumcised their sons*, thus in the following clause 5:5 וכל־העם הילדים . . . לא־מלו, and in 5:7 כי לא־מלו אותם בדרך.

In passing, it should also be noted that the Qumran evidence supports MT. Apart from the variant הראותם (MT-Josh. 5:6)—ראות (4QJosh[a])—μὴ ἰδεῖν αὐτούς (LXX, see section 7.6.4.4), 4QJosh[a] fully corresponds to MT *vis-à-vis* LXX. Contrary to E. Ulrich's claim, a reconstruction of lines 4–5 of 4QJosh[a], column I, does leave room for the MT plus שׁנית in Josh. 5:2 (*vis-à-vis* LXX section 7.5.1). The phrase עד תם כל אנשי המלחמה in the Damascus Document[B] col. XX, lines 14–15, is not a direct witness to an alleged shorter Hebrew version of Josh. 5:6 underlying LXX(-Rahlfs) διὸ ἀπερίτμητοι ἦσαν οἱ πλεῖστοι αὐτῶν τῶν μαχίμων, as argued by B. Lucassen, but only a general allusion to the theme of the death of the older generation in the desert (Num. 32:13; Deut. 2:14.16, see section 7.5.2).

The discrepancies between MT and LXX in these verses are the result of a profound reformulation of these verses (section 7.6) in which the redundancy of the Hebrew text of MT-Josh. 5:2–12 has been stylised, the inner coherence of the passage as a whole strengthened, and the links with the Pentateuch amplified. In the present context the phrase in Josh. 5:9: היום גלותי את־חרפת מצרים מעליכם (originally the sequel to Josh. 4:20, but later interrupted by the DtrH-insertion of Josh. 4:21–5:8 and therefore originally not a reference to circumcision, but to the end of the humiliating period of slavery in Egypt and wanderings through the desert) almost automatically generates the interpretation: 'at this moment the shameful foreskin has been removed from you'. This at least was how the Greek translator interpreted the clause: from the element 'Egypt' (חרפת מצרים) he inferred that there must have been Israelites in Egypt who were the object of humiliation by the Egyptians, apparently because they were not circumcised, whereas the Egyptians themselves held circumcision in high esteem (section 7.6.3.2). Accordingly, he modified the preceding verses 4–5, so that this undefined group of uncircumcised older Israelites was introduced (perhaps on the basis of separating the phrase בצאתם ממצרים לא־מלו from the beginning of the sentence וכל־העם הילדים במדבר בדרך). As a result, the Greek translator could not give a functional place in his version to the element of a 'second' circumcision (שׁנית), which originally only referred to the reinstitution of an ancient institution (section 7.4.1). Since the circumcision concerned only the male part of the Israelite population, the Greek translator modified the double mention in MT of כל־הגוי (5:6.8), either by condensation of the sentence (5:8: περιτμηθέντες δέ for ויהי כאשר־תמו כל־הגוי להמול section 7.6.6), or adaptation (5:6 οἱ πλεῖστοι αὐτῶν τῶν μαχίμων for כל־הגוי אנשי המלחמה section 7.6.4.2.3).

The Greek translator also smoothed the harsh notion of a collective enterprise of a circumcision of all Israelite males (including grown-up and aged men) by rendering the reference to the archaic instruments of stone knives (חרבות צרים) by μαχαίρας πετρίνας ἐκ πέτρας ἀκροτόμου, so that it would be clear that these primitive tools were at least sharp knives. Likewise, the Greek translator added the notion of rest (ἡσυχίαν εἶχον; αὐτόθι καθήμενοι ἐν τῇ παρεμβολῇ) and complete recovery (ἕως ὑγιάσθησαν) after this severe, hazardous and painful operation (Josh. 5:8, section 7.6.5), and stressed the interpretation of circumcision itself as an act of purification by employing the verb περι-καθαίρω for the Hebrew verb מול, alongside the standard equivalent περι-τέμνω.

This picture of a well-considered reinterpretation and reformulation of the Hebrew text by the Greek translator seems to be distorted by the clause διὸ ἀπερίτμητοι ἦσαν οἱ πλεῖστοι αὐτῶν τῶν μαχίμων τῶν ἐξεληλυθότων ἐκ γῆς Αἰγύπτου. The text as it stands contains an inner contradiction: since those Israelites are mentioned here who had left Egypt as warriors (τῶν μαχίμων), who had furthermore been disobedient and had not been allowed to enter the Promised Land, they must have died before Joshua entered the land As a result, their state of circumcision is irrelevant in the context of verse 6, which describes the period of forty years of wandering (corrected by LXX to 'forty-two' years on the basis of a calculation of the dates in Num. 10:11 and 14; see section 7.6.4.1). The problem can be solved if we assume that the text attested by all witnesses (ἀπερίτμητοι ἦσαν) is an early corruption from the graphically similar phrase ἀπηρτίσθησαν, which is an idiomatic rendering of the Hebrew verb תמם (sections 7.6.4.2.6–7). The Greek translator was apparently not so much interested in which Israelites had been or had not been circumcised before the time narrated in Joshua 5, but more concerned with the themes of individual responsibility of the older generation and the innocence of the younger generation (sections 7.6.4.3; 7.6.5).

The absence of equivalents for the temporal phrases ממחרת הפסח and ממחרת in Josh. 5:11.12 is also the result of a reformulation of the Hebrew text by the Greek translator. The Hebrew text is somewhat problematic because of the threefold stress on the proper sequence of *entry into the land of Canaan—Passover—maṣṣot—consuming of the first products of the land* by means of the references to the same day after the Passover night (14th Nisan): ממחרת הפסח—בעצם היום הזה—ממחרת באכלם מעבור הארץ. In line with the post-biblical use to apply the name Passover to the fully merged spring festivals of Passover and Feast of the Unleavened Breads (*maṣṣot*), the Greek translator understood the reference to the celebration of Passover in this sense and altered the preposition -ב (*they held the Passover sacrifice in the night of 14th Nisan*) to the more inclusive statement καὶ ἐποίησαν οἱ υἱοὶ Ισραηλ τὸ πασχα . . . ἀπὸ ἑσπέρας, *the Israelites celebrated the Passover-festival . . . from the evening onwards* . . . From the sequence 'consumption of the first fruits in the Promised Land'—'cessation of the manna' he inferred that the former must have replaced the latter, and accordingly rendered the phrase בעצם היום הזה in this relative sense (section 7.6.8.1). The Greek translator did acknowledge the references to the Pentateuch (Leviticus 23), and rendered the *pars-pro-toto* phrase קלוי in a *totum-pro-parte* sense: νέα (section 7.6.8.2). Nevertheless, most initiatives in these verses concern the geographical setting (section 7.6.8.3). The addition of the geographical details ἐν τῷ πέραν τοῦ Ιορδάνου ἐν τῷ πεδίῳ and the rendering of ויאכלו מתבואת ארץ כנען by ἐκαρπίσαντο δὲ τὴν χώραν τῶν φοινίκων (not with a capital Φ, *land of the Phoenicians*, but a small φ, *area of the date palms*), make clear that the Greek translator must have had a very vivid idea of what was described in the text, and understood the first fruits of the land as products of the date palms for which the region around Jericho was famous throughout the Hellenistic world (section 7.6.8.3).

Although in a few cases the Greek version may reflect a Hebrew *Vorlage* slightly different from MT (such as Josh. 5:6 ἐν τῇ ἐρήμῳ τῇ Μαδβαρίτιδι = במדבר המדבר? [section 7.6.4.1]; 5:6 μὴ ἰδεῖν αὐτούς = ראות [cf. 4QJosh[a]] or ראותם? *vis-à-vis* MT הראותם [section 7.6.4.4]; cf. also ἡ θαλάσση ἡ ἐσχάτης in 1:4 = הים האחרון [Deut. 11:24] *vis-à-vis* MT-Josh. 1:4 הים הגדול [section 6.4.4]), this does not imply that the Hebrew text attested by LXX is older than MT. There are good reasons to believe that also in these cases MT has preserved the older text.

In chapter 8 and 9 the two main divergencies between MT and 4QJosh[a] have been examined. A reconstruction of column V of 4QJosh[a] does not seem to leave room for most of Josh. 8:11–13, which would correspond to the minus in LXX. The shorter Hebrew text would find support from the literary-critical observation that these verses form a doublet with verses 3–9, where the sending of a group of men in ambush behind Ai has already been narrated. Yet, when the entire passage Josh. 8:1–29 is studied from an autonomous redaction-critical point of view, it becomes clear that the relevant verses are part of the older narrative (Josh. 8:10–14.16.18–20.26), which was expanded by the Deuteronomistic historian in Josh. 8:1–9.15.17.21–25.27–29 (section 8.4). Once the complete text of the columns of 4QJosh[a]—attested only by tiny fragments—is reconstructed, it becomes clear that the relevant fragment 15 could not have belonged to this column of 4QJosh[a], since not only would line 12 be four times longer than the surrounding lines, but also the surrounding lines 11 and 13 would be unusually short. If this fragment had belonged to 4QJosh[a] column V, this column with only 14 lines would have been only half as long as the preceding columns, which have 27 lines. Finally, one of the few words that have been preserved on this tiny fragment, וישׁובו, cannot be fitted into the context of Josh. 8:11, which it supposedly reflects, since in that verse the approach, not the return, of the main Israelite force is narrated (section 8.5). The minus in LXX-Josh. 8:11b–13 as well as the various other minuses in LXX-Josh. 8:1–29 *vis-à-vis* MT are the result of the Greek translator's attempt to relieve the narrative from the tensions that had resulted from the Deuteronomistic reworking of the older narrative (section 8.6).

The other main variant posed by 4QJosh[a] concerns the passage now found in MT-Josh. 8:30–35, which describes the building of an altar by Joshua on Mount Ebal, the offerings performed there, the inscribing of the *torah*, and Joshua's recitation from the *torah*. The passage clearly interrupts the sequence Josh. 8:1–29 and 9:1–27. In LXX the passage is located after Josh. 9:1–2, whereas 4QJosh[a] preserves the final words of these verses before Josh. 5:1, which would imply that the ceremonies of altar-building on the mountain and the reading from the book of the *torah* had taken place immediately after Israel had crossed the river Jordan. Although the two mountains Ebal and Gerizim are located opposite the city Shechem, Deut. 11:30 seems to locate them also in the vicinity of Gilgal and the river Jordan (section 9.1).

Once the passage itself is studied in its own right and in relation to the parallel passage in Deut. 27:1–8.11–13, it becomes clear that Josh. 8:30–35 is a relatively young addition to the book, originating from the hand of DtrN. The various traditions and literary strata in Deut. 11:29–30 and 27:1–8.11–13 have been transformed for the single purpose of placing all stress on the *torah* of Moses, one of the two main concerns of DtrN. The other main concern of this editor, abstinence from the non-Israelite indigenous population, becomes clear in the position which this addition occupies in MT. The origin of the threat posed by the continued existence of these foreign people (Josh. 23:6–7.12–13 DtrN) should be sought in Joshua 9, where the autochthonous Gibeonites manage to remain unharmed in the land by means of a ruse. As a result, the DtrN-redactor placed the blessing of the Israelite people before (בראשנה) this primeval Fall. From a redaction-critical point of view, the position of the passage in MT is more likely to be original than an alleged position before Josh. 5:2 (section 9.4).

4QJosh[a], however, does not reflect a transposition of the original MT-position to that before Josh. 5:1 (so Rofé; section 9.5), since in that case the mountains mentioned in Josh. 8:30 and 8:34 should also have been transported from their actual place to the middle of the river Jordan, since the editorial pluses in 4QJoshua[a] column I, line 2, [ ]את הירד[ן] בעברו [and [ ]אחר אשר נתקו, make clear that the recitation of the *torah* took place during Israel's passage through the Jordan, before the priests bearing the ark left their place (the use of the verb נתק links this passage to Josh. 4:18). What we find in 4QJosh[a] is not a transposition, but an expansion of the text of Josh. 4–5 on the basis of Josh. 8:32.34–35. The origin of this duplication must be sought in an interpretation of the tension between Deut. 27:4, which prescribes the erection of great stones for an altar on Mount Ebal (fulfilled in Josh. 8:30–35 by DtrN), and its Deuteronomistic correction in Deut. 27:2–3.8, in which the great stones are transformed into steles on which the *torah* should be written and in which the geographical element 'on Mount Ebal' has been replaced by the temporal element 'on the day (on which you pass through the Jordan)'. The scribe responsible for the fulfilment of this command after Israel had crossed the river Jordan (Josh. 3) and had erected great stones (Josh. 4:20), read Deut. 27:2–4 in a complementary sense. A reconstruction of columns V–VIII seems to confirm this thesis, since a reconstruction of columns VI–VII can only lead to a result that fits the number of lines and letterspaces per line, if Josh. 8:30–35 is left in its original position between Joshua 8 and Joshua 9 (section 9.5). The transposition in LXX (the only attested one) was probably motivated by the Greek translator's wish to offer a coherent and plausible historiography: Josh. 9:1–2 was understood as a temporary concentration of the hostile forces which would allow Joshua and Israel to perform their religious duties in as yet unconquered territory (section 9.6).

10.2 The History of the Text of the Book of Joshua

Although this study is mainly based on three chapters of the book of Joshua, a few conclusions with respect to the history of the text of the book of Joshua can be drawn. Of the textual witnesses, the version attested by MT is closest to the final stage of the literary formation of Joshua. Although it still remains plausible that in Joshua 20 MT does reflect a literary expansion of the shorter text attested by MT, 4QJosh[a] and LXX do not attest to such an intermediary redactional stage in the passages discussed above, but either reflect expansion or reformulation of the version attested by MT. This does not imply that on the whole MT has preserved the original text of this final stage in the literary history of the book. The absence of passages such as Josh. 13:7–8*, 15:59a, and 21:36–37, still preserved in LXX, make clear that the text that has become standardised was not completely free from scribal errors. The variants in LXX and 4QJosh[a] *vis-à-vis* MT, however, are not of the same size, nature and importance as the extensive reworkings of the older text by the Deuteronomistic, nomistic and Priestly author-redactors. Therefore, the ancient textual witnesses of Joshua do not attest to the redaction process of the book.

The text of 4QJoshua[a] contains an expansion of Josh. 4:20–5:8 on the basis of Deut. 27:2–3.8 and Josh. 8:32.34–35. This type of harmonisation resembles very much that found in the Samaritan

Pentateuch, 4QpaleoExod[m], 4QNum[b], 4QDeut[n], 4QReworkedPentateuch, the Nash Papyrus etc.). If one wishes to employ the term 'new edition' of the older composition for these expanded versions of the Pentateuch, one might use that term for 4QJosh[a] and LXX-Joshua (LXX-Josh. 21:42a–d for instance) as well. This implies that the harmonising re-editing of these biblical books was not restricted to the Pentateuch, but extended into the books of the Former Prophets as well. Several of the variants posed by 4QSam[a] *vis-à-vis* MT possibly reflect this same type of harmonising re-editing.[2] In the light of these observations it is tempting to ascribe the expansions in LXX-Josh. 6:26a (cf. MT-1 Kgs. 16:34), 16:10a (cf. MT-1 Kgs. 9:16), 19:47–48 (cf. Judg. 1:34–35), 21:42a–d (cf. MT-Josh. 19:49–50) and 24:33a–b (cf. Judg. 2:6.11–14; 3:12) to this same type of redaction and to the same school of Hebrew scribes. The harmonisations, however, are not the product of a single, comprehensive enterprise, but rather a collection of similar literary initiatives. It is therefore well possible that the Greek translator of Joshua continued this scribal tradition.

With respect to the passages that have been closely examined in the preceding chapters (6–9), there has been no reason to assume that the divergencies between MT and LXX stem from a Hebrew *Vorlage* that reflects an older stage in the literary history of the book. Although the Greek translator's *Vorlage* may from time to time have differed from MT, the scale of these variants does not exceed that of the divergencies between MT and other Hebrew witnesses such as 4QJosh[b], 4QJosh[a] (apart from the expansion in 4:20–5:1), and the Mediaeval Masoretic manuscripts. By far the majority of the MT–LXX variants can be ascribed to literary initiatives introduced by the Greek translator.

The literary heirs to the old tradition of reworking the old Joshua narratives into new literary compositions are therefore not the textual witnesses to the book of Joshua (MT, LXX, 4QJosh[a]). These versions all attest to more or less the same version of the book. In a sense the real continuation of this tradition in the first centuries BCE, i.e. the period in which the book of Joshua was translated into

[2] A. Rofé, The Nomistic Correction; A. Rofé, 4QSam[a] in the Light of Historico-literary Criticism: The Case of 2 Sam 24 and 1 Chr 21, in A. Vivian (Hg.), *Biblische und Judaistische studien. Festschrift für Paolo Sacchi.* (Judentum und Umwelt 29) Frankfurt am Main/Bern/New York/Paris 1990, pp. 109–119; A. Rofé, 4QMidrash Samuel? Observations concerning the Character of 4QSam[a], in *Textus* 19 (1998), pp. 63–74.

Greek (circa 200 BCE) and the period in which 4QJosh[a] was copied (150 BCE–50 BCE) should probably be sought in the para-biblical versions of the book of Joshua, as we find them in highly fragmentised form in 4QpaleoParaJoshua, 4QApocryphon of Joshua[a] (4Q378), 4QApocryphon of Joshua[b] (4Q379), 4QProphecy of Joshua? (4Q522), 5QWork with Place Names (5Q9) and the Masada Joshua Apocryphon (Mas 1039-211), discussed in section 3.5 above. The Samaritan version of Joshua may be a young representative of this tradition. On the next page a tentative diagram of the textual history of Joshua is offered, which summarises this section. It turns out that this model corresponds to that labelled 'the traditional model' in section 1.2.1.

10.3 The Relation Between Textual and Literary Criticism

Textual criticism attempts to account for the variant readings in extant witnesses to the text of the same literary composition. Literary criticism in its diachronic sense aims at a reconstruction of the literary history of a literary composition. Although the results of textual criticism may incidentally coincide with that of literary criticism as seems to be the case in Joshua 20, it cannot replace literary criticism. Textual and literary criticism are distinct, though complementary disciplines. When divergencies between textual witnesses seem to reflect redactional activity, the chronological relation between these alleged different editions can only be established by means of the traditional literary-critical tools. In the passages discussed in the preceding chapters, it has become clear that textual and literary history do not overlap. Nevertheless, the variants point to the vestiges of the literary formation of Joshua. In this sense, textual and literary criticism are mutually illuminating. It is to be hoped that this approach, in which justice is done to literary criticism in its own right and the ancient textual witnesses in their own context, may also be able to throw light on other passages in Joshua or other biblical books, where textual and literary history offer such dynamic and fascinating points of contact as have been examined in the present study.

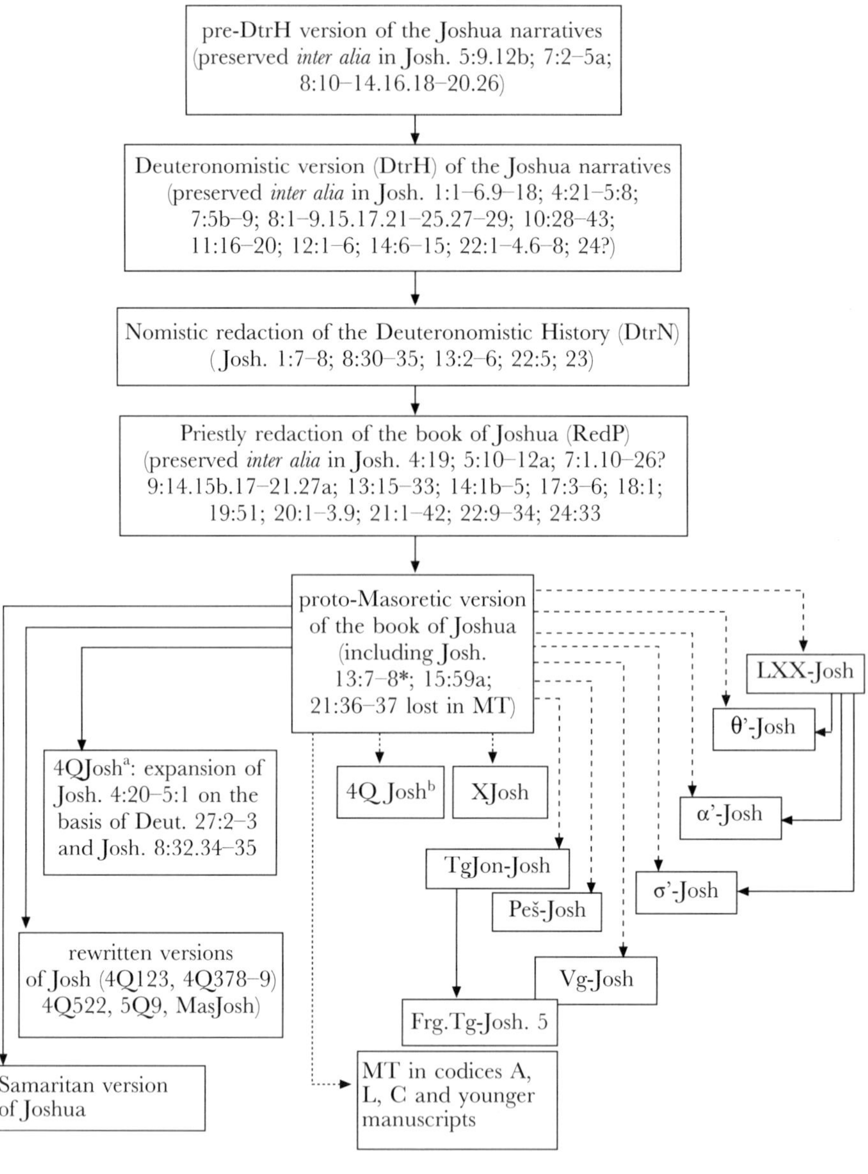
pre-DtrH version of the Joshua narratives (preserved *inter alia* in Josh. 5:9.12b; 7:2–5a; 8:10–14.16.18–20.26)
Deuteronomistic version (DtrH) of the Joshua narratives (preserved *inter alia* in Josh. 1:1–6.9–18; 4:21–5:8; 7:5b–9; 8:1–9.15.17.21–25.27–29; 10:28–43; 11:16–20; 12:1–6; 14:6–15; 22:1–4.6–8; 24?)
Nomistic redaction of the Deuteronomistic History (DtrN) (Josh. 1:7–8; 8:30–35; 13:2–6; 22:5; 23)
Priestly redaction of the book of Joshua (RedP) (preserved *inter alia* in Josh. 4:19; 5:10–12a; 7:1.10–26? 9:14.15b.17–21.27a; 13:15–33; 14:1b–5; 17:3–6; 18:1; 19:51; 20:1–3.9; 21:1–42; 22:9–34; 24:33
proto-Masoretic version of the book of Joshua (including Josh. 13:7–8*; 15:59a; 21:36–37 lost in MT)
LXX-Josh
θ'-Josh
α'-Josh
σ'-Josh
4QJosh[a]: expansion of Josh. 4:20–5:1 on the basis of Deut. 27:2–3 and Josh. 8:32.34–35
4Q Josh[b]
XJosh
TgJon-Josh
Peš-Josh
Vg-Josh
Frg.Tg-Josh. 5
rewritten versions of Josh (4Q123, 4Q378–9) 4Q522, 5Q9, MasJosh)
Samaritan version of Joshua
MT in codices A, L, C and younger manuscripts
Legenda:
reworking/redation/extensive revision of an older version
translation of the Hebrew text
direct Hebrew witness

SELECT BIBLIOGRAPHY

A. AEJMELAEUS, *Parataxis in the Septuagint. A Study of the Renderings of the Hebrew Coordinate Clauses in the Greek Pentateuch.* (AASF Dissertationes humanorum litterarum 31) Helsinki 1982.

A. AEJMELAEUS, R. SOLLAMO (eds.), I. SOISALON-SOININEN, *Studien zur Septuaginta-Syntax. Gesammelte Aufsätze.* Helsinki 1987.

A. AEJMELAEUS, *On the Trail of the Septuagint Translators.* Kampen 1993.

——. Die Septuaginta des Deuteronmiums, in T. VEIJOLA (Hg.), *Das Deuteronomium und seine Querbeziehungen.* (SFEG 62) Helsinki/Göttingen 1996, pp. 1–22.

E. ALBERS, *Die Quellenberichte in Josua I–XII. Beitrag zur Quellenkritik des Hexateuchs.* Bonn 1891.

B.J. ALFRINK, *Josue uit de grondtekst vertaald en uitgelegd.* (BOT) Roermond/Maaseik 1952.

M. ANBAR, La "reprise", in *VT* 38 (1988), pp. 385–398.

——. The Story about the Building of an Altar on Mount Ebal. The History of Its Composition and the Question of the Centralization of the Cult, in N. LOHFINK (Hg.), *Das Deuteronomium. Entstehung, Gestalt und Botschaft.* (BETL 68) Leuven 1985, pp. 304–309.

V. APTOWITZER, *Das Schriftwort in der rabbinischen Literatur.* Wien 1906, reprinted in H.M. ORLINSKY (ed.), *The Library of Biblical Studies.* New York 1970.

A.G. AULD, Judges 1 and History. A Reconsideration, in *VT* 25 (1975), pp. 261–285.

——. *Studies in Joshua: Text and Literary Relations.* (Thesis presented for the Degree of Ph.D. to the University of Edinburgh) Edinburgh 1976.

——. Joshua: The Hebrew and Greek Texts, in J.A. EMERTON (ed.), *Studies in the Historical Books of the Old Testament.* (SVT 30) Leiden 1979, pp. 1–14, reprinted in A.G. AULD, *Joshua Retold. Synoptic Perspectives.* (Old Testament Studies) Edinburgh 1998, pp. 7–18.

——. *Joshua, Moses and the Land. Tetrateuch-Pentateuch-Hexateuch in a Generation since 1938.* Edinburgh 1980.

——. *Joshua Retold. Synoptic Perspectives.* (Old Testament Studies) Edinburgh 1998.

B. BAENTSCH, *Exodus, Leviticus und Numeri übersetzt und erklärt.* (HKAT I/2) Göttingen 1903.

J. BAJARD, R.-F. POSWICK, Aspects statistiques des rapports entre la Septante et le texte massorétique, in C.E. COX (ed.), *VII Congress of the International Organization for Septuagint and Cognate Studies. Leuven 1989.* (SCS 31) Atlanta 1991, pp. 123–156.

P.D. BALDI, O.F.M., *Giosuè.* (La Sacra bibbia) Torino/Roma 1952.

D. BARTHÉLEMY, *Critique textuelle de l'ancien Testament 1. Josué, Juges, Ruth, Samuel, Rois, Chroniques, Esdras, Néhémie, Esther.* (OBO 50/1) Fribourg/Göttingen 1982.

W. BAUER, *Griechisch-Deutsches Wörterbuch zu den Schriften des Neuen Testaments und der übrigen urchristlichen Literatur.* Berlin/New York 1971[5].

G. BEER, *Pesachim (Ostern) Text, Übersetzung und Erklärung nebst einem textkritischen Anhang.* (Die Mischna. Text, Überstezung und ausführliche Erklärung mit eingehenden geschichtlichen und sprachlichen Einleitungen II. Seder. Moëd; 3. Traktat) Gießen 1912.

C.D. BENJAMIN, *The Variations between the Hebrew and Greek Texts of Joshua: Chapters 1–12.* (University of Pennsylvania. A thesis presented to the faculty of the graduate school in partial fulfillment of the requirements for the degree of doctor of philosophy) Leipzig 1921.

Biblia sacra iuxta latinam vulgatam versionem ad codicum fidem iussu Pii PP. XI cura et studio monachorum abbatiae pontificae sancti Hieronymi in urbe ordinis sancti Benedicti edita: Libri Iosue Iudicum Ruth ex interpretatione sancti Hieronymi cum praefatione et variis capitulorum seriebus. Roma 1939.

K. Bieberstein, *Lukian und Theodotion im Josuabuch. Mit einem Beitrag zu den Josuarollen von Ḫirbet Qumrān*. (Biblische Notizen. Beiheft 7) München 1994.

——. *Josua-Jordan-Jericho. Archäologie, Geschichte und Theologie der Landnahmeerzählungen Josua 1–6*. (OBO 143) Freiburg/Göttingen 1995.

A. Blaschke, *Beschneidung. Zeugnisse der Bibel und verwandter Texte*. (Texte und Arbeiten zum neutestamentlichen Zeitalter 28) Tübingen/Basel 1998.

F. Blass, A. Debrunner, F. Rehkopf, *Grammatik des neutestamentlichen Griechisch*. Göttingen 1976[14].

J. Blenkinsopp, The Structure of P, in *CBQ* 38 (1976), pp. 275–292.

E. Blum, *Studien zur Komposition des Pentateuch*. (BZAW 189) Berlin/New York 1990.

R.G. Boling, *Joshua. A New Translation with Notes and Commentary. Introduction by* G.E. Wright. (AB 6) New York/London/Toronto/Sydney/Auckland 1982.

G.J. Botterweck, H. Ringgren, G.W. Anderson, H. Cazelles, D.N. Freedman, S. Talmon, G. Wallis, H.-J. Fabry (Hg.), *Theologisches Wörterbuch zum Alten Testament*. Stuttgart/Berlin/Köln/Mainz 1973–.

C. Brekelmans, Joshua v 10–12: Another Approach, in A.S. van der Woude (ed.), *New Avenues in the Study of the Old Testament. A Collection of Old Testament Studies Published on the Occassion of the Fiftieth Anniversary of the Oudtestamentisch Werkgezelschap and the Retirement of Prof. M.J. Mulder*. (OTS 25) Leiden/New York/København/Köln 1989, pp. 89–95.

C. Brekelmans, J. Lust (eds.), *Pentateuchal and Deuteronomistic Studies. Papers Read at the XIIIth IOSOT Congress. Leuven 1989*. (BETL 94) Leuven 1990.

L.L. Brenton, *The Septuagint Version of the Old Testament with an English Translation*. London 1879.

J. Briend, *Bible et archéologie en Josué 6,1–8,29. Recherches sur la composition de Josué 1–12*. (Institut catholique de Paris U.E.R. de Théologie et de Sciences Religieuses. Cycle des études du doctorat. Thèse présentée pour l'obtention du titre de docteur en théologie.) Paris 1978.

S.P. Brock, C.T. Fritsch, S. Jellicoe, *A Classified Bibliography of the Septuagint*. (Arbeiten zur Literatur und Geschichte des hellenistischen Judentums 6) Leiden 1973.

A.E. Brooke, N. McLean (eds.), *The Old Testament in Greek. According to the Text of Codex Vaticanus, Supplemented from Other Uncial Manuscripts, with a Critical Apparatus Containing the Variants of the Chief Ancient Authorities for the Text of the Septuagint. Volume I. The Octateuch. Part IV. Joshua, Judges and Ruth*. Cambridge 1917.

G.J. Brooke, B. Lindars, s.s.f (eds.), *Septuagint, Scrolls and Cognate Writings. Papers Presented to the International Symposium on the Septuagint and Its Relations to the Dead Sea Scrolls and Other Writings (Manchester, 1990)*. (SBL-SCS 33) Atlanta 1992.

F. Brown, S.R. Driver, C.A. Briggs, *A Hebrew and English Lexicon of the Old Testament with an appendix containing the Biblical Aramaic*. Oxford 1906.

T.C. Butler, *Joshua*. (WBC 7) Waco 1983.

J.H. Charlesworth (ed.), *The Old Testament Pseudepigrapha. Volume 2. Expansions of the 'Old Testament' and Legends, Wisdom and Philosophical Literature, Prayers, Psalms, and Odes, Fragments of Lost Judeo-Hellenistic Works*. New York/London/Toronto/Sydney/Auckland 1985.

——. (ed.), XJoshua, in J. Charlesworth, N. Cohen, H. Cotton, E. Eshel, H. Eshel, P. Flint, H. Misgav, M. Morgenstern, K. Murphy, M. Segal, A. Yardeni, B. Zissu (eds.), *Miscellaneous Texts from the Judaean Desert*. (DJD 38) Oxford 2000, pp. 231–239.

E.A. CHESMAN, *Studies in the Septuagint Text of the Book of Joshua.* (Thesis Submitted in Partial Fulfillment of Requirements for the Master of Arts in Hebrew Literature Degree and Ordination. Hebrew Union College. Jewish Institute of Religion) [New York ?] 1967.
B. CHILDS, *The Book of Exodus. A Critical, Theological Commentary.* (OTL) Philadelphia 1974.
M. COHEN (ed.), *Mikra'ot Gedolot 'Haketer'. A Revised and Augmented Scientific Edition of Mikra'ot Gedolot'. Based on the Aleppo Codex and Early Medieval MSS. Joshua-Judges.* Ramat-Gan 1992.
J.W. COLENSO, *The Pentateuch and Book of Joshua.* (I–VII) London 1863–1879.
G.A. COOKE, *The Book of Joshua in the Revised Version with Introduction and Notes.* (The Cambridge Bible for Schools and Colleges) Cambridge 1918.
E. CORTESE, *Josua 13–21. Ein priesterschriftlicher Abschnitt im Deuteronomistischer Geschichtswerk.* (OBO 94) Fribourg/Göttingen 1990.
C.E. COX (ed.), *VII Congress of the International Organization for Septuagint and Cognate Studies. Leuven 1989.* (SCS 31) Atlanta 1991.
——. (ed.), *VIII Congress of the International Organization for Septuagint and Cognate Studies. Paris 1992.* (SCS 41) Atlanta 1995.
F.M. CROSS, *The Ancient Library of Qumran and Modern Biblical Studies. The Haskell Lectures 1956–1957.* New York 1961[2].
——. *Canaanite Myth and Hebrew Epic. Essays in the History of the Religion of Israel.* Cambridge, Massachusetts 1973.
F.M. CROSS, S. TALMON (eds.), *Qumran and the History of the Biblical Text.* Cambridge, Massachusetts/London 1975.
A.D. CROWN, *The Samaritans.* Tübingen 1989.
S. DANIEL, *Recherches sur le vocabulaire du culte.* Paris 1966.
R. LE DÉAUT, Le thème de la circoncision du coeur (Dt. xxx 6; Jér. iv 4) dans les versions anciennes (LXX et Targum) et à Qumrân, in J.A. EMERTON (ed.), *Congress Volume. Vienna 1980.* (SVT 32) Leiden 1981.
W. DIETRICH, *Prophetie und Geschichte: Eine redaktionsgeschichtliche Untersuchung zum deuteronomistischen Geschichtswerk* (FRLANT 108) Göttingen 1972.
A. DILLMANN, *Die Bücher Numeri, Deuteronomium und Josua.* (KeH) Leipzig 1886.
C. DOGNIEZ, M. HARL, *Le Deutéronome. Traduction du texte grec de la Septante, Introduction et Notes.* (La Bible d'Alexandrie 5) Paris 1992.
C. DOGNIEZ, *Bibliography of the Septuagint 1970–1993.* (SVT 60) Leiden/New York/Köln 1995.
G. DORIVAL, M. HARL, O. MUNNICH, *La bible grecque des Septante. Du judaïsme hellénistique au christianisme ancien.* Paris 1994[2].
G. DORIVAL, *Les Nombres. Traduction du texte grec de la Septante, Introduction et Notes.* (La Bible d'Alexandrie 4) Paris 1992.
S.R. DRIVER, *An Introduction to the Literature of the Old Testament.* Edinburgh 1909[8], reprinted Cleveland/New York 1967[9].
——. *A Critical and Exegetical Commentary on Deuteronomy.* (ICC) Edinburgh 1902[3].
J. DURHAM, J.R. PORTER (eds.), *Proclamation and Presence. Old Testament Essays in Honour of Gwyne Henton Davies.* London 1970.
A.B. EHRLICH, *Randglossen zur hebräischen Bibel. Textkritisches, Sprachliches und Sachliches. Dritter Band. Josua, Richter, I u. II. Samuelis.* Leipzig 1910.
O. EIßFELDT, *Hexateuch-Synopse. Die Erzählung der fünf Bücher Mose und des Buches Josua mit dem Anfange des Richterbuches in ihre vier Quellen zerlegt und in deutscher Übersetzung dargeboten samt einer in Einleitung und Anmerkungen gegebenen Begründung.* Leipzig 1922.
J. ERBES (ed.), *Joshua.* (The Old Testament in Syriac according to the Peshiṭta Version edited on behalf of the International Organization for the Study of the Old Testament by the Peshiṭta Institute Leiden; Part II, fascicle 1 b) Leiden 1991.

J.E. Erbes, *The Peshitta and the Versions. A Study of the Peshitta Variants in Joshua 1–5 in Relation to Their Equivalents in the Ancient Versions.* (Acta Universitatis Upsaliensis. Studia Semitica Upsaliensia 16) Uppsala 1999.

H. Eshel, The Historical Background of the Pesher Interpreting Joshua's Curse on the Rebuilder of Jericho, in *RdQ* 15 (1991–1992), pp. 409–420.

C. van den Eynde, *Commentaire d'Išoʿdad de Merv sur l'ancien Testament. III. Livres des sessions.* (CSCO 229/230. Scriptores Syri 96/97) Louvain 1962–1963.

H.-J. Fabry, Spuren des Pentateuchredaktors in Jos 4,21ff.: Anmerkungen zur Deuteronomismus-Rezeption, in N. Lohfink (Hg.), *Das Deuteronomium, Entstehung, Gestalt und Botschaft.* (BETL 68) Leuven 1985, pp. 351–356.

H. Fahr, U. Gleßmer (Hg.), *Jordandurchzug und Beschneidung als Zurechtweisung in einem Targum zu Josua 5 (Edition des MS T.-S. B 13, 12).* (Orientalia biblica et christiana 3) Glückstadt 1991.

P.A. Fernández, s.i., *Commentarius in librum Iosue.* (Cursus Scripturae Sacrae 5) Parisiis 1938.

N. Fernández Marcos, A. Sáenz-Badillos (ed.), *Theodoreti Cyrensis Quaestiones in Octateuchum.* Madrid 1979.

N. Fernández Marcos, J.R. Busto Saiz, *El Texto Antioqueno de la Biblia Griega. 1. 1–2 Samuel.* (Textos y estudios 'Cardenal Cisneros' 50) Madrid 1989.

N. Fernández Marcos, *The Septuagint in Context. Introduction to the Greek Versions of the Bible.* Leiden/Boston/Köln 2000.

F. Field, *Origenis Hexaplorum quae supersunt; sive veterum interpretum graecorum in totus Vetus Testamentum fragmenta* I–II. Oxford 1875.

J. Finkel, The Case of the Repeated Circumcision in Joshua 5:2–7: A Historical and Comparative Study, in H.L. Silverman, *Annals of the Jewish Academy of Arts and Sciences* 1974, pp. 177–213.

M. Fishbane, *Biblical Interpretation in Ancient Israel.* Oxford 1985.

P.W. Flint, J.C. VanderKam (eds.), *The Dead Sea Scrolls after Fifty Years. A Comprehensive Assessment* 1–2. Leiden/Boston/Köln 1998–1999.

V. Fritz, *Das Buch Josua.* (HAT I/7) Tübingen 1994.

A.F. von Gall (Hg.), *Der hebräische Pentateuch der Samaritaner.* Gießen 1918.

F. García Martínez, E.J.C. Tigchelaar, *The Dead Sea Scrolls Study Edition* I–II. Leiden 1997–1998.

F. García Martínez, E. Noort (eds.), *Perspectives in the Study of the Old Testament and Early Judaism. A Symposium in Honour of Adam S. van der Woude on the Occasion of his 70th Birthday.* (SVT 73) Leiden/Boston/Köln 1998.

M. Gaster, Das Buch Josua in hebräisch-samaritanischer Rezension. Entdeckt und zum ersten Male herausgegeben, in *Zeitschrift der deutschen morgenländischen Gesellschaft* 62 (1908), pp. 209–279.494–549.

W. Gesenius, E. Kautzsch, *Hebräische Grammatik.* Leipzig 1902[27].

D.W. Gooding, Traditions of Interpretation of the Circumcision at Gilgal, in A. Shinan (ed.), *Proceedings of the Sixth World Congress of Jewish Studies held at the Hebrew University of Jerusalem, 13–19 August 1973 . . . Volume One.* Jerusalem 1977, pp. 149–164.

——. On the Use of the LXX for Dating Midrashic Elements in the Targums, in *JThSt* 25 (1974), pp. 1–11.

M. Görg, *Josua.* (Die neue Echter Bibel) Würzburg 1991.

L.J. Greenspoon, *Textual Studies in the Book of Joshua.* (HSM 28) Chico 1983.

——. The Qumran Fragments of Joshua: Which Puzzle Are They Part Of and Where Do They Fit?, in G.J. Brooke, B. Lindars, s.s.f (eds.), *Septuagint, Scrolls and Cognate Writings. Papers Presented to the International Symposium on the Septuagint and Its Relations to the Dead Sea Scrolls and Other Writings (Manchester, 1990).* (SBL-SCS 33) Atlanta 1992, pp. 159–194.

L.J. Greenspoon, O. Munnich (eds.), *VIII Congress of the International Organization for Septuagint and Cognate Studies. Paris 1992.* (SBL-SCS 41) Atlanta 1995.

K. Grünwaldt, *Exil und Identität. Beschneidung, Passa und Sabbat in der Priesterschrift.* (BBB 85) Frankfurt am Main 1992.

H. Haag, *Vom alten zum neuen Pascha. Geschichte und Theologie des Osterfestes.* (SBS 49) Stuttgart 1971.

M. Harl, *La Genèse. Traduction du texte grec de la Septante, Introduction et Notes.* (La Bible d'Alexandrie 1). Paris 1994[2].

D.J. Harrington (ed.), J. Cazeaux (trad.), *Pseudo-Philon. Les Antiquités Bibliques. Tome I.* Paris 1976.

D.J. Harrington (ed.), Pseudo-Philo, in J.H Charlesworth (ed.), *The Old Testament Pseudepigrapha. Volume 2. Expansions of the 'Old Testament' and Legends, Wisdom and Philosophical Literature, Prayers, Psalms and Odes, Fragments of Lost Judeo-Hellenistic Works.* New York/London/Toronto/Sydney/Auckland 1985, pp. 297–377.

E. Hatch, H.A. Redpath, *A Concordance to the Septuagint and the Other Greek Versions of the Old Testament (including the Apocryphal Books) in Three Volumes.* Oxford 1897, reprinted in Grand Rapids, Michigan 1987.

J.D. Hawkins, Ḫatti, in D.O. Edzard (Hg.), *Reallexikon der Assyriologie* IV. Berlin/New York 1975, pp. 152–159.

C.G. den Hertog, *Studien zur griechischen Übersetzung des Buches Josua.* (Inaugural-Dissertation zur Erlangung des Doktorgrades der Philosophie des Fachbereichs 07 der Justus-Liebig-Universität Gießen) Gießen 1996.

H.W. Hertzberg, *Die Bücher Josua, Richter, Ruth übersetzt und erklärt.* (ATD 9) Göttingen 1954.

R.S. Hess, *Joshua. An Introduction and Commentary.* (Tyndale Old Testament Commentaries 6) Leicester/Downers Grove, Illinois 1996.

J. Hollenberg, Die deuteronomischen Bestandtheile des Buches Josua, in *Theologische Studien und Kritiken* 47 (1874), pp. 462–507.

——. *Der Charakter der alexandrinischen Uebersetzung des Buches Josua und ihr textkritischer Werth.* (Wissenschaftliche Beilage zu dem Oster-Programm des Gymnasiums zu Moers) Moers 1876.

——. Zur Textkritik des Buches Josua und des Buches der Richter, in *ZAW* 1 (1881), pp. 97–105.

S. Holmes, *Joshua. The Hebrew and Greek Texts.* Cambridge 1914.

H. Holzinger, *Das Buch Josua.* (Kurzer Hand-Commentar zum Alten Testament VI) Tübingen/Leipzig 1901.

M. Jastrow, *A Dictionary of the Targumim, the Talmud Babli and Yerushalmi, and the Midrashic Literature.* London 1903, reprinted in New York 1985.

A. Jaubert (éd.), *Homélies sur Josué. Texte latin, introduction, traduction et notes.* (SC 71) Paris 1960.

S. Jellicoe, *The Septuagint and Modern Study.* Oxford 1968.

E. Jenni, C. Westermann (Hg.), *Theologisches Handwörterbuch zum Alten Testament* I–II. München 1971–1976.

H.L. Jones, *The Geography of Strabo. VII. Books XV–XVI.* Cambridge, Massachusetts/London 1930.

P. Joüon, T. Muraoka, *A Grammar of Biblical Hebrew.* (Subsidia Biblica 14/I–II) Rome 1993.

R. Kasser (ed.), *Papyrus Bodmer XXI. Josué VI,16–25, VII,6–XI,23, XXII,1–2, 19-XIII,7, 15-XXIV,23.* (Bibliotheca Bodmeriana) Cologne/Genève 1965.

R. Kasser, *L'évangile selon saint Jean et les versions coptes de la Bible.* Neuchâtel/Paris 1966.

A. Kempinksi, 'בתנומת ההיסטוריה משנשנת התיאלוגיה' הערות על יהושע פרק ח' 35–30 והארכיאולוגיה של תקופת ההתנחלות. ('When History Sleeps, Theology Arises': A Note on Joshua 8:30–35 and the Archaeology of the 'Settlement Period'), in

S. Aḥituv, B.A. Levine (eds.), *Avraham Malamat Volume.* (Eretz-Israel 24) Jerusalem 1993, pp. 175–183. English abstract, p. 237*.

O. Keel, *Wirkmächtige Siegeszeichen im Alten Testament.* (OBO 5) Freiburg/Göttingen 1974.

C.F. Keil, *Josua, Richter und Ruth.* (Biblischer Commentar II/1) Leipzig 1863.

G. Kittel (Hg.), *Theologisches Wörterbuch zum Neuen Testament.* Stuttgart 1933–.

A. Knobel, *Die Bücher Numeri, Deuteronomium und Josua erklärt. Nebst einer Kritik des Pentateuch und Josua.* (Kurzgefasstes exegetisches Handbuch zum Alten Testament) Leipzig 1861.

L. Koehler, W. Baumgartner, J.J. Stamm, B. Hartmann, Z. Ben-Hayyim, E.Y. Kutscher, P. Reymond, M.E.J. Richardson, *The Hebrew and Aramaic Lexicon of the Old Testament.* Leiden/New York/Köln 1994–2000.

A. van der Kooij, *Die alten Textzeugen des Jesajabuches. Ein Beitrag zur Textgeschichte des Alten Testaments.* (OBO 35) Freiburg/Göttingen 1981.

——. Zum Verhältnis von Textkritik und Literarkritik: Überlegungen anhand einiger Beispiele, in J.A. Emerton (ed.), *Congress Volume. Cambridge 1995.* (SVT 66) Leiden/New York/Köln 1997, pp. 185–202.

——. *The Oracle of Tyre. The Septuagint of Isaiah 23 as Version and Vision.* (SVT 71) Leiden/Boston/Köln 1998

H.-J. Kraus, Gilgal. Ein Beitrag zur Kultusgeschichte Israels, in *VT* 1 (1951), pp. 181–199.

J.H. Kroeze, *Het boek Jozua.* (COT) Kampen 1968.

A. Kuenen, Bijdragen tot de critiek van Pentateuch en Jozua. III. De uitzending der verspieders, in *Theologisch Tijdschrift* 11 (1877), pp. 545–566.

——. Bijdragen tot de critiek van Pentateuch en Jozua. V. De godsdienstige vergadering bij Ebal en Gerizim. (*Deut.* XI:29, 30; XXVII; *Joz.* VIII:30–35), in *Theologisch Tijdschrift* 12 (1878), pp. 297–323.

——. *Historisch-critisch onderzoek naar het ontstaan en de verzameling van de boeken des Ouden Verbonds. Tweede, geheel omgewerkte uitgave. Eerste deel. De Thora en de historische boeken des Ouden Verbonds.* Leiden 1887[2].

G. Kuhnert, *Das Gilgalpassah. Literarische, überlieferungsgeschichtliche und geschichtliche Untersuchungen zu Jos. 3–6.* (Inaugural-Dissertation zur Erlangung der Doktorwürde des Evangelisch-Theologischen Fachbereichs der Johannes Gutenberg-Universität Mainz) Mainz 1981.

K. Latvus, *God, Anger and Ideology. The Anger of God in Joshua and Judges in Relation to Deuteronomy and the Priestly Writings.* (JSOTS 279) Sheffield 1998.

H.G. Liddell, R. Scott, H.S. Jones, R. McKenzie, *A Greek-English Lexicon. With a Revised Supplement 1996.* Oxford 1996.

G. Lisowsky, *Konkordanz zum hebräischen Alten Testament nach dem von Paul Kahle in der Biblia Hebraica edidit Rudolph Kittel besorgten Masoretische Text unter verantwortlicher Mitwerkung von Leonhard Rost ausgearbeitet und geschrieben.* Stuttgart 1981[2].

N. Lohfink, Die deuteronomistische Darstellung des Übergangs der Führung Israels von Moses auf Josue. Ein Beitrag zur alttestamentlichen Theologie des Amtes, in *Scholastik* 37 (1962), pp. 32–44; reprinted in N. Lohfink, *Studien zum Deuteronomium und zur deuteronomistischen Literatur* I. (SBAB.AT 8) Stuttgart 1990, pp. 83–98.

——. Die Priesterschrift und die Geschichte, in *Congress Volume. Göttingen 1977.* (SVT 29) Leiden 1978, pp. 189–225.

——. Kerygmata des Deuteronomistischen Geschichtswerks, in J. Jeremias, L. Perlitt (Hg.), *Die Botschaft und die Boten. Festschrift für Hans Walter Wolff zum 70. Geburtstag.* Neukirchen 1981, pp. 87–100, reprinted in N. Lohfink, *Studien zum Deuteronomium und zur deuteronomistischen Literatur* II. (SBAB 12) Stuttgart 1991, pp. 125–142.

——. Textkritisches zu jrš im Alten Testament, in P. Casetti, O. Keel, A. Schenker (éd.), *Mélanges Dominique Barthélemy. Études bibliques offertes à l'occassion de son 60e anniversaire.* (OBO 38) Freiburg/Göttingen 1981, pp. 273–288.

——. (Hg.), *Das Deuteronomium. Entstehung, Gestalt und Botschaft.* (BETL 68) Leuven 1985.

B. Lucassen, Josua, Richter und CD, in *Revue de Qumran* 18/3 (1998), pp. 373–396.

——. Possibility and Probability of Textual Reconstruction: The Transition from 4QJosh[b], frg. 2 to frg. 3 and the Transit of the Israelites through the Jordan, in *Textus* 20 (2000), pp. 71–81.

J. Lust (ed.), *The Book of Ezekiel. Textual and Literary Criticism and their Interrelation.* (BETL 74) Leuven 1986.

J. Lust, E. Eynikel, K. Hauspie, *A Greek-English Lexicon of the Septuagint. Part I–II.* Stuttgart 1992, 1996.

H. Mager, *Die Peschiṭtho zum Buche Josua.* (Freiburger Theologische Studien 9) Freiburg im Breisgau 1916.

B.J. Malina, *The Palestinian Manna Tradition. The Manna Tradition in the Palestinian Targums and Its Relationship to the New Testament Writings.* (AGJU 7) Leiden 1968.

S. Mandelkern, *Veteris Testamenti Concordantiae Hebraicae atque Chaldaicae quibus continentur cuncta quae in prioribus concordantiis reperiuntur vocabula lacunis omnibus expletis emendatis cuiusquemodi vitiis locis unique denuo excerptis atque in meliorem formam redactis vocalibus interdum adscriptis particulae omnes adhuc nondum collatae pronomina omnia hic primum congesta atque enarrata nomina propria omnia seperatim commemorata servato textu masoretico librorumque sacrorum ordine tradito.* Lipsiae 1896.

M.L. Margolis, The Grouping of Codices in the Greek Joshua, in *JQR* 1 (1910), pp. 259–263.

——. The Washington Manuscript of Joshua, in *JAOS* 31 (1911), pp. 365–367.

——. The K Text of Joshua, in *AJSL* 28 (1911–1912), pp. 1–55.

——. τῶν ενδοξῶν—Josh. iv:4, in *Studies in Jewish Literature in Honour of Prof. K. Kohler.* Berlin 1913, pp. 204–209.

——. Additions to Field from the Lyons Codex of the Old Latin, in *JAOS* 33 (1917), pp. 254–258.

——. *Andreas Masius and His Commentary on the Book of Joshua.* (Unpublished typescript finished June 15, 1923).

——. Specimen of a New Edition of the Greek Joshua, in *Jewish Studies in Memory of Israel Abrahams.* New York 1927, pp. 307–323, reprinted in S. Jellicoe (ed.), *Studies in the Septuagint: Origins, Recensions, and Interpretations.* New York 1974, pp. 434–450.

——. Textual Criticism of the Greek Old Testament, in *Proceedings of the American Philosophical Society Held at Philadelphia for Promoting Useful Knowledge* 67 (1928), pp. 187–197.

——. *The Book of Joshua in Greek. According to the Critically Restored Text with an Apparatus Containing the Variants of the Principal Recensions of the Individual Witnesses.* (Publications of the Alexander Kohut Memorial Foundation in Trust at the American Academy for Jewish Research). *Part I–IV: Joshua 1:1–19:38.* Paris 1931–1938; *Part V: Joshua 19:39–24:33. Preface by* E. Tov. Philadelphia 1992.

A. Masius, *Josuae imperatoris historia illustrata atque explicata.* Antverpiae 1574; Commentary part reprinted in *Scripturae Sacrae Cursus Completus ex commentariis omnium perfectissimis ubique habitis, et a magne parte episcoporum necnon theologorum europae catholicae, universim ad hoc interrogatorum, designatis, unice conflatus. Plurimis annotantibus presbyteris ad docendos levitas pascendosve populos alte positis. Tomus septimus. In Numeros.—In Deuteronomium.—In Josuam.* Parisiis 1838.

A.D.H. Mayes, *The Story of Israel between Settlement and Exile.* London 1983.

L. Mazor, The Origin and Evolution of the Curse upon the Rebuilder of Jericho—A Contribution of Textual Criticism to Biblical Historiography, in *Textus* 16 (1988), pp. 1–26.

——. עיונים בתרגום השבעים לספר יהושע—תרומתו להכרת המסירה הטקסטואלית של הספר ולהתפתחותו הספרותית והרעיונית (The Septuagint Translation of the Book of Joshua—Its Contribution to the Understanding of the Textual Transmission of the Book and Its Literary and Ideological Development). (Thesis Submitted for the Degree Doctor of Philosophy. Submitted to the Senate of the Hebrew University) Jerusalem 1994.

——. הסיפור אודות הנצחון על העי (יהושע ח) עיוני נוסח וספרות [A Textual and Literary Study of the Fall of Ai in Joshua 8], in S. JAPHET (ed.), *The Bible in Light of Its Interpreters. Sarah Kamin Memorial Volume*. Jerusalem 1994, pp. 73–108.

——. A Nomistic Reworking of the Jericho Conquest Narrative Reflected in LXX to Joshua 6:1–20, in *Textus* 18 (1995), pp. 47–62.

M.N. VAN DER MEER, Textual Criticism and Literary Criticism in Joshua 1:7 (MT and LXX), in B.A. TAYLOR (ed.), *X Congress of the International Organization for Septuagint and Cognate Studies, Oslo 1998*. (SBL-SCS 51) Atlanta 2001, pp. 355–371.

——. A New Spirit in an Old Corpus? Text-Critical, Literary-Critical and Linguistic Observations regarding Ezekiel 36:16–38, in F. POSTMA, K. SPRONK, E. TALSTRA (eds.), *The New Things. Eschatology in Old Testament Prophecy. Festschrift for Henk Leene*. (Amsterdamse Cahiers voor Exegese van de Bijbel en zijn Tradities Supplement Series 3) Maastricht 2002.

R. MEYER (ed.), Liber Josuae et Judicum, in K. ELLIGER, W. RUDOLPH (eds.), *Biblia Hebraica Stuttgartensia*. Stuttgart 1972.

J. MOATTI-FINE, *Jésus (Josué). Traduction du texte grec de la Septante, Introduction et notes*. (La Bible d'Alexandrie 6) Paris 1996.

S. MOWINCKEL, *Zur Frage nach dokumentarischen Quellen in Josua 13–19*. (Avhandlinger utgitt av Det Norske Videnskaps-Akademi i Olso II. Hist.-Filos. Klasse. 1946. No. 1) Oslo 1946.

——. *Tetrateuch—Pentateuch—Hexateuch. Die Berichte über die Landnahme in den drei altisraelitischen Geschichtswerken*. (BZAW 90) Berlin 1964.

M.J. MULDER, H. SYSLING (eds.), *Mikra. Text, Translation, Reading and Interpretation of the Hebrew Bible in Ancient Judaism and Early Christianity*. (CRINT II/1) Assen/Maastricht/Philadelphia 1988.

T. MURAOKA, *Hebrew/Aramaic Index to the Septuagint. Keyed to the Hatch-Redpath Concordance*. Grand Rapids, Michigan 1998.

——. *A Greek-English Lexicon of the Septuagint Chiefly of the Pentateuch and the Twelve Prophets*. Louvain/Paris/Dudley, MA 2002.

R.D. NELSON, Josiah in the Book of Joshua, in *JBL* 100 (1981), pp. 531–540.

——. *Joshua. A Commentary*. (OTL) Louisville 1997.

J. NENTEL, *Trägerschaft und Intentionen des deuteronomistischen Geschichtswerks: Untersuchungen zu den Reflexionsreden Jos 1; 23; 24; 1 Sam 12 und 1 Kön 8*. (BZAW 297) Berlin/New York 2000.

C. NEWSOM, Apocryphon of Joshua, in G.J. BROOKE, J. COLLINS, T. ELGVIN, P. FLINT, J. GREENFIELD, E. LARSON, C. NEWSOM, E. PUECH, L.H. SCHIFFMANN, M. STONE, J. TREBOLLE BARRERA, J. VANDERKAM (eds.), *Qumran Cave 4. XVII. Parabiblical Texts, Part 3*. (DJD 22) Oxford 1996, pp. 237–288.

E. NIELSEN, *Shechem. A Traditio-Historical Investigation*. (Thesis Presented for the Degree of Doctor of Theology in the University of Aarhus) Copenhagen 1955.

——. *Das Deuteronomium* (HAT I/6) Tübingen 1995.

E. NOORT, Land in zicht ? Geloofsvisie, werkelijkheid en geschiedenis in het oudtestamentische spreken van het land. Enkele opmerkingen naar aanleiding van Jozua 21:43–45, in *Tussen openbaring en ervaring. Studies aangeboden aan prof. dr. G.P. Hartvelt*. Kampen 1986, pp. 94–113.

——. *Een plek om te zijn. Over de theologie van het land van Jozua 8:30–35*. (Rede uitgesproken bij de aanvaarding van het ambt van hoogleraar in de israëlitische letterkunde, de uitlegging van het Oude Testament, de geschiedenis van Israëls godsdienst, en de intertestamentaire letterkunde aan de Rijksuniversiteit Groningen op dinsdag 8 juni 1993) Kampen 1993.

——. Josua und seine Aufgabe. Bemerkungen zu Jos. 1:1–4, in H.M. Niemann, M. Augustin, W.H. Schmidt (Hg.), *Nachdenken über Israel, Bibel und Theologie. Festschrift für Klaus-Dieter Schunck.* (BEATAJ 37) Frankfurt am Main 1994, pp. 69–87.

——. The Traditions of Ebal and Gerizim. Theological Positions in the Book of Joshua, in M. Vervenne, J. Lust (eds.), *Deuteronomy and Deuteronomic Literature. Festschrift C.H.W. Brekelmans.* (BETL 133) Leuven 1997, pp. 161–180.

——. 4QJoshua[a] and the History of Tradition in the Book of Joshua, in *JNSL* 24 (1998), pp. 127–144.

——. *Das Buch Josua. Forschungsgeschichte und Problemfelder.* (EdF 292) Darmstadt 1998.

M. Noth, *Das Buch Josua.* (HAT I/7) Tübingen 1938[1] 1953[2].

——. *Überlieferungsgeschichtliche Studien. Die sammelnden und bearbeitende Geschichtswerke im Alten Testament.* Tübingen 1957[2].

M. O'Brien, *The Deuteronomistic History Hypothesis: A Reassessment.* (OBO 92) Freiburg/Göttingen 1989.

S. Oettli, *Das Deuteronomium und die Bücher Josua und Richter mit einer Karte Palästinas.* (Kurzgefaßter Kommentar zu den heiligen Schriften Alten und Neuen Testamentes sowie den Apokryphen) München 1893.

H.M. Orlinsky, The Hebrew *Vorlage* of the Septuagint of the Book of Joshua, in *Congress Volume. Rome 1968.* (SVT 17) Leiden 1969, pp. 187–195.

E. Otto, *Das Mazzotfest in Gilgal.* (BWANT 107) Stuttgart 1975.

M. Ottoson, Tradition History, with Emphasis on the Composition of the Book of Joshua, in K. Jeppesen, B. Otzen (eds.), *The Production of Time: Tradition History in Old Testament Scholarship. A Symposium at Sandbjerg Manor, Denmark May 1982.* Sheffield 1984, pp. 81–106.

——. *Josuaboken. En programskrift för davidisk restauration.* (Studia Biblica Upsaliensia 1) Uppsala 1991.

J. Payne Smith (Mrs. Margoliouth), *A Compendious Syriac Dictionary. Founded upon the Thesaurus Syriacus by R. Payne Smith.* Oxford 1903, reprinted in Winona Lake, Indiana 1998.

L. Perlitt, *Deuteronomium.* (BKAT V) Neukirchen 1990 (Lieferung 1), 1991 (Lieferung 2).

M. Pope, *Job.* (AB 15) New York 1965.

B. Porten, A. Yardeni (eds.), *Textbook of Aramaic Documents from Ancient Egypt. 1 Letters.* Jerusalem 1986.

J.R. Porter, The Succession of Joshua, in J. Durham, J.R. Porter (eds.), *Proclamation and Presence. Old Testament Essays in Honour of Gwyne Henton Davies.* London 1970, pp. 102–132.

F. Postma, K. Spronk, E. Talstra (eds.), *The New Things. Eschatology in Old Testament Prophecy. Festschrift for Henk Leene.* (Amsterdamse Cahiers voor Exegese van de Bijbel en zijn Tradities Supplement Series 3) Maastricht 2002.

E. Power, Josue 5:9 and the Institution of Circumcision, in *Irish Theological Quarterly* 18 (1951), pp. 368–372.

O. Pretzl, Die griechischen Handschriftengruppen im Buche Josue untersucht nach ihrer Eigenart und ihrem Verhältnis zueinander, in *Biblica* 9 (1928), pp. 377–427.

H.D. Preuß, Zum deuteronomistischen Geschichtswerk, in *ThR* 58 (1993), pp. 226–264, 341–395.

G. von Rad, *Gesammelte Studien zum Alten Testament* I. (TB 8) München 1958.

——. *Theologie des Alten Testaments* I–II. München 1963–1964[3].

A. Rahlfs (ed.), *Septuaginta. Id est Vetus Testamentum graece iuxta LXX interpretes.* Stuttgart 1935.

R. Rendtorff, *Das Alte Testament. Eine Einführung.* Neukirchen 1983.

U. Robert, *Heptateuchi partis posterioris versio latina antiquissima e codice Lugdunensi. Version latine du Deutéronome, de Josué et des Juges antérieure à saint Jérôme publiée d'après le manuscript de Lyon avec un fac-simile, des observations paléographiques et philologiques sur l'origine et la valeur de ce texte.* Lyon 1900.

A. Rofé, סיומו של יהושע לפי תרגום השבעים, in *Shnaton* 2 (1977), pp. 217–227 = A. Rofé, The End of the Book of Joshua According to the Septuagint, in *Henoch* 4 (1982), pp. 17–35.

——. שיטת הביקורת הספרותית־היסטורית מודגמת ביהושע כ״, in A. Rofé, Y. Zakovitch (eds.), *Isac Leo Seeligmann Volume. Essays on the Bible and the Ancient World.* Jerusalem 1983, pp. 137–150 = A. Rofé, Joshua 20: Historico-Literary Criticism Illustrated, in J.H. Tigay (ed.), *Empirical Models for Biblical Criticism.* Philadelphia 1985, pp. 131–147.

——. The Cities of Refuge in Biblical Law, in S. Japhet (ed.), *Studies in Bible 1986.* Jerusalem 1986, pp. 285–239.

——. The Nomistic Correction in Biblical Manuscripts and its Occurrence in 4QSam[a], in *RdQ* 14 (1989), pp. 247–254.

——. The Editing of the Book of Joshua in the Light of 4QJosh[a], in G.J. Brooke, F. García Martínez (ed.), *New Qumran Texts and Studies. Proceedings of the First Meeting of the International Organization for Qumran Studies. Paris 1992.* (STDJ 15) Leiden/New York/Köln 1994, pp. 73–80.

——. המסירות ללימוד התורה בשלהי התקופה המקראית: יהו׳ א, ח ; תה׳ א, ב ; יש׳ נט, כא, in S. Japhet (ed.), *The Bible in the Light of Its Interpreters. In Memory of S. Kamin.* Jerusalem 1994, pp. 622–628. (Hebr.) = A. Rofé, The Piety of the Torah-Disciples at the Winding-Up of the Hebrew Bible: Josh. 1:8; Ps. 1:2; Isa. 59:21, in H. Merklein, K. Müller, G. Stemberger (Hg.), *Bibel in jüdischer und christlicher Tradition. Festschrift für Johann Maier zum 60. Geburtstag.* (BBB 88) Bonn 1993, pp. 78–85.

M. Rose, *Deuteronomist und Jahwist. Untersuchungen zu den Berührungspunkten beider Literaturwerke.* (AThANT 67) Zürich 1981.

H.N. Rösel, Studien zur Topographie der Kriege in den Büchern Josua und Richter, in *ZDPV* 91 (1975), pp. 159–190.

M. Rösel, The Septuagint-Version of the Book of Joshua, in *SJOT* 16/1 (2002), pp. 5–23 = M. Rösel, Die Septuaginta-Version des Josuabuches, in H.-J. Fabry, U. Offerhaus (Hg.), *Im Brennpunkt: Die Septuaginta. Studien zur Entstehung und Bedeutung der Griechischen Bibel.* (BWANT 153) Stuttgart/Berlin/Köln 2001, pp. 197–211.

J.B. de Rossi, *Variae Lectiones Veteris Testamenti Librorum. Ex immensa manuscriptorum editorumque codicum congerie haustae et ad samaritanum textum, ad vetustissimas versiones, ad accuratiores sacrae criticae fontes ac leges examinatae. Volumen II. Libri Numeri, Deuteronomium, Josue, Judices, Samuel, Reges.* Parmae 1784–1798, reprinted Amsterdam 1969.

W. Rudolph, *Der 'Elohist' von Exodus bis Josua.* (BZAW 68) Berlin 1938.

P. Sacchi, Giosuè 1,1–9: Dalla critica storica a quella letteraria, in D. Garrone, F. Israel (eds.), *Storia e tradizione di Israele. Scritti in onore di J. Alberto Soggin.* Brescia 1991, pp. 237–253.

J.M. Sasson, Circumcision in the Ancient Near East, in *JBL* 85 (1966), pp. 473–476.

Chr. Schäfer-Lichtenberger, *Josua und Salomo. Eine Studie zu Autorität und Legitimität des Nachfolgers im Alten Testament.* (SVT 58) Leiden/New York/Köln 1995.

W. Schneider, *Grammatik des biblischen Hebräisch. Völlig neue Bearbeitung der 'Hebräischen Grammatik für den akademischen Unterricht' von Oskar Grether.* München 1985[6].

L. Schwienhorst, *Die Eroberung Jerichos. Exegetische Untersuchung zu Jos. 6.* (SBS 122) Stuttgart 1986.

A.F. Shore (ed.), *Joshua i–vi and other passages in Sahidic, edited from a fourth century Sahidic codex in the Chester Beatty Library.* (Chester Beatty Monographs 9) Dublin 1963.

S. Sipilä, The Septuagint Version of Joshua 3–4, in C.E. Cox, *VII Congress of the International Organization for Septuagint and Cognate Studies. Leuven 1989.* (Society of

Biblical Literature Septuagint and Cognate Studies Series 31) Atlanta 1991, pp. 63–74.

——. The Renderings of ויהי and והיה as Formulas in the LXX of Joshua, in L. GREENSPOON, O. MUNNICH (eds.), *VIII Congress of the International Organization for Septuagint and Cognate Studies. Paris 1992.* (SBL-SCS 41) Atlanta 1995, pp. 273–289.

——. A Note to the Users of Margolis' Joshua Edition, in *BIOSCS* 26 (1993), pp. 17–21.

——. *Between Literalness and Freedom. Translation technique in the Septuagint of Joshua and Judges regarding the clause connections introduced by* ו *and* כי. (Publications of the Finnish Exegetical Society 75) Helsinki/Göttingen 1999.

R. SMEND SR., *Die Erzählung des Hexateuch auf ihre Quellen untersucht.* Berlin 1912.

R. SMEND JR., Das Gesetz und die Völker. Ein Beitrag zur deuteronomistischen Redaktionsgeschichte, in H.W. WOLFF (Hg.), *Probleme biblischer Theologie. Gerhard von Rad zum 70. Geburtstag.* München 1971.

——. Das uneroberte Land, in G. STRECKER (Hg.), *Das Land Israel in biblischer Zeit. Jerusalem-Symposium 1981 der Hebräischen Universität und der Georg-August-Universität.* Göttingen 1983, pp. 91–102.

——. *Die Entstehung des Alten Testaments.* Stuttgart/Berlin/Köln/Mainz 1989[4].

G.V. SMITH, *An Introduction to the Greek Manuscripts of Joshua: Their Classification, Characteristics and Relationships.* (A dissertation submitted in partial fulfillment of the requirements for the degree of Doctor of Philosophy. The Dropsie University for Hebrew and Cognate Learning) Philadelphia 1973.

J.A. SOGGIN, *Le livre de Josué.* (CAT Va) Neuchâtel 1970.

I. SOISALON-SOININEN, *Die Infinitive in der Septuaginta.* (AASF B 132,1) Helsinki 1965.

M. SOKOLOFF, *A Dictionary of Jewish Palestinian Aramaic.* Ramat-Gan 1990.

A. SPERBER, *The Bible in Aramaic. Volume II. The Former Prophets according to Targum Jonathan.* Leiden 1959.

C. SPICQ, O.P., *Notes de lexicographie néo-testamentaire.* (OBO 22) Fribourg/Göttingen 1978 (Tome 1/2) 1982 (Tome 3).

C. STEUERNAGEL, *Übersetzung und Erklärung der Bücher Deuteronomium und Josua und Allgemeine einleitung in den Hexateuch.* (HKAT I/3) Göttingen 1900.

H.-J. STIPP, Das Verhältnis von Textkritik und Literarkritik in neueren alttestamentlichen Veröffentlichungen, in *BZNF* 34/1 (1990), pp. 16–37.

——. Textkritik-Literarkritik-Textentwicklung. Überlegungen zur exegetischen Aspektsystematik, in *ETL* 66 (1990), pp. 143–159.

H.L. STRACK, G. STEMBERGER, *Einleitung in Talmud und Midrasch.* München 1982[7].

G. STRECKER (Hg.), *Das Land Israel in biblischer Zeit. Jerusalem-Symposium 1981 der Hebräischen Universität und der Georg-August-Universität.* Göttingen 1983.

H.B. SWETE, R.R. OTTLEY, *An Introduction to the Old Testament in Greek. With an appendix containing the Letter of Aristeas edited by* H.ST.J. THACKERAY, M.A. Cambridge 1914, reprinted in Peabody, Massachusetts 1989.

S. TALMON, Fragments of a Joshua Apocryphon. Masada 1039-211. (final photo 5254), in *JJS* 47 (1996), pp. 128–139.

S. TALMON, 1039-211; Mas 11; Joshua Apocryphon (MasapocrJosh, final photo 5254), in S. TALMON, *Hebrew fragments from Masada.* (Masada 6) Jerusalem 1999, pp. 105–116.

H. ST.J. THACKERAY, *Grammar of the Old Testament in Greek according to the Septuagint.* Cambridge 1909.

——. *Josephus III. The Jewish War. Books IV–VII.* Cambridge, Massachusetts/London 1928.

H.ST.J. THACKERAY, R. MARCUS (eds.), *Josephus V. Jewish Antiquities, Books V–VIII.* London/Cambridge, Massachusetts 1958.

J.H. TIGAY (ed.), *Empirical Models for Biblical Criticism.* Philadelphia 1985.

E. Tov, L'incidence de la critique textuelle sur la critique littéraire dans le livre de Jérémie, in *RB* 79 (1972), pp. 189–199.

——. Midrash-type Exegesis in the LXX of Joshua, in *RB* 85 (1978), pp. 50–61, reprinted in E. Tov (ed.), *The Greek and Hebrew Bible. Collected Essays on the Septuagint.* (SVT 72) Leiden/Boston/Köln 1999, pp. 153–164.

——. The Growth of the Book of Joshua in the Light of the Evidence of the LXX Translation, in S. Japhet (ed.), *Studies in Bible 1986.* (Scripta Hierosolymitana 31) Jerusalem 1986, pp. 321–339; reprinted in E. Tov, *The Greek and Hebrew Bible. Collected Essays on the Septuagint.* (SVT 72) Leiden/Boston/Köln 1999, pp. 385–396.

——. Some Sequence Differences between the MT and LXX and their Ramification for the Literary Criticism of the Bible, in *JNSL* 13 (1987), pp. 151–160, reprinted in E. Tov, *The Greek and Hebrew Bible. Collected Essays on the Septuagint.* (SVT 72) Leiden/Boston/Köln 1999, pp. 411–418.

——. 4QJosh[b], in Z.J. Kapera, *Intertestamental Essays in Honour of Józef Tadeusz Milik.* (Qumranica Mogilanensia 6). Kraków 1992, pp. 205–212.

——. *Textual Criticism of the Hebrew Bible.* Minneapolis/Assen/Maastricht 1992.

——. 4QJosh[b], in E. Ulrich, F.M. Cross, S.W. Crawford, J.A. Duncan, P.W. Skehan, E. Tov, J. Trebolle Barrera (eds.), *Qumran Cave 4.IX. Deuteronomy, Joshua, Judges, Kings.* (DJD 14) Oxford 1995, pp. 153–160.

——. *The Text-critical Use of the Septuagint in Biblical Research. Second edition, revised and enlarged.* Jerusalem 1997[2].

——. The Rewritten Book of Joshua as Found at Qumran and Masada, in M.E. Stone, E.G. Chazon (eds.), *Biblical Perspectives: Early Use and Interpretation of the Bible in Light of the Dead Sea Scrolls. Proceedings of the First International Symposium of the Orion Center for the Study of the Dead Sea Scrolls and Associated Literature, 12–14 May, 1996.* (STDJ 27) Leiden/Boston/Köln 1998, pp. 233–256.

——. *The Greek and Hebrew Bible. Collected Essays on the Septuagint.* (SVT 72) Leiden/Boston/Köln 1999.

J. Trebolle Barrera, *The Jewish Bible and the Christian Bible. An Introduction to the History of the Bible.* Leiden/New York/Köln/Grand Rapids, Michigan/Cambridge 1998.

A. Tricot, La prise d'Aï (Jos. 7,1–8,29). Notes de critique textuelle et d'histoire biblique, in *Biblica* 3 (1922), pp. 273–300.

K. de Troyer, Did Joshua Have a Crystal Ball? The Old Greek and the MT of Joshua 10:15, 17 and 23, in S.M. Paul, R.A. Kraft, L.H. Schiffman, W.W. Fields (eds.), *Emanuel. Studies in Hebrew Bible, Septuagint, and Dead Sea Scrolls in Honor of Emanuel Tov.* (SVT 94) Leiden/Boston 2003, pp. 571–589.

E. Ulrich, 4QJoshua[a] and Joshua's First Altar in the Promised Land, in G.J. Brooke, F. García Martínez (eds.), *New Qumran Texts and Studies. Proceedings of the First Meeting of the International Organization for Qumran Studies, Paris 1992.* (STDJ 15) Leiden/New York/Köln 1994, pp. 89–104.

——. 4QJosh[a], in E. Ulrich, F.M. Cross, S.W. Crawford, J.A. Duncan, P.W. Skehan, E. Tov, J. Trebolle Barrera (eds.), *Qumran Cave 4.IX. Deuteronomy, Joshua, Judges, Kings.* (DJD 14) Oxford 1995, pp. 143–152.

——. Pluriformity in the Biblical Text, Text Groups and Questions of Canon, in J. Trebolle Barrera, L. Vegas Montaner (eds.), *The Madrid Qumran Congress. Proceedings of the International Congress on the Dead Sea Scrolls Madrid 18–21 March, 1991.* (STDJ 11) Leiden/New York/Köln/Madrid 1992, pp. 23–41, reprinted in E. Ulrich (ed.), *The Dead Sea Scrolls and the Origins of the Bible.* (Studies in the Dead Sea Scrolls and Related Literature) Grand Rapids/Cambridge, Massachusetts/Leiden/Boston/Köln 1999, pp. 79–98.

——. The Canonical Process, Textual Criticism, and Latter Stages in the Composition of the Bible, in M. Fishbane, E. Tov (eds.), *Sha'arei Talmon. Studies in Bible, Qumran, and the Ancient Near East Presented to Shemaryahu Talmon.* Winona Lake 1992, pp.

267–291; reprinted in E. Ulrich (ed.), *The Dead Sea Scrolls and the Origins of the Bible.* (Studies in the Dead Sea Scrolls and Related Literature) Grand Rapids/ Cambridge, Massachusetts/Leiden/Boston/Köln 1999, pp. 51–78.

——. Multiple Literary Editions: Reflections toward a Theory of the History of the Biblical Text, in D.W. Parry, S.D. Ricks (eds.), *Current Research and Technological Developments on the Dead Sea Scrolls. Conference on the Texts from the Judaean Desert, Jerusalem, 30 April 1995.* (STDJ 20) Leiden/New York/Köln 1996, pp. 78–105; reprinted in E. Ulrich (ed.), *The Dead Sea Scrolls and the Origins of the Bible.* (Studies in the Dead Sea Scrolls and Related Literature) Grand Rapids/Cambridge, Massachusetts/Leiden/Boston/Köln 1999, pp. 99–120.

——. The Dead Sea Scrolls and the Biblical Text, in P.W. Flint, J.C. VanderKam (eds.), *The Dead Sea Scrolls after Fifty Years. A Comprehensive Assessment. Volume One.* Leiden/Boston/Köln 1998, pp. 79–100.

——. (ed.), *The Dead Sea Scrolls and the Origins of the Bible.* (Studies in the Dead Sea Scrolls and Related Literature) Grand Rapids/Cambridge, Massachusetts/Leiden/ Boston/Köln 1999.

R. de Vaux, o.p., *Les institutions de l'Ancien Testament.* I–II. Paris 1961[2].

J.G. Vink, The Date and Origin of the Priestly Code in the Old Testament, in P.A.H. de Boer (ed.), *The Priestly Code and Seven Other Studies.* (OTS 15) Leiden 1969.

J.C. de Vos, *Das Los Judas. Über Entstehung und Ziele der Landbeschreibung in Josua 15.* (SVT 95) Leiden/Boston 2003.

J. Wagenaar, The Cessation of Manna. Editorial Frames for the Wilderness Wandering in Exodus 16,35 and Joshua 5,10–12, in *ZAW* 112 (2000), pp. 192–209.

R. Weber, o.s.b. (ed.), *Biblia Sacra iuxta Vulgatam Versionem.* Stuttgart 1983[3].

M. Weinfeld, *Deuteronomy and the Deuteronomic School.* Oxford 1972.

——. *Deuteronomy 1–11.* (AB 5) New York 1991.

J. Wellhausen, *Die Composition des Hexateuchs und der historischen Bücher des Alten Testaments.* Berlin 1889[2].

J.W. Wevers, *Text History of the Greek Deuteronomy.* (MSU XIII) Göttingen 1978.

——. *Notes on the Greek Text of Exodus.* (SBL-SCS 30) Atlanta 1990.

——. *Notes on the Greek Text of Deuteronomy.* (SBL-SCS 39) Atlanta 1995.

——. The Interpretative Character and Significance of the Septuagint Version, in C. Brekelmans, M. Haran, M. Sæbø (eds.), *Hebrew Bible/Old Testament. The History of Its Interpretation. Volume I. From the Beginnings to the Middle Ages (Until 1300).* Göttingen 1996, pp. 84–107.

N. Winther-Nielsen, E. Talstra, *A Computational Display of the Book of Joshua.* (Applicatio 13) Amsterdam 1995.

N. Winther-Nielsen, *A Functional Discourse Grammar of Joshua. A Computer-Assisted Rhetorical Structure Analysis.* (Coniectanea Biblica. Old Testament Series 40) Stockholm 1995.

A.S. van der Woude, *Pluriformiteit en Uniformiteit. Overwegingen betreffende de tekstoverlevering van het Oude Testament.* (Afscheidsrede uitgesproken op 3 november 1992 door A.S. van der Woude bij het aftreden als hoogleraar in de Israëlitische letterkunde, de uitlegging van het Oude Testament, de geschiedenis van Israëls godsdienst en de intertestamentaire letterkunde) Kampen 1992 = A.S. van der Woude, Pluriformity and Uniformity. Reflections on the Transmission of the Text of the Old Testament, in J.N. Bremmer, F. García Martínez (eds.), *Sacred History and Sacred Texts in Early Judaism. A Symposium in Honour of A.S. van der Woude.* (Contributions to Biblical Exegesis and Theology 5) Kampen 1992, pp. 151–169.

INDEX OF CLASSICAL SOURCES

This index does not aim at completeness, but presents mainly those passages that receive more than incidental attention. Unless otherwise indicated all Old Testament references are to BHS without distinction between the ancient versions (Masoretic text, Qumran scrolls, Samaritan Pentateuch, Septuagint, Targumim, Pešiṭta, Vulgate). Numbering of the Septuagint verses is according to the Rahlfs edition.

Epigraphic documents

Hebrew Bible

Classical Greek and Roman literature

HELLENISTIC JEWISH LITERATURE

Hebrew and Aramaic manuscripts
(Elephantine, Qumran, Masada, Cairo, Nablus)

Rabbinic literature

Christian literature

INDEX OF MODERN AUTHORS

SUPPLEMENTS TO VETUS TESTAMENTUM

2. Pope, M.H. *El in the Ugaritic texts.* 1955. ISBN 90 04 04000 5
3. *Wisdom in Israel and in the Ancient Near East.* Presented to Harold Henry Rowley by the Editorial Board of Vetus Testamentum in celebration of his 65th birthday, 24 March 1955. Edited by M. Noth and D. Winton Thomas. 2nd reprint of the rst (1955) ed. 1969. ISBN 90 04 02326 7
4. *Volume du Congrès* [international pour l'étude de l'Ancien Testament]. *Strasbourg 1956.* 1957. ISBN 90 04 02327 5
8. Bernhardt, K.-H. *Das Problem der alt-orientalischen Königsideologie im Alten Testament.* Unter besonderer Berücksichtigung der Geschichte der Psalmenexegese dargestellt und kritisch gewürdigt. 1961. ISBN 90 04 02331 3
9. *Congress Volume, Bonn 1962.* 1963. ISBN 90 04 02332 1
11. Donner, H. *Israel unter den Völkern.* Die Stellung der klassischen Propheten des 8. Jahrhunderts v. Chr. zur Aussenpolitik der Könige von Israel und Juda. 1964. ISBN 90 04 02334 8
12. Reider, J. *An Index to Aquila.* Completed and revised by N. Turner. 1966. ISBN 90 04 02335 6
13. Roth, W.M.W. *Numerical sayings in the Old Testament.* A form-critical study. 1965. ISBN 90 04 02336 4
14. Orlinsky, H.M. *Studies on the second part of the Book of Isaiah.* — The so-called 'Servant of the Lord' and 'Suffering Servant' in Second Isaiah. — Snaith, N.H. Isaiah 40-66. A study of the teaching of the Second Isaiah and its consequences. Repr. with additions and corrections. 1977. ISBN 90 04 05437 5
15. *Volume du Congrès* [International pour l'étude de l'Ancien Testament]. *Genève 1965.* 1966. ISBN 90 04 02337 2
17. *Congress Volume, Rome 1968.* 1969. ISBN 90 04 02339 9
19. Thompson, R.J. *Moses and the Law in a century of criticism since Graf.* 1970. ISBN 90 04 02341 0
20. Redford, D.B. *A Study of the Biblical Story of Joseph.* 1970. ISBN 90 04 02342 9
21. Ahlström, G.W. *Joel and the Temple Cult of Jerusalem.* 1971. ISBN 90 04 02620 7
22. *Congress Volume, Uppsala 1971.* 1972. ISBN 90 04 03521 4
23. *Studies in the Religion of Ancient Israel.* 1972. ISBN 90 04 03525 7
24. Schoors, A. *I am God your Saviour.* A form-critical study of the main genres in Is. xl-lv. 1973. ISBN 90 04 03792 2
25. Allen, L.C. *The Greek Chronicles.* The relation of the Septuagint I and II Chronicles to the Massoretic text. Part 1. The translator's craft. 1974. ISBN 90 04 03913 9
26. *Studies on prophecy.* A collection of twelve papers. 1974. ISBN 90 04 03877 9
27. Allen, L.C. *The Greek Chronicles.* Part 2. Textual criticism. 1974. ISBN 90 04 03933 3
28. *Congress Volume, Edinburgh 1974.* 1975. ISBN 90 04 04321 7
29. *Congress Volume, Göttingen 1977.* 1978. ISBN 90 04 05835 4
30. Emerton, J.A. (ed.). *Studies in the historical books of the Old Testament.* 1979. ISBN 90 04 06017 0
31. Meredino, R.P. *Der Erste und der Letzte.* Eine Untersuchung von Jes 40-48. 1981. ISBN 90 04 06199 1
32. Emerton, J.A. (ed.). *Congress Volume, Vienna 1980.* 1981. ISBN 90 04 06514 8
33. Koenig, J. *L'herméneutique analogique du Judaïsme antique d'après les témoins textuels d'Isaïe.* 1982. ISBN 90 04 06762 0

34. BARSTAD, H.M. *The religious polemics of Amos.* Studies in the preachings of Amos ii 7B-8, iv 1-13, v 1-27, vi 4-7, viii 14. 1984. ISBN 90 04 07017 6
35. KRAŠOVEC, J. *Antithetic structure in Biblical Hebrew poetry.* 1984. ISBN 90 04 07244 6
36. EMERTON, J.A. (ed.). *Congress Volume, Salamanca 1983.* 1985. ISBN 90 04 07281 0
37. LEMCHE, N.P. *Early Israel.* Anthropological and historical studies on the Israelite society before the monarchy. 1985. ISBN 90 04 07853 3
38. NIELSEN, K. *Incense in Ancient Israel.* 1986. ISBN 90 04 07702 2
39. PARDEE, D. *Ugaritic and Hebrew poetic parallelism.* A trial cut. 1988. ISBN 90 04 08368 5
40. EMERTON, J.A. (ed.). *Congress Volume, Jerusalem 1986.* 1988. ISBN 90 04 08499 1
41. EMERTON, J.A. (ed.). *Studies in the Pentateuch.* 1990. ISBN 90 04 09195 5
42. MCKENZIE, S.L. *The trouble with Kings.* The composition of the Book of Kings in the Deuteronomistic History. 1991. ISBN 90 04 09402 4
43. EMERTON, J.A. (ed.). *Congress Volume, Leuven 1989.* 1991. ISBN 90 04 09398 2
44. HAAK, R.D. *Habakkuk.* 1992. ISBN 90 04 09506 3
45. BEYERLIN, W. *Im Licht der Traditionen.* Psalm LXVII und CXV. Ein Entwicklungszusammenhang. 1992. ISBN 90 04 09635 3
46. MEIER, S.A. *Speaking of Speaking.* Marking direct discourse in the Hebrew Bible. 1992. ISBN 90 04 09602 7
47. KESSLER, R. *Staat und Gesellschaft im vorexilischen Juda.* Vom 8. Jahrhundert bis zum Exil. 1992. ISBN 90 04 09646 9
48. AUFFRET, P. *Voyez de vos yeux.* Étude structurelle de vingt psaumes, dont le psaume 119. 1993. ISBN 90 04 09707 4
49. GARCÍA MARTÍNEZ, F., A. HILHORST and C.J. LABUSCHAGNE (eds.). *The Scriptures and the Scrolls.* Studies in honour of A.S. van der Woude on the occasion of his 65th birthday. 1992. ISBN 90 04 09746 5
50. LEMAIRE, A. and B. OTZEN (eds.). *History and Traditions of Early Israel.* Studies presented to Eduard Nielsen, May 8th, 1993. 1993. ISBN 90 04 09851 8
51. GORDON, R.P. *Studies in the Targum to the Twelve Prophets.* From Nahum to Malachi. 1994. ISBN 90 04 09987 5
52. HUGENBERGER, G.P. *Marriage as a Covenant.* A Study of Biblical Law and Ethics Governing Marriage Developed from the Perspective of Malachi. 1994. ISBN 90 04 09977 8
53. GARCÍA MARTÍNEZ, F., A. HILHORST, J.T.A.G.M. VAN RUITEN, A.S. VAN DER WOUDE. *Studies in Deuteronomy.* In Honour of C.J. Labuschagne on the Occasion of His 65th Birthday. 1994. ISBN 90 04 10052 0
54. FERNÁNDEZ MARCOS, N. *Septuagint and Old Latin in the Book of Kings.* 1994. ISBN 90 04 10043 1
55. SMITH, M.S. *The Ugaritic Baal Cycle. Volume 1.* Introduction with text, translation and commentary of KTU 1.1-1.2. 1994. ISBN 90 04 09995 6
56. DUGUID, I.M. *Ezekiel and the Leaders of Israel.* 1994. ISBN 90 04 10074 1
57. MARX, A. *Les offrandes végétales dans l'Ancien Testament.* Du tribut d'hommage au repas eschatologique. 1994. ISBN 90 04 10136 5
58. SCHÄFER-LICHTENBERGER, C. *Josua und Salomo.* Eine Studie zu Autorität und Legitimität des Nachfolgers im Alten Testament. 1995. ISBN 90 04 10064 4
59. LASSERRE, G. *Synopse des lois du Pentateuque.* 1994. ISBN 90 04 10202 7
60. DOGNIEZ, C. *Bibliography of the Septuagint – Bibliographie de la Septante (1970-1993).* Avec une préface de PIERRE-MAURICE BOGAERT. 1995. ISBN 90 04 10192 6
61. EMERTON, J.A. (ed.). *Congress Volume, Paris 1992.* 1995. ISBN 90 04 10259 0

62. SMITH, P.A. *Rhetoric and Redaction in Trito-Isaiah.* The Structure, Growth and Authorship of Isaiah 56-66. 1995. ISBN 90 04 10306 6
63. O'CONNELL, R.H. *The Rhetoric of the Book of Judges.* 1996. ISBN 90 04 10104 7
64. HARLAND, P.J. *The Value of Human Life.* A Study of the Story of the Flood (Genesis 6-9). 1996. ISBN 90 04 10534 4
65. ROLAND PAGE JR., H. *The Myth of Cosmic Rebellion.* A Study of its Reflexes in Ugaritic and Biblical Literature. 1996. ISBN 90 04 10563 8
66. EMERTON, J.A. (ed.). *Congress Volume, Cambridge 1995.* 1997. ISBN 90 04 106871
67. JOOSTEN, J. *People and Land in the Holiness Code.* An Exegetical Study of the Ideational Framework of the Law in Leviticus 17–26. 1996. ISBN 90 04 10557 3
68. BEENTJES, P.C. *The Book of Ben Sira in Hebrew.* A Text Edition of all Extant Hebrew Manuscripts and a Synopsis of all Parallel Hebrew Ben Sira Texts. 1997. ISBN 90 04 10767 3
69. COOK, J. *The Septuagint of Proverbs – Jewish and/or Hellenistic Proverbs?* Concerning the Hellenistic Colouring of LXX Proverbs. 1997. ISBN 90 04 10879 3
70,1 BROYLES, G. and C. EVANS (eds.). *Writing and Reading the Scroll of Isaiah.* Studies of an Interpretive Tradition, I. 1997. ISBN 90 04 10936 6 (*Vol.* I); ISBN 90 04 11027 5 (*Set*)
70,2 BROYLES, G. and C. EVANS (eds.). *Writing and Reading the Scroll of Isaiah.* Studies of an Interpretive Tradition, II. 1997. ISBN 90 04 11026 7 (*Vol.* II); ISBN 90 04 11027 5 (*Set*)
71. KOOIJ, A. VAN DER. *The Oracle of Tyre.* The Septuagint of Isaiah 23 as Version and Vision. 1998. ISBN 90 04 11152 2
72. TOV, E. *The Greek and Hebrew Bible.* Collected Essays on the Septuagint. 1999. ISBN 90 04 11309 6
73. GARCÍA MARTÍNEZ, F. and NOORT, E. (eds.). *Perspectives in the Study of the Old Testament and Early Judaism.* A Symposium in honour of Adam S. van der Woude on the occasion of his 70th birthday. 1998. ISBN 90 04 11322 3
74. KASSIS, R.A. *The Book of Proverbs and Arabic Proverbial Works.* 1999. ISBN 90 04 11305 3
75. RÖSEL, H.N. *Von Josua bis Jojachin.* Untersuchungen zu den deuteronomistischen Geschichtsbüchern des Alten Testaments. 1999. ISBN 90 04 11355 5
76. RENZ, Th. *The Rhetorical Function of the Book of Ezekiel.* 1999. ISBN 90 04 11362 2
77. HARLAND, P.J. and HAYWARD, C.T.R. (eds.). *New Heaven and New Earth Prophecy and the Millenium.* Essays in Honour of Anthony Gelston. 1999. ISBN 90 04 10841 6
78. KRAŠOVEC, J. *Reward, Punishment, and Forgiveness.* The Thinking and Beliefs of Ancient Israel in the Light of Greek and Modern Views. 1999. ISBN 90 04 11443 2.
79. KOSSMANN, R. *Die Esthernovelle – Vom Erzählten zur Erzählung.* Studien zur Traditions- und Redaktionsgeschichte des Estherbuches. 2000. ISBN 90 04 11556 0.
80. LEMAIRE, A. and M. SÆBØ (eds.). *Congress Volume, Oslo 1998.* 2000. ISBN 90 04 11598 6.
81. GALIL, G. and M. WEINFELD (eds.). *Studies in Historical Geography and Biblical Historiography.* Presented to Zecharia Kallai. 2000. ISBN 90 04 11608 7
82. COLLINS, N.L. *The library in Alexandria and the Bible in Greek.* 2001. ISBN 90 04 11866 7

83,1 Collins, J.J. and P.W. Flint (eds.). *The Book of Daniel.* Composition and Reception, I. 2001. ISBN 90 04 11675 3 (*Vol.* I); ISBN 90 04 12202 8 (*Set*)
83,2 Collins, J.J. and P.W. Flint (eds.). *The Book of Daniel.* Composition and Reception, II. 2001. ISBN 90 04 12200 1 (*Vol.* II); ISBN 90 04 12202 8 (*Set*).
84. Cohen, C.H.R. *Contextual Priority in Biblical Hebrew Philology.* An Application of the Held Method for Comparative Semitic Philology. 2001. ISBN 90 04 11670 2 (In preparation).
85. Wagenaar, J.A. *Judgement and Salvation.* The Composition and Redaction of Micah 2-5. 2001. ISBN 90 04 11936 1
86. McLaughlin, J.L. *The* Marzēaḥ *in sthe Prophetic Literature.* References and Allusions in Light of the Extra-Biblical Evidence. 2001. ISBN 90 04 12006 8
87. Wong, K.L. *The Idea of Retribution in the Book of Ezekiel* 2001. ISBN 90 04 12256 7
88. Barrick, W. Boyd *The King and the Cemeteries.* Toward a New Understanding of Josiah's Reform. 2002. ISBN 90 04 12171 4
89. Frankel, D. *The Murmuring Stories of the Priestly School.* A Retrieval of Ancient Sacerdotal Lore. 2002. ISBN 90 04 12368 7
90. Frydrych, T. *Living under the Sun.* Examination of Proverbs and Qoheleth. 2002. ISBN 90 04 12315 6
91. Kessel, J. *The Book of Haggai.* Prophecy and Society in Early Persian Yehud. 2002. ISBN 90 04 12368 7
92. Lemaire, A. (ed.). *Congress Volume, Basel 2001.* 2002. ISBN 90 04 12680 5
93. Rendtorff, R. and R.A. Kugler (eds.). *The Book of Leviticus.* Composition and Reception. 2003. ISBN 90 04 12634 1
94. Paul, S.M., R.A. Kraft, L.H. Schiffman and W.W. Fields (eds.). *Emanuel.* Studies in Hebrew Bible, Septuagint, and Dead Sea Scrolls in Honor of Emanuel Tov. 2003. ISBN 90 04 13007 1
95. Vos, J.C. de. *Das Los Judas.* Über Entstehung und Ziele der Landbeschreibung in Josua 15. ISBN 90 04 12953 7
96. Lehnart, B. *Prophet und König im Nordreich Israel.* Studien zur sogenannten vorklassischen Prophetie im Nordreich Israel anhand der Samuel-, Elija- und Elischa-Überlieferungen. 2003. ISBN 90 04 13237 6
97. Lo, A. *Job 28 as Rhetoric.* An Analysis of Job 28 in the Context of Job 22-31. 2003. ISBN 90 04 13320 8
98. Trudinger, P.L. *The Psalms of the Tamid Service.* A Liturgical Text from the Second Temple. 2004. ISBN 90 04 12968 5
99. Flint, P.W. and P.D. Miller, Jr. (eds.) with the assistance of A. Brunell. *The Book of Psalms.* Composition and Reception. 2003. ISBN 90 04 13842 8
100. Weinfeld, M. *The Place of the Law in the Religion of Ancient Israel.* 2004. ISBN 90 04 13749 1
101. Flint, P.W., J.C. VanderKam and E. Tov. (eds.) *Studies in the Hebrew Bible, Qumran, and the Septuagint.* Essays Presented to Eugene Ulrich on the Occasion of his Sixty-Fifth Birthday. 2003. ISBN 90 04 13738 6
102. Meer, M.N. van der. *Formation and Reformulation.* The Redaction of the Book of Joshua in the Light of the Oldest Textual Witnesses. 2004. ISBN 90 04 13125 6
103. Berman, J.A. *Narrative Analogy in the Hebrew Bible.* Battle Stories and Their Equivalent Non-battle Narratives. 2004. ISBN 90 04 13119 1